Algebra 1

Common Core

Randall I. Charles
Basia Hall
Dan Kennedy
Allan E. Bellman
Sadie Chavis Bragg
William G. Handlin
Stuart J. Murphy
Grant Wiggins

PEARSON

Boston, Massachusetts • Chandler, Arizona • Glenview, Illinois • Hoboken, New Jersey

Acknowledgments appear on page 944, which constitutes an extension of this copyright page.

PEARSON

ISBN-13: 978-0-13-328114-9
ISBN-10:   0-13-328114-0
8 9 10   18 17 16

Contents *in Brief*

Welcome to *Pearson Algebra 1 Common Core Edition* student book. Throughout this textbook, you will find content that has been developed to cover many of the High School Standards for Mathematical Content and all of the Standards for Mathematical Practice from the Common Core State Standards. The End-of-Course Assessment provides students with practice with all of the Standards for Mathematical Content listed on pages xx to xxiii.

Series *Authors*

Randall I. Charles, Ph.D., is Professor Emeritus in the Department of Mathematics and Computer Science at San Jose State University, San Jose, California. He began his career as a high school mathematics teacher, and he was a mathematics supervisor for five years. Dr. Charles has been a member of several NCTM committees and is the former Vice President of the National Council of Supervisors of Mathematics. Much of his writing and research has been in the area of problem solving. He has authored more than 90 mathematics textbooks for kindergarten through college.

Dan Kennedy, Ph.D., is a classroom teacher and the Lupton Distinguished Professor of Mathematics at the Baylor School in Chattanooga, Tennessee. A frequent speaker at professional meetings on the subject of mathematics education reform, Dr. Kennedy has conducted more than 50 workshops and institutes for high school teachers. He is coauthor of textbooks in calculus and precalculus, and from 1990 to 1994, he chaired the College Board's AP Calculus Development Committee. He is a 1992 Tandy Technology Scholar and a 1995 Presidential Award winner.

Basia Hall currently serves as Manager of Instructional Programs for the Houston Independent School District. With 33 years of teaching experience, Ms. Hall has served as a department chair, instructional supervisor, school improvement facilitator, and professional development trainer. She has developed curricula for Algebra 1, Geometry, and Algebra 2 and co-developed the Texas state mathematics standards. A 1992 Presidential Awardee, Ms. Hall is past president of the Texas Association of Supervisors of Mathematics and is a state representative for the National Council of Supervisors of Mathematics (NCSM).

Consulting *Authors*

Stuart J. Murphy is a visual learning author and consultant. He is a champion of helping students develop visual learning skills so they become more successful students. He is the author of *MathStart*, a series of children's books that presents mathematical concepts in the context of stories and *I See I Learn*, a Pre-Kindergarten and Kindergarten learning initiative that focuses on social and emotional skills. A graduate of the Rhode Island School of Design, he has worked extensively in educational publishing and has been on the authorship teams of a number of elementary and high school mathematics programs. He is a frequent presenter at meetings of the National Council of Teachers of Mathematics, the International Reading Association, and other professional organizations.

Grant Wiggins, Ed.D., is the President of Authentic Education in Hopewell, New Jersey. He earned his B.A. from St. John's College in Annapolis and his Ed.D. from Harvard University. Dr. Wiggins consults with schools, districts, and state education departments on a variety of reform matters; organizes conferences and workshops; and develops print materials and Web resources on curricular change. He is perhaps best known for being the coauthor, with Jay McTighe, of *Understanding by Design* and *The Understanding by Design Handbook*[1], the award-winning and highly successful materials on curriculum published by ASCD. His work has been supported by the Pew Charitable Trusts, the Geraldine R. Dodge Foundation, and the National Science Foundation.

[1] ASCD, publisher of "The Understanding by Design Handbook" coauthored by Grant Wiggins and registered owner of the trademark "Understanding by Design," has not authorized or sponsored this work and is in no way affiliated with Pearson or its products.

Program *Authors*

Algebra 1 and Algebra 2

Allan E. Bellman, Ph.D., is an Associate Professor of Mathematics Education at the University of Mississippi. He previously taught at the University of California, Davis for 12 years and in public school in Montgomery County, Maryland for 31. He has been an instructor for both the Woodrow Wilson National Fellowship Foundation and the Texas Instruments' T^3 program. Bellman has expertise in the use of technology in education and assessment-driven instruction, and speaks frequently on these topics. He was a 1992 Tandy Technology Scholar and has twice been listed in Who's Who Among America's Teachers.

Sadie Chavis Bragg, Ed.D., is Senior Vice President of Academic Affairs and professor of mathematics at the Borough of Manhattan Community College of the City University of New York. She is a past president of the American Mathematical Association of Two-Year Colleges (AMATYC). In recognition of her service to the field of mathematics locally, statewide, nationally, and internationally, she was awarded AMATYC's most prestigious award, the Mathematics Excellence Award for 2010. Dr. Bragg has coauthored more than 50 mathematics textbooks for kindergarten through college.

William G. Handlin, Sr., is a classroom teacher and Department Chair of Mathematics and former Department Chair of Technology Applications at Spring Woods High School in Houston, Texas. Awarded Life Membership in the Texas Congress of Parents and Teachers for his contributions to the well-being of children, Mr. Handlin is also a frequent workshop and seminar leader in professional meetings.

Geometry

Laurie E. Bass is a classroom teacher at the 9–12 division of the Ethical Culture Fieldston School in Riverdale, New York. A classroom teacher for more than 30 years, Ms. Bass has a wide base of teaching experience, ranging from Grade 6 through Advanced Placement Calculus. She was the recipient of a 2000 Honorable Mention for the Radio Shack National Teacher Awards. She has been a contributing writer for a number of publications, including software-based activities for the Algebra 1 classroom. Among her areas of special interest are cooperative learning for high school students and geometry exploration on the computer. Ms. Bass is a frequent presenter at local, regional, and national conferences.

Art Johnson, Ed.D., is a professor of mathematics education at Boston University. He is a mathematics educator with 32 years of public school teaching experience, a frequent speaker and workshop leader, and the recipient of a number of awards: the Tandy Prize for Teaching Excellence, the Presidential Award for Excellence in Mathematics Teaching, and New Hampshire Teacher of the Year. He was also profiled by the Disney Corporation in the American Teacher of the Year Program. Dr. Johnson has contributed 18 articles to NCTM journals and has authored over 50 books on various aspects of mathematics.

Reviewers *National*

Tammy Baumann
K-12 Mathematics Coordinator
School District of the City
 of Erie
Erie, Pennsylvania

Sandy Cowgill
Mathematics Department Chair
Muncie Central High School
Muncie, Indiana

Sheryl Ezze
Mathematics Chairperson
DeWitt High School
Lansing, Michigan

Dennis Griebel
Mathematics Coordinator
Cherry Creek School District
Aurora, Colorado

Bill Harrington
Secondary Mathematics
 Coordinator
State College School District
State College, Pennsylvania

Michael Herzog
Mathematics Teacher
Tucson Small School Project
Tucson, Arizona

Camilla Horton
Secondary Instruction Support
Memphis School District
Memphis, Tennessee

Gary Kubina
Mathematics Consultant
Mobile County School System
Mobile, Alabama

Sharon Liston
Mathematics Department Chair
Moore Public Schools
Oklahoma City, Oklahoma

Ann Marie Palmeri Monahan
Mathematics Supervisor
Bayonne Public Schools
Bayonne, New Jersey

Indika Morris
Mathematics Department Chair
Queen Creek School District
Queen Creek, Arizona

Jennifer Petersen
K-12 Mathematics Curriculum
 Facilitator
Springfield Public Schools
Springfield, Missouri

Tammy Popp
Mathematics Teacher
Mehlville School District
St. Louis, Missouri

Mickey Porter
Mathematics Teacher
Dayton Public Schools
Dayton, Ohio

Steven Sachs
Mathematics Department Chair
Lawrence North High School
Indianapolis, Indiana

John Staley
Secondary Mathematics
 Coordinator
Office of Mathematics, PK-12
Baltimore, Maryland

Robert Thomas, Ph.D.
Mathematics Teacher
Yuma Union High School
 District #70
Yuma, Arizona

Linda Ussery
Mathematics Consultant
Alabama Department of
 Education
Tuscumbia, Alabama

Denise Vizzini
Mathematics Teacher
Clarksburg High School
Montgomery County,
 Maryland

Marcia White
Mathematics Specialist
Academic Operations,
 Technology and Innovations
Memphis City Schools
Memphis, Tennessee

Merrie Wolf
Mathematics Department Chair
Tulsa Public Schools
Tulsa, Oklahoma

From the *Authors*

Welcome

Math is a powerful tool with far-reaching applications throughout your life. We have designed a unique and engaging program that will enable you to tap into the power of mathematics and mathematical reasoning. This award-winning program has been developed to align fully to the Common Core State Standards.

Developing mathematical understanding and problem-solving abilities is an ongoing process—a journey both inside and outside the classroom. This course is designed to help make sense of the mathematics you encounter in and out of class each day and to help you develop mathematical proficiency.

You will learn important mathematical principles. You will also learn how the principles are connected to one another and to what you already know. You will learn to solve problems and learn the reasoning that lies behind your solutions. You will also develop the key mathematical practices of the Common Core State Standards.

Each chapter begins with the "big ideas" of the chapter and some essential questions that you will learn to answer. Through this question-and-answer process you will develop your ability to analyze problems independently and solve them in different applications.

Your skills and confidence will increase through practice and review. Work through the problems so you understand the concepts and methods presented and the thinking behind them. Then do the exercises. Ask yourself how new concepts relate to old ones. Make the connections!

Everyone needs help sometimes. You will find that this program has built-in opportunities, both in this text and online, to get help whenever you need it.

This course will also help you succeed on the tests you take in class and on other tests like the SAT, ACT, and state exams. The practice exercises in each lesson will prepare you for the format and content of such tests. No surprises!

The problem-solving and reasoning habits and problem-solving skills you develop in this program will serve you in all your studies and in your daily life. They will prepare you for future success not only as a student, but also as a member of a changing technological society.

Best wishes,

[signatures: Dan Kennedy, Randy Charles, Basia Hall, Allan E. Bellman, Sadie C. Bragg, William G. Handlin, Laurie E. Bass, Art Johnson, Stuart J. Murphy, Grant Wiggins]

PowerAlgebra.com

Welcome to Algebra 1. *Pearson Algebra 1 Common Core Edition* is part of a blended digital and print environment for the study of high school mathematics. Take some time to look through the features of our mathematics program, starting with **PowerAlgebra.com,** the site of the digital features of the program.

Hi, I'm Darius. My friends and I will be showing you the great features of the Pearson Algebra 1 Common Core Edition program.

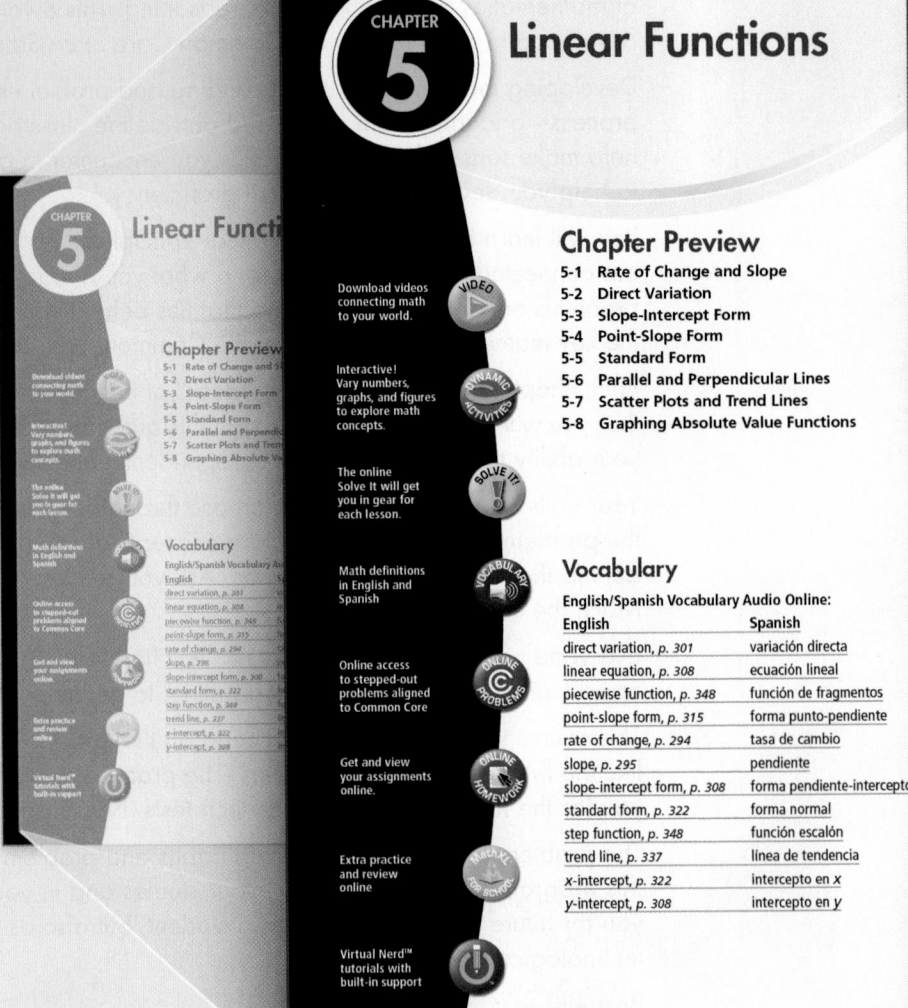

CHAPTER
5

Linear Functions

Download videos connecting math to your world.

Interactive! Vary numbers, graphs, and figures to explore math concepts.

The online Solve It will get you in gear for each lesson.

Math definitions in English and Spanish

Online access to stepped-out problems aligned to Common Core

Get and view your assignments online.

Extra practice and review online

Virtual Nerd™ tutorials with built-in support

Chapter Preview

5-1 Rate of Change and Slope
5-2 Direct Variation
5-3 Slope-Intercept Form
5-4 Point-Slope Form
5-5 Standard Form
5-6 Parallel and Perpendicular Lines
5-7 Scatter Plots and Trend Lines
5-8 Graphing Absolute Value Functions

Vocabulary

English/Spanish Vocabulary Audio Online:

English	Spanish
direct variation, p. 301	variación directa
linear equation, p. 308	ecuación lineal
piecewise function, p. 348	función de fragmentos
point-slope form, p. 315	forma punto-pendiente
rate of change, p. 294	tasa de cambio
slope, p. 295	pendiente
slope-intercept form, p. 308	forma pendiente-intercepto
standard form, p. 322	forma normal
step function, p. 348	función escalón
trend line, p. 337	línea de tendencia
x-intercept, p. 322	intercepto en x
y-intercept, p. 308	intercepto en y

On each **chapter opener,** you will find a listing of the online features of the program. Look for these buttons throughout the lessons.

Big *Ideas*

We start with **Big Ideas.** Each chapter is organized around Big Ideas that convey the key mathematics concepts you will be studying in the program. Take a look at the Big Ideas on pages xxiv and xxv.

The Common Core State Standards have a similar organizing structure. They begin with **Conceptual Categories**, such as Algebra or Functions. Within each category are **domains and clusters.**

Common Core State Standards

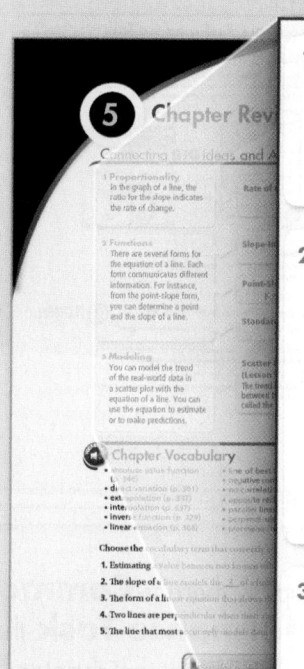

BIG ideas

1 Proportionality
Essential Question: What does the slope of a line indicate about the line?

2 Functions
Essential Question: What information does the equation of a line give you?

3 Modeling
Essential Question: How can you make predictions based on a scatter plot?

1 Proportionality
In the graph of a line, the ratio for the slope indicates the rate of change.

2 Functions
There are several forms for the equation of a line. Each form communicates different information. For instance, from the point-slope form, you can determine a point and the slope of a line.

3 Modeling
You can model the trend of the real-world data in a scatter plot with the equation of a line. You can use the equation to estimate or to make predictions.

The **Big Ideas** are organizing ideas for all of the lessons in the program. At the beginning of each chapter, we'll tell you which Big Ideas you'll be studying. We'll also present an **Essential Question** for each Big Idea.

In the **Chapter Review** at the end of the chapter, you'll find an answer to the Essential Question for each Big Idea. We'll also remind you of the lesson(s) where you studied the concepts that support the Big Ideas.

Exploring *Concepts*

The lessons offer many opportunities to explore concepts in different contexts and through different media.

Hi, I'm Serena. I never have to power down when I am in math class now.

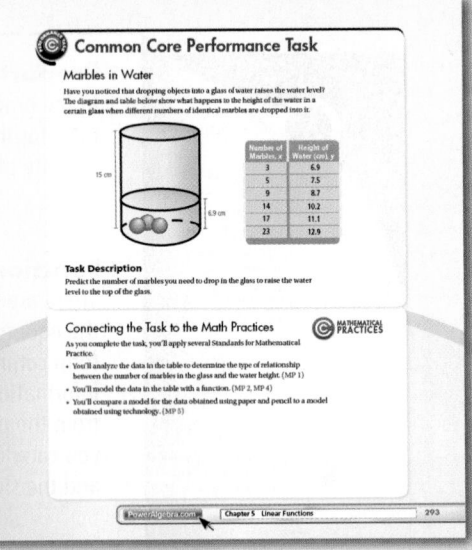

For each chapter, there is **Common Core Performance Task** that you will work on throughout the chapter. See pages xii and xiii for more information.

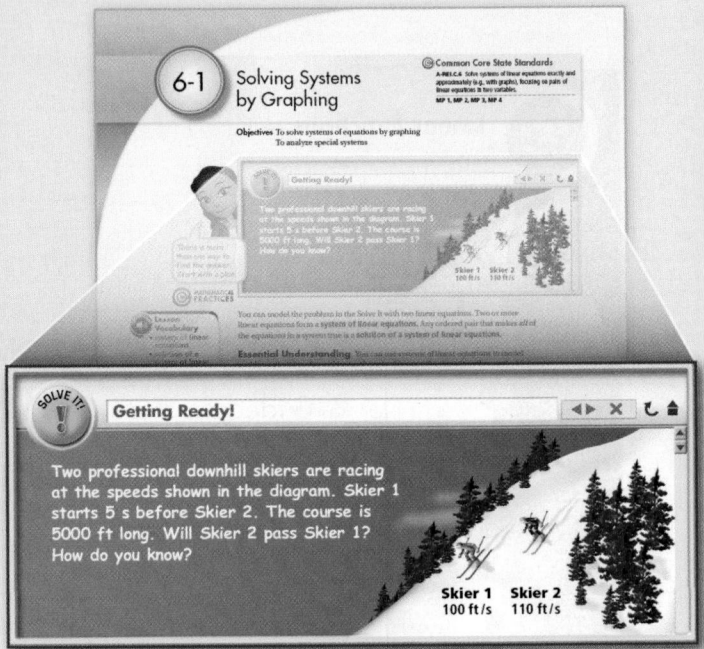

Here's another cool feature. Each lesson opens with a **Solve It,** a problem that helps you connect what you know to an important concept in the lesson. Do you notice how the Solve It frame looks like it comes from a computer? That's because all of the Solve Its can be found at **PowerAlgebra.com.**

The **Standards for Mathematical Practice** describe processes, practices, and habits of mind of mathematically proficient students. Many of the features in Algebra 1 help you become more proficient in math.

Developing Mathematical Proficiency

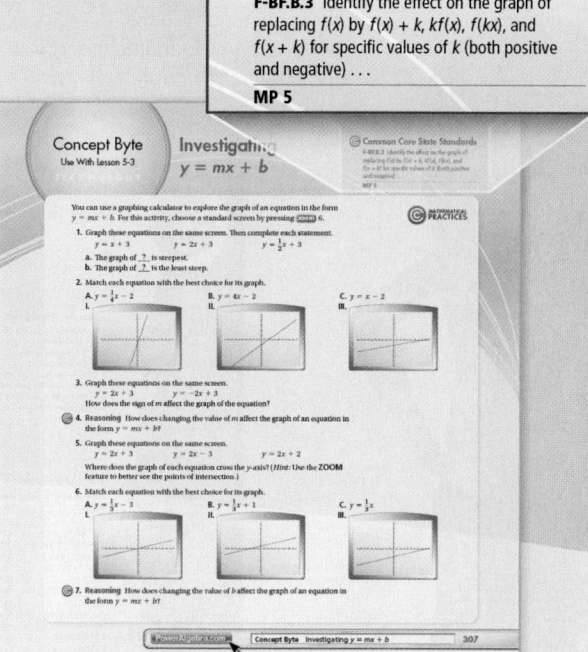

© **Common Core State Standards**

F-BF.B.3 Identify the effect on the graph of replacing $f(x)$ by $f(x) + k$, $kf(x)$, $f(kx)$, and $f(x + k)$ for specific values of k (both positive and negative) . . .

MP 5

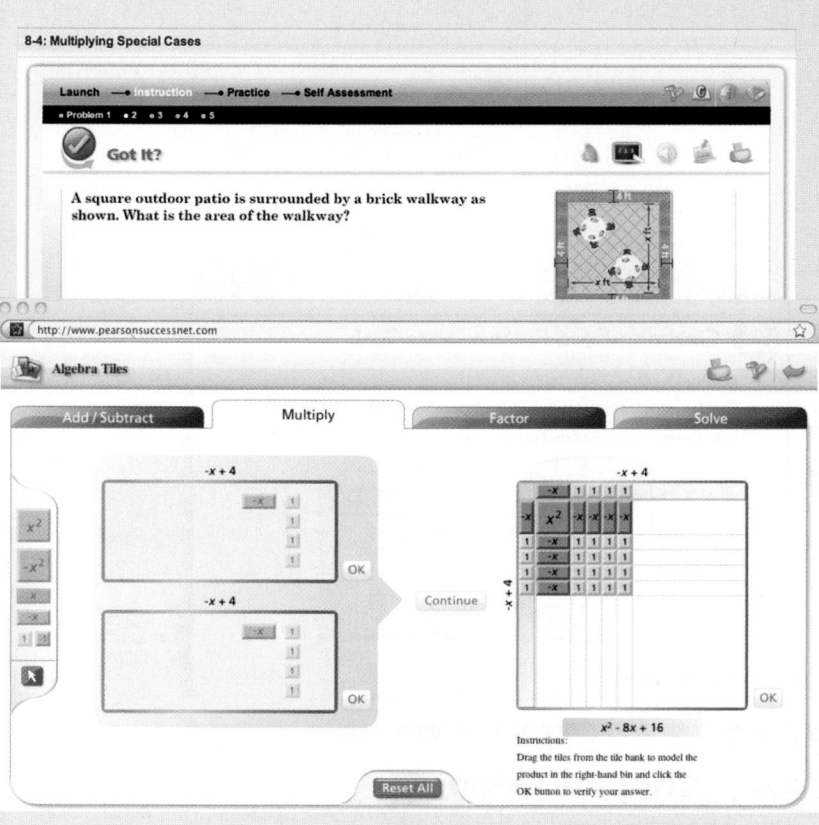

Want to do some more exploring? Try the **Math Tools** at **PowerAlgebra.com**. Click on this icon 🔧 to access these tools: Graphing Utility, Number Line, Algebra Tiles, and 2D and 3D Geometric Constructor. With the Math Tools, you can continue to explore the concepts presented in the lesson.

Try a **Concept Byte!** In a Concept Byte, you might explore technology, do a hands-on activity, or try a challenging extension.

The text in the top right corner of the first page of a lesson or Concept Byte tells you the **Standards for Mathematical Content** and the **Standards for Mathematical Practice** for the lesson.

Solving *Problems*

Pearson Algebra 1 Common Core Edition includes many opportunities to build on and strengthen your problem-solving abilities. In each chapter, you'll work through a multi-part Performance Task.

Hi, I'm Maya. These Common Core Performance Tasks will help you become a proficient problem solver.

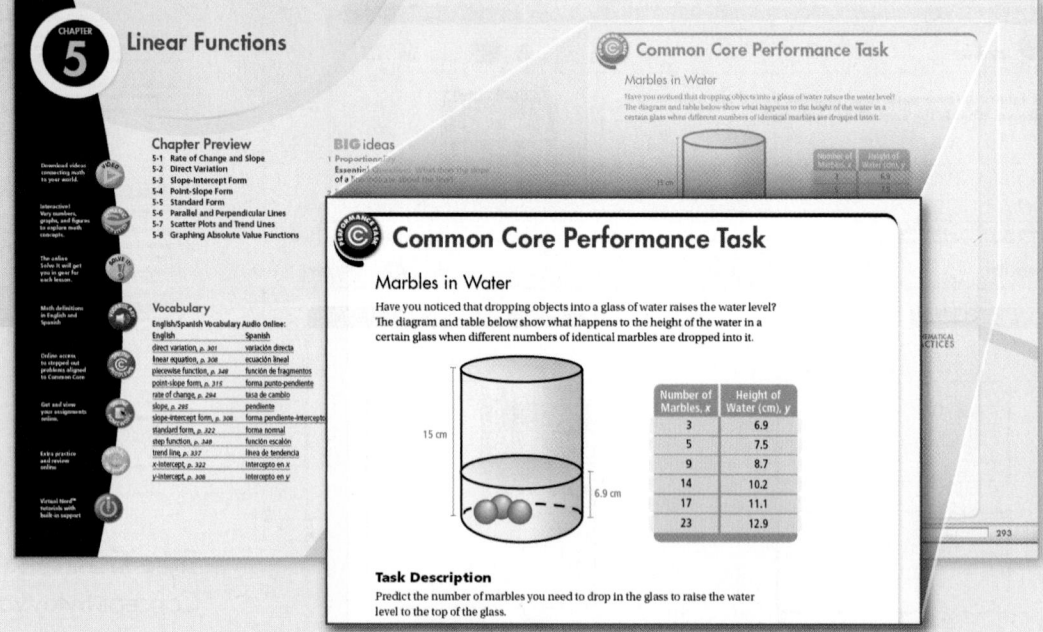

On the **Chapter Opener,** you'll be introduced to the chapter **Performance Task.** You'll start to make sense of the problem and think about solution plans.

Proficient Problem Solvers make sense of problem situations, develop workable solution plans, model the problem situation with mathematics, and communicate their thinking clearly.

Developing Proficiency with Problem Solving

49. Arithmetic Sequences Use the arithmetic sequence 10, 15, 20, 25, . . .
  a. Find the common difference of the sequence.
  b. Let $x =$ the term number, and let $y =$ the corresponding term of the sequence. Graph the ordered pairs (x, y) for the first eight terms of the sequence. Draw a line through the points.
  c. Reasoning How is the slope of a line from part (b) related to the common difference of the sequence?

Challenge Do the points in each set lie on the same line? Explain your answer.

50. $A(1, 3), B(4, 2), C(-2, 4)$ **51.** $G(3, 5), H(-1, 3), I(7, 7)$ **52.** $D(-2, 3), E(0, -1), F(2, 1)$

53. $P(4, 2), Q(-3, 2), R(2, 5)$ **54.** $G(1, -2), H(-1, -5), I(5, 4)$ **55.** $S(-3, 4), T(0, 2), X(-3, 0)$

Find the slope of the line that passes through each pair of points.

56. $(a, -b), (-a, -b)$ **57.** $(-m, n), (3m, -n)$ **58.** $(2a, b), (c, 2d)$

Apply What You've Learned

Apply What You've Learned

MATHEMATICAL PRACTICES
MP 1

The table at the right shows the height of water in a glass when different numbers of marbles are dropped into it.

  a. Find the rate of change in the water height with respect to the number of marbles from one row in the table to the next. What do you notice?

  b. For each marble you add to the glass, how much does the water level rise?

  c. What can you conclude about the type of function that models the relationship between the number of marbles and the water height? Explain.

Number of Marbles, x	Height of Water (cm), y
3	6.9
5	7.5
9	8.7
14	10.2
17	11.1
23	12.9

300 Chapter 5 Linear Functions

---

5 *Pull It* **All Together**

Completing the Performance Task

Look back at your results from the Apply What You've Learned sections in Lessons 5-1 and 5-4. Use the work you did to complete the following.

1. Solve the problem in the Task Description on page 293 by predicting the number of marbles you need to drop in the glass to raise the water level to the top of the glass.

Completing the Performance Task

Look back at your results from the Apply What You've Learned sections in Lessons 5-1 and 5-4. Use the work you did to complete the following.

  1. Solve the problem in the Task Description on page 293 by predicting the number of marbles you need to drop in the glass to raise the water level to the top of the glass. Show all your work and explain each step of your solution.

  2. Reflect Choose one of the Mathematical Practices below and explain how you applied it in your work on the Performance Task.
    MP 1: Make sense of problems and persevere in solving them.
    MP 2: Reason abstractly and quantitatively.
    MP 4: Model with mathematics.

  a. Predict the number of pieces of gravel Maria needs to drop in the glass to raise the water level to the top of the glass. Justify your prediction.

  b. Do you think your prediction from part (a) will be more or less accurate than the prediction your made when marbles were being dropped into a glass? Explain.

352 Chapter 5 Pull It All Together

Throughout the chapter, you will **Apply What You've Learned** to solve problems that relate to the Performance Task. You'll be asked to reason quantitatively and model with mathematics.

In the **Pull It All Together** at the end of the chapter, you will use the concepts and skills presented throughout the chapter to solve the Performance Task. Then you'll have another Task to solve **On Your Own.**

Thinking *Mathematically*

Mathematical reasoning is the key to making sense of math and solving problems. Throughout the program you'll learn strategies to develop mathematical reasoning habits.

Hello, I'm Tyler. These plan boxes will help me figure out where to start.

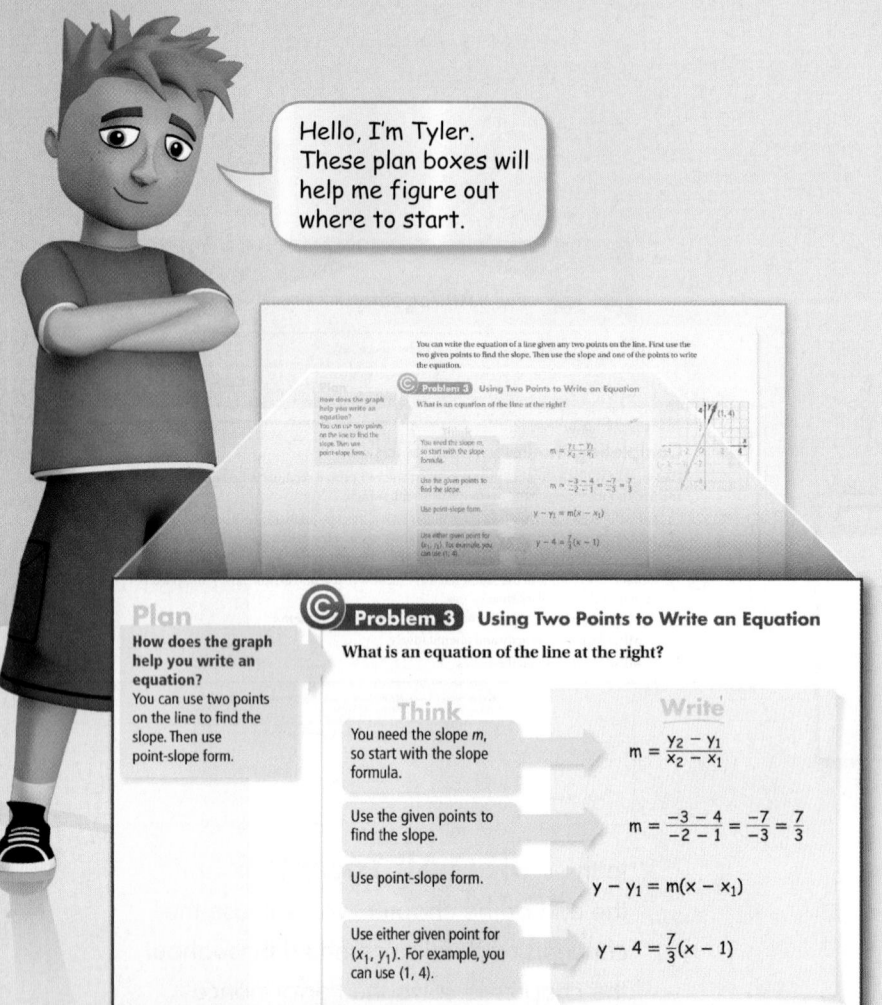

Plan

How does the graph help you write an equation?
You can use two points on the line to find the slope. Then use point-slope form.

© Problem 3   Using Two Points to Write an Equation

What is an equation of the line at the right?

Think	Write
You need the slope m, so start with the slope formula.	$m = \dfrac{y_2 - y_1}{x_2 - x_1}$
Use the given points to find the slope.	$m = \dfrac{-3 - 4}{-2 - 1} = \dfrac{-7}{-3} = \dfrac{7}{3}$
Use point-slope form.	$y - y_1 = m(x - x_1)$
Use either given point for (x_1, y_1). For example, you can use $(1, 4)$.	$y - 4 = \dfrac{7}{3}(x - 1)$

The worked-out problems include call-outs that reveal the strategies and reasoning behind the solution. Look for the boxes labeled **Plan** and **Think.**

The **Think-Write** problems model the thinking behind each step of a solution.

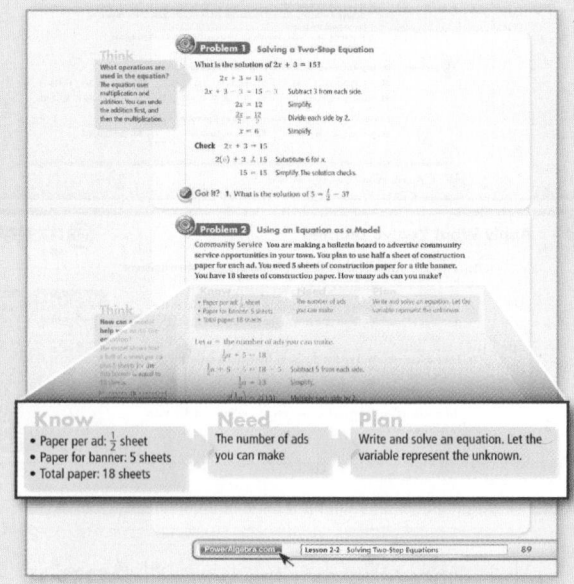

Know

- Paper per ad: $\frac{1}{2}$ sheet
- Paper for banner: 5 sheets
- Total paper: 18 sheets

Need

The number of ads you can make

Plan

Write and solve an equation. Let the variable represent the unknown.

Other worked-out problems model a problem-solving plan that includes the steps of stating what you **Know,** identifying what you **Need,** and developing a **Plan.**

The **Standards for Mathematical Practice** emphasize sense-making, reasoning, and critical reasoning. Many features in *Pearson Algebra 1* provide opportunities for you to develop these skills and dispositions.

Standards for Mathematical Practice

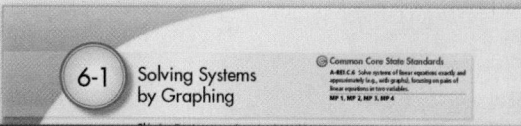

Essential Understanding You can use systems of linear equations to model problems. Systems of equations can be solved in more than one way. One method is to graph each equation and find the intersection point, if one exists.

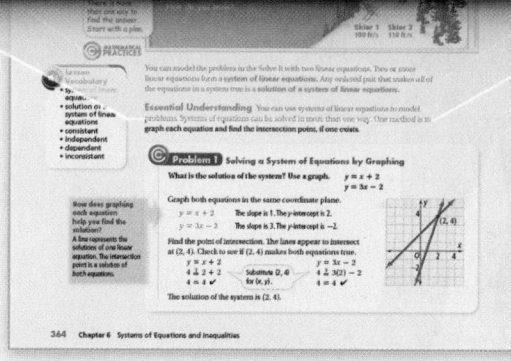

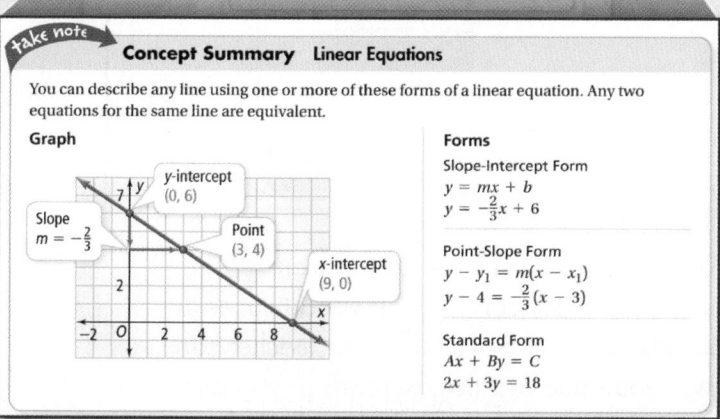

take note

Concept Summary   Linear Equations

You can describe any line using one or more of these forms of a linear equation. Any two equations for the same line are equivalent.

Graph

Slope $m = -\frac{2}{3}$

y-intercept (0, 6)

Point (3, 4)

x-intercept (9, 0)

Forms

Slope-Intercept Form
$y = mx + b$
$y = -\frac{2}{3}x + 6$

Point-Slope Form
$y - y_1 = m(x - x_1)$
$y - 4 = -\frac{2}{3}(x - 3)$

Standard Form
$Ax + By = C$
$2x + 3y = 18$

A **Take Note** box highlights key concepts in a lesson. You can use these boxes to review concepts throughout the year.

Part of thinking mathematically is making sense of the concepts that are being presented. The **Essential Understandings** help you build a framework for the Big Ideas.

Practice *Makes Perfect*

Ask any professional and you'll be told that the one requirement for becoming an expert is practice, practice, practice. *Pearson Algebra 1 Common Core Edition* offers rich and varied exercises to help you become proficient with the mathematics.

Hello, I'm Anya. I can leave my book at school and still get my homework done. All of the lessons are at PowerAlgebra.com

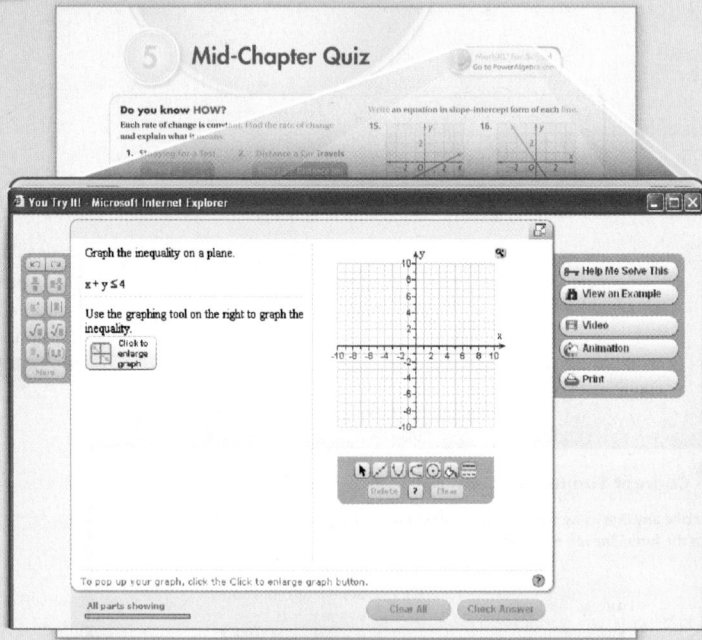

Want more practice? Look for this icon in your book. Check out all of the opportunities in **MathXL® for School.** Your teacher can assign you some practice exercises or you can choose some on your own. And you'll know right away if you got the right answer!

Acing *the Test*

Doing well on tests, whether they are chapter tests or state assessments, depends on a deep understanding of math concepts, fluency with calculations and computations, and strong problem-solving abilities.

Assessing the Common Core State Standards

All of these opportunities for practice help you prepare for assessments throughout the year including the assessments to measure your proficiency with the Common Core State Standards.

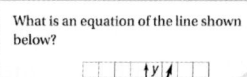

Quick Review

A function represents a **direct variation** if it has the form $y = kx$, where $k \neq 0$. The coefficient k is the **constant of variation.**

Example

Suppose y varies directly with x, and $y = 15$ when $x = 5$. Write a direct variation equation that relates x and y. What is the value of y when $x = 9$?

$y = kx$	Start with the general form of a direct variation.
$15 = k(5)$	Substitute 5 for x and 15 for y.
$3 = k$	Divide each side by 5 to solve for k.
$y = 3x$	Write an equation. Substitute 3 for k in $y = kx$.

The equation $y = 3x$ relates x and y. When $x = 9$, $y = 3(9)$, or 27.

Exercises

Suppose y varies directly with x. Write a direct variation equation that relates x and y. Then find the value of y when $x = 7$.

12. $y = 8$ when $x = -4$.   **13.** $y = 15$ when $x = 6$.

14. $y = 3$ when $x = 9$.   **15.** $y = -4$ when $x = 4$.

For the data in each table, tell whether y varies directly with x. If it does, write an equation for the direct variation.

16.

x	y
−1	−6
2	3
5	12
9	24

17.

x	y
−3	7.5
−1	2.5
2	−5
5	−12.5

At the end of the chapter, you'll find a **Quick Review** of the concepts in the chapter and a few examples and exercises so you can check your skill at solving problems related to the concepts.

In the Cumulative Standards Review at the end of the chapter, you'll also find **Tips for Success,** reminders to help with problem solving. We include problems of all different formats and types so you can feel comfortable with any test item on your state assessment.

Standards *for Mathematical Practice*

The **Common Core State Standards** are made of two separate, but equally important sets of standards:

- **Standards** *for Mathematical Content*
- **Standards** *for Mathematical Practice*

The **Math Content Standards** are grade-specific, while the **Math Practices Standards** are the same from Kindergarten through High School. The **Math Practices** describe qualities and habits of mind that strong mathematical thinkers exhibit.

The eight **Standards for Mathematical Practice,** numbered 1 through 8, can be put into the four groups shown on this page and the next. Included with the statement of each standard is a description of what the Math Practice means for you.

Making Sense of and Solving Problems

1. Make sense of problems and persevere in solving them.

When you make sense of problems, you can explain the meaning of the problem, and you are able to find an entry point to its solution and plan a solution pathway. You can look at a problem and analyze givens, constraints, relationships, and goals. You can think of similar problems or can break the problem into easier-to-solve problems. You are able to track your progress as you work through the solution and check your answer using a different method. As you work through your solution, you frequently check whether the results you are getting make sense.

6. Attend to precision.

You attend to precision when you communicate clearly and precisely the approach you used to solve a problem, and you also understand the approaches that your classmates used. You identify the meaning of symbols that you use, you specify units of measure, and you include labels on the axes of graphs. Your answers are expressed with the appropriate degree of accuracy. You are able to give clear, concise definitions of math terms.

Reasoning and Communicating

2. Reason abstractly and quantitatively.

As a strong math thinker and problem solver, you are able to make sense of quantities in problem situations. You can both represent a problem situation using symbols or equations and explain what the symbols or equations represent in relationship to the problem situation. As you represent a situation symbolically or mathematically, you can explain the meaning of the quantities.

3. Construct viable arguments and critique the reasoning of others.

You are able to communicate clearly and convincingly about your solutions to problems. You can build sound mathematical arguments, drawing on definitions, assumptions, or established solutions. You can develop and explore conjectures about mathematical situations. You make use of examples and counterexamples to support your arguments and justify your conclusions. You respond clearly and logically to the positions and conclusions of your classmates, and are able to compare two arguments, identifying any flaws in logic or reasoning that the arguments may contain. You can ask useful questions to clarify or improve the argument of a classmate.

Representing and Connecting

4. Model with mathematics.

As a strong math thinker, you are able to use mathematics to represent a problem situation and can make connections between a real-world problem situation and mathematics. You see the applicability of mathematics to everyday problems. You can explain how geometry can be used to solve a carpentry problem or algebra to solve a proportional relationship problem. You can define and map relationships among quantities in a problem, using appropriate tools to do so. You are able to analyze the relationships and draw conclusions.

5. Use appropriate tools strategically.

As you develop models to match a given problem situation, you are able to strategize about which tools would be most helpful to use to solve the problem. You consider all tools, from paper and pencil to protractors and rulers, to calculators and software applications. You can articulate the appropriateness of different tools and recognize which would best serve your needs for a given problem. You are especially insightful about technology tools and use them in ways that deepen or extend your understanding of concepts. You also make use of mental tools, such as estimation, to determine the reasonableness of a solution.

Seeing Structure and Generalizing

7. Look for and make use of structure.

You are able to go beyond simply solving problems, to see the structure of the mathematics in these problems, and to generalize mathematical principles from this structure. You are able to see complicated expressions or equations as single objects, or a being composed of many parts.

8. Look for and express regularity in repeated reasoning.

You notice when calculations are repeated and can uncover both general methods and shortcuts for solving similar problems. You continually evaluate the reasonableness of your solutions as you solve problems arising in daily life.

Standards *for Mathematical Content*
Algebra 1

Number and Quantity

The Real Number System

Extend the properties of exponents to rational exponents

N-RN.A.1*   Explain how the definition of the meaning of rational exponents follows from extending the properties of integer exponents to those values, allowing for a notation for radicals in terms of rational exponents.

N-RN.A.2*   Rewrite expressions involving radicals and rational exponents using the properties of exponents.

Use properties of rational and irrational numbers

N-RN.B.3   Explain why the sum or product of two rational numbers is rational; that the sum of a rational number and an irrational number is irrational; and that the product of a nonzero rational number and an irrational number is irrational.

Quantities

Reason quantitatively and use units to solve problems

N-Q.A.1   Use units as a way to understand problems and to guide the solution of multi-step problems; choose and interpret units consistently in formulas; choose and interpret the scale and the origin in graphs and data displays.

N-Q.A.2   Define appropriate quantities for the purpose of descriptive modeling.

N-Q.A.3   Choose a level of accuracy appropriate to limitations on measurement when reporting quantities.

Algebra

Seeing Structure in Expressions

Interpret the structure of expressions

A-SSE.A.1   Interpret expressions that represent a quantity in terms of its context.

A-SSE.A.1a   Interpret parts of an expression, such as terms, factors, and coefficients.

A-SSE.A.1b   Interpret complicated expressions by viewing one or more of their parts as a single entity.

A-SSE.A.2   Use the structure of an expression to identify ways to rewrite it.

Write expressions in equivalent forms to solve problems

A-SSE.B.3   Choose and produce an equivalent form of an expression to reveal and explain properties of the quantity represented by the expression.

A-SSE.B.3a   Factor a quadratic expression to reveal the zeros of the function it defines.

A-SSE.B.3b   Complete the square in a quadratic expression to reveal the maximum or minimum value of the function it defines.

A-SSE.B.3c   Use the properties of exponents to transform expressions for exponential functions.

Arithmetic with Polynomials and Rational Expressions

Perform arithmetic operations on polynomials

A-APR.A.1   Understand that polynomials form a system analogous to the integers, namely, they are closed under the operations of addition, subtraction, and multiplication; add, subtract, and multiply polynomials.

Understand the relationship between zeros and factors of polynomials

A-APR.B.3   Identify zeros of polynomials when suitable factorizations are available, and use the zeros to construct a rough graph of the function defined by the polynomial.

Rewrite rational expressions

A-APR.D.6*   Rewrite simple rational expressions in different forms; write $a(x)/b(x)$ in the form $q(x) + r(x)/b(x)$, where $a(x)$, $b(x)$, $q(x)$, and $r(x)$ are polynomials with the degree of $r(x)$ less than the degree of $b(x)$, using inspection, long division, or, for the more complicated examples, a computer algebra system.

A-APR.D.7*   (+) Understand that rational expressions form a system analogous to the rational numbers, closed under addition, subtraction, multiplication, and division by a nonzero rational expression; add, subtract, multiply, and divide rational expressions.

---

* These standards are not part of the PARCC Model Curriculum Framework for Algebra 1.

Creating Equations

Create equations that describe numbers or relationships

A-CED.A.1   Create equations and inequalities in one variable and use them to solve problems. *Include equations arising from linear and quadratic functions, and simple rational and exponential functions.*

A-CED.A.2   Create equations in two or more variables to represent relationships between quantities; graph equations on coordinate axes with labels and scales.

A-CED.A.3   Represent constraints by equations or inequalities, and by systems of equations and/or inequalities, and interpret solutions as viable or nonviable options in a modeling context.

A-CED.A.4   Rearrange formulas to highlight a quantity of interest, using the same reasoning as in solving equations.

Reasoning with Equations and Inequalities

Understand solving equations as a process of reasoning and explain the reasoning

A-REI.A.1   Explain each step in solving a simple equation as following from the equality of numbers asserted at the previous step, starting from the assumption that the original equation has a solution. Construct a viable argument to justify a solution method.

A-REI.A.2*   Solve simple rational and radical equations in one variable, and give examples showing how extraneous solutions may arise.

Solve equations and inequalities in one variable

A-REI.B.3   Solve linear equations and inequalities in one variable, including equations with coefficients represented by letters.

A-REI.B.4   Solve quadratic equations in one variable.

A.REI.B.4a   Use the method of completing the square to transform any quadratic equation in x into an equation of the form $(x - p)^2 = q$ that has the same solutions. Derive the quadratic formula from this form.

A.REI.B.4b   Solve quadratic equations by inspection (e.g., for $x^2 = 49$), taking square roots, completing the square, the quadratic formula and factoring, as appropriate to the initial form of the equation. Recognize when the quadratic formula gives complex solutions and write them as $a \pm bi$ for real numbers a and b.

Solve systems of equations

A-REI.C.5   Prove that, given a system of two equations in two variables, replacing one equation by the sum of that equation and a multiple of the other produces a system with the same solutions.

A-REI.C.6   Solve systems of linear equations exactly and approximately (e.g., with graphs), focusing on pairs of linear equations in two variables.

A-REI.C.7*   Solve a simple system consisting of a linear equation and a quadratic equation in two variables algebraically and graphically.

Represent and solve equations and inequalities graphically

A-REI.D.10   Understand that the graph of an equation in two variables is the set of all its solutions plotted in the coordinate plane, often forming a curve (which could be a line).

A-REI.D.11   Explain why the x-coordinates of the points where the graphs of the equations $y = f(x)$ and $y = g(x)$ intersect are the solutions of the equation $f(x) = g(x)$; find the solutions approximately, e.g., using technology to graph the functions, make tables of values, or find successive approximations. Include cases where $f(x)$ and/or $g(x)$ are linear, polynomial, rational, absolute value, exponential, and logarithmic functions.

A-REI.D.12   Graph the solutions to a linear inequality in two variables as a half-plane (excluding the boundary in the case of a strict inequality), and graph the solution set to a system of linear inequalities in two variables as the intersection of the corresponding half-planes.

Functions

Interpreting Functions

Understand the concept of a function and use function notation

F-IF.A.1   Understand that a function from one set (called the domain) to another set (called the range) assigns to each element of the domain exactly one element of the range. If f is a function and x is an element of its domain, then $f(x)$ denotes the output of f corresponding to the input x. The graph of f is the graph of the equation $y = f(x)$.

F-IF.A.2   Use function notation, evaluate functions for inputs in their domains, and interpret statements that use function notation in terms of a context.

F-IF.A.3   Recognize that sequences are functions, sometimes defined recursively, whose domain is a subset of the integers.

Interpret functions that arise in applications in terms of the context

F-IF.B.4 For a function that models a relationship between two quantities, interpret key features of graphs and tables in terms of the quantities, and sketch graphs showing key features given a verbal description of the relationship. *Key features include: intercepts; intervals where the function is increasing, decreasing, positive, or negative; relative maximums and minimums; symmetries; end behavior; and periodicity.*

F-IF.B.5 Relate the domain of a function to its graph and, where applicable, to the quantitative relationship it describes.

F-IF.B.6 Calculate and interpret the average rate of change of a function (presented symbolically or as a table) over a specified interval. Estimate the rate of change from a graph.

Analyze functions using different representations

F-IF.C.7 Graph functions expressed symbolically and show key features of the graph, by hand in simple cases and using technology for more complicated cases.

F-IF.C.7a Graph linear and quadratic functions and show intercepts, maxima, and minima.

F-IF.C.7b Graph square root, cube root, and piecewise-defined functions, including step functions and absolute value functions.

F-IF.C.7e* Graph exponential and logarithmic functions, showing intercepts and end behavior, and trigonometric functions, showing period, midline, and amplitude.

F-IF.C.8 Write a function defined by an expression in different but equivalent forms to reveal and explain different properties of the function.

F-IF.C.8a Use the process of factoring and completing the square in a quadratic function to show zeros, extreme values, and symmetry of the graph, and interpret these in terms of a context.

F-IF.C.8b* Use the properties of exponents to interpret expressions for exponential functions.

F-IF.C.9 Compare properties of two functions each represented in a different way (algebraically, graphically, numerically in tables, or by verbal descriptions).

Building Functions

Build a function that models a relationship between two quantities

F-BF.A.1 Write a function that describes a relationship between two quantities.

F-BF.A.1a Determine an explicit expression, a recursive process, or steps for calculation from a context.

F-BF.A.1b* Combine standard function types using arithmetic operations.

F-BF.A.2* Write arithmetic and geometric sequences both recursively and with an explicit formula, use them to model situations, and translate between the two forms.

Build new functions from existing functions

F-BF.B.3 Identify the effect on the graph of replacing $f(x)$ by $f(x) + k$, $k\,f(x)$, $f(kx)$, and $f(x + k)$ for specific values of k (both positive and negative); find the value of k given the graphs. Experiment with cases and illustrate an explanation of the effects on the graph using technology. *Include recognizing even and odd functions from their graphs and algebraic expressions for them.*

F-BF.B.4* Find inverse functions.

F-BF.B.4a* Solve an equation of the form $f(x) = c$ for a simple function f that has an inverse and write an expression for the inverse.

Linear, Quadratic, and Exponential Models

Construct and compare linear, quadratic, and exponential models and solve problems.

F-LE.A.1 Distinguish between situations that can be modeled with linear functions and with exponential functions.

F-LE.A.1a Prove that linear functions grow by equal differences over equal intervals, and that exponential functions grow by equal factors over equal intervals.

F-LE.A.1b Recognize situations in which one quantity changes at a constant rate per unit interval relative to another.

F-LE.A.1c Recognize situations in which a quantity grows or decays by a constant percent rate per unit interval relative to another.

F-LE.A.2 Construct linear and exponential functions, including arithmetic and geometric sequences, given a graph, a description of a relationship, or two input-output pairs (include reading these from a table).

F-LE.A.3 Observe using graphs and tables that a quantity increasing exponentially eventually exceeds a quantity increasing linearly, quadratically, or (more generally) as a polynomial function.

Interpret expressions for functions in terms of the situation they model

F-LE.B.5 Interpret the parameters in a linear or exponential function in terms of a context.

Look at the domain titles and cluster descriptions in bold to get a good idea of the topics you'll study this year.

Statistics and Probability

Interpreting Categorical and Quantitative Data

Summarize, represent, and interpret data on a single count or measurement variable

S-ID.A.1   Represent data with plots on the real number line (dot plots, histograms, and box plots).

S-ID.A.2   Use statistics appropriate to the shape of the data distribution to compare center (median, mean) and spread (interquartile range, standard deviation) of two or more different data sets.

S-ID.A.3   Interpret differences in shape, center, and spread in the context of the data sets, accounting for possible effects of extreme data points (outliers).

S-ID.A.4*   Use the mean and standard deviation of a data set to fit it to a normal distribution and to estimate population percentages. Recognize that there are data sets for which such a procedure is not appropriate. Use calculators, spreadsheets, and tables to estimate areas under the normal curve.

Summarize, represent, and interpret data on two categorical and quantitative variables

S-ID.B.5   Summarize categorical data for two categories in two-way frequency tables. Interpret relative frequencies in the context of the data (including joint, marginal, and conditional relative frequencies). Recognize possible associations and trends in the data.

S-ID.B.6   Represent data on two quantitative variables on a scatter plot, and describe how the variables are related.

S-ID.B.6a   Fit a function to the data; use functions fitted to data to solve problems in the context of the data. *Use given functions or choose a function suggested by the context. Emphasize linear, quadratic, and exponential models.*

S-ID.B.6b   Informally assess the fit of a function by plotting and analyzing residuals.

S-ID.B.6c   Fit a linear function for a scatter plot that suggests a linear association.

Interpret linear models

S-ID.C.7   Interpret the slope (rate of change) and the intercept (constant term) of a linear model in the context of the data.

S-ID.C.8   Compute (using technology) and interpret the correlation coefficient of a linear fit.

S-ID.C.9   Disinguish between correlation and causation.

Making Inferences and Justifying Conclusions

Make inferences and justify conclusions from sample surveys, experiments, and observational studies

S-IC.B.3*   Recognize the purposes of and differences among sample surveys, experiments, and observational studies; explain how randomization relates to each.

S-IC.B.5*   Use data from a randomized experiment to compare two treatments; use simulations to decide if differences between parameters are significant.

Conditional Probability and the Rules of Probability

Understand independence and conditional probability and use them to interpret data

S-CP.A.1*   Describe events as subsets of a sample space (the set of outcomes) using characteristics (or categories) of the outcomes, or as unions, intersections, or complements of other events ("or," "and," "not").

S-CP.A.4*   Construct and interpret two-way frequency tables of data when two categories are associated with each object being classified. Use the two-way table as a sample space to decide if events are independent and to approximate conditional probabilities.

Use the rules of probability to compute probabilities of compound events in a uniform probability model

S-CP.B.7*   Apply the Addition Rule, $P(A \text{ or } B) = P(A) + P(B) - P(A \text{ and } B)$, and interpret the answer in terms of the model.

S-CP.B.8*   (+) Apply the general Multiplication Rule in a uniform probability model, $P(A \text{ and } B) = P(A)P(B \mid A) = P(B)P(A \mid B)$, and interpret the answer in terms of the model.

BIGideas

These Big Ideas are the organizing ideas for the study of important areas of mathematics: algebra, geometry, and statistics.

Stay connected! These Big Ideas will help you understand how the math you study in high school fits together.

Algebra

Properties
- In the transition from arithmetic to algebra, attention shifts from arithmetic operations (addition, subtraction, multiplication, and division) to use of the *properties* of these operations.
- All of the facts of arithmetic and algebra follow from certain properties.

Variable
- Quantities are used to form expressions, equations, and inequalities.
- An expression refers to a quantity but does not make a statement about it. An equation (or an inequality) is a statement about the quantities it mentions.
- Using variables in place of numbers in equations (or inequalities) allows the statement of relationships among numbers that are unknown or unspecified.

Equivalence
- A single quantity may be represented by many different expressions.
- The facts about a quantity may be expressed by many different equations (or inequalities).

Solving Equations & Inequalities
- Solving an equation is the process of rewriting the equation to make what it says about its variable(s) as simple as possible.
- Properties of numbers and equality can be used to transform an equation (or inequality) into equivalent, simpler equations (or inequalities) in order to find solutions.
- Useful information about equations and inequalities (including solutions) can be found by analyzing graphs or tables.
- The numbers and types of solutions vary predictably, based on the type of equation.

Proportionality
- Two quantities are *proportional* if they have the same ratio in each instance where they are measured together.
- Two quantities are *inversely proportional* if they have the same product in each instance where they are measured together.

Function
- A function is a relationship between variables in which each value of the input variable is associated with a unique value of the output variable.
- Functions can be represented in a variety of ways, such as graphs, tables, equations, or words. Each representation is particularly useful in certain situations.
- Some important families of functions are developed through transformations of the simplest form of the function.
- New functions can be made from other functions by applying arithmetic operations or by applying one function to the output of another.

Modeling
- Many real-world mathematical problems can be represented algebraically. These representations can lead to algebraic solutions.
- A function that models a real-world situation can be used to make estimates or predictions about future occurrences.

Statistics and Probability

Data Collection and Analysis

- Sampling techniques are used to gather data from real-world situations. If the data are representative of the larger population, inferences can be made about that population.
- Biased sampling techniques yield data unlikely to be representative of the larger population.
- Sets of numerical data are described using measures of central tendency and dispersion.

Data Representation

- The most appropriate data representations depend on the type of data—quantitative or qualitative, and univariate or bivariate.
- Line plots, box plots, and histograms are different ways to show distribution of data over a possible range of values.

Probability

- Probability expresses the likelihood that a particular event will occur.
- Data can be used to calculate an experimental probability, and mathematical properties can be used to determine a theoretical probability.
- Either experimental or theoretical probability can be used to make predictions or decisions about future events.
- Various counting methods can be used to develop theoretical probabilities.

Geometry

Visualization

- Visualization can help you see the relationships between two figures and help you connect properties of real objects with two-dimensional drawings of these objects.

Transformations

- Transformations are mathematical functions that model relationships with figures.
- Transformations may be described geometrically or by coordinates.
- Symmetries of figures may be defined and classified by transformations.

Measurement

- Some attributes of geometric figures, such as length, area, volume, and angle measure, are measurable. Units are used to describe these attributes.

Reasoning & Proof

- Definitions establish meanings and remove possible misunderstanding.
- Other truths are more complex and difficult to see. It is often possible to verify complex truths by reasoning from simpler ones using deductive reasoning.

Similarity

- Two geometric figures are similar when corresponding lengths are proportional and corresponding angles are congruent.
- Areas of similar figures are proportional to the squares of their corresponding lengths.
- Volumes of similar figures are proportional to the cubes of their corresponding lengths.

Coordinate Geometry

- A coordinate system on a line is a number line on which points are labeled, corresponding to the real numbers.
- A coordinate system in a plane is formed by two perpendicular number lines, called the x- and y-axes, and the quadrants they form. The coordinate plane can be used to graph many functions.
- It is possible to verify some complex truths using deductive reasoning in combination with the distance, midpoint, and slope formulas.

Foundations for Algebra

Chapters 1 & 2

Number and Quantity
The Real Number System
  Use properties of rational and irrational numbers
Quantities
  Reason quantitatively and use units to solve problems

Algebra
Seeing Structure in Expressions
  Interpret the structure of expressions
Creating Equations
  Create equations that describe numbers or relationships
Reasoning with Equations and Inequalities
  Understand solving equations as a process of reasoning and
  explain the reasoning
  Solve equations and inequalities in one variable
  Represent and solve equations and inequalities graphically

2

Solving Equations

Visual See It!

Reasoning Try It!

Practice Do It!

3

Solving Inequalities

Chapters 3 & 4

Number and Quantity
Quantities
   Reason quantitatively and use units to solve problems
Algebra
Creating Equations
   Create equations that describe numbers or relationships
Reasoning with Equations and Inequalities
   Represent and solve equations and inequalities graphically

Functions
Interpreting Functions
   Understand the concept of a function and use function notation
   Interpret functions that arise in applications in terms of the context
Building Functions
   Build a function that models a relationship between two quantities
Linear and Exponential Models
   Construct and compare linear and exponential models and solve problems

4 An Introduction to Functions

Visual See It!

Reasoning Try It!

Practice Do It!

5

Linear Functions

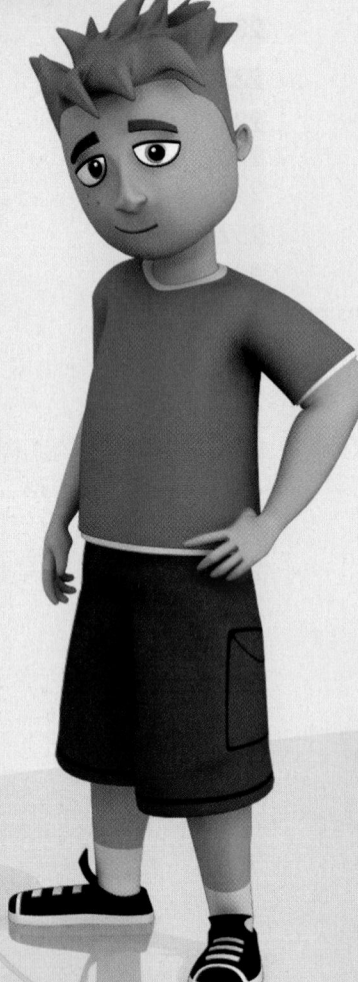

Chapters 5 & 6

Number and Quantity
Quantities
 Reason quantitatively and use units to solve problems
Algebra
Seeing Structure in Expressions
 Interpret the structure of expressions
Creating Equations
 Create equations that describe numbers or relationships
Reasoning with Equations and Inequalities
 Solve systems of equations

Functions
Interpreting Functions
 Analyze functions using different representations
Building Functions
 Build a function that models a relationship between two quantities
 Build new functions from existing functions
Linear and Exponential Models
 Construct and compare linear and exponential models and solve problems
 Interpret expressions for functions in terms of the situation they model

6

Systems of Equations and Inequalities

Visual **See It!**

Reasoning **Try It!**

Practice **Do It!**

7

Exponents and Exponential Functions

Number and Quantity

The Real Number System

    Extend the properties of exponents to rational exponents

Algebra

Seeing Structure in Expressions

    Interpret the structure of expressions

Arithmetic with Polynomials and Rational Expressions

    Perform arithmetic operations on polynomials

Creating Equations

    Create equations that describe numbers or relationships

Functions

Interpreting Functions

    Interpret functions that arise in applications in terms of the context

    Analyze functions using different representations

Building Functions

    Build a function that models a relationship between two quantities

Linear and Exponential Models

    Construct and compare linear and exponential models and solve problems

8

Polynomials and Factoring

Visual See It!

Reasoning Try It!

Practice Do It!

9 Quadratic Functions and Equations

Chapters 9 & 10

Number and Quantity
Quantities
Reason quantitatively and use units to solve problems
Algebra
Creating Equations
Create equations that describe numbers or relationships
Reasoning with Equations and Inequalities
Understand solving equations as a process of reasoning and explain the reasoning
Solve equations and inequalities in one variable

Functions
Interpreting Functions
Interpret functions that arise in applications in terms of the context
Analyze functions using different representations
Linear and Exponential Models
Construct and compare linear and exponential models and solve problems
Statistics and Probability
Interpreting Categorical and Quantitative Data
Summarize, represent, and interpret data on two categorical and quantitative variables

10 Radical Expressions and Equations

Visual See It!

Reasoning Try It!

Practice Do It!

11

Rational Expressions and Functions

Chapters 11 & 12

Number and Quantity
Quantities
   Reason quantitatively and use units to solve problems
Algebra
Creating Equations
   Create equations that describe numbers or relationships
Arithmetic with Polynomials and Rational Expressions
   Rewrite rational expressions

Functions
Interpreting Functions
   Interpret functions that arise in applications in terms of the context
Statistics and Probability
Interpreting Categorical and Quantitative Data
   Summarize, represent, and interpret data on a single count or
   measurement variable

12

Data Analysis and Probability

Visual See It!

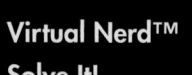

Reasoning Try It!

Practice Do It!

Entry-Level Assessment

Multiple Choice

Read each question. Then write the letter of the correct answer on your paper.

1. Sophia had $50 she put into a savings account. If she saves $15 per week for one year, how much will she have saved altogether?

- (A) $50
- (B) $65
- (C) $780
- (D) $830

2. Which set below is the domain of $\{(2, -3), (-1, 0), (0, 4), (-1, 5), (4, -2)\}$?

- (F) $\{-3, 0, 4, 5, -2\}$
- (G) $\{-3, 4, 5, -2\}$
- (H) $\{2, -1, 4\}$
- (I) $\{2, -1, 0, 4\}$

3. Which ordered pair is the solution of the system of equations graphed below?

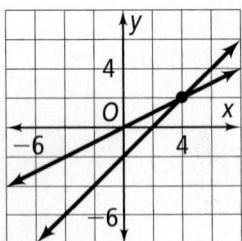

- (A) $(4, 1)$
- (B) $(1, 4)$
- (C) $(4, 2)$
- (D) $(2, 4)$

4. The Martins keep goats and chickens on their farm. If there are 23 animals with a total of 74 legs, how many of each type of animal are there?

- (F) 14 chickens, 9 goats
- (G) 19 chickens, 4 goats
- (H) 9 chickens, 14 goats
- (I) 4 chickens, 19 goats

5. Which equation represents the phrase "six more than twice a number is 72"?

- (A) $6 + x = 72$
- (B) $2x = 6 + 72$
- (C) $2 + 6x = 72$
- (D) $6 + 2x = 72$

6. Which of the following graphs best represents a person walking slowly and then speeding up?

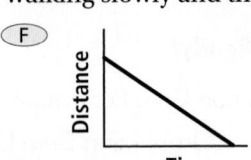
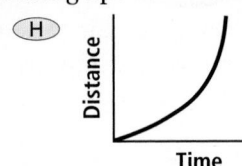
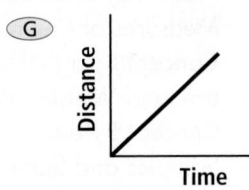

7. The graph below shows the time it takes Sam to get from his car to the mall door.

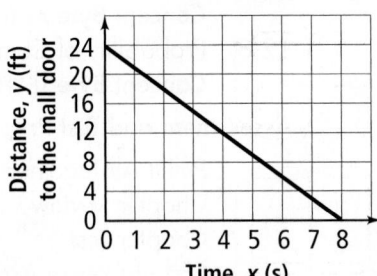

Which of the following best describes the x-intercept?

- (A) Sam's car was parked 24 ft from the mall door.
- (B) After 24 s, Sam reached the mall door.
- (C) Sam's car was parked 8 ft from the mall door.
- (D) After 8 s, Sam reached the mall door.

8. What is 23.7×10^4 written in standard notation?

- (F) 0.00237
- (G) 0.0237
- (H) 237,000
- (I) 2,370,000

9. What equation do you get when you solve $2x + 3y = 12$ for y?

- **A** $y = -\frac{2}{3}x + 4$
- **B** $y = -\frac{2}{3}x + 12$
- **C** $y = -2x + 12$
- **D** $y = 12 - 2x$

10. The formula for the circumference of a circle is $C = 2\pi r$. What is the formula solved for r?

- **F** $r = C \cdot 2\pi$
- **G** $r = \frac{C}{2\pi}$
- **H** $r = 2\pi$
- **I** $r = \frac{C\pi}{2}$

11. Which table of values was used to make the following graph?

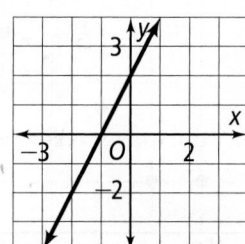

- **A**

x	−3	−1	0	1
y	−2	−1	2	4

- **B**

x	−3	−2	0	1
y	4	2	2	4

- **C**

x	−3	−1	0	1
y	−4	0	2	4

- **D**

x	−3	−2	0	1
y	−3	−2	2	4

12. A jewelry store marks up the price of a topaz ring 215%. The store paid $70 for the ring. For how much is the store selling the ring?

- **F** $91.50
- **G** $150.50
- **H** $161.50
- **I** $220.50

13. What is the solution of $-3p + 4 < 22$?

- **A** $p < -6$
- **B** $p > -6$
- **C** $p < 18$
- **D** $p > 18$

14. Which of the graphs below shows the solution of $-5 + x > 8$?

- **F** (number line, open circle at 3)
- **G** (number line, open circle at 3)
- **H** (number line, open circle at 13)
- **I** (number line, open circle at 11)

15. Between which two whole numbers does $\sqrt{85}$ fall?

- **A** 8 and 9
- **B** 9 and 10
- **C** 41 and 42
- **D** 42 and 43

16. What is the simplified form of $\frac{6 + 3^2}{(2^3)(3)}$?

- **F** $\frac{1}{3}$
- **G** $\frac{1}{2}$
- **H** $\frac{5}{8}$
- **I** $\frac{5}{6}$

17. Which of the following expressions is equivalent to $\frac{4^3}{4^6}$?

- **A** $\frac{1}{4^3}$
- **B** $\frac{1}{4^2}$
- **C** 4^2
- **D** 4^3

18. What is 40,500,000 written in scientific notation?

- **F** 4.05×10^7
- **G** 4.05×10^6
- **H** 4.05×10^{-6}
- **I** 4.05×10^{-7}

19. There are $3\frac{3}{4}$ c of flour, $1\frac{1}{2}$ c of sugar, $\frac{2}{3}$ c of brown sugar, and $\frac{1}{4}$ c of oil in a cake mix. How many cups of ingredients are there in all?

- **A** $4\frac{1}{2}$ c
- **B** $5\frac{1}{6}$ c
- **C** $5\frac{1}{2}$ c
- **D** $6\frac{1}{6}$ c

20. Cathy ran for 30 min at a rate of 5.5 mi/h. Then she ran for 15 min at a rate of 6 mi/h. How many miles did she run in all?

   (F) 2.75 mi   (H) 4.25 mi

   (G) 4.375 mi   (I) 5.75 mi

21. A 6-ft-tall man casts a shadow that is 9 ft long. At the same time, a tree nearby casts a 48 ft shadow. How tall is the tree?

   (A) 32 ft   (C) 45 ft

   (B) 36 ft   (D) 72 ft

22. Triangle *ABC* is similar to triangle *DEF*. What is *x*?

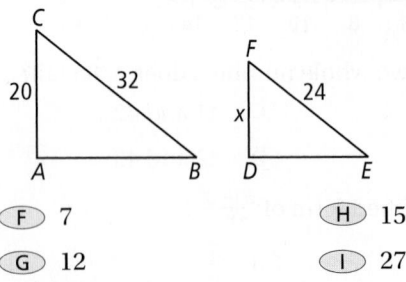

   (F) 7   (H) 15

   (G) 12   (I) 27

23. Which side lengths given below can form a right triangle?

   (A) 12, 13, 17

   (B) 3.2, 5.6, 6.4

   (C) 14, 20, 24

   (D) 10, 24, 26

24. The formula $F = \frac{9}{5}C + 32$ converts temperatures in degrees Celsius *C* to temperatures in degrees Fahrenheit *F*. What is 35°C in degrees Fahrenheit?

   (F) 20°F   (H) 95°F

   (G) 67°F   (I) 120°F

25. A bowling ball is traveling at 15 mi/h when it hits the pins. How fast is the bowling ball traveling in feet per second? (*Hint:* 1 mi = 5280 ft)

   (A) 11 ft/s

   (B) 88 ft/s

   (C) 22 ft/s

   (D) 1320 ft/s

26. What is the median of the tree height data displayed in the box-and-whisker plot below?

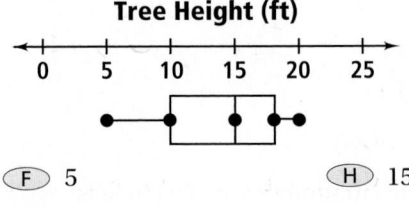

Tree Height (ft)

   (F) 5   (H) 15

   (G) 10   (I) 20

27. Helena tracked the number of hours she spent working on a science experiment each day in the scatter plot below.

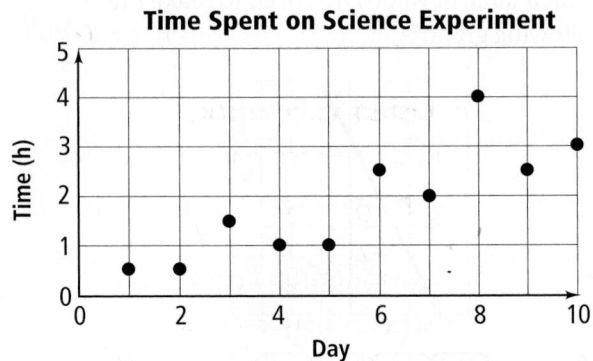

Between which two days was there the greatest increase in the number of hours Helena spent working on her science experiment?

   (A) Day 2 and 3

   (B) Day 7 and 8

   (C) Day 5 and 6

   (D) Day 9 and 10

28. Your grades on four exams are 78, 85, 97, and 92. What grade do you need on the next exam to have an average of 90 on the five exams?

   (F) 71   (H) 98

   (G) 92   (I) 100

29. The numbers of points scored by a basketball team during the first 8 games of the season are shown below.

   65 58 72 74 82 67 75 71

How much will their average game score increase by if the team scores 93 points in the next game?

   (A) 2.5   (C) 11.6

   (B) 10.5   (D) 19.5

Get Ready!

Skills
Handbook,
page 799

◆ Factors

Find the greatest common factor of each set of numbers.

1. 12, 18   **2.** 25, 35   **3.** 13, 20   **4.** 40, 80, 100

Skills
Handbook,
page 799

◆ Least Common Multiple

Find the least common multiple of each set of numbers.

5. 5, 15   **6.** 11, 44   **7.** 8, 9   **8.** 10, 15, 25

Skills
Handbook,
page 800

◆ Using Estimation

Estimate each sum or difference.

9. $956 - 542$ **10.** $1.259 + 5.312 + 1.7$ **11.** $\$14.32 + \$1.65 + \$278.05$

Skills
Handbook,
page 801

◆ Simplifying Fractions

Write in simplest form.

12. $\frac{12}{15}$ **13.** $\frac{20}{28}$ **14.** $\frac{8}{56}$ **15.** $\frac{48}{52}$

Skills
Handbook,
page 802

◆ Fractions and Decimals

Write each fraction as a decimal.

16. $\frac{7}{10}$ **17.** $\frac{3}{5}$ **18.** $\frac{13}{20}$ **19.** $\frac{93}{100}$ **20.** $\frac{7}{15}$

Skills
Handbook,
page 803

◆ Adding and Subtracting Fractions

Find the sum or difference.

21. $\frac{4}{7} + \frac{3}{14}$ **22.** $6\frac{2}{3} + 3\frac{4}{5}$ **23.** $\frac{9}{10} - \frac{4}{5}$ **24.** $8\frac{3}{4} - 4\frac{5}{6}$

 ## Looking Ahead Vocabulary

25. Several expressions may have the same meaning. For actors, the English *expression* "break a leg" means "good luck." In math, what is another *expression* for 5 • 7?

26. A beginning guitarist learns to play using *simplified* guitar music. What does it mean to write a *simplified* math expression as shown at the right?

$$5 \cdot 7 \div 5 = 7$$

27. A study *evaluates* the performance of a hybrid bus to determine its value. What does it mean to *evaluate* an expression in math?

CHAPTER 1

Foundations for Algebra

Chapter Preview

BIG ideas

- **Variable**
  Essential Question How can you represent quantities, patterns, and relationships?

- **Properties**
  Essential Question How are properties related to algebra?

Vocabulary

English/Spanish Vocabulary Audio Online:

English	Spanish
additive inverse, *p. 32*	inverso aditivo
algebraic expression, *p. 4*	expresión algebraica
coefficient, *p. 48*	coeficiente
equivalent expressions, *p. 23*	ecuaciones equivalentes
evaluate, *p. 12*	evaluar
integers, *p. 18*	números enteros
like terms, *p. 48*	términos semejantes
order of operations, *p. 11*	orden de las operaciones
real number, *p. 18*	número real
simplify, *p. 10*	simplificar
term, *p. 48*	término
variable, *p. 4*	variable

 DOMAINS
- Quantities
- Seeing Structure in Expressions

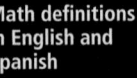
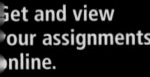
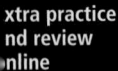
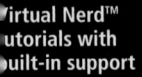

ownload videos
onnecting math
o your world.

teractive!
ary numbers,
aphs, and figures
o explore math
oncepts.

he online
olve It will get
ou in gear for
ach lesson.

Math definitions
n English and
panish

nline access
o stepped-out
roblems aligned
o Common Core

et and view
our assignments
nline.

xtra practice
nd review
nline

irtual Nerd™
utorials with
uilt-in support

Common Core Performance Task

Planning a Walk of Fame

Naomi is designing a walk of fame to honor her school's best athletes. The walkway will consist of a pattern of tiles, as shown in the figures below. There will be two rows of tiles that are inscribed with the names of athletes, and a row of plain tiles in between. In the pattern, n is the number of names on each side of the walk.

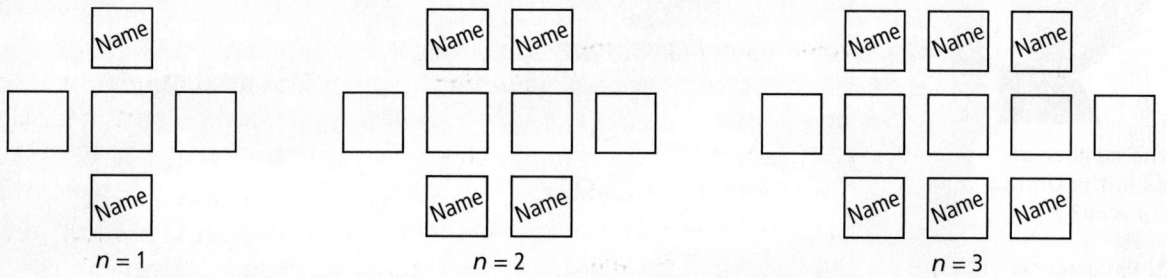

The inscribed tiles cost $15 each, and the plain tiles cost $5 each. Naomi's budget for the tiles is $500.

Task Description

Determine the number of athletes the school will be able to honor on the walk of fame.

Connecting the Task to the Math Practices

MATHEMATICAL PRACTICES

As you complete the task, you'll apply several Standards for Mathematical Practice.

- You'll determine the relationship between the number of names and the number of each type of tile. (MP 7)

- You'll write and simplify expressions using properties of real numbers. (MP 2)

- You'll solve an equation and interpret the solution to determine how many tiles are needed. (MP 4)

1-1 Variables and Expressions

© **Common Core State Standards**
A-SSE.A.1a Interpret parts of an expression, such as terms, factors, and coefficients.
MP 1, MP 3, MP 4, MP 7

Objective To write algebraic expressions

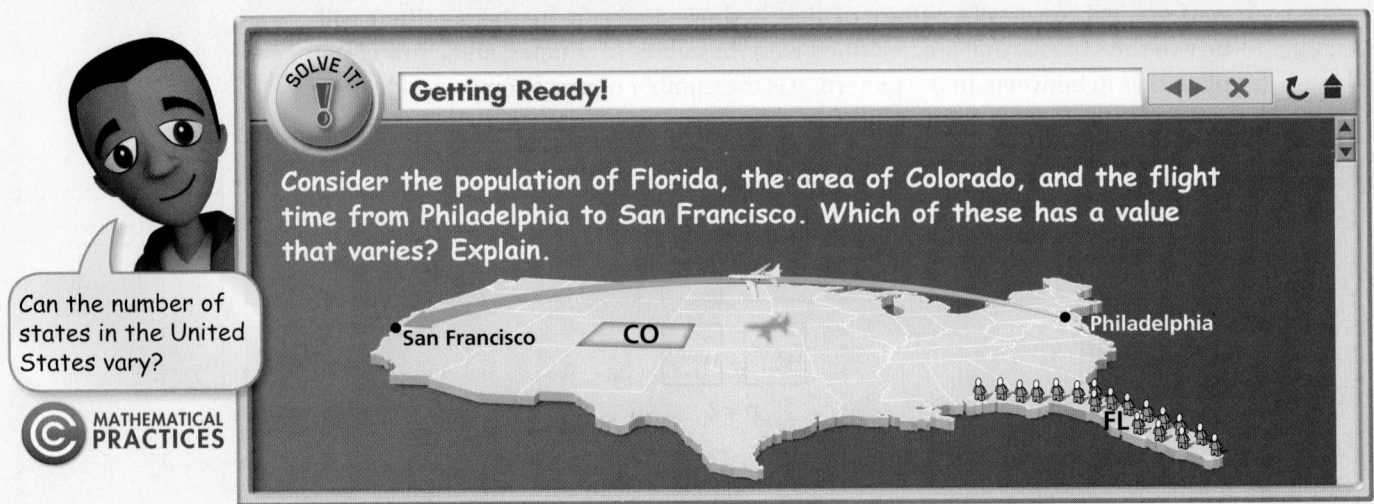

SOLVE IT!

Getting Ready!

Consider the population of Florida, the area of Colorado, and the flight time from Philadelphia to San Francisco. Which of these has a value that varies? Explain.

Can the number of states in the United States vary?

© MATHEMATICAL PRACTICES

A mathematical **quantity** is anything that can be measured or counted. Some quantities remain constant. Others change, or vary, and are called *variable quantities*.

Essential Understanding Algebra uses symbols to represent quantities that are unknown or that vary. You can represent mathematical phrases and real-world relationships using symbols and operations.

A **variable** is a symbol, usually a letter, that represents the value(s) of a variable quantity. An **algebraic expression** is a mathematical phrase that includes one or more variables. A **numerical expression** is a mathematical phrase involving numbers and operation symbols, but no variables.

Lesson Vocabulary
• quantity
• variable
• algebraic expression
• numerical expression

© **Problem 1** **Writing Expressions With Addition and Subtraction**

What is an algebraic expression for the word phrase?

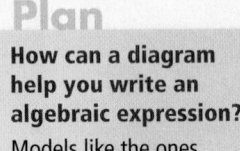

Plan

How can a diagram help you write an algebraic expression?
Models like the ones shown can help you to visualize the relationships described by the word phrases.

Word Phrase	Model	Expression
A 32 more than a number n	├-------- ? --------┤ $\begin{array}{\|c\|c\|} \hline n & 32 \\ \hline \end{array}$	$n + 32$
B 58 less a number n	├-------- 58 --------┤ $\begin{array}{\|c\|c\|} \hline n & ? \\ \hline \end{array}$	$58 - n$

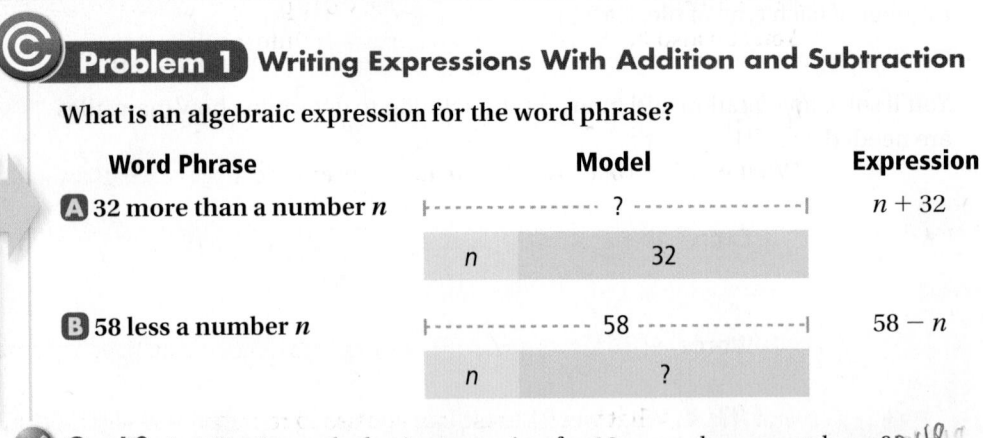

✓ **Got It?** **1.** What is an algebraic expression for 18 more than a number n? $n + 18$

What is an algebraic expression for the word phrase?

Word Phrase	Model	Expression
A 8 times a number n	$\vdash\text{------- ? -------}\dashv$ n n n n n n n	$8 \times n,\, 8 \cdot n,\, 8n$
B the quotient of a number n and 5	$\vdash\text{------- } n \text{ -------}\dashv$? ? ? ? ?	$n \div 5,\, \dfrac{n}{5}$

© ✓ **Got It?** **2.** What is an algebraic expression for each word phrase in parts (a) and (b)?

  a. 6 times a number n $6n$ **b.** the quotient of 18 and a number n $18 \div n$

  c. Reasoning Do the phrases *6 less a number y* and *6 less than a number y* mean the same thing? Explain.   No $6 - y$ $y = 6$

© **Problem 3** Writing Expressions With Two Operations

What is an algebraic expression for the word phrase?

Word Phrase	Expression
A 3 more than twice a number x	$3 + 2x$
B 9 less than the quotient of 6 and a number x	$\dfrac{6}{x} - 9$
C the product of 4 and the sum of a number x and 7	$4(x + 7)$

✓ **Got It?** **3.** What is an algebraic expression for each word phrase?

  a. 8 less than the product of a number x and 4 $4x - 8$

  b. twice the sum of a number x and 8 $2(x + 8)$

  c. the quotient of 5 and the sum of 12 and a number x $5 \div (12 + x)$

In Problems 1, 2, and 3, you were given word phrases and wrote algebraic expressions. You can also translate algebraic expressions into word phrases.

© **Problem 4** Using Words for an Expression

What word phrase can you use to represent the algebraic expression $3x$?

  Expression $3x$ ⟨ A number and a variable side by side indicate a product.
       $3 \cdot x$

  Words   three times a number x or   the product of 3 and a number x

✓ **Got It?** **4.** What word phrase can you use to represent the algebraic expression?

  a. $x + 8.1$ **b.** $10x + 9$ **c.** $\dfrac{n}{3}$ **d.** $5x - 1$

    8.1 more than x 9 more than the product of 10 and x the quotient of n and 3   1 less than 5 times x

You can use words or an algebraic expression to write a mathematical rule that describes a real-life pattern.

 Problem 5 **Writing a Rule to Describe a Pattern**

Hobbies The table below shows how the height above the floor of a house of cards depends on the number of levels.

A What is a rule for the height? Give the rule in words and as an algebraic expression.

3.5 in.

24 in.

House of Cards

Number of Levels	Height (in.)
2	$(3.5 \cdot 2) + 24$
3	$(3.5 \cdot 3) + 24$
4	$(3.5 \cdot 4) + 24$
n	?

Know

Numerical expressions for the height given several different numbers of levels

Need

A rule for finding the height given a house with n levels

Plan

Look for a pattern in the table. Describe the pattern in words. Then use the words to write an algebraic expression.

Rule in Words   Multiply the number of levels by 3.5 and add 24.

Rule as an Algebraic Expression   The variable n represents the number of levels in the house of cards.

$3.5n + 24$ ◁ This expression lets you find the height for n levels.

B A group of students built another house of cards that had 10 levels. Each card was 4 inches tall, and the height from the floor to the top of the house of cards was 70 inches. How tall would the house of cards be if they built an 11th level?

Since each card was 4 inches tall, adding 1 more level would increase the total height of the house of cards by 4 inches.

The house of cards would be 70 + 4, or 74 inches tall if the 11th level were added.

C Another group of students built a third house of cards with n levels. Each card was 5 inches tall, and the height from the floor to the top of the house of cards was $34 + 5n$ inches. How tall would the house of cards be if the group added 1 more level of cards?

Since each card was 5 inches tall, adding 1 more level would increase the total height of the house of cards by 5 inches.

The house of cards would be $34 + 5n + 5$ in. tall if the next level were added.

Got It? **5.** Suppose you draw a segment from any one vertex of a regular polygon to the other vertices. A sample for a regular hexagon is shown below. Use the table to find a pattern. What is a rule for the number of nonoverlapping triangles formed? Give the rule in words and as an algebraic expression.

n minus 2

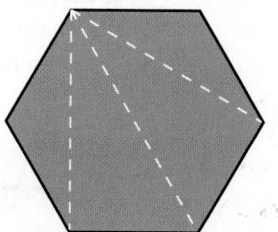

Triangles in Polygons

n =

Number of Sides of Polygon	Number of Triangles
4	4 − 2
5	5 − 2
6	6 − 2
n	■

2 less than n
n−2
n−2

6n

Lesson Check

Do you know HOW?

1. Is each expression *algebraic* or *numerical*?

a. $7 \div 2$ *numerical*   **b.** $4m + 6$ *algebraic*   **c.** $2(5 - 4)$ *numerical*

2. What is an algebraic expression for each phrase?

a. the product of 9 and a number t *9t*

b. the difference of a number x and $\frac{1}{2}$ *x − ½*

c. the sum of a number m and 7.1 *m + 7.1*

d. the quotient of 207 and a number n *207/n*

Use words to describe each algebraic expression.

3. $6c$ *6 times c*   **4.** $x - 1$ *the difference of x and 1*

5. $\frac{t}{2}$ *the quotient of t and 2*   **6.** $3t - 4$ *4 less than 3 times t*

Do you UNDERSTAND?  MATHEMATICAL PRACTICES

7. Vocabulary Explain the difference between numerical expressions and algebraic expressions. *algebraic has variables and numerical doesn't*

8. Reasoning Use the table to decide whether $49n + 0.75$ or $49 + 0.75n$ represents the total cost to rent a truck that you drive n miles. *49 + 0.75n*

Truck Rental Fees

Number of Miles	Cost
1	$49 + ($.75 × 1)$
2	$49 + ($.75 × 2)$
3	$49 + ($.75 × 3)$
n	■

Practice and Problem-Solving Exercises  MATHEMATICAL PRACTICES

A **Practice** Write an algebraic expression for each word phrase.   ◀ See Problems 1–3.

9. 4 more than p *p+4*

10. y minus 12 *y − 12*

11. the quotient of n and 8 *n/8*

12. the product of 15 and c *15c*

13. a number t divided by 82 *t/82*

14. the sum of 13 and twice a number h *13+2h*

15. 6.7 more than the product of 5 and n *6.7+5n*

16. 9.85 less than the product of 37 and t *37t−9.85*

Write a word phrase for each algebraic expression.   ◀ See Problem 4.

17. $q + 5$ *the sum of q and 5*   **18.** $\frac{y}{5}$ *y divided by 5*   **19.** $12x$ *12 times x*   **20.** $49 + m$ *49 plus m*

21. $9n + 1$ *1 more than 9 times n*   **22.** $\frac{z}{8} - 9$ *9 less than z divided by 8*   **23.** $15 - \frac{1.5}{d}$ *15 minus the quotient of 1.5 and d*   **24.** $2(5 - n)$ *2 times 5 minus n*

Write a rule in words and as an algebraic expression to model the relationship in each table.   ◀ See Problem 5.

25. Sightseeing While on vacation, you rent a bicycle. You pay $9 for each hour you use it. It costs $5 to rent a helmet while you use the bicycle.

Bike Rental

[handwritten] 5 more than 9 times n (9n)+5

[handwritten left of table] n=

Number of Hours	Rental Cost
1	($9 × 1) + $5
2	($9 × 2) + $5
3	($9 × 3) + $5
n	▓

26. Sales At a shoe store, a salesperson earns a weekly salary of $150. A salesperson is also paid $2.00 for each pair of shoes he or she sells during the week.

Shoe Sales

Pairs of Shoes Sold	Total Earned
5	$150 + ($2 × 5)
10	$150 + ($2 × 10)
15	$150 + ($2 × 15)
n	▓

[handwritten] 150+(2t)
150 more than 2 times t

B Apply   Write an algebraic expression for each word phrase.

27. 8 minus the product of 9 and r   *[handwritten]* 8−(9r)

28. the sum of 15 and x, plus 7   *[handwritten]* (15+x)+7

29. 4 less than three sevenths of y   *[handwritten]* ($\frac{3}{7}$y)−4

30. the quotient of 12 and the product of 5 and t   *[handwritten]* 12÷(5t)

© 31. Error Analysis A student writes the word phrase "the quotient of n and 5" to describe the expression $\frac{5}{n}$. Describe and correct the student's error.   *[handwritten]* it should be $\frac{n}{5}$

© 32. Think About a Plan The table at the right shows the number of bagels a shop gives you per "baker's dozen." Write an algebraic expression that gives the rule for finding the number of bagels in any number b of baker's dozens.
- What is the pattern of increase in the number of bagels?
- What operation can you perform on b to find the number of bagels?   *[handwritten]* 13b

Bagels

Baker's Dozens	Number of Bagels
1	13
2	26
3	39
b	▓

33. Tickets You and some friends are going to a museum. Each ticket costs $4.50.

a. If n is the number of tickets purchased, write an expression that gives the total cost of buying n tickets.   *[handwritten]* 4.50n

b. Suppose the total cost for n tickets is $36. What is the total cost if one more ticket is purchased?   *[handwritten]* 40.50

34. Volunteering Serena and Tyler are wrapping gift boxes at the same pace. Serena starts first, as shown in the diagram. Write an algebraic expression that represents the number of boxes Tyler will have wrapped when Serena has wrapped x boxes.   *[handwritten]* x−2

35. Multiple Choice Which expression gives the value in dollars of d dimes?

Ⓐ $0.10d$ Ⓑ $0.10 + d$ Ⓒ $\dfrac{0.10}{d}$ Ⓓ $10d$

 **Open-Ended** Describe a real-world situation that each expression might model. Tell what each variable represents.

36. $5t$ **37.** $b + 3$ **38.** $\dfrac{40}{h}$

 Challenge

39. Reasoning You write $(5 - 2) \div n$ to represent the phrase *2 less than 5 divided by a number n*. Your friend writes $(5 \div n) - 2$. Are these both reasonable interpretations? Can verbal descriptions lack precision? Explain. *the 2nd one is correct*

Write two different expressions that could both represent the given diagram.

40.

x	1	1	1	1
x	1	1	1	
x	1	1	1	1

41.

x	1	1	1	1
x	1	1		

Apply What You've Learned

MATHEMATICAL
PRACTICES
MP 7

Look back at the figures on page 3 showing the pattern of the tiles of the walkway.

Complete the table that shows the relationship between n, the number of names on each side of the walk, and the number of inscribed tiles.

Walkway Tiles

n	Number of Inscribed Tiles
1	2
a. ?	4
3	b. ?
4	c. ?

d. Write a rule in words and as an algebraic expression to model the relationship shown in the table.

e. How many plain tiles are in the walk when there are 3 names on each side? Write an expression for the number of plain tiles when there are n names on each side of the walk.

f. If $n = 8$, how many plain and inscribed tiles will there be in the walkway? Explain.

Order of Operations and Evaluating Expressions

Common Core State Standards

A-SSE.A.1a Interpret parts of an expression, such as terms, factors, and coefficients.

MP 1, MP 3, MP 4, MP 6, MP 8

Objectives To simplify expressions involving exponents
To use the order of operations to evaluate expressions

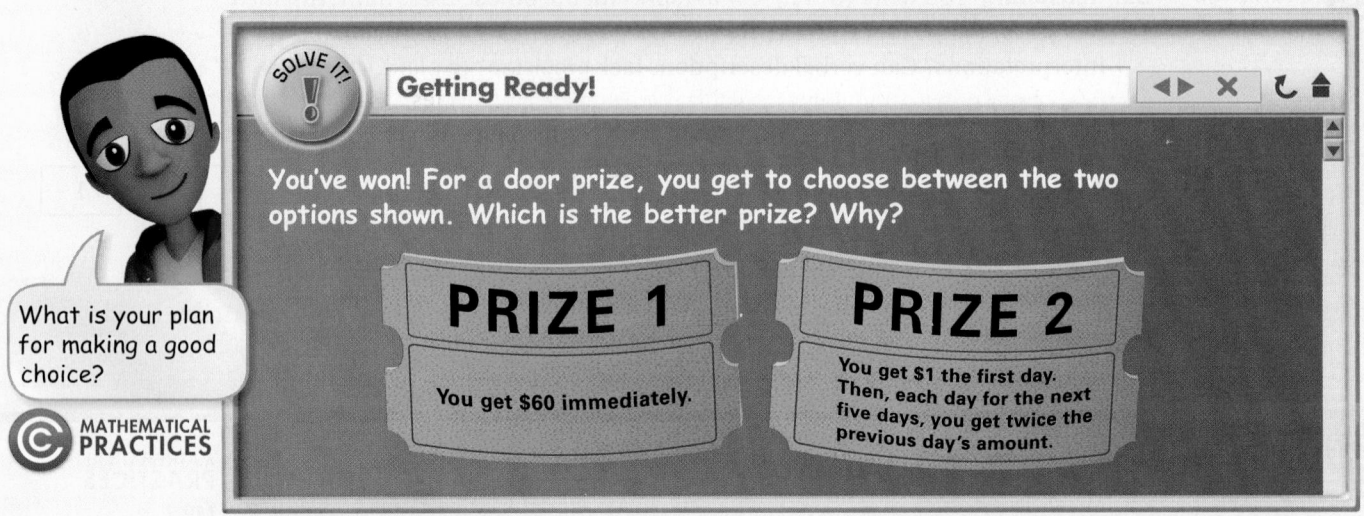

What is your plan for making a good choice?

MATHEMATICAL PRACTICES

Getting Ready!

You've won! For a door prize, you get to choose between the two options shown. Which is the better prize? Why?

PRIZE 1
You get $60 immediately.

PRIZE 2
You get $1 the first day. Then, each day for the next five days, you get twice the previous day's amount.

Essential Understanding You can use *powers* to shorten how you represent repeated multiplication, such as $2 \times 2 \times 2 \times 2 \times 2 \times 2$.

Lesson Vocabulary
• power
• exponent
• base
• simplify
• evaluate

A **power** has two parts, a *base* and an *exponent*. The **exponent** tells you how many times to use the **base** as a factor. You read the power 2^3 as "two to the third power" or "two cubed." You read 5^2 as "five to the second power" or "five squared."

You **simplify** a numerical expression when you replace it with its single numerical value. For example, the simplest form of $2 \cdot 8$ is 16. To simplify a power, you replace it with its simplest name.

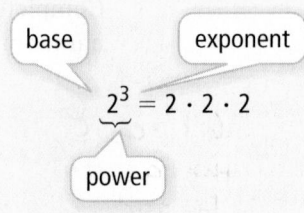

base   exponent
$$2^3 = 2 \cdot 2 \cdot 2$$
power

Problem 1 Simplifying Powers

Think

What does the exponent indicate?
It shows the number of times you use the base as a factor.

What is the simplified form of the expression?

A 10^7

$10^7 = 10 \cdot 10 \cdot 10 \cdot 10 \cdot 10 \cdot 10 \cdot 10$

$= 10,000,000$

B $(0.2)^5$

$(0.2)^5 = 0.2 \cdot 0.2 \cdot 0.2 \cdot 0.2 \cdot 0.2$

$= 0.00032$

Got It? 1. What is the simplified form of each expression?

a. 3^4 $3 \cdot 3 \cdot 3 \cdot 3$
$= 81$

b. $\left(\frac{2}{3}\right)^3$ $\frac{2}{3} \cdot \frac{2}{3} \cdot \frac{2}{3}$
$= \frac{8}{27}$

c. $(0.5)^3$ $0.5 \cdot 0.5 \cdot 0.5$
$= 0.125$

Essential Understanding When simplifying an expression, you need to perform operations in the correct order.

You might think about simplifying the expression $2 + 3 \times 5$ in two ways:

Add first.	Multiply first.

$$2 + 3 \times 5 = 5 \times 5 = 25 \text{ ✗} \qquad 2 + 3 \times 5 = 2 + 15 = 17 \text{ ✔}$$

Both results may seem sensible, but only the second result is considered correct. This is because the second way uses the order of operations that mathematicians have agreed to follow. Always use the following order of operations:

take note

Key Concept   Order of Operations

1. Perform any operation(s) inside grouping symbols, such as parentheses ( ) and brackets [ ]. A fraction bar also acts as a grouping symbol.
2. Simplify powers.
3. Multiply and divide from left to right.
4. Add and subtract from left to right.

Problem 2   **Simplifying a Numerical Expression**

What is the simplified form of each expression?

Think

How do you simplify an expression that contains a fraction?
You start by simplifying the numerator and denominator. Then you divide the numerator by the denominator.

Ⓐ $(6-2)^3 \div 2$

$$\begin{aligned}
(6-2)^3 \div 2 &= 4^3 \div 2 & \text{Subtract inside parentheses.} \\
&= 64 \div 2 & \text{Simplify the power.} \\
&= 32 & \text{Divide.}
\end{aligned}$$

Ⓑ $\dfrac{2^4 - 1}{5}$

$$\begin{aligned}
\frac{2^4 - 1}{5} &= \frac{16 - 1}{5} & \text{Simplify the power.} \\
&= \frac{15}{5} & \text{Subtract.} \\
&= 3 & \text{Divide.}
\end{aligned}$$

Got It?   2. What is the simplified form of each expression?
   a. $5 \cdot 7 - 4^2 \div 2$ 27
   b. $12 - 25 \div 5$ 7
   c. $\dfrac{4 + 3^4}{7 - 2}$ 17.8
   d. Reasoning How does a fraction bar act as a grouping symbol? Explain.
   the fraction bar groups the numerator and denomenator into seperate sections like parentheses

---

When two or more variables, or a number and variables, are written together, treat them as if they were within parentheses. So $4xy$ is equivalent to $(4xy)$, and $xy^2 = (xy^2)$. You **evaluate** an algebraic expression by replacing each variable with a given number. Then simplify the expression using the order of operations.

 Problem 3 Evaluating Algebraic Expressions

Plan

How is this Problem like ones you've seen before?
You begin by substituting numbers for the variables. After substituting, you have numerical expressions just like the ones in Problem 2.

What is the value of the expression for $x = 5$ and $y = 2$?

Ⓐ $x^2 + x - 12 \div y^2$

$$x^2 + x - 12 \div y^2 = 5^2 + 5 - 12 \div 2^2 \qquad \text{Substitute 5 for } x \text{ and 2 for } y.$$
$$= 25 + 5 - 12 \div 4 \qquad \text{Simplify powers.}$$
$$= 25 + 5 - 3 \qquad \text{Divide.}$$
$$= 27 \qquad \text{Add and subtract from left to right.}$$

Ⓑ $(xy)^2 \div (xy)$

$$(xy)^2 \div xy = (5 \cdot 2)^2 \div (5 \cdot 2) \qquad \text{Substitute 5 for } x \text{ and 2 for } y.$$
$$= 10^2 \div 10 \qquad \text{Multiply inside parentheses.}$$
$$= 100 \div 10 \qquad \text{Simplify the power.}$$
$$= 10 \qquad \text{Divide.}$$

Got It? **3.** What is the value of each expression when $a = 3$ and $b = 4$ in parts (a)–(b)?

a. $3b - a^2$ 3   **b.** $2b^2 - 7a$ 11

 Problem 4 Evaluating a Real-World Expression

Banking What is an expression for the spending money you have left after depositing $\frac{2}{5}$ of your wages in savings? Evaluate the expression for weekly wages of $40, $50, $75, and $100.

Know	Need	Plan
• Savings equals $\frac{2}{5}$ of wages. • Various weekly wages	• Expression for spending money • Amount of spending money for various weekly wages	Write an algebraic expression and evaluate it for each amount of weekly wages. Use a table to organize your results.

Think

How can a model help you write the expression?
This model shows that spending money equals your wages w minus the amount you save: $\frac{2}{5}w$.

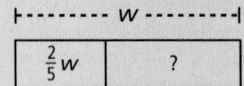

Relate   spending money equals

     $\boxed{\text{wages}}$ $\boxed{\text{minus}}$ $\boxed{\frac{2}{5}}$ $\boxed{\text{of}}$ $\boxed{\text{wages}}$

Define   Let $\boxed{w}$ = your wages.

Write $\boxed{w}$ $-$ $\boxed{\frac{2}{5}}$ $\cdot$ $\boxed{w}$

The expression $w - \frac{2}{5} \cdot w$ represents the amount of money you have left after depositing $\frac{2}{5}$ of your wages in savings.

Spending Money

Wages (w)	$w - \frac{2}{5}w$	Total Spending Money ($)
40	$40 - \frac{2}{5}(40)$	24
50	$50 - \frac{2}{5}(50)$	30
75	$75 - \frac{2}{5}(75)$	45
100	$100 - \frac{2}{5}(100)$	60

4. The shipping cost for an order at an online store is $\frac{1}{10}$ the cost of the items you order. What is an expression for the total cost of a given order? What are the total costs for orders of $43, $79, $95, and $103? $x + x \cdot \frac{1}{10}$

47.3 86.9 104.5 113.3

 Lesson Check

Do you know HOW?

What is the simplified form of each expression?

1. 5^2 $5 \cdot 5$ 25

2. 2^3 $2 \cdot 2 \cdot 2$ 8

3. $\left(\frac{3}{4}\right)^2$ $\frac{3}{4} \cdot \frac{3}{4}$ $\frac{9}{16}$

Evaluate each expression for $x = 3$ and $y = 4$.

4. $x^2 + 2(x + y)$ 23

5. $(xy)^3$ 1728

6. $4x^2 - 3xy$ 108

Do you UNDERSTAND?  MATHEMATICAL PRACTICES

7. Vocabulary Identify the exponent and the base in 4^3.
   3 4

8. Error Analysis A student simplifies an expression as shown below. Find the error and simplify the expression correctly.

$$23 - 8 \cdot 2 + 3^2 = 23 - 8 \cdot 2 + 9$$
$$= 15 \cdot 2 + 9$$
$$= 30 + 9$$
$$= 39 \quad X$$

$23 - 8 \cdot 2 + 9$
$23 - 16 + 9$
$7 + 9$
$= 16$

 Practice and Problem-Solving Exercises  MATHEMATICAL PRACTICES

 **Practice**   **Simplify each expression.**   ◀ **See Problems 1 and 2.**

9. 3^5 243

10. 4^3 64

11. 2^4 32

12. 10^8 $100,000,000$

13. $\left(\frac{2}{3}\right)^3$ $\frac{8}{27}$

14. $\left(\frac{1}{2}\right)^4$ $\frac{1}{16}$

15. $(0.4)^6$ 0.004096

16. 7^4 2401

17. $20 - 2 \cdot 3^2$ 2

18. $6 + 4 \div 2 + 3$ 11

19. $(6^2 - 3^3) \div 2$ 4.5

20. $5 \cdot 2^2 \div 2 + 8$ 18

21. $80 - (4 - 1)^3$ 53

22. $52 + 8^2 - 3(4 - 2)^3$ 68

23. $\frac{6^4 \div 3^2}{9}$ 16

24. $\frac{2 \cdot 7 + 4}{9 \div 3}$ 6

Evaluate each expression for $s = 4$ and $t = 8$.   ◀ **See Problem 3.**

25. $(s + t)^3$ 1728

26. $s^4 + t^2 + s \div 2$

27. $(st)^2 \div (st^2)$

28. $3st^2 \div (st) + 6$ 12

29. $(t - s)^5$

30. $(2s)^2 t$

31. $2st^2 - s^2$ 120

32. $2s^2 - t^3 \div 16$

33. $\frac{(3s)^3 t + t}{s}$

34. Write an expression for the amount of change you will get when you pay for a purchase p with a $20 bill. Make a table to find the amounts of change you will get for purchases of $11.59, $17.50, $19.00, and $20.00.   ◀ **See Problem 4.**

35. An object's momentum is defined as the product of its mass m and velocity v. Write an expression for the momentum of an object. Make a table to find the momentums of a vehicle with a mass of 1000 kg moving at a velocity of 15 m/s, 20 m/s, and 25 m/s.

---

36. Geometry The expression $\pi r^2 h$ represents the volume of a cylinder with radius r and height h.

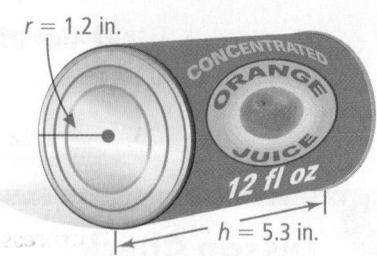

r = 1.2 in.

h = 5.3 in.

a. What is the volume, to the nearest tenth of a cubic inch, of the juice can at the right? Use 3.14 for π.

b. **Reasoning** About how many cubic inches, to the nearest tenth of a cubic inch, does a fluid ounce of juice fill?

Simplify each expression.

37. $2[(8-4)^5 \div 8]$

38. $3[(4-2)^5 - 20]$

39. $10 - (2^3 + 4) \div 3 - 1$

40. $\dfrac{22 + 1^3 + (3^4 - 7^2)}{2^3}$

41. $3[42 - 2(10^2 - 9^2)]$

42. $\dfrac{2[8 + (67 - 2^6)^3]}{9}$

43. Think About a Plan The snack bar at your school has added sushi to its menu. The ingredients for one roll include sushi rice, seaweed sheets, cucumbers, cream cheese, and 3 oz of smoked salmon. One roll can be cut into 8 servings. Write an expression for the amount of salmon needed to make s servings of sushi. How much salmon is needed to make 16 servings? 24 servings? 80 servings? 100 servings?
- What operations are needed in your calculations?
- Use a table to help you organize your results. What will you use for the column headings in your table?

44. Salary You earn $10 for each hour you work at a canoe rental shop. Write an expression for your salary for working the number of hours h. Make a table to find how much you earn for working 10 h, 20 h, 30 h, and 40 h.

Evaluate each expression for the given values of the variables.

45. $3(s-t)^2$; $s=4, t=1$

46. $2x - y^2$; $x=7, y=3.5$

47. $3m^2 - n$; $m=2, n=6$

48. $(2a+2b)^2$; $a=3, b=4$

49. $2p^2 + (2q)^2$; $p=4, q=3$

50. $(4c - d + 0.2)^2 - 10c$; $c=3.1, d=4.6$

51. $\dfrac{3g+6}{h}$; $g=5, h=7$

52. $\dfrac{2w+3v}{v^2}$; $v=6, w=1$

53. Writing Consider the expression $(1+5)^2 - (18 \div 3)$. Can you perform the operations in different orders and still get the correct answer? Explain.

54. A student wrote the expressions shown and claimed they were equal for all values of x and y.

$(x + y)^2$
$x^2 + y^2$

a. Evaluate each expression for $x=1$ and $y=0$.
b. Evaluate each expression for $x=1$ and $y=2$.
c. **Open-Ended** Choose another pair of values for x and y. Evaluate each expression for those values.
d. **Writing** Is the student's claim correct? Justify your answer.

55. Find the value of $14 + 5 \cdot 3 - 3^2$. Then change two operation signs so that the value of the expression is 8.

Use grouping symbols to make each equation true.

56. $9 + 3 - 2 + 4 = 6$

57. $16 - 4 \div 2 + 3 = 9$

58. $4^2 - 5 \cdot 2 + 1 = 1$

59. $3 \cdot 4 + 5 - 6 + 7 = 28$

60. a. Geometry A cone has a slant height ℓ of 11 cm and a radius r of 3 cm. Use the expression $\pi r(\ell + r)$ to find the surface area of the cone. Use 3.14 for π. Round to the nearest tenth of a square centimeter.

b. Reasoning Does the surface area of the cone double if the radius doubles? If the slant height doubles? Explain.

Standardized Test Prep

61. What is the simplified form of $4 + 10 \div 4 + 6$?

   A 1.4   **B** 9.5   **C** 12.5   **D** 24

62. What is the value of $(2a)^2 b - 2c^2$ for $a = 2$, $b = 4$, and $c = 3$?

   F 14   **G** 28   **H** 32   **I** 46

63. A shirt is on sale for $25 at the local department store. The sales tax equals $\frac{1}{25}$ of the shirt's price. What is the total cost of the shirt including sales tax?

   A $17   **B** $26   **C** $27   **D** $33

64. You can find the distance in feet that an object falls in t seconds using the expression $16t^2$. If you drop a ball from a tall building, how far does the ball fall in 3 s?

   F 16 ft   **G** 48 ft   **H** 96 ft   **I** 144 ft

Mixed Review

Write an algebraic expression for each word phrase.
See Lesson 1-1.

65. 4 more than p

66. 5 minus the product of y and 3

67. the quotient of m and 10

68. 3 times the difference of 7 and d

Tell whether each number is *prime* or *composite*.
See p. 798.

69. 17   **70.** 33   **71.** 43   **72.** 91

Get Ready! To prepare for Lesson 1-3, do Exercises 73–80.

Write each fraction as a decimal and each decimal as a fraction.
See p. 802.

73. $\frac{3}{5}$ **74.** $\frac{7}{8}$ **75.** $\frac{2}{3}$ **76.** $\frac{4}{7}$

77. 0.7   **78.** 0.07   **79.** 4.25   **80.** 0.425

1-3 Real Numbers and the Number Line

 Common Core State Standards

Prepares for N-RN.B.3 Explain why the sum or product of two rational numbers is rational; that the sum of a rational number and an irrational number is irrational . . .

MP 1, MP 3, MP 6

Objectives To classify, graph, and compare real numbers
To find and estimate square roots

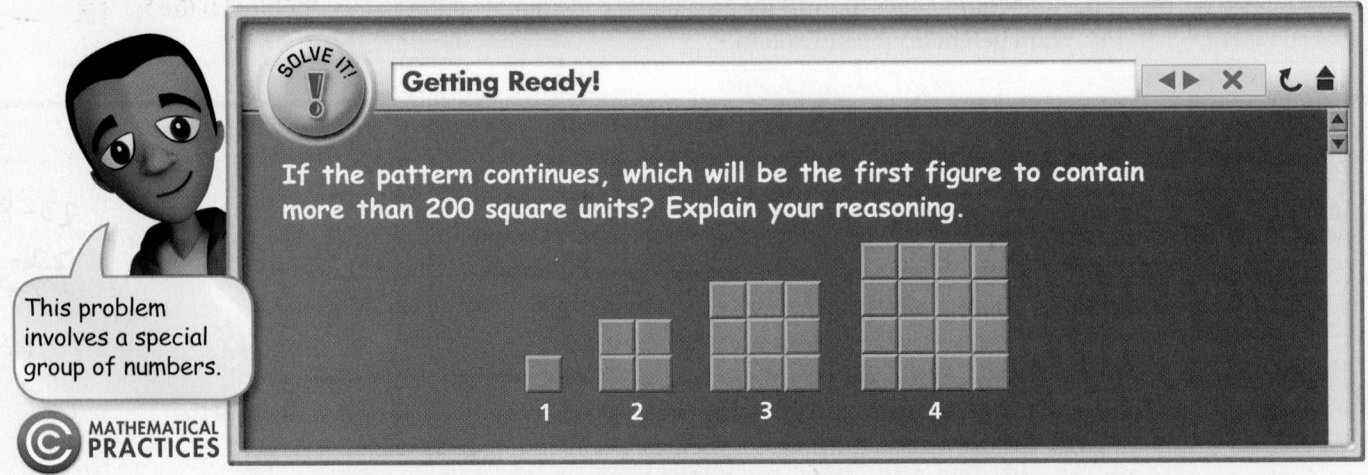

Getting Ready!

If the pattern continues, which will be the first figure to contain more than 200 square units? Explain your reasoning.

1   2   3   4

This problem involves a special group of numbers.

MATHEMATICAL PRACTICES

The diagrams in the Solve It model what happens when you multiply a number by itself to form a product. When you do this, the original number is called a *square root* of the product.

Key Concept Square Root

Algebra A number a is a **square root** of a number b if $a^2 = b$.

Example $7^2 = 49$, so 7 is a square root of 49.

Essential Understanding You can use the definition above to find the exact square roots of some nonnegative numbers. You can approximate the square roots of other nonnegative numbers.

The radical symbol $\sqrt{\ }$ indicates a nonnegative square root, also called a *principal square root*. The expression under the radical symbol is called the **radicand.**

$$\text{radical symbol} \rightarrow \sqrt{a} \leftarrow \text{radicand}$$

Together, the radical symbol and radicand form a **radical.** You will learn about negative square roots in Lesson 1-6.

Lesson Vocabulary
- square root
- radicand
- radical
- perfect square
- set
- element of a set
- subset
- rational numbers
- natural numbers
- whole numbers
- integers
- irrational numbers
- real numbers
- inequality

Problem 1 Simplifying Square Root Expressions

What is the simplified form of each expression?

A $\sqrt{81} = 9$ $9^2 = 81$, so 9 is a square root of 81.

B $\sqrt{\frac{9}{16}} = \frac{3}{4}$ $\left(\frac{3}{4}\right)^2 = \frac{9}{16}$, so $\frac{3}{4}$ is a square root of $\frac{9}{16}$.

Got It? 1. What is the simplified form of each expression?

    a. $\sqrt{64}$ 8   **b.** $\sqrt{25}$ 5   **c.** $\sqrt{\frac{1}{36}}$ $\frac{1}{6}$ **d.** $\sqrt{\frac{81}{121}}$ $\frac{9}{11}$

The square of an integer is called a **perfect square.** For example, 49 is a perfect square because $7^2 = 49$. When a radicand is not a perfect square, you can estimate the square root of the radicand.

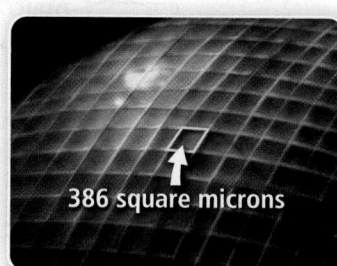
386 square microns

 Problem 2 Estimating a Square Root **STEM**

Biology Lobster eyes are made of tiny square regions. Under a microscope, the surface of the eye looks like graph paper. A scientist measures the area of one of the squares to be 386 square microns. What is the approximate side length of the square to the nearest micron?

Plan

How can you get started?
The square root of the area of a square is equal to its side length. So, find $\sqrt{386}$.

Method 1 Estimate $\sqrt{386}$ by finding the two closest perfect squares.

    The perfect squares closest to 386 are 361 and 400.

    $19^2 = 361$
          $\longleftarrow$ 386
    $20^2 = 400$

    Since 386 is closer to 400, $\sqrt{386} \approx 20$, and the side length is about 20 microns.

Method 2 Estimate $\sqrt{386}$ using a calculator.

    $\sqrt{386} \approx 19.6$ Use the square root function on your calculator.

    The side length of the square is about 20 microns.

 Got It? 2. What is the value of $\sqrt{34}$ to the nearest integer?

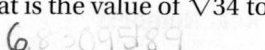   6

Essential Understanding Numbers can be classified by their characteristics. Some types of numbers can be represented on the number line.

You can classify numbers using *sets*. A **set** is a well-defined collection of objects. Each object is called an **element of the set.** A **subset** of a set consists of elements from the given set. You can list the elements of a set within braces { }.

A **rational number** is any number that you can write in the form $\frac{a}{b}$, where a and b are integers and $b \neq 0$. A rational number in decimal form is either a terminating decimal such as 5.45 or a repeating decimal such as 0.41666 . . . , which you can write as $0.41\overline{6}$. Each graph below shows a subset of the rational numbers on a number line.

Natural numbers   {1, 2, 3, . . .}

Whole numbers   {0, 1, 2, 3, . . .}

Integers   {. . . −2, −1, 0, 1, 2, 3, . . .}

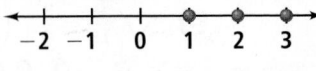

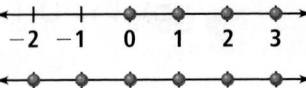

An **irrational number** cannot be represented as the quotient of two integers. In decimal form, irrational numbers do not terminate or repeat. Here are some examples.

$$0.1010010001 \ldots \qquad\qquad \pi = 3.14159265 \ldots$$

Some square roots are rational numbers and some are irrational numbers. If a whole number is not a perfect square, its square root is irrational.

Rational $\sqrt{4} = 2$ $\sqrt{25} = 5$

Irrational $\sqrt{3} = 1.73205080 \ldots$ $\sqrt{10} = 3.16227766 \ldots$

Rational numbers and irrational numbers form the set of **real numbers.**

Ⓒ Problem 3   **Classifying Real Numbers**

Think

What clues can you use to classify real numbers?
Look for negative signs, fractions, decimals that do or do not terminate or repeat, and radicands that are not perfect squares.

To which subsets of the real numbers does each number belong?

Ⓐ 15   natural numbers, whole numbers, integers, rational numbers

Ⓑ −1.4583   rational numbers (since −1.4583 is a terminating decimal)

Ⓒ $\sqrt{57}$ irrational numbers (since 57 is not a perfect square)

✓ Got It?   **3.** To which subsets of the real numbers does each number belong?

     a. $\sqrt{9}$ **b.** $\frac{3}{10}$ **c.** −0.45   **d.** $\sqrt{12}$

     N, W, In, Re, Ra   N, W, In, Ra, Re   W, In, Ra, Re   N, W, In, Re, Ir

---

take note

Concept Summary   Real Numbers

Real Numbers

Rational Numbers	Integers	Whole Numbers	Natural Numbers	Irrational Numbers
$\frac{-2}{3}$	−3			$\sqrt{10}$ $-\sqrt{123}$
$0.\overline{3}$	$-\frac{10}{5}$	0	$\sqrt{25}$	0.1010010001...
$\sqrt{0.25}$	$-\sqrt{16}$		$\frac{4}{2}$ 7	π

An **inequality** is a mathematical sentence that compares the values of two expressions using an inequality symbol. The symbols are

$<$, less than

$\le$, less than or equal to

$>$, greater than

$\ge$, greater than or equal to

 Plan

How can you compare numbers?
Write the numbers in the same form, such as decimal form.

Problem 4 Comparing Real Numbers

What is an inequality that compares the numbers $\sqrt{17}$ **and** $4\frac{1}{3}$**?**

$\sqrt{17} = 4.12310\ldots$ Write the square root as a decimal.

$4\frac{1}{3} = 4.\overline{3}$ Write the fraction as a decimal.

$\sqrt{17} < 4\frac{1}{3}$ Compare using an inequality symbol.

Got It? **4. a.** What is an inequality that compares the numbers $\sqrt{129}$ and 11.52? $\sqrt{129} < 11.52$

     b. Reasoning In Problem 4, is there another inequality you can write that compares the two numbers? Explain. Yes $4\frac{1}{3} > \sqrt{17}$

You can graph and order all real numbers using a number line.

Problem 5 Graphing and Ordering Real Numbers

Multiple Choice What is the order of $\sqrt{4}, 0.4, -\frac{2}{3}, \sqrt{2},$ and -1.5 from least to greatest?

Ⓐ $-\frac{2}{3}, 0.4, -1.5, \sqrt{2}, \sqrt{4}$ Ⓒ $-1.5, -\frac{2}{3}, 0.4, \sqrt{2}, \sqrt{4}$

Ⓑ $-1.5, \sqrt{2}, 0.4, \sqrt{4}, -\frac{2}{3}$ Ⓓ $\sqrt{4}, \sqrt{2}, 0.4, -\frac{2}{3}, -1.5$

Know	Need	Plan
Five real numbers	Order of numbers from least to greatest	Graph the numbers on a number line.

Think

Why is it useful to rewrite numbers in decimal form?
It allows you to compare numbers whose values are close, like $\frac{1}{4}$ and 0.26.

First, write the numbers that are not in decimal form as decimals: $\sqrt{4} = 2, -\frac{2}{3} \approx -0.67,$ and $\sqrt{2} \approx 1.41$. Then graph all five numbers on the number line to order the numbers, and read the graph from left to right.

From least to greatest, the numbers are $-1.5, -\frac{2}{3}, 0.4, \sqrt{2},$ and $\sqrt{4}$. The correct answer is C.

Got It? **5.** Graph $3.5, -2.1, \sqrt{9}, -\frac{7}{2},$ and $\sqrt{5}$ on a number line. What is the order of the numbers from least to greatest?

 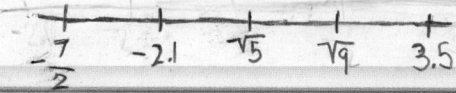

Lesson Check

Do you know HOW?

Name the subset(s) of the real numbers to which each number belongs.

1. $\sqrt{11}$ *Ir, Re Ir, Re*

2. -7 *In, Ra, Re*

3. Order $\frac{47}{10}$, 4.1, -5, and $\sqrt{16}$ from least to greatest.
$-5, \sqrt{16}, 4.1, \frac{47}{10}$

4. A square card has an area of 15 in.². What is the approximate side length of the card?
3.87

Do you UNDERSTAND?

5. **Vocabulary** What are the two subsets of the real numbers that form the set of real numbers?
Rational Irrational

6. **Vocabulary** Give an example of a rational number that is not an integer. $0.\overline{3}$

Reasoning Tell whether each square root is *rational* or *irrational*. Explain.

7. $\sqrt{100} = 10$ *Rational*

8. $\sqrt{0.29} = 0.53851648\ldots$ *Irrational*

Practice and Problem-Solving Exercises  MATHEMATICAL PRACTICES

 **Practice**

Simplify each expression.   See Problem 1.

9. $\sqrt{36}$ 6 10. $\sqrt{169}$ 13 11. $\sqrt{16}$ 4 12. $\sqrt{900}$ 30 13. $\sqrt{\frac{36}{49}}$ $\frac{6}{7}$

14. $\sqrt{\frac{25}{81}}$ $\frac{5}{9}$ 15. $\sqrt{\frac{1}{9}}$ $\frac{1}{3}$ 16. $\sqrt{\frac{121}{16}}$ $\frac{11}{4}$ 17. $\sqrt{1.96}$ 1.4 18. $\sqrt{0.25}$ 0.5

Estimate the square root. Round to the nearest integer.   See Problem 2.

19. $\sqrt{17} \approx 4$ 20. $\sqrt{35} \approx 6$ 21. $\sqrt{242} \approx 16$ 22. $\sqrt{61} \approx 8$ 23. $\sqrt{320} \approx 18$

Find the approximate side length of each square figure to the nearest whole unit.

24. a mural with an area of 18 m² ≈ 4

25. a game board with an area of 160 in.² ≈ 13

26. a helicopter launching pad with an area of 3000 ft² ≈ 55

Name the subset(s) of the real numbers to which each number belongs.   See Problem 3.

27. $\frac{2}{3}$ *Ra W, In, Ra* 28. 13 *N, W, In, Re* 29. -1 *In, Ra*   30. $-\frac{19}{100}$ *Ra, Ra* 31. π *Ir, I, Ir*

32. -2.38 *Ra Ra*   33. $\frac{17}{4573}$ *Ir, In, Ra*   34. $\sqrt{144}$ *N, W, In, Ra* 35. $\sqrt{113}$ *Ir, In, I* 36. $\frac{59}{2}$ *Ra W, In, Ra*

Compare the numbers in each exercise using an inequality symbol.   See Problem 4.

37. $5\frac{2}{3}$, $\sqrt{29}$ $5\frac{2}{3} > \sqrt{29}$ 38. -3.1, $-\frac{16}{5}$ $-3.1 > -\frac{16}{5}$ 39. $\frac{4}{3}$, $\sqrt{2}$ $\frac{4}{3} < \sqrt{2}$ 40. 9.6, $\sqrt{96}$ $9.6 < \sqrt{96}$

41. $-\frac{7}{11}$, -0.63 $-\frac{7}{11} > -0.63$ 42. $\sqrt{115}$, $10.72104\ldots$ 43. $-\frac{22}{25}$, $-0.\overline{8}$ 44. $\sqrt{184}$, $15.56987\ldots$
$\sqrt{115} > 10.72104$ $-\frac{22}{25} > -0.\overline{8}$ $\sqrt{184} < 15.56987$

Order the numbers in each exercise from least to greatest.   See Problem 5.

45. $\frac{1}{2}$, -2, $\sqrt{5}$, $-\frac{7}{4}$, 2.4 46. -3, $\sqrt{31}$, $\sqrt{11}$, 5.5, $-\frac{60}{11}$ 47. -6, $\sqrt{20}$, 4.3, $-\frac{59}{9}$

48. $\frac{10}{3}$, 3, $\sqrt{8}$, 2.9, $\sqrt{7}$ 49. $-\frac{13}{6}$, -2.1, $-\frac{26}{13}$, $-\frac{9}{4}$ 50. $-\frac{1}{6}$, -0.3, $\sqrt{1}$, $-\frac{2}{13}$, $\frac{7}{8}$

 **Apply**

Ⓒ 51. Think About a Plan A stage designer paid $4 per square foot for flooring to be used in a square room. If the designer spent $600 on the flooring, about how long is a side of the room? Round to the nearest foot.
- How is the area of a square related to its side length?
- How can you estimate the length of a side of a square?

Tell whether each statement is *true* or *false*. Explain.

52. All negative numbers are integers.

53. All integers are rational numbers.

54. All square roots are irrational numbers.

55. No positive number is an integer.

Ⓒ 56. Reasoning A restaurant owner is going to panel a square portion of the restaurant's ceiling. The portion to be paneled has an area of 185 ft². The owner plans to use square tin ceiling panels with a side length of 2 ft. What is the first step in finding out whether the owner will be able to use a whole number of panels?

Show that each number is rational by writing it in the form $\frac{a}{b}$, where a and b are integers.

57. 417   **58.** 0.37   **59.** 2.01   **60.** 2.1   **61.** 3.06

Ⓒ 62. Error Analysis A student says that $\sqrt{7}$ is a rational number because you can write $\sqrt{7}$ as the quotient $\frac{\sqrt{7}}{1}$. Is the student correct? Explain.

STEM 63. Construction A contractor is tiling a square patio that has the area shown at the right. What is the approximate side length of the patio? Round to the nearest foot.

Ⓒ 64. Open-Ended You are tutoring a younger student. How would you explain rational numbers, irrational numbers, and how they are different?

65. Geometry The irrational number π, equal to 3.14159..., is the ratio of a circle's circumference to its diameter. In the sixth century, the mathematician Brahmagupta estimated the value of π to be $\sqrt{10}$. In the thirteenth century, the mathematician Fibonacci estimated the value of π to be $\frac{864}{275}$. Which is the better estimate? Explain.

66. Home Improvement If you lean a ladder against a wall, the length of the ladder should be $\sqrt{(x)^2 + (4x)^2}$ ft to be considered safe. The distance x is how far the ladder's base is from the wall. Estimate the desired length of the ladder when the base is positioned 5 ft from the wall. Round your answer to the nearest tenth.

Ⓒ 67. Writing Is there a greatest integer on the real number line? A least fraction? Explain.

Ⓒ 68. Reasoning Choose three intervals on the real number line that contain both rational and irrational numbers. Do you think that any given interval on the real number line contains both rational and irrational numbers? Explain.

A = 136 ft²

69. Reasoning Sometimes the product of two positive numbers is less than either number. Describe the numbers for which this is true.

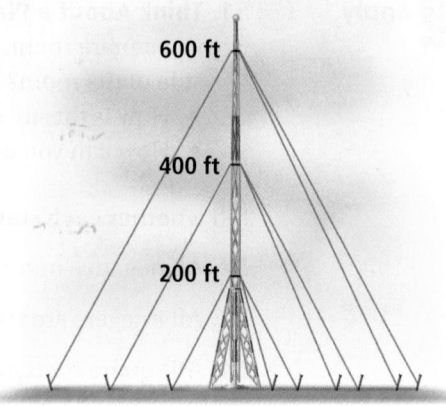
600 ft
400 ft
200 ft

STEM **70. Antennas** Guy wires are attached to an antenna tower at the heights h shown at the right. Use the expression $\sqrt{h^2 + (0.55h)^2}$ to estimate the wire length for each height. If three wires are attached at each height, what is the minimum total amount of wire needed?

71. Cube Roots The number a is the *cube root* of a number b if $a^3 = b$. For example, the cube root of 8 is 2 because $2^3 = 8$. Find the cube root of each number.

 a. 64 **b.** 1000 **c.** 343 **d.** 2197

Standardized Test Prep

72. A square picture has an area of 225 in.^{2}. What is the side length of the picture?

 Ⓐ 5 in. Ⓑ 15 in. Ⓒ 25 in. Ⓓ 225 in.

73. To simplify the expression $9 \cdot (33 - 5^2) \div 2$, what do you do first?

 Ⓕ Divide by 2. Ⓖ Subtract 5. Ⓗ Multiply by 9. Ⓘ Square 5.

74. The table at the right shows the number of pages you can read per minute. Which algebraic expression gives a rule for finding the number of pages read in any number of minutes m?

 Ⓐ m Ⓒ $2m$

 Ⓑ $m + 2$ Ⓓ $\frac{m}{2}$

Reading

Minutes	Pages Read
1	2
2	4
3	6
m	■

Mixed Review

Evaluate each expression for the given values of the variables. ◀ **See Lesson 1-2.**

75. $(r - t)^2$; $r = 11$, $t = 7$ **76.** $3m^2 + n$; $m = 5$, $n = 3$ **77.** $(2x)^2 y$; $x = 4$, $y = 8$

Write an algebraic expression for each word phrase. ◀ **See Lesson 1-1.**

78. the sum of 14 and x **79.** 4 multiplied by the sum of y and 1

80. 3880 divided by z **81.** the product of t and the quotient of 19 and 3

Get Ready! **To prepare for Lesson 1-4, do Exercises 82–85.**

Simplify each expression. ◀ **See Lesson 1-2.**

82. $4 + 7 \cdot 2$ **83.** $(7 + 1)9$ **84.** $2 + 22 \cdot 20$ **85.** $6 + 18 \div 6$

1-4 Properties of Real Numbers

© Common Core State Standards

Prepares for N-RN.B.3 Explain why the sum or product of two rational numbers is rational; that the sum of a rational number and an irrational number is irrational . . .

MP 1, MP 2, MP 3, MP 4, MP 6, MP 7

Objective To identify and use properties of real numbers

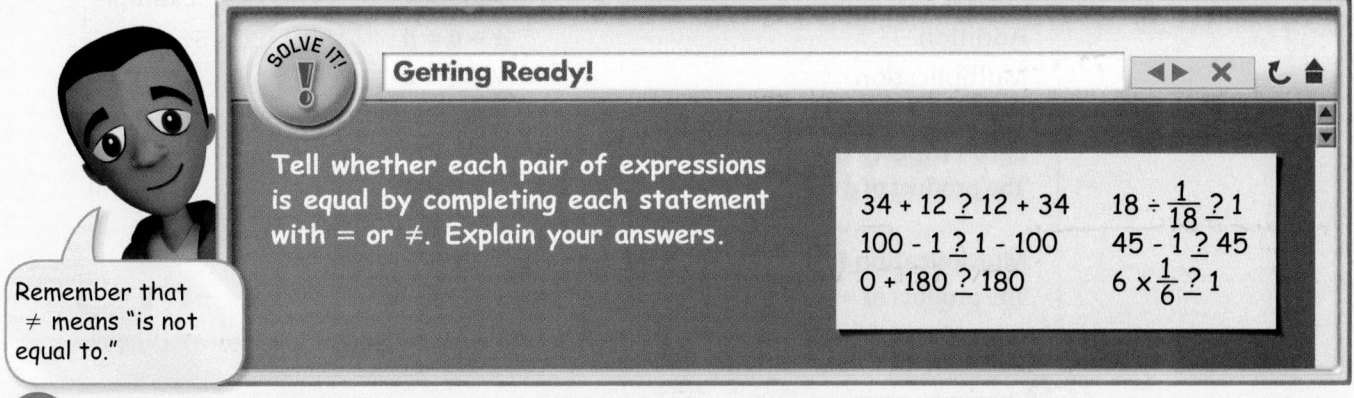

SOLVE IT!

Getting Ready!

Tell whether each pair of expressions is equal by completing each statement with = or ≠. Explain your answers.

$34 + 12 \underline{?} 12 + 34$ $18 \div \frac{1}{18} \underline{?} 1$

$100 - 1 \underline{?} 1 - 100$ $45 - 1 \underline{?} 45$

$0 + 180 \underline{?} 180$ $6 \times \frac{1}{6} \underline{?} 1$

Remember that ≠ means "is not equal to."

The Solve It illustrates numerical relationships that are always true for real numbers.

Essential Understanding Relationships that are always true for real numbers are called *properties*, which are rules used to rewrite and compare expressions.

Two algebraic expressions are **equivalent expressions** if they have the same value for all values of the variable(s). The following properties show expressions that are equivalent for all real numbers.

Lesson Vocabulary
- equivalent expressions
- deductive reasoning
- counterexample

take note

Properties   Properties of Real Numbers

Let a, b, and c be any real numbers.

Commutative Properties of Addition and Multiplication
Changing the order of the addends does not change the sum. Changing the order of the factors does not change the product.

	Algebra	Example
Addition	$a + b = b + a$	$18 + 54 = 54 + 18$
Multiplication	$a \cdot b = b \cdot a$	$12 \cdot \frac{1}{2} = \frac{1}{2} \cdot 12$

Associative Properties of Addition and Multiplication
Changing the grouping of the addends does not change the sum. Changing the grouping of the factors does not change the product.

Addition	$(a + b) + c = a + (b + c)$	$(23 + 9) + 4 = 23 + (9 + 4)$
Multiplication	$(a \cdot b) \cdot c = a \cdot (b \cdot c)$	$(7 \cdot 9) \cdot 10 = 7 \cdot (9 \cdot 10)$

 **Properties** Properties of Real Numbers

Let a be any real number.

Identity Properties of Addition and Multiplication

The sum of any real number and 0 is the original number. The product of any real number and 1 is the original number.

	Algebra	Example
Addition	$a + 0 = a$	$5\frac{3}{4} + 0 = 5\frac{3}{4}$
Multiplication	$a \cdot 1 = a$	$67 \cdot 1 = 67$

Zero Property of Multiplication

The product of a and 0 is 0. $a \cdot 0 = 0$ $18 \cdot 0 = 0$

Multiplication Property of -1

The product of -1 and a is $-a$. $-1 \cdot a = -a$ $-1 \cdot 9 = -9$

 Problem 1 Identifying Properties

Think

What math symbols give you clues about the properties?
Parentheses, operation symbols, and the numbers 0 and 1 may indicate certain properties.

What property is illustrated by each statement?

A $42 \cdot 0 = 0$ Zero Property of Multiplication

B $(y + 2.5) + 28 = y + (2.5 + 28)$ Associative Property of Addition

C $10x + 0 = 10x$ Identity Property of Addition

Got It? **1.** What property is illustrated by each statement?

    a. $4x \cdot 1 = 4x$ **b.** $x + (\sqrt{y} + z) = x + (z + \sqrt{y})$

     Identity property of Multiplication of 1   *Commutative of Addition*

You can use properties to help you solve some problems using mental math.

 **Problem 2** Using Properties for Mental Calculations

Plan

How can you make the addition easier?
Look for numbers having decimal parts you can add easily, such as 0.75 and 0.25.

Movies A movie ticket costs $7.75. A drink costs $2.40. Popcorn costs $1.25. What is the total cost for a ticket, a drink, and popcorn? Use mental math.

$(7.75 + 2.40) + 1.25 = (2.40 + 7.75) + 1.25$	Commutative Property of Addition
$= 2.40 + (7.75 + 1.25)$	Associative Property of Addition
$= 2.40 + 9$	Simplify inside parentheses.
$= 11.40$	Add.

The total cost is $11.40.

 Got It? **2.** A can holds 3 tennis balls. A box holds 4 cans. A case holds 6 boxes. How many tennis balls are in 10 cases? Use mental math. *720*

Problem 3 Writing Equivalent Expressions

Simplify each expression.

A $5(3n)$

Know	Need	Plan
An expression	Groups of numbers that can be simplified	Use properties to group or reorder parts of the expression.

$$5(3n) = (5 \cdot 3)n \quad \text{Associative Property of Multiplication}$$
$$= 15n \quad \text{Simplify.}$$

B $(4 + 7b) + 8$

$$(4 + 7b) + 8 = (7b + 4) + 8 \quad \text{Commutative Property of Addition}$$
$$= 7b + (4 + 8) \quad \text{Associative Property of Addition}$$
$$= 7b + 12 \quad \text{Simplify.}$$

C $\dfrac{6xy}{y}$

$$\frac{6xy}{y} = \frac{6x \cdot y}{1 \cdot y} \quad \text{Rewrite denominator using Identity Property of Multiplication.}$$
$$= \frac{6x}{1} \cdot \frac{y}{y} \quad \text{Use rule for multiplying fractions: } \frac{a}{b} \cdot \frac{c}{d} = \frac{ac}{bd}.$$
$$= 6x \cdot 1 \quad x \div 1 = x \text{ and } y \div y = 1.$$
$$= 6x \quad \text{Identity Property of Multiplication}$$

 Got It? 3. Simplify each expression.

    a. $2.1(4.5x)$ **b.** $6 + (4h + 3)$ **c.** $\dfrac{8m}{12mn}$

         9.45x   4h + 9 $\frac{2}{3n}$

In Problem 3, reasoning and properties were used to show that two expressions are equivalent. This is an example of *deductive reasoning*. **Deductive reasoning** is the process of reasoning logically from given facts to a conclusion.

To show that a statement is *not* true, find an example for which it is not true. An example showing that a statement is false is a **counterexample.** You need only one counterexample to prove that a statement is false.

 Problem 4 Using Deductive Reasoning and Counterexamples

Is the statement *true* or *false*? If it is false, give a counterexample.

A For all real numbers a and b, $a \cdot b = b + a$.

    False. $5 \cdot 3 \neq 3 + 5$ is a counterexample.

B For all real numbers a, b, and c, $(a + b) + c = b + (a + c)$.

    True. Use properties of real numbers to show that the expressions are equivalent.

$$(a + b) + c = (b + a) + c \quad \text{Commutative Property of Addition}$$
$$= b + (a + c) \quad \text{Associative Property of Addition}$$

Plan

Look for a counterexample to show the statement is false. If you don't find one, try to use properties to show that it is true.

 **Got It?** **4. Reasoning** Is each statement in parts (a) and (b) *true* or *false*? If it is false, give a counterexample. If true, use properties of real numbers to show the expressions are equivalent.

   a. For all real numbers j and k, $j \cdot k = (k + 0) \cdot j$. True

   b. For all real numbers m and n, $m(n + 1) = mn + 1$. False

   c. Is the statement in part (A) of Problem 4 false for *every* pair of real numbers a and b? Explain. No $0 \cdot 0 = 0 + 0$ $2 \cdot 2 = 2 + 2$

 ## Lesson Check

Do you know HOW?

Name the property that each statement illustrates.

1. $x + 12 = 12 + x$ Comm. of Add.

2. $5 \cdot (12 \cdot x) = (5 \cdot 12) \cdot x$ Assoc. of Mult.

3. You buy a sandwich for $2.95, an apple for $.45, and a bottle of juice for $1.05. What is the total cost?   4.45

4. Simplify $\frac{24cd}{c}$.   24d

Do you UNDERSTAND?  MATHEMATICAL PRACTICES

5. Vocabulary Tell whether the expressions in each pair are equivalent.

   a. $5x \cdot 1$ and $1 + 5x$ no

   b. $1 + (2t + 1)$ and $2 + 2t$ yes

6. Justify each step.

$3 \cdot (10 \cdot 12) = 3 \cdot (12 \cdot 10)$ Comm. of Mult.

$= (3 \cdot 12) \cdot 10$ Assoc. of Mult.

$= 36 \cdot 10$ Multiply

$= 360$ Multiply

 ## Practice and Problem-Solving Exercises  MATHEMATICAL PRACTICES

 **Practice**   Name the property that each statement illustrates.   ◆ **See Problem 1.**

7. $75 + 6 = 6 + 75$ Comm. of Add. **8.** $\frac{7}{9} \cdot 1 = \frac{7}{9}$ Identity of Mult. **9.** $h + 0 = h$ Identity of Add.

10. $389 \cdot 0 = 0$ 0 Property of Mult. **11.** $27 \cdot \pi = \pi \cdot 27$ Comm of Mult **12.** $9 \cdot (-1 \cdot x) = 9 \cdot (-x)$ Mult. of of Mult.

Mental Math Simplify each expression.   ◆ **See Problem 2.**

13. $21 + 6 + 9$ 36

14. $10 \cdot 2 \cdot 19 \cdot 5$ 1900

15. $0.1 + 3.7 + 5.9$ 9.7

16. $4 \cdot 5 \cdot 13 \cdot 5$ 1300

17. $55.3 + 0.2 + 23.8 + 0.7$ 80

18. $0.25 \cdot 12 \cdot 4$ 12

19. Fishing Trip The sign at the right shows the costs for a deep-sea fishing trip. How much will the total cost be for 1 adult, 2 children, and 1 senior citizen to go on a fishing trip? Use mental math. $110

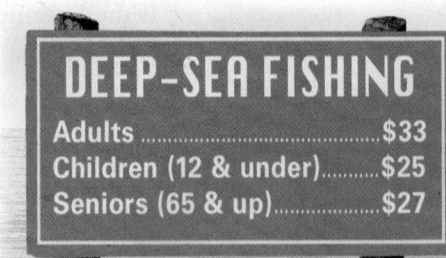

DEEP-SEA FISHING

Adults $33
Children (12 & under)..........$25
Seniors (65 & up)................$27

Simplify each expression. Justify each step. See Problem 3.

20. $8 + (9t + 4)$ **21.** $9(2x)$ **22.** $(4 + 105x) + 5$ **23.** $(10p)11$

24. $(12 \cdot r) \cdot 13$ **25.** $(2 + 3x) + 9$ **26.** $4 \cdot (x \cdot 6.3)$ **27.** $1.1 + (7d + 0.1)$

28. $\frac{56ab}{b}$ **29.** $\frac{1.5mn}{m}$ **30.** $\frac{13p}{pq}$ **31.** $\frac{33xy}{3x}$

Use deductive reasoning to tell whether each statement is *true* or *false*. See Problem 4.
If it is false, give a counterexample. If true, use properties of real numbers to show the expressions are equivalent.

32. For all real numbers r, s, and t, $(r \cdot s) \cdot t = t \cdot (s \cdot r)$.

33. For all real numbers p and q, $p \div q = q \div p$.

34. For all real numbers x, $x + 0 = 0$.

35. For all real numbers a and b, $-a \cdot b = a \cdot (-b)$.

 **Apply**

36. Error Analysis Your friend shows you the problem at the right. He says that the Associative Property allows you to change the order in which you complete two operations. Is your friend correct? Explain.

$$(5 \cdot 11) + 9 = 5 \cdot (11 + 9)$$
$$= 5 \cdot 20$$
$$= 100$$

37. Travel It is 258 mi from Tulsa, Oklahoma, to Dallas, Texas. It is 239 mi from Dallas, Texas, to Houston, Texas.
  a. What is the total distance of a trip from Tulsa to Dallas to Houston?
  b. What is the total distance of a trip from Houston to Dallas to Tulsa?
  c. Explain how you can tell whether the distances described in parts (a) and (b) are equal by using reasoning.

Tell whether the expressions in each pair are equivalent.

38. $2 + h + 4$ and $2 \cdot h \cdot 4$ **39.** $9y \cdot 0$ and 1 **40.** $3x$ and $3x \cdot 1$

41. $m(1 - 1)$ and 0 **42.** $(9 - 7) + \pi$ and 2π **43.** $(3 + 7) + m$ and $m + 10$

44. $\frac{63ab}{7a}$ and $9ab$ **45.** $\frac{11x}{(2 + 5 - 7)}$ and $11x$ **46.** $\frac{7t}{4 - 8 + \sqrt{9}}$ and $7t$

47. Think About a Plan Hannah makes a list of possible gifts for Mary, Jared, and Michael. She has two plans and can spend a total of $75 for all gifts. Which plan(s) can Hannah afford?
  • What property can you use to make it easier to find the total cost of different gifts?
  • What number do you compare to the total cost of each plan to decide whether it is affordable?

Same Gifts
DVD $22

Different Gifts
Mary: Sweater $29.26
Jared: Book $23.99
Michael: Cactus $23.74

48. Writing Suppose you are mixing red and blue paint in a bucket. Do you think the final color of the mixed paint will be the same whether you add the blue paint or the red paint to the bucket first? Relate your answer to a property of real numbers.

Simplify each expression. Justify each step.

49. $25 \cdot 3.9 \cdot 4$

50. $(4.4 \div 4.4)(x + 7)$

51. $(7^6 - 6^5)(8 - 8)$

 **Reasoning** Answer each question. Use examples to justify your answers.

52. Is subtraction commutative?

53. Is subtraction associative?

54. Is division commutative?

55. Is division associative?

Challenge

56. Patterns The Commutative Property of Addition lets you rewrite addition expressions. How many different ways can you write $a + b + c$? Show each way.

57. Reasoning Suppose you know that $a(b + c) = ab + ac$ is true for all real numbers a, b, and c. Use the properties of real numbers to prove that $(b + c)a = ba + ca$ is true for all real numbers a, b, and c.

Standardized Test Prep

SAT/ACT

58. What is the simplified form of $(1.2 + 0) + 4.6 + 3.8$?

Ⓐ 1.2
Ⓑ 8.0
Ⓒ 8.4
Ⓓ 9.6

59. Which expression is equal to $3 \cdot 3 \cdot 8 \cdot 8 \cdot 3$?

Ⓕ $3 \cdot 8$
Ⓖ 3^8
Ⓗ $3^3 \cdot 8^2$
Ⓘ $3 \cdot 3 + 2 \cdot 8$

60. There are four points plotted on the number line below.

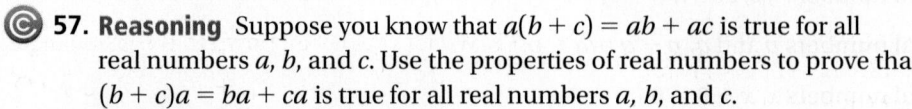

Which expression represents the greatest amount?

Ⓐ $M \div L$
Ⓑ $M - L$
Ⓒ $J + K$
Ⓓ $L - K$

61. Lane 1 at your local track is 0.25 mi long. You live 0.5 mi away from the track. Which of the following results in the shortest jog?

Ⓕ jogging 6 times around the track in Lane 1
Ⓖ jogging to the track and then 5 times around the track in Lane 1
Ⓗ jogging to the track, 3 times around the track in Lane 1, and then home
Ⓘ jogging 8 times around the track in Lane 1

Mixed Review

Order the numbers in each exercise from least to greatest.

◀ See Lesson 1-3.

62. $-6, 6^3, 1.6, \sqrt{6}$

63. $\frac{8}{5}, 1.4, -17, 10^2$

64. $1.75, -4.5, \sqrt{4}, 14^1$

Get Ready! **To prepare for Lesson 1-5, do Exercises 65–68.**

Find each sum or difference.

◀ See p. 803.

65. $3 + 11$

66. $\frac{3}{8} + \frac{5}{8}$

67. $9.7 - 8.6$

68. $\frac{5}{9} - \frac{5}{10}$

MathXL® for School
Go to PowerAlgebra.com

Do you know HOW?

Write an algebraic expression for each phrase.

1. a number n divided by 4 $\frac{n}{4}$

2. 2 less than the product of 5 and n $5n - 2$

3. The table shows how the total cost of a field trip depends on the number of students. What is a rule for the total cost of the tickets? Give the rule in words and as an algebraic expression.

Field Trip

Number of Students	Total Cost
20	$(12 \cdot 20) + 150$ $(12 \cdot n) + 150$
40	$(12 \cdot 40) + 150$
60	$(12 \cdot 60) + 150$

4. The sign shows the costs associated with a whitewater rafting trip. Write an expression to determine the cost of 3 children and 1 adult renting equipment for a whitewater rafting trip that lasts h hours.

Whitewater Tours

Adult Ticket	$53
Child Ticket	$32
Equipment Rental	$5 per hour

$(5h) + 32 \cdot 3$

$(5h) + 32 \cdot 3 + 53$

Simplify each expression.

5. $24 \div (3 + 2^2)$ $= 3.42857143\ldots$

6. $\sqrt{144}$ $= 12$

Evaluate each expression for the given values of the variables.

7. $3x \cdot 2 \div y$; $x = 3$ and $y = 6$ $= 3$

8. $(4a)^3 \div (b - 2)$; $a = 2$ and $b = 4$

9. Name the subset(s) of real numbers to which each number belongs. Then order the numbers from least to greatest.
$$\sqrt{105},\ -4,\ \frac{4}{3}$$

10. Estimate $\sqrt{14}$ to the nearest integer.

11. What property is shown in the following equation?
$$(5 + 8) + 11 = 5 + (8 + 11)$$

12. Use the table below. If the total cost for n sandwiches is $16.50, what is the total cost when 1 more sandwich is bought?

Lunch Menu

Salad	$6.25
Sandwich	$5.50
Drink	$2.75

Do you UNDERSTAND?

13. What word phrases represent the expressions $-2 + 3x$ and $3x + (-2)$? Are the two expressions equivalent? Explain.

14. Use grouping symbols to make the following equation true.
$$4^2 + 2 \cdot 3 = 54$$

15. Choose the correct word to complete the following sentence: A natural number is (*always, sometimes, never*) a whole number.

16. How many natural numbers are in the set of numbers from -10 to 10 inclusive? Explain.

17. What is the simplified form of $\frac{3abc}{abc}$, when $abc \neq 0$? Explain using the properties of real numbers.

18. Reasoning Are the associative properties true for all integers? Explain.

19. Use the Commutative Property of Multiplication to rewrite the expression $(x \cdot y) \cdot z$ in two different ways.

1-5 Adding and Subtracting Real Numbers

© Common Core State Standards

Prepares for N-RN.B.3 Explain why the sum or product of two rational numbers is rational; that the sum of a rational number and an irrational number is irrational . . .

MP 1, MP 3, MP 4

Objective To find sums and differences of real numbers

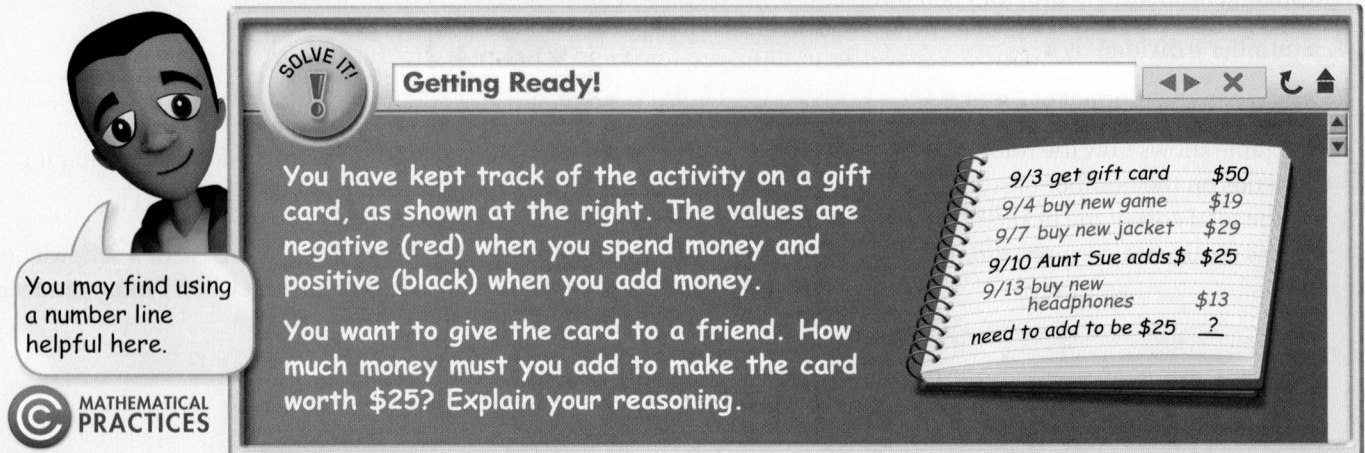

SOLVE IT!

Getting Ready!

You have kept track of the activity on a gift card, as shown at the right. The values are negative (red) when you spend money and positive (black) when you add money.

You want to give the card to a friend. How much money must you add to make the card worth $25? Explain your reasoning.

9/3 get gift card	$50
9/4 buy new game	$19
9/7 buy new jacket	$29
9/10 Aunt Sue adds $	$25
9/13 buy new headphones	$13
need to add to be $25	?

You may find using a number line helpful here.

© MATHEMATICAL PRACTICES

Essential Understanding You can add or subtract any real numbers using a number line model. You can also add or subtract real numbers using rules involving absolute value.

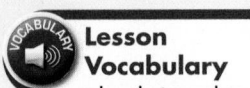

Lesson Vocabulary
• absolute value
• opposites
• additive inverses

© Problem 1 Using Number Line Models

What is each sum? Use a number line.

Think

How do you know which direction to move along the number line?
If the number added is positive, move to the right. If the number added is negative, move to the left.

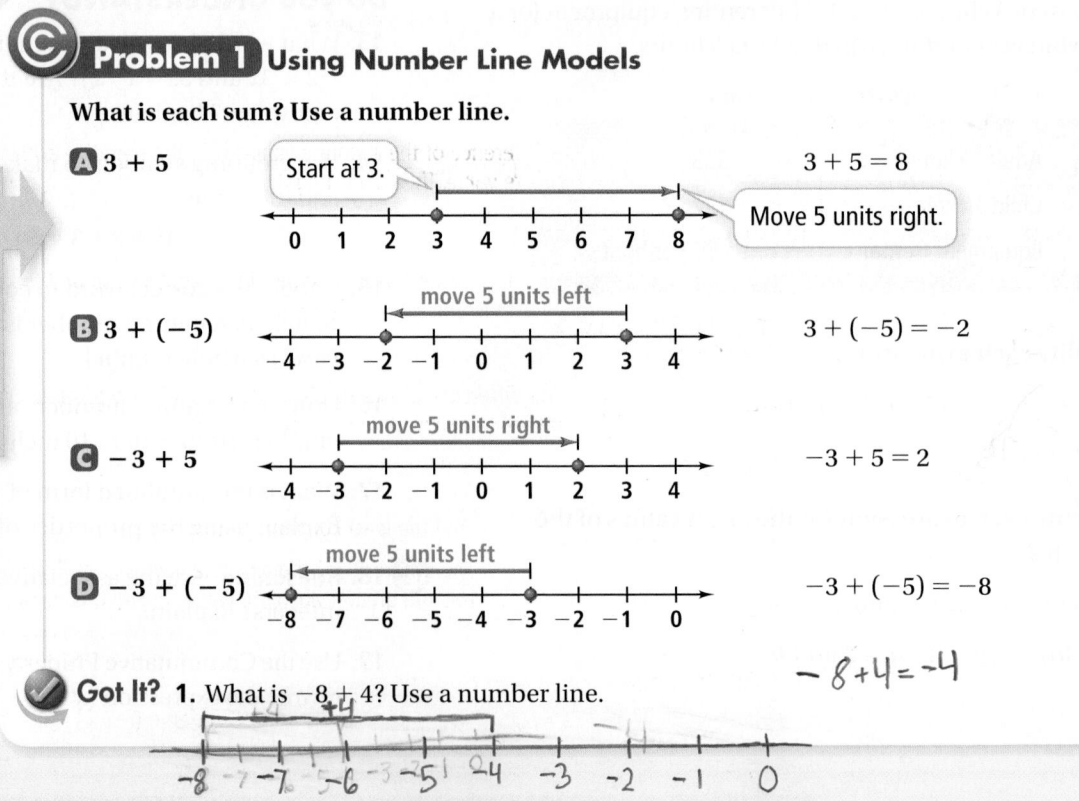

Ⓐ 3 + 5

Start at 3.   Move 5 units right.

$3 + 5 = 8$

Ⓑ 3 + (−5)   move 5 units left

$3 + (−5) = −2$

Ⓒ −3 + 5   move 5 units right

$−3 + 5 = 2$

Ⓓ −3 + (−5)   move 5 units left

$−3 + (−5) = −8$

$−8 + 4 = −4$

✓ Got It? 1. What is −8 + 4? Use a number line.

The **absolute value** of a number is its distance from 0 on a number line. Absolute value is always nonnegative since distance is always nonnegative.

For example, the absolute value of 4 is 4 and the absolute value of −4 is 4. You can write this as $|4| = 4$ and $|-4| = 4$.

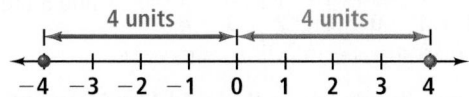

You can use absolute value when you find the sums of real numbers.

take note

Key Concept   Adding Real Numbers

Adding Numbers With the Same Sign
To add two numbers with the same sign, add their absolute values. The sum has the same sign as the addends.

Examples $3 + 4 = 7$ $-3 + (-4) = -7$

Adding Numbers With Different Signs
To add two numbers with different signs, subtract their absolute values. The sum has the same sign as the addend with the greater absolute value.

Examples $-3 + 4 = 1$ $3 + (-4) = -1$

Plan

What is the first step in finding each sum?
Identify whether the addends have the same sign or different signs. Then choose the appropriate rule to use.

Ⓒ **Problem 2** Adding Real Numbers

What is each sum?

Ⓐ $-12 + 7$

$-12 + 7 = -5$ The difference of the absolute values is 5. The negative addend has the greater absolute value. The sum is negative.

Ⓑ $-18 + (-2)$

$-18 + (-2) = -20$ The addends have the same sign (negative), so add their absolute values. The sum is negative.

Ⓒ $-4.8 + 9.5$

$-4.8 + 9.5 = 4.7$ The difference of the absolute values is 4.7. The positive addend has the greater absolute value. The sum is positive.

Ⓓ $\frac{3}{4} + \left(-\frac{5}{6}\right)$

$\frac{3}{4} + \left(-\frac{5}{6}\right) = \frac{9}{12} + \left(-\frac{10}{12}\right)$ Find the least common denominator.

$= -\frac{1}{12}$ The difference of the absolute values is $\frac{1}{12}$. The negative addend has the greater absolute value. The sum is negative.

✔ **Got It?** **2.** What is each sum?

    a. $-16 + (-8)$ **b.** $-11 + 9$ **c.** $9 + (-11)$ **d.** $-6 + (-2)$
        −24   −2   −2   −8

Two numbers that are the same distance from 0 on a number line but lie in opposite directions are **opposites.**

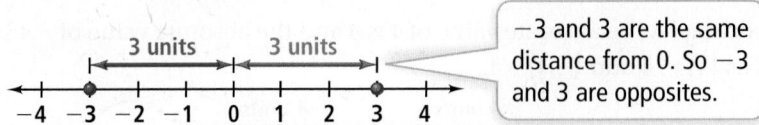

−3 and 3 are the same distance from 0. So −3 and 3 are opposites.

A number and its opposite are called **additive inverses.** To find the sum of a number and its opposite, you can use the **Inverse Property of Addition.**

take note

Property   Inverse Property of Addition

For every real number a, there is an additive inverse $-a$ such that $a + (-a) = -a + a = 0$.

Examples $14 + (-14) = 0$ $-14 + 14 = 0$

You can use opposites (additive inverses) to subtract real numbers. To see how, look at the number line below, which models $3 - 5$ and $3 + (-5)$.

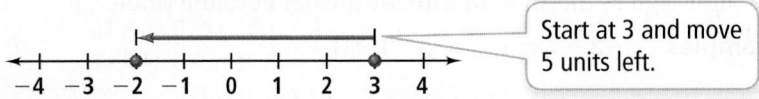

Start at 3 and move 5 units left.

$3 - 5$ and $3 + (-5)$ are equivalent expressions, illustrating the rule below.

take note

Key Concept   Subtracting Real Numbers

To subtract a real number, add its opposite: $a - b = a + (-b)$.

Examples $3 - 5 = 3 + (-5) = -2$ $3 - (-5) = 3 + 5 = 8$

© **Problem 3** Subtracting Real Numbers

Think

Why rewrite subtraction as addition?
You can simplify expressions using the rules for adding real numbers that you learned earlier in this lesson.

What is each difference?

Ⓐ $-8 - (-13) = -8 + 13$ The opposite of −13 is 13. So add 13.
   $= 5$ Use rules for addition.

Ⓑ $3.5 - 12.4 = 3.5 + (-12.4)$ The opposite of 12.4 is −12.4. So add −12.4.
   $= -8.9$ Use rules for addition.

Ⓒ $9 - 9 = 9 + (-9)$ The opposite of 9 is −9. So add −9.
   $= 0$ Inverse Property of Addition

© ✓ **Got It? 3. a.** What is $4.8 - (-8.7)$? 13.5
       b. Reasoning For what values of a and b does $a - b = b - a$?

$a = b$

All of the addition properties of real numbers that you learned in Lesson 1-4 apply to both positive and negative numbers. You can use these properties to reorder and simplify expressions.

 Problem 4 Adding and Subtracting Real Numbers

Scuba Diving A reef explorer dives 25 ft to photograph brain coral and then rises 16 ft to travel over a ridge before diving 47 ft to survey the base of the reef. Then the diver rises 29 ft to see an underwater cavern. What is the location of the cavern in relation to sea level?

Know → **Need** → **Plan**

Know	Need	Plan
Distance and direction for each change in location	Location in relation to sea level after changes	Represent the diver's trip with an expression. Reorder the values to make calculations easier.

Think

How do you represent the problem with an expression?
Start your expression with zero to represent sea level. Subtract for dives, and add for rises.

$0 - 25 + 16 - 47 + 29$ Write an expression.

$= 0 + (-25) + 16 + (-47) + 29$ Use rule for subtracting real numbers.

$= 0 + 16 + 29 + (-25) + (-47)$ Commutative Property of Addition

$= 0 + (16 + 29) + [(-25) + (-47)]$ Group addends with the same sign.

$= 0 + 45 + (-72)$ Add inside grouping symbols.

$= 45 + (-72)$ Identity Property of Addition

$= -27$ Use rule for adding numbers with different signs.

The cavern is at -27 ft in relation to sea level.

[handwritten:]
$0 + 215 + 734 + (803) + (-2619)$
$0 + (215 + 734) + [(-803) + (-2619)]$
$0 + 949 + (-3422)$
$949 + (-3422)$
$= -2473$

[handwritten:]
$0 - 803 + 215 - 2619 + 734$
$0 + (-803) + 215 + (-2619) + 734$

 Got It? 4. A robot submarine dives 803 ft to the ocean floor. It rises 215 ft as the water gets shallower. Then the submarine dives 2619 ft into a deep crevice. Next, it rises 734 ft to photograph a crack in the wall of the crevice. What is the location of the crack in relation to sea level? *-2473 ft below sea level*

 Lesson Check

Do you know HOW?

Use a number line to find each sum.

1. $-5 + 2$ *[handwritten: -2, =-3, number line -5 -4 -3 -2 -1 0]*   **2.** $-2 + (-1)$ *=-3* *[handwritten number line: -3 -2 -1 0]*

Find each sum or difference.

3. $-12 + 9$ *-3*   **4.** $-4 + (-3)$ *-7*

5. $-3 - (-5)$ *2*   **6.** $1.5 - 8.5$ *-7*

Do you UNDERSTAND?  MATHEMATICAL PRACTICES

7. Vocabulary What is the sum of a number and its opposite? *additive inverse*

8. Compare and Contrast How is subtraction related to addition? *Subtracting is the same as adding an opposite*

9. Error Analysis Your friend says that since $-a$ is the opposite of a, the opposite of a number is always negative. Describe and correct the error. *the opposite of a negative number is positive*

Practice and Problem-Solving Exercises

MATHEMATICAL PRACTICES

 **Practice**

Use a number line to find each sum. ◀ **See Problem 1.**

10. $2 + 5$ **11.** $-3 + 8$ **12.** $4 + (-3)$ **13.** $1 + (-6)$

14. $-6 + 9$ **15.** $-4 + 7$ **16.** $-6 + (-8)$ **17.** $-9 + (-3)$

Find each sum. ◀ **See Problem 2.**

18. $11 + 9$ **19.** $17 + (-28)$ **20.** $12 + (-9)$ **21.** $-2 + 7$

22. $-14 + (-10)$ **23.** $-9 + (-2)$ **24.** $3.2 + 1.4$ **25.** $5.1 + (-0.7)$

26. $-2.2 + (-3.8)$ **27.** $\frac{1}{2} + \left(-\frac{7}{2}\right)$ **28.** $-\frac{2}{3} + \left(-\frac{3}{5}\right)$ **29.** $\frac{7}{9} + \left(-\frac{5}{12}\right)$

Find each difference. ◀ **See Problem 3.**

30. $5 - 15$ **31.** $-13 - 7$ **32.** $-19 - 7$ **33.** $36 - (-12)$

34. $-29 - (-11)$ **35.** $-7 - (-5)$ **36.** $8.5 - 7.6$ **37.** $-2.5 - 17.8$

38. $-2.9 - (-7.5)$ **39.** $3.5 - 1.9$ **40.** $\frac{1}{8} - \frac{3}{4}$ **41.** $\frac{7}{16} - \left(-\frac{1}{2}\right)$

42. Bird Watching An eagle starts flying at an elevation of 42 ft. Elevation is the distance above sea level. The diagram below shows the elevation changes during the eagle's flight. Write an expression representing the eagle's flight. What is the elevation at the brook? ◀ **See Problem 4.**

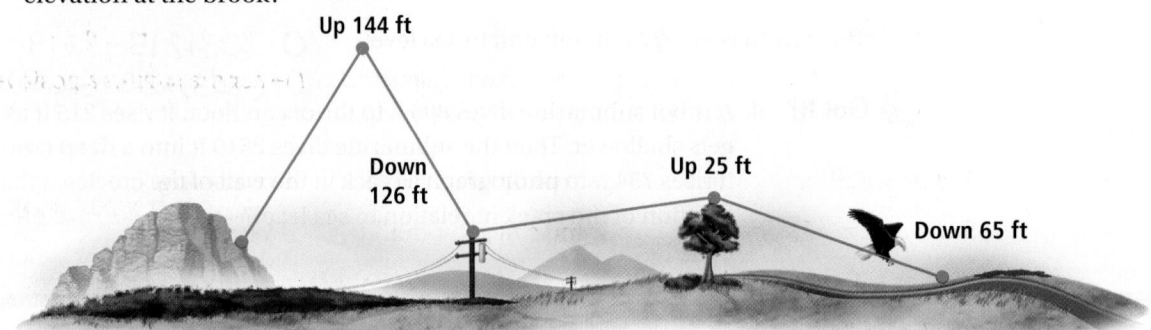

Up 144 ft

Down 126 ft

Up 25 ft

Down 65 ft

43. Stock Market A stock's starting price per share is $51.47 at the beginning of the week. During the week, the price changes by gaining $1.22, then losing $3.47, then losing $2.11, then losing $.98, and finally gaining $2.41. What is the ending stock price?

 **Apply**

Evaluate each expression for $a = -2$, $b = -4.1$, and $c = 5$.

44. $a - b + c$ **45.** $-c + b - a$ **46.** $-a + (-c)$

47. Error Analysis Describe and correct the error in finding the difference shown at the right.

48. Writing Without calculating, tell which is greater, the sum of -135 and 257 or the sum of 135 and -257. Explain your reasoning.

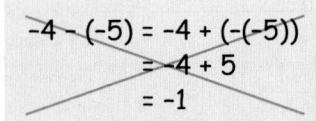

$-4 - (-5) = -4 + (-(-5))$
$= -4 + 5$
$= -1$

Simplify each expression.

49. $1 - \frac{1}{2} - \frac{1}{3} - \frac{1}{4}$ **50.** $7 + (2^2 - 3^2)$ **51.** $-2.1 - [2.3 - (3.5 - (-1.9))]$

52. Think About a Plan In golf, the expected number of strokes is called "par." When the number of strokes taken is more than par, your score is positive. When the number of strokes is less than par, your score is negative. The lowest score wins.

The scorecard shows par and one golfer's score for the first four holes played on a nine-hole golf course. The golfer's scores on the remaining five holes are -1, 0, -1, $+1$, 0. Par for the nine holes is 36. What is the golfer's total number of strokes for the nine holes?

- Can you solve the problem by adding the strokes taken on each hole?
- How is the sum of the golfer's scores related to the total number of strokes taken?

Golf Scorecard

Par	Number of Strokes	Score
4	6	+2
4	3	−1
3	3	0
5	3	−2

Reasoning Use reasoning to determine whether the value of each expression is *positive* or *negative*. Do not calculate the exact answers.

53. $-225 + 318$ **54.** $-\frac{7}{8} + \frac{1}{3}$ **55.** $34.5 + 12.9 - 50$

STEM **56. Temperature Scales** The Kelvin temperature scale is related to the degrees Celsius (°C) temperature scale by the formula $x = 273 + y$, where x is the number of kelvins and y is the temperature in degrees Celsius. What is each temperature in kelvins?

a. $-22°C$ **b.** $0°C$ **c.** $-32°C$

57. Writing Explain how you can tell without calculating whether the sum of a positive number and a negative number will be positive, negative, or zero.

Decide whether each statement is true or false. Explain your reasoning.

58. The sum of a positive number and a negative number is always negative.

59. The difference of two numbers is always less than the sum of those two numbers.

60. A number minus its opposite is twice the number.

STEM **61. Meteorology** Weather forecasters use a barometer to measure air pressure and make weather predictions. Suppose a standard mercury barometer reads 29.8 in. The mercury rises 0.02 in. and then falls 0.09 in. The mercury falls again 0.18 in. before rising 0.07 in. What is the final reading on the barometer?

62. Multiple Choice Which expression is equivalent to $x - y$?

Ⓐ $y - x$ Ⓑ $x - (-y)$ Ⓒ $x + (-y)$ Ⓓ $y + (-x)$

STEM **63. Chemistry** Atoms contain particles called protons and electrons. Each proton has a charge of $+1$ and each electron has a charge of -1. A certain sulfur ion has 18 electrons and 16 protons. The charge on an ion is the sum of the charges of its protons and electrons. What is the sulfur ion's charge?

64. Reasoning If $|x| > |y|$, does $|x - y| = |x| - |y|$? Justify your answer.

65. Reasoning A student wrote the equation $-|m| = |-m|$. Is the equation *always*, *sometimes*, or *never* true? Explain.

Simplify each expression.

66. $\frac{c}{4} - \frac{c}{4}$

67. $\frac{w}{5} + \left(-\frac{w}{10}\right)$

68. $\frac{d}{5} - \left(-\frac{d}{5}\right)$

69. Reasoning Answer each question. Justify your answers.
   a. Is $|a - b|$ always equal to $|b - a|$?
   b. Is $|a + b|$ always equal to $|a| + |b|$?

Standardized Test Prep

70. What is the value of $-b - a$ when $a = -4$ and $b = 7$?
   Ⓐ -11 Ⓑ -3 Ⓒ 3 Ⓓ 11

71. Which expression is equivalent to $19 - 41$?
   Ⓕ $|19 - 41|$ Ⓖ $|19 + 41|$ Ⓗ $-|19 - 41|$ Ⓘ $-|19 + 41|$

72. Which equation illustrates the Identity Property of Multiplication?
   Ⓐ $x \cdot 0 = 0$ Ⓑ $x \cdot 1 = x$ Ⓒ $x(yz) = (xy)z$ Ⓓ $x \cdot y = y \cdot x$

73. What is an algebraic expression for the perimeter of the triangle?
   Ⓕ $8 + x$ Ⓗ 8
   Ⓖ $4x$ Ⓘ $4 + x$

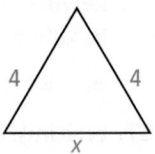

74. Which point on the number line below is the best estimate for $\sqrt{8}$?

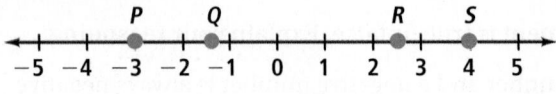

   Ⓐ P Ⓑ Q Ⓒ R Ⓓ S

Mixed Review

Tell whether the expressions in each pair are equivalent.　　　　◀ **See Lesson 1-4.**

75. $\frac{3}{4} \cdot d \cdot 4$ and $3d$

76. $(2.1 \cdot h) \cdot 3$ and $6.3 + h$

77. $(6 + b) + a$ and $6 + (a + b)$

Name the subset(s) of real numbers to which each number belongs.　　　　◀ **See Lesson 1-3.**

78. $\frac{1}{3}$ **79.** -5.333 **80.** $\sqrt{16}$ **81.** 82.0371 **82.** $\sqrt{21}$

Get Ready!   **To prepare for Lesson 1-6, do Exercises 83–85.**

Evaluate each expression for $a = 2$, $h = 5$, and $w = 8$.　　　　◀ **See Lesson 1-2.**

83. $4h - 5a \div w$

84. $a^2 w - h^2 + 2h$

85. $(w^2 h - a^2) + 12 \div 3a$

Always, Sometimes, or Never

Common Core State Standards

Prepares for A-CED.A.3 Represent constraints by equations or inequalities . . .

MP 2

A statement can be always, sometimes, or never true. For each activity, work with a group of 4 students. Take turns predicting each answer. If the predictor gives a correct answer and explanation, he or she scores 1 point. Otherwise, the first person who proves the predictor incorrect scores 1 point. Whoever has the most points at the end of an activity wins.

Activity 1

Is each description *always, sometimes,* or *never* true about the members of your group?

1. takes an algebra class

2. lives in your state

3. plays a musical instrument

4. is less than 25 years old

5. speaks more than one language

6. is taller than 5 m

7. has a sibling

8. plays basketball

Activity 2

Suppose each member of your group takes one of the four cards at the right. Will a group member *always, sometimes,* or *never* have a number that fits each description?

9. greater than 2

10. greater than 25

11. even

12. irrational number

13. prime number

14. rational number

15. divisible by 2

16. less than 10

Activity 3

Each member of your group substitutes any integer for *x* in each statement. Will a group member *always, sometimes,* or *never* have a true statement?

17. $x - 2$ is greater than x.

18. $|x|$ is less than x.

19. $7 + x = x + 7$

20. $13 - x = x - 13$

21. $x + 0 = x$

22. $-4 + (3 + x) = x + (-4 + 3)$

23. $x \cdot 0 = 0$

24. $|x|$ is greater than x.

1-6 Multiplying and Dividing Real Numbers

 Common Core State Standards

Prepares for N-RN.B.3 Explain why the sum or product of two rational numbers is rational; that the sum of a rational number and an irrational number is irrational . . .

MP 1, MP 3, MP 4, MP 6, MP 7

Objective To find products and quotients of real numbers

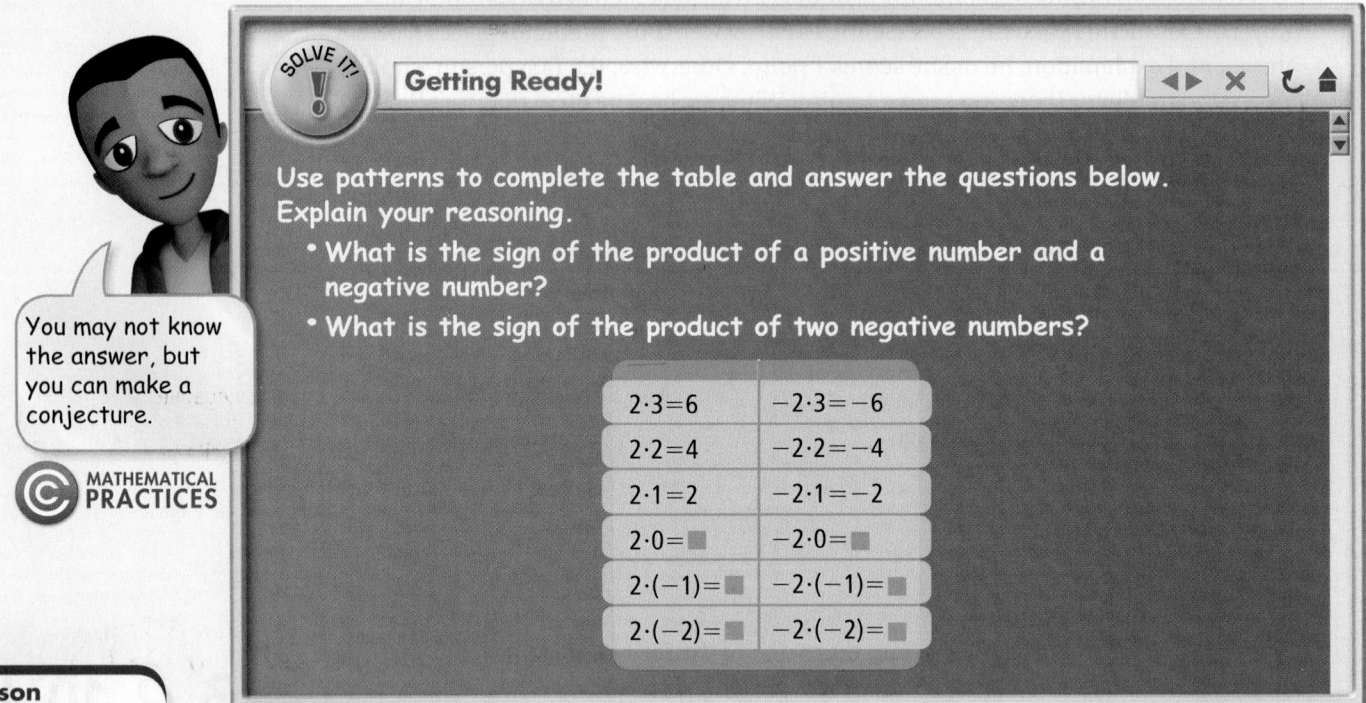

SOLVE IT!

Getting Ready!

Use patterns to complete the table and answer the questions below. Explain your reasoning.

• What is the sign of the product of a positive number and a negative number?

• What is the sign of the product of two negative numbers?

2·3=6	−2·3=−6
2·2=4	−2·2=−4
2·1=2	−2·1=−2
2·0=■	−2·0=■
2·(−1)=■	−2·(−1)=■
2·(−2)=■	−2·(−2)=■

You may not know the answer, but you can make a conjecture.

MATHEMATICAL PRACTICES

Lesson Vocabulary
• multiplicative inverse
• reciprocal

The patterns in the Solve It suggest rules for multiplying real numbers.

Essential Understanding The rules for multiplying real numbers are related to the properties of real numbers and the definitions of operations.

You know that the product of two positive numbers is positive. For example, $3(5) = 15$. You can think about the product of a positive number and a negative number in terms of groups of numbers. For example, $3(-5)$ means 3 groups of -5. So, $3(-5) = (-5) + (-5) + (-5)$, or $3(-5) = -15$.

You can also derive the product of two negative numbers, such as $-3(-5)$.

$3(-5) = -15$	Start with the product $3(-5) = -15$.
$-[3(-5)] = -(-15)$	The opposites of two equal numbers are equal.
$-1[3(-5)] = -(-15)$	Multiplication Property of -1
$[-1(3)](-5) = -(-15)$	Associative Property of Multiplication
$-3(-5) = -(-15)$	Multiplication Property of -1
$-3(-5) = 15$	The opposite of -15 is 15.

These discussions illustrate the following rules for multiplying real numbers.

> **take note**

Key Concept   Multiplying Real Numbers

Words The product of two real numbers with *different* signs is *negative*.

Examples $2(-3) = -6$ $-2 \cdot 3 = -6$

Model $2(-3) = -6$

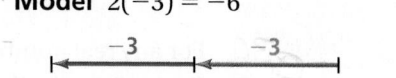

Words The product of two real numbers with the *same* sign is *positive*.

Examples $2 \cdot 3 = 6$ $-2(-3) = 6$

Model $2 \cdot 3 = 6$

Plan

What is your first step in finding a product of real numbers?
Identify the signs of the factors. Then determine the sign of the product.

© Problem 1   Multiplying Real Numbers

What is each product?

A $12(-8) = -96$ — The product of two numbers with different signs is negative.

B $24(0.5) = 12$ — The product of two numbers with the same sign is positive.

C $-\frac{3}{4} \cdot \frac{1}{2} = -\frac{3}{8}$ — The product of two numbers with different signs is negative.

D $(-3)^2 = (-3)(-3) = 9$ — The product of two numbers with the same sign is positive.

 Got It?   **1.** What is each product?

a. $6(-15) = -90$ **b.** $12(0.2) = 2.4$ **c.** $-\frac{7}{10}\left(\frac{3}{5}\right) = -\frac{21}{50}$ **d.** $(-4)^2 = 16$

Notice that $(-3)^2 = 9$ in part (d) of Problem 1. Recall from Lesson 1-3 that a is a square root of b if $a^2 = b$. So, -3 is a square root of 9. A negative square root is represented by $-\sqrt{\ }$. Every positive real number has a positive and a negative square root. The symbol $\pm$ in front of the radical indicates both square roots.

Think

How can you find a negative square root?
Look for a negative number that you can multiply by itself to get a product that is equal to the radicand.

© Problem 2   Simplifying Square Root Expressions

What is the simplified form of each expression?

A $-\sqrt{25} = -5$ $(-5)^2 = 25$, so $-\sqrt{25} = -5$.

B $\pm\sqrt{\frac{4}{49}} = \pm\frac{2}{7}$ $\left(\frac{2}{7}\right)^2 = \frac{4}{49}$ and $\left(-\frac{2}{7}\right)^2 = \frac{4}{49}$, so $\pm\sqrt{\frac{4}{49}} = \pm\frac{2}{7}$.

 Got It?   **2.** What is the simplified form of each expression?

a. $\sqrt{64}$ = 8   **b.** $\pm\sqrt{16} = \pm 4$ **c.** $-\sqrt{121}$ $-11 = -11$ **d.** $\pm\sqrt{\frac{1}{36}}$ $\pm\frac{1}{6}$

Essential Understanding Rules for dividing real numbers are related to the rules for multiplying real numbers.

For any real numbers a, b, and c where $a \neq 0$, if $a \cdot b = c$, then $b = c \div a$.
For instance, $-8(-2) = 16$, so $-2 = 16 \div (-8)$. Similarly $-8(2) = -16$, so
$2 = -16 \div (-8)$. These examples illustrate the following rules.

---

take note

Key Concept Dividing Real Numbers

Words The quotient of two real numbers with *different* signs is *negative*.
Examples $-20 \div 5 = -4$ $20 \div (-5) = -4$

Words The quotient of two real numbers with the *same* sign is *positive*.
Examples $20 \div 5 = 4$ $-20 \div (-5) = 4$

Division Involving 0

Words The quotient of 0 and any nonzero real number is 0. The quotient of any real number and 0 is undefined.

Examples $0 \div 8 = 0$ $8 \div 0$ is undefined.

© **Problem 3** **Dividing Real Numbers**

Sky Diving A sky diver's elevation changes by -3600 ft in 4 min after the parachute opens. What is the average change in the sky diver's elevation each minute?

$-3600 \div 4 = -900$ The numbers have different signs, so the quotient is negative.

The sky diver's average change in elevation is -900 ft per minute.

 Got It? 3. You make five withdrawals of equal amounts from your bank account. The total amount you withdraw is $360. What is the change in your account balance each time you make a withdrawal? $-360 \div 5 = \$72$

Think

How is dividing similar to multiplying?
You find the sign of a quotient using the signs of the numbers you're dividing, just as you find the sign of a product using the signs of the factors.

The Inverse Property of Multiplication describes the relationship between a number and its multiplicative inverse.

---

take note

Property Inverse Property of Multiplication

Words For every nonzero real number a, there is a **multiplicative inverse** $\frac{1}{a}$ such that $a\left(\frac{1}{a}\right) = 1$.

Examples The multiplicative inverse of -4 is $-\frac{1}{4}$ because $-4\left(-\frac{1}{4}\right) = 1$.

The **reciprocal** of a nonzero real number of the form $\frac{a}{b}$ is $\frac{b}{a}$. The product of a number and its reciprocal is 1, so the reciprocal of a number is its multiplicative inverse. This suggests a rule for dividing fractions.

Here's Why It Works Let a, b, c, and d be nonzero integers.

$$\frac{a}{b} \div \frac{c}{d} = \frac{\frac{a}{b}}{\frac{c}{d}}$$
Write the expression as a fraction.

$$= \frac{\frac{a}{b} \cdot \frac{d}{c}}{\frac{c}{d} \cdot \frac{d}{c}}$$
Multiply the numerator and denominator by $\frac{d}{c}$. Since this is equivalent to multiplying by 1, it does not change the quotient.

$$= \frac{\frac{a}{b} \cdot \frac{d}{c}}{1}$$
Inverse Property of Multiplication

$$= \frac{a}{b} \cdot \frac{d}{c}$$
Simplify.

This shows that dividing by a fraction is equivalent to multiplying by the reciprocal of the fraction.

Problem 4 Dividing Fractions

Multiple Choice What is the value of $\frac{x}{y}$ when $x = -\frac{3}{4}$ and $y = -\frac{2}{3}$?

Ⓐ $-\frac{9}{8}$　　　Ⓑ $-\frac{1}{2}$　　　Ⓒ $\frac{1}{2}$　　　Ⓓ $\frac{9}{8}$

Think

Rewrite the expression.

Substitute $-\frac{3}{4}$ for x and $-\frac{2}{3}$ for y.

Multiply by the reciprocal of $-\frac{2}{3}$.

Simplify. Since both factors are negative, the product is positive.

Write

$$\frac{x}{y} = x \div y$$

$$= -\frac{3}{4} \div \left(-\frac{2}{3}\right)$$

$$= -\frac{3}{4} \cdot \left(-\frac{3}{2}\right)$$

$$= \frac{9}{8}$$

The correct answer is D.

Got It? 4. a. What is the value of $\frac{3}{4} \div \left(-\frac{5}{2}\right)$? $-\frac{3}{10}$

　　b. Reasoning Is $\frac{3}{4} \div \left(-\frac{5}{2}\right)$ equivalent to $-\left(\frac{3}{4} \div \frac{5}{2}\right)$? Explain. No because then its not negative

yess

Lesson Check

Do you know HOW?

Find each product. Simplify, if necessary.

1. $-3(-12)$ — $36 25$

2. $\frac{5}{8}\left(-\frac{2}{8}\right)$ $\frac{5}{32}$

Find each quotient. Simplify, if necessary.

3. $-48 \div 3$ -16

4. $-\frac{9}{10} \div \left(-\frac{4}{5}\right)$ $\frac{9}{8}$

Do you UNDERSTAND?

 **5. Vocabulary** What is the reciprocal of $-\frac{1}{5}$? $-\frac{5}{11}$

6. Reasoning Use a number line to explain why $-15 \div 3 = -5$.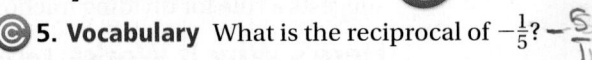

7. Reasoning Determine how many real square roots each number has. Explain your answers.

    a. 49 2 **b.** 0 1

    $= \pm 7$ $=0$

 ## Practice and Problem-Solving Exercises

MATHEMATICAL PRACTICES

Ⓐ Practice   **Find each product. Simplify, if necessary.**   **See Problem 1.**

8. $-8(12)$ **9.** $8(12)$ **10.** $7(-9)$ **11.** $5 \cdot 4.1$

12. $-7 \cdot 1.1$ **13.** $10(-2.5)$ **14.** $6\left(-\frac{1}{4}\right)$ **15.** $-\frac{1}{9}\left(-\frac{3}{4}\right)$

16. $-\frac{3}{7} \cdot \frac{9}{10}$ **17.** $-\frac{2}{11}\left(-\frac{11}{2}\right)$ **18.** $\left(-\frac{2}{9}\right)^2$ **19.** $(-1.2)^2$

Simplify each expression.   **See Problem 2.**

20. $\sqrt{400}$ **21.** $\sqrt{169}$ **22.** $-\sqrt{16}$ **23.** $-\sqrt{900}$ **24.** $\sqrt{\frac{36}{49}}$

25. $-\sqrt{\frac{25}{81}}$ **26.** $-\sqrt{\frac{1}{9}}$ **27.** $-\sqrt{\frac{121}{16}}$ **28.** $\pm\sqrt{1.96}$ **29.** $\pm\sqrt{0.25}$

Find each quotient. Simplify, if necessary.   **See Problem 3.**

30. $48 \div 3$ **31.** $-84 \div 14$ **32.** $-39 \div (-13)$ **33.** $\frac{63}{-21}$

34. $-46 \div (-2)$ **35.** $-8.1 \div 9$ **36.** $\frac{-121}{11}$ **37.** $75 \div (-0.3)$

STEM **38. Scuba Diving** A scuba diver's vertical position in relation to the surface of the water changes by -90 ft in 3 min. What is the average change in the diver's vertical position each minute?

39. Part-Time Job You earn the same amount each week at your part-time job. The total amount you earn in 4 weeks is $460. How much do you earn per week?

Find each quotient. Simplify, if necessary.   **See Problem 4.**

40. $20 \div \frac{1}{4}$ **41.** $-5 \div \left(-\frac{5}{3}\right)$ **42.** $\frac{9}{10} \div \left(-\frac{4}{5}\right)$ **43.** $-\frac{12}{13} \div \frac{12}{13}$

Find the value of the expression $\frac{x}{y}$ for the given values of x and y. Write your answer in the simplest form.

44. $x = -\frac{2}{3}; y = -\frac{1}{4}$ **45.** $x = -\frac{5}{6}; y = \frac{3}{5}$ **46.** $x = \frac{2}{7}; y = -\frac{20}{21}$ **47.** $x = \frac{3}{8}; y = \frac{3}{4}$

© **48. Think About a Plan** A lumberjack cuts 7 pieces of equal length from a log, as shown at the right. What is the change in the log's length after 7 cuts?

$2\frac{1}{4}$ ft

- What operation can you use to find the answer?
- Will your answer be a positive value or a negative value? How do you know?

49. Farmer's Market A farmer has 120 bushels of beans for sale at a farmer's market. He sells an average of $15\frac{3}{4}$ bushels each day. After 6 days, what is the change in the total number of bushels the farmer has for sale at the farmer's market?

50. Stocks The price per share of a stock changed by $-\$4.50$ on each of 5 consecutive days. If the starting price per share was $67.50, what was the ending price?

© **Open-Ended** Write an algebraic expression that uses x, y, and z and simplifies to the given value when $x = -3$, $y = -2$, and $z = -1$. The expression should involve only multiplication or division.

51. -16 **52.** 1 **53.** 12

Evaluate each expression for $m = -5$, $n = \frac{3}{2}$, and $p = -8$.

54. $-7m - 10n$ **55.** $-3mnp$

56. $8n \div (-6p)$ **57.** $2p^2(-n) \div m$

58. Look for a Pattern Extend the pattern in the diagram to six factors of -2. What rule describes the sign of the product based on the number of negative factors?

```
-2(-2) = 4
-2(-2)(-2) = -8
-2(-2)(-2)(-2) = 16
```

STEM **59. Temperature** The formula $F = \frac{9}{5}C + 32$ changes a temperature reading from the Celsius scale C to the Fahrenheit scale F. What is the temperature measured in degrees Fahrenheit when the Celsius temperature is $-25°C$?

© **60. Reasoning** Suppose a and b are integers. Describe what values of a and b make the statement true.
- **a.** Quotient $\frac{a}{b}$ is positive.
- **b.** Quotient $\frac{a}{b}$ is negative.
- **c.** Quotient $\frac{a}{b}$ is equal to 0.
- **d.** Quotient $\frac{a}{b}$ is undefined.

© **61. Writing** Explain how to find the quotient of $-1\frac{2}{3}$ and $-2\frac{1}{2}$.

© **62. Reasoning** Do you think a negative number raised to an even power will be positive or negative? Explain.

63. History The Rhind Papyrus is one of the best-known examples of Egyptian mathematics. One problem solved on the Rhind Papyrus is $100 \div 7\frac{7}{8}$. What is the solution of this problem?

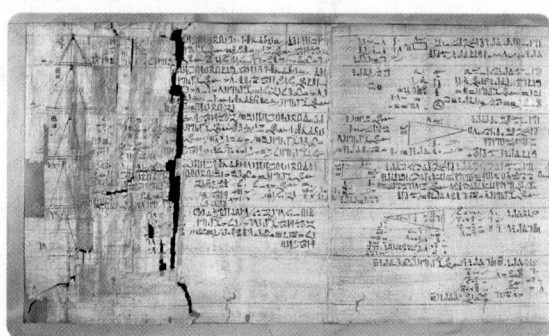

64. Error Analysis Describe and correct the error in dividing the fractions at the right.

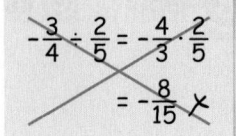

65. Reasoning You can derive the rule for division involving 0 shown on page 40.
  a. Suppose $0 \div x = y$, where $x \neq 0$. Show that $y = 0$. (*Hint*: If $0 \div x = y$, then $x \cdot y = 0$ by the definition of division.)
  b. If $x \neq 0$, show that there is no value of y such that $x \div 0 = y$. (*Hint*: Suppose there is a value of y such that $x \div 0 = y$. What would this imply about x?)

 **Challenge** Determine whether each statement is *always*, *sometimes*, or *never* true. Explain your reasoning.

66. The product of a number and its reciprocal is -1.

67. The quotient of a nonzero number and its opposite is -1.

68. If the product of two fractions is negative, then their quotient is positive.

69. Reasoning What is the greatest integer n for which $(-n)^3$ is positive and the value of the expression has a 2 in the ones place?

Standardized Test Prep

SAT/ACT

70. Which expression does NOT have the same value as $-11 + (-11) + (-11)$?
  Ⓐ -33 Ⓑ $3(-11)$ Ⓒ $(-11)^3$ Ⓓ $33 - 66$

71. Miguel measured the area of a piece of carpet and figured out that the approximate error was $3|-0.2|$. What is the decimal form of $3|-0.2|$?
  Ⓕ -0.6 Ⓖ -0.06 Ⓗ 0.06 Ⓘ 0.6

72. What is the perimeter of the triangle shown?
  Ⓐ $6y + 24$ Ⓒ $15y + 15$
  Ⓑ $21y + 9$ Ⓓ $30y$

Mixed Review

Find each difference. ◀ **See Lesson 1-5.**

73. $46 - 16$ **74.** $34 - 44$ **75.** $-37 - (-27)$

Get Ready! **To prepare for Lesson 1-7, do Exercises 76–78.**

Name the property that each statement illustrates. ◀ **See Lesson 1-4.**

76. $-x + 0 = -x$ **77.** $13(-11) = -11(13)$ **78.** $-5 \cdot (m \cdot 8) = (-5 \cdot m) \cdot 8$

Operations With Rational and Irrational Numbers

© **Common Core State Standards**

N-RN.B.3 Explain why the sum or product of two rational numbers is rational; that the sum of a rational number and an irrational number is irrational . . .

MP 2

For each sum, determine whether the result is a rational number or an irrational number.

1. $\frac{5}{8} + \frac{3}{5}$

2. $-\frac{1}{4} + \frac{2}{5}$

3. $-\frac{1}{2} + \sqrt{2}$

4. $\sqrt{5} + \left(-\frac{3}{11}\right)$

5. $\frac{1}{4} + \sqrt{12}$

6. $-\frac{3}{11} + \left(-\frac{1}{3}\right)$

For each product, determine whether the result is a rational number or an irrational number.

7. $\frac{1}{2} \cdot \frac{2}{15}$

8. $\sqrt{2} \cdot \frac{2}{5}$

9. $-\frac{3}{5} \cdot \frac{4}{9}$

10. $\frac{5}{8} \cdot \sqrt{7}$

11. $-\frac{3}{4} \cdot \frac{2}{9}$

12. $-\frac{4}{9} \cdot -\sqrt{5}$

For Exercises 13–16, predict whether the sum or product will be a rational or irrational number. Explain.

13. The sum of two rational numbers.

14. The product of a nonzero rational number and an irrational number.

15. The product of two rational numbers.

16. The sum of a rational number and an irrational number.

17. Can the sum of two irrational numbers be rational? If so, give an example. If not, explain why not.

18. Can the product of two irrational numbers be rational? If so, give an example. If not, explain why not.

The Distributive Property

 Common Core State Standards
A-SSE.A.1a Interpret parts of an expression, such as terms, factors, and coefficients.
MP 1, MP 2, MP 3, MP 4, MP 6, MP 7

Objective   To use the Distributive Property to simplify expressions

SOLVE IT!

Getting Ready!   ◀▶ ✕ ↻ ⌂

In your favorite video game, you rotate shapes as they fall to make them fit together in a rectangle. When you complete an entire row, you score 1 point for each square in that row.

The screen at the right shows your latest game in pause mode. Using only the shapes shown, what is the maximum possible score for this game? Explain your reasoning.

There's more than one way to figure this out.

MATHEMATICAL PRACTICES

 **Lesson Vocabulary**
- Distributive Property
- term
- constant
- coefficient
- like terms

To solve problems in mathematics, it is often useful to rewrite expressions in simpler forms. The **Distributive Property,** illustrated by the area model below, is another property of real numbers that helps you to simplify expressions.

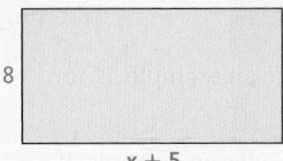

8

x + 5

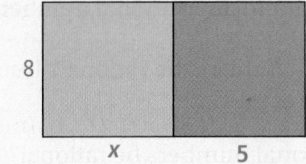

8

x   5

The model shows that $8(x + 5) = 8(x) + 8(5)$.

Essential Understanding   You can use the Distributive Property to simplify the product of a number and a sum or difference.

take note

Property   Distributive Property

Let a, b, and c be real numbers.

Algebra
$a(b + c) = ab + ac$
$(b + c)a = ba + ca$
$a(b - c) = ab - ac$
$(b - c)a = ba - ca$

Examples
$4(20 + 6) = 4(20) + 4(6)$
$(20 + 6)4 = 20(4) + 6(4)$
$7(30 - 2) = 7(30) - 7(2)$
$(30 - 2)7 = 30(7) - 2(7)$

Problem 1 Simplifying Expressions

What is the simplified form of each expression?

A $3(x + 8)$

$3(x + 8) = 3(x) + 3(8)$ Distributive Property

$= 3x + 24$ Simplify.

B $(5b - 4)(-7)$

$(5b - 4)(-7) = 5b(-7) - 4(-7)$

$= -35b + 28$

Got It? **1.** What is the simplified form of each expression?

a. $5(x + 7)$ **b.** $12\left(3 - \frac{1}{6}t\right)$ **c.** $(0.4 + 1.1c)3$ **d.** $(2y - 1)(-y)$

$5x + 35$ $36 - 2t$ $1.2 + 3.3c$ $-2y \cdot 1. -y$

Recall that a fraction bar may act as a grouping symbol. A fraction bar indicates division. Any fraction $\frac{a}{b}$ can also be written as $a \cdot \frac{1}{b}$. You can use this fact and the Distributive Property to rewrite some fractions as sums or differences.

Problem 2 Rewriting Fraction Expressions

What sum or difference is equivalent to $\frac{7x + 2}{5}$?

$\frac{7x + 2}{5} = \frac{1}{5}(7x + 2)$ Write division as multiplication.

$= \frac{1}{5}(7x) + \frac{1}{5}(2)$ Distributive Property

$= \frac{7}{5}x + \frac{2}{5}$ Simplify.

Got It? **2.** What sum or difference is equivalent to each expression?

a. $\frac{4x - 16}{3}$ **b.** $\frac{11 + 3x}{6}$ **c.** $\frac{15 + 6x}{12}$ **d.** $\frac{4 - 2x}{8}$

$\frac{4}{3}x - \frac{16}{3}$ $\frac{11}{6} + \frac{1}{2}x$ $\frac{5}{4} + \frac{1}{2}x$ $\frac{1}{2} - \frac{1}{4}x$

The Multiplication Property of -1 states that $-1 \cdot x = -x$. To simplify an expression such as $-(x + 6)$, you can rewrite the expression as $-1(x + 6)$.

Problem 3 Using the Multiplication Property of -1

Multiple Choice What is the simplified form of $-(2y - 3x)$?

Ⓐ $2y + 3x$ Ⓑ $-2y + (-3x)$ Ⓒ $-2y + 3x$ Ⓓ $2y - 3x$

$-(2y - 3x) = -1(2y - 3x)$ Multiplication Property of -1

$= (-1)(2y) + (-1)(-3x)$ Distributive Property

$= -2y + 3x$ Simplify.

The correct choice is C.

Got It? **3.** What is the simplified form of each expression?

a. $-(a + 5)$ **b.** $-(-x + 31)$ **c.** $-(4x - 12)$ **d.** $-(6m - 9n)$

$-a + (55)$ $x + 31(31)$ $-4x + 12(12)$ $-6m + 9(n9n)$

You can use the Distributive Property to make calculations easier to do with mental math. Some numbers can be thought of as simple sums or differences.

 Problem 4 Using the Distributive Property for Mental Math

Eating Out Deli sandwiches cost $4.95 each. What is the total cost of 8 sandwiches? Use mental math.

Know	Need	Plan
• Sandwiches cost $4.95. • You are buying 8 sandwiches.	Total cost of 8 sandwiches	Express $4.95 as a difference and use the Distributive Property.

The total cost is the product of the number of sandwiches you buy, 8, and the cost per sandwich, $4.95.

Think

How can you express decimals as simple sums and differences?

Think of a decimal as the sum or difference of its whole number portion and its decimal portion.

$$8(4.95) = 8(5 - 0.05) \quad \text{Think of 4.95 as } 5 - 0.05.$$
$$= 8(5) - 8(0.05) \quad \text{Distributive Property}$$
$$= 40 - 0.4 \quad \text{Multiply mentally.}$$
$$= 39.6 \quad \text{Subtract mentally.}$$

The total cost for 8 sandwiches is $39.60.

Got It? **4.** Julia commutes to work on the train 4 times each week. A round-trip ticket costs $7.25. What is her weekly cost for tickets? Use mental math.

$29.00

Essential Understanding You can simplify an algebraic expression by combining the parts of the expression that are alike.

In an algebraic expression, a **term** is a number, a variable, or the product of a number and one or more variables. A **constant** is a term that has no variable. A **coefficient** is a numerical factor of a term. Rewrite expressions as sums to identify these parts of an expression.

> $6a^2$, $-5ab$, $3b$, and -12 are terms.

$$6a^2 - 5ab + 3b - 12 = 6a^2 + (-5ab) + 3b + (-12)$$

coefficients   constant

In the algebraic expression $6a^2 - 5ab + 3b - 12$, the terms have coefficients of 6, -5, and 3. The term -12 is a constant.

Like terms have the same variable factors. To identify like terms, compare the variable factors of the terms, as shown below.

Terms	$7a$ and $-3a$	$4x^2$ and $12x^2$	$6ab$ and $-2a$	xy^2 and x^2y
Variable Factors	a and a	x^2 and x^2	ab and a	xy^2 and x^2y
Like Terms?	yes	yes	no	no

An algebraic expression in simplest form has no like terms or parentheses.

Not Simplified	Simplified
$2(3x - 5 + 4x)$	$14x - 10$

You can use the Distributive Property to help combine like terms. Think of the Distributive Property as $ba + ca = (b + c)a$.

Problem 5 Combining Like Terms

Plan

What terms can you combine?
You can combine any terms that have exactly the same variables with exactly the same exponents.

What is the simplified form of each expression?

A $8x^2 + 2x^2$

$8x^2 + 2x^2 = (8 + 2)x^2$ Distributive Property

$= 10x^2$ Simplify.

B $5x - 3 - 3x + 6y + 4$

$5x - 3 - 3x + 6y + 4 = 5x + (-3) + (-3x) + 6y + 4$ Rewrite as a sum.

$= 5x + (-3x) + 6y + (-3) + 4$ Commutative Property

$= (5 - 3)x + 6y + (-3) + 4$ Distributive Property

$= 2x + 6y + 1$ Simplify.

Got It? 5. What is the simplified form of each expression in parts (a)–(c)?

a. $3y - y = 2y$ **b.** $-7mn^4 - 5mn^4 = -12mn^4$ **c.** $7y^3z - 6yz^3 + y^3z = 8y^3z - 6yz^3$

d. Reasoning Can you simplify $8x^2 - 2x^4 - 2x + 2 + xy$ further? Explain.

no because there are no like terms to combinde

Lesson Check

Do you know HOW?

1. What is the simplified form of each expression? Use the Distributive Property.

a. $(j + 2)7 = 7j + 14$

b. $-8(x - 3) = -8x + 24$

c. $-(4 - c) = -4 + c$

d. $-(11 + 2b) = -11 - 2b$

Rewrite each expression as a sum.

2. $-8x^2 + 3xy - 9x - 3 - 8x^2 + 3xy + (-9x) + (-3)$

3. $2ab - 5ab^2 - 9a^2b$ $2ab + (-5ab^2) + (-9a^2b)$

Tell whether the terms are like terms.

4. $3a$ and $-5a$ Yes

5. $2xy^2$ and $-x^2y$ no

Do you UNDERSTAND? MATHEMATICAL PRACTICES

6. Vocabulary Does each equation demonstrate the Distributive Property? Explain.

a. $-2(x + 1) = -2x - 2$ yes

b. $(s - 4)8 = 8(s - 4)$ no

c. $5n - 45 = 5(n - 9)$ yes

d. $8 + (t + 6) = (8 + t) + 6$ no

7. Mental Math How can you express 499 to find the product 499×5 using mental math? Explain. 500 - 1

8. Reasoning Is each expression in simplified form? Justify your answer.

a. $4xy^3 + 5x^3y$ yes, no like terms

b. $-(y - 1)$ no, = -y + 1

c. $5x^2 + 12xy - 3yx$ yes, no like terms

Practice and Problem-Solving Exercises  **MATHEMATICAL PRACTICES**

 **Practice**   **Use the Distributive Property to simplify each expression.**   ◀ **See Problem 1.**

9. $6(a + 10)$ **10.** $8(4 + x)$ **11.** $(5 + w)5$ **12.** $(2t + 3)11$

13. $10(9 - t)$ **14.** $12(2j - 6)$ **15.** $16(7b + 6)$ **16.** $(1 + 3d)9$

17. $(3 - 8c)1.5$ **18.** $(5w - 15)2.1$ **19.** $\frac{1}{4}(4f - 8)$ **20.** $6\left(\frac{1}{3}h + 1\right)$

21. $(-8z - 10)(-1.5)$ **22.** $0(3.7x - 4.21)$ **23.** $1\left(\frac{3}{11} - \frac{7d}{17}\right)$ **24.** $\frac{1}{2}\left(\frac{1}{2}y - \frac{1}{2}\right)$

Write each fraction as a sum or difference.   ◀ **See Problem 2.**

25. $\frac{2x + 7}{5}$ **26.** $\frac{17 + 5n}{4}$ **27.** $\frac{8 - 9x}{3}$ **28.** $\frac{4y - 12}{2}$

29. $\frac{25 - 8t}{5}$ **30.** $\frac{18x + 51}{17}$ **31.** $\frac{22 - 2n}{2}$ **32.** $\frac{42w + 14}{7}$

Simplify each expression.   ◀ **See Problem 3.**

33. $-(20 + d)$ **34.** $-(-5 - 4y)$ **35.** $-(9 - 7c)$ **36.** $-(-x + 15)$

37. $-(18a - 17b)$ **38.** $-(2.1c - 4d)$ **39.** $-(-m + n + 1)$ **40.** $-(x + 3y - 3)$

Use mental math to find each product.   ◀ **See Problem 4.**

41. 5.1×8 **42.** 3×7.25 **43.** 299×3 **44.** 4×197

45. 3.9×6 **46.** 5×2.7 **47.** 6.15×4 **48.** 6×9.1

49. You buy 50 of your favorite songs from a Web site that charges $.99 for each song. What is the cost of 50 songs? Use mental math.

50. The perimeter of a baseball diamond is about 360 ft. If you take 12 laps around the diamond, what is the total distance you run? Use mental math.

51. One hundred and five students see a play. Each ticket costs $45. What is the total amount the students spend for tickets? Use mental math.

52. Suppose the distance you travel to school is 5 mi. What is the total distance for 197 trips from home to school? Use mental math.

Simplify each expression by combining like terms.   ◀ **See Problem 5.**

53. $11x + 9x$ **54.** $8y - 7y$ **55.** $5t - 7t$

56. $-n + 4n$ **57.** $5w^2 + 12w^2$ **58.** $2x^2 - 9x^2$

59. $-4y^2 + 9y^2$ **60.** $6c - 4 + 2c - 7$ **61.** $5 - 3x + y + 6$

62. $2n + 1 - 4m - n$ **63.** $-7h + 3h^2 - 4h - 3$ **64.** $10ab + 2ab^2 - 9ab$

 **Apply**   **Write a word phrase for each expression. Then simplify each expression.**

65. $3(t - 1)$ **66.** $4(d + 7)$ **67.** $\frac{1}{3}(6x - 1)$

STEM **68. Physiology** The recommended heart rate for exercise, in beats per minute, is given by the expression $0.8(200 - y)$ where y is a person's age in years. Rewrite this expression using the Distributive Property. What is the recommended heart rate for a 20-year-old person? For a 50-year-old person? Use mental math.

69. Error Analysis Identify and correct the error shown at the right.

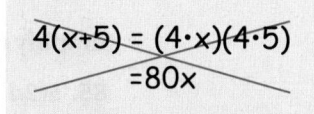

70. Error Analysis A friend uses the Distributive Property to simplify $4(2b - 5)$ and gets $8b - 5$ as the result. Describe and correct the error.

Geometry Write an expression in simplified form for the area of each rectangle.

71.

11

3x + 2

72.

5 + 2y

5

73.

7

5n − 9

74. Think About a Plan You are replacing your regular shower head with a water-saving shower head. These shower heads use the amount of water per minute shown. If you take an 8-min shower, how many gallons of water will you save?
- Which would you use to represent water saved each minute, an expression involving addition or an expression involving subtraction?
- How can you use the Distributive Property to find the total amount of water saved?

New
2.5 gallons per minute

7 gallons per minute

Simplify each expression.

75. $6yz + 2yz - 8yz$

76. $-2ab + ab + 9ab - 3ab$

77. $-9m^3n + 4m^3n + 5mn$

78. $3(-4cd - 5)$

79. $12x^2y - 8x^2y^2 + 11x^2y - 4x^3y^2 - 9xy^2$

80. $a - \frac{a}{4} + \frac{3}{4}a$

81. Reasoning The Distributive Property also applies to division, as shown.

$$\frac{a + b}{c} = \frac{a}{c} + \frac{b}{c}$$

Use the Distributive Property of Division to rewrite $\frac{9 + 12n}{3}$. Then simplify.

82. Lawn Game You play a game where you throw a pair of connected balls at a structure, as shown at the right. When a pair wraps around a bar, you earn the points shown. You toss 3 pairs, and all of them wrap around a bar. Which expression could represent your total score if a pairs of balls wrap around the blue bar?

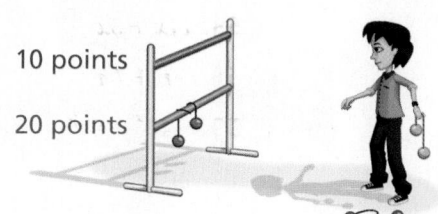

10 points

20 points

Ⓐ $30 + 10a$

Ⓒ $10a + 20(3 - a)$

Ⓑ $20a + 3 - 10a$

Ⓓ $30a + 10$

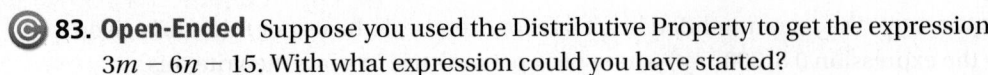

83. Open-Ended Suppose you used the Distributive Property to get the expression $3m - 6n - 15$. With what expression could you have started?

**Challenge** **84. Writing** Your friend uses the order of operations to find the value of $11(39 - 3)$. Would you prefer to use the Distributive Property instead? Explain.

Simplify each expression.

85. $5(2d + 1) + 7(5d + 3)$ **86.** $6(4t - 3) + 6(4 - 3t)$ **87.** $9(5 + t) - 7(t + 3)$

88. $4(r + 8) - 5(2r - 1)$ **89.** $-(m + 9n - 12)$ **90.** $-6(3 - 3x - 7y) + 2y - x$

 ## Apply What You've Learned

MATHEMATICAL
PRACTICES

MP 2

Look back at the information on page 3 about the walk of fame Naomi is designing. In the Apply What You've Learned in Lesson 1-1, you determined the relationship between n, the number of names on each side of the walk, and each type of tile in the design. You wrote algebraic expressions to represent these relationships.

a. Using the expression you wrote for the number of tiles with names inscribed on them, write and simplify an expression for the total cost of the inscribed tiles. List the properties you used to simplify the expression.

b. Using the expression you wrote for the number of plain tiles, write and simplify an expression for the total cost of the plain tiles. List the properties you used to simplify the expression.

c. Write and simplify an expression for the total cost of all of the tiles. Show your work.

1-8 An Introduction to Equations

© **Common Core State Standards**
A-CED.A.1 Create equations and inequalities in one variable and use them to solve problems.
MP 1, MP 3, MP 4, MP 6, MP 7, MP 8

Objective To solve equations using tables and mental math

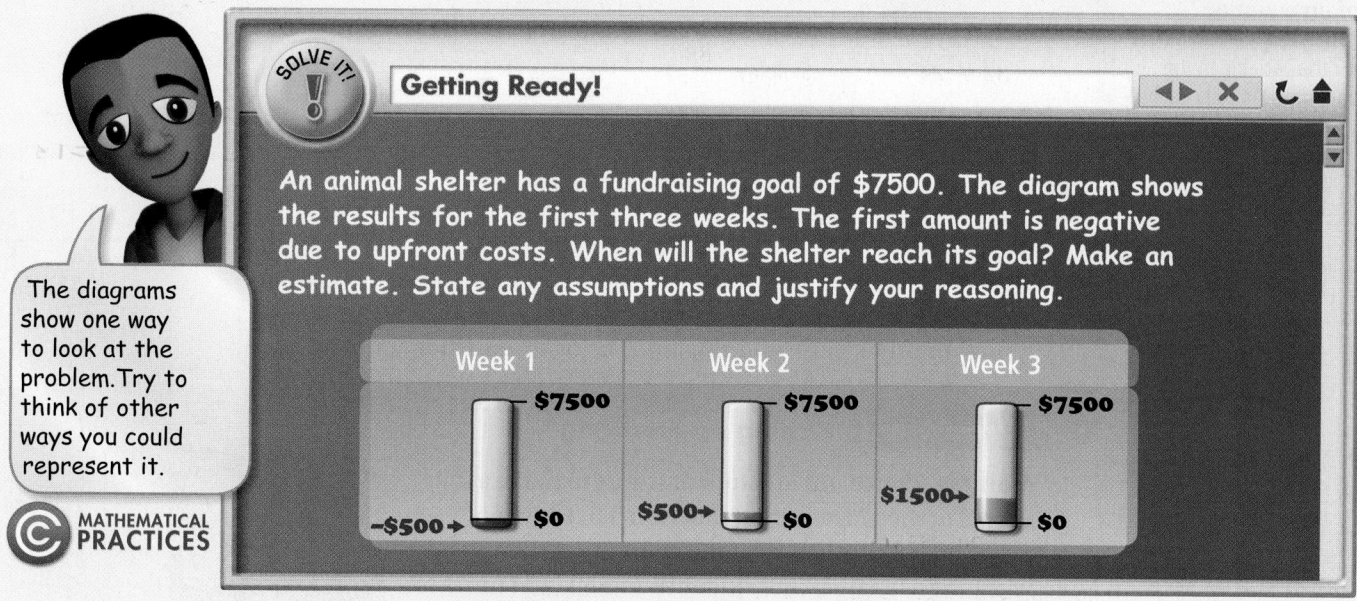

SOLVE IT!

Getting Ready!

An animal shelter has a fundraising goal of $7500. The diagram shows the results for the first three weeks. The first amount is negative due to upfront costs. When will the shelter reach its goal? Make an estimate. State any assumptions and justify your reasoning.

The diagrams show one way to look at the problem. Try to think of other ways you could represent it.

© **MATHEMATICAL PRACTICES**

Week 1	Week 2	Week 3
$7500	$7500	$7500
−$500→ $0	$500→ $0	$1500→ $0

The problem in the Solve It can be modeled by an equation. An **equation** is a mathematical sentence that uses an equal sign (=).

Essential Understanding You can use an equation to represent the relationship between two quantities that have the same value.

An equation is true if the expressions on either side of the equal sign are equal $(1 + 1 = 2, x + x = 2x)$. An equation is false if the expressions on either side of the equal sign are not equal $(1 + 1 = 3, x + x = 3x)$. An equation is an **open sentence** if it contains one or more variables and may be true or false depending on the values of its variables.

Lesson Vocabulary
- equation
- open sentence
- solution of an equation

Plan

How do you classify an equation?
If an equation contains only numbers, simplify the expressions on either side to determine if they are equal. If there is a variable in the equation, it is open.

© **Problem 1** Classifying Equations

Is the equation *true*, *false*, **or** *open*? **Explain.**

Ⓐ $24 + 18 = 20 + 22$ True, because both expressions equal 42

Ⓑ $7 \cdot 8 = 54$ False, because $7 \cdot 8 = 56$ and $56 \neq 54$

Ⓒ $2x - 14 = 54$ Open, because there is a variable

✓ **Got It?** **1.** Is the equation *true*, *false*, or *open*? Explain.

   a. $3y + 6 = 5y - 8$ **b.** $16 - 7 = 4 + 5$ **c.** $32 \div 8 = 2 \cdot 3$

   Open, because there is a variable   *True True they both = 9*   *False because*

A **solution of an equation** containing a variable is a value of the variable that makes the equation true.

 Problem 2 Identifying Solutions of an Equation

Plan

How can you tell if a number is a solution of an equation?
Substitute the number for the variable in the equation. Simplify each side to see if you get a true statement.

Is $x = 6$ a solution of the equation $32 = 2x + 12$?

$32 = 2x + 12$

$32 \stackrel{?}{=} 2(6) + 12$ Substitute 6 for x.

$32 \neq 24$ Simplify.

No, $x = 6$ is not a solution of the equation $32 = 2x + 12$.

Got It? 2. Is $m = \frac{1}{2}$ a solution of the equation $6m - 8 = -5$?

Yes $m = \frac{1}{2}$ is the solution of $6m-8=-5$

In real-world problems, the word *is* can indicate equality. You can represent some real-world situations using an equation.

 Problem 3 Writing an Equation

Multiple Choice An art student wants to make a model of the Mayan Great Ball Court in Chichén Itzá, Mexico. The length of the court is 2.4 times its width. The length of the student's model is 54 in. What should the width of the model be?

(A) 2.4 in.   (C) 22.5 in.

(B) 11.25 in.   (D) 129.6 in.

Plan

Why do you need to test each answer choice?
You should test each answer choice in case you made a calculation error. If you get two correct answers, then you know you need to double-check your work.

Relate   The length   is   2.4   times   the width

Define   Let w = the width of the model.

Write   54   =   2.4   • w

Test each answer choice in the equation to see if it is a solution.

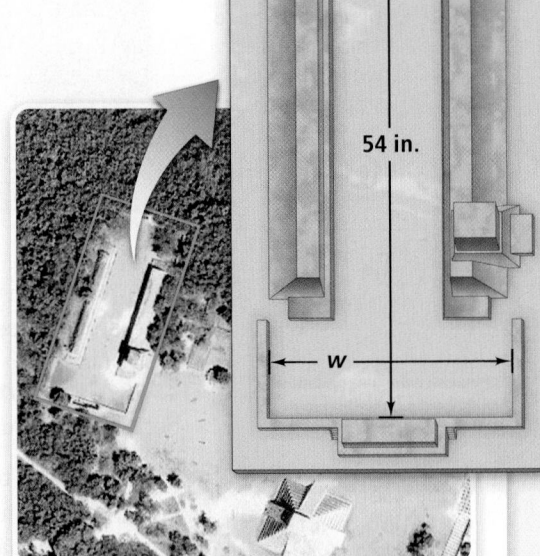

54 in.

w

Satellite view of Chichén Itzá

Check A: **Check B:**   **Check C:**   **Check D:**

$54 = 2.4w$ $54 = 2.4w$ $54 = 2.4w$ $54 = 2.4w$

$54 \stackrel{?}{=} 2.4(2.4)$ $54 \stackrel{?}{=} 2.4(11.25)$ $54 \stackrel{?}{=} 2.4(22.5)$ $54 \stackrel{?}{=} 2.4(129.6)$

$54 \neq 5.76$ $54 \neq 27$ $54 = 54$ ✔ $54 \neq 311.04$

The correct answer is C.

Got It? 3. The length of the ball court at La Venta is 14 times the height of its walls. Write an equation that can be used to find the height of a model that has a length of 49 cm. $49 = 14\ell$ $\ell = 3.5$

How can you find the solution of an equation?
You can use mental math to find a value that makes the equation true.

Problem 4 Using Mental Math to Find Solutions

What is the solution of each equation? Use mental math.

	Think	**Solution**	**Check**
A $x + 8 = 12$	What number plus 8 equals 12?	4	$4 + 8 = 12$ ✔
B $\frac{a}{8} = 9$	What number divided by 8 equals 9?	72	$\frac{72}{8} = 9$ ✔

✓ **Got It? 4.** What is the solution of $12 - y = 3$? Use mental math.

$= 9$

Problem 5 Using a Table to Find a Solution

What is the solution of $5n + 8 = 48$? Use a table.

Make a table of values. Choose a starting value using mental math. $5(1) + 8 = 13$ and $5(10) + 8 = 58$, so 1 is too low and 10 is too high.

Think

How can you start?
You can use mental math to quickly check values like 0, 1, and 10. Use these results to choose a reasonable starting value for your table.

> Try $n = 5$ and $n = 6$.

n	$5n + 8$	Value of $5n + 8$
5	$5(5) + 8$	33
6	$5(6) + 8$	38
7	$5(7) + 8$	43
8	$5(8) + 8$	48

> The value of $5n + 8$ increases as n increases, so try greater values of n.

> When $n = 8$, $5n + 8 = 48$. So the solution is 8.

P	25-3p	Value
-5	25-3(-5)	40
-6	25-3(-6)	43
-7	25-3(-7)	46
-8	25-3(-8)	49
-9	25-3(-9)	52
-10	25-3(-10)	55

✓ **Got It? 5. a.** What is the solution of $25 - 3p = 55$? Use a table. $= -10$
  b. What is a good starting value to solve part (a)? Explain your reasoning.
  $= -5$

Problem 6 Estimating a Solution

What is an estimate of the solution of $-9x - 5 = 28$? Use a table.

To estimate the solution, find the integer values of x between which the solution must lie. $-9(0) - 5 = -5$ and $-9(1) - 5 = -14$. If you try greater values of x, the value of $-9x - 5$ gets farther from 28.

Think

Can identifying a pattern help you make an estimate?
Yes. Identify how the value of the expression changes as you substitute for the variable. Use the pattern you find to work *toward* the desired value.

> Try lesser values, such as $x = -1$ and $x = -2$.

x	$-9x - 5$	Value of $-9x - 5$
-1	$-9(-1) - 5$	4
-2	$-9(-2) - 5$	13
-3	$-9(-3) - 5$	22
-4	$-9(-4) - 5$	31

> Now the values of $-9x - 5$ are getting closer to 28.

> 28 is between 22 and 31, so the solution is between -3 and -4.

X	3x+3	Value
-5	3(-5)+3	-12
-6	3(-6)+3	-15
-7	3(-7)+3	-18
-8	3(-8)+3	-21
-9	3(-9)+3	-24

✓ **Got It? 6.** What is the solution of $3x + 3 = -22$? Use a table.
between -8 and between -8 and -9

Lesson Check

Do you know HOW?

1. Is $y = -9$ a solution of $y + 1 = 8$? no

2. What is the solution of $x - 3 = 12$? Use mental math.
   = 15   15

3. **Reading** You can read 1.5 pages for every page your friend can read. Write an equation that relates the number of pages p that you can read and the number of pages n that your friend can read. p = 1.5n

Do you UNDERSTAND?

4. **Vocabulary** Give an example of an equation that is true, an equation that is false, and an open equation.
   2x+4 = 5y - 2 open   5 + 3 = 11 - 3 true

5. **Open-Ended** Write an open equation using one variable and division. $\frac{x}{3} = 15$
   4 + 6 = 5 + 9   false

6. **Compare and Contrast** Use two different methods to find the solution of the equation $x + 4 = 13$. Which method do you prefer? Explain. 4 - 13 = 9
   9 + 4 = 13

Practice and Problem-Solving Exercises

 **Practice**   Tell whether each equation is *true, false,* or *open.* Explain.   ◀ **See Problem 1.**

7. $85 + (-10) = 95$

8. $225 \div t - 4 = 6.4$

9. $29 - 34 = -5$

10. $-8(-2) - 7 = 14 - 5$

11. $4(-4) \div (-8)6 = -3 + 5(3)$

12. $91 \div (-7) - 5 = 35 \div 7 + 3$

13. $4a - 3b = 21$

14. $14 + 7 + (-1) = 21$

15. $5x + 7 = 17$

Tell whether the given number is a solution of each equation.   ◀ **See Problem 2.**

16. $8x + 5 = 29; 3$

17. $5b + 1 = 16; -3$

18. $6 = 2n - 8; 7$

19. $2 = 10 - 4y; 2$

20. $9a - (-72) = 0; -8$

21. $-6b + 5 = 1; \frac{1}{2}$

22. $7 + 16y = 11; \frac{1}{4}$

23. $14 = \frac{1}{3}x + 5; 27$

24. $\frac{3}{2}t + 2 = 4; \frac{2}{3}$

Write an equation for each sentence.   ◀ **See Problem 3.**

25. The sum of $4x$ and -3 is 8.

26. The product of 9 and the sum of 6 and x is 1.

27. **Training** An athlete trains for 115 min each day for as many days as possible. Write an equation that relates the number of days d that the athlete spends training when the athlete trains for 690 min.

28. **Salary** The manager of a restaurant earns $2.25 more each hour than the host of the restaurant. Write an equation that relates the amount h that the host earns each hour when the manager earns $11.50 each hour.

Use mental math to find the solution of each equation.   ◀ **See Problem 4.**

29. $x - 3 = 10$

30. $4 = 7 - y$

31. $18 + d = 24$

32. $2 - x = -5$

33. $\frac{m}{3} = 4$

34. $\frac{x}{7} = 5$

35. $6t = 36$

36. $20a = 100$

37. $13c = 26$

Use a table to find the solution of each equation. See Problem 5.

38. $2t - 1 = 11$ **39.** $5x + 3 = 23$ **40.** $0 = 4 + 2y$ **41.** $8a - 10 = 38$

42. $12 = 6 - 3b$ **43.** $8 - 5w = -12$ **44.** $-48 = -9 - 13n$ **45.** $\frac{1}{2}x - 5 = -1$

Use a table to find two consecutive integers between which the solution lies. See Problem 6.

46. $6x + 5 = 81$ **47.** $3.3 = 1.5 - 0.4y$ **48.** $-115b + 80 = -489$

 **Apply**

49. Bicycle Sales In the United States, the number y (in millions) of bicycles sold with wheel sizes of 20 in. or greater can be modeled by the equation $y = 0.3x + 15$, where x is the number of years since 1981. In what year were about 22 million bicycles sold?

50. Error Analysis A student checked whether $d = -2$ is a solution of $-3d + (-4) = 2$, as shown. Describe and correct the student's error.

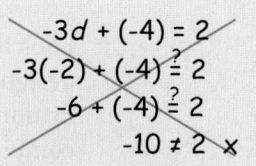

51. Writing What are the differences between an expression and an equation? Does a mathematical expression have a solution? Explain.

52. Basketball A total of 1254 people attend a basketball team's championship game. There are six identical benches in the gymnasium. About how many people would you expect each bench to seat?

Find the solution of each equation using mental math or a table. If the solution lies between two consecutive integers, identify those integers.

53. $x + 4 = -2$ **54.** $4m + 1 = 9$ **55.** $10.5 = 3n - 1$ **56.** $-3 + t = 19$

57. $5a - 4 = -16$ **58.** $9 = 4 + (-y)$ **59.** $1 = -\frac{1}{4}n + 1$ **60.** $17 = 6 + 2x$

61. Open-Ended Give three examples of equations that involve multiplication and subtraction and have a solution of -4.

62. Think About a Plan Polar researchers drill into an ice sheet. The drill is below the surface at the location shown. The drill advances at a rate of 67 m/h. About how many hours will it take the drill to reach a depth of 300 m?
- What equation models this situation?
- What integers do you need?

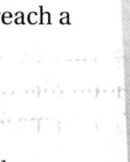

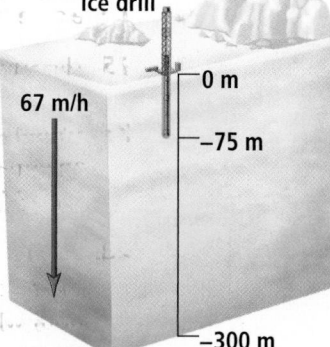

63. Deliveries The equation $25 + 0.25p = c$ gives the cost c in dollars that a store charges to deliver an appliance that weighs p pounds. Use the equation and a table to find the weight of an appliance that costs $55 to deliver.

64. Look for a Pattern Use a table. Evaluate $2x + 2$ for $x = -2, -1, 0, 1, 2,$ and 3. What pattern do you notice in your results? Use this pattern to find the solution of $2x + 2 = 28$. Check your solution.

 **Challenge**

65. Reasoning Your friend says that the solution of $15 = 4 + 2t$ is between two consecutive integers, because 15 is an odd number and 4 and 2 are both even numbers. Explain your friend's reasoning.

 66. Construction A construction crew needs to install 550 ft of curbing along a street. The crew can install curbing at a rate of 32 ft/h. Yesterday the crew installed 272 ft of curbing. Today it wants to finish the job in at most 10 h, which includes a 15-min drive to the job, an hour lunch break, and 45 min to break down the equipment. Can the crew achieve its goal? Explain.

 ## Apply What You've Learned

 MATHEMATICAL **PRACTICES**

MP 4

Look back at the information on page 3 about the walk of fame Naomi is designing, and at your work in the Apply What You've Learned sections in Lessons 1-1 and 1-7. Choose from the following numbers and expressions to complete the sentences below.

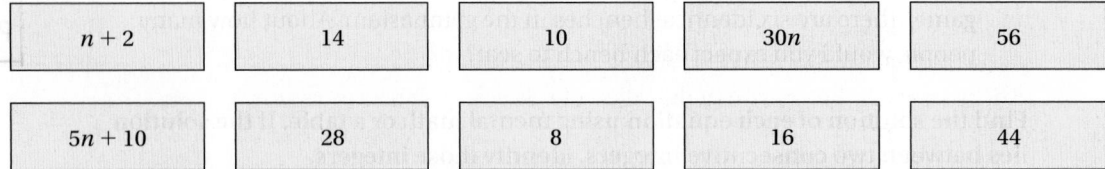

a. An equation that can be used to find the value of n that results in a walk costing $500 is $\underline{} + \underline{} = 500$.

b. Solving the equation shows that when n is equal to $\underline{}$, the walkway will cost $500.

c. The number of plain tiles Naomi should buy is $\underline{}$.

Using Tables to Solve Equations

© Common Core State Standards

Prepares for A-REI.A.1 Explain each step in solving a simple equation as following from the equality of numbers asserted at the previous step, . . .

MP 5

You can solve equations by making a table using a graphing calculator.

MATHEMATICAL PRACTICES

Activity

A raft floats downriver at 9 mi/h. The distance y the raft travels can be modeled by the equation $y = 9x$, where x is the number of hours. Make a table on a graphing calculator to find how long it takes the raft to travel 153 mi.

Step 1 Enter the equation $y = 9x$ into a graphing calculator.

* Press **y=**. The cursor appears next to Y_1.
* Press 9 **x,t,θ,n** to enter $y = 9x$.

Step 2 Access the table setup feature.

* Press **2nd** **window**.
* TblStart represents the starting value in the table. Enter 1 for TblStart.
* △Tbl represents the change in the value of x as you go from row to row. Enter 1 for △Tbl.

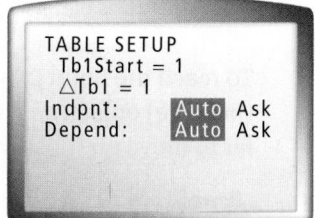

Step 3 Display the table and find the solution.

* Press **2nd** **graph**. Use ▽ to scroll through the table until you find the x-value for which $y = 153$. This x-value is 17. It takes the raft 17 h to travel 153 mi.

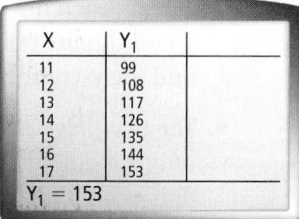

Exercises

Solve each problem by making a table on a graphing calculator.

1. A town places 560 t of waste in a landfill each month. The amount y of waste in the landfill can be modeled by the equation $y = 560x$, where x is the number of months. How many months will it take to accumulate 11,200 t of waste in the landfill?

2. A coupon gives \$15 off a customer's purchase. The total amount y of the customer's purchase can be modeled by $y = x - 15$, where x is the amount of the purchase before the coupon is used. A customer using the coupon pays \$17 for a shirt. What was the original price of the shirt?

Graphing in the Coordinate Plane

© **Common Core State Standards**

Prepares for A-CED.A.2 … graph equations on coordinate axes with labels and scales.

Two number lines that intersect at right angles form a **coordinate plane.** The horizontal axis is the **x-axis** and the vertical axis is the **y-axis.** The axes intersect at the **origin** and divide the coordinate plane into four sections called **quadrants.**

An **ordered pair** of numbers names the location of a point in the plane. These numbers are the **coordinates** of the point. Point B has coordinates $(-3, 4)$.

The first coordinate is the x-coordinate. $(-3, 4)$ The second coordinate is the y-coordinate.

To reach the point (x, y), you use the x-coordinate to tell how far to move right (positive) or left (negative) from the origin. You then use the y-coordinate to tell how far to move up (positive) or down (negative).

Activity

Play against a partner using two number cubes and a coordinate grid. One cube represents positive numbers and the other cube represents negative numbers.

- During each turn, a player rolls both cubes and adds the numbers to find an x-coordinate. Both cubes are rolled a second time, and the numbers are added to find the y-coordinate. The player graphs the resulting ordered pair on the grid.

- The two players take turns, with each player using a different color to graph points. If an ordered pair has already been graphed, the player does not graph a point, and the turn is over.

- Play ends after each player has completed 10 turns. The player with the most points graphed in a quadrant scores 1 for Quadrant I, 2 for Quadrant II, and so on. Points graphed on either axis do not count. If both players graph an equal number of points in a quadrant, both players score 0 for that quadrant.

Exercises

Describe a pair of number cube rolls that would result in a point plotted at the given location.

1. $(-3, 4)$ **2.** $(4, -3)$ **3.** in Quadrant III **4.** the origin

1-9 Patterns, Equations, and Graphs

 Common Core State Standards

A-REI.D.10 Understand that the graph of an equation in two variables is the set of all its solutions plotted in the coordinate plane, often forming a curve (which could be a line). **Also A-CED.A.2**

MP 1, MP 2, MP 3, MP 4, MP 7

Objective To use tables, equations, and graphs to describe relationships

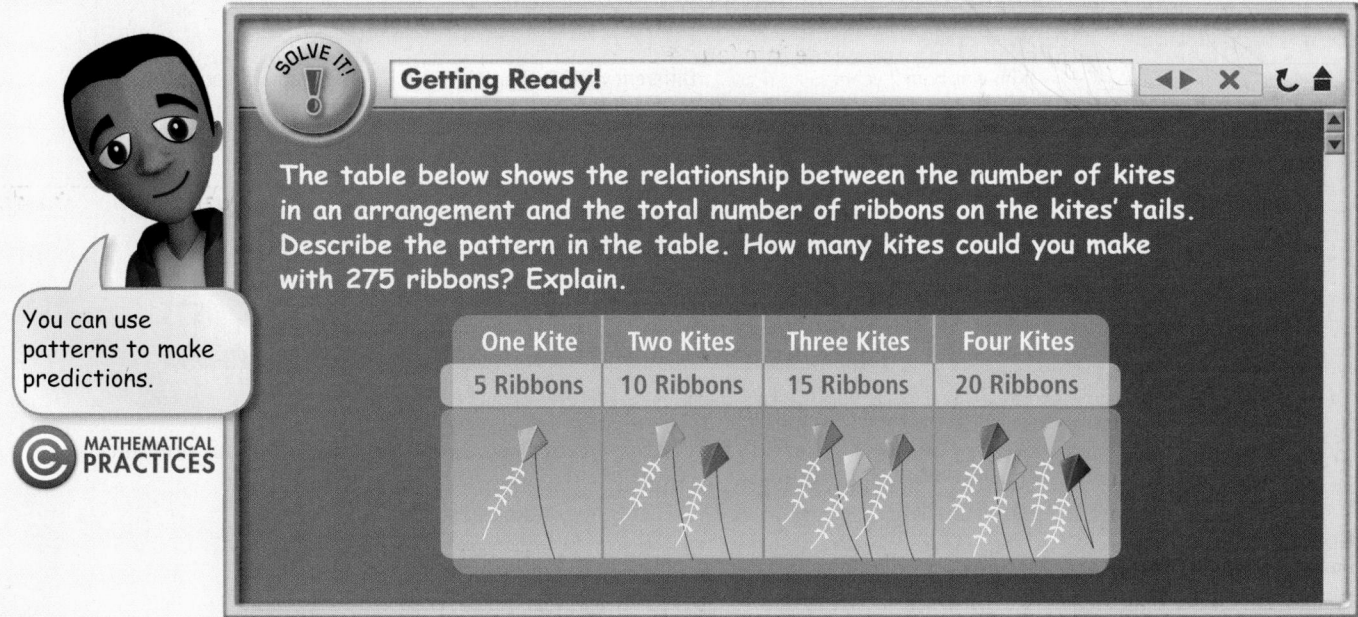

Getting Ready!

The table below shows the relationship between the number of kites in an arrangement and the total number of ribbons on the kites' tails. Describe the pattern in the table. How many kites could you make with 275 ribbons? Explain.

One Kite	Two Kites	Three Kites	Four Kites
5 Ribbons	10 Ribbons	15 Ribbons	20 Ribbons

You can use patterns to make predictions.

MATHEMATICAL PRACTICES

 **Lesson Vocabulary**
- solution of an equation
- inductive reasoning

In the Solve It, you may have described the pattern using words. You can also use an equation or a graph to describe a pattern.

Essential Understanding Sometimes the value of one quantity can be found if you know the value of another. You can represent the relationship between the quantities in different ways, including tables, equations, and graphs.

You can use an equation with two variables to represent the relationship between two varying quantities. A **solution of an equation** with two variables x and y is any ordered pair (x, y) that makes the equation true.

Plan

How can you tell whether an ordered pair is a solution?
Replace x with the first value in the ordered pair and y with the second value in the ordered pair. Is the resulting equation true?

 **Problem 1** Identifying Solutions of a Two-Variable Equation

Is (3, 10) a solution of the equation $y = 4x$?

$y = 4x$

$10 \overset{?}{=} 4 \cdot 3$ Substitute 3 for x and 10 for y.

$10 \neq 12$ So, (3, 10) is not a solution of $y = 4x$.

20 = 4·5
−20 = 4·−5
y = 4x

Got It? 1. Is the ordered pair a solution of the equation $y = 4x$?

     a. (5, 20)   **b.** (−5, −20)   **c.** (−20, −5)   **d.** (1.5, 6)

     Yes   *Yes*   *no*   *Yes*

You can represent the same relationship between two variables in several different ways.

Problem 2 Using a Table, an Equation, and a Graph

Ages Both Carrie and her sister Kim were born on October 25, but Kim was born 2 years before Carrie. How can you represent the relationship between Carrie's age and Kim's age in different ways?

Know

Kim was born 2 years before Carrie.

Need

Different ways to represent the relationship

Plan

Use a table, an equation, and a graph.

Step 1 Make a table.

Carrie's and Kim's Ages (years)										
Carrie's Age	1	2	3	4	5	6	7	8	9	10
Kim's Age	3	4	5	6	7	8	9	10	11	12

Step 2 Write an equation.

Let x = Carrie's age. Let y = Kim's age. From the table, you can see that y is always 2 greater than x.

So $y = x + 2$.

Think

Why does it make sense to connect the points on the graph?
A person's age can be any positive real number, and the ages of the girls are always 2 years apart. So every point on the line makes sense in this situation.

Step 3 Draw a graph.

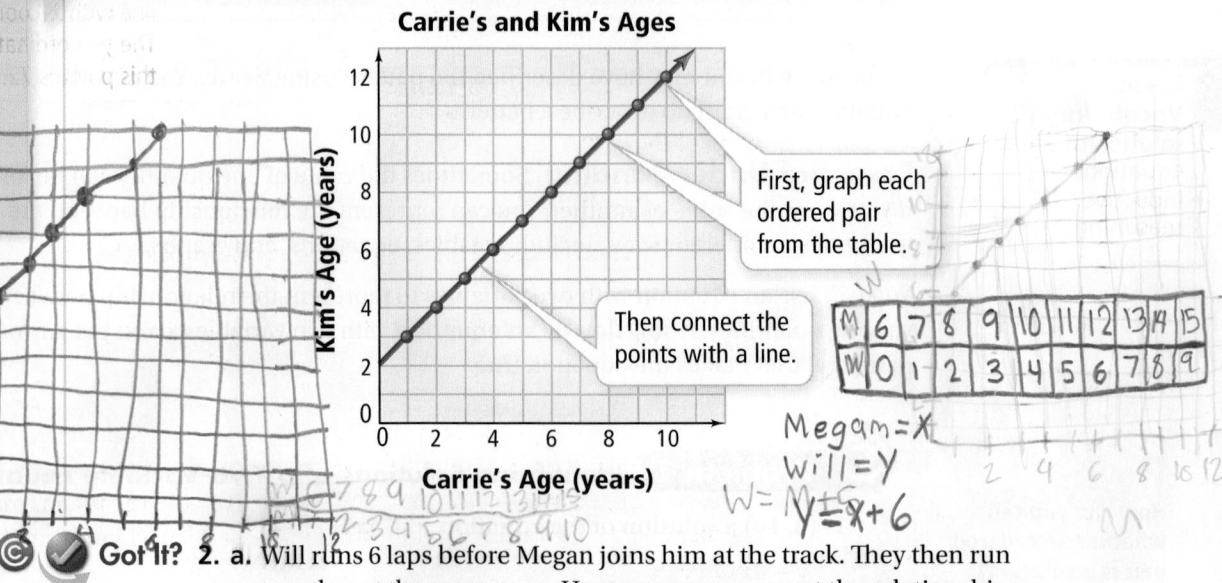

Carrie's and Kim's Ages

First, graph each ordered pair from the table.

Then connect the points with a line.

Got It? **2. a.** Will runs 6 laps before Megan joins him at the track. They then run together at the same pace. How can you represent the relationship between the number of laps Will runs and the number of laps Megan runs in different ways? Use a table, an equation, and a graph.

b. Reasoning Describe how the graph in Problem 2 above would change if the difference in ages were 5 years instead of 2 years.

Inductive reasoning is the process of reaching a conclusion based on an observed pattern. You can use inductive reasoning to predict values.

 Problem 3 **Extending a Pattern**

The table shows the relationship between the number of blue tiles and the total number of tiles in each figure. Extend the pattern. What is the total number of tiles in a figure with 8 blue tiles?

Tiles

Number of Blue Tiles, x	Total Number of Tiles, y
1	9
2	18
3	27
4	36
5	45

Think

Should you connect the points on the graph with a solid line?
No. The number of tiles must be a whole number. Use a dotted line to see the trend.

Method 1 Draw a graph.

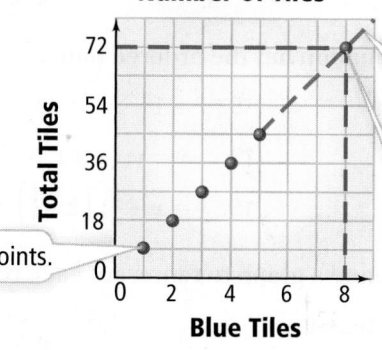

Number of Tiles

Step 1 Graph the points.

Step 2 The points fall on a line. Extend the pattern with a dashed line.

Step 3 Find the point on the line with x-coordinate 8. The y-coordinate of this point is 72.

The total number of tiles is 72.

Method 2 Write an equation.

$y = 9x$ The total number of tiles is 9 times the number of blue tiles.

$= 9(8)$ Substitute 8 for x.

$= 72$ Simplify.

The total number of tiles is 72.

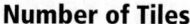

x = Orange
y = total   *x = 4   x = 12   y =*

Orange	4	6	12	16	20	24
Total	9	18	27	36	45	54

 Got It? **3.** Use the tile figure from Problem 3.

    a. Make a table showing the number of orange tiles and the total number of tiles in each figure. How many tiles in all will be in a figure with 24 orange tiles? *= 54 tiles*

    b. Make a table showing the number of blue tiles and the number of yellow tiles in each figure. How many yellow tiles will be in a figure with 24 blue tiles? *= 48 yellow tiles*

Y = 2x *2·24 = 48*
Y = 2·24   Y = 48

Blue	1	2	3	4	5	6	7	8	9	10	11
Yellow	2	4	6	8	10	12	14	16	18	20	22

Lesson Check

Do you know HOW?

1. Is (2, 4) a solution of the equation $y = x - 2$? *no*

2. Is (−3, −9) a solution of the equation $y = 3x$? *yes*

3. Drinks at the fair cost $2.50. Use a table, an equation, and a graph to represent the relationship between the number of drinks bought and the cost. *$y = 2.50x$* ✗

4. **Exercise** On a treadmill, you burn 11 Cal in 1 min, 22 Cal in 2 min, 33 Cal in 3 min, and so on. How many Calories do you burn in 10 min? *110 cal in 10 min*

Do you UNDERSTAND?

5. **Vocabulary** Describe the difference between inductive reasoning and deductive reasoning.

6. **Compare and Contrast** How is writing an equation to represent a situation involving two variables similar to writing an equation to represent a situation involving only one variable? How are they different?

7. **Reasoning** Which of (3, 5), (4, 6), (5, 7), and (6, 8) are solutions of $y = x + 2$? What is the pattern in the solutions of $y = x + 2$? *All, y is 2 more than x* ✗

Practice and Problem-Solving Exercises

 **Practice**

Tell whether the given equation has the ordered pair as a solution.

◀ **See Problem 1.**

8. $y = x + 6$; (0, 6)

9. $y = 1 - x$; (2, 1)

10. $y = -x + 3$; (4, 1)

11. $y = 6x$; (3, 16)

12. $-x = y$; (−3.1, 3.1)

13. $y = -4x$; (−2, 8)

14. $y = x + \frac{2}{3}$; $\left(1, \frac{1}{3}\right)$

15. $y = x - \frac{3}{4}$; $\left(2, 1\frac{1}{4}\right)$

16. $\frac{x}{5} = y$; (−10, −2)

Use a table, an equation, and a graph to represent each relationship.

◀ **See Problem 2.**

17. Ty is 3 years younger than Bea.

18. The number of checkers is 24 times the number of checkerboards.

19. The number of triangles is $\frac{1}{3}$ the number of sides.

20. Gavin makes $8.50 for each lawn he mows.

Use the table to draw a graph and answer the question.

◀ **See Problem 3.**

21. The table shows the height in inches of stacks of tires. Extend the pattern. What is the height of a stack of 7 tires?

Stacks of Tires

Number of Tires, x	Height of Stack, y
1	8
2	16
3	24
4	32

22. The table shows the length in centimeters of a scarf you are knitting. Suppose the pattern continues. How long is the scarf after 8 days?

Knitted Scarf

Number of Days, x	Length of Scarf, y
1	12.5
2	14.5
3	16.5
4	18.5

Use the table to write an equation and answer the question.

23. The table shows the heights in inches of trees after they have been planted. What is the height of a tree that is 64 in. tall in its pot?

Tree Height

Height in Pot, x	Height Without Pot, y
30	18
36	24
42	30
48	36

24. The table shows amounts earned for pet sitting. How much is earned for a 9-day job?

Pet Sitting

Days, x	Dollars, y
1	17
2	34
3	51
4	68

Refer to the drawing of houses for Exercises 25 and 26.

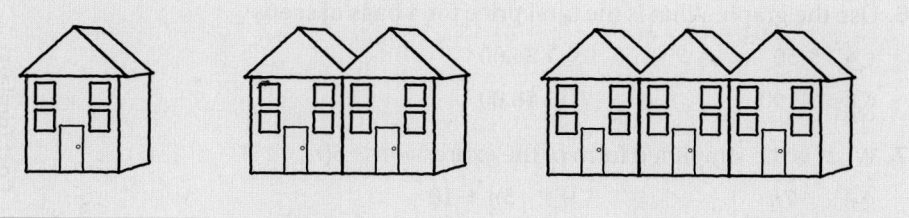

© 25. **Patterns** Make a table and draw a graph to show the relationship between the number of houses and the number of windows.

    a. What is the number of windows in 9 houses?

    b. If n houses have k windows, write an expression to represent the number of windows for $n + 1$ houses.

26. Bobby says that a subdivision similar to the one above has a total of 202 windows. Is 202 a reasonable number of windows? Explain.

B Apply

Tell whether the given ordered pair is a solution of the equation.

27. $y = 2x + 7;\ (-2, 3)$

28. $-\frac{1}{4}x + 6 = y;\ (2, 4)$

29. $y = -1.2x - 2.6;\ (3.5, 6.8)$

© 30. **Think About a Plan** The table shows how long it takes Kayla to learn new songs. How many hours does Kayla need to practice to learn 9 songs?

- From row to row, how much does the number of hours h increase? How much does the number of songs s increase?
- By how many rows would you need to extend the table to solve the problem?

Kayla's Piano Practice

Hours, h	Songs Learned, s
1.5	1
3.0	2
4.5	3
6.0	4

31. **Air Travel** Use the table at the right. How long will the jet take to travel 5390 mi?

Passenger Jet Travel

Hours, h	1	2	3	4
Miles, m	490	980	1470	1960

32. Reasoning Savannah looks at the table shown and says the equation $y = x - 6$ represents the pattern. Mary says $y = x + (-6)$ represents the pattern. Who is correct? Explain.

33. Open-Ended Think of a real-world pattern. Describe the pattern using words and an equation with two variables. Define the variables.

x	y
0	−6
1	−5
2	−4
3	−3

Challenge **34. Temperature** Suppose the temperature starts at 60°F and rises 2°F every 45 min. Use a table, an equation, and a graph to describe the relationship between the amount of time that has passed in hours and the temperature.

35. Use a table, a graph, and an equation to represent the ordered pairs $(2, -5.5)$, $(-3, -0.5)$, $(1, -4.5)$, $(0, -3.5)$, $(-3.5, 0)$, and $(-1, -2.5)$.

Standardized Test Prep

SAT/ACT

36. Use the graph. What is the total price for 4 bags of seeds?

Ⓐ $.50　　　　　　　Ⓒ $4.00

Ⓑ $2.00　　　　　　Ⓓ $8.00

Seed Cost

37. What is the simplified form of the expression $-5(n - 2)$?

Ⓕ $-7n$　　　　　　Ⓗ $-5n + 10$

Ⓖ $-5n - 2$　　　　Ⓘ $n + 10$

38. If $a = 3$ and $b = -2$, what does $-2b - a$ equal?

Ⓐ -9　　　　Ⓑ -7　　　　Ⓒ -1　　　　Ⓓ 1

39. What is the value of -3^4?

Ⓕ -81　　　　Ⓖ -12　　　　Ⓗ 12　　　　Ⓘ 81

Mixed Review

Tell whether the given number is a solution of each equation.

See Lesson 1-8.

40. $3x + 7 = 10; 0$　　　　**41.** $80 = 4a; 20$　　　　**42.** $10 = -5t; -2$

Give an example that illustrates each property.

See Lesson 1-4.

43. Commutative Property of Addition　　　　**44.** Associative Property of Multiplication

45. Identity Property of Multiplication　　　　**46.** Zero Property of Addition

Get Ready! To prepare for Lesson 2-1, do Exercises 47–54.

See Lesson 1-5.

Find each sum or difference.

47. $12 + (-3)$　　　**48.** $-7 + 4$　　　**49.** $-8 + (-6)$　　　**50.** $-42 + 15$

51. $32 - (-8)$　　　**52.** $-18 - 12$　　　**53.** $-15 - (-14)$　　　**54.** $-76 - 5$

Pull It **All Together**

To solve these problems, you will pull together many concepts and skills related to expressions, real-number properties and operations, and equations.

Completing the Performance Task

Look back at your results from the Apply What You've Learned sections in Lessons 1-1, 1-7, and 1-8. Use the work you did to complete the following.

1. Solve the problem in the Task Description on page 3 by determining the number of athletes the school will be able to honor on the walk of fame. Show all your work and explain each step of your solution.

2. **Reflect** Choose one of the Mathematical Practices below and explain how you applied it in your work on the Performance Task.

   MP 2: Reason abstractly and quantitatively.

   MP 4: Model with mathematics.

   MP 7: Look for and make use of structure.

On Your Own

Clive suggests a different design for the walk of fame. In his design, the walkway is made up of tiles and ground-cover plants. The ground-cover plants are planted in the pattern shown below. In the pattern, n is the number of names on each side of the walk. The ground-cover plants are represented by the cross-shaped figures between the tiles.

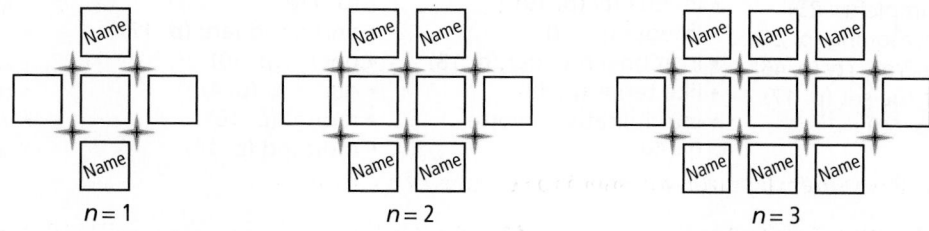

Each ground-cover plant costs $2. As before, inscribed tiles cost $15 each and plain tiles cost $5 each. Clive's total budget for the tiles and plants is the same as Naomi's ($500).

   a. Write an expression that represents the number of plants when there are n names on each side of the walk. Then, write and simplify an expression for the cost of the plants.

   b. How many athletes will the school be able to honor if Clive's design is used?

Connecting **BIG** ideas and Answering the Essential Questions

1 Variable
You can use variables to represent quantities and to write algebraic expressions and equations.

Variables and Expressions (Lesson 1-1)
a number n plus 3 $|\text{----} ? \text{----}|$
$n + 3$ $\boxed{n \mid 3}$

Patterns and Equations (Lessons 1-8 and 1-9)
1 variable: $x + 3 = 5$
2 variables: $y = 2x$

Operations With Real Numbers (Lessons 1-2, 1-5, and 1-6)
2^5 $0 \cdot 3$ $2 + (-5)$ $7(-3)$

2 Properties
The properties of real numbers describe relationships that are always true. You can use them to rewrite expressions.

Properties (Lessons 1-4 and 1-7)
$a \cdot b = b \cdot a$ $(a \cdot b) \cdot c = a \cdot (b \cdot c)$
$a(b + c) = ab + ac$

Chapter Vocabulary

- absolute value (p. 31)
- additive inverse (p. 32)
- algebraic expression (p. 4)
- base (p. 10)
- coefficient (p. 48)
- constant (p. 48)
- counterexample (p. 25)
- deductive reasoning (p. 25)
- Distributive Property (p. 46)
- element of the set (p. 17)
- equation (p. 53)

- equivalent expressions (p. 23)
- evaluate (p. 12)
- exponent (p. 10)
- inductive reasoning (p. 63)
- inequality (p. 19)
- integer (p. 18)
- irrational number (p. 18)
- like terms (p. 48)
- multiplicative inverse (p. 40)

- natural number (p. 18)
- numerical expression (p. 4)
- open sentence (p. 53)
- opposite (p. 32)
- order of operations (p. 11)
- perfect square (p. 17)
- power (p. 10)
- quantity (p. 4)
- radical (p. 16)
- radicand (p. 16)

- rational number (p. 18)
- real number (p. 18)
- reciprocal (p. 41)
- set (p. 17)
- simplify (p. 10)
- solution of an equation (p. 54, 61)
- square root (p. 16)
- subset (p. 17)
- term (p. 48)
- variable (p. 4)
- whole number (p. 18)

Choose the correct term to complete each sentence.

1. Real numbers that you cannot represent as a quotient of two integers are __?__ numbers. *irrational*

2. The sum of a number and its __?__ equals zero. *opposite*

3. You can simplify an expression by combining __?__. *like terms*

4. __?__ is a number's distance from zero on a number line. *absolut value*

5. When you make conclusions based on patterns you observe, you use __?__. *inductive resoning*

1-1 Variables and Expressions

Quick Review

A **variable** is a symbol, usually a letter, that represents values of a variable quantity. For example, d often represents distance. An **algebraic expression** is a mathematical phrase that includes one or more variables. A **numerical expression** is a mathematical phrase involving numbers and operation symbols, but no variables.

Example

What is an algebraic expression for the word phrase *3 less than half a number x*?

You can represent "half a number x" as $\frac{x}{2}$. Then subtract 3 to get $\frac{x}{2} - 3$.

Exercises

Write an algebraic expression for each word phrase.

6. the product of a number w and 737 $737w$

7. the difference of a number q and 8 $q - 8$

8. the sum of a number x and 84 $84 + x$

9. 9 more than the product of 51 and a number t $51t + 9$

10. 14 less than the quotient of 63 and a number h $\frac{63}{h} - 14$

11. a number b less the quotient of a number k and 5 $b - \frac{k}{5}$

Write a word phrase for each algebraic expression.

12. $12 + a$ 12 plus a

13. $r - 31$ 31 less than r

14. $19t$ the product of 19 and t

15. $b \div 3$ b divided by 3

16. $7c - 3$ 7 times c minus 3

17. $2 + \frac{x}{8}$ 2 plus x divided by 8

18. $\frac{y}{11} - 6$ y divided by 11 minus 6

19. $21d + 13$ 21 times d plus 13

1-2 Order of Operations and Evaluating Expressions

Quick Review

To **evaluate** an algebraic expression, first substitute a given number for each variable. Then simplify the numerical expression using the order of operations.

1. Do operation(s) inside grouping symbols.

2. Simplify powers.

3. Multiply and divide from left to right.

4. Add and subtract from left to right.

Example

A student studies with a tutor for 1 hour each week and studies alone for *h* hours each week. What is an expression for the total hours spent studying each week? Evaluate the expression for *h* = 5.

The expression is $h + 1$. To evaluate the expression for $h = 5$, substitute 5 for h: $(5) + 1 = 6$.

Exercises

Simplify each expression.

20. 9^2

21. 5^3

22. $\left(\frac{1}{6}\right)^2$

23. $7^2 \div 5$

24. $(2^4 - 6)^2$

25. $(3^3 - 4) + 5^2$

Evaluate each expression for $c = 3$ and $d = 5$.

26. $d^3 \div 15$

27. $(2 + d)^2 - 3^2$

28. $cd^2 + 4$

29. $(3c^2 - 3d)^2 - 21$

30. The expression $6s^2$ represents the surface area of a cube with edges of length s.

    a. What is the cube's surface area when $s = 6$?

    b. **Reasoning** Explain how a cube's surface area changes if you divide s by 2 in the expression $6s^2$.

31. A race car travels at 205 mi/h. How far does the car travel in 3 h?

1-3 Real Numbers and the Number Line

Quick Review

The rational numbers and irrational numbers form the **set** of **real numbers.**

A **rational number** is any number that you can write as $\frac{a}{b}$, where a and b are integers and $b \neq 0$. The rational numbers include all positive and negative integers, as well as fractions, mixed numbers, and terminating and repeating decimals.

Irrational numbers cannot be represented as the quotient of two integers. They include the square roots of all positive integers that are not perfect squares.

Example

Is the number rational or irrational?

Ⓐ -5.422 rational

Ⓑ $\sqrt{7}$ irrational

Exercises

Tell whether each number is rational or irrational.

32. π

33. $-\frac{1}{2}$

34. $\sqrt{\frac{2}{3}}$

35. $0.\overline{57}$

Estimate each square root. Round to the nearest integer.

36. $\sqrt{99}$ **37.** $\sqrt{48}$ **38.** $\sqrt{30}$

Name the subset(s) of the real numbers to which each number belongs.

39. -17 **40.** $\frac{13}{62}$ **41.** $\sqrt{94}$

42. $\sqrt{100}$ **43.** 4.288 **44.** $1\frac{2}{3}$

Order the numbers in each exercise from least to greatest.

45. $-1\frac{2}{3}, 1.6, -1\frac{4}{5}$ **46.** $\frac{7}{9}, -0.8, \sqrt{3}$

1-4 Properties of Real Numbers

Quick Review

You can use properties such as the ones below to simplify and evaluate expressions.

Commutative Properties $-2 + 7 = 7 + (-2)$

$3 \times 4 = 4 \times 3$

Associative Properties $2 \times (14 \times 3) = (2 \times 14) \times 3$

$3 + (12 + 2) = (3 + 12) + 2$

Identity Properties $-6 + 0 = -6$

$21 \times 1 = 21$

Zero Property of Multiplication $-7 \times 0 = 0$

Multiplication Property of -1 $6 \cdot (-1) = -6$

Example

Use an identity property to simplify $-\frac{7ab}{a}$.

$-\frac{7ab}{a} = -7b \cdot \frac{a}{a} = -7b \cdot 1 = -7b$

Exercises

Simplify each expression. Justify each step.

47. $-8 + 9w + (-23)$

48. $\frac{6}{5} \cdot (-10 \cdot 8)$

49. $\left(\frac{4}{3} \cdot 0\right) \cdot (-20)$

50. $53 + (-12) + (-4t)$

51. $\frac{6 + 3}{9}$

Tell whether the expressions in each pair are equivalent.

52. $(5 - 2)c$ and $c \cdot 3$

53. $41 + z + 9$ and $41 \cdot z \cdot 9$

54. $\frac{81xy}{3x}$ and $9xy$

55. $\frac{11t}{(5 + 7 - 11)}$ and t

1-5 and 1-6 Operations With Real Numbers

Quick Review

To add numbers with different signs, find the difference of their **absolute values.** Then use the sign of the addend with the greater absolute value.

$$3 + (-4) = -(4 - 3) = -1$$

To subtract, add the opposite.

$$9 - (-5) = 9 + 5 = 14$$

The product or quotient of two numbers with the same sign is positive: $5 \cdot 5 = 25 \qquad (-5) \cdot (-5) = 25$

The product or quotient of two numbers with different signs is negative: $6 \cdot (-6) = -36 \qquad -36 \div 6 = -6$

Example

Cave explorers descend to a site that has an elevation of -1.3 km. (Negative elevation means below sea level.) The explorers descend another 0.6 km before they stop to rest. What is the elevation at their resting point?

$$-1.3 + (-0.6) = -1.9$$

The elevation at their resting point is -1.9 km.

Exercises

Find each sum. Use a number line.

56. $1 + 4$ **57.** $3 + (-8)$ **58.** $-2 + (-7)$

Simplify each expression.

59. $-5.6 + 7.4$ **60.** -12^2

61. $-5(-8)$ **62.** $4.5 \div (-1.5)$

63. $-13 + (-6)$ **64.** $-9 - (-12)$

65. $(-2)(-2)(-2)$ **66.** $-54 \div (-0.9)$

Evaluate each expression for $p = 5$ and $q = -3$.

67. $-3q + 7$ **68.** $-(4q)$

69. $q - 8$ **70.** $5p - 6$

71. $-(2p)^2$ **72.** $7q - 7p$

73. $(pq)^2$ **74.** $2q \div (4p)$

1-7 The Distributive Property

Quick Review

Terms with exactly the same variable factors are **like terms.** You can combine like terms and use the Distributive Property to simplify expressions.

Distributive Property $a(b + c) = ab + ac$

                     $a(b - c) = ab - ac$

Example

Simplify $7t + (3 - 4t)$.

$$
\begin{aligned}
7t + (3 - 4t) &= 7t + (-4t + 3) && \text{Commutative Property} \\
&= (7t + (-4t)) + 3 && \text{Associative Property} \\
&= (7 + (-4))t + 3 && \text{Distributive Property} \\
&= 3t + 3 && \text{Simplify.}
\end{aligned}
$$

Exercises

Simplify each expression.

75. $5(2x - 3)$ **76.** $-2(7 - a)$

77. $(-j + 8)\frac{1}{2}$ **78.** $3v^2 - 2v^2$

79. $2(3y - 3)$ **80.** $(6y - 1)\frac{1}{4}$

81. $(24 - 24y)\frac{1}{4}$ **82.** $6y - 3 - 5y$

83. $\frac{1}{3}y + 6 - \frac{2}{3}y$ **84.** $-ab^2 - ab^2$

85. Music All 95 members of the jazz club pay $30 each to go see a jazz performance. What is the total cost of tickets? Use mental math.

86. Reasoning Are $8x^2y$ and $-5yx^2$ like terms? Explain.

1-8 An Introduction to Equations

Quick Review

An **equation** can be true or false, or it can be an **open sentence** with a variable. A **solution** of an equation is the value (or values) of the variable that makes the equation true.

Example

Is $c = 6$ a solution of the equation $25 = 3c - 2$?

$25 = 3c - 2$

$25 \overset{?}{=} 3 \cdot 6 - 2$ Substitute 6 for c.

$25 \neq 16$ Simplify.

No, $c = 6$ is not a solution of the equation $25 = 3c - 2$.

Exercises

Tell whether the given number is a solution of each equation.

87. $17 = 37 + 4f; f = -5$ **88.** $-3a^2 = 27; a = 3$

89. $3b - 9 = 21; b = -10$ **90.** $-2b + 4 = 3; b = \frac{1}{2}$

Use a table to find or estimate the solution of each equation.

91. $x + (-2) = 8$ **92.** $3m - 13 = 24$

93. $4t - 2 = 9$ **94.** $6b - 3 = 17$

1-9 Patterns, Equations, and Graphs

Quick Review

You can represent the relationship between two varying quantities in different ways, including tables, equations, and graphs. A **solution of an equation** with two variables is an **ordered pair** (x, y) that makes the equation true.

Example

Bo makes $15 more per week than Sue. How can you represent this with an equation and a table?

First write an equation. Let $b = $ Bo's earnings and $s = $ Sue's earnings. Bo makes $15 more than Sue, so $b = s + 15$. You can use the equation to make a table for $s = 25, 50, 75$, and 100.

Sue's Earnings (s)	25	50	75	100
Bo's Earnings (b)	40	65	90	115

Exercises

Tell whether the given ordered pair is a solution of each equation.

95. $3x + 5 = y; (1, 8)$

96. $y = -2(x + 3); (-6, 0)$

97. $y = (x - 1.2)(-3); (0, 1.2)$

98. $10 - 5x = y; (-4, 10)$

99. Describe the pattern in the table using words, an equation, and a graph. Extend the pattern for $x = 5, 6$, and 7.

x	y
1	15
2	25
3	35
4	45

Chapter Test

MathXL® for School
Go to PowerAlgebra.com

Do you know HOW?

1. Write an algebraic expression for the phrase *the quotient of n and 6*.

2. Write a word phrase for $-12t + 2$.

3. Evaluate the expression $-(pq)^2 \div (-8)$ for $p = 2$ and $q = 4$.

4. **Dance** The table shows how the total cost of dance classes at a studio depends on the number of classes you take. Write a rule in words and as an algebraic expression to model the relationship.

Dance Classes

Number of Classes	Total Cost
1	$(1 \times 15) + 20$
2	$(2 \times 15) + 20$
3	$(3 \times 15) + 20$

Simplify each expression.

5. $-20 - (-5) \cdot (-2^2)$

6. $\left(-\frac{1}{4}\right)^3$

7. $-\frac{7ab}{a}, a \neq 0$

8. $-|-25|$

9. $\sqrt{\frac{16}{25}}$

10. Is each statement true or false? If false, give a counterexample.

    a. For all real numbers a and b, $a \cdot b$ is equivalent to $b \cdot a$.

    b. For all real numbers a and b, $a(b \cdot c) = ab \cdot ac$

11. Is the ordered pair $(2, -5)$ a solution to the equation $4 + 3x = -2y$? Show your work.

12. Order the numbers $-\frac{7}{8}, \frac{7}{4}, -1\frac{4}{5}$, and $-\frac{13}{16}$ from least to greatest.

13. **Soccer** There are t teams in a soccer league. Each team has 11 players. Make a table, write an equation, and draw a graph to describe the total number of players p in the league. How many players are on 17 teams?

Simplify each expression.

14. $5x^2 - x^2$

15. $12 \div \left(-\frac{3}{4}\right)$

16. $-(-2 + 6t)$

17. $-3[b - (-7)]$

18. Name the subset(s) of the real numbers to which each number belongs.

    a. -2.324 b. $\sqrt{46}$

19. Identify each property.

    a. $a(b + c) = ab + ac$

    b. $(a + b) + c = a + (b + c)$

Do you UNDERSTAND?

20. Is the set of positive integers the same as the set of nonnegative integers? Explain.

21. **Error Analysis** Find and correct the error in the work shown at the right.

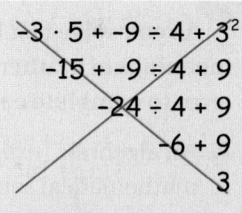

22. Is the following statement true or false? If the product of three numbers is negative, then all the numbers are negative. If false, give a counterexample.

23. **Reasoning** You notice that $10°C = 50°F$, $20°C = 68°F$, and $30°C = 86°F$. Use inductive reasoning to predict the value in degrees Fahrenheit of $40°C$.

24. **Reasoning** When is the absolute value of a difference equal to the difference of the absolute values? Explain.

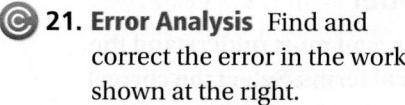

Common Core Cumulative Standards Review

 ASSESSMENT

1

TIPS FOR SUCCESS

Some test questions ask you to enter a numerical answer on a grid. In this textbook, you will record answers on a grid like the one shown below.

TIP 1
An answer may be either a fraction or a decimal. If an answer is a mixed number, rewrite it as an improper fraction or as a decimal.

What is the value of $\frac{1}{2} + \frac{3}{4}$?

Solution

$\frac{1}{2} + \frac{3}{4} = \frac{2}{4} + \frac{3}{4} = \frac{5}{4} = 1\frac{1}{4}$

Record the answer as $\frac{5}{4}$ or 1.25.

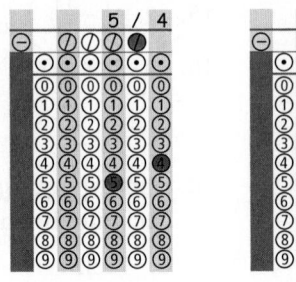

Do not record the answer as $1\frac{1}{4}$ because the test-scoring computer will read it as $\frac{11}{4}$.

TIP 2
You do not have to simplify a fraction unless the question asks for simplest form or the fraction does not fit on the grid.

Think It Through
You can add the fractions as shown in the solution on the left, or you can convert the fractions to decimals and add.

$\frac{1}{2} + \frac{3}{4} = 0.5 + 0.75 = 1.25$

Record the decimal answer on the grid.

Vocabulary Builder

As you solve test items, you must understand the meanings of mathematical terms. Select the correct term to complete each sentence.

A. An algebraic (*expression, equation*) is a mathematical sentence with an equal sign.

B. A (*coefficient, constant*) is a numerical factor of a term.

C. The (*exponent, base*) of a power tells how many times a number is used as a factor.

D. To (*simplify, evaluate*) an algebraic expression, you substitute a given number for each variable.

E. A(n) (*rational, irrational*) number is any number that you can write in the form $\frac{a}{b}$, where a and b are integers, and $b \neq 0$.

Selected Response

Read each question. Then write the letter of the correct answer on your paper.

1. Which expression shows the product of z and $x - y$?

  Ⓐ $z(x - y)$ Ⓒ $x(z - y) + x$

  Ⓑ $z \div x - y$ Ⓓ $\frac{z}{x} - xy$

2. What is the solution of the equation $7d + 7 = 14$?

  Ⓕ -3 Ⓗ 1

  Ⓖ -1 Ⓘ 3

3. What is the value of the expression $8(-9) - 6(-3)$?

  Ⓐ -90 Ⓒ 54

  Ⓑ -54 Ⓓ 90

4. You ship an 8-lb care package to your friend at college. It will cost you $.85 per pound, plus a flat fee of $12, to ship the package. Which equation can you use to find the total cost C?

(F) $C = (8 \cdot 12) + 0.85$ (H) $C = 8 \cdot (0.85 + 12)$

(G) $C = (8 + 0.85) \cdot 12$ (I) $C = (8 \cdot 0.85) + 12$

5. The graph of $y = x - 3$ is shown below. Which ordered pair is NOT a solution of the equation $y = x - 3$?

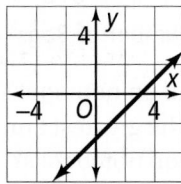

(A) $(-4, -7)$ (C) $(0, -3)$

(B) $(12, 9)$ (D) $(-8, 11)$

6. Which property does the equation $4 + x + 7 = 4 + 7 + x$ illustrate?

(F) Identity Property of Addition

(G) Distributive Property

(H) Commutative Property of Addition

(I) Associative Property of Addition

7. Bill has a $10 coupon for a party store. He needs to buy some balloons for a birthday party. If each balloon costs $2 and Bill uses his coupon, what is an equation that gives the total price y of his purchase?

(A) $y = 2x$

(B) $y = 2x - 10$

(C) $y = 2x + 10$

(D) $y = 10 - 2x$

8. You own 100 shares of Stock A and 30 shares of Stock B. On Monday, Stock A decreased by $.40 per share and Stock B increased by $.25 per share. Which equation can be used to find the total change in value of your shares?

(F) $V = (100 \cdot -0.40) + (30 \cdot 0.25)$

(G) $V = (100 \cdot -0.40) + (30 \cdot -0.25)$

(H) $V = (100 \cdot 0.40) + (30 \cdot 0.25)$

(I) $V = (100 \cdot 0.40) + (30 \cdot -0.25)$

9. The table shows the relationship between the number of laps x you swim in a pool and the distance y, in meters, that you swim. Which equation describes the pattern in the table?

Laps, x	2	4	5	8
Distance (m), y	100	200	250	400

(A) $y = 50x$ (C) $y = x + 50$

(B) $y = 100x$ (D) $y = x + 100$

10. A store is having a sale on cases of juice. The first two cases of juice cost $8 each. Any additional cases of juice cost $6 each. Which expression can be used to find the cost of buying 9 cases of juice?

(F) $(2 \cdot 8) + (9 \cdot 6)$ (H) $(2 \cdot 8) + (7 \cdot 6)$

(G) $(2 \cdot 6) + (7 \cdot 8)$ (I) $9 \cdot 14$

11. The graph below shows the depth of water in a leaking tank.

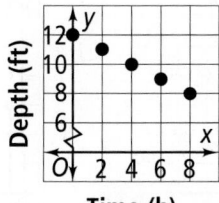

Time (h)

If the tank continues to leak at the same rate, what will be the depth of water after 10 hours?

(A) 5 ft (C) 7 ft

(B) 6 ft (D) 10 ft

12. Chris spends $3 per square foot on carpet for a square room. If he spends about $430 on carpet, what is the approximate length, in feet, of a side of the room?

(F) 12 ft (H) 72 ft

(G) 36 ft (I) 215 ft

13. What is an algebraic expression for *4 more than the product of 3 and a number x*?

(A) $(4 + 3)x$ (C) $4 - 3x$

(B) $4 + 3x$ (D) $3x - 4$

14. A blank CD can hold 80 min of music. You have burned m minutes of music onto the CD. Which equation models the amount of time t that is left on the CD?

 Ⓕ $t = 80 - m$ Ⓗ $t = 80 + m$

 Ⓖ $t = m - 80$ Ⓘ $t = 80m$

15. What is an expression for the sale price of a shirt that is sold at 40% off the original price p?

 Ⓐ $0.4p$ Ⓒ $0.4p - p$

 Ⓑ $p + 0.4p$ Ⓓ $p - 0.4p$

16. A clock originally costs x dollars. After you apply a $3 discount to a clock that costs greater than $3, the clock costs y dollars. Which graph models this situation?

Ⓕ 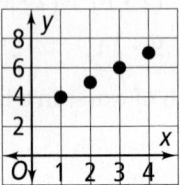   Ⓗ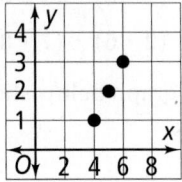

Ⓖ 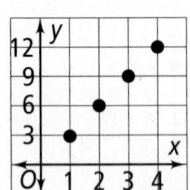   Ⓘ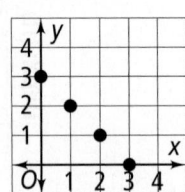

17. To order movie tickets online, John has to pay $10 per ticket plus a $2 handling fee for the whole order. Which equation can be used to determine the total cost C for t tickets?

 Ⓐ $C = 2t + 10$ Ⓒ $C = 10t + 2$

 Ⓑ $C = 10t$ Ⓓ $C = 12t$

18. The monthly cost C for a cell phone is $20 each month plus $.10 for each minute used. Which equation can be used to find the total cost (in dollars) for a month when m minutes are used?

 Ⓕ $C = m + 20$ Ⓗ $C = 10m + 20$

 Ⓖ $C = 0.1m + 20$ Ⓘ $C = 20m$

Constructed Response

19. Use the graph. What is the total cost, in dollars, for 8 bags of balloons?

Balloon Cost

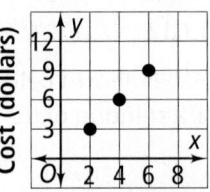

20. Cole has $15 to spend on notebooks. Each notebook costs $3.99. What is the greatest amount, in dollars, that Cole can spend on notebooks?

21. Simplify the expression $3ab + 4ab - 5ab$. What is the coefficient of the simplified expression?

22. Use mental math to find the solution of the equation $4t = 64$.

23. A student recorded the temperature change over time. The table below shows the results.

Time (h)	0.0	0.5	1.0	1.5
Temperature (°F)	76	73	70	67

If the temperature change continues at the same rate, what will the temperature be 3 hours after the start?

24. The formula $F = \frac{9}{5}C + 32$ changes a temperature reading from the Celsius scale C to the Fahrenheit scale F. What is the temperature measured in degrees Fahrenheit when the Celsius temperature is $-5°C$?

Get Ready!

Lesson 1-4 Describing a Pattern

Describe the relationship shown in each table below using words and using an equation.

1.

Number of Lawns Mowed	Money Earned
1	$7.50
2	$15.00
3	$22.50
4	$30.00

2.

Number of Hours	Pages Read
1	30
2	60
3	90
4	120

Lesson 1-5 Adding and Subtracting Real Numbers

Simplify each expression.

3. $6 + (-3)$ **4.** $-4 - 6$ **5.** $-5 - (-13)$ **6.** $-7 + (-1)$

7. $-4.51 + 11.65$ **8.** $8.5 - (-7.9)$ **9.** $\frac{3}{10} - \frac{3}{4}$ **10.** $\frac{1}{5} + \left(-\frac{2}{3}\right)$

Lesson 1-6 Multiplying and Dividing Real Numbers

Simplify each expression.

11. $-85 \div (-5)$ **12.** $7\left(-\frac{6}{14}\right)$ **13.** $4^2(-6)^2$ **14.** $22 \div (-8)$

Lesson 1-7 Combining Like Terms

Simplify each expression.

15. $14k^2 - (-2k^2)$ **16.** $4xy + 9xy$ **17.** $6t + 2 - 4t$ **18.** $9x - 4 + 3x$

Looking Ahead Vocabulary

19. If you say that two shirts are *similar,* what does that mean about the shirts? What would you expect *similar* to mean if you are talking about two similar triangles?

20. A model ship is a type of *scale model*. What is the relationship of a model ship to the actual ship that it models?

CHAPTER

2

Solving Equations

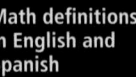

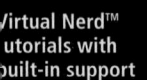

Download videos connecting math to your world.

Interactive! Vary numbers, graphs, and figures to explore math concepts.

The online Solve It will get you in gear for each lesson.

Math definitions in English and Spanish

Online access to stepped-out problems aligned to Common Core

Get and view your assignments online.

Extra practice and review online

Virtual Nerd™ tutorials with built-in support

Chapter Preview

Vocabulary

English/Spanish Vocabulary Audio Online:

English	Spanish
conversion factor, p. 117	factor de conversión
cross products, p. 125	productos cruzados
equivalent equations, p. 81	ecuaciones equivalentes
formula, p. 110	fórmula
inverse operations, p. 82	operaciones inversas
literal equation, p. 109	ecuación literal
percent change, p. 144	cambio porcentual
proportion, p. 124	proporción
rate, p. 116	tasa
ratio, p. 116	razón
scale, p. 132	escala
unit analysis, p. 117	análisis de unidades

BIG ideas

1 Equivalence
Essential Question Can equations that appear to be different be equivalent?

2 Solving Equations and Inequalities
Essential Question How can you solve equations?

3 Proportionality
Essential Question What kinds of relationships can proportions represent?

 DOMAINS

- Quantities
- Creating Equations
- Reasoning with Equations and Inequalities

Common Core Performance Task

Determining the Speed of a Monorail

An information board in an airport displays a scale drawing of the airport's new monorail route. On the information board display, the distance between the parking garage and the train station is 36 in.

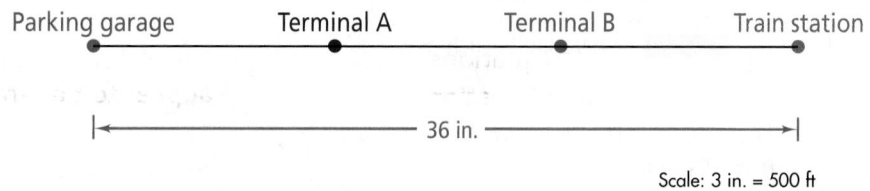

Airport Monorail Route

Parking garage   Terminal A   Terminal B   Train station

|←   36 in.   →|

Scale: 3 in. = 500 ft

Here are some facts about the new monorail.

- The trip between the parking garage and Terminal A takes 60 s.

- The trip between Terminal A and Terminal B takes 45 s.

- The monorail's average speed between Terminal A and Terminal B is 8.1 ft/s greater than its average speed between the parking garage and Terminal A.

- The distance from the parking garage to Terminal B is 3950 ft.

- The trip from Terminal B to the train station takes 10% more time than the trip from the parking garage to Terminal A.

Task Description

Determine the average speed of the monorail, in miles per hour, over each segment of the route. Round each speed to the nearest tenth of a mile per hour.

Connecting the Task to the Math Practices

MATHEMATICAL PRACTICES

As you complete the task, you'll apply several Standards for Mathematical Practice.

- You'll write and solve an equation to find the average speed of the monorail, in feet per second, between the parking garage and Terminal A. (MP 1, MP 2)

- You'll convert rates from feet per second to miles per hour. (MP 6)

- You'll use a scale drawing and a proportion to find an unknown distance. (MP 4)

Modeling One-Step Equations

 Common Core State Standards

Prepares for A-REI.A.1 Explain each step in solving a simple equation as following from the equality of numbers asserted at the previous step, . . .

MP 7

Algebra tiles can help you understand how to solve one-step equations in one variable. You can use the algebra tiles shown below to model equations. Notice that the yellow tile is positive and the red tile is negative. Together, they form a zero pair, which represents 0.

Unit tiles

$\square = +1$ $\blacksquare = -1$

$\blacksquare + \square = 0$

Variable tiles

 = a variable, such as x

 **Activity**

Model and solve $x - 2 = 4$.

Equation	Algebra tiles	Step
$x - 2 = 4$		Model the equation using tiles.
$x - 2 + 2 = 4 + 2$	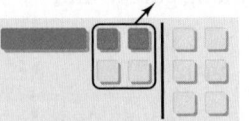	The green tile represents x. To get the green tile by itself on one side of the equation, add two yellow tiles to each side. Remember, a yellow tile and a red tile form a zero pair. Remove all zero pairs.
$x = 6$		The green tile equals six yellow tiles. This represents $x = 6$. The solution of $x - 2 = 4$ is 6.

Exercises

Write the equation modeled by the algebra tiles.

1.

2.

Use algebra tiles to model and solve each equation.

3. $x - 3 = 2$ **4.** $x - 4 = 7$ **5.** $x + 1 = 5$ **6.** $x + 4 = 7$

7. $1 + x = -3$ **8.** $5 + x = -3$ **9.** $x - 4 = -3$ **10.** $-4 + x = -8$

2-1

Solving One-Step Equations

 Common Core State Standards

A-CED.A.1 Create equations . . . in one variable and use them to solve problems. *Include equations arising from linear . . . functions.* **Also A-REI.B.3**

MP 1, MP 3, MP 4, MP 7

Objective To solve one-step equations in one variable

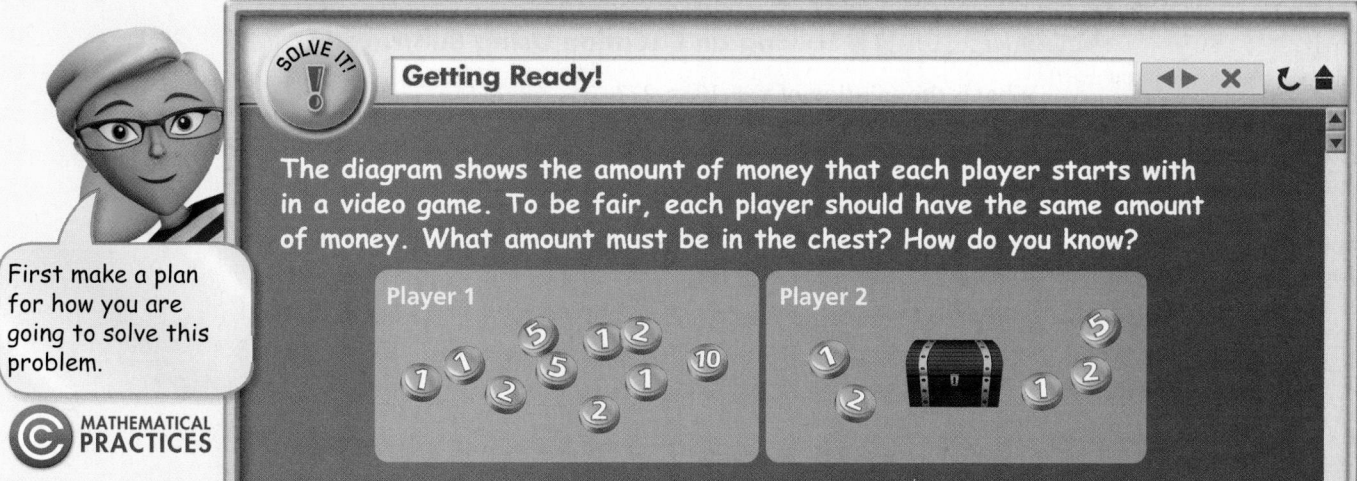

SOLVE IT!

Getting Ready!

The diagram shows the amount of money that each player starts with in a video game. To be fair, each player should have the same amount of money. What amount must be in the chest? How do you know?

Player 1

Player 2

First make a plan for how you are going to solve this problem.

 MATHEMATICAL PRACTICES

In the Solve It, you may have used reasoning to find the amount of money in the chest. In this lesson, you will learn to solve problems like the one above by using equations.

Essential Understanding **Equivalent equations** are equations that have the same solution(s). You can find the solution of a one-step equation using the properties of equality and inverse operations to write a simpler equivalent equation.

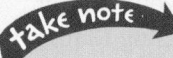 **take note**

Property **Addition and Subtraction Properties of Equality**

Addition Property of Equality Adding the same number to each side of an equation produces an equivalent equation.

Algebra
For any real numbers a, b, and c,
if $a = b$, then $a + c = b + c$.

Example
$$x - 3 = 2$$
$$x - 3 + 3 = 2 + 3$$

Subtraction Property of Equality Subtracting the same number from each side of an equation produces an equivalent equation.

Algebra
For any real numbers a, b, and c,
if $a = b$, then $a - c = b - c$.

Example
$$x + 3 = 2$$
$$x + 3 - 3 = 2 - 3$$

Lesson Vocabulary
- equivalent equations
- Addition Property of Equality
- Subtraction Property of Equality
- isolate
- inverse operations
- Multiplication Property of Equality
- Division Property of Equality

To solve an equation, you must **isolate** the variable. You do this by getting the variable with a coefficient of 1 alone on one side of the equation.

You can isolate a variable using the properties of equality and inverse operations. An **inverse operation** undoes another operation. For example, subtraction is the inverse of addition. When you solve an equation, each inverse operation you perform should produce a simpler equivalent equation.

© **Problem 1** Solving an Equation Using Subtraction

What is the solution of $x + 13 = 27$?

Plan

How can you visualize the equation?
You can *draw a diagram*. Use a model like the one below to help you visualize an equation. A model for the equation $x + 13 = 27$ is

|⌐------- 27 --------|
| x | 13 |

Think

You need to isolate *x*. Start by writing the equation.

Undo addition by subtracting the same number from each side.

Simplify each side of the equation.

Substitute your answer into the original equation to check it.

Write

$x + 13 = 27$

$x + 13 - 13 = 27 - 13$

$x = 14$

$x + 13 = 27$
$14 + 13 \overset{?}{=} 27$
$27 = 27$ ✔

© ✓ **Got It?** **1. a.** What is the solution of $y + 2 = -6$? Check your answer. $^{-2}$ $^{-2}$ $-8+2=-6$ -8

b. Reasoning In Problem 1, why does subtracting 13 from both sides of the original equation result in an equivalent equation?

© **Problem 2** Solving an Equation Using Addition

Plan

How can you get started?
Undo operations. Add 3 to each side to undo subtraction.

What is the solution of $-7 = b - 3$?

$$-7 = b - 3$$
$$-7 + 3 = b - 3 + 3 \quad \text{Add 3 to each side.}$$
$$-4 = b \quad \text{Simplify.}$$

✓ **Got It?** **2.** What is the solution of each equation? Check your answer.

a. $m - 8 = -14$

-6

b. $\frac{1}{2} = y - \frac{3}{2}$

2

You can use the Multiplication and Division Properties of Equality to solve equations. Division is the inverse of multiplication.

take note

Property   Multiplication and Division Properties of Equality

Multiplication Property of Equality Multiplying each side of an equation by the same nonzero number produces an equivalent equation.

Algebra

For any real numbers a, b, and c,
if $a = b$, then $a \cdot c = b \cdot c$.

Example

$\frac{x}{3} = 2$

$\frac{x}{3} \cdot 3 = 2 \cdot 3$

Division Property of Equality Dividing each side of an equation by the same nonzero number produces an equivalent equation.

Algebra

For any real numbers a, b, and c, such that $c \neq 0$, if $a = b$, then $\frac{a}{c} = \frac{b}{c}$.

Example

$5x = 20$

$\frac{5x}{5} = \frac{20}{5}$

Plan

How can a model help you solve the equation?
The model tells you that you must divide 6.4 by 4 in order to solve the equation $4x = 6.4$.

|------- 6.4 -------|
| x | x | x | x |

© **Problem 3** Solving an Equation Using Division   **GRIDDED RESPONSE**

What is the solution of $4x = 6.4$?

$4x = 6.4$

$\frac{4x}{4} = \frac{6.4}{4}$ Divide each side by 4.

$x = 1.6$ Simplify.

✓ **Got It? 3.** What is the solution of each equation? Check your answer.

a. $10 = 15x$ $0.67 = x$
$\frac{10}{15} = \frac{15x}{15}$

b. $-3.2z = 14$
$\frac{-3.2z}{-3.2} = \frac{14}{-3.2}$ $z = -4.375$

Plan

How can a model help you solve the equation?
The model tells you that you must multiply -9 by 4 in order to solve the equation $\frac{x}{4} = -9$.

|------- x -------|
| -9 | -9 | -9 | -9 |

© **Problem 4** Solving an Equation Using Multiplication

What is the solution of $\frac{x}{4} = -9$?

$\frac{x}{4} = -9$

$\frac{x}{4} \cdot 4 = -9 \cdot 4$ Multiply each side by 4.

$x = -36$ Simplify.

✓ **Got It? 4.** What is the solution of each equation? Check your answer.

a. $19 = \frac{r}{3}$
$19 \cdot 3 = \frac{r}{3} \cdot 3$
$57 = r$

b. $\frac{x}{-9} = 8$
$\frac{x}{-9} \cdot -9 = 8 \cdot -9$
$x = -72$

When the coefficient of the variable in an equation is a fraction, you can use the reciprocal of the fraction to solve the equation.

Problem 5 Solving Equations Using Reciprocals

What is the solution of $\frac{4}{5}m = 28$?

$$\frac{4}{5}m = 28$$

$$\frac{5}{4}\left(\frac{4}{5}m\right) = \frac{5}{4}(28) \quad \text{Multiply each side by } \frac{5}{4}, \text{ the reciprocal of } \frac{4}{5}.$$

$$m = 35 \quad \text{Simplify.}$$

Think

Why multiply by the reciprocal?
You want the coefficient of m to be 1. The product of a number and its reciprocal is 1, so multiply by the reciprocal.

Got It? **5. a.** What is the solution of $12 = \frac{3}{4}x$? Check your answer.

$12 \cdot \frac{4}{3} = \frac{3}{4}x \cdot \frac{4}{3} \qquad 16 = x$

b. Reasoning Are the equations $m = 18$ and $\frac{2}{3}m = 12$ equivalent? How do you know? Yes

$\frac{3}{2} \cdot \frac{2}{3}m = 12 \cdot \frac{3}{2} \qquad m = 18$

Problem 6 Using a One-Step Equation as a Model (STEM)

Biology Toucans and blue-and-yellow macaws are both tropical birds. The length of an average toucan is about two thirds of the length of an average blue-and-yellow macaw. Toucans are about 24 in. long. What is the length of an average blue-and-yellow macaw?

Relate length of toucan is $\frac{2}{3}$ of length of blue-and-yellow macaw

Think

How else can you solve this problem?
You can work backward. The toucan's length is $\frac{2}{3}$ the macaw's length, so the macaw's length is $\frac{3}{2}$ the toucan's length. You can multiply the length of the toucan by $\frac{3}{2}$.

Define Let ℓ = the length of an average blue-and-yellow macaw.

Write $24 = \frac{2}{3} \cdot \ell$

$$24 = \frac{2}{3}\ell$$

$$\frac{3}{2}(24) = \frac{3}{2}\left(\frac{2}{3}\ell\right) \quad \text{Multiply each side by } \frac{3}{2}.$$

$$36 = \ell \quad \text{Simplify.}$$

An average blue-and-yellow macaw is 36 in. long.

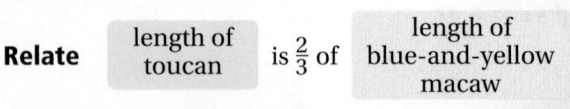

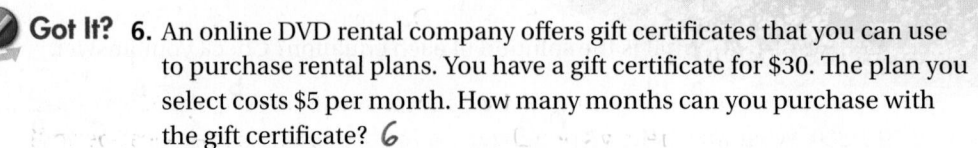

24 in

Check $24 = \frac{2}{3}\ell$

$24 \stackrel{?}{=} \frac{2}{3}(36) \quad \text{Substitute 36 for } \ell.$

$24 = 24 \quad \text{Simplify. The solution checks.}$

Got It? **6.** An online DVD rental company offers gift certificates that you can use to purchase rental plans. You have a gift certificate for $30. The plan you select costs $5 per month. How many months can you purchase with the gift certificate? 6

Lesson Check

Do you know HOW?

Solve each equation. Check your answer.

1. $x + 7 = 3$ $\quad 3-7=-4 \quad x=-4$

2. $9 = m - 4$ $\quad 9+4=13 \quad m=13$

3. $5y = 24$

4. Books You have already read 117 pages of a book. You are one third of the way through the book. Write and solve an equation to find the number of pages in the book. $117 \cdot 3 = 351$ $\quad 351$ pages

Do you UNDERSTAND?

Vocabulary Which property of equality would you use to solve each equation? Why?

5. $3 + x = -34$

6. $2x = 5$

7. $x - 4 = 9$

8. $\frac{x}{7} = 9$

9. Reasoning Write a one-step equation. Then write two equations that are equivalent to your equation. How can you prove that all three equations are equivalent?

Practice and Problem-Solving Exercises

 **Practice**

Solve each equation using addition or subtraction. Check your answer.   ◀ See Problems 1 and 2.

10. $6 = x + 2$

11. $27 + n = 46$

12. $23 = v + 5$

13. $4 = q + 13$

14. $f + 9 = 20$

15. $-5 + a = 21$

16. $-17 = 3 + k$

17. $5.5 = -2 + d$

18. $c + 4 = -9$

19. $67 = w - 65$

20. $23 = b - 19$

21. $g - 3.5 = 10$

22. $y - 19 = 37$

23. $q - 11 = -9$

24. $-2.5 = p + 7.1$

25. $j - 3 = -7$

Solve each equation using multiplication or division. Check your answer.   ◀ See Problems 3 and 4.

26. $-8n = -64$

27. $-7y = 28$

28. $5b = 145$

29. $6a = 0.96$

30. $-96 = 4c$

31. $11 = 2.2t$

32. $17.5 = 5s$

33. $7r = -\frac{7}{2}$

34. $\frac{m}{7} = 12$

35. $35 = \frac{j}{5}$

36. $\frac{k}{7} = 13$

37. $-39 = \frac{q}{3}$

38. $14 = \frac{z}{2}$

39. $\frac{q}{-9} = -9$

40. $-13 = \frac{m}{-5}$

41. $\frac{k}{4} = -\frac{17}{2}$

Solve each equation. Check your answer.   ◀ See Problem 5.

42. $\frac{2}{3}q = 18$

43. $\frac{3}{4}x = 9$

44. $\frac{5}{8}y = -1$

45. $\frac{3}{5}m = -15$

46. $\frac{1}{5}x = \frac{2}{7}$

47. $36 = \frac{4}{9}d$

48. $-6 = \frac{3}{7}n$

49. $\frac{3}{8}p = 9$

Define a variable and write an equation for each situation. Then solve.   ◀ See Problem 6.

50. Music You have a rack that can hold 30 CDs. You can fit 7 more CDs on the rack before the rack is full. How many CDs are in the rack?

51. Population In a 3-year period, a city's population decreased by 7525 to about 581,600. What was the city's population at the beginning of the 3-year period?

Apply 52. **Writing** If a one-step equation includes addition, should you expect to solve it by using addition? Why or why not?

53. **Think About a Plan** Costumes for a play at a community theater cost $1500, which is one third of the total budget. What is the total budget for the play?

⊢--------- ? ---------⊣
1500	1500	1500

- How can the model at the right help you solve the problem?
- How does the model tell you which operation to use in the equation?

54. **Entertainment** On a quiz show, a contestant was penalized 250 points for an incorrect answer, leaving the contestant with 1050 points. How many points did the contestant have before the penalty?

Solve each equation. Check your answer.

55. $\frac{2}{7} = \frac{1}{3} + a$ 56. $23 = 7x$ 57. $z - 4\frac{2}{3} = 2\frac{2}{3}$

58. $\frac{2}{3}g = -4\frac{1}{2}$ 59. $6\frac{1}{4} = \frac{r}{5}$ 60. $h + 2.8 = -3.7$

61. $\frac{3}{2}f = \frac{1}{2}$ 62. $-4 = \frac{2}{9}d$ 63. $1.6m = 1.28$

64. $4d = -2.4$ 65. $4\frac{1}{4} = 1\frac{3}{4} + p$ 66. $-5.3 + z = 8.9$

67. $-2\frac{1}{2} = \frac{t}{10}$ 68. $5b = 8.5$ 69. $\frac{3}{5}n = -\frac{3}{10}$

70. **Picnics** At a party of 102 people, 17 lb of potato salad is served.
   a. Write and solve an equation to find how many people each pound of potato salad serves.
   b. Write and solve an equation to find the average number of pounds of potato salad that each person is served. Round your answer to the nearest hundredth.

71. **Error Analysis** Describe and correct the error in solving the equation at the right.

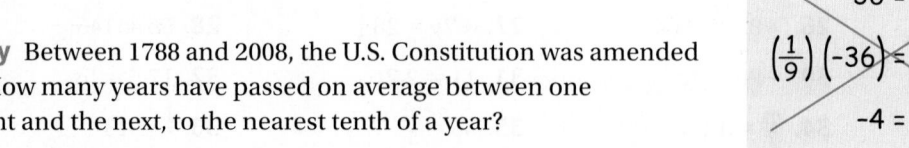

$$-36 = \frac{x}{9}$$
$$\left(\frac{1}{9}\right)(-36) = \left(\frac{1}{9}\right)\left(\frac{x}{9}\right)$$
$$-4 = x$$

72. **U.S. History** Between 1788 and 2008, the U.S. Constitution was amended 27 times. How many years have passed on average between one amendment and the next, to the nearest tenth of a year?

73. **Volleyball** In volleyball, players serve the ball to the opposing team. If the opposing team fails to hit the ball, the service is called an ace. A player's ace average is the number of aces served divided by the number of games played. A certain player has an ace average of 0.3 and has played in 70 games this season. How many aces has the player served?

74. **Open-Ended** Write a problem that you can model with a one-step equation. Write the equation and solve the problem.

75. **Language** According to one count, the letter *e* makes up one eighth of a typical document written in English. A document contains 2800 letters. About how many letters in the document are *not e*?

76. Typography A point is a unit of length that can be used to measure the distance between two lines of text. Font sizes are often stated in points. Capital letters measure two thirds of the stated point size, as shown in the diagram for a font size of 48 points. There are 72 points in 1 inch. What point size produces capital letters that are $\frac{1}{2}$ in. tall?

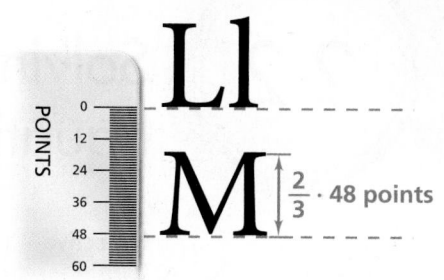

C Challenge

77. Reasoning In a school's musical, a choir member sang in the backup chorus for half the songs in the show, which was 12 songs. A student concludes that one half of 12 is 6, so there were 6 songs in the show. Write an equation that would help the student understand the correct number of songs in the musical.

78. Cooking Uncooked rice has about $\frac{4}{13}$ the weight of cooked rice. You want to make 6.5 lb of rice for a recipe. How many pounds of uncooked rice do you need?

Standardized Test Prep

SAT/ACT

79. Luis helped raise money for his school by jogging in the school jog-a-thon. The total amount of money he raised can be represented by the expression $1.75m$, where m is the number of miles he jogged. If Luis raised a total of $21, how many miles did he jog?

    Ⓐ 12   Ⓑ 19.25   Ⓒ 22.75   Ⓓ 36.75

80. What operation should you use to solve $14 + c = 39$?

    Ⓕ squaring   Ⓖ subtraction   Ⓗ multiplication   Ⓘ division

81. Sonya is checking orders at the fabric store where she works. Some of the orders are in decimals and some are in fractions. Which of the following statements is *not* true?

    Ⓐ $\frac{10}{4} = 2.5$ Ⓑ $1.3 = 1\frac{1}{3}$ Ⓒ $0.03 = \frac{3}{100}$ Ⓓ $\frac{6}{5} = 1.2$

Mixed Review

82. If the pattern shown in the table continues, what amount will have been raised by Week 5?

See Lesson 1-9.

Scholarship Funds				
Week	0	1	2	3
Amount (thousands)	0	2	4	6

Simplify each expression. Justify each step.

See Lesson 1-4.

83. $4(13x)$ **84.** $2.2 + (3.8 - x)$ **85.** $(m + 4.5) - 0.5$

Get Ready! **To prepare for Lesson 2-2, do Exercises 86–88.**

Simplify each expression.

See Lesson 1-2.

86. $2[2 - (2 - 3) - 2]$ **87.** $\left(\frac{1}{2} + \frac{1}{3}\right)^2$ **88.** $-1 + 2 \cdot 3 - 4$

2-2 Solving Two-Step Equations

Common Core State Standards

A-REI.B.3 Solve linear equations and inequalities in one variable, including equations with coefficients represented by letters. **Also A-CED.A.1, A-REI.A.1**

MP 2, MP 3, MP 4

Objective To solve two-step equations in one variable

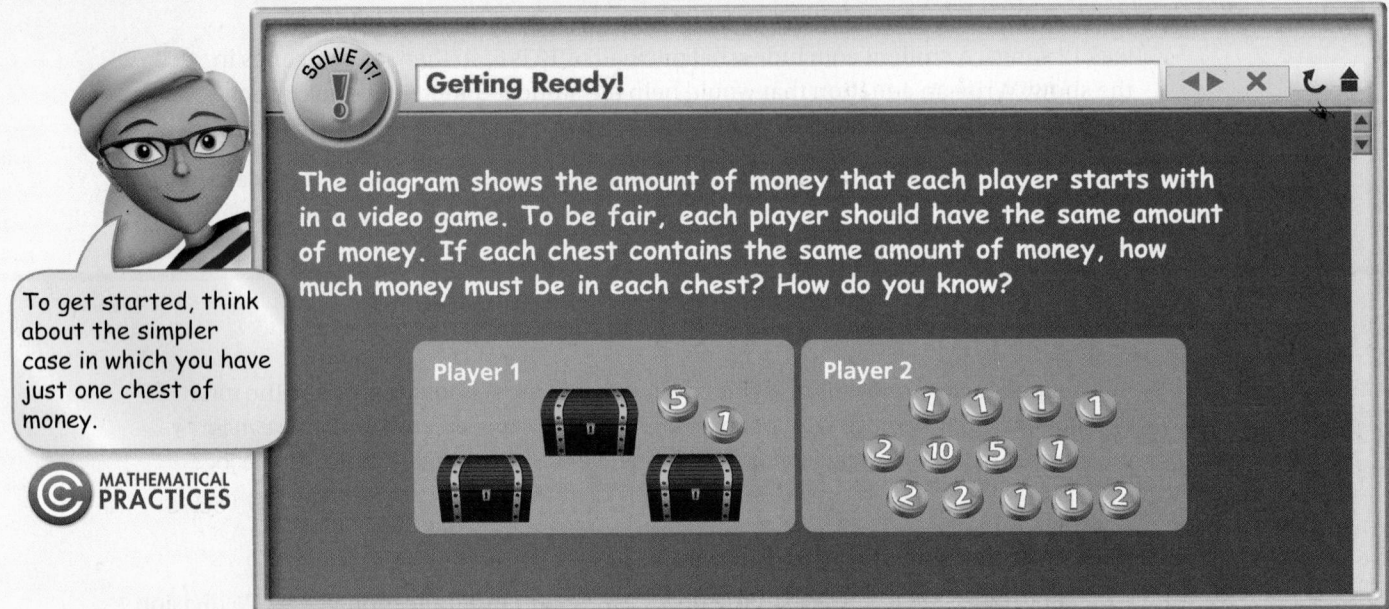

Getting Ready!

The diagram shows the amount of money that each player starts with in a video game. To be fair, each player should have the same amount of money. If each chest contains the same amount of money, how much money must be in each chest? How do you know?

To get started, think about the simpler case in which you have just one chest of money.

MATHEMATICAL PRACTICES

Player 1

Player 2

The problem in the Solve It can be modeled by an equation. The equations in this lesson are different from the equations in Lesson 2-1 because they require two steps to solve.

Essential Understanding To solve two-step equations, you can use the properties of equality and inverse operations to form a series of simpler equivalent equations. You can use the properties of equality repeatedly to isolate the variable.

A two-step equation, like the one shown below, involves two operations.

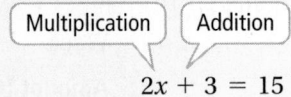

Multiplication   Addition

$$2x + 3 = 15$$

To solve a two-step equation, identify the operations and undo them using inverse operations. You can undo the operations in the reverse order of the order of operations. For example, to solve $2x + 3 = 15$, you can use subtraction first to undo the addition, and then use division to undo the multiplication.

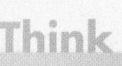

 Problem 1 Solving a Two-Step Equation

Think

What operations are used in the equation?
The equation uses multiplication and addition. You can undo the addition first, and then the multiplication.

What is the solution of $2x + 3 = 15$?

$$2x + 3 = 15$$

$2x + 3 - 3 = 15 - 3$	Subtract 3 from each side.
$2x = 12$	Simplify.
$\frac{2x}{2} = \frac{12}{2}$	Divide each side by 2.
$x = 6$	Simplify.

Check $2x + 3 = 15$

$2(6) + 3 \stackrel{?}{=} 15$	Substitute 6 for x.
$15 = 15$	Simplify. The solution checks.

 Got It? **1.** What is the solution of $5 = \frac{t}{2} - 3$?

(handwritten)
$5 = \frac{t}{2} - 3$ $2 \cdot 8 = \frac{t}{2} \cdot 2$
$5 + 3 = \frac{t}{2}$ $16 = t$
$8 = \frac{t}{2}$
$t = 16$

 Problem 2 Using an Equation as a Model

Community Service You are making a bulletin board to advertise community service opportunities in your town. You plan to use half a sheet of construction paper for each ad. You need 5 sheets of construction paper for a title banner. You have 18 sheets of construction paper. How many ads can you make?

Know	**Need**	**Plan**
• Paper per ad: $\frac{1}{2}$ sheet • Paper for banner: 5 sheets • Total paper: 18 sheets	The number of ads you can make	Write and solve an equation. Let the variable represent the unknown.

Think

How can a model help you write the equation?
The model shows that a half of a sheet per ad plus 5 sheets for the title banner is equal to 18 sheets.

|------- 18 -------|
| $\frac{1}{2}a$ | 5 |

Let a = the number of ads you can make.

$$\frac{1}{2}a + 5 = 18$$

$\frac{1}{2}a + 5 - 5 = 18 - 5$	Subtract 5 from each side.
$\frac{1}{2}a = 13$	Simplify.
$2\left(\frac{1}{2}a\right) = 2(13)$	Multiply each side by 2.
$a = 26$	Simplify.

You can make 26 community service advertisements for the bulletin board.

 Got It? **2.** Suppose you used one quarter of a sheet of paper for each ad and four full sheets for the title banner in Problem 2. How many ads could you make?

(handwritten) 18 sheets

$18 - 4 = 14$ $14 \cdot 4 = 56$ $18 = 4 + \frac{1}{4}a$
                                        $-4 \quad -4$
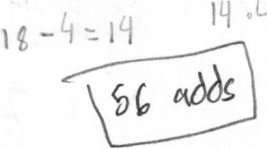 56 adds $14 = \frac{1}{4}a$
                                        $56 = a$

When one side of an equation is a fraction with more than one term in the numerator, you can still undo division by multiplying each side by the denominator.

 Problem 3 **Solving With Two Terms in the Numerator**

Plan

What operation should you perform first?
Multiplication. When you multiply by the denominator of the fraction in the equation, you get a one-step equation. So, multiplying first gets rid of the fraction.

What is the solution of $\frac{x-7}{3} = -12$?

$$\frac{x-7}{3} = -12$$

$$3\left(\frac{x-7}{3}\right) = 3(-12) \qquad \text{Multiply each side by 3.}$$

$$x - 7 = -36 \qquad \text{Simplify.}$$

$$x - 7 + 7 = -36 + 7 \qquad \text{Add 7 to each side.}$$

$$x = -29 \qquad \text{Simplify.}$$

 Got It? 3. a. What is the solution of $6 = \frac{x-2}{4}$?

$6 \cdot 4 = 24 \qquad 24 = x - 2 \qquad 24 + 2$

$26 = x$

       b. Reasoning Write the right side of the equation in part (a) as the difference of two fractions. Solve the equation. Did you find the equation in part (a) or the rewritten equation easier to solve? Why?

When you use deductive reasoning, you must state your steps and your reason for each step using properties, definitions, or rules. In Problem 4, you are asked to provide the reasons for each step of the problem using deductive reasoning.

 Problem 4 **Using Deductive Reasoning**

What is the solution of $-t + 8 = 3$? Justify each step.

Steps	Reasons
$-t + 8 = 3$	Original equation
$-t + 8 - 8 = 3 - 8$	Subtraction Property of Equality
$-t = -5$	Use subtraction to simplify.
$-1t = -5$	Multiplicative Property of -1
$\frac{-1t}{-1} = \frac{-5}{-1}$	Division Property of Equality
$t = 5$	Use division to simplify.

Think

Why isn't $-t = -5$ the solution?
When you solve for a variable, the coefficient must be 1, not -1.

Got It? 4. What is the solution of $\frac{x}{3} - 5 = 4$? Justify each step.

$$3 \cdot \frac{x}{3} = 9 \cdot 3$$

$$x = 27$$

Lesson Check

Do you know HOW?

Solve each equation. Check your answer.

1. $5x + 12 = -13$ **2.** $6 = \frac{m}{7} - 3$

3. $\frac{y - 1}{4} = -2$ **4.** $-x - 4 = 9$

5. Fundraising The junior class is selling granola bars to raise money. They purchased 1250 granola bars and paid a delivery fee of $25. The total cost, including the delivery fee, was $800. What was the cost of each granola bar?

Do you UNDERSTAND?

What properties of equality would you use to solve each equation? What operation would you perform first? Explain.

6. $-8 = \frac{s}{4} + 3$ **7.** $2x - 9 = 7$

8. $\frac{x}{3} - 8 = 4$ **9.** $-4x + 3 = -5$

ⓒ **10. Reasoning** Can you solve the equation $\frac{d - 3}{5} = 6$ by adding 3 before multiplying by 5? Explain.

Practice and Problem-Solving Exercises

 **Practice**

Solve each equation. Check your answer.

See Problem 1.

11. $2 + \frac{a}{4} = -1$ **12.** $3n - 4 = 11$ **13.** $-1 = 7 + 8x$ **14.** $\frac{y}{5} + 2 = -8$

15. $4b + 6 = -2$ **16.** $10 = \frac{x}{4} - 8$ **17.** $10 + \frac{h}{3} = 1$ **18.** $-14 = -5 + 3c$

19. $26 = \frac{m}{6} + 5$ **20.** $\frac{a}{5} - 18 = 2$ **21.** $-5x - 2 = 13$ **22.** $14 = -2k + 3$

Define a variable and write an equation for each situation. Then solve.

See Problem 2.

23. Maximum Capacity A delivery person uses a service elevator to bring boxes of books up to an office. The delivery person weighs 160 lb and each box of books weighs 50 lb. The maximum capacity of the elevator is 1000 lb. How many boxes of books can the delivery person bring up at one time?

24. Shopping You have $16 and a coupon for a $5 discount at a local supermarket. A bottle of olive oil costs $7. How many bottles of olive oil can you buy?

25. Rentals Two college friends rent an apartment. They have to pay the landlord two months' rent and a $500 security deposit when they sign the lease. The total amount they pay the landlord is $2800. What is the rent for one month?

Solve each equation. Check your answer.

See Problem 3.

26. $\frac{y - 4}{2} = 10$ **27.** $7 = \frac{x - 8}{3}$ **28.** $\frac{z + 10}{9} = 2$ **29.** $4 = \frac{a + 10}{2}$

30. $7\frac{1}{2} = \frac{x + 3}{2}$ **31.** $\frac{b + 3}{5} = -1$ **32.** $-2 = \frac{d - 7}{7}$ **33.** $\frac{g - 3}{3} = \frac{5}{3}$

Solve each equation. Justify each step.

See Problem 4.

34. $14 - b = 19$ **35.** $20 - 3h = 2$ **36.** $3 - \frac{x}{2} = 6$ **37.** $-1 = 4 + \frac{x}{3}$

Solve each equation. Check your answer.

38. $\frac{2 + y}{3} = -1$

39. $-24 = -10t + 3$

40. $10 = 0.3x - 9.1$

41. $\frac{1}{2} = \frac{1}{2}c - 2$

42. $\frac{x - 3}{3} = -4\frac{1}{2}$

43. $9.4 = -d + 5.6$

44. $\frac{d + 17}{2} = 5\frac{1}{3}$

45. $2.4 + 10m = 6.89$

46. $\frac{1}{5}t - 3 = -17$

Solve each equation. Justify each step.

47. $15 = 9 - 3p$

48. $4 - 5k = -16$

49. $9 + \frac{c}{-5} = -5$

50. $\frac{q}{-3} + 12 = 2$

51. Error Analysis Describe and correct the error in finding the solution of the equation at the right.

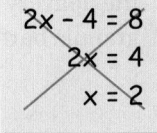

52. Writing Without solving the equation $-3x + 5 = 44$, tell whether the value of x is positive or negative. How do you know?

53. a. Solve the equation $2x - 1 = 7$ by undoing subtraction first.
  b. Solve the equation in part (a) by undoing multiplication first. Do you get the same answer you got in part (a)?
  c. Reasoning Which method from parts (a) and (b) do you prefer? Explain.

Geometry In each triangle, the measure of $\angle A$ equals the measure of $\angle B$. Find the value of x.

54.

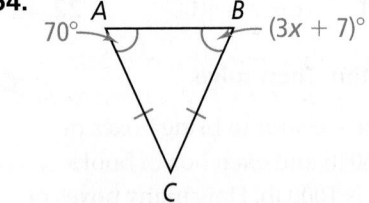

55.

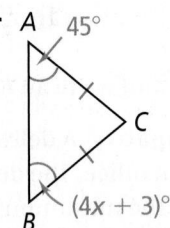

56. Think About a Plan A Web site allows musicians to post their songs online. Then people using the Web site can buy any of the posted songs. Suppose each musician must pay a one-time fee of $5 to use the Web site. Each musician earns $.09 every time a particular song of his or hers is downloaded. If a musician earned $365 for a particular song, how many times was the song downloaded?
• How can the model at the right help you solve the problem?
• How does the model tell you which operations to use in the equation?

57. Open-Ended Write a real-world problem that you can model with the two-step equation $8b + 6 = 38$. Then solve the problem.

58. Home Improvement A contractor is adding a back porch on to a house. The porch needs to hold 20 people and furniture that weighs 250 lb. The contractor calculates that the porch needs to hold 3750 lb to meet that specification. What value did the contractor use for the weight of a person?

STEM **59. Earth Science** The air temperature beneath Earth's surface increases by about 10°C per kilometer. The surface temperature and the air temperature at the bottom of a mine are shown. How many kilometers below Earth's surface is the bottom of the mine?

Surface: 18°C

Bottom of mine: 38°C
Not drawn to scale

60. Car-Sharing Program Members of a car-sharing program pay a fee of $50 per month plus $7.65 for every hour they use a car. A member's bill was $149.45 last month. How many hours did the customer use a car last month?

Challenge

61. Word Processing You format a document in three columns of equal width. The document is 8.5 in. wide. You want left and right margins of 1 in. each. Between the columns there is a "gutter" that is one eighth as wide as each column. What is the width of each column?

Tell whether each equation has a solution. If so, find the solution. If not, explain why not.

62. $2x - 0 = 0$ **63.** $0(-2x) = 4$ **64.** $\dfrac{x-2}{2} = 0$ **65.** $\dfrac{x-2}{0} = 2$

Standardized Test Prep

GRIDDED RESPONSE

SAT/ACT

66. William's age w and Jamie's age j are related by the equation $w = 2j - 12$. When William is 36.5 years old, how old is Jamie?

67. Dominique paints faces at an annual carnival. Her goal this year is to earn $100. She spends $15 on supplies and will work for 2.5 h. How much will she need to earn in dollars per hour in order to reach her goal?

68. The cost of a gallon of milk m is $.50 more than five times the cost of a gallon of water w. If a gallon of milk costs $3.75, what is the cost of a gallon of water?

Mixed Review

Solve each equation.   ◄ See Lesson 2-1.

69. $-5x = -25$ **70.** $7 = 3.2 + y$ **71.** $\dfrac{y}{4} = 36$ **72.** $z - 2 = 4.5$

Tell whether each statement is *true* or *false*. If it is false, give a counterexample.   ◄ See Lesson 1-4.

73. The difference of the absolute value of two numbers is the same as the difference of the two numbers themselves.

74. Adding 1 to a number always increases its absolute value.

Get Ready!   **To prepare for Lesson 2-3, do Exercises 75–78.**

Simplify each expression.   ◄ See Lesson 1-7.

75. $7(5 - t)$ **76.** $-2(-2x + 5)$ **77.** $-3(2 - b)$ **78.** $5(2 - 5n)$

2-3 Solving Multi-Step Equations

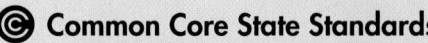
Common Core State Standards

A-CED.A.1 Create equations . . . in one variable and use them to solve problems. *Include equations arising from linear . . . functions.* **Also A-REI.A.1, A-REI.B.3**

MP 1, MP 2, MP 3, MP 4

Objective To solve multi-step equations in one variable

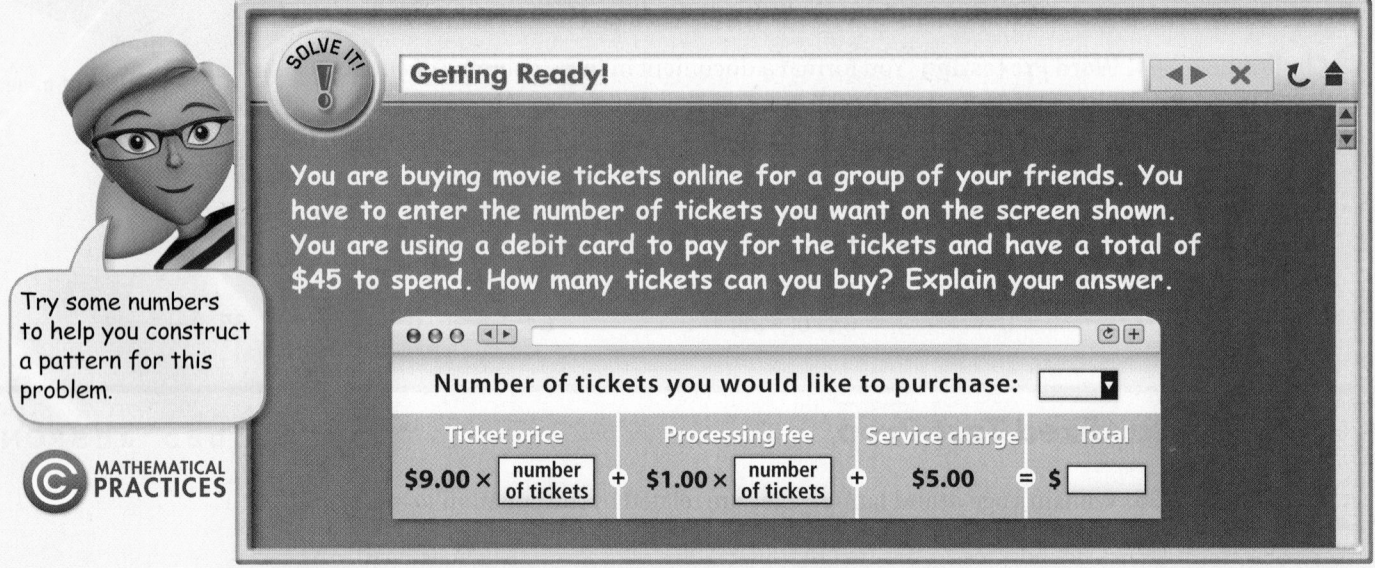

SOLVE IT!

Getting Ready!

You are buying movie tickets online for a group of your friends. You have to enter the number of tickets you want on the screen shown. You are using a debit card to pay for the tickets and have a total of $45 to spend. How many tickets can you buy? Explain your answer.

Number of tickets you would like to purchase:

Ticket price	Processing fee	Service charge	Total
$9.00 × number of tickets	+ $1.00 × number of tickets	+ $5.00	= $

Try some numbers to help you construct a pattern for this problem.

 **MATHEMATICAL PRACTICES**

In this lesson, you will learn to write and solve multi-step equations.

Essential Understanding To solve multi-step equations, you form a series of simpler equivalent equations. To do this, use the properties of equality, inverse operations, and properties of real numbers. You use the properties until you isolate the variable.

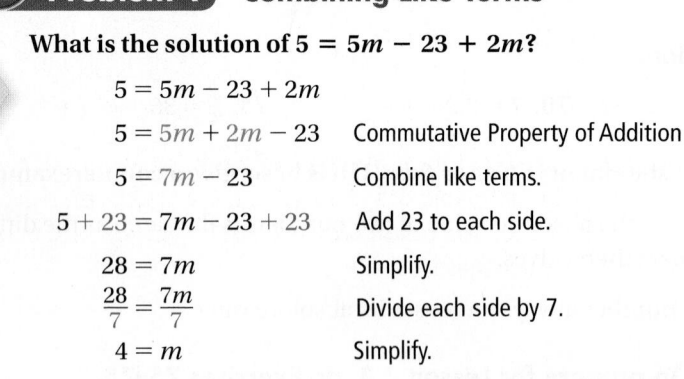 **Problem 1** **Combining Like Terms**

Think

How is this equation different from equations you've seen before?
The variable occurs in *two* terms. You can simplify the equation by grouping like terms and combining them.

What is the solution of $5 = 5m - 23 + 2m$?

$$5 = 5m - 23 + 2m$$

$5 = 5m + 2m - 23$ Commutative Property of Addition

$5 = 7m - 23$ Combine like terms.

$5 + 23 = 7m - 23 + 23$ Add 23 to each side.

$28 = 7m$ Simplify.

$\dfrac{28}{7} = \dfrac{7m}{7}$ Divide each side by 7.

$4 = m$ Simplify.

Check $5 = 5m - 23 + 2m$

$5 \overset{?}{=} 5(4) - 23 + 2(4)$ Substitute 4 for m.

$5 = 5$ ✓   Simplify. The solution checks.

Got It? **1.** What is the solution of each equation? Check each answer.

a. $11m - 8 - 6m = 22$ $m = 6$

$5m - 8 = 22$ $5m = 30 = \frac{30}{5}$

$+8 \quad +8$ $\frac{\quad}{5} \quad \frac{30}{15} \quad 17$

$5m = 30 = 30 \quad m = 6, \; 76$

b. $-2y + 5 + 5y = 14$ $y = 3$

$3y + 5 = 14$

$-5 \;\; -5$

$\frac{3y = 9}{3} \quad y = 3$

 Problem 2 Solving a Multi-Step Equation

Concert Merchandise Martha takes her niece and nephew to a concert. She buys T-shirts and bumper stickers for them. The bumper stickers cost \$1 each. Martha's niece wants 1 shirt and 4 bumper stickers, and her nephew wants 2 shirts but no bumper stickers. If Martha's total is \$67, what is the cost of one shirt?

Know
- Bumper stickers cost \$1
- Niece's items: 1 shirt, 4 bumper stickers
- Nephew's items: 2 shirts
- Total spent: \$67

Need

The cost of one shirt

Plan

Write and solve an equation that models the situation.

Think

How can a model help you write the equation?
The model shows that the cost of the niece's items plus the cost of the nephew's items is \$67.

```
|-------- 67 --------|
| s + 4  |    2s     |
```

Relate   cost of niece's items (1 shirt and 4 stickers)   plus   cost of nephew's items (2 shirts)   is   total Martha spent

Define   Let $s = $ the cost of one shirt.

Write $(s + 4)$ $+$ $2s$ $=$ 67

$(s + 4) + 2s = 67$

$s + 2s + 4 = 67$ Commutative Property of Addition

$3s + 4 = 67$ Combine like terms.

$3s + 4 - 4 = 67 - 4$ Subtract 4 from each side.

$3s = 63$ Simplify.

$\frac{3s}{3} = \frac{63}{3}$ Divide each side by 3.

$s = 21$ Simplify.

One shirt costs \$21.

 Got It? **2.** Noah and Kate are shopping for new guitar strings in a music store. Noah buys 2 packs of strings. Kate buys 2 packs of strings and a music book. The book costs \$16. Their total cost is \$72. How much is one pack of strings?

$72 = 16 + 4s$ $s = 14$

$-16 \quad -16$

$\frac{56}{4} = \frac{4s}{4}$

$14 = s$

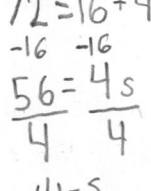

Problem 3 **Solving an Equation Using the Distributive Property**

Think

How can you make the equation easier to solve?
Remove the grouping symbols by using the Distributive Property.

What is the solution of $-8(2x - 1) = 36$?

$-8(2x - 1) = 36$	
$-16x + 8 = 36$	Distributive Property
$-16x + 8 - 8 = 36 - 8$	Subtract 8 from each side.
$-16x = 28$	Simplify.
$\dfrac{-16x}{-16} = \dfrac{28}{-16}$	Divide each side by -16.
$x = -\dfrac{7}{4}$	Simplify.

$36 = 6x$
$\dfrac{36}{6} = \dfrac{6x}{6}$
$^{+18}18 = 6x - 18^{+18}$ $x = 6$

 **Got It?** **3. a.** What is the solution of $18 = 3(2x - 6)$? Check your answer. $X = 6$

b. Reasoning Can you solve the equation in part (a) by using the Division Property of Equality instead of the Distributive Property? Explain.

You can use different methods to solve equations that contain fractions.

Problem 4 **Solving an Equation That Contains Fractions**

Plan

How do you get started?
You can either combine like terms by writing the fractions with a common denominator, or you can clear the fractions from the equation.

What is the solution of $\dfrac{3x}{4} - \dfrac{x}{3} = 10$?

Method 1 Write the like terms using a common denominator and solve.

$\dfrac{3}{4}x - \dfrac{1}{3}x = 10$	Rewrite the fractions.
$\dfrac{9}{12}x - \dfrac{4}{12}x = 10$	Write the fractions using a common denominator, 12.
$\dfrac{5}{12}x = 10$	Combine like terms.
$\dfrac{12}{5}\left(\dfrac{5}{12}x\right) = \dfrac{12}{5}(10)$	Multiply each side by $\dfrac{12}{5}$, the reciprocal of $\dfrac{5}{12}$.
$x = 24$	Simplify.

Method 2 Clear the fractions from the equation.

$12\left(\dfrac{3x}{4} - \dfrac{x}{3}\right) = 12(10)$	Multiply each side by a common denominator, 12.
$12\left(\dfrac{3x}{4}\right) - 12\left(\dfrac{x}{3}\right) = 12(10)$	Distributive Property
$9x - 4x = 120$	Multiply.
$5x = 120$	Combine like terms.
$x = 24$	Divide each side by 5 and simplify.

Got It? **4.** What is the solution of each equation? Why did you choose the method you used to solve each equation?

a. $\frac{2b}{5} + \frac{3b}{4} = 3$ **b.** $\frac{1}{9} = \frac{5}{6} - \frac{m}{3}$

You can clear decimals from an equation by multiplying by a power of 10. First, find the greatest number of digits to the right of any decimal point, and then multiply by 10 raised to that power.

 Problem 5 Solving an Equation That Contains Decimals

What is the solution of $3.5 - 0.02x = 1.24$?

Plan

The equation contains tenths (3.5) and hundredths (0.02 and 1.24). The greatest number of digits to the right of any decimal point is 2. So, multiply each side of the equation by 10^2, or 100, to clear the decimals.

Think

When you multiply a decimal by 10^n, where n is a positive integer, you can move the decimal point n places to the right. For example, $100(3.5) = 350$.

$$3.5 - 0.02x = 1.24$$

$100(3.5 - 0.02x) = 100(1.24)$	Multiply each side by 10^2, or 100.
$350 - 2x = 124$	Distributive Property
$350 - 2x - 350 = 124 - 350$	Subtract 350 from each side.
$-2x = -226$	Simplify.
$\frac{-2x}{-2} = \frac{-226}{-2}$	Divide each side by -2.
$x = 113$	Simplify.

 Got It? **5.** What is the solution of $0.5x - 2.325 = 3.95$? Check your answer.

 Lesson Check

Do you know HOW?

Solve each equation. Check your answer.

1. $7p + 8p - 12 = 59$ **2.** $-2(3x + 9) = 24$

3. $\frac{2m}{7} + \frac{3m}{14} = 1$ **4.** $1.2 = 2.4 - 0.6x$

5. Gardening There is a 12-ft fence on one side of a rectangular garden. The gardener has 44 ft of fencing to enclose the other three sides. What is the length of the garden's longer dimension?

Do you UNDERSTAND?

Explain how you would solve each equation.

6. $1.3 + 0.5x = -3.41$

7. $7(3x - 4) = 49$

8. $-\frac{2}{9}x - 4 = \frac{7}{18}$

9. Reasoning Ben solves the equation $-24 = 5(g + 3)$ by first dividing each side by 5. Amelia solves the equation by using the Distributive Property. Whose method do you prefer? Explain.

Practice and Problem-Solving Exercises

 MATHEMATICAL PRACTICES

 Practice

Solve each equation. Check your answer.

See Problem 1.

10. $7 - y - y = -1$

11. $72 + 4 - 14d = 36$

12. $13 = 5 + 3b - 13$

13. $6p - 2 - 3p = 16$

14. $x + 2 + x = 22$

15. $b - 9 + 6b = 30$

16. $9t - 6 - 6t = 6$

17. $17 = p - 3 - 3p$

18. $-23 = -2a - 10 + a$

Write an equation to model each situation. Then solve the equation.

See Problem 2.

19. Employment You have a part-time job. You work for 3 h on Friday and 6 h on Saturday. You also receive an allowance of $20 per week. You earn $92 per week. How much do you earn per hour at your part-time job?

20. Travel A family buys airline tickets online. Each ticket costs $167. The family buys travel insurance with each ticket that costs $19 per ticket. The Web site charges a fee of $16 for the entire purchase. The family is charged a total of $1132. How many tickets did the family buy?

Solve each equation. Check your answer.

See Problem 3.

21. $64 = 8(r + 2)$

22. $5(2x - 3) = 15$

23. $5(2 + 4z) = 85$

24. $2(8 + 4c) = 32$

25. $7(f - 1) = 45$

26. $15 = -2(2t - 1)$

27. $26 = 6(5 - 4f)$

28. $n + 5(n - 1) = 7$

29. $-4(r + 6) = -63$

Solve each equation. Choose the method you prefer to use. Check your answer.

See Problem 4.

30. $\frac{b}{13} - \frac{3b}{13} = \frac{8}{13}$

31. $5y - \frac{3}{5} = \frac{4}{5}$

32. $\frac{n}{5} - \frac{3n}{10} = \frac{1}{5}$

33. $\frac{2}{3} + \frac{3m}{5} = \frac{31}{15}$

34. $\frac{n}{2} - \frac{2n}{16} = \frac{3}{8}$

35. $\frac{b}{3} + \frac{1}{8} = 19$

36. $\frac{1}{4} + \frac{4x}{5} = \frac{11}{20}$

37. $\frac{11z}{16} + \frac{7z}{8} = \frac{5}{16}$

38. $\frac{x}{3} - \frac{7x}{12} = \frac{2}{3}$

Solve each equation. Check your answer.

See Problem 5.

39. $1.06g - 3 = 0.71$

40. $0.11k + 1.5 = 2.49$

41. $1.025v + 2.458 = 7.583$

42. $1.12 + 1.25g = 8.62$

43. $25.24 = 5g + 3.89$

44. $0.25n + 0.1n = 9.8$

 Apply

Solve each equation.

45. $6 + \frac{v}{-8} = \frac{4}{7}$

46. $\frac{2}{3}(c - 18) = 7$

47. $3d + d - 7 = \frac{25}{4}$

48. $0.25(d - 12) = 4$

49. $8n - (2n - 3) = 12$

50. $\frac{2}{3} + n + 6 = \frac{3}{4}$

51. $0.5d - 3d + 5 = 0$

52. $-(w + 5) = -14$

53. $\frac{a}{20} + \frac{4}{15} = \frac{9}{15}$

54. Think About a Plan Jillian and Tyson are shopping for knitting supplies. Jillian wants 3 balls of yarn and 1 set of knitting needles. Tyson wants 1 ball of yarn and 2 sets of knitting needles. Each ball of yarn costs $6.25. If their total cost is $34.60, what is the cost of 1 set of knitting needles?
- How can the model at the right help you solve the problem?
- How does the model tell you which operations to use in the equation?

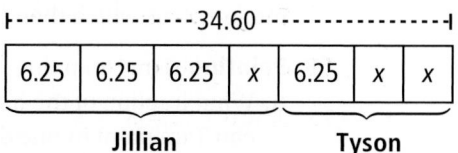

55. Online Video Games Angie and Kenny play online video games. Angie buys 1 software package and 3 months of game play. Kenny buys 1 software package and 2 months of game play. Each software package costs $20. If their total cost is $115, what is the cost of one month of game play?

56. Error Analysis Describe and correct the error in solving the equation at the right.

57. Reasoning Suppose you want to solve $-4m + 5 + 6m = -3$. What would you do as your first step? Explain.

58. Writing Describe two ways in which you can solve $-\frac{1}{2}(5x - 9) = 17$.

$$\frac{3x}{8} - 1 = \frac{5}{8}$$
$$8\left(\frac{3x}{8} - 1\right) = 8\left(\frac{5}{8}\right)$$
$$3x - 1 = 5$$
$$3x = 6$$
$$x = 2$$

59. Bowling Three friends go bowling. The cost per person per game is $5.30. The cost to rent shoes is $2.50 per person. Their total cost is $55.20. How many games did they play?

60. Moving Expenses A college student is moving into a campus dormitory. The student rents a moving truck for $19.95 plus $.99 per mile. Before returning the truck, the student fills the tank with gasoline, which costs $65.32. The total cost is $144.67. How many miles did the student drive the truck?

Geometry Find the value of x. (*Hint*: The sum of the angle measures of a quadrilateral is 360°.)

61.

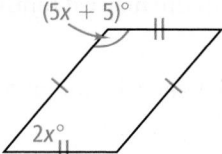

62.

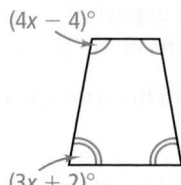

63.

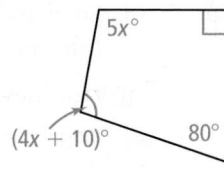

64. Dining Out You are ordering a meal and have $15 to spend. The restaurant charges 6% sales tax. You plan to leave a 15% tip. The equation $c = x + 0.06x + 0.15x$ gives the total cost c of your meal, where x is the cost before tax and tip. What is the maximum amount you can spend before tax and tip?

65. Savings You have $85 in your bank account. Each week you plan to deposit $8 from your allowance and $15 from your paycheck. The equation $b = 85 + (15 + 8)w$ gives the amount b in your bank account after w weeks. How many weeks from now will you have $175 in your bank account?

 **Challenge**

66. **Open-Ended** Find three consecutive integers with a sum of 45. Show your work.

67. **Cooking** A cook buys two identical bags of rice and uses some of the rice in each bag so that one bag is half full and the other is one-third full. The cook combines them into one bag, which then contains $3\frac{1}{3}$ cups of rice. How much rice was in a full bag?

68. **Painting** Tim can paint a house in 6 days. Tara can paint the same house in 3 days.
    a. What fraction of the house can Tim paint in one day? What fraction of the house can Tara paint in one day?
    b. What fraction of the house can Tim paint in d days? What fraction of the house can Tara paint in d days?
    c. What fraction of the house can Tim and Tara together paint in one day? What fraction of the house can Tim and Tara together paint in d days?
    d. Write and solve an equation to find the number of days it will take Tim and Tara to paint the whole house working together.

 ## Apply What You've Learned

 MATHEMATICAL PRACTICES
MP 1, MP 2

Look back at the information given about the monorail on page 79. Let r represent the average speed of the monorail, in feet per second, between the parking garage and Terminal A.

a. Write an expression for the distance the monorail travels between the parking garage and Terminal A. Then write an expression for the distance the monorail travels between Terminal A and Terminal B. (*Hint*: Use the relationship *distance = rate × time*.)

b. Write an equation that relates the total distance the monorail travels between the parking garage and Terminal B to the two expressions you wrote in part (a).

c. Solve the equation you wrote in part (b). Round your answer to the nearest tenth. Interpret your solution in terms of the situation.

d. Use your result from part (c) to find the rate of the monorail between Terminal A and Terminal B.

e. Do the rates you found in parts (c) and (d) make sense in terms of the diagram and the times given on page 79? Explain.

Modeling Equations With Variables on Both Sides

 Common Core State Standards

Prepares for A-REI.A.1 Explain each step in solving a simple equation as following from the equality of numbers asserted at the previous step, . . .

MP 7

Algebra tiles can help you understand how to solve equations with variables on both sides.

Activity

Model and solve $3b - 4 = b + 2$.

Equation	Algebra tiles	Step
$3b - 4 = b + 2$	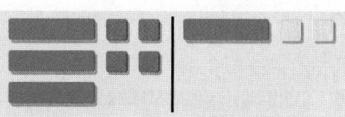	Model the equation using tiles.
$3b - 4 - b = b + 2 - b$ $2b - 4 = 2$	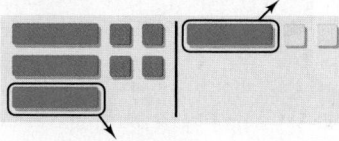	Remove one green tile from each side of the equation so that all remaining green tiles are on one side.
$2b - 4 + 4 = 2 + 4$ $2b = 6$	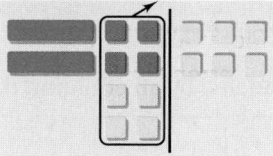	Add four yellow tiles to each side of the equation to form zero pairs that can be removed.
$\dfrac{2b}{2} = \dfrac{6}{2}$	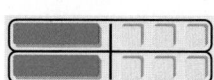	Notice that two green tiles equal six yellow tiles. You can divide the tiles on each side of the equation into two identical groups, as shown.
$b = 3$		So, one green tile equals three yellow tiles. The solution of $3b - 4 = b + 2$ is $b = 3$. You can substitute 3 for b to check.

Exercises

Write the equation modeled by the algebra tiles.

1.

2.

Use algebra tiles to model and solve each equation.

3. $3x - 5 = x + 3$ **4.** $6x - 4 = 3x + 2$ **5.** $5x - 3 = 3x + 1$ **6.** $4x + 4 = 1 + x$

Solving Equations With Variables on Both Sides

© Common Core State Standards

A-CED.A.1 Create equations . . . in one variable and use them to solve problems. *Include equations arising from linear . . . functions.* **Also A-REI.A.1, A-REI.B.3**

MP 1, MP 2, MP 3, MP 4

Objectives To solve equations with variables on both sides
To identify equations that are identities or have no solution

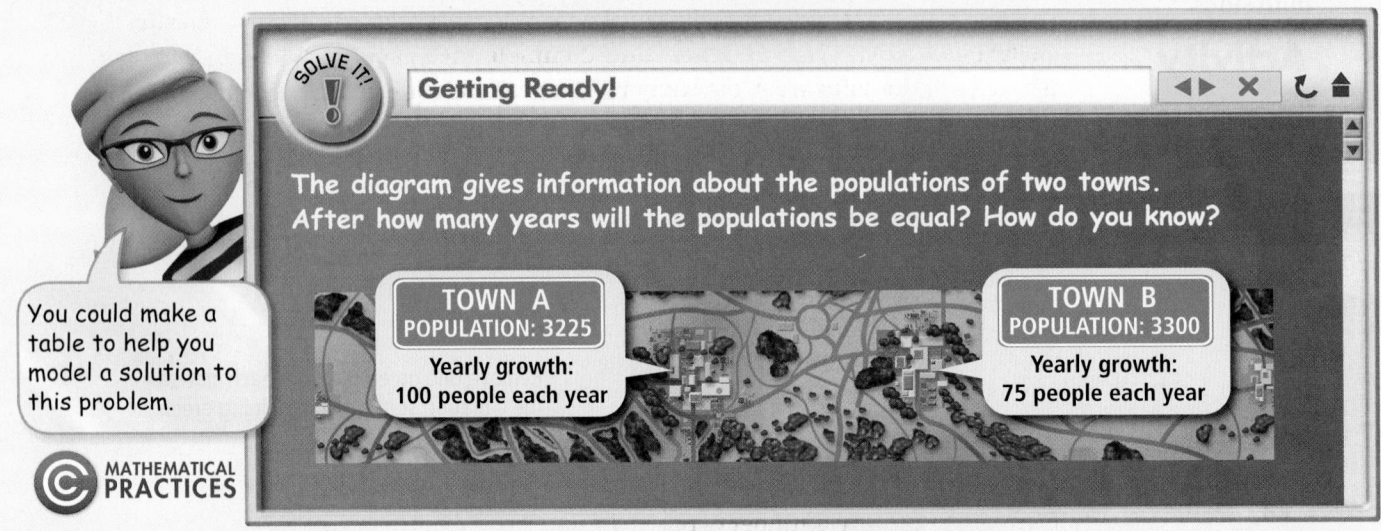

SOLVE IT!

Getting Ready!

◄► ✕ ↺ ⌂

The diagram gives information about the populations of two towns. After how many years will the populations be equal? How do you know?

You could make a table to help you model a solution to this problem.

TOWN A
POPULATION: 3225
Yearly growth:
100 people each year

TOWN B
POPULATION: 3300
Yearly growth:
75 people each year

MATHEMATICAL PRACTICES

Lesson Vocabulary
• identity

The problem in the Solve It can be modeled by an equation that has variables on *both* sides.

Essential Understanding To solve equations with variables on both sides, you can use the properties of equality and inverse operations to write a series of simpler equivalent equations.

Plan

How do you get started?
There are variable terms on both sides of the equation. Decide which variable term to add or subtract to get the variable on one side only.

© Problem 1 Solving an Equation With Variables on Both Sides

What is the solution of $5x + 2 = 2x + 14$?

$$5x + 2 = 2x + 14$$

$5x + 2 - 2x = 2x + 14 - 2x$ Subtract 2x from each side.

$3x + 2 = 14$ Simplify.

$3x + 2 - 2 = 14 - 2$ Subtract 2 from each side.

$3x = 12$ Simplify.

$\dfrac{3x}{3} = \dfrac{12}{3}$ Divide each side by 3.

$x = 4$ Simplify.

Check $5x + 2 = 2x + 14$

$5(4) + 2 \stackrel{?}{=} 2(4) + 14$ Substitute 4 for x.

$22 = 22$ ✔   Simplify. The solution checks.

Got It? **1. a.** What is the solution of $7k + 2 = 4k - 10$?

Handwritten: $3k + 2 \overset{-2}{=} -10 - 2 \quad \overset{\div 3}{3k} = \overset{\div 3}{-12} \quad k = -4$

        b. Reasoning Solve the equation in Problem 1 by subtracting $5x$ from each side instead of $2x$. Compare and contrast your solution with the solution in Problem 1.

 Problem 2 **Using an Equation With Variables on Both Sides**

Graphic Design It takes a graphic designer 1.5 h to make one page of a Web site. Using new software, the designer could complete each page in 1.25 h, but it takes 8 h to learn the software. How many Web pages would the designer have to make in order to save time using the new software?

Know	**Need**	**Plan**
• Current design time: 1.5 h per page • Time with new software: 1.25 h per page • Time to learn software: 8 h	The number of pages the designer needs to make for the new software to save time	Write and solve an equation that models the situation.

Think

How can a model help you write the equation?
The model shows that the current design time is equal to the new design time plus the 8 h needed to learn the new software.

1.5p	
1.25p	8

Relate $\underset{\text{design time}}{\text{current}}$ $=$ $\underset{\text{new software}}{\text{design time with}}$ $+$ $\underset{\text{software}}{\text{time to learn}}$

Define   Let p = the number of pages the designer needs to make.

Write $\boxed{1.5p}$ $=$ $\boxed{1.25p}$ $+$ $\boxed{8}$

$$1.5p = 1.25p + 8$$
$$1.5p - 1.25p = 1.25p + 8 - 1.25p \qquad \text{Subtract } 1.25p \text{ from each side.}$$
$$0.25p = 8 \qquad \text{Simplify.}$$
$$\frac{0.25p}{0.25} = \frac{8}{0.25} \qquad \text{Divide each side by 0.25.}$$
$$p = 32 \qquad \text{Simplify.}$$

It will take the designer the same amount of time to make 32 Web pages using either software. The designer must make 33 pages or more in order to save time using the new software.

 Got It? **2.** An office manager spent $650 on a new energy-saving copier that will reduce the monthly electric bill for the office from $112 to $88. In how many months will the copier pay for itself?

Problem 3 Solving an Equation With Grouping Symbols

Plan

How do you get started?
There are parentheses on both sides of the equation. So, remove the parentheses using the Distributive Property.

What is the solution of $2(5x - 1) = 3(x + 11)$?

$$2(5x - 1) = 3(x + 11)$$

$10x - 2 = 3x + 33$	Distributive Property
$10x - 2 - 3x = 3x + 33 - 3x$	Subtract $3x$ from each side.
$7x - 2 = 33$	Simplify.
$7x - 2 + 2 = 33 + 2$	Add 2 to each side.
$7x = 35$	Simplify.
$\frac{7x}{7} = \frac{35}{7}$	Divide each side by 7.
$x = 5$	Simplify.

✅ **Got It? 3.** What is the solution of each equation?

a. $4(2y + 1) = 2(y - 13)$ **b.** $7(4 - a) = 3(a - 4)$

An equation that is true for every possible value of the variable is an **identity.** For example, $x + 1 = x + 1$ is an identity. An equation has no solution if there is no value of the variable that makes the equation true. The equation $x + 1 = x + 2$ has no solution.

 Problem 4 Identities and Equations With No Solution

Think

How can you tell how many solutions an equation has?
If you eliminate the variable in the process of solving, the equation is either an identity with infinitely many solutions or an equation with no solution.

What is the solution of each equation?

A $10x + 12 = 2(5x + 6)$

$$10x + 12 = 2(5x + 6)$$

$10x + 12 = 10x + 12$	Distributive Property

Because $10x + 12 = 10x + 12$ is always true, there are infinitely many solutions of the equation. The original equation is an identity.

B $9m - 4 = -3m + 5 + 12m$

$9m - 4 = -3m + 5 + 12m$	
$9m - 4 = 9m + 5$	Combine like terms.
$9m - 4 - 9m = 9m + 5 - 9m$	Subtract $9m$ from each side.
$-4 = 5$ ✗	Simplify.

Because $-4 \neq 5$, the original equation has no solution.

✅ **Got It? 4.** What is the solution of each equation?

a. $3(4b - 2) = -6 + 12b$ **b.** $2x + 7 = -1(3 - 2x)$

When you solve an equation, you use reasoning to select properties of equality that produce simpler equivalent equations until you find a solution. The steps below provide a general guideline for solving equations.

take note

Concept Summary   Solving Equations

Step 1 Use the Distributive Property to remove any grouping symbols. Use properties of equality to clear decimals and fractions.

Step 2 Combine like terms on each side of the equation.

Step 3 Use the properties of equality to get the variable terms on one side of the equation and the constants on the other.

Step 4 Use the properties of equality to solve for the variable.

Step 5 Check your solution in the original equation.

Lesson Check

Do you know HOW?

Solve each equation. Check your answer.

1. $3x + 4 = 5x - 10$

2. $5(y - 4) = 7(2y + 1)$

3. $2a + 3 = \frac{1}{2}(6 + 4a)$

4. $4x - 5 = 2(2x + 1)$

5. Printing Pristine Printing will print business cards for \$.10 each plus a setup charge of \$15. The Printing Place offers business cards for \$.15 each with a setup charge of \$10. What number of business cards costs the same from either printer?

Do you UNDERSTAND?

 Vocabulary Match each equation with the appropriate number of solutions.

6. $3y - 5 = y + 2y - 9$ **A.** infinitely many

7. $2y + 4 = 2(y + 2)$ **B.** one solution

8. $2y - 4 = 3y - 5$ **C.** no solution

9. Writing A student solved an equation and found that the variable was eliminated in the process of solving the equation. How would the student know whether the equation is an identity or an equation with no solution?

Practice and Problem-Solving Exercises

 **A Practice**   Solve each equation. Check your answer.

See Problem 1.

10. $5x - 1 = x + 15$

11. $4p + 2 = 3p - 7$

12. $6m - 2 = 2m + 6$

13. $3 + 5q = 9 + 4q$

14. $8 - 2y = 3y - 2$

15. $3n - 5 = 7n + 11$

16. $2b + 4 = -18 - 9b$

17. $-3c - 12 = -5 + c$

18. $-n - 24 = 5 - n$

 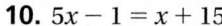

Write and solve an equation for each situation. Check your solution.

● See Problem 2.

 19. Architecture An architect is designing a rectangular greenhouse. Along one wall is a 7-ft storage area and 5 sections for different kinds of plants. On the opposite wall is a 4-ft storage area and 6 sections for plants. All of the sections for plants are of equal length. What is the length of each wall?

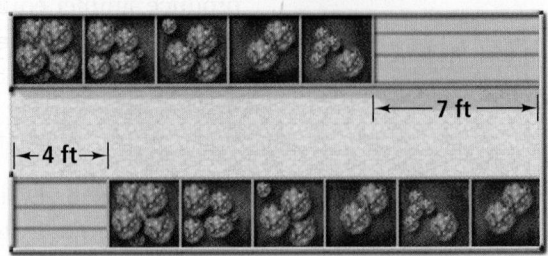

20. Business A hairdresser is deciding where to open her own studio. If the hairdresser chooses Location A, she will pay $1200 per month in rent and will charge $45 per haircut. If she chooses Location B, she will pay $1800 per month in rent and will charge $60 per haircut. How many haircuts would she have to give in one month to make the same profit at either location?

Solve each equation. Check your answer.

● See Problem 3.

21. $3(q - 5) = 2(q + 5)$

22. $8 - (3 + b) = b - 9$

23. $7(6 - 2a) = 5(-3a + 1)$

24. $(g + 4) - 3g = 1 + g$

25. $2r - (5 - r) = 13 + 2r$

26. $5g + 4(-5 + 3g) = 1 - g$

Determine whether each equation is an *identity* or whether it has *no solution*.

● See Problem 4.

27. $2(a - 4) = 4a - (2a + 4)$

28. $5y + 2 = \frac{1}{2}(10y + 4)$

29. $k - 3k = 6k + 5 - 8k$

30. $2(2k - 1) = 4(k - 2)$

31. $-6a + 3 = -3(2a - 1)$

32. $4 - d = -(d - 4)$

 **Apply**

Solve each equation. If the equation is an identity, write *identity*. If it has no solution, write *no solution*.

33. $3.2 - 4d = 2.3d + 3$

34. $3d + 4 = 2 + 3d - \frac{1}{2}$

35. $2.25(4x - 4) = -2 + 10x + 12$

36. $3a + 1 = -3.6(a - 1)$

37. $\frac{1}{2}h + \frac{1}{3}(h - 6) = \frac{5}{6}h + 2$

38. $0.5b + 4 = 2(b + 2)$

39. $-2(-c - 12) = -2c - 12$

40. $3(m + 1.5) = 1.5(2m + 3)$

41. Travel Suppose a family drives at an average rate of 60 mi/h on the way to visit relatives and then at an average rate of 40 mi/h on the way back. The return trip takes 1 h longer than the trip there.
 a. Let d be the distance in miles the family traveled to visit their relatives. How many hours did it take to drive there?
 b. In terms of d, how many hours did it take to make the return trip?
 c. Write and solve an equation to determine the distance the family drove to see their relatives. What was the average rate for the entire trip?

42. **Think About a Plan** Each morning, a deli worker has to make several pies and peel a bucket of potatoes. On Monday, it took the worker 2 h to make the pies and an average of 1.5 min to peel each potato. On Tuesday, the worker finished the work in the same amount of time, but it took 2.5 h to make the pies and an average of 1 min to peel each potato. About how many potatoes are in a bucket?
   - What quantities do you know and how are they related to each other?
   - How can you use the known and unknown quantities to write an equation for this situation?

43. **Error Analysis** Describe and correct the error in finding the solution of the equation $2x = 6x$.

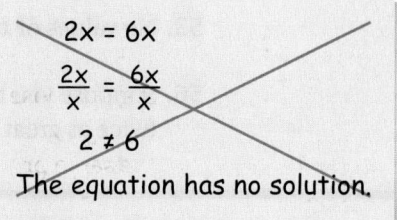

44. **Skiing** A skier is trying to decide whether or not to buy a season ski pass. A daily pass costs $67. A season ski pass costs $350. The skier would have to rent skis with either pass for $25 per day. How many days would the skier have to go skiing in order to make the season pass less expensive than daily passes?

45. **Health Clubs** One health club charges a $50 sign-up fee and $65 per month. Another club charges a $90 sign-up fee and $45 per month. For what number of months is the cost of the clubs equal?

46. **Geometry** The perimeters of the triangles shown are equal. Find the side lengths of each triangle.

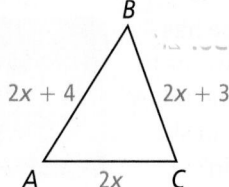
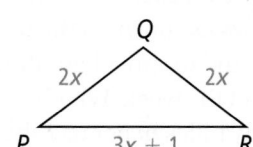

47. **Business** A small juice company spends $1200 per day on business expenses plus $1.10 per bottle of juice they make. They charge $2.50 for each bottle of juice they produce. How many bottles of juice must the company sell in one day in order to equal its daily costs?

48. **Spreadsheet** You set up a spreadsheet to solve $7(x + 1) = 3(x - 1)$.
   a. Does your spreadsheet show the solution of the equation?
   b. Between which two values of x is the solution of the equation? How do you know?
   c. For what spreadsheet values of x is $7(x + 1)$ less than $3(x - 1)$?

	A	B	C
1	x	$7(x + 1)$	$3(x - 1)$
2	−5	−28	−18
3	−3	−14	−12
4	−1	0	−6
5	1	14	0
6	3	28	6

49. Reasoning Determine whether each statement is *always*, *sometimes*, or *never* true.
   a. An equation of the form $ax + 1 = ax$ has no solution.
   b. An equation in one variable has at least one solution.
   c. An equation of the form $\frac{x}{a} = \frac{x}{b}$ has infinitely many solutions.

Challenge   **Open-Ended** Write an equation with a variable on both sides such that you get each solution.

50. $x = 5$ **51.** $x = 0$ **52.** x can be any number.

53. No values of x are solutions.   **54.** x is a negative number.   **55.** x is a fraction.

56. Suppose you have three consecutive integers. The greatest of the three integers is twice as great as the sum of the first two. What are the integers?

Standardized Test Prep

SAT/ACT

57. What is the solution of $-2(3x - 4) = -2x + 2$?
   (A) $-\frac{2}{3}$ (B) $\frac{3}{2}$ (C) 2   (D) 24

58. Two times a number plus three equals one half of the number plus 12. What is the number?
   (F) 3.6   (G) 6   (H) 8   (I) 10

59. Josie's goal is to run 30 mi each week. This week she has already run the distances shown in the table. She wants to have one day of rest and to spread out the remaining miles evenly over the rest of the week. Which equation can she use to find how many miles m per day she must run?

Miles per Day						
M	T	W	T	F	S	S
4	4.5	3.5	▪	▪	▪	▪

   (A) $4 + 4.5 + 3.5 + 3m = 30$ (C) $30 - (4 + 4.5 + 3.5) = m$
   (B) $4 + 4.5 + 3.5 + 4m = 30$ (D) $4 + 4.5 + 3.5 + m = 30$

Mixed Review

Solve each equation.   ◀ **See Lesson 2-3.**

60. $-2a + 5a - 4 = 11$ **61.** $6 = -3(x + 4)$ **62.** $3\left(c + \frac{1}{3}\right) = 4$

63. A carpenter is filling in an open entranceway with a door and two side panels of the same width. The entranceway is 3 m wide. The door will be 1.2 m wide. How wide should the carpenter make the panels on either side of the door so that the two panels and the door will fill the entranceway exactly?   ◀ **See Lesson 2-2.**

Get Ready!   **To prepare for Lesson 2-5, do Exercises 64–66.**

Evaluate each expression for the given values of the variables.   ◀ **See Lesson 1-2.**

64. $n + 2m$; $m = 12, n = -2$ **65.** $3b \div c$; $b = 12, c = 4$ **66.** xy^2; $x = 2.8, y = 2$

2-5 Literal Equations and Formulas

© Common Core State Standards

A-CED.A.4 Rearrange formulas to highlight a quantity of interest, using the same reasoning as in solving equations . . . **Also A-CED.A.1, A-REI.A.1**

MP 1, MP 2, MP 3, MP 4, MP 8

Objective To rewrite and use literal equations and formulas

Getting Ready!

You are ordering pizzas and sandwiches. You have a budget of $80. How many sandwiches can you buy if you buy 4 pizzas? 5 pizzas? Explain your answer.

MENU
Pizza $10
Sandwich $5

What happens to the number of sandwiches as the number of pizzas increases?

 **MATHEMATICAL PRACTICES** In this lesson, you will learn to solve problems using equations in more than one variable. A **literal equation** is an equation that involves two or more variables.

Essential Understanding When you work with literal equations, you can use the methods you have learned in this chapter to isolate any particular variable.

 **Lesson Vocabulary**
• literal equation
• formula

 Problem 1 Rewriting a Literal Equation

The equation $10x + 5y = 80$, where x is the number of pizzas and y is the number of sandwiches, models the problem in the Solve It. How many sandwiches can you buy if you buy 3 pizzas? 6 pizzas?

Think

Why should you rewrite the equation?
If you rewrite the equation, you have to isolate y only once. Then substitute for x. If you substitute for x first, you must isolate y twice (once for each x-value).

Step 1 Solve the equation $10x + 5y = 80$ for y.

$$10x + 5y = 80$$

$$10x + 5y - 10x = 80 - 10x \quad \text{Subtract } 10x \text{ from each side.}$$

$$5y = 80 - 10x \quad \text{Simplify.}$$

$$\frac{5y}{5} = \frac{80 - 10x}{5} \quad \text{Divide each side by 5.}$$

$$y = 16 - 2x \quad \text{Simplify.}$$

Step 2 Use the rewritten equation to find y when $x = 3$ and when $x = 6$.

$y = 16 - 2x$	$y = 16 - 2x$
$y = 16 - 2(3)$ Substitute for x.	$y = 16 - 2(6)$
$y = 10$ Simplify.	$y = 4$

If you buy 3 pizzas, you can buy 10 sandwiches. If you buy 6 pizzas, you can buy 4 sandwiches.

$5n + 4 = 2m - 5n + 5n$

$\dfrac{5+6 = 2m - 5+5}{2}$

$4 = 2m$ $\dfrac{5n+4}{2} = \dfrac{2m}{2} \cdot 2m$

$2.5n + 2 = m$ $2.5(0) + 2 = m$

$2.5(-2) + 2 = m$

  Got It? **1. a.** Solve the equation $4 = 2m - 5n$ for m. What are the values of m when $n = -2, 0,$ and 2? $-3, 2, 7$

$2.5(2) + 2 = m$

b. Reasoning Solve Problem 1 by substituting $x = 3$ and $x = 6$ into the equation $10x + 5y = 80$ and then solving for y in each case. Do you prefer this method or the method shown in Problem 1? Explain. $Y = 16 - 2x$

When you rewrite literal equations, you may have to divide by a variable or variable expression. When you do so in this lesson, assume that the variable or variable expression is not equal to zero because division by zero is not defined.

© **Problem 2** Rewriting a Literal Equation With Only Variables

Think

How can you solve a literal equation for a variable?
When a literal equation contains only variables, treat the variables you are *not* solving for as constants.

What equation do you get when you solve $ax - bx = c$ for x?

$ax - bx = c$

$x(a - b) = c$ Distributive Property

$\dfrac{x(a - b)}{a - b} = \dfrac{c}{a - b}$ Divide each side by $a - b$, where $a - b \neq 0$.

$x = \dfrac{c}{a - b}$ Simplify.

 Got It? **2.** What equation do you get when you solve $-t = r + px$ for x?

$-r - t = r + px$

$-r - t = px$ $\dfrac{-r-t}{p} = x$ $\boxed{\dfrac{-t-r}{p} = x}$

A **formula** is an equation that states a relationship among quantities. Formulas are special types of literal equations. Some common formulas are given below. Notice that some of the formulas use the same variables, but the definitions of the variables are different.

Formula Name	Formula	Definitions of Variables
Perimeter of a rectangle	$P = 2\ell + 2w$	$P =$ perimeter, $\ell =$ length, $w =$ width
Circumference of a circle	$C = 2\pi r$	$C =$ circumference, $r =$ radius
Area of a rectangle	$A = \ell w$	$A =$ area, $\ell =$ length, $w =$ width
Area of a triangle	$A = \frac{1}{2}bh$	$A =$ area, $b =$ base, $h =$ height
Area of a circle	$A = \pi r^2$	$A =$ area, $r =$ radius
Distance traveled	$d = rt$	$d =$ distance, $r =$ rate, $t =$ time
Temperature	$C = \frac{5}{9}(F - 32)$	$C =$ degrees Celsius, $F =$ degrees Fahrenheit

 **Problem 3** **Rewriting a Geometric Formula**

What is the radius of a circle with circumference 64 ft? Round to the nearest tenth. Use 3.14 for π.

Plan

Choose an appropriate formula and solve it for the variable you need to find. Substitute what you know into the rewritten formula. Simplify.

$C = 2\pi r$	Write the appropriate formula.
$\dfrac{C}{2\pi} = \dfrac{2\pi r}{2\pi}$	Divide each side by 2π.
$\dfrac{C}{2\pi} = r$	Simplify.
$\dfrac{64}{2\pi} = r$	Substitute 64 for C.
$10.2 \approx r$	Simplify. Use 3.14 for π.

The radius of the circle is about 10.2 ft.

Got It? **3.** What is the height of a triangle that has an area of 24 in.^{2} and a base with a length of 8 in.? *6 = h*

 $A = \frac{1}{2}bh$

$24 = \frac{1}{2} \cdot 8 \cdot h$ $\dfrac{48 = 8 \cdot h}{8} \quad \dfrac{}{8}$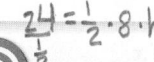

 **Problem 4** **Rewriting a Formula** STEM

Biology The monarch butterfly is the only butterfly that migrates annually north and south. The distance that a particular group of monarch butterflies travels is shown. It takes a typical butterfly about 120 days to travel one way. What is the average rate at which a butterfly travels in miles per day? Round to the nearest mile per day.

Think

How do you know which formula to use?
Read the information given in the problem. This problem gives you a measure of time and a distance. You need to find the rate, so use $d = rt$.

$d = rt$	Write the appropriate formula.
$\dfrac{d}{t} = \dfrac{rt}{t}$	Divide each side by t.
$\dfrac{d}{t} = r$	Simplify.
$\dfrac{1700}{120} = r$	Substitute 1700 for d and 120 for t.
$14 \approx r$	Simplify.

Indiana

1700 miles

Mexico

The butterflies travel at an average rate of about 14 mi per day.

Got It? **4.** Pacific gray whales migrate annually from the waters near Alaska to the waters near Baja California, Mexico, and back. The whales travel a distance of about 5000 mi each way at an average rate of 91 mi per day. About how many days does it take the whales to migrate one way? *about 55*

$d = rt$

$\dfrac{5000 = 91t}{91} \quad \dfrac{}{91}$

$55 = t$

Lesson Check

Do you know HOW?

Solve each equation for the given variable.

1. $-2x + 5y = 12$ for y

   (handwritten) $+2x \quad +2x \quad y = 2.4 + 0.4x$
   $5 \div 5y = 12 + 2x \div 5 \quad y = \frac{12 + 2x}{5}$

2. $a - 2b = -10$ for b $\quad b := \frac{-10 \cdot a}{-2}$

   (handwritten) $-a \quad -a \quad -2b = -10 - a$

3. $mx + 2nx = p$ for x

   (handwritten) $\frac{m}{m} x + 2nx = \frac{p}{m} \quad x = \frac{p}{m + 2n}$

4. $C = \frac{5}{9}(F - 32)$ for F

   (handwritten) $\frac{9}{5}C = F - 32 \quad F = \frac{9}{5}C + 32$

5. **Gardening** Jonah is planting a rectangular garden. The perimeter of the garden is 120 yd, and the width is 20 yd. What is the length of the garden? $\ell = 40$

   (handwritten) $120 = \ell 2 + 20 \cdot 2 \qquad 40 = \ell$
   $120 = \ell 2 + 40 \qquad \frac{80}{-40} = \frac{\ell 2}{2}$

Do you UNDERSTAND?

Vocabulary Classify each equation below as a formula, a literal equation, or both.

6. $c = 2d$ *literal*

7. $y = 2x - 1$ *literal*

8. $A = \frac{1}{2}bh$ *both*

9. $P = 2\ell + 2w$ *both*

10. **Compare and Contrast** How is the process of rewriting literal equations similar to the process of solving equations in one variable? How is it different?

Practice and Problem-Solving Exercises

 **Practice**

Solve each equation for y. Then find the value of y for each value of x.

See Problem 1.

11. $y + 2x = 5$; $x = -1, 0, 3$

12. $2y + 4x = 8$; $x = -2, 1, 3$

13. $3x - 5y = 9$; $x = -1, 0, 1$

14. $4x = 3y - 7$; $x = 4, 5, 6$

15. $5x = -4y + 4$; $x = 1, 2, 3$

16. $2y + 7x = 4$; $x = 5, 10, 15$

17. $x - 4y = -4$; $x = -2, 4, 6$

18. $6x = 7 - 4y$; $x = -2, -1, 0$

Solve each equation for x.

See Problem 2.

19. $mx + nx = p$

20. $ax - x = c$

21. $\frac{rx + sx}{t} = 1$

22. $y = \frac{x - v}{b}$

23. $S = C + xC$

24. $\frac{x}{a} = \frac{y}{b}$

25. $A = Bxt + C$

26. $4(x - b) = x$

27. $\frac{x + 2}{y - 1} = 2$

Solve each problem. Round to the nearest tenth, if necessary. Use 3.14 for π.

See Problem 3.

28. What is the radius of a circle with circumference 22 m?

29. What is the length of a rectangle with width 10 in. and area 45 in.^{2}?

30. A triangle has height 4 ft and area 32 ft^2. What is the length of its base?

31. A rectangle has perimeter 84 cm and length 35 cm. What is its width?

32. **Parks** A public park is in the shape of a triangle. The side of the park that forms the base of the triangle is 200 yd long, and the area of the park is 7500 yd^2. What is the length of the side of the park that forms the height of the triangle?

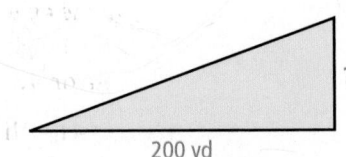
?
200 yd

Solve each problem. Round to the nearest tenth, if necessary.

See Problem 4.

33. **Travel** A vehicle travels on a highway at a rate of 65 mi/h. How long does it take the vehicle to travel 25 mi?

34. **Baseball** You can use the formula $a = \frac{h}{n}$ to find the batting average a of a batter who has h hits in n times at bat. Solve the formula for h. If a batter has a batting average of .290 and has been at bat 300 times, how many hits does the batter have?

STEM 35. **Construction** Bricklayers use the formula $n = 7\ell h$ to estimate the number n of bricks needed to build a wall of length ℓ and height h, where ℓ and h are in feet. Solve the formula for h. Estimate the height of a wall 28 ft long that requires 1568 bricks.

B **Apply**

Solve each equation for the given variable.

36. $2m - nx = x + 4$ for x

37. $\frac{x}{a} - 1 = \frac{y}{b}$ for x

38. $ax + 2xy = 14$ for y

39. $V = \frac{1}{3}\pi r^2 h$ for h

40. $A = \left(\frac{f+g}{2}\right)h$ for g

41. $2(x + a) = 4b$ for a

42. **Think About a Plan** The interior angles of a polygon are the angles formed inside a polygon by two adjacent sides. The sum S of the measures of the interior angles of a polygon with n sides can be found using the formula $S = 180(n - 2)$. The sum of a polygon's interior angle measures is $1260°$. How many sides does the polygon have?
- What information are you given in the problem?
- What variable do you need to solve for in the formula?

STEM 43. **Weather** Polar stratospheric clouds are colorful clouds that form when temperatures fall below $-78°C$. What is this temperature in degrees Fahrenheit?

STEM 44. **Science** The energy E of a moving object is called its *kinetic energy*. It is calculated using the formula $E = \frac{1}{2}mv^2$, where m is the object's mass in kilograms and v is its speed in meters per second. The units of kinetic energy are $\frac{\text{kilograms} \cdot \text{meters}^2}{\text{second}^2}$, abbreviated as $\text{kg} \cdot \text{m}^2/\text{s}^2$.
a. Solve the given formula for m.
b. What is the mass of an object moving at 10 m/s with a kinetic energy of $2500 \text{ kg} \cdot \text{m}^2/\text{s}^2$?

Polar stratospheric clouds

45. **Error Analysis** Describe and correct the error made in solving the literal equation at the right for n.

$$2m = -6n + 3$$
$$2m + 3 = -6n$$
$$\frac{2m + 3}{-6} = n$$

46. **Geometry** The formula for the volume of a cylinder is $V = \pi r^2 h$, where r is the cylinder's radius and h is its height. Solve the equation for h. What is the height of a cylinder with volume 502.4 cm^3 and radius 4 cm? Use 3.14 for π.

47. **Density** The density of an object is calculated using the formula $D = \frac{m}{V}$, where m is the object's mass and V is its volume. Gold has a density of 19.3 g/cm^3. What is the volume of an amount of gold that has a mass of 96.5 g?

48. Open-Ended Write an equation in three variables. Solve the equation for each variable. Show all your steps.

 Challenge

49. Surface Area A rectangular prism with height h and with square bases with side length s is shown.

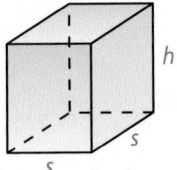

   a. Write a formula for the surface area A of the prism.

   b. Rewrite the formula to find h in terms of A and s. If s is 10 cm and A is 760 cm^2, what is the height of the prism?

   c. Writing Suppose h is equal to s. Write a formula for A in terms of s only.

50. Midpoints Suppose a segment on a number line has endpoints with coordinates a and b. The coordinate of the segment's midpoint m is given by the formula $m = \frac{a + b}{2}$.

   a. Find the midpoint of a segment with endpoints at 9.3 and 2.1.

   b. Rewrite the given formula to find b in terms of a and m.

   c. The midpoint of a segment is at 3.5. One endpoint is at 8.9. Find the other endpoint.

Standardized Test Prep

GRIDDED RESPONSE

SAT/ACT

51. What is the value of the expression $-\frac{3}{4}m + 15$ when $m = 12$?

52. What is the solution of $9p + 6 - 3p = 45$?

53. The formula $F = \frac{n}{4} + 37$ relates the number of chirps n a cricket makes in 1 min to the outside temperature F in degrees Fahrenheit. How many chirps can you expect a cricket to make in 1 min when the outside temperature is 60°F?

Mixed Review

Solve each equation. If the equation is an *identity*, write *identity*. If it has no solution, write *no solution*.

◀ **See Lesson 2-4.**

54. $3x - 3 = x + 7$ **55.** $2b - 10 = -3b + 5$

56. $4 + 12a = -2(6 - 4a)$ **57.** $2(y - 4) = -4y + 10$

58. $4c - 10 = 2(2c - 5)$ **59.** $5 + 4p = 2(2p + 1)$

Evaluate each expression for $b = 3$ and $c = 7$.

◀ **See Lesson 1-2.**

60. bc^2 **61.** $b^2 - c^2$ **62.** $(3b)^2 c$ **63.** $(b + c)^2$

Get Ready! To prepare for Lesson 2-6, do Exercises 64–66.

Simplify each product.

◀ **See p. 804.**

64. $\frac{35}{25} \times \frac{30}{14}$ **65.** $\frac{99}{108} \times \frac{96}{55}$ **66.** $\frac{21}{81} \times \frac{63}{105}$

Do you know HOW?

Solve each equation. Check your answer.

1. $38 = 2a + 54$

2. $t + 18.1 = 23.9$

3. $18.9 = 2.1x$

4. $\frac{1}{2}(b - 3) = \frac{5}{2}$

Solve each equation. Justify your steps.

5. $9 - 3r = 14$

6. $3 = \frac{1}{2}b + 11$

Solve each equation. If the equation is an identity, write *identity*. If it has no solution, write *no solution*.

7. $8(h - 1) = 6h + 4 + 2h$

8. $\frac{1}{7}(14 - 7p) - 2 = -2\left(\frac{1}{2}p + 3\right) + 6$

9. $\frac{c + 3}{5} = 15$

10. $\frac{2}{3}(x - 4) = \frac{1}{3}(2x - 6)$

11. $1.7m = 10.2$

12. $2 + \frac{1}{3}t = 1 + \frac{1}{4}t$

13. **Geometry** The formula for the area of a triangle is $A = \frac{1}{2}bh$. Solve the formula for h. A triangle has a base of 7 cm and an area of 28 cm². What is its height?

14. **Menus** A new pizza shop is going to print new menus. Each menu costs $.50 to produce. The owners have a total budget of $2500 for the new menus. How many menus can the pizza shop print?

15. **Guitars** You paid $600 for a new guitar. Your guitar cost $40 more than twice the cost of your friend's guitar. How much did your friend's guitar cost?

Define a variable and write an equation to model each situation. Then solve.

16. **Concerts** Concert tickets cost $25 each. A college student ordered some tickets online. There was a service charge of $3 per ticket. The total came to $252. How many tickets did the student order?

17. **Gyms** Membership for the Alpine rock-climbing gym costs $25 per month plus a $125 sign-up fee. Membership for Rocco's rock-climbing gym costs $30 per month plus a $50 sign-up fee.

   a. After how many months will the memberships cost the same?

   b. If you only wanted a one-year membership, which gym would you join?

Do you UNDERSTAND?

18. **Vocabulary** Complete: You can use subtraction to undo addition. Subtraction is called the _?_ of addition.

19. **Reasoning** The equation $\frac{5}{x} = \frac{2}{x} + \frac{3}{x}$ is true for all values of x where $x \neq 0$. Is the equation an identity?

20. **Writing** Would you solve the equation $10 = 4(y - 1)$ by using the Distributive Property or by dividing each side by 4? Explain.

21. **Reasoning** In the process of solving an equation, a student noticed that the variable was eliminated. The student concluded that the equation must be an identity. Is the student correct? Explain.

22. **Reasoning** You are solving the equation $0.02x - 0.004 = 0.028$. Your first step is to multiply both sides by 1000 to clear the decimals. Your classmate starts by dividing both sides by 0.02. Is there any disadvantage to your classmate's method? Explain.

2-6 Ratios, Rates, and Conversions

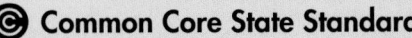
Common Core State Standards

N-Q.A.1 Use units as a way to understand problems and to guide the solution of multi-step problems; choose and interpret units consistently in formulas . . . **Also N-Q.A.2**

MP 2, MP 3, MP 4, MP 5, MP 6

Objectives To find ratios and rates
To convert units and rates

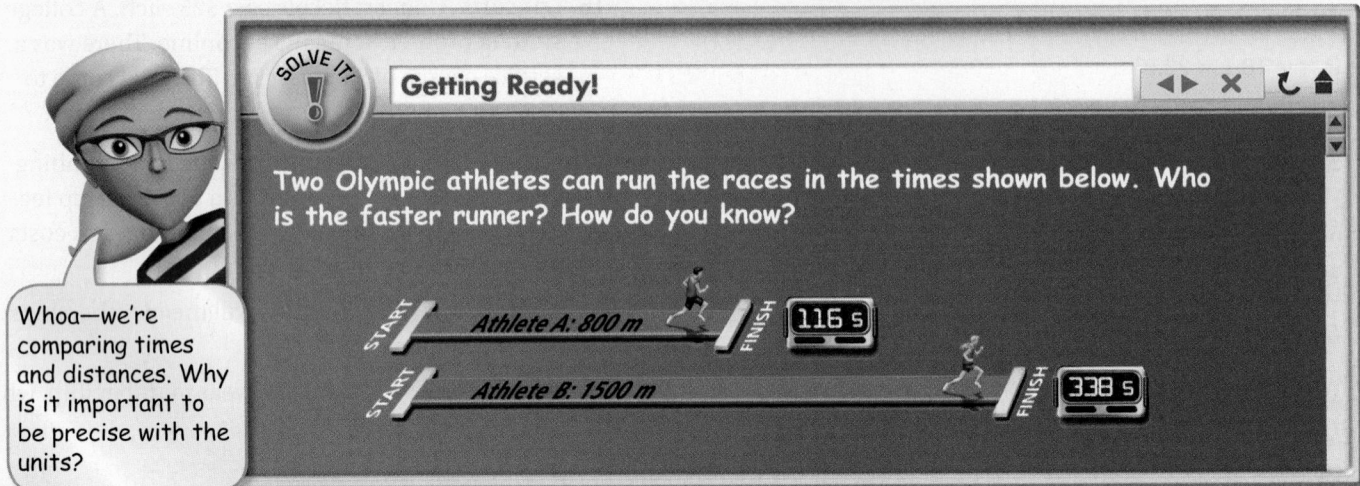

SOLVE IT!

Getting Ready!

Two Olympic athletes can run the races in the times shown below. Who is the faster runner? How do you know?

Whoa—we're comparing times and distances. Why is it important to be precise with the units?

START Athlete A: 800 m FINISH 116 s

START Athlete B: 1500 m FINISH 338 s

MATHEMATICAL PRACTICES

Lesson Vocabulary
- ratio
- rate
- unit rate
- conversion factor
- unit analysis

A **ratio** compares two numbers by division. The ratio of two numbers a and b, where $b \neq 0$, can be written in three ways: $\frac{a}{b}$, $a : b$, and a to b. For every a units of one quantity, you have b units of another quantity.

You can also think of a ratio as a multiplicative relationship. For example, if the ratio of the number of boys to the number of girls in a class is $2 : 1$, then the number of boys is *two times* the number of girls.

A ratio that compares quantities measured in different units is called a **rate.** A rate with a denominator of 1 unit is a **unit rate.** In the Solve It, you can express each athlete's speed as the number of meters traveled per 1 second of time. This is an example of a unit rate.

Essential Understanding You can write ratios and find unit rates to compare quantities. You can also convert units and rates to solve problems.

Problem 1 Comparing Unit Rates

Think

How can estimation help you?
Use estimation to *solve a simpler problem.* You can use the given information to estimate the unit rates. The estimates can help you find the solution.

Shopping You are shopping for T-shirts. Which store offers the best deal?

Store A: $25 for 2 shirts   Store B: $45 for 4 shirts   Store C: $30 for 3 shirts

Write each price as a ratio. Then write the ratio as a unit rate to compare.

Store A	Store B	Store C
$\frac{\$25}{2 \text{ shirts}} = \frac{\$12.50}{1 \text{ shirt}}$	$\frac{\$45}{4 \text{ shirts}} = \frac{\$11.25}{1 \text{ shirt}}$	$\frac{\$30}{3 \text{ shirts}} = \frac{\$10}{1 \text{ shirt}}$

Store C has the best deal because its unit rate is the lowest.

Got It? **1.** If Store B lowers its price to $42 for 4 shirts, does the solution to Problem 1 change? Explain.

To convert from one unit to another, such as feet to inches, you multiply the original unit by a *conversion factor* that produces the desired unit. A **conversion factor** is a ratio of two equivalent measures in different units. A conversion factor is always equal to 1, such as $\frac{1\text{ ft}}{12\text{ in.}}$. See the table on page 814 for some common equivalent units of measure.

Problem 2 **Converting Units**

What is the given amount converted to the given units?

Choose and multiply by the appropriate conversion factor. The appropriate factor will allow you to divide out the common units and simplify.

Plan

How do you choose the conversion factor?
Write a conversion factor that has the desired units in the numerator and the original units in the denominator.

A **330 min; hours**

$$330 \text{ min} \cdot \frac{1 \text{ h}}{60 \text{ min}}$$ ← Choose a conversion factor. →   **B** **15 kg; grams**

$$15 \text{ kg} \cdot \frac{1000 \text{ g}}{1 \text{ kg}}$$

$$= 330 \text{ min} \cdot \frac{1 \text{ h}}{60 \text{ min}}$$ ← Divide out common units. → $$= 15 \text{ kg} \cdot \frac{1000 \text{ g}}{1 \text{ kg}}$$

$$= 5.5 \text{ h}$$ ← Simplify. → $$= 15{,}000 \text{ g}$$

C **5 ft 3 in.; inches**

$$5 \text{ ft } 3 \text{ in.} = 5 \text{ ft} + 3 \text{ in.}$$

$$= 5 \text{ ft} \cdot \frac{12 \text{ in.}}{1 \text{ ft}} + 3 \text{ in.}$$

$$= 60 \text{ in.} + 3 \text{ in.} = 63 \text{ in.}$$

 Got It? **2.** What is 1250 cm converted to meters?

In Problem 2, notice that the units for each quantity are included in the calculations to help determine the units for the answers. This process is called **unit analysis**, or *dimensional analysis*.

Problem 3 **Converting Units Between Systems** **STEM**

Architecture **The CN Tower in Toronto, Canada, is about 1815 ft tall. About how many meters tall is the tower? Use the fact that 1 m ≈ 3.28 ft.**

Multiply by the appropriate conversion factor and divide out common units.

Plan

How can you convert units?
Write the conversion factor so that the original units divide out and leave only the desired units.

$$1815 \text{ ft} \cdot \frac{1 \text{ m}}{3.28 \text{ ft}} = 1815 \text{ ft} \cdot \frac{1 \text{ m}}{3.28 \text{ ft}} \approx 553 \text{ m}$$

The CN Tower is about 553 m tall.

Check   Round 1815 to 1800 and 3.28 to 3. Then divide 1800 by 3. $1800 \div 3 = 600$, and 600 is about 553. So, 553 m is a reasonable answer.

Got It? **3. a.** A building is 1450 ft tall. How many meters tall is the building? Use the fact that 1 m ≈ 3.28 ft.

b. Monetary exchange rates change from day to day. On a particular day, the exchange rate for dollars to euros was about 1 dollar = 0.63 euro. About how many euros could you get for $325 on that day?

You can also convert rates. For example, you can convert a speed in miles per hour to feet per second. Because rates compare measures in two different units, you must multiply by two conversion factors to change both of the units.

 Problem 4 **Converting Rates**

A student ran the 50-yd dash in 5.8 s. At what speed did the student run in miles per hour? Round your answer to the nearest tenth.

Know

The running speed in yards per second

Need

The running speed in miles per hour

Plan

Write the speed as a ratio. Choose conversion factors so that the original units (yards and seconds) divide out, leaving you with the units you need (miles and hours).

$$\frac{50 \text{ yd}}{5.8 \text{ s}} \cdot \frac{1 \text{ mi}}{1760 \text{ yd}} \cdot \frac{3600 \text{ s}}{1 \text{ h}} \quad \text{Use appropriate conversion factors.}$$

> This conversion factor cancels yards and leaves miles.

> This conversion factor cancels seconds and leaves hours.

$$= \frac{50 \text{ y\cancel{d}}}{5.8 \text{ \cancel{s}}} \cdot \frac{1 \text{ mi}}{1760 \text{ y\cancel{d}}} \cdot \frac{3600 \text{ \cancel{s}}}{1 \text{ h}} \quad \text{Divide common units.}$$

$$= \frac{180,000 \text{ mi}}{10,208 \text{ h}} \approx 17.6 \text{ mi/h} \quad \text{Simplify.}$$

The student ran at a speed of about 17.6 mi/h.

  Got It? **4. a.** An athlete ran a sprint of 100 ft in 3.1 s. At what speed was the athlete running in miles per hour? Round to the nearest mile per hour.

b. Reasoning In Problem 4, one student multiplied by the conversion factors $\frac{1 \text{ mi}}{1760 \text{ yd}}$, $\frac{60 \text{ s}}{1 \text{ min}}$, and $\frac{60 \text{ min}}{1 \text{ h}}$ to find the speed. Can this method work? Why or why not?

Lesson Check

Do you know HOW?

1. Which is the better buy, 6 bagels for $3.29 or 8 bagels for $4.15?

2. What is 7 lb 4 oz converted to ounces?

3. Which is longer, 12 m or 13 yd?

4. A car is traveling at 55 mi/h. What is the car's speed in feet per second?

Do you UNDERSTAND?

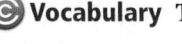 **Vocabulary** Tell whether each rate is a unit rate.

5. 20 mi every 3 h
6. 2 dollars per day

7. **Reasoning** Does multiplying by a conversion factor change the amount of what is being measured? How do you know?

8. **Reasoning** If you convert pounds to ounces, will the number of ounces be greater or less than the number of pounds? Explain.

Practice and Problem-Solving Exercises

 **Practice**

9. **Running** Trisha ran 10 km in 2.5 h. Jason ran 7.5 km in 2 h. Olga ran 9.5 km in 2.25 h. Who had the fastest average speed?

◄ **See Problem 1.**

10. **Population** Bellingham, Washington, had an area of 25.4 mi² and a population of 74,547 during one year. Bakersfield, California, had an area of 113.1 mi² and a population of 295,536 during the same year. Which city had a greater number of people per square mile?

Convert the given amount to the given unit.

◄ **See Problems 2 and 3.**

11. 63 yd; feet
12. 168 h; days
13. 2.5 lb; ounces

14. 200 cm; meters
15. 4 min; seconds
16. 1500 mL; liters

17. 9 yd; meters
18. 5 kg; pounds
19. 79 dollars; cents

20. 3 qt; liters
21. 89 cm; inches
22. 2 ft; centimeters

23. **Maintenance** The janitor at a school discovered a slow leak in a pipe. The janitor found that it was leaking at a rate of 4 fl oz per minute. How fast was the pipe leaking in gallons per hour?

◄ **See Problem 4.**

24. **Shopping** Mr. Swanson bought a package of 10 disposable razors for $6.30. He found that each razor lasted for 1 week. What was the cost per day?

Apply

Copy and complete each statement.

25. 7 ft 3 in. = ■ in.
26. 2.2 kg = ■ lb

27. 2.5 h = ■ min
28. 2 qt/min = ■ gal/s

29. 75 cents/h = ■ dollars/day
30. 60 ft/s = ■ km/h

Choose a Method Choose paper and pencil, mental math, or a calculator to tell which measurement is greater.

31. 640 ft; 0.5 mi **32.** 63 in.; 125 cm **33.** 75 g; 5 oz

34. Think About a Plan A college student is considering a subscription to a social-networking Internet site that advertises its cost as "only 87 cents per day." What is the cost of membership in dollars per year?
- How many conversion factors will you need to use to solve the problem?
- How do you choose the appropriate conversion factors?

35. Recipes Recipe A makes 5 dinner rolls using 1 c of flour. Recipe B makes 24 rolls using $7\frac{1}{2}$ c of flour. Recipe C makes 45 rolls using 10 c of flour. Which recipe requires the most flour per roll?

36. Error Analysis Find the mistake in the conversion below. Explain the mistake and convert the units correctly.

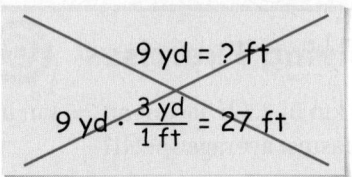

$$9 \text{ yd} = ? \text{ ft}$$
$$9 \text{ yd} \cdot \frac{3 \text{ yd}}{1 \text{ ft}} = 27 \text{ ft}$$

37. Writing Suppose you want to convert kilometers to miles. Which unit should be in the numerator of the conversion factor? Which unit should be in the denominator? Explain how you know.

38. Reasoning Without performing the conversion, determine whether the number of new units will be greater or less than the number of original units.
- **a.** 3 min 20 s converted to seconds
- **b.** 23 cm converted to inches
- **c.** kilometers per hour converted to miles per hour

39. Exchange Rates The table below shows some exchange rates on a particular day. If a sweater sells for $39.95 in U.S. dollars, what should its price be in rupees and pounds?

U.S. DOLLARS	1.00
INDIAN RUPEES	39.57
ALGERIAN DINARS	64.15
BRITISH POUNDS	.50

40. Estimation Five mi is approximately equal to 8 km. Use mental math to estimate the distance in kilometers to a town that is 30 mi away.

41. Reasoning A carpenter is building an entertainment center. She is calculating the size of the space to leave for the television. She wants to leave about a foot of space on either side of the television. Would measuring the size of the television exactly or estimating the size to the nearest inch be more appropriate? Explain.

42. Reasoning A traveler changed $300 to euros for a trip to Germany, but the trip was canceled. Three months later, the traveler changed the euros back to dollars. Would you expect that the traveler got exactly $300 back? Explain.

 **Challenge**

43. Measurement Dietrich draws a line on the blackboard whose length is given by the expression 1 mm + 1 cm + 1 in. + 1 ft + 1 yd + 1 m. What is the length of the line in millimeters?

44. Square Measurements There are 2.54 cm in 1 in.
   a. How many square centimeters are there in 1 in.^{2}? Give your answer to the nearest hundredth of a square centimeter.
   b. How many square inches are there in 129 cm^2?

 ## Apply What You've Learned

Look back at the diagram of the monorail route on page 79. In the Apply What You've Learned in Lesson 2-3, you found the average speed of the monorail between the parking garage and Terminal A and the average speed of the monorail between Terminal A and Terminal B. Select all of the following that are true. Explain your reasoning.

A. To convert the monorail's average speed from feet per second to miles per hour, multiply the speed in feet per second by $\frac{5280 \text{ ft}}{1 \text{ mi}} \cdot \frac{1 \text{ h}}{3600 \text{ s}}$.

B. Between the parking garage and Terminal A, the monorail's average speed is greater than 25 mi/h.

C. Between Terminal A and Terminal B, the monorail's average speed is greater than 25 mi/h.

D. Between Terminal A and Terminal B, the monorail's average speed is 8.1 mi/h greater than its average speed between the parking garage and Terminal A.

E. If the monorail moved at its average speed between Terminal A and Terminal B for 15 minutes, it would travel about 7.2 miles.

F. If the monorail moved at its average speed between Terminal A and Terminal B, it would take more than an hour to travel 30 miles.

Concept Byte

Use With Lesson 2-6

Unit Analysis

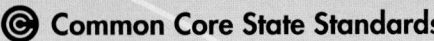 **Common Core State Standards**

N-Q.A.1 Use units as a way to understand problems and to guide the solution of multi-step problems; choose and interpret units consistently in formulas.

MP 6

In Lesson 2-6, you learned that you can use unit analysis when converting units. You can also use unit analysis to help guide you to the solution of a problem.

Activity 1

The speed of light is about 3.0×10^{10} cm/s. If a rocket car of the future can travel at the speed of light, what is this rate in miles per hour?

Step 1 **Make sense of the given information.**

     1. What units are given in the problem statement?

     2. What units of measure should you have in your answer?

Step 2 **Formulate a plan to solve the problem.**

     3. What units need to be converted to solve the problem?

     4. How do you know which conversion factors to use to solve the problem?

     5. Can you use different conversion factors to solve the problem? Explain.

Step 3 **Solve the problem.**

     6. Use unit analysis to write an expression by using the conversion factors you chose in Step 2.

     7. Simplify the expression.

Step 4 **Check your solution.**

     8. Are the units of your solution what you expected? Explain.

     9. Does your answer make sense? Explain.

You can also use unit analysis to determine the reasonableness of a solution or a claim.

Activity 2

Suppose you are a gold miner in California in 1849. You have your tools in one hand. Can you use your free hand to carry a 4-liter bucket full of gold dust? The density of gold is 19.3 g/cm^3. Use unit analysis to determine whether the bucket is too heavy to carry. (*Hint:* 1 lb $\approx$ 454 g and 1000 cm^3 = 1 L.)

Step 1 **Make sense of the given information.**

     10. What units are given in the problem statement?

     11. Describe what you need to find in order to determine whether the bucket is too heavy to carry.

12. Will the information you need to find have units of measure? If so, what do you think those units will be?

Step 2 **Formulate a plan to solve the problem.**

13. What units need to be converted to solve the problem?

14. How do you know which conversion factors to use to solve the problem?

Step 3 **Solve the problem.**

15. Use unit analysis to find what you described in Step 1.

16. Is the claim reasonable? Explain.

Step 4 **Check your solution.**

17. Are the units of your solution what you expected? Explain.

18. Does your answer make sense? Explain.

Exercises

19. The units mi/h and cm/s are units of distance/time. What do these units measure?

20. How can you use unit analysis to help you solve a problem?

Use unit analysis to help you solve each problem.

21. A popular racetrack is 2.5 miles long. A race is completed in 150 laps. One year, the winner's average speed was 161 miles per hour. During cautionary lap runs, the speed was only about 80 miles per hour. If the race had 30 cautionary laps, about how long did it take the winner to complete the race?

22. Error Analysis Your gas tank holds 13.5 gallons of gas. Your fuel gauge shows that your tank is one quarter full. Your car gets an average of 25 miles per gallon. The GPS shows that you are 85 miles from your destination. Your brother says you will make it. Is he correct? Use unit analysis to justify your response.

STEM 23. Chemistry A metal bar in the shape of a rectangular prism with dimensions 6 cm $\times$ 8 cm $\times$ 2 cm has a mass of 53 g. The density of the metal is expressed in units of g/cm^3. Use what you have learned about unit analysis to find the density of the metal.

24. According to the directions, a 12-ounce can of lemonade concentrate makes 64 ounces of lemonade. If each serving is 8 ounces, how many 12-ounce cans of concentrate are needed to make 120 servings?

2-7 Solving Proportions

© **Common Core State Standards**

A-REI.B.3 Solve linear equations and inequalities in one variable, including equations with coefficients represented by letters. **Also N-Q.A.1, A-CED.A.1**

MP 1, MP 3, MP 4, MP 8

Objective To solve and apply proportions

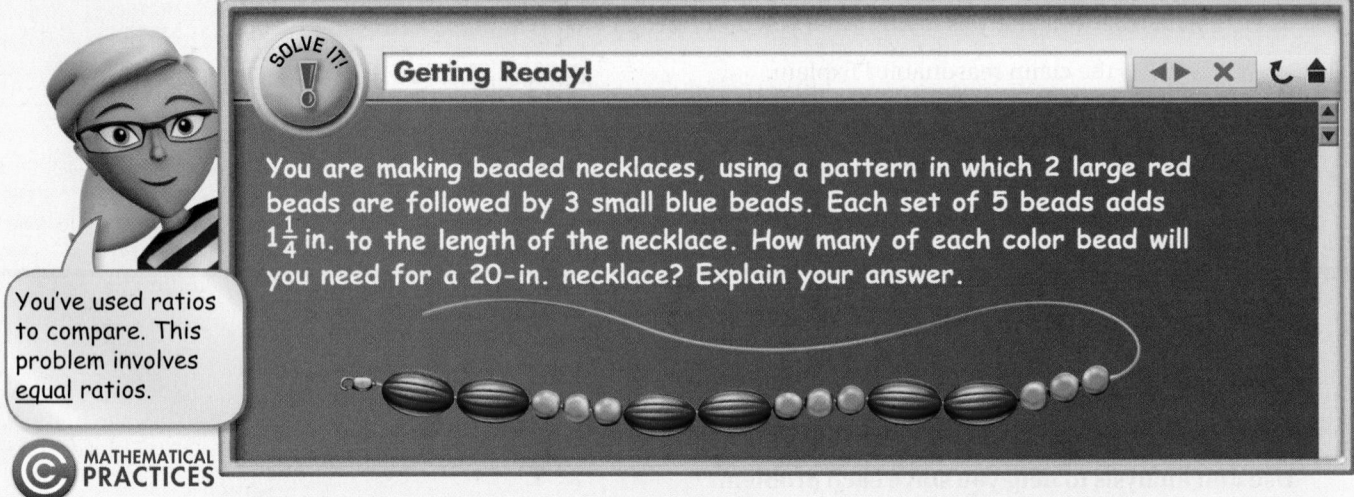

SOLVE IT!

Getting Ready!

◄► X ⟲ ▲

You are making beaded necklaces, using a pattern in which 2 large red beads are followed by 3 small blue beads. Each set of 5 beads adds $1\frac{1}{4}$ in. to the length of the necklace. How many of each color bead will you need for a 20-in. necklace? Explain your answer.

You've used ratios to compare. This problem involves <u>equal</u> ratios.

© MATHEMATICAL PRACTICES

In the Solve It, the number of red beads and the number of blue beads are quantities that have a proportional relationship. This means that the ratio of the quantities is constant even though the quantities themselves can change. For example, as you are making the necklace you will have 2 red beads and 3 blue beads, then 4 red beads and 6 blue beads, then 6 red beads and 9 blue beads, and so on. At each stage, the ratio of red beads to blue beads remains constant, 2 : 3.

Lesson Vocabulary

• proportion
• cross products
• Cross Products Property

A proportional relationship can produce an infinite number of equivalent ratios. Any two of these can be used to write a proportion. A **proportion** is an equation that states that two ratios are equal. For example, $\frac{a}{b} = \frac{c}{d}$, where $b \neq 0$ and $d \neq 0$, is a proportion. You read this as "*a* is to *b* as *c* is to *d*."

Essential Understanding If two ratios are equal and a quantity in one of the ratios is unknown, you can write and solve a proportion to find the unknown quantity.

Think

How is this problem related to problems you've solved before? Solving this proportion is similar to solving a one-step equation using multiplication. You can simply multiply by 12 to isolate *m*.

Problem 1 Solving a Proportion Using the Multiplication Property

What is the solution of the proportion $\frac{7}{8} = \frac{m}{12}$?

$$\frac{7}{8} = \frac{m}{12}$$

$$12 \cdot \frac{7}{8} = 12 \cdot \frac{m}{12}$$ Multiply each side by 12.

$$\frac{84}{8} = m$$ Simplify.

$$10.5 = m$$ Divide.

Got It? **1.** What is the solution of the proportion $\frac{x}{7} = \frac{4}{5}$?

In the proportion $\frac{a}{b} = \frac{c}{d}$, the products ad and bc are called **cross products.** You can use the following property of cross products to solve proportions.

---

take note

Property   Cross Products Property of a Proportion

Words The cross products of a proportion are equal.

Algebra If $\frac{a}{b} = \frac{c}{d}$, where $b \neq 0$ and $d \neq 0$, then $ad = bc$.

Example $\frac{3}{4} = \frac{9}{12}$, so $3(12) = 4(9)$, or $36 = 36$.

Here's Why It Works You can use the Multiplication Property of Equality to prove the Cross Products Property.

$$\frac{a}{b} = \frac{c}{d} \qquad \text{Assume this equation is true.}$$

$$bd \cdot \frac{a}{b} = bd \cdot \frac{c}{d} \qquad \text{Multiplication Property of Equality}$$

$$b\!\!/d \cdot \frac{a}{b\!\!/} = b\!\!/d\!\!/ \cdot \frac{c}{d\!\!/} \qquad \text{Divide the common factors.}$$

$$da = bc \qquad \text{Simplify.}$$

$$ad = bc \qquad \text{Commutative Property of Multiplication}$$

For this proportion, a and d are called the *extremes* of the proportion and b and c are called the *means*. Notice that in the Cross Products Property the product of the means equals the product of the extremes.

© **Problem 2** **Solving a Proportion Using the Cross Products Property**

Think

Which property should you use?
The Cross Products Property can be easier to use when the variable is in the denominator. If you use the Multiplication Property, you must multiply each side by 3x.

What is the solution of the proportion $\frac{4}{3} = \frac{8}{x}$?

$$\frac{4}{3} = \frac{8}{x}$$

$$4x = 3(8) \qquad \text{Cross Products Property}$$

$$4x = 24 \qquad \text{Multiply.}$$

$$x = 6 \qquad \text{Divide each side by 4 and simplify.}$$

Got It? **2.** **a.** What is the solution of the proportion $\frac{y}{3} = \frac{3}{5}$?

© **b. Reasoning** Would you rather use the Cross Products Property or the Multiplication Property of Equality to solve $\frac{3}{5} = \frac{13}{b}$? Explain.

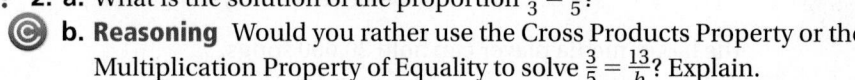

Think

How is this proportion different from others you've seen?
This proportion looks more complex, but the Cross Products Property is true for *any* proportion. Treat each numerator as a single variable when you cross-multiply.

What is the solution of the proportion $\frac{b-8}{5} = \frac{b+3}{4}$?

$$\frac{b-8}{5} = \frac{b+3}{4}$$

$4(b-8) = 5(b+3)$	Cross Products Property
$4b - 32 = 5b + 15$	Distributive Property
$4b - 32 - 4b = 5b + 15 - 4b$	Subtract $4b$ from each side.
$-32 = b + 15$	Simplify.
$-47 = b$	Subtract 15 from each side and simplify.

 Got It? **3.** What is the solution of the proportion $\frac{n}{5} = \frac{2n+4}{6}$?

When you model a real-world situation with a proportion, you must write the proportion carefully. You can write the proportion so that the numerators have the same units and the denominators have the same units.

Correct: $\frac{100 \text{ mi}}{2 \text{ h}} = \frac{x \text{ mi}}{5 \text{ h}}$ **Incorrect:** $\frac{100 \text{ mi}}{2 \text{ h}} = \frac{5 \text{ h}}{x \text{ mi}}$

 Problem 4 Using a Proportion to Solve a Problem

Music A portable media player has 2 gigabytes of storage and can hold about 500 songs. A similar but larger media player has 80 gigabytes of storage. About how many songs can the larger media player hold?

Know	Need	Plan
• Smaller media player has 2 gigabytes and can hold 500 songs • Larger media player has 80 gigabytes	The number of songs the larger player can hold	Write a proportion to model the situation. You can set up the proportion so that the numerators have the same units and the denominators have the same units. Then solve the proportion.

Think

Is there only one way to write a proportion?
No. You can write other proportions to solve the problem. For example,
$\frac{2 \text{ gigabytes}}{80 \text{ gigabytes}} = \frac{500 \text{ songs}}{s \text{ songs}}$
also works.

$\dfrac{2 \text{ gigabytes}}{500 \text{ songs}} = \dfrac{80 \text{ gigabytes}}{s \text{ songs}}$	Write a proportion.
$2s = 500(80)$	Cross Products Property
$2s = 40{,}000$	Multiply.
$s = 20{,}000$	Divide each side by 2 and simplify.

The larger media player can hold 20,000 songs.

 Got It? **4.** An 8-oz can of orange juice contains about 97 mg of vitamin C. About how many milligrams of vitamin C are there in a 12-oz can of orange juice?

Lesson Check

Do you know HOW?

Solve each proportion.

1. $\frac{b}{6} = \frac{4}{5}$

2. $\frac{5}{9} = \frac{15}{x}$

3. $\frac{w+3}{4} = \frac{w}{2}$

4. $\frac{3}{x+1} = \frac{1}{2}$

5. **Music** A band went to a recording studio and recorded 4 songs in 3 h. How long would it take the band to record 9 songs if they record at the same rate?

Do you UNDERSTAND? MATHEMATICAL PRACTICES

 Vocabulary Use the proportion $\frac{m}{n} = \frac{p}{q}$. Identify the following.

6. the extremes

7. the means

8. the cross products

 9. **Reasoning** When solving $\frac{x}{5} = \frac{3}{4}$, Lisa's first step was to write $4x = 5(3)$. Jen's first step was to write $20\left(\frac{x}{5}\right) = 20\left(\frac{3}{4}\right)$. Will both methods work? Explain.

Practice and Problem-Solving Exercises

 **Practice** Solve each proportion using the Multiplication Property of Equality.

 See Problem 1.

10. $\frac{q}{8} = \frac{4}{5}$

11. $\frac{-3}{4} = \frac{x}{26}$

12. $\frac{3}{4} = \frac{x}{5}$

13. $\frac{m}{7} = \frac{3}{5}$

14. $\frac{3}{16} = \frac{x}{12}$

15. $\frac{9}{2} = \frac{k}{25}$

16. $\frac{x}{120} = \frac{1}{24}$

17. $\frac{2}{15} = \frac{h}{125}$

Solve each proportion using the Cross Products Property.

 See Problem 2.

18. $\frac{3}{v} = \frac{8}{13}$

19. $\frac{15}{a} = \frac{3}{2}$

20. $\frac{3}{8} = \frac{30}{m}$

21. $\frac{2}{7} = \frac{4}{d}$

22. $\frac{-9}{b} = \frac{5}{6}$

23. $\frac{8}{p} = \frac{3}{10}$

24. $\frac{-3}{4} = \frac{m}{22}$

25. $\frac{2}{-5} = \frac{6}{t}$

Solve each proportion using any method.

See Problem 3.

26. $\frac{a-2}{9} = \frac{2}{3}$

27. $\frac{b+4}{5} = \frac{7}{4}$

28. $\frac{3}{7} = \frac{c+4}{35}$

29. $\frac{2c}{11} = \frac{c-3}{4}$

30. $\frac{7}{k-2} = \frac{5}{8}$

31. $\frac{3}{3b+4} = \frac{2}{b-4}$

32. $\frac{q+2}{5} = \frac{2q-11}{7}$

33. $\frac{c+1}{c-2} = \frac{4}{7}$

34. **Gardening** A gardener is transplanting flowers into a flowerbed. She has been working for an hour and has transplanted 14 flowers. She has 35 more flowers to transplant. If she works at the same rate, how many more hours will it take her?

See Problem 4.

35. **Florists** A florist is making centerpieces. He uses 2 dozen roses for every 5 centerpieces. How many dozens of roses will he need to make 20 centerpieces?

36. **Picnics** If 5 lb of pasta salad serves 14 people, how much pasta salad should you bring to a picnic with 49 people?

37. Statistics Approximately 3 people out of every 30 are left-handed. About how many left-handed people would you expect in a group of 140 people?

ⓒ **38. Think About a Plan** Maya runs 100 m in 13.4 s. Amy can run 100 m in 14.1 s. If Amy were to finish a 100-m race at the same time as Maya, how much of a head start, in meters, would Amy need?
   • What information do you know? What information is unknown?
   • What proportion can you write that will help you solve the problem?

39. Electricity The electric bill for Ferguson's Furniture is shown at the right. The cost of electricity per kilowatt-hour and the total charges for one month are given. How many kilowatt-hours of electricity did Ferguson's Furniture use in that month?

⚡ *Centerville Electric*	
Account Name: Ferguson's Furniture	
Account Number: 34-14567-89	
Cost per kilowatt-hour	$.07
Total charges	$143.32
Previous balance	$.00
Total Amount Due	$143.32

40. Video Downloads A particular computer takes 15 min to download a 45-min TV show. How long will it take the computer to download a 2-h movie?

41. Schedules You want to meet your friend at a park 4 mi away from your house. You are going to bike to the park at an average rate of 10 mi/h. Your friend lives 1.2 mi away from the park and walks at an average rate of 3 mi/h. How many minutes ahead of you should your friend start out so that you meet at the park at the same time?

Solve each proportion. Tell whether you used the Multiplication Property of Equality or the Cross Products Property for your first step. Explain your choice.

42. $\dfrac{p}{4} = \dfrac{7}{8}$ **43.** $\dfrac{m}{4.5} = \dfrac{2}{5}$ **44.** $\dfrac{3}{10} = \dfrac{b}{7}$

45. $\dfrac{r}{2.1} = \dfrac{3.6}{2.8}$ **46.** $\dfrac{9}{14} = \dfrac{3}{n}$ **47.** $\dfrac{1.5}{y} = \dfrac{2.5}{7}$

48. $\dfrac{b+13}{2} = \dfrac{-5b}{3}$ **49.** $\dfrac{3b}{b-4} = \dfrac{3}{7}$ **50.** $\dfrac{x+2}{2x-6} = \dfrac{3}{8}$

ⓒ **51. Error Analysis** Describe and correct the error in solving the proportion at the right.

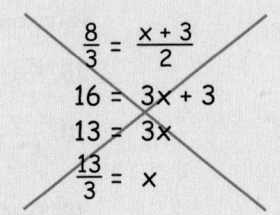

52. Bakery A bakery sells packages of 10 bagels for $3.69. If the bakery starts selling the bagels in packages of 12, how much would you expect a package of 12 to cost?

   Ⓐ $3.08 Ⓒ $4.43
   Ⓑ $4.32 Ⓓ $4.69

ⓒ **53. Open-Ended** Write a proportion that contains a variable. Name the extremes, the means, and the cross products. Solve the proportion. Tell whether you used the Multiplication Property of Equality or the Cross Products Property to solve the proportion. Explain your choice.

STEM **54. Biology** Many trees have concentric rings that can be counted to determine the tree's age. Each ring represents one year's growth. A maple tree with a diameter of 12 in. has 32 rings. If the tree continues to grow at about the same rate, how many rings will the tree have when its diameter is 20 in.?

Solve each proportion.

55. $\dfrac{4y-3}{y^2+1} = \dfrac{4}{y}$

56. $\dfrac{w^2+3}{2w+2} = \dfrac{w}{2}$

57. $\dfrac{5x}{x^3+5} = \dfrac{5}{x^2-7}$

58. Parade Floats A group of high school students is making a parade float by stuffing pieces of tissue paper into a wire frame. They use 150 tissues to fill an area 3 ft long and 2 ft wide. The total area they want to fill is 8 ft long and 7 ft wide. What is the total number of tissues they will need?

59. Insects It takes an insect 15 s to crawl 1 ft. How many hours would it take the insect to crawl 1 mi if the insect crawls at the same rate?

Standardized Test Prep

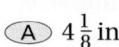

60. A high school soccer team is making trail mix to sell at a fundraiser. The recipe calls for 3 lb of raisins and 2 lb of peanuts. If the team purchases 54 lb of peanuts, how many pounds of raisins will they need?

   Ⓐ 27   Ⓑ 36   Ⓒ 81   Ⓓ 162

61. One day during flu season, $\frac{1}{3}$ of the students in a class were out sick, and only 24 students were left. How many students are in the class?

   Ⓕ 16   Ⓖ 30   Ⓗ 36   Ⓘ 72

62. An art gallery owner is framing a rectangular painting, as shown. The owner wants the width of the framed painting to be $38\frac{1}{2}$ in. How wide should each of the vertical sections of the frame be?

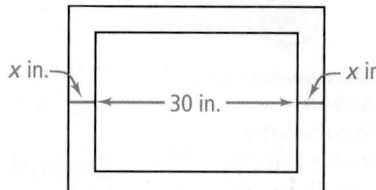

   Ⓐ $4\frac{1}{8}$ in.   Ⓒ $4\frac{1}{2}$ in.

   Ⓑ $4\frac{1}{4}$ in.   Ⓓ $8\frac{1}{2}$ in.

Mixed Review

Copy and complete each statement.   🔴 **See Lesson 2-6.**

63. 6 qt = ■ gal   **64.** 84 in. = ■ ft   **65.** $2\frac{1}{2}$ yd = ■ in.   **66.** 3 min 10 s = ■ s

Solve each equation. If the equation is an identity, write *identity*. If it has no solution, write *no solution*.   🔴 **See Lesson 2-4.**

67. $3x - (x-4) = 2x$ **68.** $4 + 6c = 6 - 4c$ **69.** $5a - 2 = 0.5(10a - 4)$

Get Ready!   **To prepare for Lesson 2-8, do Exercises 70–73.**

Solve each proportion.   🔴 **See Lesson 2-7.**

70. $\dfrac{x}{12} = \dfrac{7}{30}$ **71.** $\dfrac{y}{12} = \dfrac{8}{45}$ **72.** $\dfrac{w}{15} = \dfrac{12}{27}$ **73.** $\dfrac{n}{9} = \dfrac{n+1}{24}$

2-8 Proportions and Similar Figures

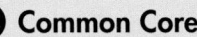
Common Core State Standards

A-CED.A.1 Create equations . . . in one variable and use them to solve problems. *Include equations arising from linear . . . functions.* **Also A-REI.B.3**

MP 1, MP 2, MP 3, MP 4, MP 6

Objectives To find missing lengths in similar figures
To use similar figures when measuring indirectly

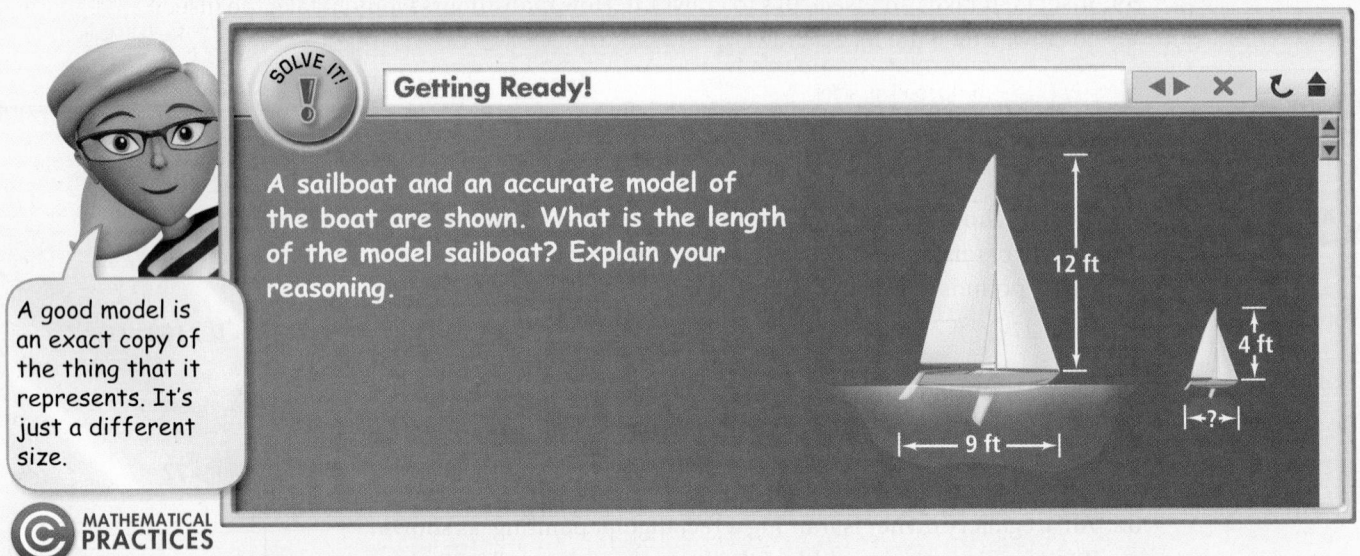

A good model is an exact copy of the thing that it represents. It's just a different size.

SOLVE IT!

Getting Ready!

A sailboat and an accurate model of the boat are shown. What is the length of the model sailboat? Explain your reasoning.

12 ft

9 ft

4 ft

?

MATHEMATICAL PRACTICES

Lesson Vocabulary
• similar figures
• scale drawing
• scale
• scale model

In the Solve It, the sailboat and its model have the same shape but they are different sizes. **Similar figures** have the same shape but not necessarily the same size.

Essential Understanding You can use proportions to find missing side lengths in similar figures. Such figures can help you measure real-world distances indirectly.

The symbol ~ means "is similar to." In the diagram, $\triangle ABC \sim \triangle FGH$.

[Diagram: Triangle ABC with sides AB = 8, AC = 10, BC = 12. Triangle FGH with sides FG = 12, FH = 15, GH = 18.]

In similar figures, the measures of corresponding angles are equal, and corresponding side lengths are in proportion. The order of the letters when you name similar figures is important because it tells which parts of the figures are corresponding parts. So, because $\triangle ABC \sim \triangle FGH$, the following is true.

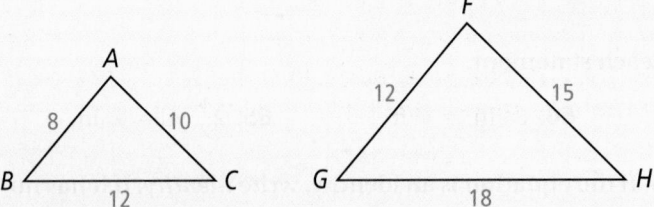

$$\angle A \cong \angle F \quad \angle B \cong \angle G \quad \angle C \cong \angle H \quad \text{and} \quad \frac{AB}{FG} = \frac{AC}{FH} = \frac{BC}{GH}$$

The symbol $\cong$ means "is congruent to." Congruent angles have the same measure.

The ratios are equal.

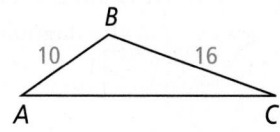

Problem 1 Finding the Length of a Side

Multiple Choice In the diagram, $\triangle ABC \sim \triangle DEF$. What is DE?

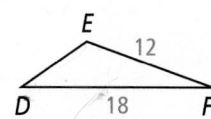

(A) 7.5   (C) 21.3

(B) 9.5   (D) 24

Know
- The length of $\overline{AB}$, which corresponds to $\overline{DE}$
- The lengths of two other corresponding sides, $\overline{BC}$ and $\overline{EF}$
- The triangles are similar.

Need

The length of $\overline{DE}$

Plan

Write a proportion involving two pairs of corresponding sides: $\overline{AB}$ and $\overline{DE}$, and $\overline{BC}$ and $\overline{EF}$. The length of $\overline{DE}$ is the only unknown, so you can solve for it.

$\dfrac{BC}{EF} = \dfrac{AB}{DE}$	Write a proportion.
$\dfrac{16}{12} = \dfrac{10}{DE}$	Substitute lengths.
$16(DE) = 12(10)$	Cross Products Property
$16DE = 120$	Multiply.
$DE = 7.5$	Divide each side by 16 and simplify.

DE is 7.5. The correct answer is A.

 Got It? **1.** Use the figures in Problem 1. What is AC?

You can also use proportions to solve indirect measurement problems like finding a distance using a map. You can use similar figures and proportions to find lengths that you cannot measure directly.

Problem 2 Applying Similarity

Indirect Measurement The sun's rays strike the building and the girl at the same angle, forming the two similar triangles shown. How tall is the building?

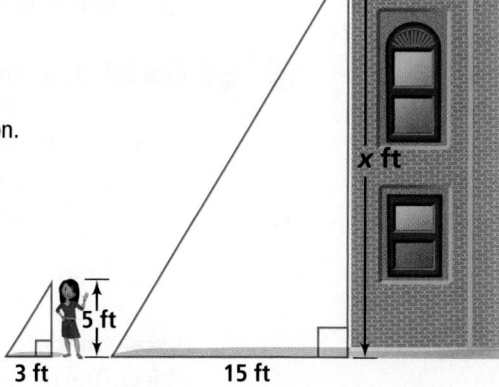

$\dfrac{\text{girl's shadow}}{\text{building's shadow}} = \dfrac{\text{girl's height}}{\text{building's height}}$	Write a proportion.
$\dfrac{3}{15} = \dfrac{5}{x}$	Substitute.
$3x = 15(5)$	Cross Products Property
$3x = 75$	Multiply.
$x = 25$	Divide each side by 3.

The building is 25 ft tall.

Got It? **2.** A man who is 6 ft tall is standing next to a flagpole. The shadow of the man is 3.5 ft and the shadow of the flagpole is 17.5 ft. What is the height of the flagpole?

A **scale drawing** is a drawing that is similar to an actual object or place. Floor plans, blueprints, and maps are all examples of scale drawings. In a scale drawing, the ratio of any length on the drawing to the actual length is always the same. This ratio is called the **scale** of the drawing.

Problem 3 **Interpreting Scale Drawings**

Maps **What is the actual distance from Jacksonville to Orlando? Use the ruler to measure the distance from Jacksonville to Orlando on the map below.**

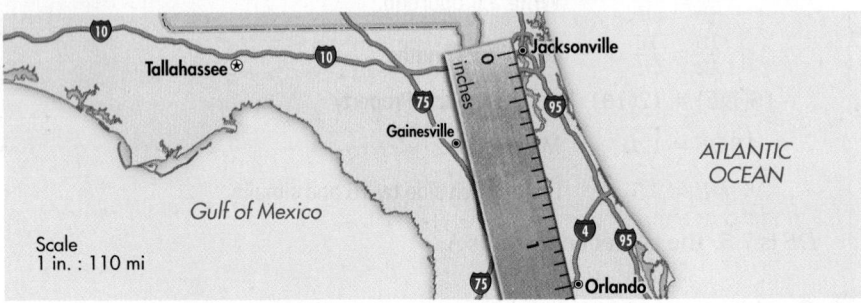

Scale
1 in. : 110 mi

Think

What does the scale of the map tell you?
The scale tells you that each inch on the map represents 110 mi of actual distance.

Relate $\text{map scale} = \dfrac{\text{map distance}}{\text{actual distance}}$

Define Let x = the total distance from Jacksonville to Orlando.

Write $\dfrac{1}{110} = \dfrac{1.25}{x}$

$1(x) = 110(1.25)$ Cross Products Property

$x = 137.5$ Multiply.

The actual distance from Jacksonville to Orlando is 137.5 mi.

  Got It? **3. a.** The distance from Jacksonville to Gainesville on the map is about 0.6 in. What is the actual distance from Jacksonville to Gainesville?

     b. Reasoning If you know that the actual distance between two cities is 250 mi and that the cities are 2 in. apart on a map, how can you find the scale of the map?

A **scale model** is a three-dimensional model that is similar to a three-dimensional object. The ratio of a linear measurement of a model to the corresponding linear measurement of the actual object is always the same. This ratio is called the scale of the model.

Science A giant model heart is shown below. The heart is the ideal size for a person who is 170 ft tall. About what size would you expect the heart of a man who is 6 ft tall to be?

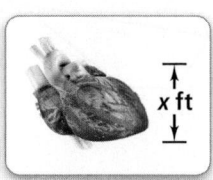

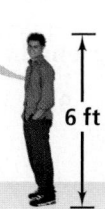

x ft

6 ft

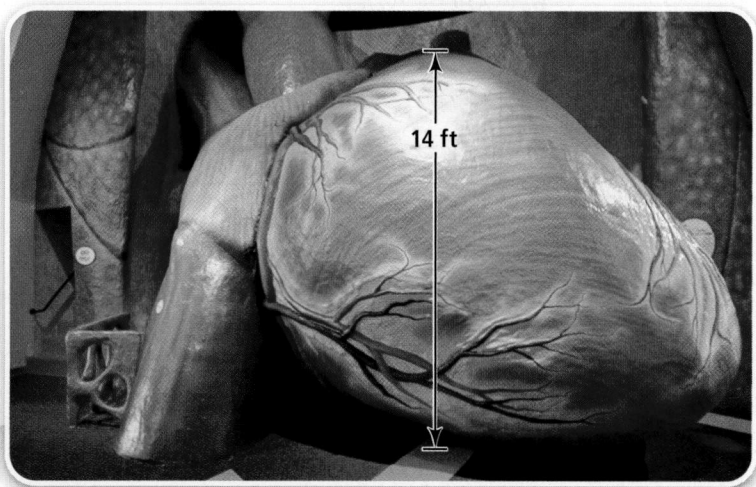

14 ft

Think

Is this problem like ones you have seen?
Yes. Scale model problems are like scale drawing problems, so you can write a proportion like you did to find the height of the building in Problem 2.

$$\frac{\text{height of giant heart}}{\text{height of man's heart}} = \frac{\text{height of giant person}}{\text{height of man}} \quad \text{Write a proportion.}$$

$$\frac{14}{x} = \frac{170}{6} \quad \text{Substitute.}$$

$$14(6) = 170x \quad \text{Cross Products Property}$$

$$0.49 \approx x \quad \text{Divide each side by 170 and simplify.}$$

The size of the man's heart would be about 0.49 ft, or 5.9 in.

 Got It? **4.** A scale model of a building is 6 in. tall. The scale of the model is 1 in. : 50 ft. How tall is the actual building?

 Lesson Check

Do you know HOW?

1. **Photocopies** You use a photocopier to enlarge a drawing of a right triangle with a base of 13 cm and a height of 7 cm. The enlarged triangle has a height of 17.5 cm.
   a. What is the base of the enlarged triangle?
   b. What is the scale of the enlargement?

2. **Maps** The scale of a map is 1 cm : 75 km. What is the actual distance between two towns that are 3 cm apart on the map?

Do you UNDERSTAND?  **MATHEMATICAL PRACTICES**

© 3. **Vocabulary** Suppose $\triangle MNP \sim \triangle RST$. How can you identify corresponding parts?

© 4. **Reasoning** Suppose $\triangle ABC \sim \triangle TUV$. Determine whether each pair of measures is equal.
   a. the measures of $\angle A$ and $\angle T$
   b. the perimeters of the two triangles
   c. the ratios of the sides $\frac{BC}{UV}$ and $\frac{AC}{TV}$

© 5. **Reasoning** The scale of a map is 1 in. : 100 mi. Is the actual distance between two towns 100 times the map distance between the two towns? Explain.

Practice and Problem-Solving Exercises

 **MATHEMATICAL PRACTICES**

 The figures in each pair are similar. Identify the corresponding sides and angles.

 **See Problem 1.**

6. △*ABC* ~ △*DEF*

7. *FGHI* ~ *KLMN*

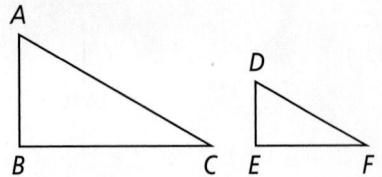

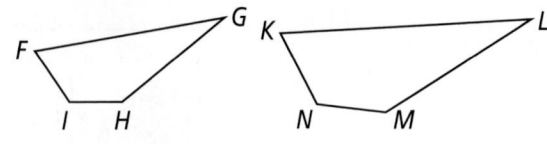

The figures in each pair are similar. Find the missing length.

8.

9.

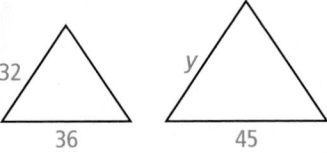

10.

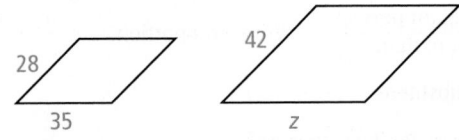

11.

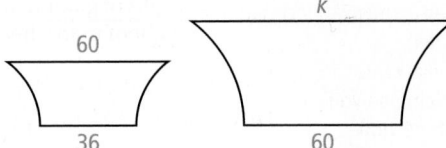

12. Bridges In the diagram of the park, △*ADF* ~ △*BCF*. The crosswalk at point *A* is about 20 yd long. A bridge across the pond will be built, from point *B* to point *C*. What will the length of the bridge be?

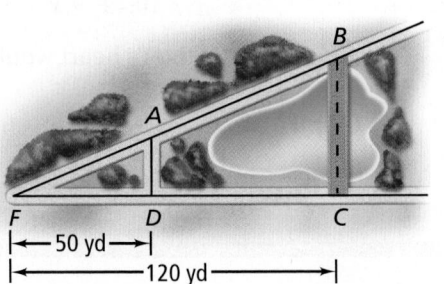

 **See Problem 2.**

The scale of a map is 1 cm : 15 km. Find the actual distance corresponding to each map distance.

 **See Problem 3.**

13. 2.5 cm

14. 0.2 cm

15. 15 cm

16. 4.6 cm

17. Movies A professional model-maker is building a giant scale model of a house fly to be used in a science fiction film. An actual fly is about 0.2 in. long with a wingspan of about 0.5 in. The model fly for the movie will be 27 ft long. What will its wingspan be?

 **See Problem 4.**

18. Maps Abbottsville and Broken Branch are 175 mi apart. On a map, the distance between the two towns is 2.5 in. What is the scale of the map?

B Apply STEM **Architecture** An architect is using the blueprint below to remodel a laundry room. The side length of each grid square represents 12 in.

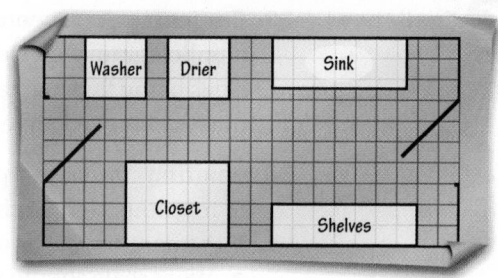

19. Find the actual length and width of the sink.

20. Find the total length and width of the actual room.

21. Will it be possible to wheel a laundry cart that is $3\frac{1}{2}$ ft wide through the room from the doorway at the left to the doorway at the right?

22. Model Rockets A particular model rocket kit uses the scale 1 : 144. The actual rocket is 168 ft tall. How tall will the model rocket be when completed?

23. Error Analysis The two figures at the right are similar. A student uses the proportion $\frac{BC}{CJ} = \frac{GH}{FN}$ to find *FN*.
   a. What mistake did the student make?
   b. What proportion should the student have used instead?

24. Think About a Plan An interior designer sketches a design for a rectangular rug. The dimensions of the sketch are 4 in. by 7.5 in. The dimensions of the actual rug will be ten times the dimensions of the drawing, so the scale of the drawing is 1 : 10. How many times the area of the sketch is the area of the actual rug?
   • Which figures in the problem are similar? What are their dimensions?
   • How can proportions help you find the dimensions of the actual rug?

25. Trucks A model of a tractor-trailer is shaped like a rectangular prism and has a width of 2 in., a length of 9 in., and a height of 4 in. The scale of the model is 1 : 34. How many times the volume of the model is the volume of the actual tractor-trailer?

26. Eiffel Tower The height of the Eiffel Tower is 324 m. Which scale was used to make the model of the Eiffel Tower shown at the right?
   Ⓐ 1 mm : 0.9 m
   Ⓑ 1 mm : 6 m
   Ⓒ 1 mm : 30 m
   Ⓓ 1 mm : 324 m

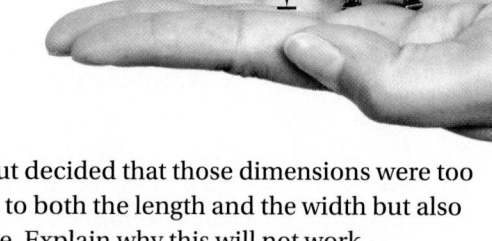

54 mm

27. Writing Are all squares similar? Explain your answer.

28. Reasoning A boat maker wanted to build a canoe 6 ft long and $2\frac{1}{2}$ ft wide but decided that those dimensions were too small. The boat maker wants to add 2 ft to both the length and the width but also wants to keep the canoe the same shape. Explain why this will not work.

29. Carpentry A carpenter is building a tabletop from a sketch. The sketch shows a parallelogram with side lengths 2 in. and 3 in. Also, the sketch specifies that the sides of the finished tabletop should be 4 ft and 6 ft. Can the carpenter be certain that the finished tabletop will be a similar parallelogram? Explain.

30. Painting You have a painting that is 30 in. wide and 22.5 in. tall. You would like to reproduce it on a sheet of paper that measures $8\frac{1}{2}$ in. by 11 in., leaving at least a 1-in. margin on all four sides.
  a. What scale should you use if you keep the sheet of paper in the normal upright orientation? Assume that the reproduction will be as large as possible.
  b. What scale should you use if you turn the paper on its side?

Apply What You've Learned

MATHEMATICAL
PRACTICES
MP 4

Look back at the information about the monorail on page 79. The scale drawing of the monorail route is shown again below.

Airport Monorail Route

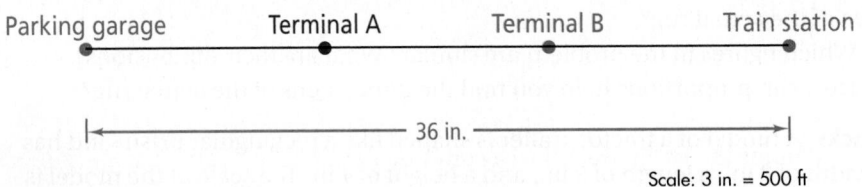

Parking garage   Terminal A   Terminal B   Train station

|← 36 in. →|

Scale: 3 in. = 500 ft

a. Write a proportion that you can use to find the total distance the monorail travels from the parking garage to the train station.

b. Determine the total distance the monorail travels from the parking garage to the train station. Explain how you know that your answer is reasonable.

c. What is the distance the monorail travels from Terminal B to the train station? Find the length that represents this distance in the scale drawing on the airport's information board.

Percents

Ⓒ Common Core State Standards

Prepares for N-Q.A.3 Choose a level of accuracy appropriate to limitations on measurement when reporting quantities.

MP 1, MP 2, MP 3, MP 4

Objectives To solve percent problems using proportions
To solve percent problems using the percent equation

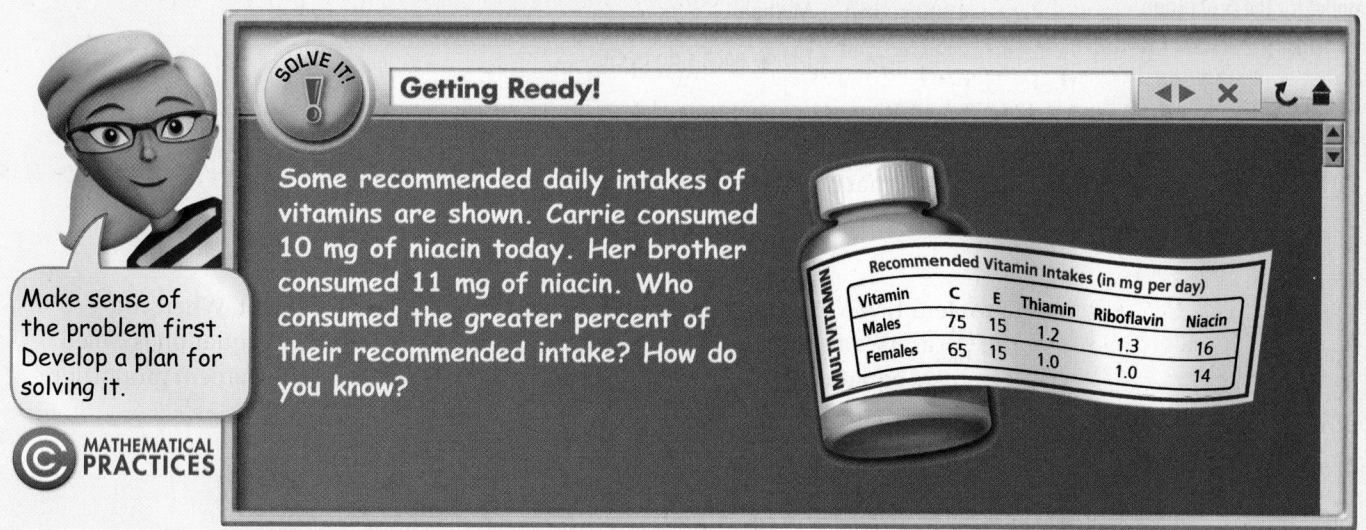

SOLVE IT!

Getting Ready!   ◀▶ ✕ ↻ ⬆

Some recommended daily intakes of vitamins are shown. Carrie consumed 10 mg of niacin today. Her brother consumed 11 mg of niacin. Who consumed the greater percent of their recommended intake? How do you know?

Recommended Vitamin Intakes (in mg per day)

Vitamin	C	E	Thiamin	Riboflavin	Niacin
Males	75	15	1.2	1.3	16
Females	65	15	1.0	1.0	14

MULTIVITAMIN

Make sense of the problem first. Develop a plan for solving it.

Ⓒ **MATHEMATICAL PRACTICES**

The problem in the Solve It involves percents. Percents are useful because they standardize comparisons to a common base of 100. In this lesson, you will solve percent problems in a variety of ways.

Essential Understanding You can solve problems involving percents using either proportions or the percent equation, which are closely related. If you write a percent as a fraction, you can use a proportion to solve a percent problem.

take note

Key Concept   The Percent Proportion

You can represent "*a* is *p* percent of *b*" using the percent proportion shown below. In the proportion, *b* is the base, and *a* is a *part* of base *b*.

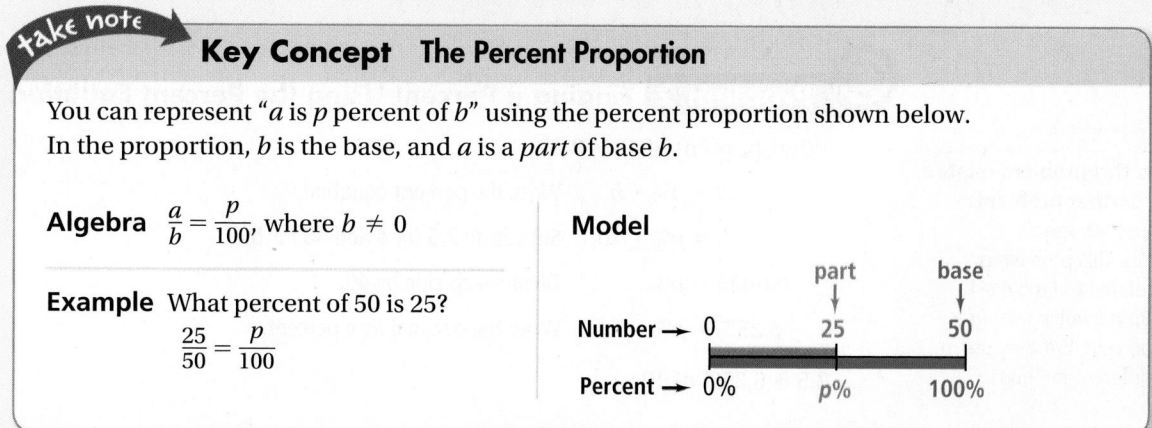

Algebra $\frac{a}{b} = \frac{p}{100}$, where $b \neq 0$

Example What percent of 50 is 25?
$$\frac{25}{50} = \frac{p}{100}$$

Model

		part	base
		↓	↓
Number ➞	0	25	50
Percent ➞	0%	*p*%	100%

 Problem 1 Finding a Percent Using the Percent Proportion

What percent of 56 is 42?

$$\frac{a}{b} = \frac{p}{100} \qquad \text{Write the percent proportion.}$$

$$\frac{42}{56} = \frac{p}{100} \qquad \text{Substitute 42 for } a \text{ and 56 for } b.$$

$$42(100) = 56p \qquad \text{Cross Products Property}$$

$$4200 = 56p \qquad \text{Multiply.}$$

$$75 = p \qquad \text{Divide each side by 56.}$$

42 is 75% of 56.

Got It? **1.** What percent of 90 is 54?

Think

How can a model help you visualize the proportion?
Use a model like the one below to visualize any percent problem. A model for the proportion $\frac{42}{56} = \frac{p}{100}$ is

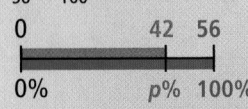

In Problem 1, you used the percent proportion $\frac{a}{b} = \frac{p}{100}$ to find a percent. When you write $\frac{p}{100}$ as $p\%$ and solve for a, you get the equation $a = p\% \cdot b$. This equation is called the percent equation. You can use either the percent equation or the percent proportion to solve any percent problem.

take note

Key Concept   The Percent Equation

You can represent "a is p percent of b" using the percent equation shown below. In the equation, a is a part of the base b.

Algebra $a = p\% \cdot b$, where $b \neq 0$

Model

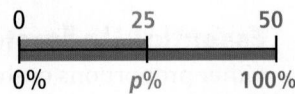

Example What percent of 50 is 25?

$$25 = p\% \cdot 50$$

 Problem 2 Finding a Percent Using the Percent Equation

What percent of 40 is 2.5?

$$a = p\% \cdot b \qquad \text{Write the percent equation.}$$

$$2.5 = p\% \cdot 40 \qquad \text{Substitute 2.5 for } a \text{ and 40 for } b.$$

$$0.0625 = p\% \qquad \text{Divide each side by 40.}$$

$$6.25\% = p\% \qquad \text{Write the decimal as a percent.}$$

2.5 is 6.25% of 40.

Think

Is this problem related to other problems you've seen?
Yes. This problem is related to Problem 1. Both involve finding a percent, but they use different methods.

  Got It? **2. Reasoning** What percent of 84 is 63? Use the percent equation to solve. Then use the percent proportion. Compare your answers.

Problem 3 **Finding a Part**

Shopping A dress shirt that normally costs $38.50 is on sale for 30% off. What is the sale price of the shirt?

Step 1 Use the percent equation to find the amount of discount.

$a = p\% \cdot b$ Write the percent equation.

$\quad = 30\% \cdot 38.50$ Substitute 30 for p and 38.50 for b.

$\quad = 0.30 \cdot 38.50$ Write the percent as a decimal.

$\quad = 11.55$ Multiply.

Step 2 Find the sale price.

$\$38.50 - \$11.55 = \$26.95$

The sale price of the shirt is $26.95.

 Got It? 3. A family sells a car to a dealership for 60% less than they paid for it. They paid $9000 for the car. For what price did they sell the car?

 Problem 4 **Finding a Base**

125% of what number is 17.5?

$a = p\% \cdot b$ Write the percent equation.

$17.5 = 125\% \cdot b$ Substitute 17.5 for a and 125 for p.

$17.5 = 1.25 \cdot b$ Write the percent as a decimal.

$14 = b$ Divide each side by 1.25.

125% of 14 is 17.5.

 Got It? 4. 30% of what number is 12.5? Solve the problem using the percent equation. Then solve the problem using the percent proportion.

Think

How can a model help you visualize finding a part or base?
Use the model below to help you visualize finding the part in the equation $a = 30\% \cdot 38.50$.

0	a	38.50

0% 30%   100%

Think

Will 125% of a number be greater than the number?
Yes. When you multiply a positive number by a percent greater than 100%, the part will be greater than the base, as shown in the model below.

0	b	17.5

0%   100% 125%

A common application of percents is simple interest, which is interest you earn on only the principal in an account.

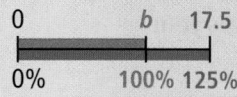

Key Concept **Simple Interest Formula**

The simple interest formula is given below, where I is the interest, P is the principal, r is the annual interest rate written as a decimal, and t is the time in years.

Algebra $I = Prt$

Example If you invest $50 at a simple interest rate of 3.5% per year for 3 years, the interest you earn is $I = 50(0.035)(3) = \$5.25$.

When you solve problems involving percents, it is helpful to know fraction equivalents for common percents. You can use the fractions to check your answers for reasonableness. Here are some common percents represented as fractions.

$1\% = \dfrac{1}{100}$ $5\% = \dfrac{1}{20}$ $10\% = \dfrac{1}{10}$ $20\% = \dfrac{1}{5}$ $25\% = \dfrac{1}{4}$

$33.\overline{3}\% = \dfrac{1}{3}$ $50\% = \dfrac{1}{2}$ $66.\overline{6}\% = \dfrac{2}{3}$ $75\% = \dfrac{3}{4}$ $100\% = 1$

Problem 5 Using the Simple Interest Formula

Finance You deposited $840 in a savings account that earns a simple interest rate of 4.5% per year. You want to keep the money in the account for 4 years. How much interest will you earn? Check your answer for reasonableness.

Think

This is a simple interest problem, so use the formula for simple interest.

Identify what you know from the problem: $P = 840$, $r = 0.045$, and $t = 4$.

Check for reasonableness by using a common percent. Since 4.5% is about 5%, use 5%.

Write

$I = Prt$

$= 840(0.045)(4)$

$= 151.2$

The account will earn $151.20.

$840 \cdot \dfrac{1}{20} \cdot 4 = 42 \cdot 4 = \$168$

So, $151.20 is reasonable. ✔

 Got It? 5. You deposited $125 in a savings account that earns a simple interest rate of 1.75% per year. You earned a total of $8.75 in interest. For how long was your money in the account?

take note

Concept Summary   Solving Percent Problems

Problem Type	Example	Proportion	Equation
Find a percent.	What percent of 6.3 is 3.5?	$\dfrac{3.5}{6.3} = \dfrac{p}{100}$	$3.5 = p\% \cdot 6.3$
Find a part.	What is 32% of 125?	$\dfrac{a}{125} = \dfrac{32}{100}$	$a = 32\% \cdot 125$
Find a base.	25% of what number is 11?	$\dfrac{11}{b} = \dfrac{25}{100}$	$11 = 25\% \cdot b$

Lesson Check

Do you know HOW?

1. What percent of 70 is 21?

2. What percent of 50 is 60?

3. What is 35% of 80?

4. 75% of what number is 36?

5. **Finance** How much interest will you earn by investing $1200 at a simple interest rate of 2.5% per year for 6 years?

Do you UNDERSTAND?

 6. **Vocabulary** Complete: p% is equivalent to a fraction with a numerator of p and a denominator of _?_ .

 7. **Reasoning** You deposited money in a savings account paying 4% simple interest per year. The first year, you earned $75 in interest. How much interest will you earn during the following year?

 8. **Open-Ended** Give an example of a percent problem where the part is greater than the base.

Practice and Problem-Solving Exercises

 **Practice**

Find each percent.

See Problems 1 and 2.

9. What percent of 75 is 15?

10. What percent of 15 is 75?

11. What percent of 16 is 10?

12. What percent of 32 is 40?

13. What percent of 48 is 20?

14. What percent of 88 is 88?

Find each part.

See Problem 3.

15. What is 25% of 144?

16. What is 63% of 150?

17. What is 12.5% of 104?

18. What is 150% of 63?

19. What is 125% of 12.8?

20. What is 1% of 1?

21. **Shopping** A tennis racket normally costs $65. The tennis racket is on sale for 20% off. What is the sale price of the tennis racket?

22. **Hair Care** A beauty salon buys bottles of styling gel for $4.50 per bottle and marks up the price by 40%. For what price does the salon sell each bottle?

Find each base.

See Problem 4.

23. 20% of what number is 80?

24. 80% of what number is 20?

25. 60% of what number is 13.5?

26. 160% of what number is 200?

27. 150% of what number is 34?

28. 1% of what number is 1?

29. **Finance** You deposit $1200 in a savings account that earns simple interest at a rate of 3% per year. How much interest will you have earned after 3 years?

See Problem 5.

30. **Finance** You deposit $150 in a savings account that earns simple interest at a rate of 5.5% per year. How much interest will you have earned after 4 years?

B Apply

Tell whether you are finding a *percent*, a *part*, or a *base*. Then solve.

31. What is 9% of 56?   **32.** What percent of 36 is 96?   **33.** What is 95% of 150?

34. What is 175% of 64?   **35.** What percent of 30 is 400?   **36.** 60 is 250% of what number?

37. Geography Water covers approximately 11,800 mi² of Florida, which is about 18% of Florida's area. What is the total area of Florida to the nearest thousand square miles?

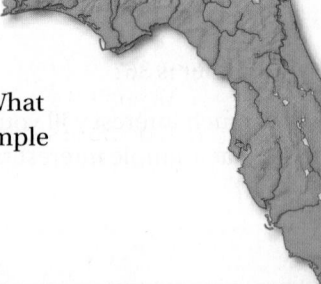

38. Finance A student has $1500 to deposit in a savings account. What is the lowest rate that would allow the student to earn $95 in simple interest in a year?

     (A) 5.5%

     (B) 6.25%

     (C) 6.33%

     (D) 7%

Solve using mental math.

39. 20% of 80 is __?__ .   **40.** 120 is 200% of __?__ .   **41.** 30 is __?__ % of 40.

Tell which is greater, *A* or *B*. Assume *A* and *B* are positive numbers.

42. *A* is 20% of *B*.   **43.** 150% of *A* is *B*.   **44.** *B* is 90% of *A*.

45. Think About a Plan The United States Mint reported at the end of 2006 that the unit cost of producing and distributing a penny was 1.21¢. What percent of the value of a penny is this cost? What can you conclude about the cost of making pennies?
- How can a model help you to visualize the problem?
- How can you use a proportion or the percent equation to solve the problem?

46. Economics Would you produce an item if the cost of producing and distributing the item were more than 100% of its value? Explain your answer.

47. Error Analysis A student was asked to make up and solve a percent problem, so the student wrote, "What percent of 1.5 is 3?" and solved it as shown at the right. Describe and correct the error in the student's solution.

48. Writing Part of a bottle of water has been consumed. Write the steps needed to determine the percent of water that has been consumed.

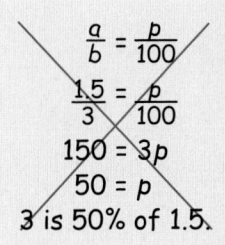

$$\frac{a}{b} = \frac{p}{100}$$
$$\frac{1.5}{3} = \frac{p}{100}$$
$$150 = 3p$$
$$50 = p$$
3 is 50% of 1.5.

49. Finance A savings account earns simple interest at a rate of 6% per year. Last year the account earned $10.86 in interest. What was the balance in the account at the beginning of last year?

50. Furniture A furniture store offers a set of furniture for $990. You can also purchase the set on an installment plan for 24 payments of $45 each. If you choose the installment plan, what percent of the original price will you have paid when you finish? Round to the nearest percent.

51. Geometry Each grid square in the figure at the right is the same size. What percent of the figure is red?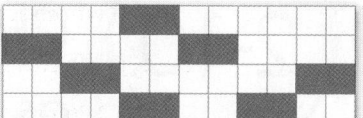

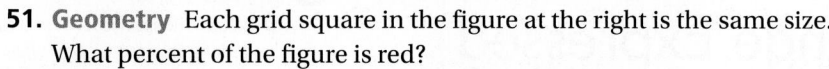

Challenge

52. Shopping Marcia buys a dress that is on sale for 15% off its original price. She uses a store coupon to obtain an additional 10% off the sale price. Marcia pays $91.80 for the dress. What was the original price of the dress?

53. Public Transportation In Mr. Ferreira's class, 80% of the students live more than half a mile from school. Of those students, 80% come to school by public transportation. Of the students using public transportation, 75% take the bus, and 75% of those students buy monthly bus passes. Nine students buy monthly bus passes. How many students are in Mr. Ferreira's class?

Standardized Test Prep

SAT/ACT

54. A rare disease has been discovered that affects 2 out of every 10,000 trees in a forest. What percent of trees are affected?

　Ⓐ 0.0002%　　　Ⓑ 0.002%　　　Ⓒ 0.02%　　　Ⓓ 0.2%

55. One kilometer equals about $\frac{5}{8}$ mi. A European racecar driver is driving at 120 km/h. Approximately what is this speed in miles per hour?

　Ⓕ 75 mi/h　　　Ⓖ 100 mi/h　　　Ⓗ 160 mi/h　　　Ⓘ 192 mi/h

56. What is the solution of $\frac{x}{2} + \frac{x}{3} - 15 = 0$?

　Ⓐ 12　　　Ⓑ 18　　　Ⓒ 24　　　Ⓓ 30

Mixed Review

57. Art A painting 36 cm wide and 22.5 cm tall is going to be reproduced on a postcard. The image on the postcard will be 9 cm tall. How wide will the image be?

◀ See Lesson 2-8.

58. Cats Alexis's cat eats 3 cans of cat food every 5 days. Alexis is going away for 30 days. A friend has offered to feed her cat. How many cans of cat food must Alexis leave for her cat while she is away?

◀ See Lesson 2-7.

59. Taxis A taxi charges $1.75 for the first $\frac{1}{8}$ mi and $.30 for each additional $\frac{1}{8}$ mi. Write an equation that gives the cost c of a taxi ride in terms of the number of miles m. How many miles did you travel if a ride cost $7.75?

◀ See Lesson 2-7.

Get Ready!　**To prepare for Lesson 2-10, do Exercises 60–62.**

Solve each percent problem.

◀ See Lesson 2-9.

60. What percent of 8 is 100?　　**61.** What is 20% of 3?　　**62.** 35 is what percent of 20?

Change Expressed as a Percent

 **Common Core State Standards**

N-Q.A.3 Choose a level of accuracy appropriate to limitations on measurement when reporting quantities.

MP 1, MP 2, MP 3, MP 4, MP 6

Objectives To find percent change
To find the relative error in linear and nonlinear measurements

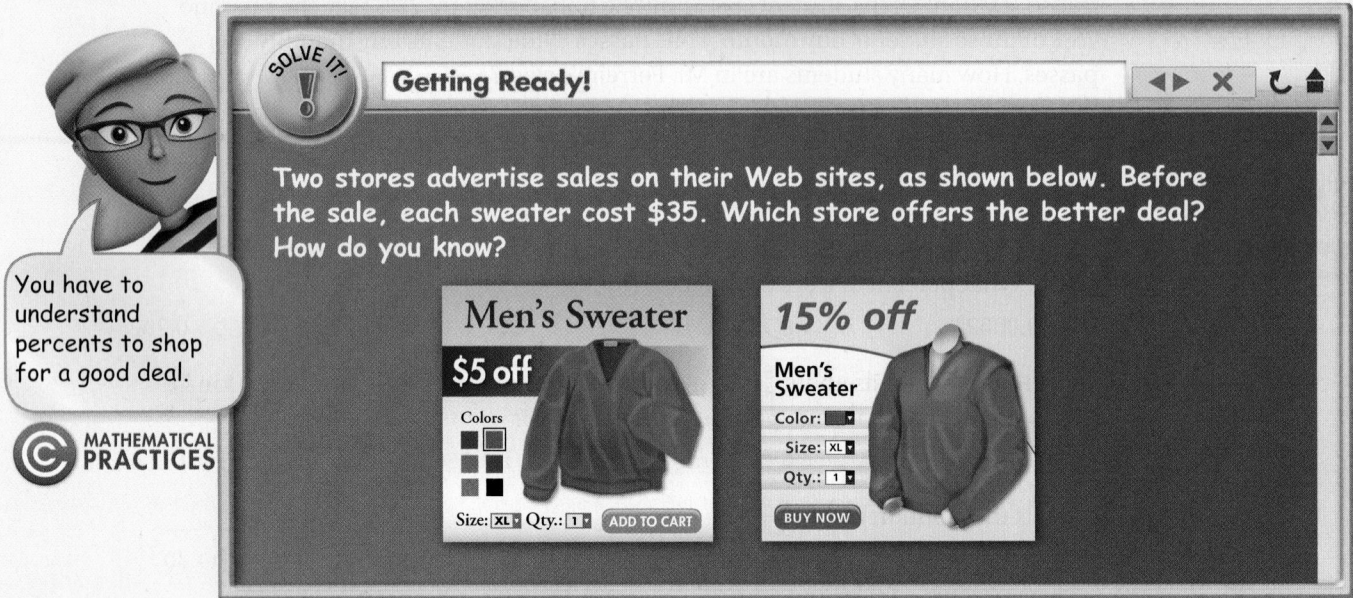

SOLVE IT!

Getting Ready!

Two stores advertise sales on their Web sites, as shown below. Before the sale, each sweater cost $35. Which store offers the better deal? How do you know?

Men's Sweater

$5 off

Colors

Size: XL   Qty.: 1   ADD TO CART

15% off

Men's Sweater

Color:
Size: XL
Qty.: 1

BUY NOW

You have to understand percents to shop for a good deal.

MATHEMATICAL PRACTICES

Lesson Vocabulary
• percent change
• percent increase
• percent decrease
• relative error
• percent error

In the Solve It, the 15% discount is a percent change in the price of the sweater. A **percent change** expresses an amount of change as a percent of an original amount. In this lesson, you will learn how to calculate a percent change.

Essential Understanding You can find a percent change when you know the original amount and how much it has changed.

If a new amount is greater than the original amount, the percent change is called a **percent increase.** If the new amount is less than the original amount, the percent change is called a **percent decrease.**

take note

Key Concept   Percent Change

Percent change is the ratio of the amount of change to the original amount.

$$\text{percent change, } p\% = \frac{\text{amount of increase or decrease}}{\text{original amount}}$$

• amount of increase = new amount − original amount
• amount of decrease = original amount − new amount

A common example of finding a percent decrease is finding a percent discount. In this lesson, round your answers to the nearest percent, if necessary.

 Problem 1 Finding a Percent Decrease

Clothing A coat is on sale. The original price of the coat is \$82. The sale price is \$74.50. What is the discount expressed as a percent change?

Think

Does this problem involve a percent decrease or a percent increase?
The new amount is less than the original amount, so the problem involves a percent decrease.

$$\text{percent change} = \frac{\text{amount of increase or decrease}}{\text{original amount}}$$

$$= \frac{\text{original amount} - \text{new amount}}{\text{original amount}}$$ This is a percent decrease. Write the appropriate ratio.

$$= \frac{82 - 74.50}{82}$$ Substitute.

$$= \frac{7.5}{82}$$ Simplify.

$$\approx 0.09, \text{ or } 9\%$$ Write the result as a percent.

The price of the coat decreased by about 9%.

 Got It? **1.** The average monthly precipitation for Chicago, Illinois, peaks in June at 4.1 in. The average monthly precipitation in December is 2.8 in. What is the percent decrease from June to December?

A common example of finding a percent increase is finding a percent markup.

 Problem 2 Finding a Percent Increase

Music A store buys an electric guitar for \$295. The store then marks up the price of the guitar to \$340. What is the markup expressed as a percent change?

Think

Have you seen a problem like this one?
Yes. Finding percent increase is like finding percent decrease. The difference is in calculating the amount of increase or decrease.

$$\text{percent change} = \frac{\text{amount of increase or decrease}}{\text{original amount}}$$

$$= \frac{\text{new amount} - \text{original amount}}{\text{original amount}}$$ This is a percent increase. Write the appropriate ratio.

$$= \frac{340 - 295}{295}$$ Substitute.

$$= \frac{45}{295}$$ Simplify.

$$\approx 0.15 \text{ or } 15\%$$ Write the result as a percent.

The price of the guitar increased by about 15%.

 Got It? **2.** In one year, the toll for passenger cars to use a tunnel rose from \$3 to \$3.50. What was the percent increase?

Essential Understanding You can use percents to compare estimated or measured values to actual or exact values.

take note

Key Concept   Relative Error

Relative error is the ratio of the absolute value of the difference of a measured (or estimated) value and an actual value compared to the actual value.

$$\text{relative error} = \frac{|\text{measured or estimated value} - \text{actual value}|}{\text{actual value}}$$

When relative error is expressed as a percent, it is called **percent error.**

© **Problem 3**   Finding Percent Error

Multiple Choice A decorator estimates that a rectangular rug is 5 ft by 8 ft. The rug is actually 4 ft by 8 ft. What is the percent error in the estimated area?

Ⓐ 0.25%   Ⓑ 20%   Ⓒ 25%   Ⓓ 80%

Think

What does the percent error tell you?
The percent error tells how accurate a measurement or estimate is.

$$\text{percent error} = \frac{|\text{estimated value} - \text{actual value}|}{\text{actual value}} \qquad \text{Write the ratio.}$$

$$= \frac{|5(8) - 4(8)|}{4(8)} \qquad \text{Substitute.}$$

$$= \frac{|40 - 32|}{32} \qquad \text{Multiply.}$$

$$= \frac{8}{32} \qquad \text{Simplify.}$$

$$= 0.25, \text{ or } 25\% \qquad \text{Write the result as a percent.}$$

The estimated area is off by 25%. The correct answer is C.

 Got It? 3. You think that the distance between your house and a friend's house is 5.5 mi. The actual distance is 4.75 mi. What is the percent error in your estimation?

In Problem 3, the actual measurements were known. Often you don't know actual measurements, but you know how precise your measurements can be.

Think about the last time you used a ruler. Because the precision of a ruler is limited, you measured to the nearest unit or fraction of a unit, such as centimeters or quarter inches. The most any measurement can be off by is one half of the unit used in measuring.

 **Problem 4** Finding Minimum and Maximum Dimensions

Posters You are framing a poster and measure the length of the poster as 18.5 in., to the nearest half inch. What are the minimum and maximum possible lengths of the poster?

You measured to the nearest 0.5 in., so the greatest possible error is 0.25 in.

Minimum length = measured value − possible error = 18.5 − 0.25 = 18.25
Maximum length = measured value + possible error = 18.5 + 0.25 = 18.75

The minimum possible length is 18.25 in. The maximum is 18.75 in.

 Got It? **4.** A student's height is measured as 66 in. to the nearest inch. What are the student's minimum and maximum possible heights?

 **Problem 5** Finding the Greatest Possible Percent Error

Crafts The diagram at the right shows the dimensions of a gift box to the nearest inch. What is the greatest possible percent error in calculating the volume of the gift box?

5 in.

12 in.

6 in.

Know
- The dimensions of the gift box to the nearest inch
- The formula for volume: $V = \ell wh$
- The greatest possible error in each dimension is 0.5 in.

Need
The greatest possible percent error in calculating the volume

Plan
Find the minimum and maximum volumes. Find the differences between the possible volumes and the measured volume. Use the greater difference to find the percent error.

Measured volume

$V = \ell wh$
$= (12)(6)(5)$
$= 360$

Minimum volume

$V = \ell wh$
$= (11.5)(5.5)(4.5)$
$= 284.625$

Maximum volume

$V = \ell wh$
$= (12.5)(6.5)(5.5)$
$= 446.875$

Find the differences.

$|\text{minimum volume} - \text{measured volume}| = |284.625 - 360| = 75.375$
$|\text{maximum volume} - \text{measured volume}| = |446.875 - 360| = 86.875$

Use the greater difference to find the greatest possible percent error.

$$\text{greatest possible percent error} = \frac{\text{greater difference in volume}}{\text{measured volume}}$$

$$= \frac{86.875}{360} \qquad \text{Substitute.}$$

$$\approx 0.24 \text{ or } 24\% \qquad \text{Write the result as a percent.}$$

The greatest possible percent error in the volume, based on measurements to the nearest inch, is about 24%.

Got It? **5. Reasoning** If the gift box's dimensions in Problem 5 were measured to the nearest half inch, how would the greatest possible error be affected?

Lesson Check

Do you know HOW?

1. **Running** Last year, an athlete's average time to run a mile was 6 min 13 s. This year, the athlete's average time is 6 min 5 s. What is the percent decrease?

2. **Cars** A used-car dealership buys a car for $2800 and then sells it for $4500. What is the percent increase?

3. **Horses** A veterinarian measures a horse to be 7.5 ft tall at the shoulder to the nearest half foot. What are the minimum and maximum possible heights of the horse?

Do you UNDERSTAND?

4. **Vocabulary** Determine whether each situation involves a percent increase or a percent decrease.

   a. A hat that originally costs $12 sold for $9.50.

   b. You buy a CD for $10 and sell it for $8.

   c. A store buys glasses wholesale for $2 per glass. The store sells them for $4.50.

5. **Reasoning** What is the greatest possible error of a measurement taken to the nearest tenth of a meter?

6. **Writing** How is calculating percent increase different from calculating percent decrease?

Practice and Problem-Solving Exercises

 **Practice** Tell whether each percent change is an increase or decrease. Then find the percent change. Round to the nearest percent.

◀ **See Problems 1 and 2.**

7. original amount: 12
   new amount: 18

8. original amount: 9
   new amount: 6

9. original amount: 15
   new amount: 14

10. original amount: 7.5
    new amount: 9.5

11. original amount: 40.2
    new amount: 38.6

12. original amount: 2008
    new amount: 1975

13. original amount: 14,500
    new amount: 22,320

14. original amount: 195.50
    new amount: 215.25

15. original amount: 1325.60
    new amount: 1685.60

16. **Employment** An employee was hired at a wage of $8 per hour. After a raise, the employee earned $8.75 per hour. What was the percent increase?

17. **Climate** On June 1, 2007, there were about 18.75 h of daylight in Anchorage, Alaska. On November 1, 2007, there were about 8.5 h of daylight. What was the percent decrease?

Find the percent error in each estimation. Round to the nearest percent.

◀ **See Problem 3.**

18. You estimate that your friend's little brother is about 8 years old. He is actually 6.5 years old.

19. You estimate that your school is about 45 ft tall. Your school is actually 52 ft tall.

A measurement is given. Find the minimum and maximum possible measurements.

See Problem 4.

20. A doctor measures a patient's weight as 162 lb to the nearest pound.

21. An ostrich egg has a mass of 1.1 kg to the nearest tenth of a kilogram.

22. The length of an onion cell is 0.4 mm to the nearest tenth of a millimeter.

23. Geometry The table below shows the measured dimensions of a prism and the minimum and maximum possible dimensions based on the greatest possible error. What is the greatest possible percent error in finding the volume of the prism?

See Problem 5.

Dimensions	Length	Width	Height
Measured	10	6	4
Minimum	9.5	5.5	3.5
Maximum	10.5	6.5	4.5

24. Geometry The side lengths of the rectangle at the right have been measured to the nearest half of a meter, as shown. What is the greatest possible percent error in finding the area of the rectangle?

7.5 m

18.5 m

B Apply

Find the percent change. Round to the nearest percent.

25. 2 ft to $5\frac{1}{2}$ ft

26. 18 lb to $22\frac{1}{4}$ lb

27. $140\frac{1}{4}$ g to $80\frac{3}{4}$ g

28. $8.99 to $15.99

29. $168.45 to $234.56

30. $4023.52 to $982.13

The measured dimensions of a rectangle are given to the nearest whole unit. Find the minimum and maximum possible areas of each rectangle.

31. 7 m by 8 m

32. 18 in. by 15 in.

33. 24 ft by 22 ft

34. Writing How are percent change and percent error similar?

35. Open-Ended Write a percent change problem that you recently experienced.

36. Think About a Plan In one season, an average of 6500 fans attended each home game played by the basketball team at a college. In the next season, the average number of fans per game increased by about 12%. What was the average number of fans per game for that season?
- What is missing—the new amount or the original amount?
- How can a percent change help you find the missing amount?

37. Error Analysis A student is trying to find the percent of change when an amount increases from 12 to 18, as shown. Describe and correct the student's error.

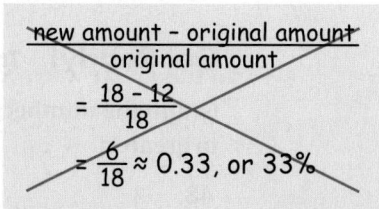

38. Rounding Error Your science class visits an aquarium. In a report on your class's visit, you sketch one of the fish tanks and round the dimensions as shown in the diagram at the right. You use the rounded dimensions to state the tank's volume is approximately $(7 \text{ m})(5 \text{ m})(3 \text{ m}) = 105 \text{ m}^3$. What is the percent error in your volume calculation due to rounding?

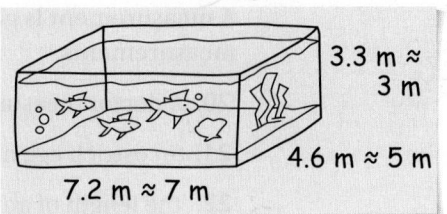

3.3 m ≈ 3 m

4.6 m ≈ 5 m

7.2 m ≈ 7 m

39. Student Discounts You show your student identification at a local restaurant in order to receive a 5% discount. You spend $12 for your meal at the restaurant. How much would your meal cost without the discount?

 **Challenge**

40. Geometry The height of a cylinder is 2 ft. The diameter of the base is 5 ft. Each dimension is accurate to the nearest foot. What is the greatest possible error in calculating the volume of the cylinder? Use 3.14 for π.

Ⓒ **41. a.** The sides of a square that measures 4 m by 4 m increased in length by 10%. Find the percent of increase in the area.

b. The sides of a square that measures 6 m by 6 m increased in length by 10%. Find the percent of increase in the area.

c. Reasoning Predict the percent of increase in the area of a square that measures 8 m by 8 m if the side lengths increase by 10%. Explain and check your answer.

Standardized Test Prep

SAT/ACT

42. Marcus bought a shirt that was marked $28, but it was on sale for 15% off the marked price. What was the price of the shirt after the discount?

Ⓐ $4.20   Ⓑ $23.80   Ⓒ $24.80   Ⓓ $32.20

43. What equation do you get when you solve $ax + bx = c$ for x?

Ⓕ $x = c - ab$ Ⓖ $x = c - a - b$ Ⓗ $x = \dfrac{c}{a - b}$ Ⓘ $x = \dfrac{c}{a + b}$

44. A teacher wants to give each student 2 pencils. A store is selling pencils in boxes of 24. If the teacher has a total of 125 students, how many boxes of pencils should he buy?

Ⓐ 5   Ⓑ 6   Ⓒ 10   Ⓓ 11

Mixed Review

Solve each percent problem.   ◀ **See Lesson 2-9.**

45. What percent of 12 is 8?   **46.** What is 35% of 185?   **47.** 20% of what number is 4.2?

Get Ready!   **To prepare for Lesson 3-1, do Exercises 48–51.**

Graph the numbers on the same number line. Then order them from least to greatest.   ◀ **See Lesson 1-3.**

48. -3 **49.** $\frac{1}{2}$ **50.** 2   **51.** -2.8

Pull It **All Together**

To solve these problems you will pull together many concepts and skills that you have studied about solving equations and working with rates and proportions.

Completing the Performance Task

Look back at your results from the Apply What You've Learned sections in Lessons 2-3, 2-6, and 2-8. Use the work you did to complete the following.

1. Solve the problem in the Task Description on page 79 by determining the average speed of the monorail, in miles per hour, over each segment of the route. Round each speed to the nearest tenth of a mile per hour. Show all your work and explain each step of your solution.

2. Reflect Choose one of the Mathematical Practices below and explain how you applied it in your work on the Performance Task.

MP 1: Make sense of problems and persevere in solving them.

MP 2: Reason abstractly and quantitatively.

MP 4: Model with mathematics.

MP 6: Attend to precision.

On Your Own

At a meeting to discuss plans for an extension of the monorail, the airport's director displays the scale drawing below.

Monorail Extension

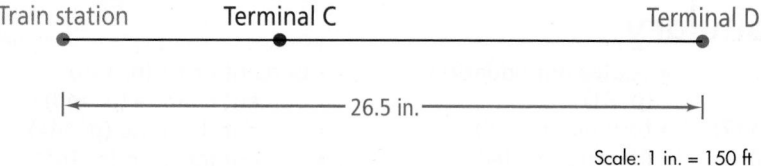

Scale: 1 in. = 150 ft

The airport's director wants to determine the speed of the monorail over each segment of the route in order to meet the following conditions.

- The trip from the train station to Terminal C should take 45 s.
- The trip from Terminal C to Terminal D should take 70 s.
- The monorail's average speed between the two terminals should be 25% greater than its average speed between the train station and Terminal C.

What is the average speed, in miles per hour, that the monorail should travel over each segment of the route? Round each speed to the nearest tenth of a mile per hour.

Connecting BIG ideas and Answering the Essential Questions

1 Equivalence
You can represent an equation in many ways. Equivalent representations have the same solution as the original equation.

Solving Equations (Lessons 2-1, 2-2, 2-3, 2-4)
Equivalent equations have the same solution(s). To solve a given equation, form a series of simpler equivalent equations that isolate the variable.

2 Solving Equations and Inequalities
You can use properties of numbers and equality to transform equations into equivalent, simpler equations and find solutions.

Solving Equations (Lessons 2-1, 2-2, 2-3, 2-4)
Use equations to model real-world situations and find unknown quantities.

Literal Equations and Formulas (Lesson 2-5)
Formulas represent reliable real-world relationships. Use them to solve problems.

3 Proportionality
In a proportional relationship, the ratios of two quantities are equal. You can use this relationship to describe similar figures, scale models, and rates.

Rates, Proportions, and Similar Figures (Lessons 2-6, 2-7, 2-8)
Use rates to model ideas like growth, speed, and unit prices. Use proportions to interpret scale drawings.

Percents (Lessons 2-9, 2-10)
Formulas represent reliable real-world relationships. Use them to solve problems.

Chapter Vocabulary

- Addition Property of Equality (p. 81)
- conversion factor (p. 117)
- cross products (p. 125)
- Cross Products Property (p. 125)
- Division Property of Equality (p. 83)

- equivalent equations (p. 81)
- formula (p. 110)
- identity (p. 104)
- inverse operations (p. 82)
- isolate (p. 82)
- literal equation (p. 109)
- Multiplication Property of Equality (p. 83)

- percent error (p. 146)
- percent change (p. 144)
- percent decrease (p. 144)
- percent increase (p. 144)
- proportion (p. 124)
- rate (p. 116)
- ratio (p. 116)
- relative error (p. 146)
- scale (p. 132)

- scale drawing (p. 132)
- scale model (p. 132)
- similar figures (p. 130)
- Subtraction Property of Equality (p. 81)
- unit analysis (p. 117)
- unit rate (p. 116)

Choose the correct term to complete each sentence.

1. Addition and subtraction are examples of __?__ because they undo each other.

2. An equation that is true for every value of the variable is a(n) __?__ .

3. A ratio of two equivalent measures given in different units is a(n) __?__ .

4. On a map, information such as "1 in. : 5 mi" is the __?__ of the map.

5. In the proportion $\frac{a}{b} = \frac{c}{d}$, ad and bc are the __?__ .

2-1 and 2-2 Solving One- and Two-Step Equations

Quick Review

To solve an equation, get the variable by itself on one side of the equation. You can use **properties of equality** and **inverse operations** to isolate the variable. For example, use multiplication to undo its inverse, division.

Example

What is the solution of $\frac{y}{2} + 5 = 8$?

$\frac{y}{2} + 5 - 5 = 8 - 5$ Subtract to undo addition.

$\frac{y}{2} = 3$ Simplify.

$2 \cdot \frac{y}{2} = 3 \cdot 2$ Multiply to undo division.

$y = 6$ Simplify.

Exercises

Solve each equation. Check your answer.

6. $x + 5 = -2$ $x = -7$

7. $a - 2.5 = 4.5$ $a = 7$

8. $3b = 42$ $b = 14$

9. $\frac{n}{5} = 13$ $n = 65$

10. $7x - 2 = 22.5$ $x = 3.5$

11. $\frac{y}{4} - 3 = -4$ $y = -4$

12. $8 + 3m = -7$ $m = -5$

13. $-\frac{3d}{4} + 5 = 11$ $d = -8$

14. Dining Five friends equally split a restaurant bill that comes to $32.50. How much does each pay? 6.50

15. Reasoning Justify each step in solving $4x - 3 = 9$.

$4x - 3 + 3 = 9 + 3$? Addition of Equality

$4x = 12$? Simplify

$\frac{4x}{4} = \frac{12}{4}$? Division of Equality

$x = 3$? Simplify

2-3 Solving Multi-Step Equations

Quick Review

To solve some equations, you may need to combine like terms or use the Distributive Property to clear fractions or decimals.

Example

What is the solution of $12 = 2x + \frac{4}{3} - \frac{2x}{3}$?

$3 \cdot 12 = 3\left(2x + \frac{4}{3} - \frac{2x}{3}\right)$ Multiply by 3.

$36 = 6x + 4 - 2x$ Simplify.

$36 = 4x + 4$ Combine like terms.

$36 - 4 = 4x + 4 - 4$ Subtract 4.

$32 = 4x$ Combine like terms.

$\frac{32}{4} = \frac{4x}{4}$ Divide each side by 4.

$8 = x$ Simplify.

Exercises

Solve each equation. Check your answer.

16. $7(s - 5) = 42$ $s = 11$

17. $3a + 2 - 5a = -14$ $a = 8$

18. $-4b - 5 + 2b = 10$ $b = -7.5$

19. $3.4t + 0.08 = 11$ $t = 3.21176...$

20. $10 = \frac{c}{3} - 4 + \frac{c}{6}$ $c = 28$

21. $\frac{2x}{7} + \frac{4}{5} = 5$ $x = 14.7$

Write an equation to model each situation. Then solve the equation.

22. Earnings You work for 4 h on Saturday and 8 h on Sunday. You also receive a $50 bonus. You earn $164. How much did you earn per hour?   h = 9.5
$164 = 50 + 8h + 4h$
$50 - 164 = 50 + 12h$ $\frac{14}{12} = \frac{12h}{12}$

23. Entertainment Online concert tickets cost $37 each, plus a service charge of $8.50 per ticket. The Web site also charges a transaction fee of $14.99 for the purchase. You paid $242.49. How many tickets did you buy?
$242.49 = 37t + 8.50t + 14.99$ 5 tickets
$242.49 = 45.5t + 14.99$
-14.99 -14.99
$\frac{227.5}{45.5} = \frac{45.5t}{45.5}$ $t = 5$

2-4 Solving Equations With Variables on Both Sides

Quick Review

When an equation has variables on both sides, you can use properties of equality to isolate the variable on one side. An equation has no solution if no value of the variable makes it true. An equation is an **identity** if every value of the variable makes it true.

Example

What is the solution of $3x - 7 = 5x + 19$?

$$3x - 7 - 3x = 5x + 19 - 3x \quad \text{Subtract } 3x.$$
$$-7 = 2x + 19 \quad \text{Simplify.}$$
$$-7 - 19 = 2x + 19 - 19 \quad \text{Subtract 19.}$$
$$-26 = 2x \quad \text{Simplify.}$$
$$\frac{-26}{2} = \frac{2x}{2} \quad \text{Divide each side by 2.}$$
$$-13 = x \quad \text{Simplify.}$$

Exercises

Solve each equation. If the equation is an identity, write *identity*. If it has no solution, write *no solution*.

24. $\frac{2}{3}x + 4 = \frac{3}{5}x - 2$ $x = -90$

25. $6 - 0.25f = f - 3$ 1.25

26. $3(h - 4) = \frac{1}{2}(24 - 6h)$ identity

27. $5n = 20(4 + 0.25n)$ no solution

28. Architecture Two buildings have the same total height. One building has 8 floors with height h. The other building has a ground floor of 16 ft and 6 other floors with height h. Write and solve an equation to find the height h of these floors.

29. Travel A train makes a trip at 65 mi/h. A plane traveling 130 mi/h makes the same trip in 3 fewer hours. Write and solve an equation to find the distance of the trip.

2-5 Literal Equations and Formulas

Quick Review

A **literal equation** is an equation that involves two or more variables. A **formula** is an equation that states a relationship among quantities. You can use properties of equality to solve a literal equation for one variable in terms of others.

Example

What is the width of a rectangle with area 91 ft² and length 7 ft?

$$A = \ell w \quad \text{Write the appropriate formula.}$$
$$\frac{A}{\ell} = w \quad \text{Divide each side by } \ell.$$
$$\frac{91}{7} = w \quad \text{Substitute 91 for } A \text{ and 7 for } \ell.$$
$$13 = w \quad \text{Simplify.}$$

The width of the rectangle is 13 ft.

Exercises

Solve each equation for x.

30. $ax + bx = -c$

31. $\frac{x + r}{t} + 1 = 0$

32. $m - 3x = 2x + p$

33. $\frac{x}{p} + \frac{x}{q} = s$

Solve each problem. Round to the nearest tenth, if necessary. Use 3.14 for π.

34. What is the width of a rectangle with length 5.5 cm and area 220 cm²?

35. What is the radius of a circle with circumference 94.2 mm?

36. A triangle has height 15 in. and area 120 in.². What is the length of its base?

2-6 Ratios, Rates, and Conversions

Quick Review

A ratio between numbers measured in different units is called a **rate**. A **conversion factor** is a ratio of two equivalent measures in different units such as $\frac{1\,h}{60\,min}$, and is always equal to 1. To convert from one unit to another, multiply the original unit by a conversion factor that has the original units in the denominator and the desired units in the numerator.

Example

A painting is 17.5 in. wide. What is its width in centimeters? Recall that 1 in. = 2.54 cm.

$$17.5\,\text{in.} \cdot \frac{2.54\,\text{cm}}{1\,\text{in.}} = 44.45\,\text{cm}$$

The painting is 44.45 cm wide.

Exercises

Convert the given amount to the given unit.

37. $6\frac{1}{2}$ ft; in.

38. 4 lb 7 oz; oz

39. 135 s; min

40. 2.25 mi; yd

41. Production A bread slicer runs 20 h per day for 30 days and slices 144,000 loaves of bread. How many loaves per hour are sliced?

42. Pets A gerbil eats about $\frac{1}{4}$ oz of food per day. About how many pounds of food can a gerbil eat in a year?

43. Sports If a baseball travels at 90 mi/h, how many seconds does it take to travel 60 ft?

2-7 and 2-8 Solving Proportions and Using Similar Figures

Quick Review

The **cross products** of a proportion are equal.

If $\frac{a}{b} = \frac{c}{d}$, where $b \neq 0$ and $d \neq 0$, then $ad = bc$.

If two figures are **similar,** then corresponding angles are congruent and corresponding side lengths are in proportion. You can use proportions to find missing side lengths in similar figures and for indirect measurement.

Example

A tree casts a shadow 10 m long. At the same time, a signpost next to the tree casts a shadow 4 m long. The signpost is 2.5 m tall. How tall is the tree?

$\frac{x}{10} = \frac{2.5}{4}$	Write a proportion.
$4x = 10(2.5)$	Cross Products Property
$4x = 25$	Simplify.
$x = 6.25$	Divide each side by 4.

Exercises

Solve each proportion.

44. $\frac{3}{7} = \frac{9}{x}$

45. $\frac{-8}{10} = \frac{y}{5}$

46. $\frac{6}{15} = \frac{a}{4}$

47. $\frac{3}{-7} = \frac{-9}{t}$

48. $\frac{b+3}{7} = \frac{b-3}{6}$

49. $\frac{5}{2c-3} = \frac{3}{7c+4}$

50. Models An airplane has a wingspan of 25 ft and a length of 20 ft. You are designing a model of the airplane with a wingspan of 15 in. What will the length of your model be?

51. Projections You project a drawing 7 in. wide and $4\frac{1}{2}$ in. tall onto a wall. The projected image is 27 in. tall. How wide is the projected image?

2-9 Percents

Quick Review

A percent is a ratio that compares a number to 100. If you write a percent as a fraction, you can use a proportion to solve a percent problem.

Example

What percent of 84 is 105?

$$\frac{105}{84} = \frac{p}{100}$$ Write the percent proportion.

$$100(105) = 84p$$ Cross Products Property

$$10{,}500 = 84p$$ Simplify.

$$125 = p$$ Divide each side by 84.

105 is 125% of 84.

Exercises

52. What percent of 37 is 111?

53. What is 72% of 150?

54. 60% of what number is 102?

55. Gardening A gardener expects that 75% of the seeds she plants will produce plants. She wants 45 plants. How many seeds should she plant?

56. Fundraising A charity sent out 700 fundraising letters and received 210 contributions in response. What was the percent of response?

57. Surveys In a survey, 60% of students prefer bagels to donuts. If 120 students were surveyed, how many students prefer bagels?

2-10 Change Expressed as a Percent

Quick Review

Percent change $p\%$ is the ratio of the amount of change to the original amount.

$$p\% = \frac{\text{amount of increase or decrease}}{\text{original amount}}$$

You can use the percent change formula to express changes as percents.

Example

A bookstore buys a book for \$16 and marks it up to \$28. What is the markup expressed as a percent change?

$$\text{percent change} = \frac{\text{new amount} - \text{original amount}}{\text{original amount}}$$

$$= \frac{28 - 16}{16}$$ Substitute.

$$= \frac{12}{16}$$ Simplify.

$$= 0.75 \text{ or } 75\%$$ Write the result as a percent.

The price of the book increased by 75%.

Exercises

Tell whether each percent change is an increase or decrease. Then find the percent change. Round to the nearest percent.

58. original amount: 27
new amount: 30

59. original amount: 250
new amount: 200

60. original amount: 873
new amount: 781

61. original amount: 4.7
new amount: 6.2

62. Demographics In 1970, the U.S. population was about 205 million people. In 2007, it was about 301 million. What was the percent increase?

63. Astronomy The time from sunrise to sunset on the shortest day of the year in Jacksonville, Florida, is about 10 h 11 min. On the longest day, the time is 14 h 7 min. What is the percent increase?

64. Weather This morning the temperature was 38°F. This afternoon it is 57°F. Did the temperature increase by 50%? Explain.

Do you know HOW?

Solve each proportion.

1. $\frac{8}{k} = -\frac{12}{30}$

2. $\frac{3}{5} = \frac{y+1}{9}$

Solve each equation. Check your answer.

3. $3w + 2 = w - 4$

4. $\frac{1}{4}(k - 1) = 7$

5. $6y = 12.8$

6. $\frac{5n+1}{8} = \frac{3n-5}{4}$

7. **Bicycling** You are riding your bicycle to prepare for a race. It takes you 12 min to go 2.5 mi. What was your speed in miles per hour?

The figures in each pair are similar. Find the missing length.

8.

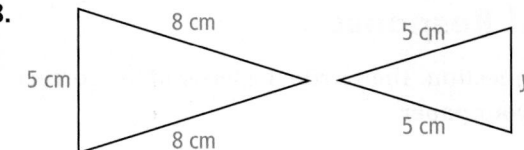

9.

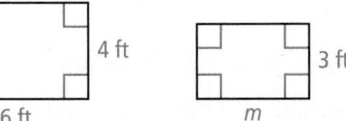

10. **Shadows** In the late afternoon, a 3.5-ft child casts a 60-in. shadow. The child is next to a telephone pole that casts a 50-ft shadow, forming similar triangles. How tall is the telephone pole?

Tell whether each percent change is an increase or decrease. Then find the percent change.

11. original amount: $5000
    new amount: $6500

12. original amount: 150 lb
    new amount: 135 lb

Define a variable and write an equation to model each situation. Then solve.

13. **Farming** You have 100 ft of fencing to build a circular sheep pen.

    a. What is the diameter of the largest pen you can build? Use 3.14 for π.

    b. What is the area of the largest pen you can build?

14. **Maps** The scale on a map is 1 in. : 25 mi. You measure 6.5 in. between two towns. What is the actual distance?

15. **Birds** In a bird sanctuary, 30% of the birds are hummingbirds. If there are about 350 birds in the sanctuary at any given time, how many are hummingbirds?

Do you UNDERSTAND?

16. **Reasoning** Explain which is more accurate: measuring to the nearest millimeter or to the nearest eighth of an inch.

17. **Writing** A 30-pack of blank CDs costs $9.50. A 50-pack of blank CDs costs $13. How can you tell which is the better buy?

18. **Error Analysis** Average attendance at a school's basketball games increased from 1000 to 1500 last year. One student said that represented a 150% increase. Explain the student's error. What was the actual percent increase?

Common Core Cumulative Standards Review

 ASSESSMENT

Vocabulary Builder

As you solve test items, you must understand the meanings of mathematical terms. Match each term with its mathematical meaning.

A. variable

B. similar

C. scale factor

D. perimeter

E. formula

I. the distance around the outside of a figure

II. two figures with exactly the same shape, but not necessarily the same size

III. a math sentence that defines the relationship between quantities

IV. a symbol that represents a number or numbers

V. the ratio of the lengths of corresponding sides in similar figures

Selected Response

Read each question. Then write the letter of the correct answer on your paper.

1. The product of an irrational number and a rational number is always a member of which classification of real numbers?

   Ⓐ whole numbers   Ⓒ integers

   Ⓑ rational numbers   Ⓓ irrational numbers

2. Belle surveyed her classmates in music class. The ratio of students who prefer playing string instruments to those who prefer wind instruments is 2 : 5. There are 28 students in Belle's class. How many students prefer playing string instruments?

   Ⓕ 5   Ⓗ 20

   Ⓖ 8   Ⓘ 25

3. What is the solution of $-30c - 6 = -9c - 3$?

(A) -7

(C) $\frac{3}{13}$

(B) $-\frac{1}{7}$

(D) $4\frac{1}{3}$

4. Jim uses 3 cups of peaches to yield 4 jars of peach jam. He also makes strawberry-peach jam. He uses equal amounts of strawberries and peaches. How many cups of strawberries does Jim need to yield 10 jars of strawberry-peach jam?

(F) $3\frac{3}{4}$ c

(H) $7\frac{1}{2}$ c

(G) $4\frac{1}{2}$ c

(I) 9 c

5. A model car kit is built to a scale of 1 : 32. The length of the actual car is 416 cm. What is the length of the model car?

(A) 384 cm

(C) 13 cm

(B) 133 cm

(D) 7 cm

6. Sabrina's car has traveled 28,000 mi. If she drives 36 mi each day, which equation can be used to find the total number of miles m Sabrina's car will have traveled after she drives it for d days?

(F) $d = 36m + 28{,}000$

(G) $m = 36d + 28{,}000$

(H) $m + 36d = 28{,}000$

(I) $d = 28{,}000m + 36$

7. Which operation should be done first to simplify the expression $12 + 6 \cdot 3 - (35 - 14 \div 7)$?

(A) $12 + 6$

(C) $35 - 14$

(B) $6 \cdot 3$

(D) $14 \div 7$

8. Erica is making feathered caps for her school play. Each cap must have 3 feathers. Which equation represents the number of feathers f Erica needs to make c caps?

(F) $c = 3f$

(H) $c = f + 3$

(G) $f = 3c$

(I) $f = c + 3$

9. Use the diagram below, which shows similar triangles formed by the shadows of a person and a tree.

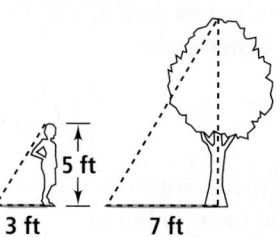

What is the approximate height of the tree?

(A) 4 ft

(C) 12 ft

(B) 9 ft

(D) 105 ft

10. In the expression $4ab + 5a - 3c$, what is the coefficient of the term $4ab$?

(F) a

(H) 4

(G) b

(I) $4ab$

11. The perimeter P of a rectangle with length ℓ and width w can be represented by the equation $P = 2\ell + 2w$. Which expression represents the width in relation to the P and ℓ?

(A) $P - 2\ell$

(C) $\frac{1}{2}P - 2\ell$

(B) $P - \ell$

(D) $\frac{P - 2\ell}{2}$

12. The equation $t = 4c$ represents the number of tires t for c cars. Which graph correctly displays this relationship?

(F)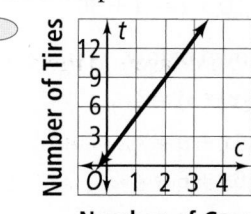

(H)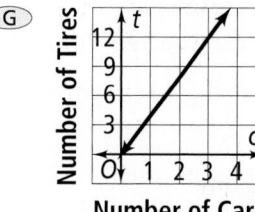

(G)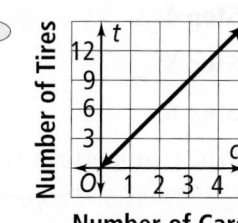

(I)

13. Last year, Conner paid 15% of his earnings in federal taxes. He paid $3000. Jose also paid 15% of his earnings in federal taxes, but he paid $3600. How much more did Jose earn than Conner?

 Ⓐ $4000   Ⓒ $20,000

 Ⓑ $6000   Ⓓ $24,000

14. The table shows the price of a bus ticket based on the number of miles traveled. Which equation represents the relationship between the ticket price p and the number of miles traveled m?

Miles	Price
100	$50
150	$70
200	$90
250	$110

 Ⓕ $p = 2m$

 Ⓖ $p = 0.5m$

 Ⓗ $p = 2m + 10$

 Ⓘ $p = 0.4m + 10$

15. During a trip, Josh recorded the amount of time it took him to travel the distances shown in the table below.

Time (hours)	2	5	7	8
Distance (miles)	60	150	210	240

Which equation represents the relationship between distance d and time t?

 Ⓐ $d = 30t$ Ⓒ $d = 30 + t$

 Ⓑ $t = 30d$ Ⓓ $t = d + 30$

16. A stepped-out solution is shown below.

$$3(3x - 1) - 3(5x - 3) = 4$$

Step 1 $9x - 3 - 15x + 9 = 4$

Step 2 $-6x + 6 = 4$

Step 3 $-6x + 6 - 6 = 4 - 6$

Step 4 $-6x = -2$

Step 5 $\dfrac{-6x}{-6} = \dfrac{-2}{-6}$

Step 6 $x = \dfrac{1}{3}$

Which property justifies Step 1?

 Ⓕ Division Property of Equality

 Ⓖ Subtraction Property of Equality

 Ⓗ Commutative Property

 Ⓘ Distributive Property

Constructed Response

17. Some two-lane rural roads in Texas have a speed limit of 75 mi/h. Convert this speed to km/h. Round to the nearest whole number. (1 mi ≈ 1.6 km)

18. When Paige left middle school and entered high school, her class size increased by 225%. There were 56 students in her middle school class. How many students are in her high school class?

19. The perimeter of a rectangle is given by the equation $2w + 33 = 54$. What is w, the width of the rectangle?

20. Pablo can wash 6 cars in 40 min. At this rate, how many cars can Pablo wash in 4 h?

21. A student performs an experiment to determine the boiling point of ethyl alcohol to be 75°C. The accepted boiling point of ethyl alcohol is 78°C. What is his percent error? Round to the nearest tenth.

22. The cost for using a phone card is 35 cents per call plus 25 cents per minute. Write an expression for the cost of a call that is n minutes long. A certain call costs $3.60. How many minutes long was the call? Show your work.

23. Travis sells black and white photos of cities across the country. Each photo's width is half its height. Write an equation to represent the area A of a photo given its height h. Use this equation to find the area of a photo that is 4 in. tall.

24. Carroll has a piece of fabric that is 4 yd long to make curtains. Each curtain requires a piece of fabric that is 16 in. long. How many curtains can Carroll make?

25. A rental car company charges $25.00 per day plus $.30 for every mile the car is driven. Dale rents a car while his own car is being repaired, and he only drives it to and from work each day. Dale drives 7 mi each way to and from work. Write an expression to represent Dale's cost of renting a car for d days. Dale rents the car for 4 days. How much does Dale owe for the rental?

Get Ready!

See Lesson 1-3 **Ordering Rational Numbers**

Complete each statement with $<$, $=$, or $>$.

1. $-3 \; \blacksquare \; -5$　　**2.** $7 \; \blacksquare \; \frac{14}{2}$　　**3.** $-8 \; \blacksquare \; -8.4$　　**4.** $-\frac{5}{2} \; \blacksquare \; 2.5$

See Lesson 1-5 **Absolute Value**

Simplify each expression.

5. $5 + |4 - 6|$　　　　**6.** $|30 - 28| - 6$　　　　**7.** $|-7 + 2| - 4$

See Lesson 2-1 **Solving One-Step Equations**

Solve each equation. Check your solution.

8. $x - 4 = -2$　　**9.** $b + 4 = 7$　　**10.** $-\frac{3}{4}y = 9$　　**11.** $\frac{m}{12} = 2.7$

12. $-8 + x = 15$　　**13.** $n - 7 = 22.5$　　**14.** $-\frac{12}{7}z = 48$　　**15.** $\frac{5y}{4} = -15$

See Lesson 2-2 **Solving Two-Step Equations**

Solve each equation. Check your solution.

16. $-5 + \frac{b}{4} = 7$　　**17.** $4.2m + 4 = 25$　　**18.** $-12 = 6 + \frac{3}{4}x$

19. $6 = -z - 4$　　**20.** $4m + 2.3 = 9.7$　　**21.** $\frac{5}{8}t - 7 = -22$

22. $-4.7 = 3y + 1.3$　　**23.** $12.2 = 5.3x - 3.7$　　**24.** $5 - \frac{1}{3}x = -15$

See Lessons 2-3 and 2-4 **Solving Multi-Step Equations**

Solve each equation. Check your solution.

25. $4t + 7 + 6t = -33$　　**26.** $2a + 5 = 9a - 16$　　**27.** $\frac{1}{3} + \frac{4y}{6} = \frac{2}{3}$

28. $6(y - 2) = 8 - 2y$　　**29.** $n + 3(n - 2) = 10.4$　　**30.** $\frac{1}{3}w + 3 = \frac{2}{3}w - 5$

Looking Ahead Vocabulary

31. You make a *compound* word, such as houseboat, by joining two words together. Why do you think $-4 < x < 7$ is called a *compound inequality*?

32. The *intersection* of two roads is the place where the roads cross. How would you define the *intersection* of two groups of objects?

CHAPTER 3

Solving Inequalities

Chapter Preview

3-1 **Inequalities and Their Graphs**

3-2 **Solving Inequalities Using Addition or Subtraction**

3-3 **Solving Inequalities Using Multiplication or Division**

3-4 **Solving Multi-Step Inequalities**

3-5 **Working With Sets**

3-6 **Compound Inequalities**

3-7 **Absolute Value Equations and Inequalities**

3-8 **Unions and Intersections of Sets**

BIG ideas

1 **Variable**

   Essential Question How do you represent relationships between quantities that are not equal?

2 **Equivalence**

   Essential Question Can inequalities that appear to be different be equivalent?

3 **Solving Equations and Inequalities**

   Essential Question How can you solve inequalities?

Vocabulary

English/Spanish Vocabulary Audio Online:

English	Spanish
complement of a set, p. 196	complemento de un conjunto
compound inequality, p. 200	desigualdade compuesta
disjoint sets, p. 215	conjuntos ajenos
empty set, p. 195	conjunto vacío
equivalent inequalities, p. 171	desigualdades equivalentes
intersection, p. 215	intersección
interval notation, p. 203	notación de intervalo
roster form, p. 194	lista
set-builder notation, p. 194	notación conjuntista
solution of an inequality, p. 165	solución de una desigualdad
union, p. 214	unión
universal set, p. 196	conjunto universal

DOMAINS

- Seeing Structure in Expressions
- Creating Equations
- Reasoning with Equations and Inequalities

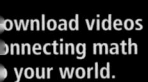
ownload videos
onnecting math
o your world.

teractive!
ry numbers,
aphs, and figures
explore math
ncepts.

e online
olve It will get
ou in gear for
ch lesson.

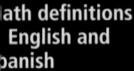
ath definitions
English and
panish

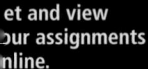
nline access
stepped-out
roblems aligned
Common Core

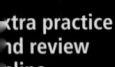
et and view
our assignments
nline.

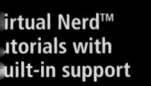
xtra practice
nd review
nline

irtual Nerd™
utorials with
uilt-in support

Common Core Performance Task

Planning for a Concession Stand

The athletic boosters for a local college raise money by selling popcorn at a concession stand. They charge customers $2.25 per box.

The popcorn machine and supplies (unpopped kernels, popping oil, and butter) are provided by a company that charges a fee of $250 per game plus $.15 per box of popcorn sold. The boosters must supply their own empty boxes to fill. Empty boxes are sold in packages of various quantities, as shown in the table below.

Empty Popcorn Boxes

Number of Boxes per Package	Price per Box
75	$.25
200	$.21
300	$.19
400	$.17

The boosters have 40 empty boxes on hand from the last game and will need to buy more for the next game. They know from previous experience that they can expect to sell no more than 310 boxes at each game.

Task Description

What is the least number of boxes of popcorn that the athletic boosters can sell at the next game to make a profit?

Connecting the Task to the Math Practices

MATHEMATICAL PRACTICES

As you complete the task, you'll apply several Standards for Mathematical Practice.

- You'll use an inequality that models the number of additional empty popcorn boxes needed for the next game. (MP 4)

- You'll manipulate symbols that represent quantities to solve an inequality. (MP 2)

Inequalities and Their Graphs

Common Core State Standards

Prepares for A-REI.B.3 Solve linear equations and inequalities in one variable, including equations with coefficients represented by letters.

MP 1, MP 2, MP 3, MP 4, MP 6

Objective To write, graph, and identify solutions of inequalities

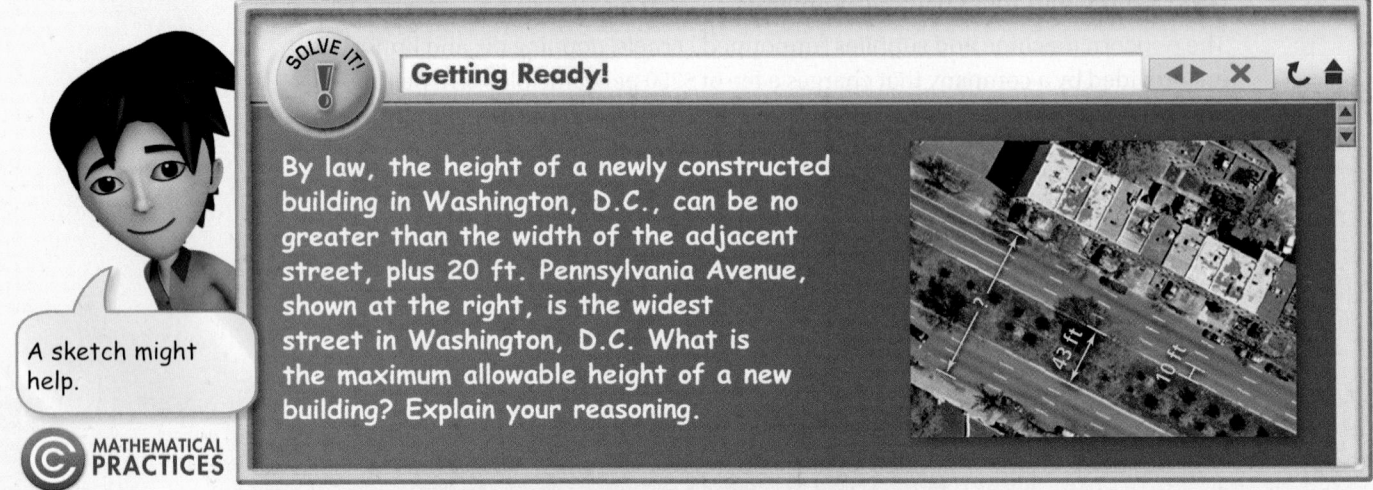

SOLVE IT!

Getting Ready!

By law, the height of a newly constructed building in Washington, D.C., can be no greater than the width of the adjacent street, plus 20 ft. Pennsylvania Avenue, shown at the right, is the widest street in Washington, D.C. What is the maximum allowable height of a new building? Explain your reasoning.

A sketch might help.

MATHEMATICAL PRACTICES

Lesson Vocabulary
• solution of an inequality

The Solve It involves comparing two quantities—the height of a building and the width of the street adjacent to it. You can use an inequality to compare such quantities.

Essential Understanding An inequality is a mathematical sentence that uses an inequality symbol to compare the values of two expressions. You can use a number line to visually represent the values that satisfy an inequality.

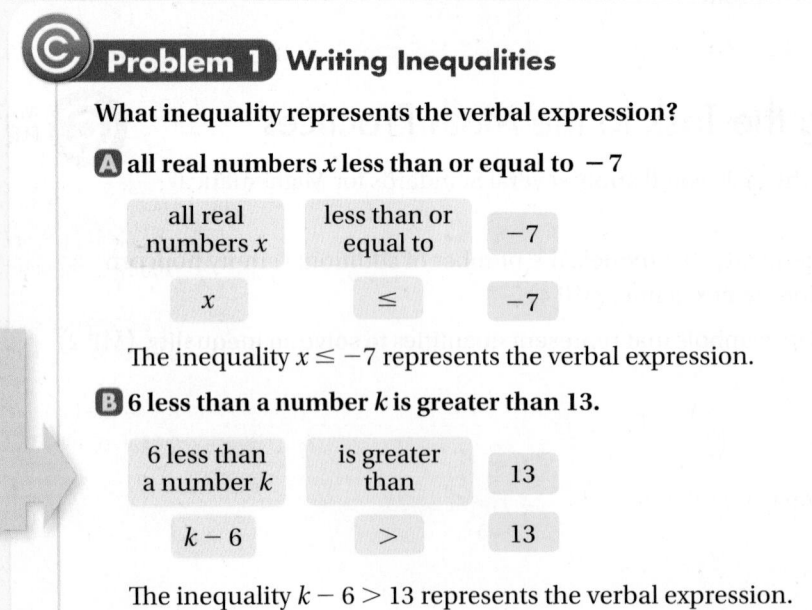

Problem 1 Writing Inequalities

What inequality represents the verbal expression?

A all real numbers x less than or equal to -7

all real numbers x	less than or equal to	-7
x	$\leq$	-7

The inequality $x \leq -7$ represents the verbal expression.

Think

Less than and *is less than* have different meanings. For example, "6 less than k" means $k - 6$, while "6 is less than k" means $6 < k$.

B 6 less than a number k is greater than 13.

6 less than a number k	is greater than	13
$k - 6$	$>$	13

The inequality $k - 6 > 13$ represents the verbal expression.

Got It? 1. What is an inequality that represents the verbal expression?

 Got It? 1. What is an inequality that represents the verbal expression?
   a. all real numbers p greater than or equal to 1.5
   b. The sum of t and 7 is less than -3.

A **solution of an inequality** is any number that makes the inequality true. The solutions of the inequality $x < 5$ are all real numbers x that are less than 5. You can evaluate an expression to determine whether a value is a solution of an inequality.

 Problem 2 **Identifying Solutions by Evaluating**

Is the number a solution of $2x + 1 > -3$?

A -3

$$2x + 1 > -3$$
$$2(-3) + 1 \overset{?}{>} -3 \quad \leftarrow \text{Substitute for } x. \rightarrow$$
$$-6 + 1 \overset{?}{>} -3 \quad \leftarrow \text{Simplify.} \rightarrow$$
$$-5 \not> -3 \quad \leftarrow \text{Compare.} \rightarrow$$

-3 does not make the original inequality true, so -3 is *not* a solution.

B -1

$$2x + 1 > -3$$
$$2(-1) + 1 \overset{?}{>} -3$$
$$-2 + 1 \overset{?}{>} -3$$
$$-1 > -3$$

-1 does make the original inequality true, so -1 is a solution.

Think

Is -1 the *only* solution to the inequality?
No. *Any* number that makes the original inequality true is a solution of the inequality. The solution -1 is one of an infinite number of solutions.

 Got It? 2. a. Consider the numbers $-1, 0, 1,$ and 3. Which are solutions of $13 - 7y \le 6$?
    b. Reasoning In Problem 2, how is the solution of the related equation $2x + 1 = -3$ related to the solutions of the inequality?

You can use a graph to indicate all of the solutions of an inequality.

Inequality   **Graph**

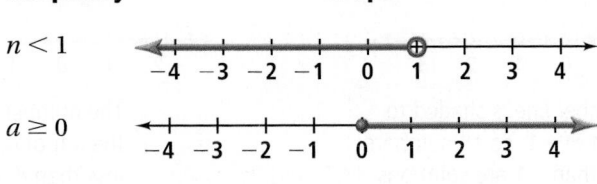

$n < 1$

The open dot shows that 1 is *not* a solution. Shade to the left of 1.

$a \ge 0$

The closed dot shows that 0 is a solution. Shade to the right of 0.

$f > -3$

The open dot shows that -3 is *not* a solution. Shade to the right of -3.

$-2 \ge x$

The closed dot shows that -2 is a solution. Shade to the left of -2.

You can also write $-2 \ge x$ as $x \le -2$.

 **Problem 3** Graphing an Inequality

What is the graph of $2 \geq a$?

Think

If 2 is greater than or equal to a, then a must be less than or equal to 2.

Write

$a \leq 2$

$a \leq 2$ means all real numbers a that are less than or equal to 2. Since 2 is a solution, draw a closed dot at 2.

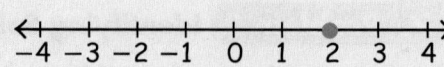

The numbers less than 2 are to the left of 2 on the number line. Shade to the left of 2.

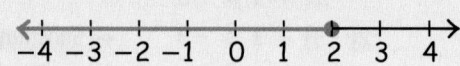

 Got It? **3.** What is the graph of each inequality?

     a. $x > -4$ **b.** $c < 0$ **c.** $3 \leq n$

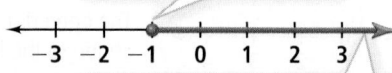 **Problem 4** Writing an Inequality From a Graph

What inequality represents the graph?

Plan

How do you know which inequality symbol to use?
Look at the arrow to see whether the solution is for quantities greater than or less than the endpoint. Look at the endpoint to see whether "equal to" is included in the solution.

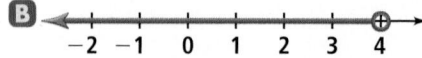

The closed dot means that -1 is a solution.

The open dot means that 4 is *not* a solution.

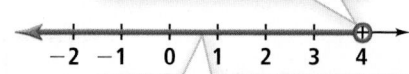

The number line is shaded to the right of -1, so all numbers greater than -1 are solutions.

The number line is shaded to the left of 4, so all numbers less than 4 are solutions.

The inequality $x \geq -1$ represents the graph.   The inequality $x < 4$ represents the graph.

 Got It? **4.** What inequality represents each graph?

    a.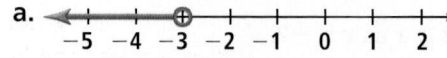

    b.

Problem 5 Writing Real-World Inequalities

What inequality describes the situation? Be sure to define a variable.

Plan

How do you know which inequality symbol to use?
The phrase "starting at $19.99" implies that the cost of a trail ride starts at $19.99 and goes up. So the cost is greater than or equal to 19.99.

A

Let c = the cost of a trail ride in dollars.

The sign indicates that $c \geq 19.99$.

B

Let s = a legal speed in miles per hour.

The sign indicates that $s \leq 8$.

  Got It? **5. Reasoning** In part (B) of Problem 5, can the speed be *all* real numbers less than or equal to 8? Explain.

---

take note

Concept Summary **Representing Inequalities**

Words	Symbols	Graph
x is less than 3.	$x < 3$	
x is greater than -2.	$x > -2$	
x is less than or equal to 0.	$x \leq 0$	
x is greater than or equal to 1.	$x \geq 1$	

 Lesson Check

Do you know HOW?

1. What algebraic inequality represents all real numbers y that are greater than or equal to 12?

2. Is the number a solution of $6x - 3 \geq 10$?
   a. -1 **b.** 0   **c.** 3   **d.** 4

3. What is the graph of $2 > p$?

4. What inequality represents the graph?

Do you UNDERSTAND? MATHEMATICAL PRACTICES

5. **Vocabulary** How do you decide whether a number is a solution of an inequality?

6. **Compare and Contrast** What are some situations you could model with $x \geq 0$? How do they differ from situations you could model with $x > 0$?

7. **Open-Ended** What is a real-world situation that you can represent with the following graph?

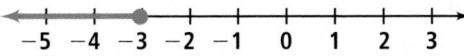

Practice and Problem-Solving Exercises  MATHEMATICAL PRACTICES

 **Practice**   Write an inequality that represents each verbal expression.   ◀ **See Problem 1.**

8. v is greater than or equal to 5.   **9.** b is less than 4.

10. 3 less than g is less than or equal to 17.   **11.** The quotient of k and 9 is greater than $\frac{1}{3}$.

Determine whether each number is a solution of the given inequality.   ◀ **See Problem 2.**

12. $3y - 8 > 22$ **a.** 2   **b.** 0   **c.** 5

13. $8m - 6 \le 10$ **a.** 2   **b.** 3   **c.** −1

14. $4x + 2 < -6$ **a.** 0   **b.** −2   **c.** 1

15. $\frac{6 - n}{n} \ge 11$ **a.** 0.5   **b.** 2   **c.** 4

16. $m(m - 3) < 54$ **a.** −10   **b.** 0   **c.** 9

Match each inequality with its graph.   ◀ **See Problem 3.**

17. $x < -1$ **18.** $x \ge -1$ **19.** $-1 < x$ **20.** $-1 \ge x$

Graph each inequality.

21. $y > 2$ **22.** $t < -4$ **23.** $z \le -5$ **24.** $v \ge -2$

25. $-3 < f$ **26.** $-\frac{9}{4} \le c$ **27.** $8 \ge b$ **28.** $5.75 > d$

Write an inequality for each graph.   ◀ **See Problem 4.**

29. 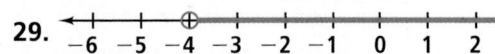   **30.**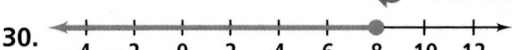

31. 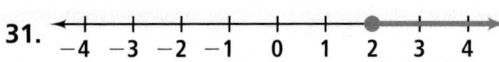   **32.**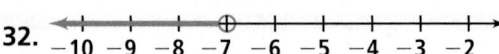

33. 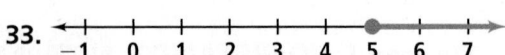   **34.**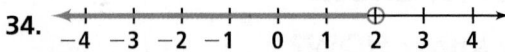

Define a variable and write an inequality to model each situation.   ◀ **See Problem 5.**

35. The restaurant can seat at most 172 people.

36. A person must be at least 35 years old to be elected President of the United States.

37. A light bulb can be no more than 75 watts to be safely used in this light fixture.

38. At least 475 students attended the orchestra concert Thursday night.

39. A law clerk has earned more than $20,000 since being hired.

© **40. Error Analysis** A student claims that the inequality $3x + 1 > 0$ is always true because multiplying a number by 3 and then adding 1 to the result always produces a number greater than 0. Explain the student's error.

© **41. Open-Ended** Describe a situation that you can model with $x \geq 25$.

42. Ticket Sales Suppose your school plans a musical. The director's goal is ticket sales of at least $4500. Adult tickets are $7.50 and student tickets are $5.00. Let a represent the number of adult tickets and s represent the number of student tickets. Which inequality represents the director's goal?

    Ⓐ $5a + 7.5s < 4500$ Ⓒ $7.5a + 5s \leq 4500$

    Ⓑ $7.5a + 5s > 4500$ Ⓓ $7.5a + 5s \geq 4500$

 43. Physics According to Albert Einstein's special theory of relativity, no object can travel faster than the speed of light, which is approximately 186,000 mi/s. What is an inequality that represents this information?

Write each inequality in words.

44. $n < 5$ **45.** $b > 0$ **46.** $7 \geq x$ **47.** $z \geq 25.6$

48. $4 > q$ **49.** $21 \geq m$ **50.** $35 \geq w$ **51.** $g - 2 < 7$

52. $a \leq 3$ **53.** $6 + r > -2$ **54.** $8 \leq h$ **55.** $1.2 > k$

56. Class Party You are making muffins for a class party. You need 2 cups of flour to make a pan of 12 muffins. You have a 5-lb bag of flour, which contains 18 cups. What is an inequality that represents the possible numbers of muffins you can make?

© **57. Writing** Explain what the phrases *no more than* and *no less than* mean when writing inequalities that model real-world situations.

Use the map at the right for Exercises 58 and 59.

© **58. Think About a Plan** You plan to go from Portland to Tucson. Let x be the distance in miles of any flight between Portland and Tucson. What is a true statement about the mileage of any route from Portland to Tucson? Assume that no route visits the same city more than once and that each route has no more than one layover.
- How many routes exist between Portland and Tucson? What are they? Which route is the shortest?
- Can you write an inequality that represents the mileage of any route from Portland to Tucson?

59. Air Travel Your travel agent is making plans for you to go from San Diego to Seattle. A direct flight is not available. Option A consists of flights from San Diego to Boise to Seattle. Option B consists of flights from San Diego to Las Vegas to Seattle. What inequality compares the flight distances of these two options?

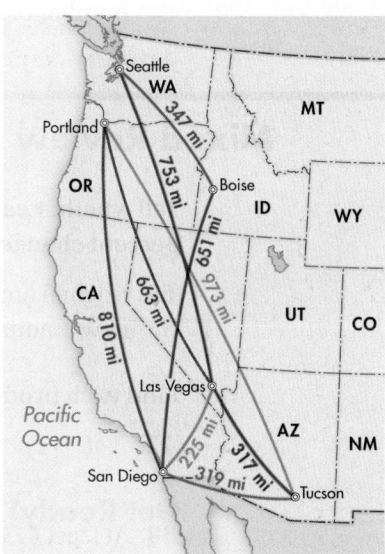

60. Reasoning Which is the correct graph of $-3 < -x$? Explain.

Ⓐ
$$\begin{array}{ccccccccc} +&+&+&+&+&+&+&\oplus&\to \\ -4&-3&-2&-1&0&1&2&3&4 \end{array}$$

Ⓒ
$$\begin{array}{cccccccccc} \leftarrow&+&\oplus&+&+&+&+&+&+&\to \\ &-4&-3&-2&-1&0&1&2&3&4 \end{array}$$

Ⓑ
$$\begin{array}{cccccccccc} +&\oplus&+&+&+&+&+&+&\to \\ -4&-3&-2&-1&0&1&2&3&4 \end{array}$$

Ⓓ
$$\begin{array}{cccccccccc} \leftarrow&+&+&+&+&+&+&\oplus&+&\to \\ &-4&-3&-2&-1&0&1&2&3&4 \end{array}$$

Ⓒ **61. Reasoning** Give a counterexample for this statement: If $x > y$, then $x^2 > y^2$.

Ⓒ **62. Reasoning** Describe the numbers x and y such that if $x > y$, then $x^2 = y^2$.

Graph on a number line.

63. all values of p such that $p > -3$ and $p \le 3$ **64.** all values of q such that $q < -2$ or $q > 5$

Standardized Test Prep

65. Which inequality has the same solutions as $k > 6$?

Ⓐ $k < -6$ Ⓑ $k < 6$ Ⓒ $6 < k$ Ⓓ $-k > -6$

66. What is the value of the expression $\dfrac{2^3 \cdot 4 - (-3)^2}{(-3)^2 + 4 \cdot 5}$?

Ⓕ $\dfrac{23}{29}$ Ⓖ $\dfrac{41}{29}$ Ⓗ $\dfrac{23}{11}$ Ⓘ $\dfrac{41}{11}$

67. Last season, Betsy scored 36 points. This is 8 less than twice the number of points that Amy scored. How many points did Amy score?

Ⓐ 22   Ⓑ 36   Ⓒ 44   Ⓓ 72

68. At an airport, a runway 1263 ft long is being repaired. The project foreman reports that less than one third of the job is complete. Draw a diagram of the runway that shows how much of it has been repaired. What is an inequality that represents the number of feet f that still need to be repaired?

Mixed Review

Tell whether each percent change is an *increase* or *decrease*. Then find the percent change. Round to the nearest percent.   ◀ See Lesson 2-10.

69. original amount: $10
new amount: $12

70. original amount: 20 in.
new amount: 18 in.

71. original amount: 36°
new amount: 12°

Find each product or quotient.   ◀ See Lesson 1-6.

72. $-4(-11)$ **73.** $\dfrac{5}{6} \cdot \left(-\dfrac{1}{4}\right)$ **74.** $-3.9 \div 1.3$ **75.** $\dfrac{4}{7} \div \left(-\dfrac{2}{5}\right)$

Get Ready! **To prepare for Lesson 3-2, do Exercises 76–79.**

Solve each equation.   ◀ See Lesson 2-1.

76. $y - 5 = 6$ **77.** $p - 4 = -6$ **78.** $v + 5 = -6$ **79.** $k + \dfrac{2}{3} = \dfrac{5}{9}$

Solving Inequalities Using Addition or Subtraction

© **Common Core State Standards**

A-REI.B.3 Solve linear equations and inequalities in one variable, including equations with coefficients represented by letters. **Also A-CED.A.1**

MP 1, MP 2, MP 3, MP 4

Objective To use addition or subtraction to solve inequalities

Make sure you understand the problem. Which numbers do you need to use?

© **MATHEMATICAL PRACTICES**

SOLVE IT!

Getting Ready!

◀▶ ✕ ↻ ⬆

In a U.S. presidential election, a candidate must win at least 270 out of 538 total electoral votes to be declared the winner. Suppose a candidate has earned 238 electoral votes in states outside the southeastern U.S.

What is the least number of states in the southeastern U.S. that the candidate could win and still become president? What are these states? Justify your reasoning.

Southeastern United States

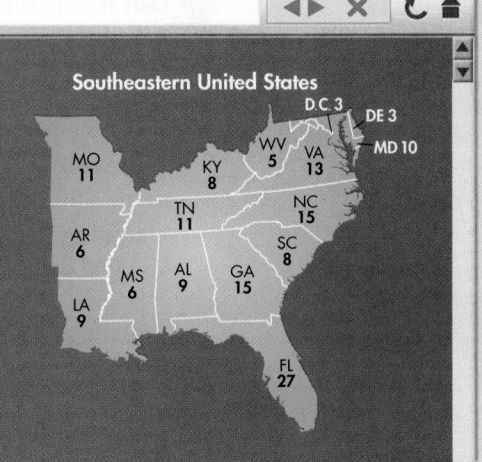

Lesson Vocabulary
• equivalent inequalities

You can model the situation in the Solve It with the inequality $238 + x \geq 270$, where x represents the number of electoral votes needed. You can find its solutions using one of the *properties of inequality*.

Essential Understanding Just as you used properties of equality to solve equations in Chapter 2, you can use properties of inequality to solve inequalities.

The Addition Property of Inequality is shown below. Applying this property to an inequality produces an equivalent inequality. **Equivalent inequalities** are inequalities that have the same solutions.

take note

Key Concept Addition Property of Inequality

Words

Let a, b, and c be real numbers.

If $a > b$, then $a + c > b + c$.

If $a < b$, then $a + c < b + c$.

This property is also true for $\geq$ and $\leq$.

Diagram

The diagram below illustrates one way to think about this rule.

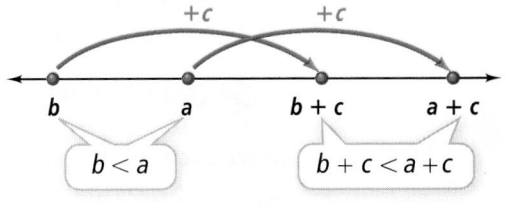

Examples

$5 > 4$, so $5 + 3 > 4 + 3$.

$-2 < 0$, so $-2 + 1 < 0 + 1$.

Think

Do you know how to solve a related problem?
Yes. You know how to solve the related equation $x - 15 = -12$ using the Addition Property of Equality.

 Problem 1 Using the Addition Property of Inequality

What are the solutions of $x - 15 > -12$? Graph the solutions.

$$x - 15 > -12$$
$$x - 15 + 15 > -12 + 15 \qquad \text{Add 15 to each side.}$$
$$x > 3 \qquad \text{Simplify.}$$

The solutions of $x > 3$ are all real numbers greater than 3.

(number line from −1 to 4 with open circle at 3, shaded to the right)

 Got It? 1. What are the solutions of $n - 5 < -3$? Graph the solutions.

In Problem 1, how can you check that the final inequality $x > 3$ describes the solutions of the original inequality $x - 15 > -12$? The original inequality has infinitely many solutions, so you cannot check them all. However, you can verify that the final inequality is correct by checking its endpoint and the direction of the inequality symbol. You will do this in Problem 2.

 Problem 2 Solving an Inequality and Checking Solutions

What are the solutions of $10 \geq x - 3$? Graph and check the solutions.

Think

Write

You need to isolate x. Undo subtraction by adding the same number to each side.

$$10 \geq x - 3$$
$$10 + 3 \geq x - 3 + 3$$
$$13 \geq x$$

The graph of $13 \geq x$ (or $x \leq 13$) contains 13 and all real numbers to the left of 13.

(number line from 2 to 14 with closed circle at 13, shaded to the left)

To check the endpoint 13 of $13 \geq x$, make sure that 13 is the solution of the related *equation* $10 = x - 3$.

$$10 = x - 3$$
$$10 \overset{?}{=} 13 - 3$$
$$10 = 10 \checkmark$$

To check the inequality symbol of $13 \geq x$, make sure that a number *less than* 13 is a solution of the original inequality.

$$10 \geq x - 3$$
$$10 \overset{?}{\geq} 12 - 3$$
$$10 \geq 9 \checkmark$$

 Got It? 2. What are the solutions of $m - 11 \geq -2$? Graph and check the solutions.

The Subtraction Property of Inequality is shown below.

take note

Key Concept   Subtraction Property of Inequality

Words

Let a, b, and c be real numbers.
If $a > b$, then $a - c > b - c$.
If $a < b$, then $a - c < b - c$.
This property is also true for $\geq$ and $\leq$.

Examples

$-3 < 5$, so $-3 - 2 < 5 - 2$.
$3 > -4$, so $3 - 1 > -4 - 1$.

Diagram

The diagram below illustrates one way to think about this rule.

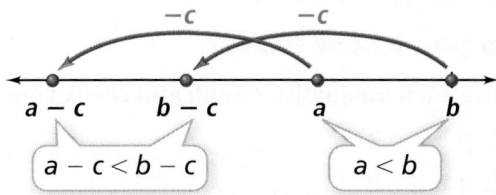

$a - c < b - c$ $a < b$

Problem 3   Using the Subtraction Property of Inequality

Think

How is this inequality different from others you have seen before?
The expression $t + 6$ involves addition, so you have to use subtraction to undo the addition and isolate the variable.

What are the solutions of $t + 6 > -4$? Graph the solutions.

$$t + 6 > -4$$

$$t + 6 - 6 > -4 - 6 \qquad \text{Subtract 6 from each side.}$$

$$t > -10 \qquad \text{Simplify.}$$

(number line from -10 to 0, open circle at -10, marks at $-10, -8, -6, -4, -2, 0$)

The solutions of $t > -10$ are all real numbers to the right of -10.

Got It? 3. What are the solutions of $-1 \geq y + 12$? Graph the solutions.

Problem 4   Writing and Solving an Inequality STEM

Think

How do you know which inequality symbol to use?
Words and phrases like *at most*, *no more than*, and *maximum* may indicate that you should use $\leq$.

Computers The hard drive on your computer has a capacity of 120 gigabytes (GB). You have used 85 GB. You want to save some home videos to your hard drive. What are the possible sizes of the home video collection you can save?

Relate   current hard drive space used   plus   size of videos   is at most   hard drive capacity

Define   Let v = the size of the video collection.

Write   85   + v $\leq$ 120

$$85 + v \leq 120$$

$$85 + v - 85 \leq 120 - 85 \qquad \text{Subtract 85 from each side.}$$

$$v \leq 35 \qquad \text{Simplify.}$$

The home video collection can be any size less than or equal to 35 GB.

Got It? **4. a.** A club has a goal to sell at least 25 plants for a fundraiser. Club members sell 8 plants on Wednesday and 9 plants on Thursday. What are the possible numbers of plants the club can sell on Friday to meet their goal?

b. Reasoning Can you use the same inequality symbol to represent phrases like *at least*, *no less than*, and *greater than or equal to*? Explain.

 Lesson Check

Do you know HOW?

Solve each inequality. Graph and check your solutions.

1. $p - 4 < 1$

2. $8 \geq d - 2$

3. $y + 5 < -7$

4. $4 + c > 7$

5. A cyclist takes her bicycle on a chairlift to the top of a slope. The chairlift can safely carry 680 lb. The cyclist weighs 124 lb, and the bicycle weighs 32 lb. What are the possible additional weights the chairlift can safely carry?

Do you UNDERSTAND?

6. Writing How can you use the addition and subtraction properties of inequality to produce equivalent inequalities?

7. Reasoning What can you do to the first inequality in each pair in order to get the second inequality?

   a. $x + 4 \leq 10; x \leq 6$

   b. $m - 1 > 3; m > 4$

   c. $5 \geq 3 + n; 2 \geq n$

   d. $-6 < y - 2; -4 < y$

8. Compare and Contrast Suppose you solve the two inequalities $y + 4 \leq 6$ and $y - 4 \leq 6$. How are your methods of solving the inequalities similar? How are they different?

 **Practice and Problem-Solving Exercises**

 **Practice**   Tell what number you would add to each side of the inequality to solve the inequality.    **See Problems 1 and 2.**

   9. $f - 6 \geq -3$ **10.** $1 < d - 7$ **11.** $a - 3.3 \geq 2.6$ **12.** $5 > -18 + m$

Solve each inequality. Graph and check your solutions.

   13. $y - 2 > 11$ **14.** $v - 4 < -3$ **15.** $-6 > c - 2$ **16.** $8 \leq f - 4$

   17. $t - 4 \geq -7$ **18.** $s - 10 \leq 1$ **19.** $9 < p - 3$ **20.** $-3 \geq x - 1$

   21. $0 < -\frac{1}{3} + f$ **22.** $z - 12 \leq -4$ **23.** $-\frac{3}{4} > r - \frac{3}{4}$ **24.** $y - 1 \geq 1.5$

   25. $4.3 > -0.4 + s$ **26.** $-2.5 > n - 0.9$ **27.** $c - \frac{4}{7} < \frac{6}{7}$ **28.** $p - 1\frac{1}{2} > 1\frac{1}{2}$

Tell what number you would subtract from each side of the inequality to solve the inequality.   **See Problem 3.**

   29. $x + 3 > 0$ **30.** $9 < \frac{7}{5} + s$ **31.** $6.8 \geq m + 4.2$ **32.** $\ell + \frac{1}{3} \geq \frac{7}{3}$

Solve each inequality. Graph and check your solutions.

33. $x + 5 \le 10$

34. $n + 6 > -2$

35. $2 < 9 + c$

36. $-1 \ge 5 + b$

37. $\frac{1}{4} + a \ge -\frac{3}{4}$

38. $8.6 + z < 14$

39. $\frac{1}{3} < n + 3$

40. $3.8 \ge b + 4$

41. $\frac{3}{5} + d \ge -\frac{2}{5}$

42. Fitness Your goal is to take at least 10,000 steps per day. According to your pedometer, you have walked 5274 steps. Write and solve an inequality to find the possible numbers of steps you can take to reach your goal.  **See Problem 4.**

43. Fundraising The environmental club is selling indoor herb gardens for Earth Day. Each member is encouraged to sell at least 10 gardens. You sell 3 gardens on Monday and 4 gardens on Tuesday. Write and solve an inequality to find the possible numbers of gardens you can sell to reach your goal.

44. Monthly Budget You earn $250 per month from your part-time job. You are in a kayaking club that costs $20 per month, and you save at least $100 each month. Write and solve an inequality to find the possible amounts you have left to spend each month.

 **Apply**

Tell what you can do to the first inequality in order to get the second.

45. $36 \le -4 + y$; $40 \le y$

46. $9 + b > 24$; $b > 15$

47. $m - \frac{1}{2} < \frac{3}{8}$; $m < \frac{7}{8}$

Tell whether the two inequalities in each pair are equivalent.

48. $45 \le -5 + z$; $40 \le z$

49. $7 + c > 33$; $c > 26$

50. $n - \frac{1}{4} < \frac{5}{4}$; $n < 1$

You can draw a model to represent an inequality. For example, the model below represents the inequality $85 + v < 120$. Draw a model to represent each inequality below.

```
|--------------- 120 ---------------|
|-------------------------------|------|
|           85                  |  v   |
|-------------------------------|------|
```

51. $17 + x < 51$

52. $12 + y > 18$

53. $-3 + m \le 13$

Solve each inequality. Justify each step.

54. $y - 4 + 2 \ge 10$

55. $\frac{3}{5} + d \le 2\frac{3}{5}$

56. $z - 1.4 < 3.9$

57. $-5 > p - \frac{1}{5}$

58. $a + 5.2 < -4.6$

59. $-3.1 > z - 1.9$

60. $\frac{5}{8} + v - \frac{7}{16} > 0$

61. $-4p - 2 + 5p > 10$

62. $5y + 5 - 4y < 8$

63. $h - \frac{1}{8} \ge -1$

64. $8v - 7v - 3 \ge -6$

65. $5 \ge m - \frac{7}{16}$

66. Government The U.S. Senate is composed of 2 senators from each of the 50 states. In order for a treaty to be ratified, at least two thirds of the senators present must approve the treaty. Suppose all senators are present and 48 of them have voted in favor of a treaty. What are the possible numbers of additional senators who must vote in favor of the treaty in order to ratify it?

67. a. If $56 + 58 = t$, does $t = 56 + 58$?

    b. If $56 + 58 \leq r$, is $r \leq 56 + 58$? Justify your answer.

    c. Explain the differences between these two examples.

68. Think About a Plan You want to qualify for a regional diving competition. At today's competition, you must score at least 53 points. Out of a possible 10 points, your scores on each of the first 5 dives are shown at the right. What scores can you earn on the armstand dive that will qualify you for the regional diving competition?

OFFICIAL SCORE CARD	
DIVE	SCORE
Front Dive	9.8
Back Dive	8.9
Reverse Dive	8.4
Inward Dive	8.2
Twisting Dive	9.4
Armstand Dive	?

    • What information do you know? What information do you need?

    • How might writing and solving an inequality help you?

    • What does the solution of the inequality mean in terms of the original situation?

69. Qualifying Scores To enter a competition, students must score a total of at least 450 points on five qualifying tests. Each test is worth 100 points. On the first four tests, your scores were 94, 88, 79, and 95. What are three possible scores you can earn on the last test to enter the competition?

Error Analysis Describe and correct the error in solving each inequality or in graphing the solution.

70.

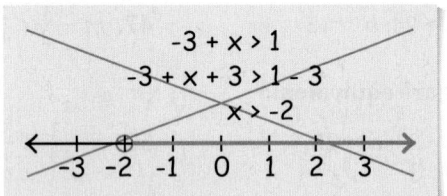

71.

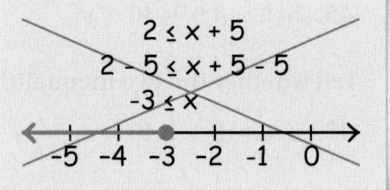

72. a. Open-Ended Use each of the inequality symbols $<$, $\leq$, $>$ and $\geq$ to write four inequalities involving addition or subtraction.

    b. Solve each inequality from part (a) and graph your solutions.

73. a. Mallory says that she can solve the inequality $a + 3.2 \geq 8.6$ by replacing a with 5, 6, and 7. When $a = 5$, the inequality is false. When $a = 6$ and when $a = 7$, the inequality is true. So Mallory says that the solution is $a \geq 6$. Is her reasoning correct? Justify your answer.

    b. Reasoning Explain why substituting values into the inequality does not guarantee that Mallory's solution is correct.

74. Geometry Suppose a triangle has side lengths a, b, and c, where c is the length of the longest side. You can use the following equation and inequalities to determine whether the triangle is right, acute, or obtuse.

    • If $a^2 + b^2 = c^2$, then the triangle is right.

    • If $a^2 + b^2 > c^2$, then the triangle is acute.

    • If $a^2 + b^2 < c^2$, then the triangle is obtuse.

Classify each triangle with the following side lengths as *right*, *acute*, or *obtuse*.

    a. 4 in., 5 in., 6 in.   **b.** 3 cm, 4 cm, 5 cm   **c.** 10 m, 15 m, 20 m

75. Banking To avoid a service fee, your checking account balance must be at least $500 at the end of each month. Your current balance is $536.45. You use your debit card to spend $125.19. What possible amounts can you deposit into your account by the end of the month to avoid paying the service fee?

 **Challenge**

Reasoning Decide whether each inequality is true for all real numbers. If the inequality is not true, give a counterexample.

76. $x + y > x - y$

77. If $x \leq y$, then $x + w \leq y + w$.

78. If $w < z$, then $x - w > x - z$.

79. If $x > y$, then $x > y + w$.

 80. Reasoning Find real numbers a, b, c, and d for which it is true that $a < b$ and $c < d$, but it is not true that $a - c < b - d$.

Apply What You've Learned

 **MATHEMATICAL PRACTICES**
MP 4

Look back at the information on page 163 about the athletic boosters' concession stand.

a. Write an inequality that relates the number of empty boxes the boosters need to buy for the next game, the number of empty boxes on hand, and the maximum number of boxes of popcorn the boosters expect to sell.

b. Solve your inequality from part (a). How can you interpret your result in the context of the situation?

c. The table from page 163 is shown again below. Which packages of empty boxes can the athletic boosters buy in order to have enough for the next game? (Consider that they might buy more than one package of empty boxes. Also note that once the boosters have enough empty boxes, they do not need to buy any additional packages.)

Empty Popcorn Boxes

Number of Boxes per Package	Price per Box
75	$.25
200	$.21
300	$.19
400	$.17

3-3

Solving Inequalities Using Multiplication or Division

© Common Core State Standards

A-CED.A.1 Create . . . inequalities in one variable and use them to solve problems . . . **Also N-Q.A.2, A-REI.B.3**

MP 1, MP 2, MP 3, MP 4, MP 7

Objective To use multiplication or division to solve inequalities

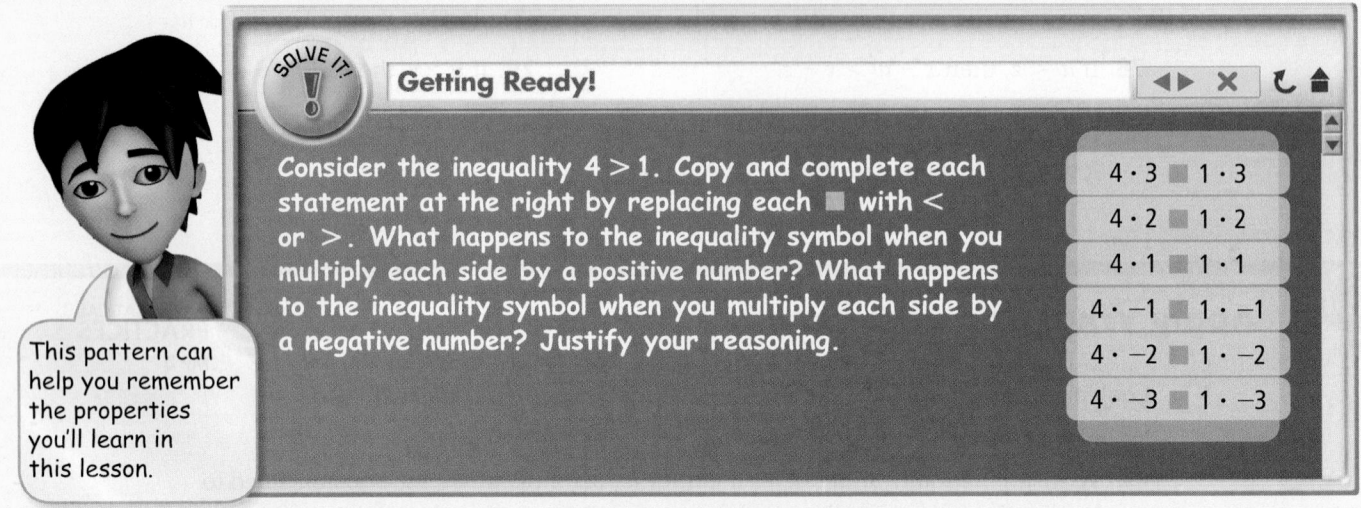

This pattern can help you remember the properties you'll learn in this lesson.

© MATHEMATICAL PRACTICES In the Solve It, you may have noticed that multiplying both sides of an inequality by a negative number affects the inequality symbol.

Essential Understanding Just as you used multiplication and division to solve equations in Chapter 2, you can use multiplication and division to solve inequalities.

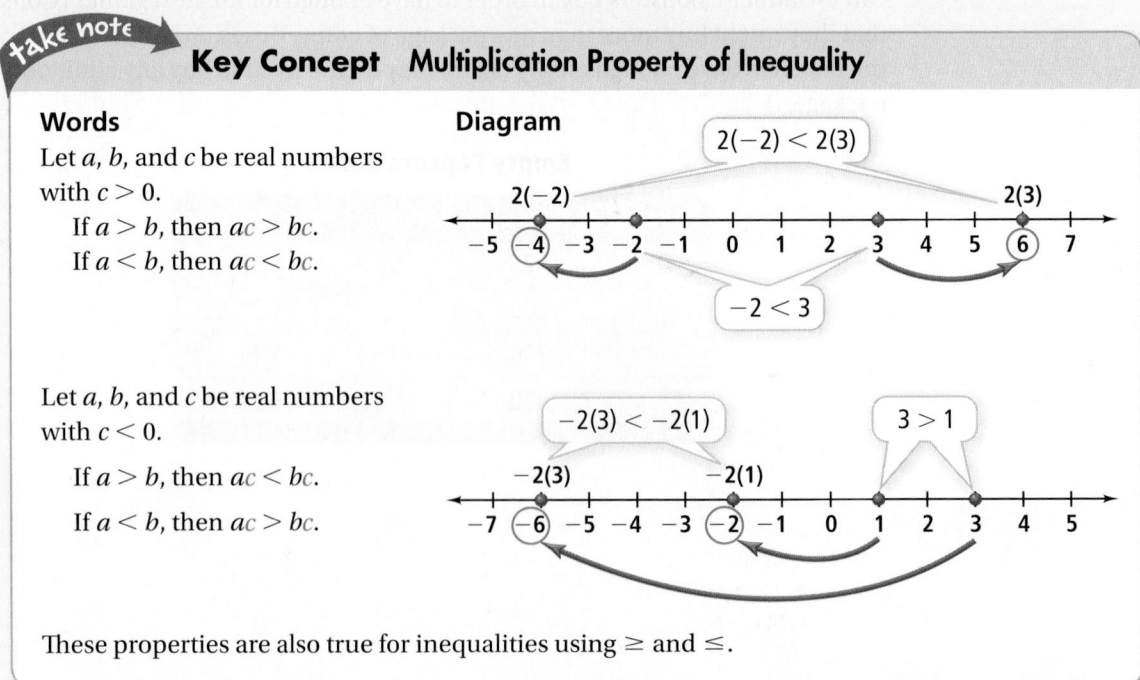

take note

Key Concept   Multiplication Property of Inequality

Words

Let a, b, and c be real numbers with $c > 0$.

If $a > b$, then $ac > bc$.

If $a < b$, then $ac < bc$.

Diagram

$2(-2) < 2(3)$

$2(-2)$

$2(3)$

$-5\ (-4)\ -3\ -2\ -1\ 0\ 1\ 2\ 3\ 4\ 5\ (6)\ 7$

$-2 < 3$

Let a, b, and c be real numbers with $c < 0$.

If $a > b$, then $ac < bc$.

If $a < b$, then $ac > bc$.

$-2(3) < -2(1)$

$3 > 1$

$-2(3)$

$-2(1)$

$-7\ (-6)\ -5\ -4\ -3\ (-2)\ -1\ 0\ 1\ 2\ 3\ 4\ 5$

These properties are also true for inequalities using $\geq$ and $\leq$.

Here's Why It Works Multiplying or dividing each side of an inequality by a negative number changes the meaning of the inequality. You need to reverse the inequality symbol to make the inequality true. Here is an example:

$$3 > 1$$

$-2(3) \; \blacksquare \; -2(1)$ Multiply by -2.

$-6 \; \blacksquare \; -2$ Simplify.

$-6 < -2$ Reverse the inequality symbol to make the inequality true.

Problem 1 **Multiplying by a Positive Number**

What are the solutions of $\frac{x}{3} < -2$? Graph the solutions.

Think

Why multiply by 3?
You can multiply by any multiple of 3. But multiplying by 3 isolates the variable.

$$\frac{x}{3} < -2$$

$3\left(\dfrac{x}{3}\right) < 3(-2)$ Multiply each side by 3.

$x < -6$ Simplify.

$$\begin{array}{ccccccccc} \leftarrow & + & + & + & \oplus & + & + & + & + & \rightarrow \\ -9 & -8 & -7 & -6 & -5 & -4 & -3 & -2 \end{array}$$

Got It? **1.** What are the solutions of $\frac{c}{8} > \frac{1}{4}$? Graph the solutions.

Problem 2 **Multiplying by a Negative Number**

What are the solutions of $-\frac{3}{4}w \geq 3$? Graph and check the solutions.

Write

Think

Multiplying by a negative number changes the inequality. Reverse the inequality symbol to make it a true statement.

$$-\frac{3}{4}w \geq 3$$

$$-\frac{4}{3}\left(-\frac{3}{4}w\right) \leq -\frac{4}{3}(3)$$

$$w \leq -4$$

$$\begin{array}{ccccccccc} \leftarrow & + & + & \bullet & + & + & + & + & + & \rightarrow \\ -6 & -5 & -4 & -3 & -2 & -1 & 0 & 1 \end{array}$$

To check the endpoint of $w \leq -4$, make sure that -4 is the solution of the equation $-\frac{3}{4}w = 3$.

$$-\frac{3}{4}(-4) \overset{?}{=} 3$$

$$3 = 3 \; ✔$$

To check the inequality symbol of $w \leq -4$, make sure that a number less than -4 is a solution of the original inequality.

$$-\frac{3}{4}(-5) \overset{?}{\geq} 3$$

$$3\frac{3}{4} \geq 3 \; ✔$$

Got It? **2.** What are the solutions of $-\frac{n}{3} < -1$? Graph and check.

Solving inequalities using division is similar to solving inequalities using multiplication. If you divide each side of an inequality by a negative number, you need to reverse the direction of the inequality symbol.

take note

Key Concept Division Property of Inequality

Let a, b, and c be real numbers with $c > 0$.

If $a > b$, then $\frac{a}{c} > \frac{b}{c}$.

If $a < b$, then $\frac{a}{c} < \frac{b}{c}$.

Let a, b, and c be real numbers with $c < 0$.

If $a > b$, then $\frac{a}{c} < \frac{b}{c}$.

If $a < b$, then $\frac{a}{c} > \frac{b}{c}$.

Examples

$6 > 3$, so $\frac{6}{3} > \frac{3}{3}$.

$9 < 12$, so $\frac{9}{3} < \frac{12}{3}$.

$6 > 3$, so $\frac{6}{-3} < \frac{3}{-3}$.

$9 < 12$, so $\frac{9}{-3} > \frac{12}{-3}$.

These properties are also true for inequalities using $\geq$ and $\leq$.

© **Problem 3** Dividing by a Positive Number

Part-Time Job You walk dogs in your neighborhood after school. You earn $4.50 per dog. How many dogs do you need to walk to earn at least $75?

Relate | cost per dog | times | number of dogs | is at least | amount wanted |

Define Let d = the number of dogs.

Write   4.50   • d $\geq$ 75

$$4.50d \geq 75$$
$$\frac{4.50d}{4.50} \geq \frac{75}{4.50} \quad \text{Divide each side by 4.50.}$$
$$d \geq 16\tfrac{2}{3} \quad \text{Simplify.}$$

Think

What types of solutions make sense for this situation?
Only whole-number solutions make sense because you cannot walk part of a dog.

However, since d represents the number of dogs, it must be a positive integer. So you must walk at least 17 dogs to earn at least $75.

© **Got It?** **3. a.** A student club plans to buy food for a soup kitchen. A case of vegetables costs $10.68. The club can spend at most $50 for this project. What are the possible numbers of cases the club can buy?

  b. Reasoning In Problem 3, why do you round to the greater whole number?

Problem 4 Dividing by a Negative Number

Think

How is this inequality different from the one in Problem 3?
The coefficient is negative. You can still use the properties of inequality to solve, but pay attention to the direction of the symbol.

What are the solutions of $-9y \le 63$? Graph the solutions.

$$-9y \le 63$$

$$\frac{-9y}{-9} \ge \frac{63}{-9} \qquad \text{Divide each side by } -9. \text{ Reverse the inequality symbol.}$$

$$y \ge -7 \qquad \text{Simplify each side.}$$

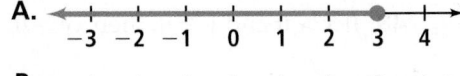

 Got It? **4.** What are the solutions of $-5x > -10$? Graph the solutions.

Lesson Check

Do you know HOW?

Match the inequality with its graph.

1. $x + 2 > -1$

2. $-\frac{x}{3} < -1$

3. $x - 4 \le -1$

4. $-3x \ge 9$

A.

B.

C.

D.

Do you UNDERSTAND?  MATHEMATICAL PRACTICES

5. Which operation would you use to solve the inequality? Explain.

a. $1 \le -\frac{x}{2}$ **b.** $y - 4 > -5$ **c.** $-6w < -36$

6. Error Analysis Describe and correct the error in the solution.

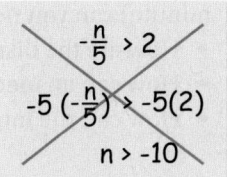

$$-\frac{n}{5} > 2$$

$$-5\left(-\frac{n}{5}\right) > -5(2)$$

$$n > -10$$

Practice and Problem-Solving Exercises  MATHEMATICAL PRACTICES

 **Practice**   Solve each inequality. Graph and check your solution.   ◀ See Problems 1 and 2.

7. $\frac{x}{5} \ge -2$ **8.** $\frac{w}{6} < 1$ **9.** $4 > \frac{p}{8}$ **10.** $1 \le -\frac{5}{4}y$

11. $-\frac{v}{2} \ge 1.5$ **12.** $-3 < \frac{x}{3}$ **13.** $-7 \le \frac{7}{3}x$ **14.** $8 > \frac{2}{3}k$

15. $0 \le -\frac{3}{11}m$ **16.** $-\frac{3}{2}b < 6$ **17.** $-\frac{3}{4} < -\frac{3}{8}m$ **18.** $-5 \ge -\frac{5}{9}y$

Solve each inequality. Graph and check your solution.   ◀ See Problems 3 and 4.

19. $3m \ge 6$ **20.** $4t < -12$ **21.** $-30 > -5c$ **22.** $-4w \le 20$

23. $11z > -33$ **24.** $56 < -7d$ **25.** $18b \le -3$ **26.** $-7y \ge 17$

27. $-5h < 65$ **28.** $8t \le 64$ **29.** $63 \ge 7q$ **30.** $-12x > 132$

31. Text Messages Text messages cost $.15 each. You can spend no more than $10. How many text messages can you send?

32. Aquarium Fish Tetras cost $3.99 each. You can spend at most $25. How many tetras can you buy for your aquarium?

 **Apply**   **Write four solutions to each inequality.**

33. $\frac{x}{2} \le -1$

34. $\frac{r}{3} \ge -4$

35. $-1 \ge \frac{r}{3}$

36. $0.5 > \frac{1}{2}c$

Tell what you can do to the first inequality in order to get the second.

37. $-\frac{c}{4} > 3; c < -12$

38. $\frac{n}{5} \le -2; n \le -10$

39. $5z > -25; z > -5$

40. $\frac{3}{4}b \le 3; b \le 4$

Replace each ▨ with the number that makes the inequalities equivalent.

41. ▨$s > 14; s < -7$

42. ▨$x \ge 25; x \le -5$

43. $-8u \le$ ▨$; u \ge -0.5$

44. $-2a >$ ▨$; a < -9$

Determine whether each statement is *always, sometimes,* or *never* true. Justify your answer.

45. If $x > 3$ and $y < 1$, then $xy > 0$.

46. If $x < 0$ and $y < 0$, then $xy > 0$.

47. If $x \ge 0$ and $y > 1$, then $xy > 0$.

48. If $x > 0$ and $y \ge 0$, then $xy > 0$.

49. Think About a Plan A friend calls you and asks you to meet at the park 2 mi away in 25 min. You set off on your skateboard after the call. At what speeds (in miles per minute) can you ride your skateboard to be at the park in at most 25 min?
  - How are the distance you travel, your speed, and time related?
  - How can an inequality help you solve the problem?
  - How can the model below help you solve the problem?

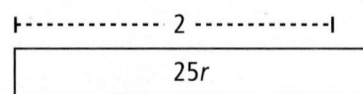

Solve each inequality. Justify each step.

50. $-4.5 > 9p$

51. $-1 \ge \frac{t}{3}$

52. $\frac{3}{4}n < 4$

53. $0.5 \le \frac{1}{2}c$

54. $-8u < 4$

55. $\frac{n}{5} \le -2$

56. $-12 > 4a$

57. $1 < -\frac{5}{7}s$

58. Trip A family is taking a cross-country trip by car. They drive at an average speed of 55 mi/h, and their goal is to travel at least 400 mi/day. How many hours per day do they need to drive?

59. Lunch You have $30. You are going to buy a sandwich and a drink for yourself and two friends from the menu at the right. You will spend the remainder on snacks. What is the least number of snacks you might buy? What is the greatest number of snacks you might buy? Explain.

60. **Open-Ended** Write an inequality that can be solved by dividing by a negative number and has the solution $x < \frac{1}{3}$.

61. **Patterns** Consider the pattern of inequalities $\frac{x}{2} < 10, \frac{x}{3} < 10, \frac{x}{4} < 10, \ldots$ Suppose a real number a is a solution of a certain inequality in the pattern. What other inequalities in the pattern do you know have a as a solution? Explain.

62. **Reasoning** If $ax \le ay$ and $ay \le az$, is $x \le z$? Explain.

Challenge

63. **Basketball** A company sells men's basketballs with a circumference of 29.5 in. They also sell youth basketballs with a circumference of 27.75 in. The company has cube-shaped packaging boxes with edges that are either 8 in., 9 in., or 10 in. long. What is the smallest box in which each ball can be packaged?

STEM 64. **Construction** A contractor is building a rectangular walkway $3\frac{1}{3}$ ft wide by 35 ft long using square cement pavers. Each paver has an area of $\frac{4}{9}$ ft². What is the least number of pavers he needs to make the walkway?

Standardized Test Prep

SAT/ACT

65. The mayor of Renee's town chose 160 students from her school to attend a city debate. This amount is no more than $\frac{1}{4}$ of the students in Renee's school. What is the least possible number of students that attend Renee's school?

Ⓐ 40   Ⓑ 160   Ⓒ 320   Ⓓ 640

66. An art teacher has a box of 100 markers. The teacher gives 7 markers to each student in the class and has 16 markers left over. How many students are in the class?

Ⓕ 11   Ⓖ 12   Ⓗ 13   Ⓘ 14

Short Response

67. The width of a rectangle is 3 in. shorter than the length. The perimeter of the rectangle is 18 in. What is the length of the rectangle? Show your work.

Mixed Review

Solve each inequality.   **See Lesson 3-2.**

68. $x + 5 \le -6$ 69. $y - 4.7 \ge 8.9$ 70. $q - 5 < 0$

71. $\frac{1}{2} > \frac{3}{4} + c$ 72. $-\frac{2}{3} < b + \frac{1}{3}$ 73. $y - 21 \le 54$

Get Ready! To prepare for Lesson 3-4, do Exercises 74–76.

Solve each equation.   **See Lesson 2-3.**

74. $-x + 8 + 4x = 14$ 75. $-6(2y + 2) = 12$ 76. $0.5t + 3.5 - 2.5t = 1.5t$

More Algebraic Properties

 Common Core State Standards

Prepares for A-REI.B.3 Solve linear equations and inequalities in one variable, including equations with coefficients represented by letters.

MP 2

The following properties can help you understand algebraic relationships.

Reflexive, Symmetric, and Transitive Properties of Equality

For all real numbers a, b, and c:

Reflexive Property	**Examples**
$a = a$	$5x = 5x$, $\$1 = \$1$
Symmetric Property	
If $a = b$, then $b = a$.	If $15 = 3t$, then $3t = 15$.
	If 1 pair = 2 socks, then 2 socks = 1 pair.
Transitive Property	
If $a = b$ and $b = c$, then $a = c$.	If $d = 3y$ and $3y = 6$, then $d = 6$.
	If 36 in. = 3 ft and 3 ft = 1 yd, then 36 in. = 1 yd.

Transitive Property of Inequality

For all real numbers a, b, and c, if $a < b$ and $b < c$, then $a < c$.

Examples If $8x < 7$ and $7 < y$, then $8x < y$.
If 1 cup < 1 qt and 1 qt < 1 gal, then 1 cup < 1 gal.

Example

Use the property given in parentheses to complete each statement.

A If $7x < y$ and $y < z + 2$, then $7x < \blacksquare$. (Transitive Property of Inequality)
    If $7x < y$ and $y < z + 2$, then $7x < z + 2$.

B If 2000 lb = 1 ton, then 1 ton = __?__ . (Symmetric Property)
    If 2000 lb = 1 ton, then 1 ton = 2000 lb.

Exercises

Name the property that each statement illustrates.

1. If $3.8 = n$, then $n = 3.8$.   **2.** 6 in. = 6 in.   **3.** If $x = 7$ and $7 = 5 + 2$, then $x = 5 + 2$.

4. If math class is earlier than art class and art class is earlier than history class, then math class is earlier than history class.

5. Complete the following sentence. If Amy is shorter than Greg and Greg is shorter than Lisa, then Amy is shorter than __?__ .

Modeling Multi-Step Inequalities

Common Core State Standards

Prepares for A-REI.B.3 Solve linear equations and inequalities in one variable, including equations with coefficients represented by letters.

MP 7

Sometimes you need to perform two or more steps to solve an inequality. Models can help you understand how to solve multi-step inequalities.

Activity

Model and solve $2x - 3 < 1$.

Inequality	Model	Think
$2x - 3 < 1$	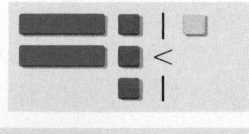	The tiles model the inequality.
$2x - 3 + 3 < 1 + 3$		Add 3 yellow tiles to each side.
$2x < 4$	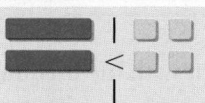	Simplify by removing the zero pairs.
$\frac{2x}{2} < \frac{4}{2}$	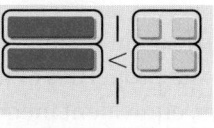	Divide each side into two equal groups.
$x < 2$	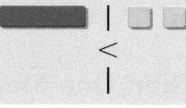	Each green tile is less than two yellow tiles, so $x < 2$.

Exercises

Write an inequality for each model. Use tiles to solve each inequality.

1.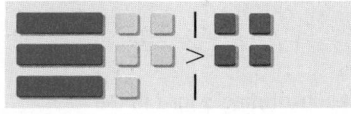

2.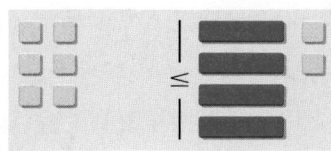

Use tiles to model and solve each inequality.

3. $2n - 5 \geq 3$

4. $-9 > 4x - 1$

5. $3w + 4 < -5$

6. $z + 6 \leq 2z + 2$

7. $3m + 7 \geq m - 5$

8. $5b + 6 > 3b - 2$

3-4 Solving Multi-Step Inequalities

 Common Core State Standards

A-REI.B.3 Solve linear equations and inequalities in one variable, including equations with coefficients represented by letters. **Also A-CED.A.1**

MP 1, MP 2, MP 3, MP 4

Objectives To solve multi-step inequalities

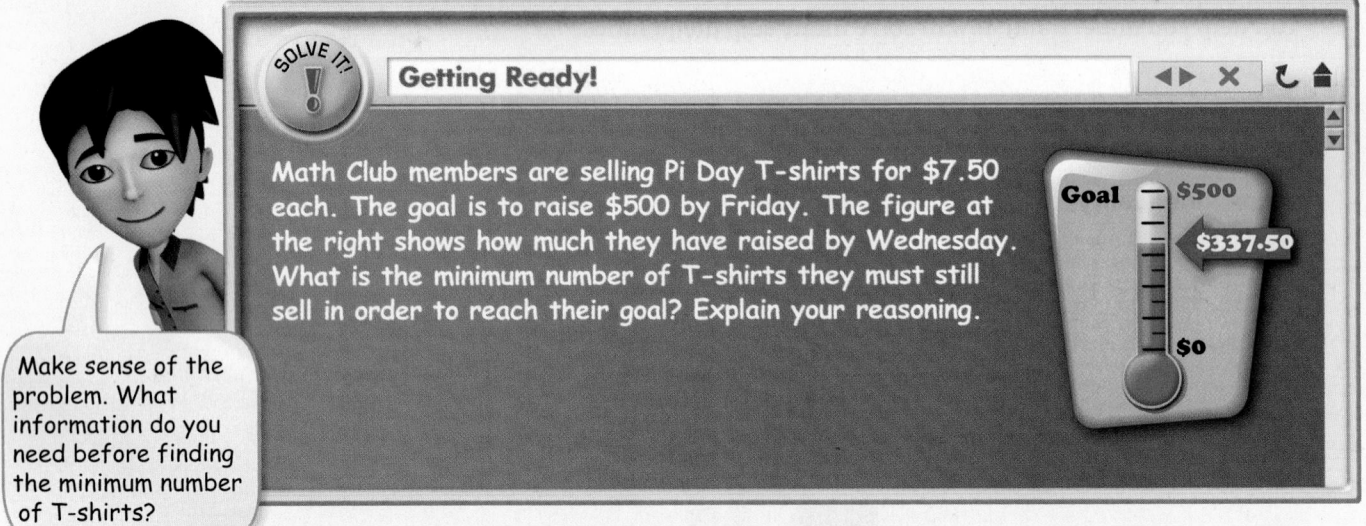

SOLVE IT!

Getting Ready! ◄► ✕ ↻ ⬆

Math Club members are selling Pi Day T-shirts for $7.50 each. The goal is to raise $500 by Friday. The figure at the right shows how much they have raised by Wednesday. What is the minimum number of T-shirts they must still sell in order to reach their goal? Explain your reasoning.

Goal — $500
◄ $337.50
$0

Make sense of the problem. What information do you need before finding the minimum number of T-shirts?

 **MATHEMATICAL PRACTICES**

You can model the situation in the Solve It with the inequality $337.50 + 7.50x \geq 500$. In this lesson, you will learn how to write and solve multi-step inequalities like this one.

Essential Understanding You solve a multi-step inequality in the same way you solve a one-step inequality. You use the properties of inequality to transform the original inequality into a series of simpler, equivalent inequalities.

Problem 1 Using More Than One Step

What are the solutions of $9 + 4t > 21$? Check the solutions.

$$9 + 4t > 21$$

$9 + 4t - 9 > 21 - 9$ Subtract 9 from each side.

$4t > 12$ Simplify.

$\dfrac{4t}{4} > \dfrac{12}{4}$ Divide each side by 4.

$t > 3$ Simplify.

Plan

How can you check the solutions?
Check the endpoint, 3. Then choose a value greater than 3 and check the inequality symbol.

Check $9 + 4(3) \stackrel{?}{=} 21$ Check the endpoint of $t > 3$ by substituting 3 for t in the related equation.

$21 = 21$ ✔   Simplify.

$9 + 4(4) \stackrel{?}{=} 21$ Check the inequality symbol of $t > 3$ by substituting 4 for t in the original inequality.

$25 > 21$ ✔   Simplify.

Got It? **1.** What are the solutions of the inequality? Check your solutions.

    a. $-6a - 7 \leq 17$ **b.** $-4 < 5 - 3n$ **c.** $50 > 0.8x + 30$

You can adapt familiar formulas to write inequalities. You use the real-world situation to determine which inequality symbol to use.

 **Problem 2** **Writing and Solving a Multi-Step Inequality**

Geometry **In a community garden, you want to fence in a vegetable garden that is adjacent to your friend's garden. You have at most 42 ft of fence. What are the possible lengths of your garden?**

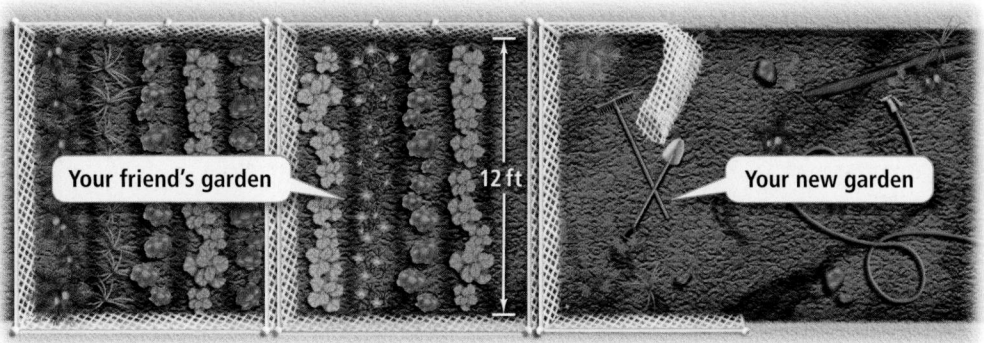

Your friend's garden   12 ft   Your new garden

Relate   Since the fence will surround the garden, you can use the perimeter formula $P = 2\ell + 2w$.

twice the length	plus	twice the width	is at most	the amount of fence

Define   Let $\ell =$ the length of the garden.

Write 2ℓ $+$ $2(12)$ $\leq$ 42

$$2\ell + 2(12) \leq 42$$

$$2\ell + 24 \leq 42 \qquad \text{Simplify.}$$

$$2\ell + 24 - 24 \leq 42 - 24 \qquad \text{Subtract 24 from each side.}$$

$$2\ell \leq 18 \qquad \text{Simplify.}$$

$$\frac{2\ell}{2} \leq \frac{18}{2} \qquad \text{Divide each side by 2.}$$

$$\ell \leq 9 \qquad \text{Simplify.}$$

The length of the garden must be 9 ft or less.

 Got It? **2.** You want to make a rectangular banner that is 18 ft long. You have no more than 48 ft of trim for the banner. What are the possible widths of the banner?

Think

You can use reasoning and *guess-and-check* to solve the problem. If either 9 or 10 is a solution, at least one other answer choice would also be a solution. So, eliminate 9 and 10 as possible answers. Guess that either 8 or 11 is correct and check your guess.

 Problem 3 Using the Distributive Property

Multiple Choice Which is a solution of $3(t + 1) - 4t \geq -5$?

  (A) 8   (B) 9   (C) 10   (D) 11

$$3(t + 1) - 4t \geq -5$$

$$3t + 3 - 4t \geq -5 \qquad \text{Distributive Property}$$

$$-t + 3 \geq -5 \qquad \text{Combine like terms.}$$

$$-t + 3 - 3 \geq -5 - 3 \qquad \text{Subtract 3 from each side.}$$

$$-t \geq -8 \qquad \text{Simplify.}$$

$$\frac{-t}{-1} \leq \frac{-8}{-1} \qquad \text{Divide each side by } -1. \text{ Reverse the inequality symbol.}$$

$$t \leq 8 \qquad \text{Simplify.}$$

8 is a solution of the inequality $t \leq 8$. The correct answer is A.

 Got It? **3.** What are the solutions of $15 \leq 5 - 2(4m + 7)$? Check your solutions.

Some inequalities have variables on both sides of the inequality symbol. You need to gather the variable terms on one side of the inequality and the constant terms on the other side.

 Problem 4 Solving an Inequality With Variables on Both Sides

What are the solutions of $6n - 1 > 3n + 8$?

Think

Why subtract 3n instead of 6n from each side of the inequality?

You can subtract either $3n$ or $6n$ from each side. However, subtracting $3n$ gives you a variable term with a positive coefficient.

$$6n - 1 > 3n + 8$$

$$6n - 1 - 3n > 3n + 8 - 3n \qquad \text{To gather variables on the left, subtract } 3n \text{ from each side.}$$

$$3n - 1 > 8 \qquad \text{Simplify.}$$

$$3n - 1 + 1 > 8 + 1 \qquad \text{To gather the constants on the right, add 1 to each side.}$$

$$3n > 9 \qquad \text{Simplify.}$$

$$\frac{3n}{3} > \frac{9}{3} \qquad \text{Divide each side by 3.}$$

$$n > 3 \qquad \text{Simplify.}$$

© ✓ **Got It?** **4. a.** What are the solutions of $3b + 12 > 27 - 2b$? Check your solutions.

   b. Reasoning The first step in solving Problem 4 was to subtract $3n$ from each side of the inequality. What else could have been the first step in solving the inequality? Explain.

Sometimes solving an inequality gives a statement that is *always* true, such as $4 > 1$. In that case, the solutions are all real numbers. If the statement is *never* true, as is $9 \leq -5$, then the inequality has no solution.

 Problem 5 Inequalities With Special Solutions

Think

Is there another way to solve this inequality?
Yes. Instead of using the Distributive Property, you can first divide each side by 2.

A **What are the solutions of $10 - 8a \geq 2(5 - 4a)$?**

$$10 - 8a \geq 2(5 - 4a)$$

$10 - 8a \geq 10 - 8a$	Distributive Property
$10 - 8a + 8a \geq 10 - 8a + 8a$	Add $8a$ to each side.
$10 \geq 10$	Simplify.

Since the inequality $10 \geq 10$ is always true, the solutions of $10 - 8a \geq 2(5 - 4a)$ are all real numbers.

B **What are the solutions of $6m - 5 > 7m + 7 - m$?**

$$6m - 5 > 7m + 7 - m$$

$6m - 5 > 6m + 7$	Simplify.
$6m - 5 - 6m > 6m + 7 - 6m$	Subtract $6m$ from each side.
$-5 > 7$	Simplify.

Think

Without solving, how can you tell that this inequality has no solution?
The variable terms on each side of the inequality are equal, but -5 is *not* greater than 7.

Since the inequality $-5 > 7$ is never true, the inequality $6m - 5 > 7m + 7 - m$ has no solution.

 Got It? **5.** What are the solutions of each inequality?

      a. $9 + 5n \leq 5n - 1$ **b.** $8 + 6x \geq 7x + 2 - x$

Lesson Check

Do you know HOW?

Solve each inequality, if possible. If the inequality has no solution, write *no solution*. If the solutions are all real numbers, write *all real numbers*.

1. $7 + 6a > 19$

2. $2(t + 2) - 3t \geq -1$

3. $6z - 15 < 4z + 11$

4. $18x - 5 \leq 3(6x - 2)$

5. The perimeter of a rectangle is at most 24 cm. Two opposite sides are both 4 cm long. What are the possible lengths of the other two sides?

Do you UNDERSTAND?

MATHEMATICAL PRACTICES

6. Reasoning How can you tell that the inequality $3t + 1 > 3t + 2$ has no solution just by looking at the terms in the inequality?

7. Reasoning Can you solve the inequality $2(x - 3) \leq 10$ *without* using the Distributive Property? Explain.

8. Error Analysis Your friend says that the solutions of the inequality $-2(3 - x) > 2x - 6$ are all real numbers. Do you agree with your friend? Explain. What if the inequality symbol were $\geq$?

Practice and Problem-Solving Exercises

 MATHEMATICAL PRACTICES

 **Practice**

Solve each inequality. Check your solutions.

See Problem 1.

9. $5f + 7 \leq 22$

10. $6n - 3 > -18$

11. $-5y - 2 < 8$

12. $6 - 3p \geq -9$

13. $9 \leq -12 + 6r$

14. $6 \leq 12 + 4j$

Write and solve an inequality.

See Problem 2.

15. Family Trip On a trip from Buffalo, New York, to St. Augustine, Florida, a family wants to travel at least 250 mi in the first 5 h of driving. What should their average speed be in order to meet this goal?

16. Geometry An isosceles triangle has at least two congruent sides. The perimeter of a certain isosceles triangle is at most 12 in. The length of each of the two congruent sides is 5 in. What are the possible lengths of the remaining side?

Solve each inequality.

See Problems 3 and 4.

17. $3(k - 5) + 9k \geq -3$

18. $-(7c - 18) - 2c > 0$

19. $-3(j + 3) + 9j < -15$

20. $-4 \leq 4(6y - 12) - 2y$

21. $30 > -(5z + 15) + 10z$

22. $-4(d + 5) - 3d > 8$

23. $4x + 3 < 3x + 6$

24. $4v + 8 \geq 6v + 10$

25. $5f + 8 \geq 2 + 6f$

26. $6 - 3p \leq 4 - p$

27. $3m - 4 \leq 6m + 11$

28. $4t + 17 > 7 + 5t$

Solve each inequality, if possible. If the inequality has no solution, write _no solution_. If the solutions are all real numbers, write _all real numbers_.

See Problem 5.

29. $-3(w - 3) \geq 9 - 3w$

30. $-5r + 6 \leq -5(r + 2)$

31. $-2(6 + s) \geq -15 - 2s$

32. $9 + 2x < 7 + 2(x - 3)$

33. $2(n - 8) < 16 + 2n$

34. $6w - 4 \leq 2(3w + 6)$

 **Apply**

Solve each inequality, if possible. If the inequality has no solution, write _no solution_. If the solutions are all real numbers, write _all real numbers_.

35. $-3(x - 3) \geq 5 - 4x$

36. $3s + 6 \leq -5(s + 2)$

37. $3(2 + t) \geq 15 - 2t$

38. $\frac{4}{3}s - 3 < s + \frac{2}{3} - \frac{1}{3}s$

39. $4 - 2n \leq 5 - n + 1$

40. $-2(0.5 - 4t) \geq -3(4 - 3.5t)$

41. $4(a - 2) - 6a \leq -9$

42. $4(3n - 1) \geq 2(n + 3)$

43. $17 - (4k - 2) \geq 2(k + 3)$

44. Think About a Plan Your cell phone plan costs $39.99 per month plus $.15 for each text message you send or receive. You have at most $45 to spend on your cell phone bill. What is the maximum number of text messages that you can send or receive next month?

- What information do you know? What information do you need?
- What inequality can you use to find the maximum number of text messages that you can send or receive?
- What are the solutions of the inequality? Are they reasonable?

45. Rental Rates The student council wants to rent a ballroom for the junior prom. The ballroom's rental rate is $1500 for 3 h and $125 for each additional half hour. Suppose the student council raises $2125. What is the maximum number of hours for which they can rent the ballroom?

Ⓒ 46. Writing Suppose a friend is having difficulty solving $3.75(q - 5) > 4(q + 3)$. Explain how to solve the inequality, showing all the necessary steps and identifying the properties you would use.

STEM 47. Biology The average normal body temperature for humans is 98.6°F. An abnormal increase in body temperature is classified as hyperthermia, or fever. Which inequality represents the body temperature in degrees Celsius of a person with hyperthermia? (*Hint*: To convert from degrees Celsius *C* to degrees Fahrenheit *F*, use the formula $F = \frac{9}{5}C + 32$.)

Ⓐ $\frac{9}{5}C + 32 \geq 98.6$ Ⓑ $\frac{9}{5}C + 32 \leq 98.6$ Ⓒ $\frac{9}{5}C + 32 < 98.6$ Ⓓ $\frac{9}{5}C + 32 > 98.6$

Ⓒ 48. Open-Ended Write two different inequalities that you can solve by subtracting 3 from each side and then dividing each side by -5. Solve each inequality.

49. a. Solve $6v + 5 \leq 9v - 7$ by gathering the variable terms on the left side and the constant terms on the right side of the inequality.
    b. Solve $6v + 5 \leq 9v - 7$ by gathering the constant terms on the left side and the variable terms on the right side of the inequality.
    c. Compare the results of parts (a) and (b).
    d. Which method do you prefer? Explain.

Ⓒ 50. Mental Math Determine whether each inequality is *always true* or *never true*.
    a. $5s + 7 \geq 7 + 5s$ **b.** $4t + 6 > 4t - 3$ **c.** $5(m + 2) < 5m - 4$

51. Commission A sales associate in a shoe store earns $325 per week, plus a commission equal to 4% of her sales. This week her goal is to earn at least $475. At least how many dollars' worth of shoes must she sell in order to reach her goal?

Ⓒ 52. A student uses the table below to help solve $7y + 2 < 6(4 - y)$.

y	7y + 2	<	6(4 − y)
0.5	7(0.5) + 2 = 5.5	True	6(4 − 0.5) = 21
1	7(1) + 2 = 9	True	6(4 − 1) = 18
1.5	7(1.5) + 2 = 12.5	True	6(4 − 1.5) = 15
2	7(2) + 2 = 16	False	6(4 − 2) = 12

    a. Reasoning Based on the table, would you expect the solution of $7y + 2 < 6(4 - y)$ to be of the form $y < c$ or $y > c$, where *c* is a real number? Explain.
    b. Estimate Based on the table, estimate the value of *c*.
    c. Solve the inequality. Compare the actual solution to your estimated solution.

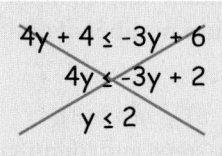 Error Analysis Describe and correct the error in each solution.

53.

$4y + 4 \leq -3y + 6$

$4y \leq -3y + 2$

$y \leq 2$

54.

$5(p + 3) > 4p + 2$

$5p + 3 > 4p + 2$

$5p > 4p - 1$

$p > -1$

 Challenge

55. Geometry The base of a triangle is 12 in. Its height is $(x + 6)$ in. Its area is no more than 72 in.^{2}. What are the possible integer values of x?

56. Part-Time Jobs You can earn money by tutoring for $8 per hour and by walking dogs for $7.50 per hour. You have 15 h available to work. What is the greatest number of hours you can spend walking dogs and still make at least $115?

57. Freight Handling The elevator of a building can safely carry no more than 4000 lb. A worker moves supplies in 50-lb boxes from the loading dock to the fourth floor of the building. The worker weighs 210 lb. The cart he uses weighs 95 lb.
a. What is the greatest number of boxes he can move in one trip?
b. The worker needs to deliver 275 boxes. How many trips must he make?

Apply What You've Learned

 MATHEMATICAL **PRACTICES**

MP 2

Look back at the information on page 163 about the athletic boosters' concession stand. In part (c) of the Apply What You've Learned section in Lesson 3-2, you listed possible combinations of packages of empty boxes the boosters can buy in order to have enough empty boxes for the next game.

a. Consider the possibility that the athletic boosters buy four packages of 75 empty boxes to augment their supply of 40 that they already have on hand. Let x be the number of boxes of popcorn that the boosters sell at the next game. Write an inequality that models the boosters making a profit (that is, where net revenue exceeds total costs).

b. Solve your inequality from part (a). Interpret your solution in terms of the situation.

Do you know HOW?

Write an inequality that represents each verbal expression or graph.

1. all real numbers y greater than or equal to 12

2. 8 more than a number m is less than 5.

3.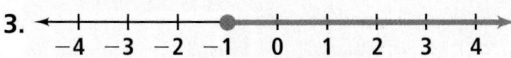

4. The product of -3 and t is greater than 11.

5. c less than 7 is less than or equal to -3.

6.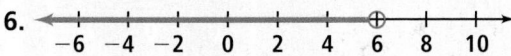

7. A cat weighs no more than 8 lb.

Solve each inequality. Graph the solutions.

8. $8d + 2 < 5d - 7$

9. $2n + 1 \geq -3$

10. $-2x + 7 \leq 45$

11. $5s - 3 + 1 < 8$

12. $5(3p - 2) > 50$

13. $\dfrac{y}{2} < -3$

14. $6 \geq -\dfrac{4}{5}n$

15. $-1.5d > 18$

16. A baseball team wants to collect at least 160 cans of food for an upcoming food drive. Team members brought 42 cans of food on Monday and 65 cans of food on Wednesday. Write and solve an inequality to describe how many cans of food the team must collect on Friday to make or exceed their goal.

17. Suppose you earn $7.25 per hour working part-time for a florist. Write and solve an inequality to find how many *full* hours you must work to earn at least $125.

Solve each inequality, if possible. If the inequality has no solution, write *no solution*. If the solutions are all real numbers, write *all real numbers*.

18. $7 - 6b \leq 19$

19. $15f + 9 > 3(5f + 3)$

20. $6z - 15 \geq 4z + 11$

21. $-3(4 - m) \geq 2(4m - 14)$

22. $8z + 5 - 2z \leq 3(2z + 1) + 2$

23. The cheerleaders are making a rectangular banner for a football game. The length of the banner is 30 ft. The cheerleaders can use no more than 96 ft of trim around the outside of the banner. What are the possible widths of the banner?

Do you UNDERSTAND?

© **24. a. Error Analysis** A student claims that the graph below represents the solutions of the inequality $-3 < x$. What error did the student make?

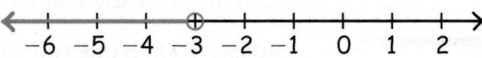

b. What inequality is actually represented by the graph?

Decide whether the two inequalities in each pair are equivalent. Explain.

25. $36 \leq -4 + y; \ 40 \leq y$

26. $9 + b > 24; \ b > 33$

27. $m - \dfrac{1}{2} < \dfrac{3}{8}; \ m < \dfrac{7}{8}$

© **28. Reasoning** A local gym offers a trial membership for 3 months. It discounts the regular monthly fee x by $25. If the total cost of the trial membership is less than $100, you will consider signing up. What inequality can you use to determine whether you should sign up?

3-5 Working With Sets

Common Core State Standards

A-REI.B.3 Solve linear equations and inequalities in one variable, including equations with coefficients represented by letters.

MP 1, MP 2, MP 6

Objectives To write sets and identify subsets
To find the complement of a set

Getting Ready!

Most numbers on a telephone keypad correspond to a set of letters. Suppose you're sending a text message. You press 4, 6, 6, and 3, in that order—one number for each letter. What word might your telephone think you're trying to spell? What words could you be trying to spell? Explain your reasoning.

How can you organize the choice of letters to help you solve this problem?

MATHEMATICAL PRACTICES

Recall from Lesson 1-3 that a *set* is a collection of distinct elements. A *subset* contains elements from a set. For example, the number 6 on the telephone keypad corresponds to the set {M, N, O}. The set {M, O} is one subset of this set.

Essential Understanding Sets are the basis of mathematical language. You can write sets in different ways and form smaller sets of elements from a larger set. You can also describe the elements that are *not* in a given set.

Lesson Vocabulary
• roster form
• set-builder notation
• empty set
• universal set
• complement of a set

Roster form is one way to write sets. Roster form lists the elements of a set within braces, { }. For example, you write the set containing 1 and 2 as {1, 2}, and you write the set of multiples of 2 as {2, 4, 6, 8, . . .}.

Set-builder notation is another way to write sets. It describes the properties an element must have to be included in a set. For example, you can write the set {2, 4, 6, 8, . . .} in set-builder notation as {$x \mid x$ is a multiple of 2}. You read this as "the set of all real numbers x, such that x is a multiple of 2."

Plan

How are roster form and set-builder notation different?
Roster form *lists* the elements of a set. Set-builder notation *describes* the properties of those elements.

 Problem 1 Using Roster Form and Set-Builder Notation

How do you write "*T* is the set of natural numbers that are less than 6" in roster form? In set-builder notation?

Roster form	Set-builder notation

Write "*T* is" as "*T* =."   List all natural numbers that are less than 6.

Use a variable.   Describe the limits on the variable.

$$T = \{1, 2, 3, 4, 5\}$$

$$T = \{x \mid x \text{ is a natural number}, x < 6\}$$

Got It? **1.** N is the set of even natural numbers that are less than or equal to 12. How do you write N in roster form? In set-builder notation?

You can use set-builder notation to write the solutions of a linear inequality.

Plan

How is this problem similar to others you've solved?
It requires using properties of inequality to solve a multi-step inequality, as you did in Lesson 3-4.

Ⓒ **Problem 2** **Inequalities and Set-Builder Notation**

Multiple Choice In set-builder notation, how do you write the solutions of $-5x + 7 \leq 17$?

Ⓐ $x \geq -2$

Ⓑ $\{x \mid x \geq -2\}$

Ⓒ $\{-2, -1, 0, \ldots\}$

Ⓓ $\{x \mid x \leq -2\}$

$$-5x + 7 \leq 17$$
$$-5x + 7 - 7 \leq 17 - 7 \qquad \text{Subtract 7 from each side.}$$
$$-5x \leq 10 \qquad \text{Simplify.}$$
$$\frac{-5x}{-5} \geq \frac{10}{-5} \qquad \text{Divide each side by } -5. \text{ Reverse the inequality symbol.}$$
$$x \geq -2 \qquad \text{Simplify.}$$

In set-builder notation, the solutions are given by $\{x \mid x \geq -2\}$. The answer is B.

 Got It? **2.** In set-builder notation, how do you write the solutions of $9 - 4n > 21$?

You know that a set A is a subset of a set B if each element of A is also an element of B. For example, if $B = \{-2, -1, 0, 1, 2, 3\}$ and $A = \{-1, 0, 2\}$, then A is a subset of B. You can write this relationship as $A \subseteq B$.

The **empty set,** or *null set*, is the set that contains no elements. The empty set is a subset of every set. Use $\varnothing$ or $\{\ \}$ to represent the empty set.

Ⓒ **Problem 3** **Finding Subsets**

What are all the subsets of the set $\{3, 4, 5\}$?

$\varnothing$	Start with the empty set.
$\{3\}, \{4\}, \{5\}$	List the subsets with one element.
$\{3, 4\}, \{3, 5\}, \{4, 5\}$	List the subsets with two elements.
$\{3, 4, 5\}$	List the original set. It is always considered a subset.

Think

Why is the original set considered a subset?
It's a subset because it contains elements from the original set. In this case, it's the subset that contains all three elements.

The eight subsets of $\{3, 4, 5\}$ are $\varnothing, \{3\}, \{4\}, \{5\}, \{3, 4\}, \{3, 5\}, \{4, 5\}$, and $\{3, 4, 5\}$.

Got It? **3. a.** What are the subsets of the set $P = \{a, b\}$? Of the set $S = \{a, b, c\}$?

Ⓒ **b. Reasoning** Let $A = \{x \mid x < -3\}$ and $B = \{x \mid x \leq 0\}$. Is A a subset of B? Explain your reasoning.

When working with sets, you call the largest set you are using the **universal set**, or universe. The **complement of a set** is the set of all elements in the universal set that are *not* in the set. You denote the complement of A by A'.

In the Venn diagrams below, U represents the universal set. Notice that $A \subseteq U$ and $A' \subseteq U$.

Set A is shaded.

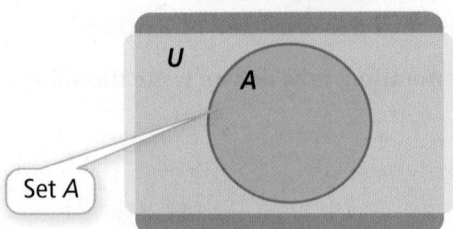

Set A

The complement of set A is shaded.

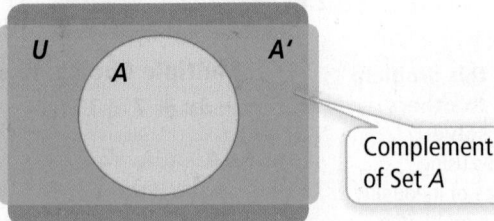

Complement of Set A

Problem 4 Finding the Complement of a Set

Universal set $U = \{$king, queen, bishop, knight, rook, pawn$\}$ and set A is the set of chess pieces that move side to side. What is the complement of set A?

King

Queen

Bishop

Knight

Rook

Pawn

Know
- The elements of set U
- The elements of set A

Need
- The elements of A'

Plan
Use a Venn diagram to find all the elements in set U that are *not* in set A.

The Venn diagram shows the relationship between sets A and U. The elements in set U that are *not* in set A are bishop, knight, and pawn.

So, $A' = \{$bishop, knight, pawn$\}$.

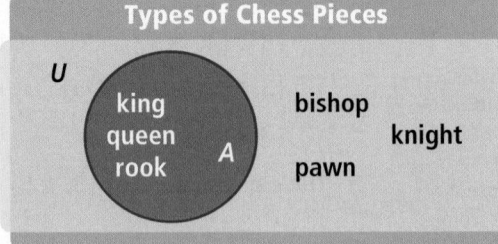

Types of Chess Pieces

U

king
queen
rook A

bishop

knight

pawn

 Got It? 4. Universal set $U = \{$months of the year$\}$ and set $A = \{$months with exactly 31 days$\}$. What is the complement of set A? Write your answer in roster form.

Lesson Check

Do you know HOW?

1. How do you write "G is the set of odd natural numbers that are less than 18" in roster form? In set-builder notation?

2. In set-builder notation, how do you write the solutions of $5 + d \leq 8$?

3. What are all the subsets of $\{4, 8, 12\}$?

4. Given the universal set $U = \{$seasons of the year$\}$ and $W = \{$winter$\}$, what is W'?

Do you UNDERSTAND?

5. **Vocabulary** What is the complement of A'? Explain.

6. Is the first set in each pair a subset of the second set? Explain.
   a. $\varnothing; \{1, 3, 5\}$ **b.** $\{1, 3, 5\}; \{1, 3\}$ **c.** $\{3\}; \{1, 3, 5\}$

7. **Reasoning** A nonempty set is a set that contains at least one element. Given nonempty sets A and B, suppose that $A \subseteq B$. Is $B \subseteq A$ *always*, *sometimes*, or *never* true?

8. **Error Analysis** A student says sets A and B below are the same. What error did the student make?
   $A = \{x \mid x$ is a whole number less than 5$\}$
   $B = \{1, 2, 3, 4\}$

 ## Practice and Problem-Solving Exercises

 **Practice**

Write each set in roster form and in set-builder notation.   ◀ **See Problem 1.**

9. M is the set of integers that are greater than -1 and less than 4.

10. N is the set of real numbers that are factors of 12.

11. P is the set of natural numbers that are less than 11.

12. R is the set of even natural numbers that are less than 2.

Write the solutions of each inequality in set-builder notation.   ◀ **See Problem 2.**

13. $4y + 7 \geq 23$ 14. $5r + 8 < 63$ 15. $13 - 9m < 58$

16. $7 - 3d \geq 28$ 17. $2(3p - 11) \geq -16$ 18. $3(2k + 12) < -42$

List all the subsets of each set.   ◀ **See Problem 3.**

19. $\{a, e, i, o\}$ 20. $\{0, 1, 2\}$ 21. $\{$dog, cat, fish$\}$

22. $\{-2, 2\}$ 23. $\{1\}$ 24. $\{+, -, \times, \div\}$

25. Suppose $U = \{1, 2, 3, 4, 5\}$ is the universal set and $A = \{2, 3\}$. What is A'?   ◀ **See Problem 4.**

26. Suppose $U = \{1, 2, 3, 4, 5, 6, 7, 8\}$ is the universal set and $P = \{2, 4, 6, 8\}$. What is P'?

27. Suppose $U = \{\ldots, -3, -2, -1, 0, 1, 2, 3, \ldots\}$ is the universal set and $R = \{\ldots, -3, -1, 1, 3, \ldots\}$. What is R'?

28. Suppose $U = \{1, 2\}$ is the universal set and $T = \{1\}$. What is T'?

C **29. Think About a Plan** Universal set U and set A are defined below. What are the
elements of A'?

$U = \{$days of the week$\}$

$A = \{$days of the week that contain the letter N$\}$

• What are the elements of the universal set?
• What are the elements of set A?
• How can you find the complement of set A?

Suppose $U = \{0, 1, 2, 3, 4, 5, 6\}$, $A = \{2, 4, 6\}$, and $B = \{1, 2, 3\}$. Tell whether
each statement is *true* or *false*. Explain your reasoning.

30. $A \subseteq U$ **31.** $U \subseteq B$ **32.** $B \subseteq A$ **33.** $\varnothing \subseteq B$

Write each set in set-builder notation.

34. $B = \{11, 12, 13, 14, \ldots\}$ **35.** $M = \{1, 3, 5, 7, 9, 11, 13, 15, 17, 19\}$

36. $S = \{1, 2, 3, 4, 6, 12\}$ **37.** $G = \{\ldots, -2, -1, 0, 1, 2, \ldots\}$

38. Universal set U and set B are defined below. What are the elements of B'?

$U = \{$states of the United States$\}$

$B = \{$states that do not start with the letter A$\}$

39. Universal set $U = \{$planets in Earth's solar system$\}$ and set $P = \{$planets farther
from the sun than Earth is from the sun$\}$. What is the complement of set P? Write
your answer in roster form.

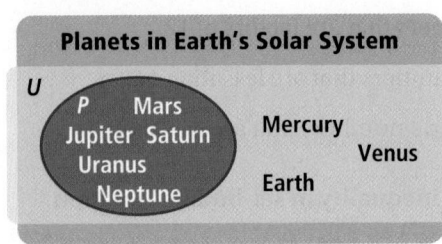

Solve each inequality. Write your solutions in set-builder notation.

40. $-2(3x + 7) > -14$ **41.** $-2(3x + 7) > -14 - 6x$

42. $-2(3x + 7) \geq -14 - 6x$ **43.** $-3(4x + 8) + 1 \geq -23$

44. $-3(4x + 8) + 1 \geq -23 - 12x$ **45.** $-3(4x + 8) + 1 < -23 - 12x$

46. Suppose $U = \{x \mid x$ is a multiple of 2, $x < 18\}$ is the universal set and
$C = \{4, 8, 12, 16\}$. What is C'?

47. Suppose $U = \{x \mid x$ is an integer, $x \leq 12\}$ is the universal set and
$T = \{x \mid x$ is a natural number, $x \leq 12\}$. What is T'?

C **48. Open-Ended** Write a two-step inequality with solutions that are given
by $\{n \mid n > 0\}$.

49. How many elements are in the set $\{x \mid x$ is an even prime number, $x < 100\}$?

50. Reasoning Without listing each subset of a set, how can you determine the number of subsets that the set has?

Use your answer from Exercise 50. Determine how many subsets each set has.

51. $R = \{\text{positive even numbers less than } 20\}$ **52.** $Q = \{0\}$

Standardized Test Prep

SAT/ACT

53. Let the universal set be $U = \{x \mid x \text{ is a natural number}\}$, and let set $E = \{2, 4, 6, 8, \ldots\}$. What is E'?

Ⓐ $\{1, 3, 5, 7, \ldots\}$ Ⓒ $\{\text{all positive integers}\}$

Ⓑ $\{0, 2, 4, 6, 8, \ldots\}$ Ⓓ $\{2, 4, 6, 8, \ldots\}$

54. Which set represents the solutions of $-9x + 17 \geq -64$?

Ⓕ $\{x \mid x \leq 9\}$ Ⓖ $\{x \mid x \geq 9\}$ Ⓗ $\left\{x \mid x \leq -\frac{47}{9}\right\}$ Ⓘ $\left\{x \mid x \geq -\frac{47}{9}\right\}$

55. In the diagram below, $\triangle ABC \sim \triangle EFG$. What is FG?

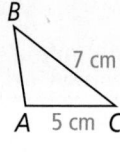
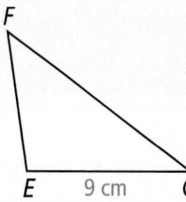

Ⓐ $3\frac{8}{9}$ Ⓑ $6\frac{3}{7}$ Ⓒ 11 Ⓓ $12\frac{3}{5}$

56. What is the least whole-number solution of $-10n \leq 5$?

Ⓕ -1 Ⓖ 0 Ⓗ 1 Ⓘ 2

Short Response

57. Mum's Florist sells two dozen roses for $24.60. First Flowers Florist sells 6 roses for $7.50. Which florist has the lower cost per rose? Explain.

Mixed Review

Solve each inequality.   ◀ See Lesson 3-4.

58. $3b + 2 > 26$ **59.** $2(t + 2) - 3t \geq -1$ **60.** $6z - 15 < 4z + 11$

Evaluate each expression for the given value of the variable.   ◀ See Lesson 1-2.

61. $3n - 6;\ n = 4$ **62.** $7 - 2b;\ b = 5$ **63.** $\frac{2d - 3}{5};\ d = 9$

Get Ready!   **To prepare for Lesson 3-6, do Exercises 64–66.**

Graph each pair of inequalities on one number line.   ◀ See Lesson 3-1.

64. $c < 8;\ c \geq 10$ **65.** $t \geq -2;\ t \leq -5$ **66.** $m \leq 7;\ m > 12$

3-6 Compound Inequalities

© **Common Core State Standards**

A-REI.B.3 Solve linear equations and inequalities in one variable, including equations with coefficients represented by letters. **Also A-CED.A.1**

MP 1, MP 2, MP 3, MP 4

Objectives To solve and graph inequalities containing the word *and*
To solve and graph inequalities containing the word *or*

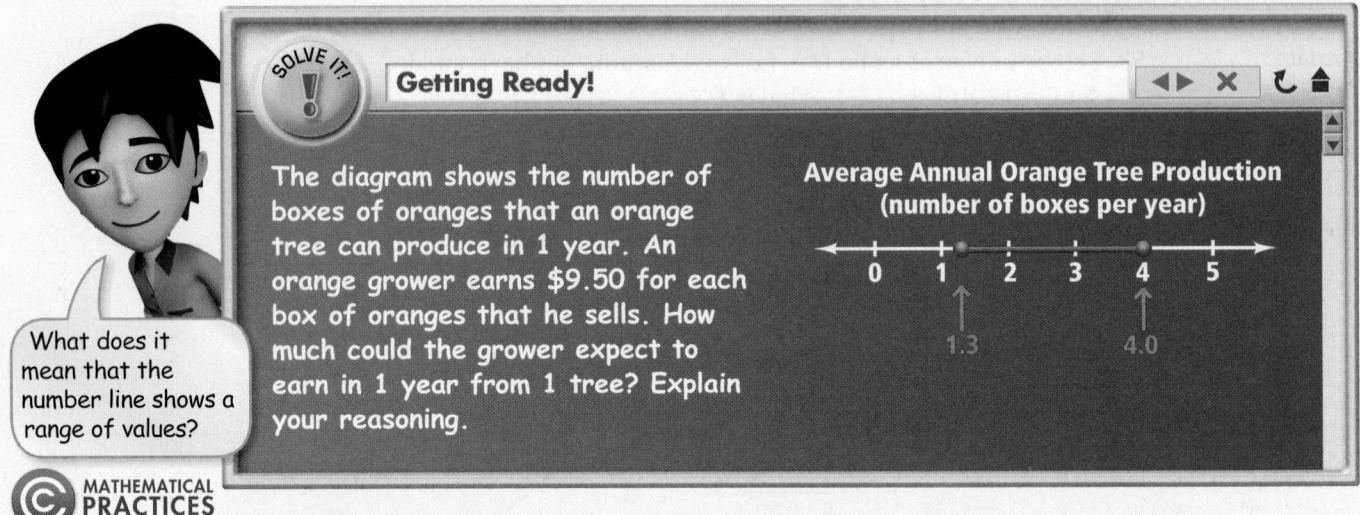

What does it mean that the number line shows a range of values?

© **MATHEMATICAL PRACTICES**

The Solve It involves a value that is between two numbers. You can use a compound inequality to represent this relationship. A **compound inequality** consists of two distinct inequalities joined by the word *and* or the word *or*.

Essential Understanding You find the solutions of a compound inequality either by identifying where the solution sets of the distinct inequalities overlap or by combining the solution sets to form a larger solution set.

Lesson Vocabulary
• compound inequality
• interval notation

The graph of a compound inequality with the word *and* contains the *overlap* of the graphs of the two inequalities that form the compound inequality.

The graph of a compound inequality with the word *or* contains *each* graph of the two inequalities that form the compound inequality.

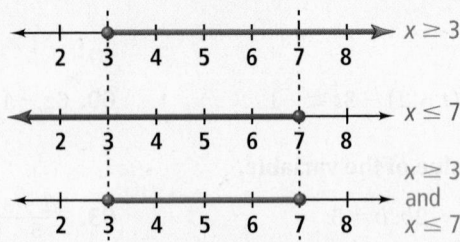

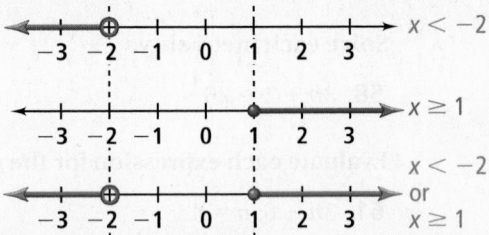

You can rewrite a compound inequality involving *and* as a single inequality. For instance, in the inequality above, you can write $x \geq 3$ and $x \leq 7$ as $3 \leq x \leq 7$. You read this as "x is greater than or equal to 3 and less than or equal to 7." Another way to read it is "x is between 3 and 7, inclusive." In this example, *inclusive* means the solutions of the inequality include both 3 and 7.

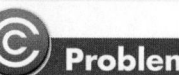

Problem 1 Writing a Compound Inequality

What compound inequality represents the phrase? Graph the solutions.

> **Think**
>
> **Why can you write an *and* inequality without the word *and*?**
> The compound inequality $-2 < n$ and $n < 6$ means n is greater than -2 *and* n is less than 6. This means n is between -2 and 6. You write this as $-2 < n < 6$.

A **all real numbers that are greater than -2 and less than 6**

$n > -2$ and $n < 6$

$-2 < n$ and $n < 6$

$-2 < n < 6$

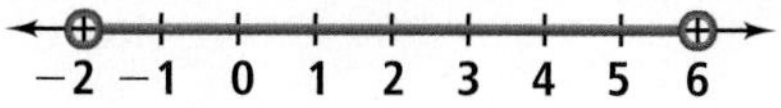

B **all real numbers that are less than 0 or greater than or equal to 5**

$t < 0$ or $t \geq 5$

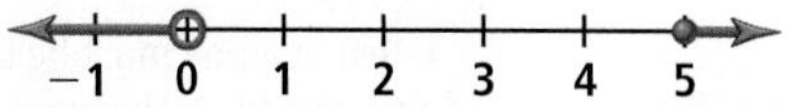

Got It? 1. For parts (a) and (b) below, write a compound inequality that represents each phrase. Graph the solutions.

a. all real numbers that are greater than or equal to -4 and less than 6

b. all real numbers that are less than or equal to $2\frac{1}{2}$ or greater than 6

c. Reasoning What is the difference between "x is between -5 and 7" and "x is between -5 and 7, inclusive"?

A solution of a compound inequality involving *and* is any number that makes *both* inequalities true. One way you can solve a compound inequality is by separating it into two inequalities.

Problem 2 Solving a Compound Inequality Involving *And*

What are the solutions of $-3 \leq m - 4 < -1$? Graph the solutions.

> **Plan**
>
> **How do you know to join the two inequalities with *and*?**
> The compound inequality $-3 \leq m - 4 < -1$ means that the quantity $m - 4$ is between -3 *and* -1, including -3. So use the word *and*.

$-3 \leq m - 4 < -1$

$-3 \leq m - 4$	and	$m - 4 < -1$	Write the compound inequality as two inequalities joined by the word *and*.
$-3 + 4 \leq m - 4 + 4$	and	$m - 4 + 4 < -1 + 4$	Add 4 to each side of each inequality.
$1 \leq m$	and	$m < 3$	Simplify.
	$1 \leq m < 3$		Write the solutions as a single inequality.

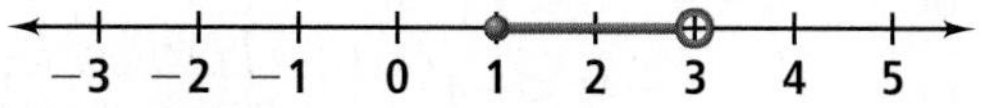

Got It? 2. What are the solutions of $-2 < 3y - 4 < 14$? Graph the solutions.

You can also solve an inequality like $-3 \leq m - 4 < -1$ by working on all three parts of the inequality at the same time. You work to isolate the variable between the inequality symbols. This method is used in Problem 3.

Test Average To earn a B in your algebra course, you must achieve an unrounded test average between 84 and 86, inclusive. You scored 86, 85, and 80 on the first three tests of the grading period. What possible scores can you earn on the fourth and final test to earn a B in the course?

Know
- Test average must be between 84 and 86, inclusive
- First 3 test scores

Need
Possible scores you can earn on the last test to get a B in the course

Plan
Write an expression for your test average. Then write and solve a compound inequality.

Think

What is another way to solve this problem?
You can *work backward* to solve this problem. You can start with the inequality $84 \leq x \leq 86$ where x represents the average of your test scores. Then rewrite the inequality in terms of the sum of your 4 test scores.

$$84 \leq \frac{86 + 85 + 80 + x}{4} \leq 86 \qquad \text{Write a compound inequality.}$$

$$4(84) \leq 4\left(\frac{251 + x}{4}\right) \leq 4(86) \qquad \text{Multiply each part by 4.}$$

$$336 \leq 251 + x \leq 344 \qquad \text{Simplify.}$$

$$336 - 251 \leq 251 + x - 251 \leq 344 - 251 \qquad \text{Subtract 251 from each part.}$$

$$85 \leq x \leq 93 \qquad \text{Simplify.}$$

Your score on the fourth test must be between 85 and 93, inclusive.

 Got It? **3. Reasoning** Suppose you scored 78, 78, and 79 on the first three tests. Is it possible for you to earn a B in the course? Assume that 100 is the maximum grade you can earn in the course and on the test. Explain.

A solution of a compound inequality involving *or* is any number that makes *either* inequality true. To solve a compound inequality involving *or*, you must solve separately the two inequalities that form the compound inequality.

 **Problem 4** Solving a Compound Inequality Involving *Or*

Plan

How is this inequality different from others you've solved?
It contains the word *or*. Unlike an *and* inequality, it's formed by two inequalities with solutions that do not overlap.

What are the solutions of $3t + 2 < -7$ or $-4t + 5 < 1$? Graph the solutions.

$$3t + 2 < -7 \qquad \text{or} \qquad -4t + 5 < 1$$

$$3t + 2 - 2 < -7 - 2 \qquad \text{or} \qquad -4t + 5 - 5 < 1 - 5$$

$$3t < -9 \qquad \text{or} \qquad -4t < -4$$

$$\frac{3t}{3} < \frac{-9}{3} \qquad \text{or} \qquad \frac{-4t}{-4} > \frac{-4}{-4}$$

$$t < -3 \qquad \text{or} \qquad t > 1$$

> Reverse the inequality symbol when you divide by a negative number.

The solutions are given by $t < -3$ or $t > 1$.

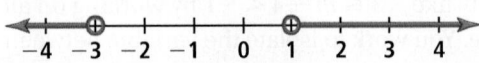

 Got It? **4.** What are the solutions of $-2y + 7 < 1$ or $4y + 3 \leq -5$? Graph the solutions.

You can use an inequality such as $x \le -3$ to describe a portion of the number line called an *interval*. You can also use *interval notation* to describe an interval on the number line. **Interval notation** includes the use of three special symbols. These symbols include

parentheses: Use (or) when a $<$ or $>$ symbol indicates that the interval's endpoints are *not* included.

brackets: Use [or] when a $\le$ or $\ge$ symbol indicates that the interval's endpoints *are* included.

infinity: Use ∞ when the interval continues forever in a *positive* direction.
Use $-\infty$ when the interval continues forever in a *negative* direction.

Inequality	Graph	Interval Notation
$x \ge 2$		$[2, \infty)$
$x < 2$		$(-\infty, 2)$
$1 < x \le 5$		$(1, 5]$
$x < -3$ or $x \ge 4$		$(-\infty, -3)$ or $[4, \infty)$

© **Problem 5** Using Interval Notation

A What is the graph of $[-4, 6)$? How do you write $[-4, 6)$ as an inequality?

The bracket indicates that -4 is included. So use a closed circle at -4.

The parenthesis indicates that 6 is *not* included. So use an open circle at 6.

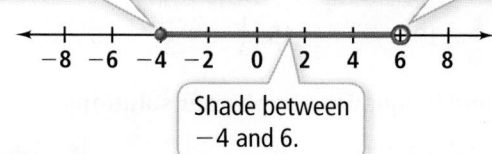

Shade between -4 and 6.

Plan

How do you write interval notation as an inequality?
It may help to read its meaning aloud first. $[-4, 6)$ means all real numbers greater than or equal to -4 and less than 6.

The inequality $-4 \le x < 6$ represents the interval notation $[-4, 6)$.

B What is the graph of $x \le -1$ or $x > 2$? How do you write $x \le -1$ or $x > 2$ in interval notation?

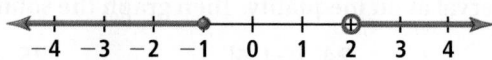

The interval notation $(-\infty, -1]$ or $(2, \infty)$ represents the inequality $x \le -1$ or $x > 2$.

✓ **Got It?** **5. a.** What is the graph of $(-2, 7]$? How do you write $(-2, 7]$ as an inequality?
  b. What is the graph of $y > 7$? How do you write $y > 7$ in interval notation?

Lesson Check

Do you know HOW?

1. What compound inequality represents the phrase "all real numbers that are greater than or equal to 0 and less than 8"? Graph the solutions.

2. What are the solutions of $-4 \le r - 5 < -1$? Graph the solutions.

3. Your test scores in science are 83 and 87. What possible scores can you earn on your next test to have a test average between 85 and 90, inclusive?

4. Write the interval represented on the number line below as an inequality and in interval notation.

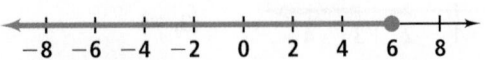

Do you UNDERSTAND?

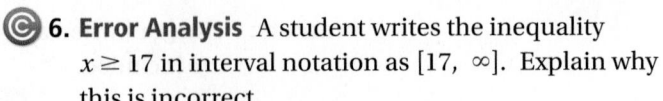 **5. Vocabulary** Which of the following are compound inequalities?

   A. $x > 4$ or $x < -4$ **B.** $x \ge 6$

   C. $8 \le 5x < 30$ **D.** $7x > 42$ or $-5x \le 10$

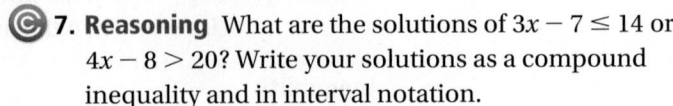 **6. Error Analysis** A student writes the inequality $x \ge 17$ in interval notation as $[17, \infty]$. Explain why this is incorrect.

7. Reasoning What are the solutions of $3x - 7 \le 14$ or $4x - 8 > 20$? Write your solutions as a compound inequality and in interval notation.

8. Writing Compare the graph of a compound inequality involving *and* with the graph of a compound inequality involving *or*.

Practice and Problem-Solving Exercises

 **Practice**   Write a compound inequality that represents each phrase. Graph the solutions.   **See Problem 1.**

9. all real numbers that are between -5 and 7

10. The circumference of a women's basketball must be between 28.5 in. and 29 in., inclusive.

Solve each compound inequality. Graph your solutions.   **See Problems 2 and 3.**

11. $-4 < k + 3 < 8$ **12.** $5 \le y + 2 \le 11$ **13.** $3 < 4p - 5 \le 15$

14. $15 \le \dfrac{20 + 11 + k}{3} \le 19$ **15.** $\dfrac{1}{4} < \dfrac{2x - 7}{2} < 5$ **16.** $-3 \le \dfrac{6 - q}{9} \le 3$

Solve each compound inequality. Graph your solutions.   **See Problem 4.**

17. $6b - 1 < -7$ or $2b + 1 > 5$ **18.** $5 + m > 4$ or $7m < -35$

19. $4d + 5 \ge 13$ or $7d - 2 < 12$ **20.** $7 - c < 1$ or $4c \le 12$

21. $5y + 7 \le -3$ or $3y - 2 \ge 13$ **22.** $5z - 3 > 7$ or $4z - 6 < -10$

Write each interval as an inequality. Then graph the solutions.   **See Problem 5.**

23. $(-\infty, 2]$ **24.** $[-4, 5]$ **25.** $(-\infty, -1]$ or $(3, \infty)$ **26.** $[6, \infty)$

Write each inequality in interval notation. Then graph the interval.

27. $x > -2$ **28.** $x \le 0$ **29.** $x < -2$ or $x \ge 1$ **30.** $-3 \le x < 4$

 Apply

Solve each inequality. Write each set in interval notation.

31. $7 < x + 6 \le 12$ **32.** $-9 < 3m + 6 \le 18$

33. $f + 14 < 9$ or $-9f \le -45$ **34.** $12h - 3 \ge 15h$ or $5 > -0.2h + 10$

Write a compound inequality that each graph could represent.

35. 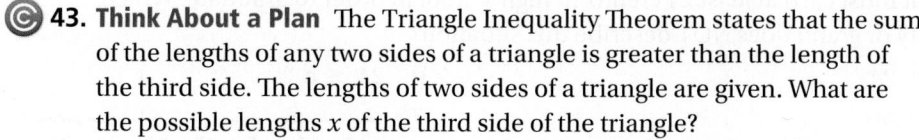   **36.**   **37.**

Solve each compound inequality. Justify each step.

38. $4r - 3 > 11$ or $4r - 3 \le -11$ **39.** $2 \le 0.75v \le 4.5$

40. $\dfrac{4y + 2}{5} - 5 > 3$ or $\dfrac{4 - 3y}{6} > 4$ **41.** $-\dfrac{4}{3} \le \dfrac{1}{7}w - \dfrac{3}{4} < 1$

STEM **42. Chemistry** The acidity of the water in a swimming pool is considered normal if the average of three pH readings is between 7.2 and 7.8, inclusive. The first two readings for a swimming pool are 7.4 and 7.9. What possible values for the third reading p will make the average pH normal?

43. Think About a Plan The Triangle Inequality Theorem states that the sum of the lengths of any two sides of a triangle is greater than the length of the third side. The lengths of two sides of a triangle are given. What are the possible lengths x of the third side of the triangle?
- Is there an upper limit on the value of x? Is there a lower limit?
- How can you use your answers to the previous question to write one or more inequalities involving x?

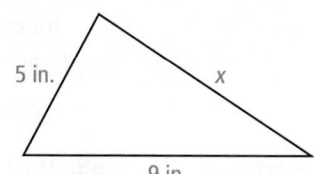

Use your answers to Exercise 43 to answer Exercises 44–47. The lengths of two sides of a triangle are given. Find the possible lengths of the third side.

44. 3.75 in., 7 in.   **45.** 15 ft, 21 ft   **46.** 14 mm, 35 mm   **47.** 6 m, 17 m

STEM **48. Physics** The force exerted on a spring is proportional to the distance the spring is stretched from its relaxed position. Suppose you stretch a spring a distance of d inches by applying a force of F pounds. For your spring, $\frac{d}{F} = 0.8$. You apply forces between 25 lb and 40 lb, inclusive. What inequality describes the distances the spring is stretched?

49. Reasoning Describe the solutions of $4x - 9 < 7$ or $3x - 10 > 2$.

50. Nutrition A sedentary 15-year-old male should consume no more than 2200 Calories per day. A moderately active 15-year-old male should consume between 2400 and 2800 Calories per day. An active 15-year-old male should consume between 2800 and 3200 Calories per day. Model these ranges on a number line. Represent each range of calories using interval notation.

51. Heart Rates Recommended heart rates during exercise vary with age and physical condition. For a healthy person doing moderate to intense exercise, such as hiking, the inequality $0.5(220 - a) \le R \le 0.9(220 - a)$ gives a target range for the heart rate R (in beats per minute), based on age a (in years).

a. What is the target range for heart rates for a person 15 years old?

b. How old is a person whose target range is between 99 and 178.2 beats per minute?

 52. Chemistry Matter is in a liquid state when its temperature is between its melting point and its boiling point. The melting point of the element mercury is $-38.87°C$, and its boiling point is $356.58°C$. What is the range of temperatures in degrees Fahrenheit for which mercury is *not* in a liquid state? (*Hint:* $C = \frac{5}{9}(F - 32)$) Express the range as an inequality and in interval notation.

Standardized Test Prep

SAT/ACT

53. A taxi traveled 5 mi to John's home and then drove him to the airport 10 mi away. Which inequality represents the possible distances d of the taxi from the airport when it started traveling toward John's home?

Ⓐ $5 \le d \le 10$ Ⓑ $5 \le d \le 15$ Ⓒ $0 \le d \le 5$ Ⓓ $0 \le d \le 10$

54. A student must earn at least 24 credits in high school in order to graduate. Which inequality or graph does NOT describe this situation?

Ⓕ $c \le 24$ Ⓗ $24 \le c$

Ⓖ $c \ge 24$ Ⓘ
$$\begin{array}{c} \xleftarrow{\hspace{0.3cm}+\hspace{0.3cm}+\hspace{0.3cm}+\hspace{0.3cm}+\hspace{0.3cm}\bullet\hspace{0.3cm}+\hspace{0.3cm}+\hspace{0.3cm}+\hspace{0.3cm}} \\ -6 \quad 0 \quad 6 \quad 12 \quad 18 \quad 24 \quad 30 \quad 36 \quad 42 \end{array}$$

Short Response

55. The County Water Department charges a monthly administration fee of $10.40 plus $.0059 for each gallon of water used, up to, but not including, 7500 gal. What are the minimum and maximum numbers of gallons of water used by customers whose monthly charge is at least $35 but no more than $50? Express amounts to the nearest gallon.

Mixed Review

Let $A = \{1, 3, 5, 7\}$, let $B = \{4, 8, 12\}$, and let the universal set be $U = \{1, 2, 3, 4, 5, 7, 8, 12, 15\}$.   **See Lesson 3-5.**

56. What are the subsets of A?   **57.** What is B'?   **58.** Is B' a subset of A?

Solve each inequality.   **See Lesson 3-4.**

59. $5 < 6b + 3$ **60.** $12n \le 3n + 27$ **61.** $2 + 4r \ge 5(r - 1)$

Get Ready! To prepare for Lesson 3-7, do Exercises 62–64.

Complete each statement with $<, =,$ or $>$.   **See Lesson 1-5.**

62. $|3 - 7| \; \blacksquare \; 4$ **63.** $|-5| + 2 \; \blacksquare \; 6$ **64.** $\left|6 - 2\frac{1}{4}\right| \; \blacksquare \; 3\frac{5}{8}$

3-7 Absolute Value Equations and Inequalities

Common Core State Standards

A-CED.A.1 Create equations . . . in one variable and use them to solve problems. *Include equations arising from linear . . . functions.* **Also A-SSE.A.1b**

MP 1, MP 2, MP 3, MP 4

Objective To solve equations and inequalities involving absolute value

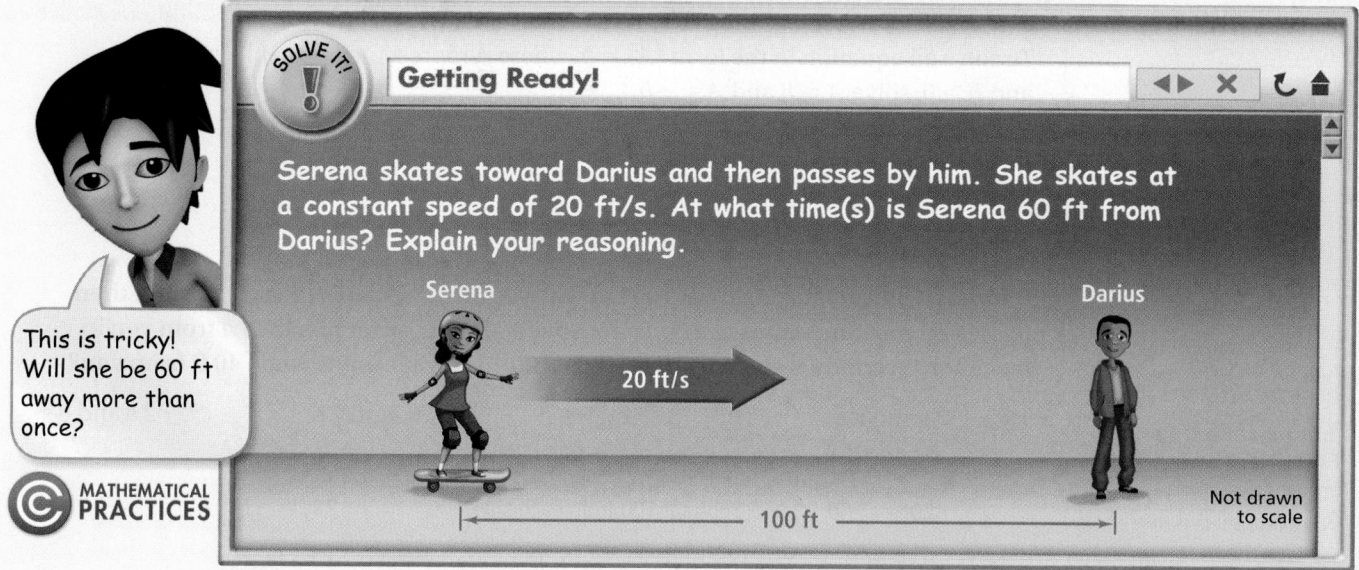

Getting Ready!

Serena skates toward Darius and then passes by him. She skates at a constant speed of 20 ft/s. At what time(s) is Serena 60 ft from Darius? Explain your reasoning.

Serena   Darius

20 ft/s

|←——————— 100 ft ———————→|

Not drawn to scale

This is tricky! Will she be 60 ft away more than once?

MATHEMATICAL PRACTICES

In the Solve It, Serena's distance from Darius decreases and then increases. You can use absolute value to model such changes.

Essential Understanding You can solve absolute value equations and inequalities by first isolating the absolute value expression, if necessary. Then write an equivalent pair of linear equations or inequalities.

Problem 1 Solving an Absolute Value Equation

What are the solutions of $|x| + 2 = 9$? Graph and check the solutions.

$$|x| + 2 = 9$$

$|x| + 2 - 2 = 9 - 2$ Subtract 2 from each side.

$|x| = 7$ Simplify.

$x = 7$ or $x = -7$ Definition of absolute value

$-8 \quad -6 \quad -4 \quad -2 \quad 0 \quad 2 \quad 4 \quad 6 \quad 8$

Check $|7| + 2 \overset{?}{=} 9$ ← Substitute 7 and −7 for x. → $|-7| + 2 \overset{?}{=} 9$

$7 + 2 = 9$ ✔ $7 + 2 = 9$ ✔

Think

How many solutions does the equation have?

There are two values on a number line that are 7 units from 0: 7 and −7. So the equation has two solutions.

Got It? 1. What are the solutions of $|n| - 5 = -2$? Graph and check the solutions.

Some equations, such as $|2x - 5| = 13$, have variable expressions within absolute value symbols. The equation $|2x - 5| = 13$ means that the distance on a number line from $2x - 5$ to 0 is 13 units. There are two points that are 13 units from 0: 13 and -13. So to find the values of x, solve the equations $2x - 5 = 13$ and $2x - 5 = -13$. You can generalize this process as follows.

take note

Key Concept Solving Absolute Value Equations

To solve an equation in the form $|A| = b$, where A represents a variable expression and $b > 0$, solve $A = b$ and $A = -b$.

 Problem 2 Solving an Absolute Value Equation

Multiple Choice Starting from 100 ft away, your friend skates toward you and then passes by you. She skates at a constant speed of 20 ft/s. Her distance d from you in feet after t seconds is given by $d = |100 - 20t|$. At what times is she 40 ft from you?

  Ⓐ -2 s and 8 s   Ⓑ -3 s and 7 s   Ⓒ 3 s and 7 s   Ⓓ 2 s and 8 s

$100 - 20t = 40$	← Write two equations. →	$100 - 20t = -40$
$-20t = -60$	← Subtract 100 from each side. →	$-20t = -140$
$t = 3$	← Divide each side by -20. →	$t = 7$

The solutions are 3 s and 7 s. The correct answer is C.

Plan

What must be true of the expression $100 - 20t$?
Its absolute value is 40, so $100 - 20t$ must equal either 40 or -40. Use this fact to write and solve two equations.

 Got It? **2.** Another friend's distance d from you (in feet) after t seconds is given by $d = |80 - 5t|$. What does the 80 in the equation represent? What does the 5 in the equation represent? At what times is she 60 ft from you?

Recall that absolute value represents distance from 0 on a number line. Distance is always nonnegative. So any equation that states that the absolute value of an expression is negative has no solutions.

Problem 3 Solving an Absolute Value Equation With No Solution

Plan

How can you make the equation look like one you've solved before?
Use properties of equality to isolate the absolute value expression on one side of the equal sign.

What are the solutions of $3|2z + 9| + 12 = 10$?

$$3|2z + 9| + 12 = 10$$
$$3|2z + 9| = -2 \quad \text{Subtract 12 from each side.}$$
$$|2z + 9| = -\frac{2}{3} \quad \text{Divide each side by 3.}$$

The absolute value of an expression cannot be negative, so there is no solution.

Got It? **3.** What are the solutions of $|3x - 6| - 5 = -7$?

You can write absolute value inequalities as compound inequalities. The graphs below show two absolute value inequalities.

$$|n - 1| < 2$$

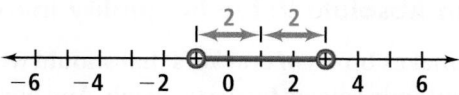

$|n - 1| < 2$ represents all numbers with a distance from 1 that is less than 2 units. So $|n - 1| < 2$ means $-2 < n - 1 < 2$.

$$|n - 1| > 2$$

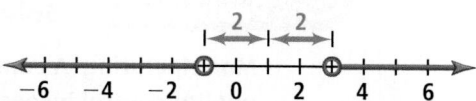

$|n - 1| > 2$ represents all numbers with a distance from 1 that is greater than 2 units. So $|n - 1| > 2$ means $n - 1 < -2$ or $n - 1 > 2$.

take note

Key Concept   Solving Absolute Value Inequalities

To solve an inequality in the form $|A| < b$, where A is a variable expression and $b > 0$, solve the compound inequality $-b < A < b$.

To solve an inequality in the form $|A| > b$, where A is a variable expression and $b > 0$, solve the compound inequality $A < -b$ or $A > b$.

Similar rules are true for $|A| \leq b$ or $|A| \geq b$.

© **Problem 4** **Solving an Absolute Value Inequality Involving ≥**

What are the solutions of $|8n| \geq 24$? Graph the solutions.

Think

The inequality says that $8n$ is at least 24 units from 0 on a number line.

Write

$$|8n| \geq 24$$

To be at least 24 units from 0, $8n$ can be less than or equal to -24 or greater than or equal to 24.

$$8n \leq -24 \text{ or } 8n \geq 24$$

You need to isolate n. Undo multiplication by dividing each side by the same number.

$$\frac{8n}{8} \leq \frac{-24}{8} \text{ or } \frac{8n}{8} \geq \frac{24}{8}$$
$$n \leq -3 \quad \text{or} \quad n \geq 3$$

Got It? **4.** What are the solutions of $|2x + 4| \geq 5$? Graph the solutions.

 **Problem 5**   **Solving an Absolute Value Inequality Involving ≤** **STEM**

Manufacturing A company makes boxes of crackers that should weigh 213 g. A quality-control inspector randomly selects boxes to weigh. Any box that varies from the weight by more than 5 g is sent back. What is the range of allowable weights for a box of crackers?

Relate   difference between actual and ideal weights   is at most   5 g

Define   Let w = the actual weight in grams.

Write $|w - 213|$ ≤   5

Think

How else could you write this inequality?

You could break the compound inequality into two parts:
$w - 213 \geq -5$ and
$w - 213 \leq 5$.

$$|w - 213| \leq 5$$
$$-5 \leq w - 213 \leq 5 \qquad \text{Write a compound inequality.}$$
$$208 \leq \quad w \quad \leq 218 \qquad \text{Add 213 to each expression.}$$

The weight of a box of crackers must be between 208 g and 218 g, inclusive.

 Got It? **5. a.** A food manufacturer makes 32-oz boxes of pasta. Not every box weighs exactly 32 oz. The allowable difference from the ideal weight is at most 0.05 oz. Write and solve an absolute value inequality to find the range of allowable weights.

b. Reasoning In Problem 5, could you have solved the inequality $|w - 213| \leq 5$ by first adding 213 to each side? Explain your reasoning.

Lesson Check

Do you know HOW?

Solve and graph each equation or inequality.

1. $|x| = 5$

2. $|n| - 3 = 4$

3. $|2t| = 6$

4. $|h - 3| < 5$

5. $|x + 2| \geq 1$

Do you UNDERSTAND?  MATHEMATICAL PRACTICES

6. Reasoning How many solutions do you expect to get when you solve an absolute value equation? Explain.

7. Writing Explain why the absolute value equation $|3x| + 8 = 5$ has no solution.

8. Compare and Contrast Explain the similarities and differences in solving the equation $|x - 1| = 2$ with solving the inequalities $|x - 1| \leq 2$ and $|x - 1| \geq 2$.

Practice and Problem-Solving Exercises

MATHEMATICAL PRACTICES

 **Practice**

Solve each equation. Graph and check your solutions.

See Problem 1.

9. $|b| = \frac{1}{2}$

10. $4 = |y|$

11. $|n| + 3 = 7$

12. $7 = |s| - 3$

13. $|x| - 10 = -2$

14. $5|d| = 20$

15. $-3|m| = -9$

16. $|y| + 3 = 3$

Solve each equation. If there is no solution, write *no solution*.

See Problems 2 and 3.

17. $|r - 8| = 5$

18. $|c + 4| = 6$

19. $2 = |g + 3|$

20. $3 = |m + 2|$

21. $-2|7d| = 14$

22. $-3|2w| = -12$

23. $3|v - 3| = 9$

24. $2|d + 4| = 8$

25. $|4f + 1| - 2 = 5$

26. $|3t - 2| + 6 = 2$

27. $4|2y - 3| - 1 = 11$

28. $3|x + 2| + 4 = 13$

29. $-4|k| = 12$

30. $|-3n| - 2 = 4$

31. $-4|k + 1| = 16$

Solve and graph each inequality.

See Problems 4 and 5.

32. $|x| \geq 3$

33. $|x| < 5$

34. $|x + 3| < 5$

35. $|y + 8| \geq 3$

36. $|y - 2| \leq 1$

37. $|p - 7| \leq 3$

38. $|2c - 5| < 9$

39. $|3t + 1| > 8$

40. $|4w + 1| > 11$

41. $|5t - 4| \geq 16$

42. $|4x + 7| > 19$

43. $|2v - 1| \leq 9$

44. $|3d - 7| > 28$

45. $|2f + 9| \leq 13$

46. $|5m - 9| \geq 24$

47. Quality Control The ideal length of one type of model airplane is 90 cm. The actual length may vary from ideal by at most 0.05 cm. What are the acceptable lengths for the model airplane?

48. Basketball The ideal circumference of a women's basketball is 28.75 in. The actual circumference may vary from the ideal by at most 0.25 in. What are the acceptable circumferences for a women's basketball?

 **Apply**

Solve each equation or inequality. If there is no solution, write *no solution*.

49. $|2d| + 3 = 21$

50. $1.2|5p| = 3.6$

51. $\left|d + \frac{1}{2}\right| + \frac{3}{4} = 0$

52. $|f| - \frac{2}{3} = \frac{5}{6}$

53. $3|5y - 7| - 6 = 24$

54. $|t| + 2.7 = 4.5$

55. $-2|c - 4| = -8.4$

56. $\frac{|y|}{-3} = 5$

57. $|n| - \frac{5}{4} < 5$

58. $\frac{7}{8} < |c + 7|$

59. $4 - 3|m + 2| > -14$

60. $|-3d| \geq 6.3$

© 61. Think About a Plan The monthly average temperature T for San Francisco, California, is usually within 7.5°F of 56.5°F, inclusive. What is the monthly average temperature in San Francisco?
- Should you model this situation with an equation or an inequality?
- How can you use the given information to write the equation or inequality?

STEM 62. Biology A horse's body temperature T is considered to be normal if it is within at least 0.9°F of 99.9°F. Find the range of normal body temperatures for a horse.

63. Biking Your friend rides his bike toward you and then passes by you at a constant speed. His distance d (in feet) from you t seconds after he started riding his bike is given by $d = |200 - 18t|$. What does the 200 in the equation represent? What does the 18 in the equation represent? At what time(s) is he 120 ft from you?

© **Error Analysis** Find and correct the mistake in solving each equation or inequality.

64.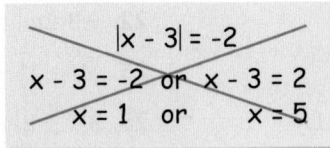

65.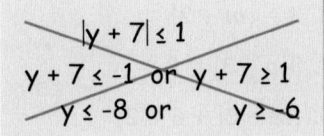

© **66. Open-Ended** Write an absolute value equation that has 2 and 6 as solutions.

© **67. Reasoning** Explain why you can rewrite $|x + 5| > 1$ as a compound inequality involving *or*.

68. Polling According to a poll for an upcoming school board election, 40% of voters are likely to vote for the incumbent. The poll shows a margin of error of ± 3 percentage points. Write and solve an absolute value equation to find the least and the greatest percents of voters v likely to vote for the incumbent.

© **69. Banking** The official weight of a nickel is 5 g, but the actual weight can vary from this amount by up to 0.194 g. Suppose a bank weighs a roll of 40 nickels. The wrapper weighs 1.5 g.
   a. What is the range of possible weights for the roll of nickels?
   b. Reasoning If all of the nickels in the roll each weigh the official amount, then the roll's weight is $40(5) + 1.5 = 201.5$ g. Is it possible for a roll to weigh 201.5 g and contain nickels that do not weigh the official amount? Explain.

STEM 70. Oil Production An oil refinery aims to process 900,000 barrels of oil per day. The daily production varies by up to 50,000 barrels from this goal, inclusive. What are the minimum and maximum numbers of barrels of oil processed each day?

Write an absolute value inequality that represents each set of numbers.

71. all real numbers less than 4 units from 0

72. all real numbers at most 7 units from 0

73. all real numbers more than 2 units from 6

74. all real numbers at least 2 units from -1

STEM 75. Manufacturing The ideal diameter of a piston for one type of car engine is 90.000 mm. The actual diameter can vary from the ideal by at most 0.008 mm. What is the range of acceptable diameters for the piston?

76. Farm Maintenance For safety, the recommended height of a horse fence is 5 ft. Because of uneven ground surfaces, the actual height of the fence can vary from this recommendation by up to 3 in. Write and solve an absolute value equation to find the maximum and minimum heights of the fence.

Solve each equation. Check your solutions.

77. $|x + 4| = 3x$

78. $|4t - 5| = 2t + 1$

79. $\frac{4}{3}|2y + 3| = 4y$

Determine whether each statement is *always*, *sometimes*, or *never* true for real numbers *a* and *b*.

80. $|ab| = |a| \cdot |b|$

81. $\left|\frac{a}{b}\right| = \frac{|a|}{|b|}, b \neq 0$

82. $|a + b| = |a| + |b|$

Standardized Test Prep

GRIDDED RESPONSE

83. The expected monthly rainfall in a certain town is shown for June, July, and August. The actual rainfall generally varies from the expected amount by up to 0.015 in. What is the maximum amount of rainfall the town can expect to receive in July?

Expected Monthly Rainfall (inches)		
June	July	August
4.12	4.25	4.41

84. What is the solution of the equation $\frac{x}{4} - 3 = 7$?

85. What is the solution of the equation $3w + 2 = 4w - 3$?

86. Jose is purchasing 4 dress shirts that cost $28 each and 2 pairs of pants that cost $38 each. The items are all on sale for 35% off. How much money will Jose save by purchasing them on sale instead of at full price?

87. 75% of what number is 90?

Mixed Review

Write a compound inequality to model each situation.

◀ **See Lesson 3-6.**

88. The highest elevation in North America is 20,310 ft above sea level at Denali in Alaska. The lowest elevation in North America is 282 ft below sea level at Death Valley, California.

89. Normal human body temperature T is within 0.3°C of 37.2°C.

Simplify each expression.

◀ **See Lesson 1-7.**

90. $2(x + 5)$

91. $-3(y - 7)$

92. $4(\ell + 3) - 7$

93. $-(m - 4) + 8$

Get Ready! **To prepare for Lesson 3-8, do Exercises 94–97.**

Write each set in set-builder notation.

◀ **See Lesson 3-5.**

94. $A = \{0, 1, 2, 3, 4, 5, 6, 7, 8, 9\}$

95. $B = \{1, 3, 5, 7\}$

Write each set in roster form.

96. $C = \{n \,|\, n \text{ is an even number between } -15 \text{ and } -5\}$

97. $D = \{k \,|\, k \text{ is a composite number between 7 and 17}\}$

3-8

Unions and Intersections of Sets

© **Common Core State Standards**

A-CED.A.1 Create equations and inequalities in one variable and use them to solve problems . . .

MP 1, MP 2, MP 3, MP 4

Objective To find the unions and intersections of sets

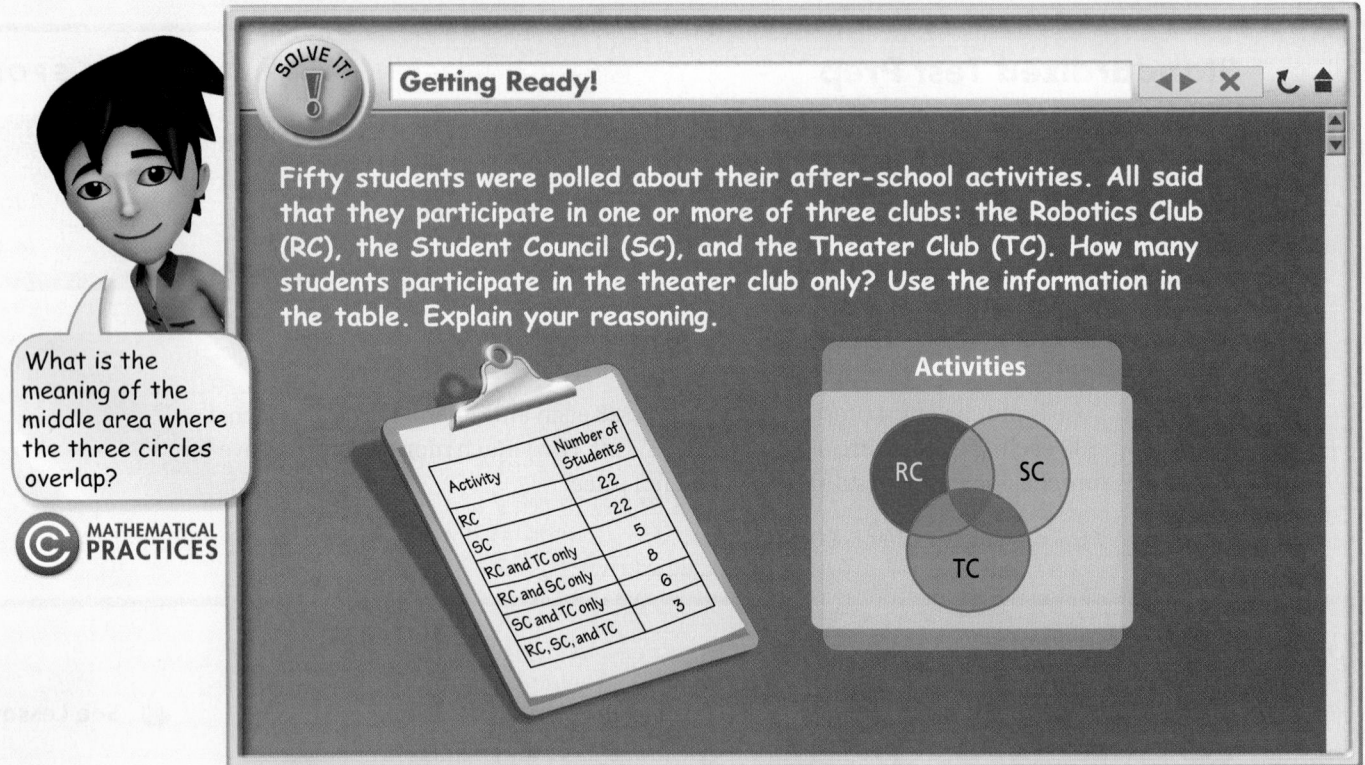

SOLVE IT!

Getting Ready!

Fifty students were polled about their after-school activities. All said that they participate in one or more of three clubs: the Robotics Club (RC), the Student Council (SC), and the Theater Club (TC). How many students participate in the theater club only? Use the information in the table. Explain your reasoning.

Activity	Number of Students
	22
RC	22
SC	5
RC and TC only	8
RC and SC only	6
SC and TC only	3
RC, SC, and TC	

Activities

What is the meaning of the middle area where the three circles overlap?

© **MATHEMATICAL PRACTICES**

Certain regions of the Venn diagram in the Solve It show *unions* and *intersections* of sets.

Essential Understanding Given two or more sets, you can describe which elements belong to *at least one* set. You can also describe which elements belong to *all* of the sets. You use symbols to represent these relationships.

The **union** of two or more sets is the set that contains all elements of the sets. The symbol for union is ∪. To find the union of two sets, list the elements that are in either set, or in both sets. An element is in the union if it belongs to *at least one* of the sets. In the Venn diagram below, $A \cup B$ is shaded.

Lesson Vocabulary
• union
• intersection
• disjoint sets

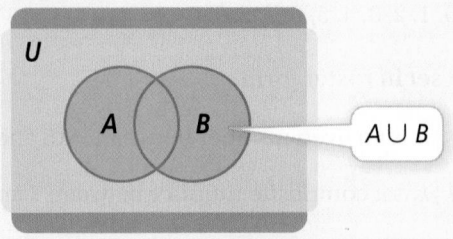

$A \cup B$

 **Problem 1** Union of Sets

In your left pocket, you have a quarter, a paper clip, and a key. In your right pocket, you have a penny, a quarter, a pencil, and a marble. What is a set that represents the different items in your pockets?

Step 1 Write sets that represent the contents of each pocket.

Left pocket: $L = \{$quarter, paper clip, key$\}$

Right pocket: $R = \{$penny, quarter, pencil, marble$\}$

Step 2 Write the union of the sets, which represents the different items that are in your pockets.

$L \cup R = \{$quarter, paper clip, key, penny, pencil, marble$\}$

Think

What if an item is in both sets?

Sets L and R each contain a quarter, so a quarter is in the union of L and R. You should list it only once, though.

Got It? **1. a.** Write sets P and Q below in roster form. What is $P \cup Q$?

$P = \{x \mid x$ is a whole number less than $5\}$

$Q = \{y \mid y$ is an even natural number less than $5\}$

b. Reasoning What is true about the union of two distinct sets if one set is a subset of the other?

The **intersection** of two or more sets is the set of elements that are common to every set. An element is in the intersection if it belongs to *all* of the sets. The symbol for intersection is ∩. When you find the intersection of two sets, list only the elements that are in both sets. In the Venn diagram below, $A \cap B$ is shaded.

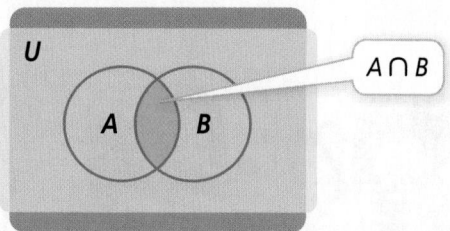

Disjoint sets have no elements in common. The intersection of disjoint sets is the empty set. The diagram below shows two disjoint sets.

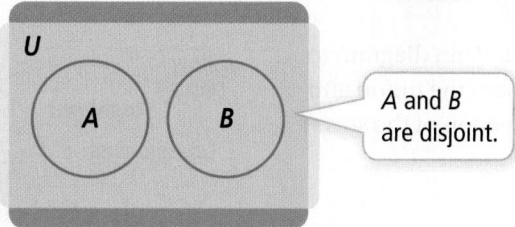

Problem 2 Intersection of Sets

Set $X = \{x \mid x$ is a natural number less than 19$\}$, set $Y = \{y \mid y$ is an odd integer$\}$,
and set $Z = \{z \mid z$ is a multiple of 6$\}$.

A What is $X \cap Z$?

List the elements that are both natural numbers less than 19 and multiples of 6:
$X \cap Z = \{6, 12, 18\}$.

B What is $Y \cap Z$?

List the elements that are both odd integers and multiples of 6. There are no
multiples of 6 that are also odd, so Y and Z are disjoint sets. They have no elements in
common. $Y \cap Z = \varnothing$, the empty set.

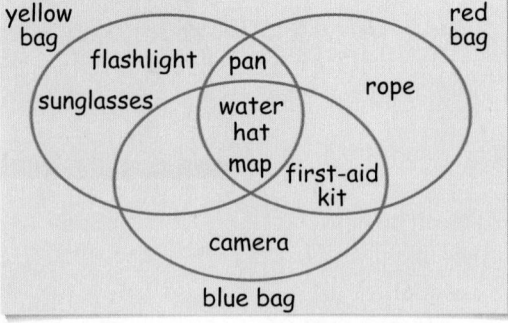

Think

Why are sets Y and Z disjoint?
Every element of Z is a multiple of 6, so every element of Z is even. Y contains only *odd* numbers. So no element of Z belongs to Y.

✔ **Got It? 2.** Let $A = \{2, 4, 6, 8\}$, $B = \{0, 2, 5, 7, 8\}$, and
$C = \{n \mid n$ is an odd whole number$\}$.
    a. What is $A \cap B$?   **b.** What is $A \cap C$?   **c.** What is $C \cap B$?

You can draw Venn diagrams to solve problems involving relationships between sets.

Problem 3 Making a Venn Diagram

Camping Three friends are going camping. The items in each of their backpacks
form a set. Which items do all three friends have in common?

Think

How do you know where in the diagram to place each item?
Items that the friends have in common belong in an intersection. Use the Venn diagram to determine the correct intersection.

Draw a Venn diagram to
represent the union and
intersection of the sets.

All three friends have a hat, a map, and a bottle of water in their backpacks.

Got It? **3.** Let $A = \{x \mid x$ is one of the first five letters in the English alphabet$\}$,
$B = \{x \mid x$ is a vowel$\}$, and $C = \{x \mid x$ is a letter in the word VEGETABLE$\}$.
Which letters are in all three sets?

You can also use Venn diagrams to show the *number* of elements in the union or
intersection of sets.

 Problem 4 **Using a Venn Diagram to Show Numbers of Elements**

Polling Of 500 commuters polled, some drive to work, some take public
transportation, and some do both. Two hundred commuters drive to work
and 125 use both types of transportation. How many commuters take
public transportation?

Know
- Number who commute: 500
- Number who drive: 200
- Number who drive *and* use public transportation: 125

Need
Number who use public transportation

Plan
- Draw a Venn diagram
- Calculate the number of commuters who only drive
- Calculate the number of commuters who only use public transportation

Step 1 Draw a Venn diagram. Let $D =$ commuters who drive
and $P =$ commuters who take public transportation.

Step 2 The intersection of D and P represents the commuters
who use both methods of transportation: $D \cap P$ has
125 commuters.

Step 3 Find the number of commuters who only drive:
$200 - 125 = 75$. Enter 75 into the Venn diagram.

Step 4 The total number of commuters is 500. Subtract to
find the number of commuters who use only public transportation:
$500 - 200 = 300$.

The number of commuters using public transportation is $300 + 125 = 425$.

 Got It? **4.** Of 30 students in student government, 20 are honor students and
9 are officers and honor students. All of the students are officers, honor
students, or both. How many are officers but not honor students?

Recall from Lesson 3-6 that the graph of a compound inequality with the word *and*
contains the *overlap* of the graphs of the two inequalities that form the compound
inequality. You can think of the overlap as the intersection of two sets. Similarly, you
can think of the solutions of an *or* inequality as the union of two sets.

 **Problem 5** **Writing Solutions of an Inequality**

What are the solutions of $|2x - 1| < 3$? Write the solutions as either the union or the intersection of two sets.

$$|2x - 1| < 3$$

$-3 < 2x - 1 < 3$	Write a compound inequality.
$-2 < \quad 2x \quad < 4$	Add 1 to each expression.
$-1 < \quad x \quad < 2$	Divide each side by 2.

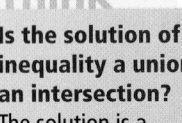 **Think**

Is the solution of the inequality a union or an intersection?
The solution is a compound inequality joined by the word *and*. So the solution is an intersection.

The solutions of the inequality are given by $-1 < x < 2$. You can write this as $x > -1$ and $x < 2$. This compound inequality is the intersection of two sets, which you can write as follows: $\{x | x > -1\} \cap \{x | x < 2\}$.

 Got It? **5.** Solve each inequality. Write the solutions as either the union or the intersection of two sets.

a. $8 \leq x + 5 < 11$

b. $|4x - 6| > 14$

 Lesson Check

Do you know HOW?

Let $X = \{2, 4, 6, 8, 10\}$, $Y = \{1, 2, 3, 4, 5, 6, 7, 8, 9, 10\}$, and $Z = \{1, 3, 5, 7, 9\}$. Find each union or intersection.

1. $X \cup Y$ **2.** $X \cap Y$ **3.** $X \cap Z$ **4.** $Y \cup Z$

5. In a survey of 80 people who use their cell phones to take pictures and play games, 49 take pictures and 35 take pictures and play games. How many people only use their cell phones to play games?

Do you UNDERSTAND?  **MATHEMATICAL PRACTICES**

6. Vocabulary Suppose A and B are nonempty sets. Which set contains more elements: $A \cup B$ or $A \cap B$? Explain your reasoning.

7. Compare and Contrast How are unions and intersections of sets different?

Determine whether each statement is *true* or *false*.

8. If x is an element of set A and x is not an element of set B, then x is an element of $A \cup B$.

9. If x is not an element of set A and x is an element of set B, then x is an element of $A \cap B$.

 Practice and Problem-Solving Exercises  **MATHEMATICAL PRACTICES**

 **Practice**   Find each union or intersection. Let $A = \{1, 3, 4\}$, $B = \{x | x \text{ is an even}$ whole number less than 9$\}$, $C = \{2, 5, 7, 10\}$, and $D = \{x | x \text{ is an odd}$ whole number less than 10$\}$.   ◀ **See Problems 1 and 2.**

10. $A \cup B$ **11.** $A \cup C$ **12.** $A \cup D$ **13.** $B \cup C$

14. $B \cup D$ **15.** $C \cup D$ **16.** $A \cap B$ **17.** $A \cap C$

18. $A \cap D$ **19.** $B \cap C$ **20.** $B \cap D$ **21.** $C \cap D$

Draw a Venn diagram to represent the union and intersection of these sets.

● See Problem 3.

22. The letters in the words ALGEBRA, GEOMETRY, and CALCULUS are represented by the sets $V = \{A, L, G, E, B, R\}$, $W = \{G, E, O, M, T, R, Y\}$, and $X = \{C, A, L, U, S\}$, respectively.

23. Let $E = \{x \mid x \text{ is a positive, composite number less than } 10\}$, $F = \{1, 2, 4, 5, 6, 8, 9\}$, and $G = \{x \mid x \text{ is a positive, even number less than or equal to } 10\}$.

24. Let $L = \{A, B, C, 1, 2, 3, \text{horse, cow, pig}\}$, $M = \{-1, 0, 1, B, Y, \text{pig, duck}, \Delta\}$, and $N = \{C, 3, \text{duck}, \Delta\}$.

25. Camping Twenty-eight girls went camping. There were two main activities: volleyball and swimming. Fourteen girls went swimming, 5 participated in both activities, and 4 girls did neither. How many girls only played volleyball?

● See Problem 4.

26. Winter Sports A ski shop owner surveys 200 people who ski or snowboard. If 196 people ski and 154 people do both activities, how many people snowboard?

Solve each inequality. Write the solutions as either the union or intersection of two sets.

● See Problem 5.

27. $|3x - 5| < 14$

28. $-6 < n + 7 \leq 21$

29. $|8w - 1| \geq 7$

30. $3 \leq |5d + 11|$

31. $2|x - 7| > 28$

32. $|4.5t - 1.5| \leq 12$

B Apply

Find each union or intersection. Let $W = \{5, 6, 7, 8\}$, $X = \{3, 6, 9\}$, $Y = \{2, 3, 7, 8\}$, and $Z = \{x \mid x \text{ is an even whole number less than } 10\}$.

33. $W \cup Y \cup Z$

34. $X \cap Y \cap Z$

35. $W \cap X \cap Z$

© 36. Writing Let $M = \{x \mid x \text{ is a multiple of } 3\}$ and $N = \{x \mid x \text{ is a multiple of } 5\}$. Describe the intersection of M and N.

© 37. Think About a Plan Blood type is determined partly by which *antigens* a red blood cell has. An antigen is a protein on the surface of a red blood cell. Type A contains the A antigen. Type B contains the B antigen. Type AB contains both A and B antigens. Type O does not have any antigens. A hospital has 25 patients with the A antigen, 17 with the B antigen, 10 with the A and B antigens, and 30 without A or B antigens. How many patients are represented by the data?
- How can a Venn diagram help you solve the problem?
- What strategies can you use to complete the Venn diagram?

38. Sports In a survey of students about favorite sports, the results include 22 who like tennis, 25 who like football, 9 who like tennis and football, 17 who like tennis and baseball, 20 who like football and baseball, 6 who like all three sports, and 4 who like none of the sports. How many students like only tennis and football? How many students like only tennis and baseball? How many students like only baseball and football?

© 39. Reasoning Suppose A and B are sets such that $A \subseteq B$. What is true about $A \cap B$?

The *cross product* of two sets A and B, denoted by $A \times B$, is the set of all ordered pairs with the first element in A and with the second element in B. In set-builder notation, you write:

$$A \times B = \{(a, b) \mid a \text{ is an element of } A, b \text{ is an element of } B\}$$

For example, suppose $A = \{1, 2\}$ and $B = \{7, 10, 12\}$. Then:

$$A \times B = \{(1, 7), (1, 10), (1, 12), (2, 7), (2, 10), (2, 12)\}$$

Given sets A and B, find $A \times B$.

40. $A = \{1, 2, 3\}$, $B = \{-3, -2, -1, 0\}$

41. $A = \{\pi, 2\pi, 3\pi, 4\pi\}$, $B = \{2, 4\}$

42. $A = \{$grape, apple, orange$\}$, $B = \{$jam, juice$\}$

43. $A = \{$reduce, reuse, recycle$\}$, $B = \{$plastic$\}$

 **Challenge**

44. Use a Venn diagram to determine whether the statement $(A \cap B)' = A' \cap B'$ is *true* or *false*.

ⓒ **45. Reasoning** Is the statement $(A \cup B) \cap C = A \cup (B \cap C)$ *always, sometimes,* or *never* true? Justify your answer.

Standardized Test Prep

SAT/ACT

46. Set $X = \{x \mid x \text{ is a factor of } 12\}$ and set $Y = \{y \mid y \text{ is a factor of } 16\}$. Which set represents $X \cap Y$?

Ⓐ $\varnothing$ Ⓑ $\{1, 2, 4\}$ Ⓒ $\{0, 1, 2, 4\}$ Ⓓ $\{1, 2, 3, 4, 6, 8, 12, 16\}$

47. Which compound inequality is equivalent to $|x + 4| < 8$?

Ⓕ $-12 < x < 4$ Ⓗ $-12 > x > 4$

Ⓖ $x < -12$ or $x > 4$ Ⓘ $x > -12$ or $x < 4$

Short Response

48. Suppose you earn $80 per week at your summer job. Your employer offers you a $20 raise or a 20% raise. Which should you take? Explain.

Mixed Review

Solve each equation or inequality.

➤ See Lesson 3-7.

49. $|x| = 4$ **50.** $|n| + 7 = 9$ **51.** $4|f - 5| = 12$ **52.** $3|3y + 2| = 18$

53. $|4d| \leq 20$ **54.** $|x - 3| \geq 7$ **55.** $|2w + 6| > 24$ **56.** $2|3x| + 1 = 9$

Tell whether the ordered pair is a solution to the given equation.

➤ See Lesson 1-9.

57. $x + 3 = y$; $(1, 4)$ **58.** $2x - 5 = y$; $(-1, 8)$ **59.** $\frac{1}{2}x + 7 = y$; $(8, 11)$

Get Ready! **To prepare for Lesson 4-1, do Exercises 60–63.**

Graph each point on the same coordinate grid.

➤ See Review p. 60.

60. $(1, 4)$ **61.** $(-1, -5)$ **62.** $(3, -6)$ **63.** $(-2, 1)$

Pull It **All Together**

Completing the Performance Task

Look back at your results from the Apply What You've Learned in Lessons 3-2 and 3-4. Use the work you did to complete the following.

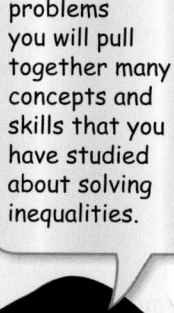

To solve these problems you will pull together many concepts and skills that you have studied about solving inequalities.

1. Solve the problem in the Task Description on page 163 by finding the least number of boxes of popcorn that the athletic boosters can sell at the next game to make a profit. Show all your work and explain each step of your solution.

2. **Reflect** Choose one of the Mathematical Practices below and explain how you applied it in your work on the Performance Task.

MP 2: Reason abstractly and quantitatively.

MP 4: Model with mathematics.

On Your Own

Use the information on page 163 about the athletic boosters' concession stand. Suppose the athletic boosters have 40 empty boxes on hand, and purchase one package of 300 empty boxes to augment their supply for the next game. At the next game, they make a profit of $165.50 from selling popcorn and have some empty boxes left over. For the following game, they need to purchase additional empty boxes again. What is the least number of boxes of popcorn they can sell at the following game and make a profit?

Connecting **BIG** ideas and Answering the Essential Questions

1 Variable
You can use algebraic inequalities to represent relationships between quantities that are not equal.

Inequalities and Their Graphs
(Lessons 3-1, 3-2, 3-3, 3-4, 3-6, 3-7)

$c \geq -2$

$$\begin{array}{ccccccc} & & \bullet & & & & \\ \hline -3 & -2 & -1 & 0 & 1 & 2 \end{array}$$

2 Equivalence
You can represent an inequality in many ways. Equivalent representations have the same solutions as the original inequality.

Solving One-Step Inequalities
(Lessons 3-2, 3-3)

The inequalities in each pair are equivalent.

$$f - 4 \geq -3 \qquad 6y < 24$$
$$f \geq 1 \qquad y < 4$$

3 Solving Equations and Inequalities
You can use properties of inequality to transform an inequality into equivalent, simpler inequalities and then find solutions.

Solving Multi-Step Inequalities
(Lesson 3-4)

$$7z + 10 \leq 24$$
$$7z + 10 - 10 \leq 24 - 10$$
$$7z \leq 14$$
$$\frac{7z}{7} \leq \frac{14}{7}$$
$$z \leq 2$$

Solving Compound and Absolute Value Inequalities
(Lessons 3-6, 3-7)

$$|3m + 2| \leq 14$$
$$-14 \leq 3m + 2 \leq 14$$
$$-16 \leq 3m \leq 12$$
$$-\frac{16}{3} \leq m \leq 4$$

Chapter Vocabulary

- complement of a set (p. 196)
- compound inequality (p. 200)
- disjoint sets (p. 215)
- empty set (p. 195)
- equivalent inequalities (p. 171)
- intersection (p. 215)
- interval notation (p. 203)
- roster form (p. 194)
- set-builder notation (p. 194)
- solution of an inequality (p. 165)
- union (p. 214)
- universal set (p. 196)

Choose the correct term to complete each sentence.

1. The set $\{5, 10, 15, 20, \dots\}$ represents the multiples of 5 written in __?__ .

2. The __?__ of two or more sets is the set that contains all elements of the sets.

3. The set that contains no elements is the __?__ .

4. The __?__ is a number that makes the inequality true.

5. The inequalities $6a \geq 12$ and $a \geq 2$ are __?__ .

3-1 Inequalities and Their Graphs

Quick Review

A **solution of an inequality** is any number that makes the inequality true. You can indicate all the solutions of an inequality on the graph. A closed dot indicates that the endpoint is a solution. An open dot indicates that the endpoint is *not* a solution.

Example

What is the graph of $x \leq -4$?

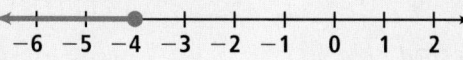

Exercises

Graph each inequality.

6. $x > 5$

7. $h \leq -1$

8. $10 \geq p$

9. $r < 3.2$

Write an inequality for each graph.

10.
```
  +---+---+---+---+---+---⊕---+---+->
 -1   0   1   2   3   4   5   6   7
```

11.
```
<-+---+---+---+---●---+---+---+---+->
 -6  -5  -4  -3  -2  -1   0   1   2
```

12.
```
<-+---+---○---+---+---+---+---+---+->
 -7  -6  -5  -4  -3  -2  -1   0   1
```

3-2 Solving Inequalities Using Addition or Subtraction

Quick Review

You can use the addition and subtraction properties of inequality to transform an inequality into a simpler, equivalent inequality.

Example

What are the solutions of $x + 4 \leq 5$?

$$x + 4 \leq 5$$
$$x + 4 - 4 \leq 5 - 4 \quad \text{Subtract 4 from each side.}$$
$$x \leq 1 \quad \text{Simplify.}$$

Exercises

Solve each inequality. Graph your solutions.

13. $w + 3 > 9$

14. $v - 6 < 4$

15. $-4 < t + 8$

16. $n - \frac{1}{2} \geq \frac{3}{4}$

17. $22.3 \leq 13.7 + h$

18. $q + 0.5 > -2$

19. **Allowance** You have at most $15.00 to spend. You want to buy a used CD that costs $4.25. Write and solve an inequality to find the possible additional amounts you can spend.

3-3 Solving Inequalities Using Multiplication or Division

Quick Review

You can use the multiplication and division properties of inequality to transform an inequality. When you multiply or divide each side of an inequality by a negative number, you have to reverse the inequality symbol.

Example

What are the solutions of $-3x > 12$?

$-3x > 12$

$\dfrac{-3x}{-3} < \dfrac{12}{-3}$ Divide each side by -3. Reverse the inequality symbol.

$x < -4$ Simplify.

Exercises

Solve each inequality. Graph your solutions.

20. $5x < 15$

21. $-6t > 18$

22. $\dfrac{y}{3} \leq 2$

23. $-\dfrac{h}{4} < 6$

24. $25.5g > 102$

25. $-\dfrac{3}{5}n \geq -9$

26. $44.5 \leq 2.7d$

27. $-17.1m < 23.8$

28. Part-Time Job You earn \$7.25 per hour baby-sitting. Write and solve an inequality to find how many full hours you must work to earn at least \$200.

3-4 Solving Multi-Step Inequalities

Quick Review

When you solve inequalities, sometimes you need to use more than one step. You need to gather the variable terms on one side of the inequality and the constant terms on the other side.

Example

What are the solutions of $3x + 5 > -1$?

$3x + 5 > -1$

$3x > -6$ Subtract 5 from each side.

$x > -2$ Divide each side by 3.

Exercises

Solve each inequality.

29. $4k - 1 \geq -3$

30. $6(c - 1) < -18$

31. $3t > 5t + 12$

32. $-\dfrac{6}{7}y - 6 \geq 42$

33. $4 + \dfrac{x}{2} > 2x$

34. $3x + 5 \leq 2x - 8$

35. $13.5a + 7.4 \leq 85.7$

36. $42w > 2(w + 7)$

37. Commission A salesperson earns \$200 per week plus a commission equal to 4% of her sales. This week her goal is to earn no less than \$450. Write and solve an inequality to find the amount of sales she must have to reach her goal.

3-5 Working With Sets

Quick Review

The **complement** of a set A is the set of all elements in the universal set that are *not* in A.

Example

Suppose $U = \{1, 2, 3, 4, 5, 6\}$ and $Y = \{2, 4, 6\}$.
What is Y'?

The elements in U that are *not* in Y are 1, 3, and 5.
So $Y' = \{1, 3, 5\}$.

Exercises

List all the subsets of each set.

38. $\{s, t\}$

39. $\{5, 10, 15\}$

40. How do you write "A is the set of even whole numbers that are less than 18" in roster form? How do you write A using set-builder notation?

41. Suppose $U = \{1, 2, 3, 4, 5, 6, 7, 8\}$ and $B = \{2, 4, 6, 8\}$. What is B'?

3-6 Compound Inequalities

Quick Review

Two inequalities that are joined by the word *and* or the word *or* are called **compound inequalities**. A solution of a compound inequality involving *and* makes both inequalities true. A solution of an inequality involving *or* makes either inequality true.

Example

What are the solutions of $-3 \leq z - 1 < 3$?

$$-3 \leq z - 1 < 3$$

$$-2 \leq z < 4 \qquad \text{Add 1 to each part of the inequality.}$$

Exercises

Solve each compound inequality.

42. $-2 \leq d + \frac{1}{2} < 4\frac{1}{2}$

43. $0 < -8b \leq 12$

44. $2t \leq -4$ or $7t \geq 49$

45. $5m < -10$ or $3m > 9$

46. $-1 \leq a - 3 \leq 2$

47. $9.1 > 1.4p \geq -6.3$

48. **Climate** A town's high temperature for a given month is 88°F and the low temperature is 65°F. Write a compound inequality to represent the range of temperatures for the given month.

3-7 Absolute Value Equations and Inequalities

Quick Review

Solving an equation or inequality that contains an absolute value expression is similar to solving other equations and inequalities. You will need to write two equations or inequalities using positive and negative values. Then solve the equations.

Example

What is the solution of $|x| - 7 = 3$?

$$|x| - 7 = 3$$

$$|x| = 10 \qquad \text{Add 7 to each side.}$$

$$x = 10 \text{ or } x = -10 \qquad \text{Definition of absolute value}$$

Exercises

Solve each equation or inequality. If there is no solution, write *no solution*.

49. $|y| = 3$

50. $|n + 2| = 4$

51. $4 + |r + 2| = 7$

52. $|x + 3| = -2$

53. $|5x| \leq 15$

54. $|3d + 5| < -2$

55. $|2x - 7| - 1 > 0$

56. $4|k + 5| > 8$

57. Manufacturing The ideal length of a certain nail is 20 mm. The actual length can vary from the ideal by at most 0.4 mm. Find the range of acceptable lengths of the nail.

3-8 Unions and Intersections of Sets

Quick Review

The **union** of two or more sets is the set that contains all elements of the sets. The **intersection** of two or more sets is the set of elements that are common to all the sets. **Disjoint sets** have no elements in common.

Example

Student Activities Of 100 students who play sports or take music lessons, 70 students play a sport and 50 students play a sport and take music lessons. How many students *only* take music lessons?

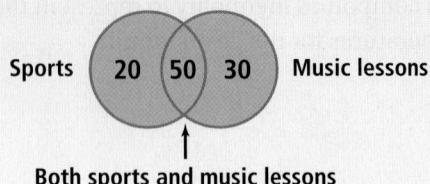

Sports 20 50 30 Music lessons

↑
Both sports and music lessons

So, 30 students take only music lessons.

Exercises

58. Given $A = \{1, 2, 3, 4, 5, 6, 7, 8, 9\}$ and $B = \{2, 4, 6, 8\}$, what is $A \cup B$?

59. Let $P = \{1, 5, 7, 9, 13\}$, $R = \{1, 2, 3, 4, 5, 6, 8\}$, and $Q = \{1, 3, 5\}$. Draw a Venn diagram that represents the intersection and union of the sets.

60. Let $N = \{x \mid x \text{ is a multiple of 2}\}$ and $P = \{x \mid x \text{ is a multiple of 6}\}$. Describe the intersection of N and P.

61. Cats There are 15 cats. Ten are striped and 7 are striped and have green eyes. The rest of the cats have green eyes but are not striped. How many cats have green eyes but are not striped?

Do you know HOW?

Write an inequality for each graph.

1.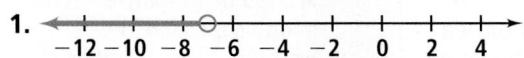

2.

3.

4.

Solve each inequality. Graph the solutions.

5. $z + 7 \leq 9$

6. $-\frac{1}{3}x < 2$

7. $5w \geq -6w + 11$

8. $-\frac{7}{2}(m - 2) < 21$

9. $|x - 5| \geq 3$

10. $9 \leq 6 - b < 12$

11. $4 + 3n \geq 1$ or $-5n > 25$

12. $10k < 75$ and $4 - k \leq 0$

List the subsets of each set.

13. $\{1, 3, 5, 7\}$

14. $\{$red, blue, yellow$\}$

15. **Quality Control** A manufacturer is cutting fabric into rectangles that are 18.55 in. long by 36.75 in. wide. Each rectangle's length and width must be within 0.05 in. of the desired size. Write and solve inequalities to find the acceptable range for the length ℓ and the width w.

Write a compound inequality that each graph could represent.

16.

17.

18. **Multiple Choice** Suppose $A = \{x \mid x > -1\}$ and $B = \{x \mid -3 \leq x \leq 2\}$. Which statement is true?

Ⓐ $A \cup B = \{\ \}$

Ⓑ $A' = \{x \mid x < -1\}$

Ⓒ $A \cap B = \{x \mid -1 < x \leq 2\}$

Ⓓ $B \subseteq \{x \mid x < 2\}$

Solve each equation. Check your solution.

19. $|4k - 2| = 11$

20. $23 = |n + 10|$

21. $|3c + 1| - 4 = 13$

22. $4|5 - t| = 20$

23. **Fundraising** A drama club wants to raise at least $500 in ticket sales for its annual show. The members of the club sold 50 tickets at a special $5 rate. The usual ticket price the day of the show is $7.50. At least how many tickets do they have to sell the day of the show to meet the goal?

24. Of 145 runners, 72 run only on weekends and 63 run on both weekends and during the week. How many of the runners run only during the week?

Do You UNDERSTAND?

25. **Open-Ended** Write an absolute value inequality that has 3 and -5 as two of its solutions.

26. **Writing** Compare and contrast the Multiplication Property of Equality and the Multiplication Property of Inequality.

27. Describe the region labeled C in terms of set A and set B.

28. Suppose set A has 9 elements. What is the greatest number of elements a subset of A can have?

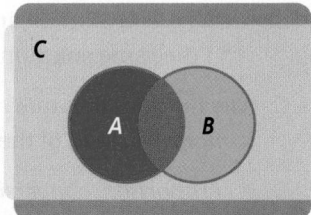

Common Core Cumulative Standards Review

 **ASSESSMENT**

TIPS FOR SUCCESS

Some questions on tests ask you to write an extended response. In this textbook, an extended response question is usually worth a maximum of 4 points. Sometimes these questions have multiple parts. To get full credit, you need to answer each part and show all your work or justify your reasoning.

TIP 1

A 1-point response might show an incorrect equation without giving the number of children who must attend to cover costs.

The Theatre Club needs to raise $440 to cover the cost of its children's play. The ticket prices are $14 for an adult and $2 for a child. The club expects that three times as many children as adults will attend the play. Write and solve an equation to find how many adult and child tickets the club needs to sell to cover the cost.

Solution

x = number of adults
$3x$ = number of children
$14(x) + 2(3x) = 440$
$14x + 6x = 440$
$20x = 440$
$x = 22$
$3x = 66$

So, 22 adults and 66 children must attend.

TIP 2

A 3-point response might approach the problem correctly, but have an error.

Think It Through

A 4–point response defines variables, shows the work, and gives a written answer to the problem. So relate what is given to what has been asked. Identify the variables and make a model that you can use to write an equation. Then show your work as you use this equation to find the solution.

Vocabulary Builder

As you solve test items, you must understand the meanings of mathematical terms. Choose the correct term to complete each sentence.

A. Two inequalities that are joined by the word *and* or the word *or* form a (*compound, connected*) inequality.

B. (*Equivalent, Similar*) inequalities are inequalities with the same solutions.

C. Any number that makes an inequality true is a (*union, solution*) of the inequality.

D. A (*proportion, conversion factor*) is an equation that states that two ratios are equal.

E. A(n) (*open, closed*) dot on the graph of an inequality shows that the point is a solution of the inequality.

Selected Response

Read each question. Then write the letter of the correct answer on your paper.

1. You are making bracelets to sell at a fair. The table shows the total cost c of making b bracelets. Which equation represents the relationship between the number of bracelets you make and the total cost?

Bracelets, b	Cost, c
10	$9.00
15	$13.50
20	$18.00
25	$22.50

   Ⓐ $c = 9b$ Ⓒ $9c = b$

   Ⓑ $c = 0.9b$ Ⓓ $0.9c = b$

2. What are the solutions of $2u + 5.2 \leq 9.4 + u$?

   Ⓕ $u \geq 4.2$ Ⓗ $u \leq 14.6$

   Ⓖ $u \leq 48.9$ Ⓘ $u \leq 4.2$

3. A baseball team can spend up to $1500 on bats. Bats cost $32 each. Which inequality represents the number of bats b they can buy?

Ⓐ $32b \leq 1500$

Ⓑ $32b \geq 1500$

Ⓒ $32b + b \leq 1500$

Ⓓ $32b + b \geq 1500$

4. What is the solution of $w - 4 = 18 + 3w$?

Ⓕ -11 Ⓗ 3.5

Ⓖ -3.5 Ⓘ 11

5. Which graph represents the solutions to the inequality $3n \leq -6$?

Ⓐ
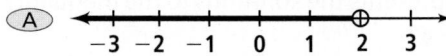

Ⓑ
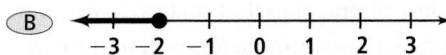

Ⓒ

Ⓓ

6. A student calculated the density of copper to be 8.37 g/cm³. The accepted value for the density of copper is 8.92 g/cm³. What is the percent error in the density?

Ⓕ 6.57% Ⓗ 5.79%

Ⓖ 6.17% Ⓘ 4.78%

7. The cost of a hardcover book x is at least $3 more than twice the cost of the paperback book y. Which inequality represents this situation?

Ⓐ $2y + 3 \geq x$ Ⓒ $2y + 3 \leq x$

Ⓑ $x + 3 \leq 2y$ Ⓓ $x + 2y \leq 3$

8. What is the solution of $\frac{18}{x} = \frac{5}{7}$?

Ⓕ 12.9 Ⓖ 20 Ⓗ 25.2 Ⓘ 35

9. A fox runs at a rate of 26 mi/h and a cat runs at a rate of 44 ft/s. What is the difference in their speeds? (*Hint:* 1 mi = 5280 ft)

Ⓐ 26 ft/s   Ⓒ 18 mi/h

Ⓑ 5.9 ft/s   Ⓓ 30 mi/h

10. When simplifying the expression $206 - 4(17 - 3^2)$, which part of the expression do you simplify first?

Ⓕ $206 - 4$

Ⓖ 3^2

Ⓗ $17 - 3$

Ⓘ $4(17)$

11. In the expression $8y - (6y - 5)$, what is the most appropriate name for $6y$?

Ⓐ coefficient

Ⓑ factor

Ⓒ term

Ⓓ variable

12. Which statement is always true?

Ⓕ The product of a nonzero rational number and an irrational number is irrational.

Ⓖ The product of two rational numbers is irrational.

Ⓗ The sum of a rational number and an irrational number is rational.

Ⓘ The sum of two rational numbers is irrational.

13. The solution to the equation below is stepped out.

$$3x - 12 = 30$$

Step 1 $3x - 12 + 12 = 30 + 12$

Step 2 $3x = 42$

Step 3 $\frac{3x}{3} = \frac{42}{3}$

Step 4 $x = 14$

Which property can be used to justify Step 3?

Ⓐ Reflexive Property

Ⓑ Subtraction Property of Equality

Ⓒ Transitive Property

Ⓓ Division Property of Equality

14. What are the solutions of $-\frac{1}{9}a + 1 < 8$?

Ⓕ $a > 7$ Ⓗ $a > -63$

Ⓖ $a < 7$ Ⓘ $a < -63$

15. What are the solutions of $4 < 6b - 2 \leq 28$?

Ⓐ $\frac{1}{3} < b \leq \frac{13}{3}$ Ⓒ $\frac{2}{3} < b \leq \frac{14}{3}$

Ⓑ $6 < b \leq 30$ Ⓓ $1 < b \leq 5$

Constructed Response

16. You can mow 400 ft² of grass if you work for 5 min, 800 ft² if you work for 10 min, 1200 ft² of grass if you work for 15 min, and so on. How many square feet can you mow in 45 min?

17. An insect flies 20 ft in 1 s. How fast does the insect fly in miles per hour? Round to the nearest hundredth if necessary.

18. Isabella is covering a square tabletop with square mosaic tiles. The tabletop is 2 ft long and 2 ft wide. Each tile is $\frac{1}{4}$ in. long and $\frac{1}{4}$ in. wide. What is the minimum number of tiles needed to cover the tabletop?

19. What is the solution of $\frac{7}{5} = \frac{9}{x}$? Round your answer to the nearest thousandth if necessary.

20. A hockey puck travels at a constant speed of 20 m/s. What is the speed in mi/h? Round to the nearest hundredth. (1 m = 3.28 ft)

21. The cost for a taxi is $2.50 plus $2.00 per mile. If the total for a taxi ride was $32.50, how many miles did the customer travel?

22. What is the value of d when $11(d + 1) = 4(d + 8)$?

23. You are making a scale model of a sports field. The actual field is a rectangle with a length of 315 ft and a width of 300 ft. Your scale model is 15 in. wide. What is its length in inches?

24. The triangles below are similar. What is the value of x?

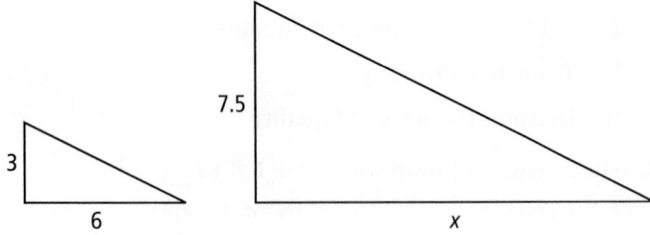

25. Colton surveyed his classmates. The ratio of students who prefer football to students who prefer baseball is 3 : 7. There are 30 students in Colton's class. How many students prefer football?

26. For safety, the weight of each rider of a certain roller coaster must fall in the range given by the inequality $10 \le \frac{w}{2} - 30 \le 70$ where w is in pounds. Solve for w to find the safe weight range.

27. You count the number of melons you use based on the number of bowls of fruit salad made, as shown in the table at the right. What is an equation that describes the relationship between the number of bowls of fruit salad f and the number of melons used m?

Fruit salad, f	Melons, m
2	1
4	2
6	3
8	4
10	5

28. What graph represents the solutions to the inequality $3(f + 2) > 2f + 4$?

29. You have a wireless phone plan that costs $25 per month. You must also pay $.10 per minute for each minute over 500 min. Your phone bill was more than $30 last month. Write an inequality to represent the number of minutes m you spent on the phone last month. Suppose you use 525 min next month. How much will your bill be?

30. An electric company charges a monthly fee of $30.60 plus $.0176 for each kilowatt-hour (kWh) of energy used. Write an equation to represent the cost of the family's electric bill each month. Suppose the family used 1327 kWh of energy. How much was their bill?

31. The volume V of a cone with radius r and height h is represented by the formula $V = \frac{1}{3}\pi r^2 h$. What equation do you get when you solve the formula for h? Show all your work.

Extended Response

32. A company has $1500 in its budget for paper this year. The regular price of paper is $32 per box, with a 10% discount for bulk orders. If the company spends at least $1400 on paper, the shipping is free. Write a compound inequality to represent the number of boxes the company can buy with the discount and receive free shipping. What are the possible numbers of boxes the company can buy with the discount and free shipping?

Get Ready!

Lesson 1-2 ◀ **Evaluating Expressions**

Evaluate each expression for the given value(s) of the variable(s).

1. $3x - 2y; x = -1, y = 2$

2. $-w^2 + 3w; w = -3$

3. $\frac{3+k}{k}; k = 3$

4. $h - \left(h^2 - 1\right) \div 2; h = -1$

Lesson 1-9 ◀ **Using Tables, Equations, and Graphs**

Use a table, an equation, and a graph to represent each relationship.

5. Bob is 9 years older than his dog.

6. Sue swims 1.5 laps per minute.

7. Each carton of eggs costs $3.

Review, page 60 ◀ **Graphing in the Coordinate Plane**

Graph the ordered pairs in the same coordinate plane.

8. $(3, -3)$

9. $(0, -5)$

10. $(-2, 2)$

11. $(-2, 0)$

Lesson 2-2 ◀ **Solving Two-Step Equations**

Solve each equation. Check your answer.

12. $5x + 3 = -12$

13. $\frac{n}{6} - 1 = 10$

14. $7 = \frac{x+8}{2}$

15. $\frac{x-1}{4} = \frac{3}{4}$

Lesson 3-7 ◀ **Solving Absolute Value Equations**

Solve each equation. If there is no solution, write *no solution*.

16. $|r + 2| = 2$

17. $-3|d - 5| = -6$

18. $-3.2 = |8p|$

19. $5|2x - 7| = 20$

🔊 Looking Ahead Vocabulary

20. The amount of money you earn from a summer job is *dependent* upon the number of hours you work. What do you think it means when a variable is *dependent* upon another variable?

21. A *relation* is a person to whom you are related. If $(1, 2)$, $(3, 4)$, and $(5, 6)$ form a mathematical *relation*, to which number is 3 related?

22. When a furnace runs *continuously*, there are no breaks or interruptions in its operation. What do you think a *continuous* graph looks like?

An Introduction to Functions

Chapter Preview

BIG ideas

1 **Functions**
Essential Question How can you represent and describe functions?

2 **Modeling**
Essential Question Can functions describe real-world situations?

Vocabulary

English/Spanish Vocabulary Audio Online:

English	Spanish
continuous graph, p. 255	gráfica continua
dependent variable, p. 240	variable dependiente
discrete graph, p. 255	gráfica discreta
domain, p. 268	dominio
function, p. 241	función
independent variable, p. 240	variable independiente
linear function, p. 241	función lineal
nonlinear function, p. 246	función no lineal
range, p. 268	rango
recursive formula, p. 275	fórmula recursiva
relation, p. 268	relación
sequence, p. 274	progresión

 DOMAINS
- Interpreting Functions
- Building Functions

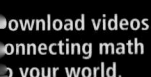

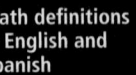

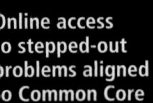

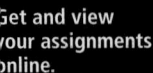

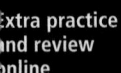

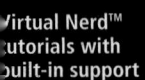

Download videos connecting math to your world.

Interactive! Vary numbers, graphs, and figures to explore math concepts.

The online Solve It will get you in gear for each lesson.

Math definitions in English and Spanish

Online access to stepped-out problems aligned to Common Core

Get and view your assignments online.

Extra practice and review online

Virtual Nerd™ tutorials with built-in support

Common Core Performance Task

Comparing the Growth of Two Blogs

Jayden and Keiko each start writing a blog at the same time. When Jayden starts his blog (Month 0), he gets 48 of his friends to subscribe. At the end of each month, he records the number of subscribers in a table. His data for the first few months are shown below.

Jayden's Blog

Number of Months	Number of Subscribers
0	48
1	56
2	64
3	72
4	80

Keiko finds that the number of subscribers K to her blog can be modeled by the function rule $K = m^2 + 10$, where m is the number of months since she started the blog.

Task Description

Determine whether Jayden's or Keiko's blog will be the first to have 200 subscribers. Assume the growth in each blog's subscribers continues to follow the established pattern.

Connecting the Task to the Math Practices

MATHEMATICAL PRACTICES

As you complete the task, you'll apply several Standards for Mathematical Practice.

- You'll analyze data to determine the type of relationship between the number of months and the number of subscribers. (MP 1)
- You'll graph the functions modeling both Jayden's and Keiko's subscriber data. (MP 4)
- You'll extend the sequence each set of data creates. (MP 8)

4-1 Using Graphs to Relate Two Quantities

Common Core State Standards

F-IF.B.4 . . . interpret key features of graphs and tables in terms of the quantities, and sketch graphs showing key features . . . of the relationship . . .

MP 1, MP 2, MP 3, MP 4

Objective To represent mathematical relationships using graphs

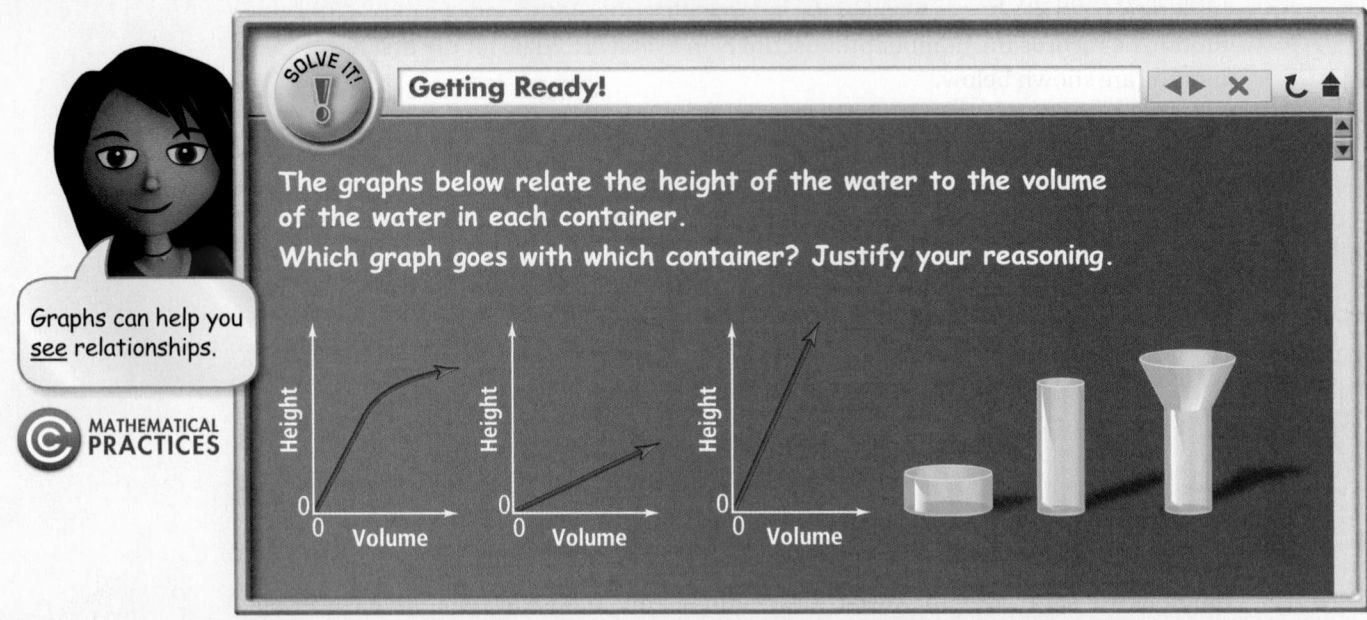

SOLVE IT!

Getting Ready!

Graphs can help you _see_ relationships.

MATHEMATICAL PRACTICES

The graphs below relate the height of the water to the volume of the water in each container.
Which graph goes with which container? Justify your reasoning.

As you may have noticed in the Solve It, the change in the height of the water as the volume increases is related to the shape of the container.

Essential Understanding You can use graphs to visually represent the relationship between two variable quantities as they both change.

Problem 1 Analyzing a Graph

Think

How can you analyze the relationship in a graph?
Read the titles. The axis titles tell you what variables are related. The graph itself represents the relationship as the variables change.

The graph shows the volume of air in a balloon as you blow it up, until it pops. What are the variables? Describe how the variables are related at various points on the graph.

The variables are volume and time. The volume increases each time you blow, and it stays constant each time you pause to breathe. When the balloon pops in the middle of the fourth blow, the volume decreases to 0.

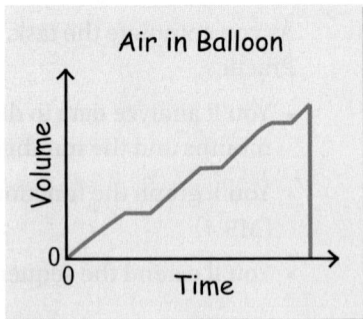

Air in Balloon

Got It? **1.** What are the variables in each graph? Describe how the variables are related at various points on the graph.

a.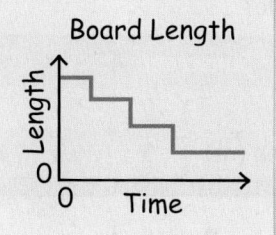

b.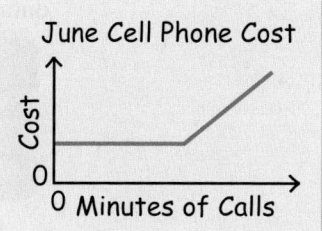

Tables and graphs can both show relationships between variables. Data from a table are often displayed using a graph to visually represent the relationship.

 Problem 2 Matching a Table and a Graph

Multiple Choice A band allowed fans to download its new video from its Web site. The table shows the total number of downloads after 1, 2, 3, and 4 days. Which graph could represent the data shown in the table?

Video Downloads

Day	Total Downloads
1	346
2	1011
3	3455
4	10,426

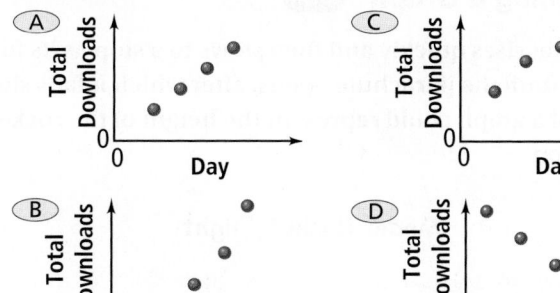

Know	Need	Plan
The relationship represented by a table	A graph that could represent the relationship	Compare the pattern of changes in the table to each graph.

In the table, the total number of downloads increases each day, and each increase is noticeably greater than the previous increase. So the graph should rise from left to right, and each rise should be steeper than the previous rise. The correct answer is B.

Got It? 2. The table shows the amount of sunscreen left in a can based on the number of times the sunscreen has been used. Which graph could represent the data shown in the table?

Sunscreen				
Number of Uses	0	1	2	3
Amount of Sunscreen (oz)	5	4.8	4.6	4.4

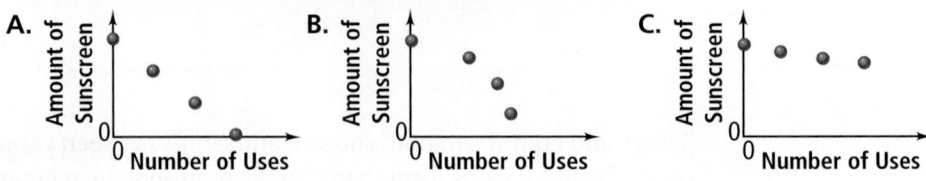

A.   B.   C.

In Problem 2, the number of downloads, which is on the vertical axis of each graph, depends on the day, which is on the horizontal axis. When one quantity depends on another, show the independent quantity on the horizontal axis and the dependent quantity on the vertical axis.

Problem 3 Sketching a Graph STEM

Rocketry A model rocket rises quickly and then slows to a stop as its fuel burns out. It begins to fall quickly until the parachute opens, after which it falls slowly back to Earth. What sketch of a graph could represent the height of the rocket during its flight? Label each section.

Think

How can you get started?
Identify the two variables that are being related, such as *height* and *time*. Then look for key words that describe the relationship, such as *rises quickly* or *falls slowly*.

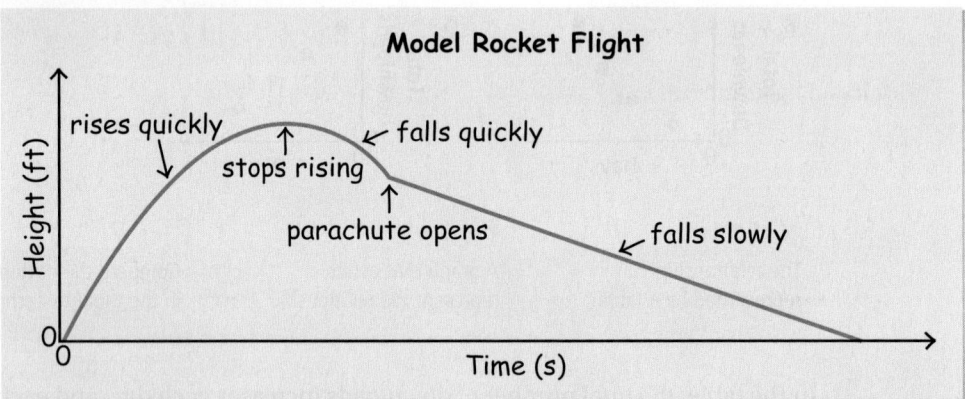

Got It? 3. a. Suppose you start to swing yourself on a playground swing. You move back and forth and swing higher in the air. Then you slowly swing to a stop. What sketch of a graph could represent how your height from the ground might change over time? Label each section.

b. Reasoning If you jumped from the swing instead of slowly swinging to a stop, how would the graph in part (a) be different? Explain.

Lesson Check

Do you know HOW?

1. What are the variables in the graph at the right? Use the graph to describe how the variables are related.

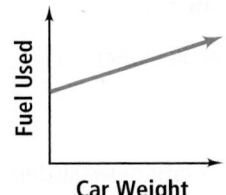

2. Describe the relationship between time and temperature in the table below.

Time (number of hours after noon)	1	3	5	7
Temperature (°F)	61	62	58	51

Do you UNDERSTAND?

MATHEMATICAL
PRACTICES

3. Match one of the labeled segments in the graph below with each of the following verbal descriptions: *rising slowly*, *constant*, and *falling quickly*.

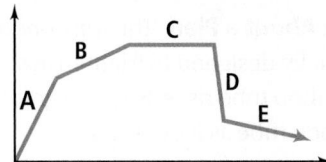

4. **Reasoning** Describe a real-world relationship that could be represented by the graph sketched above.

Practice and Problem-Solving Exercises

MATHEMATICAL
PRACTICES

 Practice

What are the variables in each graph? Describe how the variables are related at various points on the graph.

◀ See Problem 1.

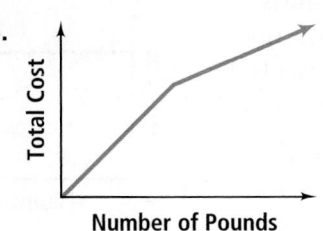

5.

6.

7.

Match each graph with its related table. Explain your answers.

◀ See Problem 2.

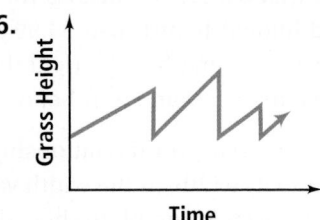

8.

9.

10.

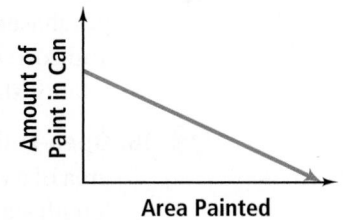

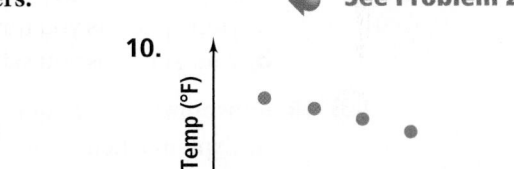

A.

Time	Temperature (°F)
1 P.M.	91°
3 P.M.	89°
5 P.M.	81°
7 P.M.	64°

B.

Time	Temperature (°F)
1 P.M.	61°
3 P.M.	60°
5 P.M.	59°
7 P.M.	58°

C.

Time	Temperature (°F)
1 P.M.	24°
3 P.M.	26°
5 P.M.	27°
7 P.M.	21°

Sketch a graph to represent each situation. Label each section.   ◀ See Problem 3.

11. hours of daylight each day over the course of one year

12. your distance from the ground as you ride a Ferris wheel

13. your pulse rate as you watch a scary movie

 **Apply**

14. Think About a Plan The *shishi-odoshi*, a popular Japanese garden ornament, was originally designed to frighten away deer. Using water, it makes a sharp rap each time a bamboo tube rises. Sketch a graph that could represent the volume of water in the bamboo tube as it operates.

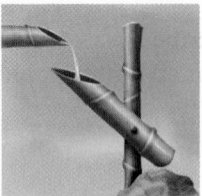   

| Tube begins filling. | Full tube begins falling. | Tube falls and empties water. | Tube rises and hits rock, making noise. |

- What quantities vary in this situation?
- How are these quantities related?

15. Error Analysis T-shirts cost $12.99 each for the first 5 shirts purchased. Each additional T-shirt costs $4.99 each. Describe and correct the error in the graph at the right that represents the relationship between total cost and number of shirts purchased.

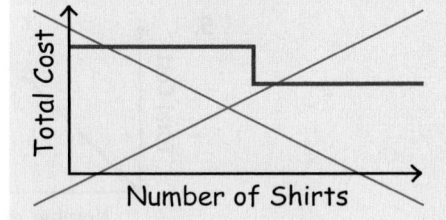

16. Open-Ended Describe a real-world relationship between the area of a rectangle and its width, as the width varies and the length stays the same. Sketch a graph to show this relationship.

17. Skiing Sketch a graph of each situation. Are the graphs the same? Explain.
   a. your speed as you travel on a ski lift from the bottom of a ski slope to the top
   b. your speed as you ski from the top of a ski slope to the bottom

18. Reasoning The diagram at the left below shows a portion of a bike trail.
   a. Explain whether the graph below is a reasonable representation of how the speed might change for the rider of the blue bike.

Blue Bike's Speed

   b. Sketch two graphs that could represent a bike's speed over time. Sketch one graph for the blue bike, and the other for the red bike.

19. Track The sketch at the right shows the distance three runners travel during a race. Describe what occurs at times A, B, C, and D. In what order do the runners finish? Explain.

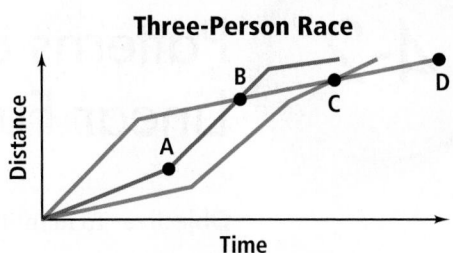

Three-Person Race

© **20. Reasoning** The graph at the right shows the vertical distance traveled as Person A walks up a set of stairs and Person B walks up an escalator next to the stairs. Copy the graph. Then draw a line that could represent the vertical distance traveled as Person C rides the escalator standing still. Explain your reasoning.

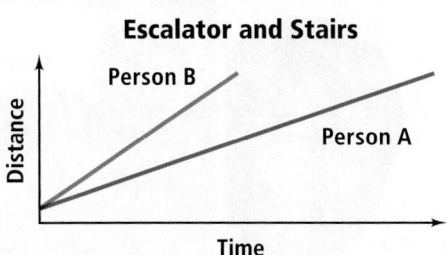

Escalator and Stairs

Standardized Test Prep

SAT/ACT

21. The graph at the right shows your distance from home as you walk to the bus stop, wait for the bus, and then ride the bus to school. Which point represents a time that you are waiting for the bus?

Ⓐ A

Ⓒ C

Ⓑ B

Ⓓ D

Distance From Home

22. What is the solution of $-2x < 4$?

Ⓕ $x < 2$ Ⓖ $x > 2$ Ⓗ $x < -2$ Ⓘ $x > -2$

Short Response

23. You earn $8.50 per hour. Then you receive a raise to $9.35 per hour. Find the percent increase. Then find your pay per hour if you receive the same percent increase two more times. Show your work.

Mixed Review

Let $A = \{-3, 1, 4\}$, $B = \{x \mid x$ is an odd number greater than -2 and less than $10\}$, and $C = \{1, 4, 7, 12\}$. Find each union or intersection.

◀ **See Lesson 3-8.**

24. $A \cup B$ **25.** $A \cap B$ **26.** $B \cup C$ **27.** $A \cap C$

Get Ready! **To prepare for Lesson 4-2, do Exercises 28 and 29.**

Use a table, an equation, and a graph to represent each relationship.

◀ **See Lesson 1-9.**

28. Donald is 4 years older than Connie.   **29.** You make 3 cards per hour.

Patterns and Linear Functions

Common Core State Standards

A-REI.D.10 Understand that the graph of an equation in two variables is the set of all its solutions plotted in the coordinate plane, often forming a curve (which could be a line). **Also F-IF.B.4**

MP 1, MP 2, MP 3, MP 4

Objective To identify and represent patterns that describe linear functions

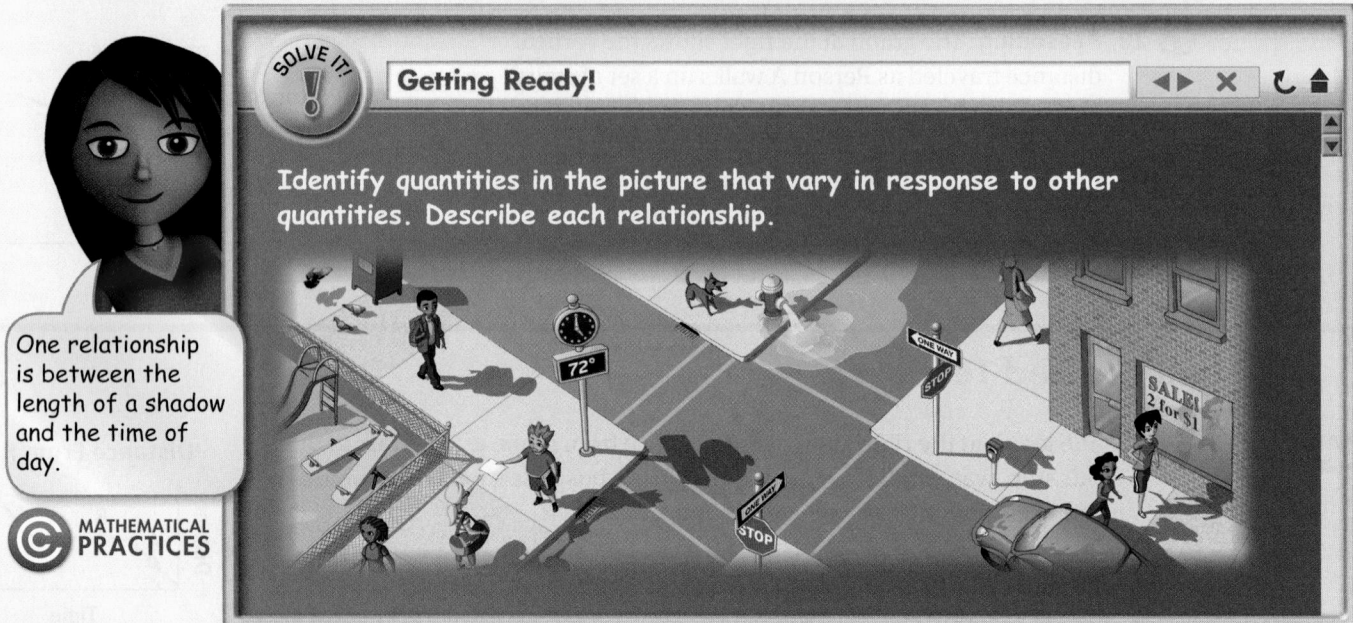

SOLVE IT!

Getting Ready!

Identify quantities in the picture that vary in response to other quantities. Describe each relationship.

One relationship is between the length of a shadow and the time of day.

MATHEMATICAL PRACTICES

Lesson Vocabulary

• dependent variable
• independent variable
• input
• output
• function
• linear function

In the Solve It, you identified variables whose value *depends* on the value of another variable. In a relationship between variables, the **dependent variable** changes in response to another variable, the **independent variable.** Values of the independent variable are called **inputs.** Values of the dependent variable are called **outputs.**

Essential Understanding The value of one variable may be uniquely determined by the value of another variable. Such relationships may be represented using tables, words, equations, sets of ordered pairs, and graphs.

Problem 1 Representing a Geometric Relationship

In the diagram below, what is the relationship between the number of rectangles and the perimeter of the figure they form? Represent this relationship using a table, words, an equation, and a graph.

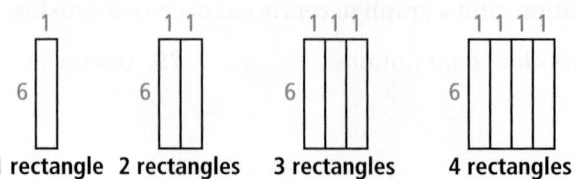

1 rectangle 2 rectangles 3 rectangles 4 rectangles

Think

Which variable is the dependent variable?
The perimeter *depends* on the number of rectangles, so perimeter is the dependent variable.

Step 1 Make a table. Use *x* as the independent variable and *y* as the dependent variable.
Let *x* = the number of rectangles.
Let *y* = the perimeter of the figure.

Write each pair of input and output values *x* and *y* as an ordered pair (*x*, *y*).

Number of Rectangles, *x*	Perimeter, *y*	Ordered Pair (*x*, *y*)
1	2(1) + 2(6) = 14	(1, 14)
2	2(2) + 2(6) = 16	(2, 16)
3	2(3) + 2(6) = 18	(3, 18)
4	2(4) + 2(6) = 20	(4, 20)

Step 2 Look for a pattern in the table. Describe the pattern in words so you can write an equation to represent the relationship.

Words Multiply the number of rectangles in each figure by 2 to get the total length of the top and bottom sides of the combined figure. Then add 2(6), or 12, for the total length of the left and right sides of the combined figure to get the entire perimeter.

Equation $y = 2x + 12$

Step 3 Use the table to make a graph.

With a graph, you can see a pattern formed by the relationship between the number of rectangles and the perimeter of the combined figure.

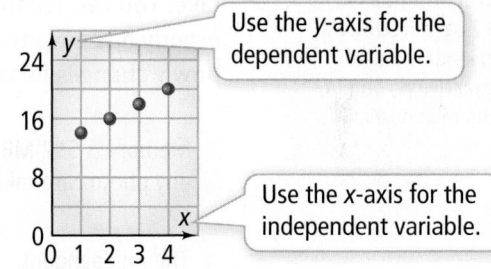

Use the *y*-axis for the dependent variable.

Use the *x*-axis for the independent variable.

Ⓒ ✓ **Got It?** **1. a.** In the diagram below, what is the relationship between the number of triangles and the perimeter of the figure they form? Represent this relationship using a table, words, an equation, and a graph.

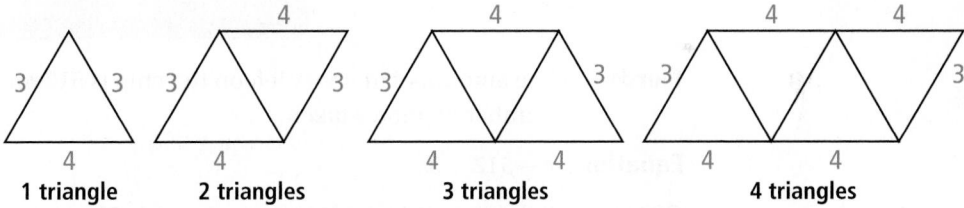

| 1 triangle | 2 triangles | 3 triangles | 4 triangles |

b. Reasoning Suppose you know the perimeter of *n* triangles. What would you do to find the perimeter of *n* + 1 triangles?

c. How does your answer to part (b) relate to the equation you wrote in part (a)?

You can describe the relationship in Problem 1 by saying that the perimeter is a function of the number of rectangles. A **function** is a relationship that pairs each input value with exactly one output value.

You have seen that one way to represent a function is with a graph. A **linear function** is a function whose graph is a nonvertical line or part of a nonvertical line.

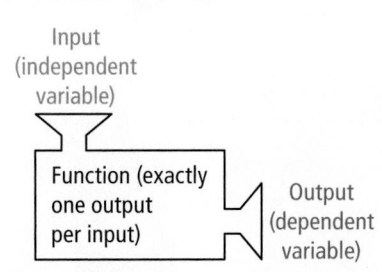

Input (independent variable)

Function (exactly one output per input)

Output (dependent variable)

Problem 2 Representing a Linear Function

Photography The table shows the relationship between the number of photos x you take and the amount of memory y in megabytes (MB) left on your camera's memory chip. Is the relationship a linear function? Describe the relationship using words, an equation, and a graph.

Camera Memory

Number of Photos, x	Memory (MB), y
0	512
1	509
2	506
3	503

Know
The amount of memory left given the number of pictures taken, as shown in the table

Need
Other representations that describe the relationship

Plan
Look for a pattern that you can describe in words to write an equation. Make a graph to show the pattern.

Think
How can you tell whether a relationship in a table is a function?
If each input is paired with *exactly* one output, then the relationship is a function.

The amount y of memory left is uniquely determined by the number x of photos you take. You can see this in the table above, where each input value of x corresponds to exactly one output value of y. So y is a function of x. To describe the relationship, look at how y changes for each change in x in the table below.

Camera Memory

Memory is 512 MB before any photos are taken.

The independent variable x increases by 1 each time.

Number of Photos, x	Memory (MB), y
0	512
1	509
2	506
3	503

$+1$ ... -3

The dependent variable y decreases by 3 each time x increases by 1.

Words The amount of memory left on the chip is 512 minus the quantity 3 times the number of photos taken.

Equation $y = 512 - 3x$

Graph You can use the table to make a graph. The points lie on a line, so the relationship between the number of photos taken and the amount of memory remaining is a linear function.

Got It? **2. a.** Is the relationship in the table below a linear function? Describe the relationship using words, an equation, and a graph.

Input, x	0	1	2	3
Output, y	8	10	12	14

b. Reasoning Does the set of ordered pairs (0, 2), (1, 4), (3, 5), and (1, 8) represent a linear function? Explain.

Lesson Check

Do you know HOW?

1. Graph each set of ordered pairs. Use words to describe the pattern shown in the graph.
   a. (0, 0), (1, 1), (2, 2), (3, 3), (4, 4)
   b. (0, 8), (1, 6), (2, 4), (3, 2), (4, 0)
   c. (3, 0), (3, 1), (3, 2), (3, 3), (3, 4)

2. Use the diagram below. Copy and complete the table showing the relationship between the number of squares and the perimeter of the figure they form.

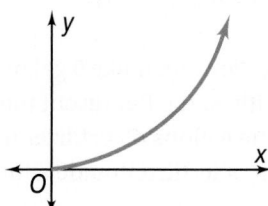

Number of Squares	Perimeter
1	4
2	6
3	■
4	■
10	■
■	62
n	■

1 square   2 squares   3 squares

Do you UNDERSTAND?

MATHEMATICAL PRACTICES

3. **Vocabulary** The amount of toothpaste in a tube decreases each time you brush your teeth. Identify the independent and dependent variables in this relationship.

4. **Reasoning** Tell whether each set of ordered pairs in Exercise 1 represents a function. Justify your answers.

5. **Reasoning** Does the graph below represent a linear function? Explain.

Practice and Problem-Solving Exercises

MATHEMATICAL PRACTICES

A Practice

For each diagram, find the relationship between the number of shapes and the perimeter of the figure they form. Represent this relationship using a table, words, an equation, and a graph.

◀ See Problem 1.

6.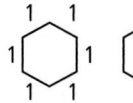

1 hexagon   2 hexagons   3 hexagons

7.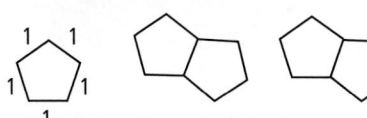

1 pentagon   2 pentagons   3 pentagons

For each table, determine whether the relationship is a linear function. Then represent the relationship using words, an equation, and a graph.

◀ See Problem 2.

8.

x	y
0	5
1	8
2	11
3	14

9.

x	y
0	−3
1	2
2	7
3	12

10.

x	y
0	43
1	32
2	21
3	10

For each table, determine whether the relationship is a linear function. Then represent the relationship using words, an equation, and a graph.

11. **Mountain Climbing**

Number of Hours Climbing, x	Elevation (ft), y
0	1127
1	1219
2	1311
3	1403

12. **Grocery Bill**

Number of Soup Cans, x	Total Bill, y
0	$52.07
1	$53.36
2	$54.65
3	$55.94

13. **Gas in Tank**

Miles Traveled, x	Gallons of Gas, y
0	11.2
17	10.2
34	9.2
51	8.2

B Apply

14. Gardening You can make 5 gal of liquid fertilizer by mixing 8 tsp of powdered fertilizer with water. Represent the relationship between the teaspoons of powder used and the gallons of fertilizer made using a table, an equation, and a graph. Is the amount of fertilizer made a function of the amount of powder used? Explain.

15. Reasoning Graph the set of ordered pairs $(-2, -3)$, $(0, -1)$, $(1, 0)$, $(3, 2)$, and $(4, 4)$. Determine whether the relationship is a linear function. Explain how you know.

16. Think About a Plan Gears are common parts in many types of machinery. In the diagram below, Gear A turns in response to the cranking of Gear B. Describe the relationship between the number of turns of Gear B and the number of turns of Gear A. Use words, an equation, and a graph.

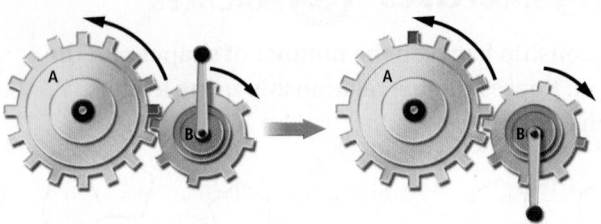

- What are the independent and dependent variables?
- How much must you turn Gear B to get Gear A to go around once?

STEM 17. Electric Car An automaker makes a car that can travel 40 mi on its charged battery before it begins to use gas. Then the car travels 50 mi per gallon of gas used. Represent the relationship between the amount of gas used and the distance traveled using a table, an equation, and a graph. Is total distance traveled a function of the amount of gas used? What are the independent and dependent variables? Explain.

18. Reasoning Suppose you know the perimeter of n octagons arranged as shown. What would you do to find the perimeter if 1 more octagon was added?

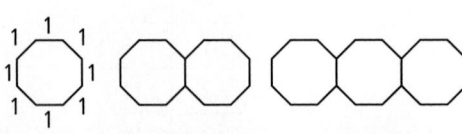

1 octagon   2 octagons   3 octagons

 **Challenge** 19. **Athletics** The graph at the right shows the distance a runner has traveled as a function of the amount of time (in minutes) she has been running. Draw a graph that shows the time she has been running as a function of the distance she has traveled.

20. **Movies** When a movie on film is projected, a certain number of frames pass through the projector per minute. You say that the length of the movie in minutes is a function of the number of frames. Someone else says that the number of frames is a function of the length of the movie. Can you both be right? Explain.

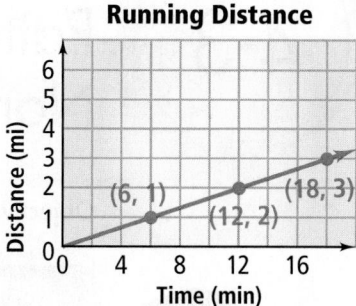

Running Distance

Distance (mi)

(6, 1)
(12, 2)
(18, 3)

Time (min)

 ## Apply What You've Learned

 **MATHEMATICAL PRACTICES**

MP 1

Look back at the table on page 233 showing the number of months and number of subscribers for Jayden's blog.

a. What is the relationship between the number of months and the number of subscribers? Explain.

b. Which column in the table represents the independent variable, and which column represents the dependent variable? Explain.

c. Is this relationship a function? Explain.

d. Look for a pattern in the table, and then write an equation to represent the relationship you find.

e. Use the pattern you found in part (d) to expand the table to 8 months. Then use your equation from part (d) to find the number of subscribers for the 8th month and compare your result with the value in the table.

f. Which method would be best to find the number of subscribers after a year? Explain.

4-3 Patterns and Nonlinear Functions

Common Core State Standards

A-REI.D.10 Understand that the graph of an equation in two variables is the set of all its solutions plotted in the coordinate plane, often forming a curve (which could be a line). **Also F-IF.B.4**

MP 1, MP 2, MP 3, MP 4, MP 6

Objective To identify and represent patterns that describe nonlinear functions

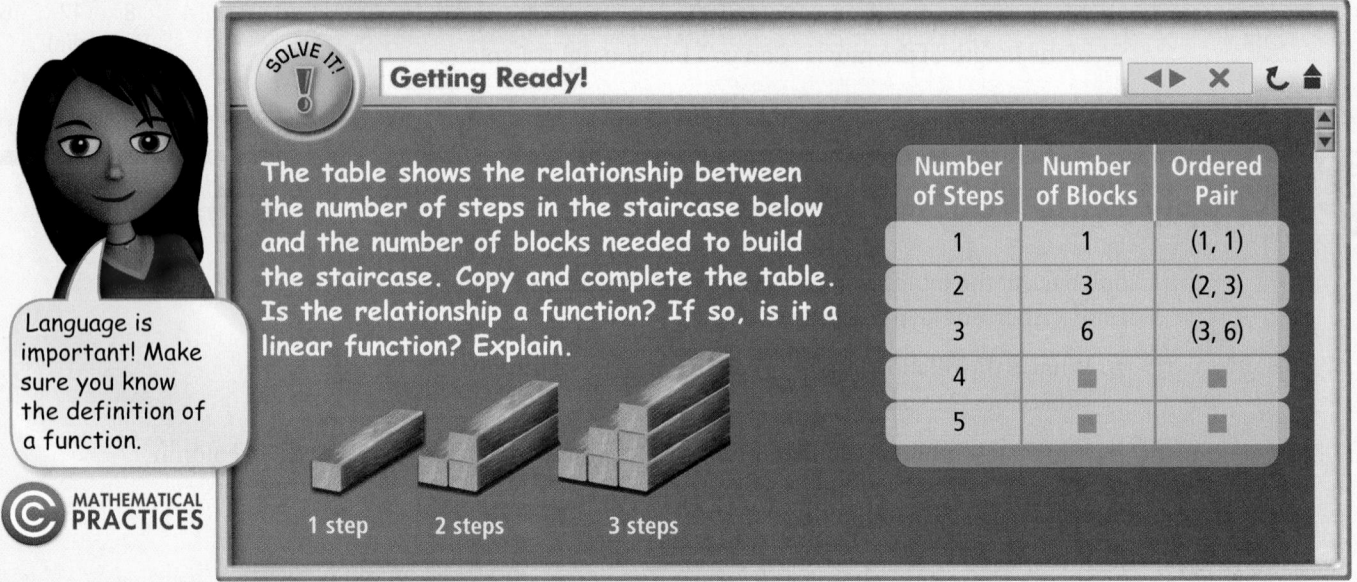

Language is important! Make sure you know the definition of a function.

MATHEMATICAL PRACTICES

Getting Ready!

The table shows the relationship between the number of steps in the staircase below and the number of blocks needed to build the staircase. Copy and complete the table. Is the relationship a function? If so, is it a linear function? Explain.

Number of Steps	Number of Blocks	Ordered Pair
1	1	(1, 1)
2	3	(2, 3)
3	6	(3, 6)
4	■	■
5	■	■

1 step 2 steps 3 steps

Lesson Vocabulary
• nonlinear function

The relationship in the Solve It is an example of a nonlinear function. A **nonlinear function** is a function whose graph is not a line or part of a line.

Essential Understanding Just like linear functions, nonlinear functions can be represented using words, tables, equations, sets of ordered pairs, and graphs.

Concept Summary   Linear and Nonlinear Functions

Linear Function
A linear function is a function whose graph is a nonvertical line or part of a nonvertical line.

Nonlinear Function
A nonlinear function is a function whose graph is not a line or part of a line.

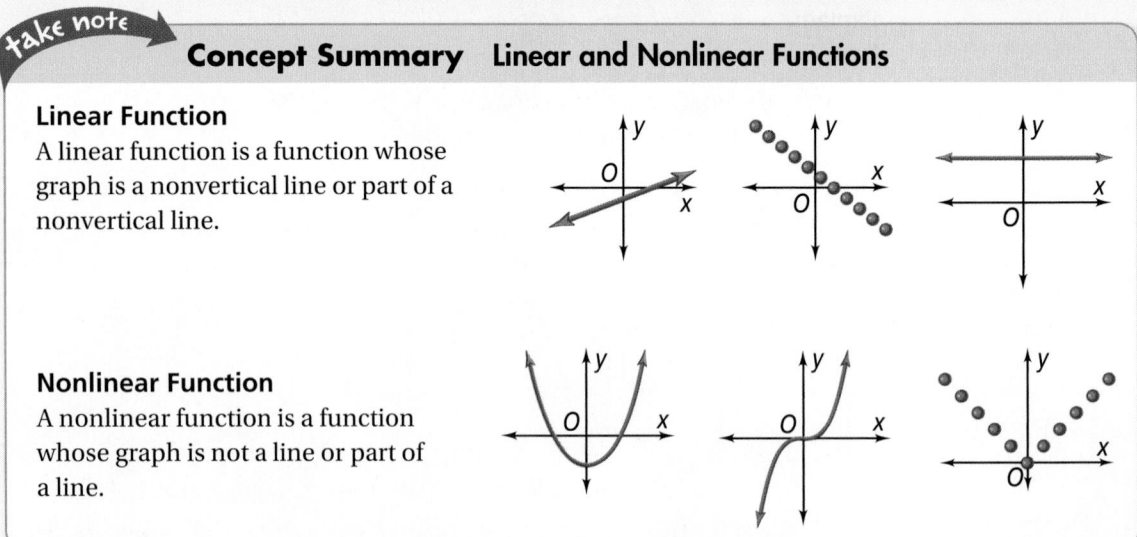

Problem 1 Classifying Functions as Linear or Nonlinear

Pizza The area A, in square inches, of a pizza is a function of its radius r, in inches. The cost C, in dollars, of the sauce for a pizza is a function of the weight w, in ounces, of sauce used. Graph these functions shown by the tables below. Is each function *linear* or *nonlinear*?

Pizza Area

Radius (in.), r	Area (in.^{2}), A
2	12.57
4	50.27
6	113.10
8	201.06
10	314.16

Sauce Cost

Weight (oz), w	Cost, C
2	$.80
4	$1.60
6	$2.40
8	$3.20
10	$4.00

Know

The relationships shown in the tables are functions.

Need

To classify the functions as *linear* or *nonlinear*

Plan

Use the tables to make graphs.

Think

How can a graph tell you if a function is linear or nonlinear?
The graph of a linear function is a nonvertical line or part of a line, but the graph of a nonlinear function is not.

Graph A as a function of r.

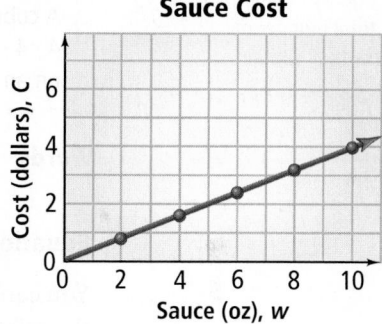

Use the vertical axis for A, the dependent variable.

Use the horizontal axis for r, the independent variable.

The graph is a curve, not a line, so the function is nonlinear.

Graph C as a function of w.

Sauce Cost

The graph is a line, so the function is linear.

  Got It? **1. a.** The table below shows the fraction A of the original area of a piece of paper that remains after the paper has been cut in half n times. Graph the function represented by the table. Is the function *linear or nonlinear*?

Cutting Paper				
Number of Cuts, n	1	2	3	4
Fraction of Original Area Remaining, A	$\frac{1}{2}$	$\frac{1}{4}$	$\frac{1}{8}$	$\frac{1}{16}$

b. Reasoning Will the area A in part (a) ever reach zero? Explain.

The table shows the total number of blocks in each figure below as a function of the number of blocks on one edge.

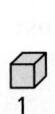  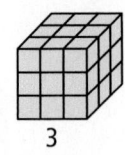

1   2   3

Number of Blocks on Edge, x	Total Number of Blocks, y	Ordered Pair (x, y)
1	1	(1, 1)
2	8	(2, 8)
3	27	(3, 27)
4	▪	▪
5	▪	▪

What is a pattern you can use to complete the table? Represent the relationship using words, an equation, and a graph.

Draw the next two figures to complete the table.

Think

How can you use a pattern to complete the table?
You can draw figures with 4 and 5 blocks on an edge. Then analyze the figures to determine the total number of blocks they contain.

4   5

A cube with 4 blocks on an edge contains 4 · 4 · 4 = 64 blocks. A cube with 5 blocks on an edge contains 5 · 5 · 5 = 125 blocks.

Number of Blocks on Edge, x	Total Number of Blocks, y	Ordered Pair (x, y)
1	1	(1, 1)
2	8	(2, 8)
3	27	(3, 27)
4	64	(4, 64)
5	125	(5, 125)

Words   The total number of blocks y is the cube of the number of blocks on one edge x.

Equation $y = x^3$

You can use the table to make a graph. The points do not lie on a line. So the relationship between the number of blocks on one edge and the total number of blocks is a nonlinear function.

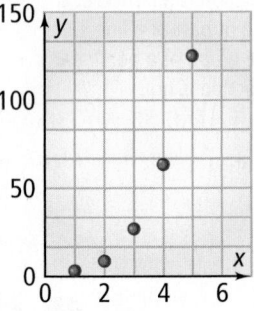

Got It? **2.** The table shows the number of new branches in each figure of the pattern below. What is a pattern you can use to complete the table? Represent the relationship using words, an equation, and a graph.

1   2   3

Number of Figure, x	1	2	3	4	5
Number of New Branches, y	3	9	27	▪	▪

A function can be thought of as a rule that you apply to the input in order to get the output. You can describe a nonlinear function with words or with an equation, just as you did with linear functions.

 Problem 3 Writing a Rule to Describe a Nonlinear Function

The ordered pairs $(1, 2)$, $(2, 4)$, $(3, 8)$, $(4, 16)$, and $(5, 32)$ represent a function. What is a rule that represents this function?

Make a table to organize the *x*- and *y*-values. For each row, identify rules that produce the given *y*-value when you substitute the *x*-value. Look for a pattern in the *y*-values.

Think

How can you use reasoning to write a rule?
You can *solve a simpler problem* by writing a rule based on the first one or two rows of the table. Then see if the rule works for the other rows.

x	y
1	2
2	4
3	8
4	16
5	32

What rule produces 2, given an *x*-value of 1? The rules $y = 2x$, $y = x + 1$, and $y = 2^x$ work for (1, 2).

$y = x + 1$ does not work for (2, 4). $y = 2x$ works for (2, 4), but not for (3, 8). $y = 2^x$ works for all three pairs.

$8 = 2 \cdot 2 \cdot 2$ and $16 = 2 \cdot 2 \cdot 2 \cdot 2$. The pattern of the *y*-values matches 2^1, 2^2, 2^3, 2^4, 2^5, or $y = 2^x$.

The function can be represented by the rule $y = 2^x$.

Got It? **3.** What is a rule for the function represented by the ordered pairs $(1, 1)$, $(2, 4)$, $(3, 9)$, $(4, 16)$, and $(5, 25)$?

Lesson Check

Do you know HOW?

1. Graph the function represented by the table below. Is the function *linear* or *nonlinear*?

x	0	1	2	3	4
y	12	13	14	15	16

2. The ordered pairs $(0, -2)$, $(1, 1)$, $(2, 4)$, $(3, 7)$, and $(4, 10)$ represent a function. What is a rule that represents this function?

3. Which rule could represent the function shown by the table below?

x	0	1	2	3	4
y	0	-1	-4	-9	-16

A. $y = x^2$ **B.** $y = -x^3$ **C.** $y = -x^2$

Do you UNDERSTAND?  MATHEMATICAL PRACTICES

4. Vocabulary Does the graph represent a *linear function* or a *nonlinear function*? Explain.

a. 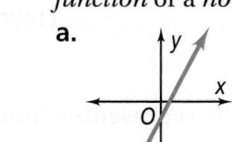   b.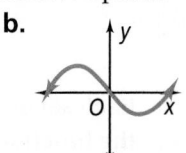

5. Error Analysis A classmate says that the function shown by the table at the right can be represented by the rule $y = x + 1$. Describe and correct your classmate's error.

x	y
0	1
1	2
2	5
3	10
4	17

 **Practice**

The cost C, in dollars, for pencils is a function of the number n of pencils purchased. The length L of a pencil, in inches, is a function of the time t, in seconds, it has been sharpened. Graph the function shown by each table below. Tell whether the function is *linear* or *nonlinear*.

◄ **See Problem 1.**

6.

Pencil Cost					
Number of Pencils, *n*	6	12	18	24	30
Cost, *C*	$1	$2	$3	$4	$5

7.

Pencil Sharpening					
Time (s), *t*	0	3	6	9	12	15
Length (in.), *L*	7.5	7.5	7.5	7.5	7.4	7.3

Graph the function shown by each table. Tell whether the function is *linear* or *nonlinear*.

8.

x	y
0	5
1	5
2	5
3	5

9.

x	y
0	−4
1	−3
2	0
3	5

10.

x	y
0	0
1	1
2	−5
3	8

11.

x	y
0	0
1	3
2	6
3	9

12. For the diagram below, the table gives the total number of small triangles y in figure number x. What pattern can you use to complete the table? Represent the relationship using words, an equation, and a graph.

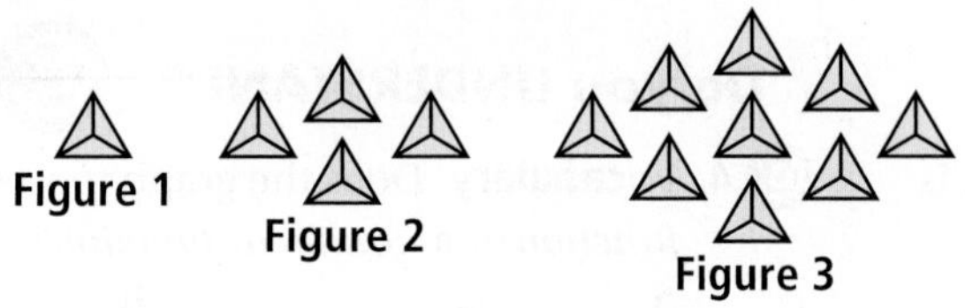

◄ **See Problem 2.**

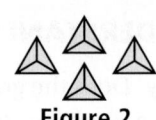

Figure 1

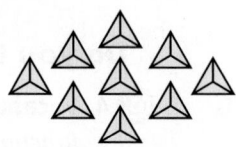

Figure 2

Figure 3

Figure Number, *x*	Total Small Triangles, *y*	Ordered Pair (*x, y*)
1	3	(1, 3)
2	12	(2, 12)
3	27	(3, 27)
4	■	■
5	■	■

Each set of ordered pairs represents a function. Write a rule that represents the function.

◄ **See Problem 3.**

13. (0, 0), (1, 4), (2, 16), (3, 36), (4, 64)

14. $\left(1, \frac{2}{3}\right), \left(2, \frac{4}{9}\right), \left(3, \frac{8}{27}\right), \left(4, \frac{16}{81}\right), \left(5, \frac{32}{243}\right)$

15. (1, 2), (2, 16), (3, 54), (4, 128), (5, 250)

16. (0, 0), (1, 0.5), (2, 2), (3, 4.5), (4, 8)

 **Apply**

Ⓒ **17. Writing** The rule $V = \frac{4}{3}\pi r^3$ gives the volume V of a sphere as a function of its radius r. Identify the independent and dependent variables in this relationship. Explain your reasoning.

Ⓒ **18. Open-Ended** Write a rule for a nonlinear function such that y is negative when $x = 1$, positive when $x = 2$, negative when $x = 3$, positive when $x = 4$, and so on.

19. Think About a Plan Concrete forming tubes are used as molds for cylindrical concrete supports. The volume V of a tube is the product of its length ℓ and the area A of its circular base. You can make $\frac{2}{3}$ft^3 of cement per bag. Write a rule to find the number of bags of cement needed to fill a tube 4 ft long as a function of its radius r. How many bags are needed to fill a tube with a 4-in. radius? A 5-in. radius? A 6-in. radius?

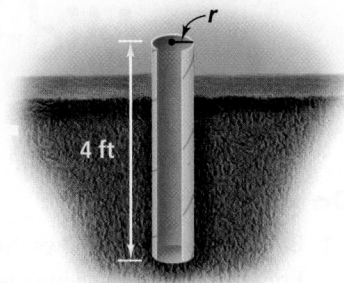

- What is a rule for the volume V of any tube?
- What operation do you use to find the number of bags needed for a given volume?

20. Fountain A designer wants to make a circular fountain inside a square of grass as shown at the right. What is a rule for the area A of the grass as a function of r?

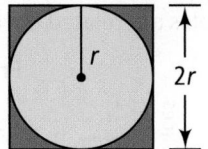

Challenge

21. Reasoning What is a rule for the function represented by $\left(0, \frac{2}{19}\right)$, $\left(1, 1\frac{2}{19}\right)$, $\left(2, 4\frac{2}{19}\right)$, $\left(3, 9\frac{2}{19}\right)$, $\left(4, 16\frac{2}{19}\right)$, and $\left(5, 25\frac{2}{19}\right)$? Explain your reasoning.

22. Reasoning A certain function fits the following description: As the value of x increases by 1 each time, the value of y continually decreases by a smaller amount each time, and never reaches a value as low as 1. Is this function *linear* or *nonlinear*? Explain your reasoning.

Standardized Test Prep

SAT/ACT

23. The ordered pairs $(-2, 1)$, $(-1, -2)$, $(0, -3)$, $(1, -2)$, and $(2, 1)$ represent a function. Which rule could represent the function?

Ⓐ $y = -3x - 5$ 　　Ⓑ $y = x^2 - 3$ 　　Ⓒ $y = x + 3$ 　　Ⓓ $y = x^2 + 5$

24. You are making a model of the library. The floor plans for the library and the plans for your model are shown. What is the value of x?

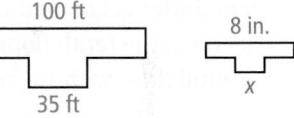

Ⓕ 1.4 in.　　　　　　　　　　Ⓗ 23.2 in.

Ⓖ 2.8 in.　　　　　　　　　　Ⓘ 437.5 in.

Short Response

25. A 15-oz can of tomatoes costs \$.89, and a 29-oz can costs \$1.69. Which can has the lower cost per ounce? Justify your answer.

Mixed Review

26. Determine whether the relationship in the table is a function. Then describe the relationship using words, an equation, and a graph.

x	0	1	2	3
y	3	5	7	9

◀ See Lesson 4-2.

Get Ready! **To prepare for Lesson 4-4, do Exercises 27–29.**

Evaluate each expression for $x = -3$, $x = 0$, and $x = 2.5$.

◀ See Lesson 1-2.

27. $7x - 3$ 　　　　　**28.** $1 + 4x$ 　　　　　**29.** $-2x^2$

Do you know HOW?

1. Buffet The graph shows the number of slices of French toast in a serving dish at a breakfast buffet as time passes. What are the variables? Describe how the variables are related at various points on the graph.

French Toast

(graph: Number of Slices of French Toast vs. Time)

Sketch a graph of the height of each object over time. Label each section.

2. Recreation You throw a flying disc into the air. It hits a tree branch on its way up and comes to rest on a roof. It stays on the roof for a minute before the wind blows it back to the ground.

3. Elevator An elevator fills with people on the ground floor. Most get off at the seventh floor, and the remainder get off at the ninth floor. Then two people get on at the tenth floor and are carried back to the ground floor without any more stops.

For each table, identify the independent and dependent variables. Then describe the relationship using words, an equation, and a graph.

4.

Ounces of Soda

Number of Cans	Soda (oz)
1	12
2	24
3	36
4	48

5.

Dog Biscuits Left

Number of Tricks	Number of Biscuits
1	20
2	17
3	14
4	11

Tell whether the function shown by each table is *linear* or *nonlinear*.

6.

x	1	2	3	4
y	6	8	10	12

7.

x	0	2	4	6
y	5	5	5	5

8.

x	0	1	2	3
y	−3	−4	−5	6

Do you UNDERSTAND?

9. Vocabulary Does each graph represent a *linear function* or a *nonlinear function*? Explain.

a.
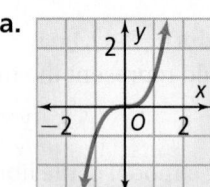

b.
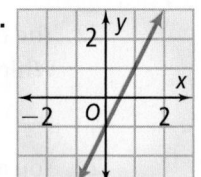

c.
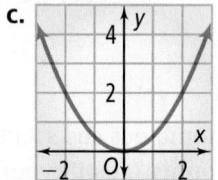

d.
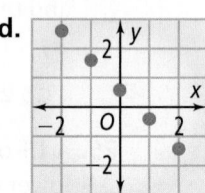

10. Writing The size of a bees' nest increases as time passes. Your friend says that time is the dependent variable because size depends on time. Is your friend correct? Explain.

11. Open-Ended With some functions, the value of the dependent variable decreases as the value of the independent variable increases. What is a real-world example of this?

Graphing a Function Rule

Common Core State Standards

F-IF.B.5 Relate the domain of a function to its graph and, where applicable, to the quantitative relationship it describes . . . **Also N-Q.A.1, A-REI.D.10**

MP 1, MP 2, MP 3, MP 4

Objective To graph equations that represent functions

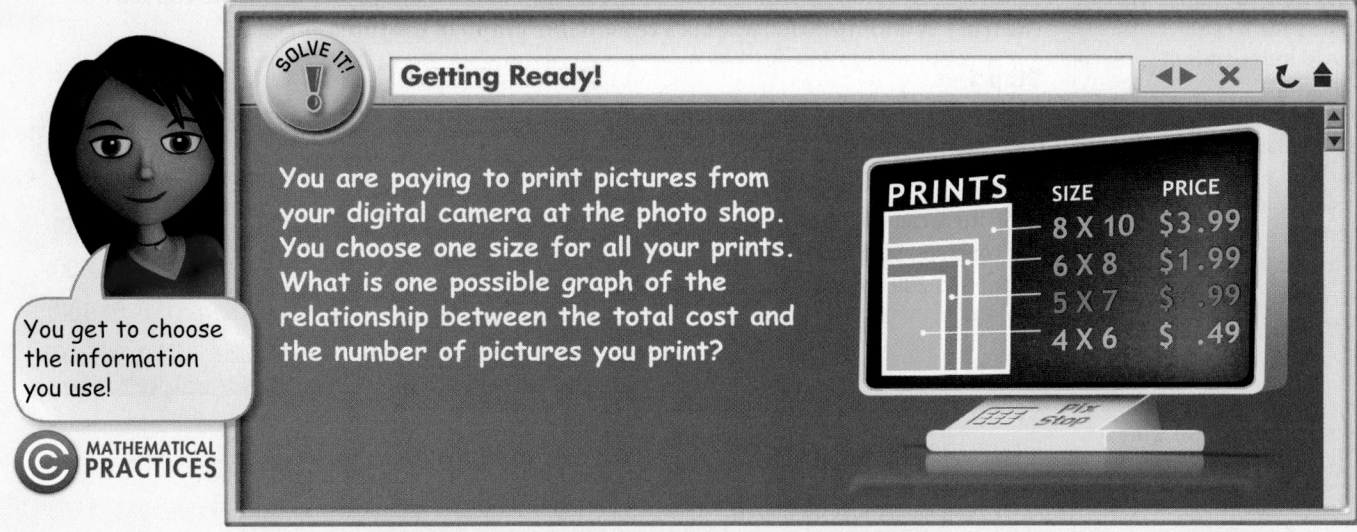

You get to choose the information you use!

MATHEMATICAL PRACTICES

Lesson Vocabulary
• continuous graph
• discrete graph

You can use a table of values to help you make a graph in the Solve It.

Essential Understanding The set of all solutions of an equation forms the equation's graph. A graph may include solutions that do not appear in a table. A real-world graph should only show points that make sense in the given situation.

Think

What input values make sense here?
It is possible to use any input x in the equation and get an output y. Choose integer values of x to produce integer values of y, which are easier to graph.

Problem 1 Graphing a Function Rule

What is the graph of the function rule $y = -2x + 1$?

Step 1 Make a table of values.

x	$y = -2x + 1$	(x, y)
-1	$y = -2(-1) + 1 = 3$	$(-1, 3)$
0	$y = -2(0) + 1 = 1$	$(0, 1)$
1	$y = -2(1) + 1 = -1$	$(1, -1)$
2	$y = -2(2) + 1 = -3$	$(2, -3)$

Step 2 Graph the ordered pairs.

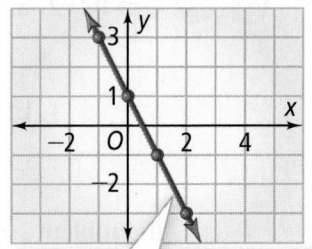

Connect the points with a line to represent *all* solutions.

Got It? **1.** What is the graph of the function rule $y = \frac{1}{2}x - 1$?

When you graph a real-world function rule, choose appropriate intervals for the units on the axes. Every interval on an axis should represent the same change in value. If all the data are nonnegative, show only the first quadrant.

Problem 2 Graphing a Real-World Function Rule

Plan

How do you choose values for a real-world independent variable?
Look for information about what the values can be. The independent variable c in this problem is limited by the capacity of the truck, 200 ft³.

Trucking The function rule $W = 146c + 30,000$ represents the total weight W, in pounds, of a concrete mixer truck that carries c cubic feet of concrete. If the capacity of the truck is about 200 ft³, what is a reasonable graph of the function rule?

Step 1
Make a table to find ordered pairs (c, W).

The truck can hold 0 to 200 ft³ of concrete. So only c-values from 0 to 200 are reasonable.

c	$W = 146c + 30,000$	(c, W)
0	$W = 146(0) + 30,000 = 30,000$	(0, 30,000)
50	$W = 146(50) + 30,000 = 37,300$	(50, 37,300)
100	$W = 146(100) + 30,000 = 44,600$	(100, 44,600)
150	$W = 146(150) + 30,000 = 51,900$	(150, 51,900)
200	$W = 146(200) + 30,000 = 59,200$	(200, 59,200)

Step 2
Graph the ordered pairs from the table.

W reaches almost 60,000 lb. So W-values from 0 to 60,000 in grid increments of 10,000 make sense.

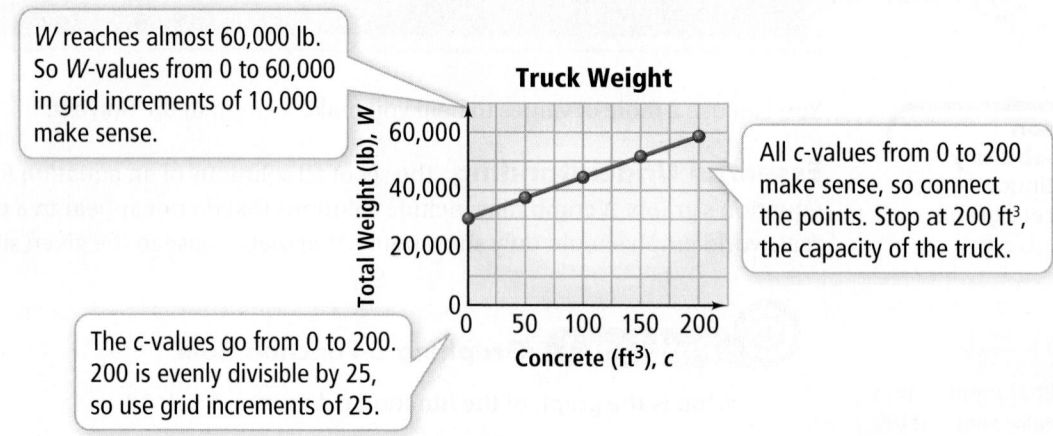

All c-values from 0 to 200 make sense, so connect the points. Stop at 200 ft³, the capacity of the truck.

The c-values go from 0 to 200. 200 is evenly divisible by 25, so use grid increments of 25.

Got It? **2. a.** The function rule $W = 8g + 700$ represents the total weight W, in pounds, of a spa that contains g gallons of water. What is a reasonable graph of the function rule, given that the capacity of the spa is 250 gal?
b. Reasoning What is the weight of the spa when empty? Explain.

In Problem 2, the truck could contain any amount of concrete from 0 to 200 ft³, such as 27.3 ft³ or $105\frac{2}{3}$ ft³. You can connect the data points from the table because any point between the data points has meaning.

Some graphs may be composed of isolated points. For example, in the Solve It you graphed only points that represent printing whole numbers of photos.

Key Concept Continuous and Discrete Graphs

take note

Continuous Graph
A **continuous graph** is a graph that is unbroken.

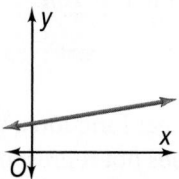

Discrete Graph
A **discrete graph** is composed of distinct, isolated points.

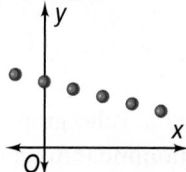

Problem 3 **Identifying Continuous and Discrete Graphs**

Farmer's Market A local cheese maker is making cheddar cheese to sell at a farmer's market. The amount of milk used to make the cheese and the price at which he sells the cheese are shown. Write a function for each situation. Graph each function. Is the graph *continuous* or *discrete*?

1 gal of milk makes 16 oz of cheddar cheese.

Each wheel of cheddar cheese costs $9.

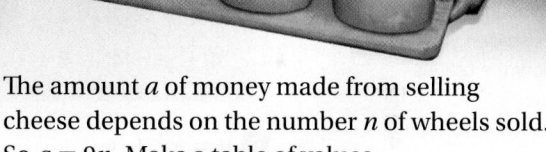

The weight *w* of cheese, in ounces, depends on the number of gallons *m* of milk used. So $w = 16m$. Make a table of values.

m	0	1	2	3	4
w	0	16	32	48	64

Graph each ordered pair (m, w).

Think

How can you decide if a graph is continuous or discrete?
Decide what values are reasonable for the independent variable. For example, if 3 and 4 make sense, do 3.3 and 3.7 make sense as well?

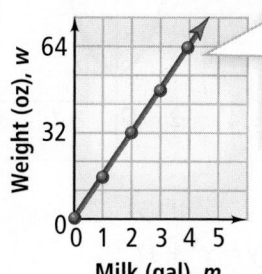

Weight of Cheese

Any amount of milk makes sense, so connect the points. The graph is continuous.

The amount *a* of money made from selling cheese depends on the number *n* of wheels sold. So $a = 9n$. Make a table of values.

n	0	1	2	3	4
a	0	9	18	27	36

Graph each ordered pair (n, a)

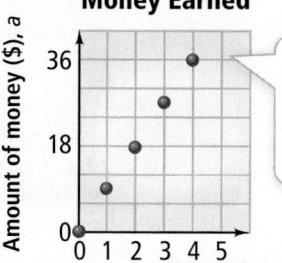

Money Earned

He can only sell whole wheels of cheese. The graph is discrete.

Got It? 3. Graph each function rule. Is the graph *continuous* or *discrete*? Justify your answer.

  a. The amount of water w in a wading pool, in gallons, depends on the amount of time t, in minutes, the wading pool has been filling, as related by the function rule $w = 3t$.

  b. The cost C for baseball tickets, in dollars, depends on the number n of tickets bought, as related by the function rule $C = 16n$.

The function rules graphed in Problems 1–3 represent linear functions. You can also graph a nonlinear function rule. When a function rule does not represent a real-world situation, graph it as a continuous function.

 Problem 4 Graphing Nonlinear Function Rules

What is the graph of each function rule?

A $y = |x| - 4$

Step 1
Make a table of values.

Think

What input values make sense for these nonlinear functions?
Include 0 as well as negative and positive values so that you can see how the graphs change.

x	y = |x| − 4	(x, y)
−4	$y = |-4| - 4 = 0$	(−4, 0)
−2	$y = |-2| - 4 = -2$	(−2, −2)
0	$y = |0| - 4 = -4$	(0, −4)
2	$y = |2| - 4 = -2$	(2, −2)
4	$y = |4| - 4 = 0$	(4, 0)

Step 2
Graph the ordered pairs.
Connect the points.

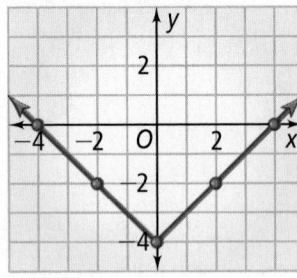

B $y = x^2 + 1$

Step 1
Make a table of values.

x	y = x² + 1	(x, y)
−2	$y = (-2)^2 + 1 = 5$	(−2, 5)
−1	$y = (-1)^2 + 1 = 2$	(−1, 2)
0	$y = 0^2 + 1 = 1$	(0, 1)
1	$y = 1^2 + 1 = 2$	(1, 2)
2	$y = 2^2 + 1 = 5$	(2, 5)

Step 2
Graph the ordered pairs.
Connect the points.

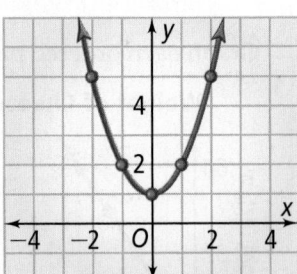

 Got It? 4. What is the graph of the function rule $y = x^3 + 1$?

Lesson Check

Do you know HOW?

Graph each function rule.

1. $y = 2x + 4$

2. $y = \frac{1}{2}x - 7$

3. $y = 9 - x$

4. $y = -x^2 + 2$

5. The function rule $h = 18 + 1.5n$ represents the height h, in inches, of a stack of traffic cones.
   a. Make a table for the function rule.
   b. Suppose the stack of cones can be no taller than 30 in. What is a reasonable graph of the function rule?

Do you UNDERSTAND?

Vocabulary Tell whether each relationship should be represented by a *continuous* or a *discrete* graph.

6. The number of bagels b remaining in a dozen depends on the number s that have been sold.

7. The amount of gas g remaining in the tank of a gas grill depends on the amount of time t the grill has been used.

8. **Error Analysis** Your friend graphs $y = x + 3$ at the right. Describe and correct your friend's error.

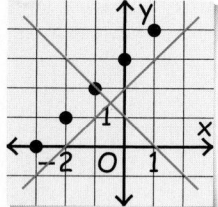

Practice and Problem-Solving Exercises

 **Practice** Graph each function rule.　　　　　　　　　　　　　　　　　◀ See Problem 1.

9. $y = x - 3$

10. $y = 2x + 5$

11. $y = 3x - 2$

12. $y = 5 + 2x$

13. $y = 3 - x$

14. $y = -5x + 12$

15. $y = 10x$

16. $y = 4x - 5$

17. $y = 9 - 2x$

18. $y = 2x - 1$

19. $y = \frac{3}{4}x + 2$

20. $y = -\frac{1}{2}x + \frac{1}{2}$

Graph each function rule. Explain your choice of intervals on the axes of the graph. Tell whether the graph is *continuous* or *discrete*.　◀ See Problems 2 and 3.

21. **Beverages** The height h, in inches, of the juice in a 20-oz bottle depends on the amount of juice j, in ounces, that you drink. This situation is represented by the function rule $h = 6 - 0.3j$.

22. **Trucking** The total weight w, in pounds, of a tractor-trailer capable of carrying 8 cars depends on the number of cars c on the trailer. This situation is represented by the function rule $w = 37,000 + 4200c$.

23. **Food Delivery** The cost C, in dollars, for delivered pizza depends on the number p of pizzas ordered. This situation is represented by the function rule $C = 5 + 9p$.

Graph each function rule.

◀ **See Problem 4.**

24. $y = |x| - 7$ **25.** $y = |x| + 2$ **26.** $y = 2|x|$

27. $y = x^3 - 1$ **28.** $y = 3x^3$ **29.** $y = -2x^2$

30. $y = |-2x| - 1$ **31.** $y = -x^3$ **32.** $y = |x - 3| - 1$

 **Apply**

Ⓒ **33. Error Analysis** The graph at the right shows the distance d you run, in miles, as a function of time t, in minutes, during a 5-mi run. Your friend says that the graph is not continuous because it stops at $d = 5$, so the graph is discrete. Do you agree? Explain.

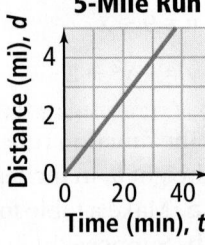

5-Mile Run

Ⓒ **34. Writing** Is the point $\left(2, 2\frac{1}{2}\right)$ on the graph of $y = x + 2$? How do you know?

35. Geometry The area A of an isosceles right triangle depends on the length ℓ of each leg of the triangle. This is represented by the rule $A = \frac{1}{2}\ell^2$. Graph the function rule. Is the graph *continuous* or *discrete*? How do you know?

36. Which function rule is graphed below?

Ⓐ $y = -\frac{1}{2}x + 1$

Ⓑ $y = \frac{1}{2}x - 1$

Ⓒ $y = \left|\frac{1}{2}x\right| - 1$

Ⓓ $y = \frac{1}{2}x + 1$

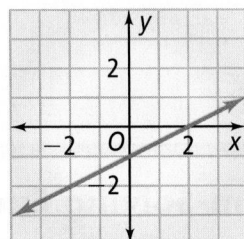

37. Sporting Goods The amount a basketball coach spends at a sporting goods store depends on the number of basketballs the coach buys. The situation is represented by the function rule $a = 15b$.
  a. Make a table of values and graph the function rule. Is the graph *continuous* or *discrete*? Explain.
  b. Suppose the coach spent $120 before tax. How many basketballs did she buy?

Ⓒ **38. Think About a Plan** The height h, in inches, of the vinegar in the jars of pickle chips shown at the right depends on the number of chips p you eat. About how many chips must you eat to lower the level of the vinegar in the jar on the left to the level of the jar on the right? Use a graph to find the answer.
  • What should the maximum value of p be on the horizontal axis?
  • What are reasonable values of p in this situation?

$h = 4.75 - 0.22p$

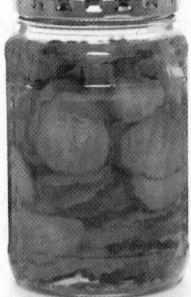

4 in.

STEM 39. Falling Objects The height h, in feet, of an acorn that falls from a branch 100 ft above the ground depends on the time t, in seconds, since it has fallen. This is represented by the rule $h = 100 - 16t^2$. About how much time does it take for the acorn to hit the ground? Use a graph and give an answer between two consecutive whole-number values of t.

 **Challenge**

40. Reasoning Graph the function rules below in the same coordinate plane.

$$y = |x| + 1 \qquad y = |x| + 4 \qquad y = |x| - 3$$

In the function rule $y = |x| + k$, how does changing the value of k affect the graph?

 41. Reasoning Make a table of values and a graph for the function rules $y = 2x$ and $y = 2x^2$. How does the value of y change when you double the value of x for each function rule?

Apply What You've Learned

 **MATHEMATICAL PRACTICES**

MP 4

In the Apply What You've Learned in Lesson 4-2, you identified the relationship shown in Jayden's blog table as a function, and you wrote a function modeling the relationship. Now look at the function on page 233 modeling the number of subscribers to Keiko's blog.

a. Make a table of values for the function that models the number of subscribers to Keiko's blog, $K = m^2 + 10$, and graph the ordered pairs from the table.

b. Graph the ordered pairs using the data about Jayden's blog, shown again below.

Jayden's Blog

Number of Months	Number of Subscribers
0	48
1	56
2	64
3	72
4	80

Graphing Functions and Solving Equations

 **Common Core State Standards**

A-REI.D.11 Explain why the *x*-coordinates . . . where the graphs of the equations $y = f(x)$ and $y = g(x)$ intersect are the solutions of the equation $f(x) = g(x)$; . . .

MP 5

You have learned to graph function rules by making a table of values. You can also use a graphing calculator to graph function rules.

MATHEMATICAL PRACTICES

Example 1

Graph $y = \frac{1}{2}x - 4$ using a graphing calculator.

Step 1   Press the **y=** key. To the right of **Y₁ =**, enter $\frac{1}{2}x - 4$ by pressing **(** 1 **÷** 2 **)** **x,θ,n** **−** 4.

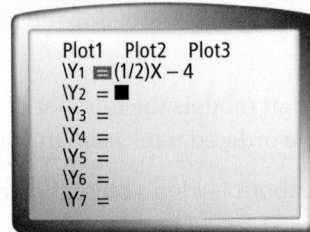

```
Plot1   Plot2   Plot3
\Y1 ■ (1/2)X − 4
\Y2 = ■
\Y3 =
\Y4 =
\Y5 =
\Y6 =
\Y7 =
```

Step 2   The screen on the graphing calculator is a "window" that lets you look at only part of the graph. Press the **window** key to set the borders of the graph. A good window for this function rule is the standard viewing window, $-10 \le x \le 10$ and $-10 \le y \le 10$.

You can have the axes show 1 unit between tick marks by setting **Xscl** and **Yscl** to 1, as shown.

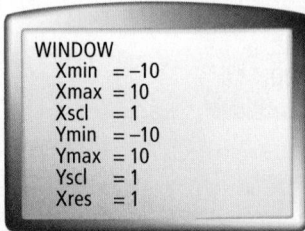

```
WINDOW
  Xmin  = −10
  Xmax  = 10
  Xscl  = 1
  Ymin  = −10
  Ymax  = 10
  Yscl  = 1
  Xres  = 1
```

Step 3   Press the **graph** key. The graph of the function rule is shown.

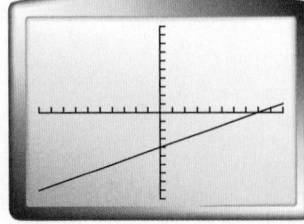

In Chapter 2 you learned how to solve equations in one variable. You can also solve equations by using a graphing calculator to graph each side of the equation as a function rule. The x-coordinate of the point where the graphs intersect is the solution of the equation.

Example 2

Solve $7 = -\frac{3}{4}k + 3$ using a graphing calculator.

Step 1 Press ⌨️ y= . Clear any equations. Then enter each side of the given equation. For $Y_1 =$, enter 7. For $Y_2 =$, enter $-\frac{3}{4}x + 3$ by pressing ((−) 3 ÷ 4) x,t,θ,n + 3. Notice that you must replace the variable k with x.

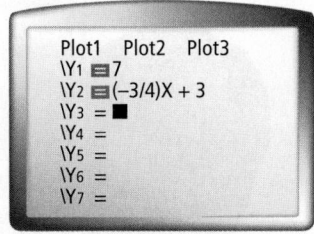

Step 2 Graph the function rules. Use a standard graphing window by pressing zoom 6. This gives a window defined by $-10 \le x \le 10$ and $-10 \le y \le 10$.

Step 3 Use the **CALC** feature. Select **INTERSECT** and press ⌨️ enter 3 times to find the point where the graphs intersect.

The calculator's value for the x-coordinate of the point of intersection is -5.333333. The actual x-coordinate is $-5\frac{1}{3}$.

The solution of the equation $7 = -\frac{3}{4}k + 3$ is $-5\frac{1}{3}$.

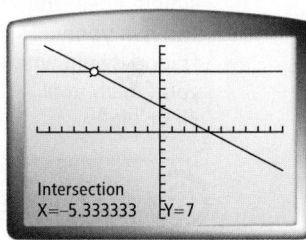

Exercises

Graph each function rule using a graphing calculator.

1. $y = 6x + 3$

2. $y = -3x + 8$

3. $y = 0.2x - 7$

4. $y = -1.8x - 6$

5. $y = -\frac{1}{3}x + 5$

6. $y = \frac{8}{3}x - 5$

7. Open-Ended Graph $y = -0.4x + 8$. Using the window screen, experiment with values for **Xmin**, **Xmax**, **Ymin**, and **Ymax** until you can see the graph crossing both axes. What values did you use for **Xmin**, **Xmax**, **Ymin**, and **Ymax**?

8. Reasoning How can you graph the equation $2x + 3y = 6$ on a graphing calculator?

Use a graphing calculator to solve each equation.

9. $8a - 12 = 6$

10. $-4 = -3t + 2$

11. $-5 = -0.5x - 2$

12. $4 + \frac{3}{2}n = -7$

13. $\frac{5}{4}d - \frac{1}{2} = 6$

14. $-3y - 1 = 3.5$

4-5 Writing a Function Rule

© **Common Core State Standards**
N-Q.A.2 Define appropriate quantities for the purpose of descriptive modeling. **Also A-SSE.A.1a, A-CED.A.2**
MP 1, MP 2, MP 3, MP 4

Objective To write equations that represent functions

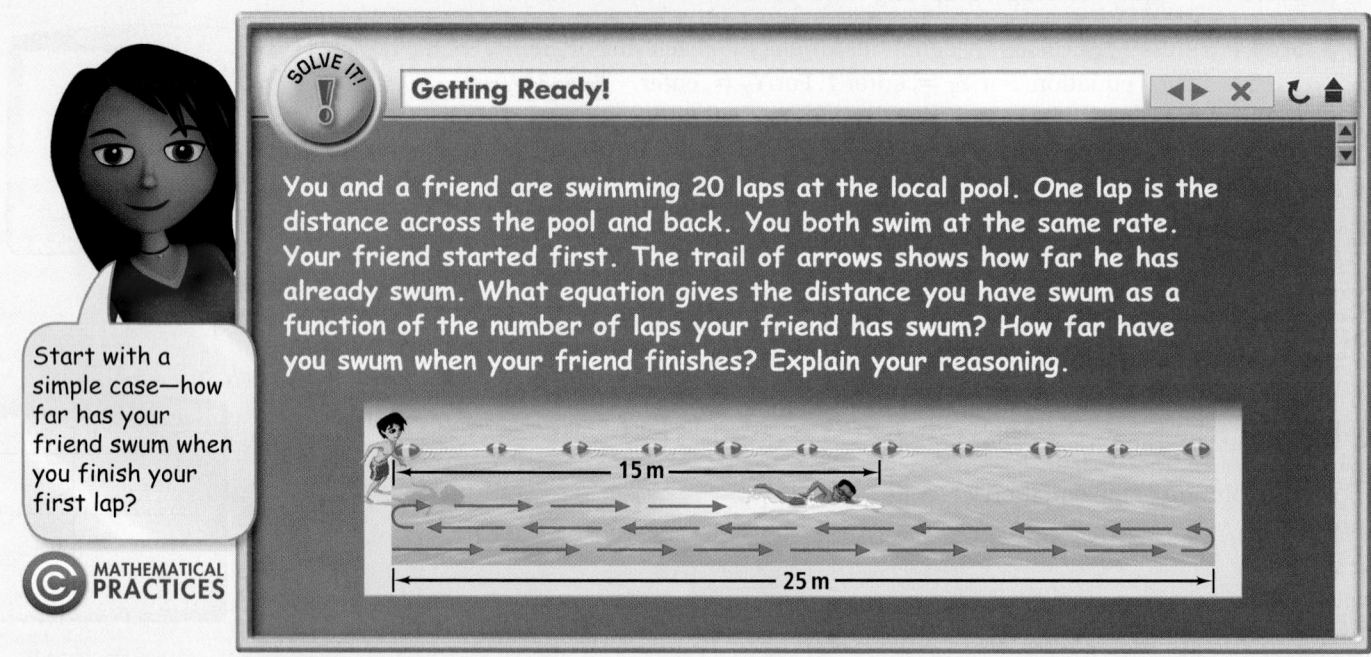

SOLVE IT!

Getting Ready!

You and a friend are swimming 20 laps at the local pool. One lap is the distance across the pool and back. You both swim at the same rate. Your friend started first. The trail of arrows shows how far he has already swum. What equation gives the distance you have swum as a function of the number of laps your friend has swum? How far have you swum when your friend finishes? Explain your reasoning.

15 m

25 m

Start with a simple case—how far has your friend swum when you finish your first lap?

© **MATHEMATICAL PRACTICES**

In the Solve It, you can see how the value of one variable depends on another. Once you see a pattern in a relationship, you can write a rule.

Essential Understanding Many real-world functional relationships can be represented by equations. You can use an equation to find the solution of a given real-world problem.

Think

How can a model help you visualize a real-world situation?
Use a model like the one below to represent the relationship that is described.

T

| $\frac{1}{4}n$ | ----40---- |

© **Problem 1** Writing a Function Rule

Insects You can estimate the temperature by counting the number of chirps of the snowy tree cricket. The outdoor temperature is about 40°F more than one fourth the number of chirps the cricket makes in one minute. What is a function rule that represents this situation?

Relate   temperature   is   40°F   more than $\frac{1}{4}$ of   the number of chirps in 1 min

Define   Let T = the temperature. Let n = the number of chirps in 1 min.

Write T =   40   + $\frac{1}{4}$ · n

A function rule that represents this situation is $T = 40 + \frac{1}{4}n$.

Got It? **1.** A landfill has 50,000 tons of waste in it. Each month it accumulates an average of 420 more tons of waste. What is a function rule that represents the total amount of waste after *m* months?

© **Problem 2** **Writing and Evaluating a Function Rule**

Concert Revenue A concert seating plan is shown below. Reserved seating is sold out. Total revenue from ticket sales will depend on the number of general-seating tickets sold. Write a function rule to represent this situation. What is the maximum possible total revenue?

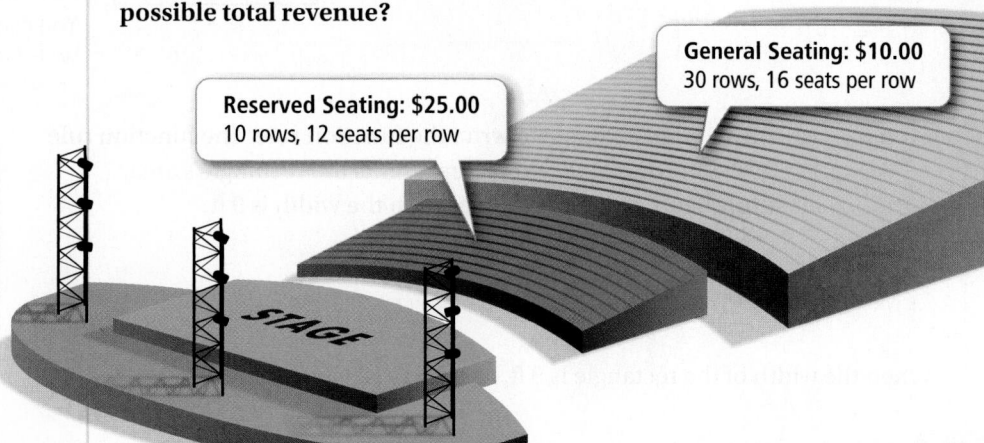

General Seating: $10.00
30 rows, 16 seats per row

Reserved Seating: $25.00
10 rows, 12 seats per row

STAGE

Plan

How can a model help you write an equation?
A model like the one below can help you write an expression for the general-seating revenue.

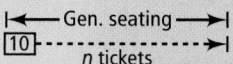

Add the reserved-seating revenue to get the total revenue.

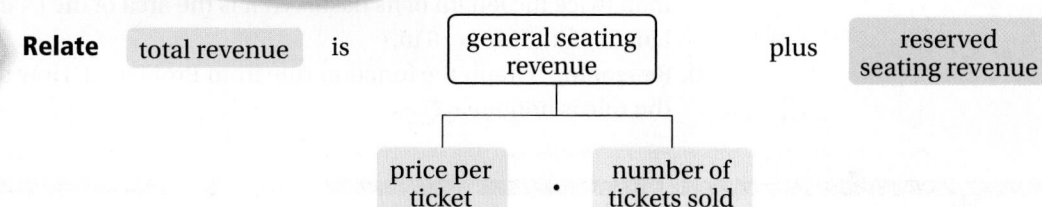

Relate total revenue   is   general seating revenue   plus   reserved seating revenue

price per ticket   •   number of tickets sold

Define Let R = the total revenue.

Let n = the number of general-seating tickets sold.

Write R =   10   • n + $(25 \cdot 10 \cdot 12)$

$$R = 10n + 3000$$

The function rule $R = 10n + 3000$ represents this situation. There are $30 \cdot 16 = 480$ general-seating tickets. Substitute 480 for *n* to find the maximum possible revenue.

$$R = 10(480) + 3000 = 7800$$

The maximum possible revenue from ticket sales is $7800.

©  **Got It?** **2. a.** A kennel charges $15 per day to board dogs. Upon arrival, each dog must have a flea bath that costs $12. Write a function rule for the total cost for *n* days of boarding plus a bath. How much does a 10-day stay cost?
     b. Reasoning Does a 5-day stay cost half as much as a 10-day stay? Explain.

 **Problem 3** **Writing a Nonlinear Function Rule**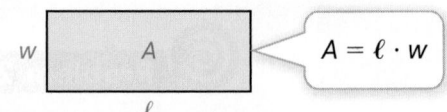

Geometry Write a function rule for the area of a rectangle whose length is 5 ft more than its width. What is the area of the rectangle when its width is 9 ft?

Think

How can *drawing a diagram* help you to write a rule?
A diagram visually represents information in the problem. It can give you a clearer understanding of how variables are related.

Step 1 Represent the general relationship first. The area A of a rectangle is the product of its length ℓ and its width w.

$A = \ell \cdot w$

Step 2 Revise the model to show that the length is 5 ft more than the width.

The length is 5 ft more than the width. You can substitute $w + 5$ for ℓ.

$w + 5$

Step 3 Use the diagram in Step 2 to write the function rule. The function rule $A = (w + 5)w$, or $A = w^2 + 5w$, represents the rectangle's area. Substitute 9 for w to find the area when the width is 9 ft.

$$A = 9^2 + 5(9)$$
$$= 81 + 45$$
$$= 126$$

When the width of the rectangle is 9 ft, its area is 126 ft^2.

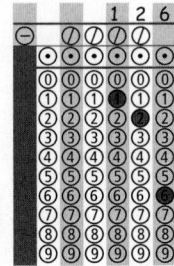

Got It? **3. a.** Write a function rule for the area of a triangle whose height is 4 in. more than twice the length of its base. What is the area of the triangle when the length of its base is 16 in.?

b. Reasoning Graph the function rule from Problem 3. How do you know the rule is nonlinear?

 Lesson Check

Do you know HOW?

Write a function rule to represent each situation.

1. the total cost C for p pounds of copper if each pound costs $3.57

2. the height f, in feet, of an object when you know the object's height h in inches

3. the amount y of your friend's allowance if the amount she receives is $2 more than the amount x you receive

4. the volume V of a cube-shaped box whose edge lengths are 1 in. greater than the diameter d of the ball that the box will hold

Do you UNDERSTAND?  MATHEMATICAL PRACTICES

5. Vocabulary Suppose you write an equation that gives a as a function of b. Which is the dependent variable and which is the independent variable?

6. Error Analysis A worker has dug 3 holes for fence posts. It will take 15 min to dig each additional hole. Your friend writes the rule $t = 15n + 3$ for the time t, in minutes, required to dig n additional holes. Describe and correct your friend's error.

7. Reasoning Is the graph of a function rule that relates a square's area to its side length *continuous* or *discrete*? Explain.

Practice and Problem-Solving Exercises  MATHEMATICAL PRACTICES

 **Practice**

Write a function rule that represents each sentence.

See Problem 1.

8. y is 5 less than the product of 4 and x.

9. C is 8 more than half of n.

10. 7 less than three fifths of b is a.

11. 2.5 more than the quotient of h and 3 is w.

Write a function rule that represents each situation.

12. Wages A worker's earnings e are a function of the number of hours n worked at a rate of $8.75 per hour.

13. Pizza The price p of a pizza is $6.95 plus $.95 for each topping t on the pizza.

14. Weight Loads The load L, in pounds, of a wheelbarrow is the sum of its own 42-lb weight and the weight of the bricks that it carries, as shown at the right.

The wheelbarrow holds n 4-lb bricks.

15. Baking The almond extract a remaining in an 8-oz bottle decreases by $\frac{1}{6}$ oz for each batch b of waffle cookies made.

16. Aviation A helicopter hovers 40 ft above the ground. Then the helicopter climbs at a rate of 21 ft/s. Write a rule that represents the helicopter's height h above the ground as a function of time t. What is the helicopter's height after 45 s?

See Problem 2.

17. Diving A team of divers assembles at an elevation of -10 ft relative to the surface of the water. Then the team dives at a rate of -50 ft/min. Write a rule that represents the team's depth d as a function of time t. What is the team's depth after 3 min?

18. Publishing A new book is being planned. It will have 24 pages of introduction. Then it will have c 12-page chapters and 48 more pages at the end. Write a rule that represents the total number of pages p in the book as a function of the number of chapters. Suppose the book has 25 chapters. How many pages will it have?

19. Write a function rule for the area of a triangle with a base 3 cm greater than 5 times its height. What is the area of the triangle when its height is 6 cm?

See Problem 3.

20. Write a function rule for the volume of the cylinder shown at the right with a height 3 in. more than 4 times the radius of the cylinder's base. What is the volume of the cylinder when it has a radius of 2 in.?

21. Write a function rule for the area of a rectangle with a length 2 ft less than three times its width. What is the area of the rectangle when its width is 2 ft?

 **Apply**

22. Open-Ended Write a function rule that models a real-world situation. Evaluate your function for an input value and explain what the output represents.

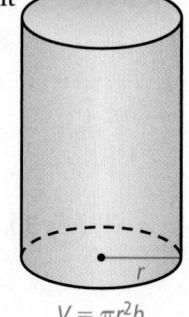

$V = \pi r^2 h$

23. Writing What advantage(s) can you see of having a rule instead of a table of values to represent a function?

24. History of Math The golden ratio has been studied and used by mathematicians and artists for more than 2000 years. A golden rectangle, constructed using the golden ratio, has a length about 1.6 times its width. Write a rule for the area of a golden rectangle as a function of its width.

25. Whales From an elevation of 3.5 m below the surface of the water, a northern bottlenose whale dives at a rate of 1.8 m/s. Write a rule that gives the whale's depth *d* as a function of time in minutes. What is the whale's depth after 4 min?

26. Think About a Plan The height *h*, in inches, of the juice in the pitcher shown at the right is a function of the amount of juice *j*, in ounces, that has been poured out of the pitcher. Write a function rule that represents this situation. What is the height of the juice after 47 oz have been poured out?
- What is the height of the juice when half of it has been poured out?
- What fraction of the juice would you pour out to make the height decrease by 1 in.?

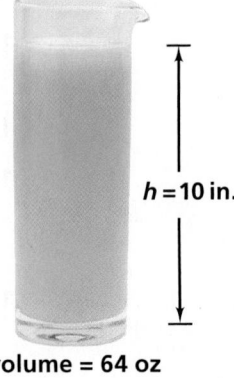

$h = 10$ in.

volume = 64 oz

27. Tips You go to dinner and decide to leave a 15% tip for the server. You had $55 when you entered the restaurant.
- **a.** Make a table showing how much money you would have left after buying a meal that costs $15, $21, $24, or $30.
- **b.** Write a function rule for the amount of money *m* you would have left if the meal costs *c* dollars before the tip.
- **c.** Graph the function rule.

28. Car Rental A car rental agency charges $29 per day to rent a car and $13.95 per day for a global positioning system (GPS). Customers are charged for their full tank of gas at $3.80 per gallon.
- **a.** A car has a 12-gal tank and a GPS. Write a rule for the total bill *b* as a function of the number of days *d* the car is rented.
- **b.** What is the bill for a 9-day rental?

29. Projectors You consult your new projector's instruction manual before mounting it on the wall. The manual says to multiply the desired image width by 1.8 to find the correct distance of the projector lens from the wall.
- **a.** Write a rule to describe the distance of the lens from the wall as a function of desired image width.
- **b.** The diagram shows the room in which the projector will be installed. Will you be able to project an image 7 ft wide? Explain.
- **c.** What is the maximum image width you can project in the room?

12 ft   ? ft

30. Reasoning Write a rule that is an example of a nonlinear function that fits the following description.

When *d* is 4, *r* is 9, and *r* is a function of *d*.

Make a table and a graph of each set of ordered pairs (x, y). Then write a function rule to represent the relationship between x and y.

31. $(-4, 7), (-3, 6), (-2, 5), (-1, 4), (0, 3), (1, 2), (2, 1), (3, 0), (4, -1)$

32. $(-4, 15), (-3, 8), (-2, 3), (-1, 0), (0, -1), (1, 0), (2, 3), (3, 8), (4, 15)$

Standardized Test Prep

SAT/ACT

33. You buy x pounds of cherries for $2.99/lb. What is a function rule for the amount of change C you receive from a $50 bill?

    Ⓐ $C = 2.99x - 50$ Ⓒ $C = 50x - 2.99$

    Ⓑ $C = 50 - 2.99x$ Ⓓ $C = 2.99 - 50x$

34. What is the solution of $-5 < h + 2 < 11$?

    Ⓕ $-3 < h < 11$ Ⓖ $-7 < h < 9$ Ⓗ $-7 > h > 9$ Ⓘ $h < -7$ or $h > 9$

35. Which equation do you get when you solve $-ax + by^2 = c$ for b?

    Ⓐ $b = \dfrac{c - ax}{y^2}$ Ⓑ $b = y^2(c + ax)$ Ⓒ $b = \dfrac{c + ax}{y^2}$ Ⓓ $b = \dfrac{c}{y^2} + ax$

Extended Response

36. The recommended dosage D, in milligrams, of a certain medicine depends on a person's body mass m, in kilograms. The function rule $D = 0.1m^2 + 5m$ represents this relationship.

    a. What is the recommended dosage for a person whose mass is 60 kg? Show your work.

    b. One pound is equivalent to approximately 0.45 kg. Explain how to find the recommended dosage for a 200-lb person. What is this dosage?

Mixed Review

Graph each function rule.   ◀ See Lesson 4-4.

37. $y = 9 - x$ **38.** $y = 4 + 3x$ **39.** $y = x + 1.5$

40. $y = 4x - 1$ **41.** $y = 6x$ **42.** $y = 12 - 3x$

Convert the given amount to the given unit.   ◀ See Lesson 2-6.

43. 8.25 lb; ounces   **44.** 450 cm; meters   **45.** 17 yd; feet

46. 90 s; minutes   **47.** 216 h; days   **48.** 9.5 km; meters

Get Ready!   **To prepare for Lesson 4-6, do Exercises 49–56.**

Find each product. Simplify if necessary.   ◀ See Lesson 1-6.

49. $-4(9)$ **50.** $-3(-7)$ **51.** $-7.2(-15.5)$ **52.** $-6(1.5)$

53. $-4\left(-\dfrac{7}{2}\right)$ **54.** $-\dfrac{4}{9}\left(-\dfrac{9}{4}\right)$ **55.** $\dfrac{25}{9}\left(\dfrac{3}{5}\right)$ **56.** $\dfrac{7}{10}\left(\dfrac{15}{8}\right)$

4-6 Formalizing Relations and Functions

Common Core State Standards

F-IF.A.1 Understand that a function from one set (called the domain) to another set (called the range) assigns to each element of the domain exactly one element of the range ... **Also F-IF.A.2**

MP 1, MP 2, MP 3, MP 4, MP 6

Objectives To determine whether a relation is a function
To find domain and range and use function notation

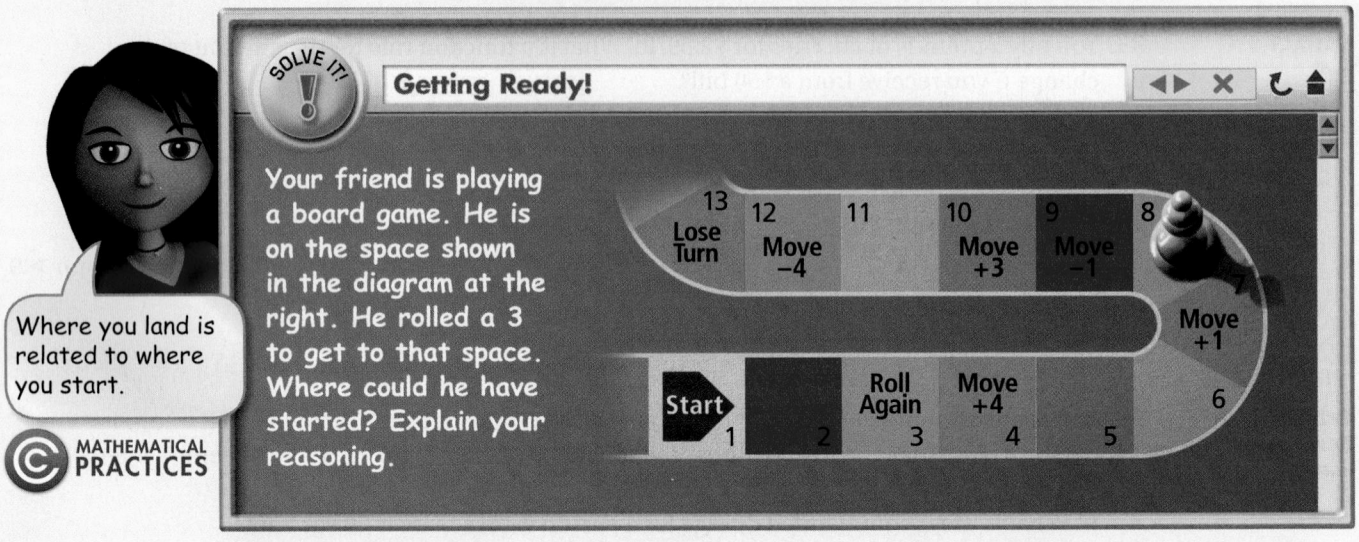

Getting Ready!

Your friend is playing a board game. He is on the space shown in the diagram at the right. He rolled a 3 to get to that space. Where could he have started? Explain your reasoning.

Where you land is related to where you start.

Lesson Vocabulary
- relation
- domain
- range
- vertical line test
- function notation

A **relation** is a pairing of numbers in one set, called the **domain,** with numbers in another set, called the **range.** A relation is often represented as a set of ordered pairs (x, y). In this case, the domain is the set of x-values and the range is the set of y-values.

Essential Understanding A function is a special type of relation in which each value in the domain is paired with exactly one value in the range.

Problem 1 Identifying Functions Using Mapping Diagrams

Think

When is a relation *not* a function?
A function maps each domain value to exactly one range value. So a relation that maps a domain value to more than one range value cannot be a function.

Identify the domain and range of each relation. Represent the relation with a mapping diagram. Is the relation a function?

A $\{(-2, 0.5), (0, 2.5), (4, 6.5), (5, 2.5)\}$
The domain is $\{-2, 0, 4, 5\}$.
The range is $\{0.5, 2.5, 6.5\}$.

B $\{(6, 5), (4, 3), (6, 4), (5, 8)\}$
The domain is $\{4, 5, 6\}$.
The range is $\{3, 4, 5, 8\}$.

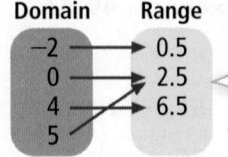

Each domain value is mapped to only one range value. The relation is a function.

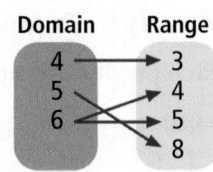

The domain value 6 is mapped to two range values. The relation is not a function.

Got It? **1.** Identify the domain and range of each relation. Represent the relation with a mapping diagram. Is the relation a function?

    a. $\{(4.2, 1.5), (5, 2.2), (7, 4.8), (4.2, 0)\}$ **b.** $\{(-1, 1), (-2, 2), (4, -4), (7, -7)\}$

Another way to decide if a relation is a function is to analyze the graph of the relation using the **vertical line test.** If any vertical line passes through more than one point of the graph, then for some domain value there is more than one range value. So the relation is not a function.

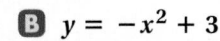 **Problem 2** **Identifying Functions Using the Vertical Line Test**

Is the relation a function? Use the vertical line test.

Ⓐ $\{(-4, 2), (-3, 1), (0, -2), (-4, -1), (1, 2)\}$ Ⓑ $y = -x^2 + 3$

Think

Use a pencil as a vertical line. Place the pencil parallel to the *y*-axis and slide it across the graph. See if the pencil intersects more than one point at any time.

The domain value −4 corresponds to two range values, 2 and −1.

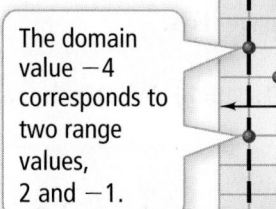

The relation is not a function.

There is no vertical line that passes through more than one point of the graph.

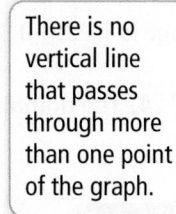
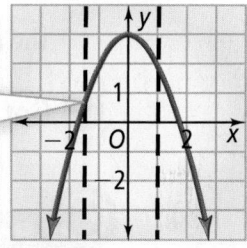

The relation is a function.

 Got It? **2.** Is the relation a function? Use the vertical line test.

    a. $\{(4, 2), (1, 2), (0, 1), (-2, 2), (3, 3)\}$ **b.** $\{(0, 2), (1 -1), (-1, 4), (0, -3), (2, 1)\}$

You have seen functions represented as equations involving x and y, such as $y = -3x + 1$. Below is the same equation written using **function notation.**

$$f(x) = -3x + 1$$

Notice that $f(x)$ replaces y. It is read "f of x." The letter f is the name of the function, not a variable. Function notation is used to emphasize that the function value $f(x)$ depends on the independent variable x. Other letters besides f can also be used, such as g and h.

Problem 3 **Evaluating a Function**

Think

How is this function like ones you've seen before?

The function $w(x) = 250x$ can be written as $y = 250x$. Remember that $w(x)$ does not mean w times x.

Reading The function $w(x) = 250x$ represents the number of words $w(x)$ you can read in x minutes. How many words can you read in 8 min?

    $w(x) = 250x$

    $w(8) = 250(8)$ Substitute 8 for *x*.

    $w(8) = 2000$ Simplify.

You can read 2000 words in 8 min.

Got It? **3.** Use the function in Problem 3. How many words can you read in 6 min?

 Problem 4 **Finding the Range of a Function**

Multiple Choice The domain of $f(x) = -1.5x + 4$ is $\{1, 2, 3, 4\}$. What is the range?

Ⓐ $\{-2, -0.5, 1, 2.5\}$ Ⓒ $\{-2.5, -1, -0.5, 2\}$

Ⓑ $\{-2.5, -1, 0.5, 2\}$ Ⓓ $\{-2.5, -0.5, 1, 2\}$

Think

What is another way to think of the domain and range?
The domain is the set of input values for the function. The range is the set of output values.

Step 1 Make a table. List the domain values as the *x*-values.

x	−1.5x + 4	f(x)
1	−1.5(1) + 4	2.5
2	−1.5(2) + 4	1
3	−1.5(3) + 4	−0.5
4	−1.5(4) + 4	−2

Step 2 Evaluate *f(x)* for each domain value. The values of *f(x)* form the range.

The range is $\{-2, -0.5, 1, 2.5\}$. The correct answer is A.

 Got It? **4.** The domain of $g(x) = 4x - 12$ is $\{1, 3, 5, 7\}$. What is the range?

 Problem 5 **Identifying a Reasonable Domain and Range**

Painting You have 3 qt of paint to paint the trim in your house. A quart of paint covers 100 ft². The function $A(q) = 100q$ represents the area $A(q)$, in square feet, that q quarts of paint cover. What domain and range are reasonable for the function? What is the graph of the function?

Know
- One quart of paint covers 100 ft².
- You have 3 qt of paint.

Need
Reasonable domain and range values in order to graph the function

Plan
Find the least and greatest amounts of paint you can use and areas of trim you can cover. Use these values to make a graph.

The least amount of paint you can use is none. So the least domain value is 0. You have only 3 qt of paint, so the most paint you can use is 3 qt. The greatest domain value is 3. The domain is $0 \le q \le 3$.

To find the range, evaluate the function using the least and greatest domain values.

$$A(0) = 100(0) = 0 \qquad A(3) = 100(3) = 300$$

The range is $0 \le A(q) \le 300$.

To graph the function, make a table of values. Choose values of q that are in the domain. The graph is a line segment that extends from (0, 0) to (3, 300).

q	A(q)
0	0
1	100
2	200
3	300

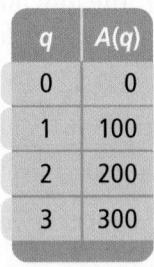

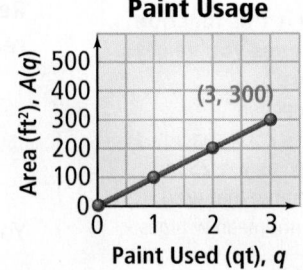

Paint Usage

Got It? **5. a.** If you have 7 qt of paint, what domain and range are reasonable for Problem 5?

b. Reasoning Why does it *not* make sense to have domain values less than 0 or greater than 3 in Problem 5?

Lesson Check

Do you know HOW?

1. Identify the domain and range of the relation $\{(-2, 3), (-1, 4), (0, 5), (1, 6)\}$. Represent the relation with a mapping diagram. Is the relation a function?

2. Is the relation in the graph shown at the right a function? Use the vertical line test.

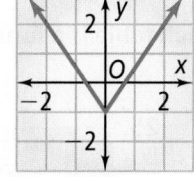

3. What is $f(2)$ for the function $f(x) = 4x + 1$?

4. The domain of $f(x) = \frac{1}{2}x$ is $\{-4, -2, 0, 2, 4\}$. What is the range?

Do you UNDERSTAND?

MATHEMATICAL PRACTICES

5. Vocabulary Write $y = 2x + 7$ using function notation.

6. Compare and Contrast You can use a mapping diagram or the vertical line test to tell if a relation is a function. Which method do you prefer? Explain.

7. Error Analysis A student drew the dashed line on the graph shown and concluded that the graph represented a function. Is the student correct? Explain.

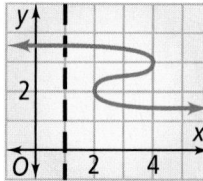

Practice and Problem-Solving Exercises

MATHEMATICAL PRACTICES

A Practice Identify the domain and range of each relation. Use a mapping diagram to determine whether the relation is a function.

See Problem 1.

8. $\{(3, 7), (3, 8), (3, -2), (3, 4), (3, 1)\}$

9. $\{(6, -7), (5, -8), (1, 4), (7, 5)\}$

10. $\{(0.04, 0.2), (0.2, 1), (1, 5), (5, 25)\}$

11. $\{(4, 2), (1, 1), (0, 0), (1, -1), (4, -2)\}$

Use the vertical line test to determine whether the relation is a function.

See Problem 2.

12.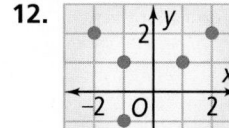

13.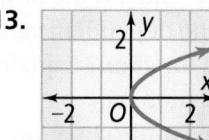

14.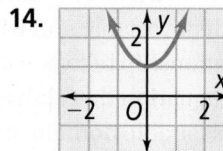

15.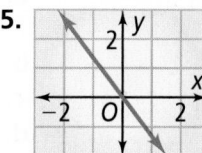

STEM 16. Physics Light travels about 186,000 mi/s. The function $d(t) = 186{,}000t$ gives the distance $d(t)$, in miles, that light travels in t seconds. How far does light travel in 30 s?

See Problem 3.

17. Shopping You are buying orange juice for $4.50 per container and have a gift card worth $7. The function $f(x) = 4.50x - 7$ represents your total cost $f(x)$ if you buy x containers of orange juice and use the gift card. How much do you pay to buy 4 containers of orange juice?

Find the range of each function for the given domain.

See Problem 4.

18. $f(x) = 2x - 7; \{-2, -1, 0, 1, 2\}$

19. $g(x) = -4x + 1; \{-5, -1, 0, 2, 10\}$

20. $h(x) = x^2; \{-1.2, 0, 0.2, 1.2, 4\}$

21. $f(x) = 8x - 3; \left\{-\dfrac{1}{2}, \dfrac{1}{4}, \dfrac{3}{4}, \dfrac{1}{8}\right\}$

Find a reasonable domain and range for each function. Then graph the function.

See Problem 5.

22. Fuel A car can travel 32 mi for each gallon of gasoline. The function $d(x) = 32x$ represents the distance $d(x)$, in miles, that the car can travel with x gallons of gasoline. The car's fuel tank holds 17 gal.

23. Nutrition There are 98 International Units (IUs) of vitamin D in 1 cup of milk. The function $V(c) = 98c$ represents the amount $V(c)$ of vitamin D, in IUs, you get from c cups of milk. You have a 16-cup jug of milk.

 **Apply**

Determine whether the relation represented by each table is a function. If the relation is a function, state the domain and range.

24.

x	0	3	3	5
y	2	1	-1	3

25.

x	-4	-1	0	3
y	-4	-4	-4	-4

26. Open-Ended Make a table that represents a relation that is not a function. Explain why the relation is not a function.

27. Reasoning If $f(x) = 6x - 4$ and $f(a) = 26$, what is the value of a? Explain.

28. Think About a Plan In a factory, a certain machine needs 10 min to warm up. It takes 15 min for the machine to run a cycle. The machine can operate for as long as 6 h per day including warm-up time. Draw a graph showing the total time the machine operates during 1 day as a function of the number of cycles it runs.
- What domain and range are reasonable?
- Is the function a linear function?

29. Carwash A theater group is having a carwash fundraiser. The group can only spend $34 on soap, which is enough to wash 40 cars. Each car is charged $5.
  a. If c is the total number of cars washed and p is the profit, which is the independent variable and which is the dependent variable?
  b. Is the relationship between c and p a function? Explain.
  c. Write an equation that shows this relationship.
  d. Find a reasonable domain and range for the situation.

30. Open-Ended What value of x makes the relation $\{(1, 5), (x, 8), (-7, 9)\}$ a function?

Determine whether each relation is a function. Assume that each different variable has a different value.

31. $\{(a, b), (b, a), (c, c), (e, d)\}$

32. $\{(b, b), (c, d), (d, c), (c, a)\}$

33. $\{(c, e), (c, d), (c, b)\}$

34. $\{(a, b), (b, c), (c, d), (d, e)\}$

35. Reasoning Can the graph of a function be a horizontal line? A vertical line? Explain.

 **36.** To form the inverse of a relation written as a set of ordered pairs, you switch the coordinates of each ordered pair. For example, the inverse of the relation $\{(1, 8), (3, 5), (7, 9)\}$ is $\{(8, 1), (5, 3), (9, 7)\}$. Give an example of a relation that is a function, but whose inverse is *not* a function.

Use the functions $f(x) = 2x$ and $g(x) = x^2 + 1$ to find the value of each expression.

37. $f(3) + g(4)$ **38.** $g(3) + f(4)$ **39.** $f(5) - 2 \cdot g(1)$ **40.** $f(g(3))$

41. What is the value of the function $f(x) = 7x$ when $x = 0.75$?

42. Andrew needs x dollars for a snack. Scott needs 2 more dollars than Andrew, but Nick only needs half as many dollars as Andrew. Altogether they need $17 to pay for their snacks. How many dollars does Nick need?

43. What is the greatest number of $.43 stamps you can buy for $5?

44. What is the greatest possible width of the rectangle, to the nearest inch?

$\ell = 35$ in.

$A < 184$ in.^{2}

Mixed Review

Write a function rule to represent each situation.

See Lesson 4-5.

45. You baby-sit for $5 per hour and get a $7 tip. Your earnings E are a function of the number of hours h you work.

46. You buy several pairs of socks for $4.50 per pair, plus a shirt for $10. The total amount a you spend is a function of the number of pairs of socks s you buy.

47. The graph shows a family's distance from home as they drive to the mountains for a vacation.
a. What are the variables in the graph?
b. Copy the graph. Describe how the variables are related at various points on the graph.

See Lesson 4-1.

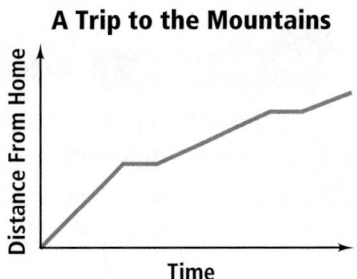

A Trip to the Mountains

Distance From Home

Time

Get Ready! **To prepare for Lesson 4-7, do Exercises 48–50.**

Evaluate each expression for $x = 1, 2, 3,$ and 4.

See Lesson 1-2.

48. $9 + 3(x - 1)$ **49.** $8 + 7(x - 1)$ **50.** $0.4 - 3(x - 1)$

4-7 Arithmetic Sequences

© Common Core State Standards

F-IF.A.3 Recognize that sequences are functions, sometimes defined recursively, . . . **Also A-SSE.A.1a, F-BF.A.1a, F-BF.A.2, F-LE.A.2**

MP 1, MP 2, MP 3, MP 4, MP 7

Objectives To identify and extend patterns in sequences
To represent arithmetic sequences using function notation

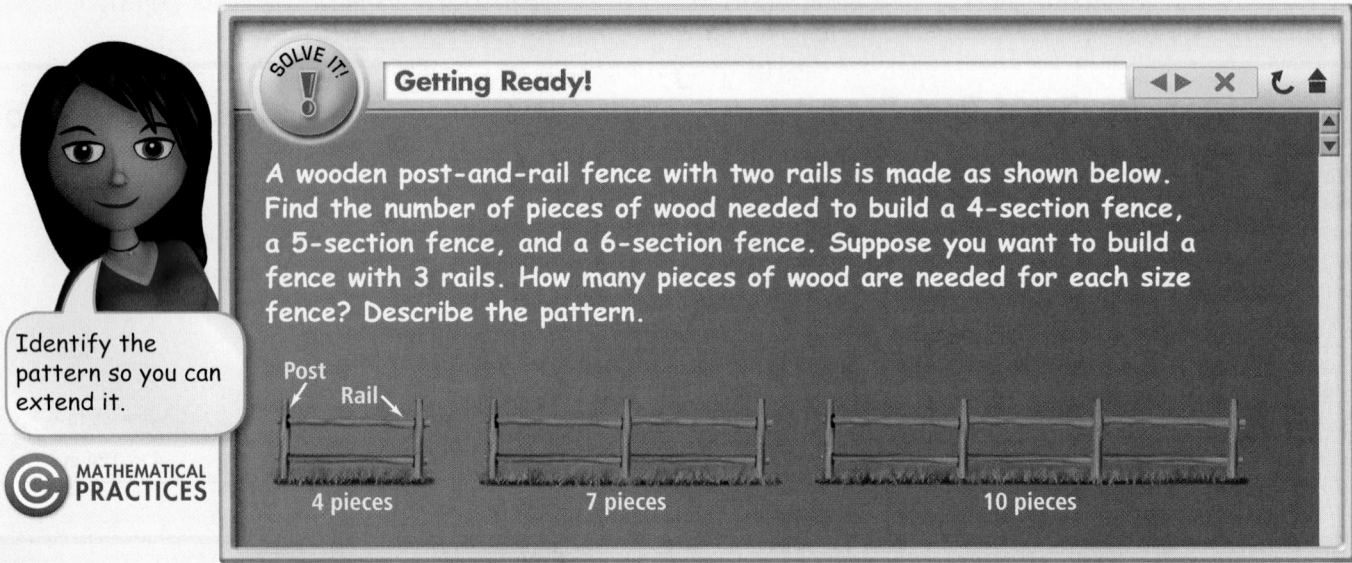

Getting Ready!

A wooden post-and-rail fence with two rails is made as shown below. Find the number of pieces of wood needed to build a 4-section fence, a 5-section fence, and a 6-section fence. Suppose you want to build a fence with 3 rails. How many pieces of wood are needed for each size fence? Describe the pattern.

Identify the pattern so you can extend it.

MATHEMATICAL PRACTICES

Post

Rail

4 pieces   7 pieces   10 pieces

Lesson Vocabulary

- sequence
- term of a sequence
- arithmetic sequence
- common difference
- recursive formula
- explicit formula

In the Solve It, the numbers of pieces of wood used for 1 section of fence, 2 sections of fence, and so on, form a pattern, or a sequence. A **sequence** is an ordered list of numbers that often form a pattern. Each number in the list is called a **term of a sequence.**

Essential Understanding When you can identify a pattern in a sequence, you can use it to extend the sequence. You can also model some sequences with a function rule that you can use to find any term of the sequence.

Plan

How can you identify a pattern?
Look at how each term of the sequence is related to the previous term. Your goal is to identify a single rule that you can apply to every term to produce the next term.

© Problem 1 Extending Sequences

Describe a pattern in each sequence. What are the next two terms of each sequence?

A 5,   8,   11,   14, . . .

+3   +3   +3

A pattern is "add 3 to the previous term." So the next two terms are $14 + 3 = 17$ and $17 + 3 = 20$.

B 2.5,   5,   10,   20, . . .
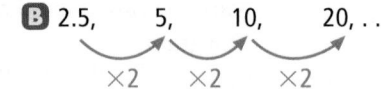
×2   ×2   ×2

A pattern is "multiply the previous term by 2." So the next two terms are $2(20) = 40$ and $2(40) = 80$.

Got It? 1. Describe a pattern in each sequence. What are the next two terms of each sequence?

a. 5, 11, 17, 23, . . .

b. 400, 200, 100, 50, . . .

c. 2, −4, 8, −16, . . .

d. −15, −11, −7, −3, . . .

In an **arithmetic sequence,** the difference between consecutive terms is constant. This difference is called the **common difference.**

 Problem 2 **Identifying an Arithmetic Sequence**

Plan

How can you identify an arithmetic sequence?
The difference between every pair of consecutive terms must be the same.

Tell whether the sequence is arithmetic. If it is, what is the common difference?

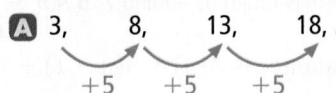

The sequence has a common difference of 5, so it is arithmetic.

The sequence does not have a common difference, so it is not arithmetic.

 Got It? 2. Tell whether the sequence is arithmetic. If it is, what is the common difference?

a. 8, 15, 22, 30, . . .

b. 7, 9, 11, 13, . . .

c. 10, 4, −2, −8, . . .

d. 2, −2, 2, −2, . . .

A sequence is a function whose domain is the natural numbers, and whose outputs are the terms of the sequence.

You can write a sequence using a recursive formula. A **recursive formula** is a function rule that relates each term of a sequence after the first to the ones before it. Consider the sequence 7, 11, 15, 19, . . . You can use the common difference of the terms of an arithmetic sequence to write a recursive formula for the sequence. For the sequence 7, 11, 15, 19, . . . , the common difference is 4.

Let n = the term number in the sequence.
Let $A(n)$ = the value of the nth term of the sequence.

value of term 1 = $A(1) = 7$ ⟵ The common difference is 4.

value of term 2 = $A(2) = A(1) + 4 = 11$

value of term 3 = $A(3) = A(2) + 4 = 15$

value of term 4 = $A(4) = A(3) + 4 = 19$ ⟵ The value of the previous term plus 4

value of term n = $A(n) = A(n − 1) + 4$

The recursive formula for the arithmetic sequence above is $A(n) = A(n − 1) + 4$, where $A(1) = 7$.

 **Problem 3** **Writing a Recursive Formula**

Write a recursive formula for the arithmetic sequence below. What is the value of the 8th term?

$$70, \quad 77, \quad 84, \quad 91, \ldots$$

$$+7 \quad +7 \quad +7$$

Step 1 $A(1) = 70$ First term of the sequence

$A(2) = A(1) + 7 = 70 + 7 = 77$ $A(2)$ is found by adding 7 to $A(1)$.

$A(3) = A(2) + 7 = 77 + 7 = 84$ $A(3)$ is found by adding 7 to $A(2)$.

$A(4) = A(3) + 7 = 84 + 7 = 91$ $A(4)$ is found by adding 7 to $A(3)$.

$A(n) = A(n - 1) + 7$ $A(n)$ is found by adding 7 to $A(n - 1)$.

The recursive formula for the arithmetic sequence is $A(n) = A(n - 1) + 7$, where $A(1) = 70$.

Step 2 To find the value of the 8th term, you need to extend the pattern.

$A(5) = A(4) + 7 = 91 + 7 = 98$

$A(6) = A(5) + 7 = 98 + 7 = 105$

$A(7) = A(6) + 7 = 105 + 7 = 112$

$A(8) = A(7) + 7 = 112 + 7 = 119$

The value of the 8th term is 119.

  Got It? **3.** Write a recursive formula for each arithmetic sequence. What is the 9th term of each sequence?

     a. 3, 9, 15, 21, . . .   **b.** 23, 35, 47, 59, . . .

     c. 7.3, 7.8, 8.3, 8.8, . . .   **d.** 97, 88, 79, 70, . . .

     e. Reasoning Is a recursive formula a useful way to find the value of an arithmetic sequence? Explain.

You can find the value of any term of an arithmetic sequence using a recursive formula. You can also write a sequence using an explicit formula. An **explicit formula** is a function rule that relates each term of a sequence to the term number.

Key Concept **Explicit Formula For an Arithmetic Sequence**

The nth term of an arithmetic sequence with first term $A(1)$ and common difference d is given by

$$A(n) = A(1) + (n - 1)d$$

         ↑   ↑   ↑

     nth term   first term   term number   common difference

Problem 4 Writing an Explicit Formula

Online Auction An online auction works as shown below. Write an explicit formula to represent the bids as an arithmetic sequence. What is the twelfth bid?

Make a table of the bids. Identify the first term and common difference.

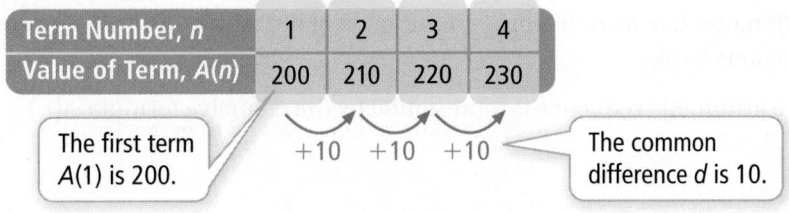

Term Number, n	1	2	3	4
Value of Term, $A(n)$	200	210	220	230

The first term $A(1)$ is 200. $+10$ $+10$ $+10$ The common difference d is 10.

Plan

What information do you need to write a rule for an arithmetic sequence?
You need the first term of the sequence and the common difference.

Substitute $A(1) = 200$ and $d = 10$ into the formula $A(n) = A(1) + (n - 1)d$. The explicit formula $A(n) = 200 + (n - 1)10$ represents the arithmetic sequence of the auction bids. To find the twelfth bid, evaluate $A(n)$ for $n = 12$.

$$A(12) = 200 + (12 - 1)10 = 310$$

The twelfth bid is $310.

Got It? **4. a.** A subway pass has a starting value of $100. After one ride, the value of the pass is $98.25. After two rides, its value is $96.50. After three rides, its value is $94.75. Write an explicit formula to represent the remaining value on the card as an arithmetic sequence. What is the value of the pass after 15 rides?

b. Reasoning How many rides can be taken with the $100 pass?

You can write an explicit formula from a recursive formula and vice versa.

Problem 5 Writing an Explicit Formula From a Recursive Formula

An arithmetic sequence is represented by the recursive formula $A(n) = A(n - 1) + 12$. If the first term of the sequence is 19, write the explicit formula.

The first term is 19, so $A(1) = 19$.   Adding 12 to the previous term means that the common difference d is 12

$A(n) = A(n - 1) + 12$

$A(n) = A(1) + (n - 1)d$ General form of an explicit formula

$A(n) = 19 + (n - 1)12$ Substitute 19 for $A(1)$ and 12 for d.

The explicit formula $A(n) = 19 + (n - 1)12$ represents the arithmetic sequence.

Got It? **5.** For each recursive formula, find an explicit formula that represents the same sequence.

 a. $A(n) = A(n - 1) + 2; A(1) = 21$

 b. $A(n) = A(n - 1) + 7; A(1) = 2$

 Problem 6 **Writing a Recursive Formula From an Explicit Formula**

An arithmetic sequence is represented by the explicit formula $A(n) = 32 + (n - 1)(22)$. What is the recursive formula?

> 32 is the first term.

$$A(n) = 32 + (n - 1)(22)$$

> 22 is the common difference.

A recursive formula relates the value of the term to the previous term using the common difference. Use $A(n)$ to represent the value of the term and $A(n - 1)$ to represent the value of the previous term.

The arithmetic sequence is represented by the recursive formula $A(n) = A(n - 1) + 22$; $A(1) = 32$.

 Got It? **6.** For each explicit formula, find a recursive formula that represents the same sequence.

 a. $A(n) = 76 + (n - 1)(10)$

 b. $A(n) = 1 + (n - 1)(3)$

 Lesson Check

Do you know HOW?

Describe a pattern in each sequence. Then find the next two terms of the sequence.

1. $3, 11, 19, 27, \ldots$

2. $3, -6, 12, -24, \ldots$

Tell whether the sequence is arithmetic. If it is, identify the common difference.

3. $1, -7, -14, -21, \ldots$

4. $11, 20, 29, 38, \ldots$

5. Write a recursive and an explicit formula for the arithmetic sequence.

$$9, 7, 5, 3, 1, \ldots$$

Do you UNDERSTAND?
MATHEMATICAL PRACTICES

6. Vocabulary Consider the following arithmetic sequence: $25, 19, 13, 7, \ldots$ Is the common difference 6 or -6? Explain.

7. Error Analysis Describe and correct the error below in finding the tenth term of the arithmetic sequence $4, 12, 20, 28, \ldots$

> first term = 4
> common difference = 8
> ~~tenth term = 4 + 10(8) = 84~~

8. Reasoning Can you use the explicit formula below to find the nth term of an arithmetic sequence with a first term $A(1)$ and a common difference d? Explain.

$$A(n) = A(1) + nd - d$$

Practice and Problem-Solving Exercises  MATHEMATICAL PRACTICES

 **Practice**

Describe a pattern in each sequence. Then find the next two terms of the sequence.

◀ See Problem 1.

9. 6, 13, 20, 27, . . .

10. 8, 4, 2, 1, . . .

11. 2, 6, 10, 14, . . .

12. 10, 4, −2, −8, . . .

13. 13, 11, 9, 7, . . .

14. 2, 20, 200, 2000, . . .

15. 1.1, 2.2, 3.3, 4.4, . . .

16. 99, 88, 77, 66, . . .

17. 4.5, 9, 18, 36, . . .

Tell whether the sequence is arithmetic. If it is, identify the common difference.

◀ See Problem 2.

18. −7, −3, 1, 5, . . .

19. −9, −17, −26, −33, . . .

20. 19, 8, −3, −14, . . .

21. 2, 11, 21, 32, . . .

22. $\frac{1}{2}, \frac{1}{3}, \frac{1}{6}, 0, \ldots$

23. 0.2, 1.5, 2.8, 4.1, . . .

24. 10, 8, 6, 4, . . .

25. 10, 24, 36, 52, . . .

26. 3, 6, 12, 24, . . .

27. 15, 14.5, 14, 13.5, 13, . . .

28. 4, 4.4, 4.44, 4.444, . . .

29. −3, −7, −10, −14, . . .

Write a recursive formula for each sequence.

◀ See Problem 3.

30. 1.1, 1.9, 2.7, 3.5, . . .

31. 99, 88, 77, 66, . . .

32. 23, 38, 53, 68, . . .

33. 13, 10, 7, 4, . . .

34. 2.3, 2.8, 3.3, 3.8, . . .

35. 4.6, 4.7, 4.8, 4.9, . . .

36. Garage After one customer buys 4 new tires, a garage recycling bin has 20 tires in it. After another customer buys 4 new tires, the bin has 24 tires in it. Write an explicit formula to represent the number of tires in the bin as an arithmetic sequence. How many tires are in the bin after 9 customers buy all new tires?

◀ See Problem 4.

37. Cafeteria You have a cafeteria card worth $50. After you buy lunch on Monday, its value is $46.75. After you buy lunch on Tuesday, its value is $43.50. Write an explicit formula to represent the amount of money left on the card as an arithmetic sequence. What is the value of the card after you buy 12 lunches?

Write an explicit formula for each recursive formula.

◀ See Problem 5.

38. $A(n) = A(n − 1) + 12; A(1) = 12$

39. $A(n) = A(n − 1) + 3.4; A(1) = 7.3$

40. $A(n) = A(n − 1) + 3; A(1) = 6$

41. $A(n) = A(n − 1) − 0.3; A(1) = 0.3$

Write a recursive formula for each explicit formula.

◀ See Problem 6.

42. $A(n) = 5 + (n − 1)(3)$

43. $A(n) = 3 + (n − 1)(−5)$

44. $A(n) = −1 + (n − 1)(−2)$

45. $A(n) = 4 + (n − 1)(1)$

Find the second, fourth, and eleventh terms of the sequence described by each explicit formula.

46. $A(n) = 5 + (n − 1)(−3)$

47. $A(n) = −3 + (n − 1)(5)$

48. $A(n) = −11 + (n − 1)(2)$

49. $A(n) = 9 + (n − 1)(8)$

50. $A(n) = 0.5 + (n - 1)(3.5)$

51. $A(n) = -7 + (n - 1)(5)$

52. $A(n) = 1 + (n - 1)(-6)$

53. $A(n) = -2.1 + (n - 1)(-1.1)$

 **Apply**

Tell whether each sequence is arithmetic. Justify your answer. If the sequence is arithmetic, write a recursive and an explicit formula to represent it.

54. $0.3, 0.9, 1.5, 2.1, \ldots$

55. $-3, -7, -11, -15, \ldots$

56. $1, 8, 27, 64, \ldots$

57. $-5, 5, -5, 5, \ldots$

58. $46, 31, 16, 2, \ldots$

59. $0.2, -0.6, -1.4, -2.2, \ldots$

Using the recursive formula for each arithmetic sequence, find the second, third, and fourth terms of the sequence. Then write the explicit formula that represents the sequence.

60. $A(n) = A(n - 1) - 4; A(1) = 8$

61. $A(n) = A(n - 1) + 1.2; A(1) = 8.8$

62. $A(n) = A(n - 1) + 3; A(1) = 13$

63. $A(n) = A(n - 1) - 2; A(1) = 0$

64. Reasoning An arithmetic sequence can be represented by the explicit function $A(n) = -10 + (n - 1)(4)$. Describe the relationship between the first term and the second term. Describe the relationship between the second term and the third term. Write a recursive formula to represent this sequence.

65. Open-Ended Write a function rule for a sequence that has 25 as the sixth term.

Write the first six terms in each sequence. Explain what the sixth term means in the context of the situation.

66. A cane of bamboo is 30 in. tall the first week and grows 6 in. per week thereafter.

67. You borrow $350 from a friend the first week and pay the friend back $25 each week thereafter.

68. Think About a Plan Suppose the first Friday of a new year is the fourth day of that year. Will the year have 53 Fridays regardless of whether or not it is a leap year?
   - What is a rule that represents the sequence of the days in the year that are Fridays?
   - How many full weeks are in a 365-day year?

69. Look For a Pattern The first five rows of Pascal's Triangle are shown at the right.
   a. Predict the numbers in the seventh row.
   b. Find the sum of the numbers in each of the first five rows. Predict the sum of the numbers in the seventh row.

70. Transportation Buses run every 9 min starting at 6:00 A.M. You get to the bus stop at 7:16 A.M. How long will you wait for a bus?

71. Multiple Representations Use the table at the right that shows an arithmetic sequence.
   a. Copy and complete the table.
   b. Graph the ordered pairs (x, y) on a coordinate plane.
   c. What do you notice about the points on your graph?

x	y
1	5
2	8
3	■
4	■

72. Number Theory The Fibonacci sequence is 1, 1, 2, 3, 5, 8, 13, . . . After the first two numbers, each number is the sum of the two previous numbers.
  a. What is the next term of the sequence? The eleventh term of the sequence?
  b. Open-Ended Choose two other numbers to start a Fibonacci-like sequence. Write the first seven terms of your sequence.

Challenge **Find the common difference of each arithmetic sequence. Then find the next term.**

73. $4, x + 4, 2x + 4, 3x + 4, . . .$

74. $a + b + c, 4a + 3b + c, 7a + 5b + c, . . .$

75. a. Geometry Draw the next figure in the pattern.

  b. Reasoning What is the color of the twentieth figure? Explain.
  c. How many sides does the twenty-third figure have? Explain.

Apply What You've Learned

MATHEMATICAL PRACTICES

MP 8

Look back to your work from the Apply What You've Learned sections on pages 245 and 259 to find the functions modeling Keiko's and Jayden's blogs. Choose from the following words and numbers to complete the sentences below.

explicit	8	−8	common difference	7
term	9	recursive	10	sequence

  a. A(n) __?__ is an ordered list of numbers that often form a pattern.

  b. The function modeling Keiko's blog is a(n) __?__ formula.

  c. The common difference in the function modeling Jayden's blog is __?__ .

  d. Jayden's blog will first have at least 100 subscribers in __?__ months.

  e. Keiko's blog will first have at least 100 subscribers in __?__ months.

  f. A function rule that relates each term of a sequence after the first term to the ones before it is called a(n) __?__ formula.

Pull It **All Together**

Completing the Performance Task

Look back at your results from the Apply What You've Learned sections in Lessons 4-2, 4-4, and 4-7. Use the work you did to complete the following.

To solve these problems, you will pull together many concepts and skills that you have studied about functions.

1. Solve the problem in the Task Description on page 233 by determining whether Jayden's or Keiko's blog will be the first to have 200 subscribers. Assume the growth in each blog's subscribers continues to follow the established pattern. Show all your work and explain each step of your solution.

 2. **Reflect** Choose one of the Mathematical Practices below and explain how you applied it in your work on the Performance Task.

   MP 1: Make sense of problems and persevere in solving them.

   MP 4: Model with mathematics.

   MP 8: Look for and express regularity in repeated reasoning.

On Your Own

Santana and Garrett started writing blogs at the same time. The number of subscribers S to Santana's blog can be modeled by the function $S = 12m + 24$, where m is the number of months since she started the blog. Data for the number of subscribers to Garrett's blog are shown in the table below.

Garrett's Blog

Number of Months	Number of Subscribers
0	84
1	90
2	96
3	102
4	108

a. Assume the growth in each blog's subscribers continues to follow the established pattern. Will Santana and Garrett ever have the same number of subscribers? If so, how many? Explain.

b. After how many months will Santana have more subscribers than Garrett? Explain.

Connecting **BIG** ideas and Answering the Essential Questions

1 Functions

A function is a relationship that pairs one input value with exactly one output value. You can use words, tables, equations, sets of ordered pairs, and graphs to represent functions.

Patterns and Functions (Lessons 4-2 and 4-3)

Linear

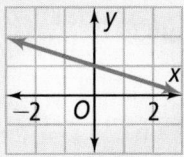

Nonlinear

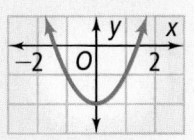

Function Notation and Sequences (Lessons 4-6 and 4-7)

n	$A(n) = 3 + (n - 1)(2)$	$A(n)$
1	$3 + (1 - 1)(2)$	3
2	$3 + (2 - 1)(2)$	5
3	$3 + (3 - 1)(2)$	7

2 Modeling

You can use functions to model real-world situations that pair one input value with a unique output value.

Using Graphs to Relate Two Quantities (Lesson 4-1)

Bus Trip

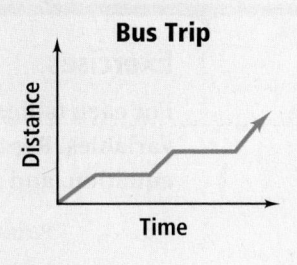

Time

Graphing a Function Rule (Lesson 4-4)

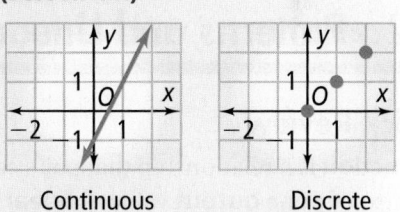

Continuous   Discrete

Writing a Function Rule (Lesson 4-5)

$$C = \frac{1}{4}n + 6 \qquad A = s^2$$

Chapter Vocabulary

- arithmetic sequence, p. 275
- common difference, p. 275
- continuous graph, p. 255
- dependent variable, p. 240
- discrete graph, p. 255
- domain, p. 268
- explicit formula, p. 276
- function, p. 241
- function notation, p. 269
- input, p. 240
- independent variable, p. 240
- linear function, p. 241
- nonlinear function, p. 246
- output, p. 240
- range, p. 268
- recursive formula, p. 275
- relation, p. 268
- sequence, p. 274
- term of a sequence, p. 274
- vertical line test, p. 269

Choose the correct term to complete each sentence.

1. If the value of a changes in response to the value of b, then b is the ___?___ .

2. The graph of a(n) ___?___ function is a nonvertical line or part of a nonvertical line.

3. The ___?___ of a function consists of the set of all output values.

4-1 Using Graphs to Relate Two Quantities

Quick Review

You can use graphs to represent the relationship between two variables.

Example

A dog owner plays fetch with her dog. Sketch a graph to represent the distance between them and the time.

Playing Fetch

Exercises

4. Travel A car's speed increases as it merges onto a highway. The car travels at 65 mi/h on the highway until it slows to exit. The car then stops at three traffic lights before reaching its destination. Draw a sketch of a graph that shows the car's speed over time. Label each section.

5. Surfing A professional surfer paddles out past breaking waves, rides a wave, paddles back out past the breaking waves, rides another wave, and paddles back to the beach. Draw a sketch of a graph that shows the surfer's possible distance from the beach over time.

4-2 Patterns and Linear Functions

Quick Review

A **function** is a relationship that pairs each **input** value with exactly one **output** value. A **linear function** is a function whose graph is a line or part of a line.

Example

The number y of eggs left in a dozen depends on the number x of 2-egg omelets you make, as shown in the table. Represent this relationship using words, an equation, and a graph.

Number of Omelets Made, x	0	1	2	3
Number of Eggs Left, y	12	10	8	6

Look for a pattern in the table. Each time x increases by 1, y decreases by 2. The number y of eggs left is 12 minus the quantity 2 times the number x of omelets made: $y = 12 - 2x$.

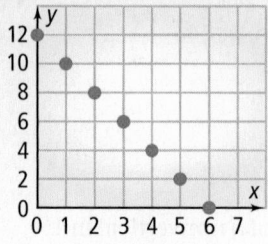

Exercises

For each table, identify the independent and dependent variables. Represent the relationship using words, an equation, and a graph.

6. **Paint in Can**

Number of Chairs Painted, p	Paint Left (oz), L
0	128
1	98
2	68
3	38

7. **Game Cost**

Number of Snacks Purchased, s	Total Cost, C
0	$18
1	$21
2	$24
3	$27

8. **Elevation**

Number of Flights of Stairs Climbed, n	0	1	2	3
Elevation (ft above sea level), E	311	326	341	356

4-3 Patterns and Nonlinear Functions

Quick Review

A **nonlinear function** is a function whose graph is *not* a line or part of a line.

Example

The area A of a square field is a function of the side length s of the field. Is the function *linear* or *nonlinear*?

Side Length (ft), s	10	15	20	25
Area (ft²), A	100	225	400	625

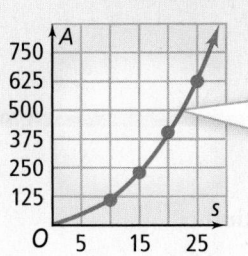

Graph the ordered pairs and connect the points. The graph is not a line, so the function is nonlinear.

Exercises

Graph the function shown by each table. Tell whether the function is *linear* or *nonlinear*.

9.

x	y
1	0
2	1
3	8
4	20

10.

x	y
1	0
2	4.5
3	9
4	13.5

11.

x	y
1	2
2	6
3	12
4	72

12.

x	y
1	−2
2	−9
3	−16
4	−23

4-4 Graphing a Function Rule

Quick Review

A **continuous graph** is a graph that is unbroken. A **discrete graph** is composed of distinct, isolated points. In a real-world graph, show only points that make sense.

Example

The total height h of a stack of cans is a function of the number n of layers of 4.5-in. cans used. This situation is represented by $h = 4.5n$. Graph the function.

n	h
0	0
1	4.5
2	9
3	13.5
4	18

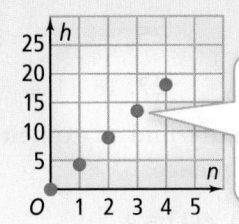

The graph is discrete because only whole numbers of layers make sense.

Exercises

Graph the function rule. Explain why the graph is *continuous* or *discrete*.

13. **Walnuts** Your cost c to buy w pounds of walnuts at $6/lb is represented by $c = 6w$.

14. **Moving** A truck originally held 24 chairs. You remove 2 chairs at a time. The number of chairs n remaining after you make t trips is represented by $n = 24 − 2t$.

15. **Flood** A burst pipe fills a basement with 37 in. of water. A pump empties the water at a rate of 1.5 in./h. The water level ℓ, in inches, after t hours is represented by $\ell = 37 − 1.5t$.

16. Graph $y = -|x| + 2$.

4-5 Writing a Function Rule

Quick Review

To write a function rule describing a real-world situation, it is often helpful to start with a verbal model of the situation.

Example

At a bicycle motocross (BMX) track, you pay $40 for a racing license plus $15 per race. What is a function rule that represents your total cost?

total cost = license fee + fee per race · number of races

$$C \quad = \quad 40 \quad + \quad 15 \quad \cdot \quad r$$

A function rule is $C = 40 + 15 \cdot r$.

Exercises

Write a function rule to represent each situation.

17. **Landscaping** The volume V remaining in a 243-ft^3 pile of gravel decreases by 0.2 ft^3 with each shovelful s of gravel spread in a walkway.

18. **Design** Your total cost C for hiring a garden designer is $200 for an initial consultation plus $45 for each hour h the designer spends drawing plans.

4-6 Formalizing Relations and Functions

Quick Review

A **relation** pairs numbers in the **domain** with numbers in the **range.** A relation may or may not be a function.

Example

Is the relation {(0, 1), (3, 3), (4, 4), (0, 0)} a function?

The x-values of the ordered pairs form the domain, and the y-values form the range. The domain value 0 is paired with two range values, 1 and 0. So the relation is not a function.

Exercises

Tell whether each relation is a function.

19. $\{(-1, 7), (9, 4), (3, -2), (5, 3), (9, 1)\}$

20. $\{(2, 5), (3, 5), (4, -4), (5, -4), (6, 8)\}$

Evaluate each function for $x = 2$ and $x = 7$.

21. $f(x) = 2x - 8$ 22. $h(x) = -4x + 61$

23. The domain of $t(x) = -3.8x - 4.2$ is $\{-3, -1.4, 0, 8\}$. What is the range?

4-7 Arithmetic Sequences

Quick Review

A **sequence** is an ordered list of numbers, called terms, that often forms a pattern. A sequence can be represented by a **recursive formula** or an **explicit formula**.

Example

Tell whether the sequence is arithmetic.

5,   2,   −1,   −4, . . .

−3   −3   −3

The sequence has a common difference of −3, so it is arithmetic.

Exercises

For each sequence, write a recursive and an explicit formula.

24. 3, 8, 13, 18, . . .   25. −2, −5, −8, −11, . . .

26. 4, 6.5, 9, 11.5, . . .   27. 18, 11, 4, −3, . . .

For each recursive formula, find an explicit formula that represents the same sequence.

28. $A(n) = A(n - 1) + 3; A(1) = 4$

29. $A(n) = A(n - 1) + 11; A(1) = 13$

30. $A(n) = A(n - 1) - 1; A(1) = 19$

Do you know HOW?

1. **Recreation** You ride your bike to the park, sit to read for a while, and then ride your bike home. It takes you less time to ride from the park to your house than it took to ride from your house to the park. Draw a sketch of a graph that shows your possible distance traveled over time. Label each section.

2. Identify the independent and dependent variables in the table below. Then describe the relationship using words, an equation, and a graph.

Speed of Sound in Air				
Temperature (°C)	10	15	20	25
Velocity (m/s)	337	340	343	346

Graph the function shown by each table. Tell whether the function is *linear* or *nonlinear*.

3.

x	y
−3	−5
−1	−1
1	3
3	7

4.

x	y
0	1
1	2
2	5
3	10

Make a table of values for each function rule. Then graph the function.

5. $y = 1.5x - 3$

6. $y = -x^2 + 4$

Identify the domain and range of each relation. Use a mapping diagram to determine whether the relation is a function.

7. $\{(-2, 5), (8, 6), (3, 12), (5, 6)\}$

8. $\{(9, 6), (3, 8), (4, 9.5), (9, 2)\}$

9. **Baking** A bottle holds 48 tsp of vanilla. The amount A of vanilla remaining in the bottle decreases by 2 tsp per batch b of cookies. Write a function rule to represent this situation. How much vanilla remains after 12 batches of cookies?

10. **Party Favors** You are buying party favors that cost $2.47 each. You can spend no more than $30 on the party favors. What domain and range are reasonable for this situation?

Find the range of each function for the domain $\{-4, -2, 0, 1.5, 4\}$.

11. $f(x) = -2x - 3$

12. $f(x) = 5x^2 + 4$

Find the second, fourth, and eleventh terms of the sequence described by each explicit formula.

13. $A(n) = 2 + (n - 1)(-2.5)$

14. $A(n) = -9 + (n - 1)(3)$

Tell whether each sequence is arithmetic. Justify your answer. If the sequence is arithmetic, write a recursive formula and an explicit formula to represent it.

15. 128, 64, 32, 16, . . .

16. 3, 3.25, 3.5, 3.75, . . .

Do you UNDERSTAND?

Ⓒ **Vocabulary** Tell whether each relationship should be represented by a *continuous* or *discrete* graph.

17. the price of turkey that sells for $.89 per pound

18. the profit you make selling flowers at $1.50 each when each flower costs you $.80

Ⓒ 19. **Reasoning** Can a function have an infinite number of values in its domain and only a finite number of values in its range? If so, describe a real-world situation that can be modeled by such a function.

Ⓒ 20. **Writing** What is the difference between a relation and a function? Is every relation a function? Is every function a relation? Explain.

Common Core Cumulative Standards Review

 ASSESSMENT

TIPS FOR SUCCESS

Some questions on standardized tests ask you to choose a graph that best represents a real-world situation. Read the question at the right. Then follow the tips to answer it.

Aiko ran at a constant speed for most of a race. Toward the end of the race, she increased her speed until she reached the finish line. Which graph best represents Aiko's distance traveled over time?

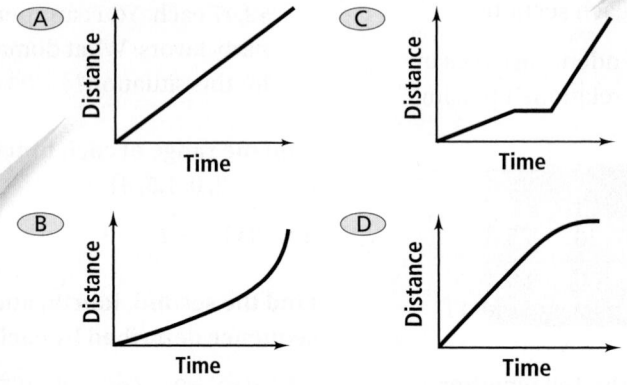

TIP 2

Aiko's speed increases toward the end of the race, so the graph should rise more quickly at the end.

Think It Through

Choice A shows a *constant* speed during the *entire* race.

Choice B shows an *increasing* speed near the race's *end*.

Choice C shows a *complete stop* in the *middle* of the race.

Choice D shows a *decreasing* speed near the race's *end*.

The correct answer is B.

TIP 1

Aiko's speed is constant for most of the race, so the graph should be a straight line most of the time.

Vocabulary Builder

As you solve test items, you must understand the meanings of mathematical terms. Match each term with its mathematical meaning.

A. dependent variable

B. equation

C. numerical expression

D. function

E. domain

I. a math sentence stating two quantities have the same value

II. a relation where each input value corresponds to exactly one output value

III. a math phrase that contains operations and numbers but no variables

IV. a variable whose value changes in response to another variable

V. the possible values for the input of a function or relation

Selected Response

Read each question. Then write the letter of the correct answer on your paper.

1. Which word phrase is represented by the algebraic expression $5(x - y)^2$?

   Ⓐ the product of 5 and $x - y^2$

   Ⓑ the product of 5 and $x^2 - y^2$

   Ⓒ the product of 5 and $(x - y)$ squared

   Ⓓ the quotient of 5 and $(x - y)$ squared

2. Angie uses the equation $E = 0.03s + 25,000$ to find her yearly earnings E based on her total sales s. What is the independent variable?

   Ⓕ E Ⓖ 0.03   Ⓗ s Ⓘ 25,000

3. The function $C = 2\pi r$ gives the circumference C of a circle with radius r. What is an appropriate domain for the function?

   Ⓐ all integers   Ⓒ positive real numbers

   Ⓑ positive integers   Ⓓ all real numbers

4. A point is missing from the graph of the relation at the the right. The relation is *not* a function. Which point is missing?

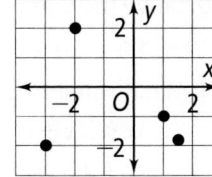

F (0, 0)   H (−1, 2)

G (1, 1)   I (2, −2)

5. The table below shows the relationship between how long an ice cube is in the sun and its weight.

Time (min)	0	1	2	3	4
Weight (g)	9	8	5	2	0

Which graph best represents the data in the table?

A 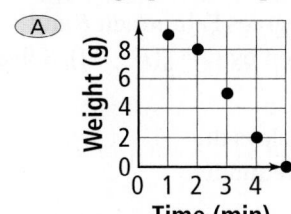   C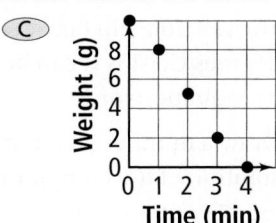

B 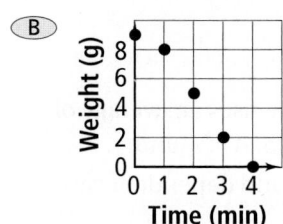   D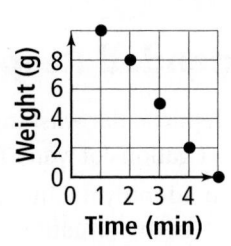

6. Which graph could represent the circumference of a balloon as the air is being let out?

F 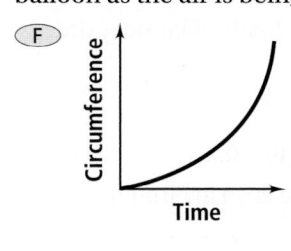   H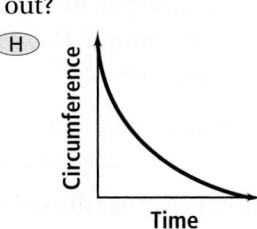

G 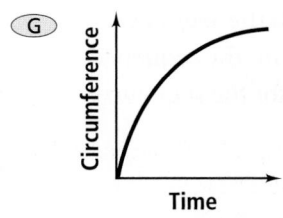   I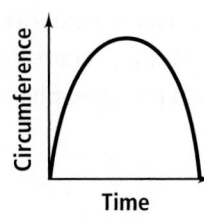

7. Mr. Washington is buying a gallon of milk for $3.99 and some number of boxes x of cereal for $4.39 each. If Mr. Washington has $20, which inequality can be used to find how many boxes of cereal can he buy?

A $3.99 + 4.39x \le 20$

B $4.39 + 3.99x \le 20$

C $3.99 + 4.39x \ge 20$

D $4.39 + 3.99x \ge 20$

8. During a clinical study, a medical company found that 3 out of 70 people experienced a side effect when using a certain medicine. The company predicts 63,000 people will use the medicine next year. How many people are expected to experience a side effect?

F 300   H 2700

G 900   I 21,000

9. Which equation can be used to generate the table of values at the right?

A $y = x + 9$

B $y = 2x + 4$

C $y = x + 3$

D $y = 3x - 2$

x	y
−3	−11
0	−2
3	7
6	16

10. In the diagram below, $\triangle ABC$ and $\triangle DEF$ are similar.

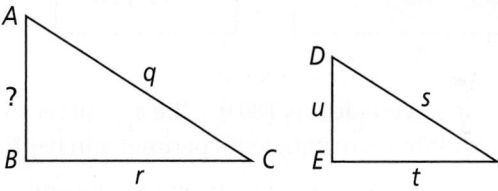

Which expression represents AB?

F $\dfrac{qu}{s}$ H $\dfrac{qr}{u}$

G $\dfrac{ru}{s}$ I $\dfrac{rs}{t}$

11. The sum of two consecutive odd integers is 24. Which equation can be used to find the first integer n?

A $n + 1 = 24$ C $2n + 1 = 24$

B $n + 2 = 24$ D $2n + 2 = 24$

Constructed Response

12. Sasha is framing a 5 in. by 7 in. picture with a frame that is 3 in. wide, as shown at the right. What is the frame's area in square inches?

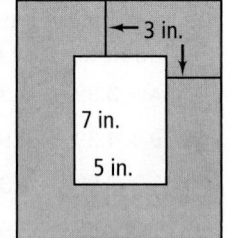

13. You are taking a plane trip that begins in Seattle and ends in Boston, with a layover in Dallas. The flight from Seattle to Dallas is 2 h 55 min. The layover in Dallas is 1 h 25 min. The flight from Dallas to Boston is 3 h 40 min. In hours, how long is the entire trip?

14. The speed of sound at sea level is approximately 340.3 m/s. What is the speed of sound in miles per hour? Round to the nearest hundredth.

15. The sum of two consecutive integers is −15. What is the product of the two integers?

16. Max writes a number pattern in which each number in the pattern is 1 less than twice the previous number. If the first number is 2, what is the fifth number?

17. The rectangles shown below are similar.

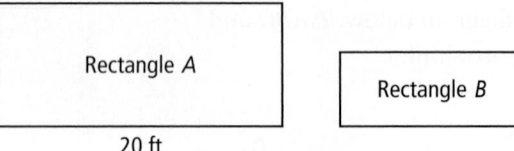

The area of rectangle A is 180 ft². The area of rectangle B is 45 ft². What is rectangle B's perimeter in feet?

18. One lap of a swimming pool is 50 m from one end of the pool to the other. Tamara swims 25 laps in a swim meet. How many kilometers does she swim?

19. An Internet company charges $8.95 per month for the first 3 months that it hosts your Web site. Then the company charges $11.95 per month for Web hosting. How much money, in dollars, will the company charge for 8 months of Web hosting?

20. Solve the equation below. Show all your work.
$$3x - 16 = 20$$

21. What values of x make both inequalities true?
$$3x < 4x + 6$$
$$2x + 1 < 15$$

22. Lindsey is using a map to find the distance between her house and Juanita's house. On the map, the distance is 2.5 in. If the map scale is $\frac{1}{8}$ in. : 1.5 mi, how far from Juanita does Lindsey live?

23. Pedro ran 2 more than $\frac{3}{4}$ the number of miles that Cierra ran. Write an equation that represents the relationship between the number of miles p that Pedro ran and the number of miles c that Cierra ran.

24. The relationship between degrees Fahrenheit F and degrees Celsius C can be given by $C = \frac{5}{9}(F - 32)$. Solve the equation for F.

25. Draw a number line that displays the solution of the compound inequality $-5 < -2x + 7 < 15$.

Extended Response

26. A particular washing machine uses an average of 41 gallons of water for every load of laundry.
  a. Identify the independent and dependent variables in this situation.
  b. Write a function rule to represent the situation.
  c. Suppose you used 533 gallons of water for laundry in one month. How many loads of laundry did you wash?

27. Look at the sequence below.
$$-3.2, -2.4, -1.6, -0.8, \ldots$$
  a. Tell whether the sequence is an arithmetic sequence.
  b. List the next three terms in the sequence.
  c. Write a recursive formula for the sequence.
  d. Write an explicit formula for the sequence.

Get Ready!

Lesson 1-9   ## Solutions of a Two-Variable Equation

Tell whether the given ordered pair is a solution of the equation.

1. $4y + 2x = 3$; $(1.5, 0)$ **2.** $y = 7x - 5$; $(0, 5)$ **3.** $y = -2x + 5$; $(2, 1)$

Lesson 2-5   ## Transforming Equations

Solve each equation for y.

4. $2y - x = 4$ **5.** $3x = y + 2$ **6.** $-2y - 2x = 4$

Lesson 2-6   ## Comparing Unit Rates

7. Transportation A car traveled 360 km in 6 h. A train traveled 400 km in 8 h. A boat traveled 375 km in 5 h. Which had the fastest average speed?

8. Plants A birch tree grew 2.5 in. in 5 months. A bean plant grew 8 in. in 10 months. A rose bush grew 5 in. in 8 months. Which grew the fastest?

Lesson 4-4   ## Graphing a Function Rule

Make a table of values for each function rule. Then graph each function.

9. $f(x) = x + 3$ **10.** $f(x) = -2x$ **11.** $f(x) = x - 4$

Lesson 4-7   ## Arithmetic Sequences

Write an explicit formula for each arithmetic sequence.

12. $2, 5, 8, 11, \ldots$ **13.** $13, 10, 7, 4, \ldots$ **14.** $-3, -0.5, 2, 4.5, \ldots$

 ## Looking Ahead Vocabulary

15. A steep hill has a greater *slope* than a flat plain. What does the *slope* of a line on a graph describe?

16. Two streets are *parallel* when they go the same way and do not cross. What does it mean in math to call two lines *parallel*?

17. John was bringing a message to the principal's office when the principal *intercepted* him and took the message. When a graph passes through the y-axis, it has a *y-intercept*. What do you think a y-intercept of a graph represents?

Linear Functions

Download videos connecting math to your world.

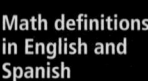

Interactive! Vary numbers, graphs, and figures to explore math concepts.

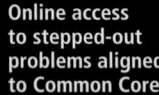

The online Solve It will get you in gear for each lesson.

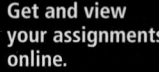

Math definitions in English and Spanish

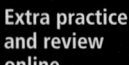

Online access to stepped-out problems aligned to Common Core

Get and view your assignments online.

Extra practice and review online

Virtual Nerd™ tutorials with built-in support

Chapter Preview

5-1 Rate of Change and Slope
5-2 Direct Variation
5-3 Slope-Intercept Form
5-4 Point-Slope Form
5-5 Standard Form
5-6 Parallel and Perpendicular Lines
5-7 Scatter Plots and Trend Lines
5-8 Graphing Absolute Value Functions

Vocabulary

English/Spanish Vocabulary Audio Online:

English	Spanish
direct variation, *p. 301*	variación directa
linear equation, *p. 308*	ecuación lineal
piecewise function, *p. 348*	función de fragmentos
point-slope form, *p. 315*	forma punto-pendiente
rate of change, *p. 294*	tasa de cambio
slope, *p. 295*	pendiente
slope-intercept form, *p. 308*	forma pendiente-intercepto
standard form, *p. 322*	forma normal
step function, *p. 348*	función escalón
trend line, *p. 337*	línea de tendencia
x-intercept, *p. 322*	intercepto en *x*
y-intercept, *p. 308*	intercepto en *y*

BIG ideas

1 Proportionality
Essential Question: What does the slope of a line indicate about the line?

2 Functions
Essential Question: What information does the equation of a line give you?

3 Modeling
Essential Question: How can you make predictions based on a scatter plot?

 DOMAINS

• Interpreting Functions
• Building Functions
• Interpreting Categorical and Quantitative Data

Common Core Performance Task

Marbles in Water

Have you noticed that dropping objects into a glass of water raises the water level? The diagram and table below show what happens to the height of the water in a certain glass when different numbers of identical marbles are dropped into it.

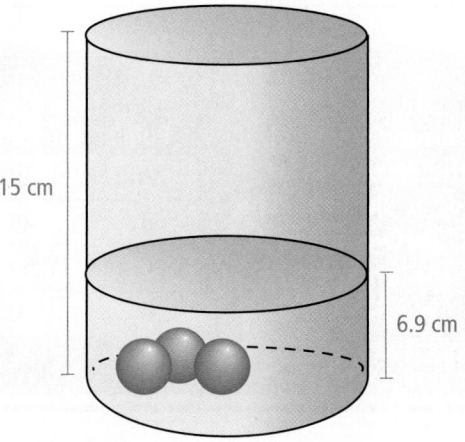

15 cm

6.9 cm

Number of Marbles, x	Height of Water (cm), y
3	6.9
5	7.5
9	8.7
14	10.2
17	11.1
23	12.9

Task Description

Predict the number of marbles you need to drop in the glass to raise the water level to the top of the glass.

Connecting the Task to the Math Practices

MATHEMATICAL PRACTICES

As you complete the task, you'll apply several Standards for Mathematical Practice.

- You'll analyze the data in the table to determine the type of relationship between the number of marbles in the glass and the water height. (MP 1)

- You'll model the data in the table with a function. (MP 2, MP 4)

5-1 Rate of Change and Slope

Common Core State Standards

F-LE.A.1b Recognize situations in which one quantity changes at a constant rate per unit interval relative to another. **Also F-IF.B.6**

MP 1, MP 2, MP 3, MP 4

Objectives To find rates of change from tables
To find slope

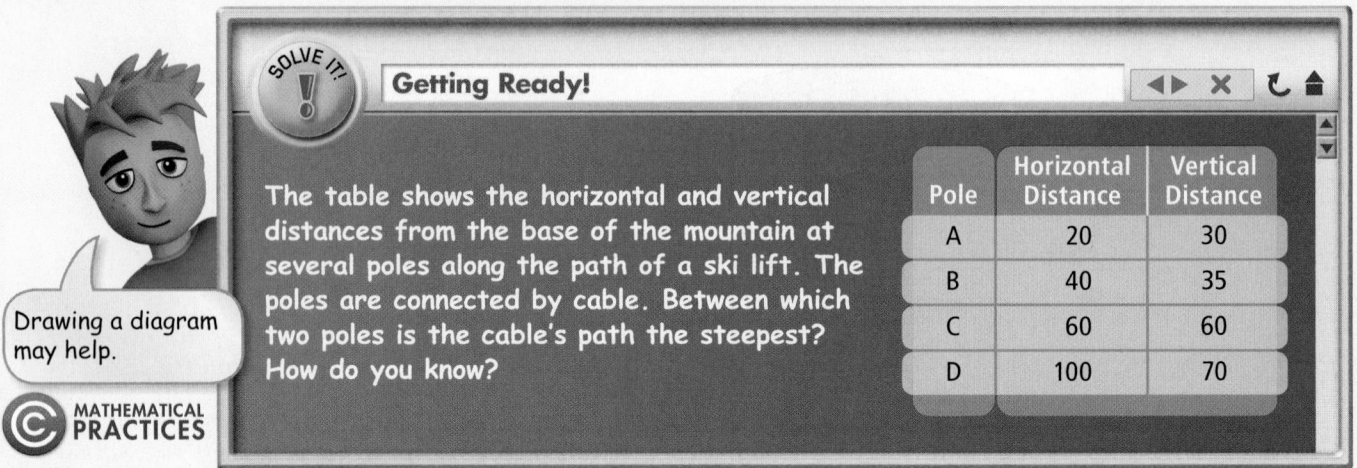

SOLVE IT!

Getting Ready!

The table shows the horizontal and vertical distances from the base of the mountain at several poles along the path of a ski lift. The poles are connected by cable. Between which two poles is the cable's path the steepest? How do you know?

Drawing a diagram may help.

MATHEMATICAL PRACTICES

Pole	Horizontal Distance	Vertical Distance
A	20	30
B	40	35
C	60	60
D	100	70

Lesson Vocabulary
• rate of change
• slope

Essential Understanding You can use ratios to show a relationship between changing quantities, such as vertical and horizontal change.

Rate of change shows the relationship between two changing quantities. When one quantity depends on the other, the following is true.

$$\text{rate of change} = \frac{\text{change in the dependent variable}}{\text{change in the independent variable}}$$

Problem 1 Finding Rate of Change Using a Table

Think

Does this problem look like one you've seen before?
Yes. In Lesson 2-6, you wrote rates and unit rates. The rate of change in Problem 1 is an example of a unit rate.

Marching Band The table shows the distance a band marches over time. Is the rate of change in distance with respect to time constant? What does the rate of change represent?

$$\text{rate of change} = \frac{\text{change in distance}}{\text{change in time}}$$

Calculate the rate of change from one row of the table to the next.

$$\frac{520 - 260}{2 - 1} = \frac{260}{1} \qquad \frac{780 - 520}{3 - 2} = \frac{260}{1} \qquad \frac{1040 - 780}{4 - 3} = \frac{260}{1}$$

The rate of change is constant and equals $\frac{260 \text{ ft}}{1 \text{ min}}$. It represents the distance the band marches per minute.

Distance Marched

Time (min)	Distance (ft)
1	260
2	520
3	780
4	1040

 Got It? 1. In Problem 1, do you get the same rate of change if you use nonconsecutive rows of the table? Explain.

The graphs of the ordered pairs (time, distance) in Problem 1 lie on a line, as shown at the right. The relationship between time and distance is linear. When data are linear, the rate of change is constant.

Notice also that the rate of change found in Problem 1 is just the ratio of the vertical change (or *rise*) to the horizontal change (or *run*) between two points on the line. The rate of change is called the *slope* of the line.

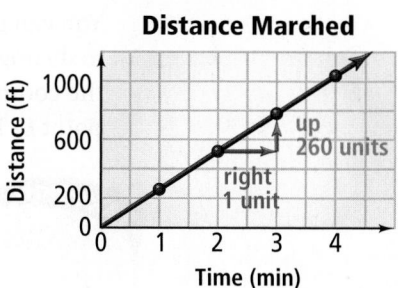

Distance Marched

$$\textbf{slope} = \frac{\text{vertical change}}{\text{horizontal change}} = \frac{\text{rise}}{\text{run}}$$

Ⓒ Problem 2 **Finding Slope Using a Graph**

Plan

What do you need to find the slope?
You need to find the rise and run. You can use the graph to count units of rise and units of run.

What is the slope of each line?

A

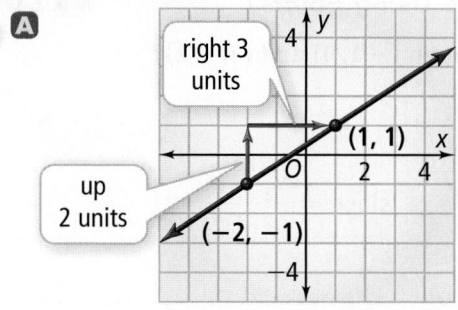

$$\text{slope} = \frac{\text{rise}}{\text{run}}$$
$$= \frac{2}{3}$$

The slope of the line is $\frac{2}{3}$.

B

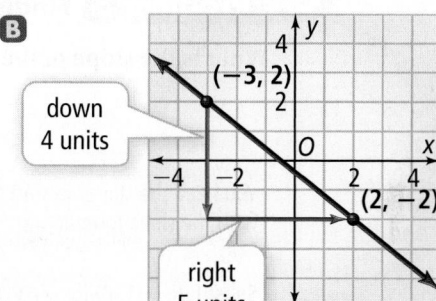

$$\text{slope} = \frac{\text{rise}}{\text{run}}$$
$$= \frac{-4}{5} = -\frac{4}{5}$$

The slope of the line is $-\frac{4}{5}$.

Ⓒ **Got It?** **2.** What is the slope of each line in parts (a) and (b)?

a.

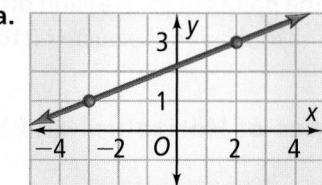

b.

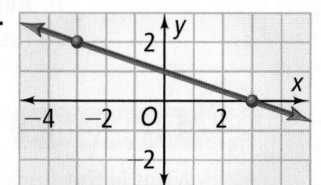

c. Reasoning In part (A) of Problem 2, pick two new points on the line to find the slope. Do you get the same slope?

Notice that the line in part (A) of Problem 2 has a positive slope and slants upward from left to right. The line in part (B) of Problem 2 has a negative slope and slopes downward from left to right.

You can use any two points on a line to find its slope. Use subscripts to distinguish between the two points. In the diagram, (x_1, y_1) are the coordinates of point A, and (x_2, y_2) are the coordinates of point B. To find the slope of $\overleftrightarrow{AB}$, you can use the *slope formula*.

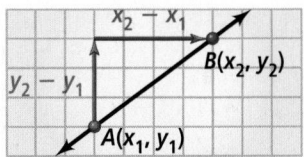

Key Concept The Slope Formula

$$\text{slope} = \frac{\text{rise}}{\text{run}} = \frac{y_2 - y_1}{x_2 - x_1}, \text{ where } x_2 - x_1 \neq 0$$

The x-coordinate you use first in the denominator must belong to the same ordered pair as the y-coordinate you use first in the numerator.

Problem 3 Finding Slope Using Points   GRIDDED RESPONSE

What is the slope of the line through $(-1, 0)$ and $(3, -2)$?

Plan

Does it matter which point is (x_1, y_1) and which is (x_2, y_2)?
No. You can pick either point for (x_1, y_1) in the slope formula. The other point is then (x_2, y_2).

Think

You need the slope, so start with the slope formula.

Substitute $(-1, 0)$ for (x_1, y_1) and $(3, -2)$ for (x_2, y_2).

Simplify to find the answer to place on the grid.

Write

$$\text{slope} = \frac{y_2 - y_1}{x_2 - x_1}$$

$$= \frac{-2 - 0}{3 - (-1)}$$

$$= \frac{-2}{4} = -\frac{1}{2}$$

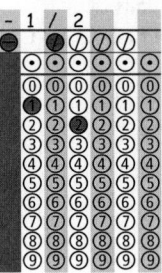

Got It? 3. a. What is the slope of the line through $(1, 3)$ and $(4, -1)$?
   b. Reasoning Plot the points in part (a) and draw a line through them. Does the slope of the line look as you expected it to? Explain.

Problem 4 Finding Slopes of Horizontal and Vertical Lines

What is the slope of each line?

Think

Can you generalize these results?
Yes. All points on a horizontal line have the same y-value, so the slope is always zero. Finding the slope of a vertical line always leads to division by zero. The slope is always undefined.

A

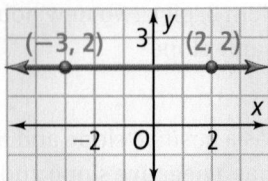

Let $(x_1, y_1) = (-3, 2)$ and $(x_2, y_2) = (2, 2)$.
$$\text{slope} = \frac{y_2 - y_1}{x_2 - x_1} = \frac{2 - 2}{2 - (-3)} = \frac{0}{5} = 0$$
The slope of the horizontal line is 0.

B

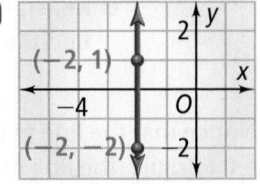

Let $(x_1, y_1) = (-2, -2)$ and $(x_2, y_2) = (-2, 1)$.
$$\text{slope} = \frac{y_2 - y_1}{x_2 - x_1} = \frac{1 - (-2)}{-2 - (-2)} = \frac{3}{0}$$
Division by zero is undefined. The slope of the vertical line is undefined.

Got It? **4.** What is the slope of the line through the given points?

a. $(4, -3), (4, 2)$　　　　　　b. $(-1, -3), (5, -3)$

The following summarizes what you have learned about slope.

take note

Concept Summary　Slopes of Lines

A line with positive slope slants upward from left to right.

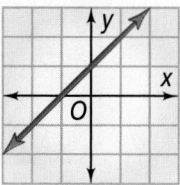

A line with negative slope slants downward from left to right.

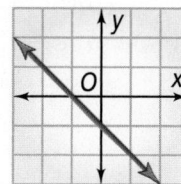

A line with a slope of 0 is horizontal.

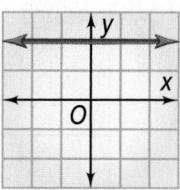

A line with an undefined slope is vertical.

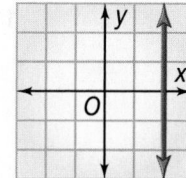

 ## Lesson Check

Do you know HOW?

1. Is the rate of change in cost constant with respect to the number of pencils bought? Explain.

Cost of Pencils				
Number of Pencils	1	4	7	12
Cost ($)	0.25	1	1.75	3

2. What is the slope of the line?

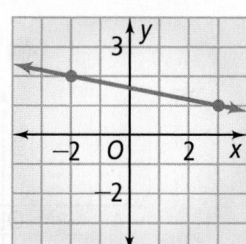

3. What is the slope of the line through $(-1, 2)$ and $(2, -3)$?

Do you UNDERSTAND? © **MATHEMATICAL PRACTICES**

© **4. Vocabulary** What characteristic of a graph represents the rate of change? Explain.

© **5. Open-Ended** Give an example of a real-world situation that you can model with a horizontal line. What is the rate of change for the situation? Explain.

© **6. Compare and Contrast** How does finding a line's slope by counting units of vertical and horizontal change on a graph compare with finding it using the slope formula?

© **7. Error Analysis** A student calculated the slope of the line at the right to be 2. Explain the mistake. What is the correct slope?

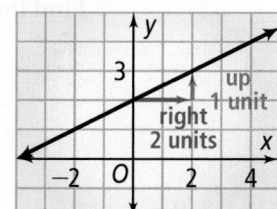

Practice and Problem-Solving Exercises

MATHEMATICAL PRACTICES

 Practice

Determine whether each rate of change is constant. If it is, find the rate of change and explain what it represents.

See Problem 1.

8. Turtle Walking

Time (min)	Distance (m)
1	6
2	12
3	15
4	21

9. Hot Dogs and Buns

Hot Dogs	Buns
1	1
2	2
3	3
4	4

10. Airplane Descent

Time (min)	Elevation (ft)
0	30,000
2	29,000
5	27,500
12	24,000

Find the slope of each line.

See Problem 2.

11.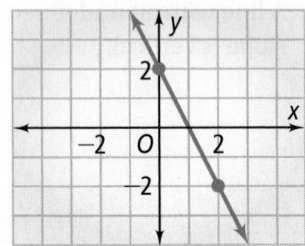

12.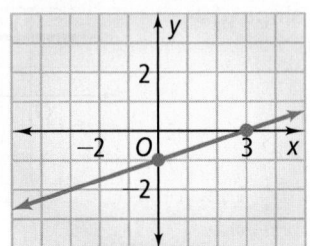

13.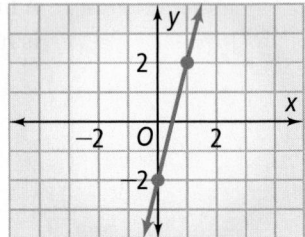

14.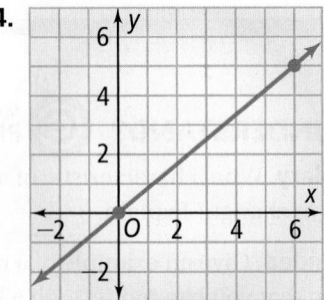

15.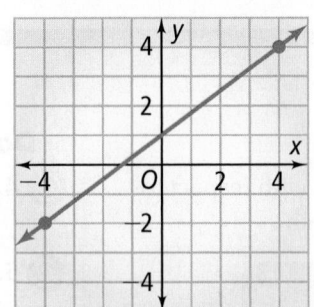

16.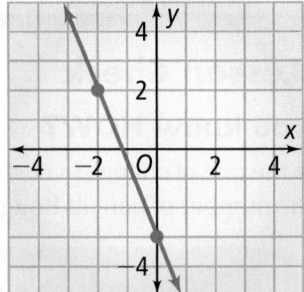

Find the slope of the line that passes through each pair of points.

See Problem 3.

17. $(0, 0), (3, 3)$

18. $(1, 3), (5, 5)$

19. $(4, 4), (5, 3)$

20. $(0, -1), (2, 3)$

21. $(-6, 1), (4, 8)$

22. $(2, -3), (5, -4)$

Find the slope of each line.

See Problem 4.

23.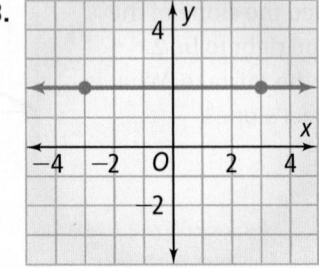

24.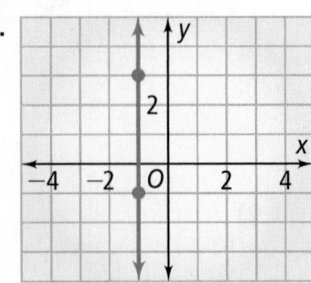

25.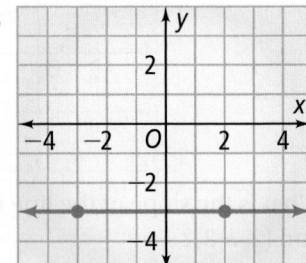

 **Apply**

Without graphing, tell whether the slope of a line that models each linear relationship is *positive*, *negative*, *zero*, or *undefined*. Then find the slope.

26. The length of a bus route is 4 mi long on the sixth day and 4 mi long on the seventeenth day.

27. A babysitter earns $9 for 1 h and $36 for 4 h.

28. A student earns a 98 on a test for answering one question incorrectly and earns a 90 for answering five questions incorrectly.

29. The total cost, including shipping, for ordering five uniforms is $66. The total cost, including shipping, for ordering nine uniforms is $114.

State the independent variable and the dependent variable in each linear relationship. Then find the rate of change for each situation.

30. Snow is 0.02 m deep after 1 h and 0.06 m deep after 3 h.

31. The cost of tickets is $36 for three people and $84 for seven people.

32. A car is 200 km from its destination after 1 h and 80 km from its destination after 3 h.

Use the slope formula to find the slope of the line that passes through each pair of points. Then plot the points and sketch the line that passes through them. Does the slope you found using the formula match the direction of the line you sketched?

33. $(-2, 1), (7, 1)$

34. $(4.25, 0), (3.5, 3)$

35. $\left(-\frac{1}{2}, \frac{4}{7}\right), \left(8, \frac{4}{7}\right)$

36. $(-5, 0.124), (-5, -0.584)$

37. $(-42.25, 5.2), (3.25, 3)$

38. $\left(-2, \frac{2}{11}\right), \left(-2, \frac{7}{13}\right)$

Ⓒ 39. Think About a Plan The graph shows the average growth rates for three different animals. Which animal's growth shows the fastest rate of change? The slowest rate of change?
- How can you use the graph to find the rates of change?
- Are your answers reasonable?

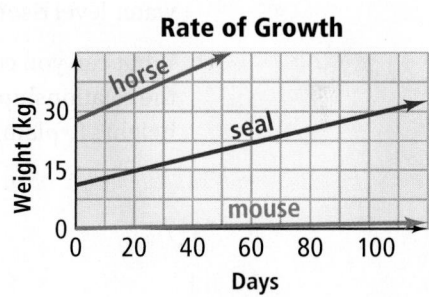

Ⓒ 40. Open-Ended Find two points that lie on a line with slope -9.

41. Profit John's business made $4500 in January and $8600 in March. What is the rate of change in his profit for this time period?

Each pair of points lies on a line with the given slope. Find *x* or *y*.

42. $(2, 4), (x, 8)$; slope $= -2$

43. $(4, 3), (5, y)$; slope $= 3$

44. $(2, 4), (x, 8)$; slope $= -\frac{1}{2}$

45. $(3, y), (1, 9)$; slope $= -\frac{5}{2}$

46. $(-4, y), (2, 4y)$; slope $= 6$

47. $(3, 5), (x, 2)$; undefined slope

Ⓒ 48. Reasoning Is it true that a line with slope 1 always passes through the origin? Explain your reasoning.

49. Arithmetic Sequences Use the arithmetic sequence 10, 15, 20, 25, . . .
   a. Find the common difference of the sequence.
   b. Let x = the term number, and let y = the corresponding term of the sequence. Graph the ordered pairs (x, y) for the first eight terms of the sequence. Draw a line through the points.
   c. Reasoning How is the slope of a line from part (b) related to the common difference of the sequence?

 **Do the points in each set lie on the same line? Explain your answer.**

50. $A(1, 3)$, $B(4, 2)$, $C(-2, 4)$ **51.** $G(3, 5)$, $H(-1, 3)$, $I(7, 7)$ **52.** $D(-2, 3)$, $E(0, -1)$, $F(2, 1)$

53. $P(4, 2)$, $Q(-3, 2)$, $R(2, 5)$ **54.** $G(1, -2)$, $H(-1, -5)$, $I(5, 4)$ **55.** $S(-3, 4)$, $T(0, 2)$, $X(-3, 0)$

Find the slope of the line that passes through each pair of points.

56. $(a, -b)$, $(-a, -b)$ **57.** $(-m, n)$, $(3m, -n)$ **58.** $(2a, b)$, $(c, 2d)$

 ## Apply What You've Learned

 **MATHEMATICAL PRACTICES**
MP 1

The table at the right shows the height of water in a glass when different numbers of marbles are dropped into it.

a. Find the rate of change in the water height with respect to the number of marbles from one row in the table to the next. What do you notice?

b. For each marble you add to the glass, how much does the water level rise?

c. What can you conclude about the type of function that models the relationship between the number of marbles and the water height? Explain.

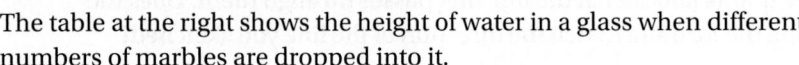

Number of Marbles, x	Height of Water (cm), y
3	6.9
5	7.5
9	8.7
14	10.2
17	11.1
23	12.9

5-2 Direct Variation

© Common Core State Standards

A-CED.A.2 Create equations in two or more variables to represent relationships between quantities; graph equations on coordinate axes with labels and scales.
Also N-Q.A.2
MP 1, MP 2, MP 3, MP 4, MP 7

Objective To write and graph an equation of a direct variation

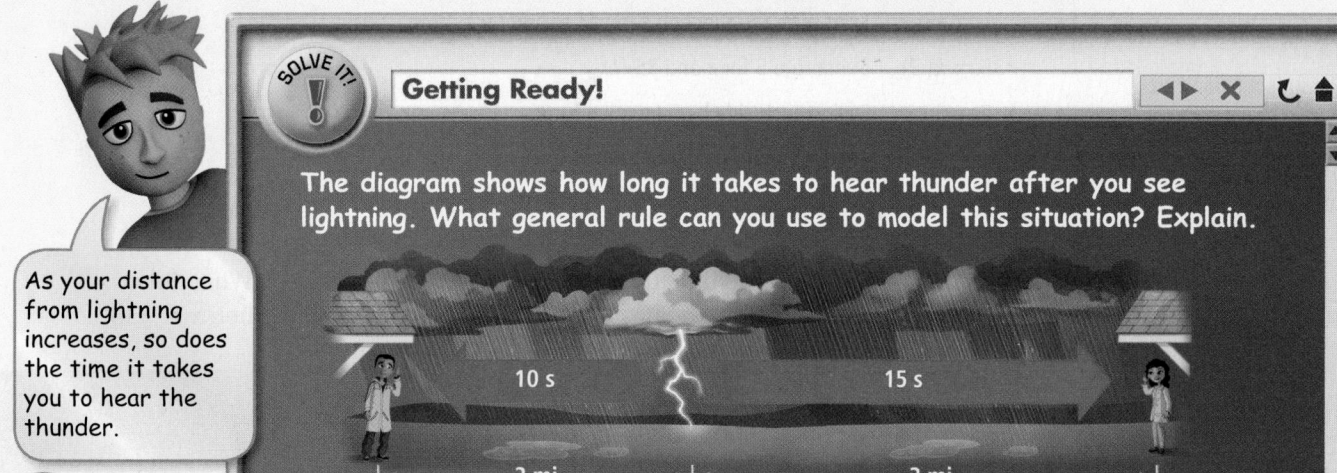

Getting Ready!

The diagram shows how long it takes to hear thunder after you see lightning. What general rule can you use to model this situation? Explain.

10 s   15 s

2 mi   3 mi

As your distance from lightning increases, so does the time it takes you to hear the thunder.

MATHEMATICAL PRACTICES

The time it takes to hear thunder *varies directly with* the distance from lightning.

Essential Understanding If the ratio of two variables is constant, then the variables have a special relationship, known as a *direct variation*.

Lesson Vocabulary
• direct variation
• constant of variation for a direct variation

A **direct variation** is a relationship that can be represented by a function in the form $y = kx$, where $k \neq 0$. The **constant of variation for a direct variation** k is the coefficient of x. By dividing each side of $y = kx$ by x, you can see that the ratio of the variables is constant: $\frac{y}{x} = k$.

To determine whether an equation represents a direct variation, solve it for y. If you can write the equation in the form $y = kx$, where $k \neq 0$, it represents a direct variation.

Problem 1 Identifying a Direct Variation

Think

Do these equations look like ones you've seen before?
Yes. They contain two variables, so they're literal equations. To determine whether they're direct variation equations, solve for y.

Does the equation represent a direct variation? If so, find the constant of variation.

A $7y = 2x$

$y = \frac{2}{7}x$ ← Solve each equation for y. →

The equation has the form $y = kx$, so the equation is a direct variation. Its constant of variation is $\frac{2}{7}$.

B $3y + 4x = 8$

$3y = 8 - 4x$

$y = \frac{8}{3} - \frac{4}{3}x$

You cannot write the equation in the form $y = kx$. It is not a direct variation.

 Got It? 1. Does $4x + 5y = 0$ represent a direct variation? If so, find the constant of variation.

To write an equation for a direct variation, first find the constant of variation k using an ordered pair, other than $(0, 0)$, that you know is a solution of the equation.

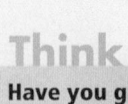 **Problem 2** **Writing a Direct Variation Equation**

Suppose y varies directly with x, and $y = 35$ when $x = 5$. What direct variation equation relates x and y? What is the value of y when $x = 9$?

$y = kx$	Start with the function form of a direct variation.
$35 = k(5)$	Substitute 5 for x and 35 for y.
$7 = k$	Divide each side by 5 to solve for k.
$y = 7x$	Write an equation. Substitute 7 for k in $y = kx$.

Think

Make sure you don't stop at $7 = k$. To write the direct variation equation, you have to substitute 7 for k in $y = kx$.

The equation $y = 7x$ relates x and y. When $x = 9$, $y = 7(9)$, or 63.

Got It? **2.** Suppose y varies directly with x, and $y = 10$ when $x = -2$. What direct variation equation relates x and y? What is the value of y when $x = -15$?

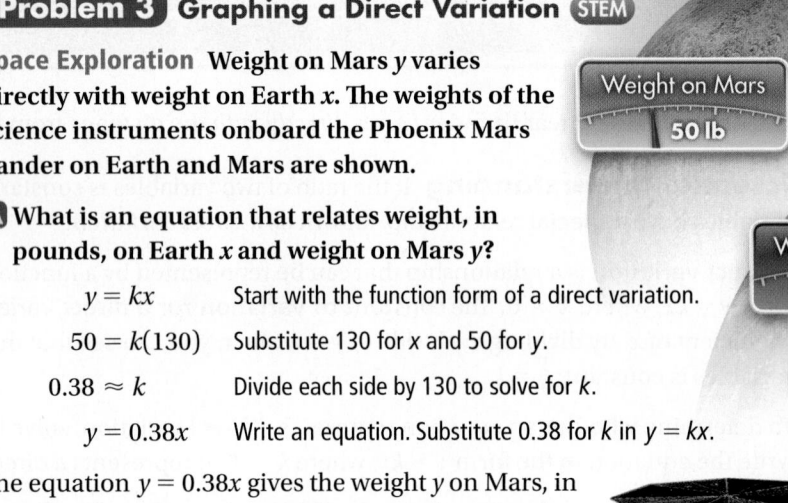 **Problem 3** **Graphing a Direct Variation** STEM

Space Exploration **Weight on Mars y varies directly with weight on Earth x. The weights of the science instruments onboard the Phoenix Mars Lander on Earth and Mars are shown.**

Weight on Mars
50 lb

Weight on Earth
130 lb

A What is an equation that relates weight, in pounds, on Earth x and weight on Mars y?

$y = kx$	Start with the function form of a direct variation.
$50 = k(130)$	Substitute 130 for x and 50 for y.
$0.38 \approx k$	Divide each side by 130 to solve for k.
$y = 0.38x$	Write an equation. Substitute 0.38 for k in $y = kx$.

The equation $y = 0.38x$ gives the weight y on Mars, in pounds, of an object that weighs x pounds on Earth.

Think

Have you graphed equations like $y = 0.38x$ before? Yes. In Chapter 4, you graphed linear functions by making a table of values and plotting points.

B What is the graph of the equation in part (A)?

Make a table of values. Then draw the graph.

x	y
0	$0.38(0) = 0$
50	$0.38(50) = 19$
100	$0.38(100) = 38$
150	$0.38(150) = 57$

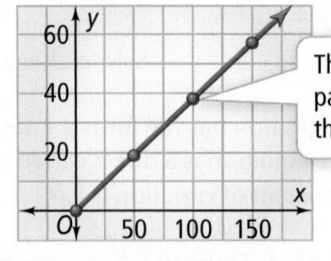

The points form a linear pattern. Draw a line through them.

Got It? **3. a.** Weight on the moon y varies directly with weight on Earth x. A person who weighs 100 lb on Earth weighs 16.6 lb on the moon. What is an equation that relates weight on Earth x and weight on the moon y? What is the graph of this equation?

b. Reasoning What is the slope of the graph of $y = 0.38x$ in Problem 3? How is the slope related to the equation?

Concept Summary **Graphs of Direct Variations**

The graph of a direct variation equation $y = kx$ is a line with the following properties.
- The line passes through $(0, 0)$.
- The slope of the line is k.

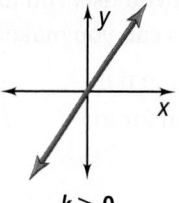 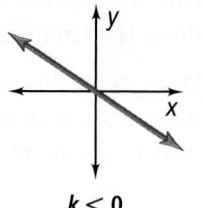

$k > 0$ $k < 0$

You can rewrite a direct variation equation $y = kx$ as $\frac{y}{x} = k$. When a set of data pairs (x, y) vary directly, $\frac{y}{x}$ is the constant of variation. It is the same for each data pair.

 Problem 4 **Writing a Direct Variation From a Table**

For the data in the table, does y vary directly with x? If it does, write an equation for the direct variation.

A

x	y
4	6
8	12
10	15

B

x	y
−2	3.2
1	2.4
4	1.6

Find $\frac{y}{x}$ for each ordered pair.

$\frac{6}{4} = 1.5$ $\frac{12}{8} = 1.5$ $\frac{15}{10} = 1.5$

The ratio $\frac{y}{x} = 1.5$ for each data pair. So y varies directly with x. The direct variation equation is $y = 1.5x$.

Find $\frac{y}{x}$ for each ordered pair.

$\frac{3.2}{-2} = -1.6$ $\frac{2.4}{1} = 2.4$ $\frac{1.6}{4} = 0.4$

The ratio $\frac{y}{x}$ is not the same for all data pairs. So y does not vary directly with x.

Plan

How can you check your answer?
Graph the ordered pairs in the coordinate plane. If you can connect them with a line that passes through $(0, 0)$, then y varies directly with x.

 Got It? **4.** For the data in the table at the right, does y vary directly with x? If it does, write an equation for the direct variation.

x	y
−3	2.25
1	−0.75
4	−3

Lesson Check

Do you know HOW?

1. Does the equation $6y = 18x$ represent a direct variation? If it does, what is its constant of variation?

2. Suppose y varies directly with x, and $y = 30$ when $x = 3$. What direct variation equation relates x and y?

3. A recipe for 12 corn muffins calls for 1 cup of flour. The number of muffins you can make varies directly with the amount of flour you use. You have $2\frac{1}{2}$ cups of flour. How many muffins can you make?

4. Does y vary directly with x? If it does, what is an equation for the direct variation?

x	y
−2	1
2	−1
4	−2

Do you UNDERSTAND?

5. **Vocabulary** Determine whether each statement is *always*, *sometimes*, or *never* true.

5. The ordered pair $(0, 0)$ is a solution of the direct variation equation $y = kx$.

6. You can write a direct variation in the form $y = k + x$, where $k \neq 0$.

7. The constant of variation for a direct variation represented by $y = kx$ is $\frac{y}{x}$.

8. **Reasoning** Suppose q varies directly with p. Does this imply that p varies directly with q? Explain.

Practice and Problem-Solving Exercises

**Practice**

Determine whether each equation represents a direct variation. If it does, find the constant of variation.

 **See Problem 1.**

9. $2y = 5x + 1$

10. $8x + 9y = 10$

11. $-12x = 6y$

12. $y + 8 = -x$

13. $-4 + 7x + 4 = 3y$

14. $0.7x - 1.4y = 0$

Suppose y varies directly with x. Write a direct variation equation that relates x and y. Then find the value of y when $x = 12$.

See Problem 2.

15. $y = -10$ when $x = 2$.

16. $y = 7\frac{1}{2}$ when $x = 3$.

17. $y = 5$ when $x = 2$.

18. $y = 125$ when $x = -5$.

19. $y = 10.4$ when $x = 4$.

20. $y = 9\frac{1}{3}$ when $x = -\frac{1}{2}$.

Graph each direct variation equation.

See Problem 3.

21. $y = 2x$

22. $y = \frac{1}{3}x$

23. $y = -x$

24. $y = -\frac{1}{2}x$

25. **Travel Time** The distance d you bike varies directly with the amount of time t you bike. Suppose you bike 13.2 mi in 1.25 h. What is an equation that relates d and t? What is the graph of the equation?

26. **Geometry** The perimeter p of a regular hexagon varies directly with the length ℓ of one side of the hexagon. What is an equation that relates p and ℓ? What is the graph of the equation?

For the data in each table, tell whether y varies directly with x. If it does, write an equation for the direct variation. Check your answer by plotting the points from the table and sketching the line.

See Problem 4.

27.

x	y
−6	9
1	−1.5
8	−12

28.

x	y
3	5.4
7	12.6
12	21.6

29.

x	y
−2	1
3	6
8	11

B Apply

Suppose y varies directly with x. Write a direct variation equation that relates x and y. Then graph the equation.

30. $y = \frac{1}{2}$ when $x = 3$.   **31.** $y = -5$ when $x = \frac{1}{4}$.   **32.** $y = \frac{6}{5}$ when $x = -\frac{5}{6}$.   **33.** $y = 7.2$ when $x = 1.2$.

34. Think About a Plan The amount of blood in a person's body varies directly with body weight. A person who weighs 160 lb has about 4.6 qt of blood. About how many quarts of blood are in the body of a 175-lb person?
  * How can you find the constant of variation?
  * Can you write an equation that relates quarts of blood to weight?
  * How can you use the equation to determine the solution?

STEM **35. Electricity** Ohm's Law $V = I \times R$ relates the voltage, current, and resistance of a circuit. V is the voltage measured in volts. I is the current measured in amperes. R is the resistance measured in ohms.
  a. Find the voltage of a circuit with a current of 24 amperes and a resistance of 2 ohms.
  b. Find the resistance of a circuit with a current of 24 amperes and a voltage of 18 volts.

ⓒ Reasoning Tell whether the two quantities vary directly. Explain your reasoning.

36. the number of ounces of cereal and the number of Calories the cereal contains

37. the time it takes to travel a certain distance and the rate at which you travel

38. the perimeter of a square and the side length of the square

39. the amount of money you have left and the number of items you purchase

ⓒ 40. a. Graph the following direct variation equations in the same coordinate plane: $y = x$, $y = 2x$, $y = 3x$, and $y = 4x$.
  b. Look for a Pattern Describe how the graphs change as the constant of variation increases.
  c. Predict how the graph of $y = \frac{1}{2}x$ would appear.

ⓒ 41. Error Analysis Use the table at the right. A student says that y varies directly with x because as x increases by 1, y also increases by 1. Explain the student's error.

ⓒ 42. Writing Suppose y varies directly with x. Explain how the value of y changes in each situation.
  a. The value of x is doubled.   **b.** The value of x is halved.

x	y
0	3
1	4
2	5

STEM **43. Physics** The force you need to apply to a lever varies directly with the weight you want to lift. Suppose you can lift a 50-lb weight by applying 20 lb of force to a certain lever.

 a. What is the ratio of force to weight for the lever?

 b. Write an equation relating force and weight. What is the force you need to lift a friend who weighs 130 lb?

 **Challenge** The ordered pairs in each exercise are for the same direct variation. Find each missing value.

44. $(3, 4)$ and $(9, y)$ **45.** $(1, y)$ and $\left(\frac{3}{2}, -9\right)$ **46.** $(-5, 3)$ and $(x, -4.8)$

47. Gas Mileage A car gets 32 mi per gallon. The number of gallons g of gas used varies directly with the number of miles m traveled.

 a. Suppose the price of gas is $3.85 per gallon. Write a function giving the cost c for g gallons of gas. Is this a direct variation? Explain your reasoning.

 b. Write a direct variation equation relating the cost of gas to the miles traveled.

 c. How much will it cost to buy gas for a 240-mi trip?

Standardized Test Prep

GRIDDED RESPONSE

SAT/ACT

48. The price p you pay varies directly with the number of pencils you buy. Suppose you buy 3 pencils for $.51. How much is each pencil, in dollars?

49. A scooter can travel 72 mi per gallon of gasoline and holds 2.3 gal. The function $d(x) = 72x$ represents the distance $d(x)$, in miles, that the scooter can travel with x gallons of gasoline. How many miles can the scooter go with a full tank of gas?

50. The table at the right shows the number of hours a clerk works per week and the amount of money she earns before taxes. If she worked 34 h per week, how much money would she earn, in dollars?

51. What is the greatest value in the range of $y = x^2 - 3$ for the domain $\{-3, 0, 1\}$?

Weekly Wages

Time (h)	Wages ($)
12	99.00
17	140.25
21	173.25
32	264.00

Mixed Review

Find the slope of the line that passes through each pair of points. ◀ See Lesson 5-1.

52. $(2, 4), (0, 2)$ **53.** $(5, 8), (-5, 8)$ **54.** $(0, 0), (3, 18)$ **55.** $(1, -2), (-2, 3)$

Get Ready! To prepare for Lesson 5-3, do Exercises 56–59.

Evaluate each expression. ◀ See Lesson 1-2.

56. $6a + 3$ for $a = 2$ **57.** $-2x - 5$ for $x = 3$ **58.** $\frac{1}{4}x + 2$ for $x = 16$ **59.** $8 - 5n$ for $n = 3$

Investigating $y = mx + b$

 Common Core State Standards

F-BF.B.3 Identify the effect on the graph of replacing $f(x)$ by $f(x) + k$, $kf(x)$, $f(kx)$, and $f(x + k)$ for specific values of k (both positive and negative) . . .

MP 5

You can use a graphing calculator to explore the graph of an equation in the form $y = mx + b$. For this activity, choose a standard screen by pressing (zoom) 6.

1. Graph these equations on the same screen. Then complete each statement.

$$y = x + 3 \qquad y = 2x + 3 \qquad y = \tfrac{1}{2}x + 3$$

   a. The graph of __?__ is steepest.

   b. The graph of __?__ is the least steep.

2. Match each equation with the best choice for its graph.

   A. $y = \tfrac{1}{4}x - 2$ **B.** $y = 4x - 2$ **C.** $y = x - 2$

   I. 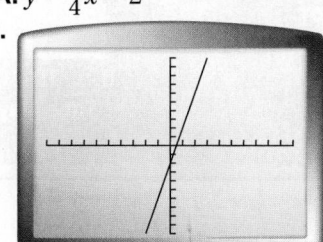   **II.** 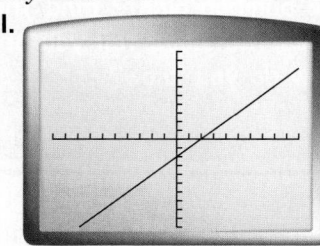   **III.**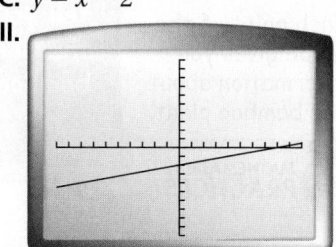

3. Graph these equations on the same screen.

$$y = 2x + 3 \qquad y = -2x + 3$$

How does the sign of m affect the graph of the equation?

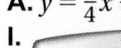 **4. Reasoning** How does changing the value of m affect the graph of an equation in the form $y = mx + b$?

5. Graph these equations on the same screen.

$$y = 2x + 3 \qquad y = 2x - 3 \qquad y = 2x + 2$$

Where does the graph of each equation cross the y-axis? (*Hint:* Use the **ZOOM** feature to better see the points of intersection.)

6. Match each equation with the best choice for its graph.

   A. $y = \tfrac{1}{3}x - 3$ **B.** $y = \tfrac{1}{3}x + 1$ **C.** $y = \tfrac{1}{3}x$

   I. 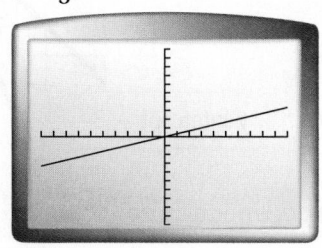   **II.** 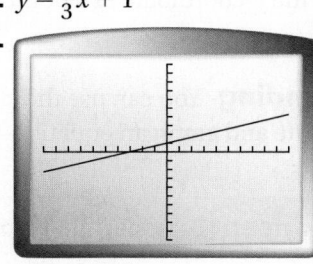   **III.**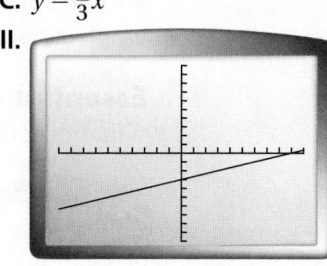

7. Reasoning How does changing the value of b affect the graph of an equation in the form $y = mx + b$?

5-3 Slope-Intercept Form

 Common Core State Standards

F-IF.C.7a Graph linear and quadratic functions and show intercepts, maxima, and minima. **Also A-SSE.A.1a, A-CED.A.2, F-IF.B.4, F-LE.A.2**

MP 1, MP 2, MP 3, MP 4

Objectives To write linear equations using slope-intercept form
To graph linear equations in slope-intercept form

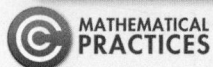

SOLVE IT!

Getting Ready!

Bamboo can grow very quickly. The graph models the growth of a bamboo plant. Find the point where the line crosses the vertical axis. What does this point tell you about the bamboo plant? Find the slope of the line. What does the slope tell you about the bamboo plant? How do you know?

Each point of the graph gives you information about the bamboo plant.

Bamboo Growth

MATHEMATICAL PRACTICES

The function in the Solve It is a linear function, but it is not a direct variation. Direct variations are only part of the family of linear functions.

A **family of functions** is a group of functions with common characteristics. A **parent function** is the simplest function with these characteristics. The **linear parent function** is $y = x$ or $f(x) = x$. The graphs of three linear functions are shown at the right.

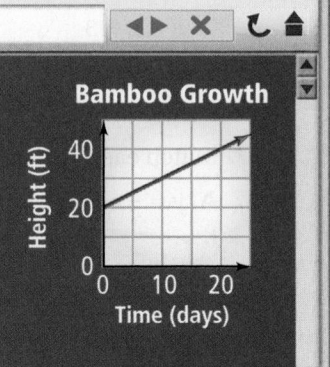

$y = -\frac{1}{2}x + 1$

$y = x$

$y = 2x$

Lesson Vocabulary
• parent function
• linear parent function
• linear equation
• *y*-intercept
• slope-intercept form

A **linear equation** is an equation that models a linear function. In a linear equation, the variables cannot be raised to a power other than 1. So $y = 2x$ is a linear equation, but $y = x^2$ and $y = 2^x$ are not. The graph of a linear equation contains all the ordered pairs that are solutions of the equation.

Graphs of linear functions may cross the *y*-axis at any point. A **y-intercept** of a graph is the *y*-coordinate of a point where the graph crosses the *y*-axis.

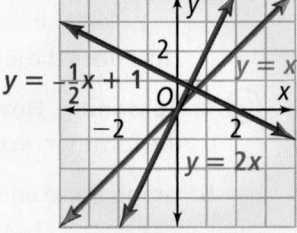

y-intercept: 0

y-intercept: −3

Essential Understanding You can use the slope and *y*-intercept of a line to write and graph an equation of the line.

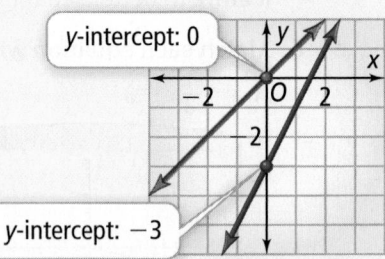

take note

Key Concept Slope-Intercept Form of a Linear Equation

The **slope-intercept form** of a linear equation of a nonvertical line is $y = mx + b$.

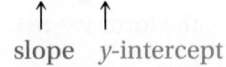

slope   *y*-intercept

 **Problem 1** **Identifying Slope and y-Intercept**

What are the slope and y-intercept of the graph of $y = 5x - 2$?

Think

Why isn't the y-intercept 2?
In slope-intercept form, the y-intercept b is added to the term mx. Instead of subtracting 2, you add the opposite, -2.

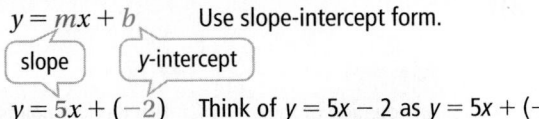

$y = mx + b$ Use slope-intercept form.

slope y-intercept

$y = 5x + (-2)$ Think of $y = 5x - 2$ as $y = 5x + (-2)$.

The slope is 5; the y-intercept is -2.

 Got It? **1. a.** What are the slope and y-intercept of the graph of $y = -\frac{1}{2}x + \frac{2}{3}$?

     b. Reasoning How do the graph of the line and the equation in part (a) change if the y-intercept is moved down 3 units?

 **Problem 2** **Writing an Equation in Slope-Intercept Form**

What is an equation of the line with slope $-\frac{4}{5}$ and y-intercept 7?

Plan

When can you use slope-intercept form?
You can write an equation of a nonvertical line in slope-intercept form if you know its slope and y-intercept.

$y = mx + b$ Use slope-intercept form.

$y = -\frac{4}{5}x + 7$ Substitute $-\frac{4}{5}$ for m and 7 for b.

An equation for the line is $y = -\frac{4}{5}x + 7$.

 Got It? **2.** What is an equation of the line with slope $\frac{3}{2}$ and y-intercept -1?

 **Problem 3** **Writing an Equation From a Graph**

Multiple Choice Which equation represents the line shown?

   Ⓐ $y = -2x + 1$ Ⓒ $y = \frac{1}{2}x - 2$

   Ⓑ $y = 2x + 1$ Ⓓ $y = 2x - 2$

Think

What does the graph tell you about the slope?
Since the line slants up from left to right, the slope of the line should be positive. The line is also fairly steep, so the slope of the line should be greater than 1.

Find the slope. Two points on the line are $(0, -2)$ and $(2, 2)$.

$$\text{slope} = \frac{2 - (-2)}{2 - 0} = \frac{4}{2} = 2$$

The y-intercept is -2. Write an equation in slope-intercept form.

$y = mx + b$

$y = 2x + (-2)$ Substitute 2 for m and -2 for b.

An equation for the line is $y = 2x - 2$. The correct answer is D.

 Got It? **3. a.** What do you expect the slope of the line to be from looking at the graph? Explain.

     b. What is an equation of the line shown at the right?

     c. Reasoning Does the equation of the line depend on the points you use to find the slope? Explain.

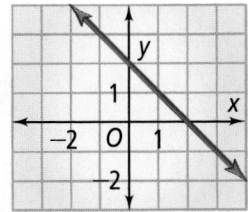

Problem 4 Writing an Equation From Two Points

What equation in slope-intercept form represents the line that passes through the points (2, 1) and (5, −8)?

Know	Need	Plan
The line passes through (2, 1) and (5, −8).	An equation of the line	Use the two points to find the slope. Then use the slope and one point to solve for the y-intercept.

Step 1 Use the two points to find the slope.

$$\text{slope} = \frac{-8-1}{5-2} = \frac{-9}{3} = -3$$

Think

Can you use either point to find the y-intercept?
Yes. You can substitute the slope and the coordinates of any point on the line into the form $y = mx + b$ and solve for b.

Step 2 Use the slope and the coordinates of one of the points to find b.

$y = mx + b$ Use slope-intercept form.

$1 = -3(2) + b$ Substitute −3 for m, 2 for x, and 1 for y.

$7 = b$ Solve for b.

Step 3 Substitute the slope and y-intercept into the slope-intercept form.

$y = mx + b$ Use slope-intercept form.

$y = -3x + 7$ Substitute −3 for m and 7 for b.

An equation of the line is $y = -3x + 7$.

 Got It? **4.** What equation in slope-intercept form represents the line that passes through the points (3, −2) and (1, −3)?

You can use the slope and y–intercept from an equation to graph a line.

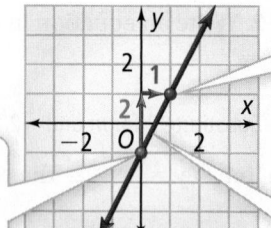 **Problem 5** Graphing a Linear Equation

Plan

What information can you use?
The slope tells you the ratio of vertical change to horizontal change. Plot the y-intercept. Then use the slope to plot another point on the line.

What is the graph of $y = 2x - 1$?

Step 2 The slope is 2, or $\frac{2}{1}$. Move up 2 units and right 1 unit. Plot another point.

Step 1 The y-intercept is −1. So plot a point at (0, −1).

Step 3 Draw a line through the two points.

 Got It? **5.** What is the graph of each linear equation?
a. $y = -3x + 4$ **b.** $y = 4x - 8$

Slope-intercept form is useful for modeling real-life situations where you are given a starting value (the *y*-intercept) and a rate of change (the slope).

At 0 meters, the pressure is 1 atm.

 Problem 6 **Modeling a Function** STEM

Physics Water pressure can be measured in atmospheres (atm). Use the information in the diagram to write an equation that models the pressure *y* at a depth of *x* meters. What graph models the pressure?

Think

How do you identify the *y*-intercept?
The *y*-intercept is the *y*-value when $x = 0$. So the *y*-intercept is the pressure at a depth of 0 m. This is the starting value, 1 atm.

Step 1 Identify the slope and the *y*-intercept.

The slope is the rate of change, 0.1 atm/m.

The *y*-intercept is the starting value, 1 atm.

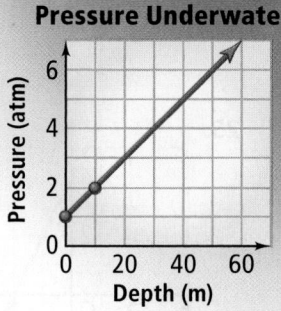

The pressure increases by 0.1 atm/m.

Step 2 Substitute the slope and *y*-intercept into the slope-intercept form.

$y = mx + b$ Use slope-intercept form.

$y = 0.1x + 1$ Substitute 0.1 for *m* and 1 for *b*.

Step 3 Graph the equation.

The *y*-intercept is 1. Plot the point (0, 1).

The slope is 0.1, which equals $\frac{1}{10}$. Plot a second point 1 unit above and 10 units to the right of the *y*-intercept. Then draw a line through the two points.

Pressure Underwater

 Got It? **6.** A plumber charges a $65 fee for a repair plus $35 per hour. Write an equation to model the total cost *y* of a repair that takes *x* hours. What graph models the total cost?

 Lesson Check

Do you know HOW?

1. What is an equation of the line with slope 6 and *y*-intercept −4?

2. What equation in slope-intercept form represents the line that passes through the points (−3, 4) and (2, −1)?

3. What is the graph of $y = 5x + 2$?

Do you UNDERSTAND?  MATHEMATICAL PRACTICES

4. Vocabulary Is $y = 5$ a linear equation? Explain.

5. Reasoning Is it *always*, *sometimes*, or *never* true that an equation in slope-intercept form represents a direct variation? Support your answer with examples.

6. Writing Describe two different methods you can use to graph the equation $y = 2x + 4$. Which method do you prefer? Explain.

Practice and Problem-Solving Exercises

 **Practice**

Find the slope and *y*-intercept of the graph of each equation. ● **See Problem 1.**

7. $y = 3x + 1$

8. $y = -x + 4$

9. $y = 2x - 5$

10. $y = -3x + 2$

11. $y = 5x - 3$

12. $y = -6x$

13. $y = 4$

14. $y = -0.2x + 3$

15. $y = \frac{1}{4}x - \frac{1}{3}$

Write an equation in slope-intercept form of the line with the given slope *m* and *y*-intercept *b*. ● **See Problem 2.**

16. $m = 1, b = -1$

17. $m = 3, b = 2$

18. $m = \frac{1}{2}, b = -\frac{1}{2}$

19. $m = 0.7, b = -2$

20. $m = -0.5, b = 1.5$

21. $m = -2, b = \frac{8}{5}$

Write an equation in slope-intercept form of each line. ● **See Problem 3.**

22.
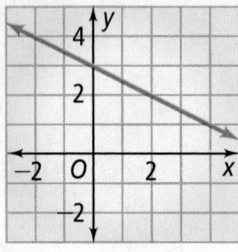

23.
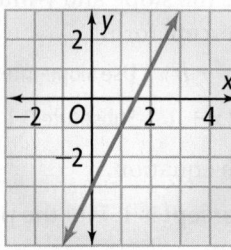

24.
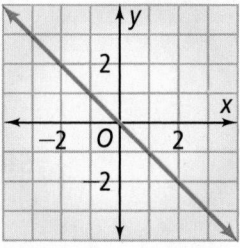

25.
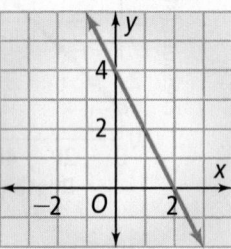

26.
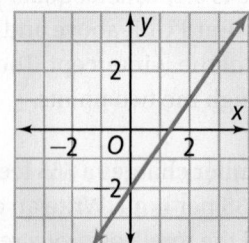

27.
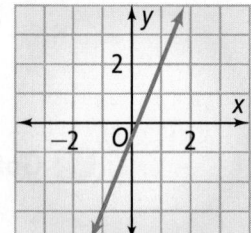

Write an equation in slope-intercept form of the line that passes through the given points. ● **See Problem 4.**

28. $(0, 3)$ and $(2, 5)$

29. $(-2, 4)$ and $(3, -1)$

30. $(-3, 3)$ and $(1, 2)$

Graph each equation. ● **See Problem 5.**

31. $y = x + 5$

32. $y = 3x + 4$

33. $y = -2x + 1$

34. Retail Sales Suppose you have a $5-off coupon at a fabric store. You buy fabric that costs $7.50 per yard. Write an equation that models the total amount of money *y* you pay if you buy *x* yards of fabric. What is the graph of the equation? ● **See Problem 6.**

35. Temperature The temperature at sunrise is 65°F. Each hour during the day, the temperature rises 5°F. Write an equation that models the temperature *y*, in degrees Fahrenheit, after *x* hours during the day. What is the graph of the equation?

36. Using the tables below, predict whether the two graphs will intersect. Plot the points and sketch the lines. Do the two lines appear to intersect? Explain.

x	y
−2	9
−1	7
0	5
1	3
2	1

x	y
−2	−18
−1	−14
0	−10
1	−6
2	−2

Find the slope and y-intercept of the graph of each equation.

37. $y - 2 = -3x$

38. $y + \frac{1}{2}x = 0$

39. $y - 9x = \frac{1}{2}$

40. $2y - 6 = 3x$

41. $-2y = 6(5 - 3x)$

42. $y - d = cx$

43. $y = (2 - a)x + a$

44. $2y + 4n = -6x$

Ⓒ 45. Think About a Plan Polar bears are listed as a threatened species. In 2005, there were about 25,000 polar bears in the world. If the number of polar bears declines by 1000 each year, in what year will polar bears become extinct?
- What equation models the number of polar bears?
- How can graphing the equation help you solve the problem?

Ⓒ 46. Error Analysis A student drew the graph at the right for the equation $y = -2x + 1$. What error did the student make? Draw the correct graph.

Ⓒ 47. Computers A computer repair service charges $50 for diagnosis and $35 per hour for repairs. Let x be the number of hours it takes to repair a computer. Let y be the total cost of the repair.
- **a.** Write an equation in slope-intercept form that relates x and y.
- **b.** Graph the equation.
- **c. Reasoning** Explain why you should draw the line only in Quadrant I.

Use the slope and y-intercept to graph each equation.

48. $y = 7 - 3x$

49. $2y + 4x = 0$

50. $3y + 6 = -2x$

51. $y + 2 = 5x - 4$

52. $4x + 3y = 2x - 1$

53. $-2(3x + 4) + y = 0$

Write a recursive formula and an explicit formula in slope-intercept form that model each arithmetic sequence. How does the recursive formula relate to the slope-intercept form?

54. $3, 5, 7, 9, \ldots$

55. $-1, 3, 7, 11, \ldots$

56. $0.7, 0.3, -0.1, -0.5, \ldots$

Ⓒ 57. Writing Describe two ways you can determine whether an equation is linear.

58. **Hobbies** Suppose you are doing a 5000-piece puzzle. You have already placed 175 pieces. Every minute you place 10 more pieces.
- **a.** Write an equation in slope-intercept form to model the number of pieces placed. Graph the equation.
- **b.** After 50 more minutes, how many pieces will you have placed?

Ⓒ Challenge Find the value of a such that the graph of the equation has the given slope m.

59. $y = 2ax + 4, m = -1$

60. $y = -\frac{1}{2}ax - 5, m = \frac{5}{2}$

61. $y = \frac{3}{4}ax + 3, m = \frac{9}{16}$

62. Sailing A sailboat begins a voyage with 145 lb of food. The crew plans to eat a total of 15 lb of food per day.

   a. Write an equation in slope-intercept form relating the remaining food supply y to the number of days x.

   b. Graph your equation.

   c. The crew plans to have 25 lb of food remaining when they end their voyage. How many days does the crew expect their voyage to last?

Standardized Test Prep

SAT/ACT

63. Which equation represents the line that has slope 5 and passes through the point $(0, -2)$?

   Ⓐ $y = x - 2$ Ⓑ $y = 5x - 2$ Ⓒ $y = -2x - 5$ Ⓓ $y = 5x$

64. What is the slope of the line that passes through the points $(-5, 3)$ and $(1, 7)$?

   Ⓕ $-\dfrac{5}{3}$ Ⓖ $-\dfrac{2}{3}$ Ⓗ $\dfrac{2}{3}$ Ⓘ $\dfrac{3}{2}$

65. Which number line shows the solution of $|2x + 5| \le 3$?

Ⓐ 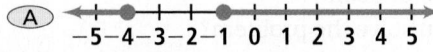   Ⓒ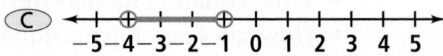

Ⓑ 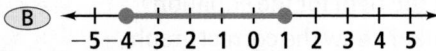   Ⓓ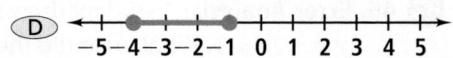

66. Which equation represents the graph at the right?

   Ⓕ $y = -\dfrac{3}{2}x + 4$ Ⓗ $y = -\dfrac{2}{3}x + 4$

   Ⓖ $y = -4x + \dfrac{3}{2}$ Ⓘ $y = 4x - \dfrac{2}{3}$

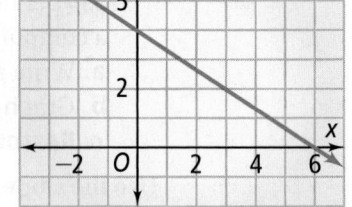

Short Response

67. If a, b, and c are real numbers, $a \ne 0$, and $b > c$, is the statement $ab > ac$ *always*, *sometimes*, or *never* true? Explain.

Mixed Review

Suppose y varies directly with x. Write a direct variation equation that relates x and y. Then find the value of y when $x = 10$.

◀ **See Lesson 5-2.**

68. $y = 5$ when $x = 1$.   **69.** $y = 8$ when $x = 4$.   **70.** $y = 9$ when $x = 3$.

Solve each equation. Justify each step.

◀ **See Lesson 2-2.**

71. $21 = -2t + 3$ **72.** $\dfrac{q}{3} - 3 = 6$ **73.** $8x + 5 = 61$

Get Ready!   **To prepare for Lesson 5-4, do Exercises 74–77.**

Simplify each expression.

◀ **See Lesson 1-7.**

74. $-3(x - 5)$ **75.** $5(x + 2)$ **76.** $-\dfrac{4}{9}(x - 6)$ **77.** $1.5(x + 12)$

5-4 Point-Slope Form

© **Common Core State Standards**

F-LE.A.2 Construct linear . . . functions . . . given a graph, a description of a relationship, or two input-output pairs. **Also A-CED.A.2, F-IF.B.4, F-IF.C.7a, F-LE.B.5**

MP 1, MP 3, MP 4

Objective To write and graph linear equations using point-slope form

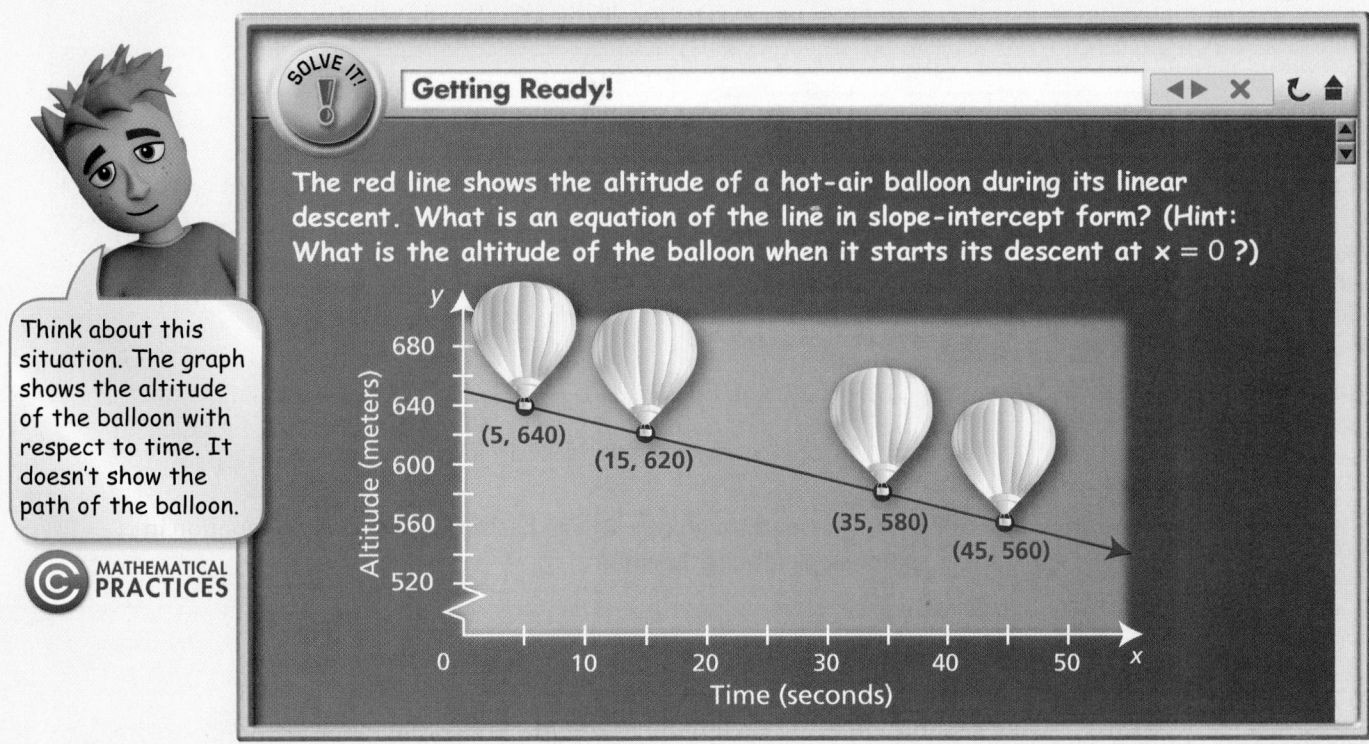

SOLVE IT!

Getting Ready!

The red line shows the altitude of a hot-air balloon during its linear descent. What is an equation of the line in slope-intercept form? (Hint: What is the altitude of the balloon when it starts its descent at $x = 0$?)

Think about this situation. The graph shows the altitude of the balloon with respect to time. It doesn't show the path of the balloon.

© MATHEMATICAL PRACTICES

You have learned how to write an equation of a line by using its y-intercept. In this lesson, you will learn how to write an equation *without* using the y-intercept.

Lesson Vocabulary
• point-slope form

Essential Understanding You can use the slope of a line and any point on the line to write and graph an equation of the line. Any two equations for the same line are equivalent.

Key Concept Point-Slope Form of a Linear Equation

Definition
The **point-slope form** of an equation of a nonvertical line with slope m and through point (x_1, y_1) is $y - y_1 = m(x - x_1)$.

Symbols
$$y - y_1 = m(x - x_1)$$
$$\uparrow \qquad \uparrow \qquad \uparrow$$
y-coordinate **slope** x-coordinate

Graph

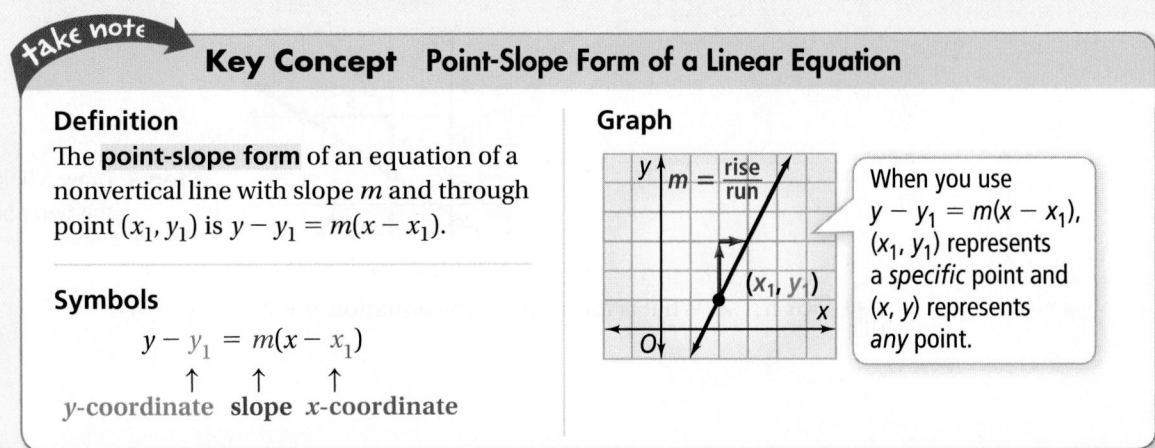

When you use $y - y_1 = m(x - x_1)$, (x_1, y_1) represents a *specific* point and (x, y) represents *any* point.

Here's Why It Works Given a point (x_1, y_1) on a line and the line's slope m, you can use the definition of slope to derive point-slope form.

$$\frac{y_2 - y_1}{x_2 - x_1} = m \qquad \text{Use the definition of slope.}$$

$$\frac{y - y_1}{x - x_1} = m \qquad \text{Let } (x, y) \text{ be any point on the line. Substitute } (x, y) \text{ for } (x_2, y_2).$$

$$\frac{y - y_1}{x - x_1} \cdot (x - x_1) = m(x - x_1) \qquad \text{Multiply each side by } (x - x_1).$$

$$y - y_1 = m(x - x_1) \qquad \text{Simplify the left side of the equation.}$$

 Problem 1 Writing an Equation in Point-Slope Form

Think

Since you know a point and the slope, use point-slope form.

A line passes through $(-3, 6)$ and has slope -5. What is an equation of the line?

$$y - y_1 = m(x - x_1) \qquad \text{Use point-slope form.}$$

$\boxed{y_1 = 6}$ $\boxed{m = -5}$ $\boxed{x_1 = -3}$

$$y - 6 = -5[x - (-3)] \qquad \text{Substitute } (-3, 6) \text{ for } (x_1, y_1) \text{ and } -5 \text{ for } m.$$

$$y - 6 = -5(x + 3) \qquad \text{Simplify inside grouping symbols.}$$

Got It? **1.** A line passes through $(8, -4)$ and has slope $\frac{2}{3}$. What is an equation in point-slope form of the line?

 Problem 2 Graphing Using Point-Slope Form

Plan

How does the equation help you make a graph?
Use the point from the equation. Use the slope from the equation to find another point. Graph using the two points.

What is the graph of the equation $y - 1 = \frac{2}{3}(x - 2)$?

The equation is in point-slope form, $y - y_1 = m(x - x_1)$. A point (x_1, y_1) on the line is $(2, 1)$, and the slope m is $\frac{2}{3}$.

Step 1 Graph a point at $(2, 1)$.

Step 2 Use the slope, $\frac{2}{3}$. Go up 2 units and right 3 units. Draw a point.

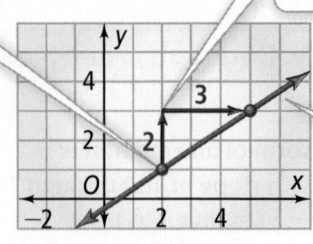

Step 3 Draw a line through the two points.

Got It? **2.** What is the graph of the equation $y + 7 = -\frac{4}{5}(x - 4)$?

You can write the equation of a line given any two points on the line. First use the two given points to find the slope. Then use the slope and one of the points to write the equation.

Plan

How does the graph help you write an equation?
You can use two points on the line to find the slope. Then use point-slope form.

 Problem 3 Using Two Points to Write an Equation

What is an equation of the line at the right?

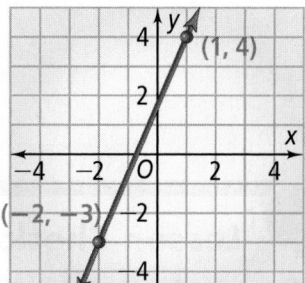

Think

You need the slope m, so start with the slope formula.

Write

$$m = \frac{y_2 - y_1}{x_2 - x_1}$$

Use the given points to find the slope.

$$m = \frac{-3 - 4}{-2 - 1} = \frac{-7}{-3} = \frac{7}{3}$$

Use point-slope form.

$$y - y_1 = m(x - x_1)$$

Use either given point for (x_1, y_1). For example, you can use (1, 4).

$$y - 4 = \frac{7}{3}(x - 1)$$

© ✔ **Got It? 3. a.** In the last step of Problem 3, use the point $(-2, -3)$ instead of $(1, 4)$ to write an equation of the line.

　　 b. Reasoning Rewrite the equations in Problem 3 and part (a) in slope-intercept form. Compare the two rewritten equations. What can you conclude?

© **Problem 4** Using a Table to Write an Equation

Recreation The table shows the altitude of a hot-air balloon during its linear descent. What equation in slope-intercept form gives the balloon's altitude at any time? What do the slope and y-intercept represent?

Hot-Air Balloon Descent

Time, x (s)	Altitude, y (m)
10	640
30	590
70	490
90	440

$m = \frac{590 - 640}{30 - 10} = -2.5$　Use two points, such as (10, 640) and (30, 590), to find the slope.

$y - y_1 = m(x - x_1)$　Use point-slope form.

$y - 640 = -2.5(x - 10)$　Use the data point (10, 640) and the slope -2.5.

$y = -2.5x + 665$　Rewrite in slope-intercept form.

The slope -2.5 represents the rate of descent of the balloon in meters per second. The y-intercept 665 represents the initial altitude of the balloon in meters.

Plan

How does the table help you write an equation?
The table gives four points. You can use any two of the points to find the slope. Then use point-slope form.

Got It? 4. a. The table shows the number of gallons of water y in a tank after x hours. The relationship is linear. What is an equation in point-slope form that models the data? What does the slope represent?

b. Reasoning Write the equation from part (a) in slope-intercept form. What does the y-intercept represent?

Volume of Water in Tank

Time, x (h)	Water, y (gal)
2	3320
3	4570
5	7070
8	10,820

Lesson Check

Do you know HOW?

1. What are the slope and one point on the graph of $y - 12 = \frac{4}{9}(x + 7)$?

2. What is an equation of the line that passes through the point $(3, -8)$ and has slope -2?

3. What is the graph of the equation $y - 4 = 3(x + 2)$?

4. What is an equation of the line that passes through the points $(-1, -2)$ and $(2, 4)$?

Do you UNDERSTAND?

5. Vocabulary What features of the graph of the equation $y - y_1 = m(x - x_1)$ can you identify?

6. Reasoning Is $y - 4 = 3(x + 1)$ an equation of a line through $(-2, 1)$? Explain.

7. Reasoning Can any equation in point-slope form also be written in slope-intercept form? Give an example to explain.

Practice and Problem-Solving Exercises

 **Practice**   Write an equation in point-slope form of the line that passes through the given point and with the given slope m.

◀ See Problem 1.

8. $(3, -4); m = 6$

9. $(4, 2); m = -\frac{5}{3}$

10. $(-2, -7); m = \frac{4}{5}$

11. $(4, 0); m = -1$

Graph each equation.

◀ See Problem 2.

12. $y + 3 = 2(x - 1)$

13. $y - 1 = -3(x + 2)$

14. $y + 5 = -(x + 2)$

15. $y - 2 = \frac{4}{9}(x - 3)$

Write an equation in point-slope form for each line.

◀ See Problem 3.

16.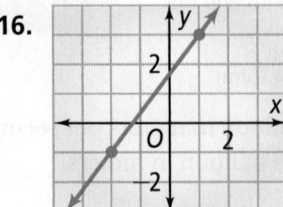

17.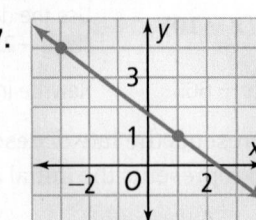

18.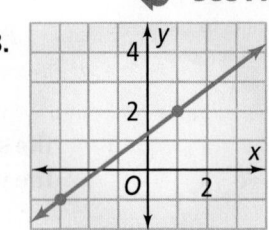

Write an equation in point-slope form of the line that passes through the given points. Then write the equation in slope-intercept form.

See Problem 4.

19. $(1, 4), (-1, 1)$ **20.** $(2, 4), (-3, -6)$ **21.** $(-6, 6), (3, 3)$

Model the data in each table with a linear equation in slope-intercept form. Then tell what the slope and *y*-intercept represent.

22.

Time Painting, *x* (days)	Volume of Paint, *y* (gal)
2	56
3	44
5	20

23.

Time Worked, *x* (h)	Wages Earned, *y* ($)
1	8.50
3	25.50
6	51.00

 **Apply**

Graph the line that passes through the given point and has the given slope *m*.

24. $(-3, -2); m = 2$ **25.** $(6, -1); m = -\frac{5}{3}$ **26.** $(-3, 1); m = \frac{1}{3}$

27. Think About a Plan The relationship of degrees Fahrenheit (°F) and degrees Celsius (°C) is linear. When the temperature is 50°F, it is 10°C. When the temperature is 77°F, it is 25°C. Write an equation giving the Celsius temperature *C* in terms of the Fahrenheit temperature *F*. What is the Celsius temperature when it is 59°F?
 • How can point-slope form help you write the equation?
 • What are two points you can use to find the slope?

28. a. Geometry Figure *ABCD* is a rectangle. Write equations in point-slope form of the lines containing the sides of *ABCD*.
 b. Reasoning Make a conjecture about the slopes of parallel lines.
 c. Use your conjecture to write an equation of the line that passes through $(0, -4)$ and is parallel to $y - 9 = -7(x + 3)$.

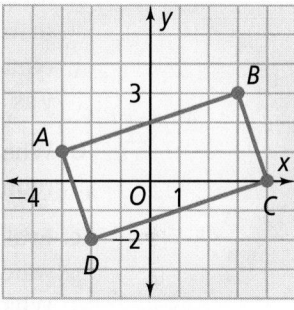

STEM 29. Boiling Point The relationship between altitude and the boiling point of water is linear. At an altitude of 8000 ft, water boils at 197.6°F. At an altitude of 4500 ft, water boils at 203.9°F. Write an equation giving the boiling point *b* of water, in degrees Fahrenheit, in terms of the altitude *a*, in feet. What is the boiling point of water at 2500 ft?

30. Using a graphing calculator, graph $f(x) = 3x + 2$.
 a. If $f(x) = 3x + 2$ and $g(x) = 4f(x)$, write the equation for $g(x)$. Graph $g(x)$ and compare it to the graph of $f(x)$.
 b. If $f(x) = 3x + 2$ and $h(x) = f(4x)$, write the equation for $h(x)$. Graph $h(x)$ and compare it to the graph of $f(x)$.
 c. Compare how multiplying a function by a number and multiplying the *x* value of a function by a number change the graphs of the functions.

31. Using a graphing calculator, graph $f(x) = 2x - 5$.
 a. If $f(x) = 2x - 5$ and $j(x) = f(x) + 3$, write the equation for $j(x)$. Graph $j(x)$ and compare it to the graph of $f(x)$.
 b. If $f(x) = 2x - 5$ and $k(x) = f(x + 3)$, write the equation for $k(x)$. Graph $k(x)$ and compare it to the graph of $f(x)$.
 c. Compare how adding a number to a function and adding a number to the *x* value of a function change the graphs of the functions.

 **Challenge**

32. Forestry A forester plants a tree and measures its circumference yearly over the next four years. The table shows the forester's measurements.

Tree Growth				
Time (yr)	1	2	3	4
Circumference (in.)	2	4	6	8

a. Show that the data are linear, and write an equation that models the data.

b. Predict the circumference of the tree after 10 yr.

c. The circumference of the tree after 10 yr was actually 43 in. After four more years, the circumference was 49 in. Based on this new information, does the relationship between time and circumference continue to be linear? Explain.

Apply What You've Learned

 MATHEMATICAL
PRACTICES
MP 2, MP 4

In the Apply What You've Learned in Lesson 5-1, you showed that there is a linear relationship between the number of marbles in the glass on page 293 and the height of the water.

a. Choose two points from the table at the right, which shows the height of the water in the glass when different numbers of marbles are dropped into it. Use the points to write an equation in slope-intercept form that gives the water height y as a function of the number of marbles x in the glass.

b. What does the y-intercept of the graph of your equation represent? What does the slope represent?

c. Evaluate the function from part (a) when $x = 40$. Does the water height given by the function make sense? Explain. What does the function value tell you about what would happen if you dropped 40 marbles in the glass?

Number of Marbles, x	Height of Water (cm), y
3	6.9
5	7.5
9	8.7
14	10.2
17	11.1
23	12.9

Do you know HOW?

Each rate of change is constant. Find the rate of change and explain what it means.

1. Studying for a Test

Study Time (h)	Grade
5	85
6	87
7	89
8	91

2. Distance a Car Travels

Time (s)	Distance (m)
3	75
6	150
9	225
12	300

Find the slope of the line that passes through each pair of points.

3. $(7, 3), (5, 1)$

4. $(-2, 1), (3, 6)$

5. $(6, -4), (6, 6)$

6. $(2, 5), (-8, 5)$

Tell whether each equation is a direct variation. If it is, find the constant of variation.

7. $y = 3x$

8. $5x + 3 = 8y + 3$

9. $-3x - 35y = 14$

Find the slope and y-intercept of the graph of each equation.

10. $y = \frac{1}{5}x + 3$

11. $3x + 4y = 12$

12. $6y = -8x - 18$

13. Credit Cards In 2000, people charged $1,243 billion on the four most-used types of credit cards. In 2005, people charged $1,838 billion on these same four types of credit cards. What was the rate of change?

14. Bicycling The distance a wheel moves forward varies directly with the number of rotations. Suppose the wheel moves 56 ft in 8 rotations. What distance does the wheel move in 20 rotations?

Write an equation in slope-intercept form of each line.

15.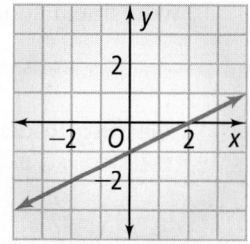

16.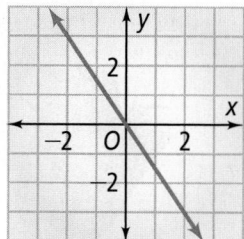

Graph each equation.

17. $y = 4x - 3$

18. $y + 3 = \frac{1}{2}(x + 2)$

Write an equation in point-slope form for the line through the given point and with the given slope m.

19. $(2, -2); m = -\frac{1}{2}$

20. $(4, 0); m = 4$

Write an equation of the line that passes through each pair of points.

21. $(4, -2)$ and $(8, -6)$

22. $(-1, -5)$ and $(2, 10)$

Do you UNDERSTAND?

© 23. Writing Describe two methods you can use to write an equation of a line given its graph.

© 24. Vocabulary How can you find the y-intercept of the graph of a linear equation?

© 25. Reasoning Can you graph a line if its slope is undefined? Explain.

© 26. Business A salesperson earns $18 per hour plus a $75 bonus for meeting her sales quota. Write and graph an equation that represents her total earnings, including her bonus. What does the independent variable represent? What does the dependent variable represent?

5-5 Standard Form

Common Core State Standards

A-CED.A.2 Create equations in two or more variables . . . graph equations on coordinate axes . . . **Also F-IF.B.4, F-IF.C.7a, F-LE.A.2, F-LE.B.5**

MP 1, MP 2, MP 3, MP 4

Objectives To graph linear equations using intercepts
To write linear equations in standard form

SOLVE IT!

Getting Ready!

An athlete wants to make a snack mix of peanuts and cashews that will contain a certain amount of protein. Cashews have 4 g of protein per ounce, and peanuts have 7 g of protein per ounce. How many grams of protein will the athlete's mix contain? What do the points (7, 0) and (0, 4) represent? Explain.

Snack Mix

Ounces of peanuts

Ounces of cashews

A point on the graph tells you (ounces of cashews, ounces of peanuts). What do you do with this information to find the grams of protein?

MATHEMATICAL PRACTICES In this lesson, you will learn to use intercepts to graph a line. Recall that a *y*-intercept is the *y*-coordinate of a point where a graph crosses the *y*-axis. The **x-intercept** is the *x*-coordinate of a point where a graph crosses the *x*-axis.

Lesson Vocabulary
• *x*-intercept
• standard form of a linear equation

Essential Understanding One form of a linear equation, called *standard form*, allows you to find intercepts quickly. You can use the intercepts to draw the graph.

take note

Key Concept   Standard Form of a Linear Equation

The **standard form of a linear equation** is $Ax + By = C$, where A, B, and C are real numbers, and A and B are not both zero.

Problem 1   Finding x- and y-Intercepts

What are the *x*- and *y*-intercepts of the graph of $3x + 4y = 24$?

Think

Why do you substitute 0 for *y* to find the *x*-intercept?
The *x*-intercept is the *x*-coordinate of a point on the *x*-axis. Any point on the *x*-axis has a *y*-coordinate of 0.

Step 1 To find the *x*-intercept, substitute 0 for *y*. Solve for *x*.

$$3x + 4y = 24$$
$$3x + 4(0) = 24$$
$$3x = 24$$
$$x = 8$$

The *x*-intercept is 8.

Step 2 To find the *y*-intercept, substitute 0 for *x*. Solve for *y*.

$$3x + 4y = 24$$
$$3(0) + 4y = 24$$
$$4y = 24$$
$$y = 6$$

The *y*-intercept is 6.

Got It? 1. What are the x- and y-intercepts of the graph of each equation?

  a. $5x - 6y = 60$ **b.** $3x + 8y = 12$

Problem 2   Graphing a Line Using Intercepts

What is the graph of $x - 2y = -2$?

Know → **Need** → **Plan**

Know	Need	Plan
An equation of the line	The coordinates of at least two points on the line	Find and plot the x- and y-intercepts. Draw a line through the points.

Think

What points do the intercepts represent?
The x-intercept is -2, so the graph crosses the x-axis at $(-2, 0)$. The y-intercept is 1, so the graph crosses the y-axis at $(0, 1)$.

Step 1   Find the intercepts.

$$x - 2y = -2$$
$$x - 2(0) = -2$$
$$x = -2$$

$$x - 2y = -2$$
$$0 - 2y = -2$$
$$-2y = -2$$
$$y = 1$$

Step 2 Plot $(-2, 0)$ and $(0, 1)$. Draw a line through the points.

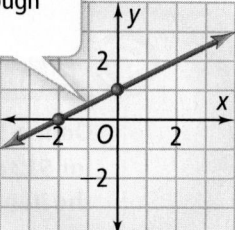

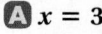 **Got It? 2.** What is the graph of $2x + 5y = 20$?

If $A = 0$ in the standard form $Ax + By = C$, then you can write the equation in the form $y = b$, where b is a constant. If $B = 0$, you can write the equation in the form $x = a$, where a is a constant. The graph of $y = b$ is a horizontal line, and the graph of $x = a$ is a vertical line.

Problem 3   Graphing Horizontal and Vertical Lines

What is the graph of each equation?

Think

Why write $x = 3$ in standard form?
When you write $x = 3$ in standard form, you can see that, for any value of y, $x = 3$. This form of the equation makes graphing the line easier.

A $x = 3$
$$1x + 0y = 3$$

  ← Write in standard form. →

B $y = 3$
$$0x + 1y = 3$$

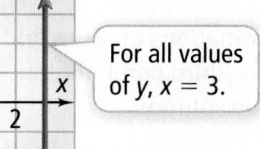

For all values of y, $x = 3$.

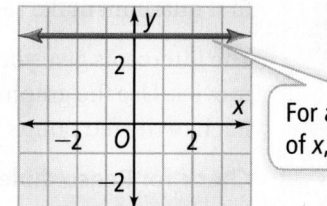

For all values of x, $y = 3$.

 Got It? 3. What is the graph of each equation?

  a. $x = 4$ **b.** $x = -1$ **c.** $y = 0$ **d.** $y = 1$

Given an equation in slope-intercept form or point-slope form, you can rewrite the equation in standard form using only integers.

 Problem 4 Transforming to Standard Form

What is $y = -\frac{3}{7}x + 5$ written in standard form using integers?

Plan

How can you get started?
You need to clear the fraction. So, multiply each side of the equation by the denominator of the fraction.

$$y = -\frac{3}{7}x + 5$$

$$7y = 7\left(-\frac{3}{7}x + 5\right) \quad \text{Multiply each side by 7.}$$

$$7y = -3x + 35 \quad \text{Distributive Property}$$

$$3x + 7y = 35 \quad \text{Add } 3x \text{ to each side.}$$

 Got It? **4.** Write $y - 2 = -\frac{1}{3}(x + 6)$ in standard form using integers.

 Problem 5 Using Standard Form as a Model

Online Shopping A media download store sells songs for $1 each and movies for $12 each. You have $60 to spend. Write and graph an equation that describes the items you can purchase. What are three combinations of numbers of songs and movies you can purchase?

Relate $\boxed{\text{cost of a song}}$ times $\boxed{\text{number of songs}}$ plus $\boxed{\text{cost of a movie}}$ times $\boxed{\text{number of movies}}$ equals $\boxed{\$60}$

Define Let $\boxed{x}$ = the number of songs purchased.

Let $\boxed{y}$ = the number of movies purchased.

Write $\boxed{1}$ • $\boxed{x}$ + $\boxed{12}$ • $\boxed{y}$ = $\boxed{60}$

Think

Is there another way to find solutions?
You can *guess and check* by substituting values for one variable and solving for the other. Then check if your solution makes sense in the context of the problem. Graphing is the quickest way to see *all* the solutions.

An equation for this situation is $x + 12y = 60$.
Find the intercepts.

$$x + 12y = 60 \qquad\qquad x + 12y = 60$$
$$x + 12(0) = 60 \qquad\qquad 0 + 12y = 60$$
$$x = 60 \qquad\qquad y = 5$$

Use the intercepts to draw the graph. Only points in the first quadrant make sense.

The intercepts give you two combinations of songs and movies. Use the graph to identify a third combination. Each of the red points is a possible solution.

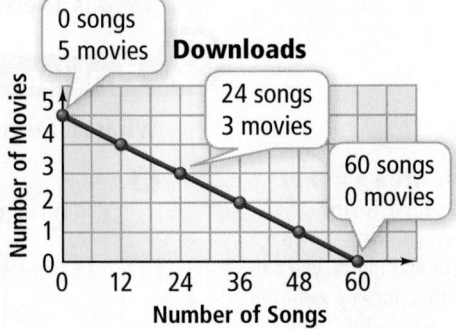

Check for Reasonableness You cannot buy a fraction of a song or movie. The graph is a line, but only points with integer coordinates are solutions.

Got It? **5. a.** In Problem 5, suppose the store charged $15 for each movie. What equation describes the numbers of songs and movies you can purchase for $60?

b. Reasoning What domain and range are reasonable for the equation in part (a)? Explain.

take note

Concept Summary   Linear Equations

You can describe any line using one or more of these forms of a linear equation. Any two equations for the same line are equivalent.

Graph

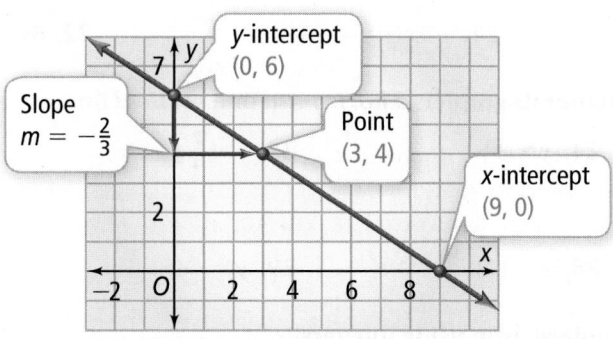

Forms

Slope-Intercept Form
$y = mx + b$
$y = -\frac{2}{3}x + 6$

Point-Slope Form
$y - y_1 = m(x - x_1)$
$y - 4 = -\frac{2}{3}(x - 3)$

Standard Form
$Ax + By = C$
$2x + 3y = 18$

Lesson Check

Do you know HOW?

1. What are the *x*- and *y*-intercepts of the graph of $3x - 4y = 9$?

2. What is the graph of $5x + 4y = 20$?

3. Is the graph of $y = -0.5$ a *horizontal line*, a *vertical line*, or *neither*?

4. What is $y = \frac{1}{2}x + 3$ written in standard form using integers?

5. A store sells gift cards in preset amounts. You can purchase gift cards for $10 or $25. You have spent $285 on gift cards. Write an equation in standard form to represent this situation. What are three combinations of gift cards you could have purchased?

Do you UNDERSTAND?

6. Vocabulary Tell whether each linear equation is in *slope-intercept form*, *point-slope form*, or *standard form*.
   a. $y + 5 = -(x - 2)$
   b. $y = -2x + 5$
   c. $y - 10 = -2(x - 1)$
   d. $2x + 4y = 12$

7. Reasoning Which form would you use to write an equation of the line at the right: *slope-intercept form*, *point-slope form*, or *standard form*? Explain.

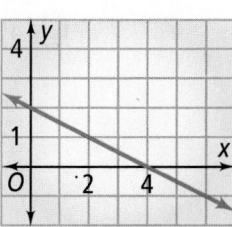

Practice and Problem-Solving Exercises

A Practice

Find the *x*- and *y*-intercepts of the graph of each equation.　　　　　◀ **See Problem 1.**

8. $x + y = 9$　　　　　　**9.** $x - 2y = 2$　　　　　　**10.** $-3x + 3y = 7$

11. $3x - 5y = -20$　　　　**12.** $7x - y = 21$　　　　　**13.** $-5x + 3y = -7.5$

Draw a line with the given intercepts.　　　　　　　　　　　　　◀ **See Problem 2.**

14. *x*-intercept: 3　　　　**15.** *x*-intercept: -1　　　　**16.** *x*-intercept: 4
　　y-intercept: 5　　　　　　　*y*-intercept: -4　　　　　　　*y*-intercept: -3

Graph each equation using *x*- and *y*-intercepts.

17. $x + y = 4$　　　　　　**18.** $x + y = -3$　　　　　**19.** $x - y = -8$

20. $-2x + y = 8$　　　　　**21.** $-4x + y = -12$　　　　**22.** $6x - 2y = 18$

For each equation, tell whether its graph is a *horizontal* or a *vertical* line.　　◀ **See Problem 3.**

23. $y = -4$　　　**24.** $x = 3$　　　**25.** $y = \frac{7}{4}$　　　**26.** $x = -1.8$

Graph each equation.

27. $y = 6$　　　**28.** $x = -3$　　　**29.** $y = -2$　　　**30.** $x = 7$

Write each equation in standard form using integers.　　　　　　　◀ **See Problem 4.**

31. $y = 2x + 5$　　　　　　**32.** $y + 3 = 4(x - 1)$　　　　**33.** $y - 4 = -2(x - 3)$

34. $y = \frac{1}{4}x - 2$　　　　　**35.** $y = -\frac{2}{3}x - 1$　　　　**36.** $y + 2 = \frac{2}{3}(x + 4)$

37. **Video Games** In a video game, you earn 5 points for each jewel you find. You　　◀ **See Problem 5.**
earn 2 points for each star you find. Write and graph an equation that represents
the numbers of jewels and stars you must find to earn 250 points. What are three
combinations of jewels and stars you can find that will earn you 250 points?

38. **Clothing** A store sells T-shirts for \$12 each and sweatshirts for \$15 each. You
plan to spend \$120 on T-shirts and sweatshirts. Write and graph an equation that
represents this situation. What are three combinations of T-shirts and sweatshirts
you can buy for \$120?

B Apply　　　**39.** **Writing** The three forms of linear equations you have studied are slope-intercept
form, point-slope form, and standard form. Explain when each form is most useful.

Ⓒ **40.** **Think About a Plan** You are preparing a fruit salad. You want the total
carbohydrates from pineapple and watermelon to equal 24 g. Pineapple has 3 g of
carbohydrates per ounce and watermelon has 2 g of carbohydrates per ounce. What
is a graph that shows all possible combinations of ounces of pineapple and ounces
of watermelon?
- Can you write an equation to model the situation?
- What domain and range are reasonable for the graph?

41. Compare and Contrast Graph $3x + y = 6$, $3x - y = 6$, and $-3x + y = 6$. How are the graphs similar? How are they different?

42. Reasoning What are the slope and y-intercept of the graph of $Ax + By = C$?

43. Error Analysis A student says the equation $y = 4x + 1$ can be written in standard form as $4x - y = 1$. Describe and correct the student's error.

44. Reasoning The coefficients of x and y in the standard form of a linear equation cannot both be zero. Explain why.

Graphing Calculator **Use a graphing calculator to graph each equation. Make a sketch of the graph. Include the x- and y-intercepts.**

45. $2x - 8y = -16$ **46.** $-3x - 4y = 0$ **47.** $x + 3.5y = 7$

48. $-x + 2y = -8$ **49.** $3x + 3y = -15$ **50.** $4x - 6y = 9$

51. Compare and Contrast The graph below represents one function, and the table represents a different function. How are the functions similar? How are they different?

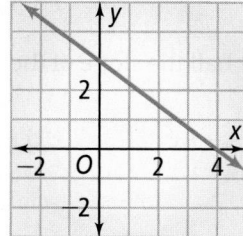

x	−4	−2	0	2	4
y	5	4	3	2	1

Find the x- and y-intercepts of the line that passes through the given points.

52. $(-6, 4), (3, -5)$ **53.** $(-5, -5), (4, -2)$ **54.** $(-7, 6), (-4, 11)$

55. $(-2, 8), (4, 2)$ **56.** $(3, -8), (-4, 13)$ **57.** $(5, 0.4), (-1, -2)$

58. Sports The scoreboard for a football game is shown at the right. All of the points the home team scored came from field goals worth 3 points and touchdowns with successful extra-point attempts worth 7 points. Write and graph a linear equation that represents this situation. List every possible combination of field goals and touchdowns the team could have scored.

Challenge

59. Geometry Graph $x + 4y = 8$, $4x - y = -1$, $x + 4y = -12$, and $4x - y = 20$ in the same coordinate plane. What figure do the four lines appear to form?

Write an equation of each line in standard form.

60. The line contains the point $(-4, -7)$ and has the same slope as the graph of $y + 3 = 5(x + 4)$.

61. The line has the same slope as $4x - y = 5$ and the same y-intercept as the graph of $3y - 13x = 6$.

62. a. Graph $2x + 3y = 6$, $2x + 3y = 12$, and $2x + 3y = 18$ in the same coordinate plane.

    b. How are the lines from part (a) related?

    c. As C increases, what happens to the graph of $2x + 3y = C$?

Ⓒ **63. a. Fundraising** Suppose your school is having a talent show to raise money for new band supplies. You think that 200 students and 150 adults will attend. It will cost $200 to put on the talent show. What is an equation that describes the ticket prices you can set for students and adults to raise $1000?

    b. Open-Ended Graph your equation. What are three possible prices you could set for student and adult tickets?

Standardized Test Prep

SAT/ACT

64. What is $y = -\frac{3}{4}x + 2$ written in standard form using integers?

    Ⓐ $\frac{3}{4}x + y = 2$ Ⓑ $3x + 4y = 2$ Ⓒ $3x + 4y = 8$ Ⓓ $-3x - 4y = 8$

65. Which of the following is an equation of a horizontal line?

    Ⓕ $3x + 6y = 0$ Ⓖ $2x + 7 = 0$ Ⓗ $-3y = 29$ Ⓘ $x - 2y = 4$

66. Which equation models a line with the same y-intercept but half the slope of the line $y = 6 - 8x$?

    Ⓐ $y = -4x + 3$ Ⓑ $y = 6 - 4x$ Ⓒ $y = 3 - 8x$ Ⓓ $y = -16x + 6$

67. What is the solution of $\frac{7}{2}x - 19 = -13 + 2x$?

    Ⓕ -9 Ⓖ -4 Ⓗ 4 Ⓘ 9

Short Response

68. The drama club plans to attend a professional production. Between 10 and 15 students will go. Each ticket costs $25 plus a $2 surcharge. There is a one-time handling fee of $3 for the entire order. What is a linear function that models this situation? What domain and range are reasonable for the function?

Mixed Review

Write an equation in point-slope form of the line that passes through the given points. Then write the equation in slope-intercept form.

 See Lesson 5-4.

69. $(5, -1), (-3, 4)$ **70.** $(0, -2), (3, 2)$ **71.** $(-2, -1), (1, 2)$

Solve each compound inequality. Graph your solution.

See Lesson 3-6.

72. $-6 < 3t \le 9$ **73.** $-9.5 < 3 - y \le 1.3$ **74.** $3x + 1 > 10$ or $5x + 3 \le -2$

Get Ready!   **To prepare for Lesson 5-6, do Exercises 75–77.**

Find the slope of the line that passes through each pair of points.

See Lesson 5-1.

75. $(0, -4), (2, 0)$ **76.** $(5, 5), (3, -1)$ **77.** $(-4, 2), (5, 2)$

Inverse of a Linear Function

 Common Core State Standards

F-BF.B.4a Solve an equation of the form $f(x) = c$ for a simple function f that has an inverse and write an expression for the inverse.

MP 3

Let f be a function. If there is another function that pairs b with a whenever f pairs a with b, then functions are called **inverse functions.**

You can find the inverse function algebraically.

Example

Find the inverse of the function $f(x) = -2x + 4.$

Step 1 Replace $f(x)$ with y. Then switch x for y and y for x.

$y = -2x + 4$ Write f(x) as y.

$x = -2y + 4$ Switch x and y.

Step 2 Solve for y.

$x - 4 = -2y$ Subtract 4 from each side.

$\dfrac{x-4}{-2} = \dfrac{-2y}{-2}$ Divide by −2.

$-\dfrac{1}{2}x + 2 = y$ Simplify.

Step 3 Write in function notation, using f^{-1} to represent the inverse of the function f.

$f^{-1}(x) = -\dfrac{1}{2}x + 2$

Exercises

Find the inverse of each function.

1. $f(x) = 4x - 2$ **2.** $f(x) = 3x + 2$ **3.** $f(x) = -2x - 3$

4. $f(x) = \frac{1}{2}x + 1$ **5.** $f(x) = 4x + 8$ **6.** $f(x) = -4x$

7. $f(x) = 2 - 7x$ **8.** $f(x) = \frac{1}{4}x - 4$ **9.** $f(x) = -\frac{2}{3}x + 1$

10. $f(x) = 2x + 8$ **11.** $f(x) = -4x + 8$ **12.** $f(x) = -1 - 2x$

13. $f(x) = -7 + x$ **14.** $f(x) = 4x - 5$ **15.** $f(x) = \frac{3}{4}x - 1$

16. $f(x) = x - 1$ **17.** $f(x) = -2 - \frac{3}{2}x$ **18.** $f(x) = -\frac{1}{6}x + 1$

19. Reasoning Why does interchanging the x and y match the definition of an inverse function?

5-6 Parallel and Perpendicular Lines

Common Core State Standards

G-GPE.B.5 Prove the slope criteria for parallel and perpendicular lines and use them to solve geometric problems.

MP 1, MP 2, MP 3, MP 4, MP 7

Objectives To determine whether lines are parallel, perpendicular, or neither
To write equations of parallel lines and perpendicular lines

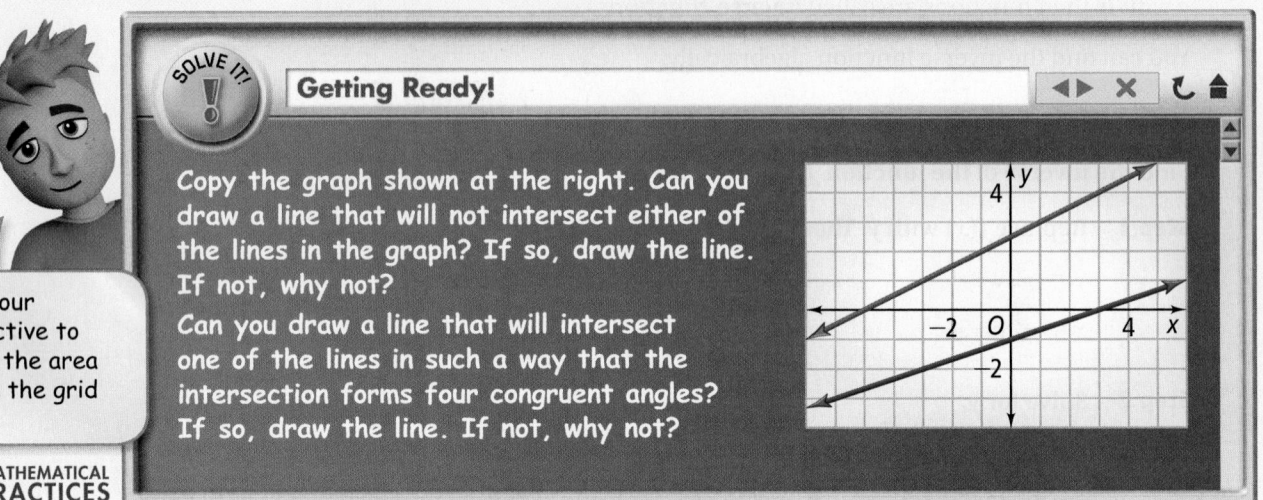

SOLVE IT!

Getting Ready!

Copy the graph shown at the right. Can you draw a line that will not intersect either of the lines in the graph? If so, draw the line. If not, why not?

Can you draw a line that will intersect one of the lines in such a way that the intersection forms four congruent angles? If so, draw the line. If not, why not?

Shift your perspective to include the area outside the grid as well.

MATHEMATICAL PRACTICES

Lesson Vocabulary
- parallel lines
- perpendicular lines
- opposite reciprocals

Two distinct lines in a coordinate plane either intersect or are *parallel*. **Parallel lines** are lines in the same plane that never intersect.

Essential Understanding You can determine the relationship between two lines by comparing their slopes and y-intercepts.

Key Concept Slopes of Parallel Lines

Words
Nonvertical lines are parallel if they have the same slope and different y-intercepts. Vertical lines are parallel if they have different x-intercepts.

Graph

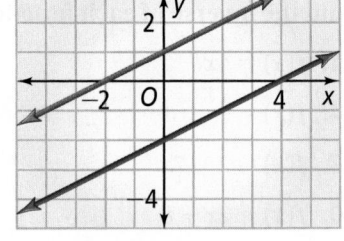

Example
The graphs of $y = \frac{1}{2}x + 1$ and $y = \frac{1}{2}x - 2$ are lines that have the same slope, $\frac{1}{2}$, and different y-intercepts. The lines are parallel.

You can use the fact that the slopes of parallel lines are the same to write the equation of a line parallel to a given line.

Problem 1 **Writing an Equation of a Parallel Line**

A line passes through (12, 5) and is parallel to the graph of $y = \frac{2}{3}x - 1$. What equation represents the line in slope-intercept form?

Step 1 Identify the slope of the given line. The slope of the graph of $y = \frac{2}{3}x - 1$ is $\frac{2}{3}$. The parallel line has the same slope.

Step 2 Write an equation in slope-intercept form of the line through (12, 5) with slope $\frac{2}{3}$.

Think

Why start with point-slope form?
You know a point on the line. You can use what you know about parallel lines to find the slope. So, point-slope form is convenient to use.

$y - y_1 = m(x - x_1)$	Start with point-slope form.
$y - 5 = \frac{2}{3}(x - 12)$	Substitute (12, 5) for (x_1, y_1) and $\frac{2}{3}$ for m.
$y - 5 = \frac{2}{3}x - \frac{2}{3}(12)$	Distributive Property
$y - 5 = \frac{2}{3}x - 8$	Simplify.
$y = \frac{2}{3}x - 3$	Add 5 to each side.

The graph of $y = \frac{2}{3}x - 3$ passes through (12, 5) and is parallel to the graph of $y = \frac{2}{3}x - 1$.

 Got It? **1.** A line passes through $(-3, -1)$ and is parallel to the graph of $y = 2x + 3$. What equation represents the line in slope-intercept form?

You can also use slope to determine whether two lines are *perpendicular*. **Perpendicular lines** are lines that intersect to form right angles.

 Key Concept **Slopes of Perpendicular Lines**

Words

Two nonvertical lines are perpendicular if the product of their slopes is -1. A vertical line and a horizontal line are also perpendicular.

Graph

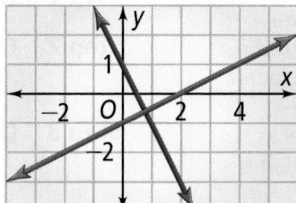

Example
The graph of $y = \frac{1}{2}x - 1$ has a slope of $\frac{1}{2}$.
The graph of $y = -2x + 1$ has a slope of -2.
Since $\frac{1}{2}(-2) = -1$, the lines are perpendicular.

Two numbers whose product is -1 are **opposite reciprocals.** So, the slopes of perpendicular lines are opposite reciprocals. To find the opposite reciprocal of $-\frac{3}{4}$, for example, first find the reciprocal, $-\frac{4}{3}$. Then write its opposite, $\frac{4}{3}$. Since $-\frac{3}{4} \cdot \frac{4}{3} = -1$, $\frac{4}{3}$ is the opposite reciprocal of $-\frac{3}{4}$.

Problem 2 **Classifying Lines**

Are the graphs of $4y = -5x + 12$ and $y = \frac{4}{5}x - 8$ *parallel*, *perpendicular*, or *neither*? Explain.

Think

Why write each equation in slope-intercept form?
You can easily identify the slope of an equation in slope-intercept form. Just look at the coefficient of *x*.

Step 1 Find the slope of each line by writing its equation in slope-intercept form, if necessary. Only the first equation needs to be rewritten.

$$4y = -5x + 12 \quad \text{Write the first equation.}$$

$$\frac{4y}{4} = \frac{-5x + 12}{4} \quad \text{Divide each side by 4.}$$

$$y = -\frac{5}{4}x + 3 \quad \text{Simplify.}$$

The slope of the graph of $y = -\frac{5}{4}x + 3$ is $-\frac{5}{4}$.

The slope of the graph of $y = \frac{4}{5}x - 8$ is $\frac{4}{5}$.

Step 2 The slopes are not the same, so the lines cannot be parallel. Multiply the slopes to see if they are opposite reciprocals.

$$-\frac{5}{4} \cdot \frac{4}{5} = -1$$

The slopes are opposite reciprocals, so the lines are perpendicular.

 Got It? **2.** Are the graphs of the equations *parallel*, *perpendicular*, or *neither*? Explain.

a. $y = \frac{3}{4}x + 7$ and $4x - 3y = 9$ **b.** $6y = -x + 6$ and $y = -\frac{1}{6}x + 6$

 Problem 3 **Writing an Equation of a Perpendicular Line**

Multiple Choice Which equation represents the line that passes through $(2, 4)$ and is perpendicular to the graph of $y = \frac{1}{3}x - 1$?

Ⓐ $y = \frac{1}{3}x + 10$ Ⓑ $y = 3x + 10$ Ⓒ $y = -3x - 2$ Ⓓ $y = -3x + 10$

Think

How do you know you have found the opposite reciprocal?
Multiply the two numbers together as a check. If the product is -1, the numbers are opposite reciprocals:
$\frac{1}{3}(-3) = -1$.

Step 1 Identify the slope of the graph of the given equation. The slope is $\frac{1}{3}$.

Step 2 Find the opposite reciprocal of the slope from Step 1. The opposite reciprocal of $\frac{1}{3}$ is -3. So, the perpendicular line has a slope of -3.

Step 3 Use point-slope form to write an equation of the perpendicular line.

$$y - y_1 = m(x - x_1) \quad \text{Write point-slope form.}$$

$$y - 4 = -3(x - 2) \quad \text{Substitute } (2, 4) \text{ for } (x_1, y_1) \text{ and } -3 \text{ for } m.$$

$$y - 4 = -3x + 6 \quad \text{Distributive Property}$$

$$y = -3x + 10 \quad \text{Add 4 to each side.}$$

The equation is $y = -3x + 10$. The correct answer is D.

 Got It? **3.** A line passes through $(1, 8)$ and is perpendicular to the graph of $y = 2x + 1$. What equation represents the line in slope-intercept form?

 **Problem 4** **Solving a Real-World Problem** (STEM)

Architecture An architect uses software to design the ceiling of a room. The architect needs to enter an equation that represents a new beam. The new beam will be perpendicular to the existing beam, which is represented by the red line. The new beam will pass through the corner represented by the blue point. What is an equation that represents the new beam?

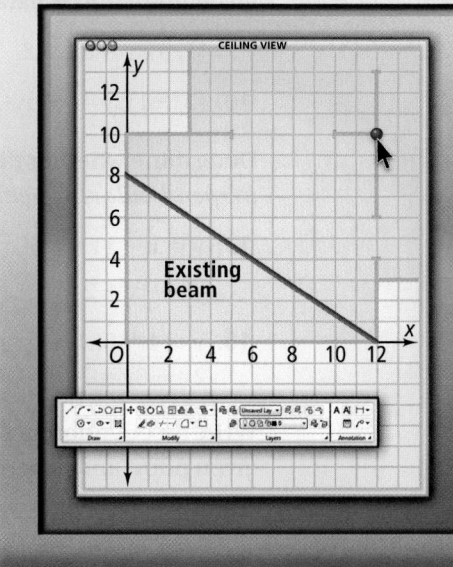

Plan

Have you seen a problem like this before?
Yes. You wrote the equation of a perpendicular line in Problem 3. Follow the same steps here after you calculate the slope of the line from the graph.

Step 1 Use the slope formula to find the slope of the red line that represents the existing beam.

$$m = \frac{4-6}{6-3} \qquad \text{Points (3, 6) and (6, 4)}$$
are on the red line.

$$= -\frac{2}{3} \qquad \text{Simplify.}$$

The slope of the line that represents the existing beam is $-\frac{2}{3}$.

Step 2 Find the opposite reciprocal of the slope from Step 1. The opposite reciprocal of $-\frac{2}{3}$ is $\frac{3}{2}$.

Step 3 Use point-slope form to write an equation. The slope of the line that represents the new beam is $\frac{3}{2}$. It will pass through (12, 10). An equation that represents the new beam is $y - 10 = \frac{3}{2}(x - 12)$ or, in slope-intercept form, $y = \frac{3}{2}x - 8$.

 Got It? **4.** What equation could the architect enter to represent a second beam whose graph will pass through the corner at (0, 10) and be parallel to the existing beam? Give your answer in slope-intercept form.

 Lesson Check

Do you know HOW?

1. Which equations below have graphs that are parallel to one another? Which have graphs that are perpendicular to one another?

$$y = -\frac{1}{6}x \qquad y = 6x \qquad y = 6x - 2$$

2. What is an equation of the line that passes through (3, −1) and is parallel to $y = -4x + 1$? Give your answer in slope-intercept form.

3. What is an equation of the line that passes through (2, −3) and is perpendicular to $y = x - 5$? Give your answer in slope-intercept form.

Do you UNDERSTAND? (C) **MATHEMATICAL PRACTICES**

(C) **4. Vocabulary** Tell whether the two numbers in each pair are opposite reciprocals.

   a. $-2, \frac{1}{2}$ **b.** $\frac{1}{4}, 4$ **c.** $5, -5$

(C) **5. Open-Ended** Write equations of two parallel lines.

(C) **6. Compare and Contrast** How is determining if two lines are parallel similar to determining if they are perpendicular? How are the processes different?

Practice and Problem-Solving Exercises

Ⓐ Practice

Write an equation in slope-intercept form of the line that passes through the given point and is parallel to the graph of the given equation.

◀ See Problem 1.

7. $(1, 3); y = 3x + 2$

8. $(2, -2); y = -x - 2$

9. $(1, -3); y + 2 = 4(x - 1)$

10. $(2, -1); y = -\frac{3}{2}x + 6$

11. $(0, 0); y = \frac{2}{3}x + 1$

12. $(4, 2); x = -3$

Determine whether the graphs of the given equations are *parallel*, *perpendicular*, or *neither*. **Explain.**

◀ See Problem 2.

13. $y = x + 11$
$y = -x + 2$

14. $y = \frac{3}{4}x - 1$
$y = \frac{3}{4}x + 29$

15. $y = -2x + 3$
$2x + y = 7$

16. $y - 4 = 3(x + 2)$
$2x + 6y = 10$

17. $y = -7$
$x = 2$

18. $y = 4x - 2$
$-x + 4y = 0$

Write an equation in slope-intercept form of the line that passes through the given point and is perpendicular to the graph of the given equation.

◀ See Problem 3.

19. $(0, 0); y = -3x + 2$

20. $(-2, 3); y = \frac{1}{2}x - 1$

21. $(1, -2); y = 5x + 4$

22. $(-3, 2); x - 2y = 7$

23. $(5, 0); y + 1 = 2(x - 3)$

24. $(1, -6); x - 2y = 4$

25. Urban Planning A path for a new city park will connect the park entrance to Main Street. The path should be perpendicular to Main Street. What is an equation that represents the path?

◀ See Problem 4.

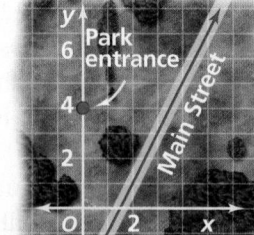

26. Bike Path A bike path is being planned for the park in Exercise 25. The bike path will be parallel to Main Street and will pass through the park entrance. What is an equation of the line that represents the bike path?

Ⓑ Apply

27. Identify each pair of parallel lines. Then identify each pair of perpendicular lines.

line *a*: $y = 3x + 3$

line *b*: $x = -1$

line *c*: $y - 5 = \frac{1}{2}(x - 2)$

line *d*: $y = 3$

line *e*: $y + 4 = -2(x + 6)$

line *f*: $9x - 3y = 5$

Determine whether each statement is *always*, *sometimes*, or *never* true. **Explain.**

28. A horizontal line is parallel to the *x*-axis.

29. Two lines with positive slopes are parallel.

30. Two lines with the same slope and different *y*-intercepts are perpendicular.

Ⓒ 31. Reasoning For an arithmetic sequence, the first term is $A(1) = 3$. Each successive term adds 2 to the previous term. Another arithmetic sequence has the rule $B(n) = 5 + (n - 1)d$, where *n* is the term number and *d* is the common difference. If the graphs of the two sequences are parallel, what is the value of *d*? **Explain.**

Ⓒ 32. Reasoning Will the graph of the line represented by the table intersect the graph of $y = 4x + 5$? **Explain.**

x	−1	0	1	2
y	−1	3	7	11

33. Think About a Plan A designer is creating a new logo, as shown at the right. The designer wants to add a line to the logo that will be perpendicular to the blue line and pass through the red point. What equation represents the new line?
- What is the slope of the blue line?
- What is the slope of the new line?

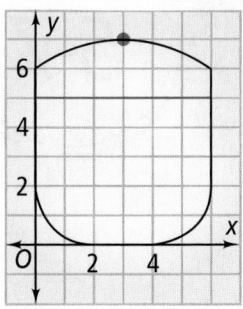

34. Reasoning For what value of k are the graphs of $12y = -3x + 8$ and $6y = kx - 5$ parallel? For what value of k are they perpendicular?

35. Agriculture Two farmers use combines to harvest corn from their fields. One farmer has 600 acres of corn, and the other has 1000 acres of corn. Each farmer's combine can harvest 100 acres per day. Write two equations for the number of acres y of corn *not* harvested after x days. Are the graphs of the equations *parallel*, *perpendicular*, or *neither*? How do you know?

Challenge

36. Geometry In a rectangle, opposite sides are parallel and adjacent sides are perpendicular. Figure $ABCD$ has vertices $A(-3, 3)$, $B(-1, -2)$, $C(4, 0)$, and $D(2, 5)$. Show that $ABCD$ is a rectangle.

37. Geometry A right triangle has two sides that are perpendicular to each other. Triangle PQR has vertices $P(4, 3)$, $Q(2, -1)$, and $R(0, 1)$. Determine whether PQR is a right triangle. Explain your reasoning.

Standardized Test Prep

SAT/ACT

38. Which equation represents the graph of a line parallel to the line at the right?

Ⓐ $y = \frac{1}{2}x + 5$　　　　　　Ⓒ $y = -2x + 4$

Ⓑ $y = 2x - 6$　　　　　　　Ⓓ $y = -\frac{1}{2}x - 2$

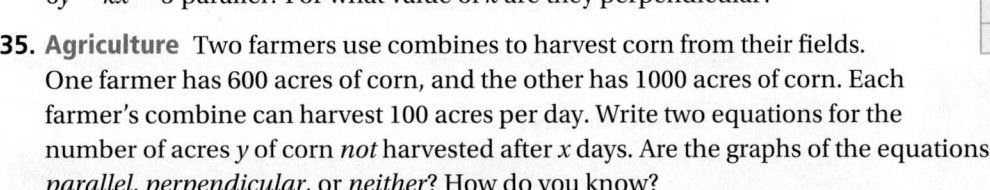

39. What is the solution of $(5x - 1) + (-2x + 7) = 9$?

Ⓕ $\frac{3}{7}$　　　　Ⓖ 1　　　　Ⓗ 3　　　　Ⓘ 5

Short Response

40. Sal's Supermarket sells cases of twenty-four 12-oz bottles of water for $15.50. Shopper's World sells 12-packs of 12-oz bottles of water for $8.15. Which store has the better price per bottle? Explain.

Mixed Review

Graph each equation using x- and y-intercepts.

See Lesson 5-5.

41. $x + y = 8$　　　　**42.** $2x + y = -3$　　　　**43.** $x - 3y = -6$

Get Ready! To prepare for Lesson 5-7, do Exercises 44–47.

Write an equation in slope-intercept form of the line that passes through the given points.

See Lesson 5-3.

44. $(1, 1)$, $(3, 7)$　　　**45.** $(2, 5)$, $(12, 1)$　　　**46.** $(0.5, 2)$, $(4.5, 3)$　　　**47.** $(13, 20)$, $(6, 60)$

5-7 Scatter Plots and Trend Lines

Common Core State Standards

S-ID.B.6c Fit a linear function for a scatter plot that suggests a linear association. **Also S-ID.B.6a, S-ID.C.7, S-ID.C.8, S-ID.C.9**

MP 1, MP 2, MP 3, MP 4

Objectives To write an equation of a trend line and of a line of best fit
To use a trend line and a line of best fit to make predictions

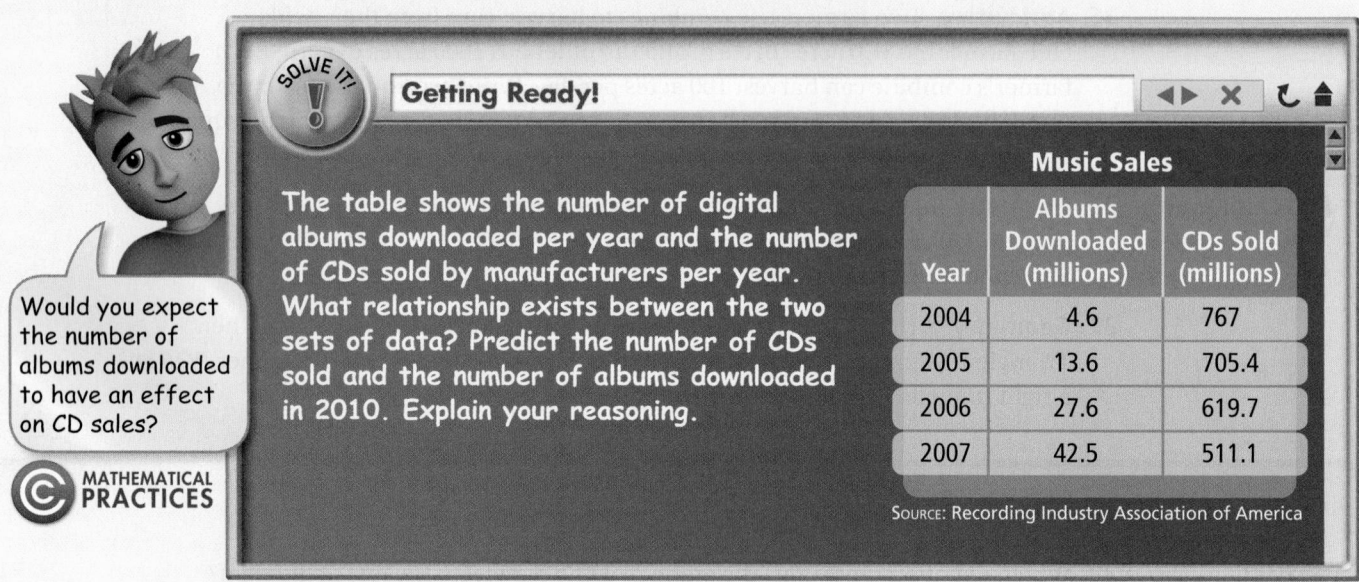

Would you expect the number of albums downloaded to have an effect on CD sales?

MATHEMATICAL PRACTICES

Getting Ready!

The table shows the number of digital albums downloaded per year and the number of CDs sold by manufacturers per year. What relationship exists between the two sets of data? Predict the number of CDs sold and the number of albums downloaded in 2010. Explain your reasoning.

Music Sales

Year	Albums Downloaded (millions)	CDs Sold (millions)
2004	4.6	767
2005	13.6	705.4
2006	27.6	619.7
2007	42.5	511.1

SOURCE: Recording Industry Association of America

In the Solve It, the number of albums downloaded per year and the number of CDs sold per year are related.

Essential Understanding You can determine whether two sets of numerical data are related by graphing them as ordered pairs. If the two sets of data are related, you may be able to use a line to estimate or predict values.

A **scatter plot** is a graph that relates two different sets of data by displaying them as ordered pairs. Most scatter plots are in the first quadrant of the coordinate plane because the data are usually positive numbers.

You can use scatter plots to find trends in data. The scatter plots below show the three types of relationships that two sets of data may have.

Lesson Vocabulary

- scatter plot
- positive correlation
- negative correlation
- no correlation
- trend line
- interpolation
- extrapolation
- line of best fit
- correlation coefficient
- causation

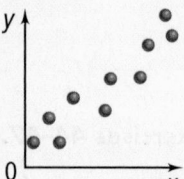

When y tends to increase as x increases, the two sets of data have a **positive correlation.**

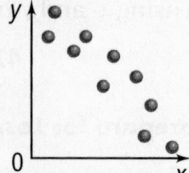

When y tends to decrease as x increases, the two sets of data have a **negative correlation.**

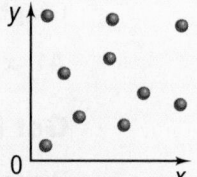

When x and y are not related, the two sets of data have **no correlation.**

 **Problem 1** Making a Scatter Plot and Describing Its Correlation

Temperature The table shows the altitude of an airplane and the temperature outside the plane.

Plane Altitude and Outside Temperature											
Altitude (m)	0	500	1000	1500	2000	2500	3000	3500	4000	4500	5000
Temperature (°F)	59.0	59.2	61.3	55.5	41.6	29.8	29.9	18.1	26.2	12.4	0.6

Think

The highest altitude is 5000 m. So a reasonable scale on the altitude axis is 0 to 5500 with every 1000 m labeled. You can use similar reasoning to label the temperature axis.

A **Make a scatter plot of the data.**

Treat the data as ordered pairs. For the altitude of 1500 m and the temperature of 55.5°F, plot (1500, 55.5).

B **What type of relationship does the scatter plot show?**

The temperature outside the plane tends to decrease as the altitude of the plane increases. So the data have a negative correlation.

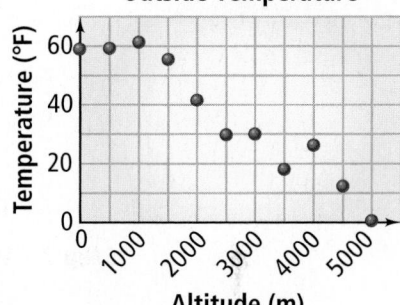

Got It? **1. a.** Make a scatter plot of the data in the table below. What type of relationship does the scatter plot show?

Gasoline Purchases								
Dollars Spent	10	11	9	10	13	5	8	4
Gallons Bought	2.5	2.8	2.3	2.6	3.3	1.3	2.2	1.1

b. Reasoning Consider the population of a city and the number of letters in the name of the city. Would you expect a *positive correlation*, a *negative correlation*, or *no correlation* between the two sets of data? Explain your reasoning.

When two sets of data have a positive or negative correlation, you can use a trend line to show the correlation more clearly. A **trend line** is a line on a scatter plot, drawn near the points, that shows a correlation.

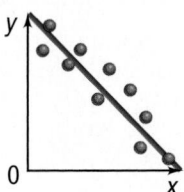

You can use a trend line to estimate a value between two known data values or to predict a value outside the range of known data values. **Interpolation** is estimating a value between two known values. **Extrapolation** is predicting a value outside the range of known values.

 **Problem 2** **Writing an Equation of a Trend Line**

Biology Make a scatter plot of the data at the right. What is the approximate weight of a 7-month-old panda?

Weight of a Panda	
Age (months)	Weight (lb)
1	2.5
2	7.6
3	12.5
4	17.1
6	24.3
8	37.9
10	49.2
12	54.9

Step 1 Make a scatter plot and draw a trend line. Estimate the coordinates of two points on the line.

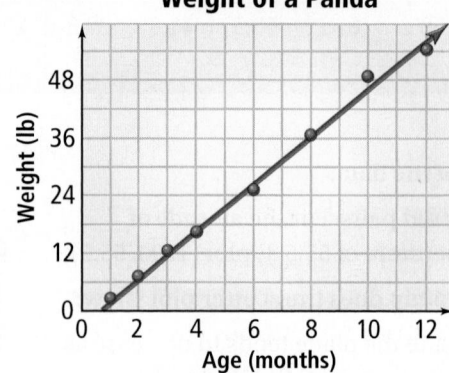

Two points on the trend line are (4, 17.1) and (8, 37.9).

Step 2 Write an equation of the trend line.

$$m = \frac{y_2 - y_1}{x_2 - x_1} = \frac{37.9 - 17.1}{8 - 4} = \frac{20.8}{4} = 5.2 \qquad \text{Find the slope of the trend line.}$$

$y - y_1 = m(x - x_1)$ Use point-slope form.

$y - 17.1 = 5.2(x - 4)$ Substitute 5.2 for m and (4, 17.1) for (x_1, y_1).

$y - 17.1 = 5.2x - 20.8$ Distributive Property

$y = 5.2x - 3.7$ Add 17.1 to each side.

Step 3 Estimate the weight of a 7-month-old panda.

$y = 5.2(7) - 3.7$ Substitute 7 for x.

$y = 32.7$ Simplify.

The weight of a 7-month-old panda is about 32.7 lb.

Plan

How do you draw an accurate trend line?
An accurate trend line should fit the data closely. There should be about the same number of points above the line as below it.

Think

How can you check the reasonableness of your answer?
Since $x = 7$ is visible on the graph, find its corresponding y-value. When $x = 7$, $y \approx 32.7$. So the estimate is reasonable.

  Got It? **2. a.** Make a scatter plot of the data below. Draw a trend line and write its equation. What is the approximate body length of a 7-month-old panda?

Body Length of a Panda								
Age (months)	1	2	3	4	5	6	8	9
Body Length (in.)	8.0	11.75	15.5	16.7	20.1	22.2	26.5	29.0

b. Reasoning Do you think you can use your model to extrapolate the body length of a 3-year-old panda? Explain.

The trend line that shows the relationship between two sets of data most accurately is called the **line of best fit.** A graphing calculator computes the equation of the line of best fit using a method called linear regression.

The graphing calculator also gives you the **correlation coefficient** r, a number from -1 to 1, that tells you how closely the equation models the data.

$r = -1$ $r = 0$ $r = 1$

strong negative correlation   no correlation   strong positive correlation

The nearer r is to 1 or -1, the more closely the data cluster around the line of best fit. If r is near 1, the data lie close to a line of best fit with positive slope. If r is near -1, the data lie close to a line of best fit with negative slope.

Problem 3   Finding the Line of Best Fit

College Tuition Use a graphing calculator to find the equation of the line of best fit for the data at the right. What is the correlation coefficient to three decimal places? Predict the cost of attending in the 2012–2013 academic year.

Average Tuition and Fees at Public 4-Year Colleges

Academic Year	Cost ($)
2000–2001	3508
2001–2002	3766
2002–2003	4098
2003–2004	4645
2004–2005	5126
2005–2006	5492
2006–2007	5836

SOURCE: The College Board

Step 1 Press **stat** . From the **EDIT** menu, choose **Edit**. Enter the years into L_1. Let $x = 2000$ represent academic year 2000–2001, $x = 2001$ represent 2001–2002, and so on. Enter the costs into L_2.

Step 2 Press **stat** . Choose **LinReg($ax + b$)** from the **CALC** menu. Press **enter** to find the equation of the line of best fit and the correlation coefficient. The calculator uses the form $y = ax + b$ for the equation.

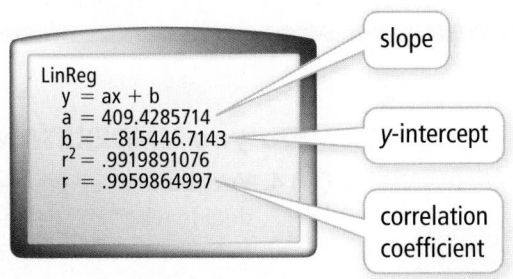

slope

y-intercept

correlation coefficient

Think

What does the value of the correlation coefficient mean?
The correlation coefficient of 0.996 is close to 1. So there is a strong positive correlation between the academic year and the cost of attending college.

Round to the nearest hundredth. The equation of the line of best fit is $y = 409.43x - 815,446.71$. The correlation coefficient is about 0.996.

Step 3 Predict the cost of attending in the 2012–2013 academic year.

$y = 409.43x - 815,446.71$ Use the equation of the line of best fit.

$y = 409.43(2012) - 815,446.71$ Substitute 2012 for x.

$y \approx 8326$ Simplify. Round to the nearest whole number.

The cost of attending a four-year public college in the 2012–2013 academic year is predicted to be about $8326.

Got It? **3. a.** Predict the cost of attending in the 2016–2017 academic year.

b. Reasoning What does the slope of the line of best fit in Problem 3 tell you about the rate of change in the cost?

Causation is when a change in one quantity causes a change in a second quantity. A correlation between quantities does not always imply causation.

 Problem 4 **Identifying Whether Relationships Are Causal**

In the following situations, is there likely to be a correlation? If so, does the correlation reflect a causal relationship? Explain.

Ⓐ the number of loaves of bread baked and the amount of flour used

There is a positive correlation and also a causal relationship. As the number of loaves of bread baked increases, the amount of flour used increases.

Ⓑ the number of mailboxes and the number of firefighters in a city

There is likely to be a positive correlation because both the number of mailboxes and the number of firefighters tend to increase as the population of a city increases. However, installing more mailboxes will not *cause* the number of firefighters to increase, so there is no causal relationship.

Think

Causal relationships always have a correlation. However, two data sets that have a correlation may not have a causal relationship.

Got It? **4.** In the following situations, is there likely to be a correlation? If so, does the correlation reflect a causal relationship? Explain.

a. the cost of a family's vacation and the size of their house

b. the time spent exercising and the number of Calories burned

---

 Lesson Check

Do you know HOW?

Use the table.

Average Maximum Daily Temperature in January for Northern Latitudes							
Latitude (° N)	35	33	30	25	43	40	39
Temperature (°F)	46	52	67	76	32	37	44

SOURCE: U.S. Department of Commerce

1. Make a scatter plot of the data. What type of relationship does the scatter plot show?

2. Draw a trend line and write its equation.

3. Predict the average maximum daily temperature in January at a latitude of 50° N.

Do you UNDERSTAND?  MATHEMATICAL PRACTICES

4. Vocabulary Given a set of data pairs, how would you decide whether to use interpolation or extrapolation to find a certain value?

5. Compare and Contrast How are a trend line and the line of best fit for a set of data pairs similar? How are they different?

6. Error Analysis Refer to the table below. A student says that the data have a negative correlation because as x decreases, y also decreases. What is the student's error?

x	10	7	5	4	1	0
y	1	0	−2	−4	−7	−9

Practice and Problem-Solving Exercises

MATHEMATICAL PRACTICES

 **Practice**

For each table, make a scatter plot of the data. Describe the type of correlation the scatter plot shows.

◀ **See Problem 1.**

7.

Jeans Sales				
Average Price ($)	21	28	36	40
Number Sold	130	112	82	65

8.

Gasoline Purchases					
Dollars Spent	10	11	9	8	13
Gallons Bought	2.6	3	2.4	2.2	3.5

Theme Parks Use the table below for Exercises 9 and 10.

◀ **See Problem 2.**

Attendance and Revenue at U.S. Theme Parks									
Year	1990	1992	1994	1996	1998	2000	2002	2004	2006
Attendance (millions)	253	267	267	290	300	317	324	328	335
Revenue (billions of dollars)	5.7	6.5	7.0	7.9	8.7	9.6	9.9	10.8	11.5

SOURCE: International Association of Amusement Parks and Attractions

9. Make a scatter plot of the data pairs (year, attendance). Draw a trend line and write its equation. Estimate the attendance at U.S. theme parks in 2005.

10. Make a scatter plot of the data pairs (year, revenue). Draw a trend line and write its equation. Predict the revenue at U.S. theme parks in 2012.

11. Entertainment Use a graphing calculator to find the equation of the line of best fit for the data in the table. Find the value of the correlation coefficient r to three decimal places. Then predict the number of movie tickets sold in the U.S. in 2014.

◀ **See Problem 3.**

Movie Tickets Sold in U.S. by Year										
Year	1998	1999	2000	2001	2002	2003	2004	2005	2006	2007
Tickets Sold (millions)	1289	1311	1340	1339	1406	1421	1470	1415	1472	1470

SOURCE: Motion Picture Association of America

In each situation, tell whether a correlation is likely. If it is, tell whether the correlation reflects a causal relationship. Explain your reasoning.

◀ **See Problem 4.**

12. the amount of time you study for a test and the score you receive

13. a person's height and the number of letters in the person's name

14. the shoe size and the salary of a teacher

15. the price of hamburger at a grocery store and the amount of hamburger sold

 **Apply**

© **16. Open-Ended** Describe three real-world situations: one with a positive correlation, one with a negative correlation, and one with no correlation.

17. Writing Give two data sets that are correlated but do *not* have a causal relationship.

18. Business During one month at a local deli, the amount of ham sold decreased as the amount of turkey sold increased. Is this an example of *positive correlation*, *negative correlation*, or *no correlation*?

19. Think About a Plan Students measured the diameters and circumferences of the tops of a variety of cylinders. Below are the data that they collected. Estimate the diameter of a cylinder with circumference 22 cm.

Cylinder Tops										
Diameter (cm)	3	3	5	6	8	8	9.5	10	10	12
Circumference (cm)	9.3	9.5	16	18.8	25	25.6	29.5	31.5	30.9	39.5

- How can you use a scatter plot to find an equation of a trend line?
- How can you use the equation of the trend line to make an estimate?

20. U.S. Population Use the data below.

Estimated Population of the United States (thousands)							
Year	2000	2001	2002	2003	2004	2005	2006
Male	138,482	140,079	141,592	142,937	144,467	145,973	147,512
Female	143,734	145,147	146,533	147,858	149,170	150,533	151,886

SOURCE: U.S. Census Bureau

a. Make a scatter plot of the data pairs (male population, female population).
b. Draw a trend line and write its equation.
c. Use your equation to predict the U.S. female population if the U.S. male population increases to 150,000,000.
d. Reasoning Consider a scatter plot of the data pairs (year, male population). Would it be reasonable to use this scatter plot to predict the U.S. male population in 2035? Explain your reasoning.

21. a. Graphing Calculator Use a graphing calculator to find the equation of the line of best fit for the data below. Let $x = 8$ represent 1998, $x = 9$ represent 1999, and so on.

U.S. Computer and Video Game Unit Sales										
Year	1998	1999	2000	2001	2002	2003	2004	2005	2006	2007
Unit Sales (millions)	152.4	184.5	196.3	210.3	225.8	240.9	249.5	229.5	241.6	267.9

SOURCE: The NPD Group/Retail Tracking Service

b. What is the slope of the line of best fit? What does the slope mean in terms of the number of computer and video game units sold?
c. What is the *y*-intercept of the line of best fit? What does the *y*-intercept mean in terms of the number of computer and video game units sold?

 **Challenge**

22. a. Make a scatter plot of the data below. Then find the equation of the line of best fit. Draw the line of best fit on your scatter plot.

Car Stopping Distances								
Speed (mi/h)	10	15	20	25	30	35	40	45
Stopping Distance (ft)	27	44	63	85	109	136	164	196

b. Use your equation to predict the stopping distance at 90 mi/h.

 c. Reasoning The actual stopping distance at 90 mi/h is close to 584 ft. Why do you think this distance is not close to your prediction?

d. Suppose you plot (90, 584) on your scatter plot. What effect would it have on the slope and y-intercept of the line of best fit you found in part (a)?

Standardized Test Prep

SAT/ACT

23. Suppose you survey each school in your state. What relationship would you expect between the number of students and the number of teachers in each school?

    Ⓐ positive correlation   Ⓒ no correlation

    Ⓑ negative correlation   Ⓓ none of the above

24. A horizontal line passes through $(5, -2)$. Which other point is also on the line?

    Ⓕ $(5, 2)$ Ⓖ $(-5, -2)$ Ⓗ $(-5, 2)$ Ⓘ $(5, 0)$

25. When 18 gal of water are pumped into an empty tank, the tank is filled to three fourths of its capacity. How many gallons of water does the tank hold?

    Ⓐ 12   Ⓑ 13.5   Ⓒ 18.5   Ⓓ 24

Short Response

26. The table shows the balance of a student's bank account at various times. Estimate how much money is in the student's bank account in Week 6. Justify your answer.

Weekly Account Balance					
Week	1	3	4	7	9
Account Balance	$35	$68	$85	$105	$136

Mixed Review

Write an equation of the line in slope-intercept form that passes through the given point and is parallel to the graph of the given equation.

◀ See Lesson 5-6.

27. $y = 5x + 1$; $(2, -3)$ **28.** $y = -x - 9$; $(0, 5)$ **29.** $2x + 3y = 9$; $(-1, 4)$

Get Ready! To prepare for Lesson 5-8, do Exercises 30–33.

Find each absolute value.

◀ See Lesson 1-5.

30. $|2 - 7|$ **31.** $|7 - 7|$ **32.** $|56 - 38|$ **33.** $|-24 + 12|$

Using Residuals

Common Core State Standards

S-ID.B.6b Informally assess the fit of a function by plotting and analyzing residuals.

MP 7

In Lesson 5-7, you learned how to assess the line of best fit by using the correlation coefficient r. In this activity you will learn how to determine whether the best linear function is a good fit for the data. As you learn different types of functions in future chapters, residual plots will help you analyze the fit of other models.

A **residual** is the difference between the y-value of a data point and the corresponding y-value of a model for the data set.

You can find a residual by calculating $y - \hat{y}$, where y represents the y-value of the data set and $\hat{y}$ represents the corresponding y-value predicted from the model.

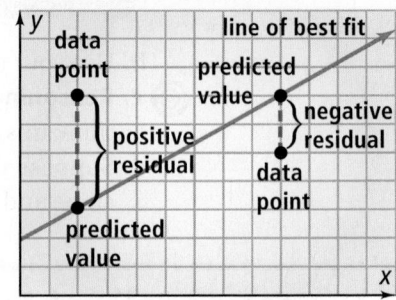

Activity

The linear function $\hat{y} = 2.3x + 33.4$ models the data shown below.

Mean Heights of Boys Ages 5 to 13

Age (yr)	5	6	7	8	9	10	11	12	13
Height (in.)	44.5	46.9	49.7	52.2	54.4	55.7	58.5	60.9	63.1

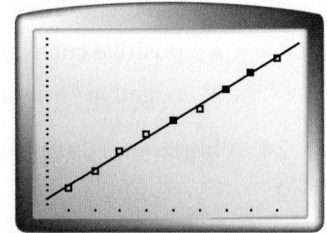

1. Complete a table like the one started below to calculate the residuals.

Age (x)	Height (y)	Predicted value $\hat{y} = 2.3x + 33.4$	Residual $y - \hat{y}$
5	44.5	$2.3(5) + 33.4 = 44.9$	$44.5 - 44.9 = -0.4$
⋮	⋮	⋮	⋮
13	■	■	■

You can plot each of the points $(x, y - \hat{y})$ on a coordinate plane, and analyze the residual plot to assess whether the function is a good fit for the data. For a good fit, the points appear to have a random pattern.

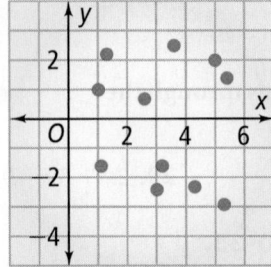

There is no apparent pattern in the residual plot. This indicates that the model function is a good fit for the data.

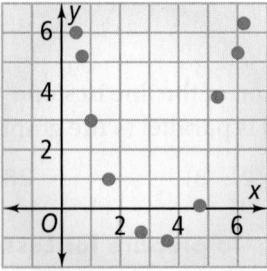

The points in the residual plot form a pattern. This indicates that the model function is not a good fit for the data.

2. Plot the points $(x, y - \hat{y})$ on a coordinate plane similar to the one shown.

3. Do the points appear to follow a pattern?

Ⓒ **4. Writing** Explain how you can use the residual plot to determine whether the model function is a good fit for the data.

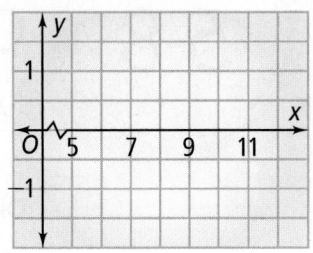

Exercises

5. You model two data sets using linear models. The resulting residual plots are shown below. Which residual plot indicates that the linear model is a good fit for the data? Justify your answer.

Plot A

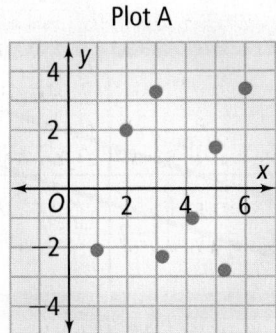

Plot B

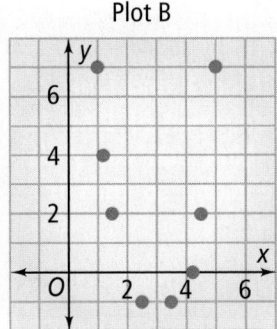

6. Use a graphing calculator to determine the line of best fit for the data set below. Then use a residual plot to determine whether the line of best fit is a good model. Explain.

Latitude and Temperature in Selected Cities

City	Latitude (°N)	Mean High Temperature in April (°F)
Lagos, Nigeria	6	89
San Juan, Puerto Rico	18	84
Calcutta, India	23	97
Cairo, Egypt	30	83
Tokyo, Japan	35	63
Rome, Italy	42	68
Belgrade, Serbia	45	45
London, England	52	56
Copenhagen, Denmark	56	50
Moscow, Russia	56	47

5-8 Graphing Absolute Value Functions

© **Common Core State Standards**

F-BF.B.3 Identify the effect on the graph of replacing $f(x)$ by $f(x) + k$, $kf(x)$, $f(kx)$, and $f(x + k)$ for specific values of k (both positive and negative); find the value of k given the graphs . . . **Also F-IF.C.7b**

MP 1, MP 2, MP 3, MP 4

Objectives   To graph an absolute value function
    To translate the graph of an absolute value function

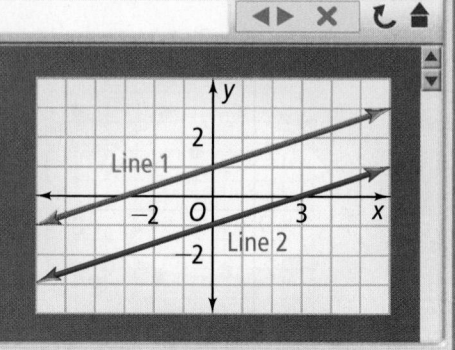

SOLVE IT!

Getting Ready!

Write the equations of Line 1 and Line 2. How can you transform the equation of Line 1 into the equation of Line 2? How can you slide Line 1 in the coordinate plane so that it becomes Line 2? Explain.

Remember what you have learned about families of functions.

In the Solve It you described how one line could be shifted to result in a second line. You can use a similar method to graph *absolute value functions*. An **absolute value function** has a V-shaped graph that opens up or down. The parent function for the family of absolute value functions is $y = |x|$.

A **translation** is a shift of a graph horizontally, vertically, or both. The result is a graph of the same size and shape, but in a different position.

Lesson Vocabulary
• absolute value function
• piecewise function
• step function
• translation

Essential Understanding   You can quickly graph absolute value equations by shifting the graph of $y = |x|$.

Plan

How can you compare the graphs?
Look for the characteristics that you've studied with other graphs, such as shape, size, or individual points.

© **Problem 1**   **Describing Translations**

Below are the graphs of $y = |x|$ and $y = |x| - 2$. How are the graphs related?

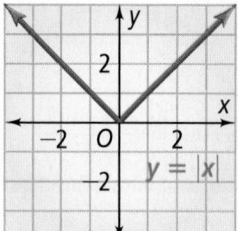

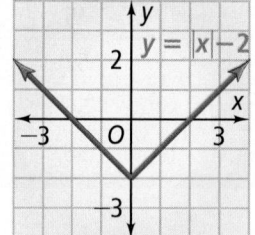

The graphs have the same shape. Notice each point on $y = |x| - 2$ is 2 units lower than the corresponding point on $y = |x|$. The graph of $y = |x| - 2$ is the graph of $y = |x|$ translated down 2 units.

Got It? **1. a.** How is the graph at the right related to the graph of
$y = |x|$?

b. Reasoning What are the domain and range of each
function in Problem 1?

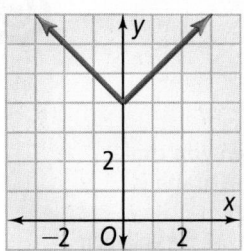

The graph of $y = |x| + k$ is a translation of $y = |x|$. Let k be a positive number. Then
$y = |x| + k$ translates the graph of $y = |x|$ up k units, while $y = |x| - k$ translates the
graph of $y = |x|$ down k units.

 Problem 2 **Graphing a Vertical Translation**

What is the graph of $y = |x| + 2$?

Know
- The equation of an absolute value function
- The graph of $y = |x|$

Need
The graph of the function

Plan
Identify the direction and amount of the translation. Translate the y-intercept point and one point on each side of it. Draw the graph.

Think

Why start with the graph of $y = |x|$?
Since $y = |x|$ is the parent function of $y = |x| + 2$, you can start with the graph of $y = |x|$ and shift it up.

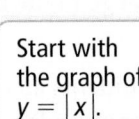 Start with the graph of $y = |x|$.

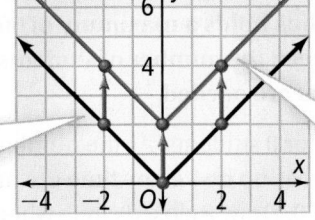 Draw the graph of $y = |x| + 2$ by translating the graph of $y = |x|$ up 2 units.

 Got It? **2.** What is the graph of $y = |x| - 7$?

The graphs below show what happens when you graph $y = |x + 2|$ and $y = |x - 2|$.

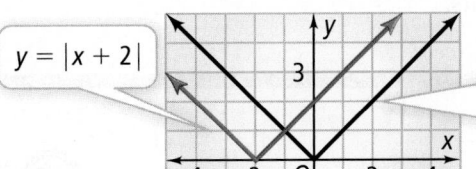

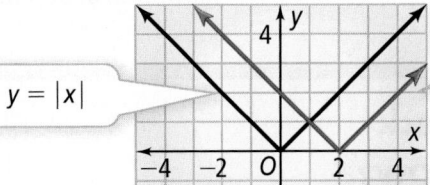

For a positive number h, $y = |x + h|$ translates the graph of $y = |x|$ left h units, and
$y = |x - h|$ translates the graph of $y = |x|$ right h units.

What is the graph of $y = |x + 5|$?

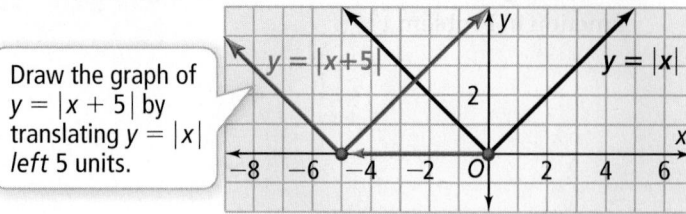

Draw the graph of $y = |x + 5|$ by translating $y = |x|$ *left* 5 units.

 Got It? 3. What is the graph of $y = |x - 5|$?

The absolute value function is an example of a piecewise function. A **piecewise function** is a function that has different rules for different parts of its domain. For example, when $x \geq 0$, $|x| = x$. When $x < 0$, $|x| = -x$. Another example of a piecewise function is a step function. A **step function** is a function that pairs every number in an interval with a single value. The graph of a step function can look like the steps of a staircase.

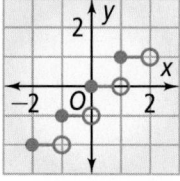

Each piece of the graph is a horizontal segment that is missing its right endpoint, indicated by an open circle.

Transportation A school will charter buses so that the student body can attend a football game. Each bus holds a maximum of 60 students. Make a graph that models the relationship between the number of students x that go to the game by bus and the number of buses y that are needed.

You will need 0 buses for 0 students. As the number of students increases, the number of buses goes up by 1 every time the number of students exceeds a multiple of 60. Draw a closed circle when the endpoints are part of the graph, and then draw an open point when they are not.

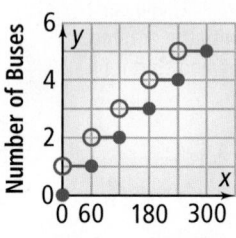

 Got It? 4. Make a graph that models the relationship between the number of students x that go to the game by bus and the number of buses y that are needed if each bus holds a maximum of 50 students.

Lesson Check

Do you know HOW?

1. How is the graph of $y = |x| - 8$ different from the graph of $y = |x|$? How is it the same?

2. What is the equation for the translation of $y = |x|$ 9 units up?

3. What is the graph of $y = |x + 7|$?

Do you UNDERSTAND?

© **4. Compare and Contrast** How are the graphs of $y = |x| - 4$ and $y = |x - 4|$ the same? How are they different?

© **5. Error Analysis** A student is graphing the equation $y = |x - 10|$ and translates the graph of $y = |x|$ 10 units left. Describe the student's error.

Practice and Problem-Solving Exercises

A Practice

Describe how each graph is related to the graph of $y = |x|$.

See Problem 1.

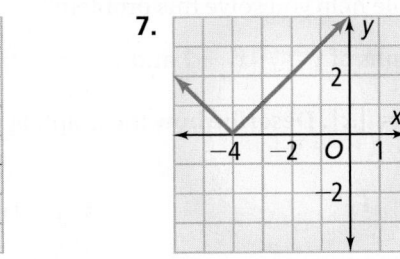

6.   7.   8.

Graph each function by translating $y = |x|$.

See Problem 2.

9. $y = |x| - 3$ 10. $y = |x| + 7$ 11. $y = |x| + 3$

12. $y = |x| - 6$ 13. $y = |x| + 6$ 14. $y = |x| - 2.5$

Graph each function by translating $y = |x|$.

See Problem 3.

15. $y = |x - 3|$ 16. $y = |x + 3|$ 17. $y = |x - 1|$

18. $y = |x + 6|$ 19. $y = |x - 7|$ 20. $y = |x + 2.5|$

21. **Postage** The table lists postage for letters weighing as much as 3 oz. You want to mail a letter that weighs 2.7 oz. Graph the step function. How much will you pay in postage?

See Problem 4.

First-Class Postage

Weight x	Price y
0 < Weight < 1 oz	$.44
1 oz ≤ Weight < 2 oz	$.61
2 oz ≤ Weight ≤ 3 oz	$.78

B Apply

At the right is the graph of $y = -|x|$. Graph each function by translating $y = -|x|$.

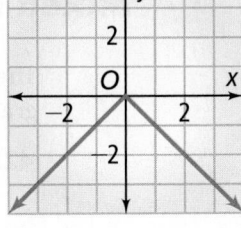

22. $y = -|x| + 3$ 23. $y = -|x| - 3$

24. $y = -|x + 3|$ 25. $y = -|x - 3|$

Write an equation for each translation of $y = -|x|$.

26. 2 units up   27. 2.25 units left

28. 15 units down   29. 4 units right

30. **Writing** Explain how the relationship between $y = |x|$ and $y = |x| + k$ is similar to the relationship between $y = mx$ and $y = mx + b$.

31. **Think About a Plan** What point(s) do the graphs of $y = |x - 2|$ and $y = |x + 4|$ have in common?
- How are these graphs related?
- Could a graph or a table help you solve this problem?

32. What point(s) do the graphs of $y = -|x| + 7$ and $y = |x - 3|$ have in common?

Graph each translation of $y = |x|$. Describe how the graph is related to the graph of $y = |x|$.

33. $y = |x - 1| + 2$ 34. $y = |x + 2| - 1$

35. **a.** Graph $y = |x - 2| + 3$.
    b. The *vertex* of an absolute value function is the point at which its graph changes direction. What is the vertex of the graph of $y = |x - 2| + 3$?
    c. Reasoning What relationship do you see between the vertex and the equation? What is the vertex of the graph of $y = |x - h| + k$?

 **Challenge**

36. **a.** Graph $y = |2x|$ by making a table of values.
    b. Translate $y = |2x|$ to graph $y = |2x| + 3$.
    c. Translate $y = |2x|$ to graph $y = |2(x - 1)|$.
    d. Translate $y = |2x|$ to graph $y = |2(x - 1)| + 3$.

37. Graph $y = -|x + 4| - 7$.

Standardized Test Prep

GRIDDED RESPONSE

SAT/ACT

38. For $f(x) = 5x - 7$, what value of x gives $f(x) = -3$?

39. What is the slope of the line at the right?

40. What is the value of $f(x) = x^2 - 4x + 6$ when $x = -3$?

41. What is the x-intercept of the line $y = -4x + 2$?

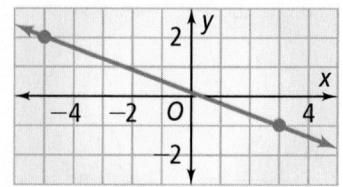

Mixed Review

The data below follow a linear model. Write an equation of a trend line or use a graphing calculator to find an equation of the line of best fit.   ◀ See Lesson 5-7.

42.

Year	1	2	3	4
Price	$5.30	$5.57	$5.82	$6.05

43.

Ounces	8	12	16	20
Calories	100	151	202	250

Get Ready! To prepare for Lesson 6-1, do Exercises 44–47.

Graph each equation.   ◀ See Lesson 5-3.

44. $y = 2x - 1$ 45. $y = -3x + 5$ 46. $y = \frac{1}{3}x + 2$ 47. $y = -\frac{5}{2}x - 7$

Characteristics of Absolute Value Graphs

© Common Core
State Standards

F-IF.C.7b Graph square root, cube root, and piecewise-defined functions, including step functions and absolute value functions.

MP 7

In previous lessons you explored characteristics of linear graphs. Here you will explore characteristics of absolute value graphs of the form $y = a|x - h| + k$.

For a linear graph you can identify the x- and y-intercepts, the domain and range, and the slope. For an absolute value graph, you can also identify the direction the graph opens and the *vertex*. The vertex of an absolute value graph is the point at which the graph changes direction. The graph of $y = a|x - h| + k$ has vertex (h, k).

The graph of an absolute value function will always have one y-intercept, but it can have zero, one, or two x-intercepts. An absolute value graph has a different slope for each *branch*. The branches are the two rays on either side of the vertex.

Example

Graph $y = |x + 1| - 2$. What are the slope of each branch, the x- and y-intercepts, the vertex, and the domain and range?

Step 1 Plot the vertex $(-1, -2)$.

Step 2 Use the equation to find a point on either side of the vertex.

Step 3 Draw the two branches of the graph.

The domain is all real numbers. The range is all real numbers greater than or equal to -2.

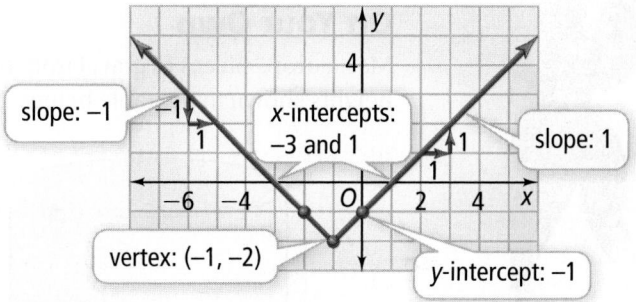

slope: −1

x-intercepts: −3 and 1

slope: 1

vertex: (−1, −2)

y-intercept: −1

Exercises

© **1.** **a.** Graph $y = -|x - 3| - 4$, $y = |x - 3| - 4$, $y = -2|x + 3| - 4$, and $y = 2|x + 3| - 4$.

   b. Which graphs open up and which graphs open down?

   c. Reasoning How does the sign of a affect the direction the graph opens?

   d. What are the slopes of the left and right branches of each graph?

   e. Reasoning How does the slope of the left branch relate to the slope of the right branch? How does a relate to the slope of the branches?

© **2.** **a.** Graph $y = -2|x - 1| + 4$.

   b. What is the vertex of the graph?

   c. What are the domain and range of the function?

   d. What are the x- and y-intercepts?

   e. Reasoning How can you use the vertex and the sign of a to determine the range of the absolute value function?

5

Pull It **All Together**

Completing the Performance Task

Look back at your results from the Apply What You've Learned sections in Lessons 5-1 and 5-4. Use the work you did to complete the following.

> To solve these problems you will pull together many concepts and skills that you have studied about linear functions.

1. Solve the problem in the Task Description on page 293 by predicting the number of marbles you need to drop in the glass to raise the water level to the top of the glass. Show all your work and explain each step of your solution.

2. **Reflect** Choose one of the Mathematical Practices below and explain how you applied it in your work on the Performance Task.

   MP 1: Make sense of problems and persevere in solving them.

   MP 2: Reason abstractly and quantitatively.

   MP 4: Model with mathematics.

On Your Own

Maria drops pieces of gravel from her driveway into a glass of water and records the water heights shown in the table below. The pieces of gravel vary in size.

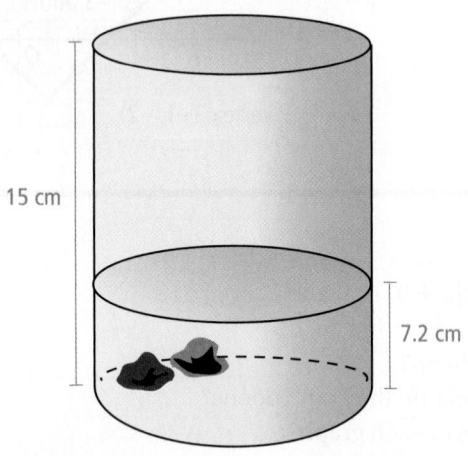

15 cm

7.2 cm

Pieces of Gravel, x	Height of Water (cm), y
2	7.2
6	8.5
11	9.0
13	9.8
16	10.0
20	11.4

a. Predict the number of pieces of gravel Maria needs to drop in the glass to raise the water level to the top of the glass. Justify your prediction.

b. Do you think your prediction from part (a) will be more or less accurate than the prediction your made when marbles were being dropped into a glass? Explain.

Connecting **BIG** ideas and Answering the Essential Questions

1 Proportionality
In the graph of a line, the ratio for the slope indicates the rate of change.

Rate of Change and Slope (Lesson 5-1)
$$\text{slope} = \frac{\text{rise}}{\text{run}} = \frac{y_2 - y_1}{x_2 - x_1}$$

Parallel and Perpendicular Lines (Lesson 5-6)
Parallel lines have the same slope. The product of the slopes of perpendicular lines is -1.

2 Functions
There are several forms for the equation of a line. Each form communicates different information. For instance, from the point-slope form, you can determine a point and the slope of a line.

Slope-Intercept Form (Lesson 5-3)
$$y = mx + b$$

Point-Slope Form (Lesson 5-4)
$$y - y_1 = m(x - x_1)$$

Standard Form (Lesson 5-5)
$$Ax + By = C$$

3 Modeling
You can model the trend of the real-world data in a scatter plot with the equation of a line. You can use the equation to estimate or to make predictions.

Scatter Plots and Trend Lines (Lesson 5-7)
The trend line that shows the relationship between two sets of data most accurately is called the line of best fit.

Chapter Vocabulary

- absolute value function (p. 346)
- direct variation (p. 301)
- extrapolation (p. 337)
- interpolation (p. 337)
- inverse function (p. 329)
- linear equation (p. 308)
- line of best fit (p. 339)
- negative correlation (p. 336)
- no correlation (p. 337)
- opposite reciprocals (p. 331)
- parallel lines (p. 330)
- perpendicular lines (p. 331)
- piecewise function (p. 348)
- point-slope form (p. 315)
- positive correlation (p. 336)
- rate of change (p. 294)
- residual (p. 344)
- scatter plot (p. 336)
- slope (p. 295)
- slope-intercept form (p. 308)
- standard form of a linear equation (p. 322)
- step function (p. 348)
- trend line (p. 337)
- x-intercept (p. 322)
- y-intercept (p. 308)

Choose the vocabulary term that correctly completes the sentence.

1. Estimating a value between two known values in a data set is called ? .

2. The slope of a line models the ? of a function.

3. The form of a linear equation that shows the slope and one point is the ? .

4. Two lines are perpendicular when their slopes are ? .

5. The line that most accurately models data in a scatter plot is the ? .

5-1 Rate of Change and Slope

Quick Review

Rate of change shows the relationship between two changing quantities. The **slope** of a line is the ratio of the vertical change (the rise) to the horizontal change (the run).

$$\text{slope} = \frac{\text{rise}}{\text{run}} = \frac{y_2 - y_1}{x_2 - x_1}$$

The slope of a horizontal line is 0, and the slope of a vertical line is undefined.

Example

What is the slope of the line that passes through the points (1, 12) and (6, 22)?

$$\text{slope} = \frac{y_2 - y_1}{x_2 - x_1} = \frac{22 - 12}{6 - 1} = \frac{10}{5} = 2$$

Exercises

Find the slope of the line that passes through each pair of points.

6. (2, 2), (3, 1) **7.** (4, 2), (0, 2)

8. (−1, 2), (0, 5) **9.** (−3, −2), (−3, 2)

Find the slope of each line.

10.

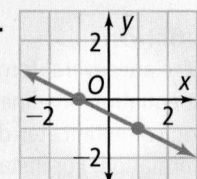

11.

5-2 Direct Variation

Quick Review

A function represents a **direct variation** if it has the form $y = kx$, where $k \neq 0$. The coefficient k is the **constant of variation**.

Example

Suppose y varies directly with x, and $y = 15$ when $x = 5$. Write a direct variation equation that relates x and y. What is the value of y when $x = 9$?

$y = kx$	Start with the general form of a direct variation.
$15 = k(5)$	Substitute 5 for x and 15 for y.
$3 = k$	Divide each side by 5 to solve for k.
$y = 3x$	Write an equation. Substitute 3 for k in $y = kx$.

The equation $y = 3x$ relates x and y. When $x = 9$, $y = 3(9)$, or 27.

Exercises

Suppose y varies directly with x. Write a direct variation equation that relates x and y. Then find the value of y when $x = 7$.

12. $y = 8$ when $x = -4$. **13.** $y = 15$ when $x = 6$.

14. $y = 3$ when $x = 9$. **15.** $y = -4$ when $x = 4$.

For the data in each table, tell whether y varies directly with x. If it does, write an equation for the direct variation.

16.

x	y
−1	−6
2	3
5	12
9	24

17.

x	y
−3	7.5
−1	2.5
2	−5
5	−12.5

5-3, 5-4, and 5-5 Forms of Linear Equations

Quick Review

The graph of a linear equation is a line. You can write a linear equation in different forms.

The **slope-intercept form** of a linear equation is $y = mx + b$, where m is the slope and b is the **y-intercept**.

The **point-slope form** of a linear equation is $y - y_1 = m(x - x_1)$, where m is the slope and (x_1, y_1) is a point on the line.

The **standard form** of a linear equation is $Ax + By = C$, where A, B, and C are real numbers, and A and B are not both zero.

Example

What is an equation of the line that has slope -4 and passes through the point $(-1, 7)$?

$y - y_1 = m(x - x_1)$	Use point-slope form.
$y - 7 = -4(x - (-1))$	Substitute $(-1, 7)$ for (x_1, y_1) and -4 for m.
$y - 7 = -4(x + 1)$	Simplify inside grouping symbols.

An equation of the line is $y - 7 = -4(x + 1)$.

Exercises

Write an equation in slope-intercept form of the line that passes through the given points.

18. $(-3, 4), (1, 4)$ **19.** $(3, -2), (6, 1)$

Write an equation of each line.

20. 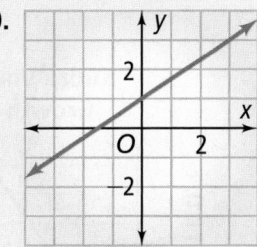   **21.**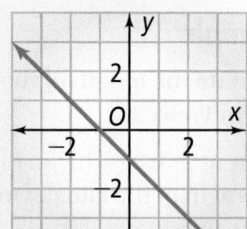

Graph each equation.

22. $y = 4x - 3$ **23.** $y = 2$

24. $y + 3 = 2(x - 1)$ **25.** $x + 4y = 10$

5-6 Parallel and Perpendicular Lines

Quick Review

Parallel lines are lines in the same plane that never intersect. Two lines are **perpendicular** if they intersect to form right angles.

Example

Are the graphs of $y = \frac{4}{3}x + 5$ and $y = -\frac{3}{4}x + 2$ *parallel*, *perpendicular*, or *neither*? Explain.

The slope of the graph of $y = \frac{4}{3}x + 5$ is $\frac{4}{3}$.

The slope of the graph of $y = -\frac{3}{4}x + 2$ is $-\frac{3}{4}$.

$$\frac{4}{3}\left(-\frac{3}{4}\right) = -1$$

The slopes are opposite reciprocals, so the graphs are perpendicular.

Exercises

Write an equation of the line that passes through the given point and is parallel to the graph of the given equation.

26. $(2, -1); y = 5x - 2$ **27.** $(0, -5); y = 9x$

Determine whether the graphs of the two equations are *parallel*, *perpendicular*, or *neither*. Explain.

28. $y = 6x + 2$ **29.** $2x - 5y = 0$
     $18x - 3y = 15$ $y + 3 = \frac{5}{2}x$

Write an equation of the line that passes through the given point and is perpendicular to the graph of the given equation.

30. $(3, 5); y = -3x + 7$ **31.** $(4, 10); y = 8x - 1$

5-7 Scatter Plots and Trend Lines

Quick Review

A **scatter plot** displays two sets of data as ordered pairs. A **trend line** for a scatter plot shows the correlation between the two sets of data. The most accurate trend line is the **line of best fit**. To estimate or predict values on a scatter plot, you can use **interpolation** or **extrapolation**.

Example

Estimate the length of the kudzu vine in Week 3.

When $w = 3$, $\ell \approx 10$. So in Week 3, the length of the kudzu vine was about 10 ft.

Kudzu Vine Growth

Predict the length of the kudzu vine in Week 11.

$\ell = 3.5w$ Use the equation of the trend line.

$\ell = 3.5(11)$ Substitute 11 for w.

$\ell = 38.5$ Simplify.

The length of the vine in Week 11 will be about 38.5 ft.

Exercises

Describe the type of correlation the scatter plot shows.

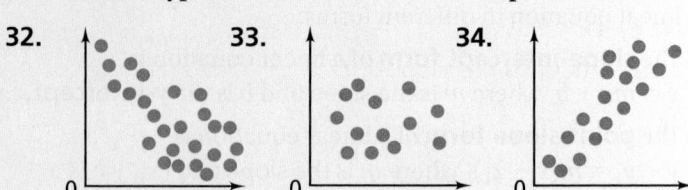

32.   **33.**   **34.**

35. a. Make a scatter plot of the data below.

Heights and Arm Spans						
Height (m)	1.5	1.8	1.7	2.0	1.7	2.1
Arm Span (m)	1.4	1.7	1.7	1.9	1.6	2.0

b. Write an equation of a reasonable trend line or use a graphing calculator to find the equation of the line of best fit.

c. Estimate the arm span of someone who is 1.6 m tall.

d. Predict the arm span of someone who is 2.2 m tall.

5-8 Graphing Absolute Value Functions

Quick Review

The graph of an **absolute value function** is a V-shaped graph that opens upward or downward.

A **translation** shifts a graph either vertically, horizontally, or both. To graph an absolute value function, you can translate $y = |x|$.

Example

Graph the absolute value function $y = |x - 4|$.

Start with the graph of $y = |x|$. Translate the graph right 4 units.

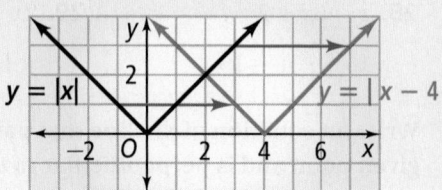

Exercises

Graph each function by translating $y = |x|$.

36. $y = |x| + 2$ **37.** $y = |x| - 7$

38. $y = |x + 3|$ **39.** $y = |x - 5|$

40. The table below shows the income tax for a single person's monthly income. Graph the step function for this information.

Tax Rates for Single Persons

If Monthly Income Is . . .	Computed Tax is . . .
$0–$504.00	0%
$504.01–$869.00	10%
$869.01–$3,004.00	15%
$3,004.01–$5,642.00	25%
$5,642.01–$7,038.00	30%

Do you know HOW?

Write an equation in slope-intercept form of each line.

1. 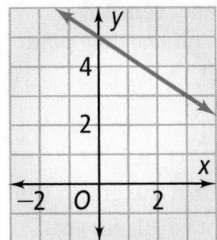   2.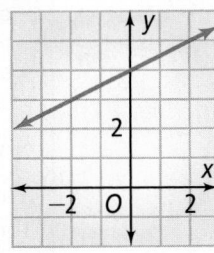

Write an equation in point-slope form of the line through the given point and with the given slope.

3. $(5, 1); m = \frac{1}{3}$

4. $(-2, 3); m = -2$

Write each equation in standard form using integers.

5. $y = \frac{3}{4}x + 5$

6. $y + 4 = \frac{1}{3}(x + 6)$

Graph each equation.

7. $y = 4x - 3$

8. $y = 7$

9. $y + 3 = \frac{1}{2}(x + 2)$

10. $-3x + 5y = 15$

Determine whether each equation represents a direct variation. If it does, find the constant of variation.

11. $2x + 3y = 0$

12. $4x + 6y = 3$

Graph each function.

13. $y = |x - 4|$

14. $y = |x| + 3$

15. **Pet Grooming** You start a pet grooming service. You spend $30 on supplies. You plan to charge $5 to groom each pet.
   a. Write an equation to relate your profit y to the number of pets x you groom.
   b. Graph the equation. What are the x- and y-intercepts?

16. Make a scatter plot and draw a trend line for the data in the table. Interpolate or extrapolate to estimate the number of inventors applying for patents in 2006 and in 2015.

Number of Inventors Applying for Patents

Year	Inventors
1999	22,052
2001	20,588
2003	18,462
2005	14,039
2007	13,748

SOURCE: U.S. Patent Office

17. What is an equation of the line parallel to $y = -x + 1$ and through $(4, 4)$?

18. What is an equation of the line perpendicular to $y = -x - 2$ and through $(-2, 4)$?

Do you UNDERSTAND?

19. **Writing** How are lines of best fit and other trend lines used with scatter plots?

20. **Open-Ended** Write an equation whose graph is parallel to the graph of $y = 0.5x - 10$.

21. **Compare and Contrast** Is an equation that represents a direct variation a type of linear equation? Explain.

22. **Vocabulary** What does it mean when a line of best fit has a correlation coefficient close to 1?

23. **Reasoning** How many lines can you draw that are parallel to the line and through the point shown at the right? Explain.

Common Core Cumulative Standards Review

 **ASSESSMENT**

TIPS FOR SUCCESS

Some questions on standardized tests ask you to use a graph. Read the sample question at the right. Then follow the tips to answer it.

What is an equation of the line shown below?

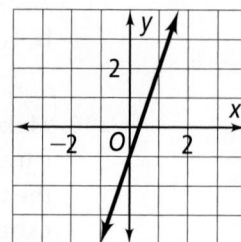

Ⓐ $y = \frac{1}{3}x - 1$ Ⓒ $y = 3x - 1$

Ⓑ $y = \frac{1}{3}x + \frac{1}{2}$ Ⓓ $y = 3x + \frac{1}{2}$

TIP 1

Identifying the y-intercept may help eliminate some possibilities.

TIP 2

Find the slope by using the point that represents the y-intercept and another point on the line.

Think It Through

You can see from the graph that the y-intercept is −1. So you can eliminate choices B and D. To get from $(0, -1)$ to $(1, 2)$, move 3 units up and 1 unit to the right. The slope is $\frac{3}{1} = 3$. So an equation is $y = 3x - 1$. The correct answer is C.

Vocabulary Builder

As you solve test items, you must understand the meanings of mathematical terms. Choose the correct term to complete each sentence.

A. The (*dependent, independent*) variable provides the output values of a function.

B. The set of all possible values for the dependent variable is called the (*domain, range*).

C. The (*slope, y-intercept*) of a line is determined by the ratio $\frac{\text{rise}}{\text{run}}$.

D. An (*equation, inequality*) is a math sentence that shows the relationship between two quantities that may not have the same value.

E. (*Parallel, Perpendicular*) lines are lines in the same plane that never intersect.

Selected Response

Read each question. Then write the letter of the correct answer on your paper.

1. Which is an equation of a line with slope 3?

Ⓐ $y = 3x - 4$ Ⓒ $y = 4x - 3$

Ⓑ $y = -3x + 3$ Ⓓ $y = -3x - 5$

2. Ben has a cell phone plan where he pays $12 per month plus $.10 per minute of talk time. The equation $y = 0.10x + 12$ can be used to find his monthly phone bill y given the number of minutes x he spends talking. Which set or inequality represents a reasonable range of the function?

Ⓕ $\{0, 12\}$ Ⓗ $12 \leq y$

Ⓖ $0 \leq y \leq 12$ Ⓘ $0 \leq y$

3. What is the slope of the line at the right?

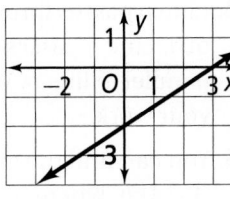

Ⓐ -2

Ⓑ $\frac{2}{3}$

Ⓒ $\frac{3}{2}$

Ⓓ 3

4. Tim uses the function $g = 0.05d$ to find how much money g he needs for gasoline based on the number of miles d he travels. Which statement is true?

Ⓕ The number of miles Tim travels depends on how much money he needs for gasoline.

Ⓖ The number of miles Tim travels depends on the price of a gallon of gasoline.

Ⓗ The amount of money Tim needs for gasoline depends on the number of miles he travels.

Ⓘ The amount of money Tim needs for gasoline is constant.

5. The perimeter P of a rectangle can be found using the formula $P = 2(\ell + w)$, where ℓ represents the length and w represents the width. Which equation represents the width in terms of P and ℓ?

Ⓐ $w = 2(P - \ell)$ Ⓒ $w = 2P - \ell$

Ⓑ $w = \dfrac{P - \ell}{2}$ Ⓓ $w = \dfrac{P}{2} - \ell$

6. Use the graph at the right. If the y-intercept increases by 2 and the slope remains the same, what will the x-intercept be?

Ⓕ -3 Ⓗ 1

Ⓖ -2 Ⓘ 4

7. The U.S. Mint charges \$25 for a limited edition coin, plus a \$6 shipping charge. The cost c of purchasing n coins can be found using the function $c = 25n + 6$. There is a limit of 5 coins per purchase. What is a reasonable domain of the function?

Ⓐ $\{5\}$

Ⓑ $\{1, 2, 3, 4, 5\}$

Ⓒ $\{25, 50, 75, 100, 125\}$

Ⓓ $\{31, 56, 81, 106, 131\}$

8. A financial advisor collected data on the amount of money earned and saved each year by people ages 20–29. The results are shown in the scatter plot. Which best describes the slope of the line of best fit?

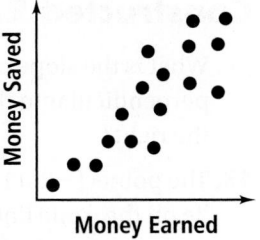

Ⓕ positive   Ⓗ zero

Ⓖ negative   Ⓘ undefined

9. Which graph shows a line with slope $\frac{1}{3}$ and y-intercept -1?

Ⓐ 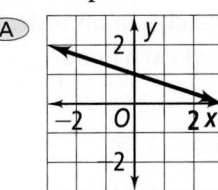   Ⓒ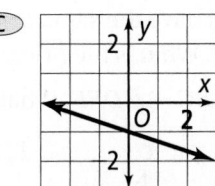

Ⓑ 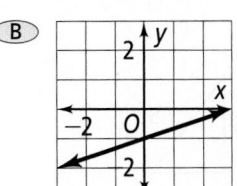   Ⓓ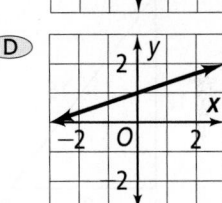

10. The graph shows the relationship between the total price of tomatoes and the number of pounds of tomatoes purchased. Which statement is true?

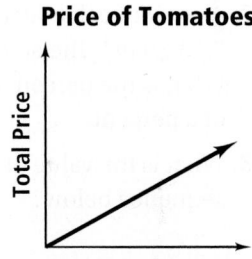

Price of Tomatoes

Ⓕ The number of pounds depends on the total price.

Ⓖ The number of tomatoes depends on the total price.

Ⓗ The total price depends on the number of pounds.

Ⓘ The number of tomatoes depends on the number of pounds.

11. A line passes through the point $(2, 1)$ and has a slope of $-\frac{3}{5}$. What is an equation of the line?

Ⓐ $y - 1 = -\frac{3}{5}(x - 2)$

Ⓑ $y - 1 = -\frac{5}{3}(x - 2)$

Ⓒ $y - 2 = -\frac{3}{5}(x - 1)$

Ⓓ $y - 2 = -\frac{5}{3}(x - 1)$

Constructed Response

12. What is the slope of a line that is perpendicular to the line shown at the right?

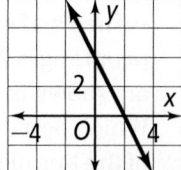

13. The points $(-2, 11)$ and $(6, 3)$ lie on the same line. What is the x-intercept of the line?

14. What is the solution of the equation $4x + 7 = 9x + 2$?

15. An online bookseller charges \$3 per order plus \$1 per book for shipping. John places an order for four books that have the same price. The total cost of his order is \$30. What is the price, in dollars, of each book?

16. $\triangle ABC \sim \triangle DEF$. What is DE?

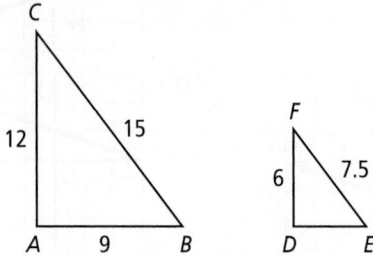

17. A student calculated the density of nickel to be 7.59 g/cm^3. The actual density of nickel is 8.9 g/cm^3. What is the percent error? Round to the nearest tenth of a percent.

18. What is the value of the 8th term for the arithmetic sequence below?

$$12, 18, 24, 30, \ldots$$

19. What is the slope of a line perpendicular to the line $2x + 4y = 12$?

20. What is the y-intercept of the line $-3x - 2y = 18$?

21. What is the solution of the equation $\frac{h}{3} = 18$?

22. What is the slope of a line that is parallel to the line $y = 4x - 10$?

23. A builder measured the perimeter of the foundation of a new house to be 330 ft. He must order the steel beams for the foundation in meters. How many meters should the builder order? Round to the nearest tenth of a meter.

24. Line p passes through the point $(5, -2)$ and has a slope of 0. Line q passes through the point $(-13, -9)$ and is parallel to line p. What is an equation of line q? Show your work.

25. You can find the area of a triangle using the formula $A = \frac{1}{2}bh$, where b is the length of the base, and h is the height. Write the equation for b in terms of A and h. Show all your work.

26. A student reads 40 pages of a book in 50 minutes. At this rate, how many pages can the student read in 80 minutes?

27. What are the solutions of the equation $|x + 6| = 7$?

28. Write an equation in point-slope form of the line that passes through the point $(-2, 7)$ and has a slope of -1.

29. Tell whether the graph is a function.

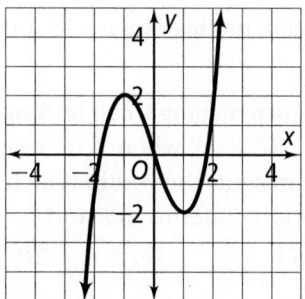

30. Solve the inequality $8 \le x + 2 < 13$.

Extended Response

31. The perimeter of a square is 16 in. A trapezoid has the same area and height as the square. The area of a trapezoid is $\frac{1}{2}h(b_1 + b_2)$, where h is the height and b_1 and b_2 are the lengths of the bases. If one base of the trapezoid is 3 in. long, what is the length of the other base? Show your work.

32. Solve the equation below. Show all your work and give the property that justifies each step.

$$6(2x - 5) = 4x + 2$$

Get Ready!

Lesson 2-4 ◀◗ **Solving Equations**

Solve each equation. If the equation is an identity, write *identity*. If it has no solution, write *no solution*.

1. $3(2 - 2x) = -6(x - 1)$ **2.** $3p + 1 = -p + 5$

3. $4x - 1 = 3(x + 1) + x$ **4.** $\frac{1}{2}(6c - 4) = 4 + c$

5. $5x = 2 - (x - 7)$ **6.** $v + 5 = v - 5$

Lesson 3-4 ◀◗ **Solving Inequalities**

Solve each inequality.

7. $5x + 3 < 18$ **8.** $-\frac{r}{5} + 1 \geq -6$

9. $-3t - 5 < 34$ **10.** $-(7f + 18) - 2f \leq 0$

11. $8s + 7 > -3(5s - 4)$ **12.** $\frac{1}{2}(x + 6) + 1 \geq -5$

Lesson 4-5 ◀◗ **Writing Functions**

13. The height of a triangle is 1 cm less than twice the length of the base. Let $x =$ the length of the base.
     a. Write an expression for the height of the triangle.
     b. Write a function rule for the area of the triangle.
     c. What is the area of such a triangle if the length of its base is 16 cm?

Lessons 5-3, 5-4, and 5-5 ◀◗ **Graphing Linear Equations**

Graph each equation.

14. $2x + 4y = -8$ **15.** $y = -\frac{2}{3}x + 3$ **16.** $y + 5 = -2(x - 2)$

 Looking Ahead Vocabulary

17. Two answers to a question are said to be *inconsistent* if they could not both be true. Two answers to a question are said to be *consistent* if they could both be true. If there is no solution that makes both equations in a system of two linear equations true, do you think the system is *inconsistent* or *consistent*?

18. After a team loses a game, they're *eliminated* from a tournament. The *elimination method* is a way to solve a system of equations. Do you think using the elimination method adds or deletes a variable from a system of equations?

Systems of Equations and Inequalities

Download videos connecting math to your world.

Interactive! Vary numbers, graphs, and figures to explore math concepts.

The online **Solve It** will get you in gear for each lesson.

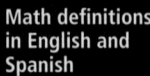

Math definitions in English and Spanish

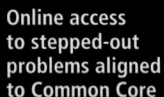

Online access to stepped-out problems aligned to Common Core

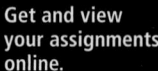

Get and view your assignments online.

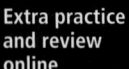

Extra practice and review online

Virtual Nerd™ tutorials with built-in support

Chapter Preview

BIG ideas

1 Solving Equations and Inequalities
Essential Question: How can you solve a system of equations or inequalities?

2 Modeling
Essential Question: Can systems of equations model real-world situations?

Vocabulary

English/Spanish Vocabulary Audio Online:

English	Spanish
consistent, *p. 365*	consistente
dependent, *p. 365*	dependiente
elimination method, *p. 378*	eliminación
inconsistent, *p. 365*	inconsistente
independent, *p. 365*	independiente
linear inequality, *p. 394*	desigualdad lineal
solution of an inequality, *p. 394*	solución de una desigualdad
solution of a system of linear equations, *p. 364*	solución de un sistema de ecuaciones lineales
solution of a system of linear inequalities, *p. 400*	solución de un sistema de desigualdades lineales
substitution method, *p. 372*	método de sustitución

 DOMAINS

- Creating Equations
- Reasoning with Equations and Inequalities
- Interpreting Categorical and Quantitative Data

Common Core Performance Task

Planning an Exercise Program

Ashley uses the rowing machine and the stair machine at the gym for an exercise program. Her trainer wants her to do an exercise program that meets these two conditions:

(1) Ashley will exercise for 40 minutes, dividing her time between the stair machine and the rowing machine.

(2) Ashley will spend twice as much time on the stair machine as on the rowing machine.

Miguel also uses the stair machine and the rowing machine at the gym for an exercise program. His trainer wants him on an exercise program that meets these three conditions:

(1) Miguel will spend at most 60 minutes working out at the gym.

(2) Miguel will exercise for at least 30 minutes, dividing his time between the stair machine and the rowing machine.

(3) Miguel will spend at least twice as much time on the stair machine as on the rowing machine.

Task Description

Find the number of minutes Ashley should use each exercise machine, and the maximum number of minutes Miguel can use the rowing machine.

Connecting the Task to the Math Practices

MATHEMATICAL PRACTICES

As you complete the task, you'll apply several Standards for Mathematical Practice.

- You'll analyze given information and constraints to write equations that model Ashley's exercise program. (MP 1, MP 4)

- You'll find inequalities that describe how the amounts of time Miguel spends on the two machines are related. (MP 2)

6-1 Solving Systems by Graphing

Common Core State Standards

A-REI.C.6 Solve systems of linear equations exactly and approximately (e.g., with graphs), focusing on pairs of linear equations in two variables.

MP 1, MP 2, MP 3, MP 4

Objectives To solve systems of equations by graphing
To analyze special systems

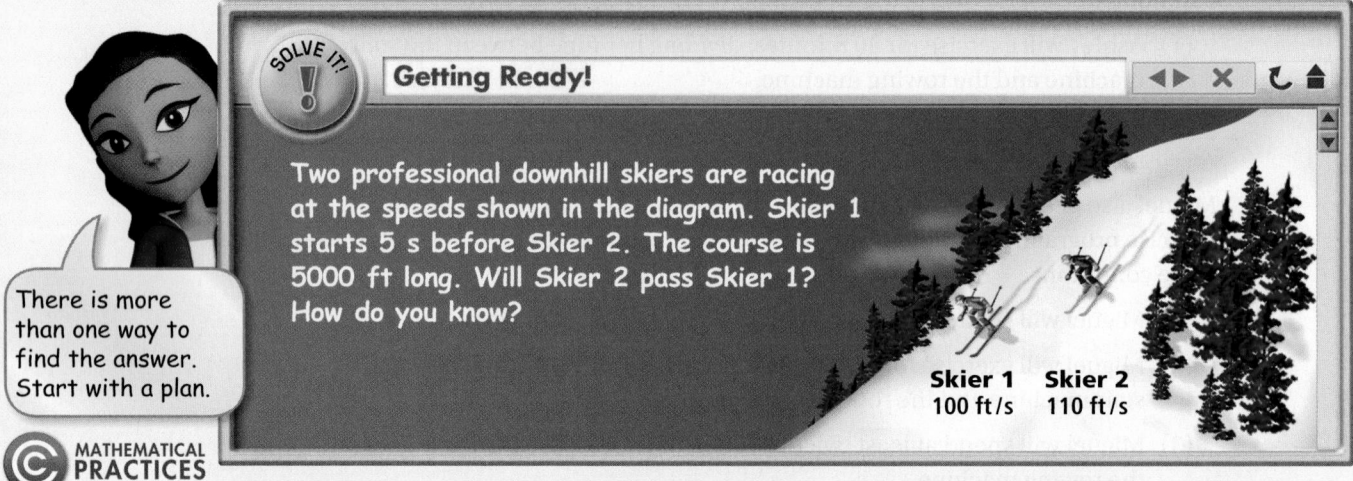

Getting Ready!

Two professional downhill skiers are racing at the speeds shown in the diagram. Skier 1 starts 5 s before Skier 2. The course is 5000 ft long. Will Skier 2 pass Skier 1? How do you know?

Skier 1	Skier 2
100 ft/s	110 ft/s

There is more than one way to find the answer. Start with a plan.

MATHEMATICAL PRACTICES

Lesson Vocabulary

- system of linear equations
- solution of a system of linear equations
- consistent
- independent
- dependent
- inconsistent

You can model the problem in the Solve It with two linear equations. Two or more linear equations form a **system of linear equations.** Any ordered pair that makes *all* of the equations in a system true is a **solution of a system of linear equations.**

Essential Understanding You can use systems of linear equations to model problems. Systems of equations can be solved in more than one way. One method is to graph each equation and find the intersection point, if one exists.

Problem 1 Solving a System of Equations by Graphing

What is the solution of the system? Use a graph. $y = x + 2$
                                                              $y = 3x - 2$

Think

How does graphing each equation help you find the solution?
A line represents the solutions of *one* linear equation. The intersection point is a solution of *both* equations.

Graph both equations in the same coordinate plane.

$y = x + 2$ The slope is 1. The y-intercept is 2.
$y = 3x - 2$ The slope is 3. The y-intercept is -2.

Find the point of intersection. The lines appear to intersect at $(2, 4)$. Check to see if $(2, 4)$ makes both equations true.

$y = x + 2$ $y = 3x - 2$
$4 \stackrel{?}{=} 2 + 2$ $4 \stackrel{?}{=} 3(2) - 2$
$4 = 4$ ✔ $4 = 4$ ✔

Substitute $(2, 4)$ for (x, y).

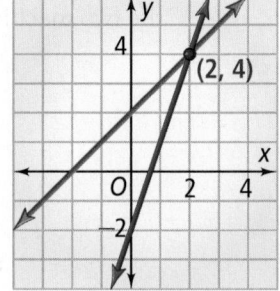

The solution of the system is $(2, 4)$.

Got It? **1.** What is the solution of the system? Use a graph. $\quad y = 2x + 4$
Check your answer. $\qquad\qquad\qquad\qquad\qquad\qquad y = x + 2$

© **Problem 2** **Writing a System of Equations** (STEM)

Biology Scientists studied the weights of two alligators over a period of 12 months. The initial weight and growth rate of each alligator are shown below. After how many months did the alligators weigh the same amount?

ALLIGATOR 1
Initial Weight: 4 lb
Rate of Growth:
1.5 lb per month

ALLIGATOR 2
Initial Weight: 6 lb
Rate of Growth:
1 lb per month

Relate | alligator weight | is | initial weight | plus | growth rate | times | time

Define Let w = alligator weight.
Let t = time in months.

Write Alligator 1: $\quad w \;=\; 4 \;+\; 1.5 \;\cdot\; t$

Alligator 2: $\quad w \;=\; 6 \;+\; 1 \;\cdot\; t$

Think

Is there another way to solve this problem?
Yes. You can *make a table*. Show the weight of each alligator after 1 month, 2 months, and so on.

Graph both equations in the same coordinate plane.

$w = 4 + 1.5t$ The slope is 1.5. The w-intercept is 4.

$w = 6 + t$ The slope is 1. The w-intercept is 6.

The lines intersect at (4, 10).

After 4 months, both alligators weighed 10 lb.

Alligator Weights

Weight, w (lb)

(4, 10)

Time, t (months)

 Got It? **2.** One satellite radio service charges $10 per month plus an activation fee of $20. A second service charges $11 per month plus an activation fee of $15. In what month was the cost of the service the same?

A system of equations that has at least one solution is **consistent.** A consistent system can be either *independent* or *dependent*.

A consistent system that is **independent** has exactly one solution. For example, the systems in Problems 1 and 2 are consistent and independent. A consistent system that is **dependent** has infinitely many solutions.

A system of equations that has no solution is **inconsistent.**

Problem 3 Systems With Infinitely Many Solutions or No Solution

Think

If two equations have the same slope and y-intercept, their graphs will be the same line. If two equations have the same slope but different y-intercepts, their graphs will be parallel lines.

What is the solution of each system? Use a graph.

A $2y - x = 2$

$y = \frac{1}{2}x + 1$

Graph the equations $2y - x = 2$ and $y = \frac{1}{2}x + 1$ in the same coordinate plane.

The equations represent the same line. Any point on the line is a solution of the system, so there are infinitely many solutions. The system is consistent and dependent.

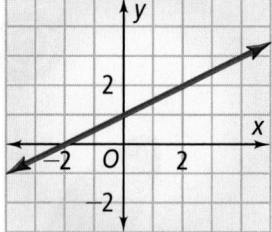

B $y = 2x + 2$

$y = 2x - 1$

Graph the equations $y = 2x + 2$ and $y = 2x - 1$ in the same coordinate plane.

The lines are parallel, so there is no solution. The system is inconsistent.

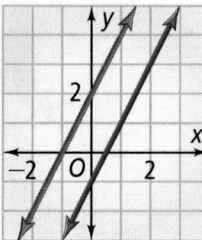

Got It? **3.** What is the solution of each system in parts (a) and (b)? Use a graph. Describe the number of solutions.

a. $y = -x - 3$

$y = -x + 5$

b. $y = 3x - 3$

$3y = 9x - 9$

c. Reasoning Before graphing the equations, how can you determine whether a system of equations has exactly one solution, infinitely many solutions, or no solution?

take note

Concept Summary **Systems of Linear Equations**

One solution

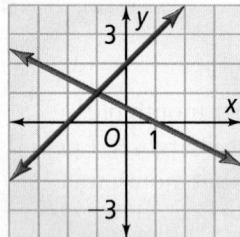

The lines intersect at one point. The lines have different slopes. The equations are consistent and independent.

Infinitely many solutions

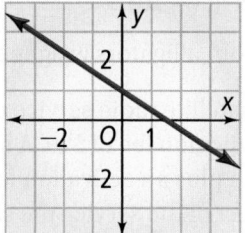

The lines are the same. The lines have the same slope and y-intercept. The equations are consistent and dependent.

No solution

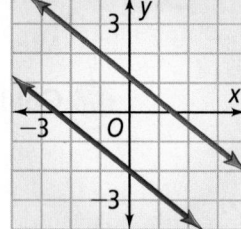

The lines are parallel. The lines have the same slope and different y-intercepts. The equations are inconsistent.

Lesson Check

Do you know HOW?

Solve each system by graphing.

1. $y = x + 7$
$y = 2x + 1$

2. $y = \frac{1}{2}x + 6$
$y = x - 2$

3. $y = -3x - 3$
$y = 2x + 2$

4. $y = -x - 4$
$4x - y = -1$

5. Concert Tickets Tickets for a concert cost $10 each if you order them online, but you must pay a service charge of $8 per order. The tickets are $12 each if you buy them at the door on the night of the concert.

   a. Write a system of equations to model the situation. Let c be the total cost. Let t be the number of tickets.

   b. Graph the equations and find the intersection point. What does this point represent?

Do you UNDERSTAND?

6. Vocabulary Match each type of system with the number of solutions the system has.

   A. inconsistent
   B. consistent and dependent
   C. consistent and independent

   I. exactly one
   II. infinitely many
   III. no solution

7. Writing Suppose you graph a system of linear equations. If a point is on only one of the lines, is it a solution of the system? Explain.

8. Reasoning Can a system of two linear equations have exactly two solutions? Explain.

9. Reasoning Suppose you find that two linear equations are true when $x = -2$ and $y = 3$. What can you conclude about the graphs of the equations? Explain.

Practice and Problem-Solving Exercises

 **Practice**

Solve each system by graphing. Check your solution.

See Problem 1.

10. $y = 2x$
$y = -2x + 8$

11. $y = \frac{1}{2}x + 7$
$y = \frac{3}{2}x + 3$

12. $y = \frac{1}{3}x + 1$
$y = -3x + 11$

13. $y = x - 4$
$y = -x$

14. $y = -x + 3$
$y = x + 1$

15. $4x - y = -1$
$-x + y = x - 5$

16. $y = -\frac{1}{2}x + 2$
$y = \frac{1}{2}x + 6$

17. $2x - y = -5$
$-2x - y = -1$

18. $x = -3$
$y = 5$

19. Student Statistics The number of right-handed students in a mathematics class is nine times the number of left-handed students. The total number of students in the class is 30. How many right-handed students are in the class? How many left-handed students are in the class?

See Problem 2.

20. Plants A plant nursery is growing a tree that is 3 ft tall and grows at an average rate of 1 ft per year. Another tree at the nursery is 4 ft tall and grows at an average rate of 0.5 ft per year. After how many years will the trees be the same height?

21. Fitness At a local fitness center, members pay a $20 membership fee and $3 for each aerobics class. Nonmembers pay $5 for each aerobics class. For what number of aerobics classes will the cost for members and nonmembers be the same?

Solve each system by graphing. Tell whether the system has *one solution,* *infinitely many solutions,* or *no solution.*

See Problem 3.

22. $y = x + 3$
$y = x - 1$

23. $y = 2x - 1$
$3y = 6x - 5$

24. $3x + y = 2$
$4y = 12 - 12x$

25. $2x - 2y = 5$
$y = x - 4$

26. $y = 2x - 2$
$2y = 4x - 4$

27. $y - x = 5$
$3y = 3x + 15$

28. $2x + 2y = 4$
$12 - 3x = 3y$

29. $2y = x - 2$
$3y = \frac{3}{2}x - 3$

30. $3x - y = 2$
$4y = -x + 5$

B Apply

31. Think About a Plan You are looking for an after-school job. One job pays $9 per hour. Another pays $12 per hour, but you must buy a uniform that costs $39. After how many hours of work would your net earnings from either job be the same?
- What equations can you write to model the situation?
- How will graphing the equations help you solve the problem?

32. Error Analysis A student graphs the system $y = -x + 3$ and $y = -2x - 1$ as shown at the right. The student concludes there is no solution. Describe and correct the student's error.

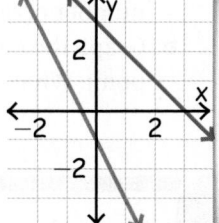

33. Reasoning Suppose you graph a system of linear equations and the intersection point appears to be (3, 7). Can you be sure that the ordered pair (3, 7) is the solution? What must you do to be sure?

34. Cell Phone Plans A cell phone provider offers a plan that costs $40 per month plus $.20 per text message sent or received. A comparable plan costs $60 per month but offers unlimited text messaging.
a. How many text messages would you have to send or receive in order for the plans to cost the same each month?
b. If you send or receive an average of 50 text messages each month, which plan would you choose? Why?

Without graphing, decide whether each system has *one solution, infinitely many solutions,* or *no solution.* Justify your answer.

35. $y = x - 4$
$y = x - 3$

36. $x - y = -\frac{1}{2}$
$2x - 2y = -1$

37. $y = 5x - 1$
$10x = 2y + 2$

38. $3x + 2y = 1$
$4y = 6x + 2$

39. Banking The graph at the right shows the balances in two bank accounts over time. Use the graph to write a system of equations giving the amount in each account over time. Let t = the time in weeks and let b = the balance in dollars. If the accounts continue to grow as shown, when will they have the same balance?

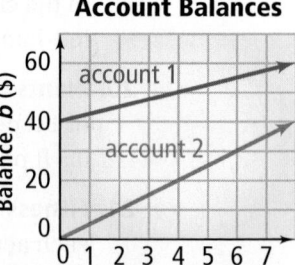

Account Balances

40. Open-Ended One equation in a system is $y = \frac{1}{2}x - 2$.
a. Write a second equation so that the system has one solution.
b. Write a second equation so that the system has no solution.
c. Write a second equation so that the system has infinitely many solutions.

41. Reasoning Consider the system at the right.

$$y = gx + 3$$
$$y = hx + 7$$

a. If $g \geq h$, will the system *always*, *sometimes*, or *never* have exactly one solution? Explain your reasoning.

b. If $g \leq h$, will the system *always*, *sometimes*, or *never* have infinitely many solutions? Explain your reasoning.

42. Hiking Two hikers are walking along a marked trail. The first hiker starts at a point 6 mi from the beginning of the trail and walks at a speed of 4 mi/h. At the same time, the second hiker starts 1 mi from the beginning and walks at a speed of 3 mi/h.

a. What is a system of equations that models the situation?

b. Graph the two equations and find the intersection point.

c. Is the intersection point meaningful in this situation? Explain.

Standardized Test Prep

SAT/ACT

43. Which ordered pair is the solution of the system?

$$2x + 3y = -17$$
$$3x + 2y = -8$$

Ⓐ $(2, -7)$ Ⓑ $(-4, 2)$ Ⓒ $(-2, -1)$ Ⓓ $\left(-\frac{4}{3}, -2\right)$

44. Which expression is equivalent to $5(m - 12) + 8$?

Ⓕ $5m - 68$ Ⓖ $5m - 20$ Ⓗ $5m - 4$ Ⓘ $5m - 52$

Extended Response

45. The costs for parking in two different parking garages are given in the table at the right.

a. What is a system of equations that models the situation?

b. How many hours of parking would cost the same parking in either garage?

c. If you needed to park a car for 3 h, which garage would you choose? Why?

Garage Parking Fees

Garage	Flat Fee	Hourly Fee
A	$5	$2.50
B	$20	$0

Mixed Review

Graph each function by translating the graph of $y = |x|$.   ◀ **See Lesson 5-8.**

46. $y = |x| - 2$ **47.** $y = |x| - 1$ **48.** $y = |x + 3|$ **49.** $y = |x + 2|$

Find the slope of a line that is parallel to the graph of the equation.   ◀ **See Lesson 5-6.**

50. $y = x + 3$ **51.** $y = -\frac{1}{2}x - 4$ **52.** $3y + 2x = 7$ **53.** $3x = 5y + 10$

Get Ready!   **To prepare for Lesson 6-2, do Exercises 54–57.**

Solve each equation for y.   ◀ **See Lesson 2-5.**

54. $4x + 2y = 38$ **55.** $\frac{1}{2}x + \frac{1}{3}y = 5$ **56.** $\frac{3}{2}y = \frac{4}{5}x$ **57.** $1.5x - 4.5y = 21$

Solving Systems Using Tables and Graphs

Common Core State Standards

A-REI.D.11 Explain why the *x*-coordinates . . . where the graphs of the equations $y = f(x)$ and $y = g(x)$ intersect are the solutions of the equation $f(x) = g(x)$ . . . using technology to graph the functions . . .

MP 5

Activity

MATHEMATICAL PRACTICES

Solve the system using a table. $y = 3x - 7$
$y = -0.5x + 7$

Step 1
Enter the equations in the screen.

Step 2
Use the (tblset) function. Set TblStart to 0 and △Tbl to 1.

Step 3
Press (table) to show the table on the screen.

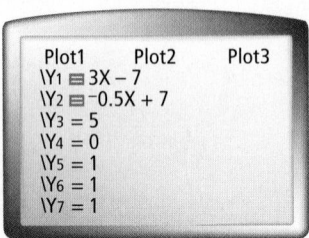

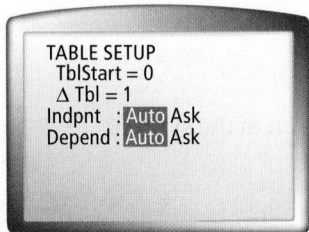

1. Which *x*-value gives the same value for Y_1 and Y_2?

2. What ordered pair is the solution of the system?

Activity

Solve the system using a graph. $y = -5x + 6$
$y = -x - 2$

Step 1   Enter the equations in the screen.

Step 2   Graph the equations. Use a standard graphing window.

Step 3   Use the (calc) feature. Choose **INTERSECT** to find the point where the lines intersect.

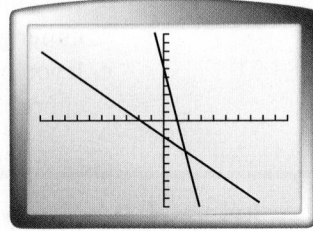

3. Copy and complete: The lines intersect at (__?__ , __?__), so this point is the solution of the system.

4. How can you use the graph to find the solution of the equation $-5x + 6 = -x - 2$?

Exercises

Use a table and a graph to solve each system. Sketch your graph.

5. $y = 5x - 3$
$y = 3x + 1$

6. $y = 2x - 13$
$y = x - 9$

7. $2x - y = 1.5$
$y = -\frac{1}{2}x - 1.5$

8. How can you use the graph of a system to find the solution of the equation $5x - 3 = 3x + 1$?

Solving Systems Using Algebra Tiles

© Common Core State Standards

Prepares for A-REI.C.6 Solve systems of linear equations exactly and approximately (e.g., with graphs), focusing on pairs of linear equations in two variables.

MP 7

Just as algebra tiles can help you solve linear equations in one variable, they can also help you solve systems of linear equations in two variables.

Activity

Model and solve the system. $-x + 2y = 4$
$y = x + 1$

Since $y = x + 1$, use tiles for $x + 1$ to model y.
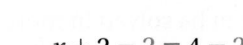

Equation	Algebra Tiles	Steps
$-x + 2y = 4$ $-x + 2(x + 1) = 4$ $-x + 2x + 2 = 4$		Substitute $x + 1$ for y in the first equation.
$(-x + x) + x + 2 = 4$ $x + 2 = 4$	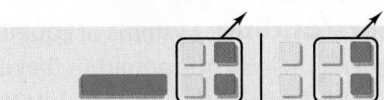	Remove the zero pair x and $-x$.
$x + 2 - 2 = 4 - 2$	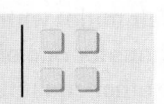	Subtract 2 from each side. Remove zero pairs.
$x = 2$		Solve for x.
$y = x + 1$	y 	Model the second equation.
$y = 2 + 1$ $y = 3$	y 	Substitute 2 for x and simplify.

The solution of the system is (2, 3).

Exercises

Model and solve each system.

1. $y = x + 1$
$2x + y = 10$

2. $x + 4y = 1$
$x + 4 = y$

3. $y = 2x - 1$
$y = x + 2$

6-2 Solving Systems Using Substitution

© **Common Core State Standards**

A-REI.C.6 Solve systems of linear equations exactly and approximately (e.g., with graphs), focusing on pairs of linear equations in two variables.

MP 1, MP 2, MP 3, MP 4

Objective To solve systems of equations using substitution

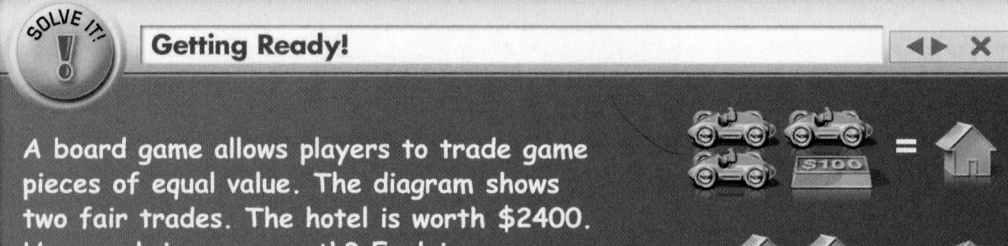

Getting Ready!

A board game allows players to trade game pieces of equal value. The diagram shows two fair trades. The hotel is worth $2400. How much is a car worth? Explain your reasoning.

How can you get started? One house equals 3 cars plus $100. Two houses equal . . .

© **MATHEMATICAL PRACTICES**

You can model fair trades with a linear system. You can solve linear systems by solving one of the equations for one of the variables. Then substitute the expression for the variable into the other equation. This is called the **substitution method.**

Lesson Vocabulary
• substitution method

Essential Understanding Systems of equations can be solved in more than one way. When a system has at least one equation that can be solved quickly for a variable, the system can be solved efficiently using substitution.

 Problem 1 Using Substitution

What is the solution of the system? Use substitution. $y = 3x$
$x + y = -32$

Plan

How can you get started?
If one equation is already solved for one variable, use it for the substitution. If both equations are solved for a variable, you can use either one.

Step 1 Because $y = 3x$, you can substitute $3x$ for y in $x + y = -32$.

$x + y = -32$	Write the second equation.
$x + 3x = -32$	Substitute $3x$ for y.
$4x = -32$	Simplify.
$x = -8$	Divide each side by 4.

Step 2 Substitute -8 for x in either equation and solve for y.

$y = 3x$	Write either equation.
$y = 3(-8) = -24$	Substitute -8 for x and solve.

The solution is $(-8, -24)$. Check by substituting $(-8, -24)$ into each equation.

Check

$$y = 3x \qquad\qquad x + y = -32$$
$$-24 \overset{?}{=} 3(-8) \qquad -8 + (-24) \overset{?}{=} -32$$
$$-24 = -24 ✔ \qquad\qquad -32 = -32 ✔$$

 Got It? **1.** What is the solution of the system? Use substitution. $\quad y = 2x + 7$
Check your answer. $\qquad\qquad\qquad\qquad\qquad\qquad\qquad\qquad y = x - 1$

To use substitution to solve a system of equations, one of the equations must be solved for a variable.

 Problem 2 **Solving for a Variable and Using Substitution**

What is the solution of the system? Use substitution. $\quad 3y + 4x = 14$
$\qquad\qquad\qquad\qquad\qquad\qquad\qquad\qquad\qquad\qquad\qquad -2x + y = -3$

Know	Need	Plan
Neither equation is solved for one of the variables.	The solution of the system	Solve one of the equations for one of the variables. Then use the substitution method to find the solution of the system.

Think

Which variable should you solve for?
If one equation has a variable with a coefficient of 1 or −1, solve for that variable. It is generally easier to solve for a variable with a coefficient of 1 or −1.

Step 1 Solve one of the equations for one of the variables.
$$-2x + y = -3 \qquad \text{Write the second equation.}$$
$$-2x + y + 2x = -3 + 2x \quad \text{Add } 2x \text{ to each side.}$$
$$y = 2x - 3 \qquad \text{Simplify.}$$

Step 2 Substitute $2x - 3$ for y in the other equation and solve for x.
$$3y + 4x = 14 \qquad \text{Write the first equation.}$$
$$3(2x - 3) + 4x = 14 \qquad \text{Substitute } 2x - 3 \text{ for } y. \text{ Use parentheses.}$$
$$6x - 9 + 4x = 14 \qquad \text{Distributive Property}$$
$$10x = 23 \qquad \text{Add 9 to each side. Simplify.}$$
$$x = 2.3 \qquad \text{Divide each side by 10.}$$

Step 3 Substitute 2.3 for x in either equation and solve for y.
$$-2x + y = -3 \qquad \text{Write either equation.}$$
$$-2(2.3) + y = -3 \qquad \text{Substitute 2.3 for } x.$$
$$-4.6 + y = -3 \qquad \text{Simplify.}$$
$$y = 1.6 \qquad \text{Add 4.6 to each side.}$$

The solution is (2.3, 1.6).

 Got It? **2. a.** What is the solution of the system? Use substitution. $\quad 6y + 5x = 8$
$\qquad\qquad\qquad\qquad\qquad\qquad\qquad\qquad\qquad\qquad\qquad\qquad\qquad x + 3y = -7$

b. Reasoning In your first step in part (a), which variable did you solve for? Which equation did you use to solve for the variable?

Problem 3 Using Systems of Equations   **GRIDDED RESPONSE**

Snack Bar A snack bar sells two sizes of snack packs. A large snack pack is $5, and a small snack pack is $3. In one day, the snack bar sold 60 snack packs for a total of $220. How many small snack packs did the snack bar sell?

Step 1   Write the system of equations. Let x = the number of large $5 snack packs, and let y = the number of small $3 snack packs.

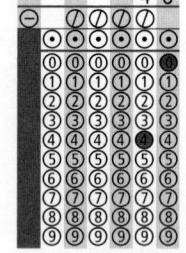

$x + y = 60$ Represent the total number of snack packs.

$5x + 3y = 220$ Represent the amount earned from 60 snack packs.

Step 2 $x + y = 60$ Use the first equation to solve for y.

$y = 60 - x$ Subtract x from each side.

Step 3 $5x + 3(60 - x) = 220$ Substitute $60 - x$ for y in the second equation.

$5x + 180 - 3x = 220$ Distributive Property

$2x = 40$ Simplify.

$x = 20$ Divide each side by 2.

Step 4 $20 + y = 60$ Substitute 20 for x in the first equation.

$y = 40$ Subtract 20 from each side.

The system's solution is (20, 40). The snack bar sold 40 small snack packs.

> **Think**
>
> **What does the solution represent in the real world?**
> Check what the assigned variables represent. Here, (20, 40) represents 20 large snack packs and 40 small snack packs.

 Got It?   **3.** You pay $22 to rent 6 video games. The store charges $4 for new games and $2 for older games. How many new games did you rent?

If you get an identity, like $2 = 2$, when you solve a system of equations, then the system has infinitely many solutions. If you get a false statement, like $8 = 2$, then the system has no solution.

 Problem 4 Systems With Infinitely Many Solutions or No Solution

How many solutions does each system have?

> **Think**
>
> **How many solutions can a system of linear equations have?**
> A system can have exactly one solution, infinitely many solutions, or no solution.

Ⓐ $x = -2y + 4$
$3.5x + 7y = 14$

Substitute $-2y + 4$ for x in
$3.5x + 7y = 14$.

$3.5x + 7y = 14$

$3.5(-2y + 4) + 7y = 14$

$-7y + 14 + 7y = 14$

$14 = 14$ ✔

The system has infinitely many solutions.

Ⓑ $y = 3x - 11$
$y - 3x = -13$

Substitute $3x - 11$ for y in
$y - 3x = -13$.

$y - 3x = -13$

$(3x - 11) - 3x = -13$

$-11 = -13$ ✗

The system has no solution.

 Got It?   **4.** How many solutions does the system have? $6y + 5x = 8$
$2.5x + 3y = 4$

374   **Chapter 6**   Systems of Linear Equations and Inequalities

Lesson Check

Do you know HOW?

Solve each system using substitution. Check your solution.

1. $4y = x$
$3x - y = 70$

2. $-2x + 5y = 19$
$3x - 4 = y$

Tell whether the system has *one solution, infinitely many solutions*, or *no solution*.

3. $y = 2x + 1$
$4x - 2y = 6$

4. $-x + \frac{1}{2}y = 13$
$x + 15 = \frac{1}{2}y$

5. Talent Show In a talent show of singing and comedy acts, singing acts are 5 min long and comedy acts are 3 min long. The show has 12 acts and lasts 50 min. How many singing acts and how many comedy acts are in the show?

Do you UNDERSTAND?

 6. Vocabulary When is the substitution method a better method than graphing for solving a system of linear equations?

For each system, tell which equation you would first use to solve for a variable in the first step of the substitution method. Explain your choice.

7. $-2x + y = -1$
$4x + 2y = 12$

8. $2.5x - 7y = 7.5$
$6x - y = 1$

Tell whether each statement is *true* or *false*. Explain.

9. When solving a system using substitution, if you obtain an identity, then the system has no solution.

10. You cannot use substitution to solve a system that does not have a variable with a coefficient of 1 or -1.

Practice and Problem-Solving Exercises

 **Practice**   Solve each system using substitution. Check your answer.   ◀ **See Problems 1 and 2.**

11. $x + y = 8$
$y = 3x$

12. $2x + 2y = 38$
$y = x + 3$

13. $x + 3 = y$
$3x + 4y = 7$

14. $y = 8 - x$
$7 = 2 - y$

15. $y = -2x + 6$
$3y - x + 3 = 0$

16. $3x + 2y = 23$
$\frac{1}{2}x - 4 = y$

17. $y - 2x = 3$
$3x - 2y = 5$

18. $4x = 3y - 2$
$18 = 3x + y$

19. $2 = 2y - x$
$23 = 5y - 4x$

20. $4y + 3 = 3y + x$
$2x + 4y = 18$

21. $7x - 2y = 1$
$2y = x - 1$

22. $4y - x = 5 + 2y$
$3x + 7y = 24$

23. Theater Tickets Adult tickets to a play cost $22. Tickets for children cost $15. Tickets for a group of 11 people cost a total of $228. Write and solve a system of equations to find how many children and how many adults were in the group.   ◀ **See Problem 3.**

24. Transportation A school is planning a field trip for 142 people. The trip will use six drivers and two types of vehicles: buses and vans. A bus can seat 51 passengers. A van can seat 10 passengers. Write and solve a system of equations to find how many buses and how many vans will be needed.

25. Geometry The measure of one acute angle in a right triangle is four times the measure of the other acute angle. Write and solve a system of equations to find the measures of the acute angles.

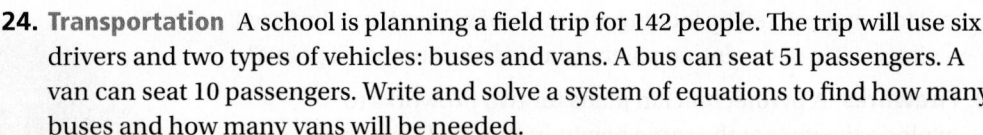

◀ See Problem 4.

Tell whether the system has *one solution, infinitely many solutions,* or *no solution.*

26. $y = \frac{1}{2}x + 3$
$2y - x = 6$

27. $6y = -5x + 24$
$2.5x + 3y = 12$

28. $x = -7y + 34$
$x + 7y = 32$

29. $5 = \frac{1}{2}x + 3y$
$10 - x = 6y$

30. $17 = 11y + 12x$
$12x + 11y = 14$

31. $1.5x + 2y = 11$
$3x + 6y = 22$

 **Apply**

32. Geometry The rectangle shown has a perimeter of 34 cm and the given area. Its length is 5 more than twice its width. Write and solve a system of equations to find the dimensions of the rectangle.

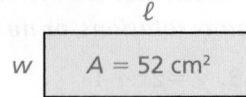

ℓ

w $\boxed{A = 52 \text{ cm}^2}$

© **33. Writing** What would your first step be in solving the system below? Explain.

$1.2x + y = 2$
$1.4y = 2.8x + 1$

34. Coins You have $3.70 in dimes and quarters. You have 5 more quarters than dimes. How many of each type of coin do you have?

© **35. Error Analysis** Describe and correct the error at the right in finding the solution of the following system:

$7x + 5y = 14$
$x + 8y = 21$

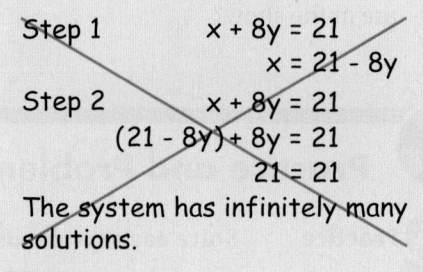

Step 1   x + 8y = 21
           x = 21 - 8y
Step 2   x + 8y = 21
           (21 - 8y) + 8y = 21
           21 = 21
The system has infinitely many solutions.

36. Art An artist is going to sell two sizes of prints at an art fair. The artist will charge $20 for a small print and $45 for a large print. The artist would like to sell twice as many small prints as large prints. The booth the artist is renting for the day costs $510. How many of each size print must the artist sell in order to break even at the fair?

© **37. Think About a Plan** At a certain high school, 350 students are taking an algebra course. The ratio of boys to girls taking algebra is 33 : 37. How many more girls are taking algebra than boys?
- How can you write a system of equations to model the situation?
- Which equation will you solve for a variable in the first step of solving the system? Why?
- How can you interpret the solution in the context of the problem?

© **38. a. Compare and Contrast** Using a graph, how can you tell when a system of linear equations has no solution?
b. Using substitution, how can you tell when a system of linear equations has no solution?
c. How can you tell by looking at a table of values if two lines will intersect in one point, no points, or an infinite number of points?

39. Fireworks A pyrotechnician plans for two fireworks to explode together at the same height in the air. They travel at speeds shown at the right. Firework B is launched 0.25 s before Firework A. How many seconds after Firework B launches will both fireworks explode?

Firework A   Firework B
220 ft/s   200 ft/s

40. Writing Let a be any real number. Will the system at the right *always*, *sometimes*, or *never* have a solution? Explain.

$$y = ax$$
$$y = ax + 4$$

41. Reasoning Explain how you can use substitution to show that the system at the right has no solution.

$$y + x = x$$
$$\frac{3x}{2y} = 4$$

 Challenge

42. Agriculture A farmer grows corn, tomatoes, and sunflowers on a 320-acre farm. This year, the farmer wants to plant twice as many acres of tomatoes as acres of sunflowers. The farmer also wants to plant 40 more acres of corn than of tomatoes. How many acres of each crop should the farmer plant?

43. Track and Field Michelle and Pam are running a 200-m race. Michelle runs at an average of 7.5 m/s. Pam averages 7.8 m/s, but she starts 1 s after Michelle.
a. How long will it take Pam to catch up to Michelle?
b. Will Pam overtake Michelle before the finish line? Explain.

Apply What You've Learned

 **MATHEMATICAL PRACTICES**
MP 1, MP 4

Look back at the information on page 363 about the amounts of time Ashley uses the stair machine and rowing machine at the gym.

a. Define two variables to represent the amounts of time Ashley can spend on the two exercise machines.

b. Write a system of two equations that describes the relationships between the amounts of time Ashley spends on the two machines.

c. Solve the system of equations.

d. Interpret the solution of the system.

6-3 Solving Systems Using Elimination

 Common Core State Standards

A-REI.C.5 Prove that, given . . . two equations . . . replacing one equation by the sum of that equation and a multiple of the other produces a system with the same solutions. **Also A-REI.C.6**

MP 1, MP 2, MP 3, MP 4, MP 6

Objective To solve systems by adding or subtracting to eliminate a variable

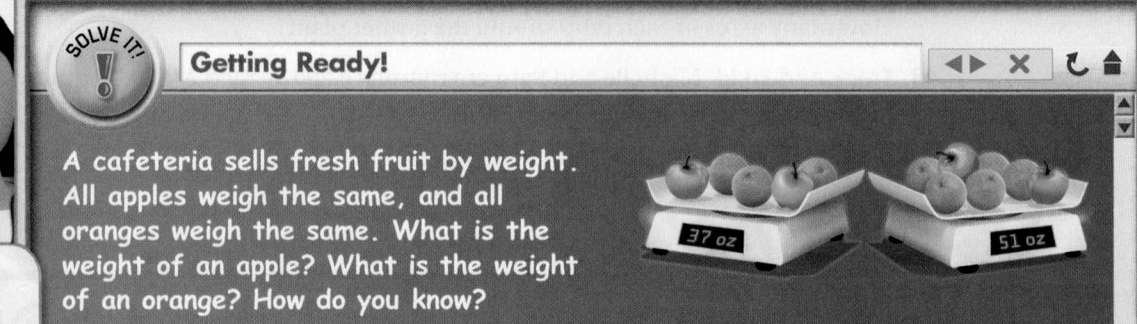

Getting Ready!

A cafeteria sells fresh fruit by weight. All apples weigh the same, and all oranges weigh the same. What is the weight of an apple? What is the weight of an orange? How do you know?

37 oz   51 oz

Hmm . . . Can the methods from earlier lessons be used to solve this?

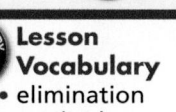 **MATHEMATICAL PRACTICES**

By the Addition and Subtraction Properties of Equality, if $a = b$ and $c = d$, then $a + c = b + d$ and $a - c = b - d$. For example, $5 + 1 = 6$ and $3 + 4 = 7$, so $(5 + 1) + (3 + 4) = 6 + 7$. In the **elimination method,** you use these properties to add or subtract equations in order to eliminate a variable in a system.

Lesson Vocabulary
• elimination method

Essential Understanding There is more than one way to solve a system of equations. Some systems are written in a way that makes eliminating a variable a good method to use.

 Problem 1   **Solving a System by Adding Equations**

Plan

Which variable should you eliminate?
You can eliminate either variable. Since the coefficients of y are opposites, you can add the equations to eliminate y in one step.

What is the solution of the system? Use elimination.

$$2x + 5y = 17$$
$$6x - 5y = -9$$

Step 1 Eliminate one variable. Since the sum of the coefficients of y is 0, add the equations to eliminate y.

$$2x + 5y = 17$$
$$\underline{6x - 5y = -9}$$
$$8x + 0 = 8 \qquad \text{Add the two equations.}$$
$$x = 1 \qquad \text{Solve for } x.$$

Step 2 Substitute 1 for x to solve for the eliminated variable.

$$2x + 5y = 17 \qquad \text{You can use the first equation.}$$
$$2(1) + 5y = 17 \qquad \text{Substitute 1 for } x.$$
$$2 + 5y = 17 \qquad \text{Simplify.}$$
$$y = 3 \qquad \text{Solve for } y.$$

Since $x = 1$ and $y = 3$, the solution is (1, 3).

Got It? **1.** What is the solution of each system? Use elimination.

a. $5x - 6y = -32$

$3x + 6y = 48$

b. $-3x - 3y = 9$

$3x - 4y = 5$

Problem 2 Solving a System by Subtracting Equations

Multiple Choice The theater club sells a total of 101 tickets to its first play. A student ticket costs $1. An adult ticket costs $2.50. Total ticket sales are $164. How many student tickets were sold?

Ⓐ 25 Ⓑ 42 Ⓒ 59 Ⓓ 76

Define Let a = the number of adult tickets sold.

Let s = the number of student tickets sold.

Relate total number of tickets   total ticket sales

Write $a + s = 101$ $2.5a + s = 164$

Step 1 Eliminate one variable. Since the difference of the coefficients of s is 0, eliminate s.

$$a + s = 101$$

$$\underline{2.5a + s = 164}$$

$$-1.5a + 0 = -63 \quad \text{Subtract the equations.}$$

$$a = 42 \quad \text{Solve for } a.$$

Step 2 Solve for the eliminated variable. Use either equation.

$$a + s = 101 \quad \text{You can use the first equation.}$$

$$42 + s = 101 \quad \text{Substitute 42 for } a.$$

$$s = 59 \quad \text{Solve for } s.$$

There were 59 student tickets sold. The correct answer is C.

Check 42 is close to 40 and 59 is close to 60. The total number of tickets is about $40 + 60 = 100$, which is close to 101. The total sales are about $\$2.50(40) + \$60 = \$160$, which is close to $164. The solution is reasonable.

Think

How is this problem similar to Problem 1? In each problem, you are looking for coefficients of one variable that are either the same or opposites. Here, the coefficients of s are the same, so eliminate s.

 Got It? **2.** Washing 2 cars and 3 trucks takes 130 min. Washing 2 cars and 5 trucks takes 190 min. How long does it take to wash each type of vehicle?

In Problems 1 and 2, a variable is eliminated because the sum or difference of its coefficients is zero. From the Multiplication Property of Equality, you know that you can multiply each side of an equation to get a new equation that is equivalent to the original. That is, $a + b = c$ is equivalent to $d(a + b) = dc$, or $da + db = dc$. Since this is true, you can eliminate a variable by adding or subtracting, if you first multiply an equation by an appropriate number. You can prove that the results are the same simply by substituting the values for the variables in the original equations to show that the equations are true.

Problem 3 Solving a System by Multiplying One Equation

What is the solution of the system? Use elimination. $-2x + 15y = -32$
$7x - 5y = 17$

Know	Need	Plan
A system of equations that can't quickly be solved by graphing or substitution	The solution of the system	Multiply one or both equations by a constant so that the coefficients of one variable are the same or opposites. Then eliminate the variable.

Step 1 To eliminate one variable, you can multiply $7x - 5y = 17$ by 3 and then add.

$$-2x + 15y = -32 \qquad\qquad -2x + 15y = -32$$
$$7x - 5y = 17 \quad \boxed{\text{Multiply by 3.}} \quad \underline{21x - 15y = 51}$$
$$19x + 0 = 19 \qquad \text{Add the equations.}$$
$$x = 1 \qquad \text{Solve for } x.$$

Step 2 Solve for the eliminated variable. Use either of the original equations.

$$7x - 5y = 17 \qquad \text{You can use the second equation.}$$
$$7(1) - 5y = 17 \qquad \text{Substitute 1 for } x.$$
$$y = -2 \qquad \text{Solve for } y.$$

Think

How can you show that this is a solution to the original system?
Substitute (–1, 2) in the original system.

The solution is $(1, -2)$.

 Got It? **3. a.** How can you use the Multiplication Property of Equality to change an equation in this system in order to solve it using elimination? $-5x - 2y = 6$
$3x + 6y = 6$

   b. Write and solve a revised system.

   c. Show that the solution of the revised system is a solution of the original system.

 Problem 4 Solving a System by Multiplying Both Equations

What is the solution of the system? Use elimination. $3x + 2y = 1$
$4x + 3y = -2$

Plan

How can you get started?
Find the LCM of the coefficients of the variable that you want to eliminate. Multiply to make the coefficients equal to the LCM.

Step 1 Multiply each equation so you can eliminate one variable.

$$3x + 2y = 1 \quad \boxed{\text{Multiply by 3.}} \quad 9x + 6y = 3$$
$$4x + 3y = -2 \quad \boxed{\text{Multiply by 2.}} \quad \underline{8x + 6y = -4}$$
$$x + 0 = 7 \qquad \text{Subtract the equations.}$$

Step 2 Solve for the eliminated variable. Use either of the original equations.

$$3x + 2y = 1 \qquad \text{You can use the first equation.}$$
$$3(7) + 2y = 1 \qquad \text{Substitute 7 for } x.$$
$$2y = -20 \qquad \text{Subtract 21 from each side. Simplify.}$$
$$y = -10 \qquad \text{Solve for } y.$$

The solution is $(7, -10)$.

Got It? 4. a. How can you use the Multiplication Property of Equality to change the equations in this system in order to solve it using elimination?
$4x + 3y = -19$
$3x - 2y = -10$

b. Write and solve a revised system.

c. Show that the solution of the revised system is a solution of the original system.

Recall that if you get a false statement as you solve a system, then the system has no solution. If you get an identity, then the system has infinitely many solutions.

 Problem 5 Finding the Number of Solutions

How many solutions does the system have?
$2x + 6y = 18$
$x + 3y = 9$

Think

Could you have solved this problem another way?
Yes. For example, you could have multiplied the second equation by 2 and subtracted.

Multiply the second equation by -2.

$2x + 6y = 18$ $2x + 6y = 18$
$x + 3y = 9$ Multiply by -2.→ $-2x - 6y = -18$

                          $0 = 0$ Add the equations.

Because $0 = 0$ is an identity, there are infinitely many solutions.

 Got It? 5. How many solutions does the system have?
$-2x + 5y = 7$
$-2x + 5y = 12$

The flowchart below can help you decide which steps to take when solving a system of equations using elimination.

Can I eliminate a variable by adding or subtracting the given equations? *yes* → Do so.

no ↓

Can I multiply one of the equations by a number, and then add or subtract the equations? *yes* → Do so.

no ↓

Multiply both equations by different numbers. Then add or subtract the equations.

 Lesson Check

Do you know HOW?

Solve each system using elimination.

1. $3x - 2y = 0$
$4x + 2y = 14$

2. $3p + q = 7$
$2p - 2q = -6$

3. $3x - 2y = 1$
$8x + 3y = 2$

Do you UNDERSTAND?  **MATHEMATICAL PRACTICES**

4. Vocabulary If you add two equations in two variables and the sum is an equation in one variable, what method are you using to solve the system? Explain.

5. Reasoning Explain how the Addition Property of Equality allows you to add equations.

6. Writing Explain how you would solve a system of equations using elimination.

Practice and Problem-Solving Exercises

 MATHEMATICAL PRACTICES

 **Practice**   **Solve each system using elimination.**   ◀ **See Problems 1 and 2.**

7. $3x + 3y = 27$
   $x - 3y = -11$

8. $-x + 5y = 13$
   $x - y = 15$

9. $2x + 4y = 22$
   $2x - 2y = -8$

10. $4x - 7y = 3$
   $x - 7y = -15$

11. $5x - y = 0$
   $3x + y = 24$

12. $6x + 5y = 39$
   $3x + 5y = 27$

13. Talent Show Your school's talent show will feature 12 solo acts and 2 ensemble acts. The show will last 90 min. The 6 solo performers judged best will give a repeat performance at a second 60-min show, which will also feature the 2 ensemble acts. Each solo act lasts x minutes, and each ensemble act lasts y minutes.
   a. Write a system of equations to model the situation.
   b. Solve the system from part (a). How long is each solo act? How long is each ensemble act?

14. Furniture A carpenter is designing a drop-leaf table with two drop leaves of equal size. The lengths of the table when one leaf is folded up and when both leaves are folded up are shown. How long is the table when no leaves are folded up?

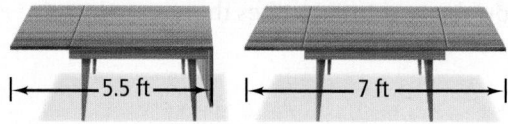

|← 5.5 ft →| |← 7 ft →|

Solve each system using elimination.   ◀ **See Problems 3 and 4.**

15. $2x + 3y = 9$
   $x + 5y = 8$

16. $3x + y = 5$
   $2x - 2y = -2$

17. $6x + 4y = 42$
   $-3x + 3y = -6$

18. $3x + 2y = 17$
   $2x + 5y = 26$

19. $6x - 3y = 15$
   $7x + 4y = 10$

20. $5x - 9y = -43$
   $3x + 8y = 68$

Tell whether the system has *one solution, infinitely many solutions,* or *no solution.*   ◀ **See Problem 5.**

21. $9x + 8y = 15$
   $9x + 8y = 30$

22. $3x + 4y = 24$
   $6x + 8y = 24$

23. $5x - 3y = 10$
   $10x + 6y = 20$

24. $2x - 5y = 17$
   $6x - 15y = 51$

25. $4x - 7y = 15$
   $-8x + 14y = -30$

26. $4x - 8y = 15$
   $-5x + 10y = -30$

 **Apply**   © **27. Think About a Plan** A photo studio offers portraits in 8×10 and wallet-sized formats. One customer bought two 8×10 portraits and four wallet-sized portraits and paid $52. Another customer bought three 8×10 portraits and two wallet-sized portraits and paid $50. What is the cost of an 8×10 portrait? What is the cost of a wallet-sized portrait?
   • Can you eliminate a variable simply by adding or subtracting?
   • If not, how many of the equations do you need to multiply by a constant?

28. Reasoning A toy store worker packed two boxes of identical dolls and plush toys for shipping in boxes that weigh 1 oz when empty. One box held 3 dolls and 4 plush toys. The worker marked the weight as 12 oz. The other box held 2 dolls and 3 plush toys. The worker marked the weight as 10 oz. Explain why the worker must have made a mistake.

29. Error Analysis A student solved a system of equations by elimination. Describe and correct the error made in the part of the solution shown.

$$5x + 4y = 2 \quad - \times 3 \rightarrow \quad 15x + 12y = 6$$
$$3x + 3y = -3 \quad - \times 4 \rightarrow \quad \underline{12x + 12y = -3}$$
$$3x + 0 = 9$$
$$x = 3$$

30. Nutrition Half a pepperoni pizza plus three fourths of a ham-and-pineapple pizza contains 765 Calories. One fourth of a pepperoni pizza plus a whole ham-and-pineapple pizza contains 745 Calories. How many Calories are in a whole pepperoni pizza? How many Calories are in a whole ham-and-pineapple pizza?

31. Open-Ended Write a system of equations that can be solved efficiently by elimination. Explain what you would do to eliminate one of the variables. Then solve the system.

Solve each system using any method. Explain why you chose the method you used.

32. $y = 2.5x$
$2y + 3x = 32$

33. $2x + y = 4$
$6x + 7y = 12$

34. $3x + 2y = 5$
$4x + 5y = 16$

35. $y = \frac{2}{3}x + 1$
$2x + 3y = 27$

36. $x + y = 1.5$
$2x + y = 1$

37. $\frac{1}{3}x + \frac{1}{2}y = 0$
$\frac{1}{2}x + \frac{1}{5}y = \frac{11}{5}$

38. Compare and Contrast What do the substitution method and the elimination method have in common? Explain. Give an example of a system that you would prefer to solve using one method instead of the other. Justify your choice.

39. Vacations A hotel offers two activity packages. One costs $192 and includes 3 h of horseback riding and 2 h of parasailing. The second costs $213 and includes 2 h of horseback riding and 3 h of parasailing. What is the cost for 1 h of each activity?

40. Geometry Each of the squares in the figures shown at the right has the same area, and each of the triangles has the same area. The total area of Figure A is 141 cm². The total area of Figure B is 192 cm². What is the area of each square and each triangle?

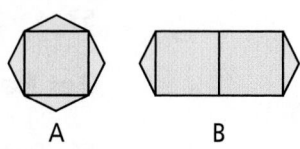

A   B

Challenge **Solve each system using elimination.**

41. $\frac{2}{x} - \frac{3}{y} = -5$
$\frac{4}{x} + \frac{6}{y} = 14$

42. $2x = 5(2 - y)$
$y = 3(-x + 5)$

43. $2x - 3y + z = 0$
$2x + y + z = 12$
$y - z = 4$

44. Reasoning Use the dartboard at the right. Can you score exactly 100 points with seven darts that all land on the board? Explain.

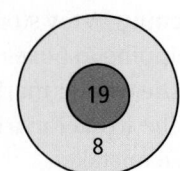

Standardized Test Prep

SAT/ACT

45. What is the value of the y-coordinate of the solution of the given system?

$$4x + 3y = 33$$
$$3x + 2y = 23$$

46. What is the y-intercept of $2x + 5y = 15$?

47. You buy a toothbrush for \$2.83 and a tube of toothpaste for \$2.37. There is a 5% sales tax. Including the tax, what is the total cost in dollars of your purchases?

48. Three fire trucks and 4 ambulances can fit into a parking lane 152 ft long. Two fire trucks and 5 ambulances can fit into a lane 136 ft long. How many feet long must a parking lane be for 1 fire truck and 5 ambulances? Assume there is 1 ft of space between each vehicle.

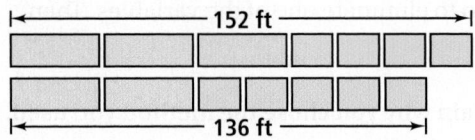

49. You are competing in a mountain bike race. Your average speed is 10 mi/h. If the racecourse is 65 mi long, how many minutes will it take you to finish the race?

Mixed Review

Solve each system using substitution.

See Lesson 6-2.

50. $y = \frac{1}{2}x$
$2y + 3x = 28$

51. $x - 7 = y$
$2x - y = 41$

52. $x + 2y = -1$
$3x - 5y = 30$

Solve each inequality.

See Lesson 3-4.

53. $4 - 2a < 3a - 1$

54. $3(2x - 1) \geq 5x + 4$

55. $2.7 + 2b > 3.4 - 1.5b$

Get Ready! **To prepare for Lesson 6-4, do Exercise 56.**

56. Two trains run on two sets of parallel tracks. The first train leaves a city $\frac{1}{2}$ h before the second train. The first train travels at 55 mi/h. The second train travels at 65 mi/h. How long does it take for the second train to pass the first train?

See Lesson 2-4.

Matrices and Solving Systems

Common Core State Standards

Extends A-REI.C.6 Solve systems of linear equations exactly and approximately (e.g., with graphs), focusing on pairs of linear equations in two variables.

MP 6

A *matrix* is a rectangular arrangement of numbers in rows and columns. The plural of *matrix* is *matrices*. You will learn more about matrix operations, including adding and subtracting matrices, in Chapter 12.

You can use a special type of matrix, called an *augmented matrix*, to solve a system of linear equations. An augmented matrix is formed using the coefficients and constants in the equations in a system. The equations must be written in standard form.

System of Equations

$$7x + 6y = 10$$

$$4x + 5y = -5$$

Augmented Matrix

$$\begin{bmatrix} 7 & 6 & | & 10 \\ 4 & 5 & | & -5 \end{bmatrix}$$

Recall the operations you performed when you solved systems using elimination. You can perform similar operations on the rows of an augmented matrix.

You can perform any of the following row operations on an augmented matrix to produce an equivalent augmented matrix.

Interchange two rows. $\begin{bmatrix} 7 & 6 & | & 10 \\ 4 & 5 & | & -5 \end{bmatrix} \rightarrow \begin{bmatrix} 4 & 5 & | & -5 \\ 7 & 6 & | & 10 \end{bmatrix}$

Multiply a row by any constant except 0. $\begin{bmatrix} 7 & 6 & | & 10 \\ 4 & 5 & | & -5 \end{bmatrix} \rightarrow \begin{bmatrix} 7 & 6 & | & 10 \\ 2(4) & 2(5) & | & 2(-5) \end{bmatrix} \rightarrow \begin{bmatrix} 7 & 6 & | & 10 \\ 8 & 10 & | & -10 \end{bmatrix}$

Add a multiple of one row to another row.

$$\begin{bmatrix} 7 & 6 & | & 10 \\ 4 & 5 & | & -5 \end{bmatrix} \rightarrow \begin{bmatrix} 7+2(4) & 6+2(5) & | & 10+2(-5) \\ 4 & 5 & | & -5 \end{bmatrix} \rightarrow \begin{bmatrix} 15 & 16 & | & 0 \\ 4 & 5 & | & -5 \end{bmatrix}$$

To solve a system using an augmented matrix, choose row operations that will transform the augmented matrix into a matrix with 1's along the main diagonal (top left to lower right) and 0's above and below the main diagonal, as shown below.

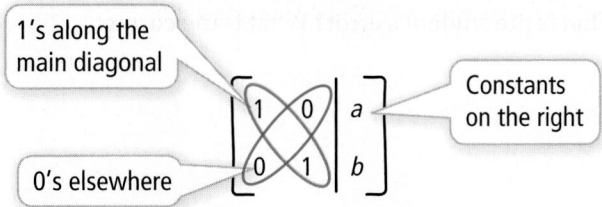

1's along the main diagonal

Constants on the right

0's elsewhere

$$\begin{bmatrix} 1 & 0 & | & a \\ 0 & 1 & | & b \end{bmatrix}$$

Example

Solve the system using an augmented matrix.

$$3x + 2y = 11$$
$$4x + y = 18$$

$$\begin{bmatrix} 3 & 2 & | & 11 \\ 4 & 1 & | & 18 \end{bmatrix}$$

Write the system as an augmented matrix.

$$\begin{bmatrix} 3 + (-2)(4) & 2 + (-2)(1) & | & 11 + (-2)(18) \\ 4 & 1 & | & 18 \end{bmatrix} \rightarrow \begin{bmatrix} -5 & 0 & | & -25 \\ 4 & 1 & | & 18 \end{bmatrix}$$

Multiply row 2 by -2 and add to row 1.

$$\begin{bmatrix} -\frac{1}{5}(-5) & -\frac{1}{5}(0) & | & -\frac{1}{5}(-25) \\ 4 & 1 & | & 18 \end{bmatrix} \rightarrow \begin{bmatrix} 1 & 0 & | & 5 \\ 4 & 1 & | & 18 \end{bmatrix}$$

Multiply row 1 by $-\frac{1}{5}$.

$$\begin{bmatrix} 1 & 0 & | & 5 \\ 4 + (-4)(1) & 1 + (-4)(0) & | & 18 + (-4)(5) \end{bmatrix} \rightarrow \begin{bmatrix} 1 & 0 & | & 5 \\ 0 & 1 & | & -2 \end{bmatrix}$$

Multiply row 1 by -4 and add to row 2.

$$x = 5$$
$$y = -2$$

Write each row of the matrix as an equation.

The solution of the system is $(5, -2)$.

Exercises

Solve each system using an augmented matrix.

1. $3x + 2y = 26$
$x + y = 7$

2. $-4x - 4y = 16$
$4x + 5y = 14$

3. $2x + 2y = 14$
$-x - 2y = -13$

Ⓒ **4. Compare and Contrast** Solve the system of equations in the example above using the elimination method. How are the row operations you have used in this activity like the operations you performed using the elimination method? How are they different?

Ⓒ **5. Writing** Are the row operations more like the substitution method or the elimination method? Explain.

6. Cosmetology A hairdresser finds that he can give 3 haircuts and 2 hair dyes in 315 min. Giving 2 haircuts and 4 hair dyes takes 450 min. How long does it take him to give a haircut? How long does it take him to dye a customer's hair? Write a system of equations and solve it using an augmented matrix.

Ⓒ **7. Error Analysis** A student says the augmented matrix at the right shows that the solution of the system is $(5, 3)$. What is the student's error? What is the correct solution of the system?

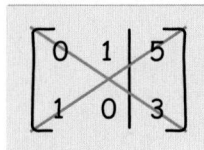

6-4 Applications of Linear Systems

© Common Core State Standards
A-REI.C.6 Solve systems of linear equations exactly and approximately, focusing on pairs of linear equations in two variables. **Also N-Q.A.3, A-CED.A.3**
MP 1, MP 2, MP 3, MP 4

Objective To choose the best method for solving a system of linear equations

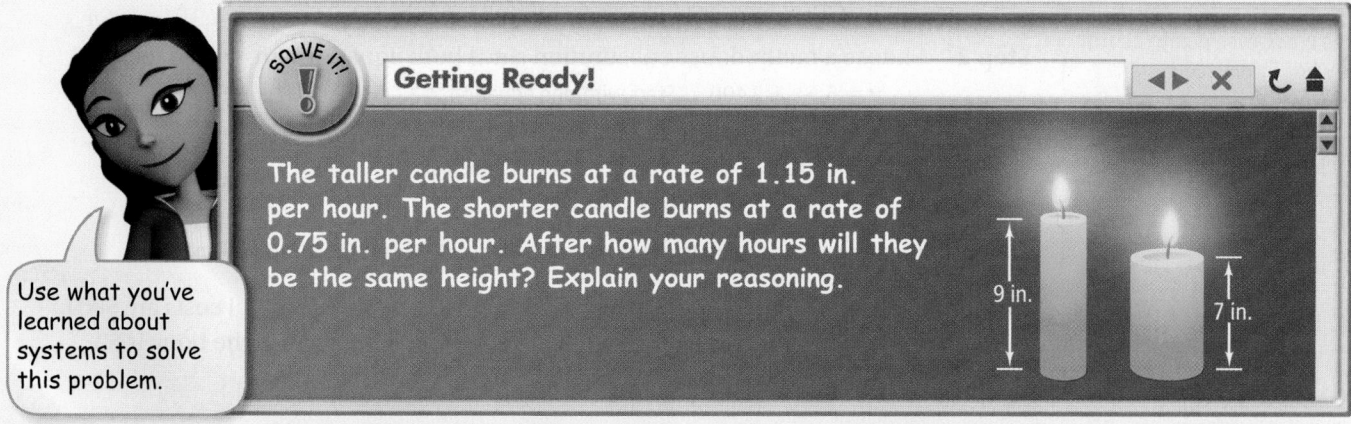

SOLVE IT!

Getting Ready!

The taller candle burns at a rate of 1.15 in. per hour. The shorter candle burns at a rate of 0.75 in. per hour. After how many hours will they be the same height? Explain your reasoning.

9 in.   7 in.

Use what you've learned about systems to solve this problem.

MATHEMATICAL PRACTICES

Essential Understanding You can solve systems of linear equations using a graph, the substitution method, or the elimination method. The best method to use depends on the forms of the given equations and how precise the solution should be.

take note

Concept Summary   Choosing a Method for Solving Linear Systems

Method	When to Use
Graphing	When you want a visual display of the equations, or when you want to estimate a solution
Substitution	When one equation is already solved for one of the variables, or when it is easy to solve for one of the variables
Elimination	When the coefficients of one variable are the same or opposites, or when it is not convenient to use graphing or substitution

Systems of equations are useful for modeling problems involving mixtures, rates, and break-even points.

The break-even point for a business is the point at which income equals expenses. The graph shows the break-even point for one business.

Notice that the values of *y* on the red line represent dollars spent on expenses. The values of *y* on the blue line represent dollars received as income. So *y* is used to represent both expenses and income.

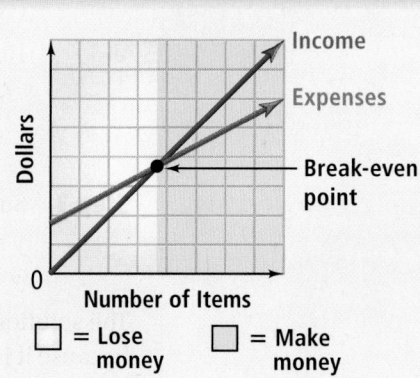

Income

Expenses

Dollars

Break-even point

0   Number of Items

☐ = Lose money   ☐ = Make money

 **Problem 1** Finding a Break-Even Point

Business A fashion designer makes and sells hats. The material for each hat costs $5.50. The hats sell for $12.50 each. The designer spends $1400 on advertising. How many hats must the designer sell to break even?

Think

What equations should you write?
The break-even point is when income equals expenses, so write one equation for income and one equation for expenses.

Step 1 Write a system of equations. Let x = the number of hats sold, and let y = the number of dollars of expense or income.

Expense: $y = 5.5x + 1400$ Income: $y = 12.5x$

Step 2 Choose a method. Use substitution since both equations are solved for y.

$y = 5.5x + 1400$	Start with one equation.
$12.5x = 5.5x + 1400$	Substitute $12.5x$ for y.
$7x = 1400$	Subtract $5.5x$ from each side.
$x = 200$	Divide each side by 7.

Since x is the number of hats, the designer must sell 200 hats to break even.

 Got It? **1.** A puzzle expert wrote a new sudoku puzzle book. His initial costs are $864. Binding and packaging each book costs $.80. The price of the book is $2. How many copies must be sold to break even?

In real-world situations, you need to consider the constraints described in the problem in order to write equations. Once you solve an equation, you need to consider the viability of the solution. For example, a solution that has a negative number of hours is not a viable solution.

 Problem 2 Identifying Constraints and Viable Solutions

Zoo The local zoo is filling two water tanks for the elephant exhibit. One water tank contains 50 gal of water and is filled at a constant rate of 10 gal/h. The second water tank contains 29 gal of water and is filled at a constant rate of 3 gal/h. When will the two tanks have the same amount of water? Explain.

Think

What are the constraints of the system?
If x represents time, then $x \geq 0$. If y represents the number of gallons, then $y \geq 0$.

Step 1 Write a system of equations. Let x = the number of hours the tanks are filling and let y = the number of gallons in the tank.

Tank 1: $y = 10x + 50$ Tank 2: $y = 3x + 29$

Step 2 The system is easy to solve using substitution. Substitute $10x + 50$ for y in the second equation and solve for x.

$y = 3x + 29$	Write the second equation.
$10x + 50 = 3x + 29$	Substitute $10x + 50$ for y.
$7x + 50 = 29$	Subtract $3x$ from each side. Then simplify.
$7x = -21$	Subtract 50 from each side. Then simplify.
$x = -3$	Divide each side by 7.

Step 3 Substitute -3 for x in either equation and solve for y.

$y = 10(-3) + 50$	Substitute -3 for x in the first equation.
$y = 20$	Simplify.

The solution to the system is $(-3, 20)$. The solution $(-3, 20)$ is not a viable solution because it is not possible to have time be -3 hours. So, the tanks never have the same amount of water.

Got It? **2.** The zoo has two other water tanks that are leaking. One tank contains 10 gal of water and is leaking at a constant rate of 2 gal/h. The second tank contains 6 gal of water and is leaking at a constant rate of 4 gal/h. When will the tanks have the same amount of water? Explain.

When a plane travels from west to east across the United States, the steady west-to-east winds act as tailwinds. This increases the plane's speed relative to the ground. When a plane travels from east to west, the winds act as headwinds. This decreases the plane's speed relative to the ground.

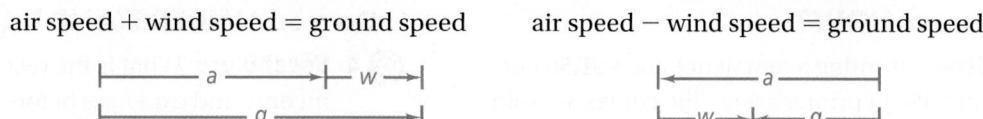

From West to East	**From East to West**
air speed + wind speed = ground speed	air speed − wind speed = ground speed

 Problem 3 **Solving a Wind or Current Problem**

Travel A traveler flies from Charlotte, North Carolina, to Los Angeles, California. At the same time, another traveler flies from Los Angeles to Charlotte. The air speed of each plane is the same. The ground speeds are shown below. What is the air speed? What is the wind speed?

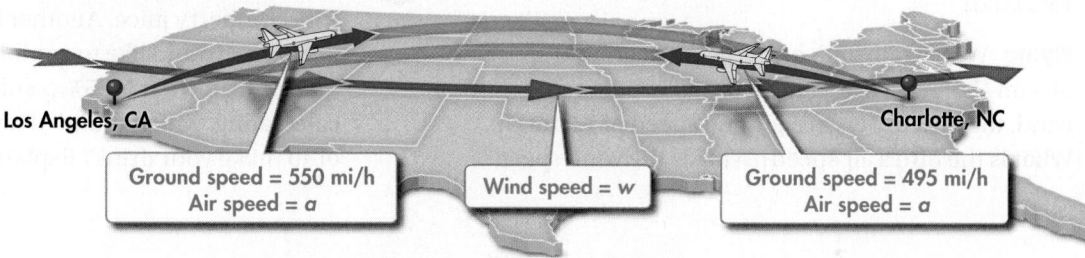

Los Angeles, CA

Charlotte, NC

Ground speed = 550 mi/h
Air speed = a

Wind speed = w

Ground speed = 495 mi/h
Air speed = a

Use the ground speed with the tailwind and with the headwind to write the system. Let a = the air speed of the planes. Let w = the wind speed.

Think

How are the speeds related?
The air speed is a plane's speed with no wind. Add wind speed and air speed to get the ground speed with a tailwind. Subtract wind speed from air speed to find the ground speed with a headwind.

air speed	+	wind speed	=	ground speed with tailwind		air speed	−	wind speed	=	ground speed with headwind
a	+	w	=	550		a	−	w	=	495

Choose a method to solve the system. Use elimination.

$$a + w = 550$$
$$\underline{a - w = 495}$$
$$2a + 0 = 1045 \quad \text{Add the equations.}$$
$$a = 522.5 \quad \text{Solve for } a.$$

Substitute 522.5 for a in either equation and solve for w.

$$522.5 + w = 550 \quad \text{Substitute 522.5 for } a \text{ in the first equation.}$$

$$w = 27.5 \quad \text{Solve for } w.$$

The air speed is 522.5 mi/h. The wind speed is 27.5 mi/h.

Got It? **3. a.** You row upstream at a speed of 2 mi/h. You travel the same distance downstream at a speed of 5 mi/h. What would be your rowing speed in still water? What is the speed of the current?

b. **Reasoning** Suppose your rowing speed in still water is 3 mi/h and the speed of the current is 4 mi/h. What happens when you try to row upstream?

Lesson Check

Do you know HOW?

1. Newsletters Printing a newsletter costs $1.50 per copy plus $450 in printer's fees. The copies are sold for $3 each. How many copies of the newsletter must be sold to break even?

2. Jewelry A metal alloy is a metal made by blending 2 or more types of metal. A jeweler has supplies of two metal alloys. One alloy is 30% gold and the other is 10% gold. How much of each alloy should the jeweler combine to create 4 kg of an alloy containing 15% gold?

3. Flying With a tailwind, a bird flew at a ground speed of 3 mi/h. Flying the same path against the same wind, the bird travels at a ground speed of 1.5 mi/h. What is the bird's air speed? What is the wind speed?

Do you UNDERSTAND?

4. Vocabulary What is the relationship between income and expenses before a break-even point is reached? What is the relationship between income and expenses after a break-even point is reached?

5. Reasoning Which method would you use to solve the following system? Explain.
$$3x + 2y = 9$$
$$-2x + 3y = 5$$

6. Reasoning One brand of cranberry-apple drink is 15% cranberry juice. Another brand is 40% cranberry juice. You would like to combine the brands to make a drink that is 25% cranberry juice. Without calculating, which brand of juice will you need more of to make your drink? Explain.

Practice and Problem-Solving Exercises

 **Practice**

7. Business A bicycle store costs $2400 per month to operate. The store pays an average of $60 per bike. The average selling price of each bicycle is $120. How many bicycles must the store sell each month to break even?

◀ **See Problem 1.**

8. Theater Producing a musical costs $88,000 plus $5900 per performance. One sold-out performance earns $7500 in revenue. If every performance sells out, how many performances are needed to break even?

9. Investment You split $1500 between two savings accounts. Account A pays annual 5% interest and Account B pays 4% annual interest. After one year, you have earned a total of $69.50 in interest. How much money did you invest in each account? Explain.

◀ **See Problem 2.**

STEM 10. Biology A group of scientists studied the effect of a chemical on various strains of bacteria. Strain A started with 6000 cells and decreased at a constant rate of 2000 cells per hour after the chemical was applied. Strain B started with 2000 cells and decreased at a constant rate of 1000 cells per hour after the chemical was applied. When will the strains have the same number of cells? Explain.

11. **Airports** A traveler is walking on a moving walkway in an airport. The traveler must walk back on the walkway to get a bag he forgot. The traveler's groundspeed is 2 ft/s against the walkway and 6 ft/s with the walkway. What is the traveler's speed off the walkway? What is the speed of the moving walkway?

◀ **See Problem 3.**

12. **Kayaking** A kayaker paddles upstream from camp to photograph a waterfall and returns. The kayaker's speed while traveling upstream and downstream is shown below. What is the kayaker's speed in still water? What is the speed of the current?

 **Apply**

13. **Money** You have a jar of pennies and quarters. You want to choose 15 coins that are worth exactly $4.35.
    a. Write and solve a system of equations that models the situation.
    b. Is your solution reasonable in terms of the original problem? Explain.

Solve each system. Explain why you chose the method you used.

14. $4x + 5y = 3$
    $3x - 2y = 8$

15. $2x + 7y = -20$
    $y = 3x + 7$

16. $5x + 2y = 17$
    $x - 2y = 8$

17. **Reasoning** Find A and B so that the system below has the solution $(2, 3)$.
    $$Ax - 2By = 6$$
    $$3Ax - By = -12$$

18. **Think About a Plan** A tugboat can pull a boat 24 mi downstream in 2 h. Going upstream, the tugboat can pull the same boat 16 mi in 2 h. What is the speed of the tugboat in still water? What is the speed of the current?
    • How can you use the formula $d = rt$ to help you solve the problem?
    • How are the tugboat's speeds when traveling upstream and downstream related to its speed in still water and the speed of the current?

Open-Ended Without solving, decide which method you would use to solve each system: *graphing*, *substitution*, or *elimination*. Explain.

19. $y = 3x - 1$
    $y = 4x$

20. $3m - 4n = 1$
    $3m - 2n = -1$

21. $4s - 3t = 8$
    $t = -2s - 1$

22. **Business** A perfume maker has stocks of two perfumes on hand. Perfume A sells for $15 per ounce. Perfume B sells for $35 per ounce. How much of each should be combined to make a 3-oz bottle of perfume that can be sold for $63?

STEM 23. **Chemistry** In a chemistry lab, you have two vinegars. One is 5% acetic acid, and one is 6.5% acetic acid. You want to make 200 mL of a vinegar with 6% acetic acid. How many milliliters of each vinegar do you need to mix together?

24. Boating A boat is traveling in a river with a current that has a speed of 1.5 km/h. In one hour, the boat can travel twice the distance downstream that it can travel upstream. What is the boat's speed in still water?

 **25. Reasoning** A student claims that the best way to solve the system at the right is by substitution. Do you agree? Explain.

$$y - 3x = 4$$
$$y - 6x = 12$$

26. Entertainment A contestant on a quiz show gets 150 points for every correct answer and loses 250 points for each incorrect answer. After answering 20 questions, the contestant has 200 points. How many questions has the contestant answered correctly? Incorrectly?

Challenge

27. Number Theory You can represent the value of any two-digit number with the expression $10a + b$, where a is the tens' place digit and b is the ones' place digit. For example, if a is 5 and b is 7, then the value of the number is $10(5) + 7$, or 57. What two-digit number is described below?
- The ones' place digit is one more than twice the tens' place digit.
- The value of the number is two more than five times the ones' place digit.

28. Mixed Nuts You want to sell 1-lb jars of mixed peanuts and cashews for $5. You pay $3 per pound for peanuts and $6 per pound for cashews. You plan to combine 4 parts peanuts and 1 part cashews to make your mix. You have spent $70 on materials to get started. How many jars must you sell to break even?

Standardized Test Prep

SAT/ACT

29. Last year, one fourth of the students in your class played an instrument. This year, 6 students joined the class. Four of the new students play an instrument. Now, one third of the students play an instrument. How many students are in your class now?

   Ⓐ 18   Ⓑ 24   Ⓒ 30   Ⓓ 48

30. Which answer choice shows $2x - y = z$ correctly solved for y?

   Ⓕ $y = 2x + z$ Ⓖ $y = 2x - z$ Ⓗ $y = -2x + z$ Ⓘ $y = -2x - z$

Short Response

31. What is an equation of a line passing through the points (3, 1) and (4, 3) written in slope-intercept form?

Mixed Review

Solve each system using elimination.   ◀ See Lesson 6-3.

32. $x + 3y = 11$
    $2x + 3y = 4$

33. $2x + 4y = -12$
    $-6x + 5y = 2$

34. $5x + 8y = 40$
    $3x - 10y = -13$

Get Ready!   To prepare for Lesson 6-5, do Exercises 35–37.

Solve each inequality. Check your solution.   ◀ See Lesson 3-4.

35. $3a + 5 > 20$ **36.** $2d - 3 \geq 4d + 2$ **37.** $3(q + 4) \leq -2q - 8$

Do you know HOW?

Solve each system by graphing. Tell whether the system has *one solution, infinitely many solutions,* or *no solution.*

1. $y = x - 1$
  $y = -3x - 5$

2. $y = \frac{4}{3}x - 2$
  $3y - 4x = -6$

3. $y = 3x - 4$
  $y - 3x = 1$

4. $y = 3x - 14$
  $y - x = 10$

Solve each system using substitution.

5. $y = 2x + 5$
  $y = 6x + 1$

6. $x = y + 7$
  $y - 8 = 2x$

7. $4x + y = 2$
  $3y + 2x = -1$

8. $4x + 9y = 24$
  $y = -\frac{1}{3}x + 2$

Solve each system using elimination.

9. $2x + 5y = 2$
  $3x - 5y = 53$

10. $4x + 2y = 34$
  $10x - 4y = -5$

11. $11x - 13y = 89$
  $-11x + 13y = 107$

12. $3x + 6y = 42$
  $-7x + 8y = -109$

Write and solve a system of equations to solve each problem. Explain why you chose the method you used.

13. Geometry The length of a rectangle is 3 times the width. The perimeter is 44 cm. What are the dimensions of the rectangle?

14. Farming A farmer grows only pumpkins and corn on her 420-acre farm. This year she wants to plant 250 more acres of corn than pumpkins. How many acres of each crop should the farmer plant?

15. Coins You have a total of 21 coins, all nickels and dimes. The total value is $1.70. How many nickels and how many dimes do you have?

16. Business Suppose you start an ice cream business. You buy a freezer for $200. It costs you $.45 to make each single-scoop ice cream cone. You sell each cone for $1.25. How many cones do you need to sell to break even?

Do you UNDERSTAND?

Ⓒ **Reasoning** Without solving, tell which method you would choose to solve each system: *graphing, substitution,* or *elimination.* Explain your answer.

17. $y = 2x - 5$
  $4y + 8x = 15$

18. $2y + 7x = 3$
  $y - 7x = 9$

Ⓒ **19. Reasoning** If a system of linear equations has infinitely many solutions, what do you know about the slopes and *y*-intercepts of the graphs of the equations?

Ⓒ **20. Open-Ended** Write a system of equations that you would solve using substitution.

Ⓒ **21. Reasoning** Suppose you write a system of equations to find a break-even point for a business. You solve the system and find that it has no solution. What would that mean in terms of the business?

Linear Inequalities

 **Common Core State Standards**

A-REI.D.12 Graph the solutions to a linear inequality in two variables as a half-plane . . . **Also A-CED.A.3**

MP 1, MP 2, MP 3, MP 4, MP 6

Objectives To graph linear inequalities in two variables
To use linear inequalities when modeling real-world situations

 **Getting Ready!**   ◄► ✕ ↻ ⌂

One of these and one of those . . . no, wait. Three of these . . .

You are buying paperback and hardcover books at a book sale. You can spend at most $20. What are the possible combinations of paperback and hardcover books that you can buy? Explain.

Paperback $2.50   Hardcover $4.50

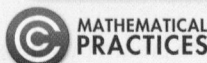 **MATHEMATICAL PRACTICES**

 **Lesson Vocabulary**
• linear inequality
• solution of an inequality

A **linear inequality** in two variables, such as $y > x - 3$, can be formed by replacing the equal sign in a linear equation with an inequality symbol. A **solution of an inequality** in two variables is an ordered pair that makes the inequality true.

Essential Understanding A linear inequality in two variables has an infinite number of solutions. These solutions can be represented in the coordinate plane as the set of all points on one side of a boundary line.

Think

Have you tested solutions before?
Yes. You have tested whether ordered pairs are solutions of equations. Now you will test ordered pairs to see whether they satisfy an inequality.

 **Problem 1** **Identifying Solutions of a Linear Inequality**

Is the ordered pair a solution of $y > x - 3$?

Ⓐ $(1, 2)$

$y > x - 3$ ← Write the inequality. →
$2 \overset{?}{>} 1 - 3$ ← Substitute. →
$2 > -2$ ✔ ← Simplify. →

$(1, 2)$ is a solution.

Ⓑ $(-3, -7)$

$y > x - 3$
$-7 \overset{?}{>} -3 - 3$
$-7 > -6$ ✘

$(-3, -7)$ is *not* a solution.

Got lt? **1. a.** Is $(3, 6)$ a solution of $y \le \frac{2}{3}x + 4$?
b. Reasoning Suppose an ordered pair is not a solution of $y > x + 10$. Must it be a solution of $y < x + 10$? Explain.

The graph of a linear inequality in two variables consists of all points in the coordinate plane that represent solutions. The graph is a region called a *half-plane* that is bounded by a line. All points on one side of the boundary line are solutions, while all points on the other side are not solutions.

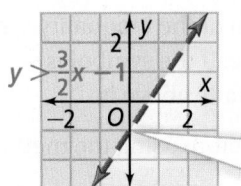

$y > \frac{3}{2}x - 1$

Each point on a *dashed* line is not a solution. A dashed line is used for inequalities with > or <.

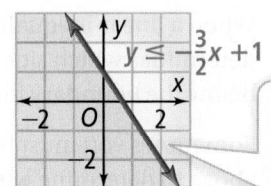

$y \le -\frac{3}{2}x + 1$

Each point on a *solid* line is a solution. A solid line is used for inequalities with ≥ or ≤.

ⒸProblem 2 **Graphing an Inequality in Two Variables**

Think

Why does $y = x - 2$ represent the boundary line?
For any value of x, the corresponding value of y is the boundary between values of y that are greater than $x - 2$ and values of y that are less than $x - 2$.

What is the graph of $y > x - 2$?

First, graph the boundary line $y = x - 2$. Since the inequality symbol is >, the points on the boundary line are *not* solutions. Use a dashed line to indicate that the points are not included in the solution.

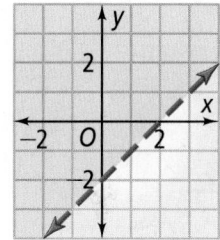

To determine which side of the boundary line to shade, test a point that is not on the line. For example, test the point $(0, 0)$.

$y > x - 2$

$0 \overset{?}{>} 0 - 2$ Substitute $(0, 0)$ for (x, y).

$0 > -2$ ✔ $(0, 0)$ is a solution.

Because the point $(0, 0)$ is a solution of the inequality, so are all the points on the same side of the boundary line as $(0, 0)$. Shade the area above the boundary line.

 Got It? 2. What is the graph of $y \le \frac{1}{2}x + 1$?

An inequality in one variable can be graphed on a number line or in the coordinate plane. The boundary line will be a horizontal or vertical line.

ⒸProblem 3 **Graphing a Linear Inequality in One Variable**

Think

Have you graphed inequalities like these before?
Yes. In Lesson 3-1, you graphed inequalities in one variable on a number line. Here you graph them in the coordinate plane.

What is the graph of each inequality in the coordinate plane?

Ⓐ $x > -1$

Graph $x = -1$ using a dashed line. Use $(0, 0)$ as a test point.

$x > -1$

$0 > -1$ ✔

Shade on the side of the line that contains $(0, 0)$.

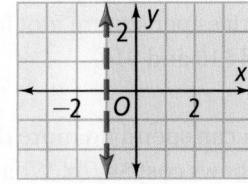

Ⓑ $y \ge 2$

Graph $y = 2$ using a solid line. Use $(0, 0)$ as a test point.

$y \ge 2$

$0 \ge 2$ ✗

Shade on the side of the line that does *not* contain $(0, 0)$.

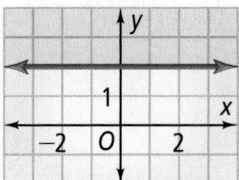

Got It? **3.** What is the graph of each inequality?

     a. $x < -5$ **b.** $y \leq 2$

When a linear inequality is solved for y, the direction of the inequality symbol determines which side of the boundary line to shade. If the symbol is $<$ or $\leq$, shade below the boundary line. If the symbol is $>$ or $\geq$, shade above it.

Sometimes you must first solve an inequality for y before using the method described above to determine where to shade.

ⓒ **Problem 4** **Rewriting to Graph an Inequality**

Interior Design An interior decorator is going to remodel a kitchen. The wall above the stove and the counter is going to be redone as shown. The owners can spend $420 or less. Write a linear inequality and graph the solutions. What are three possible prices for the wallpaper and tiles?

Tiled Area
3 ft · 4 ft = 12 ft²

Papered Area
3 ft · 8 ft = 24 ft²

Let $x =$ the cost per square foot of the paper.

Let $y =$ the cost per square foot of the tiles.

Think

Which inequality symbol should you use?
You must read the problem statement carefully. Here "$420 or less" means that the solution includes, but cannot exceed, $420, so use $\leq$.

Write an inequality and solve it for y.

$24x + 12y \leq 420$	Total cost is $420 or less.
$12y \leq -24x + 420$	Subtract $24x$ from each side.
$y \leq -2x + 35$	Divide each side by 12.

Graph $y \leq -2x + 35$. The inequality symbol is $\leq$, so the boundary line is solid and you shade below it. The graph only makes sense in the first quadrant. Three possible prices per square foot for wallpaper and tile are $5 and $25, $5 and $15, and $10 and $10.

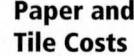

Paper and Tile Costs

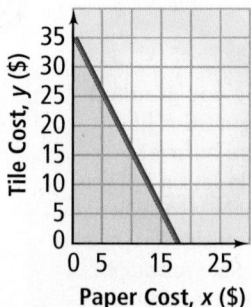

 Got It? **4.** For a party, you can spend no more than $12 on nuts. Peanuts cost $2/lb. Cashews cost $4/lb. What are three possible combinations of peanuts and cashews you can buy?

 **Problem 5** Writing an Inequality From a Graph

Think

Can you eliminate choices?
Yes. The boundary line is solid and the region below it is shaded, so you know the inequality symbol must be ≤. You can eliminate choices C and D.

Multiple Choice Which inequality represents the graph at the right?

Ⓐ $y \leq 2x + 1$

Ⓒ $y \geq 2x + 1$

Ⓑ $y \leq x + 1$

Ⓓ $y < 2x + 1$

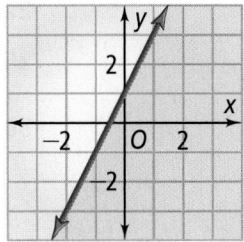

The slope of the line is 2 and the y-intercept is 1, so the equation of the boundary line is $y = 2x + 1$. The boundary line is solid, so the inequality symbol is either ≤ or ≥. The symbol must be ≤, because the region below the boundary line is shaded. The inequality is $y \leq 2x + 1$.

The correct answer is A.

Got It? **5.** You are writing an inequality from a graph. The boundary line is dashed and has slope $\frac{1}{3}$ and y-intercept -2. The area above the line is shaded. What inequality should you write?

Lesson Check

Do you know HOW?

1. Is $(-1, 4)$ a solution of the inequality $y < 2x + 5$?

Graph each linear inequality.

2. $y \leq -2x + 3$

3. $x < -1$

4. What is an inequality that represents the graph at the right?

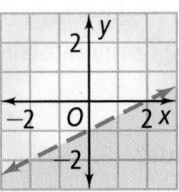

Do you UNDERSTAND?

5. Vocabulary How is a linear inequality in two variables like a linear equation in two variables? How are they different?

6. Writing To graph the inequality $y < \frac{3}{2}x + 3$, do you shade above or below the boundary line? Explain.

7. Reasoning Write an inequality that describes the region of the coordinate plane *not* included in the graph of $y < 5x + 1$.

Practice and Problem-Solving Exercises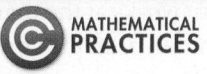

Ⓐ Practice Determine whether the ordered pair is a solution of the linear inequality. ◀ See Problem 1.

8. $y \leq -2x + 1$; $(2, 2)$

9. $x < 2$; $(-1, 0)$

10. $y \geq 3x - 2$; $(0, 0)$

11. $y > x - 1$; $(0, 1)$

12. $y \geq -\frac{2}{5}x + 4$; $(0, 0)$

13. $3y > 5x - 12$; $(-6, 1)$

Graph each linear inequality. ◀ See Problem 2.

14. $y \leq x - 1$

15. $y \geq 3x - 2$

16. $y < -4x - 1$

17. $y > 2x - 6$

18. $y < 5x - 5$

19. $y \leq \frac{1}{2}x - 3$

20. $y > -3x$

21. $y \geq -x$

Graph each inequality in the coordinate plane.

◀ See Problems 3 and 4.

22. $x \leq 4$ **23.** $y \geq -1$ **24.** $x > -2$ **25.** $y < -4$

26. $-2x + y \geq 3$ **27.** $x + 3y < 15$ **28.** $4x - y > 2$ **29.** $-x + 0.25y \leq -1.75$

30. Carpentry You budget $200 for wooden planks for outdoor furniture. Cedar costs $2.50 per foot and pine costs $1.75 per foot. Let $x =$ the number of feet of cedar and let $y =$ the number of feet of pine. What is an inequality that shows how much of each type of wood can be bought? Graph the inequality. What are three possible amounts of each type of wood that can be bought within your budget?

31. Business A fish market charges $9 per pound for cod and $12 per pound for flounder. Let $x =$ the number of pounds of cod. Let $y =$ the number of pounds of flounder. What is an inequality that shows how much of each type of fish the store must sell today to reach a daily quota of at least $120? Graph the inequality. What are three possible amounts of each fish that would satisfy the quota?

Write a linear inequality that represents each graph.

◀ See Problem 5.

32. 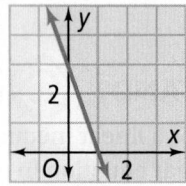 **33.** 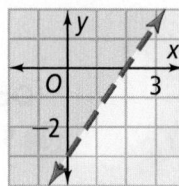 **34.**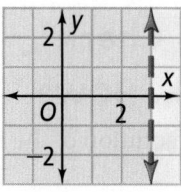

 **Apply**

Ⓒ 35. Think About a Plan A truck that can carry no more than 6400 lb is being used to transport refrigerators and upright pianos. Each refrigerator weighs 250 lb and each piano weighs 475 lb. Write and graph an inequality to show how many refrigerators and how many pianos the truck could carry. Will 12 refrigerators and 8 pianos overload the truck? Explain.
- What inequality symbol should you use?
- Which side of the boundary line should you shade?

36. Employment A student with two summer jobs earns $10 per hour at a cafe and $8 per hour at a market. The student would like to earn at least $800 per month.
a. Write and graph an inequality to represent the situation.
b. The student works at the market for 60 h per month and can work at most 90 h per month. Can the student earn at least $800 each month? Explain how you can you use your graph to determine this.

Ⓒ 37. Error Analysis A student graphed $y \geq 2x + 3$ as shown at the right. Describe and correct the student's error.

Ⓒ 38. Writing When graphing an inequality, can you always use $(0, 0)$ as a test point to determine where to shade? If not, how would you choose a test point?

Ⓒ Challenge

39. Music Store A music store sells used CDs for $5 each and buys used CDs for $1.50 each. You go to the store with $20 and some CDs to sell. You want to have at least $10 left when you leave the store. Write and graph an inequality to show how many CDs you could buy and sell.

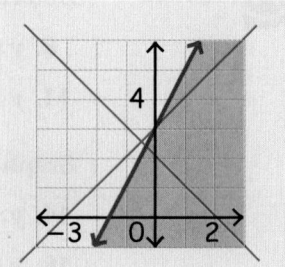

40. Groceries At your grocery store, milk normally costs $3.60 per gallon. Ground beef costs $3 per pound. Today there are specials: Milk is discounted $.50 per gallon, and ground beef is 20% off. You want to spend no more than $20. Write and graph a linear inequality to show how many gallons of milk and how many pounds of ground beef you can buy today.

41. Reasoning You are graphing a linear inequality of the form $y > mx + b$. The point $(1, 2)$ is not a solution, but $(3, 2)$ is. Is the slope of the boundary line *positive, negative, zero,* or *undefined*? Explain.

Standardized Test Prep

SAT/ACT

42. What is the equation of the graph shown?

Ⓐ $y + x \geq -3$

Ⓑ $y - x \geq 3$

Ⓒ $x - y > -3$

Ⓓ $y > -x + 3$

43. You secure pictures to your scrapbook using 3 stickers. You started with 24 stickers. There are now 2 pictures in your scrapbook. You write the equation $3(x + 2) = 24$ to find the number x of additional pictures you can put in your scrapbook. How many more pictures can you add?

Ⓕ 4

Ⓖ 6

Ⓗ 8

Ⓘ 12

Short Response

44. At Market A, 1-lb packages of rice are sold for the price shown. At Market B, rice is sold in bulk for the price shown. For each market, write a function describing the cost of buying rice in terms of the weight. How are the domains of the two functions different?

RICE
$2.00

BULK RICE
$2.00/lb

Mixed Review

45. Small Business An electrician spends $12,000 on initial costs to start a new business. He estimates his expenses at $25 per day. He expects to earn $150 per day. If his estimates are correct, after how many working days will he break even?

◄ See Lesson 6-4.

46. What compound inequality represents the phrase "all real numbers that are greater than 2 and less than or equal to 7"? Graph the solutions.

◄ See Lesson 3-6.

Get Ready! **To prepare for Lesson 6-6, do Exercises 47–49.**

Solve each system by graphing. Tell whether the system has *one solution, infinitely many solutions,* or *no solution.*

◄ See Lesson 6-1.

47. $y = \frac{3}{2}x$
$-2x + y = 3$

48. $3x + y = 6$
$2x - y = 4$

49. $x + y = 11$
$x + y = 16$

6-6 Systems of Linear Inequalities

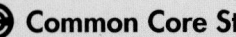 **Common Core State Standards**

A-REI.D.12 Graph . . . the solution set to a system of linear inequalities in two variables as the intersection of the corresponding half-planes.

MP 1, MP 2, MP 3, MP 4, MP 7

Objectives To solve systems of linear inequalities by graphing
To model real-world situations using systems of linear inequalities

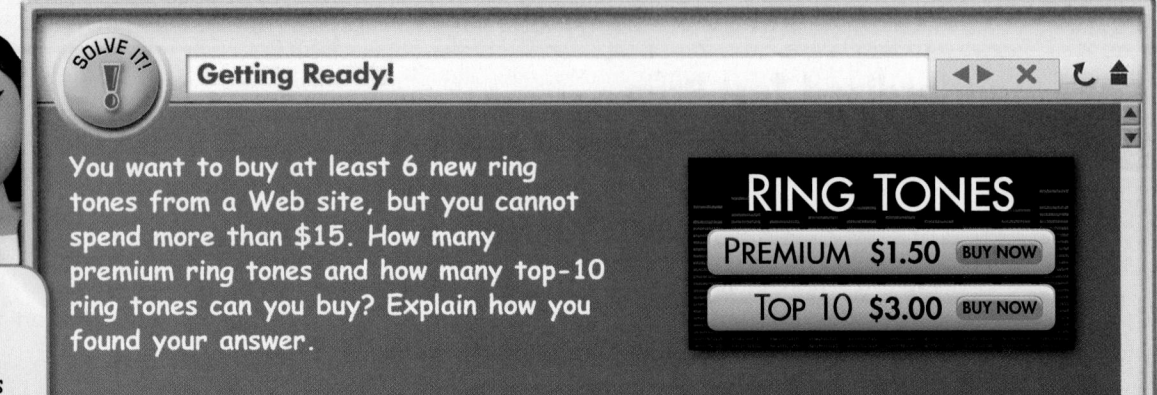

Getting Ready!

You want to buy at least 6 new ring tones from a Web site, but you cannot spend more than $15. How many premium ring tones and how many top-10 ring tones can you buy? Explain how you found your answer.

RING TONES
PREMIUM **$1.50** BUY NOW
TOP 10 **$3.00** BUY NOW

See how many combinations you can find that satisfy this situation.

MATHEMATICAL PRACTICES

A **system of linear inequalities** is made up of two or more linear inequalities. A **solution of a system of linear inequalities** is an ordered pair that makes *all* the inequalities in the system true. The graph of a system of linear inequalities is the set of points that represent all of the solutions of the system.

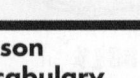

Lesson Vocabulary
- system of linear inequalities
- solution of a system of linear inequalities

Essential Understanding You can graph the solutions of a system of linear inequalities in the coordinate plane. The graph of the system is the region where the graphs of the individual inequalities overlap.

Problem 1 Graphing a System of Inequalities

Think

Have you seen a problem like this before?
Yes. The solution of a system of equations is shown by the intersection of two lines. The solutions of a system of inequalities are shown by the intersection of two shaded areas.

What is the graph of the system? $y < 2x - 3$
$2x + y > 2$

Graph $y < 2x - 3$ and $2x + y > 2$.

The blue region represents solutions of $2x + y > 2$.

The green region represents solutions of *both* inequalities.

The yellow region represents solutions of $y < 2x - 3$.

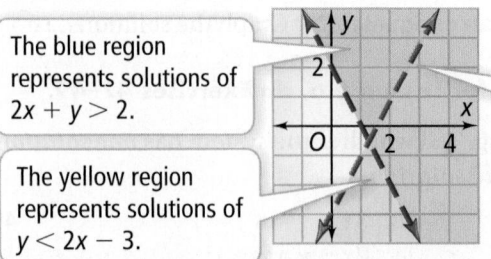

The system's solutions lie in the green region where the graphs overlap.

Check (3, 0) is in the green region. See if (3, 0) satisfies both inequalities.

$y \overset{?}{\leq} 2x - 3$ ← Write both inequalities. → $2x + y \overset{?}{\geq} 2$

$0 \overset{?}{\leq} 2(3) - 3$ ← Substitute (3, 0) for (x, y). → $2(3) + 0 \overset{?}{\geq} 2$

$0 < 3$ ✔ ← Simplify. The solution checks. → $6 > 2$ ✔

 Got It? 1. What is the graph of the system? $y \geq -x + 5$
$-3x + y \leq -4$

You can combine your knowledge of linear equations with your knowledge of inequalities to describe a graph using a system of inequalities.

Think

Have you seen a problem like this one before?
Yes. You wrote an inequality from a graph in Lesson 6-5. Now you'll write two inequalities.

© **Problem 2** Writing a System of Inequalities From a Graph

What system of inequalities is represented by the graph below?

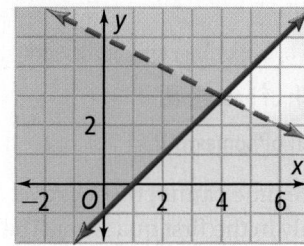

To write a system that is represented by the graph, write an inequality that represents the yellow region and an inequality that represents the blue region.

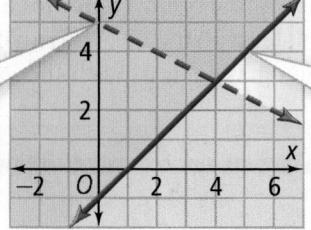

The red boundary line is $y = -\frac{1}{2}x + 5$. The region does not include the line, only points below. The inequality is $y < -\frac{1}{2}x + 5$.

The blue boundary line is $y = x - 1$. The region includes the boundary line and points above. The inequality is $y \geq x - 1$.

The graph shows the intersection of the system $y < -\frac{1}{2}x + 5$ and $y \geq x - 1$.

© **Got It? 2. a.** What system of inequalities is represented by the graph?

     b. Reasoning In part (a), is the point where the boundary lines intersect a solution of the system? Explain.

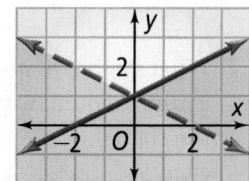

You can model many real-world situations by writing and graphing systems of linear inequalities. Some real-world situations involve three or more restrictions, so you must write a system of at least three inequalities.

Problem 3 Using a System of Inequalities

Time Management You are planning what to do after school. You can spend at most 6 h daily playing basketball and doing homework. You want to spend less than 2 h playing basketball. You must spend at least $1\frac{1}{2}$ h on homework. What is a graph showing how you can spend your time?

Know	Need	Plan
• At most 6 h playing basketball and doing homework • Less than 2 h playing basketball • At least $1\frac{1}{2}$ h doing homework	To find different ways you can spend your time	Write and graph an inequality for each restriction. Find the region where all three restrictions are met.

Let x = the number of hours playing basketball.

Let y = the number of hours doing homework.

Write a system of inequalities.

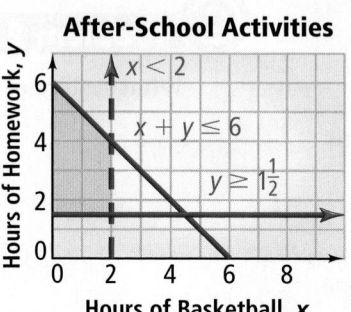

After-School Activities

$x + y \leq 6$ At most 6 h of basketball and homework

$x < 2$ Less than 2 h of basketball

$y \geq 1\frac{1}{2}$ At least $1\frac{1}{2}$ h of homework

Graph the system. Because time cannot be negative, the graph makes sense only in the first quadrant. The solutions of the system are all of the points in the shaded region, including the points on the solid boundary lines.

Got It?   **3.** You want to build a fence for a rectangular dog run. You want the run to be at least 10 ft wide. The run can be at most 50 ft long. You have 126 ft of fencing. What is a graph showing the possible dimensions of the dog run?

Lesson Check

Do you know HOW?

1. What is the graph of the system? $y > 3x - 2$
$$2y - x \leq 6$$

2. What system of inequalities is represented by the graph at the right?

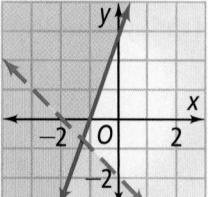

3. Cherries cost \$4/lb. Grapes cost \$2.50/lb. You can spend no more than \$15 on fruit, and you need at least 4 lb in all. What is a graph showing the amount of each fruit you can buy?

Do you UNDERSTAND?  MATHEMATICAL PRACTICES

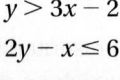 **4. Vocabulary** How can you determine whether an ordered pair is a solution of a system of linear inequalities?

5. Reasoning Suppose you are graphing a system of two linear inequalities, and the boundary lines for the inequalities are parallel. Does that mean that the system has no solution? Explain.

6. Writing How is finding the solution of a system of inequalities different from finding the solution of a system of equations? How is it the same? Explain.

Practice and Problem-Solving Exercises

MATHEMATICAL PRACTICES

 **Practice**   Determine whether the ordered pair is a solution of the given system.   ◀ **See Problem 1.**

7. (2, 12);
$y > 2x + 4$
$y < 3x + 7$

8. (8, 2);
$3x - 2y \le 17$
$0.3x + 4y > 9$

9. (−3, 17);
$y > -5x + 2$
$y \ge -3x + 7$

Solve each system of inequalities by graphing.

10. $y < 2x + 4$
$-3x - 2y \ge 6$

11. $y < 2x + 4$
$2x - y \le 4$

12. $y > 2x + 4$
$2x - y \le 4$

13. $y > \frac{1}{4}x$
$y \le -x + 4$

14. $y < 2x - 3$
$y > 5$

15. $y \le -\frac{1}{3}x + 7$
$y \ge -x + 1$

16. $x + 2y \le 10$
$x + 2y \ge 9$

17. $y \ge -x + 5$
$y \le 3x - 4$

18. $y \le 0.75x - 2$
$y > 0.75x - 3$

19. $8x + 4y \ge 10$
$3x - 6y > 12$

20. $2x - \frac{1}{4}y < 1$
$4x + 8y > 4$

21. $6x - 5y < 15$
$x + 2y \ge 7$

Write a system of inequalities for each graph.   ◀ **See Problem 2.**

22.
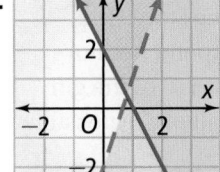

23.
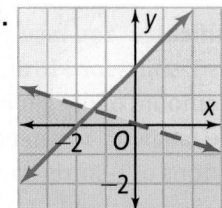

24.
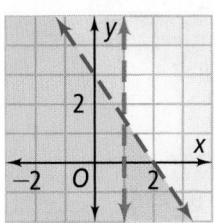

25.
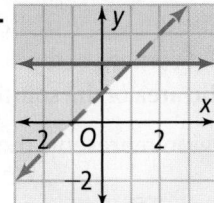

26. Earnings Suppose you have a job mowing lawns that pays $12 per hour. You   ◀ **See Problem 3.**
also have a job at a clothing store that pays $10 per hour. You need to earn at least
$350 per week, but you can work no more than 35 h per week. You must work a
minimum of 10 h per week at the clothing store. What is a graph showing how
many hours per week you can work at each job?

27. Driving Two friends agree to split the driving on a road trip from Philadelphia,
Pennsylvania, to Denver, Colorado. One friend drives at an average speed of
60 mi/h. The other friend drives at an average speed of 55 mi/h. They want to drive
at least 500 mi per day. They plan to spend no more than 10 h driving each day. The
friend who drives slower wants to drive fewer hours. What is a graph showing how
they can split the driving each day?

C **28. Think About a Plan** You are fencing in a rectangular area for a garden. You have only 150 ft of fence. You want the length of the garden to be at least 40 ft. You want the width of the garden to be at least 5 ft. What is a graph showing the possible dimensions your garden could have?
- What variables will you use? What will they represent?
- How many inequalities do you need to write?

C **29. a.** Graph the system $y > 3x + 3$ and $y \le 3x - 5$.
  b. Writing Will the boundary lines $y = 3x + 3$ and $y = 3x - 5$ ever intersect? How do you know?
  c. Do the shaded regions in the graph from part (a) overlap?
  d. Does the system of inequalities have any solutions? Explain.

C **30. Error Analysis** A student graphs the system as shown below. Describe and correct the student's error.

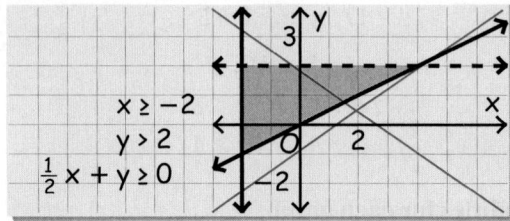

31. Gift Certificates You received a $100 gift certificate to a clothing store. The store sells T-shirts for $15 and dress shirts for $22. You want to spend no more than the amount of the gift certificate. You want to leave at most $10 of the gift certificate unspent. You need at least one dress shirt. What are all of the possible combinations of T-shirts and dress shirts you could buy?

32. a. Geometry Graph the system of linear inequalities. $x \ge 2$
  b. Describe the shape of the solution region. $y \ge -3$
  c. Find the vertices of the solution region. $x + y \le 4$
  d. Find the area of the solution region.

33. Which region represents the solution of the system? $y \le -\frac{3}{2}x - 2$
  Ⓐ I   Ⓒ III $3y - 9x \ge 6$
  Ⓑ II   Ⓓ IV

C **Open-Ended** Write a system of linear inequalities with the given characteristic.

34. All solutions are in Quadrant III.   **35.** There are no solutions.

36. Business A jeweler plans to produce a ring made of silver and gold. The price of gold is about $25 per gram. The price of silver is approximately $.40 per gram. She considers the following in deciding how much gold and silver to use in the ring.
- The total mass must be more than 10 g but less than 20 g.
- The ring must contain at least 2 g of gold.
- The total cost of the gold and silver must be less than $90.
  a. Write and graph the inequalities that describe this situation.
  b. For one solution, find the mass of the ring and the cost of the gold and silver.

37. Solve $|y| \geq x$. (*Hint:* Write two inequalities and then graph them.)

38. Student Art A teacher wants to post a row of student artwork on a wall that is 20 ft long. Some pieces are 8.5 in. wide. Other pieces are 11 in. wide. She is going to leave 3 in. of space to the left of each art piece. She wants to post at least 16 pieces of art. Write and graph a system of inequalities that describes how many pieces of each size she can post.

Apply What You've Learned

Look back at the information on page 363 about Miguel's exercise program at the gym. Choose from the following inequalities to complete the sentences below. In each inequality, x represents the number of minutes Miguel spends on the stair machine and y represents the number of minutes Miguel spends on the rowing machine.

$x + y \leq 60$	$2y \leq x$	$x - y \geq 30$	$x + y \geq 30$
$2y \geq x$	$y \geq 2x$	$x + 2y \geq 30$	$x + y \geq 60$

a. An inequality representing the first condition given by Miguel's trainer is __?__ .

b. An inequality representing the second condition given by Miguel's trainer is __?__ .

c. An inequality representing the third condition given by Miguel's trainer is __?__ .

Concept Byte

Use With Lesson 6-6

TECHNOLOGY

Graphing Linear Inequalities

© Common Core State Standards

A-REI.D.12 Graph the solutions to a linear inequality in two variables as a half-plane . . . and graph the solution set to a system of linear inequalities . . .

MP 5

A graphing calculator can show the solutions of an inequality or a system of inequalities. To enter an inequality, press **apps** and scroll down to select **INEQUAL**. Move the cursor over the = symbol for one of the equations. Notice the inequality symbols at the bottom of the screen, above the keys labeled **F2–F5**. Change the = symbol to an inequality symbol by pressing **alpha** followed by one of **F2–F5**.

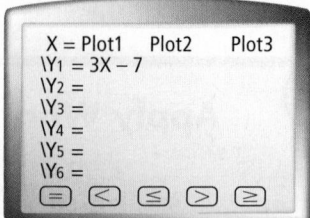

Activity 1

Graph the inequality $y < 3x - 7$.

1. Move the cursor over the = symbol for **Y₁**. Press **alpha** and **F2** to select the < symbol.

2. Enter the given inequality as **Y₁**.

3. Press **graph** to graph the inequality.

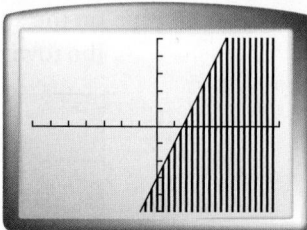

Activity 2

Graph the system. $y < -2x - 3$
$y \geq x + 4$

4. Move the cursor over the = symbol for **Y₁**. Press **alpha** and **F2** to select the < symbol. Enter the first inequality as **Y₁**.

5. Then move the cursor over the = symbol for **Y₂**, and press **alpha** and **F5** to select the ≥ symbol. Enter the second inequality as **Y₂**.

6. Press **graph** to graph the system of inequalities.

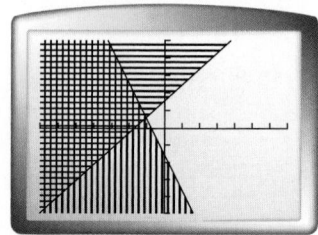

Exercises

Use a graphing calculator to graph each inequality. Sketch your graph.

7. $y \leq x$

8. $y > 5x - 9$

9. $y \geq -1$

10. $y < -x + 8$

Use a graphing calculator to graph each system of inequalities. Sketch your graph.

11. $y \geq -x + 3$
$y \leq x + 2$

12. $y > x$
$y \geq -2x + 5$

13. $y \geq -1$
$y < 0.5x - 2$

14. $y \geq 2x - 2$
$y \leq 2x - 4$

Pull It **All Together**

To solve these problems you will pull together many concepts and skills that you have studied about systems of equations and inequalities.

Completing the Performance Task

Look back at your results from the Apply What You've Learned section in Lessons 6-2 and 6-6. Use the work you did to complete the following.

1. Solve the problem in the Task Description on page 363 by finding the number of minutes Ashley should use each exercise machine, and the maximum number of minutes Miguel can use the rowing machine. Show all your work and explain each step of your solution.

 2. Reflect Choose one of the Mathematical Practices below and explain how you applied it in your work on the Performance Task.

> MP 1: Make sense of problems and persevere in solving them.
>
> MP 2: Reason abstractly and quantitatively.
>
> MP 4: Model with mathematics.

On Your Own

Brittany uses the ski machine and the treadmill at the gym for an exercise program. Her trainer wants her on an exercise program that meets these two conditions:

- Brittany will exercise for at least 45 minutes and at most 1 hour and 15 minutes, dividing her time between the ski machine and the treadmill.

- Brittany will spend at least three times as much time on the treadmill as on the ski machine.

a. Write a system of inequalities that models the relationships between the amounts of time Brittany spends on the two machines.

b. Find the minimum number of minutes Brittany can spend on the treadmill.

Connecting **BIG** ideas and Answering the Essential Questions

1 Solving Equations and Inequalities

There are several ways to solve systems of equations and inequalities, including graphing and using equivalent forms of equations and inequalities within the system. The number of solutions depends on the type of system.

Solving Systems of Equations (Lessons 6-1, 6-2, and 6-3)

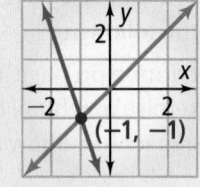

$y = x$
$y = -3x - 4$

The solution is $(-1, -1)$.

Linear Inequalities (Lessons 6-5 and 6-6)

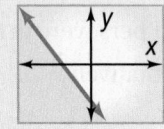

2 Modeling

You can represent many real-world mathematical problems algebraically. When you need to find two unknowns, you may be able to write and solve a system of equations.

Applying Linear Systems (Lesson 6-4)

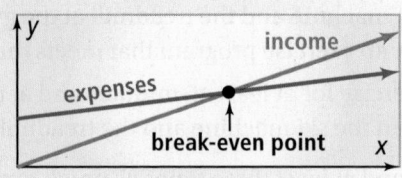

income

expenses

break-even point

Chapter Vocabulary

- consistent (p. 365)
- dependent (p. 365)
- elimination method (p. 378)
- inconsistent (p. 365)
- independent (p. 365)
- linear inequality (p. 394)
- solution of an inequality (p. 394)
- solution of a system of linear equations (p. 364)
- solution of a system of linear inequalities (p. 400)
- substitution method (p. 372)
- system of linear equations (p. 364)
- system of linear inequalities (p. 400)

Choose the correct term to complete each sentence.

1. A system of equations that has no solution is said to be __?__ .

2. You can solve a system of equations by adding or subtracting the equations in such a way that one variable drops out. This is called the __?__ method.

3. Two or more linear equations together form a(n) __?__ .

6-1 Solving Systems by Graphing

Quick Review

One way to solve a system of linear equations is by graphing each equation and finding the intersection point of the graph, if one exists.

Example

What is the solution of the system? $y = -2x + 2$
$y = 0.5x - 3$

$y = -2x + 2$ Slope is -2; y-intercept is 2.

$y = 0.5x - 3$ Slope is 0.5; y-intercept is -3.

The lines appear to intersect at $(2, -2)$. Check if $(2, -2)$ makes both equations true.

$-2 = -2(2) + 2$ ✔

$-2 = 0.5(2) - 3$ ✔

So, the solution is $(2, -2)$.

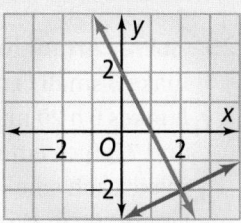

Exercises

Solve each system by graphing. Check your answer.

4. $y = 3x + 13$
   $y = x - 3$

5. $y = -x + 4$
   $y = 3x + 12$

6. $y = 2x + 3$
   $y = \frac{1}{3}x - 2$

7. $y = 1.5x + 2$
   $4.5x - 3y = -9$

8. $y = -2x - 21$
   $y = x - 7$

9. $y = x + 1$
   $2x - 2y = -2$

10. **Songwriting** Jay has written 24 songs to date. He writes an average of 6 songs per year. Jenna started writing songs this year and expects to write about 12 songs per year. How many years from now will Jenna have written as many songs as Jay? Write and graph a system of equations to find your answer.

11. **Reasoning** Describe the graph of a system of equations that has no solution.

6-2 Solving Systems Using Substitution

Quick Review

You can solve a system of equations by solving one equation for one variable and then substituting the expression for that variable into the other equation.

Example

What is the solution of the system? $y = -\frac{1}{3}x$
$3x + 3y = -18$

$3x + 3y = -18$ Write the second equation.

$3x + 3(-\frac{1}{3}x) = -18$ Substitute $-\frac{1}{3}x$ for y.

$2x = -18$ Simplify.

$x = -9$ Solve for x.

$y = -\frac{1}{3}(-9)$ Substitute -9 for x in the first equation.

$y = 3$

The solution is $(-9, 3)$.

Exercises

Solve each system using substitution. Tell whether the system has *one solution, infinitely many solutions*, or *no solution*.

12. $y = 2x - 1$
    $2x + 2y = 22$

13. $-x + y = -13$
    $3x - y = 19$

14. $2x + y = -12$
    $-4x - 2y = 30$

15. $\frac{1}{3}y = \frac{7}{3}x + \frac{5}{3}$
    $x - 3y = 5$

16. $y = x - 7$
    $3x - 3y = 21$

17. $3x + y = -13$
    $-2x + 5y = -54$

18. **Business** The owner of a hair salon charges $20 more per haircut than the assistant. Yesterday the assistant gave 12 haircuts. The owner gave 6 haircuts. The total earnings from haircuts were $750. How much does the owner charge for a haircut? Solve by writing and solving a system of equations.

6-3 and 6-4 Solving Systems Using Elimination; Applications of Systems

Quick Review

You can add or subtract equations in a system to eliminate a variable. Before you add or subtract, you may have to multiply one or both equations by a constant to make eliminating a variable possible.

Example

What is the solution of the system? $3x + 2y = 41$
$5x - 3y = 24$

$$3x + 2y = 41 \quad \text{Multiply by 3.} \quad 9x + 6y = 123$$
$$5x - 3y = 24 \quad \text{Multiply by 2.} \quad \underline{10x - 6y = 48}$$
$$19x + 0 = 171$$
$$x = 9$$

$3x + 2y = 41$ Write the first equation.

$3(9) + 2y = 41$ Substitute 9 for x.

$y = 7$ Solve for y.

The solution is (9, 7).

Exercises

Solve each system using elimination. Tell whether the system has *one solution, infinitely many solutions,* or *no solution.*

19. $x + 2y = 23$
$5x + 10y = 55$

20. $7x + y = 6$
$5x + 3y = 34$

21. $5x + 4y = -83$
$3x - 3y = -12$

22. $9x + \frac{1}{2}y = 51$
$7x + \frac{1}{3}y = 39$

23. $4x + y = 21$
$-2x + 6y = 9$

24. $y = 3x - 27$
$x - \frac{1}{3}y = 9$

25. Flower Arranging It takes a florist 3 h 15 min to make 3 small centerpieces and 3 large centerpieces. It takes 6 h 20 min to make 4 small centerpieces and 7 large centerpieces. How long does it take to make each small centerpiece and each large centerpiece? Write and solve a system of equations to find your answer.

6-5 and 6-6 Linear Inequalities and Systems of Inequalities

Quick Review

A **linear inequality** describes a region of the coordinate plane with a boundary line. Two or more inequalities form a **system of inequalities.** The system's solutions lie where the graphs of the inequalities overlap.

Example

What is the graph of the system? $y > 2x - 4$
$y \leq -x + 2$

Graph the boundary lines
$y = 2x - 4$ and $y = -x + 2$.
For $y > 2x - 4$, use a dashed
boundary line and shade above
it. For $y \leq -x + 2$, use a solid
boundary line and shade below. The
green region of overlap contains the
system's solutions.

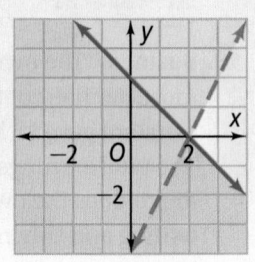

Exercises

Solve each system of inequalities by graphing.

26. $y \geq x + 4$
$y < 2x - 1$

27. $4y < -3x$
$y < -\frac{3}{4}x$

28. $2x - y > 0$
$3x + 2y \leq -14$

29. $x + 0.5y \geq 5.5$
$0.5x + y < 6.5$

30. $y < 10x$
$y > x - 5$

31. $4x + 4 > 2y$
$3x - 4y \geq 1$

32. Downloads You have 60 megabytes (MB) of space left on your portable media player. You can choose to download song files that use 3.5 MB or video files that use 8 MB. You want to download at least 12 files. What is a graph showing the numbers of song and video files you can download?

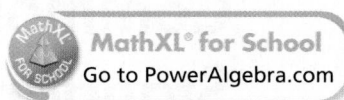
Do you know HOW?

Solve each system by graphing. Tell whether the system has *one solution, infinitely many solutions,* or *no solution.*

1. $y = 3x - 7$
   $y = -x + 1$

2. $x + 3y = 12$
   $x = y - 8$

3. $x + y = 5$
   $x + y = -2$

Solve each system using substitution.

4. $y = 4x - 7$
   $y = 2x + 9$

5. $8x + 2y = -2$
   $y = -5x + 1$

6. $y + 2x = -1$
   $y - 3x = -16$

Solve each system using elimination.

7. $4x + y = 8$
   $-3x - y = 0$

8. $2x + 5y = 20$
   $3x - 10y = 37$

9. $3x + 2y = -10$
   $2x - 5y = 3$

Solve each system of inequalities by graphing.

10. $y > 4x - 1$
   $y \le -x + 4$

11. $x > -3$
   $-3x + y \ge 6$

12. Garage Sale You go to a garage sale. All the items cost $1 or $5. You spend less than $45. Write and graph a linear inequality that models the situation.

13. Gardening A farmer plans to create a rectangular garden that he will enclose with chicken wire. The garden can be no more than 30 ft wide. The farmer would like to use at most 180 ft of chicken wire.
   a. Write a system of linear inequalities that models this situation.
   b. Graph the system to show all possible solutions.

Write a system of equations to model each situation. Solve by any method.

14. Education A writing workshop enrolls novelists and poets in a ratio of 5 : 3. There are 24 people at the workshop. How many novelists are there? How many poets are there?

STEM 15. Chemistry A chemist has one solution containing 30% insecticide and another solution containing 50% insecticide. How much of each solution should the chemist mix to get 200 L of a 42% insecticide?

Do you UNDERSTAND?

16. Open-Ended Write a system of two linear equations that has no solution.

17. Error Analysis A student concluded that $(-2, -1)$ is a solution of the inequality $y < 3x + 2$, as shown below. Describe and correct the student's error.

$$y < 3x + 2$$
$$-2 \stackrel{?}{<} 3(-1) + 2$$
$$-2 < -1 \checkmark$$

18. Reasoning Consider a system of two linear equations in two variables. If the graphs of the equations are not the same line, is it possible for the system to have infinitely many solutions? Explain.

Reasoning Suppose you add two linear equations that form a system, and you get the result shown below. How many solutions does the system have?

19. $x = 8$ **20.** $0 = 4$ **21.** $0 = 0$

TIPS FOR SUCCESS

Some questions on tests ask you to solve a problem that involves a system of equations. Read the sample question at the right. Then follow the tips to answer the question.

Melissa keeps a jar for holding change. The jar holds 21 coins. All of the coins are quarters and nickels. The total amount in the jar is $3.85. How many quarters are in the jar?

- (A) 3
- (B) 7
- (C) 14
- (D) 21

TIP 1

When writing an equation, try to use variables that make sense for the problem. Instead of using x and y, use q for quarters and n for nickels.

TIP 2

Make sure to answer the question asked. Here you only need to find the number of quarters.

Think It Through

Write a system of equations.

$$q + n = 21$$
$$0.25q + 0.05n = 3.85$$

Solve the first equation for n and substitute to find q.

$$0.25q + 0.05n = 3.85$$
$$0.25q + 0.05(21 - q) = 3.85$$
$$0.2q + 1.05 = 3.85$$
$$q = 14$$

The correct answer is C.

Vocabulary Builder

As you solve test items, you must understand the meanings of mathematical terms. Choose the correct term to complete each sentence.

A. The (*substitution*, *elimination*) method is a way to solve a system of equations in which you replace one variable with an equivalent expression containing the other variable.

B. A linear (*equation*, *inequality*) is a mathematical sentence that describes a region of the coordinate plane having a boundary line.

C. A(n) (*x-intercept*, *y-intercept*) is the coordinate of a point where a graph intersects the *y*-axis.

D. The (*area*, *perimeter*) of a figure is the distance around the outside of the figure.

E. A (*function rule*, *relation*) is an equation that can be used to find a unique range value given a domain value.

Selected Response

Read each question. Then write the letter of the correct answer on your paper.

1. A group of students are going on a field trip. If the group takes 3 vans and 1 car, 22 students can be transported. If the group takes 2 vans and 4 cars, 28 students can be transported. How many students can fit in each van?

- (A) 2
- (B) 4
- (C) 6
- (D) 10

2. Greg's school paid $1012.50 for 135 homecoming T-shirts. How much would it cost the school to purchase 235 T-shirts?

- (F) $750.00
- (G) $1762.50
- (H) $2025.00
- (I) $2775.00

3. What is the solution of $12(x + 1) = 36$?

   (A) 12   (C) 2

   (B) 8   (D) −2

4. Which equation describes a line with slope 12 and y-intercept 4?

   (F) $y = 12x + 4$ (H) $y = 4x + 12$

   (G) $y = 12(x + 4)$ (I) $y = x + 3$

5. What is the solution of the system of equations shown at the right?

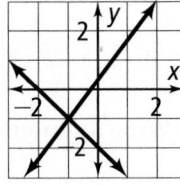

   (A) $(1, -1)$

   (B) $(-1, 1)$

   (C) $(-1, -1)$

   (D) $(1, 1)$

6. The width of Ben's rectangular family room is 3 ft less than the length. The perimeter is 70 ft. Which equation can be used to find the length ℓ of the room?

   (F) $70 = \ell - 3$ (H) $70 = 2(\ell - 3)$

   (G) $70 = 2\ell - 3$ (I) $70 = 2(2\ell - 3)$

7. Marisa's Flower Shop charges $3 per rose plus $16 for a delivery. Chris wants to have a bouquet of roses delivered to his mother. Which value is in the range of the function that gives the bouquet's cost in terms of the number of roses?

   (A) $16   (C) $34

   (B) $27   (D) $48

8. Which number is a solution of $8 > 3x - 1$?

   (F) 0   (H) 4

   (G) 3   (I) 6

9. The formula for the area A of a trapezoid is $A = \frac{1}{2}(b_1 + b_2)h$, where b_1 and b_2 represent the lengths of the bases and h represents the height. Which equation can be used to find the height of a trapezoid?

   (A) $h = 2A - b_1 - b_2$

   (B) $h = \dfrac{2A}{b_1 + b_2}$

   (C) $h = \dfrac{A(b_1 + b_2)}{2}$

   (D) $h = \dfrac{A - 2}{b_1 + b_2}$

10. Martin used 400 ft of fencing to enclose a rectangular area in his backyard. Isabella wants to enclose a similar area that is twice as long and twice as wide as the one in Martin's backyard. How much fencing does Isabella need?

   (F) 800 ft   (H) 1600 ft

   (G) 1200 ft   (I) 2000 ft

11. At the Conic Company, a new employee's earnings E, in dollars, can be calculated using the function $E = 0.05s + 30{,}000$, where s represents the employee's total sales, in dollars. All of the new employees earned between $50,000 and $60,000 last year. Which value is in the domain of the function?

   (A) $34,000   (C) $430,000

   (B) $300,000   (D) $3,400,000

12. Hilo's class fund has $65. The class is having a car wash to raise more money for a trip. The graph below models the amount of money the class will have if it charges $4 for each car washed.

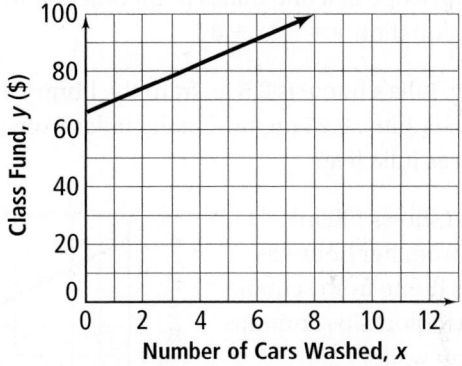

How would the graph change if the class charged $5 per car washed?

   (F) The y-intercept would increase.

   (G) The slope would increase.

   (H) The y-intercept would decrease.

   (I) The slope would decrease.

13. A system has two linear equations in two variables. The graphs of the equations have the same slope but different y-intercepts. How many solutions does the system have?

   (A) 0   (C) 2

   (B) 1   (D) infinitely many

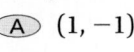

Constructed Response

14. Rhonda has 25 coins in her pocket. All of the coins are either dimes or nickels. If Rhonda has a total of $2.30, how many dimes does she have?

15. What is the value of x in the proportion?

$$\frac{2}{5} = \frac{x}{21 - x}$$

16. An artist is adding a frame to a rectangular painting that is 12 in. wide and 19 in. long. The frame is 3 in. wide on each side. To the nearest square inch, what is the area of the painting with the frame?

17. What is the solution of $4(-3x + 6) - 1 = -13$?

18. In a regular polygon, all sides have the same length. Suppose a regular hexagon has a perimeter of 25.2 in. What is the length of each side in inches?

19. The sum of four consecutive integers is 250. What is the greatest of these integers?

20. What is the slope of a line that is perpendicular to the line with equation $y = -5x + 8$?

21. On a map, Julia's home is 8.5 in. from the library. If the map scale is 1 in. : 0.25 mi, how many miles from the library does Julia live?

22. The graph shows Jillian's distance from her house as she walks home from school. How many blocks per minute does Jillian walk?

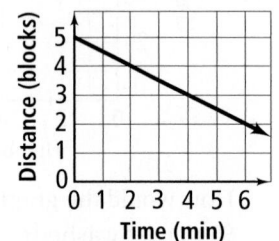

23. Sam is ordering pizza. Tony's Pizza charges $7 for a large cheese pizza plus $.75 for each additional topping. Maria's Pizza charges $8 for a large cheese pizza plus $.50 for each additional topping. For what number of toppings will the cost of a large pizza be the same at either restaurant?

24. The graph below is the solution of a linear system. How many solutions does the system have?

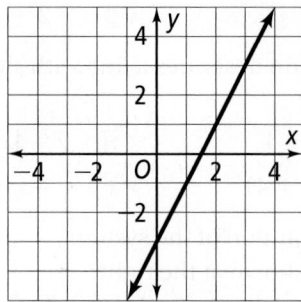

25. Write a system of inequalities for the graph below.

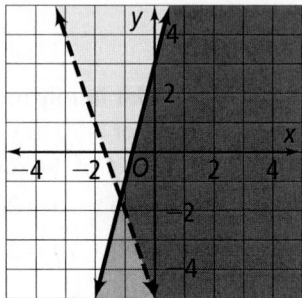

26. The volume V of a cube is given by the formula $V = s^3$, where s represents the length of an edge of the cube. Suppose the edge length is 24 in. What is the volume of the cube in cubic feet?

27. You plan to mail surveys to different households. A box of 50 envelopes costs $3.50, and a postage stamp costs $.44. How much will it cost you to mail 400 surveys?

Extended Response

28. The vertices of quadrilateral $ABCD$ are $A(1, 1)$, $B(1, 5)$, $C(5, 5)$, and $D(7, 1)$.

  a. A trapezoid is a four-sided figure with exactly one pair of parallel sides. Is $ABCD$ a trapezoid? Explain your answer.

  b. You want to transform $ABCD$ into a parallelogram by only moving point B. A parallelogram is a four-sided figure with both pairs of opposite sides parallel. What should be the new coordinates of point B? Explain.

Get Ready!

Skills
Handbook,
page 802 ◀◆ Converting Fractions to Decimals

Write as a decimal.

1. $\frac{7}{10}$ **2.** $6\frac{2}{5}$ **3.** $\frac{8}{1000}$ **4.** $\frac{7}{2}$ **5.** $\frac{3}{11}$

Lesson 1-2 ◀◆ Using Order of Operations

Simplify each expression.

6. $(9 \div 3 + 4)^2$ **7.** $5 + (0.3)^2$ **8.** $3 - (1.5)^2$ **9.** $64 \div 2^4$

10. $4 \div (0.5)^2$ **11.** $(0.25)4^2$ **12.** $2(3 + 7)^3$ **13.** $-3(4 + 6 \div 2)^2$

Lesson 1-2 ◀◆ Evaluating Expressions

Evaluate each expression for $a = -2$ and $b = 5$.

14. $(ab)^2$ **15.** $(a - b)^2$ **16.** $a^3 + b^3$ **17.** $b - (3a)^2$

Lesson 2-10 ◀◆ Finding Percent Change

Tell whether each percent change is an increase or decrease. Then find the percent change. Round to the nearest percent.

18. $15 to $20   **19.** $20 to $15

20. $600 to $500   **21.** $2000 to $2100

Lesson 4-6 ◀◆ Understanding Domain and Range

Find the range of each function with domain $\{-2, 0, 3.5\}$.

22. $f(x) = -2x^2$ **23.** $g(x) = 10 - x^3$ **24.** $y = 5x - 1$

 ## Looking Ahead Vocabulary

25. If you say that a plant has new growth, has the size of the plant changed? What do you think the *growth factor* of the plant describes?

26. In a mathematical expression, an exponent indicates repeated multiplication by the same number. How would you expect a quantity to change when it experiences *exponential growth*?

27. Tooth decay occurs when tooth enamel wears away over time. If *exponential decay* models the change in the number of dentists in the United States over time, do you think the number of dentists in the United States is increasing or decreasing?

CHAPTER 7

Exponents and Exponential Functions

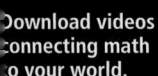
Download videos connecting math to your world.

Interactive! Vary numbers, graphs, and figures to explore math concepts.

The online Solve It will get you in gear for each lesson.

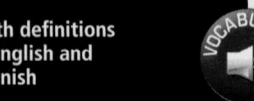

Math definitions in English and Spanish

Online access to stepped-out problems aligned to Common Core

Get and view your assignments online.

Extra practice and review online

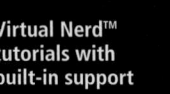

Virtual Nerd™ tutorials with built-in support

Chapter Preview

Vocabulary

English/Spanish Vocabulary Audio Online:

English	Spanish
compound interest, *p. 461*	interés compuesto
decay factor, *p. 462*	factor de decremento
exponential decay, *p. 462*	decremento exponencial
exponential function, *p. 453*	función exponencial
exponential growth, *p. 460*	incremento exponencial
geometric sequence, *p. 467*	progresión geométrica
growth factor, *p. 460*	factor incremental

BIG ideas

1 Equivalence
Essential Question: How can you represent numbers less than 1 using exponents?

2 Properties
Essential Question: How can you simplify expressions involving exponents?

3 Function
Essential Question: What are the characteristics of exponential functions?

 DOMAINS
- The Real Number System
- Seeing Structure in Expressions
- Linear, Quadratic, and Exponential Models

Common Core Performance Task

Investing Prize Money

Emilio wants to invest $15,820 that he has just received as a prize from a contest he entered. He researches certificates of deposit (CDs) at two different banks. The details for his two best options are in the table below. Both CDs earn *compound interest*, which you will work with in Lesson 7-7. When interest is compounded, it is added to the account's principal to become part of the money that earns interest.

Bank	CD Length	Annual Interest Rate	Frequency of Compounding
Bank West	6 years	3.8%	Quarterly
First Bank	5 years	4.3%	Monthly

Task Description

Determine which investment will earn Emilio more interest. How much more interest will he earn with that investment?

Connecting the Task to the Math Practices

As you complete the task, you'll apply several Standards for Mathematical Practice.

- You'll find the value of a compound interest account after one year. (MP 1)
- You'll write algebraic expressions that will help you understand a formula for the value of a compound interest account. (MP 7)
- You'll use a formula to model Emilio's investment choices. (MP 4)

Zero and Negative Exponents

@ **Common Core State Standards**

Prepares for N-RN.A.1 Explain how the definition of the meaning of rational exponents follows from extending the properties of integer exponents to those values . . . **Also prepares for N-RN.A.2**

MP 1, MP 2, MP 3, MP 4, MP 7

Objective   To simplify expressions involving zero and negative exponents

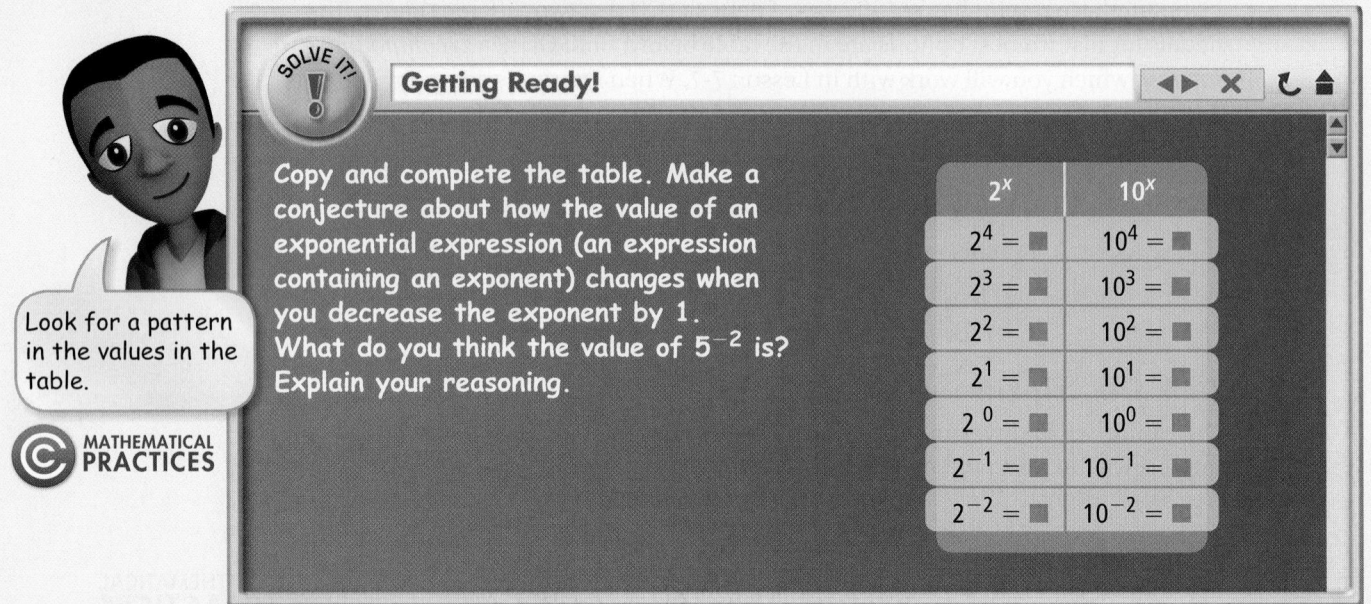

SOLVE IT!

Getting Ready!

Copy and complete the table. Make a conjecture about how the value of an exponential expression (an expression containing an exponent) changes when you decrease the exponent by 1. What do you think the value of 5^{-2} is? Explain your reasoning.

Look for a pattern in the values in the table.

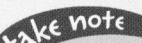

MATHEMATICAL PRACTICES

2^x	10^x
$2^4 = \blacksquare$	$10^4 = \blacksquare$
$2^3 = \blacksquare$	$10^3 = \blacksquare$
$2^2 = \blacksquare$	$10^2 = \blacksquare$
$2^1 = \blacksquare$	$10^1 = \blacksquare$
$2^0 = \blacksquare$	$10^0 = \blacksquare$
$2^{-1} = \blacksquare$	$10^{-1} = \blacksquare$
$2^{-2} = \blacksquare$	$10^{-2} = \blacksquare$

The patterns you found in the Solve It illustrate the definitions of zero and negative exponents.

Essential Understanding   You can extend the idea of exponents to include zero and negative exponents.

Consider 3^3, 3^2, and 3^1. Decreasing the exponents by 1 is the same as dividing by 3. If you continue the pattern, 3^0 equals 1 and 3^{-1} equals $\frac{1}{3}$.

take note

Properties   Zero and Negative Exponents

Zero as an Exponent   For every nonzero number a, $a^0 = 1$.

Examples $4^0 = 1$ $(-3)^0 = 1$ $(5.14)^0 = 1$

Negative Exponent   For every nonzero number a and integer n, $a^{-n} = \frac{1}{a^n}$.

Examples $7^{-3} = \frac{1}{7^3}$ $(-5)^{-2} = \frac{1}{(-5)^2}$

Why can't you use 0 as a base with zero exponents? The first property on the previous page implies the following pattern.

$$3^0 = 1 \qquad 2^0 = 1 \qquad 1^0 = 1 \qquad 0^0 = 1$$

However, consider the following pattern.

$$0^3 = 0 \qquad 0^2 = 0 \qquad 0^1 = 0 \qquad 0^0 = 0$$

It is not possible for 0^0 to equal both 1 and 0. Therefore 0^0 is undefined.

Why can't you use 0 as a base with a negative exponent? Using 0 as a base with a negative exponent will result in division by zero, which is undefined.

 Problem 1 Simplifying Powers

Think

Can you use the definition of zero as an exponent when the base is a negative number?
Yes, the definition of zero as an exponent is true for all nonzero bases.

What is the simplified form of each expression?

A 9^{-2}

$$9^{-2} = \frac{1}{9^2} \qquad \text{Use the definition of negative exponent.}$$
$$= \frac{1}{81} \qquad \text{Simplify.}$$

B $(-3.6)^0 = 1$ Use the definition of zero as an exponent.

Got It? **1.** What is the simplified form of each expression?

    a. 4^{-3} **b.** $(-5)^0$ **c.** 3^{-2} **d.** 6^{-1} **e.** $(-4)^{-2}$

An algebraic expression is in simplest form when powers with a variable base are written with only positive exponents.

 Problem 2 Simplifying Exponential Expressions

Think

Which part of the expression do you need to rewrite?
The base b has a negative exponent, so you need to rewrite it with a positive exponent.

What is the simplified form of each expression?

A $5a^3b^{-2}$

$$5a^3b^{-2} = 5a^3\left(\frac{1}{b^2}\right) \qquad \text{Use the definition of negative exponent.}$$
$$= \frac{5a^3}{b^2} \qquad \text{Simplify.}$$

B $\frac{1}{x^{-5}}$

$$\frac{1}{x^{-5}} = 1 \div x^{-5} \qquad \text{Rewrite using a division symbol.}$$
$$= 1 \div \frac{1}{x^5} \qquad \text{Use the definition of negative exponent.}$$
$$= 1 \cdot x^5 \qquad \text{Multiply by the reciprocal of } \frac{1}{x^5}, \text{ which is } x^5.$$
$$= x^5 \qquad \text{Identity Property of Multiplication}$$

Got It? **2.** What is the simplified form of each expression?

    a. x^{-9} **b.** $\frac{1}{n^{-3}}$ **c.** $4c^{-3}b$ **d.** $\frac{2}{a^{-3}}$ **e.** $\frac{n^{-5}}{m^2}$

When you evaluate an exponential expression, you can simplify the expression before substituting values for the variables.

 Problem 3 Evaluating an Exponential Expression

Plan

How do you simplify the expression?
Use the definition of negative exponent to rewrite the expression with only positive exponents.

What is the value of $3s^3t^{-2}$ for $s = 2$ and $t = -3$?

Method 1 Simplify first.

$$3s^3t^{-2} = \frac{3(s)^3}{t^2}$$

$$= \frac{3(2)^3}{(-3)^2}$$

$$= \frac{24}{9} = 2\frac{2}{3}$$

Method 2 Substitute first.

$$3s^3t^{-2} = 3(2)^3(-3)^{-2}$$

$$= \frac{3(2)^3}{(-3)^2}$$

$$= \frac{24}{9} = 2\frac{2}{3}$$

 Got It? **3.** What is the value of each expression in parts (a)–(d) for $n = -2$ and $w = 5$?

     a. $n^{-4}w^0$ **b.** $\dfrac{n^{-1}}{w^2}$ **c.** $\dfrac{n^0}{w^6}$ **d.** $\dfrac{1}{nw^{-1}}$

     e. Reasoning Is it easier to evaluate n^0w^0 for $n = -2$ and $w = 3$ by simplifying first or by substituting first? Explain.

 Problem 4 Using an Exponential Expression   **STEM**

Population Growth A population of marine bacteria doubles every hour under controlled laboratory conditions. The number of bacteria is modeled by the expression $1000 \cdot 2^h$, where h is the number of hours after a scientist measures the population size. Evaluate the expression for $h = 0$ and $h = -3$. What does each value of the expression represent in the situation?

Know	Need	Plan
$1000 \cdot 2^h$ models the population.	Values of the expression for $h = 0$ and $h = -3$	Substitute each value of h into the expression and simplify.

$$1000 \cdot 2^h = 1000 \cdot 2^0 \qquad \text{Substitute 0 for } h.$$

$$= 1000 \cdot 1 = 1000 \qquad \text{Simplify.}$$

The value of the expression for $h = 0$ is 1000. There were 1000 bacteria at the time the scientist measured the population.

$$1000 \cdot 2^h = 1000 \cdot 2^{-3} \qquad \text{Substitute } -3 \text{ for } h.$$

$$= 1000 \cdot \frac{1}{8} = 125 \qquad \text{Simplify.}$$

The value of the expression for $h = -3$ is 125. There were 125 bacteria 3 h before the scientist measured the population.

Got It? **4.** A population of insects triples every week. The number of insects is modeled by the expression $5400 \cdot 3^w$, where w is the number of weeks after the population was measured. Evaluate the expression for $w = -2$, $w = 0$, and $w = 1$. What does each value of the expression represent in the situation?

 Lesson Check

Do you know HOW?

Simplify each expression.

1. 2^{-5}

2. m^0

3. $5s^2t^{-1}$

4. $\dfrac{4}{x^{-3}}$

Evaluate each expression for $a = 2$ and $b = -4$.

5. a^3b^{-1}

6. $2a^{-4}b^0$

Do you UNDERSTAND?

 **7. Vocabulary** A positive exponent shows repeated multiplication. What repeated operation does a negative exponent show?

8. Error Analysis A student incorrectly simplified $\dfrac{x^n}{a^{-n}b^0}$ as shown below. Find and correct the student's error.

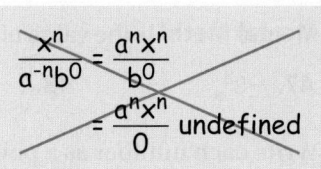

$$\frac{x^n}{a^{-n}b^0} = \frac{a^n x^n}{b^0}$$

$$= \frac{a^n x^n}{0} \text{ undefined}$$

  Practice and Problem-Solving Exercises

A **Practice**   Simplify each expression.   **See Problem 1.**

9. 3^{-2}	**10.** $(-4.25)^0$	**11.** $(-5)^{-2}$
12. -5^{-2}	**13.** $(-4)^{-2}$	**14.** 2^{-6}
15. -3^0	**16.** -12^{-1}	**17.** $\dfrac{1}{2^0}$
18. 58^{-1}	**19.** 1.5^{-2}	**20.** $(-5)^{-3}$

Simplify each expression.   **See Problem 2.**

21. $4ab^0$	**22.** $\dfrac{1}{x^{-7}}$	**23.** $5x^{-4}$	**24.** $\dfrac{1}{c^{-1}}$
25. $\dfrac{3^{-2}}{n}$	**26.** $k^{-4}j^0$	**27.** $\dfrac{3x^{-2}}{y}$	**28.** $\dfrac{7ab^{-2}}{3w}$
29. $c^{-5}d^{-7}$	**30.** $c^{-5}d^7$	**31.** $\dfrac{8}{2s^{-3}}$	**32.** $\dfrac{7s}{5t^{-3}}$
33. $\dfrac{6a^{-1}c^{-3}}{d^0}$	**34.** $2^{-3}x^2z^{-7}$	**35.** $12^0t^7u^{-11}$	**36.** $\dfrac{7s^0t^{-5}}{2^{-1}m^2}$

Evaluate each expression for $r = -3$ and $s = 5$.

See Problem 3.

37. r^{-3} **38.** s^{-3} **39.** $\dfrac{3r}{s^{-2}}$ **40.** $\dfrac{s^0}{r^{-2}}$

41. $4s^{-1}$ **42.** $r^0 s^{-2}$ **43.** $r^{-4}s^2$ **44.** $2^{-4}r^3 s^{-2}$

45. Internet Traffic The number of visitors to a certain Web site triples every month. See Problem 4.
The number of visitors is modeled by the expression $8100 \cdot 3^m$, where m is the
number of months after the number of visitors was measured.
Evaluate the expression $m = -4$. What does the value of the expression
represent in the situation?

 **46. Population Growth** A Galápagos cactus finch population increases
by half every decade. The number of finches is modeled by the
expression $45 \cdot 1.5^d$, where d is the number of decades after the
population was measured. Evaluate the expression for $d = -2$, $d = 0$,
and $d = 1$. What does each value of the expression represent in the
situation?

Galápagos cactus finch

B Apply   **Mental Math** Is the value of each expression *positive* or *negative*?

47. -2^2 **48.** $(-2)^2$ **49.** $(-2)^3$ **50.** $(-2)^{-3}$

Write each number as a power of 10 using negative exponents.

51. $\dfrac{1}{10}$ **52.** $\dfrac{1}{100}$ **53.** $\dfrac{1}{1000}$ **54.** $\dfrac{1}{10,000}$

55. a. Patterns Complete the pattern using powers of 5.
$$\dfrac{1}{5^2} = \blacksquare \qquad \dfrac{1}{5^1} = \blacksquare \qquad \dfrac{1}{5^0} = \blacksquare \qquad \dfrac{1}{5^{-1}} = \blacksquare \qquad \dfrac{1}{5^{-2}} = \blacksquare$$
  b. Write $\dfrac{1}{5^{-4}}$ using a positive exponent.
  c. Rewrite $\dfrac{1}{a^{-n}}$ as a power of a.

Rewrite each fraction with all the variables in the numerator.

56. $\dfrac{a}{b^{-2}}$ **57.** $\dfrac{4g}{h^3}$ **58.** $\dfrac{5m^6}{3n}$ **59.** $\dfrac{8c^5}{11d^4 e^{-2}}$

60. Think About a Plan Suppose your drama club's budget doubles every year. This
year the budget is \$500. How much was the club's budget 2 yr ago?
  • What expression models what the budget of the club will be in 1 yr?
    In 2 yr? In y years?
  • What value of y can you substitute into your expression to find the budget of the
    club 2 yr ago?

61. Copy and complete the table at the right.

62. a. Simplify $a^n \cdot a^{-n}$.
  b. Reasoning What is the mathematical
    relationship between a^n and a^{-n}? Explain.

n	3	$\blacksquare$	$\blacksquare$	$\frac{5}{8}$	$\blacksquare$
n^{-1}	$\blacksquare$	6	$\frac{1}{7}$	$\blacksquare$	0.5

63. Open-Ended Choose a fraction to use as a value for the variable a. Find the values of a^{-1}, a^2, and a^{-2}.

STEM **64. Manufacturing** A company is making metal rods with a target diameter of 1.5 mm. A rod is acceptable when its diameter is within 10^{-3} mm of the target diameter. Write an inequality for the acceptable range of diameters.

65. Reasoning Are $3x^{-2}$ and $3x^2$ reciprocals? Explain.

Challenge Simplify each expression.

66. $\left(\dfrac{r^{-7}b^{-8}}{t^{-4}w^1}\right)^0$

67. $(-5)^2 - (0.5)^{-2}$

68. $\dfrac{6}{m^2} + \dfrac{5m^{-2}}{3^{-3}}$

69. $2^3\left(5^0 - 6m^2\right)$

70. $\dfrac{2x^{-5}y^3}{n^2} \div \dfrac{r^2y^5}{2n}$

71. $2^{-1} - \dfrac{1}{3^{-2}} + 5\left(\dfrac{1}{2^2}\right)$

72. For what value or values of n is $n^{-3} = \left(\dfrac{1}{n}\right)^5$?

Standardized Test Prep

GRIDDED RESPONSE

SAT/ACT

73. What is the simplified form of $-6(-6)^{-1}$?

74. Segment CD represents the flight of a bird that passes through the points $(1, 2)$ and $(5, 4)$. What is the slope of a line that represents the flight of a second bird that flew perpendicular to the first bird?

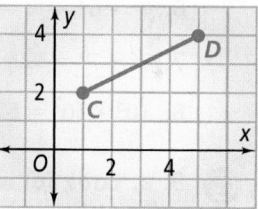

75. What is the solution of the equation $1.5(x - 2.5) = 3$?

76. What is the simplified form of $|3.5 - 4.7| + 5.6$?

77. What is the y-intercept of the graph of $3x - 2y = -8$?

Mixed Review

Solve each system by graphing.

◀ See Lesson 6-6.

78. $y > 3x + 4$
$y \le -3x + 1$

79. $y \le -2x + 1$
$y < 2x - 1$

80. $y \ge 0.5x$
$y \le x + 2$

Write an equation in slope-intercept form for the line with the given slope m and y-intercept b.

◀ See Lesson 5-3.

81. $m = -1, b = 4$

82. $m = 5, b = -2$

83. $m = \dfrac{2}{5}, b = -3$

84. $m = -\dfrac{3}{11}, b = -17$

85. $m = \dfrac{5}{9}, b = \dfrac{1}{3}$

86. $m = 1.25, b = -3.79$

Get Ready! To prepare for Lesson 7-2, do Exercises 87–91.

Simplify each expression.

◀ See Lesson 7-1.

87. $6 \cdot 10^4$

88. $7 \cdot 10^{-2}$

89. $8.2 \cdot 10^5$

90. $3 \cdot 10^{-3}$

91. $3.4 \cdot 10^5$

Multiplying Powers

Common Core State Standards

Prepares for N-RN.A.1 Explain how the definition of the meaning of rational exponents follows from extending the properties of integer exponents to those values . . .

MP 7

You can use patterns to find a shortcut for multiplying powers.

Activity 1

Copy and complete each statement in Exercises 1–8.

1. $2^2 \cdot 2^2 = 2 \cdot 2 \cdot 2 \cdot 2 = 2^4 = 2^{2+\blacksquare}$

2. $3^2 \cdot 3^2 = 3 \cdot 3 \cdot 3 \cdot 3 = 3^4 = 3^{2+\blacksquare}$

3. $3^3 \cdot 3^2 = 3 \cdot 3 \cdot 3 \cdot 3 \cdot 3 = 3^{\blacksquare} = 3^{\blacksquare+\blacksquare}$

4. $4^3 \cdot 4^2 = 4 \cdot 4 \cdot 4 \cdot 4 \cdot 4 = 4^{\blacksquare} = 4^{\blacksquare+\blacksquare}$

5. $5^1 \cdot 5^2 = 5 \cdot 5 \cdot 5 = 5^{\blacksquare} = 5^{\blacksquare+\blacksquare}$

6. $6^3 \cdot 6^3 = \blacksquare = 6^{\blacksquare} = 6^{\blacksquare+\blacksquare}$

7. $7^2 \cdot 7^6 = \blacksquare = 7^{\blacksquare} = 7^{\blacksquare+\blacksquare}$

8. $10^3 \cdot 10^7 = \blacksquare = 10^{\blacksquare} = 10^{\blacksquare+\blacksquare}$

9. a. Look for a Pattern What pattern do you see in your answers to Exercises 1–8?
  b. Predict Use your pattern to predict the solution to $7^5 \cdot 7^6 = 7^{\blacksquare}$.
  c. Generalize Use your pattern to predict the value of $x^n \cdot x^m$.

You can find a similar pattern when multiplying powers with negative exponents.

Activity 2

Copy and complete each statement in Exercises 10–15.

10. $2^2 \cdot 2^{-1} = 2 \cdot 2 \cdot \frac{1}{2} = 2^1 = 2^{2+\blacksquare}$

11. $2^4 \cdot 2^{-2} = 2 \cdot 2 \cdot 2 \cdot 2 \cdot \frac{1}{2} \cdot \frac{1}{2} = 2^{\blacksquare} = 2^{4+\blacksquare}$

12. $3^3 \cdot 3^{-2} = 3 \cdot 3 \cdot 3 \cdot \frac{1}{3} \cdot \frac{1}{3} = 3^{\blacksquare} = 3^{3+\blacksquare}$

13. $4^{-3} \cdot 4^3 = \frac{1}{4} \cdot \frac{1}{4} \cdot \frac{1}{4} \cdot 4 \cdot 4 \cdot 4 = 4^{\blacksquare} = 4^{\blacksquare+\blacksquare}$

14. $8^{-4} \cdot 8^6 = \blacksquare = 8^{\blacksquare} = 8^{\blacksquare+\blacksquare}$

15. $12^{-3} \cdot 12^7 = \blacksquare = 12^{\blacksquare} = 12^{\blacksquare+\blacksquare}$

16. a. Look for a Pattern What pattern do you see in your answers to Exercises 10–15?
  b. Predict Use your pattern to predict the solution to $9^5 \cdot 9^{-7} = 9^{\blacksquare}$.
  c. Generalize Use your pattern to predict the value of $x^n \cdot x^{-m}$.

Multiplying Powers With the Same Base

© Common Core State Standards

N-RN.A.1 Explain how the definition of the meaning of rational exponents follows from extending the properties of integer exponents to those values . . .

MP 1, MP 2, MP 3, MP 4, MP 7

Objective To multiply powers with the same base

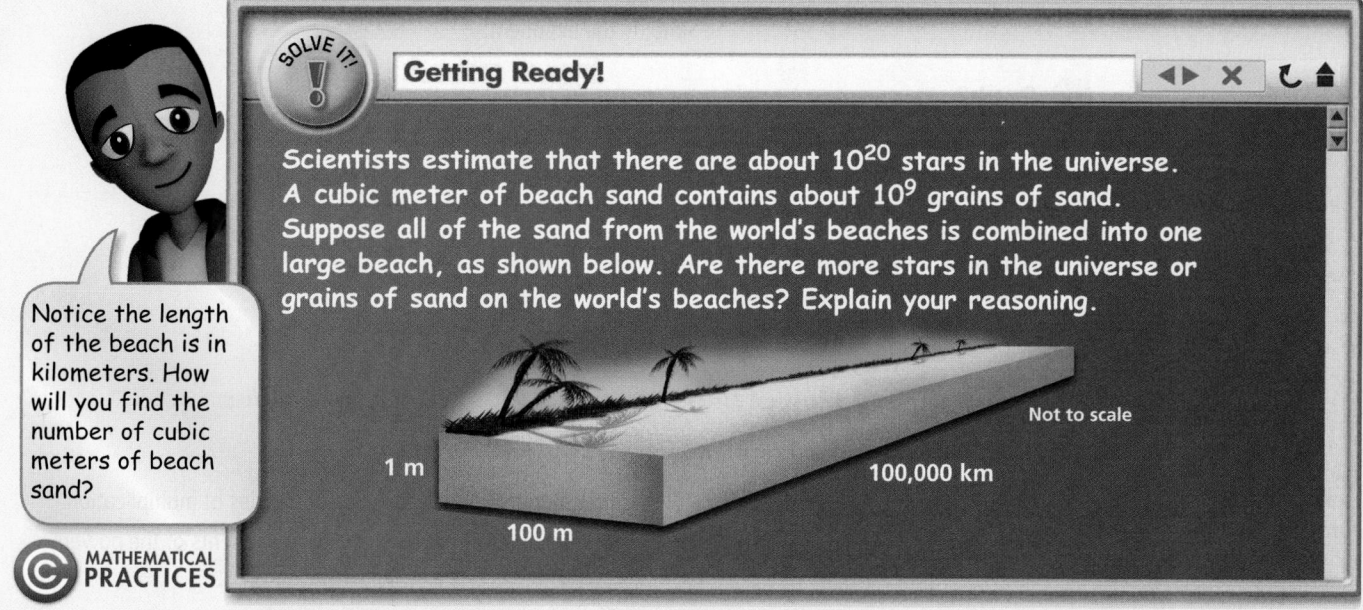

SOLVE IT!

Getting Ready!

◄► ✕ ↻ ⬆

Scientists estimate that there are about 10^{20} stars in the universe. A cubic meter of beach sand contains about 10^9 grains of sand. Suppose all of the sand from the world's beaches is combined into one large beach, as shown below. Are there more stars in the universe or grains of sand on the world's beaches? Explain your reasoning.

Not to scale

1 m

100 m

100,000 km

Notice the length of the beach is in kilometers. How will you find the number of cubic meters of beach sand?

© MATHEMATICAL PRACTICES

All of the numbers in the Solve It are powers of 10. In this lesson, you will learn a method for multiplying powers that have the same base.

Essential Understanding You can use a property of exponents to multiply powers with the same base.

You can write a product of powers with the same base, such as $3^4 \cdot 3^2$, using one exponent.

$$3^4 \cdot 3^2 = (3 \cdot 3 \cdot 3 \cdot 3) \cdot (3 \cdot 3) = 3^6$$

Notice that the sum of the exponents in the expression $3^4 \cdot 3^2$ equals the exponent of 3^6.

In general, an equation such as $3^4 \cdot 3^2 = 3^6$ can be written using variables: $a^m \cdot a^n = a^{m+n}$.

Here's Why It Works You can use repeated multiplication to rewrite a product of powers.

$$a^m \cdot a^n = \underbrace{(a \cdot a \cdot \ldots \cdot a)}_{m \text{ factors of } a} \cdot \underbrace{(a \cdot a \cdot \ldots \cdot a)}_{n \text{ factors of } a} = \underbrace{a \cdot a \cdot \ldots \cdot a}_{m + n \text{ factors of } a} = a^{m+n}$$

 **Problem 1** Multiplying Powers

 **Think**

When can you use the property for multiplying powers?
You can use the property for multiplying powers when the bases of the powers are the same.

What is each expression written using each base only once?

A $12^4 \cdot 12^3 = 12^{4+3}$ Add the exponents of the powers with the same base.

$\quad\quad = 12^7$ Simplify the exponent.

B $(-5)^{-2}(-5)^7 = (-5)^{-2+7}$ Add the exponents of the powers with the same base.

$\quad\quad = (-5)^5$ Simplify the exponent.

Got It? **1.** What is each expression written using each base only once?

a. $8^3 \cdot 8^6$ **b.** $(0.5)^{-3}(0.5)^{-8}$ **c.** $9^{-3} \cdot 9^2 \cdot 9^6$

When variable factors have more than one base, be careful to combine only those powers with the same base.

 Problem 2 Multiplying Powers in Algebraic Expressions

Plan

Which parts of the expression can you combine?
You can group the coefficients and multiply. You can also write any powers that have the same base with a single exponent.

What is the simplified form of each expression?

A $4z^5 \cdot 9z^{-12} = (4 \cdot 9)\left(z^5 \cdot z^{-12}\right)$ Commutative and associative properties of multiplication

$\quad\quad = 36\left(z^{5+(-12)}\right)$ Multiply the coefficients. Add the exponents of the powers with the same base.

$\quad\quad = 36z^{-7}$ Simplify the exponent.

$\quad\quad = \dfrac{36}{z^7}$ Rewrite using a positive exponent.

B $2a \cdot 9b^4 \cdot 3a^2 = (2 \cdot 9 \cdot 3)\left(a \cdot a^2\right)\left(b^4\right)$ Commutative and associative properties of multiplication

$\boxed{a = a^1}$

$\quad\quad = 54\left(a^1 \cdot a^2\right)\left(b^4\right)$ Multiply the coefficients. Write a as a^1.

$\quad\quad = 54\left(a^{1+2}\right)\left(b^4\right)$ Add exponents of powers with the same base.

$\quad\quad = 54a^3b^4$ Simplify.

 Got It? **2.** What is the simplified form of each expression in parts (a)–(c)?

a. $5x^4 \cdot x^9 \cdot 3x$ **b.** $-4c^3 \cdot 7d^2 \cdot 2c^{-2}$ **c.** $j^2 \cdot k^{-2} \cdot 12j$

d. Reasoning Explain how to simplify the expression $x^a \cdot x^b \cdot x^c$.

You can use the property for multiplying powers with the same base to multiply two numbers written in scientific notation.

Recall that you can use powers of 10 to make writing very large and very small numbers more convenient. In scientific notation, you can write any number as $a \times 10^b$, where $1 \le |a| < 10$. For example, 256,000 is written in scientific notation as 2.56×10^5.

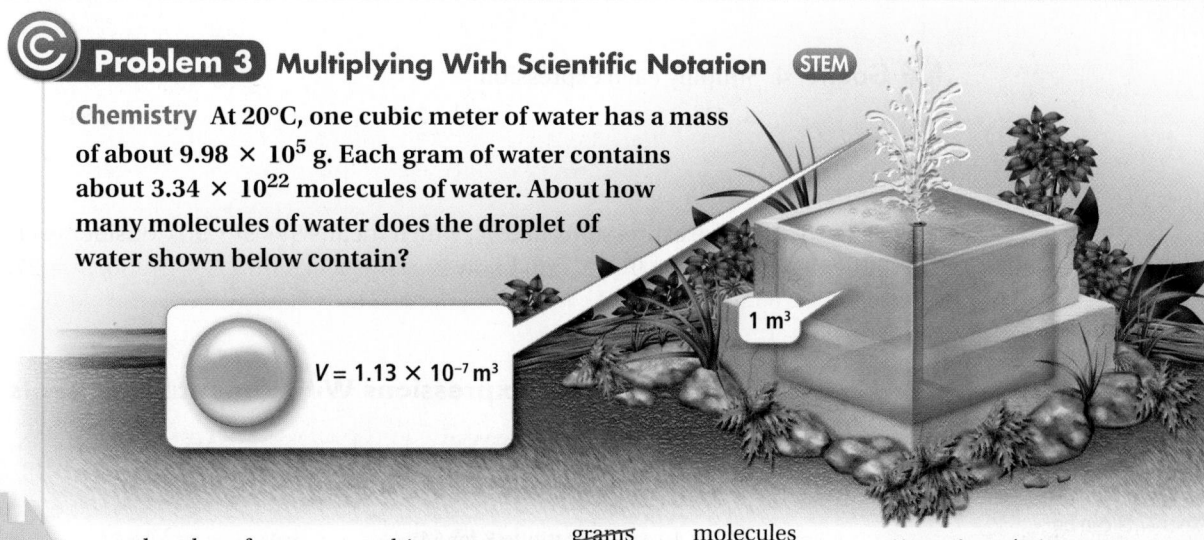

Problem 3 Multiplying With Scientific Notation STEM

Chemistry At 20°C, one cubic meter of water has a mass of about 9.98×10^5 g. Each gram of water contains about 3.34×10^{22} molecules of water. About how many molecules of water does the droplet of water shown below contain?

1 m³

$V = 1.13 \times 10^{-7}\,m^3$

Plan

How do you find the number of molecules?
Use unit analysis. Divide out the common units.

$$\text{molecules of water} = \cancel{\text{cubic meters}} \cdot \frac{\text{grams}}{\cancel{\text{cubic meters}}} \cdot \frac{\text{molecules}}{\cancel{\text{grams}}} \qquad \text{Use unit analysis.}$$

$$= \left(1.13 \times 10^{-7}\right) \cdot \left(9.98 \times 10^5\right) \cdot \left(3.34 \times 10^{22}\right) \qquad \text{Substitute.}$$

$$= (1.13 \cdot 9.98 \cdot 3.34) \times \left(10^{-7} \cdot 10^5 \cdot 10^{22}\right) \qquad \begin{array}{l}\text{Commutative and} \\ \text{associative properties} \\ \text{of multiplication}\end{array}$$

$$\approx 37.7 \times 10^{-7+5+22} \qquad \text{Multiply. Add exponents.}$$

$$= 37.7 \times 10^{20} \qquad \text{Simplify.}$$

$$= 3.77 \times 10^{21} \qquad \text{Write in scientific notation.}$$

The droplet contains about 3.77×10^{21} molecules of water.

Got It? **3.** About how many molecules of water are in a swimming pool that holds 200 m³ of water? Write your answer in scientific notation.

Exponents can also be expressed as fractions. Fractional exponents are called rational exponents.

Recall that 3^2 means $3 \cdot 3$, which equals 9. You can write the same expression using rational exponents: $9^{\frac{1}{2}}$. The equation $9^{\frac{1}{2}} = b$ indicates that b is the positive number that when multiplied by itself, equals 9.

$$9^{\frac{1}{2}} = 3 \text{ since } 3 \cdot 3 = 9.$$

In general, $a^{\frac{1}{m}} = b$ means that b multiplied as a factor m times equals a.

Think

What number
multiplied by itself
4 times equals 81?
$9 \cdot 9 = 81$ and
$(3 \cdot 3)(3 \cdot 3) = 81$.

 Problem 4 Simplifying Expressions With Rational Exponents

Simplify the expression $81^{\frac{1}{4}}$.

$81^{\frac{1}{4}}$ Find the number that when multiplied by itself four times gives 81.

$81^{\frac{1}{4}} = 3$ $3 \cdot 3 \cdot 3 \cdot 3 = 81$

✔ **Got It?** **4.** Simplify each expression.

     a. $16^{\frac{1}{4}}$ **b.** $27^{\frac{1}{3}}$ **c.** $64^{\frac{1}{2}}$

You can also have expressions like $9^{\frac{3}{2}}$, which means $9^{\frac{1}{2}} \cdot 9^{\frac{1}{2}} \cdot 9^{\frac{1}{2}}$. Consider each factor individually. Because $9^{\frac{1}{2}} = 3$, you know $9^{\frac{1}{2}} \cdot 9^{\frac{1}{2}} \cdot 9^{\frac{1}{2}} = 3 \cdot 3 \cdot 3 = 27$. So, $9^{\frac{3}{2}} = 27$.

Think

How can the
fractional exponent
be rewritten?
Exponents can be
rewritten as multiple
factors if the base of
each exponential factor
is the same.

 Problem 5 Simplifying Expressions With Rational Exponents

Simplify the expression $64^{\frac{3}{2}}$.

$64^{\frac{3}{2}} = 64^{\frac{1}{2}} \cdot 64^{\frac{1}{2}} \cdot 64^{\frac{1}{2}}$ Rewrite the expression.

     $= 8 \cdot 8 \cdot 8$ Substitute 8 for $64^{\frac{1}{2}}$.

     $= 512$ Simplify.

✔ **Got It?** **5.** Simplify each expression.

     a. $25^{\frac{3}{2}}$ **b.** $27^{\frac{2}{3}}$ **c.** $16^{\frac{3}{4}}$

You can use the properties of multiplying powers with the same base to simplify expressions with rational exponents.

 take note

Property   **Multiplying Powers With the Same Base**

Words To multiply powers with the same base, add the exponents.

Algebra $a^m \cdot a^n = a^{m+n}$, where $a \neq 0$ and m and n are rational numbers

Examples $4^{\frac{1}{3}} \cdot 4^{\frac{1}{3}} = 4^{\frac{1}{3} + \frac{1}{3}} = 4^{\frac{2}{3}}$ $b^7 \cdot b^{-4} = b^{7+(-4)} = b^3$

Problem 6 **Simplifying Expressions With Rational Exponents**

Think

Why must like variables be grouped together?
To simplify by adding exponents, the bases must be the same.

Simplify the expression $\left(2a^{\frac{2}{3}} \cdot 3b^{\frac{1}{4}}\right)\left(a^{\frac{1}{3}} \cdot 5b^{\frac{1}{2}}\right)$.

$$= (2 \cdot 3 \cdot 5)\left(a^{\frac{2}{3}} \cdot a^{\frac{1}{3}}\right)\left(b^{\frac{1}{4}} \cdot b^{\frac{1}{2}}\right) \quad \text{Commutative and associative properties of multiplication}$$

$$= 30\left(a^{\frac{2}{3}} \cdot a^{\frac{1}{3}}\right)\left(b^{\frac{1}{4}} \cdot b^{\frac{1}{2}}\right) \quad \text{Simplify.}$$

$$= 30\left(a^{\frac{3}{3}}\right)\left(b^{\frac{3}{4}}\right) \quad \text{Add exponents that have the same base.}$$

$$= 30ab^{\frac{3}{4}} \quad \text{Simplify.}$$

 Got It? **6.** Simplify each expression.

a. $2c^{\frac{3}{5}} \cdot 2c^{\frac{1}{5}}$

b. $n^{\frac{1}{3}} \cdot n^{\frac{4}{3}}$

c. $\left(b^{\frac{2}{3}} \cdot c^{\frac{2}{5}}\right)\left(b^{\frac{4}{9}} \cdot c^{\frac{9}{10}}\right)$

d. $\left(3j^{\frac{2}{3}} \cdot 7m^{\frac{1}{4}}\right)\left(3j^{\frac{1}{6}} \cdot 7m^{\frac{3}{2}}\right)$

Lesson Check

Do you know HOW?

1. What is $8^4 \cdot 8^8$ written using each base only once?

2. What is the simplified form of $2n^{\frac{2}{3}} \cdot 3n^{\frac{3}{4}}$?

3. What is $\left(3 \times 10^5\right)\left(8 \times 10^4\right)$ written in scientific notation?

4. Measurement The diameter of a penny is about 1.9×10^{-5} km. It would take about 2.1×10^9 pennies placed end to end to circle the equator once. What is the approximate length of the equator?

Do you UNDERSTAND?  MATHEMATICAL PRACTICES

5. Writing Can $x^8 \cdot y^3$ be written as a single power? Explain your reasoning.

6. Reasoning Suppose $a \times 10^m$ and $b \times 10^n$ are two numbers in scientific notation. Is their product $ab \times 10^{m+n}$ *always*, *sometimes*, or *never* a number in scientific notation? Justify your answer.

7. Error Analysis Your friend says $4a^{\frac{1}{2}} \cdot 3a^{\frac{1}{5}} = 7a^{\frac{1}{7}}$. Explain your friend's error. What is the correct answer?

 ## Practice and Problem-Solving Exercises  MATHEMATICAL PRACTICES

 **A Practice** Rewrite each expression using each base only once. ◀ **See Problem 1.**

8. $7^3 \cdot 7^4$

9. $(-6)^{12} \cdot (-6)^5 \cdot (-6)^2$

10. $9^6 \cdot 9^{-4} \cdot 9^{-2}$

11. $2^2 \cdot 2^7 \cdot 2^0$

12. $5^{-2} \cdot 5^{-4} \cdot 5^8$

13. $(-8)^5 \cdot (-8)^{-5}$

Simplify each expression. ◀ **See Problem 2.**

14. $m^3 m^4$

15. $5c^4 \cdot c^6$

16. $4t^{-5} \cdot 2t^{-3}$

17. $\left(x^5 y^2\right)\left(x^{-6} y\right)$

18. $\left(5x^5\right)\left(3y^6\right)\left(3x^2\right)$

19. $-m^2 \cdot 4r^3 \cdot 12r^{-4} \cdot 5m$

Write each answer in scientific notation. ◀ **See Problem 3.**

STEM **20. Biology** A human body contains about 2.7×10^4 microliters (μL) of blood for each pound of body weight. Each microliter of blood contains about 7×10^4 white blood cells. About how many white blood cells are in the body of a 140-lb person?

21. Astronomy The distance light travels in one second (one light-second) is about 1.86×10^5 mi. Saturn is about 475 light-seconds from the sun. About how many miles from the sun is Saturn?

Simplify each expression. **See Problem 4.**

22. $8^{\frac{1}{3}}$ **23.** $625^{\frac{1}{4}}$ **24.** $1000^{\frac{1}{3}}$

Simplify each expression. **See Problem 5.**

25. $16^{\frac{3}{4}}$ **26.** $9^{\frac{5}{2}}$ **27.** $64^{\frac{7}{3}}$

Simplify each expression. **See Problem 6.**

28. $\left(8b^{\frac{2}{3}} \cdot 9t^{\frac{1}{5}}\right)\left(8b^{\frac{5}{3}} \cdot 9t^{\frac{3}{5}}\right)$ **29.** $\left(7d^{\frac{3}{2}} \cdot 2g^{\frac{5}{6}}\right)\left(2g^{\frac{3}{2}} \cdot 7d^{\frac{5}{6}}\right)$ **30.** $\left(4r^{\frac{2}{5}} \cdot 5s^{\frac{2}{7}}\right)\left(5s^{\frac{5}{7}} \cdot 4r^{\frac{3}{5}}\right)$

 **Apply**

Complete each equation.

31. $5^2 \cdot 5^{\blacksquare} = 5^{11}$ **32.** $m^{\blacksquare} \cdot m^{-4} = m^{-9}$ **33.** $2^{\blacksquare} \cdot 2^{\frac{1}{2}} = 2^1$

34. $a^{\blacksquare} \cdot a^4 = 1$ **35.** $a^{\frac{2}{3}} \cdot a^{\blacksquare} = a^{\frac{5}{6}}$ **36.** $x^3 y^{\blacksquare} \cdot x^{\blacksquare} = y^2$

37. Think About a Plan A liter of water contains about 3.35×10^{25} molecules. The Mississippi River discharges about 1.7×10^7 L of water every second. About how many molecules does the Mississippi River discharge every minute? Write your answer in scientific notation.
- How can you use unit analysis to help you find the answer?
- What properties can you use to make the calculation easier?

38. When you simplify an algebraic expression like $c^{\frac{3}{5}} \cdot c^{\frac{1}{2}}$, you know that the bases of the expressions must be the same. You also need to rewrite the exponents so that they have a common denominator.
   a. Explain why you need to find the common denominator to simplify.
   b. Simplify the expression $c^{\frac{3}{5}} \cdot c^{\frac{1}{2}}$.

Simplify each expression. Write each answer in scientific notation.

39. $\left(9 \times 10^7\right)\left(3 \times 10^{-16}\right)$ **40.** $\left(0.5 \times 10^{-6}\right)\left(0.3 \times 10^{-2}\right)$ **41.** $\left(0.2 \times 10^5\right)\left(4 \times 10^{-12}\right)$

 42. Chemistry In chemistry, a *mole* is a unit of measure equal to 6.02×10^{23} atoms of a substance. The mass of a single neon atom is about 3.35×10^{-23} g. What is the mass of 2 moles of neon atoms? Write your answer in scientific notation.

Simplify each expression.

43. $\dfrac{1}{a^4 \cdot a^{-3}}$ **44.** $8m^{\frac{1}{3}}\left(m^{\frac{1}{3}} + 2\right)$ **45.** $-4x^3\left(3x^3 - 10x\right)$

 46. a. Open-Ended Write y^6 as a product of two powers with the same base in four different ways. Use only positive exponents.
   b. Write y^6 as a product of two powers with the same base in four different ways, using negative or zero exponents in each product.
   c. Reasoning How many ways can you write y^6 as the product of two powers? Explain your reasoning.

Simplify each expression.

47. $3^x \cdot 3^{2-x} \cdot 3^2$

48. $2^n \cdot 2^{n+2} \cdot 2$

49. $3^{\frac{1}{4}} \cdot 2^y \cdot 3^2 \cdot 2^x$

50. $(a+b)^2(a+b)^{-3}$

51. $(t+3)^{\frac{4}{5}}(t+3)^{\frac{2}{5}}$

52. $5^{x+1} \cdot 5^{1-x}$

53. Nature A book shows an enlarged photo of a carpenter bee. A carpenter bee is about 6×10^{-3} m long. The photo is 13.5 cm long. About how many times as long as a carpenter bee is the photo?

Standardized Test Prep

SAT/ACT

54. What is the simplified form of $\left(2x^{\frac{1}{2}}y^{\frac{2}{3}}\right)\left(4x^{\frac{1}{4}}y^{\frac{5}{6}}\right)$?

Ⓐ $6x^{\frac{1}{2}}y^{\frac{2}{3}}$ Ⓑ $6xy$ Ⓒ $8x^{\frac{1}{2}}y^{\frac{7}{9}}$ Ⓓ $8x^{\frac{3}{4}}y^{\frac{3}{2}}$

55. What is the x-intercept of the graph of $5x - 3y = 30$?

Ⓕ -10 Ⓖ -6 Ⓗ 6 Ⓘ 10

56. At the Athens Olympics, the winning time for the women's 100-m hurdles was 2.06×10^{-1} min. Which number is another way to express this time in minutes?

Ⓐ 0.206 Ⓑ 20.6 Ⓒ 206×10^1 Ⓓ 206×10^{-2}

57. What is the solution of $4x - 5 = 2x + 13$?

Ⓕ 3 Ⓖ 4 Ⓗ 9 Ⓘ 32

Extended Response

58. Bill's company packages its circular mirrors in boxes with square bottoms, as shown at the right. Show your work for each answer.
  a. What is an expression for the area of the bottom of the box?
  b. If the mirror has a radius of 4 in., what is the area of the bottom of the box?
  c. The area of the bottom of a second box is 196 in.^{2}. What is the diameter of the largest mirror the box can hold?

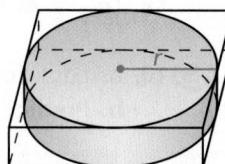

Mixed Review

Solve each system.   ◀ **See Lesson 6-3.**

59. $2x + 3y = 12$
$-3x + y = -7$

60. $2x - y = -3$
$x - y = 1$

61. $2x + y = 15$
$-\frac{1}{2}x + y = 5$

Find the third, seventh, and tenth terms of the sequence described by each rule.   ◀ **See Lesson 4-7.**

62. $A(n) = 10 + (n - 1)(4)$

63. $A(n) = -5 + (n - 1)(2)$

64. $A(n) = 1.2 + (n - 1)(-4)$

Get Ready!   To prepare for Lesson 7-3, do Exercises 65–68.

Simplify each expression.   ◀ **See Lesson 7-1.**

65. $(-2)^{-4}$

66. $5xy^0$

67. $4m^{-1}n^2$

68. $-3x^{\frac{1}{3}}y^{-\frac{1}{2}}z^6$

Powers of Powers and Powers of Products

© **Common Core State Standards**

Prepares for N-RN.A.1 Explain how the definition of the meaning of rational exponents follows from extending the properties of integer exponents to those values . . .

MP 7

You can use patterns to find a shortcut for simplifying a power raised to a power or a product raised to a power.

Activity 1

Copy and complete each statement in Exercises 1–9.

1. $(4^5)^2 = 4^5 \cdot 4^5 = 4^{\blacksquare + \blacksquare} = 4^{5 \cdot \blacksquare} = 4^{\blacksquare}$

2. $(3^6)^3 = 3^6 \cdot 3^6 \cdot 3^6 = 3^{\blacksquare + \blacksquare + \blacksquare} = 3^{6 \cdot \blacksquare} = 3^{\blacksquare}$

3. $(5^8)^4 = 5^8 \cdot 5^8 \cdot 5^8 \cdot 5^8 = 5^{\blacksquare + \blacksquare + \blacksquare + \blacksquare} = 5^{8 \cdot \blacksquare} = 5^{\blacksquare}$

4. $(4^{\frac{1}{3}})^3 = 4^{\frac{1}{3}} \cdot 4^{\frac{1}{3}} \cdot 4^{\frac{1}{3}} = 4^{\blacksquare + \blacksquare + \blacksquare} = 4^{\frac{1}{3} \cdot \blacksquare} = 4^{\blacksquare}$

5. $(5^{\frac{1}{2}})^4 = 5^{\frac{1}{2}} \cdot 5^{\frac{1}{2}} \cdot 5^{\frac{1}{2}} \cdot 5^{\frac{1}{2}} = 5^{\blacksquare + \blacksquare + \blacksquare + \blacksquare} = 5^{\frac{1}{2} \cdot \blacksquare} = 5^{\blacksquare}$

6. $(a^4)^2 = a^4 \cdot a^4 = a^{\blacksquare + \blacksquare} = a^{4 \cdot \blacksquare} = a^{\blacksquare}$

7. $(n^2)^3 = \blacksquare \cdot \blacksquare \cdot \blacksquare = n^{\blacksquare + \blacksquare + \blacksquare} = n^{2 \cdot \blacksquare} = n^{\blacksquare}$

8. $(x^5)^4 = \blacksquare \cdot \blacksquare \cdot \blacksquare \cdot \blacksquare = x^{\blacksquare + \blacksquare + \blacksquare + \blacksquare} = x^{5 \cdot \blacksquare} = x^{\blacksquare}$

9. $(a^{\frac{1}{4}})^4 = \blacksquare \cdot \blacksquare \cdot \blacksquare \cdot \blacksquare = a^{\blacksquare + \blacksquare + \blacksquare + \blacksquare} = a^{\frac{1}{4} \cdot \blacksquare} = a^{\blacksquare}$

© **10. a. Look for a Pattern** What pattern do you see in your answers to Exercises 1–9?

    b. Predict Use your pattern to simplify $(y^{11})^{33}$.

Activity 2

Copy and complete each statement in Exercises 11–15.

11. $(3n)^2 = 3n \cdot 3n = (3 \cdot 3)(n \cdot n) = 3^{\blacksquare} n^{\blacksquare}$

12. $(2x)^3 = 2x \cdot 2x \cdot 2x = (2 \cdot 2 \cdot 2)(x \cdot x \cdot x) = 2^{\blacksquare} x^{\blacksquare}$

13. $(ab)^2 = ab \cdot ab = (a \cdot a)(b \cdot b) = a^{\blacksquare} b^{\blacksquare}$

14. $(xy)^3 = xy \cdot xy \cdot xy = (\blacksquare \cdot \blacksquare \cdot \blacksquare)(\blacksquare \cdot \blacksquare \cdot \blacksquare) = x^{\blacksquare} y^{\blacksquare}$

15. $(pq)^4 = \blacksquare \cdot \blacksquare \cdot \blacksquare \cdot \blacksquare = (\blacksquare \cdot \blacksquare \cdot \blacksquare \cdot \blacksquare)(\blacksquare \cdot \blacksquare \cdot \blacksquare \cdot \blacksquare) = p^{\blacksquare} q^{\blacksquare}$

© **16. a. Look for a Pattern** What pattern do you see in your answers to Exercises 11–15?

    b. Predict Use your pattern to simplify $(rs)^{20}$.

More Multiplication Properties of Exponents

© Common Core State Standards

N-RN.A.1 Explain how the definition of the meaning of rational exponents follows from extending the properties of integer exponents to those values, allowing for a notation for radicals in terms of rational exponents.

MP 1, MP 2, MP 3, MP 4, MP 7

Objectives To raise a power to a power
To raise a product to a power

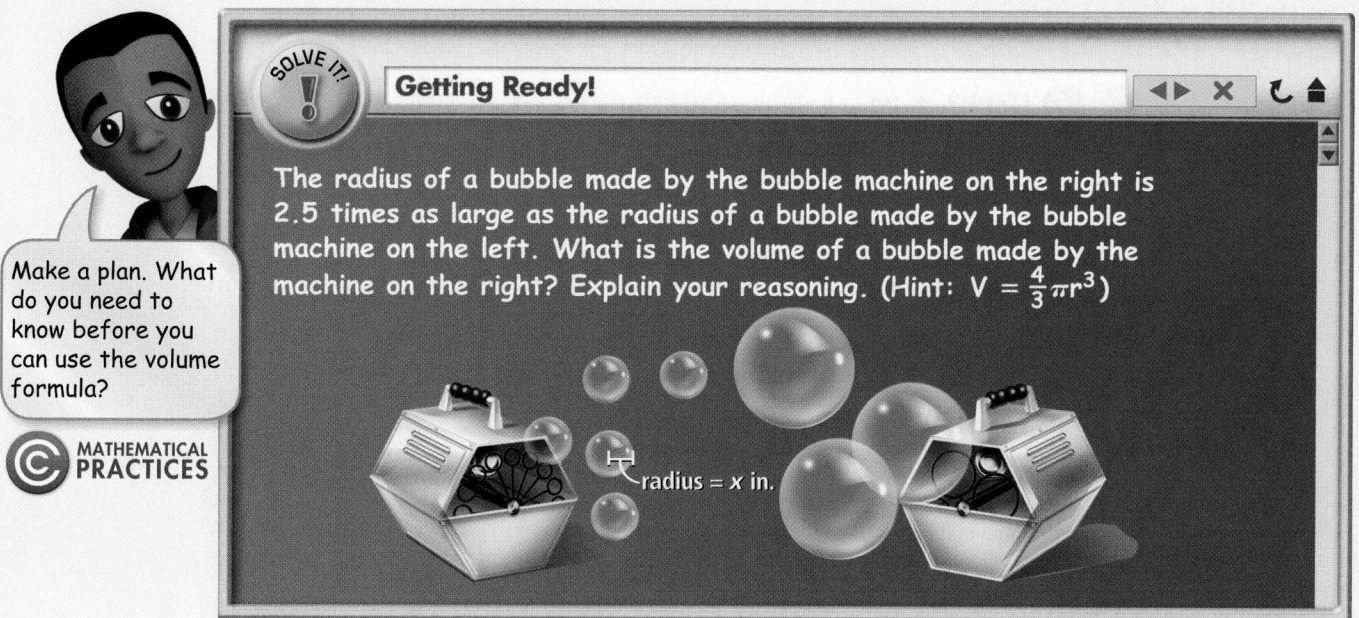

Make a plan. What do you need to know before you can use the volume formula?

© MATHEMATICAL PRACTICES

SOLVE IT!

Getting Ready!

The radius of a bubble made by the bubble machine on the right is 2.5 times as large as the radius of a bubble made by the bubble machine on the left. What is the volume of a bubble made by the machine on the right? Explain your reasoning. (Hint: $V = \frac{4}{3}\pi r^3$)

radius = x in.

In the Solve It, the expression for the volume of the larger bubble involves a product raised to a power. In this lesson, you will use properties of exponents to simplify similar expressions.

Essential Understanding You can use properties of exponents to simplify a power raised to a power or a product raised to a power.

You can use repeated multiplication to simplify a power raised to a power.

$$(x^5)^2 = x^5 \cdot x^5 = x^{5+5} = x^{5 \cdot 2} = x^{10}$$

Notice that $(x^5)^2 = x^{5 \cdot 2}$. Raising a power to a power is the same as raising the base to the product of the exponents.

take note

Property   Raising a Power to a Power

Words To raise a power to a power, multiply the exponents.

Algebra $(a^m)^n = a^{mn}$, where $a \neq 0$ and m and n are rational numbers

Examples $(5^4)^2 = 5^{4 \cdot 2} = 5^8$ $(m^3)^5 = m^{3 \cdot 5} = m^{15}$

$(a^{\frac{3}{2}})^3 = a^{\frac{3}{2} \cdot 3} = a^{\frac{9}{2}}$ $(x^{\frac{1}{2}})^{\frac{3}{5}} = x^{\frac{1}{2} \cdot \frac{3}{5}} = x^{\frac{3}{10}}$

 Problem 1 Simplifying a Power Raised to a Power

Think

Should you add or multiply the exponents to simplify the expression?
You multiply the exponents when raising a power to a power.

Ⓐ What is the simplified form of $(n^4)^7$?

$(n^4)^7 = n^{4 \cdot 7}$ Multiply exponents when raising a power to a power.

$= n^{28}$ Simplify.

Ⓑ What is the simplified form of $(x^{\frac{2}{3}})^{\frac{1}{2}}$?

$(x^{\frac{2}{3}})^{\frac{1}{2}} = x^{\frac{2}{3} \cdot \frac{1}{2}}$ Multiply exponents when raising a rational power to a rational power.

$= x^{\frac{2}{6}} = x^{\frac{1}{3}}$ Simplify.

 Got It? **1.** What is the simplified form of each expression in parts (a)–(d)?

     a. $(p^5)^4$ **b.** $(p^4)^5$ **c.** $(p^{\frac{1}{2}})^{\frac{1}{4}}$ **d.** $(p^{\frac{1}{4}})^{\frac{1}{2}}$

     e. Reasoning Is $(a^m)^n = (a^n)^m$ true for all integers m and n? Explain.

Use the order of operations when you simplify an exponential expression.

Problem 2 Simplifying an Expression With Powers

What is the simplified form of $y^3(y^{\frac{5}{2}})^{-2}$?

Plan

What is the first step in simplifying the expression?
By the order of operations, you simplify powers before you multiply.

Think

You multiply exponents when raising a power to a power.

You add exponents when multiplying powers with the same base.

Write the expression using only positive exponents.

Write

$y^3(y^{\frac{5}{2}})^{-2} = y^3 y^{\frac{5}{2} \cdot (-2)}$

$= y^3 y^{-\frac{10}{2}}$

$= y^{3+(-5)}$

$= y^{-2}$

$= \dfrac{1}{y^2}$

 Got It? **2.** What is the simplified form of each expression?

     a. $x^2(x^6)^{-4}$ **b.** $w^{-2}(w^{\frac{5}{3}})^3$ **c.** $(s^{-5})^{-\frac{1}{2}}(s^{\frac{3}{2}})$

You can use repeated multiplication to simplify an expression like $(4m^{\frac{1}{2}})^3$.

$(4m^{\frac{1}{2}})^3 = 4m^{\frac{1}{2}} \cdot 4m^{\frac{1}{2}} \cdot 4m^{\frac{1}{2}}$

$= 4 \cdot 4 \cdot 4 \cdot m^{\frac{1}{2}} \cdot m^{\frac{1}{2}} \cdot m^{\frac{1}{2}}$

$= 4^3 m^{\frac{3}{2}}$

$= 64m^{\frac{3}{2}}$

Notice that $(4m^{\frac{1}{2}})^3 = 4^3 m^{\frac{3}{2}}$. This example illustrates another property of exponents.

Property   Raising a Product to a Power

Words To raise a product to a power, raise each factor to the power and multiply.

Algebra $(ab)^n = a^n b^n$, where $a \neq 0$, $b \neq 0$, and n is a rational number

Examples $(3x)^4 = 3^4 x^4 = 81x^4$ $\qquad\qquad$ $(4b)^{\frac{3}{2}} = 4^{\frac{3}{2}} b^{\frac{3}{2}} = 8b^{\frac{3}{2}}$

Problem 3 Simplifying a Product Raised to a Power

Multiple Choice Which expression represents the area of the square?

$5x^3$

Ⓐ $10x^3$ $\qquad\qquad\qquad\qquad\qquad$ Ⓒ $25x^5$

Ⓑ $5x^6$ $\qquad\qquad\qquad\qquad\qquad$ Ⓓ $25x^6$

$(5x^3)^2 = 5^2(x^3)^2$ $\qquad$ Raise each factor to the second power.

$\qquad\quad = 5^2 x^6$ $\qquad\quad$ Multiply the exponents of a power raised to a power.

$\qquad\quad = 25x^6$ $\qquad\quad$ Simplify.

The correct answer is D.

Got It? 3. What is the simplified form of each expression?

$\qquad$ **a.** $(7m^9)^3$ $\qquad\qquad$ **b.** $(2z)^{-4}$ $\qquad\qquad$ **c.** $(3g^4)^{-2}$

Plan

How do you find the area of the square?
The area of a square with side length s is s^2. Square the side length of the square to find the area.

Problem 4 Simplifying an Expression With Products

Think

What is the exponent of m?
It has an implied exponent of 1. Similar to coefficients, exponents of 1 don't need to be written.

What is the simplified form of $(n^{\frac{1}{2}})^{10}(4mn^{-\frac{2}{3}})^3$?

$(n^{\frac{1}{2}})^{10}(4mn^{-\frac{2}{3}})^3 = (n^{\frac{1}{2}})^{10} 4^3 m^3 (n^{-\frac{2}{3}})^3$ $\qquad$ Raise each factor of $4mn^{-\frac{2}{3}}$ to the third power.

$\qquad\qquad\qquad\quad = n^5 4^3 m^3 n^{-2}$ $\qquad\qquad$ Multiply the exponents of a power raised to a power.

$\qquad\qquad\qquad\quad = 4^3 m^3 n^5 n^{-2}$ $\qquad\qquad$ Commutative Property of Multiplication

$\qquad\qquad\qquad\quad = 4^3 m^3 n^{5+(-2)}$ $\qquad\quad$ Add the exponents of powers with the same base.

$\qquad\qquad\qquad\quad = 64m^3 n^3$ $\qquad\qquad\quad$ Simplify.

Got It? 4. What is the simplified form of each expression?

$\qquad$ **a.** $(x^{-2})^2(3xy^5)^4$ $\qquad\qquad$ **b.** $(3c^{\frac{5}{2}})^4(c^2)^3$ $\qquad\qquad$ **c.** $(6ab)^3(5a^{-3})^2$

You can use the property of raising a product to a power to solve problems involving scientific notation. For example, to simplify the expression $(3 \times 10^8)^2$, you raise both 3 and 10^8 to the second power. Then multiply the two powers.

Problem 5 Raising a Number in Scientific Notation to a Power **STEM**

Aircraft The expression $\frac{1}{2}mv^2$ gives the kinetic energy, in joules, of an object with a mass of m kg traveling at a speed of v meters per second. What is the kinetic energy of an experimental unmanned jet with a mass of 1.3×10^3 kg traveling at a speed of about 3.1×10^3 m/s?

Plan

How do you raise a number in scientific notation to a power?
A number written in scientific notation is a product. Use the property for raising a product to a power.

$$\frac{1}{2}mv^2 = \frac{1}{2} \cdot (1.3 \times 10^3)(3.1 \times 10^3)^2 \qquad \text{Substitute the values for } m \text{ and } v \text{ into the expression.}$$

$$= \frac{1}{2} \cdot 1.3 \cdot 10^3 \cdot 3.1^2 \cdot (10^3)^2 \qquad \text{Raise the two factors to the second power.}$$

$$= \frac{1}{2} \cdot 1.3 \cdot 10^3 \cdot 3.1^2 \cdot 10^6 \qquad \text{Multiply the exponents of a power raised to a power.}$$

$$= \frac{1}{2} \cdot 1.3 \cdot 3.1^2 \cdot 10^3 \cdot 10^6 \qquad \text{Use the Commutative Property of Multiplication.}$$

$$= \frac{1}{2} \cdot 1.3 \cdot 3.1^2 \cdot 10^{3+6} \qquad \text{Add exponents of powers with the same base.}$$

$$= 6.2465 \times 10^9 \qquad \text{Simplify. Write in scientific notation.}$$

The aircraft has a kinetic energy of about 6.2×10^9 joules.

 Got It? **5.** What is the kinetic energy of an aircraft with a mass of 2.5×10^5 kg traveling at a speed of 3×10^2 m/s?

 Lesson Check

Do you know HOW?

Simplify each expression.

1. $(n^3)^6$

2. $(b^{-7})^3$

3. $(3a^{\frac{1}{2}})^4$

4. $(9x^{\frac{1}{2}})^2(x^2)^5$

Simplify each expression. Write each answer in scientific notation.

5. $(4 \times 10^5)^2$

6. $(2 \times 10^{-3})^5$

Do you UNDERSTAND?  MATHEMATICAL PRACTICES

7. Vocabulary Compare and contrast the property for raising a power to a power and the property for multiplying powers with the same base.

8. Error Analysis One student simplified $x^5 + x^5$ to x^{10}. A second student simplified $x^5 + x^5$ to $2x^5$. Which student is correct? Explain.

9. Open-Ended Write four different expressions that are equivalent to $(x^{\frac{2}{3}})^3$.

  **Practice and Problem-Solving Exercises**  MATHEMATICAL PRACTICES

A Practice Simplify each expression. **See Problems 1 and 2.**

10. $(n^8)^4$

11. $(n^4)^8$

12. $(c^2)^{\frac{1}{4}}$

13. $(x^{\frac{2}{5}})^{10}$

14. $(w^7)^{-1}$

15. $(x^{\frac{3}{5}})^{-\frac{1}{2}}$

16. $d(d^{-2})^{-9}$

17. $(z^8)^0 z^{\frac{1}{2}}$

18. $(a^{\frac{2}{3}})^3 c^4$

19. $(c^3)^{\frac{1}{9}}(d^3)^0$

20. $(t^2)^{-2}(t^2)^{-5}$

21. $(m^3)^{-1}(x^{\frac{1}{3}})^{\frac{1}{4}}$

Simplify each expression.

◀ See Problems 3 and 4.

22. $(3n^{-6})^{-4}$ **23.** $(7a)^{-2}$ **24.** $(5y^{\frac{1}{2}})^4$ **25.** $(36g^4)^{-\frac{1}{2}}$

26. $(2x^{\frac{1}{6}})^3x^2$ **27.** $(2y^{\frac{7}{9}})^{-3}$ **28.** $(r^{\frac{2}{5}}s)^5$ **29.** $(y^2z^{-3})^{\frac{1}{6}}(y^3)^2$

30. $(3b^{-2})^2(a^2b^4)^3$ **31.** $4j^2k^6(2j^{11})^3k^5$ **32.** $(mg^4)^{-1}(mg^4)$ **33.** $(2j^2k^4)^{-5}(k^{-1}j^7)^6$

Simplify. Write each answer in scientific notation.

◀ See Problem 5.

34. $(3 \times 10^5)^2$ **35.** $(4 \times 10^2)^5$ **36.** $(2 \times 10^{-10})^3$ **37.** $(2 \times 10^{-3})^3$

38. $(7.4 \times 10^4)^2$ **39.** $(6.25 \times 10^{-12})^{-2}$ **40.** $(3.5 \times 10^{-4})^3$ **41.** $(2.37 \times 10^8)^3$

42. Geometry The radius of a cylinder is 7.8×10^{-4} m. The height of the cylinder is 3.4×10^{-2} m. What is the volume of the cylinder? Write your answer in scientific notation. (*Hint:* $V = \pi r^2 h$)

 **Apply**

Complete each equation.

43. $(b^2)^{\blacksquare} = b^8$ **44.** $(m^{\blacksquare})^{\frac{1}{3}} = m^{-12}$ **45.** $(x^{\blacksquare})^7 = x^6$

46. $(n^9)^{\blacksquare} = n$ **47.** $(y^{-4})^{\blacksquare} = y^{\frac{1}{2}}$ **48.** $7(c^1)^{\blacksquare} = 7c^{\frac{2}{3}}$

49. $(5x^{\blacksquare})^2 = 25x^{-4}$ **50.** $(3x^3y^{\blacksquare})^3 = 27x^9$ **51.** $(m^2n^3)^{\blacksquare} = \dfrac{1}{m^6n^9}$

52. Think About a Plan How many times the volume of the small cube is the volume of the large cube?
- What expression can you write for the volume of the small cube? For the volume of the large cube?
- What property of exponents can you use to simplify the volume expressions?

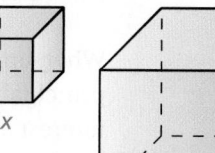

$3x$

$6x$

Simplify each expression.

53. $3^2(3x)^3$ **54.** $(4.1)^5(4.1)^{-5}$ **55.** $(b^{\frac{1}{6}})^3b^{\frac{1}{6}}$

56. $(-5x)^2 + 5x^2$ **57.** $(-2a^{\frac{2}{3}}b)^3(ab^{\frac{1}{3}})^3$ **58.** $(2x^{-3})^2(0.2x)^2$

59. $4xy^20^4(-y)^{-3}$ **60.** $(10^3)^4(4.3 \times 10^{-8})$ **61.** $(3^7)^2(3^{-4})^3$

62. Reasoning Simplify $(x^2)^3$ and x^{2^3}. Are the expressions equivalent? Explain.

63. a. Error Analysis What mistake did the student make in simplifying the expression at the right?
   b. What is the correct simplified form of the expression?

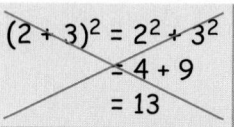
$(2 + 3)^2 = 2^2 + 3^2$
$= 4 + 9$
$= 13$

64. Wind Energy The power generated by a wind turbine depends on the wind speed. The expression $800v^3$ gives the power in watts for a certain wind turbine at wind speed v in meters per second. If the wind speed triples, by what factor does the power generated by the wind turbine increase?

65. Can you write the expression $49x^2y^2z^2$ using only one exponent? Show how or explain why not.

66. a. Geography Earth has a radius of about 6.4×10^6 m. What is the approximate surface area of Earth? Use the formula for the surface area of a sphere, S.A. $= 4\pi r^2$. Write your answer in scientific notation.

     b. Oceans cover about 70% of the surface of the Earth. About how many square meters of Earth's surface are covered by ocean water?

     c. The oceans have an average depth of 3790 m. Estimate the volume of water in Earth's oceans.

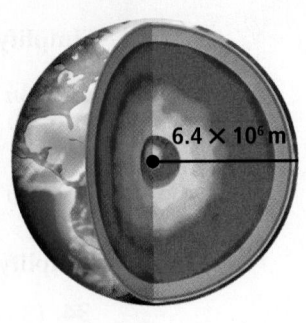
6.4×10^6 m

Challenge **Solve each equation. Use the fact that if $a^x = a^y$, then $x = y$.**

67. $5^6 = 25^x$ **68.** $3^x = 27^4$ **69.** $8^{\frac{1}{3}} = 2^x$

70. $4^x = 2^{\frac{1}{2}}$ **71.** $3^{2x} = 9^4$ **72.** $2^x = \frac{1}{32}$

73. Reasoning How many different ways are there to rewrite the expression $16x^4$ using only the property of raising a product to a power? Show the ways.

Apply What You've Learned

MATHEMATICAL PRACTICES
MP 1

Look back at the information on page 417 about the two CDs that Emilio is considering for the investment of his prize money.

When interest is compounded quarterly, interest is added to the account's principal every three months (one-quarter of a year). The bank calculates the interest using a rate that is $\frac{1}{4}$ of the annual interest rate.

     a. How many times per year is the interest from the Bank West investment compounded? What is the interest rate used to calculate the interest?

     b. Suppose Emilio chooses the Bank West CD. Confirm the values in the table below, and then complete the table. What is the value of the CD after one year?

Bank West CD

Quarter	Starting Principal	Interest Earned	Ending Principal
1	$15,820.00	$150.29	$15,970.29
2	$15,970.29	■	■
3	■	■	■
4	■	■	■

     c. If the Bank West CD earned simple interest instead of compound interest, what would the value of Emilio's CD be after one year?

7-4 Division Properties of Exponents

© Common Core State Standards

N-RN.A.1 Explain how the definition of the meaning of rational exponents follows from extending the properties of integer exponents to those values, allowing for a notation for radicals in terms of rational exponents.

MP 1, MP 2, MP 3, MP 4, MP 7

Objectives To divide powers with the same base
To raise a quotient to a power

Solve a simpler problem first. Use a value for x to understand all of the relationships in this problem.

© MATHEMATICAL PRACTICES

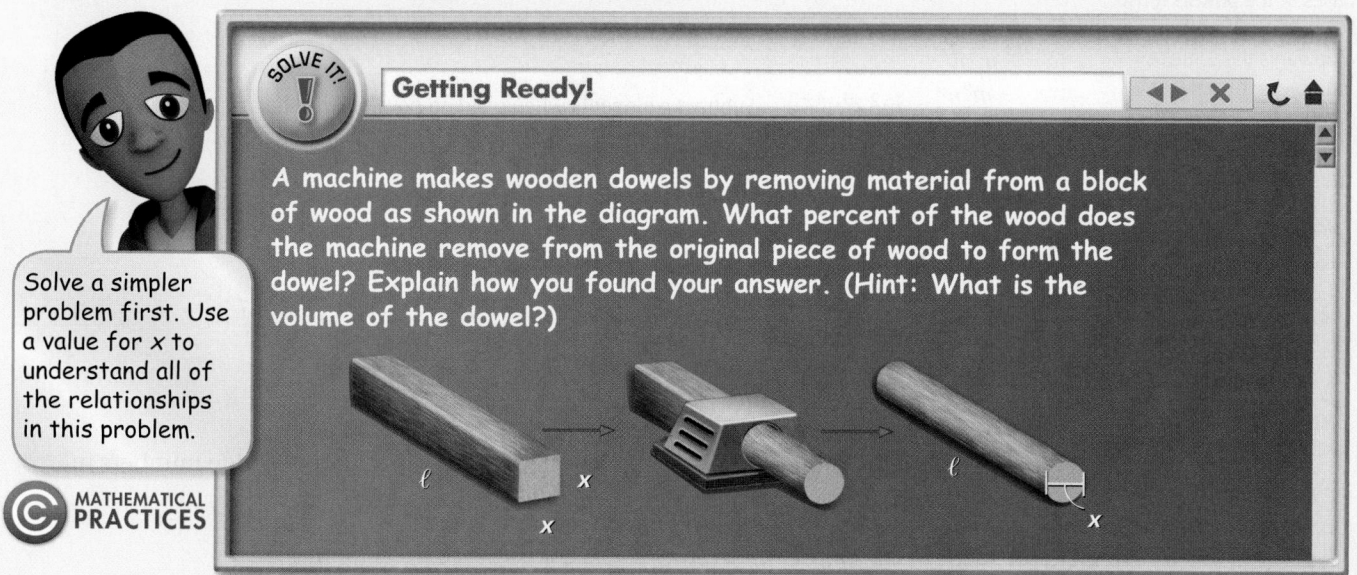

Getting Ready!

A machine makes wooden dowels by removing material from a block of wood as shown in the diagram. What percent of the wood does the machine remove from the original piece of wood to form the dowel? Explain how you found your answer. (Hint: What is the volume of the dowel?)

In the Solve It, the expression for the volume of the dowel involves a quotient raised to a power.

Essential Understanding You can use properties of exponents to divide powers with the same base.

You can use repeated multiplication to simplify quotients of powers with the same base. Expand the numerator and the denominator. Then divide out the common factors.

$$\frac{4^5}{4^3} = \frac{4 \cdot 4 \cdot 4 \cdot 4 \cdot 4}{4 \cdot 4 \cdot 4} = 4^2$$

This example suggests the following property of exponents.

take note

Property Dividing Powers With the Same Base

Words To divide powers with the same base, subtract the exponents.

Algebra $\frac{a^m}{a^n} = a^{m-n}$, where $a \neq 0$ and m and n are rational numbers

Examples $\frac{2^6}{2^2} = 2^{6-2} = 2^4$ $\frac{x^4}{x^7} = x^{4-7} = x^{-3} = \frac{1}{x^3}$ $\frac{s^{\frac{3}{4}}}{s^{\frac{1}{2}}} = s^{\frac{3}{4}-\frac{1}{2}} = s^{\frac{3}{4}-\frac{2}{4}} = s^{\frac{1}{4}}$

Think

How are the properties for dividing powers and multiplying powers similar?
For both properties, the bases of the powers must be the same. Dividing a power is the same as multiplying by a negative exponent.

 **Problem 1** Dividing Algebraic Expressions

What is the simplified form of each expression?

A $\dfrac{x^{\frac{5}{2}}}{x^2}$

$\dfrac{x^{\frac{5}{2}}}{x^2} = x^{\frac{5}{2}-2}$ Subtract exponents when dividing powers with the same base.

$= x^{\frac{1}{2}}$ Simplify.

B $\dfrac{m^2 n^4}{m^5 n^3}$

$\dfrac{m^2 n^4}{m^5 n^3} = m^{2-5} n^{4-3}$ Subtract exponents when dividing powers with the same base.

$= m^{-3} n^1$ Simplify the exponents.

$= \dfrac{n}{m^3}$ Rewrite using positive exponents.

 Got It? 1. What is the simplified form of each expression?

a. $\dfrac{y^{\frac{3}{4}}}{y^{\frac{1}{2}}}$ b. $\dfrac{d^{\frac{7}{2}}}{d^3}$ c. $\dfrac{k^6 j^2}{k j^5}$ d. $\dfrac{a^{-3} b^7}{a^5 b^2}$ e. $\dfrac{x^4 y^{-1} z^8}{x^4 y^{-5} z}$

You can use the property of dividing powers with the same base to divide numbers in scientific notation.

 **Problem 2** Dividing Numbers in Scientific Notation

Demographics Population density describes the number of people per unit area. During one year, the population of Angola was 1.21×10^7 people. The area of Angola is $4.81 \times 10^5 \text{ mi}^2$. What was the population density of Angola that year?

Know
• The population
• The area

Need
The population density

Plan
Write the ratio of population to area.

$\dfrac{1.21 \times 10^7}{4.81 \times 10^5} = \dfrac{1.21}{4.81} \times 10^{7-5}$ Subtract exponents when dividing powers with the same base.

$= \dfrac{1.21}{4.81} \times 10^2$ Simplify the exponent.

$\approx 0.252 \times 10^2$ Divide. Round to the nearest thousandth.

$= 25.2$ Write in standard notation.

The population density of Angola was about 25.2 people per square mile.

 Got It? 2. During one year, Honduras had a population of 7.33×10^6 people. The area of Honduras is $4.33 \times 10^4 \text{ mi}^2$. What was the population density of Honduras that year?

You can use repeated multiplication to simplify a quotient raised to a power.

$$\left(\frac{x}{y}\right)^3 = \frac{x}{y} \cdot \frac{x}{y} \cdot \frac{x}{y} = \frac{x \cdot x \cdot x}{y \cdot y \cdot y} = \frac{x^3}{y^3}$$

This suggests another property of exponents.

Property Raising a Quotient to a Power

Words To raise a quotient to a power, raise the numerator and the denominator to the power and simplify.

Algebra $\left(\frac{a}{b}\right)^n = \frac{a^n}{b^n}$, where $a \neq 0$, $b \neq 0$, and n is an rational number

Examples $\left(\frac{3}{5}\right)^3 = \frac{3^3}{5^3} = \frac{27}{125}$ $\left(\frac{x}{y}\right)^5 = \frac{x^5}{y^5}$ $\left(\frac{a}{b}\right)^{\frac{1}{2}} = \frac{a^{\frac{1}{2}}}{b^{\frac{1}{2}}}$

Problem 3 Raising a Quotient to a Power

Multiple Choice What is the simplified form of $\left(\frac{z^{\frac{2}{3}}}{5}\right)^3$?

Ⓐ $\dfrac{z^{\frac{11}{3}}}{15}$ Ⓑ $\dfrac{z^2}{15}$ Ⓒ $\dfrac{z^{\frac{11}{3}}}{125}$ Ⓓ $\dfrac{z^2}{125}$

$$\left(\frac{z^{\frac{2}{3}}}{5}\right)^3 = \frac{\left(z^{\frac{2}{3}}\right)^3}{5^3} \quad \text{Raise the numerator and the denominator to the third power.}$$

$$= \frac{z^{\frac{2}{3} \cdot 3}}{5^3} \quad \text{Multiply the exponents in the numerator.}$$

$$= \frac{z^2}{125} \quad \text{Simplify.}$$

The correct answer is D.

Think

How can you check your answer?
Substitute the same number for the variable in the original expression and the simplified expression. The expressions should be equal.

Got It? 3. a. What is the simplified form of $\left(\frac{4}{x^3}\right)^2$?

Ⓒ **b. Reasoning** Describe two different ways to simplify the expression $\left(\frac{a^{\frac{3}{4}}}{a^5}\right)^4$. Which method do you prefer? Explain.

You can write an expression of the form $\left(\frac{a}{b}\right)^{-n}$ using positive exponents.

$$\left(\frac{a}{b}\right)^{-n} = \frac{1}{\left(\frac{a}{b}\right)^n} \quad \text{Use the definition of negative exponent.}$$

$$= \frac{1}{\left(\frac{a^n}{b^n}\right)} \quad \text{Raise the quotient to a power.}$$

$$= 1 \cdot \frac{b^n}{a^n} \quad \text{Multiply by the reciprocal of } \frac{a^n}{b^n} \text{ which is } \frac{b^n}{a^n}.$$

$$= \frac{b^n}{a^n} = \left(\frac{b}{a}\right)^n \quad \text{Simplify. Write the quotient using one exponent.}$$

So, $\left(\frac{a}{b}\right)^{-n} = \left(\frac{b}{a}\right)^n$ for all nonzero numbers a and b and positive integers n.

Problem 4 Simplifying an Exponential Expression

What is the simplified form of $\left(\frac{2x^6}{y^4}\right)^{-3}$?

$$\left(\frac{2x^6}{y^4}\right)^{-3} = \left(\frac{y^4}{2x^6}\right)^3 \quad \text{Rewrite using the reciprocal of } \frac{2x^6}{y^4}.$$

$$= \frac{(y^4)^3}{(2x^6)^3} \quad \text{Raise the numerator and denominator to the third power.}$$

$$= \frac{y^{12}}{8x^{18}} \quad \text{Simplify.}$$

Plan

How do you write an expression in simplified form?
Use the properties of exponents to write each variable with a single positive exponent.

✓ **Got It?** **4.** What is the simplified form of $\left(\frac{a}{5b}\right)^{-2}$?

Lesson Check

Do you know HOW?

Simplify each expression.

1. $\frac{y^3}{y^{10}}$

2. $\left(\frac{x^{\frac{1}{3}}}{3}\right)^3$

3. $\left(\frac{m}{n}\right)^{-3}$

4. $\left(\frac{3x^2}{5y^4}\right)^{-4}$

5. A large cube is made up of many small cubes. The volume of the large cube is 7.506×10^5 mm³. The volume of each small cube is 2.78×10^4 mm³. How many small cubes make up the large cube?

Do you UNDERSTAND?

MATHEMATICAL PRACTICES

ⓒ **6. Vocabulary** How is the property for raising a quotient to a power similar to the property for raising a product to a power?

ⓒ **7. a. Reasoning** Ross simplifies $\frac{a^3}{a^7}$ as shown at the right. Explain why Ross's method works.

$$\frac{a^3}{a^7} = \frac{1}{a^{7-3}} = \frac{1}{a^4}$$

b. Open-Ended Write a quotient of powers and use Ross's method to simplify it.

Practice and Problem-Solving Exercises

MATHEMATICAL PRACTICES

Ⓐ **Practice**　Copy and complete each equation.　　　　　　　　　　　　◀ **See Problem 1.**

8. $\frac{5^9}{5^2} = 5^{\blacksquare}$

9. $\frac{2^{\frac{7}{3}}}{2^2} = 2^{\blacksquare}$

10. $\frac{3^2}{3^5} = 3^{\blacksquare}$

11. $\frac{5^2 5^3}{5^3 5^2} = 5^{\blacksquare}$

Simplify each expression.

12. $\frac{3^8}{3^6}$

13. $\frac{9^{\frac{3}{4}}}{9^{\frac{1}{4}}}$

14. $\frac{d^{14}}{d^{17}}$

15. $\frac{n^{-1}}{n^{-4}}$

16. $\frac{5s^{-7}}{10s^{-9}}$

17. $\frac{x^{11}y^3}{x^{11}y}$

18. $\frac{c^{\frac{2}{3}}d^{-5}}{c^{\frac{1}{6}}d^{-1}}$

19. $\frac{10m^6n^3}{5m^2n^7}$

20. $\frac{m^{\frac{2}{3}}n^2}{m^{-1}n^3}$

21. $\frac{3^2m^5t^6}{3^5m^7t^{-5}}$

22. $\frac{x^5y^{-\frac{9}{2}}z^3}{xy^{-4}z^3}$

23. $\frac{12a^{-1}b^6c^{-3}}{4a^5b^{-1}c^5}$

Simplify each quotient. Write each answer in scientific notation. 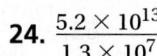 **See Problem 2.**

24. $\dfrac{5.2 \times 10^{13}}{1.3 \times 10^7}$

25. $\dfrac{3.6 \times 10^{-10}}{9 \times 10^{-6}}$

26. $\dfrac{6.5 \times 10^4}{5 \times 10^6}$

27. $\dfrac{8.4 \times 10^{-5}}{2 \times 10^{-8}}$

28. $\dfrac{4.65 \times 10^{-4}}{3.1 \times 10^2}$

29. $\dfrac{3.5 \times 10^6}{5 \times 10^8}$

30. Computers The average time it takes a computer to execute one instruction is measured in picoseconds. There are 3.6×10^{15} picoseconds per hour. What fraction of a second is a picosecond?

31. Wildlife Data from a deer count in a forested area show that an estimated 3.16×10^3 deer inhabit 7.228×10^4 acres of land. What is the density of the deer population?

 **32. Astronomy** The sun's mass is 1.998×10^{30} kg. Saturn's mass is 5.69×10^{26} kg. How many times as great as the mass of Saturn is the mass of the sun?

Simplify each expression. **See Problems 3 and 4.**

33. $\left(\dfrac{3}{8}\right)^2$

34. $\left(\dfrac{1}{a}\right)^3$

35. $\left(\dfrac{3x}{y}\right)^4$

36. $\left(\dfrac{2x}{3y}\right)^5$

37. $\left(\dfrac{6}{5^2}\right)^3$

38. $\left(\dfrac{2^2}{2^3}\right)^5$

39. $\left(\dfrac{8}{n^5}\right)^6$

40. $\left(\dfrac{2p}{9}\right)^3$

41. $\left(\dfrac{2}{5}\right)^{-1}$

42. $\left(\dfrac{5}{4}\right)^{-4}$

43. $\left(-\dfrac{7x^{\frac{3}{2}}}{5y^4}\right)^{-2}$

44. $\left(-\dfrac{2x^{\frac{1}{6}}}{3y^4}\right)^{-3}$

45. $\left(\dfrac{3x^{\frac{1}{2}}}{15}\right)^2$

46. $\left(\dfrac{6n^2}{3n}\right)^{-3}$

47. $\left(\dfrac{b^{\frac{4}{5}}}{b^7}\right)^{-5}$

48. $\left(\dfrac{3}{5c^2}\right)^0$

B Apply

Explain why each expression is *not* in simplest form.

49. $5^3 m^3$

50. $x^5 y^{-2}$

51. $(2c)^4$

52. $x^0 y$

53. $\dfrac{d^7}{d}$

© 54. Think About a Plan During one year, about 163 million adults over 18 years old in the United States spent a total of about 93 billion hours online at home. On average, how many hours per day did each adult spend online at home?
- How do you write each number in scientific notation?
- How do you convert the units to hours per day?

55. Television During one year, people in the United States older than 18 years old watched a total of 342 billion hours of television. The population of the United States older than 18 years old was about 209 million people.
- **a.** On average, how many hours of television did each person older than 18 years old watch that year? Round to the nearest hour.
- **b.** On average, how many hours per week did each person older than 18 years old watch that year? Round to the nearest hour.

Which property or properties of exponents would you use to simplify each expression?

56. 2^{-3}

57. $\dfrac{2^2}{2^5}$

58. $\dfrac{1}{2^{-4}2^7}$

59. $\dfrac{(2^{\frac{2}{3}})^3}{2^{15}}$

Simplify each expression.

60. $\dfrac{3n^2(5^0)}{2n^3}$

61. $\left(\dfrac{2m^4}{m^2}\right)^{-4}$

62. $\dfrac{3x^3}{(3x)^3}$

63. $\dfrac{(2a^6)(4a)}{8a^3}$

64. $\left(\dfrac{9t^{\frac{2}{3}}}{36t}\right)^3$

65. $\left(\dfrac{a^4a}{a^2}\right)^{-3}$

66. $\left(\dfrac{2x^2}{5x^3}\right)^{-2}$

67. $\dfrac{4x^{-2}y^4}{8x^3(y^{-2})^3}$

 68. a. Open-Ended Write three numbers greater than 1000 in scientific notation.
  b. Divide each number by 2.
  c. Reasoning Is the exponent of the power of 10 divided by 2 when you divide a number in scientific notation by 2? Explain.

69. Simplify the expression $\left(\dfrac{3}{x^2}\right)^{-3}$ in three different ways. Justify each step.

70. Geometry The area of the rectangle is $72a^3b^4$. What is the length of the rectangle?

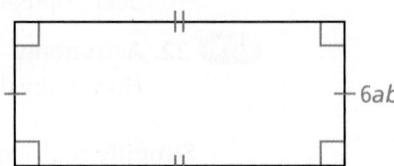

  A $\dfrac{a^3b^4}{12}$

  C $\dfrac{12}{a^3b^4}$

  B $12a^2b^3$

  D $12a^3b^4$

Simplify each expression.

71. $\left(\dfrac{3xy^5}{x^4y}\right)^{-2}$

72. $\dfrac{m^4n^3p^{-3}}{m^{-2}n^7p^{-8}}$

73. $\dfrac{\left(\frac{1}{4}\right)^{-2}}{\left(\frac{1}{6}\right)^{-3}}$

74. $\dfrac{0.2^3\cdot0.2^4}{0.2^7}$

75. $\left(\dfrac{a^{-1}b^3c}{a^2b^4}\right)^6$

76. $\left(\dfrac{(-4)^2}{(-3)^{-3}}\right)^2$

77. $\left(\dfrac{(4x)^2y}{xy^4}\right)^{-2}$

78. $\dfrac{(6a^3)(8b^4)}{(2a^4)(36b^{-1})}$

STEM 79. Physics The wavelength of a radio wave is defined as speed divided by frequency. An FM radio station has a frequency of 9×10^7 waves per second. The speed of the waves is about 3×10^8 meters per second. What is the wavelength of the station?

 80. a. Error Analysis What mistake did the student make in simplifying the expression at the right?
  b. What is the correct simplified form of the expression?

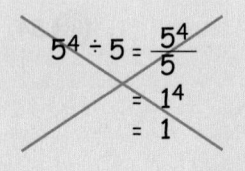

$54 \div 5 = \dfrac{5^4}{5}$
$= 1^4$
$= 1$

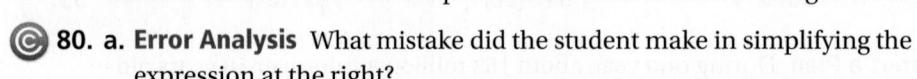 **81. Writing** Suppose $\dfrac{a^x}{a^y} = a^3$ and $\dfrac{a^x}{a^{3y}} = a^{-5}$. Find the values of x and y. Explain how you found your answer.

82. a. Finance In 2000, the United States government owed about \$5.63 trillion to its creditors. The population of the United States was 282.4 million people. How much did the government owe per person in 2000? Round to the nearest dollar.
  b. In 2005, the debt had grown to \$7.91 trillion, with a population of 296.9 million. How much did the government owe per person? Round to the nearest dollar.
  c. What was the percent increase in the average amount owed per person from 2000 to 2005?

Write each expression with only one exponent. You may need to use parentheses.

83. $\dfrac{m^7}{n^7}$

84. $\dfrac{10^7\cdot10^0}{10^{-3}}$

85. $\dfrac{27x^3}{8y^3}$

86. $\dfrac{4m^2}{169m^4}$

 **87. a.** Use the property for dividing powers with the same base to write $\frac{a^0}{a^n}$ as a power of a.

b. Use the definition of a zero exponent to simplify $\frac{a^0}{a^n}$.

c. Reasoning Explain how your results from parts (a) and (b) justify the definition of a negative exponent.

Challenge   Simplify each expression.

88. $n^{x+2} \div n^x$ **89.** $n^{5x} \div n^x$ **90.** $\left(\dfrac{x^n}{x^{n-2}}\right)^3$ **91.** $\dfrac{\left(\frac{m^4}{m^5}\right)}{m^2}$

92. Reasoning Use the division property of exponents to show why 0^0 is undefined.

STEM **93. Astronomy** The density of an object is the ratio of its mass to its volume. Neptune has a mass of 1.02×10^{26} kg. The radius of Neptune is 2.48×10^4 km. What is the density of Neptune in grams per cubic meter? (*Hint:* $V = \frac{4}{3}\pi r^3$)

Standardized Test Prep

SAT/ACT

94. Which expression is equivalent to $\dfrac{(2x)^5}{x^3}$?

   Ⓐ $2x^2$ Ⓑ $32x^2$ Ⓒ $2x^8$ Ⓓ $32x^{-2}$

95. Which equation is an equation of the line that contains the point $(8, -3)$ and is perpendicular to the line $y = -4x + 5$?

   Ⓕ $y = -\frac{1}{4}x - 1$ Ⓖ $y = \frac{1}{4}x + \frac{35}{4}$ Ⓗ $y = \frac{1}{4}x - 5$ Ⓘ $y = 4x - 35$

96. What is the solution of the system of equations $y = -3x + 5$ and $y = -4x - 1$?

   Ⓐ $(23, 6)$ Ⓑ $(6, 23)$ Ⓒ $(-6, 23)$ Ⓓ $(-6, -23)$

Short Response

97. You have 8 bags of grass seed. Each bag covers 1200 ft^2 of ground. The function $A(b) = 1200b$ represents the area $A(b)$, in square feet, that b bags cover. What domain and range are reasonable for the function? Explain.

Mixed Review

Simplify each expression.   ◀ **See Lesson 7-3.**

98. $\left(2m^{\frac{2}{3}}\right)^3$ **99.** $2(3s^{-2})^{-3}$ **100.** $\left(4^3c^2\right)^{\frac{1}{6}}$ **101.** $(-3)^2\left(r^{\frac{1}{4}}\right)^2$ **102.** $(7^0n^{-3})^2(n^7)^3$

Solve each system by graphing.   ◀ **See Lesson 6-1.**

103. $y = 3x$
$y = -2x$

104. $y = 2x + 1$
$y = x - 3$

105. $y = 5$
$x = 3$

106. $y = 7$
$y = 8$

Get Ready!   **To prepare for Lesson 7-5, do Exercises 107–110.**

Graph each function.   ◀ **See Lesson 4-4.**

107. $y = 4x$ **108.** $y = 5x$ **109.** $y = -3x$ **110.** $y = 1.5x$

Do you know HOW?

Simplify each expression.

1. $5^{-1}(3^{-2})$

2. $\dfrac{mn^{-4}}{p^0 q^{-2}}$

3. $3x^{-4}$

4. $d^{-4}t^3$

5. $3^0 s^{-2} t^2$

Write each expression in simplest form.

6. $(2x^5)(3x^{\frac{3}{5}})$

7. $a^2 b^0 (a^{-3})$

8. $6x^{\frac{1}{3}} \cdot 5x^{\frac{2}{3}}$

9. $b^{\frac{1}{2}} \cdot b^{\frac{1}{2}}$

10. $(a^3)(a^3)$

Simplify each expression.

11. $(x^{\frac{1}{4}} y^{\frac{3}{4}})^4$

12. $(3t^{\frac{1}{6}})^3 (2t^0)^{-3}$

13. $(a^3)^4$

14. $(a^{\frac{3}{5}})^5$

15. $(xy^3 z^5)^2$

Simplify each quotient.

16. $\dfrac{7b^6}{b^4}$

17. $\dfrac{a^4}{a^6}$

18. $\dfrac{6x^7}{3x^4}$

19. $\dfrac{-25a^{\frac{3}{4}} b^6}{5a^{\frac{1}{2}} b^4}$

20. $\dfrac{12s^{\frac{5}{2}} t^{\frac{7}{3}}}{s^2 t^2}$

STEM 21. **Astronomy** The radius of Mars is about 3.4×10^3 km. What is the approximate surface area of Mars? Use the formula for the surface area of a sphere, S.A. $= 4\pi r^2$. Write your answer in scientific notation.

22. **Geometry** A box has a square bottom with sides of length $3x^2$ cm. The height of the box is $4xy$ cm. What is the volume of the box?

23. Evaluate $\frac{1}{2} a^{-4} b^2$ for $a = -2$ and $b = 4$.

Do you UNDERSTAND?

24. **Reasoning** A population of bacteria triples every week in a laboratory. The number of bacteria is modeled by the expression $900 \cdot 3^x$, where x is the number of weeks after a scientist measures the population size. When $x = -2$, what does the value of the expression represent?

25. Use the properties of exponents to explain whether each of the following expressions is equal to 64.

  a. $2^5 \cdot 2$ b. $2^2 \cdot 2^3$ c. $(2^2)(2^2)^2$

26. **Reasoning** Can you simplify $(b^{\frac{2}{3}} \cdot c^{\frac{3}{4}})(b^{\frac{5}{9}} \cdot c^{\frac{1}{2}})$? Explain.

27. **Writing** Is the following statement *always, sometimes,* or *never* true? Explain your choice.

  A number raised to a negative exponent is negative.

28. **Error Analysis** Identify and correct the error in the student's work below.

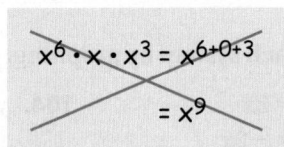

Relating Radicals to Rational Exponents

 Common Core State Standards

Prepares for N-RN.A.2 Rewrite expressions involving radicals and rational exponents using the properties of exponents.

MP 7

You can use patterns to explore the relationship between radicals and rational exponents.

Activity 1

Copy and complete the table. Round to the nearest thousandth if necessary.

	Square Root	Power
1. 9	$\sqrt{9} = \blacksquare$	$9^{\frac{1}{2}} = \blacksquare$
2. 36	$\sqrt{36} = \blacksquare$	$36^{\frac{1}{2}} = \blacksquare$
3. 15	$\sqrt{15} \approx \blacksquare$	$15^{\frac{1}{2}} \approx \blacksquare$
4. 24	$\sqrt{24} \approx \blacksquare$	$24^{\frac{1}{2}} \approx \blacksquare$

A calculator can help with fractional powers. On most calculators, the ⊙ key is used to enter an exponent. For instance, $27^{\frac{1}{3}}$ would be entered as 27 ⊙ (1 ÷ 3).

 5. Look for a Pattern What appears to be the relationship between the square root of a number and the $\frac{1}{2}$ power of the number?

 6. a. Make a Conjecture What do you think the relationship is between the cube root of a number and the $\frac{1}{3}$ power of the number?

    b. Test your conjecture for the numbers 8 and 27, which have integer cube roots. Describe your results.

You can also find a pattern when placing powers with rational exponents on a number line.

Activity 2

For Exercises 7–10, use a calculator to find the approximate value of each expression. Then plot each number on a number line.

7. $3^{\frac{1}{2}}, 3^{\frac{1}{3}}, 3^{0}, 3^{1}, 3^{\frac{2}{3}}$

8. $5^{\frac{1}{4}}, 5^{\frac{1}{2}}, 5^{0}, 5^{\frac{1}{3}}, 5^{\frac{3}{4}}$

9. $25^{\frac{7}{8}}, 25^{\frac{2}{3}}, 25^{\frac{1}{2}}, 25^{\frac{3}{4}}, 25^{\frac{4}{5}}$

10. $10^{\frac{1}{4}}, 10^{\frac{1}{3}}, 10^{\frac{3}{4}}, 10^{\frac{2}{3}}, 10^{\frac{1}{5}}$

 11. Look for a Pattern For a set of powers with the same base that is greater than 1, how can you predict their order on a number line?

Exercises

Predict answers for the following problems using the patterns you have discovered.

12. If $a > 1$ and $x < y$, which is greater, a^x or a^y?

13. If $1 < x < y$ and $a > 1$, which is greater, x^a or y^a?

14. If $a > 1$ and $x > 1$, which is greater, a^x or a^{-x}?

7-5 Rational Exponents and Radicals

 Common Core State Standards

N-RN.A.2 Rewrite expressions involving radicals and rational exponents using the properties of exponents.

MP 1, MP 3, MP 4, MP 6, MP 7

Objective To rewrite expressions involving radicals and rational exponents

SOLVE IT!

Getting Ready!

The figure at the right is made up of squares. The side of a larger square is bisected by the vertices of the square that is one size smaller. What are the values of a, b, and c? (Hint: The hypotenuse of an isosceles right triangle equals a smaller side times $\sqrt{2}$.)

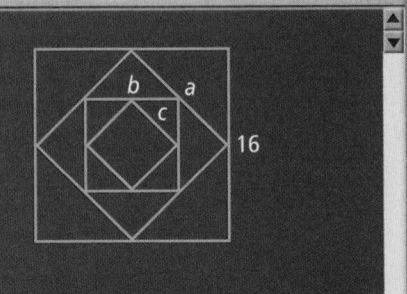

Make a sketch and look for right triangles. Look for a pattern in your answers and predict the value of c before finding the value of c.

 **MATHEMATICAL PRACTICES**

In this lesson, you will learn the relationship between radical expressions and expressions using rational exponents.

Essential Understanding You can use rational exponents to represent radicals.

 **Lesson Vocabulary**
• index

In a radical expression, the number under the radical sign a is the *radicand*. The number n in the crook of the radical sign is the *index*. The **index** gives the degree of the root. For a cube root, the degree is 3. If there is no index, the degree is 2, which means square root.

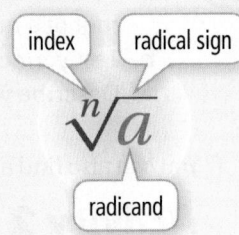

Recall what you know about square roots. Since $5^2 = 25$, you know that $\sqrt{25} = 5$. You also know that $25^{\frac{1}{2}} = 5$. Using the transitive property of equality, you can conclude that $\sqrt{25} = 25^{\frac{1}{2}}$. Similarly, $\sqrt[3]{8} = 8^{\frac{1}{3}}$.

You can simplify radical expressions by finding like factors, just as when simplifying powers with rational exponents.

Think

How do you find $\sqrt[n]{a}$ for any number a?
You look for n equal factors of a.

Problem 1 Finding Roots

What is the simplified form of each expression?

A $\sqrt[3]{125}$

B $\sqrt[4]{16}$

Method 1

$\sqrt[3]{125} = \sqrt[3]{5 \cdot 5 \cdot 5}$

$\qquad = 5$

Method 2

$\sqrt[4]{16} = 16^{\frac{1}{4}}$

$\qquad = (2 \cdot 2 \cdot 2 \cdot 2)^{\frac{1}{4}}$

$\qquad = 2$

Got It? **1.** What is the simplified form of each expression?

    a. $\sqrt[3]{27}$ **b.** $\sqrt[5]{32}$ **c.** $\sqrt[3]{64}$ **d.** $\sqrt[2]{36}$

You can also write expressions that have rational exponents like $\frac{2}{3}$ in radical form.

$8^{\frac{2}{3}} = 8^{2 \cdot \frac{1}{3}} = (8^2)^{\frac{1}{3}} = \sqrt[3]{8^2}$

$8^{\frac{2}{3}} = 8^{\frac{1}{3} \cdot 2} = (8^{\frac{1}{3}})^2 = (\sqrt[3]{8})^2$

So, $8^{\frac{2}{3}} = \sqrt[3]{8^2} = (\sqrt[3]{8})^2$.

take note

Key Concept   Equivalence of Radicals and Rational Exponents

If the nth root of a is a real number and m and n are positive integers, then

$a^{\frac{1}{n}} = \sqrt[n]{a}$ and $a^{\frac{m}{n}} = \sqrt[n]{a^m} = (\sqrt[n]{a})^m$.

Plan

In radical form, do you use the numerator or denominator as the index?
You use the denominator of the rational exponent as the index of the radical.

Ⓒ Problem 2   **Converting to Radical Form**

Ⓐ What is $12a^{\frac{2}{3}}$ in radical form?

$12a^{\frac{2}{3}} = 12\sqrt[3]{a^2}$ Rewrite $a^{\frac{2}{3}}$ in radical form.

Ⓑ What is $(64a)^{\frac{4}{5}}$ in radical form?

$(64a)^{\frac{4}{5}} = (32 \cdot 2a)^{\frac{4}{5}}$ Since 32 is the 5th power of 2, write $64a$ as a product of 32 and $2a$.

$= 32^{\frac{4}{5}}(2a)^{\frac{4}{5}}$ Power of a product

$= 2^{5 \cdot \frac{4}{5}} \cdot (2a)^{\frac{4}{5}}$ Rewrite 32 as 2^5.

$= 2^4 \cdot (2a)^{\frac{4}{5}}$ Simplify $5 \cdot \frac{4}{5}$.

$= 16\sqrt[5]{(2a)^4}$ Simplify and write $(2a)^{\frac{4}{5}}$ in radical form.

 Got It? **2.** What is each exponential expression in radical form?

    a. $a^{\frac{5}{6}}$ **b.** $5x^{\frac{1}{3}}$ **c.** $(54y)^{\frac{2}{3}}$

Think

Can you write $\sqrt[3]{27d^5}$ as $27d^{\frac{5}{3}}$?
No. Since the coefficient 27 is under the radical, the index operates on the coefficient as well as the variable.

Ⓒ Problem 3   **Converting to Exponential Form**

Ⓐ What is $\sqrt[5]{b^3}$ in exponential form?

$\sqrt[5]{b^3} = b^{\frac{3}{5}}$ Rewrite using exponential form.

Ⓑ What is $\sqrt[3]{27d^5}$ in exponential form? Simplify.

$\sqrt[3]{27d^5} = (27d^5)^{\frac{1}{3}}$ Rewrite the radical expression in exponential form.

$= 27^{\frac{1}{3}}(d^5)^{\frac{1}{3}}$ Power of a product

$= 3d^{\frac{5}{3}}$ Simplify.

Got It? **3.** Write each radical expression in exponential form.

a. $\sqrt[3]{s^2}$ **b.** $12\sqrt[3]{x^4}$ **c.** $\sqrt{(4y)^5}$ **d.** $\sqrt[4]{256a^8}$

 Problem 4 **Using a Radical Expression** STEM

Biology You can estimate the metabolic rate of living organisms based on body mass using Kleiber's law. The formula $R = 73.3\sqrt[4]{M^3}$ relates metabolic rate R measured in Calories per day to body mass M measured in kilograms. What is the metabolic rate of a dog with a body mass of 18 kg?

Think

How can you find the approximate value of the expression?
You can use 18^(3/4) to simplify the radical using a calculator.

$R = 73.3\sqrt[4]{M^3}$

$= 73.3\sqrt[4]{18^3}$ Substitute 18 for M.

≈ 640.5578436 Use a calculator to simplify.

The metabolic rate is about 641 Calories per day.

 Got It? **4.** What is the metabolic rate of a man with a body mass of 75 kg?

 Lesson Check

Do you know HOW?

Simplify each expression.

1. $\sqrt[6]{64}$ **2.** $\sqrt[4]{81}$ **3.** $\left(\sqrt[3]{125}\right)^4$

Write each expression using rational exponents in radical form and each radical expression in exponential form.

4. $\sqrt{x}$ **5.** $c^{\frac{1}{5}}$ **6.** $(8d)^{\frac{2}{3}}$ **7.** $\sqrt[4]{16y^3}$

Do you UNDERSTAND? **MATHEMATICAL PRACTICES**

8. Error Analysis What is the error in the problem at the right? What is the correct answer?

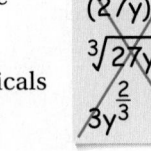

9. Write a rule for multiplying two radicals with the same radicand. Justify why your rule works.

10. Does $\sqrt{4^3} - \sqrt{4} = 4$? Explain why or why not.

 Practice and Problem-Solving Exercises  **MATHEMATICAL PRACTICES**

 **Practice** What is the value of each expression? **See Problem 1.**

11. $\sqrt[2]{49}$ **12.** $\sqrt[5]{1}$ **13.** $\sqrt[4]{625}$

14. $\sqrt[2]{81}$ **15.** $\sqrt[3]{216}$ **16.** $\sqrt[4]{81}$

Write each expression in radical form. **See Problem 2.**

17. $a^{\frac{2}{3}}$ **18.** $(64b)^{\frac{3}{4}}$ **19.** $25x^{\frac{1}{2}}$

20. $z^{\frac{3}{4}}$ **21.** $(25x)^{\frac{1}{2}}$ **22.** $27a^{\frac{2}{3}}$

23. $(98d)^{\frac{1}{2}}$ **24.** $18b^{\frac{1}{4}}$ **25.** $(24c)^{\frac{2}{3}}$

Write each expression in exponential form.

See Problem 3.

26. $\sqrt[5]{a^3}$

27. $\sqrt{(2c)^4}$

28. $\sqrt[4]{256a^3}$

29. $\sqrt[3]{(8x)^2}$

30. $\sqrt[3]{27c^2}$

31. $\sqrt[4]{625y^3}$

32. $\sqrt{36x}$

33. $\sqrt[4]{x^3}$

34. $\sqrt[3]{8b^5}$

35. Manufacturing A company that manufactures memory chips for digital cameras uses the formula $c = 120\sqrt[3]{n^2} + 1300$ to determine the cost c, in dollars, of producing n chips. How much will it cost to produce 250 chips?

See Problem 4.

STEM 36. Archaeology Carbon-14 is present in all living organisms and decays at a predictable rate. To estimate the age of an organism, archaeologists measure the amount of carbon-14 left in its remains. The approximate amount of carbon-14 remaining after 5000 years can be found using the formula $A = A_0(2.7)^{-\frac{3}{5}}$, where A_0 is the initial amount of carbon-14 in the sample that is tested. How much carbon-14 is left in a sample that is 5000 years old and originally contained 7.0×10^{-12} grams of carbon-14?

Apply

Simplify each expression using the properties of exponents, and then write the expression in radical form.

37. $\left(x^{\frac{3}{4}}\right)\left(x^{\frac{1}{2}}\right)$

38. $\left(a^{\frac{2}{3}}\right)\left(a^{\frac{1}{4}}\right)$

39. $(cd)^{\frac{1}{2}}\left(d^{\frac{1}{3}}\right)$

40. $(3x^{\frac{1}{3}})(8x^2)$

41. $\left(36x\right)^{\frac{1}{2}}\left(49x\right)^{\frac{1}{2}}$

42. $\left(x^{\frac{2}{3}}\right)\left(8x\right)^{\frac{1}{3}}$

Write each expression in exponential form. Simplify when possible.

43. $\sqrt[3]{b^2} - \sqrt[3]{b}$

44. $3\sqrt[4]{a^3} - 2\sqrt[4]{a^3}$

45. $\left(\sqrt[3]{8b^5}\right) - \left(\sqrt[4]{256a^3}\right)$

46. $\sqrt[4]{(9x)^2} + \sqrt[4]{625y^3}$

47. $\left(\sqrt[3]{y}\right)\left(\sqrt[3]{y}\right)\left(\sqrt[3]{y}\right)$

48. $\sqrt{(2c)^4} + \sqrt[3]{c^6}$

49. Sports The radius r of a sphere that has volume V is $r = \sqrt[3]{\frac{3V}{4\pi}}$. The volume of a basketball is approximately 434.67 in.^{3}. The radius of a tennis ball is about one fourth the radius of a basketball. Find the radius of the tennis ball.

50. a. Show that $\sqrt{x^2} = x$ by rewriting $\sqrt{x^2}$ in exponential form.

b. Show that $\sqrt[4]{x^2} = \sqrt{x}$ by rewriting $\sqrt[4]{x^2}$ in exponential form.

51. Think about a Plan You want to simplify the expression $4x^{\frac{3}{2}} + 3\sqrt{x^3}$.
- How can you write the radical expression using a rational exponent?
- Can you add the resulting terms?
- What is the result in simplest form?
- Can you write the result in two equivalent forms?

52. Open-Ended Write an expression using rational exponents. Then write an equivalent expression using radicals.

53. Inflation The formula $C = c(1 + r)^n$ can be used to estimate the future cost C of an item due to inflation. Here c represents the current cost of the item, r is the rate of inflation, and n is the number of years for the projection. Suppose a video game system costs $299 now. How much will the price increase in nine months with an annual inflation rate of 3.2%?

 **Challenge**

54. Cells The number of cells in a cell culture grows exponentially. The number of cells in the culture as a function of time is given by the expression $N\left(\frac{6}{5}\right)^t$, where t is measured in hours and N is the initial size of the culture.

  a. After 2 hours, there were 144 cells in the culture. What was N?

  b. How many cells were in the culture after 20 minutes?

  c. How many cells were in the culture after 2.5 hours?

Standardized Test Prep

55. Which of the following expressions is equivalent to $(8x)^{\frac{4}{3}}$?

  (A) $16\sqrt[3]{x^4}$

  (B) $\sqrt[4]{16x^3}$

  (C) $\sqrt[3]{8x^4}$

  (D) $8\sqrt[4]{x^3}$

56. Which of the following expressions is equivalent to $4\sqrt{b^5}$?

  (F) $2b^{\frac{2}{5}}$

  (G) $(4b)^{\frac{5}{2}}$

  (H) $(2b)^{\frac{2}{5}}$

  (I) $4b^{\frac{5}{2}}$

Short Response

57. Write the expression $\sqrt{9s^3} + \sqrt{16s^3}$ with rational exponents.

Mixed Review

Simplify the following expressions.

⬤ See Lesson 7-3.

58. $5(t^2)^3$

59. $(-2x^4)^5$

60. $-6(a^0)^9$

61. $\left((9d)^{\frac{1}{2}}\right)^3$

62. $-12(c^2)^1$

63. $(10a^3)^2$

64. $-4(y^4)^2$

65. $\left((27t)^{\frac{1}{3}}\right)^2$

Write each equation in standard form.

⬤ See Lesson 5-5.

66. $y = 4x + 7$

67. $y + 3 = 2(x - 5)$

68. $-3y + 6 = \frac{7x}{2}$

69. $3y - 5 = 6(x + 2)$

70. $x = 6y + 3$

71. $9y = \frac{9x}{4} + 27$

Get Ready! **To Prepare for Lesson 7-6, do Exercises 72–77.**

Describe the pattern for each sequence. Then write the next three numbers in the sequence.

⬤ See Lesson 4-7.

72. $3, 6, 9, \ldots$

73. $10, 4, -2, \ldots$

74. $\frac{1}{2}, \frac{1}{3}, \frac{1}{4}, \ldots$

75. $2, 7, 12, \ldots$

76. $3, -1, -5, \ldots$

77. $1, 4, 9, \ldots$

Exponential Functions

© Common Core State Standards

F-IF.C.7e Graph exponential . . . functions, showing intercepts and end behavior . . . **Also F-IF.B.4, F-IF.B.5, F-IF.C.9, F-LE.A.2**

MP 1, MP 2, MP 3, MP 4, MP 7

Objective To evaluate and graph exponential functions

Step back and think. Are these plans reasonable?

MATHEMATICAL PRACTICES

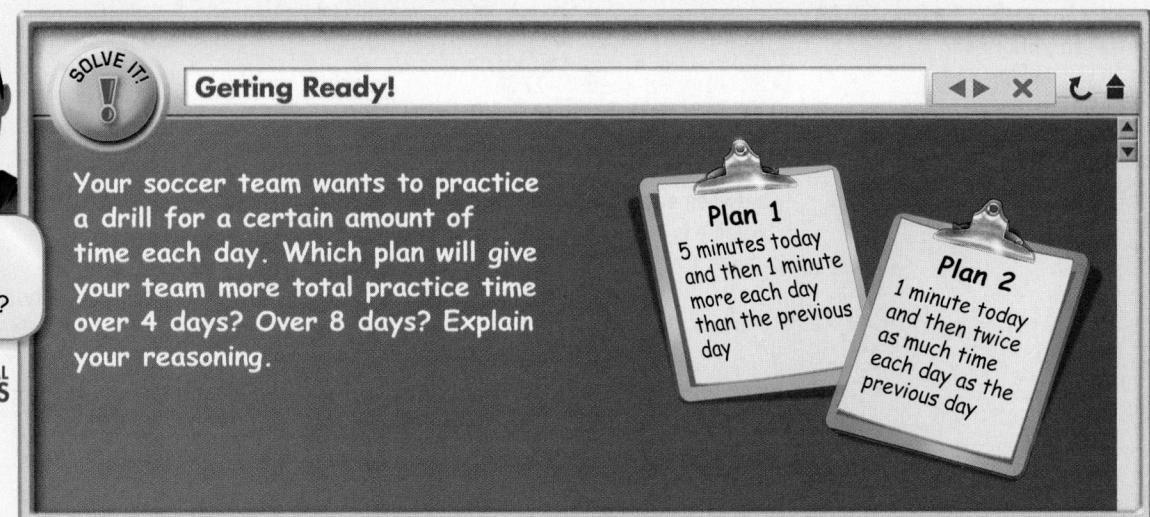

SOLVE IT!

Getting Ready!

Your soccer team wants to practice a drill for a certain amount of time each day. Which plan will *give* your team more total practice time over 4 days? Over 8 days? Explain your reasoning.

Plan 1
5 minutes today and then 1 minute more each day than the previous day

Plan 2
1 minute today and then twice as much time each day as the previous day

The two plans in the Solve It have different patterns of growth. You can model each type of growth with a different type of function.

Lesson Vocabulary
• exponential function

Essential Understanding Some functions model an initial amount that is repeatedly multiplied by the same positive number. In the rules for these functions, the independent variable is an exponent.

Key Concept   Exponential Function

Definition
An **exponential function** is a function of the form $y = a \cdot b^x$, where $a \neq 0$, $b > 0$, $b \neq 1$, and x is a real number.

Examples

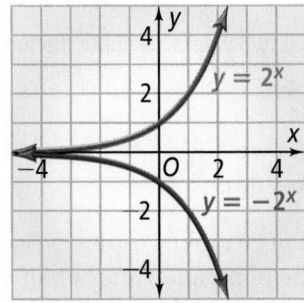
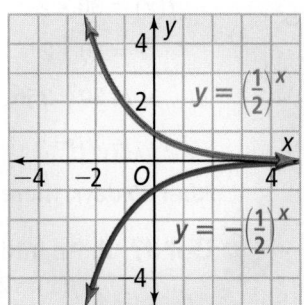

Suppose all the x-values in a table have a common difference. If all the y-values have a common difference, then the table represents a linear function. If all of the y-values have a common ratio, then the table represents an exponential function.

 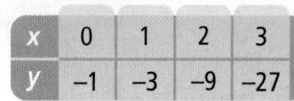 **Problem 1** Identifying Linear and Exponential Functions

Think

How can you identify a constant ratio between y-values?
When you multiply each y-value by the same constant and get the next y-value, there is a constant ratio between the values.

Does the table or rule represent a linear or an exponential function? Explain.

A

x	0	1	2	3
y	−1	−3	−9	−27

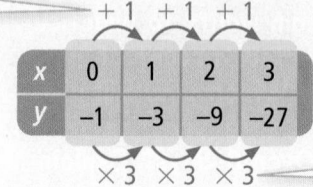

The difference between each x-value is 1.

$+1$ $+1$ $+1$

x	0	1	2	3
y	−1	−3	−9	−27

$\times 3$ $\times 3$ $\times 3$

The ratio between each y-value is 3.

The table represents an exponential function. There is a common difference between x-values and a common ratio between y-values.

B $y = 3x$

The rule represents a linear function. The independent variable x is not an exponent.

 Got It? **1.** Does the table or rule represent a linear or an exponential function? Explain.

a.

x	1	2	3	4
y	−1	1	3	5

b. $y = 3 \cdot 6^x$

 Problem 2 Evaluating an Exponential Function   GRIDDED RESPONSE

Think

Why is the function $30 \cdot 2^x$ not $2 \cdot 30^x$?
In an exponential function, a is the starting value and b is the common ratio.

Population Growth Suppose 30 flour beetles are left undisturbed in a warehouse bin. The beetle population doubles each week. The function $f(x) = 30 \cdot 2^x$ gives the population after x weeks. How many beetles will there be after 56 days?

$f(x) = 30 \cdot 2^x$

$\qquad = 30 \cdot 2^8 \qquad$ 56 days is equal to 8 weeks. Evaluate the function for $x = 8$.

$\qquad = 30 \cdot 256 \qquad$ Simplify the power.

$\qquad = 7680 \qquad$ Simplify.

After 56 days, there will be 7680 beetles.

 Got It? **2.** An initial population of 20 rabbits triples every half year. The function $f(x) = 20 \cdot 3^x$ gives the population after x half-year periods. How many rabbits will there be after 3 yr?

Problem 3 **Graphing an Exponential Function**

What are the domain and range of the function?
Any value substituted for *x* results in a positive *y*-value. The domain is all real numbers. The range is all positive real numbers.

What is the graph of $y = 3 \cdot 2^x$?

Make a table of *x*- and *y*-values.

x	$y = 3 \cdot 2^x$	(x, y)
-2	$3 \cdot 2^{-2} = \frac{3}{2^2} = \frac{3}{4}$	$\left(-2, \frac{3}{4}\right)$
-1	$3 \cdot 2^{-1} = \frac{3}{2^1} = 1\frac{1}{2}$	$\left(-1, 1\frac{1}{2}\right)$
0	$3 \cdot 2^0 = 3 \cdot 1 = 3$	$(0, 3)$
1	$3 \cdot 2^1 = 3 \cdot 2 = 6$	$(1, 6)$
2	$3 \cdot 2^2 = 3 \cdot 4 = 12$	$(2, 12)$

Plot the points.

Connect the points with a smooth curve.

✓ **Got It?** **3.** What is the graph of each function?

    a. $y = 0.5 \cdot 3^x$ **b.** $y = -0.5 \cdot 3^x$

Problem 4 **Graphing an Exponential Model**

Maps Computer mapping software allows you to zoom in on an area to view it in more detail. The function $f(x) = 100 \cdot 0.25^x$ models the percent of the original area the map shows after zooming in *x* times. Graph the function.

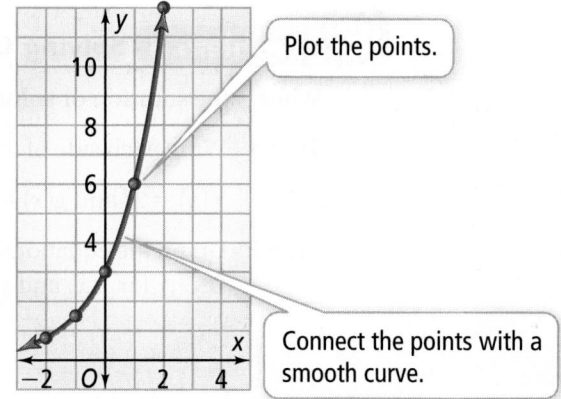

ORIGINAL AREA

Should you connect the points of the graph?
No. The number of times you zoom in must be a nonnegative integer.

x	$f(x) = 100 \cdot 0.25^x$	$(x, f(x))$
0	$100 \cdot 0.25^0 = 100$	$(0, 100)$
1	$100 \cdot 0.25^1 = 25$	$(1, 25)$
2	$100 \cdot 0.25^2 = 6.25$	$(2, 6.25)$
3	$100 \cdot 0.25^3 \approx 1.56$	$(3, 1.56)$
4	$100 \cdot 0.25^4 \approx 0.39$	$(4, 0.39)$

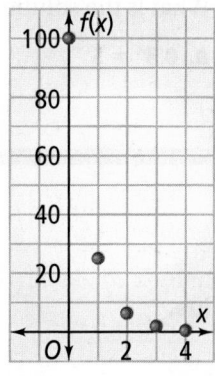

ZOOMED IN 1 TIME

© ✓ **Got It?** **4. a.** You can also zoom out to view a larger area on the map. The function $f(x) = 100 \cdot 4^x$ models the percent of the original area the map shows after zooming out *x* times. Graph the function.

    b. Reasoning What is the percent change in area each time you zoom out in part (a)?

ZOOMED IN 2 TIMES

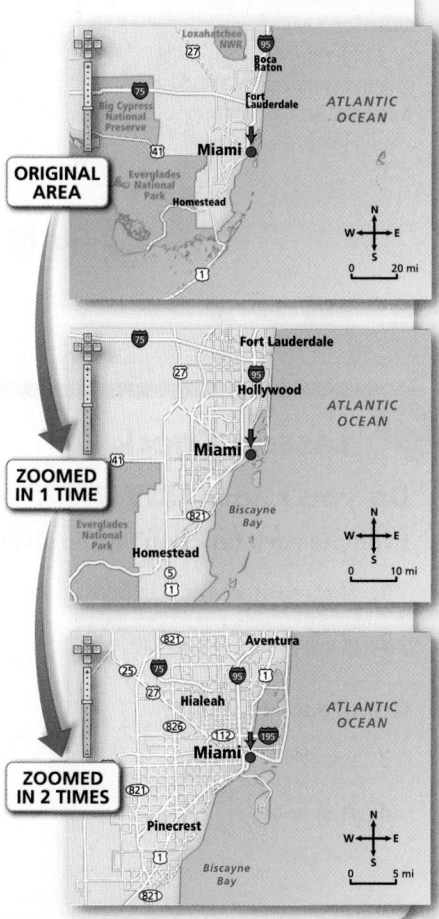

In the Concept Byte after Lesson 6-1, you solved one-variable linear equations using graphs and a graphing calculator. In the next example, you will write each side of the equation as a function and graph the functions. The *x*-value where the functions intersect is a solution.

Problem 5 Solving One-Variable Equations

What is the solution or solutions of $2^x = 0.5x + 2$?

Step 1 Write each side of the equation as a function equation.

$f(x) = 2^x$ and $g(x) = 0.5x + 2$

Step 2 Graph the equations using a graphing calculator. Use y_1 for $f(x)$ and y_2 for $g(x)$.

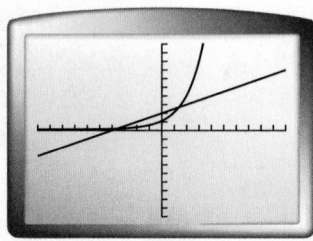

Think

How can you check that the *x*-value is a solution?
Substitute for *x* in the original equation. Make sure you use the same *x*-value for each instance of *x*.

Step 3 Use the **CALC** feature. Chose **INTERSECT** to find the points where the lines intersect.

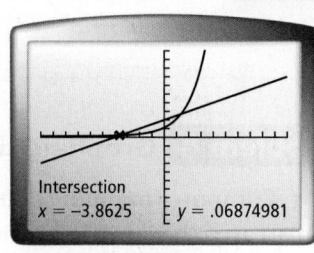
Intersection
x = −3.8625   y = .06874981

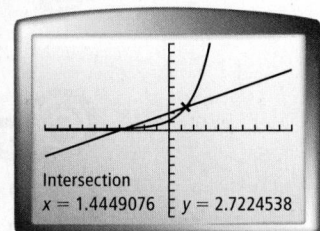
Intersection
x = 1.4449076   y = 2.7224538

The solutions of $2^x = 0.5x + 2$ are about −3.86 and 1.45.

 Got It? **5.** What is the solution or solutions of each equation?

a. $0.3^x = 5$ 　　　　 **b.** $1.25^x = -2x$ 　　　　 **c.** $-(2^x) = \frac{3}{4}x - 4$

Lesson Check

Do you know HOW?

Evaluate each function for the given value.

1. $f(x) = 6 \cdot 2^x$ for $x = 3$

2. $g(w) = 45 \cdot 3^w$ for $w = -2$

Graph each function.

3. $y = 3^x$

4. $f(x) = 4\left(\frac{1}{2}\right)^x$

Do you UNDERSTAND? ⓒ MATHEMATICAL PRACTICES

ⓒ **5. Vocabulary** Describe the differences between a linear function and an exponential function.

ⓒ **6. Reasoning** Is $y = (-2)^x$ an exponential function? Justify your answer.

ⓒ **7. Error Analysis** A student evaluated the function $f(x) = 3 \cdot 4^x$ for $x = -1$ as shown at the right. Describe and correct the student's mistake.

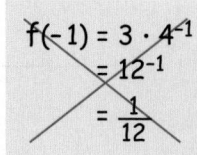

Practice and Problem-Solving Exercises

MATHEMATICAL
PRACTICES

 **Practice**

Determine whether each table or rule represents a linear or an exponential function. Explain why or why not.

◀ See Problem 1.

8.

x	1	2	3	4
y	2	8	32	128

9.

x	0	1	2	3
y	6	9	12	15

10. $y = 4 \cdot 5^x$

11. $y = 12 \cdot x$

12. $y = -5 \cdot 0.25^x$

13. $y = 7x + 3$

Evaluate each function for the given value.

◀ See Problem 2.

14. $f(x) = 6^x$ for $x = 2$

15. $g(t) = 2 \cdot 0.4^t$ for $t = -2$

16. $y = 20 \cdot 0.5^x$ for $x = 3$

17. $h(w) = -0.5 \cdot 4^w$ for $w = 18$

18. Finance An investment of \$5000 doubles in value every decade. The function $f(x) = 5000 \cdot 2^x$, where x is the number of decades, models the growth of the value of the investment. How much is the investment worth after 30 yr?

19. Wildlife Management A population of 75 foxes in a wildlife preserve quadruples in size every 15 yr. The function $y = 75 \cdot 4^x$, where x is the number of 15-yr periods, models the population growth. How many foxes will there be after 45 yr?

Graph each exponential function.

◀ See Problem 3.

20. $y = 4^x$

21. $y = -4^x$

22. $y = \left(\frac{1}{3}\right)^x$

23. $y = -\left(\frac{1}{3}\right)^x$

24. $y = 10 \cdot \left(\frac{3}{2}\right)^x$

25. $y = 0.1 \cdot 2^x$

26. $y = \frac{1}{4} \cdot 2^x$

27. $y = 1.25^x$

28. Admissions A new museum had 7500 visitors this year. The museum curators expect the number of visitors to grow by 5% each year. The function $y = 7500 \cdot 1.05^x$ models the predicted number of visitors each year after x years. Graph the function.

◀ See Problem 4.

29. Environment A solid waste disposal plan proposes to reduce the amount of garbage each person throws out by 2% each year. This year, each person threw out an average of 1500 lb of garbage. The function $y = 1500 \cdot 0.98^x$ models the average amount of garbage each person will throw out each year after x years. Graph the function.

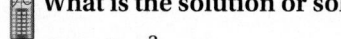 What is the solution or solutions of each equation?

◀ See Problem 5.

30. $4^x = \frac{3}{2}x + 5$

31. $x + 3 = 3^x$

 **Apply**

Evaluate each function over the domain $\{-2, -1, 0, 1, 2, 3\}$. As the values of the domain increase, do the values of the range *increase* or *decrease*?

32. $f(x) = 5^x$

33. $y = 2.5^x$

34. $h(x) = 0.1^x$

35. $f(x) = 5 \cdot 4^x$

36. $y = 0.5^x$

37. $y = 8^x$

38. $g(x) = 4 \cdot 10^x$

39. $y = 100 \cdot 0.3^x$

40. Compare the rule and the function table below. Which function has the greater value when $x = 12$? Explain.

Function 1

$y = 4^x$

Function 2

x	1	2	3	4
y	5	25	125	625

41. You have just read a journal article about a population of fungi that doubles every 3 weeks. The beginning population was 10. The function $y = 10 \cdot 2^{\frac{n}{3}}$ represents the population after n weeks.
   a. You have a population of 15 of the same fungi. Assuming the journal articles gives the correct rate of increase, write the function that represents the population of fungi after n weeks.
   b. Suppose you find another article that states that the fungi population triples every 4 weeks. If there are currently 15 fungi in your population, write the function that represents the population after n weeks.

42. Think About a Plan Hydra are small freshwater animals. They can double in number every two days in a laboratory tank. Suppose one tank has an initial population of 60 hydra. When will there be more than 5000 hydra?
   • How can a table help you identify a pattern?
   • What function models the situation?

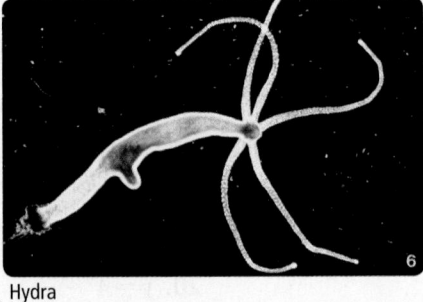

Hydra

43. a. Graph $y = 2^x$, $y = 4^x$, and $y = 0.25^x$ on the same axes.
   b. What point is on all three graphs?
   c. Does the graph of an exponential function intersect the x-axis? Explain.
   d. Reasoning How does the graph of $y = b^x$ change as the base b increases or decreases?

Which function has the greater value for the given value of x?

44. $y = 4^x$ or $y = x^4$ for $x = 2$

45. $f(x) = 10 \cdot 2^x$ or $f(x) = 200 \cdot x^2$ for $x = 7$

46. $y = 3^x$ or $y = x^3$ for $x = 5$

47. $f(x) = 2^x$ or $f(x) = 100x^2$ for $x = 10$

48. Computers A computer valued at $1500 loses 20% of its value each year.
   a. Write a function rule that models the value of the computer.
   b. Find the value of the computer after 3 yr.
   c. In how many years will the value of the computer be less than $500?

49. a. Graph the functions $y = x^2$ and $y = 2^x$ on the same axes.
   b. What do you notice about the graphs for the values of x between 1 and 3?
   c. Reasoning How do you think the graph of $y = 8^x$ would compare to the graphs of $y = x^2$ and $y = 2^x$?

50. Writing Find the range of the function $f(x) = 500 \cdot 1^x$ using the domain $\{1, 2, 3, 4, 5\}$. Explain why the definition of *exponential function* states that $b \neq 1$.

 **Challenge** Solve each equation.

51. $2^x = 64$ **52.** $3^x = \frac{1}{27}$ **53.** $3 \cdot 2^x = 24$ **54.** $5 \cdot 2^x - 152 = 8$

55. Suppose $(0, 4)$ and $(2, 36)$ are on the graph of an exponential function.

    a. Use $(0, 4)$ in the general form of an exponential function, $y = a \cdot b^x$, to find the value of the constant a.

    b. Use your answer from part (a) and $(2, 36)$ to find the value of the constant b.

    c. Write a rule for the function.

    d. Evaluate the function for $x = -2$ and $x = 4$.

 ## Apply What You've Learned

MP 7

Look back at the information on page 417 about the two CDs that Emilio is considering for the investment of his prize money, and at your work in the Apply What You've Learned in Lesson 7-3.

Let r be the annual interest rate, expressed as a decimal, of an account for which interest is compounded n times per year, and let P represent the starting principal (the initial deposit).

    a. Write an expression in terms of r and n for the interest rate used to calculate the interest for each compounding period.

    b. Write an expression in terms of P, r, and n for the value of the account after the first compounding period.

    c. Explain how you can use the Distributive Property to rewrite your expression from part (b).

    d. Using a process similar to the one you used to complete the table on page 438, you can show that the formula $A = P\left(1 + \frac{r}{n}\right)^x$ gives the value of the account after x compounding periods. Use this formula to confirm your result in part (b) of the Apply What You've Learned on page 438.

    e. Suppose Emilio chooses the First Bank CD. Use the formula given in part (d) to find the value of the CD after one year.

    f. Is the formula given in part (d) an exponential function? Explain.

7-7

Exponential Growth and Decay

 Common Core State Standards

F-IF.C.8b Use the properties of exponents to interpret expressions for exponential functions . . .
Also A-SSE.B.3c, A-CED.A.2, F-LE.A.1c, F-LE.B.5
MP 1, MP 2, MP 3, MP 4, MP 8

Objective To model exponential growth and decay

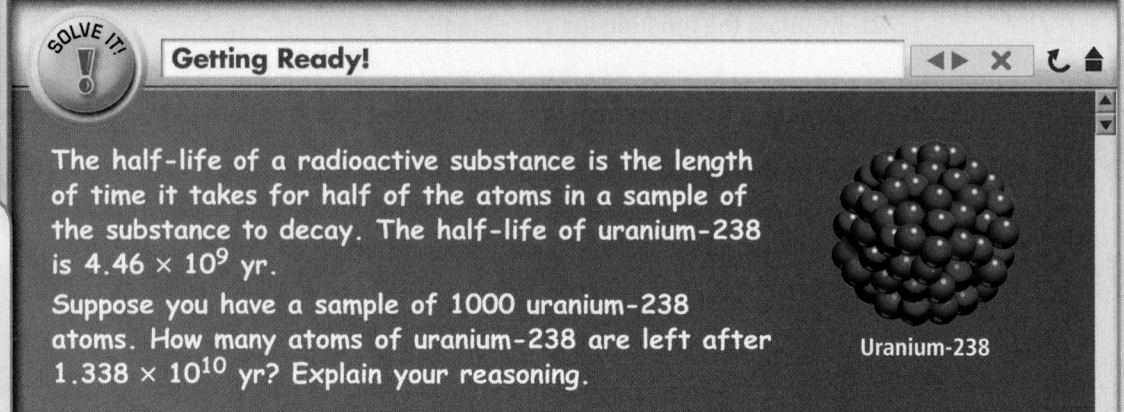

Getting Ready!

The half-life of a radioactive substance is the length of time it takes for half of the atoms in a sample of the substance to decay. The half-life of uranium-238 is 4.46×10^9 yr.

Suppose you have a sample of 1000 uranium-238 atoms. How many atoms of uranium-238 are left after 1.338×10^{10} yr? Explain your reasoning.

Uranium-238

Try a simpler problem. How many atoms are left after 4.46×10^9 years? Will the result for 1.338×10^{10} be greater or less than the result for 4.46×10^9 years?

 **MATHEMATICAL PRACTICES**

In the Solve It, the number of uranium-238 atoms decreases exponentially. In this lesson, you will use exponential functions to model similar situations.

Essential Understanding An exponential function can model growth or decay of an initial amount.

 Lesson Vocabulary
• exponential growth
• growth factor
• compound interest
• exponential decay
• decay factor

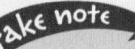

Key Concept   Exponential Growth

Definitions
Exponential growth can be modeled by the function $y = a \cdot b^x$, where $a > 0$ and $b > 1$. The base b is the **growth factor**, which equals 1 plus the percent rate of change expressed as a decimal.

Algebra

initial amount (when $x = 0$)
↓
$y = a \cdot b^x$ ← exponent
↑
The base, which is greater than 1, is the growth factor.

Graph

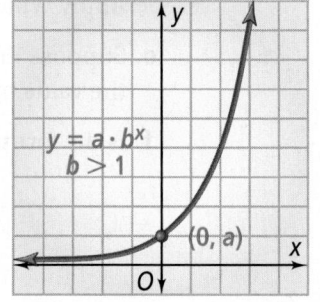

$y = a \cdot b^x$
$b > 1$

$(0, a)$

Problem 1 Modeling Exponential Growth

Economics Since 2005, the amount of money spent at restaurants in the United States has increased about 7% each year. In 2005, about $360 billion was spent at restaurants.

Think

When can you use an exponential growth function?
You can use an exponential growth function when an initial amount increases by a fixed percent each time period.

A If the trend continues, about how much will be spent at restaurants in 2015?

Relate $y = a \cdot b^x$ Use an exponential function.

Define   Let x = the number of years since 2005.
Let y = the annual amount spent at restaurants (in billions of dollars).
Let a = the initial amount spent (in billions of dollars), 360.
Let b = the growth factor, which is $1 + 0.07 = 1.07$.

Write $y = 360 \cdot 1.07^x$

Use the equation to predict the annual spending in 2015.

$y = 360 \cdot 1.07^x$

$\quad = 360 \cdot 1.07^{10}$ 2015 is 10 yr after 2005, so substitute 10 for x.

$\quad \approx 708$ Round to the nearest billion dollars.

About $708 billion will be spent at restaurants in the United States in 2015 if the trend continues.

B What is an expression that represents the equivalent monthly increase of spending at U.S. restaurants in 2005?

You will need to find an expression of the form r^m, where r is approximately the monthly growth factor and m is the number of months. You know that 1.07^x represents the yearly increase where x is the number of years.

$1.07^x = 1.07^{\frac{12x}{12}}$ There are $12x$ months in x years.

$\quad = \left(1.07^{\frac{1}{12}}\right)^{12x}$ Power raised to a power

$\quad \approx 1.0057^{12x}$ Simplify.

$\quad = 1.0057^m$ Let $12x = m$, the number of months.

The expression 1.0057^m represents the equivalent monthly increase of spending at restaurants.

 Got It? **1.** Suppose that in 1985, there were 285 cell phone subscribers in a small town. The number of subscribers increased by 75% each year after 1985. How many cell phone subscribers were in the small town in 1994? Write an expression to represent the equivalent monthly cell phone subscription increase.

When a bank pays interest on both the principal *and* the interest an account has already earned, the bank is paying **compound interest.** Compound interest is an example of exponential growth.

You can use the following formula to find the balance of an account that earns compound interest.

$$A = P\left(1 + \frac{r}{n}\right)^{nt}$$

A = the balance
P = the principal (the initial deposit)
r = the annual interest rate (expressed as a decimal)
n = the number of times interest is compounded per year
t = the time in years

 Problem 2 **Compound Interest**

Finance Suppose that when your friend was born, your friend's parents deposited $2000 in an account paying 4.5% interest compounded quarterly. What will the account balance be after 18 yr?

Know	Need	Plan
• $2000 principal • 4.5% interest • interest compounded quarterly	Account balance in 18 yr	Use the compound interest formula.

Think

Is the formula an exponential growth function?
Yes. You can rewrite the formula as $A = P\left[\left(1 + \frac{r}{n}\right)^n\right]^t$. So it is an exponential function with initial amount P and growth factor $\left(1 + \frac{r}{n}\right)^n$.

$$A = P\left(1 + \frac{r}{n}\right)^{nt}$$ Use the compound interest formula.

$$= 2000\left(1 + \frac{0.045}{4}\right)^{4 \cdot 18}$$ Substitute the values for P, r, n, and t.

$$= 2000(1.01125)^{72}$$ Simplify.

The balance will be $4475.53 after 18 yr.

 Got It? **2.** Suppose the account in Problem 2 pays interest compounded monthly. What will the account balance be after 18 yr?

The function $y = a \cdot b^x$ can model *exponential decay* as well as exponential growth. In both cases, b is determined by the percent rate of change. The value of b tells if the equation models exponential growth or decay.

take note

Key Concept **Exponential Decay**

Definitions
Exponential decay can be modeled by the function $y = a \cdot b^x$, where $a > 0$ and $0 < b < 1$. The base b is the **decay factor,** which equals 1 minus the percent rate of change expressed as a decimal.

Algebra

initial amount (when $x = 0$)
↓
$$y = a \cdot b^x \leftarrow \text{exponent}$$
↑
The base is the decay factor.

Graph

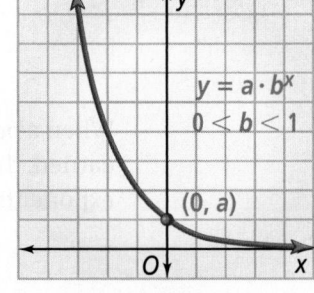

$y = a \cdot b^x$
$0 < b < 1$
$(0, a)$

 **Problem 3** Modeling Exponential Decay **STEM**

Physics The kilopascal is a unit of measure for atmospheric pressure. The atmospheric pressure at sea level is about 101 kilopascals. For every 1000-m increase in altitude, the pressure decreases about 11.5%. What is the approximate pressure at an altitude of 3000 m?

Think

Will the pressure ever be negative?
No. The range of an exponential decay function is all positive real numbers. The graph of an exponential decay function approaches but does not cross the x-axis.

Relate $y = a \cdot b^x$ Use an exponential function.

Define Let x = the altitude (in thousands of meters).
Let y = the atmospheric pressure (in kilopascals).
Let a = the initial pressure (in kilopascals), 101.
Let b = the decay factor, which is $1 - 0.115 = 0.885$.

Write $y = 101 \cdot 0.885^x$

Use the equation to estimate the pressure at an altitude of 3000 m.

$y = 101 \cdot 0.885^x$

$= 101 \cdot 0.885^3$ Substitute 3 for x.

≈ 70 Round to the nearest kilopascal.

The pressure at an altitude of 3000 m is about 70 kilopascals.

 Got It? **3. a.** What is the atmospheric pressure at an altitude of 5000 m?

b. Reasoning Why do you subtract the percent decrease from 1 to find the decay factor?

 Lesson Check

Do you know HOW?

1. What is the growth factor in the equation $y = 34 \cdot 4^x$?

2. What is the initial amount in the function $y = 15 \cdot 3^x$?

3. What is the decay factor in the function $y = 17 \cdot 0.2^x$?

4. A population of fish in a lake decreases 6% annually. What is the decay factor?

5. Suppose your friend's parents invest $20,000 in an account paying 5% interest compounded annually. What will the balance be after 10 yr?

Do you UNDERSTAND? © **MATHEMATICAL PRACTICES**

© **6. Vocabulary** How can you tell if an exponential function models growth or decay?

© **7. Reasoning** How can you simplify the compound interest formula when the interest is compounded annually? Explain.

© **8. Error Analysis** A student deposits $500 into an account that earns 3.5% interest compounded quarterly. Describe and correct the student's error in calculating the account balance after 2 yr.

$A = 500 \left(1 + \dfrac{3.5}{4}\right)^{4 \cdot 2}$

$= 500 \left(1.875\right)^8$

$\approx 76,380.09$

Practice and Problem-Solving Exercises

**A** **Practice** Identify the initial amount a and the growth factor b in each exponential function.

See Problem 1.

9. $g(x) = 14 \cdot 2^x$

10. $y = 150 \cdot 1.0894^x$

11. $y = 25{,}600 \cdot 1.01^x$

12. $f(t) = 1.4^t$

13. College Enrollment The number of students enrolled at a college is 15,000 and grows 4% each year.
 a. The initial amount a is ■.
 b. The percent rate of change is 4%, so the growth factor b is $1 + ■ = ■$.
 c. To find the number of students enrolled after one year, you calculate $15{,}000 \cdot ■$.
 d. Complete the equation $y = ■ \cdot ■$ to find the number of students enrolled after x years.
 e. Use your equation to predict the number of students enrolled after 25 yr.

14. Population A population of 100 frogs increases at an annual rate of 22%. How many frogs will there be in 5 years? Write an expression to represent the equivalent monthly population increase rate.

Find the balance in each account after the given period.

See Problem 2.

15. $4000 principal earning 6% compounded annually, after 5 yr

16. $12,000 principal earning 4.8% compounded annually, after 7 yr

17. $500 principal earning 4% compounded quarterly, after 6 yr

18. $20,000 deposit earning 3.5% compounded monthly, after 10 yr

19. $5000 deposit earning 1.5% compounded quarterly, after 3 yr

20. $13,500 deposit earning 3.3% compounded monthly, after 1 yr

21. $775 deposit earning 4.25% compounded annually, after 12 yr

22. $3500 deposit earning 6.75% compounded monthly, after 6 months

Identify the initial amount a and the decay factor b in each exponential function.

See Problem 3.

23. $y = 5 \cdot 0.5^x$ **24.** $f(x) = 10 \cdot 0.1^x$ **25.** $g(x) = 100\left(\frac{2}{3}\right)^x$ **26.** $y = 0.1 \cdot 0.9^x$

27. Population The population of a city is 45,000 and decreases 2% each year. If the trend continues, what will the population be after 15 yr?

**B** **Apply** State whether the equation represents *exponential growth*, *exponential decay*, or *neither*.

28. $y = 0.93 \cdot 2^x$ **29.** $y = 2 \cdot 0.68^x$ **30.** $y = 68 \cdot x^2$ **31.** $y = 68 \cdot 0.2^x$

32. **Sports** In a single-elimination tournament starting with 128 teams, half of the remaining teams are eliminated in each round.
   a. Make a table, a scatter plot, and a function rule to represent the situation.
   b. Is it possible for 24 teams to remain after a round? Which representation in part (a) made it the easiest to answer the question?
   c. What is the domain of the function? What does the domain represent?
   d. How many teams will be left after 5 rounds?

33. **Car Value** A family buys a car for $20,000. The value of the car decreases about 20% each year. After 6 yr, the family decides to sell the car. Should they sell it for $4000? Explain.

Ⓒ 34. **Think About a Plan** You invest $100 and expect your money to grow 8% each year. About how many years will it take for your investment to double?
   • What function models the growth of your investment?
   • How can you use a table to find the approximate amount of time it takes for your investment to double?
   • How can you use a graph to find the approximate amount of time it takes for your investment to double?

Ⓒ 35. **Reasoning** · Give an example of an exponential function in the form $y = a \cdot b^x$ that is neither an exponential growth function nor an exponential decay function. Explain your reasoning.

State whether each graph shows an *exponential growth function,* an *exponential decay function,* or *neither.*

36. 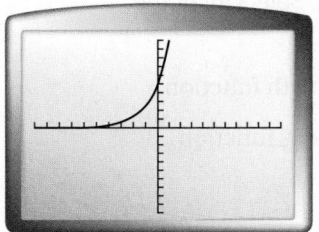   37.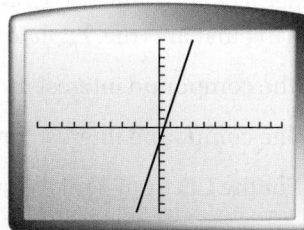

38. Use a table and a scatter plot to answer each question.
   a. You play a game of musical chairs in which 32 players start and you remove 2 chairs in each round. How many rounds will you play before two players are left?
   b. In another game of musical chairs, you take away half of the chairs each time. If the game begins with 32 players, how many rounds will it take to get down to two players?
   c. Will a game where you remove half of the chairs always end more quickly than one in which you take the same number of chairs each time? Give an example.

39. **Business** Suppose you start a lawn-mowing business and make a profit of $400 in the first year. Each year, your profit increases 5%.
   a. Write a function that models your annual profit.
   b. If you continue your business for 10 yr, what will your *total* profit be?

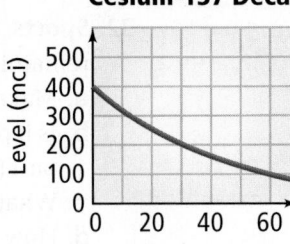

STEM **40. Medicine** Cesium-137 is a radioisotope used in radiology where levels are measured in millicuries (mci). Use the graph at the right. What is a reasonable estimate of the half-life of cesium-137?

 Challenge

41. Credit Suppose you use a credit card to buy a new suit for $250. If you do not pay the entire balance after one month, you are charged 1.8% monthly interest on your account balance. Suppose you can make a $30 payment each month.

   a. What is your balance after your first monthly payment?

   b. How much interest are you charged on the remaining balance after your first payment?

   c. What is your balance just before you make your second payment?

   d. What is your balance after your second payment?

   e. How many months will it take for you to pay off the entire bill?

   f. How much interest will you have paid in all?

42. Open-Ended Write two exponential growth functions $f(x)$ and $g(x)$ such that $f(x) < g(x)$ for $x < 3$ and $f(x) > g(x)$ for $x > 3$.

Apply What You've Learned

MATHEMATICAL
PRACTICES
MP 4

Use the compound interest formula $A = P\left(1 + \frac{r}{n}\right)^{nt}$ and the information on page 417 about the two CDs that Emilio is considering. Select all of the following that are true. Explain your reasoning.

   A. The compound interest formula is an exponential growth function.

   B. The compound interest formula is an exponential decay function.

   C. For the CD from Bank West, $n = 12$.

   D. For the CD from First Bank, $nt = 60$.

   E. The growth/decay factor for the CD from Bank West is $\left(1 + \frac{0.038}{4}\right)^{24}$.

   F. The growth/decay factor for the CD from Bank West is $\left(1 + \frac{0.038}{4}\right)^{4}$.

   G. The growth/decay factor for the CD from First Bank is $0.0031\overline{6}$.

7-8

Geometric Sequences

© **Common Core State Standards**

F-BF.A.2 Write . . . geometric sequences both recursively and with an explicit formula, use them to model situations, and translate between the two forms. **Also F-BF.A.1a, F-LE.A.2**

MP 1, MP 2, MP 3, MP 4, MP 6

Objective To write and use recursive formulas for geometric sequences

What happens as a number grows or shrinks by the same factor? Try it here, and this lesson will show you an easier way to find out.

SOLVE IT!

Getting Ready!

Imagine working part time at a clothing store. Each week a coat doesn't sell, its price is marked down 20%. What will the sale price for the coat shown at the right be after three weeks?

$80.00

© **MATHEMATICAL PRACTICES** In the Solve It, the sales prices form a *geometric sequence*.

Essential Understanding In a **geometric sequence**, the ratio of any term to its preceding term is a constant value.

Lesson Vocabulary
• geometric sequence

Key Concept Geometric Sequence

A geometric sequence with a *starting value a* and a *common ratio r* is a sequence of the form
$$a, ar, ar^2, ar^3, \ldots$$

A *recursive definition* for the sequence has two parts:
$a_1 = a$ Initial condition
$a_n = a_{n-1} \cdot r$, for $n \geq 2$ Recursive formula

An *explicit definition* for this sequence is a single formula:
$a_n = a_1 \cdot r^{n-1}$, for $n \geq 1$

Every geometric sequence has a starting value and a common ratio. The starting value and common ratio define a unique geometric sequence.

Think

How do you find the common ratio between two adjacent terms?
Divide each term by the previous term.

 Problem 1 Identifying Geometric Sequences

Which of the following are geometric sequences?

A 20   200   2,000   20,000   200,000, . . .

$\times 10$ $\times 10$ $\times 10$ $\times 10$

There is a common ratio, $r = 10$. So, the sequence is geometric.

B 2   4   6   8   10, . . .

$\times 2$ $\times 1.5$ $\times 1.33$ $\times 1.25$

There is no common ratio. So, the sequence is not geometric.

C 5 -5 5 -5 5, . . .

$\times -1$ $\times -1$ $\times -1$ $\times -1$

There is a common ratio, $r = -1$. So, the sequence is geometric.

Got It? **1.** Which of the following are geometric sequences? If the sequence is not geometric, is it arithmetic?

a. 3, 6, 12, 24, 48, . . .

b. 3, 6, 9, 12, 15, . . .

c. $\frac{1}{3}, \frac{1}{9}, \frac{1}{27}, \frac{1}{81}, \ldots$

d. 4, 7, 11, 16, 22, . . .

Any geometric sequence can be written with both an explicit and a recursive formula. The recursive formula is useful for finding the next term in the sequence. The explicit formula is more convenient when finding the nth term.

 Problem 2 Finding Recursive and Explicit Formulas

Find the recursive and explicit formulas for the sequence 7, 21, 63, 189, . . .

Plan

What do you need to know in order to write recursive and explicit formulas for a geometric sequence?
You need the common ratio and the starting value.

The starting value a_1 is 7. The common ratio r is $\frac{21}{7} = 3$.

$a_1 = a; a_n = a_{n-1} \cdot r$	Use the formula.
$a_1 = 7; a_n = a_{n-1} \cdot r$	Substitute the starting value for a_1.
$a_1 = 7; a_n = a_{n-1} \cdot 3$	Substitute the common ratio for r.

$a_n = a_1 \cdot r^{n-1}$

$a_n = 7 \cdot r^{n-1}$

$a_n = 7 \cdot 3^{n-1}$

The recursive formula is
$a_1 = 7; a_n = a_{n-1} \cdot 3$.

The explicit formula is
$a_n = 7 \cdot 3^{n-1}$.

Got It? **2.** Find the recursive and explicit formulas for each of the following.

a. 2, 4, 8, 16, . . .

b. 40, 20, 10, 5, . . .

Problem 3 Using Sequences

Two managers at a clothing store created sequences to show the original price and the marked-down prices of an item. Write a recursive formula and an explicit formula for each sequence. What will the price of the item be after the 6th markdown?

First Sequence		Second Sequence
\$60, \$51, \$43.35, \$36.85, . . .		\$60, \$52, \$44, \$36, . . .
common ratio $= 0.85$		common difference $= -8$

$a_1 = 60$		$a_1 = 60$
$a_n = a_{n-1} \cdot 0.85$	Recursive formula	$a_n = a_{n-1} - 8$
$a_n = 60 \cdot 0.85^{n-1}$	Explicit formula	$a_n = -8(n-1) + 60$
$a_7 = 60 \cdot 0.85^{7-1}$	Substitute 7 for n.	$a_7 = -8(7-1) + 60$
$a_7 \approx \$22.63$	Simplify.	$a_7 = \$12$

The price continuing the first sequence is \$22.63 after the 6th markdown.

The price continuing the second sequence is \$12 after the 6th markdown.

Got It? 3. Write a recursive formula and an explicit formula for each sequence. Find the 8th term of each sequence.

    a. 14, 84, 504, 3024, . . .   **b.** 648, 324, 162, 81, . . .

You can also represent a sequence by using function notation. This allows you to plot the sequence using the points (n, a_n), where n is the term number and a_n is the term.

Problem 4 Writing Geometric Sequences as Functions

A geometric sequence has an initial value of 6 and a common ratio of 2. Write a function to represent the sequence. Graph the function.

    $a_n = a_1 \cdot r^{n-1}$ Explicit formula

    $f(x) = 6 \cdot 2^{x-1}$ Substitute $f(x)$ for a_n, 6 for a_1, and 2 for r.

The function $f(x) = 6 \cdot 2^{x-1}$ represents the geometric sequence.

Determine the first few terms of the sequence by using the function.

$f(2) = 6 \cdot 2^{2-1} = 12$ $f(4) = 6 \cdot 2^{4-1} = 48$

$f(3) = 6 \cdot 2^{3-1} = 24$ $f(5) = 6 \cdot 2^{5-1} = 96$

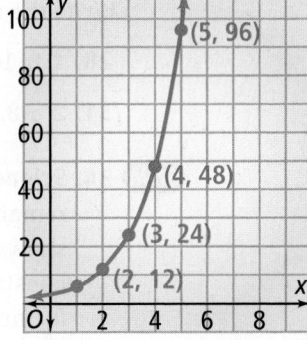

Plot the points $(1, 6)$, $(2, 12)$, $(3, 24)$, $(4, 48)$, and $(5, 96)$.

Got It? 4. A geometric sequence has an initial value of 2 and a common ratio of 3. Write a function to represent the sequence. Graph the function.

Lesson Check

Do you know HOW?

Are the following geometric sequences? If so, find the common ratio.

1. $3, 9, 27, 81, \ldots$

2. $200, 50, 12.5, 3.125, \ldots$

3. $10, 8, 6, 4, \ldots$

Write the explicit and recursive formulas for each geometric sequence.

4. $5, 20, 80, 320, \ldots$ **5.** $4, -8, 16, -32, \ldots$

6. $162, 108, 72, 48, \ldots$ **7.** $3, 6, 12, 24, \ldots$

Do you UNDERSTAND?

8. Error Analysis A friend says that the recursive formula for the geometric sequence $1, -1, 1, -1, 1, \ldots$ is $a_n = 1 \cdot (-1)^{n-1}$. Explain your friend's error and give the correct recursive formula for the sequence.

9. Critical Thinking Describe the similarities and differences between arithmetic and geometric sequences.

Practice and Problem-Solving Exercises

 Determine whether the sequence is a geometric sequence. Explain.   ◀ See Problem 1.

10. $2, 8, 32, 128, \ldots$ **11.** $5, 10, 15, 20, \ldots$ **12.** $162, 54, 18, 6, \ldots$

13. $256, 192, 144, 108, \ldots$ **14.** $6, -12, 24, -48, \ldots$ **15.** $10, 20, 40, 80, \ldots$

Find the common ratio for each geometric sequence.

16. $3, 6, 12, 24, \ldots$ **17.** $81, 27, 9, 3, \ldots$ **18.** $128, 96, 72, 54, \ldots$

19. $5, 20, 80, 320, \ldots$ **20.** $7, -7, 7, -7, \ldots$ **21.** $2, -6, 18, -54, \ldots$

Write the explicit formula for each geometric sequence.   ◀ See Problem 2.

22. $2, 6, 18, 54, \ldots$ **23.** $3, 6, 12, 24, \ldots$ **24.** $200, 40, 8, 1\frac{3}{5}, \ldots$

25. $3, -12, 48, -192, \ldots$ **26.** $8, -8, 8, -8, \ldots$ **27.** $686, 98, 14, 2, \ldots$

Write the recursive formula for each geometric sequence.

28. $4, 8, 16, 32, \ldots$ **29.** $1, 5, 25, 125, \ldots$ **30.** $100, 50, 25, 12.5, \ldots$

31. $2, -8, 32, -64, \ldots$ **32.** $-\frac{1}{36}, \frac{1}{12}, -\frac{1}{4}, \frac{3}{4}, \ldots$ **33.** $192, 128, 85\frac{1}{3}, 56\frac{8}{9}, \ldots$

 34. Science When a radioactive substance decays, measurements of the amount remaining over constant intervals of time form a geometric sequence. The table shows the amount of Fl-18, remaining after different constant intervals. Write the explicit and recursive formulas for the geometric sequence formed by the amount of Fl-18 remaining.   ◀ See Problem 3.

Fluorine-18 Remaining				
Time (min)	0	110	220	330
Fl-18 (picograms)	260	130	65	32.5

35. A store manager plans to offer discounts on some sweaters according to this sequence: $48, $36, $27, $20.25, . . . Write the explicit and recursive formulas for the sequence.

36. A geometric sequence has an initial value of 18 and a common ratio of $\frac{1}{2}$. Write a function to represent this sequence. Graph the function.  **See Problem 4.**

37. Write and graph the function that represents the sequence in the table.

x	1	2	3	4
f(x)	8	16	32	64

B **Apply**

Determine if each sequence is a geometric sequence. If it is, find the common ratio and write the explicit and recursive formulas.

38. 5, 10, 20, 40, . . . **39.** 20, 15, 10, 5, . . . **40.** 3, −9, 27, −81, . . .

41. 98, 14, 2, $\frac{2}{7}$, . . . **42.** −3, −1, 1, 3, . . . **43.** 200, −100, 50, −25, . . .

Identify each sequence as *arithmetic*, *geometric*, or *neither*.

44. 1.5, 4.5, 13.5, 40.5, . . . **45.** 42, 38, 34, 30, . . . **46.** 4, 9, 16, 25, . . .

47. −4, 1, 6, 11, . . . **48.** 1, 2, 3, 5, . . . **49.** 2, 8, 32, 128, . . .

© **50. Think about a Plan** Suppose you are rehearsing for a concert. You plan to rehearse the piece you will perform four times the first day and then to double the number of times you rehearse the piece each day until the concert. What are two formulas you can write to describe the sequence of how many times you will rehearse the piece each day?
* How can you write a sequence of numbers to represent this situation?
* Is the sequence arithmetic, geometric, or neither?
* How can you write explicit and recursive formulas for this sequence?

© **51. Open-Ended** Write a geometric sequence. Then write the explicit and recursive formulas for your sequence.

 52. Science A certain culture of yeast increases by 50% every three hours. A scientist places 9 grams of the yeast in a culture dish. Write the explicit and recursive formulas for the geometric sequence formed by the growth of the yeast.

C **Challenge**

53. The differences between consecutive terms in a geometric sequence form a new geometric sequence. For instance, when you take the differences between the consecutive terms of the geometric sequence 5, 15, 45, 135, . . . you get 15 − 5, 45 − 15, 135 − 45, . . . The new geometric sequence is 10, 30, 90, . . . Compare the two sequences. How are they similar, and how do they differ?

54. Which of the following is the explicit formula for the geometric sequence 15, 3, 0.6, 0.12, . . .?

   (A) $a_n = 15 \cdot 0.2^{n-1}$ (C) $a_1 = 15; a_n = 0.2 \cdot a^{n-1}$

   (B) $a_1 = 0.12; a_n = 5 \cdot a^{n-1}$ (D) $a_n = 0.2 \cdot 15^{n-1}$

55. Which of the following is the recursive formula for the geometric sequence 2, 12, 72, 432, . . .?

   (F) $a_n = 2 \cdot 6^{n-1}$ (H) $a_1 = 6; a_n = 2 \cdot a^{n-1}$

   (G) $a_1 = 2; a_n = 6 \cdot a^{n-1}$ (I) $a_n = 6 \cdot 2^{n-1}$

56. Which of the following is the explicit formula for the geometric sequence 12, 18, 27, 40.5, . . .?

   (A) $a_n = 15 \cdot 1.2^{n-1}$ (C) $a_1 = 12; a_n = 1.5 \cdot a^{n-1}$

   (B) $a_1 = 12; a_n = 0.5 \cdot a^{n-1}$ (D) $a_n = 12 \cdot 1.5^{n-1}$

57. Which of the following is both an arithmetic sequence and a geometric sequence?

   (F) $1, -1, 1, -1, \ldots$ (H) $1, 4, 9, 16, \ldots$

   (G) $16, 24, 36, 54, \ldots$ (I) $5, 5, 5, 5, \ldots$

Short Response

58. Write the explicit and recursive formulas for the geometric sequence 27, 36, 48, 64, . . .

Mixed Review

Write the recursive and explicit formulas for each arithmetic sequence.   ◀ See Lesson 4-7.

59. $0, 9, 18, 27, \ldots$ **60.** $5, 3, 1, -1, \ldots$ **61.** $-7, -3, 1, 5, \ldots$

Solve each equation.   ◀ See Lesson 2-3.

62. $3x + 7 = 2x - 1$ **63.** $\frac{y}{2} + 5 = -y + 2$ **64.** $5(a - 3) = 20 + a$

Solve the following problems.   ◀ See Lesson 2-10.

65. A price changes from $40 to $70. What is the percent change?

66. The value 25 is increased by 50%. What is the new value?

Get Ready!   To prepare for Lesson 8-1, do Exercises 67–69.

Simplify the following expressions.   ◀ See Lesson 1-8.

67. $(2x + 3y) + 2y$ **68.** $(4a + 5b) - 3b$ **69.** $(-6c + 5d) + 2c$

Pull It **All Together**

Completing the Performance Task

Look back at your results from the Apply What You've Learned sections in Lessons 7-3, 7-6, and 7-7. Use the work you did to complete the following.

1. Solve the problem in the Task Description on page 417 by determining which investment will earn Emilio more interest. How much more interest will Emilio earn with that investment? Show all your work and explain each step of your solution.

 2. **Reflect** Choose one of the Mathematical Practices below and explain how you applied it in your work on the Performance Task.

    MP 1: Make sense of problems and persevere in solving them.

    MP 4: Model with mathematics.

    MP 7: Look for and make use of structure.

On Your Own

Kristi has $19,000 to invest. Reliable Bank is offering a 4-year CD with a 3.5% annual interest rate, compounded semi-annually (once every 6 months).

a. Kristi wants to earn at least $2750 in total interest. Can she earn this much with the 4-year CD from Reliable Bank? Explain.

b. Reliable Bank also offers a 6-year CD at the same interest rate as the 4-year CD. What will be the value of Kristi's investment after 6 years if she chooses the 6-year CD?

Connecting **BIG** ideas and Answering the Essential Questions

1 Equivalence
One way to represent numbers is to use exponents. A number raised to the 0 power is equal to 1.

→

Zero and Negative Exponents (Lesson 7-1)
$10^0 = 1$
$10^{-3} = \dfrac{1}{10^3}$

2 Properties
Just as there are properties that describe how to rewrite expressions involving addition and multiplication, there are properties that describe how to rewrite and simplify exponential and radical expressions.

→

Properties of Exponents (Lessons 7-2, 7-3, and 7-4)
$5^2 \cdot 5^4 = 5^{2+4} = 5^6$
$\left(3^{\frac{3}{4}}\right)^4 = 3^{\frac{3}{4} \cdot 4} = 3^3$
$\dfrac{7^8}{7^5} = 7^{8-5} = 7^3$

→

Rational Exponents and Radicals (Lesson 7-5)
$4^{\frac{1}{2}} = \sqrt{4}$
$x^{\frac{1}{3}} = \sqrt[3]{x}$
$b^{\frac{2}{3}} = \sqrt[3]{b^2}$

3 Function
The family of exponential functions has equations of the form $y = a \cdot b^x$. They can be used to model exponential growth or decay and to model geometric sequences.

→

Exponential Functions (Lessons 7-6 and 7-7)
Exponential Growth
$y = 2 \cdot \left(\dfrac{5}{4}\right)^x$
Exponential Decay
$y = 3 \cdot \left(\dfrac{1}{4}\right)^x$

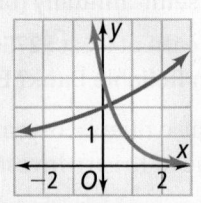

→

Geometric Sequences (Lesson 7-8)
An *explicit formula* is a function rule that relates each term of a sequence to the term number.
A *recursive formula* is a function rule that relates each term of a sequence to the ones before it.

Chapter Vocabulary

- compound interest (p. 461)
- decay factor (p. 462)
- exponential decay (p. 462)
- exponential function (p. 453)
- exponential growth (p. 460)
- geometric sequence (p. 467)
- growth factor (p. 460)
- index (p. 448)

Choose the correct term to complete each sentence.

1. A _?_ is a number sequence that has a common ratio between terms.

2. For a function $y = a \cdot b^x$, where $a > 0$ and $b > 1$, b is the _?_ .

3. For a function $y = a \cdot b^x$, where $a > 0$ and $0 < b < 1$, b is the _?_ .

4. The function $y = a \cdot b^x$ models _?_ for $a > 0$ and $b > 1$.

5. The function $y = a \cdot b^x$ models _?_ for $a > 0$ and $0 < b < 1$.

7-1 Zero and Negative Exponents

Quick Review

You can use zero and negative integers as exponents. For every nonzero number a, $a^0 = 1$. For every nonzero number a and any integer n, $a^{-n} = \frac{1}{a^n}$. When you evaluate an exponential expression, you can simplify the expression before substituting values for the variables.

Example

What is the value of $a^2b^{-4}c^0$ for $a = 3$, $b = 2$, and $c = -5$?

$$a^2b^{-4}c^0 = \frac{a^2c^0}{b^4} \quad \text{Use the definition of negative exponents.}$$

$$= \frac{a^2(1)}{b^4} \quad \text{Use the definition of zero exponent.}$$

$$= \frac{3^2}{2^4} \quad \text{Substitute.}$$

$$= \frac{9}{16} \quad \text{Simplify.}$$

Exercises

Simplify each expression.

6. 5^0

7. 7^{-2}

8. $\frac{4x^{-2}}{y^{-8}}$

9. $\frac{1}{p^2q^{-4}r^0}$

Evaluate each expression for $x = 2$, $y = -3$, and $z = -5$.

10. x^0y^2

11. $(-x)^{-4}y^2$

12. x^0z^0

13. $\frac{5x^0}{y^{-2}}$

14. $y^{-2}z^2$

15. $\frac{2x}{y^2z^{-1}}$

16. Reasoning Is it true that $(-3b)^4 = -12b^4$? Explain why or why not.

7-2 Multiplying Powers With the Same Base

Quick Review

To multiply powers with the same base, add the exponents.

$a^m \cdot a^n = a^{m+n}$, where $a \neq 0$ and m and n are real numbers

Example

What is the simplified form of each expression?

a. $3^{10} \cdot 3^4 = 3^{10+4} = 3^{14}$

b. $\left(a^4\right)\left(a^3\right) = a^{4+3} = a^7$

c. $\left(x^{\frac{3}{5}}\right)\left(x^{\frac{1}{5}}\right) = x^{\frac{3}{5}+\frac{1}{5}} = x^{\frac{4}{5}}$

d. $\left(b^{\frac{3}{4}}\right)\left(b^{\frac{1}{2}}\right) = b^{\frac{3}{4}+\frac{1}{2}} = b^{\frac{3}{4}+\frac{2}{4}} = b^{\frac{5}{4}}$

Exercises

Complete each equation.

17. $3^2 \cdot 3^{\blacksquare} = 3^{10}$

18. $a^6 \cdot a^{\blacksquare} = a^8$

19. $x^2y^5 \cdot x^{\blacksquare}y^{\blacksquare} = x^5y^{11}$

20. $a^{\frac{1}{2}} \cdot a^{\blacksquare} = a$

21. $x^{\frac{2}{3}} \cdot x^{\blacksquare} = x^{\frac{11}{12}}$

22. $m^{\frac{3}{4}}n^{\frac{1}{2}} \cdot m^{\blacksquare}n^{\blacksquare} = m^{\frac{5}{4}}n$

Simplify each expression.

23. $2d^2 \cdot d^3$

24. $(x^3)(x^4)$

25. $\left(x^3y^5\right)\left(-y^7x\right)$

26. $\left(s^{\frac{3}{5}}\right)\left(s^{\frac{2}{3}}\right)$

27. $\left(p^{\frac{1}{3}}q\right)\left(q^{\frac{1}{2}}p\right)$

28. $2m^{\frac{1}{4}}n^2 \cdot 3m^{\frac{1}{4}}n$

29. Estimation Each square inch of your body has about 6.5×10^2 pores. Suppose the back of your hand has an area of about 0.12×10^2 in.^{2}. About how many pores are on the back of your hand? Write your answer in scientific notation.

7-3 More Multiplication Properties of Exponents

Quick Review

To raise a power to a power, multiply the exponents.

$(a^m)^n = a^{mn}$, where $a \neq 0$ and m and n are real numbers

To raise a product to a power, raise each factor in the product to the power.

$(ab)^n = a^n b^n$, where $a \neq 0$, $b \neq 0$, and n are real numbers

Example

What is the simplified form of each expression?

a. $(x^5)^7 = x^{5 \cdot 7} = x^{35}$

b. $(pq)^8 = p^8 q^8$

c. $\left(x^{\frac{1}{3}}\right)^3 = x^{\frac{1}{3} \cdot 3} = x^{\frac{3}{3}} = x$

d. $(ab)^{\frac{2}{3}} = a^{\frac{2}{3}} b^{\frac{2}{3}}$

Exercises

Complete each equation.

30. $(5^5)^{\blacksquare} = 5^{15}$

31. $(b^{-4})^{\blacksquare} = b^{20}$

32. $(4x^3 y^5)^{\blacksquare} = 16x^6 y^{10}$

33. $\left(x^{\frac{2}{3}}\right)^{\blacksquare} = x^2$

34. $\left(a^{\frac{1}{2}}\right)^{\blacksquare} = a^{\frac{1}{4}}$

35. $\left(2x^2 y^{\frac{1}{4}}\right)^{\blacksquare} = 4x^4 y^{\frac{1}{2}}$

Simplify each expression.

36. $(q^3 r)^4$

37. $(1.34^2)^5 (1.34)^{-8}$

38. $(12x^2 y^{-2})^5 (4xy^{-3})^{-7}$

39. $(-2r^{-4})^2 (-3r^2 z^8)^{-1}$

40. $\left(x^{\frac{4}{7}}\right)^7$

41. $\left(a^{\frac{3}{4}} b^{\frac{7}{8}}\right)^4$

7-4 Division Properties of Exponents

Quick Review

To divide powers with the same base, subtract the exponents.

$\dfrac{a^m}{a^n} = a^{m-n}$, where $a \neq 0$ and m and n are integers

To raise a quotient to a power, raise the numerator and the denominator to the power.

$\left(\dfrac{a}{b}\right)^n = \dfrac{a^n}{b^n}$, where $a \neq 0$, $b \neq 0$, and n is an integer

Example

What is the simplified form of $\left(\dfrac{5x^4}{z^2}\right)^3$?

$$\left(\frac{5x^4}{z^2}\right)^3 = \frac{(5x^4)^3}{(z^2)^3} = \frac{5^3 x^{4 \cdot 3}}{z^{2 \cdot 3}} = \frac{125x^{12}}{z^6}$$

Exercises

Simplify each expression.

42. $\dfrac{w^2}{w^5}$

43. $\dfrac{21x^3}{3x^{-1}}$

44. $\left(\dfrac{n^5}{v^3}\right)^7$

45. $\left(\dfrac{3c^3}{e^5}\right)^{-4}$

Simplify each quotient. Write your answer in scientific notation.

46. $\dfrac{4.2 \times 10^8}{2.1 \times 10^{11}}$

47. $\dfrac{3.1 \times 10^4}{1.24 \times 10^2}$

48. $\dfrac{4.5 \times 10^3}{9 \times 10^7}$

49. $\dfrac{5.1 \times 10^5}{1.7 \times 10^2}$

50. **Writing** List the steps that you would use to simplify $\left(\dfrac{5a^8}{10a^6}\right)^{-3}$.

7-5 Rational Exponents and Radicals

Quick Review

If the nth root of a is a real number, m is an integer, and $\frac{m}{n}$ is in lowest terms, then $a^{\frac{1}{n}} = \sqrt[n]{a}$ and $a^{\frac{m}{n}} = \sqrt[n]{a^m} = \left(\sqrt[n]{a}\right)^m$.

Example

Write the expression $(8x)^{\frac{1}{3}}$ in radical form.

$(8x)^{\frac{1}{3}} = 8^{\frac{1}{3}}x^{\frac{1}{3}} = 2\sqrt[3]{x}$

Write the expression $\sqrt[3]{b^2}$ as a power with a rational exponent.

$\sqrt[3]{b^2} = b^{\frac{2}{3}}$

Exercises

Write each expression in radical form.

51. $m^{\frac{1}{2}}$ **52.** $p^{\frac{2}{3}}r^{\frac{4}{5}}$

53. $\left(36x^4\right)^{\frac{1}{2}}$ **54.** $(125x)^{\frac{1}{3}}$

55. $(64)^{\frac{1}{2}}x^{\frac{3}{4}}$ **56.** $25^{\frac{1}{3}}\left(x^2y\right)^{\frac{1}{2}}$

Write each expression as a power with a rational exponent.

57. $\sqrt{xy}$ **58.** $\sqrt[4]{a}$

59. $\sqrt[3]{b^2}$ **60.** $\sqrt[3]{x^6y^9}$

61. $\sqrt[4]{81x^2}$ **62.** $\sqrt[5]{x^2y^3}$

7-6 Exponential Functions

Quick Review

An **exponential function** involves repeated multiplication of an initial amount a by the same positive number b. The general form of an exponential function is $y = a \cdot b^x$, where $a \neq 0$, $b > 0$, and $b \neq 1$.

Example

What is the graph of $y = \frac{1}{2} \cdot 5^x$?

Make a table of values. Graph the ordered pairs.

x	y
−2	$\frac{1}{50}$
−1	$\frac{1}{10}$
0	$\frac{1}{2}$
1	$\frac{5}{2}$
2	$\frac{25}{2}$

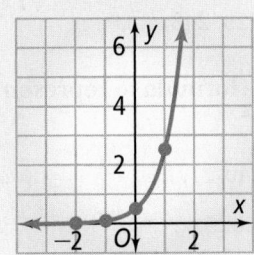

Exercises

Evaluate each function for the domain $\{1, 2, 3\}$.

63. $f(x) = 4^x$ **64.** $y = 0.01^x$

65. $y = 40\left(\frac{1}{2}\right)^x$ **66.** $f(x) = 3 \cdot 2^x$

Graph each function.

67. $f(x) = 2.5^x$ **68.** $y = 0.5(0.5)^x$

69. $f(x) = \frac{1}{2} \cdot 3^x$ **70.** $y = 0.1^x$

71. Biology A population of 50 bacteria in a laboratory culture doubles every 30 min. The function $p(x) = 50 \cdot 2^x$ models the population, where x is the number of 30-min periods.
   a. How many bacteria will there be after 2 h?
   b. How many bacteria will there be after 1 day?

7-7 Exponential Growth and Decay

Quick Review

When $a > 0$ and $b > 1$, the function $y = a \cdot b^x$ models **exponential growth**. The base b is called the **growth factor**. When $a > 0$ and $0 < b < 1$, the function $y = a \cdot b^x$ models **exponential decay**. In this case the base b is called the **decay factor**.

Example

The population of a city is 25,000 and decreases 1% each year. Predict the population after 6 yr.

$$y = 25{,}000 \cdot 0.99^x \quad \text{Exponential decay function}$$
$$= 25{,}000 \cdot 0.99^6 \quad \text{Substitute 6 for } x.$$
$$\approx 23{,}537 \quad \text{Simplify.}$$

The population will be about 23,537 after 6 yr.

Exercises

Tell whether the function represents *exponential growth* or *exponential decay*. Identify the growth or decay factor.

72. $y = 5.2 \cdot 3^x$

73. $f(x) = 7 \cdot 0.32^x$

74. $y = 0.15\left(\dfrac{3}{2}\right)^x$

75. $g(x) = 1.3\left(\dfrac{1}{4}\right)^x$

76. Finance Suppose $2000 is deposited in an account paying 2.5% interest compounded quarterly. What will the account balance be after 12 yr?

77. Music A band performs a free concert in a local park. There are 200 people in the crowd at the start of the concert. The number of people in the crowd grows 15% every half hour. How many people are in the crowd after 3 h? Round to the nearest person.

7-8 Geometric Sequences

Quick Review

In a geometric sequence the ratio of any term to its preceding term is a constant value.

Example

Find the common ratio of the geometric sequence.

2, 6, 18, 54, . . .

$\times 3 \quad \times 3 \quad \times 3$

The common ratio of the geometric sequence is 3.

Write a recursive formula to represent the geometric sequence.

256, 64, 16, 4, . . .

$a_1 = 265; a_n = a_{n-1} \cdot \dfrac{1}{4}$

Exercises

Find the common ratio of each geometric sequence.

78. 10, 20, 40, 80, . . .

79. 1, 10, 100, 1000, . . .

80. 100, 20, 4, 0.8, . . .

81. 6561, 2187, 729, 243, . . .

Write a recursive formula to represent the geometric sequence.

82. 20, 60, 180, 540, . . .

83. 5, 2.5, 1.25, 0.625, . . .

84. 3, 12, 48, 192, . . .

85. 10, 1, 0.1, 0.01, . . .

Do you know HOW?

Simplify each expression.

1. $\dfrac{r^3 t^{-7}}{t^5}$

2. $\left(\dfrac{a^3}{5m}\right)^{-4}$

3. $c^3 v^9 c^{-1} c^0$

4. $2y^{\frac{3}{4}} h^2 \left(2y^{\frac{1}{3}} h^{-4}\right)^6$

5. $(1.2)^5 (1.2)^{-2}$

6. $\left(27q^{\frac{1}{2}}\right)^{\frac{1}{3}}$

7. Write the expression $(4x)^{\frac{1}{2}}$ in radical form.

8. Write the expression $\sqrt[5]{a^4}$ as a power with a rational exponent.

Write a recursive definition for each geometric sequence.

9. 10, 40, 160, 640, . . .

10. 25, 5, 1, 0.2, . . .

Simplify each expression. Write each answer in scientific notation.

11. $\left(6 \times 10^4\right)\left(4.8 \times 10^2\right)$

12. $\dfrac{1.5 \times 10^7}{5 \times 10^{-2}}$

13. **Medicine** The human body normally produces about 2×10^6 red blood cells per second.

   a. Use scientific notation to express how many red blood cells your body produces in one day.

   b. One pint of blood contains about 2.4×10^{12} red blood cells. How many seconds will it take your body to replace the red blood cells lost by donating one pint of blood? How many days?

Evaluate each function for $x = -1, 2,$ and 3.

14. $y = 3 \cdot 5^x$

15. $f(x) = \frac{1}{2} \cdot 4^x$

16. $f(x) = 4(0.95)^x$

Graph each function.

17. $y = \frac{1}{2} \cdot 2^x$

18. $y = 2 \cdot \left(\frac{1}{2}\right)^x$

19. **Banking** A customer deposits $2000 in a savings account that pays 5.2% interest compounded quarterly. How much money will the customer have in the account after 2 yr? After 5 yr?

20. **Automobiles** Suppose a new car is worth $30,000. You can use the function $y = 30{,}000(0.85)^x$ to estimate the car's value after x years.

   a. What is the decay factor? What does it mean?

   b. Estimate the car's value after 1 yr.

   c. Estimate the car's value after 4 yr.

Do you UNDERSTAND?

21. **Error Analysis** Find and correct the error in the work shown below.

$$3^4 \cdot 3^3 = 9^7$$

22. **Reasoning** Show that $\sqrt[3]{x^9} = x^3$ by rewriting $\sqrt[3]{x^9}$ in exponential form.

23. **Writing** Explain when a function in the form $y = a \cdot b^x$ models exponential growth and when it models exponential decay.

24. Simplify the expression $\left(\dfrac{a^6}{a^4}\right)^2$ in two different ways. Justify each step.

25. **Reasoning** Explain how you can use the property for dividing powers with the same base to justify the definition of a zero exponent.

TIPS FOR SUCCESS

Some questions on tests ask you to solve problems involving exponents. Read the sample question at the right. Then follow the tips to answer it.

If the side length of a square can be represented by the expression $4x^2y^6$, which expression could represent the area of the square?

Ⓐ $2xy^3$

Ⓑ $8x^4y^{12}$

Ⓒ $16x^4y^{12}$

Ⓓ $16x^4y^{36}$

TIP 1

Look to eliminate answer choices. You need to square 4, so you can eliminate A and B.

TIP 2

Use properties of exponents to help you solve the problem.

Think It Through

The side length of the square is $4x^2y^6$, so the area is $(4x^2y^6)^2$. Multiply the exponents when you are raising a power to a power.

$$(4x^2y^6)^2 = 4^2x^{2\cdot2}y^{6\cdot2}$$
$$= 16x^4y^{12}$$

The correct answer is C.

Vocabulary Builder

As you solve test items, you must understand the meanings of mathematical terms. Choose the correct term to complete each sentence.

A. The values of the (*independent, dependent*) variable are the output values of the function.

B. The (*base, exponent*) of a power is the number that is multiplied repeatedly.

C. A number in (*scientific, standard*) notation is a shorthand way to write numbers using powers of 10.

D. The (*slope, y-intercept*) of a line is the ratio of the vertical change to the horizontal change.

E. A system of two equations has exactly one solution if the lines are (*parallel, intersecting*) lines.

Selected Response

Read each question. Then write the letter of the correct answer on your paper.

1. Which expression is equivalent to $(27x^2)^{\frac{1}{3}}$?

Ⓐ $27\sqrt[3]{x^2}$ Ⓒ $3\sqrt{x}$

Ⓑ $3\sqrt[3]{x^2}$ Ⓓ $27\sqrt[3]{x}$

2. Which equation has $(2, -6)$ and $(-3, 4)$ as solutions?

Ⓕ $y = \frac{1}{2}x - 7$ Ⓗ $y = -\frac{1}{2}x - 5$

Ⓖ $y = 2x - 10$ Ⓘ $y = -2x - 2$

3. Which equation best represents the statement *two more than twice a number is the number tripled*?

Ⓐ $2 + n = 3n$ Ⓒ $2(2 + n) = 3n$

Ⓑ $2n + 2 = 3n$ Ⓓ $2n + 2 = 3 + n$

4. The graph at the right shows how Manuel's height changed during the past year. Which conclusion can you make from the graph?

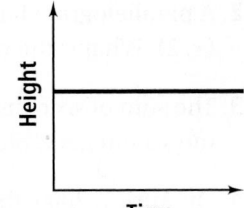

Height / Time

- **F** His height is average.
- **G** He will grow more next year.
- **H** His height did not change during the year.
- **I** His height steadily increased during the year.

5. What is the y-intercept of the graph at the right?

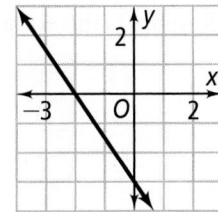

- **A** -3
- **B** -2
- **C** $-\frac{3}{2}$
- **D** 0

6. Which *cannot* be represented by a linear function?

- **F** the area of a square, given its side length
- **G** the price of fruit, given the weight of the fruit
- **H** the number of steps on a ladder, given the height
- **I** the number of inches, given the number of yards

7. A light-year is the distance light travels in one year. One light-year is about 5.9×10^{12} mi. If it takes light 3 months to travel from one star to another, about how far apart are the stars?

- **A** 2×10^3 mi
- **B** 1.5×10^4 mi
- **C** 1.5×10^{12} mi
- **D** 2×10^{12} mi

8. Use the graph at the right. Suppose the y-intercept increases by 2 and the slope stays the same. What will the x-intercept be?

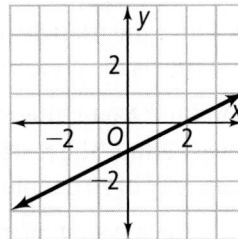

- **F** -3
- **G** -2
- **H** 1
- **I** 4

9. Which expression is equivalent to $\sqrt[4]{81x^3}$?

- **A** $81x^{\frac{3}{4}}$
- **B** $3x^{\frac{3}{4}}$
- **C** $3x^3$
- **D** $(3x)^{\frac{3}{4}}$

10. The dimensions of a rectangular prism are shown in the diagram at the right. Which expression represents the volume of the rectangular prism?

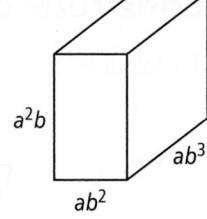

a^2b / ab^3 / ab^2

- **F** a^2b^5
- **G** a^2b^6
- **H** a^4b^5
- **I** a^4b^6

11. Suppose you are buying apples and bananas. The price of apples is \$.40 each and the price of bananas is \$.25 each. Which equation models the number of apples and bananas you can buy for \$2?

- **A** $40x + 25y = 200$
- **B** $40x - 25y = 2$
- **C** $5x + 8y = 200$
- **D** $5x + 8y = 2$

12. At lunchtime, Mitchell cast a shadow 0.5 ft long while a nearby flagpole cast a shadow 2.5 ft long. If Mitchell is 5 ft 3 in. tall, how tall is the flagpole?

- **F** 26 ft 3 in.
- **G** 26 ft 4 in.
- **H** 26 ft 5 in.
- **I** 26 ft 6 in.

13. Laura rented a car that cost \$20 for the day plus \$.12 for each mile driven. She returned the car later that day. Laura gave the salesperson \$50 and received change. Which inequality represents the possible numbers of miles m that she could have driven?

- **A** $50 > 0.12m + 20$
- **B** $50 < 0.12m + 20$
- **C** $50 > 0.12m - 20$
- **D** $50 < 0.12m - 20$

14. A doctor did a 6-month study on resting heart rate and exercise in healthy adults. The doctor found that for every 20 min of exercise added to a daily routine, the resting heart rate decreased by 1 beat per minute. According to the doctor's study, what does the resting heart rate depend on?

- **F** the 6-month study
- **G** minutes of exercise
- **H** a daily routine
- **I** diet

Constructed Response

15. What is the area, in square units, of the triangle below?

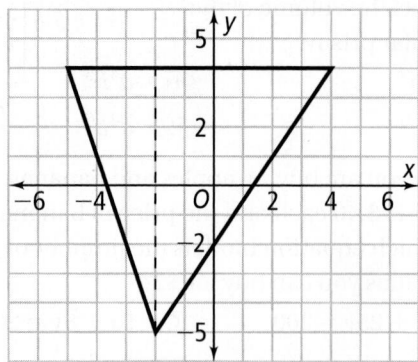

16. Charles purchased 50 shares of a stock at $23 per share. He paid a $15 commission to his broker for the purchase. How much money, in dollars, did he spend for the purchase and commission combined?

17. What is the value of the expression $\left(8^{\frac{1}{3}}\right)^2$?

18. A designer tested 50 jackets in a clothing warehouse and found that 4% of the jackets were labeled with the wrong size. How many jackets did the designer find that were labeled the wrong size?

19. If $b = 2a - 16$ and $b = a + 2$, what is $a + b$?

20. Alejandro bought 6 notebooks and 2 binders for $23.52. Cassie bought 3 notebooks and 4 binders for $25.53. What was the cost, in dollars, of 1 notebook?

21. Ashley surveyed 200 students in her school to find out whether they liked mustard or mayo on a turkey sandwich. Her results are shown in the diagram below.

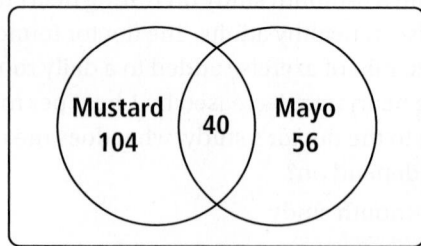

What fraction of the students surveyed liked mustard but not mayo? Write your answer in lowest terms.

22. A parallelogram has vertices $(-3, 2)$, $(0, 7)$, $(7, 7)$, and $(x, 2)$. What is the value of x?

23. The sum of six consecutive integers is 165. What are the six integers? Show your work.

24. On April 1, 2000, the day of the 2000 national census, the population of the United States was 281,421,906 people. This was a 13.2% increase from the 1990 census. What was the 1990 population of the United States?

25. What is the equation of the graph in standard form?

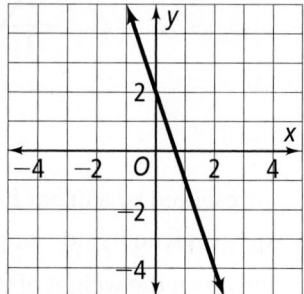

Extended Response

26. A triangle is enclosed by the following lines:
$$x - y = -1$$
$$y = 2$$
$$-0.4x - y = -5.2$$

  a. What are the coordinates of the vertices of the triangle? Use algebraic methods to justify your answers.

  b. Draw the triangle using your answers in part (a). What is the area, in square units, of the triangle?

27. On Kids' Night, there must be at least one child with every adult. The restaurant has a maximum seating capacity of 75 people.

  a. Write a system of inequalities to represent the constraints in this situation.

  b. Graph the solution. Is it possible for 50 children to escort 10 adults to the restaurant?

Get Ready!

Skills
Handbook,
page 798

Finding Factors of Composite Numbers

List all the factors of each number.

1. 12   **2.** 18   **3.** 100   **4.** 81

5. 72   **6.** 300   **7.** 250   **8.** 207

Lesson 1-7

Simplifying Expressions

Simplify each expression.

9. $3x^2 - 4x - 2x^2 - 5x$ **10.** $-2d + 7 + 5d + 8$

11. $3(2r + 4r^2 - 7r + 4r^2)$ **12.** $-2(m + 1) + 9(4m - 3)$

13. $6(a - 3a^2 - 2a - 3a^2)$ **14.** $s - 4 - (s^2 - 2) - 8s$

Lessons 7-2
and 7-3

Multiplying Expressions With Exponents

Simplify each expression.

15. $(5x)^2$ **16.** $(-3v^2)(-3v^{\frac{1}{2}})$ **17.** $(4c^2)^3$ **18.** $(8m^{\frac{3}{5}})(7m^5)$

19. $(9b^3)^2$ **20.** $(-6pq)^2$ **21.** $7(n^{\frac{1}{2}})^2$ **22.** $(-5t^4)^3$

Lesson 7-4

Dividing Expressions With Exponents

Simplify each expression.

23. $\dfrac{p^4 q^9}{p^2 q^6}$ **24.** $\dfrac{(5x)^2}{5x}$ **25.** $\dfrac{-3n}{(6n^4)(4n^2)}$ **26.** $\dfrac{(2y)(9y^4)}{6y^3}$

 Looking Ahead Vocabulary

27. Both of the words *tricycle* and *triangle* begin with the prefix *tri-*. A *trinomial* is a type of mathematical expression. How many terms do you think a trinomial has?

28. Use your knowledge of the meaning of the words *binocular* and *bicycle* to guess at the meaning of the word *binomial*.

29. Which of the following products do you think is a *perfect-square trinomial* when multiplied? Explain your reasoning.

a. $(x + 4)(x + 7)$ **b.** $(x + 4)(x + 4)$

Polynomials and Factoring

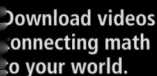

Download videos connecting math to your world.

Interactive! Vary numbers, graphs, and figures to explore math concepts.

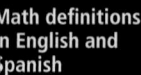

The online Solve It will get you in gear for each lesson.

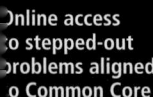

Math definitions in English and Spanish

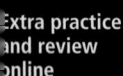

Online access to stepped-out problems aligned to Common Core

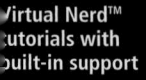

Get and view your assignments online.

Extra practice and review online

Virtual Nerd™ tutorials with built-in support

Chapter Preview

Vocabulary

English/Spanish Vocabulary Audio Online:

English	Spanish
binomial, *p. 487*	binomio
degree of a monomial, *p. 486*	grado de un monomio
degree of a polynomial, *p. 487*	grado de un polinomio
difference of two squares, *p. 525*	diferencia de dos cuadrados
factoring by grouping, *p. 529*	factor común por agrupación de términos
monomial, *p. 486*	monomio
perfect-square trinomial, *p. 523*	trinomio cuadrado perfecto
polynomial, *p. 487*	polinomio
standard form of a polynomial, *p. 487*	forma normal de un polinomio
trinomial, *p. 487*	trinomio

BIG ideas

1 Equivalence
Essential Question Can two algebraic expressions that appear to be different be equivalent?

2 Properties
Essential Question How are the properties of real numbers related to polynomials?

 DOMAINS

- Seeing Structure in Expressions
- Arithmetic with Polynomials and Rational Expressions

Common Core Performance Task

Planning a Garden Plot

Each rectangular plot in a community garden consists of a planting area surrounded by a border of wood chips. Kelly and Roberto each design a plot for the community garden. They use identical square flower beds in their plots, but they design different borders, as shown below.

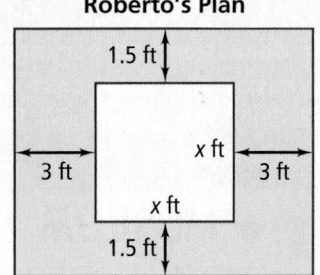

After some discussion, Kelly and Roberto decide to scrap their original plans and combine their plots to make one larger rectangular plot. They plan to place the two x ft-by-x ft square flower beds side by side to make a $2x$ ft-by-x ft flower bed, centered inside a rectangular border. The area of the new plot will equal the sum of the areas of the two original plots.

Task Description

Draw and label a sketch of the new flower bed and border. Include expressions for the length and width of the new plot. Each expression must be a linear polynomial with integer coefficients.

Connecting the Task to the Math Practices

MATHEMATICAL PRACTICES

As you complete the task, you'll apply several Standards for Mathematical Practice.

- You'll analyze the polynomials that describe Kelly's and Roberto's original plots. (MP 6)
- You'll write an expression for the area of each of the original plots. (MP 2, MP 3)
- You'll write and factor an expression for the area of the new plot. (MP 7)

8-1 Adding and Subtracting Polynomials

Common Core State Standards

A-APR.A.1 Understand that polynomials form a system analogous to the integers, namely, they are closed under the operations of addition, subtraction, and multiplication; add, subtract, and multiply polynomials.

MP 1, MP 2, MP 3, MP 4, MP 6

Objective To classify, add, and subtract polynomials

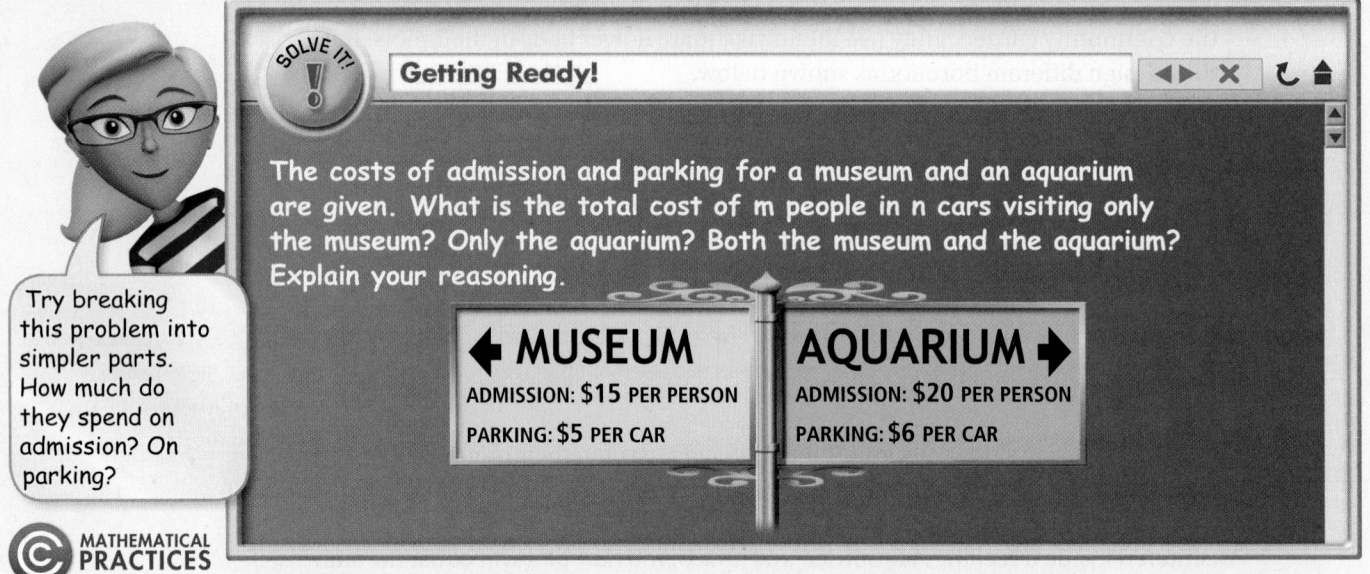

SOLVE IT!

Getting Ready!

The costs of admission and parking for a museum and an aquarium are given. What is the total cost of m people in n cars visiting only the museum? Only the aquarium? Both the museum and the aquarium? Explain your reasoning.

Try breaking this problem into simpler parts. How much do they spend on admission? On parking?

◀ MUSEUM
ADMISSION: $15 PER PERSON
PARKING: $5 PER CAR

AQUARIUM ▶
ADMISSION: $20 PER PERSON
PARKING: $6 PER CAR

MATHEMATICAL PRACTICES

In some cases, you can model a situation with an expression composed of *monomials*. A **monomial** is a real number, a variable, or a product of a real number and one or more variables with whole-number exponents. Here are some examples of monomials.

$$18 \qquad z \qquad -4x^2 \qquad 2.5xy^3 \qquad \frac{a}{3}$$

Essential Understanding You can use monomials to form larger expressions called *polynomials*. Polynomials can be added and subtracted.

The **degree of a monomial** is the sum of the exponents of its variables. The degree of a nonzero constant is 0. Zero has no degree.

Lesson Vocabulary

- monomial
- degree of a monomial
- polynomial
- standard form of a polynomial
- degree of a polynomial
- binomial
- trinomial

Problem 1 Finding the Degree of a Monomial

What is the degree of each monomial?

A $5x$ Degree: 1 $5x = 5x^1$. The exponent is 1.

B $6x^3y^2$ Degree: 5   The exponents are 3 and 2. Their sum is 5.

C 4 Degree: 0 $4 = 4x^0$. The degree of a nonzero constant is 0.

Think

Why is the degree of a nonzero constant 0?
You can write a nonzero constant c as cx^0. The exponent is 0, so the degree is 0 also.

Got It? **1.** What is the degree of each monomial?
   a. $8xy$ **b.** $-7y^4z$ **c.** 11

You can add or subtract monomials by adding or subtracting like terms.

Think

Will the sum of two monomials always be a monomial?
No. The monomials must be like terms.

© **Problem 2** Adding and Subtracting Monomials

What is the sum or difference?

A $3x^2 + 5x^2 = 8x^2$ Combine like terms.   B $4x^3y - x^3y = 3x^3y$ Combine like terms.

✓ **Got It?** **2.** What is the sum $-6x^4 + 11x^4$? What is the difference $2x^2y^4 - 7x^2y^4$?

A **polynomial** is a monomial or a sum of monomials. The following polynomial is the sum of the monomials $3x^4$, $5x^2$, $-7x$, and 1.

$$3x^4 + 5x^2 - 7x + 1$$

Degree of each monomial   4   2   1   0

The polynomial shown above is in *standard form*. **Standard form of a polynomial** means that the degrees of its monomial terms decrease from left to right. The **degree of a polynomial** in one variable is the same as the degree of the monomial with the greatest exponent. The degree of $3x^4 + 5x^2 - 7x + 1$ is 4.

You can name a polynomial based on its degree or the number of monomials it contains.

Polynomial	Degree	Name Using Degree	Number of Terms	Name Using Number of Terms
6	0	Constant	1	Monomial
$5x + 9$	1	Linear	2	**Binomial**
$4x^2 + 7x + 3$	2	Quadratic	3	**Trinomial**
$2x^3$	3	Cubic	1	Monomial
$8x^4 - 2x^3 + 3x$	4	Fourth degree	3	Trinomial

© **Problem 3** Classifying Polynomials

Think

Why do you need to combine like terms in part (B)?
To name a polynomial correctly based on its number of terms, you must first combine all like terms.

Write each polynomial in standard form. What is the name of the polynomial based on its degree and number of terms?

A $3x + 4x^2$

$4x^2 + 3x$ Place terms in order.

This is a quadratic binomial.

B $4x - 1 + 5x^3 + 7x$

$5x^3 + 4x + 7x - 1$ Place terms in order.

$5x^3 + 11x - 1$ Combine like terms.

This is a cubic trinomial.

✓ **Got It?** **3. a.** Write $2x - 3 + 8x^2$ in standard form. What is the name of the polynomial based on its degree and number of terms?

© **b. Reasoning** How does writing a polynomial in standard form help you name the polynomial?

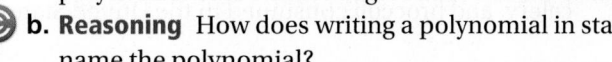

You can add polynomials by adding like terms.

Problem 4 Adding Polynomials

Travel A researcher studied the number of overnight stays in U.S. National Park Service campgrounds and in the backcountry of the national park system over a 5-yr period. The researcher modeled the results, in thousands, with the following polynomials.

Campgrounds: $-7.1x^2 - 180x + 5800$

Backcountry: $21x^2 - 140x + 1900$

In each polynomial, $x = 0$ corresponds to the first year in the 5-yr period. What polynomial models the total number of overnight stays in both campgrounds and backcountry?

Know	Need	Plan
• Overnight stays in campgrounds: $-7.1x^2 - 180x + 5800$ • Overnight stays in backcountry: $21x^2 - 140x + 1900$	A polynomial for the total number of overnight stays in campgrounds and backcountry	The word *both* implies addition, so add the two polynomials to find a polynomial that represents the total.

Method 1 Add vertically.
Line up like terms. Then add the coefficients.

$$-7.1x^2 - 180x + 5800$$
$$\underline{+\ 21x^2 - 140x + 1900}$$
$$13.9x^2 - 320x + 7700$$

Method 2 Add horizontally.
Group like terms. Then add the coefficients.

$$\left(-7.1x^2 - 180x + 5800\right) + \left(21x^2 - 140x + 1900\right)$$
$$= \left(-7.1x^2 + 21x^2\right) + \left(-180x - 140x\right) + \left(5800 + 1900\right)$$
$$= 13.9x^2 - 320x + 7700$$

A polynomial that models the number of stays (in thousands) in campgrounds and backcountry over the 5-yr period is $13.9x^2 - 320x + 7700$.

 Got It? **4.** A nutritionist studied the U.S. consumption of carrots and celery and of broccoli over a 6-yr period. The nutritionist modeled the results, in millions of pounds, with the following polynomials.

Carrots and celery: $-12x^3 + 106x^2 - 241x + 4477$

Broccoli: $14x^2 - 14x + 1545$

In each polynomial, $x = 0$ corresponds to the first year in the 6-yr period. What polynomial models the total number of pounds, in millions, of carrots, celery, and broccoli consumed in the United States during the 6-yr period?

Recall that subtraction means to add the opposite. So when you subtract a polynomial, change each of the terms to its opposite. Then add the coefficients.

 Problem 5 **Subtracting Polynomials**

What is a simpler form of $(x^3 - 3x^2 + 5x) - (7x^3 + 5x^2 - 12)$?

Think

Is the sum or difference of two polynomials always a polynomial?
Yes. The set of polynomials is *closed* under addition and subtraction, which means that adding or subtracting polynomials always gives you another polynomial.

Method 1 Subtract vertically.

$$x^3 - 3x^2 + 5x \qquad \text{Line up like terms.}$$
$$\underline{- \left(7x^3 + 5x^2 \qquad - 12\right)}$$

$$x^3 - 3x^2 + 5x$$
$$\underline{-7x^3 - 5x^2 \qquad + 12}$$
$$-6x^3 - 8x^2 + 5x + 12$$

Then add the opposite of each term in the polynomial being subtracted.

Method 2 Subtract horizontally.

$$\left(x^3 - 3x^2 + 5x\right) - \left(7x^3 + 5x^2 - 12\right)$$

$$= x^3 - 3x^2 + 5x - 7x^3 - 5x^2 + 12 \qquad \text{Write the opposite of each term in the polynomial being subtracted.}$$

$$= \left(x^3 - 7x^3\right) + \left(-3x^2 - 5x^2\right) + 5x + 12 \qquad \text{Group like terms.}$$

$$= -6x^3 - 8x^2 + 5x + 12 \qquad \text{Simplify.}$$

 Got It? **5.** What is a simpler form of $\left(-4m^3 - m + 9\right) - \left(4m^2 + m - 12\right)$?

 Lesson Check

Do you know HOW?

Find the degree of each monomial.

1. $-7x^4$ **2.** $8y^2z^3$

Simplify each sum or difference.

3. $\left(5r^3 + 8\right) + \left(6r^3 + 3\right)$

4. $\left(x^2 - 2\right) - \left(3x + 5\right)$

Do you UNDERSTAND?  **MATHEMATICAL PRACTICES**

 Vocabulary Name each polynomial based on its degree and number of terms.

5. $5x^2 + 2x + 1$ **6.** $3z - 2$

 7. Compare and Contrast How are the processes of adding monomials and adding polynomials alike? How are the processes different?

 **Practice and Problem-Solving Exercises**  **MATHEMATICAL PRACTICES**

A **Practice**   Find the degree of each monomial.   ◀ **See Problem 1.**

8. $3x$ **9.** $8a^3$ **10.** 20 **11.** $2b^8c^2$

12. $-7y^3z$ **13.** -3 **14.** $12w^4$ **15.** 0

Simplify. See Problem 2.

16. $12p^2 + 8p^2$ **17.** $2m^3n^3 + 9m^3n^3$ **18.** $8w^2x + w^2x$ **19.** $3t^4 + 11t^4$

20. $x^3 - 9x^3$ **21.** $30v^4w^3 - 12v^4w^3$ **22.** $7x^2 - 2x^2$ **23.** $5bc^4 - 13bc^4$

Write each polynomial in standard form. Then name each polynomial based on its degree and number of terms. See Problem 3.

24. $5y - 2y^2$ **25.** $-2q + 7$ **26.** $x^2 + 4 - 3x$

27. $6x^2 - 13x^2 - 4x + 4$ **28.** $c + 8c^3 - 3c^7$ **29.** $3z^4 - 5z - 2z^2$

Simplify. See Problem 4.

30. $4w - 5$
$\underline{+\ 9w + 2}$

31. $6x^2 + 7$
$\underline{+\ 3x^2 + 1}$

32. $2k^2 - k + 3$
$\underline{+\ 5k^2 + 3k - 7}$

33. $\left(5x^2 + 3\right) + \left(15x^2 + 2\right)$ **34.** $\left(2g^4 - 3g + 9\right) + \left(-g^3 + 12g\right)$

35. Education The number of students at East High School and the number of students at Central High School over a 10-year period can be modeled by the following polynomials.

East High School: $-11x^2 + 133x + 1200$
Central High School: $-7x^2 + 95x + 1100$

In each polynomial, $x = 0$ corresponds to the first year in the 10-year period. What polynomial models the total number of students at both high schools?

Simplify. See Problem 5.

36. $5n - 2$
$\underline{-(3n + 8)}$

37. $6x^3 + 17$
$\underline{-\left(4x^3 + 9\right)}$

38. $2c^2 + 7c - 1$
$\underline{-\left(c^2 - 10c + 4\right)}$

39. $\left(14h^4 + 3h^3\right) - \left(9h^4 + 2h^3\right)$ **40.** $\left(-6w^4 + w^2\right) - \left(-2w^3 + 4w^2 - w\right)$

 **Apply**

41. Think About a Plan The perimeter of a triangular park is $16x + 3$. What is the missing length?

• What is the sum of the two given side lengths?
• What operation should you use to find the remaining side length?

42. Geometry The perimeter of a trapezoid is $39a - 7$. Three sides have the following lengths: $9a$, $5a + 1$, and $17a - 6$. What is the length of the fourth side?

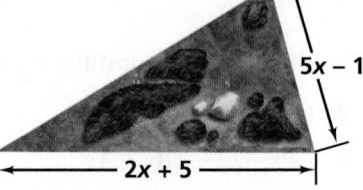

5x − 1

2x + 5

43. Error Analysis Describe and correct the error in finding the difference of the polynomials.

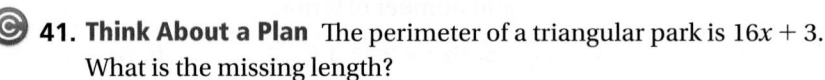

$(4x^2 - x + 3) - (3x^2 - 5x - 6) = 4x^2 - x + 3 - 3x^2 - 5x - 6$
$= 4x^2 - 3x^2 - x - 5x + 3 - 6$
$= x^2 - 6x - 3$

Simplify. Write each answer in standard form.

44. $\left(5x^2 - 3x + 7x\right) + \left(9x^2 + 2x^2 + 7x\right)$

45. $\left(y^3 - 4y^2 - 2\right) - \left(6y^3 + 4 - 6y^2\right)$

46. $\left(-9r^3 + 2r - 1\right) - \left(-5r^2 + r + 8\right)$

47. $\left(3z^3 - 4z + 7z^2\right) + \left(8z^2 - 6z - 5\right)$

48. a. Is the sum of two polynomials always a polynomial? Explain.

   b. Is the difference of two polynomials always a polynomial? Explain.

 Challenge **49. a.** Write the equations for line p and line q. Use slope-intercept form.

   b. Use your equations from part (a) to write a function for the vertical distance $D(x)$ between points on lines p and q with the same x-value.

   c. For what value of x does $D(x)$ equal zero?

   d. Reasoning How does the x-value in part (c) relate to the graph?

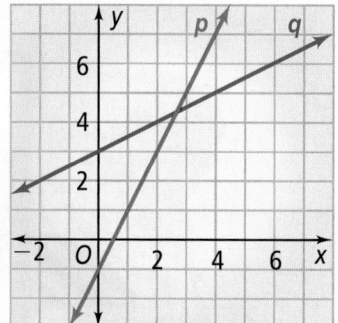

Simplify each expression.

50. $\left(ab^2 + ba^3\right) + \left(4a^3b - ab^2 - 5ab\right)$

51. $\left(9pq^6 - 11p^4q\right) - \left(-5pq^6 + p^4q^4\right)$

Apply What You've Learned

 MATHEMATICAL
PRACTICES

MP 6

Look back at Kelly's and Roberto's original plots on page 485. Choose from the following words, numbers, and expressions to complete the sentences below.

monomial	binomial	trinomial	1	2

x^2	$x + 2$	$x^2 + 2$	$x + 6$	$2x + 6$

Two polynomials that represent the length and width of Kelly's plot are
a. _?_ and **b.** _?_ . Each of these polynomials is an example of a **c.** _?_ . The polynomial that represents the area of Roberto's flower bed is **d.** _?_ . This polynomial is an example of a **e.** _?_ . The degree of this polynomial is **f.** _?_ .

8-2

Multiplying and Factoring

© **Common Core State Standards**

A-APR.A.1 Understand that polynomials form a system analogous to the integers, namely, they are closed under the operations of addition, subtraction, and multiplication; add, subtract, and multiply polynomials.

MP 1, MP 2, MP 3, MP 4

Objectives To multiply a monomial by a polynomial
To factor a monomial from a polynomial

Getting Ready!

You set aside part of a rectangular plot of land for a garden and seed the rest of the plot with grass, as shown. Grass seed costs $.03 per square foot. Write an expression for the total cost of the seed. Suppose you buy $50 worth of seed. How wide can the section of grass be? Explain your reasoning.

Sketch a diagram. A diagram can help you understand all the parts of this problem.

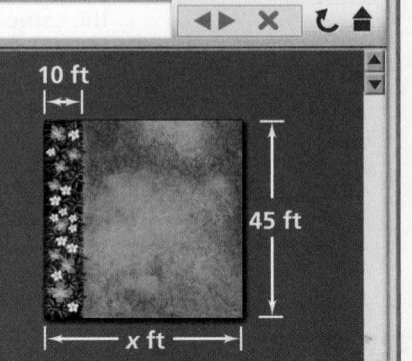

Essential Understanding You can use the Distributive Property to multiply a monomial by a polynomial.

For example, consider the product $2x(3x + 1)$.

$$2x(3x + 1) = 2x(3x) + 2x(1)$$
$$= 6x^2 + 2x$$

You can show why the multiplication makes sense using the area model at the right.

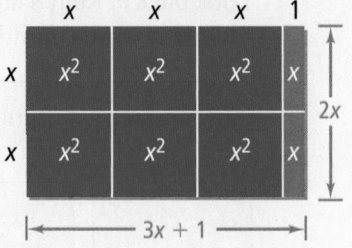

© **Problem 1** **Multiplying a Monomial and a Trinomial**

Multiple Choice What is a simpler form of $-x^3(9x^4 - 2x^3 + 7)$?

Ⓐ $-9x^{12} + 2x^9 - 7x^3$

Ⓒ $-9x^7 - 2x^3 + 7$

Ⓑ $9x^7 - 2x^6 + 7x^3$

Ⓓ $-9x^7 + 2x^6 - 7x^3$

Plan

What should I keep in mind when multiplying?
Remember to distribute $-x^3$ to *all* of the terms. Also remember to add the exponents instead of multiplying them.

$-x^3(9x^4 - 2x^3 + 7) = -x^3(9x^4) - x^3(-2x^3) - x^3(7)$ Use the Distributive Property.

$= -9x^{3+4} + 2x^{3+3} - 7x^3$ Multiply coefficients and add exponents.

$= -9x^7 + 2x^6 - 7x^3$ Simplify.

The correct answer is D.

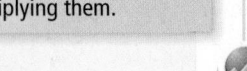 **Got It? 1.** What is a simpler form of $5n(3n^3 - n^2 + 8)$?

Essential Understanding Factoring a polynomial reverses the multiplication process. When factoring a monomial from a polynomial, the first step is to find the greatest common factor (GCF) of the polynomial's terms.

 Problem 2 Finding the Greatest Common Factor

What is the GCF of the terms of $5x^3 + 25x^2 + 45x$?

List the prime factors of each term. Identify the factors common to all terms.

$$5x^3 = 5 \cdot x \cdot x \cdot x$$

$$25x^2 = 5 \cdot 5 \cdot x \cdot x$$

Remember to list only the prime factors of the variables.

$$45x = 3 \cdot 3 \cdot 5 \cdot x$$

The GCF is $5 \cdot x$, or $5x$.

Think

Why use the factors 5 and x to form the GCF, but not 3?
Both 5 and x are factors of *every* term of the polynomial, but 3 is only a factor of the last term.

Got It? 2. What is the GCF of the terms of $3x^4 - 9x^2 - 12x$?

Once you find the GCF of a polynomial's terms, you can factor it out of the polynomial.

 Problem 3 Factoring Out a Monomial

What is the factored form of $4x^5 - 24x^3 + 8x$?

Think

To factor the polynomial, first factor each term.

Write

$$4x^5 = 2 \cdot 2 \cdot x \cdot x \cdot x \cdot x \cdot x$$

$$24x^3 = 2 \cdot 2 \cdot 2 \cdot 3 \cdot x \cdot x \cdot x$$

$$8x = 2 \cdot 2 \cdot 2 \cdot x$$

Find the GCF of the three terms.

The GCF is $2 \cdot 2 \cdot x$, or $4x$.

Factor out the GCF from each term. Then factor it out of the polynomial.

$$4x^5 - 24x^3 + 8x = 4x(x^4) + 4x(-6x^2) + 4x(2)$$
$$= 4x(x^4 - 6x^2 + 2)$$

The factored form of the polynomial is $4x(x^4 - 6x^2 + 2)$.

Got It? 3. a. What is the factored form of $9x^6 + 15x^4 + 12x^2$?

b. Reasoning What is $-6x^4 - 18x^3 - 12x^2$ written as the product of a polynomial with positive coefficients and a monomial?

Problem 4 Factoring a Polynomial Model

Helipads A helicopter landing pad, or helipad, is sometimes marked with a circle inside a square so that it is visible from the air. What is the area of the shaded region of the helipad at the right? Write your answer in factored form.

Plan

How can you find the shaded region's area?
The shaded region is the entire square except for the circular portion. So, subtract the area of the circle from the area of the square.

Step 1 Find the area of the shaded region.

$$A_1 = s^2 \qquad \text{Area of a square}$$
$$= (2x)^2 \qquad \text{Substitute } 2x \text{ for } s.$$
$$= 4x^2 \qquad \text{Simplify.}$$
$$A_2 = \pi r^2 \qquad \text{Area of a circle}$$
$$= \pi x^2 \qquad \text{Substitute } x \text{ for } r.$$

The area of the shaded region is $A_1 - A_2$, or $4x^2 - \pi x^2$.

Step 2 Factor the expression.

First find the GCF.

$$4x^2 = 2 \cdot 2 \cdot x \cdot x$$

$$\pi x^2 = \pi \cdot x \cdot x$$

The GCF is $x \cdot x$, or x^2.

Step 3 Factor out the GCF.

$$4x^2 - \pi x^2 = x^2(4) + x^2(-\pi)$$
$$= x^2(4 - \pi)$$

The factored form of the area of the shaded region is $x^2(4 - \pi)$.

 Got It? **4.** In Problem 4, suppose the side length of the square is $6x$ and the radius of the circle is $3x$. What is the factored form of the area of the shaded region?

 Lesson Check

Do you know HOW?

1. What is a simpler form of $6x(2x^3 + 7x)$?

2. What is the GCF of the terms in $4a^4 + 6a^2$?

Factor each polynomial.

3. $6m^2 - 15m$

4. $4x^3 + 8x^2 + 12x$

Do you UNDERSTAND? **MATHEMATICAL PRACTICES**

Match each pair of monomials with its GCF.

5. $14n^2, 35n^4$ **A.** 1

6. $21n^3, 18n^2$ **B.** $7n^2$

7. $7n^2, 9$ **C.** $3n^2$

8. Reasoning Write a binomial with $9x^2$ as the GCF of its terms.

Practice and Problem-Solving Exercises  MATHEMATICAL PRACTICES

 **Practice**

Simplify each product.

🔹 See Problem 1.

9. $7x(x + 4)$

10. $(b + 11)2b$

11. $3m^2(10 + m)$

12. $-w^2(w - 15)$

13. $4x(2x^3 - 7x^2 + x)$

14. $-8y^3(7y^2 - 4y - 1)$

Find the GCF of the terms of each polynomial.

🔹 See Problem 2.

15. $12x + 20$

16. $8w^2 - 18w$

17. $45b + 27$

18. $a^3 + 6a^2 - 11a$

19. $4x^3 + 12x - 28$

20. $14z^4 - 42z^3 + 21z^2$

Factor each polynomial.

🔹 See Problem 3.

21. $9x - 6$

22. $t^2 + 8t$

23. $14n^3 - 35n^2 + 28$

24. $5k^3 + 20k^2 - 15$

25. $14x^3 - 2x^2 + 8x$

26. $g^4 + 24g^3 + 12g^2 + 4g$

27. Art A circular mirror is surrounded by a square metal frame. The radius of the mirror is $5x$. The side length of the metal frame is $15x$. What is the area of the metal frame? Write your answer in factored form.

🔹 See Problem 4.

28. Design A circular table is painted yellow with a red square in the middle. The radius of the tabletop is $6x$. The side length of the red square is $3x$. What is the area of the yellow part of the tabletop? Write your answer in factored form.

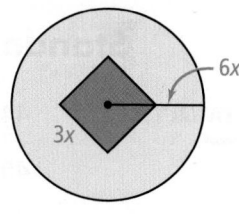

Apply

Simplify. Write in standard form.

29. $-2x(5x^2 - 4x + 13)$

30. $-5y^2(-3y^3 + 8y)$

31. $10a(-6a^2 + 2a - 7)$

32. $p(p + 2) - 3p(p - 5)$

33. $t^2(t + 1) - t(2t^2 - 1)$

34. $3c(4c^2 - 5) - c(9c)$

ⓒ **35. Think About a Plan** A rectangular wooden frame has side lengths $5x$ and $7x + 1$. The rectangular opening for a picture has side lengths $3x$ and $5x$. What is the area of the wooden part of the frame? Write your answer in factored form.
  • How can drawing a diagram help you solve the problem?
  • How can you express the area of the wooden part of the frame as a difference of areas?

ⓒ **36. Error Analysis** Describe and correct the error made in multiplying.

$$-3x(2x - 5) = -3x(2x) - 3x(5)$$
$$= -6x^2 - 15x$$

Factor each polynomial.

37. $17xy^4 + 51x^2y^3$

38. $9m^4n^5 - 27m^2n^3$

39. $31a^6b^3 + 63a^5$

ⓒ **40. a.** Factor $n^2 + n$.
  b. Writing Suppose n is an integer. Is $n^2 + n$ *always*, *sometimes*, or *never* an even integer? Justify your answer.

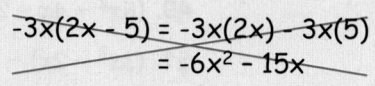

 **41. Reasoning** The GCF of two numbers p and q is 7. What is the GCF of p^2 and q^2? Justify your answer.

Challenge **42. a. Geometry** How many sides does the polygon have? How many of its diagonals come from one vertex?

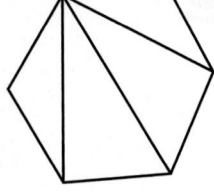

   b. A polygon has n sides. How many diagonals will it have from one vertex?

   c. The number of diagonals from all the vertices is $\frac{n}{2}(n-3)$. Write this polynomial in standard form.

   d. A polygon has 8 sides. How many diagonals does it have?

STEM 43. Manufacturing The diagram shows a cube of metal with a cylinder cut out of it. The formula for the volume of a cylinder is $V = \pi r^2 h$, where r is the radius and h is the height.

   a. Write a formula for the volume of the cube in terms of s.

   b. Write a formula for the volume of the cylinder in terms of s.

   c. Write a formula in terms of s for the volume V of the metal left after the cylinder has been removed.

   d. Factor your formula from part (c).

   e. Find V in cubic inches for $s = 15$ in. Use $\pi = 3.14$.

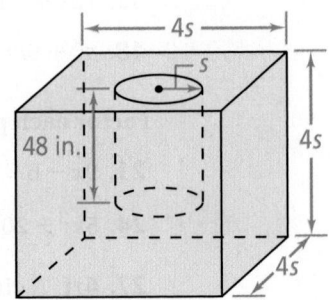

Standardized Test Prep

GRIDDED RESPONSE

SAT/ACT

44. Simplify the product $4x(5x^2 + 3x + 7)$. What is the coefficient of the x^2-term?

45. What is the slope of the line that passes through $\overline{CD}$?

46. What is the solution of the equation $7x - 11 = 3$?

47. Simplify the product $8x^3(2x^2)$. What is the exponent?

48. The expression $9x^3 - 15x$ can be factored as $ax(3x^2 - 5)$. What is the value of a?

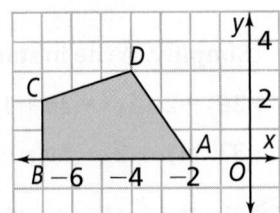

Mixed Review

Simplify each sum or difference.

   See Lesson 8-1.

49. $(5x^2 + 4x - 2) + (3x^2 + 7)$

50. $(4x^4 - 3x^2 - 1) + (3x^4 + 6x^2)$

51. $(3x^3 - 2x) - (8x^3 + 4x)$

52. $(7x^4 + 3x^3 - 5x + 1) - (x^3 + 8x^2 - 5x - 3)$

Solve each inequality for y. Then graph the inequality.

   See Lesson 6-5.

53. $4x - 5y \geq 10$

54. $7x - 2y \leq 8$

55. $-3y - x > 9$

Get Ready! **To prepare for Lesson 8-3, do Exercises 56–58.**

Use the Distributive Property to simplify each expression.

   See Lesson 1-7.

56. $8(x - 5)$

57. $-3(w + 4)$

58. $0.25(6c + 16)$

Using Models to Multiply

© Common Core State Standards

Prepares for A-APR.A.1 Understand that polynomials form a system analogous to the integers, namely, they are closed under the operations of addition, subtraction, and multiplication; add, subtract, and multiply polynomials.

MP 7

You can use algebra tiles to model the multiplication of two binomials.

Activity

Find the product $(x + 4)(2x + 3)$.

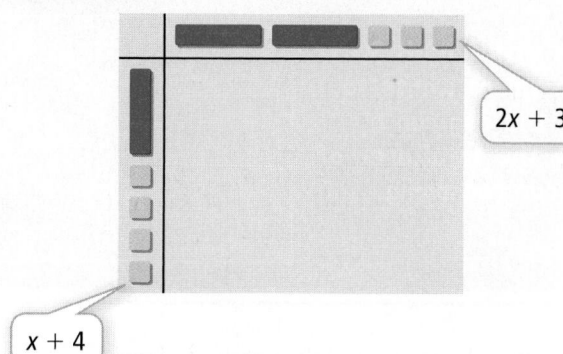

2x + 3

x + 4

$2x^2 + 3x + 8x + 12$

$2x^2 + 11x + 12$ Add coefficients of like terms.

The product is $2x^2 + 11x + 12$.

You can also model products that involve subtraction. Red tiles indicate negative variables and negative numbers.

Activity

Find the product $(x - 1)(2x + 1)$.

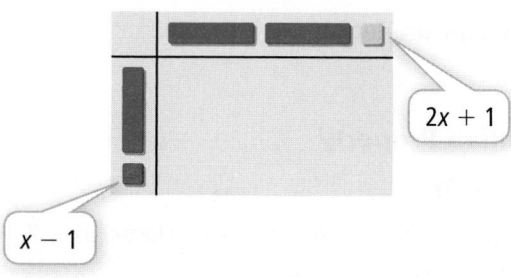

2x + 1

x − 1

$2x^2 + x - 2x - 1$

$2x^2 - x - 1$ Add coefficients of like terms.

The product is $2x^2 - x - 1$.

Exercises

Use algebra tiles to find each product.

1. $(x + 4)(x + 2)$ **2.** $(x + 2)(x - 3)$ **3.** $(x + 1)(3x - 2)$ **4.** $(3x + 2)(2x + 1)$

Multiplying Binomials

 Common Core State Standards

A-APR.A.1 Understand that polynomials form a system analogous to the integers, namely, they are closed under the operations of addition, subtraction, and multiplication; add, subtract, and multiply polynomials.

MP 1, MP 2, MP 3, MP 4, MP 7, MP 8

Objective To multiply two binomials or a binomial by a trinomial

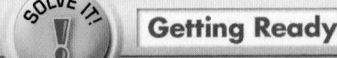

Getting Ready!

A park has a rectangular dog run with length 30 ft and width 20 ft. The parks department wants to expand each end of each side of the dog run by the same amount x. What will be the total area of the expanded dog run? Justify your reasoning.

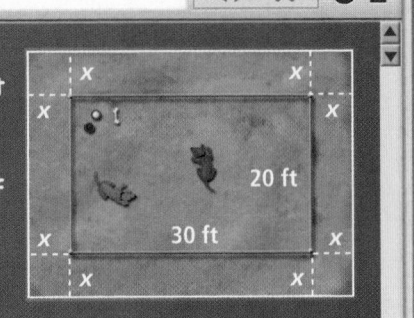

You've got a diagram. How can you use it to create expressions for the width and for the length?

 **Essential Understanding** There are several ways to find the product of two binomials, including models, algebra, and tables.

One way to find the product of two binomials is to use an area model, as shown below.

This model shows that $(2x + 1)(x + 2)$ can be written in standard form as $2x^2 + 5x + 2$.

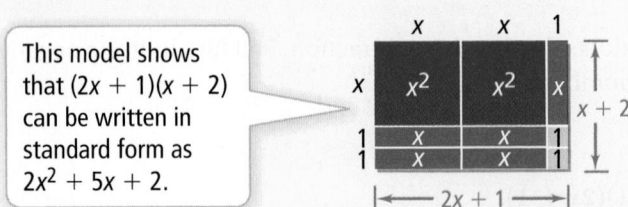

You can also use the Distributive Property to find the product of two binomials.

Think

Is the product of two polynomials always a polynomial?
Yes. The set of polynomials is *closed* under multiplication, which means that multiplying polynomials always gives you another polynomial.

Problem 1 Using the Distributive Property

What is a simpler form of $(2x + 4)(3x - 7)$?

$$(2x + 4)(3x - 7) = 2x(3x - 7) + 4(3x - 7)$$ Distribute the second factor, $3x - 7$.

$$= 6x^2 - 14x + 4(3x - 7)$$ Distribute $2x$.

$$= 6x^2 - 14x + 12x - 28$$ Distribute 4.

$$= 6x^2 - 2x - 28$$ Combine like terms.

Got It? **1.** What is a simpler form of $(x - 6)(4x + 3)$?

When you use the Distributive Property to multiply binomials, notice that you multiply each term of the first binomial by each term of the second binomial. A table can help you organize your work.

 **Problem 2** Using a Table

What is a simpler form of $(x - 3)(4x - 5)$?

Know	Need	Plan
Binomial factors	Product of binomials written in standard form	Use a table.

Make a table of products.

Think

Is this the only table you can make?
No. You can write the terms of $x - 3$ in a row and the terms of $4x - 5$ in a column.

	$4x$	-5
x	$4x^2$	$-5x$
-3	$-12x$	15

When labeling the rows and columns, think of $x - 3$ as $x + (-3)$. Think of $4x - 5$ as $4x + (-5)$.

The product is $4x^2 - 5x - 12x + 15$, or $4x^2 - 17x + 15$.

 Got It? **2.** What is a simpler form of $(3x + 1)(x + 4)$? Use a table.

There is a shortcut you can use to multiply two binomials. Consider the product of $2x + 2$ and $x + 3$. The large rectangle below models this product. You can divide the large rectangle into four smaller rectangles.

The area of the large rectangle is the sum of the areas of the four smaller rectangles.

$$(2x + 2)(x + 3) = (2x)(x) + (2x)(3) + (2)(x) + (2)(3)$$
$$= 2x^2 + 6x + 2x + 6$$
$$= 2x^2 + 8x + 6$$

The area of each rectangle is the product of one term of $2x + 2$ and one term of $x + 3$.

This model illustrates another way to find the product of two binomials. You find the sum of the products of the First terms, the Outer terms, the Inner terms, and the Last terms of the binomials. The acronym FOIL may help you remember this method.

 **Problem 3** Using FOIL

What is a simpler form of $(5x - 3)(2x + 1)$?

Plan

How can a diagram help you multiply two binomials?
Draw arrows from each term of the first binomial to each term of the second binomial. This will help you organize the products of the terms.

$$
\begin{array}{ccccc}
 & \textbf{First} & \textbf{Outer} & \textbf{Inner} & \textbf{Last} \\
(5x - 3)(2x + 1) = & (5x)(2x) & + \; (5x)(1) & + \; (-3)(2x) & + \; (-3)(1) \\
= & 10x^2 & + \quad 5x & - \quad 6x & - \quad 3 \\
= & 10x^2 & - \quad x & - \quad 3 &
\end{array}
$$

The product is $10x^2 - x - 3$.

 Got It? **3.** What is a simpler form of each product? Use the FOIL method.

a. $(3x - 4)(x + 2)$ **b.** $(n - 6)(4n - 7)$ **c.** $(2p^2 + 3)(2p - 5)$

 **Problem 4** Applying Multiplication of Binomials

Multiple Choice A cylinder has the dimensions shown in the diagram. Which polynomial in standard form best describes the total surface area of the cylinder?

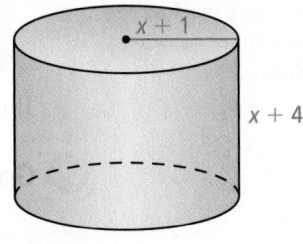

- Ⓐ $2\pi x^2 + 4\pi x + 2\pi$
- Ⓒ $4\pi x^2 + 14\pi x + 10\pi$
- Ⓑ $2\pi x^2 + 10\pi x + 8\pi$
- Ⓓ $2\pi x^2 + 2\pi x + 10\pi$

The total surface area (S.A.) of a cylinder is given by the formula
S.A. $= 2\pi r^2 + 2\pi rh$, where r is the radius of the cylinder and h is the height.

Think

How can you simplify $(x + 1)^2$?
Write the expression as $(x + 1)(x + 1)$ and multiply the binomials. You do not "distribute" the exponent to each term: $(x + 1)^2 \neq x^2 + 1^2$.

S.A. $= 2\pi r^2 + 2\pi rh$	Surface area of a cylinder
$= 2\pi(x + 1)^2 + 2\pi(x + 1)(x + 4)$	Substitute $x + 1$ for r and $x + 4$ for h.
$= 2\pi(x + 1)(x + 1) + 2\pi(x + 1)(x + 4)$	Write $(x + 1)^2$ as $(x + 1)(x + 1)$.
$= 2\pi\left(x^2 + x + x + 1\right) + 2\pi\left(x^2 + 4x + x + 4\right)$	Multiply binomials.
$= 2\pi\left(x^2 + 2x + 1\right) + 2\pi\left(x^2 + 5x + 4\right)$	Combine like terms.
$= 2\pi\left(x^2 + 2x + 1 + x^2 + 5x + 4\right)$	Factor out 2π.
$= 2\pi\left(2x^2 + 7x + 5\right)$	Combine like terms.
$= 4\pi x^2 + 14\pi x + 10\pi$	Write in standard form.

The correct answer is C.

 Got It? **4.** What is the total surface area of a cylinder with radius $x + 2$ and height $x + 4$? Write your answer as a polynomial in standard form.

You can use the FOIL method when you multiply two binomials, but it is not helpful when multiplying a trinomial and a binomial. In this case, you can use a vertical method to distribute each term.

Problem 5 Multiplying a Trinomial and a Binomial

What is a simpler form of $(3x^2 + x - 5)(2x - 7)$?

Multiply by arranging the polynomials vertically as shown.

Plan

How should you align the polynomials?
Write the polynomials so that like terms are vertically aligned.

$$3x^2 + x - 5$$
$$\underline{ 2x - 7}$$
$$-21x^2 - 7x + 35 \qquad \text{Multiply by } -7.$$
$$\underline{6x^3 + 2x^2 - 10x } \qquad \text{Multiply by } 2x.$$
$$6x^3 - 19x^2 - 17x + 35 \qquad \text{Add like terms.}$$

The product is $6x^3 - 19x^2 - 17x + 35$.

 Got It? **5. a.** What is a simpler form of $(2x^2 - 3x + 1)(x - 3)$?

b. Reasoning How can you use the Distributive Property to find the product of a trinomial and a binomial?

 ## Lesson Check

Do you know HOW?

Simplify each product.

1. $(x + 3)(x + 6)$

2. $(2x - 5)(x + 3)$

3. $(x + 2)(x^2 + 3x - 4)$

4. A rectangle has length $x + 5$ and width $x - 3$. What is the area of the rectangle? Write your answer as a polynomial in standard form.

Do you UNDERSTAND?

5. Reasoning Explain how to use the FOIL method to find the product of two binomials.

6. Compare and Contrast Simplify $(3x + 8)(x + 1)$ using a table, the Distributive Property, and the FOIL method. Which method is most efficient? Explain.

7. Writing How is the degree of the product of two polynomials $p(x)$ and $q(x)$ related to the degrees of $p(x)$ and $q(x)$?

 ## Practice and Problem-Solving Exercises

 **Practice** **Simplify each product using the Distributive Property.**  See Problem 1.

8. $(x + 7)(x + 4)$ **9.** $(y - 3)(y + 8)$ **10.** $(m + 6)(m - 7)$

11. $(c - 10)(c - 5)$ **12.** $(2r - 3)(r + 1)$ **13.** $(2x + 7)(3x - 4)$

Simplify each product using a table. 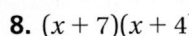 See Problem 2.

14. $(x + 5)(x - 4)$ **15.** $(a - 1)(a - 11)$ **16.** $(w - 2)(w + 6)$

17. $(2h - 7)(h + 9)$ **18.** $(x - 8)(3x + 1)$ **19.** $(3p + 4)(2p + 5)$

Simplify each product using the FOIL method.

See Problem 3.

20. $(a + 8)(a - 2)$ **21.** $(x + 4)(4x - 5)$ **22.** $(k - 6)(k + 8)$

23. $(b - 3)(b - 9)$ **24.** $(5m - 2)(m + 3)$ **25.** $(9z + 4)(5z - 3)$

26. $(3h + 2)(6h - 5)$ **27.** $(4w + 13)(w + 2)$ **28.** $(8c - 1)(6c - 7)$

29. Geometry What is the total surface area of the cylinder? Write your answer as a polynomial in standard form.

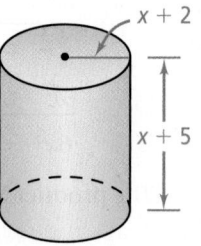

See Problem 4.

30. Design The radius of a cylindrical gift box is $(2x + 3)$ in. The height of the gift box is twice the radius. What is the surface area of the cylinder? Write your answer as a polynomial in standard form.

Simplify each product.

See Problem 5.

31. $(x + 5)(x^2 - 3x + 1)$ **32.** $(k^2 - 4k + 3)(k - 2)$

33. $(2a^2 + 4a + 5)(5a - 4)$ **34.** $(2g + 7)(3g^2 - 5g + 2)$

35. Sports A school's rectangular athletic fields currently have a length of 125 yd and a width of 75 yd. The school plans to expand both the length and the width of the fields by x yards. What polynomial in standard form represents the area of the expanded athletic field?

 **Apply**

Simplify each product. Write in standard form.

36. $(x^2 + 1)(x - 3)$ **37.** $(-n^2 - 1)(n + 3)$ **38.** $(b^2 - 1)(b^2 + 3)$

39. $(2m^2 + 1)(m + 5)$ **40.** $(c^2 - 4)(2c + 3)$ **41.** $(4z^2 + 1)(z + 3z^2)$

ⓒ 42. Error Analysis Describe and correct the error made in finding the product.

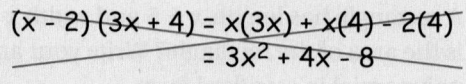

ⓒ 43. Reasoning Is the product of two polynomials always a polynomial? Explain.

ⓒ 44. Think About a Plan You are planning a rectangular dining pavilion. Its length is three times its width x. You want a stone walkway that is 3 ft wide around the pavilion. You have enough stones to cover 396 ft^2 and want to use them all in the walkway. What should the dimensions of the pavilion be?
- Can you draw a diagram that represents this situation?
- How can you write a variable expression for the area of the walkway?

ⓒ 45. a. Simplify each pair of products.

    i. $(x + 1)(x + 1)$ **ii.** $(x + 1)(x + 2)$ **iii.** $(x + 1)(x + 3)$
      $11 \cdot 11$ $11 \cdot 12$ $11 \cdot 13$

    b. Reasoning What are the similarities between your two answers in each pair of products?

46. Geometry The dimensions of a rectangular prism are n, $n + 7$, and $n + 8$. Use the formula $V = \ell wh$ to write a polynomial in standard form for the volume of the prism.

 **Challenge** For Exercises 47–49, each expression represents the side length of a cube. Write a polynomial in standard form for the surface area of each cube.

47. $x + 2$

48. $3a + 1$

49. $2c^2 + 3$

50. Financial Planning Suppose you deposit $1500 for college in a savings account that has an annual interest rate r (expressed as a decimal). At the end of 3 years, the value of your account will be $1500(1 + r)^3$ dollars.
   a. Rewrite the expression $1500(1 + r)^3$ by finding the product $1500(1 + r)(1 + r)(1 + r)$. Write your answer in standard form.
   b. How much money is in the account after 3 yr if the interest rate is 3% per year?

 ## Apply What You've Learned

MATHEMATICAL PRACTICES
MP 2, MP 3

Look back at the information on page 485 about a community garden. Kelly's and Roberto's plans for their original plots are shown again below. In the Apply What You've Learned in Lesson 8-1, you wrote binomials for the length and width of Kelly's plot.

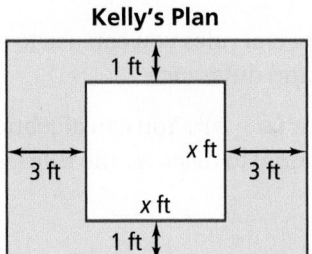

Kelly's Plan

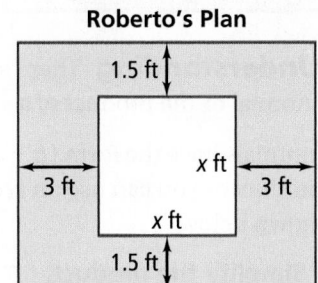

Roberto's Plan

a. Use a product of two binomials to find a polynomial that represents the area of Kelly's plot.

b. Use a product of two binomials to find a polynomial that represents the area of Roberto's plot.

c. Explain how you can use a specific value of x to check that you found the products in parts (a) and (b) correctly.

d. Based on the polynomials you wrote in parts (a) and (b), can you conclude that the area of Roberto's plot is greater than the area of Kelly's plot for any value of x? Give an argument to support your answer.

8-4 Multiplying Special Cases

© **Common Core State Standards**

A-APR.A.1 Understand that polynomials form a system analogous to the integers, namely, they are closed under the operations of addition, subtraction, and multiplication; add, subtract, and multiply polynomials.

MP 1, MP 2, MP 3, MP 4, MP 7, MP 8

Objectives To find the square of a binomial and to find the product of a sum and difference

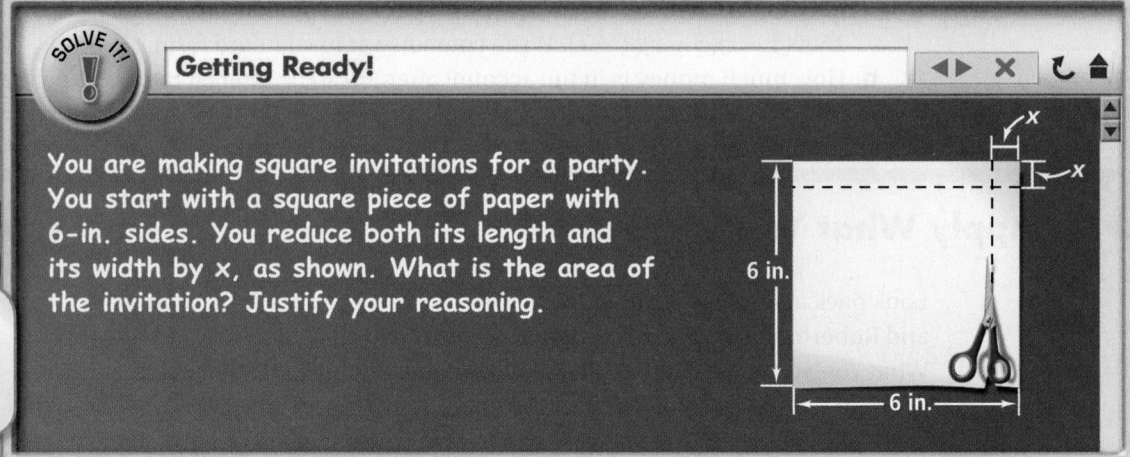

Getting Ready!

You are making square invitations for a party. You start with a square piece of paper with 6-in. sides. You reduce both its length and its width by x, as shown. What is the area of the invitation? Justify your reasoning.

6 in.

6 in.

How is this Solve It like the one for Lesson 8-3? How is it different?

© MATHEMATICAL PRACTICES

Essential Understanding There are special rules you can use to simplify the square of a binomial or the product of a sum and difference.

Squares of binomials have the form $(a + b)^2$ or $(a - b)^2$. You can algebraically simplify the product or you can use an area model to discover the rule for simplifying $(a + b)^2$, as shown below.

Simplify the product.

$(a + b)^2 = (a + b)(a + b)$

$= a^2 + ab + ba + b^2$ Multiply the binomials.

$= a^2 + 2ab + b^2$ Simplify.

Area Model

	a	b
a	a^2	ab
b	ab	b^2

$a^2 + 2ab + b^2$

Key Concept   The Square of a Binomial

Words The square of a binomial is the square of the first term plus twice the product of the two terms plus the square of the last term.

Algebra

$(a + b)^2 = a^2 + 2ab + b^2$

$(a - b)^2 = a^2 - 2ab + b^2$

Examples

$(x + 4)^2 = x^2 + 8x + 16$

$(x - 3)^2 = x^2 - 6x + 9$

Plan

What rule can you use to simplify this product?
$(2m - 3)^2$ may not look like $(a - b)^2$, but it has the same form. Use the rule for $(a - b)^2$ and let $a = 2m$ and $b = 3$.

 Problem 1 **Squaring a Binomial**

What is a simpler form of each product?

A $(x + 8)^2 = x^2 + 2x(8) + 8^2$ Square the binomial.

$= x^2 + 16x + 64$ Simplify.

B $(2m - 3)^2 = (2m)^2 - 2(2m)(3) + 3$ Square the binomial.

$= 4m^2 - 12m + 9$ Simplify.

Got It? **1.** What is a simpler form of each product?

a. $(n - 7)^2$ **b.** $(2x + 9)^2$

Plan

How do you find the area of the walkway?
The area of the walkway is the difference of the total area and the area of the patio.

 Problem 2 **Applying Squares of Binomials**

Exterior Design A square outdoor patio is surrounded by a brick walkway as shown. What is the area of the walkway?

Step 1 Find the total area of the patio and walkway.

$(x + 6)^2 = x^2 + 2(x)(6) + 6^2$ Square the binomial.

$= x^2 + 12x + 36$ Simplify.

Step 2 Find the area of the patio.

The area of the patio is $x \cdot x$, or x^2.

Step 3 Find the area of the walkway.

Area of walkway = Total area − Area of patio

$= (x^2 + 12x + 36) - x^2$ Substitute.

$= (x^2 - x^2) + 12x + 36$ Group like terms.

$= 12x + 36$ Simplify.

The area of the walkway is $(12x + 36)$ ft^2.

Got It? **2.** In Problem 2, suppose the brick walkway is 4 ft wide. What is its area?

Using mental math, you can square a binomial to find the square of a number.

Think

What number close to 39 can you square mentally?
The nearest multiple of 10 to 39 is 40, which is a number you should be able to square mentally.

Problem 3 **Using Mental Math**

What is 39^2? Use mental math.

$39^2 = (40 - 1)^2$ Write 39^2 as the square of a binomial.

$= 40^2 - 2(40)(1) + 1^2$ Square the binomial.

$= 1600 - 80 + 1$ Simplify.

$= 1521$ Simplify.

Got It? 3. a. What is 85^2? Use mental math.

b. Reasoning Is there more than one way to find 85^2 using mental math? Explain your reasoning.

The product of the sum and difference of the same two terms also produces a pattern.

$$(a + b)(a - b) = a^2 - ab + ba - b^2$$

> Notice that the sum of $-ab$ and ba is 0, leaving $a^2 - b^2$.

$$= a^2 - b^2$$

take note

Key Concept The Product of a Sum and Difference

Words The product of the sum and difference of the same two terms is the difference of their squares.

Algebra	**Examples**
$(a + b)(a - b) = a^2 - b^2$	$(x + 2)(x - 2) = x^2 - 2^2 = x^2 - 4$

Ⓒ Problem 4 Finding the Product of a Sum and Difference

What is a simpler form of $(x^3 + 8)(x^3 - 8)$?

Plan

How do you choose which rule to use?
The first factor in the product is the sum of x^3 and 8. The second factor is the difference of x^3 and 8. So, use the rule for the product of a sum and difference.

Think

Write the original product.

Identify which terms correspond to a and b in the rule for the product of a sum and difference.

Substitute for a and b in the rule.

Simplify.

Write

$(x^3 + 8)(x^3 - 8)$

$a = x^3; b = 8$

$(x^3 + 8)(x^3 - 8) = (x^3)^2 - (8)^2$

$= x^6 - 64$

 Got It? 4. What is a simpler form of each product?

a. $(x + 9)(x - 9)$ **b.** $(6 + m^2)(6 - m^2)$ **c.** $(3c - 4)(3c + 4)$

You can use the rule for the product of a sum and difference to calculate products using mental math.

 Problem 5 **Using Mental Math**

What is 64 · 56?

$$64 \cdot 56 = (60 + 4)(60 - 4)$$ Write as a product of a sum and a difference.

$$= 60^2 - 4^2$$ Use $(a + b)(a - b) = a^2 - b^2$.

$$= 3600 - 16$$ Simplify powers.

$$= 3584$$ Simplify.

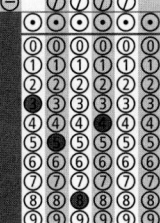

 Got It? **5.** What is 52 · 48? Use mental math.

Think

How can you write 64 · 56 as the product of a sum and difference?
Find the number halfway between the factors. 60 is 4 units from each factor. Write the factors in terms of 60 and 4.

 ## Lesson Check

Do you know HOW?

Simplify each product.

1. $(c + 3)(c + 3)$

2. $(g - 4)^2$

3. $(2r - 3)(2r + 3)$

4. A square has side length $(2x + 3)$ in. What is the area of the square?

Do you UNDERSTAND?

What rule would you use to find each product? Why?

5. $(3x - 1)^2$

6. $(4x - 9)(4x + 9)$

7. $(7x + 2)(7x + 2)$

 **8. Reasoning** How do you know whether it is convenient to use the rule for the product of a sum and difference to mentally multiply two numbers?

 ## Practice and Problem-Solving Exercises

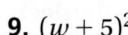 **Practice** Simplify each expression.

See Problem 1.

9. $(w + 5)^2$ **10.** $(h + 2)^2$ **11.** $(3s + 9)^2$ **12.** $(2n + 7)^2$

13. $(a - 8)^2$ **14.** $(k - 11)^2$ **15.** $(5m - 2)^2$ **16.** $(4x - 6)^2$

Geometry The figures below are squares. Find an expression for the area of each shaded region. Write your answers in standard form.

See Problem 2.

17.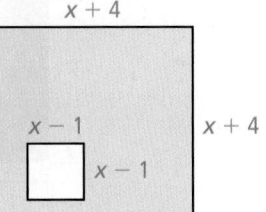

$x + 4$

$x - 1$ $x + 4$

$x - 1$

18.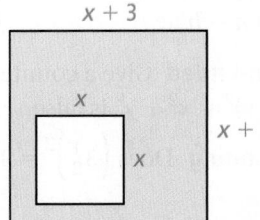

$x + 3$

x

$x + 3$

x

---

19. Interior Design A square green rug has a blue square in the center. The side length of the blue square is x inches. The width of the green band that surrounds the blue square is 6 in. What is the area of the green band?

 **Mental Math** Simplify each product. See Problem 3.

20. 61^2 **21.** 79^2 **22.** 48^2 **23.** 403^2 **24.** 302^2

Simplify each product. See Problem 4.

25. $(v+6)(v-6)$ **26.** $(b+1)(b-1)$ **27.** $(z-5)(z+5)$

28. $(x-3)(x+3)$ **29.** $(10+y)(10-y)$ **30.** $(t-13)(t+13)$

Mental Math Simplify each product. See Problem 5.

31. $42 \cdot 38$ **32.** $79 \cdot 81$ **33.** $63 \cdot 57$ **34.** $399 \cdot 401$ **35.** $303 \cdot 297$

B Apply   Simplify each product.

36. $(m+3n)^2$ **37.** $(2a+b)^2$ **38.** $(4s-t)^2$ **39.** $(g-7h)^2$

40. $(9k+2q)^2$ **41.** $(8r-5s)^2$ **42.** $(s+6t^2)^2$ **43.** $(p^4-9q^2)^2$

44. $(4x+7y)(4x-7y)$ **45.** $(a-6b)(a+6b)$ **46.** $(2g+9h)(2g-9h)$

47. $(r^2+3s)(r^2-3s)$ **48.** $(2p^2+7q)(2p^2-7q)$ **49.** $(3w^3-z^2)(3w^3+z^2)$

50. Error Analysis Describe and correct the error made in simplifying the product.

$$(3a - 7)^2 = 9a^2 - 21a + 49$$

51. Think About a Plan A company logo is a white square inside a red square. The side length of the white square is $x+2$. The side length of the red square is three times the side length of the white square. What is the area of the red part of the logo? Write your answer in standard form.
- How can drawing a diagram help you solve the problem?
- How can you express the area of the red part of the logo as a difference of areas?

STEM 52. Construction A square deck has a side length of $x+5$. You are expanding the deck so that each side is four times as long as the side length of the original deck. What is the area of the new deck? Write your answer in standard form.

53. Reasoning Use the area model at the right to write a second expression for the area of the square labeled $(a-b)^2$. Then simplify the expression to derive the rule for the square of a binomial of the form $a-b$.

54. Open-Ended Give a counterexample to show that $(x+y)^2 = x^2 + y^2$ is false.

55. Reasoning Does $\left(3\frac{1}{2}\right)^2 = 9\frac{1}{4}$? Explain.

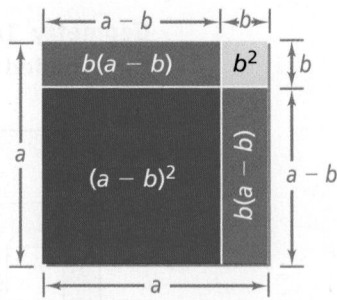

56. Simplify $(a + b + c)^2$.

57. Number Theory You can use factoring to show that the sum of two multiples of 3 is also a multiple of 3.

If m and n are integers, then $3m$ and $3n$ are multiples of three.
$3m + 3n = 3(m + n)$
Since $m + n$ is an integer, $3(m + n)$ is a multiple of three.

a. Show that if an integer is one more than a multiple of 3, then its square is also one more than a multiple of 3.

b. Reasoning If an integer is two more than a multiple of 3, is its square also two more than a multiple of 3? Explain.

58. The formula $V = \frac{4}{3}\pi r^3$ gives the volume of a sphere with radius r. Find the volume of a sphere with radius $x + 3$. Write your answer in standard form.

Standardized Test Prep

SAT/ACT

59. What is a simpler form of $(2x + 5)(2x - 5)$?

    Ⓐ $4x^2 - 20x - 25$ Ⓑ $4x^2 + 20x + 25$ Ⓒ $4x^2 - 25$ Ⓓ $2x^2 - 5$

60. Sara and Nick sold tickets to a play. Sara sold 20 student tickets and 3 adult tickets for more than $60. Nick sold 15 student tickets and 5 adult tickets for less than $75. This information can be represented by $20x + 3y > 60$ and $15x + 5y < 75$, where x is the price of a student ticket and y is the price of an adult ticket. The inequalities are graphed at the right. Which could be the price of a student ticket?

Ticket Sales

    Ⓕ $1   Ⓗ $5.50

    Ⓖ $2.75   Ⓘ $6

Short
Response

61. Graph the solutions of the system. $5x + 4y \geq 20$
    $5x + 4y \leq 20$

Mixed Review

Simplify each product.   ◀ See Lesson 8-3.

62. $(3x + 2)(2x - 5)$ **63.** $(4m - 1)(6m - 7)$ **64.** $(x + 9)(5x + 8)$

Find each percent change. Describe the percent change as an *increase* or *decrease*. If necessary, round to the nearest tenth.   ◀ See Lesson 2-10.

65. $4 to $3   **66.** 4 ft to 5 ft   **67.** 12 lb to 15 lb   **68.** $40 to $35

Get Ready!   **To prepare for Lesson 8-5, do Exercises 69–71.**

Factor each polynomial.   ◀ See Lesson 8-2.

69. $12x^4 + 30x^3 + 42x$ **70.** $72x^3 + 54x^2 + 27$ **71.** $35x^3 + 7x^2 + 63x$

Do you know HOW?

Find the degree of each monomial.

1. $-5a^8$

2. $4x^2y^3$

Write each polynomial in standard form. Then name each polynomial based on its degree and number of terms.

3. $4x + 3x^2$

4. $7p^2 - 3p + 2p^3$

Simplify each sum or difference.

5. $\left(x^2 + 6x + 11\right) + \left(3x^2 + 7x + 4\right)$

6. $\left(5w^3 + 3w^2 + 8w + 2\right) + \left(7w^2 + 3w + 1\right)$

7. $\left(4q^2 + 10q + 7\right) - \left(2q^2 + 7q + 5\right)$

8. $\left(9t^4 + 5t + 8\right) - \left(3t^2 - 6t - 4\right)$

Simplify each product.

9. $6x^2\left(4x^2 + 3\right)$

10. $-8c^3\left(3c^2 + 2c - 9\right)$

Factor each polynomial.

11. $16b^4 + 8b^2 + 20b$

12. $77x^3 + 22x^2 - 33x - 88$

Simplify each product.

13. $(x + 2)(x + 9)$

14. $(4b - 1)(b - 8)$

15. $(h + 2)\left(3h^2 + h - 7\right)$

16. $(z - 1)\left(z^2 - 4z + 9\right)$

17. Design You are designing a rectangular rubber stamp. The length of the stamp is $2r + 3$. The width of the stamp is $r - 4$. What polynomial in standard form represents the area of the stamp?

Simplify each product.

18. $(r + 3)^2$

19. $(k - 3)(k + 3)$

20. $(3d + 10)^2$

21. $(g + 10)(g - 10)$

22. $(2m - 7)^2$

23. $(7h - 2)(7h + 2)$

24. Woodworking A birdhouse has a square base with side length $3x - 4$. What polynomial in standard form represents the area of the base?

Do you UNDERSTAND?

ⓒ 25. Writing Can the degree of a monomial ever be negative? Explain.

26. Geometry The figures below are rectangles. What polynomial in standard form represents the area of the shaded region?

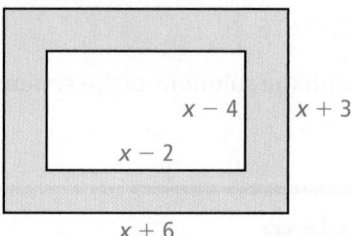

ⓒ 27. Open-Ended Write a trinomial that has $9x^2$ as the GCF of its terms.

ⓒ 28. Open-Ended Write a trinomial of degree 4 such that the GCF of its terms is 1.

ⓒ 29. Reasoning Suppose n represents an even number. Write a simplified expression that represents the product of the next two even numbers.

ⓒ 30. Writing Describe how to simplify $\left(8k^2 + k - 1\right) - \left(k^3 - 4k^2 - 7k + 15\right)$. Write your answer as a polynomial in standard form.

Using Models to Factor

Common Core State Standards

Prepares for A-SSE.A.2 Use the structure of an expression to identify ways to rewrite it.

MP 7

You can sometimes write a trinomial as the product of two binomial factors. You can use algebra tiles to find the factors by arranging all of the tiles to form a rectangle. The lengths of the sides of the rectangle are the factors of the trinomial.

Activity

Write $x^2 + 7x + 12$ as the product of two binomial factors.

Model of polynomial

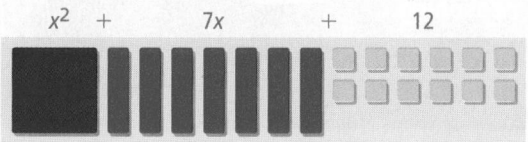

Use the tiles to form a rectangle.

First try:

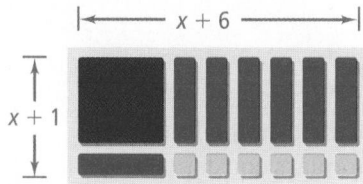

There are six ☐ tiles left over.

Second try:

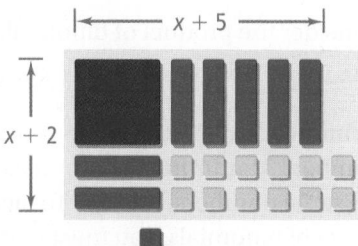

There is one ▮ tile too few.

Third try:

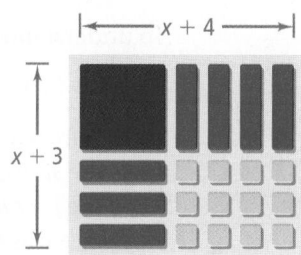

Correct! There is the exact number of tiles needed.
$x^2 + 7x + 12 = (x + 3)(x + 4)$

Exercises

Use algebra tiles to find binomial factors of each trinomial.

1. $x^2 + 4x + 4$ **2.** $x^2 + 5x + 6$ **3.** $x^2 + 10x + 9$

4. $x^2 + 7x + 10$ **5.** $x^2 + 9x + 14$ **6.** $x^2 + 8x + 16$

ⓒ **7. Reasoning** Explain why you cannot use algebra tiles to represent the trinomial $x^2 + 2x + 3$ as a rectangle.

Factoring $x^2 + bx + c$

 Common Core State Standards

A-SSE.A.1a Interpret parts of an expression, such as terms, factors, and coefficients.

MP 1, MP 3, MP 4, MP 7, MP 8

Objective To factor trinomials of the form $x^2 + bx + c$

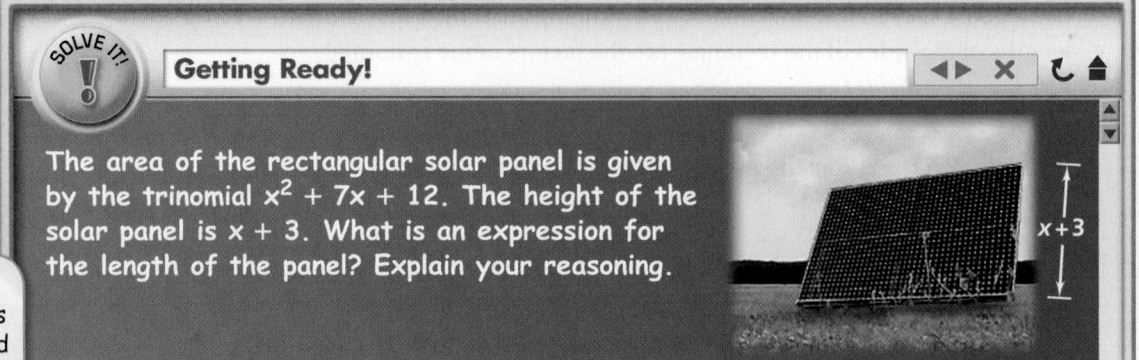

SOLVE IT!

Getting Ready!

The area of the rectangular solar panel is given by the trinomial $x^2 + 7x + 12$. The height of the solar panel is $x + 3$. What is an expression for the length of the panel? Explain your reasoning.

$x + 3$

Here's a hint. What two numbers have a sum of 7 and a product of 12?

MATHEMATICAL PRACTICES **Essential Understanding** You can write some trinomials of the form $x^2 + bx + c$ as the product of two binomials.

To understand how, consider the product of binomials below.

$$(x + 3)(x + 7) = x^2 + (7 + 3)x + 3 \cdot 7 = x^2 + 10x + 21$$

The coefficient of the trinomial's x^2-term is 1. The coefficient of the trinomial's x-term, 10, is the *sum* of the numbers 3 and 7 in the binomials. The trinomial's constant term, 21, is the *product* of the same numbers, 3 and 7. To factor a trinomial of the form $x^2 + bx + c$ as the product of binomials, you must find two numbers that have a sum of b and a product of c.

Problem 1 Factoring $x^2 + bx + c$ Where $b > 0, c > 0$

Plan

What is an easy way to organize your factoring?
Use a table to list the pairs of factors of the constant term c and the sums of those pairs of factors.

What is the factored form of $x^2 + 8x + 15$?

List the pairs of factors of 15. Identify the pair that has a sum of 8.

Factors of 15	Sum of Factors
1 and 15	16
3 and 5	8 ✔

$x^2 + 8x + 15 = (x + 3)(x + 5)$

Check $(x + 3)(x + 5) = x^2 + 5x + 3x + 15$

$= x^2 + 8x + 15$ ✔

Got It? **1.** What is the factored form of $r^2 + 11r + 24$?

Some factorable trinomials have a negative coefficient of x and a positive constant term. In this case, you need to inspect the negative factors of c to find the factors of the trinomial.

© **Problem 2** Factoring $x^2 + bx + c$ Where $b < 0, c > 0$

What is the factored form of $x^2 - 11x + 24$?

List the pairs of negative factors of 24. Identify the pair that has a sum of -11.

Factors of 24	Sum of Factors
-1 and -24	-25
-2 and -12	-14
-3 and -8	-11 ✔
-4 and -6	-10

$$x^2 - 11x + 24 = (x - 3)(x - 8)$$

Check $\quad (x - 3)(x - 8) = x^2 - 8x - 3x + 24$
$$= x^2 - 11x + 24 \ ✔$$

© ✓ **Got It?** **2. a.** What is the factored form of $y^2 - 6y + 8$?

b. Reasoning Can you factor $x^2 - x + 2$? Explain.

When you factor trinomials with a negative constant term, you need to inspect pairs of positive and negative factors of c.

© **Problem 3** Factoring $x^2 + bx + c$ Where $c < 0$

What is the factored form of $x^2 + 2x - 15$?

Identify the pair of factors of -15 that has a sum of 2.

Factors of -15	Sum of Factors
1 and -15	-14
-1 and 15	14
3 and -5	-2
-3 and 5	2 ✔

$$x^2 + 2x - 15 = (x - 3)(x + 5)$$

✓ **Got It?** **3.** What is the factored form of each polynomial?

a. $n^2 + 9n - 36$ **b.** $c^2 - 4c - 21$

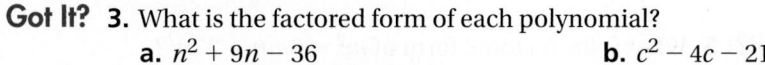

Problem 4 Applying Factoring Trinomials

Geometry The area of a rectangle is given by the trinomial $x^2 - 2x - 35$. What are the possible dimensions of the rectangle? Use factoring.

Know

The area of the rectangle

Need

Possible dimensions of the rectangle

Plan

Area = length × width, so factor the trinomial for area as the product of binomials that represent the length and width.

To factor $x^2 - 2x - 35$, identify the pair of factors of -35 that has a sum of -2.

Factors of −35	Sum of Factors
1 and −35	−34
−1 and 35	34
5 and −7	−2 ✔
−5 and 7	2

$x^2 - 2x - 35 = (x + 5)(x - 7)$

So the possible dimensions of the rectangle are $x + 5$ and $x - 7$.

 Got It? 4. A rectangle's area is $x^2 - x - 72$. What are possible dimensions of the rectangle? Use factoring.

You can also factor some trinomials that have more than one variable. Consider the product $(p + 9q)(p + 7q)$.

$(p + 9q)(p + 7q) = p^2 + 7pq + 9pq + 9q(7q)$
$= p^2 + 16pq + 63q^2$

This suggests that a trinomial with two variables may be factorable if the first term includes the square of one variable, the middle term includes both variables, and the last term includes the square of the other variable.

 Problem 5 Factoring a Trinomial With Two Variables

Plan

Is this problem similar to one you've seen before?
Yes. This problem is similar to factoring a trinomial in one variable of the form $x^2 + bx + c$, where $c < 0$.

What is the factored form of $x^2 + 6xy - 55y^2$?

List the pairs of factors of -55. Identify the pair that has a sum of 6.

Factors of −55	Sum of Factors
1 and −55	−54
−1 and 55	54
5 and −11	−6
−5 and 11	6 ✔

$x^2 + 6xy - 55y^2 = (x - 5y)(x + 11y)$

 Got It? 5. What is the factored form of $m^2 + 6mn - 27n^2$?

Lesson Check

Do you know HOW?

Factor each expression. Check your answer.

1. $x^2 + 7x + 12$

2. $r^2 - 13r + 42$

3. $p^2 + 3p - 40$

4. $a^2 + 12ab + 32b^2$

5. The area of a rectangle is given by the trinomial $n^2 - 3n - 28$. What are the possible dimensions of the rectangle? Use factoring.

Do you UNDERSTAND?  MATHEMATICAL PRACTICES

Tell whether the sum of the factors of the constant term should be *positive* or *negative* when you factor the trinomial.

6. $s^2 + s - 30$

7. $w^2 + 11w + 18$

8. $x^2 - x - 20$

 9. **Reasoning** Under what circumstances should you look at pairs of negative factors of the constant term when factoring a trinomial of the form $x^2 + bx + c$?

Practice and Problem-Solving Exercises  MATHEMATICAL PRACTICES

Ⓐ Practice

Complete.

See Problems 1 and 2.

10. $k^2 + 5k + 6 = (k + 2)(k + \blacksquare)$

11. $x^2 - 7x + 10 = (x - 5)(x - \blacksquare)$

12. $t^2 - 10t + 24 = (t - 4)(t - \blacksquare)$

13. $v^2 + 12v + 20 = (v + 10)(v + \blacksquare)$

Factor each expression. Check your answer.

14. $y^2 + 6y + 5$

15. $t^2 + 10t + 16$

16. $x^2 + 15x + 56$

17. $n^2 - 15n + 56$

18. $r^2 - 11r + 24$

19. $q^2 - 8q + 12$

Complete.

See Problem 3.

20. $q^2 + 3q - 54 = (q - 6)(q + \blacksquare)$

21. $z^2 - 2z - 48 = (z - 8)(z + \blacksquare)$

22. $n^2 - 5n - 50 = (n + 5)(n - \blacksquare)$

23. $y^2 + 8y - 9 = (y + 9)(y - \blacksquare)$

Factor each expression. Check your answer.

24. $r^2 + 6r - 27$

25. $w^2 - 7w - 8$

26. $z^2 + 2z - 8$

27. $x^2 + 5x - 6$

28. $v^2 + 5v - 36$

29. $n^2 - 3n - 10$

STEM 30. **Carpentry** The area of a rectangular desk is given by the trinomial $d^2 - 7d - 18$. What are the possible dimensions of the desk? Use factoring.

See Problem 4.

31. **Design** The area of a rectangular rug is given by the trinomial $r^2 - 3r - 4$. What are the possible dimensions of the rug? Use factoring.

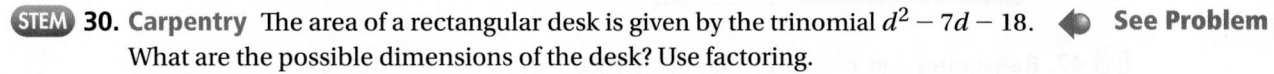

Choose the correct factored form for each expression.

See Problem 5.

32. $k^2 + 5kn - 84n^2$ **A.** $(k - 7n)(k - 12n)$ **B.** $(k - 7n)(k + 12n)$

33. $p^2 - 8pq - 33q^2$ **A.** $(p + 3q)(p - 11q)$ **B.** $(p - 3q)(p + 11q)$

34. $x^2 - 16xy + 48y^2$ **A.** $(x - 4y)(x + 12y)$ **B.** $(x - 4y)(x - 12y)$

Factor each expression.

35. $r^2 + 19rs + 90s^2$ **36.** $g^2 - 12gh + 35h^2$ **37.** $m^2 - 3mn - 28n^2$

38. $x^2 + 3xy - 18y^2$ **39.** $w^2 - 14wz + 40z^2$ **40.** $p^2 + 11pq + 24q^2$

B Apply

41. Writing Suppose you can factor $x^2 + bx + c$ as $(x + p)(x + q)$.
  a. Explain what you know about p and q when $c > 0$.
  b. Explain what you know about p and q when $c < 0$.

42. Error Analysis Describe and correct the error made in factoring the trinomial.

$$x^2 - 10x - 24 = (x - 6)(x - 4)$$

43. Think About a Plan The area of a parallelogram is given by the trinomial $x^2 - 14x + 24$. The base of the parallelogram is $x - 2$. What is an expression for the height of the parallelogram?
  • What is the formula for the area of a parallelogram?
  • How can you tell whether the binomial that represents the height has a positive or negative constant term?

44. Recreation A rectangular skateboard park has an area of $x^2 + 15x + 54$. What are the possible dimensions of the park? Use factoring.

Write the standard form of each polynomial modeled below. Then factor each expression.

45.

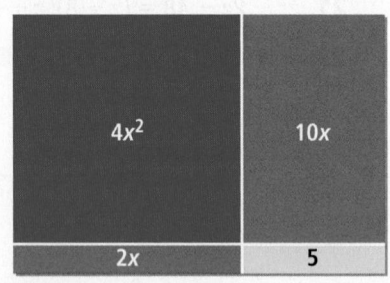

46.

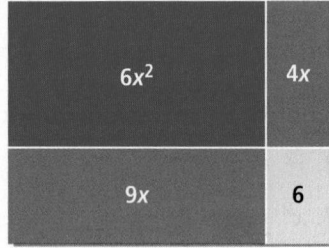

47. Reasoning Let $x^2 - 13x - 30 = (x + p)(x + q)$.
  a. What do you know about the signs of p and q?
  b. Suppose $|p| > |q|$. Which number, p or q, is a negative integer? Explain.

48. Reasoning Let $x^2 + 13x - 30 = (x + p)(x + q)$.
  a. What do you know about the signs of p and q?
  b. Suppose $|p| > |q|$. Which number, p or q, is a negative integer? Explain.

Factor each expression.

49. $x^2 + 27x + 50$

50. $g^2 - 18g + 45$

51. $k^2 - 18k - 63$

52. $d^2 + 30d - 64$

53. $s^2 - 10st - 75t^2$

54. $h^2 + 9hj - 90j^2$

 **Challenge**   Factor each trinomial.

Sample $n^6 + n^3 - 42 = (n^3)^2 + n^3 - 42$
$$= (n^3 - 6)(n^3 + 7)$$

55. $x^{12} + 12x^6 + 35$

56. $t^8 + 5t^4 - 24$

57. $r^6 - 21r^3 + 80$

58. $m^{10} + 18m^5 + 17$

59. $x^{12} - 19x^6 - 120$

60. $p^6 + 14p^3 - 72$

Standardized Test Prep

SAT/ACT

61. What is the factored form of $x^2 + x - 42$?

Ⓐ $(x - 7)(x - 6)$ Ⓑ $(x - 7)(x + 6)$ Ⓒ $(x + 7)(x - 6)$ Ⓓ $(x + 7)(x + 6)$

62. What is the solution of the equation $6x + 7 = 25$?

Ⓕ 2   Ⓖ 3   Ⓗ $5\frac{1}{3}$ Ⓘ 8

63. A museum charges an admission price of $12 per person when you buy tickets online. There is also a $5 charge per order. You spend $65 purchasing p tickets online. Which equation best represents this situation?

Ⓐ $12p + 5 = 65$ Ⓑ $5p + 12 = 65$ Ⓒ $12p - 5 = 65$ Ⓓ $65p + 12 = 5$

Short Response

64. You and your friend bike to school at the rates shown. Who is faster? Show your work.

You: 7 mi/h   Your friend: 11 ft/s

Mixed Review

Simplify each product.   ◀ See Lesson 8-4.

65. $(c + 4)^2$

66. $(2v - 9)^2$

67. $(3w + 7)(3w - 7)$

Solve each equation for x.   ◀ See Lesson 2-5.

68. $\frac{a}{b} = \frac{x}{d}$

69. $8(x - d) = x$

70. $m = \frac{(c + x)}{n}$

Get Ready!   To prepare for Lesson 8-6, do Exercises 71–73.

Find the GCF of the terms of each polynomial.   ◀ See Lesson 8-2.

71. $14x^2 + 7x$

72. $24x^2 - 30x + 12$

73. $6x^3 + 45x^2 + 15$

8-6   Factoring $ax^2 + bx + c$

 Common Core State Standards

A-SSE.A.1a Interpret parts of an expression, such as terms, factors, and coefficients.

MP 1, MP 2, MP 3, MP 4

Objective   To factor trinomials of the form $ax^2 + bx + c$

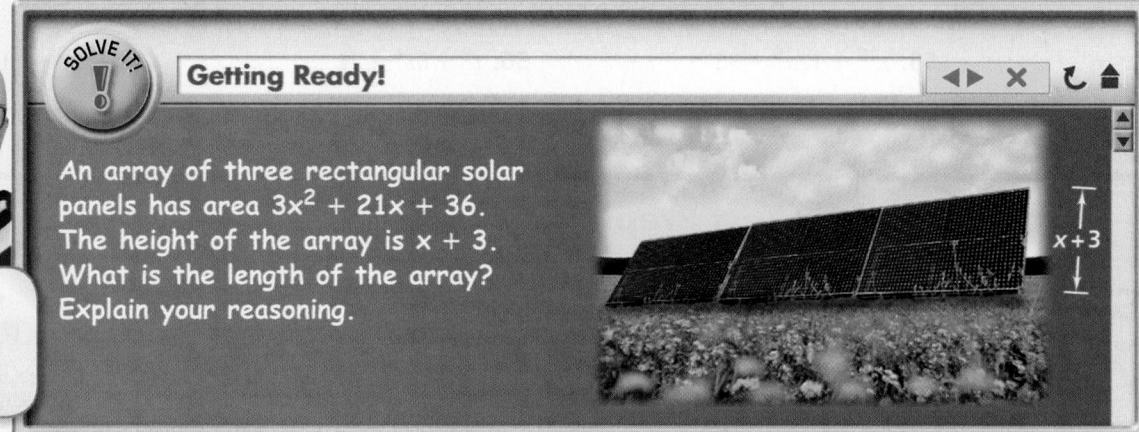

Getting Ready!

An array of three rectangular solar panels has area $3x^2 + 21x + 36$. The height of the array is $x + 3$. What is the length of the array? Explain your reasoning.

You did this for one panel in Lesson 8-5—now there are more.

$x + 3$

Essential Understanding You can write some trinomials of the form $ax^2 + bx + c$ as the product of two binomials.

Consider the trinomial $6x^2 + 23x + 7$. To factor it, think of $23x$ as $2x + 21x$.

$$6x^2 + 23x + 7 = 6x^2 + 2x + 21x + 7 \qquad \text{Rewrite } 23x \text{ as } 2x + 21x.$$
$$= 2x(3x + 1) + 7(3x + 1) \qquad \text{Factor out the GCF of each pair of terms.}$$
$$= (2x + 7)(3x + 1) \qquad \text{Distributive Property}$$

How do you know to rewrite $23x$ as $2x + 21x$? Notice that multiplying 2 and 21 gives 42, which is the product of the x^2-coefficient 6 and the constant term 7. This example suggests that, to factor a trinomial of the form $ax^2 + bx + c$, you should look for factors of the product ac that have a sum of b.

 Problem 1   **Factoring When ac Is Positive**

What is the factored form of $5x^2 + 11x + 2$?

Think

Will the process still work if you write $5x^2 + 10x + x + 2$? Yes. You can rewrite this alternate expression as $5x(x + 2) + (x + 2)$, which equals $(5x + 1)(x + 2)$.

Step 1   Find factors of ac that have sum b. Since $ac = 10$ and $b = 11$, find positive factors of 10 that have sum 11.

Factors of 10	1, 10	2, 5
Sum of Factors	11 ✔	7

Step 2   To factor the trinomial, use the factors you found to rewrite bx.

$$5x^2 + 11x + 2 = 5x^2 + 1x + 10x + 2 \qquad \text{Rewrite } bx: 11x = 1x + 10x.$$
$$= x(5x + 1) + 2(5x + 1) \qquad \text{Factor out the GCF of each pair of terms.}$$
$$= (x + 2)(5x + 1) \qquad \text{Distributive Property}$$

Got It? **1. a.** What is the factored form of $6x^2 + 13x + 5$?

b. Reasoning In $ax^2 + bx + c$, suppose ac is positive and b is negative. What do you know about the factors of ac? Explain.

 Problem 2 Factoring When ac Is Negative

What is the factored form of $3x^2 + 4x - 15$?

Plan

Can you apply the steps for Problem 1 to this problem?
Yes. Your goal is still to find factors of ac that have sum b. Because $ac < 0$, the factors must have different signs.

Step 1 Find factors of ac that have sum b. Since $ac = -45$ and $b = 4$, find factors of -45 that have sum 4.

Factors of −45	1, −45	−1, 45	3, −15	−3, 15	5, −9	−5, 9
Sum of Factors	−44	44	−12	12	−4	4 ✔

Step 2 To factor the trinomial, use the factors you found to rewrite bx.

$3x^2 + 4x - 15 = 3x^2 - 5x + 9x - 15$ Rewrite bx: $4x = -5x + 9x$.

$\qquad\qquad\quad = x(3x - 5) + 3(3x - 5)$ Factor out the GCF of each pair of terms.

$\qquad\qquad\quad = (3x - 5)(x + 3)$ Distributive Property

 Got It? **2.** What is the factored form of $10x^2 + 31x - 14$?

 Problem 3 Applying Trinomial Factoring

Geometry The area of a rectangle is $2x^2 - 13x - 7$. What are the possible dimensions of the rectangle? Use factoring.

Plan

How can you find the dimensions of the rectangle?
Factor the rectangle's area as the product of two binomials, one of which is the width. The other must be the length since area = length · width.

Step 1 Find factors of ac that have sum b. Since $ac = -14$ and $b = -13$, find factors of -14 that have sum -13.

Factors of −14	1, −14	−1, 14	2, −7	−2, 7
Sum of Factors	−13 ✔	13	−5	5

Step 2 To factor the trinomial, use the factors you found to rewrite bx.

$2x^2 - 13x - 7 = 2x^2 + x - 14x - 7$ Rewrite bx: $-13x = x - 14x$.

$\qquad\qquad\quad = x(2x + 1) - 7(2x + 1)$ Factor out the GCF of each pair of terms.

$\qquad\qquad\quad = (2x + 1)(x - 7)$ Distributive Property

The possible dimensions of the rectangle are $2x + 1$ and $x - 7$.

 Got It? **3.** The area of a rectangle is $8x^2 + 22x + 15$. What are the possible dimensions of the rectangle? Use factoring.

To factor a polynomial completely, first factor out the GCF of the polynomial's terms. Then factor the remaining polynomial until it is written as the product of polynomials that cannot be factored further.

 Problem 4 Factoring Out a Monomial First

What is the factored form of $18x^2 - 33x + 12$?

Plan

How can you simplify this problem?
Factor out the GCF of the trinomial's terms. The trinomial that remains is similar to those in Problems 1–3.

Think **Write**

Factor out the GCF.

$$18x^2 - 33x + 12 = 3(6x^2 - 11x + 4)$$

Factor $6x^2 - 11x + 4$. Since $ac = 24$ and $b = -11$, find negative factors of 24 that have sum -11.

Factors of 24	$-1, -24$	$-2, -12$	$-3, -8$	$-4, -6$
Sum of Factors	-25	-14	-11 ✔	-10

Rewrite the term bx. Then use the Distributive Property to finish factoring.

$3(6x^2 - 3x - 8x + 4)$
$3[3x(2x - 1) - 4(2x - 1)]$
$3(3x - 4)(2x - 1)$

 Got It? **4.** What is the factored form of $8x^2 - 36x - 20$?

 Lesson Check

Do you know HOW?

Factor each expression.

1. $3x^2 + 16x + 5$

2. $10q^2 + 9q + 2$

3. $4w^2 + 4w - 3$

4. The area of a rectangle is $6x^2 - 11x - 72$. What are the possible dimensions of the rectangle? Use factoring.

Do you UNDERSTAND?  MATHEMATICAL PRACTICES

5. Reasoning Explain why you cannot factor the trinomial $2x^2 + 7x + 10$.

6. Reasoning To factor $8x^2 + bx + 3$, a student correctly rewrites the trinomial as $8x^2 + px + qx + 3$. What is the value of pq?

7. Compare and Contrast How is factoring a trinomial $ax^2 + bx + c$ when $a \neq 1$ different from factoring a trinomial when $a = 1$? How is it similar?

 **Practice and Problem-Solving Exercises**  MATHEMATICAL PRACTICES

A Practice Factor each expression.

See Problem 1.

8. $2x^2 + 13x + 6$

9. $3d^2 + 23d + 14$

10. $4n^2 - 8n + 3$

11. $4p^2 + 7p + 3$

12. $6r^2 - 23r + 20$

13. $8g^2 - 14g + 3$

Factor each expression.

See Problem 2.

14. $5z^2 + 19z - 4$

15. $2k^2 - 13k - 24$

16. $6t^2 + 7t - 5$

17. $3x^2 + 23x - 36$

18. $4w^2 - 5w - 6$

19. $4d^2 - 4d - 35$

20. Interior Design The area of a rectangular kitchen tile is $8x^2 + 30x + 7$. What are the possible dimensions of the tile? Use factoring.

See Problem 3.

21. Crafts The area of a rectangular knitted blanket is $15x^2 - 14x - 8$. What are the possible dimensions of the blanket? Use factoring.

Factor each expression completely.

See Problem 4.

22. $12p^2 + 20p - 8$

23. $8v^2 + 34v - 30$

24. $6s^2 + 57s + 72$

25. $20w^2 - 45w + 10$

26. $12x^2 - 46x - 8$

27. $9r^2 + 3r - 30$

B Apply  **Open-Ended** Find two different values that complete each expression so that the trinomial can be factored into the product of two binomials. Factor your trinomials.

28. $4s^2 + \blacksquare s + 10$

29. $15v^2 + \blacksquare v - 24$

30. $35m^2 + \blacksquare m - 16$

31. $9g^2 + \blacksquare g + 4$

32. $6n^2 + \blacksquare n + 28$

33. $8r^2 + \blacksquare r - 42$

34. Error Analysis Describe and correct the error made in factoring the expression at the right.

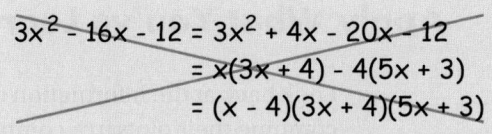

$$3x^2 - 16x - 12 = 3x^2 + 4x - 20x - 12$$
$$= x(3x + 4) - 4(5x + 3)$$
$$= (x - 4)(3x + 4)(5x + 3)$$

35. Think About a Plan A triangle has area $9x^2 - 9x - 10$. The base of the triangle is $3x - 5$. What is the height of the triangle?

- What is the formula for the area of a triangle?
- How does factoring the given trinomial help you solve the problem?

STEM 36. Carpentry The top of a rectangular table has an area of $18x^2 + 69x + 60$. The width of the table is $3x + 4$. What is the length of the table?

37. a. Write each area as a product of two binomials.

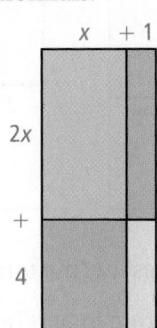

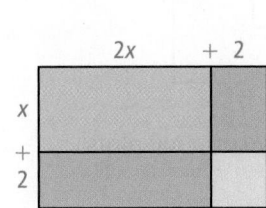

b. Are the products equal?

c. Writing Explain how the two products you found in part (a) can equal the same trinomial.

Factor each expression.

38. $54x^2 + 87x + 28$

39. $66k^2 + 57k + 12$

40. $14z^2 - 53z + 14$

41. $28h^2 + 28h - 56$

42. $21y^2 + 72y - 48$

43. $55n^2 - 52n + 12$

44. $36p^2 + 114p - 20$

45. $63g^2 - 89g + 30$

46. $99v^2 - 92v + 9$

47. Reasoning If a and c in $ax^2 + bx + c$ are prime numbers and the trinomial is factorable, how many positive values are possible for b? Explain your reasoning.

 Challenge **Factor each expression.**

48. $56x^3 + 43x^2 + 5x$

49. $49p^2 + 63pq - 36q^2$

50. $108g^2h - 162gh + 54h$

51. The graph of the function $y = x^2 + 5x + 6$ is shown at the right.
  a. What are the x-intercepts?
  b. Factor $x^2 + 5x + 6$.
  c. Reasoning Describe the relationship between the binomial factors you found in part (b) and the x-intercepts.

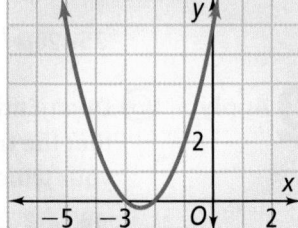

Apply What You've Learned

MATHEMATICAL PRACTICES

MP 7

Look back at the information on page 485 about Kelly's and Roberto's plan to combine their plots in a community garden. Kelly's and Roberto's plans for their original plots are shown again below. In the Apply What You've Learned in Lesson 8-3, you wrote trinomials for the area of Kelly's original plot and the area of Roberto's original plot.

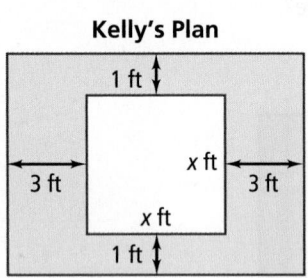

Kelly's Plan

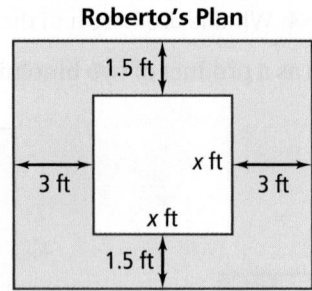

Roberto's Plan

a. Write a trinomial that represents the total area of the two original plots.

b. Factor the trinomial you wrote in part (a).

c. What do the factors in your answer to part (b) represent in relation to the new plot? Explain how you know.

Objective To factor perfect-square trinomials and the differences of two squares

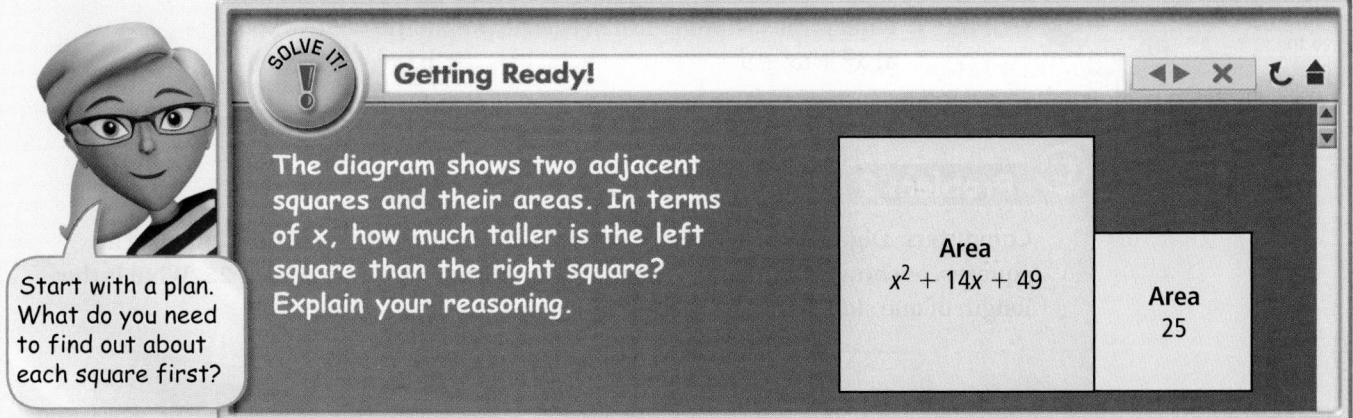

SOLVE IT!

Getting Ready!

The diagram shows two adjacent squares and their areas. In terms of x, how much taller is the left square than the right square? Explain your reasoning.

Area
$x^2 + 14x + 49$

Area
25

Start with a plan. What do you need to find out about each square first?

MATHEMATICAL
PRACTICES

Essential Understanding You can factor some trinomials by "reversing" the rules for multiplying special case binomials that you learned in Lesson 8-4.

For example, recall the rules for finding squares of binomials.

$$(a + b)^2 = (a + b)(a + b) = a^2 + 2ab + b^2$$

$$(a - b)^2 = (a - b)(a - b) = a^2 - 2ab + b^2$$

Any trinomial of the form $a^2 + 2ab + b^2$ or $a^2 - 2ab + b^2$ is a **perfect-square trinomial** because it is the result of squaring a binomial. Reading the equations above from right to left gives you rules for factoring perfect-square trinomials.

Lesson Vocabulary
- perfect-square trinomial
- difference of two squares

take note

Key Concept   Factoring Perfect-Square Trinomials

Algebra   For every real number a and b:

$$a^2 + 2ab + b^2 = (a + b)(a + b) = (a + b)^2$$
$$a^2 - 2ab + b^2 = (a - b)(a - b) = (a - b)^2$$

Examples $x^2 + 8x + 16 = (x + 4)(x + 4) = (x + 4)^2$

$4n^2 - 12n + 9 = (2n - 3)(2n - 3) = (2n - 3)^2$

Here is how to recognize a perfect-square trinomial:

- The first and the last terms are perfect squares.
- The middle term is twice the product of one factor from the first term and one factor from the last term.

Will the answer have the form $(a + b)^2$ or $(a - b)^2$?
The middle term $-12x$ has a negative coefficient, so the factored expression will have the form $(a - b)^2$.

What is the factored form of $x^2 - 12x + 36$?

$$x^2 - 12x + 36 = x^2 - 12x + 6^2 \qquad \text{Write the last term as a square.}$$
$$= x^2 - 2(x)(6) + 6^2 \qquad \text{Does middle term equal } -2ab? \ -12x = -2(x)(6) \ ✔$$
$$= (x - 6)^2 \qquad \text{Write as the square of a binomial.}$$

Got It? **1.** What is the factored form of each expression?
  a. $x^2 + 6x + 9$ **b.** $x^2 - 14x + 49$

 Problem 2 Factoring to Find a Length **STEM**

Computers Digital images are composed of thousands of tiny pixels rendered as squares, as shown below. Suppose the area of a pixel is $4x^2 + 20x + 25$. What is the length of one side of the pixel?

One Pixel
$A = 4x^2 + 20x + 25$

How can you find the side length?
Since the pixel's area is its side length squared, factor the expression for area as the square of a binomial. The binomial is the side length.

$$4x^2 + 20x + 25 = (2x)^2 + 20x + 5^2 \qquad \text{Write first and last terms as squares.}$$
$$= (2x)^2 + 2(2x)(5) + 5^2 \qquad \text{Does middle term equal } 2ab? \ 20x = 2(2x)(5) \ ✔$$
$$= (2x + 5)^2 \qquad \text{Write as the square of a binomial.}$$

The length of one side of the pixel is $2x + 5$.

Got It? **2.** You are building a square patio. The area of the patio is $16m^2 - 72m + 81$. What is the length of one side of the patio?

Recall from Lesson 8-4 that $(a + b)(a - b) = a^2 - b^2$. So you can factor a **difference of two squares,** $a^2 - b^2$, as $(a + b)(a - b)$.

Key Concept Factoring a Difference of Two Squares

Algebra   For all real numbers a and b:
$$a^2 - b^2 = (a + b)(a - b)$$

Examples $x^2 - 64 = (x + 8)(x - 8)$
$25x^2 - 36 = (5x + 6)(5x - 6)$

 Problem 3   **Factoring a Difference of Two Squares**

What is the factored form of $z^2 - 9$?

Plan

Can you use the rule for the difference of two squares?
Yes. The binomial is a difference *and* both its terms are perfect squares.

Think

Rewrite 9 as a square.

Factor using the rule for a difference of two squares.

Check your answer by multiplying the factored form.

Write

$z^2 - 9 = z^2 - 3^2$

$= (z + 3)(z - 3)$

$(z + 3)(z - 3) = z^2 - 3z + 3z - 9$
$= z^2 - 9$ ✔

Got It?   **3.** What is the factored form of each expression?
   a. $v^2 - 100$ **b.** $s^2 - 16$

 Problem 4   **Factoring a Difference of Two Squares**

Think

When is a term of the form ax^2 a perfect square?
ax^2 is a perfect square when a is a perfect square. For example, $16x^2$ is a perfect square but $17x^2$ is not.

What is the factored form of $16x^2 - 81$?

$16x^2 - 81 = (4x)^2 - 9^2$ Write each term as a square.

$= (4x + 9)(4x - 9)$ Use the rule for the difference of squares.

Got It?   **4. a.** What is the factored form of $25d^2 - 64$?
    b. Reasoning The expression $25d^2 + 64$ contains two perfect squares. Can you use the method in Problem 4 to factor it? Explain your reasoning.

When you factor out the GCF of a polynomial, sometimes the expression that remains is a perfect-square trinomial or the difference of two squares. You can then factor this expression further using the rules from this lesson.

 Problem 5 Factoring Out a Common Factor

What is the factored form of $24g^2 - 6$?

$$24g^2 - 6 = 6(4g^2 - 1) \qquad \text{Factor out the GCF, 6.}$$
$$= 6[(2g)^2 - 1^2] \qquad \text{Write the difference as } a^2 - b^2.$$
$$= 6(2g + 1)(2g - 1) \quad \text{Use the rule for the difference of squares.}$$

Got It? **5.** What is the factored form of each expression?

    a. $12t^2 - 48$ **b.** $12x^2 + 12x + 3$

Lesson Check

Do you know HOW?

Factor each expression.

1. $y^2 - 16y + 64$

2. $9q^2 + 12q + 4$

3. $p^2 - 36$

4. The area of a square is $36w^2 + 60w + 25$. What is the side length of the square?

Do you UNDERSTAND?

Identify the rule you would use to factor each expression.

5. $81r^2 - 90r + 25$

6. $k^2 + 12k + 36$

7. $9h^2 - 64$

8. Reasoning Explain how to determine whether a binomial is a difference of two squares.

Practice and Problem-Solving Exercises 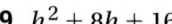 MATHEMATICAL PRACTICES

Practice   Factor each expression.   **See Problems 1 and 2.**

    9. $h^2 + 8h + 16$ **10.** $v^2 - 10v + 25$ **11.** $d^2 - 20d + 100$

    12. $m^2 + 18m + 81$ **13.** $q^2 + 2q + 1$ **14.** $p^2 - 4p + 4$

    15. $64x^2 + 112x + 49$ **16.** $4r^2 + 36r + 81$ **17.** $9n^2 - 42n + 49$

    18. $36s^2 - 60s + 25$ **19.** $25z^2 + 40z + 16$ **20.** $49g^2 - 84g + 36$

The given expression represents the area. Find the side length of the square.

21.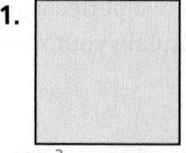

$100r^2 - 220r + 121$

22.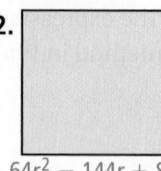

$64r^2 - 144r + 81$

23.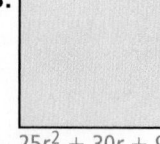

$25r^2 + 30r + 9$

Factor each expression. See Problems 3–5.

24. $w^2 - 144$ **25.** $a^2 - 49$ **26.** $y^2 - 121$

27. $t^2 - 25$ **28.** $k^2 - 64$ **29.** $m^2 - 225$

30. $4p^2 - 49$ **31.** $81r^2 - 1$ **32.** $36v^2 - 25$

33. $64q^2 - 81$ **34.** $16x^2 - 121$ **35.** $9n^2 - 400$

36. $2h^2 - 2$ **37.** $27w^2 - 12$ **38.** $80g^2 - 45$

 **Apply**

39. Rewrite the expression $x^4 - y^4$ so that it is a difference of squares. Then factor the expression completely.

40. Error Analysis Describe and correct the error made in factoring.

$$\cancel{9x^2 - 49 = (9x + 7)(9x - 7)}$$

41. Writing Summarize the procedure for factoring a difference of two squares. Give at least two examples.

42. Think About a Plan Two square windows and their areas are shown at the right. What is an expression that represents the difference of the areas of the windows? Show two different ways to find the solution.
- How can you solve the problem without factoring?
- How can you use the factored forms of the areas to find the difference of the areas of the windows?

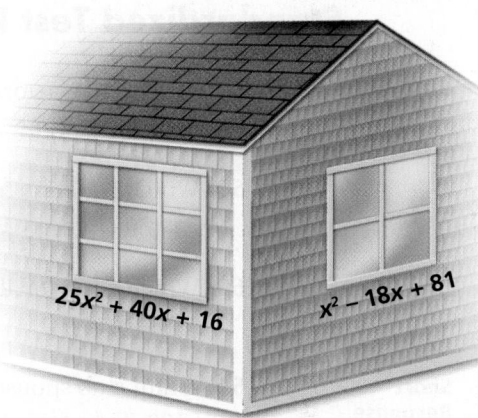

$25x^2 + 40x + 16$ $x^2 - 18x + 81$

43. Interior Design A square rug has an area of $49x^2 - 56x + 16$. A second square rug has an area of $16x^2 + 24x + 9$. What is an expression that represents the difference of the areas of the rugs? Show two different ways to find the solution.

Mental Math For Exercises 44–48, find a pair of factors for each number by using the difference of two squares.

Sample	$117 = 121 - 4$	Write 117 as the difference of two squares.
	$= 11^2 - 2^2$	Write each term as a square.
	$= (11 + 2)(11 - 2)$	Use the rule for the difference of squares.
	$= (13)(9)$	Simplify.

44. 143 **45.** 99 **46.** 224 **47.** 84 **48.** 91

49. a. Open-Ended Write an expression that is a perfect-square trinomial.
b. Explain how you know your trinomial is a perfect-square trinomial.

 **50. a.** Factor $4x^2 - 100$ by removing the common monomial factor and then using the difference-of-squares rule to factor the remaining expression.

   b. Factor $4x^2 - 100$ by using the difference-of-squares rule and removing the common monomial factors.

   c. Reasoning Why can you factor $4x^2 - 100$ in two different ways?

   d. Can you factor $3x^2 - 75$ in the two ways you factored $4x^2 - 100$ in parts (a) and (b)? Explain your answer.

 Challenge Factor each expression.

51. $64r^6 - 144r^3 + 81$ **52.** $p^6 + 40p^3q + 400q^2$ **53.** $36m^4 + 84m^2 + 49$

54. $108n^6 - 147$ **55.** $x^{20} - 4x^{10}y^5 + 4y^{10}$ **56.** $256g^4 - 100h^6$

57. The binomial $16 - 81n^4$ can be factored twice using the difference-of-squares rule.

   a. Factor $16 - 81n^4$ completely.

   b. Reasoning What characteristics do 16 and $81n^4$ share that make this possible?

   c. Open-Ended Write another binomial that can be factored twice using the difference of squares rule.

Standardized Test Prep

SAT/ACT

58. What is the factored form of $4x^2 - 20x + 25$?

   Ⓐ $(2x + 5)(2x - 5)$ Ⓑ $(2x - 5)(2x - 5)$ Ⓒ $(4x - 5)(4x - 5)$ Ⓓ $(4x + 5)(4x - 5)$

59. Which equation has -2 as its solution?

   Ⓕ $x + 3 = 2x + 1$ Ⓖ $x - 5 = 2x - 7$ Ⓗ $2x + 5 = 5x + 11$ Ⓘ $3x + 1 = x - 5$

60. Which equation illustrates the Commutative Property of Multiplication?

   Ⓐ $ab = ba$ Ⓑ $a(bc) = (ab)c$ Ⓒ $ab = ab$ Ⓓ $a(b + c) = ab + ac$

Short Response

61. A film club sponsors a film fest at a local movie theater. Renting the theater costs $190. The admission is $2 per person.

   a. Write an equation that relates the film club's total cost c and the number of people p who attend the film fest.

   b. Graph the equation you wrote in part (a).

Mixed Review

Factor each expression.   ◀ **See Lesson 8-6.**

62. $18x^2 + 9x - 14$ **63.** $8x^2 + 18x + 9$ **64.** $12x^2 - 41x + 35$

Get Ready!   **To prepare for Lesson 8-8, do Exercises 65–67.**

Find the GCF of the terms of each polynomial.   ◀ **See Lesson 8-2.**

65. $6t^2 + 12t - 4$ **66.** $9m^3 + 15m^2 - 21m$ **67.** $16h^4 - 12h^3 - 36h^2$

Factoring by Grouping

© Common Core State Standards

A-SSE.A.1a Interpret parts of an expression, such as terms, factors, and coefficients. **Also A-SSE.A.1b, A-SSE.A.2**

MP 1, MP 2, MP 3, MP 4, MP 7

Objective To factor higher-degree polynomials by grouping

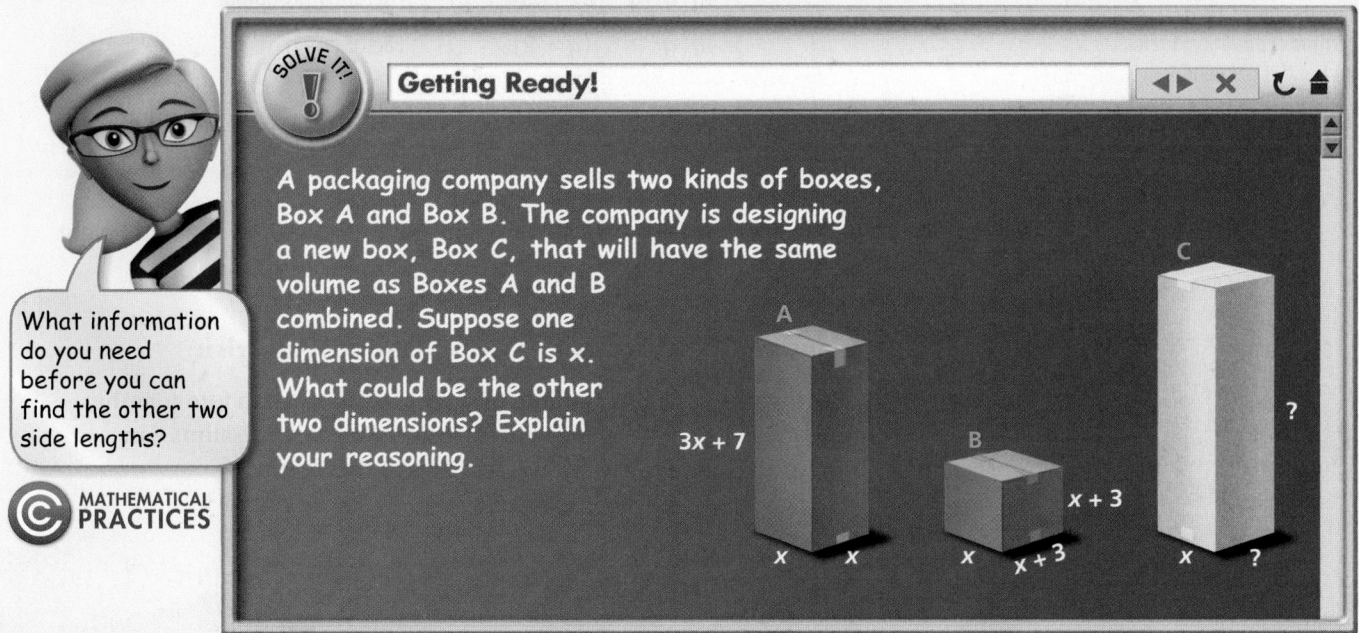

SOLVE IT!

Getting Ready!

A packaging company sells two kinds of boxes, Box A and Box B. The company is designing a new box, Box C, that will have the same volume as Boxes A and B combined. Suppose one dimension of Box C is x. What could be the other two dimensions? Explain your reasoning.

A
$3x + 7$
x x

B
$x + 3$
x $x + 3$

C
?
x ?

What information do you need before you can find the other two side lengths?

© MATHEMATICAL PRACTICES

Lesson Vocabulary
• factoring by grouping

Essential Understanding Some polynomials of a degree greater than 2 can be factored.

In Lesson 8-6, you factored trinomials of the form $ax^2 + bx + c$ by rewriting bx as a sum of two monomials. You then grouped the terms in pairs, factored the GCF from each pair, and looked for a common binomial factor. This process is called **factoring by grouping.** You can extend this technique to higher-degree polynomials.

Plan

How should you group the terms of the polynomial?
First group the two terms with the highest degrees. If that doesn't work, try another grouping. Your goal is to find a common binomial factor.

© Problem 1 Factoring a Cubic Polynomial

What is the factored form of $3n^3 - 12n^2 + 2n - 8$?

$$3n^3 - 12n^2 + 2n - 8 = 3n^2(n - 4) + 2(n - 4)$$ Factor out the GCF of each group of two terms.

$$= (3n^2 + 2)(n - 4)$$ Factor out the common factor $n - 4$.

Check $(3n^2 + 2)(n - 4) = 3n^3 - 12n^2 + 2n - 8$ ✔

Got It? **1. a.** What is the factored form of $8t^3 + 14t^2 + 20t + 35$?

© b. Reasoning How is the factoring method used in Problem 1 like the method used in Lesson 8-6? How is it different?

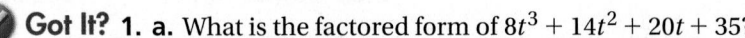

Before factoring by grouping, you may need to factor out the GCF of all the terms.

Problem 2 Factoring a Polynomial Completely

Think

Do the terms share any numerical or variable factors?
Yes. The terms have a common numerical factor of 4 and a common variable factor of q. The GCF is $4q$.

What is the factored form of $4q^4 - 8q^3 + 12q^2 - 24q$? Factor completely.

$$4q^4 - 8q^3 + 12q^2 - 24q = 4q(q^3 - 2q^2 + 3q - 6) \qquad \text{Factor out the GCF.}$$
$$= 4q[q^2(q - 2) + 3(q - 2)] \qquad \text{Factor by grouping.}$$
$$= 4q(q^2 + 3)(q - 2) \qquad \text{Factor again.}$$

Got It? 2. What is the factored form of $6h^4 + 9h^3 + 12h^2 + 18h$? Factor completely.

You can sometimes factor to find possible expressions for the length, width, and height of a rectangular prism.

Problem 3 Finding the Dimensions of a Rectangular Prism

Entertainment The toy shown below is made of several bars that can fold together to form a rectangular prism or unfold to form a "ladder." What expressions can represent the dimensions of the toy when it is folded up? Use factoring.

$$V = 6x^3 + 19x^2 + 15x$$

Plan

How can you find the prism's dimensions?
Factor the cubic expression for the volume of the prism as the product of three linear expressions. Each linear expression is a dimension.

Step 1 Factor out the GCF.
$$6x^3 + 19x^2 + 15x = x(6x^2 + 19x + 15)$$

Step 2 To factor the trinomial, find factors of ac that have sum b.
Since $ac = 90$ and $b = 19$, find factors of 90 that have sum 19.

Factors of 90	1, 90	2, 45	3, 30	5, 18	6, 15	9, 10
Sum of Factors	91	47	33	23	21	19 ✔

Step 3 To factor the trinomial, use the factors you found to rewrite bx.
$$x(6x^2 + 19x + 15) = x(6x^2 + 9x + 10x + 15) \qquad \text{Rewrite } bx: 19x = 9x + 10x.$$
$$= x[3x(2x + 3) + 5(2x + 3)] \qquad \text{Factor by grouping.}$$
$$= x(3x + 5)(2x + 3) \qquad \text{Distributive Property}$$

The possible dimensions are x, $3x + 5$, and $2x + 3$.

Got It? **3. Geometry** A rectangular prism has volume $60x^3 + 34x^2 + 4x$. What expressions can represent the dimensions of the prism? Use factoring.

Here is a summary of what to remember as you factor polynomials.

take note

Summary   Factoring Polynomials

1. Factor out the greatest common factor (GCF).

2. If the polynomial has two terms or three terms, look for a difference of two squares, a perfect-square trinomial, or a pair of binomial factors.

3. If the polynomial has four or more terms, group terms and factor to find common binomial factors.

4. As a final check, make sure there are no common factors other than 1.

 ## Lesson Check

Do you know HOW?

Factor each expression.

1. $20r^3 + 8r^2 + 15r + 6$

2. $6d^3 + 3d^2 - 10d - 5$

3. $24x^3 + 60x^2 + 36x + 90$

4. A rectangular prism has a volume of $36x^3 + 36x^2 + 8x$. What expressions can represent the dimensions of the prism? Use factoring.

Do you UNDERSTAND?

**Vocabulary** Tell whether you would factor the polynomial by grouping. Explain your answer.

5. $x^2 - 6x + 9$

6. $4w^2 + 23w + 15$

7. $24t^3 - 42t^2 - 28t + 49$

8. Reasoning Can you factor the polynomial $6q^3 + 2q^2 + 12q - 3$ by grouping? Explain.

 ## Practice and Problem-Solving Exercises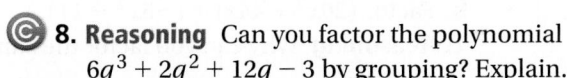

**Practice**   Find the GCF of the first two terms and the GCF of the last two terms for each polynomial.

See Problem 1.

9. $2z^3 + 6z^2 + 3z + 9$

10. $10g^3 - 25g^2 + 4g - 10$

11. $2r^3 + 12r^2 - 5r - 30$

12. $6p^3 + 3p^2 + 2p + 1$

Factor each expression.

13. $15q^3 + 40q^2 + 3q + 8$

14. $14y^3 + 8y^2 + 7y + 4$

15. $14z^3 - 35z^2 + 16z - 40$

16. $11w^3 - 9w^2 + 11w - 9$

17. $8m^3 + 12m^2 - 2m - 3$

18. $12k^3 - 27k^2 - 40k + 90$

19. $20v^3 + 24v^2 - 25v - 30$

20. $18h^3 + 45h^2 - 8h - 20$

21. $12y^3 + 4y^2 - 9y - 3$

Factor completely.

◀ **See Problem 2.**

22. $8p^3 - 32p^2 + 28p - 112$ **23.** $3w^4 - 2w^3 + 18w^2 - 12w$ **24.** $5g^4 - 5g^3 + 20g^2 - 20g$

25. $6q^4 + 3q^3 - 24q^2 - 12q$ **26.** $36v^3 - 126v^2 + 48v - 168$ **27.** $4d^3 - 6d^2 + 16d - 24$

Find expressions for the possible dimensions of each rectangular prism.

◀ **See Problem 3.**

28.

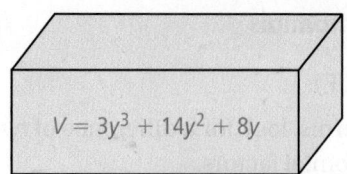

$V = 3y^3 + 14y^2 + 8y$

29.

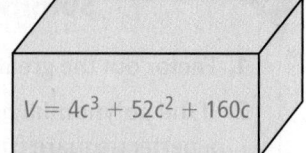

$V = 4c^3 + 52c^2 + 160c$

STEM **30. Carpentry** A trunk in the shape of a rectangular prism has a volume of $6x^3 + 38x^2 - 28x$. What expressions can represent the dimensions of the trunk?

Ⓑ Apply **Factor completely.**

31. $9t^3 - 90t^2 + 144t$ **32.** $60y^4 - 300y^3 - 42y^2 + 210y$

33. $8m^3 + 32m^2 + 40m + 160$ **34.** $10p^2 - 5pq - 180q^2$

Ⓒ **35. Error Analysis** Describe and correct the error made in factoring completely.

$$4x^4 + 12x^3 + 8x^2 + 24x = 4(x^4 + 3x^3 + 2x^2 + 6x)$$
$$= 4[x^3(x + 3) + 2x(x + 3)]$$
$$= 4(x^3 + 2x)(x + 3)$$

Ⓒ **36. a.** Factor $(20x^3 - 5x^2) + (44x - 11)$.
   b. Factor $(20x^3 + 44x) + (-5x^2 - 11)$.
   c. Reasoning Why can you factor the same polynomial using different pairs of terms?

Ⓒ **37. Writing** Describe how to factor the expression $6x^5 + 4x^4 + 12x^3 + 8x^2 + 9x + 6$.

Ⓒ **38. Think About a Plan** Bat houses, such as the one at the right, are large wooden structures that people mount on buildings to attract bats. What expressions can represent the dimensions of the bat house?
   • Into how many factors should you factor the expression for the volume?
   • What is the first step in factoring this expression?

Ⓒ **39. Open-Ended** Write a four-term polynomial that you can factor by grouping. Factor your polynomial.

40. Art The pedestal of a sculpture is a rectangular prism with a volume of $63x^3 - 28x$. What expressions can represent the dimensions of the pedestal? Use factoring.

$V = 4x^3 + 22x^2 + 24x$

Factor by grouping.

41. $y^3 + 11y^2 - 4y - 44$ **42.** $p^2m + p^2n^5 + qm + qn^5$ **43.** $30g^5 + 24g^3h - 35g^2h^2 - 28h^3$

44. Geometry The polynomial $2\pi x^3 + 12\pi x^2 + 18\pi x$ represents the volume of a cylinder. The formula for the volume V of a cylinder with radius r and height h is $V = \pi r^2 h$.

     a. Factor $2\pi x^3 + 12\pi x^2 + 18\pi x$.

     b. Based on your answer to part (a), write an expression for a possible radius of the cylinder.

You can write the number 63 as $2^5 + 2^4 + 2^3 + 2^2 + 2^1 + 2^0$. For Exercises 45 and 46, factor each expression by grouping. Then simplify the powers of 2 to write 63 as the product of two numbers.

45. $\left(2^5 + 2^4 + 2^3\right) + \left(2^2 + 2^1 + 2^0\right)$ **46.** $\left(2^5 + 2^4\right) + \left(2^3 + 2^2\right) + \left(2^1 + 2^0\right)$

Standardized Test Prep

SAT/ACT

47. What is $30z^3 - 12z^2 + 120z - 48$ factored completely?

     Ⓐ $2(15z^3 - 6z^2 + 60z - 24)$ Ⓒ $6(5z^3 - 2z^2 + 20z - 8)$

     Ⓑ $(6z^2 + 24)(5z - 2)$ Ⓓ $6(z^2 + 4)(5z - 2)$

48. What is the simplified form of $2x^3 \cdot x^8$?

     Ⓕ $2x^{11}$ Ⓖ $8x^{11}$ Ⓗ $2x^{24}$ Ⓘ $8x^{24}$

49. Which equation represents the line with slope -3 that passes through $(2, 5)$?

     Ⓐ $y = -3x + 17$ Ⓑ $y = -3x + 11$ Ⓒ $y = 4x - 3$ Ⓓ $y = x - 3$

50. What is the solution of the inequality $7 < -2x + 5$?

     Ⓕ $x > -1$ Ⓖ $x < -1$ Ⓗ $x > 1$ Ⓘ $x < 1$

Short Response

51. Factor $10r^4 + 30r^3 + 5r^2 + 15r$ completely. Show your work.

Mixed Review

Factor each expression.   ◀ **See Lesson 8-7.**

52. $m^2 + 12m + 36$ **53.** $64x^2 - 144x + 81$ **54.** $49p^2 - 4$

Use a mapping diagram to determine whether each relation is a function.   ◀ **See Lesson 4-6.**

55. $\{(4, 3), (3, 4), (4, 7), (7, 4)\}$ **56.** $\{(-1, 8), (1, 8), (3, 8), (5, 8)\}$ **57.** $\{(2, 7), (4, -7), (6, 7), (8, -7)\}$

Get Ready!   To prepare for Lesson 9-1, do Exercises 58–61.

Use the slope and y-intercept to graph each equation.   ◀ **See Lesson 5-3.**

58. $y = \frac{1}{2}x + 3$ **59.** $y = -4x - 1$ **60.** $y = 2x - 3$ **61.** $y = -\frac{5}{3}x + 2$

Pull It All Together

Completing the Performance Task

> To solve these problems you will pull together many concepts and skills that you have studied about polynomials and factoring.

Look back at your results from the Apply What You've Learned sections in Lessons 8-1, 8-3, and 8-6. Use the work you did to complete the following.

1. Solve the problem in the Task Description on page 485 by drawing and labeling a sketch of the new flower bed and border. Include expressions for the length and width of the new plot. Each expression must be a linear polynomial with integer coefficients. Show all your work and explain each step of your solution.

© **2. Reflect** Choose one of the Mathematical Practices below and explain how you applied it in your work on the Performance Task.

MP 2: Reason abstractly and quantitatively.

MP 3: Construct viable arguments and critique the reasoning of others.

MP 6: Attend to precision.

MP 7: Look for and make use of structure.

On Your Own

Three members of the community garden design the plots shown below. Each plan shows a flower bed inside a rectangular border.

DeShawn's Plan

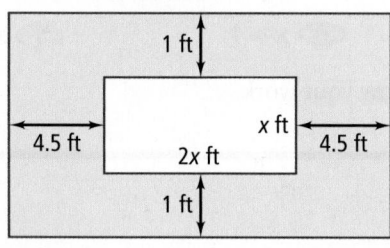

Christy's Plan

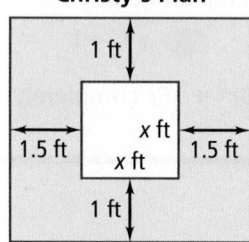

Nick's Plan

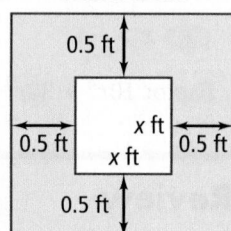

The three members decide to combine their plots to make one large rectangular plot. They plan to place the three flower beds together to make one $2x$ ft-by-$2x$ ft square flower bed, centered inside a rectangular border. The area of the new plot will equal the sum of the areas of the three original plots.

Draw and label a sketch of the new flower bed and border. Include expressions for the length and width of the new plot. Each expression must be a linear polynomial with integer coefficients.

Connecting BIG ideas and Answering the Essential Questions

1 Equivalence
You can represent algebraic expressions in many ways. When you add, subtract, multiply, divide, and factor polynomials, you replace one expression with an equivalent expression.

Adding and Subtracting Polynomials (Lesson 8-1)
$$\left(3x^2 + 4x + 1\right) + \left(2x^2 + 5x + 8\right)$$
$$= \left(3x^2 + 2x^2\right) + (4x + 5x) + (1 + 8)$$
$$= 5x^2 + 9x + 9$$

Multiplying Binomials (Lesson 8-3)
$$(m + 4)(2m - 5) = 2m^2 - 5m + 8m - 20$$
$$= 2m^2 + 3m - 20$$

Multiplying Special Cases (Lesson 8-4)
$$(2x + 3)(2x - 3) = 4x^2 - 9$$

2 Properties
The properties of real numbers are the basis of the laws of algebra. You can apply properties of real numbers, such as the Distributive Property, to polynomials.

Factoring Trinomials (Lessons 8-5 and 8-6)
$$x^2 - 6x + 8 = (x - 2)(x - 4)$$

Factoring Special Cases (Lesson 8-7)
$$49p^2 - 16 = (7p + 4)(7p - 4)$$

Factoring by Grouping (Lesson 8-8)
$$3x^2 - 10x - 8 = 3x^2 - 12x + 2x - 8$$
$$= \left(3x^2 - 12x\right) + \left(2x - 8\right)$$
$$= 3x(x - 4) + 2(x - 4)$$
$$= (3x + 2)(x - 4)$$

Chapter Vocabulary

- binomial (p. 487)
- degree of a monomial (p. 486)
- degree of a polynomial (p. 487)
- difference of two squares (p. 525)
- factoring by grouping (p. 529)
- monomial (p. 486)
- perfect-square trinomial (p. 523)
- polynomial (p. 487)
- standard form of a polynomial (p. 487)
- trinomial (p. 487)

Choose the correct term to complete each sentence.

1. A polynomial that has two terms is a(n) _?_ .

2. A monomial or the sum of two or more monomials is a(n) _?_ .

3. A(n) _?_ is an expression that is a number, a variable, or a product of a number and one or more variables.

4. A polynomial that is the product of two identical binomial factors is a(n) _?_ .

5. The sum of the exponents of the variables in a monomial is the _?_ .

8-1 Adding and Subtracting Polynomials

Quick Review

A **monomial** is a number, a variable, or a product of a number and one or more variables. A **polynomial** is a monomial or the sum of two or more monomials. The **degree of a polynomial** in one variable is the same as the degree of the monomial with the greatest exponent. To add two polynomials, add the like terms of the polynomials. To subtract a polynomial, add the opposite of the polynomial.

Example

What is the difference of $3x^3 - 7x^2 + 5$ and $2x^2 - 9x - 1$?

$$\left(3x^3 - 7x^2 + 5\right) - \left(2x^2 - 9x - 1\right)$$
$$= 3x^3 - 7x^2 + 5 - 2x^2 + 9x + 1$$
$$= 3x^3 + \left(-7x^2 - 2x^2\right) + 9x + (1 + 5)$$
$$= 3x^3 - 9x^2 + 9x + 6$$

Exercises

Write each polynomial in standard form. Then name each polynomial based on its degree and number of terms.

6. $4r + 3 - 9r^2 + 7r$ **7.** $3 + b^3 + b^2$

8. $3 + 8t^2$ **9.** $n^3 + 4n^5 + n - n^3$

10. $7x^2 + 8 + 6x - 7x^2$ **11.** p^3q^3

Simplify. Write each answer in standard form.

12. $\left(2v^3 - v + 8\right) + \left(-v^3 + v - 3\right)$

13. $\left(6s^4 + 7s^2 + 7\right) + \left(8s^4 - 11s^2 + 9s\right)$

14. $\left(4h^3 + 3h + 1\right) - \left(-5h^3 + 6h - 2\right)$

15. $\left(8z^3 - 3z^2 - 7\right) - \left(z^3 - z^2 + 9\right)$

8-2 Multiplying and Factoring

Quick Review

You can multiply a monomial and a polynomial using the Distributive Property. You can factor a polynomial by finding the greatest common factor (GCF) of the terms of the polynomial.

Example

What is the factored form of $10y^4 - 12y^3 + 4y^2$?

First find the GCF of the terms of the polynomial.

$$10y^4 = 2 \cdot 5 \cdot y \cdot y \cdot y \cdot y$$
$$12y^3 = 2 \cdot 2 \cdot 3 \cdot y \cdot y \cdot y$$
$$4y^2 = 2 \cdot 2 \cdot y \cdot y$$

The GCF is $2 \cdot y \cdot y$ or $2y^2$.

Then factor out the GCF.

$$10y^4 - 12y^3 + 4y^2 = 2y^2\left(5y^2\right) + 2y^2(-6y) + 2y^2(2)$$
$$= 2y^2\left(5y^2 - 6y + 2\right)$$

Exercises

Simplify each product. Write in standard form.

16. $5k(3 - 4k)$ **17.** $4m\left(2m + 9m^2 - 6\right)$

18. $6g^2(g - 8)$ **19.** $3d\left(6d + d^2\right)$

20. $-2n^2\left(5n - 9 + 4n^2\right)$ **21.** $q\left(11 + 8q - 2q^2\right)$

Find the GCF of the terms of each polynomial. Then factor the polynomial.

22. $12p^4 + 16p^3 + 8p$ **23.** $3b^4 - 9b^2 + 6b$

24. $45c^5 - 63c^3 + 27c$ **25.** $4g^2 + 8g$

26. $3t^4 - 6t^3 - 9t + 12$ **27.** $30h^5 - 6h^4 - 15h^3$

28. Reasoning The GCF of two numbers p and q is 5. Can you find the GCF of $6p$ and $6q$? Explain your answer.

8-3 and 8-4 Multiplying Binomials

Quick Review

You can use algebra tiles, tables, or the Distributive Property to multiply polynomials. The FOIL method (First, Outer, Inner, Last) can be used to multiply two binomials. You can also use rules to multiply special case binomials.

Example

What is the simplified form of $(4x + 3)(3x + 2)$?

Use FOIL to multiply the binomials. Find the product of the first terms, the outer terms, the inner terms, and the last terms. Then add.

$$(4x + 3)(3x + 2) = (4x)(3x) + (4x)(2) + (3)(3x) + (3)(2)$$
$$= 12x^2 + 8x + 9x + 6$$
$$= 12x^2 + 17x + 6$$

Exercises

Simplify each product. Write in standard form.

29. $(w + 1)(w + 12)$ **30.** $(2s - 3)(5s + 4)$

31. $(3r - 2)^2$ **32.** $(6g + 7)(g - 8)$

33. $(7q + 2)(3q + 8)$ **34.** $(4n^3 + 5)(3n + 5)$

35. $(t + 9)(t - 3)$ **36.** $(6c + 5)^2$

37. $(7h - 3)(7h + 3)$ **38.** $(y - 6)(3y + 7)$

39. $(4a - 7)(8a + 3)$ **40.** $(4b - 3)(4b + 3)$

41. Geometry A rectangle has dimensions $3x + 5$ and $x + 7$. Write an expression for the area of the rectangle as a product and as a polynomial in standard form.

8-5 and 8-6 Factoring Quadratic Trinomials

Quick Review

You can write some quadratic trinomials as the product of two binomial factors. When you factor a polynomial, be sure to factor out the GCF first.

Example

What is the factored form of $x^2 + 7x + 12$?

List the pairs of factors of 12. Identify the pair with a sum of 7.

Factors of 12	Sum of Factors
1, 12	13
2, 6	8
3, 4	7 ✔

$x^2 + 7x + 12 = (x + 3)(x + 4)$

Exercises

Factor each expression.

42. $g^2 - 5g - 14$ **43.** $2n^2 + 3n - 2$

44. $6k^2 - 10k\ell + 4\ell^2$ **45.** $p^2 + 8p + 12$

46. $r^2 + 6r - 40$ **47.** $6m^2 + 25mn + 11n^2$

48. $t^2 - 13t - 30$ **49.** $2g^2 - 35g + 17$

50. $3x^2 + 3x - 6$ **51.** $d^2 - 18d + 45$

52. $w^2 - 15w - 54$ **53.** $21z^2 - 70z + 49$

54. $-2h^2 + 4h + 70$ **55.** $x^2 + 21x + 38$

56. $10v^2 + 11v - 8$ **57.** $5g^2 + 15g + 10$

58. Reasoning Can you factor the expression $2x^2 + 15x + 9$? Explain why or why not.

8-7   Factoring Special Cases

Quick Review

When you factor a perfect-square trinomial, the two binomial factors are the same.

$$a^2 + 2ab + b^2 = (a + b)(a + b) = (a + b)^2$$
$$a^2 - 2ab + b^2 = (a - b)(a - b) = (a - b)^2$$

When you factor a difference of squares of two terms, the two binomial factors are the sum and the difference of the two terms.

$$a^2 - b^2 = (a + b)(a - b)$$

Example

What is the factored form of $81t^2 - 90t + 25$?

First rewrite the first and last terms as squares. Then determine if the middle term equals $-2ab$.

$$81t^2 - 90t + 25 = (9t)^2 - 90t + 5^2$$
$$= (9t)^2 - 2(9t)(5) + 5^2$$
$$= (9t - 5)^2$$

Exercises

Factor each expression.

59. $s^2 - 20s + 100$ 60. $16q^2 + 56q + 49$

61. $r^2 - 64$ 62. $9z^2 - 16$

63. $25m^2 + 80m + 64$ 64. $49n^2 - 4$

65. $g^2 - 225$ 66. $9p^2 - 42p + 49$

67. $36h^2 - 12h + 1$ 68. $w^2 + 24w + 144$

69. $32v^2 - 8$ 70. $25x^2 - 36$

71. **Geometry** Find an expression for the length of a side of a square with an area of $9n^2 + 54n + 81$.

72. **Reasoning** Suppose you are using algebra tiles to factor a quadratic trinomial. What do you know about the factors of the trinomial when the tiles form a square?

8-8   Factoring by Grouping

Quick Review

When a polynomial has four or more terms, you may be able to group the terms and find a common binomial factor. Then you can use the Distributive Property to factor the polynomial.

Example

What is the factored form of $2r^3 - 12r^2 + 5r - 30$?

First factor out the GCF from each group of two terms. Then factor out a common binomial factor.

$$2r^3 - 12r^2 + 5r - 30 = 2r^2(r - 6) + 5(r - 6)$$
$$= (2r^2 + 5)(r - 6)$$

Exercises

Find the GCF of the first two terms and the GCF of the last two terms for each polynomial.

73. $6y^3 - 3y^2 + 2y - 1$

74. $8m^3 + 40m^2 + 6m + 15$

Factor completely.

75. $6d^4 + 4d^3 - 6d^2 - 4d$

76. $11b^3 - 6b^2 + 11b - 6$

77. $45z^3 + 20z^2 + 9z + 4$

78. $9a^3 - 12a^2 + 18a - 24$

Do you know HOW?

Write each polynomial in standard form.

1. $2x - 3x^2 + 6 + 5x^3$

2. $7 + 9x + 2x^2 + 8x^5$

Simplify. Write each answer in standard form.

3. $(4x^2 + 9x + 1) + (2x^2 + 7x + 13)$

4. $(8x^2 + 5x + 7) - (5x^2 + 8x - 6)$

5. $(5x^4 + 7x + 2) - (3x^2 - 2x + 9)$

6. $(-7x^3 + 4x - 6) + (6x^3 + 10x^2 + 3)$

Simplify each product. Write in standard form.

7. $-p(8p^2 + 3p)$

8. $(r + 8)(r + 6)$

9. $(5w - 6)(2w + 7)$

10. $(4s + 5)(7s^2 - 4s + 3)$

11. $(q - 1)^2$

12. $(3g - 5)(3g + 5)$

13. Camping A rectangular campground has length $4x + 7$ and width $3x - 2$. What is the area of the campground?

Find the GCF of the terms of each polynomial.

14. $16x^6 + 22x^2 + 30x^5$

15. $7v^3 - 10v^2 + 9v^4$

Factor each expression.

16. $x^2 + 17x + 72$

17. $4v^2 - 16v + 7$

18. $n^2 - 16n + 64$

19. $6t^2 - 54$

20. $y^2 - 121$

Factor completely.

21. $7h^4 - 4h^3 + 28h^2 - 16h$

22. $15t^3 + 2t^2 - 45t - 6$

23. $6n^4 + 15n^3 - 9n^2$

24. $9v^4 + 12v^3 - 18v^2 - 24v$

25. Art The area of a square painting is $81p^2 + 90p + 25$. What is the side length of the painting?

Do you UNDERSTAND?

26. Open-Ended Write a trinomial with degree 5.

27. Writing Explain how to use the Distributive Property to multiply two binomials. Include an example.

28. Geometry What is an expression for the area of the figure? Write your answer as a polynomial in standard form.

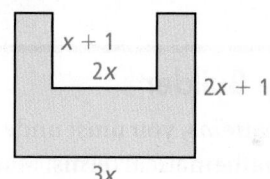

29. Open-Ended What are three different values that complete the expression $x^2 + \blacksquare x + 24$ so that you can factor it into the product of two binomials? Show each factorization.

Write the missing value in each perfect-square trinomial.

30. $n^2 + \blacksquare n + 81$

31. $16y^2 - 56y + \blacksquare$

32. $\blacksquare p^2 + 30p + 25$

33. Reasoning The expression $(x - 2)^2 - 9$ has the form $a^2 - b^2$.
  a. Identify a and b.
  b. Factor $(x - 2)^2 - 9$. Then simplify.

TIPS FOR SUCCESS

Some questions on tests ask you to use polynomials to represent perimeter, area, and volume. Read the sample question at the right. Then follow the tips to answer it.

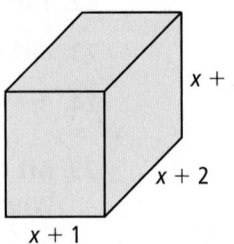

The figure below is a rectangular prism.

$x + 3$

$x + 2$

$x + 1$

Which expression represents the volume of the prism?

Ⓐ $x^3 + 6$

Ⓑ $x^2 + 2x + 2$

Ⓒ $x^3 + x^2 + 10x + 6$

Ⓓ $x^3 + 6x^2 + 11x + 6$

TIP 1

Make sure you look at the figure and understand it. This figure is a rectangular prism. The expressions $x + 1$, $x + 2$, and $x + 3$ represent the lengths of its edges.

TIP 2

Be sure to answer the question being asked. In this problem, you need to find the volume of the prism.

Think It Through

The volume of a rectangular prism is given by $V = \ell wh$. Substitute the edge lengths into the formula. Then simplify the product.

$$V = \ell wh$$
$$= (x + 1)(x + 2)(x + 3)$$
$$= (x^2 + 3x + 2)(x + 3)$$
$$= x^3 + 6x^2 + 11x + 6$$

The correct answer is D.

Vocabulary Builder

As you solve test items, you must understand the meanings of mathematical terms. Match each term with its mathematical meaning.

A. polynomial

B. power

C. area

D. volume

E. scale

I. an expression of the form a^n, where a is the base and n is the exponent

II. the ratio of a distance in a drawing and the actual distance

III. the number of cubic units contained in a space figure

IV. a monomial or the sum of two or more monomials

V. the number of square units contained in a planar figure

Selected Response

Read each question. Then write the letter of the correct answer on your paper.

1. What is $y = \frac{2}{7}x - 4$ written in standard form?

Ⓐ $2x + 7y = -28$ Ⓒ $-2x - 7y = -28$

Ⓑ $2x - 7y = 28$ Ⓓ $-2x + 7y = 28$

2. Which expression is equivalent to $\frac{3x^3 y}{(3y)^{-2}}$?

Ⓕ $9x^3 y^3$ Ⓗ $27x^3 y^3$

Ⓖ $\frac{x^3}{y}$ Ⓘ $\frac{x^3 y^3}{3}$

3. Which expression is equivalent to $10x - (5x - 1)$?

Ⓐ $2x - 1$ Ⓒ $5x - 1$

Ⓑ $2x + 1$ Ⓓ $5x + 1$

4. The area of a rectangle is $6n^2 + n - 2$. Which expression could represent the perimeter of the rectangle?

F $\;$ $2n - 1$ $\qquad$ H $\;$ $5n + 1$

G $\;$ $3n + 2$ $\qquad$ I $\;$ $10n + 2$

5. A company sells calculators for \$35 each. Businesses must order a minimum of 100 calculators, and they must pay a shipping cost of \$50. Which amount of money represents a reasonable sum that a business might spend to purchase calculators?

A $\;$ \$750 $\qquad$ C $\;$ \$2990

B $\;$ \$1070 $\qquad$ D $\;$ \$3585

6. The formula for the volume V of a pyramid is $V = \frac{1}{3}Bh$, where B is the area of the base of the pyramid and h is the height of the pyramid. Which equation represents the height of the pyramid in terms of V and B?

F $\;$ $h = \dfrac{3V}{B}$ $\qquad$ H $\;$ $h = 3VB$

G $\;$ $h = \dfrac{V}{3B}$ $\qquad$ I $\;$ $h = \dfrac{B}{3V}$

7. You are using a map to find the distance between your house and a friend's house. On the map, the distance is 2.5 in. Suppose the map's scale is $\frac{1}{8}$ in. = 1.5 mi. How far do you live from your friend?

A $\;$ 0.08 mi $\qquad$ C $\;$ 3.75 mi

B $\;$ 0.2 mi $\qquad$ D $\;$ 30 mi

8. Which expression represents the volume of the prism?

F $\;$ $x^3 + 4$

G $\;$ $x^3 + 6x^2 + 9x + 4$

H $\;$ $x^3 + 9x^2 + 6x + 4$

I $\;$ $x^3 + 4x^2 + x + 4$

9. Which equation models a line with positive slope and a positive x-intercept?

A $\;$ $5x - 2y = 14$

B $\;$ $-5x - 2y = 14$

C $\;$ $-5x + 2y = 14$

D $\;$ $5x + 2y = -14$

10. You can represent the width of a certain rectangle with the expression $x + 2$. The length of the rectangle is twice the width. What is the area of the rectangle?

F $\;$ $2x + 4$ $\qquad$ H $\;$ $2x^2 + 8x + 8$

G $\;$ $2x^2 + 8$ $\qquad$ I $\;$ $4x^2 + 16x + 16$

11. Which equation represents a line with slope that is greater than the slope of the line with equation $y = \frac{3}{4}x - 1$?

A $\;$ $y = -\frac{3}{4}x - 2$ $\qquad$ C $\;$ $y = \frac{2}{3}x - 1$

B $\;$ $y = \frac{4}{3}x - 2$ $\qquad$ D $\;$ $y = \frac{3}{4}x + 2$

12. What is the x-intercept of the line that passes through $(0, -4)$ and $(1, 4)$?

F $\;$ -4 $\qquad$ H $\;$ $\frac{1}{2}$

G $\;$ $\frac{1}{4}$ $\qquad$ I $\;$ 2

13. Megan earns \$20,000 per year plus 5% commission on her sales. Laurie earns \$32,000 per year plus 1% commission on her sales. Which system of equations can you use to determine the amounts that Megan and Laurie must sell s to receive equal pay p?

A $\;$ $p = 5s + 20{,}000$ $\qquad$ C $\;$ $p + 0.5s = 20{,}000$
$\quad\;\;\; p = s + 32{,}000$ $\qquad\qquad\;\; p + 0.1s = 32{,}000$

B $\;$ $p + 5s = 20{,}000$ $\qquad$ D $\;$ $p = 0.05s + 20{,}000$
$\quad\;\;\; p + s = 32{,}000$ $\qquad\qquad\;\;\; p = 0.01s + 32{,}000$

14. Your family is driving to the beach. The graph at the right relates your distance from the beach to the amount of time you spend driving.

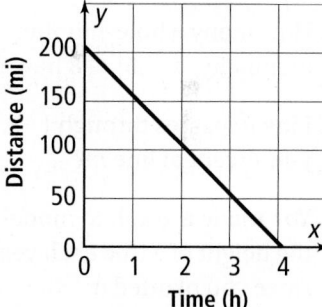

What does the y-intercept of the graph represent?

F $\;$ a stop on the way to the beach

G $\;$ your average speed in miles per hour

H $\;$ your distance from the beach before you started driving

I $\;$ the amount of time it takes to get to the beach

Constructed Response

15. Suppose $b = 2a - 16$ and $b = a + 2$. What is the value of a?

16. A student's score on a history test varies directly with the number of questions the student correctly answers. A student who correctly answers 14 questions receives a score of 70. What score would a student receive for correctly answering 15 questions?

17. You bought a candlestick holder for $11.78 and several candles for $.62 each. You spent a total of $18.60. How many candles did you buy?

18. An artist is making a scale model of a ladybug for an insect museum. What is the length in millimeters of the actual ladybug that the artist is using to make this model?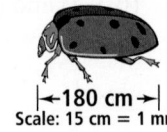

|←180 cm→|
Scale: 15 cm = 1 mm

19. A flagpole casts a shadow that is 9.1 m long. At the same time, a meter stick casts a shadow that is 1.4 m long. How tall is the flagpole in meters?

20. What is the seventh term in the following sequence?
$$81, 27, 9, 3, 1, \ldots$$

21. Suppose you have $200. Sweaters cost $45 each. What is the greatest number of sweaters you can buy?

22. How many whole-number solutions does the inequality $|x - 5| \le 8$ have?

23. Line m passes through $(-9, 4)$ and $(9, 6)$. What is the y-intercept of line m?

24. You made a graph to model the height of a tree each year since you planted it.

Suppose the tree had been 5 ft tall when you planted it. How tall would the tree be in 6 yr? Assume its growth rate did not change.

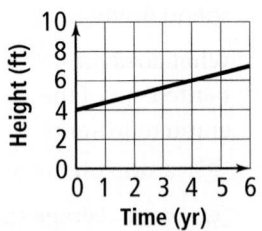

25. A laundromat charges $2.25 to wash one load of clothes and $1.75 to dry one load. The machines accept only quarters. To wash and dry one load of clothes, how many quarters would you need?

26. The formula for the area A of a trapezoid is $A = \frac{1}{2}h(b_1 + b_2)$, where h is the height of the trapezoid and b_1 and b_2 are the lengths of its two bases.

Suppose the height of a trapezoid is $x - 2$. The lengths of the bases are $x + 2$ and $3x - 2$. What polynomial in standard form represents the area of the trapezoid? Show your work.

27. A monthly subway pass costs $60. A one-ride ticket costs $1.80. You plan to ride the subway to school and back for 21 days this month. How much more money would you spend to buy one-ride tickets than to buy a monthly pass? Show your work.

28. Write a system of inequalities for the graph.

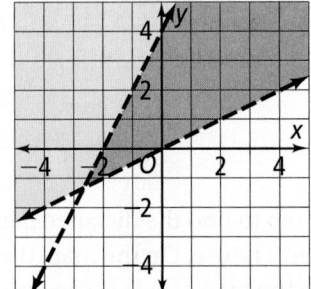

29. Write the expression $\sqrt[3]{8a^2}$ using rational exponents.

30. Simplify the expression $(3x - 5)(2x + 5)$.

Extended Response

31. You sell hot dogs and sodas at basketball games. Each hot dog costs $1.50 and each soda costs $.50. At one game, you made a total of $78.50. In all, you sold 87 hot dogs and sodas.
  a. Write a system of linear equations to solve the problem.
  b. How many hot dogs did you sell? How many sodas did you sell?

32. If $A(2, 1)$, $B(5, 4)$, $C(8, 12)$, and $D(5, 9)$ are the coordinates of the vertices of a quadrilateral, verify that the quadrilateral $ABCD$ is a parallelogram.

Get Ready!

Lesson 1-2 ◆ **Evaluating Expressions**

Evaluate each expression for $a = -1$, $b = 3$, and $c = -2$.

1. $2a - b^2 + c$

2. $\dfrac{c^2 - ab}{2a}$

3. $bc - 3a^2$

4. $\dfrac{b^2 - 4ac}{2a}$

5. $5a + 2b(c - 1)$

6. $c^2 + 2ab - 1$

Lesson 4-4 ◆ **Graphing Functions**

Graph each function.

7. $y = x$

8. $y = -x^2$

9. $y = |x|$

10. $y = 2x - 5$

11. $y = 2|x|$

12. $y = -4x + 3$

Lesson 4-6 ◆ **Evaluating Function Rules**

Evaluate each function rule for $x = -6$.

13. $f(x) = -3x^2$

14. $h(x) = x^2 + 6x$

15. $g(x) = (x - 1)^2$

16. $f(x) = (1 + x)^2$

17. $g(x) = \frac{2}{3}x^2$

18. $h(x) = (2x)^2$

Lessons 8-5 and 8-6 ◆ **Factoring**

Factor each expression.

19. $4x^2 + 4x + 1$

20. $5x^2 + 32x - 21$

21. $8x^2 - 10x + 3$

22. $x^2 - 18x + 81$

23. $12y^2 + 8y - 15$

24. $m^2 - 7m - 18$

Looking Ahead Vocabulary

25. Use your knowledge of the definition of a quadratic polynomial to make a conjecture about the definition of a *quadratic function*.

26. The graph of a quadratic function is a U-shaped curve that has an *axis of symmetry*. What do you think this means?

27. The following is an example of the *Zero-Product Property*.
$(x + 3)(x - 4) = 0$, so $x + 3 = 0$ or $x - 4 = 0$.
What do you think this means?

CHAPTER
9

Quadratic Functions and Equations

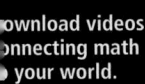
ownload videos
onnecting math
your world.

teractive!
ry numbers,
aphs, and figures
explore math
ncepts.

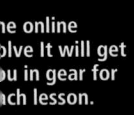
e online
olve It will get
ou in gear for
ch lesson.

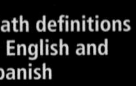
ath definitions
English and
panish

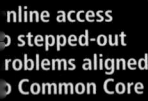
nline access
stepped-out
roblems aligned
Common Core

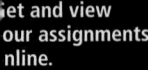
et and view
our assignments
nline.

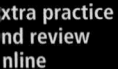
xtra practice
nd review
nline

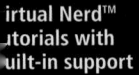
irtual Nerd™
utorials with
uilt-in support

Chapter Preview

Vocabulary

English/Spanish Vocabulary Audio Online:

English	Spanish
axis of symmetry, *p. 546*	eje de simetría
completing the square, *p. 576*	completar el cuadrado
discriminant, *p. 585*	discriminante
maximum, *p. 547*	valor máximo
minimum, *p. 547*	valor mínimo
parabola, *p. 546*	parábola
quadratic equation, *p. 561*	ecuación cuadrática
quadratic formula, *p. 582*	fórmula cuadrática
quadratic function, *p. 546*	función cuadrática
root of an equation, *p. 561*	raíz de una ecuación
vertex, *p. 547*	vértice

BIG ideas

1 Function
Essential Question What are the characteristics of quadratic functions?

2 Solving Equations and Inequalities
Essential Question How can you solve a quadratic equation?

3 Modeling
Essential Question How can you use functions to model real-world situations?

 DOMAINS
• Seeing Structure in Expressions
• Reasoning with Equations and Inequalities
• Interpreting Functions

Common Core Performance Task

Maximizing the Area of a Sign

The Ski Barn is having its annual sale. The manager asks you to order a large rectangular sign to hang on the outside of the store. The sign must fit on a wall that is in the shape of an isosceles triangle. The manager wants the sign to be as large as possible so that it can be seen clearly from far away. One side of the sign will align with the bottom of the wall, and the endpoints of the opposite side will be on the legs of the isosceles triangle, as shown in the figure below.

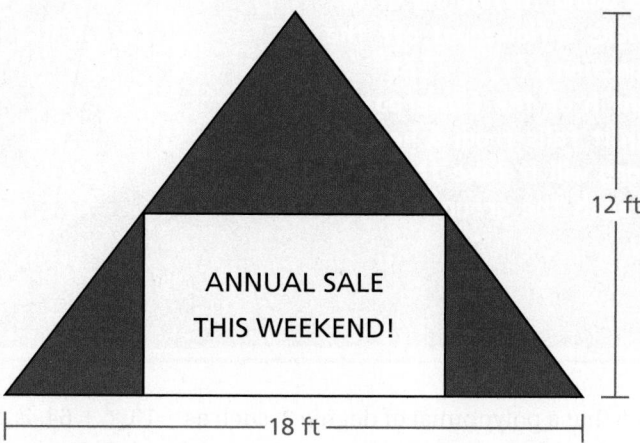

Task Description

Find the dimensions of the sign that will have the greatest possible area. What is this area?

Connecting the Task to the Math Practices

 **MATHEMATICAL PRACTICES**

As you complete the task, you'll apply several Standards for Mathematical Practice.

- You'll model the height of the sign and the area of the sign with functions. (MP 4)

- You'll use a graphing calculator or other graphing utility to analyze the graph of the area function. (MP 5)

- You'll consider how to use the zeros of the area function to determine the maximum area of the sign. (MP 2)

9-1 Quadratic Graphs and Their Properties

 Common Core State Standards

F-IF.C.7a Graph linear and quadratic functions and show intercepts, maxima, and minima. **Also A-CED.A.2, F-IF.B.4, F-IF.B.5, F-BF.B.3**

MP 1, MP 2, MP 3, MP 4, MP 5, MP 6

Objective To graph quadratic functions of the form $y = ax^2$ and $y = ax^2 + c$

Getting Ready!

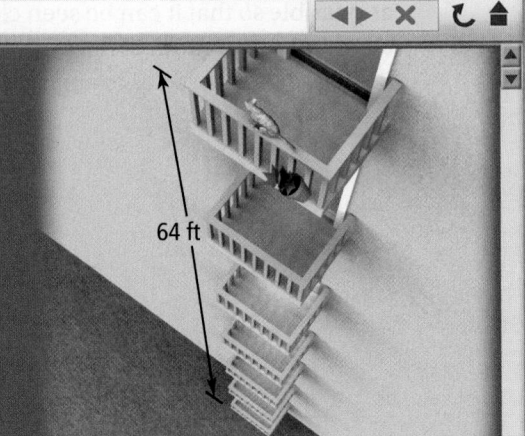

As a cat walks along the railing of a balcony, it knocks a flowerpot off the railing. The function $h(t) = -16t^2 + c$ gives the height h of the flowerpot after t seconds when it falls from a height of c feet. How long will it take the flowerpot to reach the ground? Explain your reasoning.

64 ft

Make sense of the situation. What is the value of h(t) when the flowerpot hits the ground?

 **MATHEMATICAL PRACTICES**

Lesson Vocabulary
- quadratic function
- standard form of a quadratic function
- quadratic parent function
- parabola
- axis of symmetry
- vertex
- minimum
- maximum

Recall from Chapter 8 that a polynomial of degree 2, such as $-16x^2 + 64$, is called a quadratic polynomial. You can use a quadratic polynomial to define a *quadratic function* like the one in the Solve It.

Essential Understanding A quadratic function is a type of nonlinear function that models certain situations where the rate of change is not constant. The graph of a quadratic function is a symmetric curve with a highest or lowest point corresponding to a maximum or minimum value.

take note

Key Concept   Standard Form of a Quadratic Function

A **quadratic function** is a function that can be written in the form $y = ax^2 + bx + c$, where $a \neq 0$. This form is called the **standard form of a quadratic function.**

Examples $y = 3x^2$ $y = x^2 + 9$ $y = x^2 - x - 2$

The simplest quadratic function $f(x) = x^2$ or $y = x^2$ is the **quadratic parent function.**

The graph of a quadratic function is a U-shaped curve called a **parabola.** The parabola with equation $y = x^2$ is shown at the right.

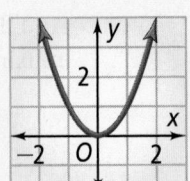

You can fold a parabola so that the two sides match exactly. This property is called *symmetry*. The fold or line that divides the parabola into two matching halves is called the **axis of symmetry.**

The highest or lowest point of a parabola is its **vertex,** which is on the axis of symmetry.

If $a > 0$ in $y = ax^2 + bx + c$, the parabola opens upward.
↓
The vertex is the **minimum** point, or lowest point, of the parabola.

If $a < 0$ in $y = ax^2 + bx + c$, the parabola opens downward.
↓
The vertex is the **maximum** point, or highest point, of the parabola.

 Problem 1 Identifying a Vertex

What are the coordinates of the vertex of each graph? Is it a minimum or a maximum?

Think

Can a parabola have both a minimum and a maximum point?
No. A parabola either opens upward and has a minimum point or opens downward and has a maximum point.

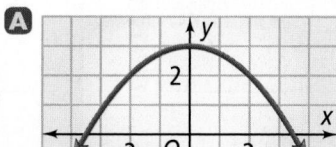

The vertex is $(0, 3)$. It is a maximum.

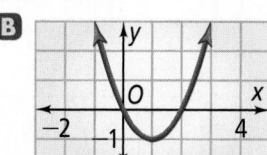

The vertex is $(1, -1)$. It is a minimum.

 Got It? 1. What is the vertex of the graph at the right? Is it a minimum or a maximum?

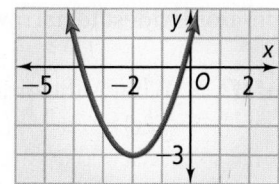

You can use the fact that a parabola is symmetric to graph it quickly. First, find the coordinates of the vertex and several points on one side of the vertex. Then reflect the points across the axis of symmetry. For graphs of functions of the form $y = ax^2$, the vertex is at the origin. The axis of symmetry is the y-axis, or $x = 0$.

 Problem 2 Graphing $y = ax^2$

Graph the function $y = \frac{1}{3}x^2$. Make a table of values. What are the domain and range?

Plan

What are good values to choose for x when making the table?
Choose values of x that make x^2 divisible by 3 so that the y-values will be integers.

x	$y = \frac{1}{3}x^2$	(x, y)
0	$\frac{1}{3}(0)^2 = 0$	$(0, 0)$
3	$\frac{1}{3}(3)^2 = 3$	$(3, 3)$
6	$\frac{1}{3}(6)^2 = 12$	$(6, 12)$

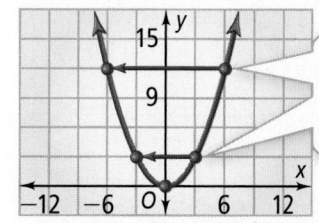

Reflect the points from the table over the axis of symmetry, $x = 0$, to find more points on the graph.

The domain is all real numbers. The range is $y \geq 0$.

 Got It? 2. Graph the function $y = -3x^2$. What are the domain and range?

The coefficient of the x^2-term in a quadratic function affects the width of a parabola as well as the direction in which it opens. When $|m| < |n|$, the graph of $y = mx^2$ is wider than the graph of $y = nx^2$.

 Problem 3 Comparing Widths of Parabolas

Use the graphs below. What is the order, from widest to narrowest, of the graphs of the quadratic functions $f(x) = -4x^2$, $f(x) = \frac{1}{4}x^2$, and $f(x) = x^2$?

$f(x) = -4x^2$ $f(x) = \frac{1}{4}x^2$ $f(x) = x^2$

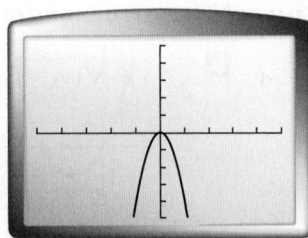   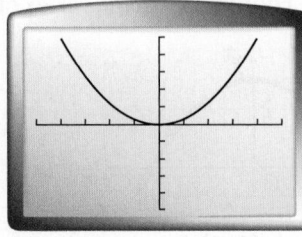   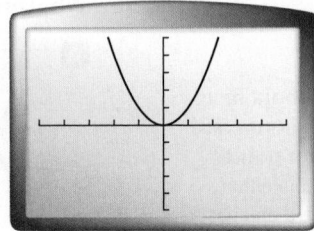

Of the three graphs, $f(x) = \frac{1}{4}x^2$ is the widest and $f(x) = -4x^2$ is the narrowest. So, the order from widest to narrowest is $f(x) = \frac{1}{4}x^2$, $f(x) = x^2$, and $f(x) = -4x^2$.

 Got It? 3. What is the order, from widest to narrowest, of the graphs of the functions $f(x) = -x^2$, $f(x) = 3x^2$, and $f(x) = -\frac{1}{3}x^2$?

The y-axis is the axis of symmetry for graphs of functions of the form $y = ax^2 + c$. The value of c translates the graph up or down.

 Problem 4 Graphing $y = ax^2 + c$

Multiple Choice How is the graph of $y = 2x^2 + 3$ different from the graph of $y = 2x^2$?

    Ⓐ It is shifted 3 units up.   Ⓒ It is shifted 3 units to the right.

    Ⓑ It is shifted 3 units down.   Ⓓ It is shifted 3 units to the left.

x	$y = 2x^2$	$y = 2x^2 + 3$
-2	8	11
-1	2	5
0	0	3
1	2	5
2	8	11

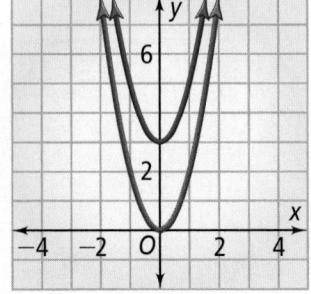

The graph of $y = 2x^2 + 3$ has the same shape as the graph of $y = 2x^2$ but is shifted up 3 units. The correct answer is A.

 Got It? 4. Graph $y = x^2$ and $y = x^2 - 3$. How are the graphs related?

As an object falls, its speed continues to increase, so its height above the ground decreases at a faster and faster rate. Ignoring air resistance, you can model the object's height with the function $h = -16t^2 + c$. The height h is in feet, the time t is in seconds, and the object's initial height c is in feet.

 Problem 5 Using the Falling Object Model

Nature An acorn drops from a tree branch 20 ft above the ground. The function $h = -16t^2 + 20$ gives the height h of the acorn (in feet) after t seconds. What is the graph of this quadratic function? At about what time does the acorn hit the ground?

Know
• The function for the acorn's height
• The initial height is 20 ft.

Need
The function's graph and the time the acorn hits the ground

Plan
Use a table of values to graph the function. Use the graph to estimate when the acorn hits the ground.

Think

Can you choose negative values for t?
No. t represents time, so it cannot be negative.

t	$h = -16t^2 + 20$
0	20
0.5	16
1	4
1.5	−16

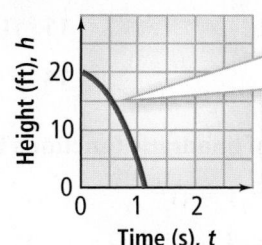

Graph the function using the first three ordered pairs from the table. Do not plot $(1.5, -16)$ because height cannot be negative.

The acorn hits the ground when its height above the ground is 0 ft. From the graph, you can see that the acorn hits the ground after slightly more than 1 s.

 Got It? **5. a.** In Problem 5 above, suppose the acorn drops from a tree branch 70 ft above the ground. The function $h = -16t^2 + 70$ gives the height h of the acorn (in feet) after t seconds. What is the graph of this function? At about what time does the acorn hit the ground?

   b. Reasoning What are a reasonable domain and range for the original function in Problem 5? Explain your reasoning.

Lesson Check

Do you know HOW?

Graph the parabola. Identify the vertex.

1. $y = -3x^2$

2. $y = 4x^2$

3. $y = \frac{1}{2}x^2 + 2$

4. $y = -2x^2 - 1$

Do you UNDERSTAND?  MATHEMATICAL PRACTICES

 5. Vocabulary When is the vertex of a parabola the minimum point? When is it the maximum point?

 6. Compare and Contrast How are the graphs of $y = -\frac{1}{2}x^2$ and $y = -\frac{1}{2}x^2 + 1$ similar? How are they different?

Practice and Problem-Solving Exercises  MATHEMATICAL PRACTICES

 **Practice**   Identify the vertex of each parabola. Tell whether it is a minimum or a maximum.   ◀ **See Problem 1.**

7.
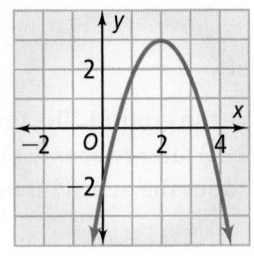

8.
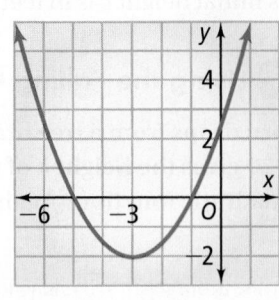

9.

x	y
0	8
1	2
2	0
3	2
4	8

Graph each function. Then identify the domain and range of the function.   ◀ **See Problem 2.**

10. $y = -4x^2$ **11.** $f(x) = 1.5x^2$ **12.** $f(x) = 3x^2$

13. $f(x) = \frac{2}{3}x^2$ **14.** $y = -\frac{1}{2}x^2$ **15.** $y = -\frac{1}{3}x^2$

Order each group of quadratic functions from widest to narrowest graph.   ◀ **See Problem 3.**

16. $y = 3x^2, y = 2x^2, y = 4x^2$ **17.** $f(x) = 5x^2, f(x) = -3x^2, f(x) = x^2$

18. $y = -\frac{1}{2}x^2, y = 5x^2, y = -\frac{1}{4}x^2$ **19.** $f(x) = -2x^2, f(x) = -\frac{2}{3}x^2, f(x) = -4x^2$

Graph each function.   ◀ **See Problem 4.**

20. $f(x) = x^2 + 4$ **21.** $y = x^2 - 7$ **22.** $y = \frac{1}{2}x^2 + 2$

23. $f(x) = -x^2 - 3$ **24.** $y = -2x^2 + 4$ **25.** $f(x) = 4x^2 - 5$

26. Dropped Object A person walking across a bridge accidentally drops an   ◀ **See Problem 5.**
orange into the river below from a height of 40 ft. The function $h = -16t^2 + 40$
gives the orange's approximate height h above the water, in feet, after t seconds.
Graph the function. In how many seconds will the orange hit the water?

27. Nature A bird drops a stick to the ground from a height of 80 ft. The function
$h = -16t^2 + 80$ gives the stick's approximate height h above the ground, in feet,
after t seconds. Graph the function. At about what time does the stick hit the
ground?

 **Apply**   **28. Error Analysis** Describe and correct the error
made in graphing the function $y = -2x^2 + 1$.

Identify the domain and range of each function.

29. $f(x) = 3x^2 + 6$ **30.** $y = -2x^2 - 1$

31. $y = -\frac{3}{4}x^2 - 9$ **32.** $y = \frac{2}{3}x^2 + 12$

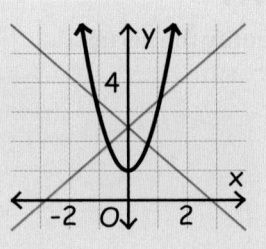

ⓒ **33. Writing** What information do the numbers a and c
give you about the graph of $y = ax^2 + c$?

Match each function with its graph.

34. $f(x) = x^2 - 1$ **35.** $f(x) = -3x^2 + 8$ **36.** $f(x) = -0.2x^2 + 5$

A. 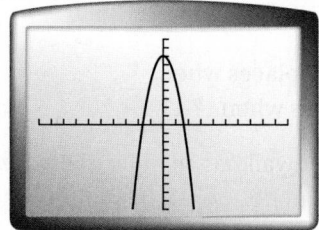   **B.** 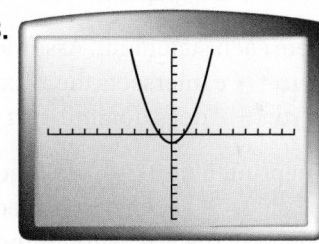   **C.**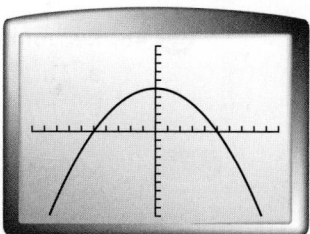

37. Using a graphing calculator, graph $f(x) = x^2 + 2$.
  a. If $f(x) = x^2 + 2$ and $g(x) = 3f(x)$, write the equation for $g(x)$. Graph $g(x)$ and compare it to the graph of $f(x)$.
  b. If $f(x) = x^2 + 2$ and $h(x) = f(3x)$, write the equation for $h(x)$. Graph $h(x)$ and compare it to the graph of $f(x)$.
  c. Compare how multiplying a quadratic function by a number and multiplying the x value of a quadratic function by a number change the graphs of the quadratic functions.

© **38. Think About a Plan** Suppose a person is riding in a hot-air balloon, 154 ft above the ground. He drops an apple. The height h, in feet, of the apple above the ground is given by the formula $h = -16t^2 + 154$, where t is the time in seconds. To the nearest tenth of a second, at what time does the apple hit the ground?

  • How can you use a table to approximate the answer between two consecutive whole numbers of seconds?
  • How can you use a second table to make your approximation more accurate?

 Graphing Calculator Use a graphing calculator to graph each function. Identify the vertex and axis of symmetry.

39. $y = \frac{1}{4}x^2 + 3$ **40.** $f(x) = -1.5x^2 + 5$ **41.** $y = -3x^2 - 6$

Three graphs are shown at the right. Identify the graph or graphs that fit each description.

42. $a > 0$ **43.** $a < 0$

44. $|a|$ has the greatest value.   **45.** $|a|$ has the least value.

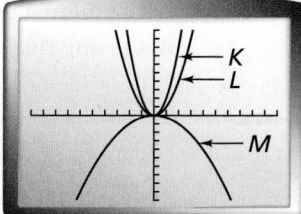

STEM **46. Physics** In a physics class demonstration, a ball is dropped from the roof of a building, 72 ft above the ground. The height h, in feet, of the ball above the ground is given by the function $h = -16t^2 + 72$, where t is the time in seconds.
  a. Graph the function.
  b. How far has the ball fallen from time $t = 0$ to $t = 1$?
© **c. Reasoning** Does the ball fall the same distance from time $t = 1$ to $t = 2$ as it does from $t = 0$ to $t = 1$? Explain.

 **Challenge**

47. Consider the graphs of $y = ax^2$ and $y = (ax)^2$. Assume $a \neq 0$.
   a. For what values of a will both graphs lie in the same quadrant(s)?
   b. For what values of a will the graph of $y = ax^2$ be wider than the graph of $y = (ax)^2$?

 48. Reasoning Complete each statement. Assume $a \neq 0$.
   a. The graph of $y = ax^2 + c$ intersects the x-axis in two places when   ? .
   b. The graph of $y = ax^2 + c$ does not intersect the x-axis when   ? .

STEM 49. Construction A blueprint for a 15 ft-by-9 ft rectangular wall has a square window in the center. If each side of the window is x feet, the function $y = 135 - x^2$ gives the area (in square feet) of the wall without the window.
   a. Graph the function.
   b. What is a reasonable domain for the function? Explain.
   c. What is the range of the function? Explain.
   d. Estimate the side length of the window if the area of the wall is 117 ft^2.

Standardized Test Prep

SAT/ACT

50. Which equation has a graph that is narrower than the graph of $y = 4x^2 + 5$?
   Ⓐ $y = 4x^2 - 5$ Ⓒ $y = 0.75x^2 + 5$
   Ⓑ $y = -5x^2 + 4$ Ⓓ $y = -0.75x^2 - 4$

51. Kristina is evaluating some formulas as part of a science experiment. One of the formulas involves the expression $24 - (-17)$. What is the value of this expression?
   Ⓕ -41 Ⓖ -7 Ⓗ 7 Ⓘ 41

52. Which expression is equivalent to $8(x + 9)$?
   Ⓐ $x + 72$ Ⓑ $8x + 72$ Ⓒ $8x + 17$ Ⓓ $8x + 9$

53. What is the solution of the equation $2(x + 3) + 7 = -11$?
   Ⓕ -12 Ⓖ -1 Ⓗ 1 Ⓘ 12

Short Response

54. A rectangular dog run has an area of $x^2 - 22x - 48$. What are possible dimensions of the dog run? Use factoring. Explain how you found the dimensions.

Mixed Review

Factor completely.   **See Lesson 8-8.**

55. $30r^3 + 51r^2 + 9r$ **56.** $15q^3 - 18q^2 - 10q + 12$ **57.** $7b^4 + 14b^3 + b + 2$

Get Ready! **To prepare for Lesson 9-2, do Exercises 58–63.**

Evaluate the expression $\frac{-b}{2a}$ for the following values of a and b.   **See Lesson 1-6.**

58. $a = -2, b = 3$ **59.** $a = -5, b = -4$ **60.** $a = 8, b = 6$

61. $a = 10, b = -7$ **62.** $a = -4, b = 1$ **63.** $a = -12, b = -48$

Quadratic Functions

© **Common Core State Standards**
F-IF.C.7a Graph linear and quadratic functions and show intercepts, maxima, and minima. **Also A-CED.A.2, F-IF.B.4, F-IF.C.8a, F-IF.C.9**
MP 1, MP 2, MP 3, MP 4, MP 7

Objective To graph quadratic functions of the form $y = ax^2 + bx + c$

Getting Ready!

You throw a ball straight up into the air and catch it at the same height you released it. The parabola at the right shows the height h of the ball in feet after t seconds. What is the total distance the ball travels? For how long does the ball travel up? Explain your reasoning.

Be careful! The graph shows the height of the ball, not the path of the ball.

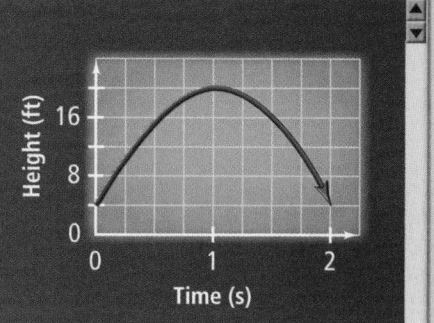

MATHEMATICAL PRACTICES

The parabola in the Solve It has the equation $h = -16t^2 + 32t + 4$. Unlike the quadratic functions you saw in previous lessons, this function has a linear term, $32t$.

Essential Understanding In the quadratic function $y = ax^2 + bx + c$, the value of b affects the position of the axis of symmetry.

Consider the graphs of the following functions.

$y = 2x^2 + 2x$

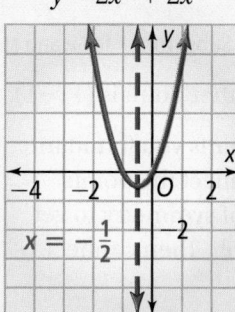

$y = 2x^2 + 4x$

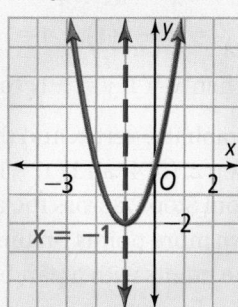

$y = 2x^2 + 6x$

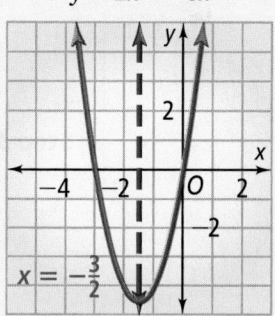

Notice that the axis of symmetry changes with each change in the b-value. The equation of the axis of symmetry is related to the ratio $\frac{b}{a}$.

equation:	$y = 2x^2 + 2x$	$y = 2x^2 + 4x$	$y = 2x^2 + 6x$
$\frac{b}{a}$:	$\frac{2}{2} = 1$	$\frac{4}{2} = 2$	$\frac{6}{2} = 3$
axis of symmetry:	$x = -\frac{1}{2}$	$x = -1$, or $-\frac{2}{2}$	$x = -\frac{3}{2}$

The equation of the axis of symmetry is $x = -\frac{1}{2}\left(\frac{b}{a}\right)$, or $x = \frac{-b}{2a}$.

take note

Key Concept   Graph of a Quadratic Function

The graph of $y = ax^2 + bx + c$, where $a \neq 0$, has the line $x = \frac{-b}{2a}$ as its axis of symmetry. The x-coordinate of the vertex is $\frac{-b}{2a}$.

When you substitute $x = 0$ into the equation $y = ax^2 + bx + c$, you get $y = c$. So the y-intercept of a quadratic function is c. You can use the axis of symmetry and the y-intercept to help you graph a quadratic function.

Ⓒ **Problem 1** **Graphing $y = ax^2 + bx + c$**

What is the graph of the function $y = x^2 - 6x + 4$?

Step 1 Find the axis of symmetry and the coordinates of the vertex.

Think

How are the vertex and the axis of symmetry related?
The vertex is on the axis of symmetry. You can use the equation for the axis of symmetry to find the x-coordinate of the vertex.

$$x = \frac{-b}{2a} = \frac{-(-6)}{2(1)} = 3 \qquad \text{Find the equation of the axis of symmetry.}$$

The axis of symmetry is $x = 3$. So the x-coordinate of the vertex is 3.

$$\begin{aligned} y &= x^2 - 6x + 4 \\ &= 3^2 - 6(3) + 4 \qquad \text{Substitute 3 for } x \text{ to find the } y\text{-coordinate of the vertex.} \\ &= -5 \qquad\qquad\quad \text{Simplify.} \end{aligned}$$

The vertex is $(3, -5)$.

Step 2 Find two other points on the graph.

Find the y-intercept. When $x = 0$, $y = 4$, so one point is $(0, 4)$.

Find another point by choosing a value for x on the same side of the vertex as the y-intercept. Let $x = 1$.

$$\begin{aligned} y &= x^2 - 6x + 4 \\ &= 1^2 - 6(1) + 4 = -1 \qquad \text{Substitute 1 for } x \text{ and simplify.} \end{aligned}$$

When $x = 1$, $y = -1$, so another point is $(1, -1)$.

Step 3 Graph the vertex and the points you found in Step 2, $(0, 4)$ and $(1, -1)$. Reflect the points from Step 2 across the axis of symmetry to get two more points on the graph. Then connect the points with a parabola.

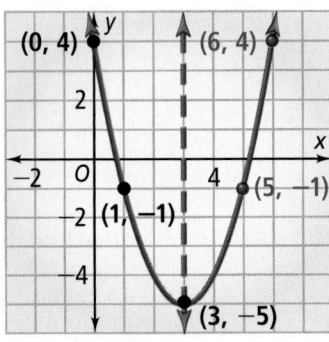

Ⓒ ✓ **Got It?** **1. a.** What is the graph of the function $y = -x^2 + 4x - 2$?

   b. Reasoning In Step 2 of Problem 1, why do you think it was useful to use the y-intercept as one point on the graph?

In Lesson 9-1, you used $h = -16t^2 + c$ to find the height h above the ground of an object falling from an initial height c at time t. If an object projected into the air given an initial upward velocity v continues with no additional force acting on it, the formula $h = -16t^2 + vt + c$ gives its approximate height above the ground.

 Problem 2 Using the Vertical Motion Model

Entertainment During halftime of a basketball game, a slingshot launches T-shirts at the crowd. A T-shirt is launched with an initial upward velocity of 72 ft/s. The T-shirt is caught 35 ft above the court. How long will it take the T-shirt to reach its maximum height? What is its maximum height? What is the range of the function that models the height of the T-shirt over time?

5 ft

Plan

What are the values of v and c?
The T-shirt is launched from a height of 5 ft, so $c = 5$. The T-shirt has an initial upward velocity of 72 ft/s, so $v = 72$.

The function $h = -16t^2 + 72t + 5$ gives the T-shirt's height h, in feet, after t seconds. Since the coefficient of t^2 is negative, the parabola opens downward, and the vertex is the maximum point.

Method 1 Use a formula.

$$t = \frac{-b}{2a} = \frac{-72}{2(-16)} = 2.25$$ Find the t-coordinate of the vertex.

$$h = -16(2.25)^2 + 72(2.25) + 5 = 86$$ Find the h-coordinate of the vertex.

The T-shirt will reach its maximum height of 86 ft after 2.25 s. The range describes the height of the T-shirt during its flight. The T-shirt starts at 5 ft, peaks at 86 ft, and then is caught at 35 ft. The height of the T-shirt at any time is between 5 ft and 86 ft, inclusive, so the range is $5 \le h \le 86$.

Method 2 Use a graphing calculator.

Enter the function $h = -16t^2 + 72t + 5$ as $y = -16x^2 + 72x + 5$ on the **Y=** screen and graph the function.

Use the **CALC** feature and select **MAXIMUM**. Set left and right bounds on the maximum point and calculate the point's coordinates. The coordinates of the maximum point are (2.25, 86).

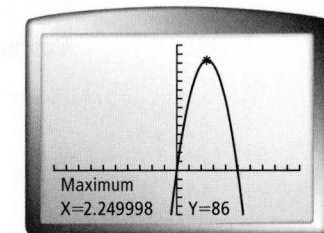

Maximum
X=2.249998   Y=86

The T-shirt will reach its maximum height of 86 ft after 2.25 s. The range of the function is $5 \le h \le 86$.

Got It? **2.** In Problem 2, suppose a T-shirt is launched with an initial upward velocity of 64 ft/s and is caught 35 ft above the court. How long will it take the T-shirt to reach its maximum height? How far above court level will it be? What is the range of the function that models the height of the T-shirt over time?

Lesson Check

Do you know HOW?

Graph each function.

1. $y = x^2 - 4x + 1$

2. $y = -2x^2 - 8x - 3$

3. $y = 3x^2 + 6x + 2$

4. $f(x) = -x^2 + 2x - 5$

Do you UNDERSTAND?

© **5. Reasoning** How does each of the numbers a, b, and c affect the graph of a quadratic function $y = ax^2 + bx + c$?

© **6. Writing** Explain how you can use the y-intercept, vertex, and axis of symmetry to graph a quadratic function. Assume the vertex is not on the y-axis.

Practice and Problem-Solving Exercises

A **Practice**

Find the equation of the axis of symmetry and the coordinates of the vertex of the graph of each function.

◀ **See Problem 1.**

7. $y = 2x^2 + 3$

8. $y = -3x^2 + 12x + 1$

9. $f(x) = 2x^2 + 4x - 1$

10. $y = x^2 - 8x - 7$

11. $f(x) = 3x^2 - 9x + 2$

12. $y = -4x^2 + 11$

13. $f(x) = -5x^2 + 3x + 2$

14. $y = -4x^2 - 16x - 3$

15. $f(x) = 6x^2 + 6x - 5$

Match each function with its graph.

16. $y = -x^2 - 6x$

17. $y = -x^2 + 6$

18. $y = x^2 - 6$

19. $y = x^2 + 6x$

A.

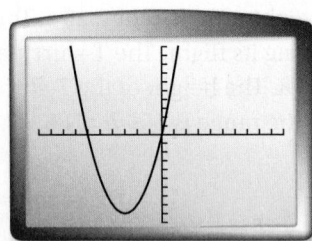

C.

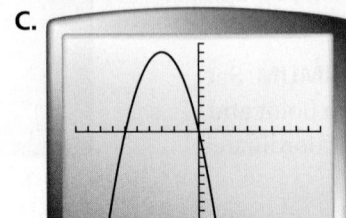

B.

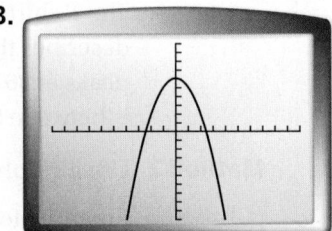

D.

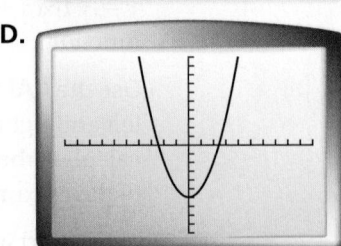

Graph each function. Label the axis of symmetry and the vertex.

20. $f(x) = x^2 + 4x - 5$

21. $y = 3x^2 - 20x$

22. $y = -2x^2 + 8x + 9$

23. $f(x) = -x^2 + 4x + 3$

24. $y = -2x^2 - 10x$

25. $y = 2x^2 - 6x + 1$

26. Sports A baseball is thrown into the air with an upward velocity of 30 ft/s. Its height h, in feet, after t seconds is given by the function $h = -16t^2 + 30t + 6$. How long will it take the ball to reach its maximum height? What is the ball's maximum height? What is the range of the function? ◀ **See Problem 2.**

27. School Fair Suppose you have 100 ft of string to rope off a rectangular section for a bake sale at a school fair. The function $A = -x^2 + 50x$ gives the area of the section in square feet, where x is the width in feet. What width gives you the maximum area you can rope off? What is the maximum area? What is the range of the function?

 **Apply**

28. a. What is the vertex of the function $y = x^2 + 4$?
b. What is the vertex of the function given in the table?

x	−2	−1	0	1	2
y	−14	−8	−6	−8	−14

29. a. What is the vertex of the function $y = 5x^2 + 10x + 24$?
b. What is the vertex of the function given in the table?

x	−4	−3	−2	−1	0
y	3	−3	−5	−3	3

30. Think About a Plan The Riverside Geyser in Yellowstone National Park erupts about every 6.25 h. When the geyser erupts, the water has an initial upward velocity of 69 ft/s. What is the maximum height of the geyser? Round your answer to the nearest foot.
- What is the initial height of the geyser?
- What function gives the geyser's height h (in feet) t seconds after it starts erupting?

31. Business A cell phone company sells about 500 phones each week when it charges $75 per phone. It sells about 20 more phones per week for each $1 decrease in price. The company's revenue is the product of the number of phones sold and the price of each phone. What price should the company charge to maximize its revenue?

32. Graph the function $f(x) = x^2 + 2x - 3$. Then graph the following transformations of the function. Describe how the parent function changes with each transformation.
a. $f(x) + 3$
b. $2[f(x)]$
c. $f(4x)$
d. $f(x + 5)$

33. Error Analysis Describe and correct the error made in finding the axis of symmetry for the graph of $y = -x^2 - 6x + 2$.

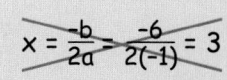

34. Reasoning What do you know about the value of b in the function $y = ax^2 + bx + c$ when the x-coordinate of the vertex is an integer?

35. Sports Suppose a tennis player hits a ball over the net. The ball leaves the racket 0.5 m above the ground. The equation $h = -4.9t^2 + 3.8t + 0.5$ gives the ball's height h in meters after t seconds.

    a. When will the ball be at the highest point in its path? Round to the nearest tenth of a second.

    b. Reasoning If you double your answer from part (a), will you find the amount of time the ball is in the air before it hits the court? Explain.

36. The parabola at the right is of the form $y = x^2 + bx + c$.

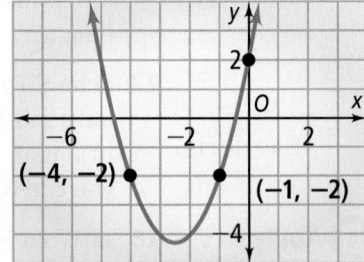

    a. Use the graph to find the y-intercept.

    b. Use the graph to find the equation of the axis of symmetry.

    c. Use the formula $x = \frac{-b}{2a}$ to find b.

    d. Write the equation of the parabola.

    e. Test one point using your equation from part (d).

    f. Reasoning Would this method work if the value of a were not known? Explain.

Apply What You've Learned

MATHEMATICAL
PRACTICES
MP 4

Look back at the information on page 545 about the sale sign on the wall of the Ski Barn.

    a. Copy the figure from page 545. Label the width of the rectangular sign x, and label the height y.

    b. The triangle above the sign is an isosceles triangle that is similar to the triangular wall. Use the similar triangles to write a proportion. Solve your proportion for y in terms of x to find a function that models the height of the rectangular sign.

    c. Using the formula for the area of a rectangle and your height function from part (b), determine an equation for the function $A(x)$ that represents the area of the rectangular sign.

    d. What kind of function is the function you found in part (c)? Explain.

Common Core State Standards

F-LE.A.3 Observe using graphs and tables that a quantity increasing exponentially eventually exceeds a quantity increasing linearly, quadratically, or (more generally) as a polynomial function. **Also F-IF.B.6**

MP 8

Concept Byte

Use With Lesson 9-2

ACTIVITY

Rates of Increase

In this activity, you will use functions, tables, and graphs to determine and compare rates of change presented in various forms.

Activity 1

The function $h(t) = 20t - 5t^2$ represents the approximate height of a ball that is thrown upward with an initial velocity of 20 m/s, where $h(t)$ is the height (in meters) of the ball after t seconds.

1. Graph the function on a graphing calculator.

2. Copy and complete the tables.

Time (s)	Height (m)
0	
1	
2	
3	
4	

Time Interval	Average Rate of Change (m/s)
0 s to 1 s	
1 s to 2 s	
2 s to 3 s	
3 s to 4 s	

3. Does the average rate of change increase or decrease from 0 s to 2 s? Justify your answer using your graph.

4. Does the average rate of change increase or decrease from 2 s to 4 s? Justify your answer using your graph.

5. Make a conjecture What do the positive and negative signs of the average rate of change indicate? Use the scenario and the graph to check your conjecture.

Exercises

A toy car is traveling up an inclined plane. The graph shows the distance the car has traveled at t seconds. Use the graph to answer Exercises 6–9.

6. Estimate the distance the car has traveled at 1 second, at 3 seconds, and at 5 seconds.

7. What is the average rate of change from 1 s to 3 s?

8. What is the average rate of change from 3 s to 5 s?

9. Does the average rate of change increase or decrease? Explain how the graph can help you answer this question.

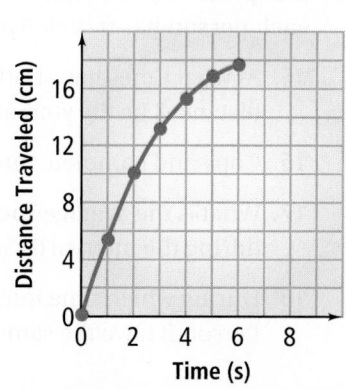

Activity 2

Use the graphs below to answer Exercises 10–14.

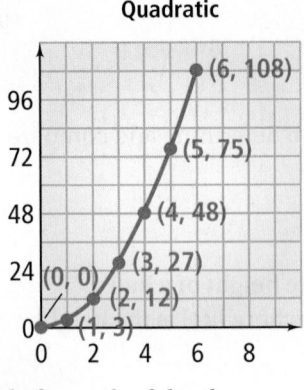

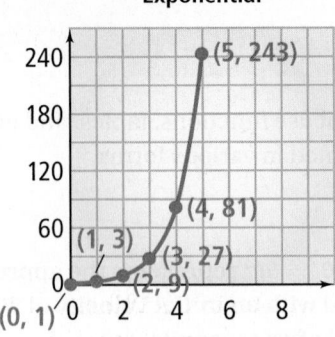

10. Copy and complete the table for each of the three graphs.

Interval	Average Rate of Change
0 to 1	
1 to 2	
2 to 3	
3 to 4	
4 to 5	

11. What do you notice about the average rate of change for the linear function?

12. What do you notice about the average rate of change for the quadratic function?

13. What do you notice about the average rate of change for the exponential function?

14. Compare the average rate of change for the quadratic function and the exponential function. Which average rate of change increases more quickly?

Exercises

Two people are running along parallel, straight tracks. Person A slowly increases his speed while Person B runs at a constant speed. The graph shows the distance each person has traveled at *t* seconds. Use the graph to answer Exercises 15–18.

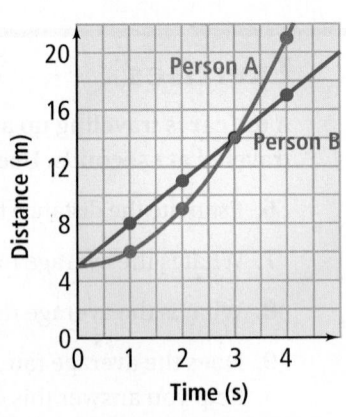

15. At what times have both runners traveled the same distance? Justify your answer using the graph.

16. Copy and complete the table for each runner.

17. What is the average speed of each person during the interval 0 s to 4 s?

18. During which time interval do Person A and Person B have the same average speed?

Time Interval	Average Rate of Change
0 s to 1 s	
1 s to 2 s	
2 s to 3 s	
3 s to 4 s	

9-3 Solving Quadratic Equations

Common Core State Standards

A-REI.B.4b Solve quadratic equations by inspection (e.g., for $x^2 = 49$), taking square roots . . . **Also A-APR.B.3, A-CED.A.1, A-CED.A.4**

MP 1, MP 2, MP 3, MP 4, MP 7

Objective To solve quadratic equations by graphing and using square roots

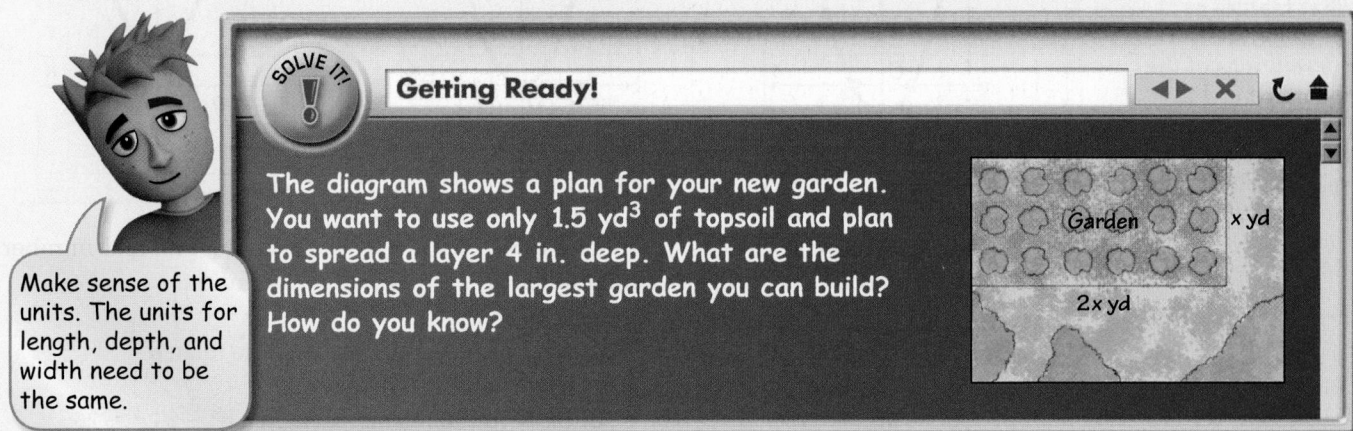

SOLVE IT!

Getting Ready!

The diagram shows a plan for your new garden. You want to use only 1.5 yd³ of topsoil and plan to spread a layer 4 in. deep. What are the dimensions of the largest garden you can build? How do you know?

Garden   x yd

2x yd

Make sense of the units. The units for length, depth, and width need to be the same.

MATHEMATICAL PRACTICES The situation in the Solve It can be modeled by a *quadratic equation*.

Lesson Vocabulary

- quadratic equation
- standard form of a quadratic equation
- root of an equation
- zero of a function

take note

Key Concept   Standard Form of a Quadratic Equation

A **quadratic equation** is an equation that can be written in the form $ax^2 + bx + c = 0$, where $a \neq 0$. This form is called the **standard form of a quadratic equation.**

Essential Understanding Quadratic equations can be solved by a variety of methods, including graphing and finding square roots.

One way to solve a quadratic equation $ax^2 + bx + c = 0$ is to graph the related quadratic function $y = ax^2 + bx + c$. The solutions of the equation are the x-intercepts of the related function.

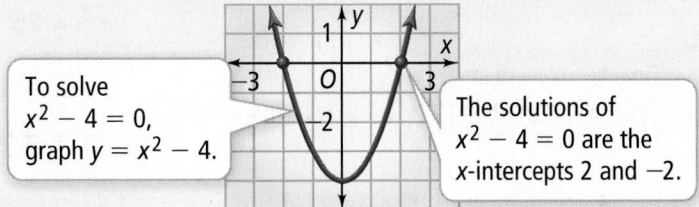

To solve
$x^2 - 4 = 0$,
graph $y = x^2 - 4$.

The solutions of
$x^2 - 4 = 0$ are the
x-intercepts 2 and -2.

A quadratic equation can have two, one, or no real-number solutions. In a future course you will learn about solutions of quadratic equations that are not real numbers. In this course, *solutions* refers to real-number solutions.

The solutions of a quadratic equation and the x-intercepts of the graph of the related function are often called **roots of the equation** or **zeros of the function.**

 **Problem 1** Solving by Graphing

What are the solutions of each equation? Use a graph of the related function.

Ⓐ $x^2 - 1 = 0$

Graph $y = x^2 - 1$.

Ⓑ $x^2 = 0$

Graph $y = x^2$.

Ⓒ $x^2 + 1 = 0$

Graph $y = x^2 + 1$.

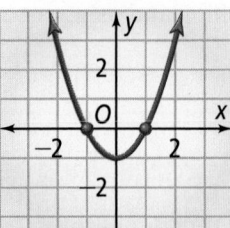

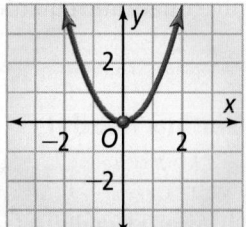

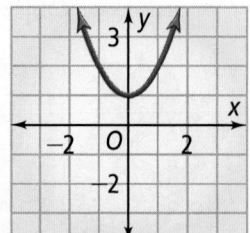

There are two
solutions, ± 1.

There is one
solution, 0.

There is no real-number
solution.

 Got It? **1.** What are the solutions of each equation? Use a graph of the related function.

    a. $x^2 - 16 = 0$ **b.** $3x^2 + 6 = 0$ **c.** $x^2 - 25 = -25$

You can solve equations of the form $x^2 = k$ by finding the square roots of each side.
For example, the solutions of $x^2 = 81$ are $\pm \sqrt{81}$, or ± 9.

 **Problem 2** Solving Using Square Roots

What are the solutions of $3x^2 - 75 = 0$?

Think

Write the original equation.

Isolate x^2 on one side of the equation.

Find the square roots of each side and simplify.

Write

$3x^2 - 75 = 0$

$3x^2 = 75$

$x^2 = 25$

$x = \pm\sqrt{25}$

$x = \pm 5$

 Got It? **2.** What are the solutions of each equation?

    a. $m^2 - 36 = 0$ **b.** $3x^2 + 15 = 0$ **c.** $4d^2 + 16 = 16$

You can solve some quadratic equations that model real-world problems by finding square roots. In many cases, the negative square root may not be a reasonable solution.

 Problem 3 Choosing a Reasonable Solution

Aquarium An aquarium is designing a new exhibit to showcase tropical fish. The exhibit will include a tank that is a rectangular prism with a length ℓ that is twice the width w. The volume of the tank is 420 ft³. What is the width of the tank to the nearest tenth of a foot?

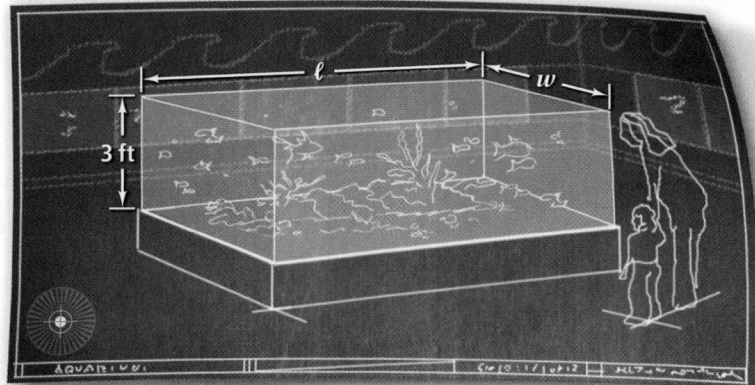

How can you write the length of the tank?
The length ℓ is twice the width w, so write the length as $2w$.

$V = \ell w h$	Use the formula for volume of a rectangular prism.
$420 = (2w)w(3)$	Substitute 420 for V, $2w$ for ℓ, and 3 for h.
$420 = 6w^2$	Simplify.
$70 = w^2$	Divide each side by 6.
$\pm\sqrt{70} = w$	Find the square roots of each side.
$\pm 8.366600265 \approx w$	Use a calculator.

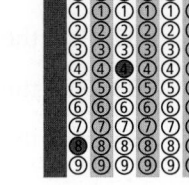

A tank cannot have a negative width, so only the positive square root makes sense. The tank will have a width of about 8.4 ft.

  Got It? **3. a.** Suppose the tank in Problem 3 will have a height of 4 ft and a volume of 500 ft³. What is the width of the tank to the nearest tenth of a foot?

   b. Reasoning What are the disadvantages of using a graph to approximate the solution to Problem 3? Explain.

 Lesson Check

Do you know HOW?

Solve each equation by graphing the related function or by finding square roots.

1. $x^2 - 25 = 0$

2. $2x^2 - 8 = 0$

3. $t^2 = 144$

4. $y^2 - 225 = 0$

Do you UNDERSTAND? MATHEMATICAL PRACTICES

5. Vocabulary What are the zeros of a function? Give an example of a quadratic function and its zeros.

6. Compare and Contrast When is it easier to solve a quadratic equation of the form $ax^2 + c = 0$ using square roots than to solve it using a graph?

7. Reasoning Consider the equation $ax^2 + c = 0$, where $a \neq 0$. What is true of a and c if the equation has two solutions? Only one solution? No solutions?

Practice and Problem-Solving Exercises

MATHEMATICAL PRACTICES

Practice

Solve each equation by graphing the related function. If the equation has no real-number solution, write *no solution*.

◀ See Problem 1.

8. $x^2 - 9 = 0$

9. $x^2 + 7 = 0$

10. $3x^2 = 0$

11. $3x^2 - 12 = 0$

12. $x^2 + 4 = 0$

13. $\frac{1}{3}x^2 - 3 = 0$

14. $\frac{1}{2}x^2 + 1 = 0$

15. $x^2 + 5 = 5$

16. $\frac{1}{4}x^2 - 1 = 0$

17. $x^2 + 25 = 0$

18. $x^2 - 10 = -10$

19. $2x^2 - 18 = 0$

Solve each equation by finding square roots. If the equation has no real-number solution, write *no solution*.

◀ See Problem 2.

20. $n^2 = 81$

21. $a^2 = 324$

22. $k^2 - 196 = 0$

23. $r^2 + 49 = 49$

24. $w^2 - 36 = -64$

25. $4g^2 = 25$

26. $64b^2 = 16$

27. $5q^2 - 20 = 0$

28. $144 - p^2 = 0$

29. $2r^2 - 32 = 0$

30. $3a^2 + 12 = 0$

31. $5z^2 - 45 = 0$

Model each problem with a quadratic equation. Then solve. If necessary, round to the nearest tenth.

◀ See Problem 3.

32. Find the length of a side of a square with an area of 169 m^2.

33. Find the length of a side of a square with an area of 75 ft^2.

34. Find the radius of a circle with an area of 90 cm^2.

35. Painting You have enough paint to cover an area of 50 ft^2. What is the side length of the largest square that you could paint? Round your answer to the nearest tenth of a foot.

36. Gardening You have enough shrubs to cover an area of 100 ft^2. What is the radius of the largest circular region you can plant with these shrubs? Round your answer to the nearest tenth of a foot.

Apply

© **Mental Math** Tell how many solutions each equation has.

37. $h^2 = -49$

38. $c^2 - 18 = 9$

39. $s^2 - 35 = -35$

© **40. Think About a Plan** A circular above-ground pool has a height of 52 in. and a volume of 1100 ft^3. What is the radius of the pool to the nearest tenth of a foot? Use the equation $V = \pi r^2 h$, where V is the volume, r is the radius, and h is the height.
- How can drawing a diagram help you solve this problem?
- Do you need to convert any of the given measurements to different units?

© **41. Reasoning** For what values of n will the equation $x^2 = n$ have two solutions? Exactly one solution? No solution?

42. Quilting You are making a square quilt with the design shown at the right. Find the side length x of the inner square that would make its area equal to 50% of the total area of the quilt. Round to the nearest tenth of a foot.

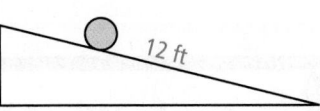

6 ft

Solve each equation by finding square roots. If the equation has no real-number solution, write *no solution*. If a solution is irrational, round to the nearest tenth.

43. $1.2z^2 - 7 = -34$ **44.** $49p^2 - 16 = -7$ **45.** $3m^2 - \frac{1}{12} = 0$

46. $\frac{1}{2}t^2 - 4 = 0$ **47.** $7y^2 + 0.12 = 1.24$ **48.** $-\frac{1}{4}x^2 + 3 = 0$

49. Find the value of c such that the equation $x^2 - c = 0$ has 12 and -12 as solutions.

STEM **50. Physics** The equation $d = \frac{1}{2}at^2$ gives the distance d that an object starting at rest travels given acceleration a and time t. Suppose a ball rolls down the ramp shown at the right with acceleration $a = 2 \text{ ft/s}^2$. Find the time it will take the ball to roll from the top of the ramp to the bottom. Round to the nearest tenth of a second.

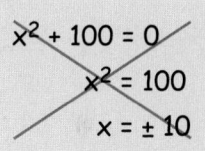

12 ft

© 51. Error Analysis Describe and correct the error made in solving the equation.

$x^2 + 100 = 0$
$x^2 = 100$
$x = \pm 10$

© 52. Open-Ended Write and solve an equation in the form $ax^2 + c = 0$, where $a \neq 0$, that satisfies the given condition.
  a. The equation has no solution.
  b. The equation has exactly one solution.
  c. The equation has two solutions.

Geometry Find the value of h for each triangle. If necessary, round to the nearest tenth.

53.

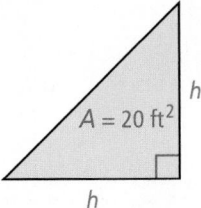

$A = 20 \text{ ft}^2$
h
h

54.

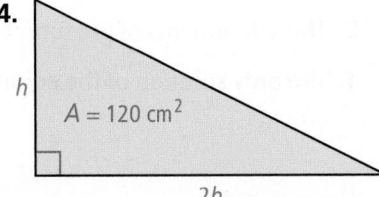

h
$A = 120 \text{ cm}^2$
$2h$

© 55. You can use a spreadsheet like the one at the right to solve a quadratic equation.
  a. What spreadsheet formula would you use to find the value in cell B2?
  b. Use a spreadsheet to find the solutions of the quadratic equation $6x^2 - 24 = 0$. Explain how you used the spreadsheet to find the solutions.
  c. Reasoning Suppose a quadratic equation has solutions that are not integers. How could you use a spreadsheet to approximate the solutions?

	A	B	
1	x	6x^2 − 24 = 0	
2	−3	▦	
3	−2	▦	
4	−1	▦	
5	0	▦	
6	1	▦	
7	2	▦	
8	3	▦	

 **Challenge**

56. a. Solve the equation $(x - 7)^2 = 0$.

    b. Find the vertex of the graph of the related function $y = (x - 7)^2$.

    c. Open-Ended Choose a value for h and repeat parts (a) and (b) using $(x - h)^2 = 0$ and $y = (x - h)^2$.

    d. Where would you expect to find the vertex of the graph of $y = (x + 4)^2$? Explain.

57. Geometry The trapezoid has an area of 1960 cm². Use the formula $A = \frac{1}{2}h(b_1 + b_2)$, where A represents the area of the trapezoid, h represents its height, and b_1 and b_2 represent its bases, to find the value of y.

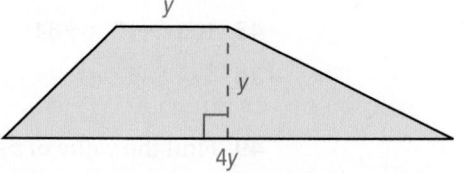

Apply What You've Learned

MATHEMATICAL
PRACTICES

MP 5

In the Apply What You've Learned in Lesson 9-2, you found a function that represents the area of the rectangular sign described on page 545. Use a graphing calculator or other graphing utility to graph the function. Select all of the following that are true. Explain your reasoning.

    A. The graph of the function is a parabola that has a maximum point.

    B. The graph of the function is a line with a positive slope.

    C. The axis of symmetry of the graph is $x = 4.5$.

    D. The axis of symmetry of the graph is $x = 9$.

    E. The x-intercepts of the function are 0 and 18.

    F. The only solution of the equation $0 = -\frac{2}{3}x^2 + 12x$ is 0.

Finding Roots

 **Common Core State Standards**

F-IF.C.7a Graph linear and quadratic functions and show intercepts, maxima, and minima. **Also A-REI.B.4**

MP 5

The solutions of a quadratic equation are the x-intercepts of the graph of the related quadratic function. Recall that the solutions and the related x-intercepts are often called roots of the equation or zeros of the function.

Activity

Use a graphing calculator to solve $x^2 - 6x + 3 = 0$.

Step 1   Enter $y = x^2 - 6x + 3$ on the **Y=** screen. Use the **CALC** feature. Select **ZERO**. The calculator will graph the function.

Step 2

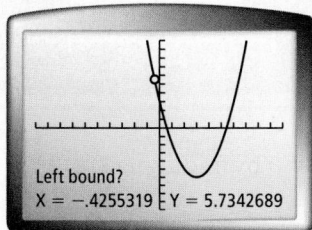

Left bound?
X = −.4255319   Y = 5.7342689

Move the cursor to the left of the first x-intercept. Press **enter** to set the left bound.

Step 3

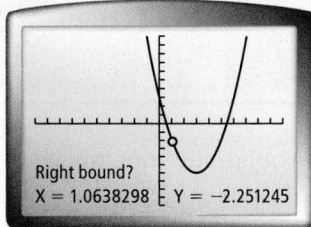

Right bound?
X = 1.0638298   Y = −2.251245

Move the cursor slightly to the right of the intercept. Press **enter** to set the right bound.

Step 4

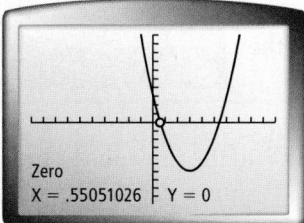

Zero
X = .55051026   Y = 0

Press **enter** to display the first root, which is about 0.55.

Repeat Steps 2–4 for the second x-intercept. The second root is about 5.45. So the solutions are about 0.55 and 5.45.

Suppose you cannot see both of the x-intercepts on your graph. You can find the values of y that are close to zero by using the **TABLE** feature. Use the **TBLSET** feature to control how the table behaves. Set △**TBL** to 0.5. Set **INDPNT:** and **DEPEND:** to **AUTO**. The calculator screen at the right shows part of the table for $y = 2x^2 - 48x + 285$.

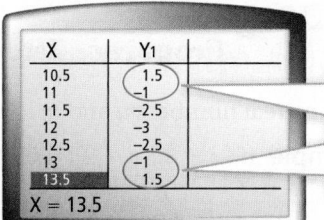

X	Y1
10.5	1.5
11	−1
11.5	−2.5
12	−3
12.5	−2.5
13	−1
13.5	1.5

X = 13.5

The graph crosses the x-axis when the values for y change signs. So the range of x-values should include 10.5 and 13.5.

Exercises

Use a graphing calculator to solve each equation. Round your solutions to the nearest hundredth.

1. $x^2 - 6x - 16 = 0$

2. $2x^2 + x - 6 = 0$

3. $\frac{1}{3}x^2 + 8x - 3 = 0$

4. $x^2 - 18x + 5 = 0$

5. $0.25x^2 - 8x - 45 = 0$

6. $0.5x^2 + 3x - 36 = 0$

9-4

Factoring to Solve Quadratic Equations

Common Core State Standards

A-REI.B.4b Solve quadratic equations by . . . factoring . . . **Also A-SSE.B.3a, A-CED.A.1, F-IF.C.8a**

MP 1, MP 2, MP 3, MP 4, MP 7

Objective To solve quadratic equations by factoring

Getting Ready!

You are finishing a stained glass hanging that your friend has started. You have enough supplies to add 6 ft² to the hanging. You are planning to add the same amount to the length and width. What will be the dimensions of the hanging when you are finished? How do you know?

Analyze the situation. What expressions can you use for the length and for the width?

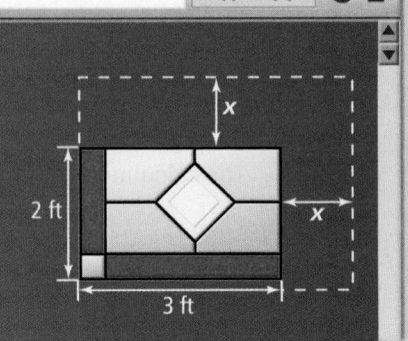

MATHEMATICAL PRACTICES In the previous lesson, you solved quadratic equations $ax^2 + bx + c = 0$ by finding square roots. This method works if $b = 0$.

Lesson Vocabulary
• Zero-Product Property

Essential Understanding You can solve some quadratic equations, including equations where $b \neq 0$, by using the *Zero-Product Property*.

The Multiplication Property of Zero states that for any real number a, $a \cdot 0 = 0$. This is equivalent to the following statement: For any real numbers a and b, if $a = 0$ or $b = 0$, then $ab = 0$. The Zero-Product Property reverses this statement.

take note

Property   Zero-Product Property

For any real numbers a and b, if $ab = 0$, then $a = 0$ or $b = 0$.

Example If $(x + 3)(x + 2) = 0$, then $x + 3 = 0$ or $x + 2 = 0$.

Problem 1   Using the Zero-Product Property

What are the solutions of the equation $(4t + 1)(t - 2) = 0$?

$$(4t + 1)(t - 2) = 0$$

$4t + 1 = 0$	or	$t - 2 = 0$

Use the Zero-Product Property.

$4t = -1$ or $t = 2$ Solve for t.

$t = -\dfrac{1}{4}$ or $t = 2$

Think

How else can you write the solutions?
You can write the solutions as a set in roster form: $\{-\frac{1}{4}, 2\}$.

Got It? **1.** What are the solutions of each equation?

    a. $(x + 1)(x - 5) = 0$ **b.** $(2x + 3)(x - 4) = 0$

    c. $(2y + 1)(y + 14) = 0$ **d.** $(7n - 2)(5n - 4) = 0$

You can also use the Zero-Product Property to solve equations of the form $ax^2 + bx + c = 0$ if the quadratic expression $ax^2 + bx + c$ can be factored.

 Problem 2 **Solving by Factoring**

Multiple Choice What are the solutions of the equation $x^2 + 8x + 15 = 0$?

    Ⓐ $-5, -3$ Ⓒ $-3, 5$

    Ⓑ $-5, 3$ Ⓓ $3, 5$

Plan

How can you factor $x^2 + 8x + 15$?
Find two integers with a product of 15 and a sum of 8.

$x^2 + 8x + 15 = 0$	
$(x + 3)(x + 5) = 0$	Factor $x^2 + 8x + 15$.
$x + 3 = 0$ or $x + 5 = 0$	Use the Zero-Product Property.
$x = -3$ or $x = -5$	Solve for x.

The solutions are -3 and -5. The correct answer is A.

 Got It? **2.** What are the solutions of each equation?

    a. $m^2 - 5m - 14 = 0$ **b.** $p^2 + p - 20 = 0$ **c.** $2a^2 - 15a + 18 = 0$

Before solving a quadratic equation, you may need to add or subtract terms from each side in order to write the equation in standard form. Then factor the quadratic expression.

Problem 3 **Writing in Standard Form First**

What are the solutions of $4x^2 - 21x = 18$?

Think

Why do you need to subtract 18 from each side before you factor?
To use the Zero-Product Property, one side of the equation must be zero.

$4x^2 - 21x = 18$	
$4x^2 - 21x - 18 = 0$	Subtract 18 from each side.
$(4x + 3)(x - 6) = 0$	Factor $4x^2 - 21x - 18$.
$4x + 3 = 0$ or $x - 6 = 0$	Use the Zero-Product Property.
$4x = -3$ or $x = 6$	Solve for x.
$x = -\dfrac{3}{4}$ or $x = 6$	

The solutions are $-\dfrac{3}{4}$ and 6.

 Got It? **3. a.** What are the solutions of $x^2 + 14x = -49$?

    b. Reasoning Why do quadratic equations of the form $x^2 + 2ax + a^2 = 0$ or $x^2 - 2ax + a^2 = 0$ have only one real-number solution?

Problem 4 Using Factoring to Solve a Real-World Problem

Photography You are constructing a frame for the rectangular photo shown. You want the frame to be the same width all the way around and the total area of the frame and photo to be 315 in.^{2}. What should the outer dimensions of the frame be?

11 in.

17 in.

Know → **Need** → **Plan**

The size of the photo is 11 in. by 17 in. The total area is 315 in.^{2}.

The outer dimensions of the frame

Write the frame's outer dimensions in terms of its width x. Use these dimensions to write an equation for the area of the frame and photo.

Think

Why can you ignore the factor of 4?
By the Zero-Product Property, one of the factors, 4, $x + 16$, or $x - 2$, must equal 0. Since $4 \neq 0$, either $x + 16$ or $x - 2$ equals 0.

$(2x + 11)(2x + 17) = 315$ Width $\times$ Length = Area

$4x^2 + 56x + 187 = 315$ Find the product $(2x + 11)(2x + 17)$.

$4x^2 + 56x - 128 = 0$ Subtract 315 from each side.

$4(x^2 + 14x - 32) = 0$ Factor out 4.

$4(x + 16)(x - 2) = 0$ Factor $x^2 + 14x - 32$.

$x + 16 = 0$ or $x - 2 = 0$ Use the Zero-Product Property.

$x = -16$ or $x = 2$ Solve for x.

The only reasonable solution is 2. So the outer dimensions of the frame are $2(2) + 11$ in. by $2(2) + 17$ in., or 15 in. by 21 in.

Got It? **4.** In Problem 4, suppose the total area of the frame and photo were 391 in.^{2}. What would the outer dimensions of the frame be?

Lesson Check

Do you know HOW?

Solve each equation.

1. $(v - 4)(v - 7) = 0$

2. $t^2 + 3t - 54 = 0$

3. $3y^2 - 17y + 24 = 0$

STEM **4. Carpentry** You are making a rectangular table. The area of the table should be 10 ft^2. You want the length of the table to be 1 ft shorter than twice its width. What should the dimensions of the table be?

Do you UNDERSTAND?

5. Vocabulary Give an example of how the Zero-Product Property can be used to solve a quadratic equation.

6. Compare and Contrast How is factoring the expression $x^2 - 6x + 8$ similar to solving the equation $x^2 - 6x + 8 = 0$? How is it different?

7. Reasoning Can you extend the Zero-Product Property to nonzero products of numbers? For example, if $ab = 8$, is it always true that $a = 8$ or $b = 8$? Explain.

Practice and Problem-Solving Exercises

 **Practice**

Use the Zero-Product Property to solve each equation.   ◀ **See Problem 1.**

8. $(x - 9)(x - 8) = 0$ **9.** $(4k + 5)(k + 7) = 0$ **10.** $n(n + 2) = 0$

11. $-3n(2n - 5) = 0$ **12.** $(7x + 2)(5x - 4) = 0$ **13.** $(4a - 7)(3a + 8) = 0$

Solve by factoring.   ◀ **See Problems 2 and 3.**

14. $x^2 + 11x + 10 = 0$ **15.** $g^2 + 4g - 32 = 0$ **16.** $s^2 - 14s + 45 = 0$

17. $2z^2 - 21z - 36 = 0$ **18.** $3q^2 + q - 14 = 0$ **19.** $4m^2 - 27m - 40 = 0$

20. $x^2 + 13x = -42$ **21.** $p^2 - 4p = 21$ **22.** $c^2 = 5c$

23. $2w^2 - 11w = -12$ **24.** $3h^2 + 17h = -10$ **25.** $9b^2 = 16$

26. Geometry A box shaped like a rectangular prism has a volume of 280 in.^{3}.   ◀ **See Problem 4.**
Its dimensions are 4 in. by $(n + 2)$ in. by $(n + 5)$ in. Find n.

27. Knitting You are knitting a blanket. You want the area of the blanket to be 24 ft^2.
You want the length of the blanket to be 2 ft longer than its width. What should the
dimensions of the blanket be?

STEM 28. Construction You are building a rectangular deck. The area of the deck should be
250 ft^2. You want the length of the deck to be 5 ft longer than twice its width. What
should the dimensions of the deck be?

 **Apply**

Use the Zero-Product Property to solve each equation. Write your solutions as a
set in roster form.

29. $x^2 + 6x + 8 = 0$ **30.** $a^2 + 8a + 12 = 0$ **31.** $k^2 + 7k + 10 = 0$

Write each equation in standard form. Then solve.

32. $7n^2 + 16n + 15 = 2n^2 + 3$ **33.** $4q^2 + 3q = 3q^2 - 4q + 18$

© **34. Think About a Plan** You have a rectangular koi pond that measures
6 ft by 8 ft. You have enough concrete to cover 72 ft^2 for a walkway,
as shown in the diagram. What should the width of the walkway be?
• How can you write the outer dimensions of the walkway?
• How can you represent the total area of the walkway and pond in
two ways?

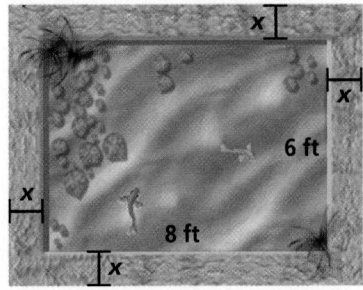

© **35. Reasoning** Find the zeros of the function $f(x) = x^2 - 3x + 2$ by
factoring. How can you verify the zeros of the function are correct by
looking at the graph?

© **36. Error Analysis** Describe and correct the error made in solving the equation.

© **37. Reasoning** How many solutions does an equation of the form
$x^2 - k^2 = 0$ have? Explain.

$2x^2 + 3x = 20$
$x(2x + 3) = 20$
$x = 0$ or $2x + 3 = 0$
$x = 0$ or $x = -\dfrac{3}{2}$

38. Sports You throw a softball into the air with an initial upward velocity of 38 ft/s and an initial height of 5 ft.

    a. Use the vertical motion model to write an equation that gives the ball's height h, in feet, at time t, in seconds.

    b. The ball's height is 0 ft when it is on the ground. Solve the equation you wrote in part (a) for $h = 0$ to find when the ball lands.

Solve each cubic equation by factoring out the GCF first.

39. $x^3 - 10x^2 + 24x = 0$ **40.** $x^3 - 5x^2 + 4x = 0$ **41.** $3x^3 - 9x^2 = 0$

 **Challenge**   **42.** Find an equation that has the given numbers as solutions. For example, 4 and -3 are solutions of $x^2 - x - 12 = 0$.

    a. $-5, 8$ **b.** $3, -2$ **c.** $\frac{1}{2}, -10$ **d.** $\frac{2}{3}, -\frac{5}{7}$

Solve. Factor by grouping.

43. $x^3 + 5x^2 - x - 5 = 0$ **44.** $x^3 + x^2 - 4x - 4 = 0$ **45.** $x^3 + 2x^2 - 9x - 18 = 0$

Apply What You've Learned

 **MATHEMATICAL PRACTICES**

MP 2

In the Apply What You've Learned in Lesson 9-2, you found a function that represents the area of the rectangular sign described on page 545.

    a. Write the function for the area of the rectangular sign in factored form.

    b. Find the zeros of the function.

    c. Describe how you can use the zeros to help you determine the maximum area of the rectangle.

Writing Quadratic Equations

© **Common Core State Standards**

A-CED.A.2 Create equations in two variables to represent the relationships between quantities . . .

MP 2

In Lesson 9-2, you learned the standard form of a quadratic equation, $ax^2 + bx + c = 0$. You have also learned how to find the roots of quadratic equations, and how to find the zeros of the related function.

Activity 1

1. Write the quadratic equation $x^2 - 2x - 15 = 0$ in factored form.

2. What are the roots of the equation?

3. Graph the quadratic function $y = x^2 - 2x - 15$. What are the zeros of the function?

4. How are the roots of the equation $x^2 - 2x - 15 = 0$ related to the zeros of the function $y = x^2 - 2x - 15$?

Activity 2

5. The roots of a quadratic equation are -2 and 8. How can the roots be used to write a quadratic equation in factored form? What are the factors of the quadratic expression?

6. What is this equation in standard form?

7. What is the related quadratic function in standard form?

8. How do you know the zeros of this function without graphing?

9. Graph the function on a graphing calculator. How can you use the calculator to check that the graph has the zeros you found in Exercise 8?

Activity 3

10. The graph of a quadratic function is shown at the right. What are the zeros of the function?

11. Write a quadratic function with the zeros you found in Exercise 10.

12. Choose another point on the graph and test whether it satisfies the equation you wrote in Exercise 11.

13. How can you use a graphing calculator to check that the function is correct? Explain, and check your work by using a graphing calculator.

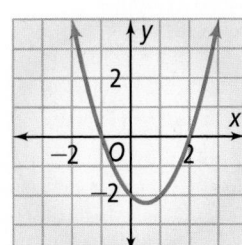

Activity 4

14. What are the zeros of the quadratic function at the right?

15. Write a quadratic function with the zeros you found in Exercise 14. Does your function match the graph at the right? Explain.

16. Let $a \neq 0$ and $a \neq 1$. If you multiply the function you found in Exercise 15 by a, you have a new function. What are its zeros?

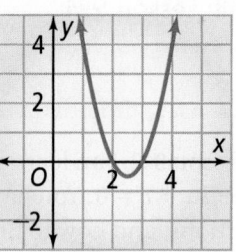

17. Let $g(x)$ be the function you found in Exercise 15 times some number a, where $a \neq 0$ and $a \neq 1$. If $g(x)$ represents the graph at the right, what must a be? Explain.

18. Using the value of a that you found in Exercise 17, write $g(x)$ in standard form.

19. Using a graphing calculator, verify that $g(x)$ matches the graph at the right.

Activity 5

20. Write a quadratic function with zeros -1 and 8.

21. How can you write other quadratic functions that have the same zeros? Explain.

22. Now write two other quadratic functions with the same zeros.

Ⓒ 23. Compare and Contrast Use a graphing calculator to graph all three functions on the same screen. Describe what is the same and what is different about the graphs.

Ⓒ 24. Reasoning How can you write a quadratic function with zeros -1 and 8 with a graph that opens down? Make a conjecture about how to write a quadratic function with a graph that opens down. Explain your reasoning.

Do you know HOW?

Order each group of quadratic functions from widest to narrowest graph.

1. $y = 2x^2, y = 0.5x^2, y = -x^2$

2. $f(x) = 4x^2, f(x) = \frac{2}{3}x^2, f(x) = 3x^2$

3. $f(x) = 0.6x^2, f(x) = 0.3x^2, f(x) = 0.2x^2$

4. $y = -2x^2, y = x^2, y = -0.25x^2$

Graph each function. Label the axis of symmetry and the vertex.

5. $y = \frac{1}{2}x^2$

6. $y = -2x^2 - 1$

7. $y = 3x^2 - 6x$

8. $y = x^2 + 2x + 4$

9. $y = -0.5x^2 + 2x + 1$

Solve each equation by graphing the related function. If the equation has no real-number solution, write *no solution.*

10. $x^2 - 16 = 0$

11. $x^2 + 9 = 0$

12. $0.25x^2 = 0$

Solve each equation by finding square roots. If the equation has no real-number solution, write *no solution.*

13. $m^2 = 81$ **14.** $t^2 - 7 = -18$

15. $5r^2 - 180 = 0$ **16.** $36n^2 = 9$

17. Sewing You have 324 ft^2 of fabric to make a circular play parachute for kids. What is the radius of the largest parachute you could make? Round to the nearest tenth of a foot.

Solve by factoring.

18. $b^2 + 3b - 4 = 0$

19. $n^2 + n - 12 = 0$

20. $2x^2 - 5x - 3 = 0$

21. $t^2 - 3t = 28$

22. $3n^2 = 6n$

STEM 23. Construction You are building a rectangular planter for your school garden. You want the area of the bottom to be 90 ft^2. You want the length of the planter to be 3 ft longer than twice its width. What should the dimensions of the bottom of the planter be?

Do you UNDERSTAND?

24. Writing Describe the steps you would use to graph the function $y = 2x^2 + 5$.

25. Reasoning Does the value of c in the quadratic function $y = ax^2 + bx + c$ affect the horizontal position of the vertex of the graph? Explain why or why not.

26. Writing Describe how the graph of $y = 3x^2$ differs from the graph of $y = x^2$.

Open-Ended Give an example of a quadratic function that matches each description.

27. The axis of symmetry is to the left of the y-axis.

28. Its graph lies entirely below the x-axis.

29. Its graph opens upward and has its vertex at $(0, 0)$.

30. a. Solve $x^2 - 4 = 0$ and $2x^2 - 8 = 0$ by graphing their related functions.

   b. Reasoning Why does it make sense that the graphs have the same x-intercepts?

Completing the Square

© **Common Core State Standards**

A-REI.B.4a Use the method of completing the square to transform any quadratic equation in x into an equation of the form $(x - p)^2 = q$ . . . **Also A-REI.A.1, A-REI.B.4b**

MP 1, MP 2, MP 3, MP 4

Objective To solve quadratic equations by completing the square

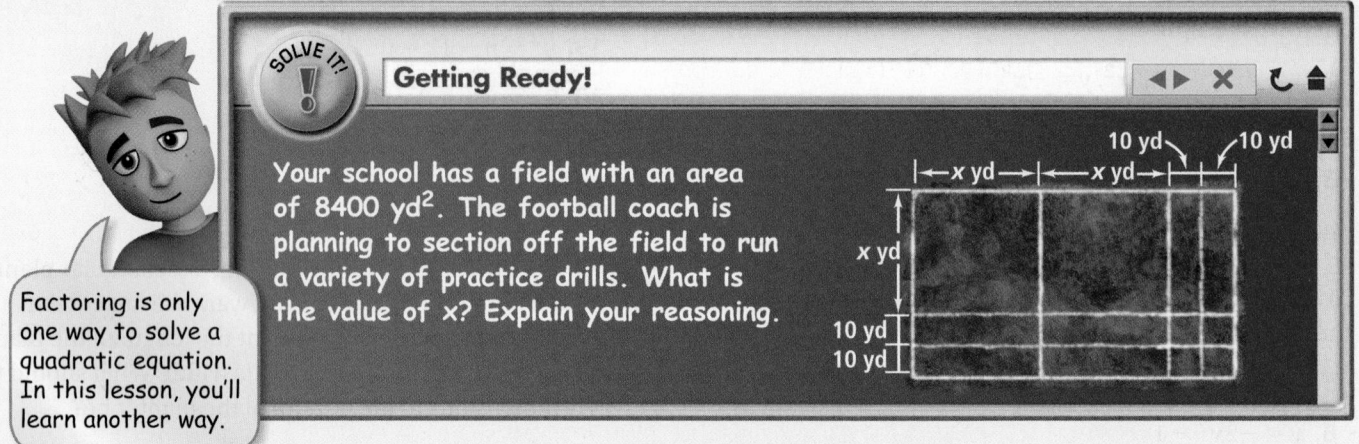

SOLVE IT!

Getting Ready!

Your school has a field with an area of 8400 yd². The football coach is planning to section off the field to run a variety of practice drills. What is the value of x? Explain your reasoning.

Factoring is only one way to solve a quadratic equation. In this lesson, you'll learn another way.

© **MATHEMATICAL PRACTICES**

In previous lessons, you solved quadratic equations by finding square roots and by factoring. These methods work in some cases, but not all.

Essential Understanding You can solve any quadratic equation by first writing it in the form $m^2 = n$.

You can model this process using algebra tiles. The algebra tiles at the right represent the expression $x^2 + 8x$.

Lesson Vocabulary
• completing the square

Here is the same expression rearranged to form part of a square. Notice that the x-tiles have been split evenly into two groups of four.

You can complete the square by adding 4^2, or 16, 1-tiles. The completed square is $x^2 + 8x + 16$, or $(x + 4)^2$.

In general, you can change the expression $x^2 + bx$ into a perfect-square trinomial by adding $\left(\frac{b}{2}\right)^2$ to $x^2 + bx$. This process is called **completing the square**. The process is the same whether b is positive or negative.

Problem 1 Finding *c* to Complete the Square

Think

Can *c* be negative?
No. *c* is the square of a real number, which is never negative.

What is the value of *c* such that $x^2 - 16x + c$ is a perfect-square trinomial?

The value of *b* is -16. The term to add to $x^2 - 16x$ is $\left(\frac{-16}{2}\right)^2$, or 64. So $c = 64$.

 Got It? **1.** What is the value of *c* such that $x^2 + 20x + c$ is a perfect-square trinomial?

To solve an equation in the form $x^2 + bx + c = 0$, first subtract the constant term *c* from each side of the equation.

 Problem 2 Solving $x^2 + bx + c = 0$

What are the solutions of the equation $x^2 - 14x + 16 = 0$?

Think

Why do you write $x - 7 \approx \pm 5.74$ as two equations?
Recall that the symbol $\pm$ means "plus or minus." That means $x - 7$ equals 5.74 or -5.74.

$x^2 - 14x + 16 = 0$		
$x^2 - 14x = -16$		Subtract 16 from each side.
$x^2 - 14x + 49 = -16 + 49$		Add $\left(\frac{-14}{2}\right)^2$, or 49, to each side.
$(x - 7)^2 = 33$		Write $x^2 - 14x + 49$ as a square.
$x - 7 = \pm\sqrt{33}$		Find square roots of each side.
$x - 7 \approx \pm 5.74$		Use a calculator to approximate $\sqrt{33}$.
$x - 7 \approx 5.74$ or $x - 7 \approx -5.74$		Write as two equations.
$x \approx 5.74 + 7$ or $x \approx -5.74 + 7$		Add 7 to each side.
$x \approx 12.74$ or $x \approx 1.26$		Simplify.

 Got It? **2. a.** What are the solutions of the equation $x^2 + 9x + 15 = 0$?
b. Reasoning Could you use factoring to solve part (a)? Explain.

The equation $y = (x - h)^2 + k$ represents a parabola with vertex (h, k). You can use the method of completing the square to find the vertex of quadratic functions of the form $y = x^2 + bx + c$.

Problem 3 Finding the Vertex by Completing the Square

Find the vertex of $y = x^2 + 6x + 8$ by completing the square.

Think

Why do you need to add the same number to each side?
You need to add the same number to each side to keep the equation balanced.

$y = x^2 + 6x + 8$	
$y - 8 = x^2 + 6x$	Subtract 8 from each side.
$y - 8 + 9 = x^2 + 6x + 9$	Add $\left(\frac{6}{2}\right)^2$, or 9, to each side.
$y + 1 = (x + 3)^2$	Simplify the left side and write the right side as a square.
$y = (x + 3)^2 - 1$	Subtract 1 from each side so that equation is in vertex form.

The vertex of $y = x^2 + 6x + 8$ is $(-3, -1)$.

The method of completing the square works when $a = 1$ in $ax^2 + bx + c = 0$. To solve an equation when $a \neq 1$, divide each side by a before completing the square.

 Problem 4 **Completing the Square When $a \neq 1$**

Gardening You are planning a flower garden consisting of three square plots surrounded by a 1-ft border. The total area of the garden and the border is 100 ft². What is the side length x of each square plot?

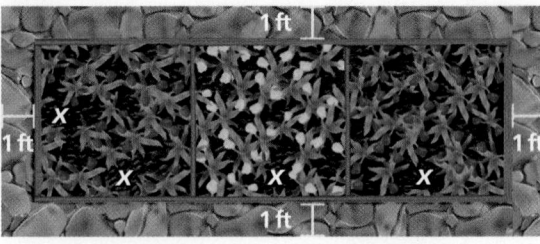

🌱 **Red tulips**   🌱 **Yellow tulips**

Know
- Area of garden and border
- Expressions for the dimensions of the garden and border.

Need
The side length x of each square plot

Plan
Write and solve an equation that relates the dimensions and area of the garden and border.

Step 1   Write an equation that you can use to solve the problem.

$$(3x + 2)(x + 2) = 100 \quad \text{Length} \times \text{Width} = \text{Area}$$

$$3x^2 + 8x + 4 = 100 \quad \text{Find the product } (3x + 2)(x + 2).$$

$$3x^2 + 8x = 96 \quad \text{Subtract 4 from each side.}$$

$$x^2 + \frac{8}{3}x = 32 \quad \text{Divide each side by 3.}$$

Step 2   Complete the square.

$$x^2 + \frac{8}{3}x + \frac{16}{9} = 32 + \frac{16}{9} \quad \text{Add } \left(\frac{4}{3}\right)^2\text{, or } \frac{16}{9}\text{, to each side.}$$

$$\left(x + \frac{4}{3}\right)^2 = \frac{304}{9} \quad \text{Write left side as a square and right side as a fraction.}$$

Step 3   Solve the equation.

$$x + \frac{4}{3} = \pm\sqrt{\frac{304}{9}} \quad \text{Find square roots of each side.}$$

$$x + \frac{4}{3} \approx \pm 5.81 \quad \text{Use a calculator to approximate } \sqrt{\frac{304}{9}}.$$

$$x + \frac{4}{3} \approx 5.81 \quad \text{or} \quad x + \frac{4}{3} \approx -5.81 \quad \text{Write as two equations.}$$

$$x \approx 4.48 \quad \text{or} \quad x \approx -7.14 \quad \text{Solve for } x.$$

The negative answer does not make sense in this problem. So the side length of each square plot is about 4.48 ft.

Think

Why do you need to find $\frac{1}{2}\left(\frac{8}{3}\right)$?

To make a perfect-square trinomial on the left side of $x^2 + \frac{8}{3}x = 32$, find $\frac{1}{2}\left(\frac{8}{3}\right)$. Then square the result and add to each side of the equation.

Got It? **4.** Suppose the total area of the garden and border in Problem 4 is 150 ft^2. What is the side length x of each square plot? Round to the nearest hundredth.

 Lesson Check

Do you know HOW?

Solve each equation by completing the square.

1. $x^2 + 8x = 180$

2. $t^2 - 4t - 165 = 0$

3. $m^2 + 7m - 294 = 0$

4. $2z^2 + 3z = 135$

Do you UNDERSTAND?

5. Vocabulary Tell whether you would use square roots, factoring, or completing the square to solve each equation. Explain your choice of method.

a. $k^2 - 3k = 304$ **b.** $t^2 - 6t + 16 = 0$

6. Compare and Contrast How is solving a quadratic equation using square roots like completing the square? How is it different?

 **Practice and Problem-Solving Exercises**

 **Practice** Find the value of c such that each expression is a perfect-square trinomial. **See Problem 1.**

7. $x^2 + 18x + c$ **8.** $z^2 + 22z + c$ **9.** $p^2 - 30p + c$

10. $k^2 - 5k + c$ **11.** $g^2 + 17g + c$ **12.** $q^2 - 4q + c$

Solve each equation by completing the square. If necessary, round to the nearest hundredth. **See Problem 2.**

13. $g^2 + 7g = 144$ **14.** $r^2 - 4r = 30$ **15.** $m^2 + 16m = -59$

16. $a^2 - 2a - 35 = 0$ **17.** $m^2 + 12m + 19 = 0$ **18.** $w^2 - 14w + 13 = 0$

Find the vertex of each parabola by completing the square. **See Problem 3.**

19. $y = x^2 + 4x - 16$ **20.** $y = x^2 + 18x - 307$ **21.** $y = x^2 - 2x - 323$

22. $y = x^2 + 6x - 7$ **23.** $y = x^2 + 2x - 28$ **24.** $y = x^2 + 12x - 468$

Solve each equation by completing the square. If necessary, round to the nearest hundredth. **See Problem 4.**

25. $4a^2 - 8a = 24$ **26.** $2y^2 - 8y - 10 = 0$ **27.** $5n^2 - 3n - 15 = 10$

28. $4w^2 + 12w - 44 = 0$ **29.** $3r^2 + 18r = 21$ **30.** $2v^2 - 10v - 20 = 8$

31. Art The painting shown at the right has an area of 420 in.^{2}. What is the value of x?

x in.

$(2x + 5)$ in.

B Apply

© 32. Think About a Plan A park is installing a rectangular reflecting pool surrounded by a concrete walkway of uniform width. The reflecting pool will measure 42 ft by 26 ft. There is enough concrete to cover 460 ft² for the walkway. What is the maximum width x of the walkway?

- How can drawing a diagram help you solve this problem?
- How can you write an expression in terms of x for the area of the walkway?

33. Landscaping A school is fencing in a rectangular area for a playground. It plans to enclose the playground using fencing on three sides, as shown at the right. The school has budgeted enough money for 75 ft of fencing material and would like to make a playground with an area of 600 ft².

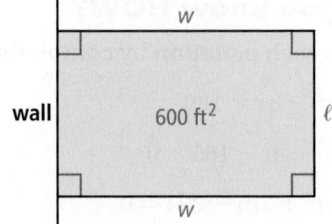

a. Let w represent the width of the playground. Write an expression in terms of w for the length of the playground.

b. Write and solve an equation to find the width w. Round to the nearest tenth of a foot.

c. What should the length of the playground be?

Solve each equation. If necessary, round to the nearest hundredth. If there is no real-number solution, write *no solution*.

34. $q^2 + 3q + 1 = 0$ **35.** $s^2 + 5s = -11$ **36.** $w^2 + 7w - 40 = 0$

37. $z^2 - 8z = -13$ **38.** $4p^2 - 40p + 56 = 0$ **39.** $m^2 + 4m + 13 = -8$

40. $2p^2 - 15p + 8 = 43$ **41.** $3r^2 - 27r = 3$ **42.** $s^2 + 9s + 20 = 0$

© 43. Error Analysis A classmate was completing the square to solve $4x^2 + 10x = 8$. For her first step she wrote $4x^2 + 10x + 25 = 8 + 25$. What was her error?

© 44. Reasoning Explain why completing the square is a better strategy for solving $x^2 - 7x - 9 = 0$ than graphing or factoring.

© 45. Open-Ended Write a quadratic equation and solve it by completing the square. Show your work.

Use each graph to estimate the values of x for which $f(x) = 5$. Then write and solve an equation to find the values of x such that $f(x) = 5$. Round to the nearest hundredth.

46. $f(x) = x^2 - 2x - 1$ **47.** $f(x) = -\frac{1}{2}x^2 + 2x + 6$

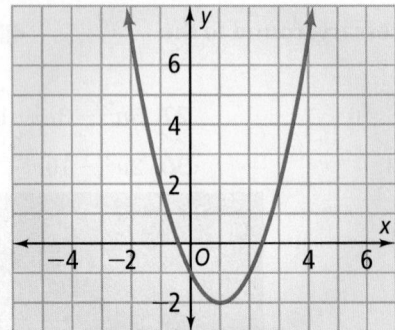   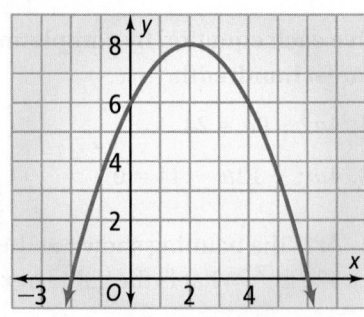

 **Challenge**

48. Geometry Suppose the prism at the right has the same surface area as a cube with edges 8 in. long.
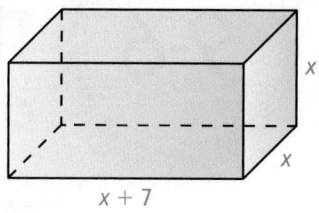

a. Write an expression for the surface area of the prism shown.

b. Write an equation that relates the surface area of the prism to the surface area of the 8-in. cube.

c. Solve the equation you wrote in part (b). What are the dimensions of the prism?

49. a. Solve the equation $x^2 - 6x + 4 = 0$, but leave the solutions in the form $p \pm \sqrt{q}$.

b. Use the formula $x = \frac{-b}{2a}$ to find the coordinates of the vertex of the graph of $y = x^2 - 6x + 4$.

c. Reasoning Explain the relationship between your answers to parts (a) and (b).

Standardized Test Prep

 SAT/ACT

50. The rectangular poster has an area 40 ft². What is the value of x to the nearest tenth of a foot?

51. The width of a notebook is 2.15×10^{-2} m. In decimal form, how many meters wide is the notebook?

52. What is the solution of the equation $19 + x = 35$?

53. How many elements are in the intersection of the two sets $M = \{2, 3, 4, 5\}$ and $N = \{1, 3, 5, 9\}$?

54. A ribbon with straight edges has an area of 24 in.². Its width is x and its length is $2x + 13$. What is the width of the ribbon in inches?

55. What is the x-intercept of the graph of $2x + 3y = 9$?

56. The sum of two numbers is 20. The difference between three times the larger number and twice the smaller number is 40. What is the larger number?

$(x+1)$ ft

$(x+2)$ ft

Mixed Review

Solve by factoring.

◀ **See Lesson 9-4.**

57. $n^2 + 11n + 30 = 0$

58. $9v^2 - 64 = 0$

59. $12w^2 = 28w + 5$

Simplify.

◀ **See Lesson 7-3.**

60. $(m^3)^4$

61. $-b^7(b^8)^{-1}$

62. $t(t^2)^6$

63. $y^8(y^{-7})^{-3}$

Get Ready! **To prepare for Lesson 9-6, do Exercises 64–66.**

Evaluate $b^2 - 4ac$ for the given values of a, b, and c.

◀ **See Lesson 1-2.**

64. $a = 2, b = 5, c = -7$

65. $a = 2, b = 4, c = 2$

66. $a = 1, b = 3, c = 6$

9-6

The Quadratic Formula and the Discriminant

© Common Core State Standards

A-REI.B.4a Use the method of completing the square to transform any quadratic equation in *x* into an equation of the form $(x - p)^2 = q$ ... Derive the quadratic formula from this form. **Also A-REI.B.4b**

MP 1, MP 2, MP 3, MP 4, MP 7, MP 8

Objectives To solve quadratic equations using the quadratic formula
To find the number of solutions of a quadratic equation

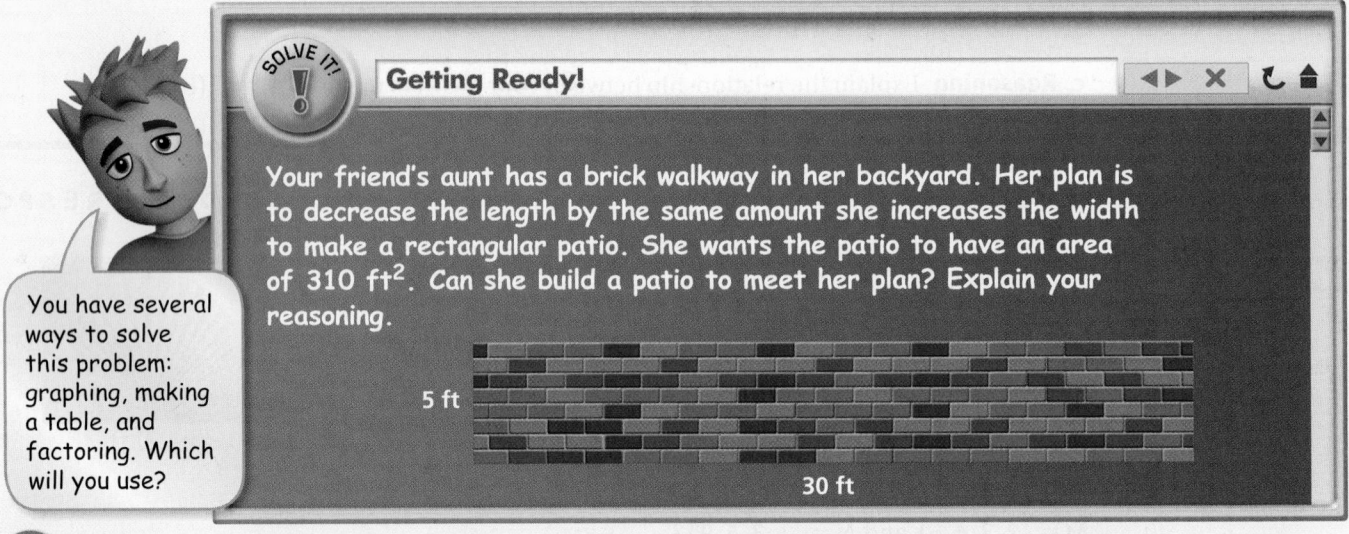

SOLVE IT!

Getting Ready!

Your friend's aunt has a brick walkway in her backyard. Her plan is to decrease the length by the same amount she increases the width to make a rectangular patio. She wants the patio to have an area of 310 ft². Can she build a patio to meet her plan? Explain your reasoning.

5 ft

30 ft

You have several ways to solve this problem: graphing, making a table, and factoring. Which will you use?

 **MATHEMATICAL PRACTICES**

Recall that quadratic equations can have two, one, or no real-number solutions. A quadratic equation can never have more than two solutions.

Lesson Vocabulary
• quadratic formula
• discriminant

Essential Understanding You can find the solution(s) of *any* quadratic equation using the **quadratic formula**.

---

take note

Key Concept   Quadratic Formula

Algebra

If $ax^2 + bx + c = 0$, and $a \neq 0$, then
$$x = \frac{-b \pm \sqrt{b^2 - 4ac}}{2a}$$

Example

Suppose $2x^2 + 3x - 5 = 0$. Then $a = 2$, $b = 3$, and $c = -5$. Therefore
$$x = \frac{-(3) \pm \sqrt{(3)^2 - 4(2)(-5)}}{2(2)}$$

Here's Why It Works If you complete the square for the general equation $ax^2 + bx + c = 0$, you can derive the quadratic formula.

Step 1 Write $ax^2 + bx + c = 0$ so the coefficient of x^2 is 1.

$$ax^2 + bx + c = 0$$

$$x^2 + \frac{b}{a}x + \frac{c}{a} = 0 \qquad \text{Divide each side by } a.$$

Step 2 Complete the square.

$$x^2 + \frac{b}{a}x = -\frac{c}{a} \qquad \text{Subtract } \frac{c}{a} \text{ from each side.}$$

$$x^2 + \frac{b}{a}x + \left(\frac{b}{2a}\right)^2 = -\frac{c}{a} + \left(\frac{b}{2a}\right)^2 \qquad \text{Add } \left(\frac{b}{2a}\right)^2 \text{ to each side.}$$

$$\left(x + \frac{b}{2a}\right)^2 = -\frac{c}{a} + \frac{b^2}{4a^2} \qquad \text{Write the left side as a square.}$$

$$\left(x + \frac{b}{2a}\right)^2 = -\frac{4ac}{4a^2} + \frac{b^2}{4a^2} \qquad \text{Multiply } -\frac{c}{a} \text{ by } \frac{4a}{4a} \text{ to get like denominators.}$$

$$\left(x + \frac{b}{2a}\right)^2 = \frac{b^2 - 4ac}{4a^2} \qquad \text{Simplify the right side.}$$

Step 3 Solve the equation for x.

$$\sqrt{\left(x + \frac{b}{2a}\right)^2} = \pm\sqrt{\frac{b^2 - 4ac}{4a^2}} \qquad \text{Take square roots of each side.}$$

$$x + \frac{b}{2a} = \pm\frac{\sqrt{b^2 - 4ac}}{2a} \qquad \text{Simplify the right side.}$$

$$x = -\frac{b}{2a} \pm \frac{\sqrt{b^2 - 4ac}}{2a} \qquad \text{Subtract } \frac{b}{2a} \text{ from each side.}$$

$$x = \frac{-b \pm \sqrt{b^2 - 4ac}}{2a} \qquad \text{Simplify.}$$

> This step uses the property $\sqrt{\frac{m}{n}} = \frac{\sqrt{m}}{\sqrt{n}}$, which you will study in Lesson 10-2.

Be sure to write a quadratic equation in standard form before using the quadratic formula.

Problem 1 Using the Quadratic Formula

What are the solutions of $x^2 - 8 = 2x$? Use the quadratic formula.

$$x^2 - 2x - 8 = 0 \qquad \text{Write the equation in standard form.}$$

$$x = \frac{-b \pm \sqrt{b^2 - 4ac}}{2a} \qquad \text{Use the quadratic formula.}$$

$$x = \frac{-(-2) \pm \sqrt{(-2)^2 - 4(1)(-8)}}{2(1)} \qquad \text{Substitute 1 for } a, -2 \text{ for } b, \text{ and } -8 \text{ for } c.$$

$$x = \frac{2 \pm \sqrt{36}}{2} \qquad \text{Simplify.}$$

$$x = \frac{2 + 6}{2} \qquad \text{or} \qquad x = \frac{2 - 6}{2} \qquad \text{Write as two equations.}$$

$$x = 4 \qquad \text{or} \qquad x = -2 \qquad \text{Simplify.}$$

Think

Why do you need to write the equation in standard form?
You can only use the quadratic formula with equations in the form $ax^2 + bx + c = 0$.

✔ **Got It? 1.** What are the solutions of $x^2 - 4x = 21$? Use the quadratic formula.

When the radicand in the quadratic formula is not a perfect square, you can use a calculator to approximate the solutions of an equation.

Problem 2 Finding Approximate Solutions

Sports In the shot put, an athlete throws a heavy metal ball through the air. The arc of the ball can be modeled by the equation $y = -0.04x^2 + 0.84x + 2$, where x is the horizontal distance, in meters, from the athlete and y is the height, in meters, of the ball. How far from the athlete will the ball land?

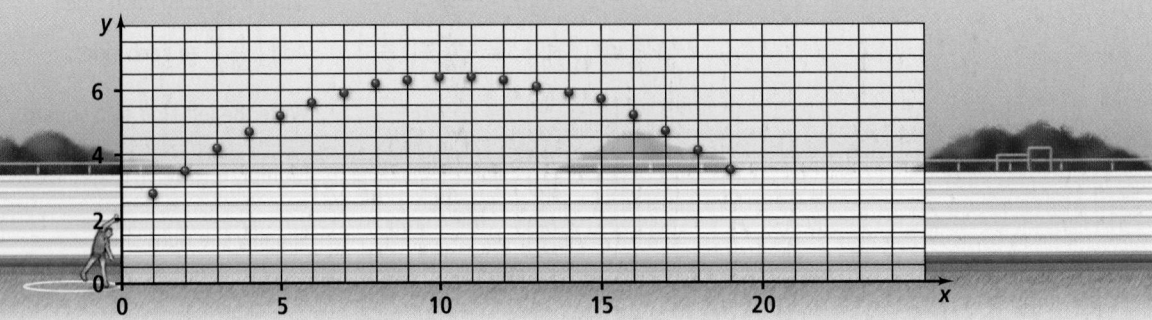

Think

Why do you substitute 0 for y?
When the ball hits the ground, its height will be 0.

$0 = -0.04x^2 + 0.84x + 2$	Substitute 0 for y in the given equation.
$x = \dfrac{-b \pm \sqrt{b^2 - 4ac}}{2a}$	Use the quadratic formula.
$x = \dfrac{-0.84 \pm \sqrt{0.84^2 - 4(-0.04)(2)}}{2(-0.04)}$	Substitute -0.04 for a, 0.84 for b, and 2 for c.
$x = \dfrac{-0.84 \pm \sqrt{1.0256}}{-0.08}$	Simplify.

$$x = \frac{-0.84 + \sqrt{1.0256}}{-0.08} \quad \text{or} \quad x = \frac{-0.84 - \sqrt{1.0256}}{-0.08} \qquad \text{Write as two equations.}$$

$$x \approx -2.16 \quad \text{or} \quad x \approx 23.16 \qquad \text{Simplify.}$$

Only the positive answer makes sense in this situation. The ball will land about 23.16 m from the athlete.

 Got It? **2.** A batter strikes a baseball. The equation $y = -0.005x^2 + 0.7x + 3.5$ models its path, where x is the horizontal distance, in feet, the ball travels and y is the height, in feet, of the ball. How far from the batter will the ball land? Round to the nearest tenth of a foot.

There are many methods for solving a quadratic equation.

Method	When to Use
Graphing	Use if you have a graphing calculator handy.
Square roots	Use if the equation has no x-term.
Factoring	Use if you can factor the equation easily.
Completing the square	Use if the coefficient of x^2 is 1, but you cannot easily factor the equation.
Quadratic formula	Use if the equation cannot be factored easily or at all.

Think

Can you use the quadratic formula to solve part (A)?
Yes. You can use the quadratic formula with $a = 3$, $b = 0$, and $c = -9$. However, it is faster to use square roots.

© **Problem 3** **Choosing an Appropriate Method**

Which method(s) would you choose to solve each equation? Explain your reasoning.

A $3x^2 - 9 = 0$ Square roots; there is no x-term

B $x^2 - x - 30 = 0$ Factoring; the equation is easily factorable

C $6x^2 + 13x - 17 = 0$ Quadratic formula, graphing; the equation cannot be factored

D $x^2 - 5x + 3 = 0$ Quadratic formula, completing the square, or graphing; the coefficient of the x^2-term is 1, but the equation cannot be factored

E $-16x^2 - 50x + 21 = 0$ Quadratic formula, graphing; the equation cannot be factored easily since the numbers are large

 Got It? **3.** Which method(s) would you choose to solve each equation? Justify your reasoning.

     a. $x^2 - 8x + 12 = 0$ **b.** $169x^2 = 36$ **c.** $5x^2 + 13x - 1 = 0$

Quadratic equations can have two, one, or no real-number solutions. Before you solve a quadratic equation, you can determine how many real-number solutions it has by using the discriminant. The **discriminant** is the expression under the radical sign in the quadratic formula.

$$x = \frac{-b \pm \sqrt{b^2 - 4ac}}{2a} \longleftarrow \text{the discriminant}$$

The discriminant of a quadratic equation can be positive, zero, or negative.

take note

Key Concept **Using the Discriminant**

Discriminant	$b^2 - 4ac > 0$	$b^2 - 4ac = 0$	$b^2 - 4ac < 0$
Example	$x^2 - 6x + 7 = 0$ The discriminant is $(-6)^2 - 4(1)(7) = 8$, which is positive.	$x^2 - 6x + 9 = 0$ The discriminant is $(-6)^2 - 4(1)(9) = 0$.	$x^2 - 6x + 11 = 0$ The discriminant is $(-6)^2 - 4(1)(11) = -8$, which is negative.
Number of Solutions	There are two real-number solutions.	There is one real-number solution.	There are no real-number solutions.

Problem 4 Using the Discriminant

How many real-number solutions does $2x^2 - 3x = -5$ have?

Plan

Can you solve this problem another way?
Yes. You could actually solve the equation to find any solutions. However, you only need to know the number of solutions, so use the discriminant.

Think

Write the equation in standard form.

Evaluate the discriminant by substituting 2 for a, -3 for b, and 5 for c.

Draw a conclusion.

Write

$2x^2 - 3x + 5 = 0$

$b^2 - 4ac = (-3)^2 - 4(2)(5)$
$= -31$

Because the discriminant is negative, the equation has no real-number solutions.

  Got It? **4. a.** How many real-number solutions does $6x^2 - 5x = 7$ have?
   b. Reasoning If a is positive and c is negative, how many real-number solutions will the equation $ax^2 + bx + c = 0$ have? Explain.

 Lesson Check

Do you know HOW?

Use the quadratic formula to solve each equation. If necessary, round answers to the nearest hundredth.

1. $-3x^2 - 11x + 4 = 0$

2. $7x^2 - 2x = 8$

3. How many real-number solutions does the equation $-2x^2 + 8x - 5 = 0$ have?

Do you UNDERSTAND?

 **4. Vocabulary** Explain how the discriminant of the equation $ax^2 + bx + c = 0$ is related to the number of x-intercepts of the graph of $y = ax^2 + bx + c$.

5. Reasoning What method would you use to solve the equation $x^2 + 9x + c = 0$ if $c = 14$? If $c = 7$? Explain.

6. Writing Explain how completing the square is used to derive the quadratic formula.

 Practice and Problem-Solving Exercises

 **Practice** Use the quadratic formula to solve each equation. 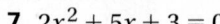 **See Problem 1.**

7. $2x^2 + 5x + 3 = 0$ **8.** $5x^2 + 16x - 84 = 0$ **9.** $4x^2 + 7x - 15 = 0$

10. $3x^2 - 41x = -110$ **11.** $18x^2 - 45x - 50 = 0$ **12.** $3x^2 + 44x = -96$

13. $3x^2 + 19x = 154$ **14.** $2x^2 - x - 120 = 0$ **15.** $5x^2 - 47x = 156$

Use the quadratic formula to solve each equation. Round your answer to the nearest hundredth.

See Problem 2.

16. $x^2 + 8x + 11 = 0$

17. $5x^2 + 12x - 2 = 0$

18. $2x^2 - 16x = -25$

19. $8x^2 - 7x - 5 = 0$

20. $6x^2 + 9x = 32$

21. $3x^2 + 5x = 4$

22. Football A football player punts a ball. The path of the ball can be modeled by the equation $y = -0.004x^2 + x + 2.5$, where x is the horizontal distance, in feet, the ball travels and y is the height, in feet, of the ball. How far from the football player will the ball land? Round to the nearest tenth of a foot.

Which method(s) would you choose to solve each equation? Justify your reasoning.

See Problem 3.

23. $x^2 + 4x - 15 = 0$

24. $9x^2 - 49 = 0$

25. $4x^2 - 41x = 73$

26. $3x^2 - 7x + 3 = 0$

27. $x^2 + 4x - 60 = 0$

28. $-4x^2 + 8x + 1 = 0$

Find the number of real-number solutions of each equation.

See Problem 4.

29. $x^2 - 2x + 3 = 0$

30. $x^2 + 7x - 5 = 0$

31. $x^2 + 3x + 11 = 0$

32. $x^2 - 15 = 0$

33. $x^2 + 2x = 0$

34. $9x^2 + 12x + 4 = 0$

 **Apply**

Use any method to solve each equation. If necessary, round your answer to the nearest hundredth.

35. $3w^2 = 48$

36. $3x^2 + 2x - 4 = 0$

37. $6g^2 - 18 = 0$

38. $3p^2 + 4p = 10$

39. $k^2 - 4k = -4$

40. $13r^2 - 117 = 0$

41. Think About a Plan You operate a dog-walking service. You have 50 customers per week when you charge $14 per walk. For each $1 decrease in your fee for walking a dog, you get 5 more customers per week. Can you ever earn $750 in a week? Explain.
- What quadratic equation in standard form can you use to model this situation?
- How can the discriminant of the equation help you solve the problem?

42. Sports Your school wants to take out an ad in the paper congratulating the basketball team on a successful season, as shown below. The area of the photo will be half the area of the entire ad. What is the value of x?

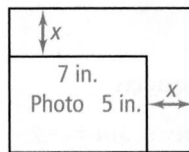

43. Writing How can you use the discriminant to write a quadratic equation that has two solutions?

44. Error Analysis Describe and correct the error at the right that a student made in finding the discriminant of $2x^2 + 5x - 6 = 0$.

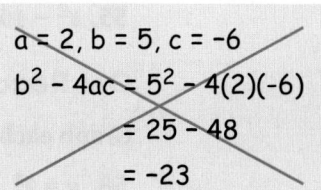

$a = 2, b = 5, c = -6$
$b^2 - 4ac = 5^2 - 4(2)(-6)$
$= 25 - 48$
$= -23$

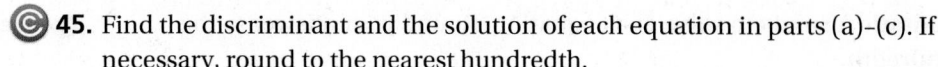 **45.** Find the discriminant and the solution of each equation in parts (a)–(c). If necessary, round to the nearest hundredth.

    a. $x^2 - 6x + 5 = 0$ **b.** $x^2 + x - 20 = 0$ **c.** $2x^2 - 7x - 3 = 0$

    d. Reasoning When the discriminant is a perfect square, are the solutions rational or irrational? Explain.

 **Challenge**   **46. Reasoning** The solutions of any quadratic equation $ax^2 + bx + c = 0$ are

$$\frac{-b + \sqrt{b^2 - 4ac}}{2a} \text{ and } \frac{-b - \sqrt{b^2 - 4ac}}{2a}.$$

    a. Find a formula for the sum of the solutions.

    b. One solution of $2x^2 + 3x - 104 = 0$ is -8. Use the formula you found in part (a) to find the second solution.

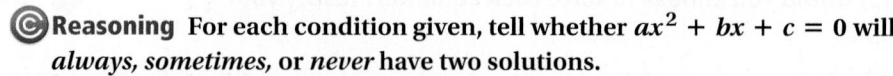 **Reasoning** For each condition given, tell whether $ax^2 + bx + c = 0$ will *always, sometimes,* or *never* have two solutions.

    47. $b^2 < 4ac$ **48.** $b^2 = 0$ **49.** $ac < 0$

Standardized Test Prep

SAT/ACT

50. What are the approximate solutions of the equation $x^2 - 7x + 3 = 0$?

    Ⓐ $-6.54, 0.46$ Ⓑ $-6.54, -0.46$ Ⓒ $-0.46, 6.54$ Ⓓ $0.46, 6.54$

51. Which of the following relations is a function?

    Ⓕ $\{(1, 2), (3, 5), (1, 4), (2, 3)\}$ Ⓗ $\{(8, 2), (6, 3), (6, 11), (-8, 2)\}$

    Ⓖ $\{(-5, 6), (0, 9), (-1, 2), (0, 6)\}$ Ⓘ $\{(-1, 3), (7, 3), (-7, 2), (4, 5)\}$

52. What equation do you get when you solve $3a - b = 2c$ for b?

    Ⓐ $b = -3a + 2c$ Ⓑ $b = 3a - 2c$ Ⓒ $b = 3a + 2c$ Ⓓ $b = -3a - 2c$

53. What are the approximate solutions of the equation $\frac{1}{3}x^2 - \frac{5}{4}x + 1 = 0$? Use a graphing calculator.

    Ⓕ $1.07, 2.77$ Ⓖ $1.16, 2.59$ Ⓗ $0.87, 10.38$ Ⓘ $0.19, 16.01$

Short Response

54. Suppose the line through points $(n, 6)$ and $(1, 2)$ is parallel to the graph of $2x + y = 3$. Find the value of n. Show your work.

Mixed Review

Solve each equation by completing the square.   ◀ **See Lesson 9-5.**

55. $s^2 - 10s + 13 = 0$ **56.** $m^2 + 3m = -2$ **57.** $3w^2 + 18w - 1 = 0$

Get Ready!   **To prepare for Lesson 9-7, do Exercises 58–61.**

Graph each function.   ◀ **See Lesson 7-6.**

58. $y = 2^x$ **59.** $y = 3^x$ **60.** $y = \left(\frac{1}{3}\right)^x$ **61.** $y = \left(\frac{1}{2}\right)^x$

9-7

Linear, Quadratic, and Exponential Models

© **Common Core State Standards**

F-LE.A.1a Prove that linear functions grow by equal differences . . . and that exponential functions grow by equal factors over equal intervals. **Also F-LE.A.2, F-LE.A.3**

MP 1, MP 2, MP 3, MP 4, MP 7

Objective To choose a linear, quadratic, or exponential model for data

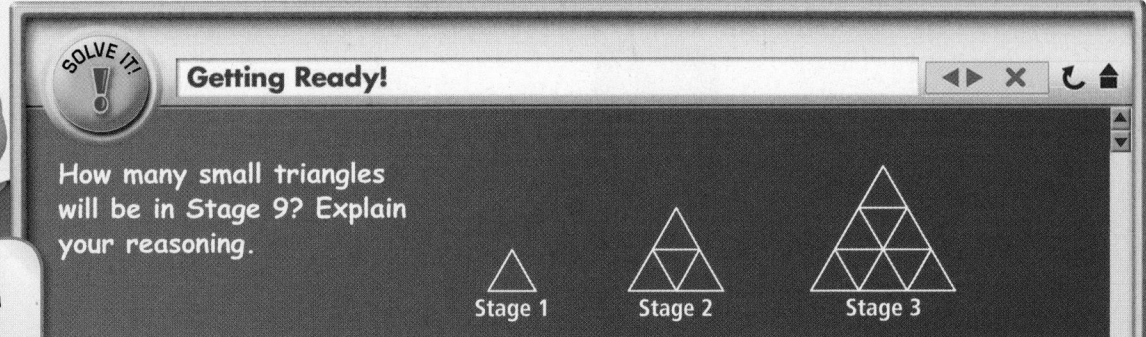

Do you see the pattern? You can model it with a function.

SOLVE IT!

Getting Ready!

How many small triangles will be in Stage 9? Explain your reasoning.

Stage 1   Stage 2   Stage 3

© **MATHEMATICAL PRACTICES** **Essential Understanding** You can use the linear, quadratic, or exponential functions you have studied to model some sets of data.

take note

Concept Summary   Linear, Quadratic, and Exponential Functions

Linear: $y = mx + b$ Quadratic: $y = ax^2 + bx + c$ Exponential: $y = a \cdot b^x$

© **Problem 1** Choosing a Model by Graphing

Graph each set of points. Which model is most appropriate for each set?

A $(1, 3), (0, 0), (-3, 3),$ $(-1, -1), (-2, 0)$

B $(0, 2), (-1, 4),$ $(1, 1), (2, 0.5)$

C $(-1, -2), (0, -1),$ $(1, 0), (3, 2)$

Think

Can you eliminate possibilities?
Yes. For example, you know that a linear model isn't appropriate in parts (A) and (B) because the slope between any two points is not constant.

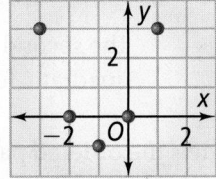

Quadratic model

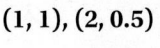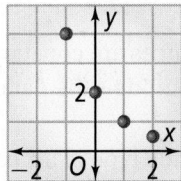

Exponential model

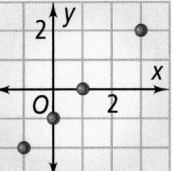

Linear model

When the x-values in a set of data pairs have a common difference, you can analyze data numerically to find the best model. You can use a linear function to model data pairs with y-values that have a common difference. You can use an exponential function to model data pairs with y-values that have a common ratio.

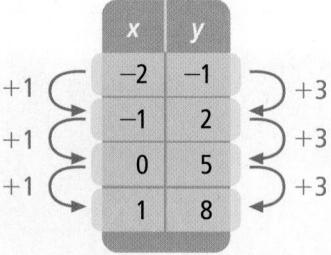

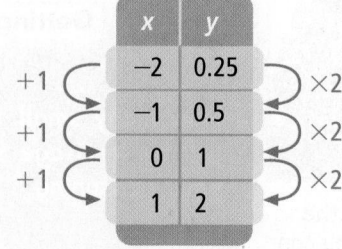

The y-values have a common difference of 3. A linear model fits the data.

The y-values have a common ratio of 2. An exponential model fits the data.

For quadratic functions, the second differences are constant.

In the table at the right, the second differences of the y-values are all 4, so a quadratic model fits the data.

	x	y	First differences	
+1	−1	1	−2	
+1	0	−1	+2	+4
+1	1	1	+6	+4
+1	2	7	+10	+4
	3	17		

Second differences

© **Problem 2** **Choosing a Model Using Differences or Ratios**

Which type of function best models the data? Use differences or ratios.

Plan

How can you get started?
Begin by checking the first differences of the y-values. Then check the second differences and ratios, if necessary.

A

	x	y	
+1	−3	9	−4
+1	−2	5	−4
+1	−1	1	−4
+1	0	−3	−4
	1	−7	

B

	x	y		
+1	0	0	−0.25	
+1	1	−0.25	−0.75	−0.5
+1	2	−1	−1.25	−0.5
+1	3	−2.25	−1.75	−0.5
	4	−4		

The first differences are constant, so a linear function models the data.

The second differences are constant, so a quadratic function models the data.

 Got It? **2.** Which type of function best models the ordered pairs
$(-1, 0.5), (0, 1), (1, 2), (2, 4),$ and $(3, 8)$? Use differences or ratios.

Real-world data seldom fall exactly into linear, exponential, or quadratic patterns. However, you can determine which type of function represents the best possible model for the data.

 Problem 3 Modeling Real-World Data

Transportation The data at the right give the value of a used car over time. Which type of function best models the data? Write an equation to model the data.

Value of Used Car

Years	Value ($)
0	12,575
1	11,065
2	9750
3	8520
4	7540

Know
The value of a used car over time

Need
The most appropriate model for the data

Plan
Graph the data and then use differences or ratios to find a model for the situation.

Step 1
Graph the data.

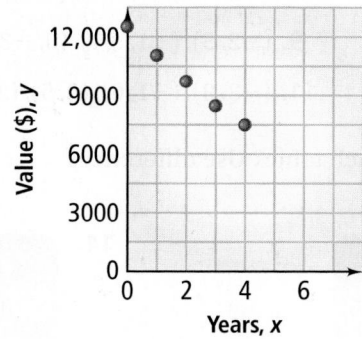

The graph curves and does not look quadratic. It may be exponential.

Step 2
Test for a common ratio.

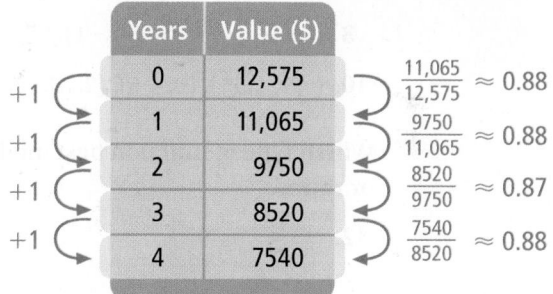

The value of the car is roughly 0.88 times its value the previous year.

Step 3
Write an exponential model.

Relate $y = a \cdot b^x$

Define Let a = the initial value, 12,575.
Let b = the decay factor, 0.88.

Write $y = 12{,}575 \cdot 0.88^x$

Step 4
Test two points other than (0, 12,575).

Test (2, 9750):

$y = 12{,}575 \cdot 0.88^2$

$y \approx 9738$

Test (4, 7540):

$y = 12{,}575 \cdot 0.88^4$

$y \approx 7541$

The point (2, 9738) is close to the data point (2, 9750). The point (4, 7541) is close to the data point (4, 7540). The equation $y = 12{,}575 \cdot 0.88^x$ models the data.

 Got It? **3.** The table shows the annual income of a small theater company. Which type of function best models the data? Write an equation to model the data.

Theater Company Annual Income

Year	0	1	2	3	4
Income ($)	18,254	18,730	19,215	19,695	20,175

Lesson Check

Do you know HOW?

Which type of function best models each set of data points?

1. $(0, 11), (1, 5), (2, 3), (3, 5), (4, 11)$

2. $(-4, -10), (-2, -7), (0, -4), (2, -1), (4, 2)$

3. $(-1, 8), (0, 4), (2, 1), (3, 0.5)$

Do you UNDERSTAND?

 4. Reasoning Can the y-values in a set of data pairs have both a common ratio and a common difference? Explain why or why not.

5. Writing Explain how to decide whether a linear, exponential, or quadratic function is the most appropriate model for a set of data.

 ## Practice and Problem-Solving Exercises

 Graph each set of points. Which model is most appropriate for each set?　　**See Problem 1.**

6. $(-2, -3), (-1, 0), (0, 1), (1, 0), (2, -3)$ 　　**7.** $(-2, -8), (0, -4), (3, 2), (5, 6)$

8. $(-3, 6), (-1, 0), (0, -1), (1, -1.5)$ 　　**9.** $(-2, 5), (-1, -1), (0, -3), (1, -1), (2, 5)$

10. $(-1, -5\frac{2}{3}), (0, -5), (2, 3), (3, 27)$ 　　**11.** $(-3, 8), (-1, 6), (0, 5), (2, 3), (3, 2)$

Which type of function best models the data in each table? Use differences or ratios.　　**See Problem 2.**

12.

x	y
0	0
1	1.5
2	6
3	13.5
4	24

13.

x	y
0	-5
1	-3
2	-1
3	1
4	3

14.

x	y
0	1
1	1.2
2	1.44
3	1.728
4	2.0736

Which type of function best models the data in each table? Write an equation to model the data.　　**See Problem 3.**

15.

x	y
0	0
1	3
2	11.3
3	24.7
4	43.3

16.

x	y
0	5
1	2
2	0.79
3	0.32
4	0.128

17.

x	y
0	2
1	1.52
2	1
3	0.49
4	0

18. Sports The number of people attending a school's first five football games is shown in the table below. Which type of function best models the data? Write an equation to model the data.

Game	1	2	3	4	5
Attendance	248	307	366	425	484

19. Banking The average monthly balance of a savings account is shown in the table at the right. Which type of function best models the data? Write an equation to model the data.

Month	Balance ($)
0	540
1	556.20
2	572.89
3	590.07
4	607.77

Ⓑ Apply

Ⓒ 20. Error Analysis Tom claims that, because the data pairs $(1, 4)$, $(2, 6)$, $(3, 9)$, and $(4, 13.5)$ have y-value with a common ratio, they are best modeled by a quadratic function. What is his error?

Ⓒ 21. a. Make a table of five ordered pairs for each function using consecutive x-values. Find the common second difference.
  i. $f(x) = x^2 - 3$ **ii.** $f(x) = 3x^2$ **iii.** $f(x) = 4x^2 - 5x$
  b. What is the relationship between the common second difference and the coefficient of the x^2-term?
  c. Reasoning Explain how you could use this relationship to model data.

Ⓒ 22. Think About a Plan The number of visitors at a Web site over several days is shown in the table at the right. What is an equation that models the data?
  • Does the graph of the data suggest a type of function to use?
  • Will your equation fit the data exactly? How do you know?

Day	Visitors
1	52
2	197
3	447
4	805
5	1270

Ⓒ 23. Open-Ended Write a set of data pairs that you could model with a quadratic function.

STEM 24. Zoology A conservation organization collected the data on the number of frogs in a local wetland, shown in the table at the right. Which type of function best models the data? Write an equation to model the data.

Year	Number of Frogs
0	120
1	101
2	86
3	72
4	60

25. The table below shows the projected population of a small town. Let $t = 0$ correspond to the year 2020.
  a. Graph the data. Does the graph suggest a linear, exponential, or quadratic model?
  b. Find the rate of change in population with respect to time from one data pair to the next. How do the results support your answer to part (a)?
  c. Write a function that models the data shown in the table.
  d. Use the function from part (c) to predict the town's population in 2050.
  e. Suppose the projected population s of another small town is represented by the function $s = 50t + 1300$. Let $t = 0$ correspond to the year 2020. Write an expression that can be used to find the difference in population of the two towns.

Year, t	0	5	10	15
Population, p	5100	5700	6300	6900

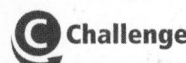 Challenge

26. Reasoning Write a quadratic function $y = ax^2 + bx + c$ whose graph passes through the points $(0, 7)$, $(2, 13)$, and $(4, 35)$.

 27. Reasoning The diagram at the right shows the differences for the cubic function $f(x) = x^3 - 2x + 5$ for the x-values 0, 1, 2, 3, 4, and 5.

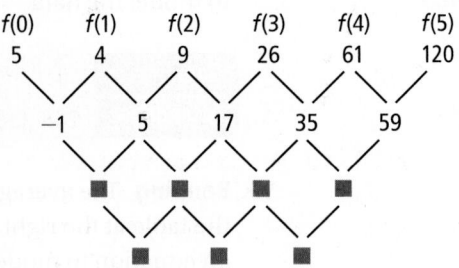

a. Write the second and third differences in the appropriate locations in the diagram.

b. What do you predict the third difference would be if $f(6)$ were added to the diagram?

c. Do you think that the third differences will be constant for other cubic functions? Explain why or why not.

Standardized Test Prep

SAT/ACT

28. The graph at the right shows the number y of visitors to a museum over x days. Which function models the number of visitors?

Ⓐ $y = -100x + 900$

Ⓒ $y = -100x + 800$

Ⓑ $y = 900(0.875)^x$

Ⓓ $y = -50x^2 - 400x + 1300$

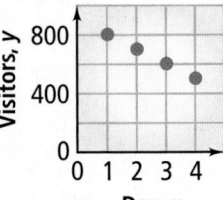

29. Which expression is equivalent to $(4x^3 + 2x^2 + 1) + (3x^2 + 8x + 2)$?

Ⓕ $7x^2 + 10x + 3$ Ⓖ $7x^3 + 10x^2 + 3$ Ⓗ $4x^3 + 5x^2 + 3$ Ⓘ $4x^3 + 5x^2 + 8x + 3$

30. Which line passes through the point $(1, 3)$ and is parallel to the line graphed at the right?

Ⓐ $y = 2x + 1$

Ⓒ $y = 2x - 5$

Ⓑ $y = 2x + 3$

Ⓓ $y = -5x + 8$

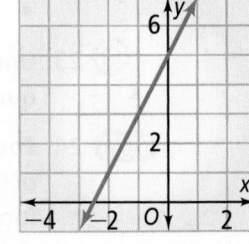

Short Response

31. What are the factors of $10x^2 - x - 2$? Show your work.

Mixed Review

Use the quadratic formula to solve each equation. If necessary, round to the nearest hundredth.

 **See Lesson 9-6.**

32. $4x^2 + 4x - 3 = 0$ **33.** $x^2 + 2x - 7 = 0$ **34.** $3x^2 - 8x = -1$

Get Ready! To prepare for Lesson 9-8, do Exercises 35–37.

Solve by elimination.

 **See Lesson 6-3.**

35. $x + y = 10$
    $x - y = 2$

36. $5x - 6y = -32$
    $3x + 6y = 48$

37. $-2x + 15y = -32$
    $7x - 5y = 17$

Analyzing Residual Plots

 **Common Core State Standards**

S-ID.B.6b Informally assess the fit of a function by plotting and analyzing residuals.

MP 5

Recall that in the Concept Byte Using Residuals in Chapter 5, you used a residual plot to determine whether the best linear model is a good fit for the data. You can also use residual plots to analyze the fit of other models.

Activity

Analyze the residual plot to determine whether the model is a good fit for the data.

x	0.3	0.7	1.0	1.8	2.3	3.6	4.6	5.9	7.3	8.7	9.0	11.3	13.5	14.7
y	0.6	0.5	0.5	0.7	1.0	2.2	3.8	6.4	10.1	14.4	15.5	25.1	36.1	42.9

Step 1   Using a graphing calculator, create a scatter plot of the data.

The data appear to be best modeled by either a quadratic function or an exponential function. Find both functions and then analyze the residual plots to determine which function is a better fit for the data.

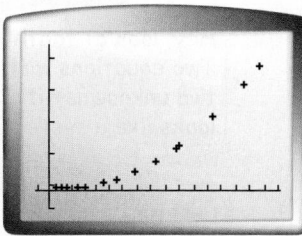

Step 2   Perform a quadratic regression.

Press **stat** . Select CALC and QUADREG to find the model.
$y = 0.22x^2 - 0.28x + 0.55$

Step 3   Plot the residuals.

Press **stat plot** 1. Turn on Plot 1 using L_1 for the Xlist. Place the cursor to select the Ylist. Press LIST (2nd STAT) and select RESID. Press **zoom** 9 to graph.

There is no apparent pattern in the residual plot.

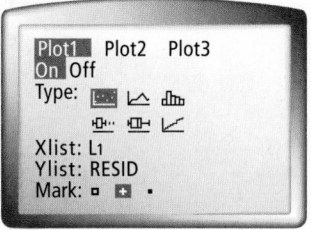

Step 4   Check the exponential function.

1. Using a graphing calculator, perform an exponential regression. Press **stat** . Select CALC and EXPREG.

What is the exponential function that models the data?

2. Using a graphing calculator, plot the residuals.

Does the residual plot appear to follow a pattern? Sketch the residual plot.

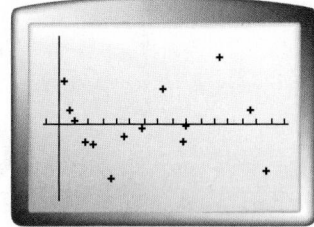

3. Using what you know about residual plots, which type of model best fits the data? Explain.

Exercise

4. By analyzing the residual plots, determine whether the data are best modeled by a quadratic, an exponential, or a linear function. Explain.

x	0.43	0.78	1.10	2.05	3.14	4.60	6.23	7.51	8.83	9.03	10.20	11.51
y	0.84	0.90	0.95	1.13	1.38	1.80	2.43	3.07	3.90	4.05	5.01	6.36

Systems of Linear and Quadratic Equations

© Common Core State Standards

A-REI.C.7 Solve a simple system consisting of a linear equation and a quadratic equation in two variables algebraically and graphically . . . **Also A-CED.A.3, A-REI.D.11**

MP 1, MP 3, MP 4, MP 5

Objective To solve systems of linear and quadratic equations

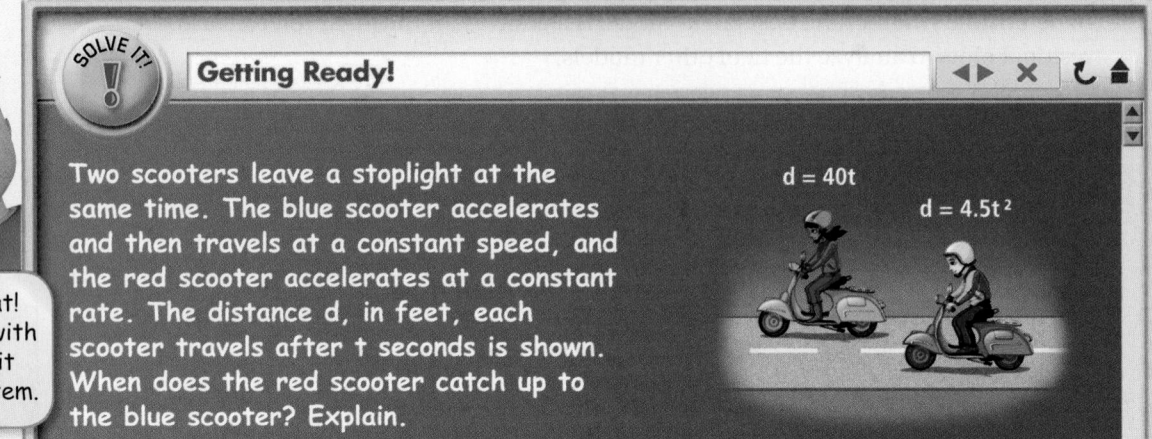

SOLVE IT!

Getting Ready!

Two scooters leave a stoplight at the same time. The blue scooter accelerates and then travels at a constant speed, and the red scooter accelerates at a constant rate. The distance d, in feet, each scooter travels after t seconds is shown. When does the red scooter catch up to the blue scooter? Explain.

$d = 40t$

$d = 4.5t^2$

Hey, look at that! Two equations with two unknowns—it looks like a system.

© MATHEMATICAL PRACTICES

Essential Understanding You can solve systems of linear and quadratic equations graphically and algebraically. This type of system can have two solutions, one solution, or no solutions.

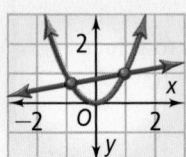

Two solutions

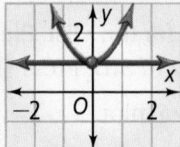

One solution

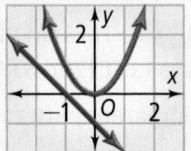

No solutions

Plan

How can you solve this system by graphing?
The points where the two graphs intersect are the solutions of the system.

 Problem 1 Solving by Graphing

What are the solutions of the system? Solve by graphing. $y = x^2 - x - 2$
$y = -x + 2$

Step 1   Graph both equations in the same coordinate plane.

Step 2   Identify the point(s) of intersection, if any. The points of intersection are $(-2, 4)$ and $(2, 0)$.

The solutions of the system are $(-2, 4)$ and $(2, 0)$.

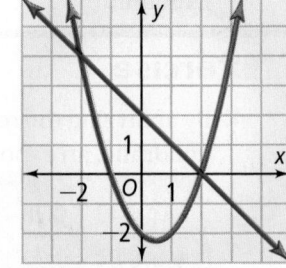

Got It? **1.** What are the solutions of each system? Solve by graphing.

    a. $y = 2x^2 + 1$
          $y = -2x + 5$

    b. $y = x^2 + x + 3$
          $y = -x$

In Lesson 6-3, you solved linear systems using elimination. The same technique can be applied to systems of linear and quadratic equations.

 Problem 2 **Using Elimination**

Recreation Since opening day, attendance at Pool A has increased steadily, while attendance at Pool B first rose and then fell. Equations modeling the daily attendance *y* at each pool are shown below, where *x* is the number of days since opening day. On what day(s) was the attendance the same at both pools? What was the attendance?

    Pool A: $y = 28x + 4$
    Pool B: $y = -x^2 + 39x + 64$

Know	Need	Plan
Equations giving the attendance at each pool	The day(s) when the attendance was the same	Use elimination to solve the system formed by the equations.

Step 1 Eliminate *y*.

$$y = -x^2 + 39x + 64$$
$$\underline{-(y = \qquad 28x + 4)}$$ Subtract the two equations.
$$0 = -x^2 + 11x + 60$$ Subtraction Property of Equality

Step 2 Factor and solve for *x*.

$$0 = -x^2 + 11x + 60$$
$$0 = -(x^2 - 11x - 60)$$ Factor out -1.
$$0 = -(x + 4)(x - 15)$$ Factor.
$$x + 4 = 0 \quad \text{or} \quad x - 15 = 0$$ Zero-Product Property
$$x = -4 \quad \text{or} \quad x = 15$$ Solve for *x*.

Step 3 Eliminate the impossible solution. The pools cannot be open a negative number of days, so $x \neq -4$.

Step 4 Use the viable solution to find the corresponding *y*-value. Use either equation.

$$y = -x^2 + 39x + 64 \qquad\qquad y = 28x + 4$$
$$y = -(15)^2 + 39(15) + 64 \qquad y = 28(15) + 4$$
$$y = -225 + 585 + 64 \qquad\quad y = 424$$
$$y = 424$$

The pools had the same attendance on Day 15 with 424 people.

 Got It? **2.** In Problem 2, suppose the daily attendance *y* at Pool A can be modeled by the equation $y = 36x + 54$. On what day(s) was the attendance the same at both pools? What was the attendance?

Substitution is another method you have used to solve linear systems. This method also works with systems of linear and quadratic equations.

 Problem 3 Using Substitution

What are the solutions of the system? $y = x^2 - 6x + 10$
                                              $y = 4 - x$

Plan

Which variable should you substitute for?
Substitute for y since both equations are already solved for y.

Step 1   Write a single equation containing only one variable.

$$y = x^2 - 6x + 10$$

$$4 - x = x^2 - 6x + 10 \qquad \text{Substitute } 4 - x \text{ for } y.$$

$$4 - x - (4 - x) = x^2 - 6x + 10 - (4 - x) \qquad \text{Subtract } 4 - x \text{ from each side.}$$

$$0 = x^2 - 5x + 6 \qquad \text{Write in standard form.}$$

Step 2   Factor and solve for x.

$$0 = (x - 2)(x - 3) \qquad \text{Factor.}$$

$$x - 2 = 0 \quad \text{or} \quad x - 3 = 0 \qquad \text{Zero-Product Property}$$

$$x = 2 \quad \text{or} \quad x = 3 \qquad \text{Solve for } x.$$

Step 3   Find corresponding y-values. Use either original equation.

$$y = 4 - x = 4 - 2 = 2 \qquad\qquad y = 4 - x = 4 - 3 = 1$$

The solutions of the system are $(2, 2)$ and $(3, 1)$.

 Got It? 3. What are the solutions of the system? $y - 30 = 12x$
                                                                              $y = x^2 + 11x - 12$

 Problem 4 Solving With a Graphing Calculator

What are the solutions of the system? $y = -x + 5$
Use a graphing calculator. $y = -x^2 + 4x + 1$

Step 1   Enter the equations on the **Y=** screen. Press **graph** to display the system.

Step 2

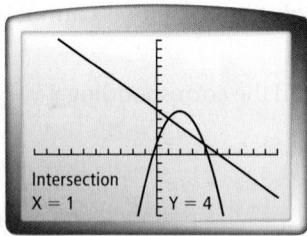

Intersection
X = 1   Y = 4

Step 3

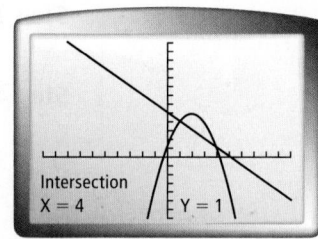

Intersection
X = 4   Y = 1

Think

How can you check your solutions?
Substitute them into the original equations and simplify.

Use the **CALC** feature. Select **INTERSECT.** Move the cursor close to a point of intersection. Press **enter** three times to find the point of intersection.

Repeat Step 2 to find the second intersection point.

The solutions are $(1, 4)$ and $(4, 1)$.

 **Got It?** **4. a.** What are the solutions of the system? $y = x^2 - 2$
Use a graphing calculator. $y = -x$

b. Reasoning How else can you solve the system in part (a)? Explain.

 ## Lesson Check

Do you know HOW?

1. Use a graph to solve the system $y = x^2 + x - 2$ and $y = x + 2$.

2. Use elimination to solve the system $y = x^2 - 13x + 52$ and $y = -14x + 94$.

3. Use substitution to solve the system $y = x^2 - 6x + 9$ and $y + x = 5$.

4. Use a graphing calculator to solve the system $y = -x^2 + 4x + 1$ and $y = 2x + 2$.

Do you UNDERSTAND?

5. Use two different methods to solve the system $y = x$ and $y = 2x^2 + 10x + 9$. Which method do you prefer? Explain.

6. Open-Ended Write a system of linear and quadratic equations with the given number of solutions.
a. two   **b.** exactly one   **c.** none

7. Compare and Contrast How are solving systems of linear equations and solving systems of linear and quadratic equations alike? How are they different?

 ## Practice and Problem-Solving Exercises

 **A Practice**   Solve each system by graphing.   **See Problem 1.**

8. $y = x^2 + 1$
     $y = x + 1$

9. $y = x^2 + 4$
     $y = 4x$

10. $y = x^2 - 5x - 4$
      $y = -2x$

11. $y = x^2 + 2x + 1$
      $y = x + 1$

12. $y = x^2 + 2x + 5$
      $y = -2x + 1$

13. $y = 3x + 4$
      $y = -x^2 + 4$

Solve each system using elimination.   **See Problem 2.**

14. $y = -x + 3$
      $y = x^2 + 1$

15. $y = x^2$
      $y = x + 2$

16. $y = -x - 7$
      $y = x^2 - 4x - 5$

17. Sales The equations at the right model the numbers y of two portable music players sold x days after both players were introduced. On what day(s) did the company sell the same number of each player? How many players of each type were sold?

Music Player A: $y = 191x - 32$
Music Player B: $y = -x^2 + 200x + 20$

Solve each system using substitution.   **See Problem 3.**

18. $y = x^2 - 2x - 6$
      $y = 4x + 10$

19. $y = 3x - 20$
      $y = -x^2 + 34$

20. $y = x^2 + 7x + 100$
      $y + 10x = 30$

21. $-x^2 - x + 19 = y$
      $x = y + 80$

22. $3x - y = -2$
      $2x^2 = y$

23. $y = 3x^2 + 21x - 5$
      $-10x + y = -1$

Graphing Calculator Solve each system using a graphing calculator.
See Problem 4.

24. $y = x^2 - 2x - 2$
$y = -2x + 2$

25. $y = -x^2 + 2$
$y = 4 - 0.5x$

26. $y = x - 5$
$y = x^2 - 6x + 5$

27. $y = -0.5x^2 - 2x + 1$
$y + 3 = -x$

28. $y = 2x^2 - 24x + 76$
$y + 7 = 11$

29. $-x^2 - 8x - 15 = y$
$-x + y = 3$

 **Apply**

30. The equation $x^2 + y^2 = 25$ defines a circle with center at the origin and radius 5. The line $y = x + 1$ passes through the circle. Using the substitution method, find the point(s) at which the circle and the line intersect.

31. Think About a Plan A company's logo consists of a parabola and a line. The parabola in the logo can be modeled by the function $y = 3x^2 - 4x + 2$. The line intersects the parabola when $x = 0$ and when $x = 2$. What is an equation of the line?
- How can you find the coordinates of the points of intersection?
- Can you write an equation of the line given the points of intersection?

32. Business The daily number of customers y at a coffee shop can be modeled by the function $y = 0.25x^2 - 5x + 80$, where x is the number of days since the beginning of the month. The daily number of customers at a second shop can be modeled by a linear function. Both shops have the same number of customers on days 10 and 20. What function models the number of customers at the second shop?

33. Error Analysis A classmate says that the system $y = x^2 + 2x + 4$ and $y = x + 1$ has one solution. Explain the classmate's error.

34. Writing Explain why a system of linear and quadratic equations cannot have an infinite number of solutions.

Challenge

35. Geometry The figures below show rectangles that are centered on the y-axis with bases on the x-axis and upper vertices defined by the function $y = -0.3x^2 + 4$. Find the area of each rectangle.

a.

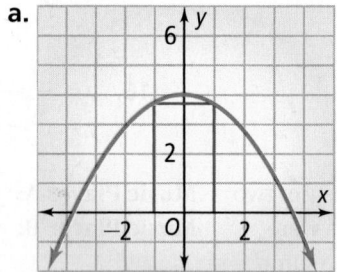

b.

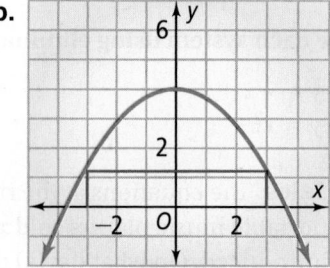

c. Find the coordinates of the vertices of the square constructed in the same manner. Round to the nearest hundredth.

d. Find the area of the square. Round to the nearest hundredth.

36. What are the solutions of the system $y = x^2 + x + 6$ and $y = 2x^2 - x + 3$? Explain how you solved the system.

Standardized Test Prep

SAT/ACT

37. A designer sketches a design for a tabletop on graph paper. The table is bounded by a parabola and a line. The parabola can be modeled by the function $y = 2x^2 - 3x + 2$. The line intersects the parabola when $x = -1$ and when $x = 3$. What is an equation of the line?

   Ⓐ $y = -x + 8$ Ⓒ $y = 2x + 5$

   Ⓑ $y = x + 8$ Ⓓ $y = -2x + 5$

38. Which equation illustrates the Distributive Property?

   Ⓕ $4(x + 2) = 4x + 8$ Ⓗ $4(x + 2) = 4(2 + x)$

   Ⓖ $4(x + 2) = (x + 2)4$ Ⓘ $4(x + 2) = 4(x + 2)$

39. Which rate is equivalent to 30 m/s?

   Ⓐ 3 km/h   Ⓑ 108 km/h   Ⓒ 3000 km/h   Ⓓ 108,000 km/h

40. Which of the following is equivalent to 0.05%?

   Ⓕ 0.00005   Ⓖ 0.0005   Ⓗ 0.005   Ⓘ 0.05

Short Response

41. A box with 4 balls weighs 5 lb. The same box with 10 balls weighs 11 lb. Write an equation in slope-intercept form for the weight y of a box containing x balls. Then rewrite the equation in standard form using integer coefficients.

Mixed Review

Which type of function best models the data in each table? Write an equation to model the data.

                                               ◀ See Lesson 9-7.

42.

x	y
−1	0.2
0	0
1	0.2
2	0.8
3	1.8
4	3.2

43.

x	y
−1	1.6
0	4
1	10
2	25
3	62.5
4	156.25

44.

x	y
−1	11.2
0	7
1	2.8
2	−1.4
3	−5.6
4	−9.8

Get Ready! To prepare for Lesson 10-1, do Exercises 45–50.

Simplify each expression.   ◀ See Lesson 1-3.

45. $\sqrt{196}$ **46.** $\sqrt{\dfrac{25}{49}}$ **47.** $\sqrt{1.44}$

48. $\sqrt{81}$ **49.** $\sqrt{0.36}$ **50.** $\sqrt{400}$

Pull It **All Together**

Completing the Performance Task

Look back at your results from the Apply What You've Learned sections in Lessons 9-2, 9-3, and 9-4. Use the work you did to complete the following.

To solve these problems you will pull together many concepts and skills that you have studied about quadratic functions and equations.

1. Solve the problem in the Task Description on page 545 by finding the dimensions of the sign that will have the greatest possible area. What is this area? Show all your work and explain each step of your solution.

 2. **Reflect** Choose one of the Mathematical Practices below and explain how you applied it in your work on the Performance Task.

MP 2: Reason abstractly and quantitatively.

MP 4: Model with mathematics.

MP 5: Use appropriate tools strategically.

On Your Own

Another store has a wall that is a right triangle with a base of 10 m and a height of 15 m. The manager plans to order a rectangular sign to hang on this wall. Two sides of the sign will align with the perpendicular sides of the wall. The fourth corner of the sign will be on the third side of the wall, as shown in the figure below.

a. What are the dimensions of the sign that will have the greatest possible area?

b. What is the maximum area of the sign?

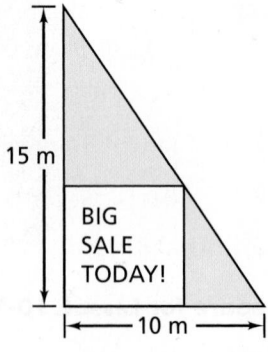

15 m

BIG
SALE
TODAY!

10 m

9 Chapter Review

Connecting **BIG** ideas and Answering the Essential Questions

1 Function
The family of quadratic functions has equations of the form $y = ax^2 + bx + c$, where $a \neq 0$. The graph of a quadratic function is a parabola.

Graphing Quadratic Functions (Lessons 9-1 and 9-2)

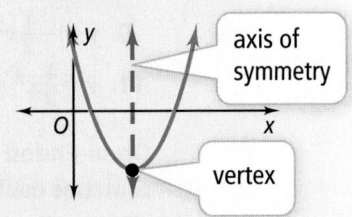

axis of symmetry

vertex

2 Solving Equations and Inequalities
You can solve quadratic equations using several methods.

Solving Quadratic Equations (Lessons 9-3, 9-4, 9-5, and 9-6)
$$ax^2 + bx + c = 0$$
$$x = \frac{-b \pm \sqrt{b^2 - 4ac}}{2a}$$

Systems of Linear and Quadratic Equations (Lesson 9-8)

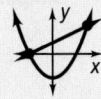

Two solutions   One solution   No solution

Choosing a Model (Lesson 9-7)

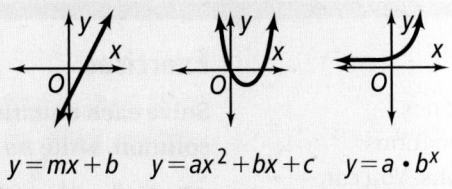

$$y = mx + b \qquad y = ax^2 + bx + c \qquad y = a \cdot b^x$$

3 Modeling
To model a data set, choose a function that most closely matches the pattern in the data or graph.

Chapter Vocabulary

- axis of symmetry (p. 546)
- completing the square (p. 576)
- discriminant (p. 585)
- maximum (p. 547)
- minimum (p. 547)
- parabola (p. 546)
- quadratic equation (p. 561)
- quadratic formula (p. 582)
- quadratic function (p. 546)
- root of an equation (p. 561)
- vertex (p. 547)
- zero of a function (p. 561)

Choose the correct term to complete each sentence.

1. The U-shaped graph of a quadratic function is a(n) ? .

2. The line that divides a parabola in half is the ? .

3. The ? can be used to determine the number of real-number solutions of a quadratic equation.

4. The ? of a parabola is the point at which the parabola intersects the axis of symmetry.

9-1 and 9-2 Graphing Quadratic Functions

Quick Review

A function of the form $y = ax^2 + bx + c$, where $a \neq 0$, is a **quadratic function**. Its graph is a **parabola**. The **axis of symmetry** of a parabola divides it into two matching halves. The **vertex** of a parabola is the point at which the parabola intersects the axis of symmetry.

Example

What is the vertex of the graph of $y = x^2 + 6x - 2$?

The x-coordinate of the vertex is given by $x = \frac{-b}{2a}$.

$$x = \frac{-b}{2a} = \frac{-6}{2(1)} = -3$$

Find the y-coordinate of the vertex.

$y = (-3)^2 + 6(-3) - 2$ Substitute -3 for x.

$y = -11$ Simplify.

The vertex is $(-3, -11)$.

Exercises

Graph each function. Label the axis of symmetry and the vertex.

5. $y = \frac{2}{3}x^2$ **6.** $y = -x^2 + 1$

7. $y = x^2 - 4$ **8.** $y = 5x^2 + 8$

9. $y = -\frac{1}{2}x^2 + 4x + 1$ **10.** $y = -2x^2 - 3x + 10$

11. $y = \frac{1}{2}x^2 + 2x - 3$ **12.** $y = 3x^2 + x - 5$

Open-Ended Give an example of a quadratic function that matches each description.

13. Its graph opens downward.

14. The vertex of its graph is at the origin.

15. Its graph opens upward.

16. Its graph is wider than the graph of $y = x^2$.

9-3 and 9-4 Solving Quadratic Equations

Quick Review

The **standard form of a quadratic equation** is $ax^2 + bx + c = 0$, where $a \neq 0$. Quadratic equations can have two, one, or no real-number solutions. You can solve a quadratic equation by graphing the related function and finding the x-intercepts. Some quadratic equations can also be solved using square roots. If the left side of $ax^2 + bx + c = 0$ can be factored, you can use the **Zero-Product Property** to solve the equation.

Example

What are the solutions of $2x^2 - 72 = 0$?

$2x^2 - 72 = 0$

$2x^2 = 72$ Add 72 to each side.

$x^2 = 36$ Divide each side by 2.

$x = \pm\sqrt{36}$ Find the square roots of each side.

$x = \pm 6$ Simplify.

Exercises

Solve each equation. If the equation has no real-number solution, write *no solution*.

17. $6(x^2 - 2) = 12$ **18.** $-5m^2 = -125$

19. $9(w^2 + 1) = 9$ **20.** $3r^2 + 27 = 0$

21. $4 = 9k^2$ **22.** $4n^2 = 64$

Solve by factoring.

23. $x^2 + 7x + 12 = 0$ **24.** $5x^2 - 10x = 0$

25. $2x^2 - 9x = x^2 - 20$ **26.** $2x^2 + 5x = 3$

27. $3x^2 - 5x = -3x^2 + 6$ **28.** $x^2 - 5x + 4 = 0$

29. Geometry The area of a circle A is given by the formula $A = \pi r^2$, where r is the radius of the circle. Find the radius of a circle with area 16 in.^{2}. Round to the nearest tenth of an inch.

9-5 Completing the Square

Quick Review

You can solve any quadratic equation by writing it in the form $x^2 + bx = c$, **completing the square,** and finding the square roots of each side of the equation.

Example

What are the solutions of $x^2 + 8x = 513$?

$x^2 + 8x + 16 = 513 + 16$	Add $\left(\frac{8}{2}\right)^2$, or 16, to each side.
$(x + 4)^2 = 529$	Write $x^2 + 8x + 16$ as a square.
$x + 4 = \pm\sqrt{529}$	Find the square roots.
$x + 4 = \pm 23$	Simplify.
$x + 4 = 23$ or $x + 4 = -23$	Write as two equations.
$x = 19$ or $x = -27$	Solve for x.

Exercises

Solve each equation by completing the square. If necessary, round to the nearest hundredth.

30. $x^2 + 6x - 5 = 0$ **31.** $x^2 = 3x - 1$

32. $2x^2 + 7x = -6$ **33.** $x^2 + 10x = -8$

34. $4x^2 - 8x = 24$ **35.** $x^2 - 14x + 16 = 0$

36. Construction You are planning a rectangular patio with length that is 7 ft less than three times its width. The area of the patio is 120 ft^2. What are the dimensions of the patio?

37. Design You are designing a rectangular birthday card for a friend. You want the card's length to be 1 in. more than twice the card's width. The area of the card is 88 in.^{2}. What are the dimensions of the card?

9-6 The Quadratic Formula and the Discriminant

Quick Review

You can solve the quadratic equation $ax^2 + bx + c = 0$, where $a \neq 0$, by using the **quadratic formula** $x = \frac{-b \pm \sqrt{b^2 - 4ac}}{2a}$. The **discriminant** is $b^2 - 4ac$. The discriminant tells you how many real-number solutions the equation has.

Example

How many real-number solutions does the equation $x^2 + 3 = 2x$ have?

$x^2 - 2x + 3 = 0$	Write in standard form.
$b^2 - 4ac = (-2)^2 - 4(1)(3)$	Evaluate discriminant.
$= -8$	Simplify.

Because the discriminant is negative, the equation has no real-number solutions.

Exercises

Find the number of real-number solutions of each equation.

38. $x^2 + 7x - 10 = 3$ **39.** $3x^2 - 2 = 5x$

Solve each equation using the quadratic formula. Round to the nearest hundredth.

40. $4x^2 + 3x - 8 = 0$ **41.** $2x^2 - 3x = 20$

42. $-x^2 + 8x + 4 = 5$ **43.** $64x^2 + 12x - 1 = 0$

Solve each equation using any method. Explain why you chose the method you used.

44. $5x^2 - 10 = x^2 + 90$ **45.** $x^2 - 6x + 9 = 0$

46. Vertical Motion A ball is thrown into the air. The height h, in feet, of the ball can be modeled by the equation $h = -16t^2 + 20t + 6$, where t is the time, in seconds, the ball is in the air. When will the ball hit the ground?

9-7 Linear, Quadratic, and Exponential Models

Quick Review

Graphing data points or analyzing data numerically can help you find the best model. Linear data have a common first difference. Exponential data have a common ratio. Quadratic data have a common second difference.

Example

Graph the points $(1, 4)$, $(4, 2)$, $(2, 3)$, $(5, 3.5)$, and $(6, 5)$. Which model is most appropriate?

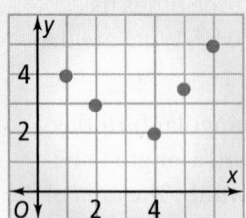

A quadratic model is most appropriate.

Exercises

Graph each set of points. Which model is most appropriate for each data set?

47. $(-3, 0)$, $(1, 4)$, $(-1, 6)$, $(2, 0)$

48. $(0, 6)$, $(5, 2)$, $(1, 4)$, $(8, 1.5)$, $(2, 3)$

Write an equation to model the data.

49.

x	y
−1	−5
0	−2
1	1
2	4
3	7

50.

x	y
−1	2.5
0	5
1	10
2	20
3	40

9-8 Systems of Linear and Quadratic Equations

Quick Review

Systems of linear and quadratic equations can have two solutions, one solution, or no solution. These systems can be solved graphically or algebraically.

Example

What are the solutions of the system?

$$y = x^2 - 7x - 40$$
$$y = -3x + 37$$

$y = x^2 - 7x - 40$	Use elimination.
$- (y = -3x + 37)$	Subtract the equations.
$0 = x^2 - 4x - 77$	
$0 = (x - 11)(x + 7)$	Factor.
$x - 11 = 0$ or $x + 7 = 0$	Zero-Product Property
$x = 11$ or $x = -7$	Solve for x.

Find the corresponding y-values.

$$y = -3(11) + 37 = 4 \qquad y = -3(-7) + 37 = 58$$

The solutions are $(11, 4)$ and $(-7, 58)$.

Exercises

Solve each system by graphing.

51. $y = x^2 - 4x + 3$
$y = -3x + 5$

52. $y = x^2 - 2x - 1$
$y = -x - 1$

53. $y = -2x^2 + x + 2$
$y = x$

54. $y = x^2 + x - 6$
$y = 2x$

Solve each system algebraically.

55. $y = x^2 + 2x - 45$
$y = 6x + 51$

56. $y = x^2 - 12x + 33$
$y = 4x - 30$

57. $y = x^2 + 19x + 39$
$y - 11 = 8x$

58. $y = x^2 + 5x - 40$
$y + 1 = -5x$

59. $y = x^2 + 3x + 15$
$y + 45 = 19x$

60. $y = x^2 + 11x + 51$
$y = -10x - 57$

61. Writing Explain how you can use graphing to determine the number of solutions of a system of linear and quadratic equations.

Do you know HOW?

Graph each function.

1. $y = 3x^2 - 7$

2. $y = -x^2 - 2$

3. $y = -2x^2 + 10x - 1$

4. $y = x^2 - 3x + 2$

Solve each equation.

5. $x^2 + 11x - 26 = 0$

6. $x^2 - 25 = 0$

7. $x^2 - 19x + 80 = -8$

8. $x^2 - 5x = -4x$

9. $4x^2 - 100 = 0$

10. $5x^2 - 8x = 8 - 5x$

11. **Design** You are creating a rectangular banner for a school pep rally. You have 100 ft^2 of paper, and you want the length to be 15 ft longer than the width. What should be the dimensions of the banner?

Find the number of real-number solutions of each equation.

12. $x^2 + 4x = -4$

13. $x^2 + 8 = 0$

14. $3x^2 - 9x = -5$

Solve each equation. If necessary, round to the nearest hundredth.

15. $-3x^2 + 7x = -10$

16. $x^2 + 4x = 1$

17. $12x^2 + 16x - 28 = 0$

18. $x^2 + 6x + 9 = 25$

19. **Vertical Motion** You throw a ball upward. Its height h, in feet, after t seconds can be modeled by the function $h = -16t^2 + 30t + 6$. After how many seconds will it hit the ground?

20. Identify the graph at the right as *linear*, *quadratic*, or *exponential*. Write an equation that models the data points shown.

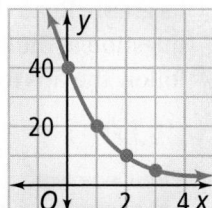

Solve each system.

21. $y = x^2 + 3x - 23$
    $y = 25 - 5x$

22. $y = x^2 + 2x - 2$
    $y = x + 10$

Do you UNDERSTAND?

23. **Writing** Explain what you can determine about the shape of a parabola from its equation alone.

24. **Open-Ended** Write an equation of a parabola that has two x-intercepts and a maximum value. Include a graph of your parabola.

25. Find a nonzero value of k such that $kx^2 - 10x + 25 = 0$ has one real-number solution.

26. **Reasoning** The graph of a quadratic function $y = ax^2 + bx + c$ is shown. What do you know about the values of a, b, and c just by looking at the graph?

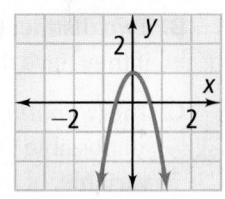

27. **Geometry** Suppose a rectangle has an area of 60 ft^2 and dimensions, in feet, of x and $x + 1$.
    a. Estimate each dimension of the rectangle to the nearest foot.
    b. Write a quadratic equation and use the quadratic formula to find each dimension to the nearest hundredth of a foot.

Common Core Cumulative Standards Review

 ASSESSMENT

T I P S   F O R   S U C C E S S

Some questions on standardized tests ask you to describe how changing an equation affects its graph. Read the sample question at the right. Then follow the tips to answer it.

How would the graph of $y = x^2 - 1$ change if the equation became $y = x^2 + 2$?

- Ⓐ The graph would shift 3 units down.
- Ⓑ The graph would shift 3 units up.
- Ⓒ The graph would shift 2 units down.
- Ⓓ The graph would shift 2 units up.

TIP 1

You may want to sketch the graphs of both equations and compare the graphs.

TIP 2

Think about what operation you would use to change $y = x^2 - 1$ to $y = x^2 + 2$.

Think It Through

To change the equation $y = x^2 - 1$ to $y = x^2 + 2$, you add 3 to the expression $x^2 - 1$:

$$y = x^2 - 1 + 3 = x^2 + 2$$

Adding 3 to the constant term of a quadratic function causes the graph to shift 3 units up.

The correct answer is B.

Vocabulary Builder

As you solve test items, you must understand the meanings of mathematical terms. Choose the correct term to complete each sentence.

A. The (*vertex, axis of symmetry*) is the highest or lowest point of a parabola.

B. Two distinct lines are (*parallel, perpendicular*) if they have the same slope.

C. The (*domain, range*) of a function is the set of all possible values for the input, or independent variable, of the function.

D. A (*proportion, rate*) is an equation that states that two ratios are equal.

E. A(n) (*quadratic, exponential*) function is a function of the form $y = ax^2 + bx + c$.

Selected Response

Read each question. Then write the letter of the correct answer on your paper.

1. Manuela can type about 150 words in 4 minutes. At this rate, about how long will she take to type 2000 words?

- Ⓐ 10 minutes
- Ⓒ 75 minutes
- Ⓑ 50 minutes
- Ⓓ 750 minutes

2. The graphs of $y = -7x + 12$ and $y = -\frac{2}{3}x - \frac{2}{3}$ are shown. Which region describes the solutions of the system of inequalities $y \le -7x + 12$ and $y \le -\frac{2}{3}x - \frac{2}{3}$?

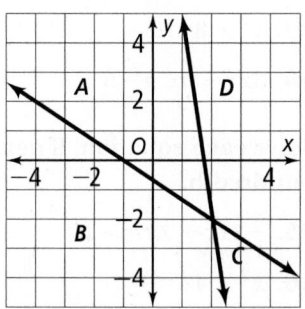

- Ⓕ Region A
- Ⓗ Region C
- Ⓖ Region B
- Ⓘ Region D

3. Which expression is equivalent to $\left(m^4 n^{-1}\right)\left(mp^2\right)\left(np^{-6}\right)$?

  (A) $m^5 p^{-4}$

  (B) $m^5 n p^{-4}$

  (C) $m^3 n p^4$

  (D) $m^4 n p^{-12}$

4. How would the graph of the function $y = x^2 - 5$ change if the function became $y = x^2 + 2$?

  (F) The graph would shift 2 units down.

  (G) The graph would shift 3 units up.

  (H) The graph would shift 7 units up.

  (I) The graph would shift 10 units down.

5. Which of the following is a function rule for the sequence 3, 8, 13, 18, 23, . . . ?

  (A) $A(n) = 5 + (n - 1)(3)$

  (B) $A(n) = 3 + (n - 1)(5)$

  (C) $A(n) = 1 + (n - 1)(5)$

  (D) $A(n) = 1 + (n - 1)(3)$

6. What are the solutions of $4v + 18 \geq 6v + 10$?

  (F) $v \leq 4$

  (G) $v \geq 4$

  (H) $v < 4$

  (I) $v > 4$

7. What are the solutions of $2x^2 - 11x + 5 = 0$?

  (A) $2, 5$

  (B) $-5, -0.5$

  (C) $0.5, 5$

  (D) $-5, -2$

8. The difference of Ann's and Jay's heights is half of Jay's height. Which equation represents Ann's height a in terms of Jay's height j?

  (F) $a = \frac{1}{2}j - j$

  (G) $a = j - \frac{1}{2}j$

  (H) $a = \frac{1}{2}j + j$

  (I) $a = 2j - j$

9. Keisha's grandmother gave her a doll that she paid $6 for 60 years ago. The doll's current value is $96. Its value doubles every 15 years. What will the doll be worth in 60 years?

  (A) $570   (C) $1536

  (B) $768   (D) $3072

10. The length of a rectangle is represented by the expression $n - 3$. The width of the rectangle is represented by the expression $4n + 5$. Which expression represents the area of the rectangle?

  (F) $4n^2 - 12n - 15$ (H) $-3n - 15$

  (G) $4n^2 - 17n - 15$ (I) $4n^2 - 7n - 15$

11. Which expression is equivalent to $\left(\dfrac{x^4 y^{-2}}{z^3}\right)^{-3}$?

  (A) $\dfrac{y^6 z^3}{x^{12}}$ (C) $\dfrac{y^6 z^9}{x^{12}}$

  (B) $\dfrac{y^6}{x^{12} z^9}$ (D) $\dfrac{y^6}{x^{12} z^3}$

12. The table shows the number of volunteers v needed based on the number of children c who will go on a field trip. Which equation best represents the relationship between the number of volunteers and the number of children?

c	v
20	6
25	7
30	8
35	9

  (F) $v = 0.25c + 10$ (H) $v = 0.2c + 2$

  (G) $v = 5c - 10$ (I) $v = 4c + 2$

13. Which graph shows a line that is parallel to the line with equation $4x - 8y = 10$?

  (A) 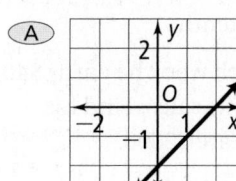   (C)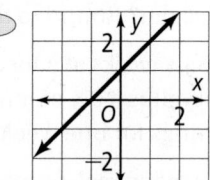

  (B) 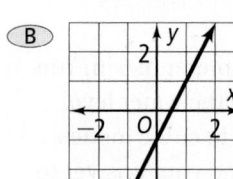   (D)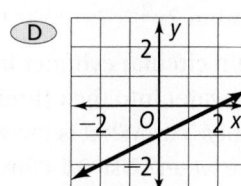

Constructed Response

14. Alan is tiling a 6 ft-by-8 ft rectangular floor with square tiles that measure 4 in. on each side. How many tiles does Alan need to cover the floor?

15. A library is having a used book sale. All hardcover books have the same price and all softcover books have the same price. You buy 4 hardcover books and 2 softcover books for $24. Your friend buys 3 hardcover books and 3 softcover books for $21. What is the cost in dollars of a hardcover book?

16. The two triangles below are similar.

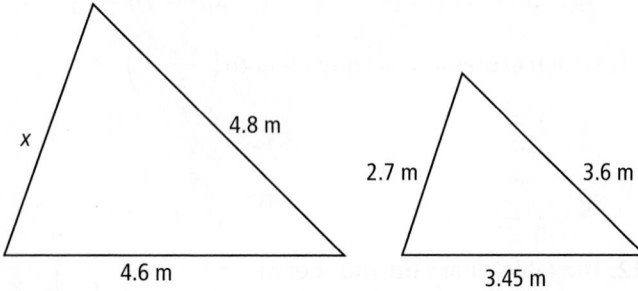

What is the length, in meters, of the side labeled x?

17. A soup company sells chicken broth in a container shaped like a rectangular prism. The container is 3.5 in. long, 2.5 in. wide, and 6.5 in. high. One cubic inch of broth weighs about 0.56 oz. To the nearest whole number, how many ounces does the container hold?

18. One model of a jumbo jet is approximately 230 ft long and has a wingspan of 195 ft. If a scale model of the plane is about 40 cm long, what is the model's wingspan? Round to the nearest tenth.

19. Marcus works at a local store. Each week he earns $400 salary plus a 3% commission on his sales. Find his earnings for one week if his sales are $2500.

20. How many real-number solutions does the quadratic equation $2x^2 + 7x + 9 = 0$ have?

21. A right circular cylinder has a diameter of 6 in. You pour water into the cylinder until the water level reaches 3 in. What is the volume, in cubic inches, of the water? Use 3.14 for π. Round your answer to the nearest cubic inch.

22. Terry says that a quadratic equation has two real solutions. Is this statement *always*, *sometimes*, or *never* true? Give two examples to support your answer.

23. An equation of line p is $y = 4x - 3$. Line n is perpendicular to line p and contains the point $(8, -1)$. What is an equation of line n? Show your work.

24. A caterer charges a $50 fee plus $12 per person for an event. Write a function to represent the total cost C for n people.

25. Suppose you deposit $1000 in an account that pays 3.5% interest compounded quarterly. What will the account balance be after 5 years?

26. Factor the expression $3x^2 + 23x + 14$.

27. What is an inequality that represents the graph?

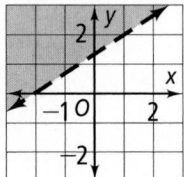

28. What is an equation of the line?

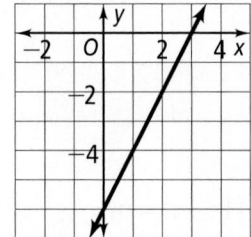

Extended Response

29. A system of equations is shown below.

$$y = 2x + 5$$
$$y = -x + 11$$

  a. Graph the equations in the same coordinate plane.
  b. What is the point of intersection of the two graphs?

30. Graph the function $y = 2x^2$. Make a table of values. What are the domain and range?

Get Ready!

Lesson 2-7 ◆ **Solving Proportions**

Solve each proportion.

1. $\frac{2}{3} = \frac{x}{15}$ **2.** $\frac{3}{a} = \frac{1}{6}$ **3.** $\frac{4}{3} = \frac{6}{m}$

Lesson 1-3 ◆ **Estimating Square Roots**

Estimate the square root. Round to the nearest integer.

4. $\sqrt{61}$ **5.** $\sqrt{94}$ **6.** $\sqrt{15}$ **7.** $\sqrt{148}$ **8.** $\sqrt{197}$

Lesson 8-3 ◆ **Multiplying Binomials**

Simplify each product.

9. $(2h + 3)(4 - h)$ **10.** $(3b^2 + 7)(3b^2 - 7)$ **11.** $(5x + 2)(-3x - 1)$

Lesson 9-1 ◆ **Quadratic Graphs**

Graph each function.

12. $y = 3x^2$ **13.** $y = x^2 + 4$ **14.** $y = 2x^2 + 3$

Lesson 9-6 ◆ **The Quadratic Formula and the Discriminant**

Find the number of real-number solutions of each equation.

15. $x^2 + 6x + 1 = 0$ **16.** $x^2 - 5x - 6 = 0$ **17.** $x^2 - 2x + 9 = 0$

18. $4x^2 - 4x = -1$ **19.** $6x^2 + 5x - 2 = -3$ **20.** $(2x - 5)^2 = 121$

 Looking Ahead Vocabulary

21. Things are *alike* if part of them is the same. Why would $2\sqrt{3}$ and $6\sqrt{3}$ be *like radicals*?

22. The *conclusion* is the end of a book. Which part is the *conclusion* of the statement, "If I had a lot of money, I would be rich"?

CHAPTER 10

Radical Expressions and Equations

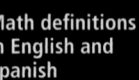
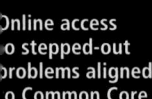
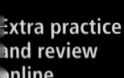
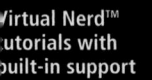

Download videos connecting math to your world.

Interactive! Vary numbers, graphs, and figures to explore math concepts.

The online Solve It will get you in gear for each lesson.

Math definitions in English and Spanish

Online access to stepped-out problems aligned to Common Core

Get and view your assignments online.

Extra practice and review online

Virtual Nerd™ tutorials with built-in support

Chapter Preview

Vocabulary

English/Spanish Vocabulary Audio Online:

English	Spanish
conditional, *p. 615*	condicional
conjugates, *p. 628*	valores conjugados
extraneous solution, *p. 635*	solución extraña
hypotenuse, *p. 614*	hipotenusa
like radicals, *p. 626*	radicales semejantes
Pythagorean Theorem, *p. 614*	Teorema de Pitágoras
radical expression, *p. 619*	expresión radical
square root function, *p. 639*	función de raíz cuadrada
trigonometric ratios, *p. 645*	razones trigonométricas

BIG ideas

1 Equivalence
Essential Question How are radical expressions represented?

2 Functions
Essential Question What are the characteristics of square root functions?

3 Solving Equations and Inequalities
Essential Question How can you solve a radical equation?

DOMAINS

- Reasoning with Equations and Inequalities
- Interpreting Functions
- Similarity, Right Triangles, and Trigonometry

Common Core Performance Task

Using Skid Marks to Find the Speed of a Car

A driver on Pine Street applies his car's brakes to avoid an accident. His car leaves skid marks from Sanchez Street to Market Street, as shown in the diagram below. Pine Street is paved with asphalt and the speed limit along Pine Street is 50 mi/h.

You can use the formula $s = \sqrt{30\,fd}$ to determine the approximate speed of a car when it begins to skid, where s is the speed of the car in miles per hour, f is the coefficient of friction, and d is the length of the skid marks in feet. The coefficient of friction is a value that depends on the surface material of the road, as shown in the table below.

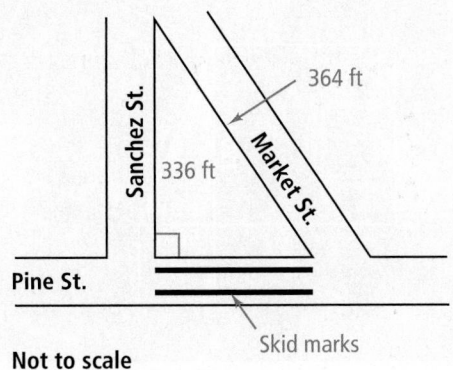

Not to scale

Typical Coefficients of Friction

Surface Material	Coefficient of Friction
Gravel	0.6
Asphalt	0.7
Cement	0.9

Task Description

Determine whether the driver on Pine Street was traveling within the speed limit. Then determine the maximum length of the skid marks left on Pine Street by a car that travels within the speed limit. Round your answer to the nearest foot.

Connecting the Task to the Math Practices

MATHEMATICAL PRACTICES

As you complete the task, you'll apply several Standards for Mathematical Practice.

- You'll use a triangle relationship to determine the length of the skid marks. (MP 1, MP 4)
- You'll write and simplify a radical expression to find the speed of the car. (MP 6)
- You'll graph a square root function to analyze the relationship between skid-mark length and speed. (MP 5)

10-1 The Pythagorean Theorem

Common Core State Standards

G-SRT.C.8 Use trigonometric ratios and the Pythagorean Theorem to solve right triangles in applied problems.

MP 1, MP 2, MP 3, MP 4

Objectives To solve problems using the Pythagorean Theorem
To identify right triangles

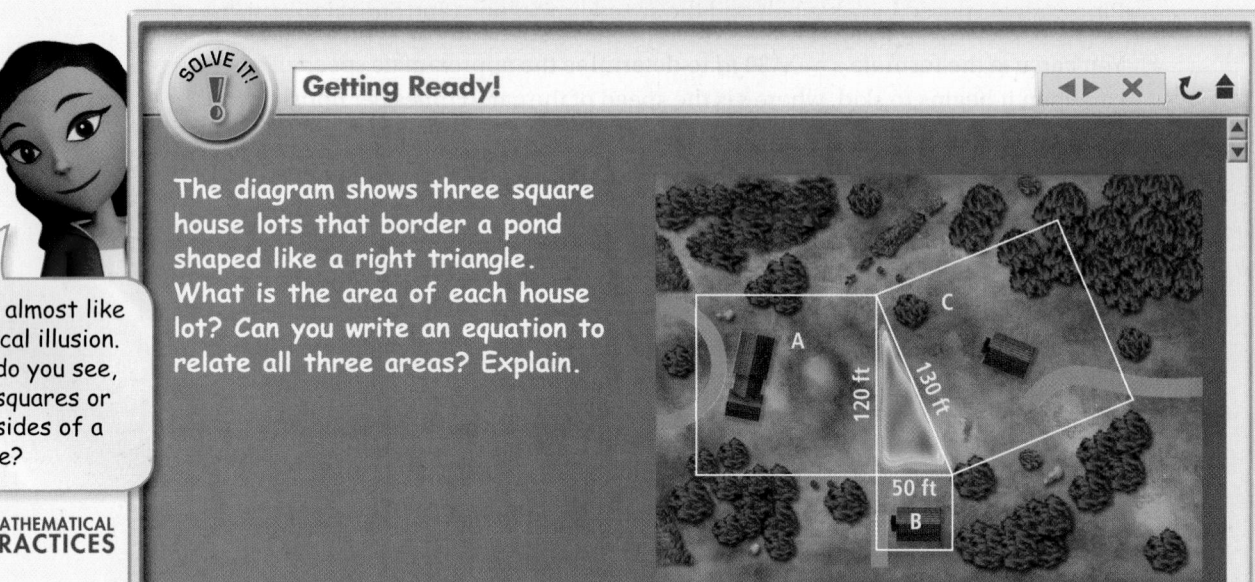

SOLVE IT!

Getting Ready!

The diagram shows three square house lots that border a pond shaped like a right triangle. What is the area of each house lot? Can you write an equation to relate all three areas? Explain.

This is almost like an optical illusion. What do you see, three squares or three sides of a triangle?

MATHEMATICAL PRACTICES

Lesson Vocabulary
- hypotenuse
- leg
- Pythagorean Theorem
- conditional
- hypothesis
- conclusion
- converse

There are special names for the sides of a right triangle like the one in the Solve It. The side opposite the right angle is the **hypotenuse.** It is the longest side. Each of the sides forming the right angle is a **leg.** The **Pythagorean Theorem,** named after the Greek mathematician Pythagoras, relates the lengths of the legs and the length of the hypotenuse.

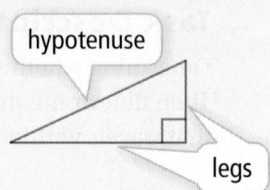

Essential Understanding The lengths of the sides of a right triangle have a special relationship. If you know the lengths of any two of the sides, you can find the length of the third side.

take note

Theorem The Pythagorean Theorem

Words
In any right triangle, the sum of the squares of the lengths of the legs is equal to the square of the length of the hypotenuse.

Algebra
$a^2 + b^2 = c^2$

Diagram

You can use the Pythagorean Theorem to find the length of a right triangle's hypotenuse given the lengths of its legs. Using the Pythagorean Theorem to solve for a side length involves finding a principal square root, because side lengths are always positive.

 **Problem 1** Finding the Length of a Hypotenuse

The tiles at the right are squares with 6-in. sides. What is the length of the hypotenuse of the right triangle shown?

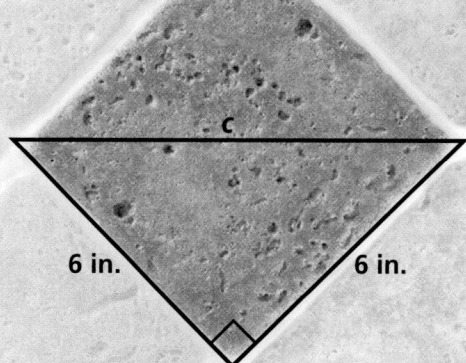

$a^2 + b^2 = c^2$	Pythagorean Theorem
$6^2 + 6^2 = c^2$	Substitute 6 for a and b.
$72 = c^2$	Simplify.
$\sqrt{72} = c$	Find the principal square root.
$8.5 \approx c$	Use a calculator.

The length of the hypotenuse is about 8.5 in.

6 in.   **6 in.**

 Got It? **1.** What is the length of the hypotenuse of a right triangle with legs of lengths 9 cm and 12 cm?

Plan

What do you know? What do you need?
You know the lengths a and b of the two legs. You need to find the length c of the hypotenuse. Substitute for a and b in $a^2 + b^2 = c^2$, and then solve for c.

You can also use the Pythagorean Theorem to find the length of a leg of a right triangle.

 Problem 2 Finding the Length of a Leg

What is the side length b in the triangle at the right?

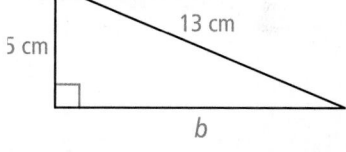

$a^2 + b^2 = c^2$	Pythagorean Theorem
$5^2 + b^2 = 13^2$	Substitute 5 for a and 13 for c.
$25 + b^2 = 169$	Simplify.
$b^2 = 144$	Subtract 25 from each side.
$b = 12$	Find the principal square root of each side.

The side length b is 12 cm.

Think

How is this problem different from Problem 1?
In Problem 1, the length of the hypotenuse was unknown. In this problem, the length of a leg is unknown.

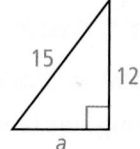

 Got It? **2.** What is the side length a in the triangle at the right?

An *if-then* statement such as "If an animal is a horse, then it has four legs" is called a **conditional.** Conditionals have two parts. The part following *if* is the **hypothesis.** The part following *then* is the **conclusion.**

The **converse** of a conditional switches the hypothesis and the conclusion. Sometimes the converse of a true conditional is not true.

You can write the Pythagorean Theorem as a conditional: "If a triangle is a right triangle with legs of lengths a and b and hypotenuse of length c, then $a^2 + b^2 = c^2$." The converse of the Pythagorean Theorem is always true.

 take note

> **Property   The Converse of the Pythagorean Theorem**
>
> If a triangle has sides of lengths a, b, and c, and $a^2 + b^2 = c^2$, then the triangle is a right triangle with hypotenuse of length c.

You can use the Pythagorean Theorem and its converse to determine whether a triangle is a right triangle. If the side lengths satisfy the equation $a^2 + b^2 = c^2$, then the triangle is a right triangle. If they do not, then it is not a right triangle.

Ⓒ **Problem 3 Identifying Right Triangles**

Multiple Choice Which set of lengths could be the side lengths of a right triangle?

Ⓐ 6 in., 24 in., 25 in.　Ⓑ 4 m, 8 m, 10 m　Ⓒ 10 in., 24 in., 26 in.　Ⓓ 8 ft, 15 ft, 16 ft

Plan

Why should you check each answer choice?
If you find two answer choices that appear to be correct, then you know you have made a mistake.

Determine whether the lengths satisfy $a^2 + b^2 = c^2$. The greatest length is c.

$6^2 + 24^2 \overset{?}{=} 25^2$　　$4^2 + 8^2 \overset{?}{=} 10^2$　　$10^2 + 24^2 \overset{?}{=} 26^2$　　$8^2 + 15^2 \overset{?}{=} 16^2$

$36 + 576 \overset{?}{=} 625$　　$16 + 64 \overset{?}{=} 100$　　$100 + 576 \overset{?}{=} 676$　　$64 + 225 \overset{?}{=} 256$

$612 \neq 625$　　　$80 \neq 100$　　　$676 = 676$ ✔　　$289 \neq 256$

By the Converse of the Pythagorean Theorem, the lengths 10 in., 24 in., and 26 in. could be the side lengths of a right triangle. The correct answer is C.

Ⓒ ✓ **Got It? 3. a.** Could the lengths 20 mm, 47 mm, and 52 mm be the side lengths of a right triangle? Explain.

b. Reasoning If a, b, and c satisfy the equation $a^2 + b^2 = c^2$, are $2a$, $2b$, and $2c$ also possible side lengths of a right triangle? How do you know?

✓ **Lesson Check**

Do you know HOW?

Find each missing side length.

1.

2.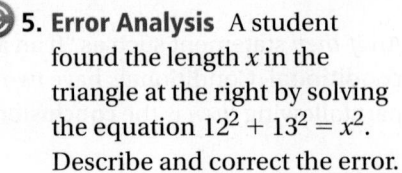

3. Could the lengths 12 cm, 35 cm, and 37 cm be the side lengths of a right triangle? Explain.

Do you UNDERSTAND? Ⓒ MATHEMATICAL PRACTICES

Ⓒ **4. Vocabulary** What is the converse of the conditional, "If you study math, then you are a student"?

Ⓒ **5. Error Analysis** A student found the length x in the triangle at the right by solving the equation $12^2 + 13^2 = x^2$. Describe and correct the error.

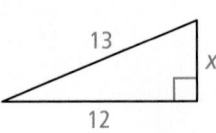

Practice and Problem-Solving Exercises

MATHEMATICAL PRACTICES

 **Practice**

Use the triangle at the right. Find the missing side length. If necessary, round to the nearest tenth.

See Problems 1 and 2.

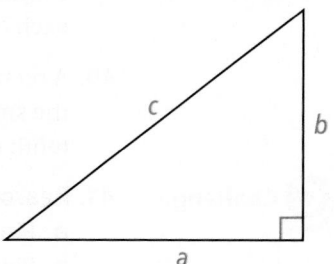

6. $a = 3, b = 4$
7. $a = 6, c = 10$
8. $b = 1, c = \frac{5}{4}$

9. $a = 5, c = 13$
10. $a = 0.3, b = 0.4$
11. $a = 8, b = 15$

12. $a = 1, c = \frac{5}{3}$
13. $b = 6, c = 7.5$
14. $b = 3.5, c = 3.7$

15. $a = 1.1, b = 6$
16. $a = 8, c = 17$
17. $a = 9, b = 40$

18. $b = 2.4, c = 7.4$
19. $a = 4, b = 7.5$
20. $a = 0.9, c = 4.1$

21. Fitness A jogger goes half a mile north and then turns west. If the jogger finishes 1.3 mi from the starting point, how far west did the jogger go?

 22. Construction A construction worker is cutting along the diagonal of a rectangular board 15 ft long and 8 ft wide. What will be the length of the cut?

Determine whether the given lengths can be side lengths of a right triangle. See Problem 3.

23. 15 ft, 36 ft, 39 ft
24. 12 m, 60 m, 61 m
25. 13 in., 35 in., 38 in.

26. 16 cm, 63 cm, 65 cm
27. 14 in., 48 in., 50 in.
28. 16 yd, 30 yd, 34 yd

 **Apply**

29. Swimming A swimmer asks a question to a lifeguard sitting on a tall chair, as shown in the diagram. The swimmer needs to be close to the lifeguard to hear the answer. What is the distance between the swimmer's head and the lifeguard's head?

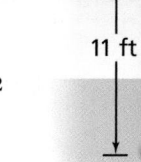

Any set of three positive integers that satisfies the equation $a^2 + b^2 = c^2$ is a *Pythagorean triple*. Determine whether each set of numbers is a Pythagorean triple.

30. 11, 60, 61
31. 13, 84, 85
32. 40, 41, 58

33. 50, 120, 130
34. 32, 126, 130
35. 28, 45, 53

36. Think About a Plan A banner shaped like a right triangle has a hypotenuse of length 26 ft and a leg of length 10 ft. What is the area of the banner?
  • What information do you need to find the area of a triangle?
  • How can you find the length of the other leg?

37. History Originally, each face of the Great Pyramid of Giza was a triangle with the dimensions shown. How far was a corner of the base from the pyramid's top? Round to the nearest foot.

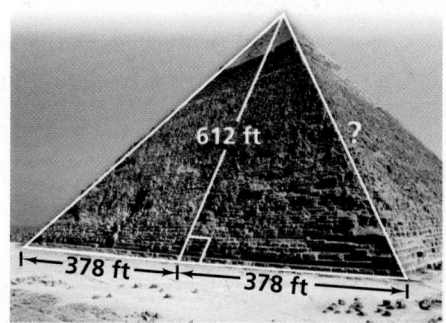

38. Two sides of a right triangle measure 10 in. and 8 in.
  a. Writing Explain why this is not enough information to be sure of the length of the third side.
  b. Give two possible values for the length of the third side.

39. Physics If two forces pull at right angles to each other, the resultant force can be represented by the diagonal of a rectangle, as shown at the right. This diagonal is a hypotenuse of a right triangle. A 50-lb force and a 120-lb force combine for a resultant force of 130 lb. Are the forces pulling at right angles to each other? Explain.

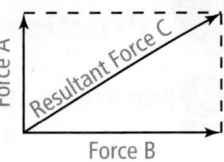

40. A rectangular box is 4 cm wide, 4 cm tall, and 10 cm long. What is the diameter of the smallest circular opening through which the box will fit? Round to the nearest tenth of a centimeter.

 **41. Reasoning** Use the diagram at the right.
  a. Find the area of the larger square. Write your answer as a trinomial.
  b. Find the area of the smaller square.
  c. Find the area of each triangle in terms of a and b.
  d. The area of the larger square equals the sum of the area of the smaller square and the areas of the four triangles. Write this equation and simplify. What do you notice?

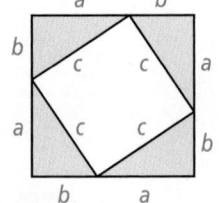

42. Geometry The lengths of the sides of a right triangle are three consecutive integers. Write and solve an equation to find the three integers.

Apply What You've Learned

MATHEMATICAL PRACTICES
MP 1, MP 4

Look back at the information on page 613 about the car skidding on Pine Street. The diagram showing the streets and the skid marks is shown again below.

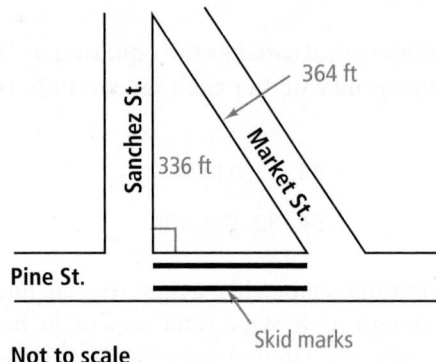

Not to scale

a. Write an equation that you can use to find the length of the skid marks. Explain how you wrote the equation.

b. Find the length of the skid marks.

c. How do you know that your answer in part (b) is reasonable?

10-2 Simplifying Radicals

© **Common Core State Standards**

Prepares for A-REI.A.2 Solve simple rational and radical equations in one variable, and give examples showing how extraneous solutions may arise.

MP 1, MP 2, MP 3, MP 4, MP 7

Objective To simplify radicals involving products and quotients

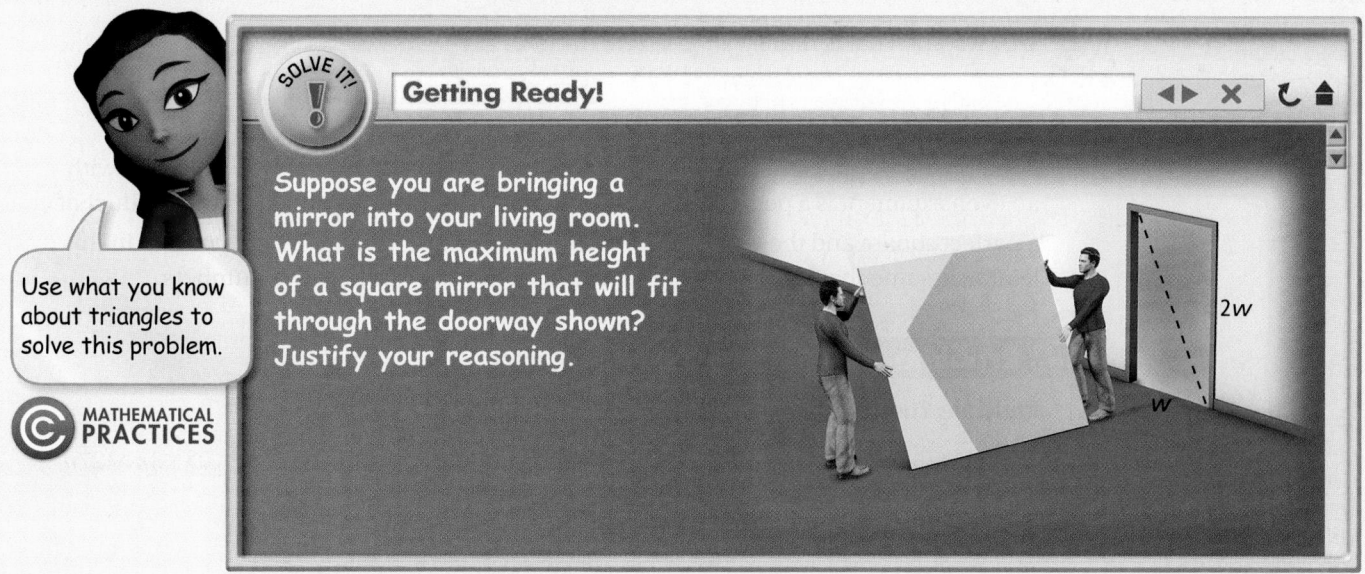

SOLVE IT!

Getting Ready!

Suppose you are bringing a mirror into your living room. What is the maximum height of a square mirror that will fit through the doorway shown? Justify your reasoning.

Use what you know about triangles to solve this problem.

 MATHEMATICAL PRACTICES

Lesson Vocabulary
• radical expression
• rationalize the denominator

In the Solve It, the maximum height of the mirror is a *radical expression*. A **radical expression,** such as $2\sqrt{3}$ or $\sqrt{x + 3}$, is an expression that contains a radical. A radical expression is simplified if the following statements are true.

• The radicand has no perfect-square factors other than 1.
• The radicand contains no fractions.
• No radicals appear in the denominator of a fraction.

Simplified

$3\sqrt{5}$ $9\sqrt{x}$ $\dfrac{\sqrt{2}}{4}$

Not Simplified

$3\sqrt{12}$ $\sqrt{\dfrac{x}{2}}$ $\dfrac{5}{\sqrt{7}}$

Essential Understanding You can simplify radical expressions using multiplication and division properties of square roots.

take note

Property Multiplication Property of Square Roots	
Algebra	**Example**
For $a \geq 0$ and $b \geq 0$, $\sqrt{ab} = \sqrt{a} \cdot \sqrt{b}$.	$\sqrt{48} = \sqrt{16} \cdot \sqrt{3} = 4\sqrt{3}$

You can use the Multiplication Property of Square Roots to simplify radicals by removing perfect-square factors from the radicand.

Problem 1 Removing Perfect-Square Factors

What is the simplified form of $\sqrt{160}$?

$\sqrt{160} = \sqrt{16 \cdot 10}$ 16 is the greatest perfect-square factor of 160.

$\quad\quad\quad = \sqrt{16} \cdot \sqrt{10}$ Use the Multiplication Property of Square Roots.

$\quad\quad\quad = 4\sqrt{10}$ Simplify $\sqrt{16}$.

Got It? **1.** What is the simplified form of $\sqrt{72}$?

Sometimes you can simplify radical expressions that contain variables. A variable with an even exponent is a perfect square. A variable with an odd exponent is the product of a perfect square and the variable. For example, $n^3 = n^2 \cdot n$, so $\sqrt{n^3} = \sqrt{n^2 \cdot n}$. In this lesson, assume that all variables in radicands represent nonnegative numbers.

 Problem 2 Removing Variable Factors

Think

How is this problem similar to Problem 1?
In both problems, you need to remove a perfect-square factor from the radicand. In this problem, however, the factor you remove contains a variable.

Multiple Choice What is the simplified form of $\sqrt{54n^7}$?

  Ⓐ $n^3\sqrt{54n}$ Ⓑ $9n^6\sqrt{6n}$ Ⓒ $3n^3\sqrt{6n}$ Ⓓ $3n\sqrt{27n}$

$\sqrt{54n^7} = \sqrt{9n^6 \cdot 6n}$ $9n^6$, or $(3n^3)^2$, is a perfect-square factor of $54n^7$.

$\quad\quad\quad = \sqrt{9n^6} \cdot \sqrt{6n}$ Use the Multiplication Property of Square Roots.

$\quad\quad\quad = 3n^3\sqrt{6n}$ Simplify $\sqrt{9n^6}$.

The correct answer is C.

Got It? **2.** What is the simplified form of $-m\sqrt{80m^9}$?

You can use the Multiplication Property of Square Roots to write $\sqrt{a} \cdot \sqrt{b} = \sqrt{ab}$.

 Problem 3 Multiplying Two Radical Expressions

Think

What property allows you to multiply the whole numbers first?
The Commutative Property of Multiplication allows you to change the order of the factors.

What is the simplified form of $2\sqrt{7t} \cdot 3\sqrt{14t^2}$?

$2\sqrt{7t} \cdot 3\sqrt{14t^2} = 6\sqrt{7t \cdot 14t^2}$ Multiply the whole numbers and use the Multiplication Property of Square Roots.

$\quad\quad\quad = 6\sqrt{98t^3}$ Simplify under the radical symbol.

$\quad\quad\quad = 6\sqrt{49t^2 \cdot 2t}$ $49t^2$, or $(7t)^2$, is a perfect-square factor of $98t^3$.

$\quad\quad\quad = 6\sqrt{49t^2} \cdot \sqrt{2t}$ Use the Multiplication Property of Square Roots.

$\quad\quad\quad = 6 \cdot 7t\sqrt{2t}$ Simplify $\sqrt{49t^2}$.

$\quad\quad\quad = 42t\sqrt{2t}$ Simplify.

Got It? **3.** What is the simplified form of each expression in parts (a)–(c)?

     a. $3\sqrt{6} \cdot \sqrt{18}$ **b.** $\sqrt{2a} \cdot \sqrt{9a^3}$ **c.** $7\sqrt{5x} \cdot 3\sqrt{20x^5}$

     d. Reasoning In Problem 3, can you simplify the given product by first simplifying $\sqrt{14t^2}$? Explain.

 Problem 4 **Writing a Radical Expression**

Art A rectangular door in a museum is three times as tall as it is wide. What is a simplified expression for the maximum length of a painting that fits through the door?

Know

The door is w units wide and $3w$ units high.

→

Need

The diagonal length d of the doorway

Plan

Use the Pythagorean Theorem.

Think

How is this like problems you have done before?
The width and height of the door are two legs of a right triangle. This is like finding the hypotenuse of a right triangle using the Pythagorean Theorem.

$d^2 = w^2 + (3w)^2$ Pythagorean Theorem

$d^2 = w^2 + 9w^2$ Simplify $(3w)^2$.

$d^2 = 10w^2$ Combine like terms.

$d = \sqrt{10w^2}$ Find the principal square root of each side.

$d = \sqrt{w^2} \cdot \sqrt{10}$ Multiplication Property of Square Roots

$d = w\sqrt{10}$ Simplify $\sqrt{w^2}$.

An expression for the maximum length of the painting is $w\sqrt{10}$, or about $3.16w$.

Got It? **4.** A door's height is four times its width w. What is the maximum length of a painting that fits through the door?

You can simplify some radical expressions using the following property.

take note

Property **Division Property of Square Roots**

Algebra

For $a \geq 0$ and $b > 0$, $\sqrt{\dfrac{a}{b}} = \dfrac{\sqrt{a}}{\sqrt{b}}$.

Example

$\sqrt{\dfrac{36}{49}} = \dfrac{\sqrt{36}}{\sqrt{49}} = \dfrac{6}{7}$

When a radicand has a denominator that is a perfect square, it is easier to apply the Division Property of Square Roots first and then simplify the numerator and denominator of the result. When the denominator of a radicand is not a perfect square, it may be easier to simplify the fraction first.

Problem 5 Simplifying Fractions Within Radicals

What is the simplified form of each radical expression?

Think

Which method should you use?
If the denominator is a perfect square, apply the Division Property of Square Roots first. If not, simplify the fraction first.

Ⓐ $\sqrt{\dfrac{64}{49}}$

$\sqrt{\dfrac{64}{49}} = \dfrac{\sqrt{64}}{\sqrt{49}}$ Use the Division Property of Square Roots.

$= \dfrac{8}{7}$ Simplify $\sqrt{64}$ and $\sqrt{49}$.

Ⓑ $\sqrt{\dfrac{8x^3}{50x}}$

$\sqrt{\dfrac{8x^3}{50x}} = \sqrt{\dfrac{4x^2}{25}}$ Divide the numerator and denominator by $2x$.

$= \dfrac{\sqrt{4x^2}}{\sqrt{25}}$ Use the Division Property of Square Roots.

$= \dfrac{\sqrt{4} \cdot \sqrt{x^2}}{\sqrt{25}}$ Use the Multiplication Property of Square Roots.

$= \dfrac{2x}{5}$ Simplify $\sqrt{4}$, $\sqrt{x^2}$, and $\sqrt{25}$.

Got It? **5.** What is the simplified form of each radical expression?

   a. $\sqrt{\dfrac{144}{9}}$ **b.** $\sqrt{\dfrac{36a}{4a^3}}$ **c.** $\sqrt{\dfrac{25y^3}{z^2}}$

When a radicand in a denominator is not a perfect square, you may need to **rationalize the denominator** to remove the radical. To do this, multiply the numerator and denominator by the same radical expression. Choose an expression that makes the radicand in the denominator a perfect square. It may be helpful to start by simplifying the original radical in the denominator.

 Problem 6 Rationalizing Denominators

What is the simplified form of each expression?

Think

Does multiplying an expression by $\dfrac{\sqrt{7}}{\sqrt{7}}$ change its value?
No. The fraction $\dfrac{\sqrt{7}}{\sqrt{7}}$ is equal to 1. Multiplying an expression by 1 won't change its value.

Ⓐ $\dfrac{\sqrt{3}}{\sqrt{7}}$ Ⓑ $\dfrac{\sqrt{7}}{\sqrt{8n}}$

$\dfrac{\sqrt{3}}{\sqrt{7}} = \dfrac{\sqrt{3}}{\sqrt{7}} \cdot \dfrac{\sqrt{7}}{\sqrt{7}}$ Multiply by $\dfrac{\sqrt{7}}{\sqrt{7}}$.

$= \dfrac{\sqrt{21}}{\sqrt{49}}$

$= \dfrac{\sqrt{21}}{7}$ Multiply by $\dfrac{\sqrt{2n}}{\sqrt{2n}}$.

$\dfrac{\sqrt{7}}{\sqrt{8n}} = \dfrac{\sqrt{7}}{2\sqrt{2n}}$

$= \dfrac{\sqrt{7}}{2\sqrt{2n}} \cdot \dfrac{\sqrt{2n}}{\sqrt{2n}}$

$= \dfrac{\sqrt{14n}}{2\sqrt{4n^2}}$

$= \dfrac{\sqrt{14n}}{4n}$

Got It? **6.** What is the simplified form of each radical expression?

   a. $\dfrac{\sqrt{2}}{\sqrt{3}}$ **b.** $\dfrac{\sqrt{5}}{\sqrt{18m}}$ **c.** $\sqrt{\dfrac{7s}{3}}$

Lesson Check

Do you know HOW?

Simplify each radical expression.

1. $\sqrt{98}$

2. $\sqrt{16b^5}$

3. $3\sqrt{5m} \cdot 4\sqrt{\frac{1}{5}m^3}$

4. $\sqrt{\frac{15x}{x^3}}$

5. $\frac{\sqrt{5}}{\sqrt{3}}$

6. $\frac{\sqrt{6}}{\sqrt{2n}}$

Do you UNDERSTAND?

7. Vocabulary Is the radical expression in simplified form? Explain.

   a. $\frac{\sqrt{31}}{3}$ **b.** $7\sqrt{\frac{6}{11}}$ **c.** $-5\sqrt{175}$

8. Compare and Contrast Simplify $\frac{3}{\sqrt{12}}$ two different ways. Which way do you prefer? Explain.

9. Writing Explain how you can tell whether a radical expression is in simplified form.

Practice and Problem-Solving Exercises

 Simplify each radical expression.

                                              See Problems 1 and 2.

10. $\sqrt{225}$ **11.** $\sqrt{99}$ **12.** $\sqrt{128}$ **13.** $-\sqrt{60}$

14. $-4\sqrt{117}$ **15.** $5\sqrt{700}$ **16.** $\sqrt{192s^2}$ **17.** $\sqrt{50t^5}$

18. $3\sqrt{18a^2}$ **19.** $-21\sqrt{27x^9}$ **20.** $3\sqrt{150b^8}$ **21.** $-2\sqrt{243y^3}$

Simplify each product.

                                              See Problem 3.

22. $\sqrt{8} \cdot \sqrt{32}$ **23.** $\frac{1}{3}\sqrt{6} \cdot \sqrt{24}$ **24.** $4\sqrt{10} \cdot 2\sqrt{90}$

25. $5\sqrt{6} \cdot \frac{1}{6}\sqrt{216}$ **26.** $-5\sqrt{21} \cdot (-3\sqrt{42})$ **27.** $\sqrt{18n} \cdot \sqrt{98n^3}$

28. $3\sqrt{5c} \cdot 7\sqrt{15c^2}$ **29.** $\sqrt{2y} \cdot \sqrt{128y^5}$ **30.** $-6\sqrt{15s^3} \cdot 2\sqrt{75}$

31. $-9\sqrt{28a^2} \cdot \frac{1}{3}\sqrt{63a}$ **32.** $10\sqrt{12x^3} \cdot 2\sqrt{6x^3}$ **33.** $-\frac{1}{3}\sqrt{18c^5} \cdot \left(-6\sqrt{8c^9}\right)$

STEM 34. Construction Students are building rectangular wooden frames for the set of a school play. The height of a frame is 6 times the width w. Each frame has a brace that connects two opposite corners of the frame. What is a simplified expression for the length of a brace?   **See Problem 4.**

35. Park A park is shaped like a rectangle with a length 5 times its width w. What is a simplified expression for the distance between opposite corners of the park?

Simplify each radical expression.

                                              See Problems 5 and 6.

36. $\sqrt{\frac{16}{25}}$ **37.** $7\sqrt{\frac{6}{32}}$ **38.** $-4\sqrt{\frac{100}{729}}$ **39.** $\sqrt{\frac{3x^3}{64x^2}}$

40. $-5\sqrt{\frac{162t^3}{2t}}$ **41.** $11\sqrt{\frac{49a^5}{4a^3}}$ **42.** $\frac{1}{\sqrt{11}}$ **43.** $\frac{\sqrt{5}}{\sqrt{8x}}$

44. $\frac{3\sqrt{6}}{\sqrt{15}}$ **45.** $\frac{22}{\sqrt{11}}$ **46.** $\frac{2\sqrt{24}}{\sqrt{48t^4}}$ **47.** $\frac{8\sqrt{7s}}{\sqrt{28s^3}}$

**Apply**

48. Look for a Pattern From a viewing height of h feet, the approximate distance d to the horizon, in miles, is given by the equation $d = \sqrt{\frac{3h}{2}}$.

 a. To the nearest mile, what is the distance to the horizon from a height of 150 ft? 225 ft? 300 ft?

 b. How does the distance to the horizon increase as the height increases?

49. Think About a Plan A square picture on the front page of a newspaper occupies an area of 24 in.^{2}. What is the length of each side of the picture? Write your answer as a radical in simplified form.

 • How can you find the side length of a square if you know the area?

 • What property can you use to write your answer in simplified form?

Explain why each radical expression is or is not in simplified form.

50. $\dfrac{13x}{\sqrt{4}}$ **51.** $\dfrac{3}{\sqrt{3}}$ **52.** $-4\sqrt{5}$ **53.** $5\sqrt{30}$

54. Error Analysis A student simplified the radical expression at the right. What mistake did the student make? What is the correct answer?

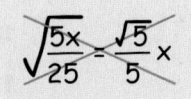

55. Reasoning You can simplify radical expressions with negative exponents by first rewriting the expressions using positive exponents. What are the simplified forms of the following radical expressions?

 a. $\dfrac{\sqrt{3}}{\sqrt{f^{-3}}}$ **b.** $\dfrac{\sqrt{x^{-3}}}{\sqrt{x}}$ **c.** $\dfrac{\sqrt{5a^{-2}}}{\sqrt{10a^{-1}}}$ **d.** $\dfrac{\sqrt{(2m)^{-3}}}{m^{-1}}$

56. Sports The bases in a softball diamond are located at the corners of a 3600-ft^2 square. How far is a throw from second base to home plate?

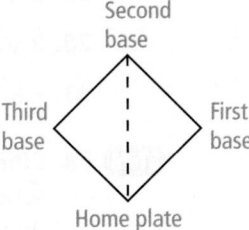

57. Suppose a and b are positive integers.

 a. Verify that if $a = 18$ and $b = 10$, then $\sqrt{a} \cdot \sqrt{b} = 6\sqrt{5}$.

 b. Open-Ended Find two other pairs of positive integers a and b such that $\sqrt{a} \cdot \sqrt{b} = 6\sqrt{5}$.

Simplify each radical expression.

58. $\sqrt{12} \cdot \sqrt{75}$ **59.** $\sqrt{26 \cdot 2}$ **60.** $\dfrac{\sqrt{72}}{\sqrt{64}}$ **61.** $\dfrac{-2}{\sqrt{a^3}}$

62. $\dfrac{\sqrt{180}}{\sqrt{3}}$ **63.** $\dfrac{\sqrt{x^2}}{\sqrt{y^3}}$ **64.** $\dfrac{-3\sqrt{2}}{\sqrt{6}}$ **65.** $\sqrt{8} \cdot \sqrt{10}$

66. $\sqrt{20a^2b^3}$ **67.** $\sqrt{a^3b^5c^3}$ **68.** $\sqrt{\dfrac{3m}{16m^2}}$ **69.** $\dfrac{16a}{\sqrt{6a^3}}$

Solve each equation. Leave your answer in simplified radical form.

70. $x^2 + 6x - 9 = 0$ **71.** $n^2 - 2n + 1 = 5$ **72.** $3y^2 - 4y - 2 = 0$

73. Open-Ended What are three numbers whose square roots can be written in the form $a\sqrt{3}$ for some integer value of a?

   Simplify each radical expression.

74. $\sqrt{24} \cdot \sqrt{2x} \cdot \sqrt{3x}$ **75.** $2b(\sqrt{5b})^2$ **76.** $\sqrt{45a^7} \cdot \sqrt{20a}$

77. Geometry The equation $r = \sqrt{\frac{A}{\pi}}$ gives the radius r of a circle with area A. What is the radius of a circle with the given area? Write your answer as a simplified radical and as a decimal rounded to the nearest hundredth.

    a. 50 ft^2 **b.** 32 in.^{2} **c.** 10 m^2

78. For a linear equation in standard form $Ax + By = C$, where $A \neq 0$ and $B \neq 0$, the distance d between the x- and y-intercepts is given by $d = \sqrt{\left(\frac{C}{A}\right)^2 + \left(\frac{C}{B}\right)^2}$. What is the distance between the x- and y-intercepts of the graph of $4x - 3y = 2$?

Apply What You've Learned

 MATHEMATICAL PRACTICES

MP 6

Look back at the information about the formula $s = \sqrt{30fd}$ on page 613. The table giving several coefficients of friction is shown again below.

Typical Coefficients of Friction

Surface Material	Coefficient of Friction
Gravel	0.6
Asphalt	0.7
Cement	0.9

  a. Based on the surface material of Pine Street, write and simplify a formula that gives the speed s of a car in terms of the length d of the skid marks, where s is in miles per hour and d is in feet.

  b. In the Apply What You've Learned in Lesson 10-1, you found the length of the skid marks left by the car described on page 613. Use this value and the formula you found in part (a) to write a radical expression that gives the speed, in miles per hour, of the car. Give your answer in simplest radical from.

  c. Suppose Pine Street was paved with gravel instead of asphalt. How would this change your answers to parts (a) and (b)? Does a decrease in the coefficient of friction lead to an increase or a decrease in the calculated speed of the car? Explain.

10-3 Operations With Radical Expressions

Common Core State Standards

Prepares for A-REI.A.2 Solve simple rational and radical equations in one variable, and give examples showing how extraneous solutions may arise.

MP 1, MP 2, MP 3, MP 4, MP 7

Objectives To simplify sums and differences of radical expressions
To simplify products and quotients of radical expressions

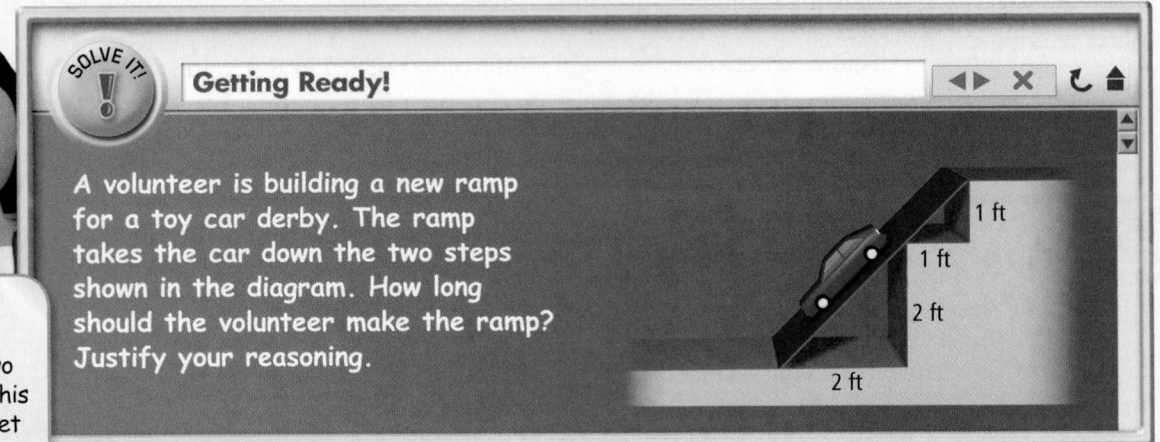

SOLVE IT!

Getting Ready!

A volunteer is building a new ramp for a toy car derby. The ramp takes the car down the two steps shown in the diagram. How long should the volunteer make the ramp? Justify your reasoning.

1 ft
1 ft
2 ft
2 ft

Notice that the ramp is the hypotenuse of two right triangles. This should help you get started.

MATHEMATICAL PRACTICES

Essential Understanding You can use properties of real numbers to perform operations with radical expressions.

For example, you can use the Distributive Property to simplify sums or differences of radical expressions by combining *like radicals*. **Like radicals,** such as $3\sqrt{5}$ and $7\sqrt{5}$, have the same radicand. **Unlike radicals,** such as $4\sqrt{3}$ and $-2\sqrt{2}$, have different radicands.

Lesson Vocabulary
- like radicals
- unlike radicals
- conjugates

Think

Have you seen a problem like this before?
Yes. Combining like radicals is similar to combining like terms. For example, simplifying the expression in part (A) is similar to simplifying $6x + 9x$.

 **Problem 1** Combining Like Radicals

What is the simplified form of each expression?

A $6\sqrt{11} + 9\sqrt{11}$

$\quad 6\sqrt{11} + 9\sqrt{11} = (6 + 9)\sqrt{11}$ Use the Distributive Property to combine like radicals.

$\quad\quad\quad\quad\quad\quad = 15\sqrt{11}$ Simplify.

B $\sqrt{3} - 5\sqrt{3}$

$\quad \sqrt{3} - 5\sqrt{3} = 1\sqrt{3} - 5\sqrt{3}$ Write $\sqrt{3}$ as $1\sqrt{3}$.

$\quad\quad\quad\quad\quad = (1 - 5)\sqrt{3}$ Use the Distributive Property to combine like radicals.

$\quad\quad\quad\quad\quad = -4\sqrt{3}$ Simplify.

 Got It? **1.** What is the simplified form of each expression?

     a. $7\sqrt{2} - 8\sqrt{2}$ **b.** $5\sqrt{5} + 2\sqrt{5}$

You may need to simplify radical expressions first to determine if they can be added or subtracted by combining like radicals.

 **Problem 2** Simplifying to Combine Like Radicals

Think

How do you know if radical expressions can be combined?
Simplify all radicals. Although $\sqrt{3}$ and $\sqrt{12}$ are unlike radicals, they can be combined after $\sqrt{12}$ is simplified.

What is the simplified form of $5\sqrt{3} - \sqrt{12}$?

$$5\sqrt{3} - \sqrt{12} = 5\sqrt{3} - \sqrt{4 \cdot 3}$$ 4 is a perfect-square factor of 12.

$$= 5\sqrt{3} - \sqrt{4} \cdot \sqrt{3}$$ Multiplication Property of Square Roots

$$= 5\sqrt{3} - 2\sqrt{3}$$ Simplify $\sqrt{4}$.

$$= (5 - 2)\sqrt{3}$$ Use the Distributive Property to combine like radicals.

$$= 3\sqrt{3}$$ Simplify.

Got It? **2.** What is the simplified form of each expression in parts (a) and (b)?

a. $4\sqrt{7} + 2\sqrt{28}$ **b.** $5\sqrt{32} - 4\sqrt{18}$

c. Reasoning Can you combine two unlike radicals when the radicands have no common factors other than 1? Explain.

When simplifying a product like $\sqrt{10}(\sqrt{6} + 3)$, you can use the Distributive Property to multiply $\sqrt{10}$ times $\sqrt{6}$ and $\sqrt{10}$ times 3. If both factors in the product have two terms, as in $(\sqrt{6} - 2\sqrt{3})(\sqrt{6} + \sqrt{3})$, you can use FOIL to multiply just as you do when multiplying binomials.

 **Problem 3** Multiplying Radical Expressions

Think

Have you seen a problem like this before?
Yes. Parts (A) and (B) are similar to simplifying products like $3(x + 2)$ and $(2x + 1)(x - 5)$.

What is the simplified form of each expression?

A $\sqrt{10}(\sqrt{6} + 3)$

$$\sqrt{10}(\sqrt{6} + 3) = (\sqrt{10} \cdot \sqrt{6}) + (\sqrt{10} \cdot 3)$$ Distributive Property

$$= \sqrt{60} + 3\sqrt{10}$$ Multiplication Property of Square Roots

$$= \sqrt{4} \cdot \sqrt{15} + 3\sqrt{10}$$ 4 is a perfect-square factor of 60.

$$= 2\sqrt{15} + 3\sqrt{10}$$ Simplify $\sqrt{4}$.

B $(\sqrt{6} - 2\sqrt{3})(\sqrt{6} + \sqrt{3})$

$$(\sqrt{6} - 2\sqrt{3})(\sqrt{6} + \sqrt{3}) = \sqrt{36} + \sqrt{18} - 2\sqrt{18} - 2\sqrt{9}$$ Use FOIL.

$$= 6 - \sqrt{18} - 2(3)$$ Combine like radicals and simplify.

$$= 6 - \sqrt{9} \cdot \sqrt{2} - 6$$ 9 is a perfect-square factor of 18.

$$= -3\sqrt{2}$$ Simplify.

 Got It? **3.** What is the simplified form of each expression?

a. $\sqrt{2}(\sqrt{6} + 5)$ **b.** $(\sqrt{11} - 2)^2$ **c.** $(\sqrt{6} - 2\sqrt{3})(4\sqrt{3} + 3\sqrt{6})$

Conjugates are the sum and difference of the same two terms. For example, $\sqrt{7} + \sqrt{3}$ and $\sqrt{7} - \sqrt{3}$ are conjugates. The product of conjugates is a difference of squares.

$$(\sqrt{7} + \sqrt{3})(\sqrt{7} - \sqrt{3}) = (\sqrt{7})^2 - (\sqrt{3})^2$$

$$= 7 - 3 = 4 \quad \boxed{\text{The product of the conjugates has no radicals.}}$$

You can use conjugates to simplify a quotient whose denominator is a sum or difference of radicals.

© **Problem 4** Rationalizing a Denominator Using Conjugates

Plan

How do you rationalize the denominator?
Multiply by the conjugate of the denominator. If the denominator has the form $a - b$, the conjugate is $a + b$.

What is the simplified form of $\dfrac{10}{\sqrt{7} - \sqrt{2}}$?

$$\dfrac{10}{\sqrt{7} - \sqrt{2}} = \dfrac{10}{\sqrt{7} - \sqrt{2}} \cdot \dfrac{\sqrt{7} + \sqrt{2}}{\sqrt{7} + \sqrt{2}} \qquad \text{Multiply the numerator and denominator by the conjugate of the denominator.}$$

$$= \dfrac{10(\sqrt{7} + \sqrt{2})}{7 - 2} \qquad \text{Multiply in the denominator.}$$

$$= \dfrac{10(\sqrt{7} + \sqrt{2})}{5} \qquad \text{Simplify the denominator.}$$

$$= 2(\sqrt{7} + \sqrt{2}) \qquad \text{Divide 10 and 5 by the common factor 5.}$$

$$= 2\sqrt{7} + 2\sqrt{2} \qquad \text{Simplify the expression.}$$

✔ **Got It?** **4.** What is the simplified form of $\dfrac{-3}{\sqrt{10} + \sqrt{5}}$?

Golden rectangles appear frequently in nature and art. The ratio of the length to the width of a golden rectangle is $(1 + \sqrt{5}) : 2$.

© **Problem 5** Solving a Proportion Involving Radicals **STEM**

Think

How do you begin this problem?
Since the rectangle is a golden rectangle, the length divided by the width has to equal $\dfrac{1 + \sqrt{5}}{2}$.

Biology Fiddlehead ferns naturally grow in spirals that fit into golden rectangles. What is the width w of the fern shown?

$$\dfrac{1 + \sqrt{5}}{2} = \dfrac{4}{w} \qquad \text{Write a proportion.}$$

$$w(1 + \sqrt{5}) = 8 \qquad \text{Cross Products Property}$$

$$w = \dfrac{8}{1 + \sqrt{5}} \qquad \text{Divide each side by } 1 + \sqrt{5}.$$

$$w = \dfrac{8}{1 + \sqrt{5}} \cdot \dfrac{1 - \sqrt{5}}{1 - \sqrt{5}} \qquad \text{Multiply the numerator and denominator by the conjugate of the denominator.}$$

$$w = \dfrac{8 - 8\sqrt{5}}{1 - 5} \qquad \text{Multiply.}$$

$$w = \dfrac{8 - 8\sqrt{5}}{-4} \qquad \text{Simplify the denominator.}$$

$$w = -2 + 2\sqrt{5} \approx 2.5 \qquad \text{Simplify. Use a calculator.}$$

The width of the fern is about 2.5 cm.

Got It? **5.** A golden rectangle is 12 in. long. What is the width of the rectangle? Write your answer in simplified radical form. Round to the nearest tenth of an inch.

 ## Lesson Check

Do you know HOW?

Simplify each radical expression.

1. $4\sqrt{3} + \sqrt{3}$

2. $3\sqrt{6} - \sqrt{24}$

3. $\sqrt{7}(\sqrt{3} - 2)$

4. $(\sqrt{5} - 6)^2$

5. $\dfrac{7\sqrt{5}}{3 + \sqrt{2}}$

6. $\dfrac{6}{\sqrt{7} + 2}$

Do you UNDERSTAND?  MATHEMATICAL PRACTICES

7. Vocabulary What is the conjugate of each expression?

a. $\sqrt{13} - 2$ **b.** $\sqrt{6} + \sqrt{3}$ **c.** $\sqrt{5} - \sqrt{10}$

8. Error Analysis A student simplified an expression, as shown below. Describe and correct the error.

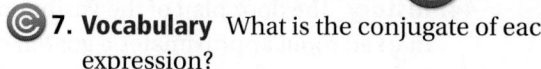
$$\frac{1}{\sqrt{3}-1} = \frac{1}{\sqrt{3}-1} \cdot \frac{\sqrt{3}+1}{\sqrt{3}+1} = \frac{\sqrt{3}+1}{9-1} = \frac{\sqrt{3}+1}{8}$$

 ## Practice and Problem-Solving Exercises  MATHEMATICAL PRACTICES

 **Practice**

Simplify each sum or difference.

◀ See Problems 1 and 2.

9. $\sqrt{5} + 6\sqrt{5}$

10. $12\sqrt{5} - 3\sqrt{5}$

11. $7\sqrt{3} + \sqrt{3}$

12. $4\sqrt{2} - 7\sqrt{2}$

13. $3\sqrt{7} - \sqrt{63}$

14. $4\sqrt{128} + 5\sqrt{18}$

15. $3\sqrt{45} - 8\sqrt{20}$

16. $\sqrt{28} - 5\sqrt{7}$

17. $-6\sqrt{10} + 5\sqrt{90}$

18. $3\sqrt{3} - 2\sqrt{12}$

19. $-\frac{1}{2}\sqrt{5} + 2\sqrt{125}$

20. $5\sqrt{8} + 2\sqrt{72}$

Simplify each product.

◀ See Problem 3.

21. $\sqrt{6}(\sqrt{2} + \sqrt{3})$

22. $\sqrt{5}(\sqrt{15} - 3)$

23. $3\sqrt{7}(1 - \sqrt{7})$

24. $-\sqrt{12}(4 - 2\sqrt{3})$

25. $5\sqrt{11}(\sqrt{3} - 3\sqrt{2})$

26. $(3\sqrt{11} + \sqrt{7})^2$

27. $(2 + \sqrt{10})(2 - \sqrt{10})$

28. $(\sqrt{6} + \sqrt{3})(\sqrt{2} - 2)$

29. $(5\sqrt{2} - 2\sqrt{3})^2$

Simplify each quotient.

◀ See Problem 4.

30. $\dfrac{5}{\sqrt{2} - 1}$

31. $\dfrac{3}{\sqrt{7} - \sqrt{3}}$

32. $\dfrac{-2}{\sqrt{6} + \sqrt{11}}$

33. $\dfrac{\sqrt{5}}{2 - \sqrt{5}}$

34. $\dfrac{-1}{2 - 2\sqrt{3}}$

35. $\dfrac{7}{\sqrt{5} + \sqrt{13}}$

STEM **36. Biology** A shell fits into a golden rectangle with a length of 8 in. What is the shell's width? Write your answer in simplified radical form and rounded to the nearest tenth of an inch.

◀ See Problem 5.

STEM **37. Architecture** A room is approximately shaped like a golden rectangle. Its length is 23 ft. What is the room's width? Write your answer in simplified radical form and rounded to the nearest tenth of a foot.

B Apply

Find the exact solution for each equation. Find the approximate solution to the nearest tenth.

38. $\dfrac{5\sqrt{2}}{\sqrt{2}-1} = \dfrac{x}{\sqrt{2}}$

39. $\dfrac{3}{1+\sqrt{5}} = \dfrac{1-\sqrt{5}}{x}$

40. $\dfrac{\sqrt{2}-1}{\sqrt{2}+1} = \dfrac{x}{2}$

41. $\dfrac{x}{2+\sqrt{7}} = \dfrac{3-\sqrt{7}}{4}$

42. $\dfrac{4\sqrt{15}}{1+\sqrt{3}} = \dfrac{1+\sqrt{3}}{x}$

43. $\dfrac{2+\sqrt{2}}{2-\sqrt{2}} = \dfrac{x}{3+\sqrt{10}}$

44. History The floor plan of the Parthenon in Athens, Greece, is shown below. The marked room approximates a golden rectangle. What is the width of the room? Write your answer in simplified radical form. Round to the nearest tenth of a meter.

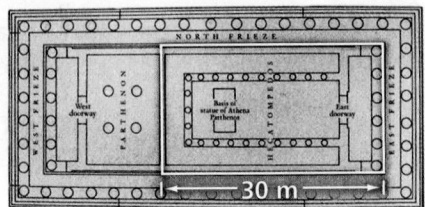

45. Writing Are $\sqrt{3}$ and $\sqrt{12}$ like radicals? Can their sum be simplified? Explain.

46. Error Analysis A student added two radical expressions as shown at the right. Describe and correct the student's mistake.

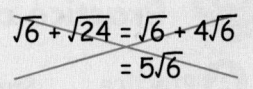

Simplify each expression.

47. $\sqrt{40} + \sqrt{90}$

48. $3\sqrt{2}(2+\sqrt{6})$

49. $\sqrt{12} + 4\sqrt{75} - \sqrt{36}$

50. $(\sqrt{3}+\sqrt{5})^2$

51. $\dfrac{\sqrt{13}+\sqrt{10}}{\sqrt{13}-\sqrt{5}}$

52. $(\sqrt{7}+\sqrt{8})(\sqrt{7}+\sqrt{8})$

53. $2\sqrt{2}(-2\sqrt{32}+\sqrt{8})$

54. $4\sqrt{50} - 7\sqrt{18}$

55. $\dfrac{2\sqrt{12}+3\sqrt{6}}{\sqrt{9}-\sqrt{6}}$

STEM 56. Chemistry The ratio of the diffusion rates of two gases is given by the formula $\dfrac{r_1}{r_2} = \dfrac{\sqrt{m_2}}{\sqrt{m_1}}$, where m_1 and m_2 are the masses of the molecules of the gases. Find $\dfrac{r_1}{r_2}$ if $m_1 = 12$ units and $m_2 = 30$ units. Write your answer in simplified radical form.

57. Reasoning The diagram at the right shows the dimensions of a kite. The length of the vertical blue crosspiece is s. What is the length of the horizontal red crosspiece in terms of s?

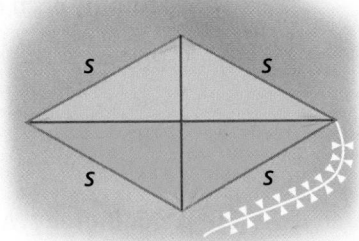

58. Think About a Plan The formula $r = \sqrt{\dfrac{A}{P}} - 1$ gives the interest rate r, expressed as a decimal, that will allow principal P to grow into amount A in 2 yr, if the interest is compounded annually. If you invest \$10,000 and want to make \$2000 in interest over 2 yr, what interest rate do you need?
- What amount do you want in the account after 2 yr?
- What radical expression gives the interest rate you need?

59. a. Suppose n is an even number. Simplify $\sqrt{x^n}$.
 b. Suppose n is an odd number greater than 1. Simplify $\sqrt{x^n}$.

60. Reasoning Simplify $\dfrac{a\sqrt{b}}{b\sqrt{a}}$.

 **Challenge**

61. Geometry A square has sides with length n. How much must be added to the length of one side to transform the square into a golden rectangle?

Ⓒ **62. Reasoning** What are three fractions that you can multiply $\frac{1}{\sqrt{2}+3}$ by to rationalize the denominator? Will the resulting products be the same? Explain.

63. Geometry Find the length of each hypotenuse. Write your answer in simplified radical form.

a.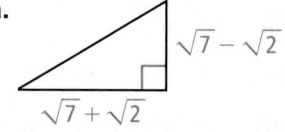

b.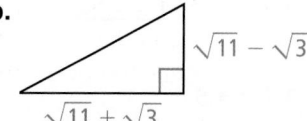

c.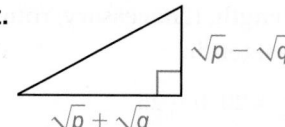

Standardized Test Prep

 SAT/ACT

64. What is the simplified form of $2\sqrt{18} - \sqrt{32} + 4\sqrt{8}$?

Ⓐ $8\sqrt{3}$ Ⓑ $10\sqrt{2}$ Ⓒ $18\sqrt{2}$ Ⓓ $10\sqrt{18}$

65. A surveyor is calculating the areas of lots that are going to be sold. The dimensions of one lot are shown at the right. What is the area of the lot shown?

Ⓕ $8.82 \times 10^6 \text{ m}^2$ Ⓗ $4.41 \times 10^5 \text{ m}^2$
Ⓖ $8.82 \times 10^5 \text{ m}^2$ Ⓘ $4.41 \times 10^6 \text{ m}^2$

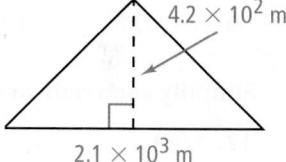

66. What are the approximate solutions of the equation $\frac{5}{2}x^2 + \frac{3}{4}x - 5 = 0$? Use a graphing calculator.

Ⓐ $-5, 0$ Ⓑ $-1.57, 1.27$ Ⓒ $-1.36, 0.71$ Ⓓ $-0.96, 0.84$

Short Response

67. What are the domain and range of the function $y = |x|$? Show how you find your answer.

Mixed Review

Simplify each radical expression. ◀ **See Lesson 10-2.**

68. $\sqrt{108}$ **69.** $3\sqrt{150}$ **70.** $\dfrac{4}{\sqrt{18c^2}}$ **71.** $\sqrt{5} \cdot \sqrt{45}$

Rewrite each expression using each base only once. ◀ **See Lesson 7-2.**

72. $8^5 \cdot 8^{11}$ **73.** $2^{24} \cdot 2^{-13}$ **74.** $5^{11} \cdot 5^{16}$ **75.** $3^7 \cdot 3^{-4}$

Get Ready!   To prepare for Lesson 10-4, do Exercises 76–81.

Solve by factoring. ◀ **See Lesson 9-4.**

76. $x^2 + 2x + 1 = 0$ **77.** $x^2 + x - 12 = 0$ **78.** $x^2 + 2x - 15 = 0$

79. $3x^2 + 7x - 6 = 0$ **80.** $2x^2 + 3x - 2 = 0$ **81.** $x^2 + 14x + 49 = 0$

Do you know HOW?

Use the triangle at the right. Find the missing side length. If necessary, round to the nearest tenth.

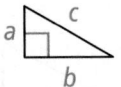

1. $a = 20, b = 25$ **2.** $a = 0.8, b = 1.5$

3. $a = 5, b = 12$ **4.** $a = 2.2, b = 12$

5. $a = 14, c = 50$ **6.** $a = 9, c = 41$

7. $b = 40, c = 41$ **8.** $b = 36, c = 39$

Determine whether the given lengths can be side lengths of a right triangle.

9. 8, 15, 17   **10.** 5, 24, 25   **11.** 60, 80, 100

Simplify each radical expression.

12. $\sqrt{80}$ **13.** $\sqrt{10} \cdot \sqrt{18}$

14. $\sqrt{6x} \cdot \sqrt{2x}$ **15.** $-2\sqrt{3b^2} \cdot \sqrt{12b}$

16. $\sqrt{\dfrac{64}{81}}$ **17.** $-\dfrac{\sqrt{5c}}{\sqrt{45c^3}}$

18. $\dfrac{-3\sqrt{14x^3}}{-\sqrt{21x}}$ **19.** $\dfrac{\sqrt{13f^3}}{\sqrt{5f^2}}$

20. Sports A rectangular soccer field is $6w$ yards wide and $10w$ yards long. What is an expression for the distance from one corner to the opposite corner?

Find the area of each figure.

21.

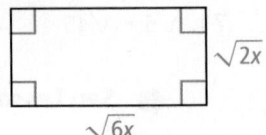

22.

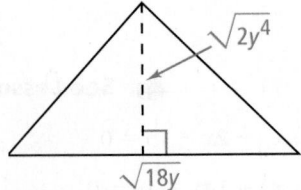

Simplify each radical expression.

23. $5\sqrt{5} + 3\sqrt{5}$

24. $2\sqrt{28} - 3\sqrt{7}$

25. $\sqrt{3}(\sqrt{6} - 4)$

26. $(2\sqrt{21} + 4\sqrt{3})(5\sqrt{21} - \sqrt{3})$

27. $\dfrac{1}{\sqrt{3} - 2}$

28. $\dfrac{3 + \sqrt{2}}{4\sqrt{2} + 2}$

Find the exact solution for each equation. Find the approximate solution to the nearest tenth.

29. $\dfrac{5}{\sqrt{8} - 2} = \dfrac{\sqrt{8} + 2}{x}$

30. $\dfrac{x}{\sqrt{10}} = \dfrac{3\sqrt{2}}{\sqrt{2} + 1}$

31. Transportation A bus leaves the bus station and drives 3.75 mi east. The bus then turns and drives 5 mi south. How far is the bus from the bus station?

Do you UNDERSTAND?

32. What type of angle is formed by the two legs of a right triangle?

33. Writing How do you use a conjugate to simplify a fraction with a radical expression in its denominator?

34. Reasoning Is the equation $\sqrt{a} + \sqrt{b} = \sqrt{a + b}$ *always*, *sometimes*, or *never* true? Justify your answer.

35. Error Analysis Describe and correct the error shown below in simplifying the radical expression.

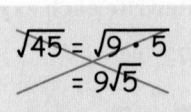

36. Open-Ended Give the side lengths of a triangle that is not a right triangle. Explain why these lengths cannot be the side lengths of a right triangle.

10-4 Solving Radical Equations

© Common Core State Standards

A-REI.A.2 Solve simple rational and radical equations in one variable, and give examples showing how extraneous solutions may arise.

MP 1, MP 2, MP 3, MP 4

Objectives To solve equations containing radicals
To identify extraneous solutions

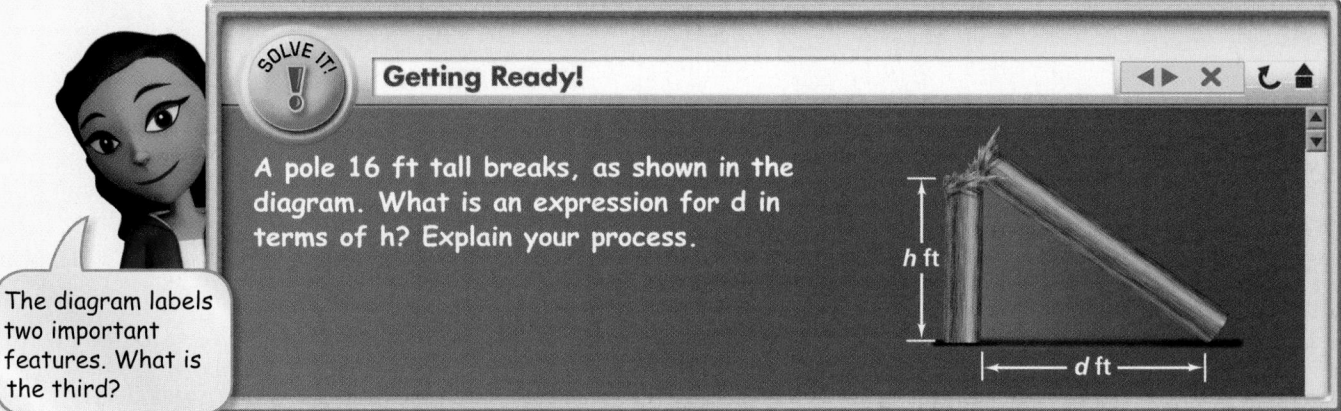

Getting Ready!

A pole 16 ft tall breaks, as shown in the diagram. What is an expression for d in terms of h? Explain your process.

h ft

d ft

The diagram labels two important features. What is the third?

Lesson Vocabulary
• radical equation
• extraneous solution

The expression for d in the Solve It has a variable in a radicand. A **radical equation** is an equation that has a variable in a radicand. Examples include $\sqrt{x} - 5 = 3$ and $\sqrt{x-2} = 1$. To solve a radical equation, get the radical by itself on one side of the equation. Then square both sides. The expression under the radical must be nonnegative.

Essential Understanding You can solve some radical equations by squaring each side of the equation and testing the solutions.

Plan

How do you start when solving a radical equation?
Use the properties of equality to get the radical by itself on one side of the equation.

© Problem 1 Solving by Isolating the Radical

What is the solution of $\sqrt{x} + 7 = 16$?

$$\sqrt{x} + 7 = 16$$

$$\sqrt{x} = 9 \quad \text{Get the radical by itself on one side of the equation.}$$

$$(\sqrt{x})^2 = 9^2 \quad \text{Square each side.}$$

$$x = 81 \quad \text{Simplify.}$$

Check $\sqrt{x} + 7 = 16$

$$\sqrt{81} + 7 \stackrel{?}{=} 16 \quad \text{Substitute 81 for } x.$$

$$9 + 7 = 16 \ ✔$$

✔ Got It? 1. What is the solution of $\sqrt{x} - 5 = -2$?

Problem 2 Using a Radical Equation

Clocks The time t in seconds it takes for a pendulum of a clock to complete a full swing is approximated by the equation $t = 2\sqrt{\frac{\ell}{3.3}}$, where ℓ is the length of the pendulum, in feet. If the pendulum of a clock completes a full swing in 3 s, what is the length of the pendulum? Round to the nearest tenth of a foot.

Know
- A function relating t and ℓ
- The value of t

Need
The value for ℓ, the length of the pendulum

Plan
Substitute for t in the function and solve for ℓ.

Think

Have you solved problems like this before?
Yes. You have substituted a value for one variable in a function and then solved for the other variable.

$$t = 2\sqrt{\frac{\ell}{3.3}}$$

$$3 = 2\sqrt{\frac{\ell}{3.3}} \qquad \text{Substitute 3 for } t.$$

$$1.5 = \sqrt{\frac{\ell}{3.3}} \qquad \text{Divide each side by 2 to isolate the radical.}$$

$$(1.5)^2 = \left(\sqrt{\frac{\ell}{3.3}}\right)^2 \qquad \text{Square each side.}$$

$$2.25 = \frac{\ell}{3.3} \qquad \text{Simplify.}$$

$$7.425 = \ell \qquad \text{Multiply each side by 3.3.}$$

Check $\quad 3 \overset{?}{=} 2\sqrt{\frac{7.425}{3.3}} \qquad$ Substitute 7.425 for ℓ.

$$3 \overset{?}{=} 2\sqrt{2.25}$$

$$3 = 3 ✔$$

The pendulum is about 7.4 ft long.

 Got It? **2.** How long is a pendulum if each swing takes 1 s?

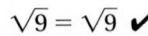 **Problem 3** Solving With Radical Expressions on Both Sides

Think

How can you make the equation simpler to solve?
You can *solve a simpler problem* by squaring each side of the equation. You know how to solve equations like $5t - 11 = t + 5$.

What is the solution of $\sqrt{5t - 11} = \sqrt{t + 5}$**?**

$$\sqrt{5t - 11} = \sqrt{t + 5}$$

$$(\sqrt{5t - 11})^2 = (\sqrt{t + 5})^2 \qquad \text{Square each side.}$$

$$5t - 11 = t + 5 \qquad \text{Simplify.}$$

$$4t - 11 = 5 \qquad \text{Subtract } t \text{ from each side.}$$

$$4t = 16 \qquad \text{Add 11 to each side.}$$

$$t = 4 \qquad \text{Divide each side by 4.}$$

Check $\quad \sqrt{5(4) - 11} \overset{?}{=} \sqrt{4 + 5} \qquad$ Substitute 4 for t.

$$\sqrt{9} = \sqrt{9} ✔$$

 Got It? **3.** What is the solution of $\sqrt{7x - 4} = \sqrt{5x + 10}$?

When you solve an equation by squaring each side, you create a new equation. The new equation may have solutions that do not satisfy the original equation.

Original Equation	**Square each side.**	**New Equation**	**Apparent Solutions**
$x = 3$	$x^2 = 3^2$	$x^2 = 9$	$3, -3$

In the example above, -3 does not satisfy the original equation. It is an *extraneous* solution. An **extraneous solution** is an apparent solution that does not satisfy the original equation. Always substitute each apparent solution into the original equation to check for extraneous solutions.

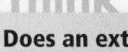 **Problem 4** Identifying Extraneous Solutions

What is the solution of $n = \sqrt{n + 12}$?

$$n = \sqrt{n + 12}$$
$$n^2 = (\sqrt{n + 12})^2 \qquad \text{Square each side.}$$
$$n^2 = n + 12 \qquad \text{Simplify.}$$
$$n^2 - n - 12 = 0 \qquad \text{Subtract } n + 12 \text{ from each side.}$$
$$(n - 4)(n + 3) = 0 \qquad \text{Factor the quadratic equation.}$$
$$n - 4 = 0 \quad \text{or} \quad n + 3 = 0 \qquad \text{Use the Zero-Product Property.}$$
$$n = 4 \quad \text{or} \quad n = -3 \qquad \text{Solve for } n.$$

Check $\quad 4 \stackrel{?}{=} \sqrt{4 + 12} \qquad$ Substitute 4 and -3 for n. $\qquad -3 \stackrel{?}{=} \sqrt{-3 + 12}$

$\qquad\qquad 4 = 4$ ✔ $\qquad\qquad\qquad\qquad\qquad\qquad\qquad\qquad -3 \neq 3$

The solution of the original equation is 4. The value -3 is an extraneous solution.

Think

Does an extraneous solution solve the problem?
No. An extraneous solution solves only the new equation formed after squaring both sides. It is not a solution to the problem.

 Got It? 4. What is the solution of $-y = \sqrt{y + 6}$?

Sometimes you get only extraneous solutions after squaring each side of an equation. In that case, the original equation has no solution.

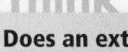 **Problem 5** Identifying Equations With No Solution

What is the solution of $\sqrt{3y} + 8 = 2$?

$$\sqrt{3y} + 8 = 2$$
$$\sqrt{3y} = -6 \qquad \text{Subtract 8 from each side.}$$
$$3y = 36 \qquad \text{Square each side.}$$
$$y = 12 \qquad \text{Divide each side by 3.}$$

Check $\quad \sqrt{3(12)} + 8 \stackrel{?}{=} 2 \qquad$ Substitute 12 for y.

$\qquad\qquad\qquad 14 \neq 2 \qquad y = 12$ does not satisfy the original equation.

The apparent solution 12 is extraneous. The original equation has no solution.

Think

Have you seen other equations with no solutions?
Yes. You learned that equations such as $x + 1 = x$ have no solution.

Got It? **5. a.** What is the solution of $6 - \sqrt{2x} = 10$?

b. Reasoning How can you determine that the equation $\sqrt{x} = -5$ does not have a solution without going through all the steps of solving the equation?

 ## Lesson Check

Do you know HOW?

Solve each radical equation. Check your solution. If there is no solution, write *no solution.*

1. $\sqrt{3x} + 10 = 16$

2. $\sqrt{r+5} = 2\sqrt{r-1}$

3. $\sqrt{2x-1} = x$

4. $\sqrt{x-3} = \sqrt{x+5}$

Do you UNDERSTAND?

5. Vocabulary Which is an extraneous solution of $s = \sqrt{s+2}$?

Ⓐ 2   Ⓒ −1

Ⓑ 0   Ⓓ −2

6. Reasoning What is the converse of the conditional statement "If $x = y$, then $x^2 = y^2$"? Is the converse of this statement always true? Explain.

 ## Practice and Problem-Solving Exercises

 **Practice**

Solve each radical equation. Check your solution.

See Problem 1.

7. $\sqrt{x} + 3 = 5$

8. $\sqrt{t} + 2 = 9$

9. $\sqrt{z} - 1 = 5$

10. $\sqrt{n} - 3 = 6$

11. $\sqrt{2b} + 4 = 8$

12. $3 - \sqrt{t} = -2$

13. $\sqrt{3a+1} = 7$

14. $\sqrt{10b+6} = 6$

15. $1 = \sqrt{-2v-3}$

16. $\sqrt{x-3} = 4$

17. Recreation You are making a tire swing for a playground. The time t in seconds for the tire to make one swing is given by $t = 2\sqrt{\frac{\ell}{3.3}}$, where ℓ is the length of the swing in feet. You want one swing to take 2.5 s. How many feet long should the swing be?

See Problem 2.

18. Geometry The length s of one edge of a cube is given by $s = \sqrt{\frac{A}{6}}$, where A represents the cube's surface area. Suppose a cube has an edge length of 9 cm. What is its surface area? Round to the nearest hundredth.

Solve each radical equation. Check your solution.

See Problem 3.

19. $\sqrt{3x+1} = \sqrt{5x-8}$

20. $\sqrt{2y} = \sqrt{9-y}$

21. $\sqrt{7v-4} = \sqrt{5v+10}$

22. $\sqrt{s+10} = \sqrt{6-s}$

23. $\sqrt{n+5} = \sqrt{5n-11}$

24. $\sqrt{3m+1} = \sqrt{7m-9}$

Tell which solutions, if any, are extraneous for each equation.    **See Problems 4 and 5.**

25. $-z = \sqrt{-z + 6}$; $z = -3$, $z = 2$

26. $\sqrt{12 - n} = n$; $n = -4$, $n = 3$

27. $y = \sqrt{2y}$; $y = 0$, $y = 2$

28. $2a = \sqrt{4a + 3}$; $a = \frac{3}{2}$, $a = -\frac{1}{2}$

29. $x = \sqrt{28 - 3x}$; $x = 4$, $x = -7$

30. $-t = \sqrt{-6t - 5}$; $t = -5$, $t = -1$

Solve each radical equation. Check your solution. If there is no solution, write *no solution*.

31. $x = \sqrt{2x + 3}$

32. $n = \sqrt{4n + 5}$

33. $\sqrt{3b} = -3$

34. $2y = \sqrt{5y + 6}$

35. $-2\sqrt{2r + 5} = 6$

36. $\sqrt{d + 12} = d$

B **Apply**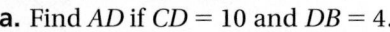

37. Error Analysis A student solved the equation $r = \sqrt{-6r - 5}$ and found the solutions -1 and -5. Describe and correct the student's error.

38. Think About a Plan The total surface area A of Earth, in square kilometers, is related to Earth's radius r, in kilometers, by $r = \sqrt{\dfrac{A}{4\pi}}$. Earth's radius is about 6378 km. What is its surface area? Round to the nearest square kilometer.
- What equation in one variable can you solve to find Earth's surface area?
- How can you check the reasonableness of your solution?

39. Geometry In the right triangle $\triangle ABC$, the altitude $\overline{CD}$ is at a right angle to the hypotenuse. You can use $CD = \sqrt{(AD)(DB)}$ to find missing lengths.
a. Find AD if $CD = 10$ and $DB = 4$.
b. Find DB if $AD = 20$ and $CD = 15$.

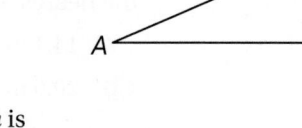

40. Packaging The radius r of a cylindrical can with volume V and height h is given by $r = \sqrt{\dfrac{V}{\pi h}}$. What is the height of a can with a radius of 2 in. and a volume of 75 in.^{3}?

41. Writing Explain how you would solve the equation $\sqrt{2y} - \sqrt{y + 2} = 0$.

42. Open-Ended Write two radical equations that have 3 for a solution.

Solve each radical equation. Check your solution. If there is no solution, write *no solution*.

43. $\sqrt{5x + 10} = 5$

44. $-6 - \sqrt{3y} = -3$

45. $\sqrt{7p + 5} = \sqrt{p - 3}$

46. $a = \sqrt{7a - 6}$

47. $\sqrt{y + 12} = 3\sqrt{y}$

48. $3 - \sqrt{4a + 1} = 12$

STEM **49. Physics** The formula $t = \sqrt{\dfrac{n}{16}}$ gives the time t in seconds for an object that is initially at rest to fall n feet. What is the distance an object falls in the first 10 s?

50. Packaging The diagram at the right shows a piece of cardboard that makes a box when sections of it are folded and taped. The ends of the box are x inches by x inches, and the body of the box is 10 in. long.

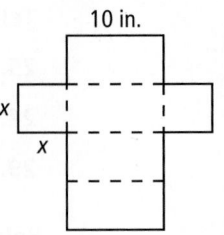

   a. Write an equation for the volume V of the box.

   b. Solve the equation in part (a) for x.

   c. Find the integer values of x that would give the box a volume between 40 in.^{3} and 490 in.^{3}, inclusive.

Challenge   **51. Reasoning** Explain the difference between squaring $\sqrt{x-1}$ and $\sqrt{x}-1$.

   52. a. Reasoning What is the solution of $\sqrt{7y+18}=y$? What is the extraneous solution?

     b. Multiply one side of $\sqrt{7y+18}=y$ by -1. What is the solution of the new equation? What is an extraneous solution of the new equation?

     c. What do you think will happen to the solutions and extraneous solutions of $\sqrt{y+2}=y$ if you multiply one side by -1? Explain.

Standardized Test Prep

SAT/ACT   **53.** What are the solutions of $\sqrt{c^2-17}=8$?

    Ⓐ 6, 9   Ⓑ 8, -8 Ⓒ 8, 0   Ⓓ 9, -9

54. Sam is building a fence around a triangular flower garden. What is the perimeter of the garden? Round your answer to the nearest tenth of a meter.

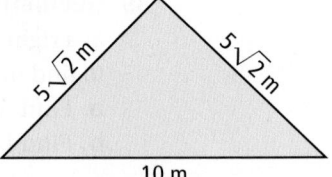

    Ⓕ 14.1 m   Ⓗ 24.1 m

    Ⓖ 20.0 m   Ⓘ 50.0 m

55. What is the slope-intercept form of the equation $2x + 5y = 40$?

    Ⓐ $y = -2x + 8$ Ⓑ $y = -\frac{2}{5}x + 8$ Ⓒ $y = \frac{2}{5}x + 8$ Ⓓ $y = 2x + 8$

Short Response   **56.** Write the equation of the line passing through $(1, -1)$ with a slope of $\frac{1}{2}$ in three different forms. When would each of the forms be useful?

Mixed Review

Simplify each expression.   ◀ **See Lesson 10-3.**

57. $\sqrt{8} + 3\sqrt{2}$ **58.** $(2\sqrt{5} - 6)(9 + 3\sqrt{5})$ **59.** $\dfrac{2}{\sqrt{3} + \sqrt{8}}$

Use the quadratic formula to solve each equation.   ◀ **See Lesson 9-6.**

60. $3a^2 + 4a + 3 = 0$ **61.** $2f^2 - 8 = 0$ **62.** $6m^2 + 13m + 6 = 0$

Get Ready!   **To prepare for Lesson 10-5, do Exercises 63–65.**

Graph each function by translating $y = |x|$.   ◀ **See Lesson 5-8.**

63. $y = |x + 2|$ **64.** $y = |x| - 3$ **65.** $y = |x - 4|$

10-5 Graphing Square Root Functions

 Common Core State Standards

F-IF.C.7b Graph square root, cube root, and piecewise-defined functions, including step functions and absolute value functions. **Also A-CED.A.2**

MP 1, MP 2, MP 3, MP 4, MP 6

Objectives To graph square root functions
To translate graphs of square root functions

Look at your graph. How is it similar to and different from a parabola?

MATHEMATICAL PRACTICES

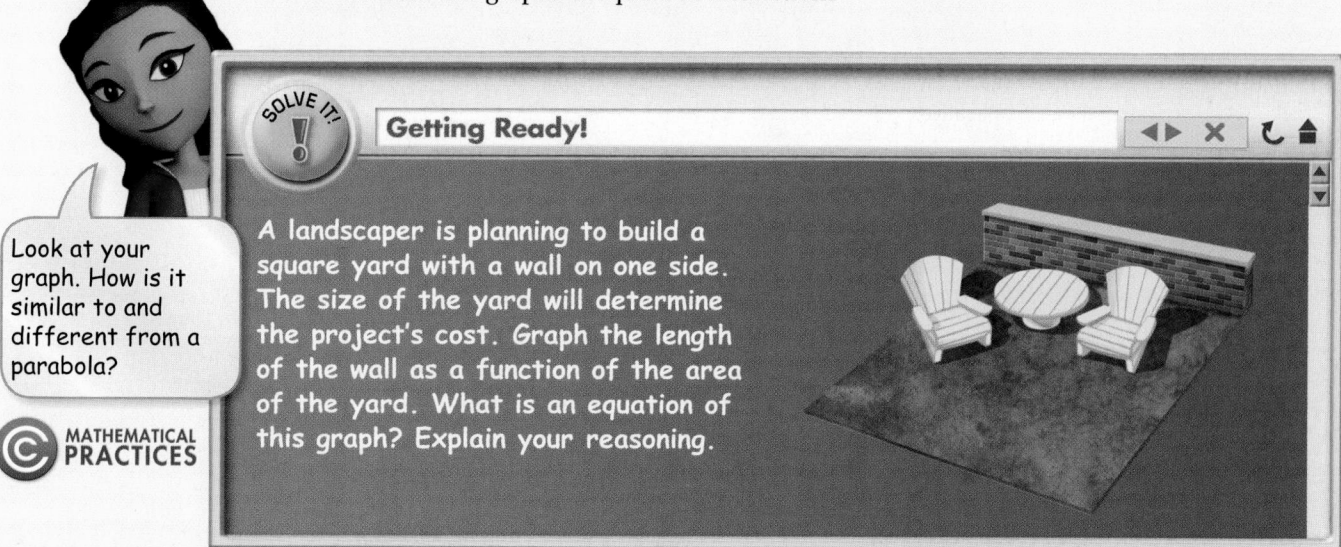

SOLVE IT!

Getting Ready!

A landscaper is planning to build a square yard with a wall on one side. The size of the yard will determine the project's cost. Graph the length of the wall as a function of the area of the yard. What is an equation of this graph? Explain your reasoning.

The Solve It involves a *square root function*. Square root functions are examples of radical functions.

Lesson Vocabulary
• square root function

take note

Key Concept   Square Root Functions

A **square root function** is a function containing a square root with the independent variable in the radicand. The parent square root function is $y = \sqrt{x}$.

The table and graph below show the parent square root function.

x	y
0	0
1	1
2	1.4
4	2
9	3

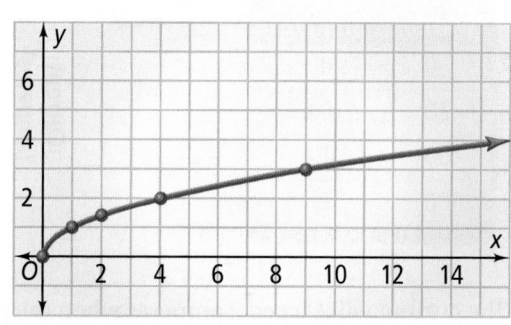

Essential Understanding You can graph a square root function by plotting points or using a translation of the parent square root function.

For real numbers, the value of the radicand cannot be negative. So the domain of a square root function is limited to values of x for which the radicand is greater than or equal to 0.

 **Problem 1** Finding the Domain of a Square Root Function

What is the domain of the function $y = 2\sqrt{3x - 9}$?

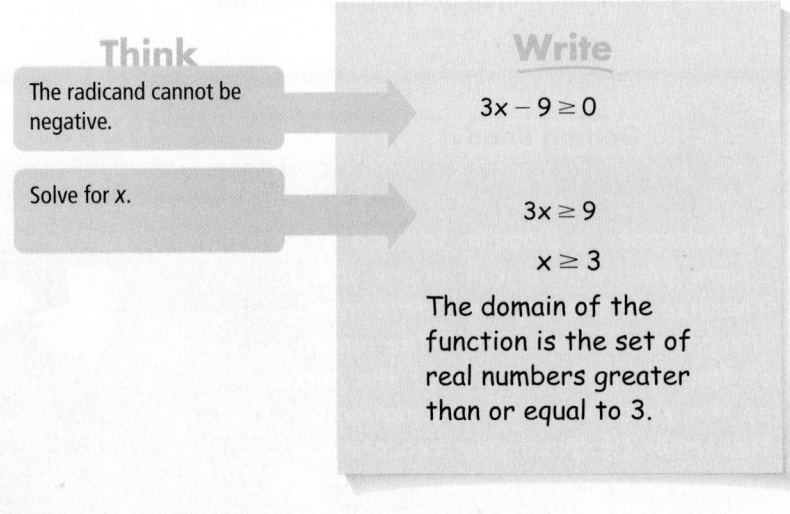

Think

The radicand cannot be negative.

Solve for x.

Write

$3x - 9 \geq 0$

$3x \geq 9$

$x \geq 3$

The domain of the function is the set of real numbers greater than or equal to 3.

Got It? 1. What is the domain of $y = \sqrt{-2x + 5}$?

 **Problem 2** Graphing a Square Root Function (STEM)

Engineering Graph the function $I = \frac{1}{5}\sqrt{P}$, which gives the current I in amperes for a certain circuit with P watts of power. When will the current exceed 2 amperes?

Plan

How can you solve this problem?
Make a chart of ordered pairs that satisfy the equation. Then plot the ordered pairs on a graph.

Step 1 Make a table.

Current in Circuit

Power (watts)	Current (amperes)
0	0
10	0.6
50	1.4
100	2

Step 2 Plot the points on a graph.

Current in Circuit

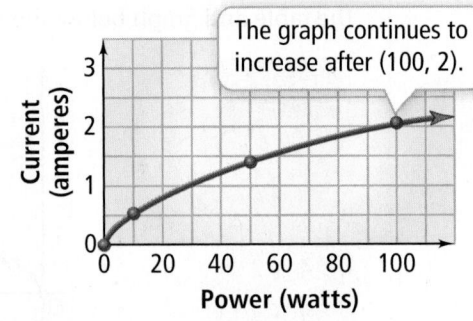

The graph continues to increase after (100, 2).

The current will exceed 2 amperes when the power is more than 100 watts.

Got It? 2. a. When will the current in Problem 2 exceed 1.5 amperes?

b. Reasoning By how many times must you increase the power to double the current?

For any positive number k, graphing $y = \sqrt{x} + k$ translates the graph of $y = \sqrt{x}$ up k units. Graphing $y = \sqrt{x} - k$ translates the graph of $y = \sqrt{x}$ down k units.

Problem 3 Graphing a Vertical Translation

What is the graph of $y = \sqrt{x} + 2$?

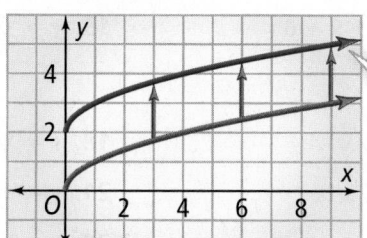

For the graph of $y = \sqrt{x} + 2$, the graph of $y = \sqrt{x}$ is shifted 2 units up.

Think

Is this similar to a problem you've seen before?
Yes. You have graphed functions of the form $y = |x| + k$ by translating the graph of $y = |x|$.

Got It? **3.** What is the graph of $y = \sqrt{x} - 3$?

For any positive number h, graphing $y = \sqrt{x + h}$ translates the graph of $y = \sqrt{x}$ to the left h units. Graphing $y = \sqrt{x - h}$ translates the graph of $y = \sqrt{x}$ to the right h units.

Problem 4 Graphing a Horizontal Translation

What is the graph of $y = \sqrt{x + 3}$?

Think

Is there another way to solve this problem?
Yes. You could make a table of ordered pairs that satisfy the equation and then plot them.

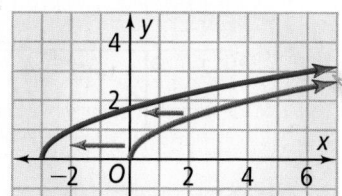

For the graph of $y = \sqrt{x + 3}$, the graph of $y = \sqrt{x}$ is shifted 3 units to the left.

Got It? **4.** What is the graph of $y = \sqrt{x - 3}$?

Lesson Check

Do you know HOW?

1. What is the domain of the function $y = \sqrt{x} + 3$?

Graph each function.

2. $y = 2\sqrt{x}$

3. $y = \sqrt{x} - 6$

Do you UNDERSTAND? MATHEMATICAL PRACTICES

4. Vocabulary Is $y = x\sqrt{5}$ a square root function? Explain.

5. Writing Explain how the graph of $y = \sqrt{x - 1}$ is related to the graph of $y = \sqrt{x}$.

6. Reasoning Can the domain of a square root function include negative numbers? Explain.

Practice and Problem-Solving Exercises

MATHEMATICAL PRACTICES

 **Practice**

Find the domain of each function.

See Problem 1.

7. $y = \frac{1}{2}\sqrt{x}$

8. $y = \sqrt{x} + 2$

9. $y = \sqrt{x - 7}$

10. $y = 3\sqrt{\frac{x}{3}}$

11. $y = 2.7\sqrt{x + 2} + 11$

12. $y = \sqrt{4x - 13}$

13. $y = \frac{4}{7}\sqrt{18 - x}$

14. $y = \sqrt{3x + 9} - 6$

15. $y = \sqrt{3(x - 4)}$

Make a table of values and graph each function.

See Problem 2.

16. $y = \sqrt{2x}$

17. $f(x) = 4\sqrt{x}$

18. $y = \sqrt{4x - 8}$

19. $y = \sqrt{3x}$

20. $f(x) = 3\sqrt{x}$

21. $y = -3\sqrt{x}$

22. $f(x) = \frac{1}{3}\sqrt{x}$

23. $y = \sqrt{\frac{x}{2}}$

24. $y = 2\sqrt{x - 3}$

 25. Physics The function $v = \sqrt{19.6h}$ models an object's velocity v in meters per second after it has fallen h meters, ignoring the effects of air resistance. Make a table and graph the function. For what values of h will the object's velocity be more than 10 m/s?

Match each function with its graph.

See Problems 3 and 4.

26. $y = \sqrt{x} + 4$

27. $y = \sqrt{x} - 2$

28. $y = \sqrt{x + 4}$

29. $y = \sqrt{x - 2}$

A.

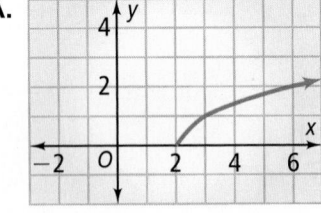

B.

 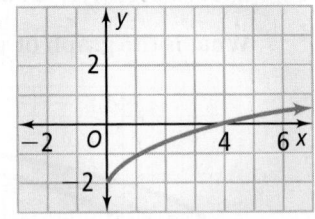

C.

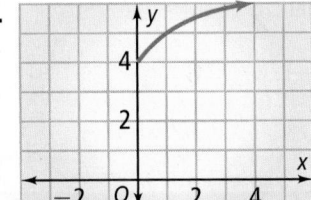

D.

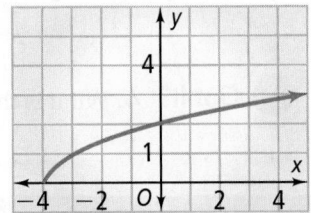

Graph each function by translating the graph of $y = \sqrt{x}$.

30. $y = \sqrt{x} + 5$

31. $y = \sqrt{x} - 5$

32. $y = \sqrt{x} - 1$

33. $y = \sqrt{x + 2}$

34. $f(x) = \sqrt{x - 5}$

35. $f(x) = \sqrt{x - 4}$

36. $y = \sqrt{x + 1}$

37. $y = \sqrt{x + 1}$

38. $y = \sqrt{x - 1}$

 **Apply**

39. What are the domain and the range of the function $y = \sqrt{2x - 8}$?

40. What are the domain and the range of the function $y = \sqrt{8 - 2x}$?

41. Firefighting When firefighters are trying to put out a fire, the rate at which they can spray water on the fire depends on the nozzle pressure. You can find the flow rate f in gallons per minute using the function $f = 120\sqrt{p}$, where p is the nozzle pressure in pounds per square inch.

a. Graph the function.

b. What nozzle pressure gives a flow rate of 800 gal/min?

42. Error Analysis A student graphed the function $y = \sqrt{x-2}$ at the right. What mistake did the student make? Draw the correct graph.

43. Think About a Plan The velocity v in meters per second of a 2,000,000-kg rocket is given by the function $v = \sqrt{E}$, where E is the rocket's kinetic energy in megajoules (MJ). When the rocket's kinetic energy is 8,000,000 MJ, what is its velocity?

• How can you use a graph to solve the problem?

• How can you check your answer?

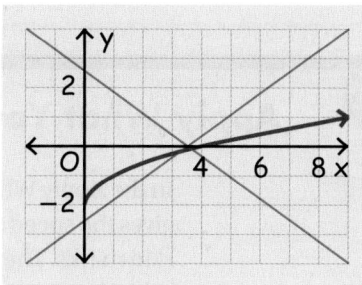

Make a table of values and graph each function.

44. $y = \sqrt{x - 2.5}$ **45.** $f(x) = 4\sqrt{x}$ **46.** $y = \sqrt{x + 6}$

47. $y = \sqrt{0.5x}$ **48.** $y = \sqrt{x - 2} + 3$ **49.** $f(x) = \sqrt{x + 2} - 4$

50. $y = \sqrt{2x} + 3$ **51.** $y = \sqrt{2x + 6} + 1$ **52.** $y = \sqrt{3x - 3} - 2$

53. The graph of $x = y^2$ is shown at the right.

a. Is this the graph of a function?

b. How does $x = y^2$ relate to the square root function $y = \sqrt{x}$?

c. Reasoning What is a function for the part of the graph that is shown in Quadrant IV? Explain.

54. Reasoning Without graphing, determine which graph rises more steeply, $y = \sqrt{3x}$ or $y = 3\sqrt{x}$. Explain your answer.

Graph each function by translating the graph of $y = \sqrt{x}$.

55. $y = \sqrt{x + 4} - 1$ **56.** $y = \sqrt{x + 1} + 5$

57. $y = \sqrt{x - 3} - 2$ **58.** $y = \sqrt{x - 6} + 3$

59. $y = \sqrt{x + 2.5} - 1$ **60.** $y = \sqrt{x - 4.5} + 1.5$

 **61. a.** Graph $y = \sqrt{x^2} + 5$.

b. Write a function for the graph you drew that does not require a radical.

62. In parts (a)–(d), graph each function.

a. $y = \sqrt{4x}$

b. $y = \sqrt{5x}$

c. $y = \sqrt{6x}$

d. $y = \sqrt{-6x}$

e. Reasoning Describe how the graph of $y = \sqrt{nx}$ changes as the value of n varies.

63. Data Collection Mark at least 6 places on a ramp that is at least 6 ft long. For each mark, measure the distance *d* from the mark to the bottom of the ramp. Measure the time *t* it takes a ball to roll from each mark to the bottom of the ramp.

  a. Graph the data points (d, t). Connect the points with a smooth curve.

  b. Describe your graph. What function does it resemble?

  c. Is the graph linear? Why or why not?

Apply What You've Learned

MATHEMATICAL
PRACTICES
MP 5

In the Apply What You've Learned in Lesson 10-2, you wrote a formula that gives the speed *s* of the car described on page 613, in terms of the length *d* of the skid marks. The formula is a square root function, $s = \sqrt{21d}$. Use a graphing calculator to graph this function. Then select all of the following that are true. Explain your reasoning.

  A. The domain of the function $s = \sqrt{21d}$ is the set of all real numbers greater than or equal to 0.

  B. The graph of $s = \sqrt{21d}$ lies entirely in Quadrant I.

  C. The graph of $s = \sqrt{21d}$ is a vertical translation of the graph of the parent square root function.

  D. The graph of $s = \sqrt{21d}$ is a horizontal translation of the graph of the parent square root function.

  E. The graph of $s = \sqrt{21d}$ shows that the speed of the car increases as the length of the skid marks increases.

  F. The graph of $s = \sqrt{21d}$ intersects the horizontal line $s = 50$.

Trigonometric Ratios

© **Common Core State Standards**

G-SRT.C.8 Use trigonometric ratios and the Pythagorean Theorem to solve right triangles in applied problems. **Also G-SRT.C.6**

MP 1, MP 3, MP 4, MP 5, MP 5, MP 6

Objective To find and use trigonometric ratios

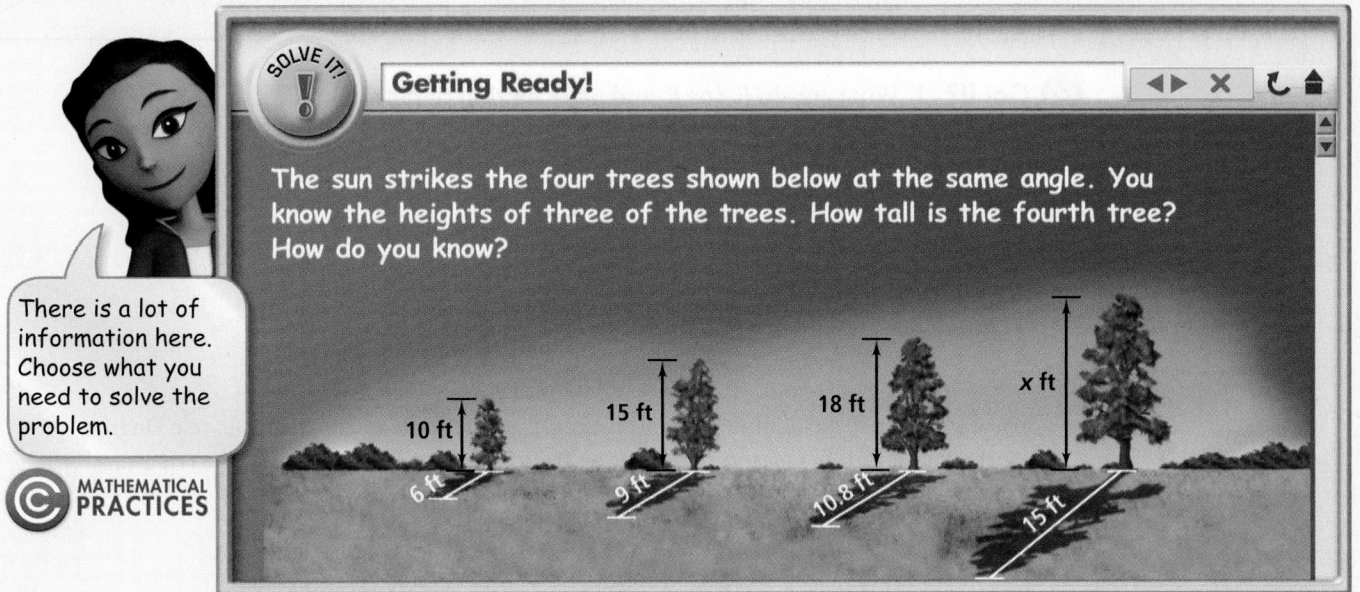

Getting Ready!

The sun strikes the four trees shown below at the same angle. You know the heights of three of the trees. How tall is the fourth tree? How do you know?

There is a lot of information here. Choose what you need to solve the problem.

10 ft   15 ft   18 ft   x ft

6 ft   9 ft   10.8 ft   15 ft

MATHEMATICAL PRACTICES

Lesson Vocabulary
• trigonometric ratios
• sine
• cosine
• tangent
• angle of elevation
• angle of depression

The Solve It involves ratios and right triangles. Ratios of the side lengths of a right triangle are called **trigonometric ratios.** Below are the definitions of three trigonometric ratios.

take note

Key Concept   Trigonometric Ratios

Name	Written	Definition	
sine of $\angle A$	**sin** A	$\dfrac{\text{length of leg opposite } \angle A}{\text{length of hypotenuse}}$	
cosine of $\angle A$	**cos** A	$\dfrac{\text{length of leg adjacent to } \angle A}{\text{length of hypotenuse}}$	
tangent of $\angle A$	**tan** A	$\dfrac{\text{length of leg opposite } \angle A}{\text{length of leg adjacent to } \angle A}$	

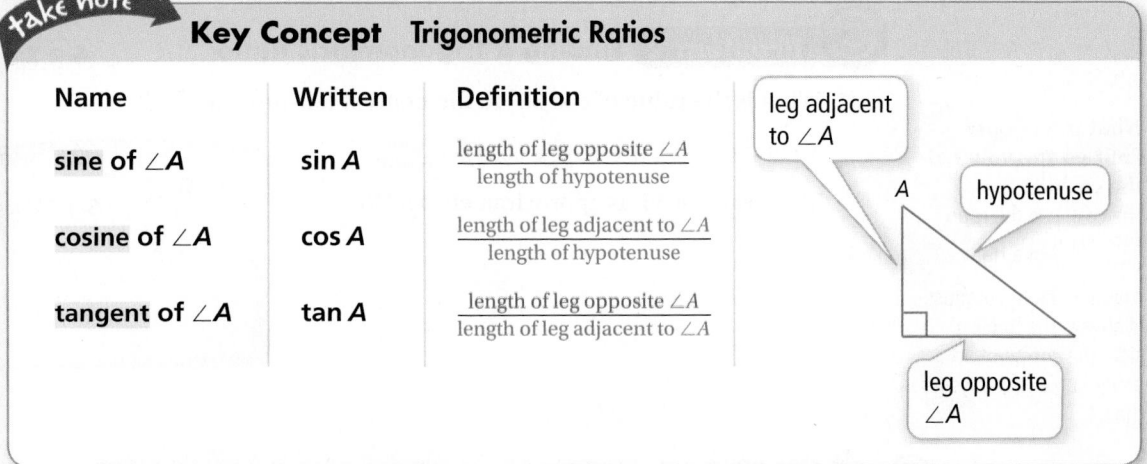

leg adjacent to $\angle A$

A   hypotenuse

leg opposite $\angle A$

Essential Understanding You can use the sine, cosine, and tangent ratios to find the measurements of sides and angles of right triangles.

Plan

How do you calculate trigonometric ratios?
Calculate a trigonometric ratio by substituting the lengths of the appropriate sides into the ratio.

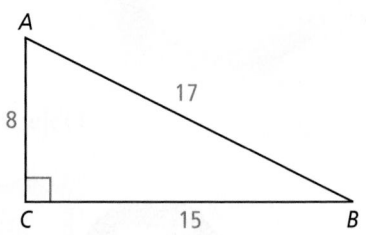

Problem 1 Finding Trigonometric Ratios

What are sin A, cos A, and tan A for the triangle shown?

$$\sin A = \frac{\text{opposite leg}}{\text{hypotenuse}} = \frac{15}{17}$$

$$\cos A = \frac{\text{adjacent leg}}{\text{hypotenuse}} = \frac{8}{17}$$

$$\tan A = \frac{\text{opposite leg}}{\text{adjacent leg}} = \frac{15}{8}$$

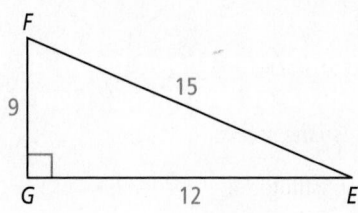

Got It? 1. What are sin E, cos E, and tan E for the triangle below?

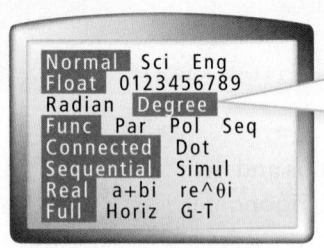

You can also use a calculator to find trigonometric ratios. In this chapter, use Degree mode when finding trigonometric ratios. That allows you to enter angles in degrees.

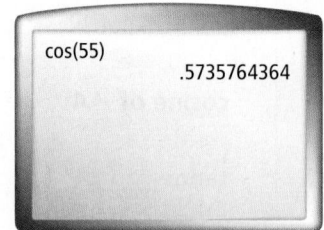

Set your calculator to Degree mode.

Think

What is an upper limit on the value of the cosine?
The cosine is the ratio $\frac{\text{adjacent leg}}{\text{hypotenuse}}$ in a right triangle. The hypotenuse is always the longest side. The cosine of an acute angle is always less than 1.

Problem 2 Finding a Trigonometric Ratio

GRIDDED RESPONSE

What is the value of cos 55° to the nearest ten-thousandth?

To find cos 55°, press [cos] 55 [)] [enter].

The cosine of 55° is approximately 0.5736.

cos(55)
    .5735764364

 Got It? 2. What is the value of each expression in parts (a)–(d)?

    a. sin 80°   **b.** tan 45°   **c.** cos 15°   **d.** sin 9°

    e. Reasoning Describe the relationship between sin 45° and cos 45°. Explain why this is true.

You can use trigonometry to find missing lengths in a right triangle when you know the length of one side and the measure of an acute angle.

 Problem 3 Finding a Missing Side Length

To the nearest tenth, what is the value of x in the triangle at the right?

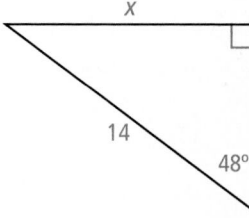

Know	Need	Plan
• The measure of an acute angle • The length of the hypotenuse	The length of the opposite leg	Use the sine ratio.

Write an equation and solve.

$\sin 48° = \dfrac{\text{opposite leg}}{\text{hypotenuse}}$ Use the definition of sine.

$\sin 48° = \dfrac{x}{14}$ Substitute x and 14 from the diagram.

$x = 14(\sin 48°)$ Solve for x.

$x \approx 10.40402756$ Use a calculator.

$x \approx 10.4$ Round to the nearest tenth.

The value of x is about 10.4.

 Got It? 3. To the nearest tenth, what is the value of x in the triangle at the right?

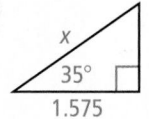

If you know the lengths of two sides of a right triangle, you can find a trigonometric ratio for each acute angle of the triangle. If you know a trigonometric ratio for an angle, you can use the inverse of the trigonometric ratio to find the measure of the angle. Use the $\sin^{-1}$, $\cos^{-1}$, or $\tan^{-1}$ feature on your calculator.

 Problem 4 Finding the Measures of Angles

What is the measure of each angle in the triangle at the right?

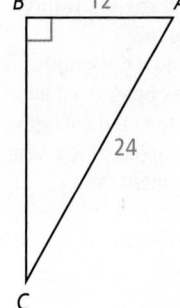

Step 1 Since you know the length of the side adjacent to $\angle A$ and the length of the hypotenuse, use the cosine ratio.

Step 2 Write an equation and solve.

$\cos A = \dfrac{12}{24}$ Use the definition of cosine.

$\cos A = 0.5$ Divide.

measure of $\angle A = \cos^{-1}(0.5)$ Use the inverse of cosine.

measure of $\angle A = 60°$ Use a calculator.

$\angle A$ measures 60°. The right angle B measures 90°. $\angle C$ measures $180° - 90° - 60° = 30°$.

Think

How can you find the measure of the third angle of the triangle?
The sum of the measures of the angles of a triangle is 180°. You can subtract the measures of the two known angles from 180° to find the third angle's measure.

Got It? **4.** In a right triangle, the side opposite $\angle A$ is 8 mm long and the hypotenuse is 12 mm long. What is the measure of $\angle A$?

You can use trigonometric ratios to measure some distances indirectly. To measure such distances, it is often convenient to use an *angle of elevation* or an *angle of depression*.

An **angle of elevation** is an angle from the horizontal up to a line of sight.

An **angle of depression** is an angle from the horizontal down to a line of sight.

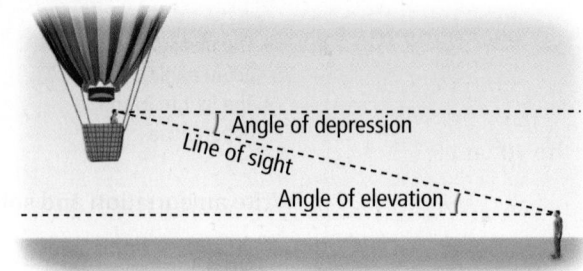

When you solve real-world problems using trigonometric ratios, you often need to round your answers. The problem may tell you how to round. Otherwise, round your answers to the precision of the measurements used in the problem. For instance, if the problem has measurements to the nearest 10 ft, round your answer to the nearest 10 ft.

© **Problem 5** **Using an Angle of Elevation or Depression**

Rides Suppose you are waiting in line for a ride. You see your friend at the top of the ride. How far are you from the base of the ride?

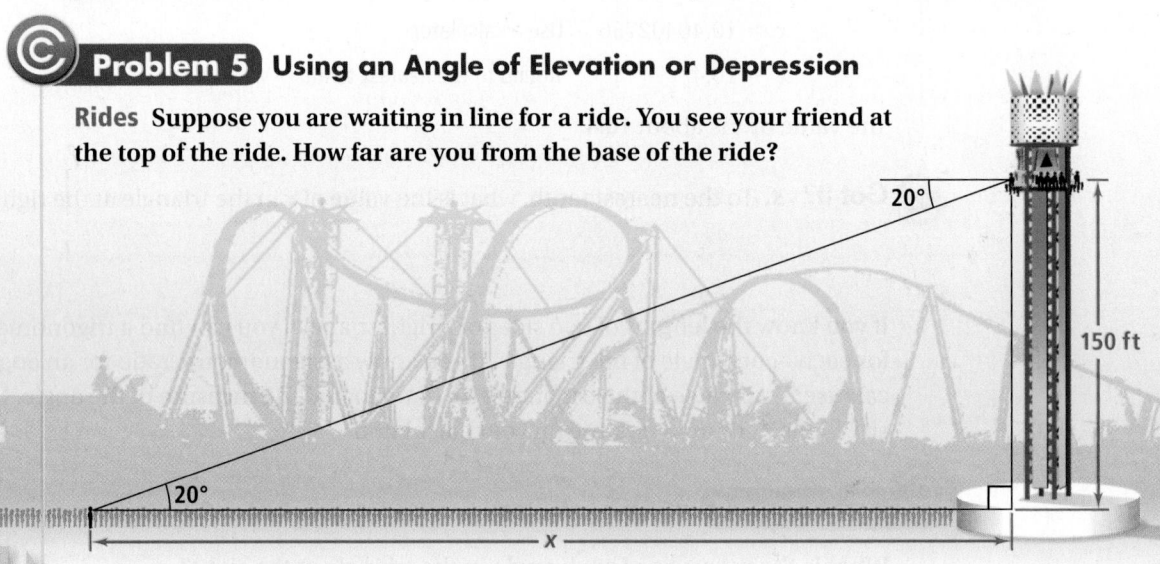

Think

Which ratio should you use?
You know the length of the opposite leg and want to find the length of the adjacent leg. Use the tangent ratio.

$\tan 20° = \dfrac{\text{opposite leg}}{\text{adjacent leg}}$ Use the tangent ratio.

$\tan 20° = \dfrac{150}{x}$ Substitute 150 and x from the diagram.

$x\,(\tan 20°) = 150$ Multiply each side by x.

$x = \dfrac{150}{\tan 20°}$ Divide each side by tan 20°.

$x \approx 412.1216129$ Use a calculator.

$x \approx 410$ Round to the nearest 10 ft.

You are about 410 ft from the base of the ride.

 Got It? **5.** After you move forward in the line, the angle of elevation to the top of the ride becomes 50°. How far are you from the base of the ride now?

Lesson Check

Do you know HOW?

Find each trigonometric ratio for angle A in the triangle at the right.

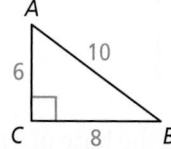

1. $\sin A$ **2.** $\cos A$ **3.** $\tan A$

Solve using trigonometric ratios.

4. A right triangle has a 40° angle. The hypotenuse is 10 cm long. What is the length of the side opposite the 40° angle?

5. A right triangle's legs are 7 in. and 24 in. long. What is the measure of the angle opposite the 24-in. leg?

Do you UNDERSTAND?

 MATHEMATICAL PRACTICES

 6. Vocabulary Describe the difference between finding the sine of an angle and the cosine of an angle.

7. Error Analysis In a right triangle, the hypotenuse is 5 in. long, and the side opposite $\angle A$ is 4.5 in. long. A student found the measure of $\angle A$ as shown on the calculator screen at the right. Describe and correct the student's error.

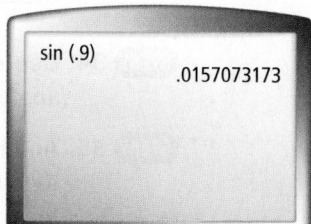

Practice and Problem-Solving Exercises

MATHEMATICAL PRACTICES

A Practice   For $\triangle FGH$ and $\triangle LMN$, find the value of each expression.   **See Problem 1.**

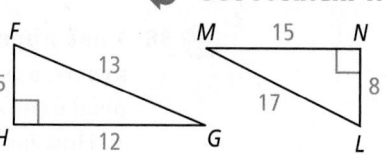

8. $\sin F$ **9.** $\cos F$ **10.** $\tan G$

11. $\cos L$ **12.** $\tan M$ **13.** $\sin M$

14. $\tan F$ **15.** $\sin G$ **16.** $\tan L$

Find the value of each expression. Round to the nearest ten-thousandth.   **See Problem 2.**

17. $\sin 10°$ **18.** $\tan 25°$

19. $\cos 85°$ **20.** $\tan 12°$

21. $\sin 70°$ **22.** $\cos 22°$

23. $\sin 71°$ **24.** $\tan 30°$

Find the value of x to the nearest tenth.   **See Problem 3.**

25.   **26.**   **27.**

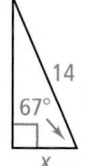   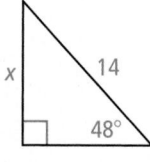   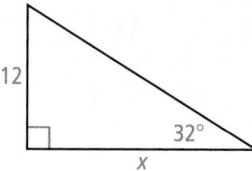

28.   **29.**   **30.**

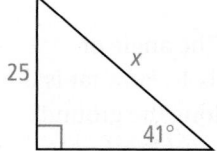   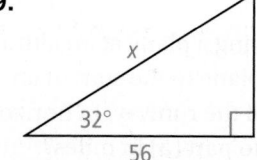   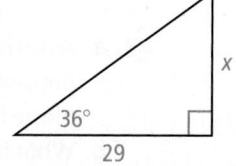

Find the value of *x* to the nearest degree.

See Problem 4.

31.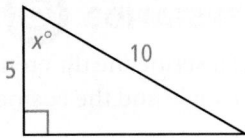

32.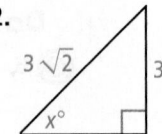

33.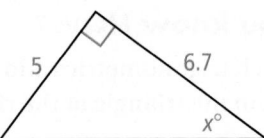

STEM **34. Geology** From an observation point 20 ft from the base of a geyser, the angle of elevation to the top of the geyser is 50°. How tall is the geyser?

See Problem 5.

STEM **35. Architecture** The wheelchair ramp shown is being planned for a new building. The ramp will rise a total of 2.5 ft and form a 3° angle with the ground. How far from the base of the building should the wheelchair ramp start?

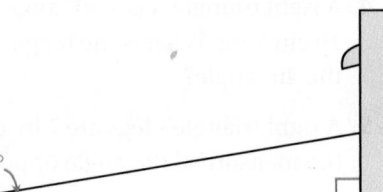

B **Apply**

ⓒ 36. a. Find the values of each pair of expressions.
    i. $\sin 80°$, $\cos 10°$ **ii.** $\cos 25°$, $\sin 65°$
  b. What do you notice about your values and the angles in each pair?
  c. Reasoning Explain why your results make sense.

ⓒ 37. Writing Describe how you can find the length of the hypotenuse of a right triangle if you know the measure of one of the acute angles and the length of the leg adjacent to that angle.

ⓒ 38. Think About a Plan A boat is passing between two towers, as shown in the diagram. How far does the boat need to move to be in the middle of the channel?
  • How far is the center of the boat from each tower?
  • What is the distance from the base of a tower to the middle of the channel?

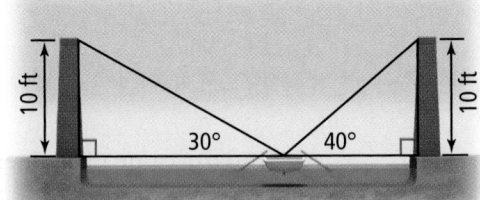

Find the value of each variable in each figure to the nearest tenth.

39.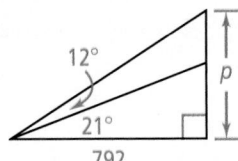

40.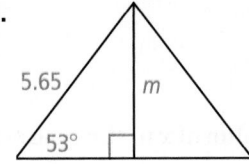

41.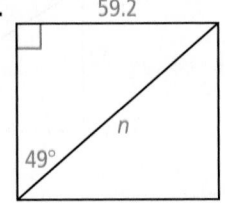

42.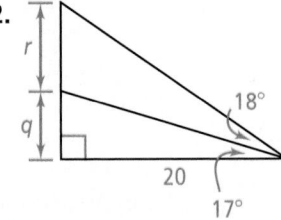

43. a. Aviation A pilot is flying a plane at an altitude of 30,000 ft. The angle of depression from the plane to the start of an airport runway is 1°. How far is the plane from the start of the runway, in horizontal distance along the ground?
  b. What is your answer to part (a) in miles?

44. Hobbies Suppose you are flying a kite. The kite string is 60 m long, and the angle of elevation of the string is 65° from your hand. Your hand is 1 m above the ground. How high above the ground is the kite?

 **Challenge**

45. At a certain point in a large, level park, the angle of elevation to the top of an office building is 30°. If you move 400 ft closer to the building, the angle of elevation is 45°. To the nearest 10 ft, how tall is the building?

46. A line passes through the origin of a coordinate plane and forms a 14° angle with the positive x-axis. What is the slope of the line? Round to the nearest hundredth.

47. Reasoning Use the definitions of sine, cosine, and tangent to simplify each expression.

   a. $\cos A \cdot \tan A$ **b.** $\sin A \div \tan A$ **c.** $\sin A \div \cos A$

Standardized Test Prep

SAT/ACT

48. What is the value of b in the proportion $\frac{3}{7} = \frac{2b}{4b + 2}$?

  Ⓐ 3   Ⓒ 12

  Ⓑ 6   Ⓓ 28

49. The profits of a large corporation can be graphed as a line that passes through $(-3, 6)$ and $(4, -1)$. Which equation represents the line?

  Ⓕ $y = 3 - x$ Ⓗ $y = -3x + 1$

  Ⓖ $y = 3x + 1$ Ⓘ $y = x + 3$

50. Which expression is equivalent to $3\sqrt{12} + 2\sqrt{3}$?

  Ⓐ $5\sqrt{3}$ Ⓒ $5\sqrt{15}$

  Ⓑ $8\sqrt{3}$ Ⓓ $8\sqrt{12}$

Short Response

51. Graph the solutions of the inequality $-2x \geq 1$ on a number line.

Mixed Review

Graph each function.   ◀ See Lesson 10-5.

52. $y = \sqrt{x} + 8$ **53.** $y = \sqrt{x - 6}$ **54.** $y = 4\sqrt{x}$

Determine whether the given lengths can be side lengths of a right triangle.   ◀ See Lesson 10-1.

55. 15, 36, 39   **56.** $\frac{7}{9}, \frac{24}{9}, \frac{25}{9}$ **57.** 12, 35, 36

Get Ready!   **To prepare for Lesson 11-1, do Exercises 58–61.**

Factor each expression.   ◀ See Lesson 8-5.

58. $x^2 + x - 12$ **59.** $x^2 + 6x + 8$ **60.** $x^2 - 2x - 15$ **61.** $x^2 + 9x + 18$

Pull It **All Together**

Completing the Performance Task

Look back at your results from the Apply What You've Learned sections in Lessons 10-1, 10-2, and 10-5. Use the work you did to complete the following.

1. Solve the problem in the Task Description on page 613 by determining whether the driver on Pine Street was traveling within the speed limit. Then determine the maximum length of the skid marks left on Pine Street by a car that travels within the speed limit. Round your answer to the nearest foot. Show all your work and explain each step of your solution.

2. Reflect Choose one of the Mathematical Practices below and explain how you applied it in your work on the Performance Task.

> MP 1: Make sense of problems and persevere in solving them.
>
> MP 4: Model with mathematics.
>
> MP 5: Use appropriate tools strategically.
>
> MP 6: Attend to precision.

To solve these problems you will pull together many concepts and skills that you have studied about radical expressions and equations.

On Your Own

Use the information about the formula $s = \sqrt{30fd}$ and the table of coefficients of friction on page 613.

The speed limit on Lincoln Street is 45 mi/h. The street is paved with cement. A car left skid marks from Ashton Road to Mulberry Avenue, as shown in the diagram below.

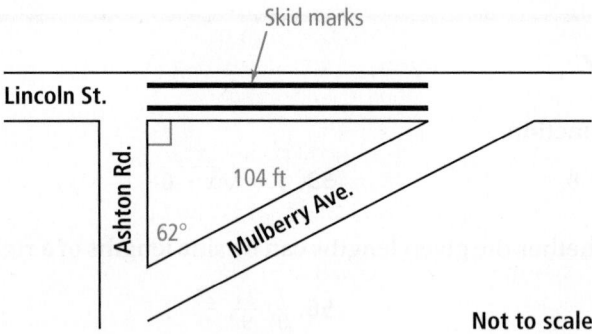

Determine whether the car was traveling within the speed limit when the driver applied the brakes. Justify your response.

Connecting **BIG** ideas and Answering the Essential Questions

1 Equivalence
Radical expressions can be represented in many ways. To simplify a square root, factor out perfect squares from the radicand.

Simplifying Radicals (Lesson 10-2)
$$\sqrt{12} = \sqrt{4} \cdot \sqrt{3} = 2\sqrt{3}$$

Operations With Radical Expressions (Lesson 10-3)
$$\sqrt{5} \cdot \sqrt{10} = \sqrt{50} = 5\sqrt{2}$$

2 Functions
Square root functions contain a variable in the radicand. The parent square root function is $y = \sqrt{x}$.

Graphing Square Root Functions (Lesson 10-5)
Graph of the parent square root function

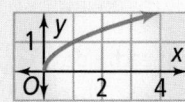

3 Solving Equations and Inequalities
To isolate the variable in a radical equation, first isolate the radical and then square both sides.

Solving Radical Equations (Lesson 10-4)
$$2x = \sqrt{4x + 3}$$

Chapter Vocabulary

- angle of depression (p. 648)
- angle of elevation (p. 648)
- conclusion (p. 615)
- conditional (p. 615)
- conjugates (p. 628)
- converse (p. 616)
- cosine (p. 645)

- extraneous solution (p. 635)
- hypotenuse (p. 614)
- hypothesis (p. 615)
- leg (p. 614)
- like radicals (p. 626)
- Pythagorean Theorem (p. 614)
- radical equation (p. 633)

- radical expression (p. 619)
- rationalize the denominator (p. 622)
- sine (p. 645)
- square root function (p. 639)
- tangent (p. 645)
- trigonometric ratios (p. 645)
- unlike radicals (p. 626)

Choose the correct term to complete each sentence.

1. Sine, cosine, and tangent are ? .

2. A(n) ? is an apparent solution that does not make the original equation true.

3. The radical expressions $2\sqrt{3}$ and $3\sqrt{2}$ contain ? .

4. You ? of a radical expression by rewriting it without radicals in the denominator.

5. The radical expressions $5 + \sqrt{5}$ and $5 - \sqrt{5}$ are ? .

10-1 The Pythagorean Theorem

Quick Review

Given the lengths of two sides of a right triangle, you can use the **Pythagorean Theorem** to find the length of the third side. Given the lengths of all three sides of a triangle, you can determine whether it is a right triangle.

Example

What is the side length x in the triangle at the right?

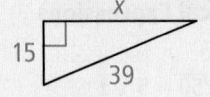

$$a^2 + b^2 = c^2 \quad \text{Pythagorean Theorem}$$

$$15^2 + x^2 = 39^2 \quad \text{Substitute 15 for } a, x \text{ for } b, \text{ and 39 for } c.$$

$$225 + x^2 = 1521 \quad \text{Simplify.}$$

$$x^2 = 1296 \quad \text{Subtract 225 from each side.}$$

$$x = 36 \quad \text{Find the principal square root of each side.}$$

Exercises

Use the triangle at the right. Find the missing side length. If necessary, round to the nearest tenth.

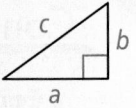

6. $a = 2.5, b = 6$ **7.** $a = 3.5, b = 12$

8. $a = 1.1, b = 6$ **9.** $a = 13, c = 85$

10. $a = 6, c = 18.5$ **11.** $b = 2.4, c = 2.5$

12. $b = 8.8, c = 11$ **13.** $a = 1, c = 2.6$

Determine whether the given lengths can be side lengths of a right triangle.

14. 4, 7.5, 8.5 **15.** 22, 120, 122 **16.** 8, 40, 41

17. 1.6, 3, 3.4 **18.** 6, 24, 25 **19.** 18, 52.5, 55.5

20. 1.2, 6, 6.1 **21.** 0.7, 2.3, 2.5 **22.** 1.3, 8.4, 8.5

10-2 Simplifying Radicals

Quick Review

A **radical expression** is simplified if the following statements are true.
- The radicand has no perfect-square factors other than 1.
- The radicand contains no fractions.
- No radicals appear in the denominator of a fraction.

Example

What is the simplified form of $\frac{\sqrt{3x}}{\sqrt{2}}$?

$$\frac{\sqrt{3x}}{\sqrt{2}} = \frac{\sqrt{3x}}{\sqrt{2}} \cdot \frac{\sqrt{2}}{\sqrt{2}} \quad \text{Multiply by } \frac{\sqrt{2}}{\sqrt{2}}.$$

$$= \frac{\sqrt{6x}}{\sqrt{4}} \quad \text{Multiply numerators and denominators.}$$

$$= \frac{\sqrt{6x}}{2} \quad \text{Simplify.}$$

Exercises

Simplify each radical expression.

23. $3\sqrt{14} \cdot (-2\sqrt{21})$ **24.** $\sqrt{8} \cdot \frac{1}{4}\sqrt{6}$

25. $\sqrt{\frac{25a^3}{4a}}$ **26.** $\frac{\sqrt{8s}}{\sqrt{18s^3}}$

27. $-2\sqrt{7x^2} \cdot \frac{1}{3}\sqrt{28x^3}$ **28.** $6\sqrt{5t^3} \cdot \sqrt{15t^5}$

29. Open-Ended Write three radical expressions that have $4\sqrt{2s}$ as their simplified form. What do the three expressions have in common? Explain.

30. Geometry The width of a rectangle is s. Its length is $3s$. How long is a diagonal of the rectangle? Express your answer in simplified radical form.

10-3 Operations With Radical Expressions

Quick Review

You can use the properties of real numbers to combine radical expressions. To simplify radical expressions such as $\frac{2}{\sqrt{5}+3}$, multiply the numerator and denominator by the **conjugate** of the denominator, $\sqrt{5}-3$.

Example

What is the simplified form of $\frac{2\sqrt{5}}{\sqrt{5}+2}$?

$\frac{2\sqrt{5}}{\sqrt{5}+2} = \frac{2\sqrt{5}}{\sqrt{5}+2} \cdot \frac{\sqrt{5}-2}{\sqrt{5}-2}$ Multiply by $\frac{\sqrt{5}-2}{\sqrt{5}-2}$.

$= \frac{2\sqrt{5}(\sqrt{5}-2)}{(\sqrt{5}+2)(\sqrt{5}-2)}$ Multiply fractions.

$= \frac{10-4\sqrt{5}}{1}$ Simplify the numerator and denominator.

$= 10 - 4\sqrt{5}$ Simplify the fraction.

Exercises

Simplify each radical expression.

31. $5\sqrt{6} - 3\sqrt{6}$

32. $\sqrt{2}(\sqrt{8} + \sqrt{6})$

33. $(3\sqrt{2} - 2\sqrt{5})(4\sqrt{2} + 2\sqrt{5})$

34. $\frac{3}{\sqrt{2}-3}$

35. $\frac{\sqrt{3}-3}{\sqrt{3}+3}$

36. Geometry A golden rectangle is 3 in. long. The ratio of its length to its width is $(1 + \sqrt{5}) : 2$. What is the width of the rectangle? Write your answer in simplified radical form.

10-4 Solving Radical Equations

Quick Review

You can solve some **radical equations** by isolating the radicals, squaring both sides of the equation, and then testing the solutions.

Some solutions may be extraneous. Some equations may have no solution.

Example

What is the solution of $\sqrt{x + 16} = \sqrt{9x}$?

$\sqrt{x+16} = \sqrt{9x}$

$(\sqrt{x+16})^2 = (\sqrt{9x})^2$ Square each side.

$x + 16 = 9x$ Simplify.

$16 = 8x$ Subtract x from each side.

$2 = x$ Divide each side by 8.

Check $\sqrt{2 + 16} \overset{?}{=} \sqrt{9(2)}$ Substitute 2 for x.

$\sqrt{18} = \sqrt{18}$ ✔

The solution is 2.

Exercises

Solve each radical equation. Check your solution. If there is no solution, write *no solution*.

37. $\sqrt{x} - 5 = 8$

38. $4 + \sqrt{y} = 7$

39. $\sqrt{w - 2} = 4$

40. $\sqrt{f + 4} = 5$

41. $\sqrt{2 + d} = d$

42. $2\sqrt{r} = \sqrt{3r + 1}$

43. $n\sqrt{2} = \sqrt{9 - 3n}$

44. $2x = \sqrt{2 - 2x}$

45. Geometry The radius r of a cylinder is given by the equation $r = \sqrt{\frac{V}{\pi h}}$, where V is the volume and h is the height. If the radius of a cylinder is 3 cm and the height is 2 cm, what is the volume of the cylinder? Round to the nearest tenth of a cubic centimeter.

10-5 Graphing Square Root Functions

Quick Review

Graph a **square root function** by plotting points or translating the parent square root function $y = \sqrt{x}$.

The graphs of $y = \sqrt{x} + k$ and $y = \sqrt{x} - k$ are vertical translations of $y = \sqrt{x}$. The graphs of $y = \sqrt{x - h}$ and $y = \sqrt{x + h}$ are horizontal translations of $y = \sqrt{x}$.

Example

What is the graph of the square root function $y = \sqrt{x - 2}$?

The graph of $y = \sqrt{x - 2}$ is the graph of $y = \sqrt{x}$ shifted 2 units right.

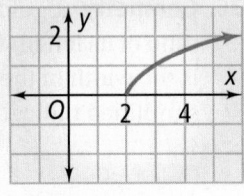

Exercises

Find the domain of each function.

46. $y = \sqrt{x} - 5$

47. $y = \sqrt{x + 4}$

Graph each function.

48. $y = \sqrt{x} + 6$

49. $y = \sqrt{x - 8}$

50. $y = \sqrt{x - 2.5}$

51. $y = \frac{1}{4}\sqrt{x}$

52. $y = 3\sqrt{x}$

10-6 Trigonometric Ratios

Quick Review

You can use the **sine, cosine,** and **tangent** ratios to find the measurements of sides or angles of right triangles.

$$\sin A = \frac{\text{opposite leg}}{\text{hypotenuse}}$$

$$\cos A = \frac{\text{adjacent leg}}{\text{hypotenuse}}$$

$$\tan A = \frac{\text{opposite leg}}{\text{adjacent leg}}$$

Example

What are the trigonometric ratios of angle A?

$$\sin A = \frac{3}{\sqrt{13}} = \frac{3\sqrt{13}}{13}$$

$$\cos A = \frac{2}{\sqrt{13}} = \frac{2\sqrt{13}}{13}$$

$$\tan A = \frac{3}{2}$$

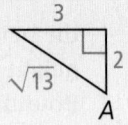

Exercises

Find the trigonometric ratios for $\angle A$.

53.

8, 17

54.

A, 12, 6

55.

A, 15, 20

Suppose a right triangle ABC has right angle C. Find the measures of the other sides to the nearest tenth.

56. length of $\overline{AB} = 12$, measure of $\angle A = 34°$

57. length of $\overline{AC} = 8$, measure of $\angle B = 52°$

58. length of $\overline{BC} = 18$, measure of $\angle A = 42°$

59. length of $\overline{AB} = 25$, measure of $\angle A = 12°$

Do you know HOW?

Use the triangle below. Find the missing side length. If necessary, round to the nearest tenth.

1. $a = 28$, $b = 35$

2. $a = 12$, $b = 35$

3. $b = 4.0$, $c = 4.1$

4. $a = 10$, $c = 26$

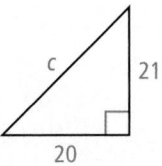

State whether segments of the given lengths can be sides of a right triangle.

5. 7, 24, 25

6. 0.9, 1.2, 1.5

7. 8, 16, 17

Simplify each radical expression.

8. $\sqrt{3} + \sqrt{12}$

9. $\sqrt{300}$

10. $4\sqrt{10} - \sqrt{10}$

11. $\dfrac{-\sqrt{18}}{\sqrt{12}}$

12. $\dfrac{1}{\sqrt{3} + 4}$

13. $\dfrac{\sqrt{6}}{4 - \sqrt{6}}$

14. $\dfrac{\sqrt{2}}{\sqrt{2} + 3}$

15. $-3\sqrt{5x^3} \cdot \sqrt{10x^3}$

Solve the following radical equations. Check your solutions.

16. $\sqrt{2x} + 4 = 7$

17. $\sqrt{k} - 8 = 28$

18. $\dfrac{\sqrt{3m + 2}}{3} = 1$

19. $\sqrt{2x + 4} = \sqrt{3x}$

20. $\sqrt{2 - x} = x$

21. $\sqrt{-5a + 6} = -a$

Graph each function.

22. $y = \sqrt{x} + 2$

23. $y = \sqrt{x} - 3$

24. $y = \sqrt{x} + 5$

For each triangle, find the missing side length.

25.

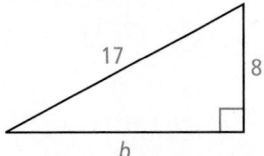

26.

27. A right triangle has a 50° angle. The hypotenuse is 10 cm long. To the nearest tenth, what is the length of the side opposite the 50° angle?

Do you UNDERSTAND?

ⓒ 28. Reasoning Draw right $\triangle ABC$ with $\angle B$ as the right angle. What is the relationship between sin A and cos C? Explain.

ⓒ 29. Open-Ended Give an example of a radical equation for which all solutions are extraneous. What is the solution to the equation? How do you know?

ⓒ 30. Reasoning Is the following conditional statement always true? "If a right triangle has a leg that is 3 in. long and a leg that is 4 in. long, then the hypotenuse is 5 in. long." Is its converse always true? Explain.

ⓒ 31. Writing Explain how you would simplify the radical expression $\dfrac{2}{\sqrt{5} + 2}$.

32. Geometry Find the length of a diagonal of a square with a side length of 3 in. Is the length of the diagonal a rational number? Explain.

Common Core Cumulative Standards Review

 ASSESSMENT

Vocabulary Builder

As you solve test items, you must understand the meanings of mathematical terms. Match each term with its mathematical meaning.

A. square root

B. arithmetic sequence

C. function

D. literal equation

I. a number pattern formed by adding a fixed number to each previous term

II. a relation that pairs each input value with exactly one output value

III. an equation involving two or more variables

IV. a number a such that $a^2 = b$

Selected Response

Read each question. Then write the letter of the correct answer on your paper.

1. If the graph of the function $y = x^2 - 6$ were shifted 3 units down, which equation could represent the shifted graph?

  Ⓐ $y = 3x^2 - 6$ Ⓒ $y = x^2 - 9$

  Ⓑ $y = x^2 - 3$ Ⓓ $y = 3x^2 - 3$

2. Which ordered pair is a solution of $3x - y < 20$?

  Ⓕ $(7, 1)$ Ⓗ $(8, 0)$

  Ⓖ $(5, -6)$ Ⓘ $(-1, -4)$

3. Brianna has a cylindrical glass that is 15 cm tall. The diameter of the base is 5 cm. About how much water can the glass hold?

  Ⓐ 75 cm^3 Ⓒ 295 cm^3

  Ⓑ 118 cm^3 Ⓓ 1178 cm^3

4. What is the solution of this system of equations?

$$-3x + y = -2$$
$$x + y = -6$$

(F) $(-2, -6)$

(H) $(1, 5)$

(G) $(-1, -5)$

(I) $(-3, -2)$

5. Jeremiah made the graph at the right to show how much money he saved after working for a few months. Which of the following represents the amount of money Jeremiah had when he started working?

Savings

(A) x-intercept

(B) y-intercept

(C) slope

(D) domain

6. What is the value of x in the equation below?

$$\sqrt{x - 8} = 12$$

(F) 11.4

(H) 136

(G) 20

(I) 152

7. What is the value of x in the equation below?

$$\sqrt{4x + 8} = \sqrt{3x + 13}$$

(A) 5

(C) 21

(B) 13

(D) 35

8. Eduardo is drawing the graph of a function. Each time the x-value increases by 3, the y-value decreases by 4. The function includes the point $(1, 3)$. Which could be Eduardo's graph?

(F)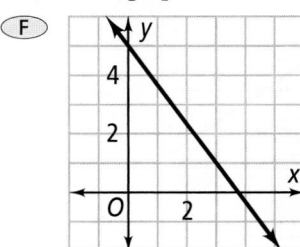

(H)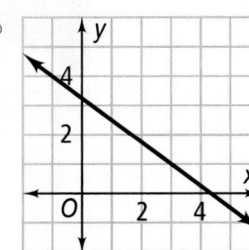

(G)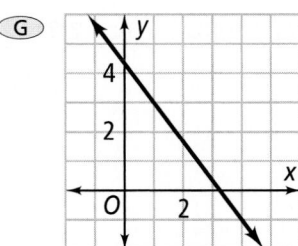

(I)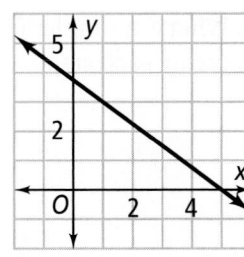

9. The data shown in the table at the right represent points on a line. What is the y-intercept of the line?

(A) -5

(B) -3

(C) 0

(D) 2.5

x	y
2	−1
3	1
4	3
5	5

10. What is the factored form of $3x^2 + 2xy - 8y^2$?

(F) $(x + y)(3x - 8y)$

(G) $(x + 4y)(3x - 2y)$

(H) $(x + 2y)(3x - 4y)$

(I) $(3x + 2y)(x - 4y)$

11. The formula for the area A of a circle is $A = \pi r^2$, where r is the radius of the circle. Which equation can be used to find the radius?

(A) $r = \frac{\sqrt{A\pi}}{\pi}$

(C) $r = \frac{A^2}{\pi}$

(B) $r = \frac{A}{\pi}$

(D) $r = \sqrt{A\pi}$

12. Which function has y-values that always increase when the corresponding x-values increase?

(F) $y = |x| + 2$

(G) $y = x^2 + 2$

(H) $y = x + 2$

(I) $y = -x - 1$

13. What is the solution of this system of equations?

$$x + 2y = 23$$
$$4x - y = -7$$

(A) $(1, 11)$

(C) $(-1, -11)$

(B) $(-11, 1)$

(D) $(11, 1)$

14. If the graph of $y = 5x - 4$ is translated up 3 units, which of the following is true?

(F) The resulting line will have a slope that is greater than the slope of the graph of $y = 5x - 4$.

(G) The resulting line will have the same x-intercept as the graph of $y = 5x - 4$.

(H) The resulting line will be parallel to the graph of $y = 5x - 4$.

(I) The resulting line will have a slope of -1.

Constructed Response

15. What is the solution of the following proportion?
$$\frac{-a}{4} = \frac{-3(a-2)}{6}$$

16. Mariah made a model of a square pyramid. The height h of the pyramid is 6 in. The area of the base B is 36 in.^{2}. What is the volume V, in cubic inches, of the pyramid? Use the formula $V = \frac{1}{3}Bh$.

17. The list below shows the heights, in inches, of the students in Corey's class.

60, 64, 58, 57, 60, 65, 51, 53, 57, 56

How many students are more than 5 ft tall?

18. What is the fifth term in the sequence below?

3.25, 4, 4.75, 5.5, . . .

19. Mr. Wong drove to the grocery store. The graph at the right shows his distance from home during the drive. How many times did Mr. Wong stop the car before reaching the grocery store?

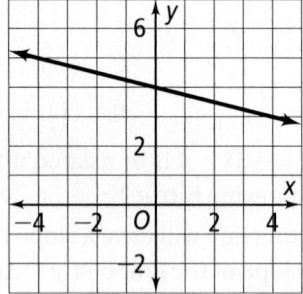

20. The volume of a rectangular prism is 720 in.^{3}. The height of the prism is 10 in. The width is 4 in. What is the length, in inches?

21. What is the slope of the line below?

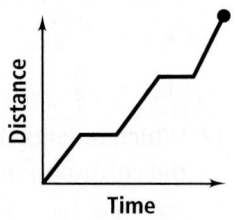

22. Your cell phone plan costs $39.99 per month plus $.10 for every text message that you receive or send. This month, you receive 7 text messages and send 10 text messages. What is your bill, in dollars, for this month?

23. Rosita states that the solutions of the equation $x = \sqrt{x + 12}$ are -3 and 4. Is Rosita's statement correct? Explain your answer by solving the equation and checking the possible solutions.

24. The formula $h = -16t^2 + c$ can be used to find the height h, in feet, of a falling object t seconds after it is dropped from a height of c feet. Suppose an object falls from a height of 40 ft. How long will the object take to reach the ground? Round your answer to the nearest tenth of a second.

25. A 25-foot ladder rests against a wall. The top of the ladder reaches 20 feet high on the wall. How far away from the wall is the bottom of the ladder?

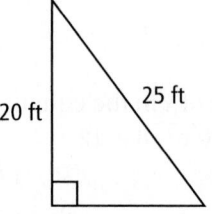

26. The formula $I = \frac{1}{5}\sqrt{P}$ gives the current I in amperes for a certain circuit with P watts of power. Solve for P.

Extended Response

27. Write the system of inequalities for the graph below. Show your work.

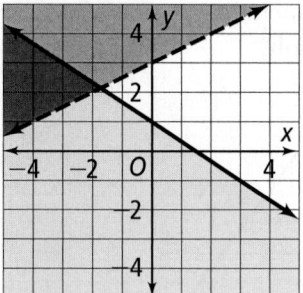

28. What is a simpler form of $(2x + 6)(3x^2 + 5x + 7)$? Justify each step.

Get Ready!

Skills Handbook, page 803

Adding and Subtracting Fractions

Find each sum or difference.

1. $\frac{6}{5} + \frac{5}{6}$

2. $\frac{5}{2} + \frac{3}{4}$

3. $\frac{7}{24} - \frac{9}{10}$

4. $\frac{3}{5} - \frac{2}{7}$

Lesson 7-4

Simplifying Expressions

Simplify each expression.

5. $\dfrac{m^2 p^{-3} q^4}{m^2 p^2 q^{-2}}$

6. $\dfrac{(3a^2)^3 (2b^{-1})^2}{(7a^3)^2 (3b^2)^{-1}}$

7. $\dfrac{\left(\frac{2}{3}\right)^4}{\left(\frac{3}{2}\right)^2}$

8. $\dfrac{8x^{-3} y^2 z^4}{5x^3 y z^{-2}}$

Lesson 9-4

Factoring to Solve Quadratic Equations

Solve each equation by factoring.

9. $x^2 - 2x - 63 = 0$

10. $12y^2 - y = 35$

11. $z^2 + 26z + 169 = 0$

12. $w^2 - 3w = 0$

13. $11p + 20 = 3p^2$

14. $6r^2 + 20 = -34r$

15. $3m^2 + 33m + 30 = 0$

16. $5d^2 - 20d = 105$

17. $6g^2 - 7g = 5$

Lesson 10-4

Solving Radical Equations

Solve each equation. If there is no solution, write *no solution*.

18. $\sqrt{x+1} = \sqrt{x-2}$

19. $2b = \sqrt{b+3}$

20. $\sqrt{x} + 2 = x$

Looking Ahead Vocabulary

21. If tickets are required for admission to a show, anyone without a ticket will be *excluded*. What do you think it means when some input values of a function are allowed but other input values are *excluded*?

22. When people are *rational*, they make sense. When a number is *rational*, it can be written as the ratio of two integers. Do you think that the term *rational expression* refers to an expression that makes sense or to an expression that involves a ratio?

23. *Inverting* a cup or glass means changing its orientation to the opposite direction. If positive values x and y are related by an *inverse variation*, do you think they increase and decrease together? Or do you think they move in opposite directions, one decreasing as the other increases?

CHAPTER

11

Rational Expressions and Functions

Download videos connecting math to your world.

Interactive! Vary numbers, graphs, and figures to explore math concepts.

The online Solve It will get you in gear for each lesson.

Math definitions in English and Spanish

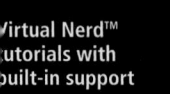

Online access to stepped-out problems aligned to Common Core

Get and view your assignments online.

Extra practice and review online

Virtual Nerd™ tutorials with built-in support

Chapter Preview

Vocabulary

English/Spanish Vocabulary Audio Online:

English	Spanish
asymptote, *p. 706*	asíntota
constant of variation for an inverse variation, *p. 698*	constante de variación en variaciones inversas
excluded value, *p. 664*	valor excluido
inverse variation, *p. 698*	variación inversa
rational equation, *p. 691*	ecuación racional
rational expression, *p. 664*	expresión racional
rational function, *p. 705*	función racional

BIG ideas

1 **Equivalence**
   Essential Question How are rational expressions represented?

2 **Functions**
   Essential Question What are the characteristics of rational functions?

3 **Solving Equations and Inequalities**
   Essential Question How can you solve a rational equation?

 DOMAINS

- Arithmetic with Polynomials and Rational Expressions
- Reasoning with Equations and Inequalities
- Interpreting Functions

Common Core Performance Task

Packaging Lunches

Sandra's Deli is a very popular lunch spot in the downtown area. After a great deal of planning, Sandra decides to sell two of the most popular types of lunches boxed in a container made of cardboard lined with aluminum foil. She will first sell the boxed lunches at her deli, and if things go well she would like to sell them in grocery stores.

Sandra is deciding on the dimensions to use for the new lunch box. She sketches the rectangular box shown in the diagram at the right. She needs the box to hold 355 in.^{3}. The cardboard lined with aluminum foil is expensive, so Sandra wants the box to use the least amount of cardboard possible.

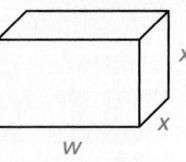

Task Description

Find the dimensions Sandra should use for the lunch box. Round the dimensions to the nearest hundredth of an inch.

Connecting the Task to the Math Practices

MATHEMATICAL
PRACTICES

As you complete the task, you'll apply several Standards for Mathematical Practice.

- You'll write expressions to model the surface area and volume of the box in terms of its dimensions. (MP 4)

- You'll rewrite an expression for the surface area in an equivalent form. (MP 2)

- You'll use a graphing calculator to analyze a function for the surface area, and relate your results to the original context. (MP 2, MP 5)

11-1 Simplifying Rational Expressions

Common Core State Standards

Prepares for A-APR.D.7 . . . add, subtract, multiply, and divide rational expressions.

MP 1, MP 2, MP 3, MP 4

Objective To simplify rational expressions

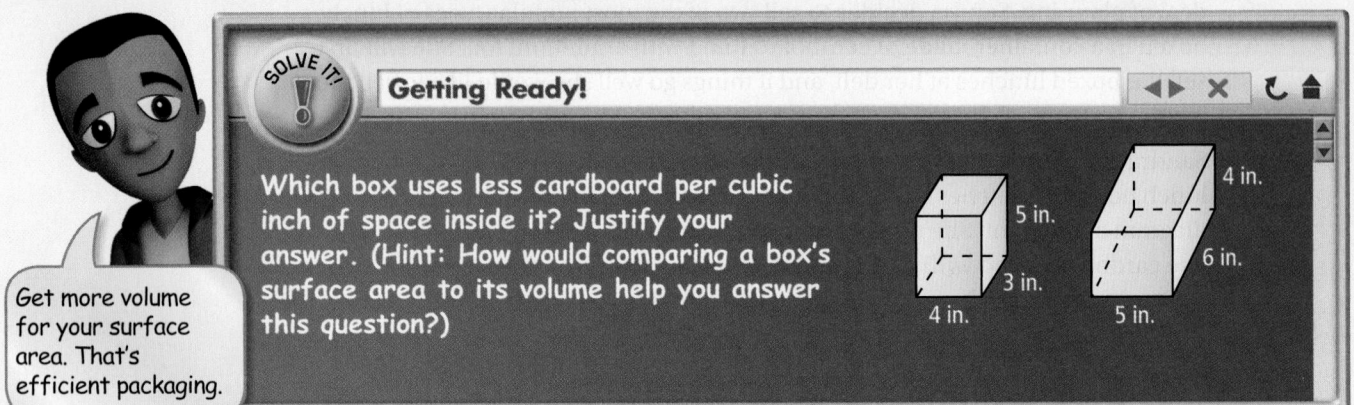

Getting Ready!

Which box uses less cardboard per cubic inch of space inside it? Justify your answer. (Hint: How would comparing a box's surface area to its volume help you answer this question?)

Get more volume for your surface area. That's efficient packaging.

MATHEMATICAL PRACTICES An expression of the form $\frac{\text{polynomial}}{\text{polynomial}}$ is a **rational expression**.

Lesson Vocabulary
• rational expression
• excluded value

Essential Understanding The simplified form of a rational expression is like the simplified form of a numerical fraction. The numerator and denominator have no common factor other than 1. To simplify a rational expression, divide out common factors from the numerator and denominator.

Like a numerical fraction, a rational expression is undefined when the denominator is 0. A value of a variable for which a rational expression is undefined is an **excluded value.**

Problem 1 Simplifying a Rational Expression

What is the simplified form of $\frac{x-1}{5x-5}$? State any excluded values.

$$\frac{x-1}{5x-5} = \frac{x-1}{5(x-1)}$$ Factor the denominator. The numerator cannot be factored.

$$= \frac{\cancel{x-1}^{1}}{5_{1}\cancel{(x-1)}}$$ Divide out the common factor $x-1$.

$$= \frac{1}{5}$$ Simplify.

The denominator of the original expression is 0 when $x = 1$. The simplified form is $\frac{1}{5}$, where $x \neq 1$.

Think

Should you use the simplified form to find excluded values?
No. You must check the original expression to see which values of x make the denominator 0.

Got It? **1.** What is the simplified form of the expression? State any excluded values.

a. $\frac{21a^2}{7a^3}$ b. $\frac{18d^2}{4d+8}$ c. $\frac{2n-3}{6n-9}$ d. $\frac{26c^3+91c}{2c^2+7}$

Problem 2 **Simplifying a Rational Expression Containing a Trinomial**

What is the simplified form of $\frac{3x - 6}{x^2 + x - 6}$? State any excluded values.

Think

Write

To see if there are any common factors, factor the numerator and the denominator.

$$\frac{3x - 6}{x^2 + x - 6} = \frac{3(x - 2)}{(x + 3)(x - 2)}$$

Divide out the common factor $x - 2$. Simplify.

$$= \frac{3(x - 2)^1}{(x + 3)_1(x - 2)}$$

$$= \frac{3}{(x + 3)}$$

State the simplified form with any restrictions on the variable.

The denominator of the original expression is 0 when $x = -3$ or $x = 2$. So the simplified form is $\frac{3}{x + 3}$, where $x \neq -3$ and $x \neq 2$.

Think

Could you also find the restricted values *before* simplifying?
Yes. You use the original expression to find the restrictions on x, so you don't need to simplify first.

 Got It? **2.** What is the simplified form of the expression? State any excluded values.

a. $\frac{2x - 8}{x^2 - 2x - 8}$ **b.** $\frac{a^2 - 3a + 2}{3a - 3}$ **c.** $\frac{6z + 12}{2z^2 + 7z + 6}$ **d.** $\frac{c^2 - c - 6}{c^2 + 5c + 6}$

The numerator and denominator of $\frac{x - 3}{3 - x}$ are opposites. To simplify the expression, you can factor -1 from $3 - x$ to get $-1(-3 + x)$, which you can rewrite as $-1(x - 3)$. Then simplify $\frac{x - 3}{-1(x - 3)}$.

Problem 3 **Recognizing Opposite Factors**

What is the simplified form of $\frac{4 - x^2}{7x - 14}$? State any excluded values.

$$\frac{4 - x^2}{7x - 14} = \frac{(2 - x)(2 + x)}{7(x - 2)} \qquad \text{Factor the numerator and the denominator.}$$

$$= \frac{-1(x - 2)(2 + x)}{7(x - 2)} \qquad \text{Factor } -1 \text{ from } 2 - x.$$

$$= \frac{-1(x - 2)^1(2 + x)}{7_1(x - 2)} \qquad \text{Divide out the common factor } x - 2.$$

$$= -\frac{x + 2}{7} \qquad \text{Simplify.}$$

The denominator of the original expression is 0 when $x = 2$. The simplified form is $-\frac{x + 2}{7}$, where $x \neq 2$.

Plan

When should you factor -1 from an expression?
You should factor -1 from $a - x$ when factoring -1 results in a common factor.

You can use rational expressions to model some real-world situations.

 Problem 4 **Using a Rational Expression**

Shopping You are choosing between the two wastebaskets that have the shape of the figures at the right. They both have the same volume. What is the height h of the rectangular wastebasket? Give your answer in terms of a.

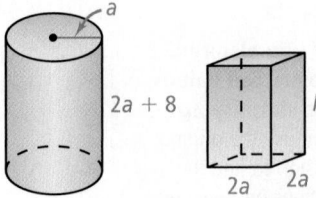

Plan

Is there another way to solve the problem?
Yes. You can set the volumes equal to each other and then solve for h.

Step 1 Find the volume of the cylinder.

$$V = \pi r^2 h \qquad \text{Formula for volume of a cylinder}$$
$$= \pi a^2(2a + 8) \quad \text{Substitute } a \text{ for } r \text{ and } 2a + 8 \text{ for } h.$$

Step 2 Find the height of a rectangular prism with volume $\pi a^2(2a + 8)$ and base area $B = (2a)^2 = 4a^2$.

$$V = Bh \qquad \text{Formula for volume of a prism}$$

$$h = \frac{V}{B} \qquad \text{Solve for } h.$$

$$= \frac{\pi a^2(2a + 8)}{4a^2} \qquad \begin{array}{l}\text{Substitute the volume of the cylinder for the volume of the}\\\text{rectangular prism and } 4a^2 \text{ for } B.\end{array}$$

$$= \frac{\pi a^2(2)(a + 4)}{4a^2} \qquad \text{Factor.}$$

$$= \frac{\pi a^{2^1}(2)^1(a + 4)}{{}_2 4_1 a^2} \qquad \text{Divide out common factors 2 and } a^2.$$

$$= \frac{\pi(a + 4)}{2} \qquad \text{Simplify.}$$

The height of the rectangular prism is $\dfrac{\pi(a + 4)}{2}$.

  Got It? 4. a. A square has side length $6x + 2$. A rectangle with width $3x + 1$ has the same area as the square. What is the length of the rectangle?

  b. **Reasoning** Suppose the dimensions of the wastebaskets in Problem 4 are measured in feet. Is it possible for the height of the rectangular wastebasket to be 1 ft? What are the possible heights? Explain.

Lesson Check

Do you know HOW?

Simplify each expression. State any excluded values.

1. $\dfrac{3x + 9}{x + 3}$

2. $\dfrac{5 - x}{x^2 - 2x - 15}$

3. The two rectangles below have the same area. What is a simplified expression for the length ℓ of the rectangle on the right?

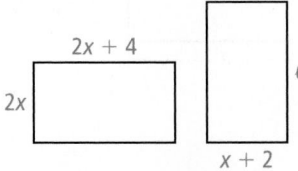

Do you UNDERSTAND?

MATHEMATICAL PRACTICES

4. **Vocabulary** Is each expression a rational expression? Explain your reasoning.

   a. $\dfrac{\sqrt{x} + 2}{x^2 + 4}$

   b. $\dfrac{y}{y - 1}$

5. **Writing** When simplifying a rational expression, why may it be necessary to exclude values? Explain.

6. **Reasoning** Suppose neither the numerator nor the denominator of a rational expression can be factored. Is the expression necessarily in simplified form? Explain.

7. Are the given factors opposites? Explain.

   a. $3 - x$; $x - 3$

   b. $2 - y$; $-y + 2$

Practice and Problem-Solving Exercises

MATHEMATICAL PRACTICES

 **Practice**

Simplify each expression. State any excluded values.

See Problems 1, 2, and 3.

8. $\dfrac{6a + 9}{12}$

9. $\dfrac{4x^3}{28x^4}$

10. $\dfrac{2m - 5}{6m - 15}$

11. $\dfrac{2p - 24}{4p - 48}$

12. $\dfrac{3x^2 - 9x}{x - 3}$

13. $\dfrac{3x + 6}{3x^2}$

14. $\dfrac{2x^2 + 2x}{3x^2 + 3x}$

15. $\dfrac{2b - 8}{b^2 - 16}$

16. $\dfrac{m + 6}{m^2 - m - 42}$

17. $\dfrac{w^2 + 7w}{w^2 - 49}$

18. $\dfrac{a^2 + 2a + 1}{5a + 5}$

19. $\dfrac{m^2 + 7m + 12}{m^2 + 6m + 8}$

20. $\dfrac{c^2 - 6c + 8}{c^2 + c - 6}$

21. $\dfrac{b^2 + 8b + 15}{b + 5}$

22. $\dfrac{m + 4}{m^2 + 2m - 8}$

23. $\dfrac{5 - 4n}{4n - 5}$

24. $\dfrac{12 - 4t}{t^2 - 2t - 3}$

25. $\dfrac{4m - 8}{4 - 2m}$

26. $\dfrac{m - 2}{4 - 2m}$

27. $\dfrac{v - 5}{25 - v^2}$

28. $\dfrac{4 - w}{w^2 - 8w + 16}$

29. **Geometry** The length of a rectangular prism is 5 more than twice the width w. The volume of the prism is $2w^3 + 7w^2 + 5w$. What is a simplified expression for the height of the prism?

See Problem 4.

30. **Geometry** Rectangle A has length $2x + 6$ and width $3x$. Rectangle B has length $x + 2$ and an area 12 square units greater than Rectangle A's area. What is a simplified expression for the width of Rectangle B?

Simplify each expression. State any excluded values.

31. $\dfrac{2r^2 + 9r - 5}{r^2 + 10r + 25}$

32. $\dfrac{7z^2 + 23z + 6}{z^2 + 2z - 3}$

33. $\dfrac{5t^2 + 6t - 8}{3t^2 + 5t - 2}$

34. $\dfrac{32a^3}{16a^2 - 8a}$

35. $\dfrac{3z^2 + 12z}{z^4}$

36. $\dfrac{2s^2 + s}{s^3}$

37. $\dfrac{4a^2 - 8a - 5}{15 - a - 2a^2}$

38. $\dfrac{16 + 16m + 3m^2}{m^2 - 3m - 28}$

39. $\dfrac{10c + c^2 - 3c^3}{5c^2 - 6c - 8}$

© **40. Think About a Plan** In the figure at the right, what is the ratio of the area of the shaded triangle to the area of the rectangle? Write your answer in simplified form.
- What is an expression for the length of the rectangle?
- How do you find the area of a triangle?

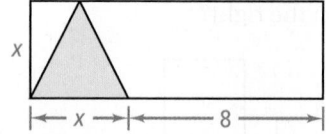

© **41. Writing** Is $\dfrac{x^2 - 9}{x + 3}$ the same as $x - 3$? Explain.

STEM **42. a. Construction** To keep heating costs down for a building, architects want the ratio of surface area to volume to be as small as possible. What is an expression for the ratio of surface area to volume for each figure?

    i. square prism

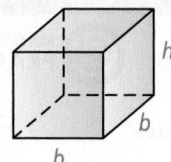

    ii. cylinder

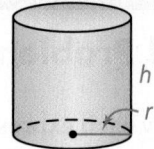

    b. For each figure, what is the ratio of surface area to volume when $b = 12$ ft, $h = 18$ ft, and $r = 6$ ft?

© **43. Error Analysis** A student simplified a rational expression as shown at the right. Describe and correct the error.

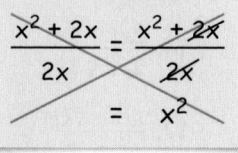

44. Banking A bank account with principal P earns interest at rate r (expressed as a decimal), compounded annually. What is the ratio of the balance after 3 yr to the balance after 1 yr? Write r as a decimal.

© **45. Open-Ended** Write a rational expression that has 4 and -3 as excluded values.

Write a ratio in simplified form of the area of the shaded figure to the area of the figure that encloses it.

46.

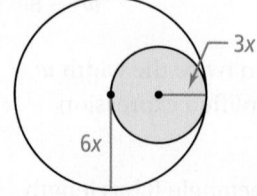

47.

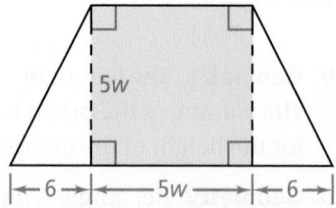

© **Challenge** **Simplify each expression. State any excluded values.**

48. $\dfrac{m^2 - n^2}{m^2 + 11mn + 10n^2}$

49. $\dfrac{a^2 - 5ab + 6b^2}{a^2 + 2ab - 8b^2}$

50. $\dfrac{36v^2 - 49w^2}{18v^2 + 9vw - 14w^2}$

Reasoning Determine whether each statement is *always, sometimes,* or *never* true for real numbers a and b. Explain.

51. $\dfrac{2b}{b} = 2$

52. $\dfrac{ab^3}{b^4} = ab$

53. $\dfrac{a^2 + 6a + 5}{2a + 2} = \dfrac{a + 5}{2}$

Apply What You've Learned

MP 4

Look back at the information on page 663 about Sandra's plans for a new lunch box. Sandra's diagram of the lunch box is shown again below.

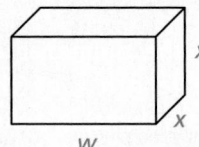

a. What is an algebraic expression for the volume of the box? Write an equation that relates this expression to the given volume, 355 in.^{3}.

b. Solve for w in the equation from part (a).

c. Write an expression in terms of x and w to represent the surface area of the lunch box.

d. Substitute for w in the expression for the surface area of the lunch box, using your result from part (b). Simplify the expression.

11-2 Multiplying and Dividing Rational Expressions

Common Core State Standards

A-APR.D.7 . . . add, subtract, multiply, and divide rational expressions.

MP 1, MP 2, MP 3, MP 4, MP 7

Objectives To multiply and divide rational expressions
To simplify complex fractions

Getting Ready!

In the figure at the right, the diameter of the sphere is equal to the edge length x of the cube. What percent of the cube's volume is taken up by the sphere? Justify your reasoning.

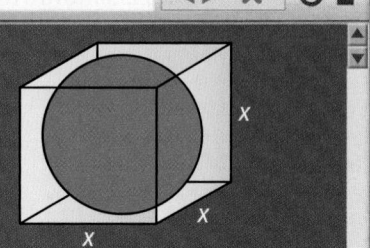

Solve a simpler problem. Use a value for x to understand what is going on.

MATHEMATICAL PRACTICES

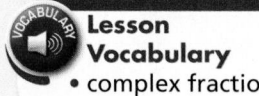
Lesson Vocabulary
• complex fraction

Many problems require finding products and quotients of rational expressions.

Essential Understanding You can multiply and divide rational expressions using the same properties you use to multiply and divide numerical fractions.

If a, b, c, and d represent polynomials (where $b \neq 0$ and $d \neq 0$), then $\frac{a}{b} \cdot \frac{c}{d} = \frac{ac}{bd}$.

Problem 1 Multiplying Rational Expressions

What is the product? State any excluded values.

Ⓐ $\dfrac{6}{a^2} \cdot \dfrac{-2}{a^3}$

$\dfrac{6}{a^2} \cdot \dfrac{-2}{a^3} = \dfrac{6(-2)}{a^2(a^3)}$ Multiply numerators and multiply denominators.

$= \dfrac{-12}{a^5}$ Simplify.

The product is $\dfrac{-12}{a^5}$, where $a \neq 0$.

Think

Are products of rational expressions defined for all real numbers?
No. The products may have excluded values. In part (A), the excluded value is 0. In part (B), the excluded values are 0 and −3.

Ⓑ $\dfrac{x-7}{x} \cdot \dfrac{x-5}{x+3}$

$\dfrac{x-7}{x} \cdot \dfrac{x-5}{x+3} = \dfrac{(x-7)(x-5)}{x(x+3)}$ Multiply numerators and multiply denominators. Leave the product in factored form.

The product is $\dfrac{(x-7)(x-5)}{x(x+3)}$, where $x \neq 0$ and $x \neq -3$.

Got It? **1.** What is the product? State any excluded values.

a. $\dfrac{5}{y} \cdot \dfrac{3}{y^3}$

b. $\dfrac{x}{x-2} \cdot \dfrac{x+1}{x-3}$

As Problem 1 indicates, products of rational expressions may have excluded values. For the rest of this chapter, it is not necessary to state excluded values unless you are asked.

Sometimes the product $\frac{ac}{bd}$ of two rational expressions may not be in simplified form. You may need to divide out common factors.

 **Problem 2** Using Factoring

What is the product $\frac{x+5}{7x-21} \cdot \frac{14x}{x^2+3x-10}$**?**

$$\frac{x+5}{7x-21} \cdot \frac{14x}{x^2+3x-10} = \frac{x+5}{7(x-3)} \cdot \frac{14x}{(x+5)(x-2)}$$ Factor denominators.

$$= \frac{x+5^{\,1}}{{}_1 7(x-3)} \cdot \frac{14^{\,2}x}{{}_1(x+5)(x-2)}$$ Divide out the common factors 7 and $x+5$.

$$= \frac{1}{x-3} \cdot \frac{2x}{x-2}$$ Simplify.

$$= \frac{2x}{(x-3)(x-2)}$$ Multiply numerators and multiply denominators. Leave the product in factored form.

Got It? **2. a.** What is the product $\frac{3x^2}{x+2} \cdot \frac{x^2+3x+2}{x}$?

    b. Reasoning In Problem 2, suppose you multiply the numerators and denominators *before* you factor. Will you still get the same product? Explain.

You can also multiply a rational expression by a polynomial. Leave the product in factored form.

 Problem 3 Multiplying a Rational Expression by a Polynomial

What is the product $\frac{2m+5}{3m-6} \cdot \left(m^2+m-6\right)$**?**

$$\frac{2m+5}{3m-6} \cdot \left(m^2+m-6\right) = \frac{2m+5}{3(m-2)} \cdot \frac{(m-2)(m+3)}{1}$$ Factor.

$$= \frac{(2m+5)}{3_1(m-2)} \cdot \frac{(m-2)^{\,1}(m+3)}{1}$$ Divide out the common factor $m-2$.

$$= \frac{(2m+5)(m+3)}{3}$$ Multiply. Leave the product in factored form.

Got It? **3.** What is the product?

    a. $\frac{2x-14}{4x-6} \cdot (6x^2-13x+6)$ **b.** $\frac{x^2+2x+1}{x^2-1} \cdot (x^2+2x-3)$

Recall that $\frac{a}{b} \div \frac{c}{d} = \frac{a}{b} \cdot \frac{d}{c}$, where $b \neq 0$, $c \neq 0$, and $d \neq 0$. When you divide rational expressions, first rewrite the quotient as a product using the reciprocal before dividing out common factors.

Problem 4 Dividing Rational Expressions

What is the quotient $\frac{x^2 - 25}{4x + 28} \div \frac{x - 5}{x^2 + 9x + 14}$?

Think

To divide by a rational expression, multiply by its reciprocal.

Before multiplying, factor.

Divide out the common factors $x - 5$ and $x + 7$.

Multiply numerators and multiply denominators. Leave the quotient in factored form.

Write

$$\frac{x^2 - 25}{4x + 28} \div \frac{x - 5}{x^2 + 9x + 14}$$

$$= \frac{x^2 - 25}{4x + 28} \cdot \frac{x^2 + 9x + 14}{x - 5}$$

$$= \frac{(x + 5)(x - 5)}{4(x + 7)} \cdot \frac{(x + 7)(x + 2)}{x - 5}$$

$$= \frac{(x + 5)(x - 5)^1}{4_1(x + 7)} \cdot \frac{(x + 7)^1(x + 2)}{{}_1 x - 5}$$

$$= \frac{(x + 5)(x + 2)}{4}$$

 Got It? **4.** What is the quotient?

a. $\frac{x}{x + y} \div \frac{xy}{x + y}$

b. $\frac{4k + 8}{6k - 10} \div \frac{k^2 + 6k + 8}{9k - 15}$

The reciprocal of a polynomial such as $x^2 + 3x + 2$ is $\frac{1}{x^2 + 3x + 2}$.

 Problem 5 Dividing a Rational Expression by a Polynomial

Multiple Choice What is the quotient $\frac{3x^2 - 12x}{5x} \div (x^2 - 3x - 4)$?

Ⓐ $\frac{3x}{(x - 4)(x + 1)}$ 　　 Ⓑ $\frac{3x}{5x^2 + 5}$ 　　 Ⓒ $\frac{3(x - 4)^2(x + 1)}{5x}$ 　　 Ⓓ $\frac{3}{5(x + 1)}$

Plan

Why write the polynomial as a rational expression?
To divide a rational expression by a polynomial, you have to multiply by the reciprocal of the polynomial. Writing the polynomial over 1 may help you find its reciprocal.

$$\frac{3x^2 - 12x}{5x} \div \frac{x^2 - 3x - 4}{1} = \frac{3x^2 - 12x}{5x} \cdot \frac{1}{x^2 - 3x - 4}$$ 　　 Multiply by the reciprocal.

$$= \frac{3x(x - 4)}{5x} \cdot \frac{1}{(x - 4)(x + 1)}$$ 　　 Factor.

$$= \frac{3x^1(x - 4)^1}{5_1 x} \cdot \frac{1}{{}_1(x - 4)(x + 1)}$$ 　　 Divide out the common factors x and $x - 4$.

$$= \frac{3}{5(x + 1)}$$ 　　 Simplify.

The correct answer is D.

 Got It? **5.** What is the quotient $\frac{z^2 - 2z + 1}{z^2 + 2} \div (z - 1)$?

A **complex fraction** is a fraction that contains one or more fractions in its numerator, in its denominator, or in both. You can simplify a complex fraction by dividing its numerator by its denominator.

Any complex fraction of the form $\dfrac{\frac{a}{b}}{\frac{c}{d}}$ (where $b \neq 0$, $c \neq 0$, and $d \neq 0$) can be expressed as $\dfrac{a}{b} \div \dfrac{c}{d}$.

 Problem 6 Simplifying a Complex Fraction

What is the simplified form of $\dfrac{\frac{1}{x-2}}{\frac{x+3}{x^2-4}}$?

$\dfrac{\frac{1}{x-2}}{\frac{x+3}{x^2-4}} = \dfrac{1}{x-2} \div \dfrac{x+3}{x^2-4}$ Write as a quotient.

$= \dfrac{1}{x-2} \cdot \dfrac{x^2-4}{x+3}$ Multiply by the reciprocal.

$= \dfrac{1}{x-2} \cdot \dfrac{(x+2)(x-2)}{x+3}$ Factor.

$= \dfrac{1}{{}_1\cancel{x-2}} \cdot \dfrac{(x+2)\cancel{(x-2)}^{\,1}}{x+3}$ Divide out the common factor $x-2$.

$= \dfrac{x+2}{x+3}$ Simplify.

Think

Have you solved a similar problem before?
Yes. In Problem 4, you found the quotient of two rational expressions. You simplify this complex fraction in the same way, but first write it as a quotient.

 Got It? 6. What is the simplified form of $\dfrac{\frac{1}{q+4}}{\frac{2q^2}{2q+8}}$?

 Lesson Check

Do you know HOW?

Multiply.

1. $\dfrac{2}{5t} \cdot \dfrac{3}{t^5}$ **2.** $\dfrac{2x+5}{4x-12} \cdot (x^2 - 8x + 15)$

Divide.

3. $\dfrac{k^2 + k}{5k} \div \dfrac{1}{15k^2}$ **4.** $\dfrac{8x^2 - 12x}{x+7} \div (4x^2 - 9)$

Simplify each complex fraction.

5. $\dfrac{\frac{a^2 + 2a - 8}{3a}}{\frac{a+4}{a-2}}$

6. $\dfrac{\frac{x^2 + 6x}{x+6}}{x}$

Do you UNDERSTAND?  MATHEMATICAL PRACTICES

7. Reasoning Are the complex fractions $\dfrac{\frac{a}{b}}{c}$ and $\dfrac{a}{\frac{b}{c}}$ equivalent? Explain.

8. Compare and Contrast How are multiplying rational expressions and multiplying numerical fractions similar? How are they different?

9. Reasoning Consider that $\dfrac{a}{b} \div \dfrac{c}{d} = \dfrac{a}{b} \cdot \dfrac{d}{c}$. Why must it be true that $b \neq 0$, $c \neq 0$, and $d \neq 0$?

10. a. Writing Explain how to multiply a rational expression by a polynomial.
     b. Explain how to divide a rational expression by a polynomial.

Practice and Problem-Solving Exercises

 Practice   Multiply.

See Problems 1, 2, and 3.

11. $\frac{7}{3} \cdot \frac{5x}{12}$

12. $\frac{3}{t} \cdot \frac{4}{t}$

13. $\frac{5}{3a^2} \cdot \frac{8}{a^3}$

14. $\frac{m-2}{m+2} \cdot \frac{m}{m-1}$

15. $\frac{2x}{x+1} \cdot \frac{x-1}{3}$

16. $\frac{6x^2}{5} \cdot \frac{2}{x+1}$

17. $\frac{4c}{2c+2} \cdot \frac{c^2+3c+2}{c-1}$

18. $\frac{b^2+4b+4}{2b^2-8} \cdot \frac{3b-6}{4b}$

19. $\frac{r^2+5r+6}{2r} \cdot \frac{r-2}{r+3}$

20. $\frac{m-2}{3m+9} \cdot \frac{2m+6}{2m-4}$

21. $\frac{t^2-t-12}{t+1} \cdot \frac{t+1}{t+3}$

22. $\frac{4x+1}{5x+10} \cdot \frac{30x+60}{2x-2}$

23. $\frac{4t+4}{t-3} \cdot (t^2-t-6)$

24. $\frac{2m+1}{3m-6} \cdot (9m^2-36)$

25. $(x^2-1) \cdot \frac{x-2}{3x+3}$

26. $\frac{2y+9}{4y+12} \cdot \left(y^2+y-6\right)$

27. $\frac{h-1}{6h+3} \cdot \left(2h^2+9h+4\right)$

28. $\left(w^2-8w+15\right) \cdot \frac{w+3}{4w-20}$

Find the reciprocal of each expression.

See Problems 4 and 5.

29. $\frac{2}{x+1}$

30. $\frac{-6d^2}{2d-5}$

31. c^2-1

Divide.

32. $\frac{x-1}{x+4} \div \frac{x+3}{x+4}$

33. $\frac{3t+12}{5t} \div \frac{t+4}{10t}$

34. $\frac{x-3}{6} \div \frac{3-x}{2}$

35. $\frac{y-4}{10} \div \frac{4-y}{5}$

36. $\frac{x^2+6x+8}{x^2+x-2} \div \frac{x+4}{2x+4}$

37. $\frac{2n^2-5n-3}{4n^2-12n-7} \div \frac{4n+5}{2n-7}$

38. $\frac{3x+9}{x} \div (x+3)$

39. $\frac{11k+121}{7k-15} \div (k+11)$

40. $\frac{x^2+10x-11}{x^2+12x+11} \div (x-1)$

Simplify each complex fraction.

See Problem 6.

41. $\dfrac{\frac{4b-1}{b^2+2b+1}}{\frac{12b-3}{b^2-1}}$

42. $\dfrac{\frac{3x^2+2x+1}{8x}}{12x^2+8x+4}$

43. $\dfrac{\frac{6s+12}{s+2}}{3}$

44. $\dfrac{\frac{t^2-t-6}{t-3}}{t+2}$

45. $\dfrac{\frac{x^2-25}{x^2+6x+5}}{2x-10}$

46. $\dfrac{\frac{3}{3d^2+5d-2}}{\frac{3}{2d+4}}$

47. $\dfrac{\frac{g+2}{3g-1}}{\frac{g^2+2g}{6g+2}}$

48. $\dfrac{\frac{5f^2}{10f}}{f^2+1}$

49. $\dfrac{\frac{z-10}{z+10}}{3z^2-30z}$

50. $\dfrac{\frac{c+4}{c^2+5c+6}}{\frac{3c^2+12c}{2c^2+5c-3}}$

B Apply

Multiply or divide.

51. $\dfrac{t^2 + 5t + 6}{t - 3} \cdot \dfrac{t^2 - 2t - 3}{t^2 + 3t + 2}$

52. $\dfrac{c^2 + 3c + 2}{c^2 - 4c + 3} \div \dfrac{c + 2}{c - 3}$

53. $\dfrac{7t^2 - 28t}{2t^2 - 5t - 12} \cdot \dfrac{6t^2 - t - 15}{49t^3}$

54. $\dfrac{5x^2 + 10x - 15}{5 - 6x + x^2} \div \dfrac{2x^2 + 7x + 3}{4x^2 - 8x - 5}$

55. $\dfrac{x^2 + x - 6}{x^2 - x - 6} \div \dfrac{x^2 + 5x + 6}{x^2 + 4x + 4}$

56. $\left(\dfrac{x^2 - 25}{x^2 - 4x}\right)\left(\dfrac{x^2 + x - 20}{x^2 + 10x + 25}\right)$

Loan Payments The formula below gives the monthly payment m on a loan as a function of the amount borrowed A, the annual rate of interest r (expressed as a decimal), and the number of months n of the loan. Use this formula and a calculator for Exercises 57–60.

$$m = \dfrac{A\left(\frac{r}{12}\right)\left(1 + \frac{r}{12}\right)^n}{\left(1 + \frac{r}{12}\right)^n - 1}$$

57. What is the monthly payment on a loan of $1500 at 8% annual interest paid over 18 months?

58. What is the monthly payment on a loan of $3000 at 6% annual interest paid over 24 months?

© 59. Think About a Plan Suppose a family wants to buy the house advertised at the right. They have $60,000 for a down payment. Their mortgage will have an annual interest rate of 6%. The loan is to be repaid over a 30-yr period. How much will it cost the family to repay this mortgage over the 30 yr?
- What information can you obtain from the formula above?
- How can you use the information given by the formula to solve the problem?

60. Auto Loans You want to purchase a car that costs $18,000. The car dealership offers two different 48-month financing plans. The first plan offers 0% interest for 4 yr. The second plan offers a $2000 discount, but you must finance the rest of the purchase price at an interest rate of 7.9% for 4 yr. For which financing plan will your total cost be less? How much less will it be?

© 61. Error Analysis In the work shown at the right, what error did the student make in dividing the rational expressions?

© 62. Open-Ended Write two rational expressions. Find their product.

© 63. Reasoning For what values of x is the expression $\dfrac{2x^2 - 5x - 12}{6x} \div \dfrac{-3x - 12}{x^2 - 16}$ undefined? Explain your reasoning.

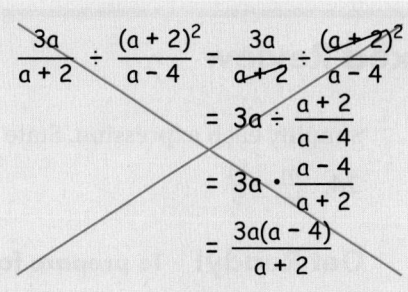

Geometry Find the volume of each rectangular prism.

64.

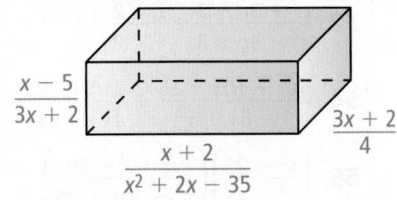

$\dfrac{x-5}{3x+2}$

$\dfrac{x+2}{x^2+2x-35}$

$\dfrac{3x+2}{4}$

65.

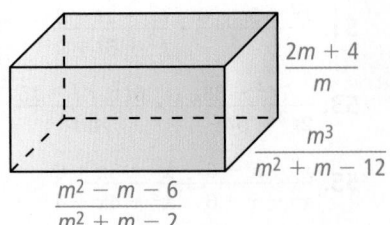

$\dfrac{2m+4}{m}$

$\dfrac{m^3}{m^2+m-12}$

$\dfrac{m^2-m-6}{m^2+m-2}$

Challenge Multiply or divide.

66. $\dfrac{3m^3-3m}{4m^2+4m-8}\cdot(6m^2+12m)$

67. $\dfrac{t^2-r^2}{t^2+tr-2r^2}\cdot\dfrac{t^2+3tr+2r^2}{t^2+2tr+r^2}$

68. $\dfrac{5x^2}{y^2-25}\div\dfrac{5xy-25x}{y^2-10y+25}$

69. $\dfrac{2a^2-ab-6b^2}{2b^2+9ab-5a^2}\div\dfrac{2a^2-7ab+6b^2}{a^2-4b^2}$

Standardized Test Prep

SAT/ACT

70. What is the simplified form of $(2x-5)\cdot\dfrac{2x}{2x^2-9x+10}$?

Ⓐ 1　　　　Ⓑ $\dfrac{2x}{x-2}$　　　　Ⓒ $\dfrac{x-5}{-4x+5}$　　　　Ⓓ $\dfrac{2x-5}{-8x-10}$

71. The volume of the rectangular prism is $4x^3+6x^2$.
What is the width w of the prism?

Ⓕ $4x^3+6x^2-2x$

Ⓖ $2x+3$

Ⓗ $2x+4$

Ⓘ $2x+6$

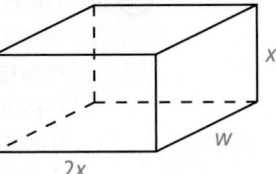

72. What is the vertex of the parabola with the equation $y=2x^2+3x-1$?

Ⓐ $(-0.75,-2.125)$

Ⓑ $(0.75,2.125)$

Ⓒ $(-2.125,-0.75)$

Ⓓ $(-0.75,2.125)$

Short Response

73. A soccer ball is kicked with an initial upward velocity of 35 ft/s from a starting height of 2.5 ft. If no one touches the ball, how long will it be in the air? Use the formula $h=-16t^2+vt+c$, where h is the ball's height at time t, v is the initial upward velocity, and c is the starting height. Show your work.

Mixed Review

Simplify each expression. State any excluded values.

◀ See Lesson 11-1.

74. $\dfrac{7m-14}{3m-6}$

75. $\dfrac{5a^2}{10a^4-15a^2}$

76. $\dfrac{4c^2-36c+81}{4c^2-2c-72}$

Get Ready!　To prepare for Lesson 11-3, do Exercises 77–79.

Find each product.

◀ See Lesson 8-3.

77. $(2x+4)(x+3)$

78. $(-3n-4)(n-5)$

79. $(3a^2+1)(2a-7)$

Dividing Polynomials Using Algebra Tiles

© **Common Core State Standards**
Prepares for A-APR.D.7 . . . add, subtract, multiply, and divide rational expressions.
MP 7

You can use algebra tiles to model polynomial division.

Activity

What is $(x^2 + 4x + 3) \div (x + 3)$? Use algebra tiles.

Step 1 Use algebra tiles to model the dividend, $x^2 + 4x + 3$.

Step 2 Use the x^2-tile and the 1-tiles to form a figure with length $x + 3$, the divisor.

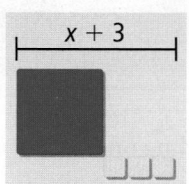

Step 3 Use the remaining tiles to fill in the rectangle.

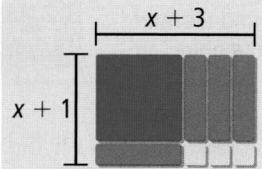

Since $(x + 1)(x + 3) = x^2 + 4x + 3$, you can write $(x^2 + 4x + 3) \div (x + 3) = x + 1$.

Check Check your result by multiplying $x + 1$ and $x + 3$. The product should be the dividend, $x^2 + 4x + 3$.

$$(x + 1)(x + 3) = (x)(x) + (x)(3) + (1)(x) + (1)(3)$$
$$= x^2 + 3x + x + 3$$
$$= x^2 + 4x + 3 ✔$$

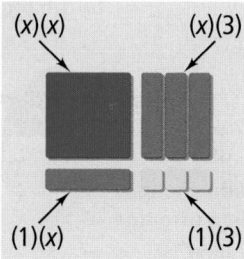

Exercises

Use algebra tiles to find each quotient. Check your result.

1. $(x^2 + 6x + 8) \div (x + 4)$ **2.** $(x^2 + 5x + 6) \div (x + 2)$

3. $(x^2 + 8x + 12) \div (x + 6)$ **4.** $(x^2 + 8x + 7) \div (x + 1)$

© **5. Reasoning** In Exercises 1–4, the divisor is a factor of the dividend. How do you know? Can you use algebra tiles to represent polynomial division when the divisor is *not* a factor of the dividend? Explain.

11-3 Dividing Polynomials

© **Common Core State Standards**

A-APR.D.6 Rewrite simple rational expressions in different forms; write $a(x)/b(x)$ in the form $q(x) + r(x)/b(x)$, where $a(x)$, $b(x)$, $q(x)$, and $r(x)$ are polynomials with the degree of $r(x)$ less than the degree of $b(x) \ldots$

MP 1, MP 2, MP 3, MP 4, MP 6, MP 7

Objective To divide polynomials

Solve a simpler problem. Use values for r and h to understand what is going on.

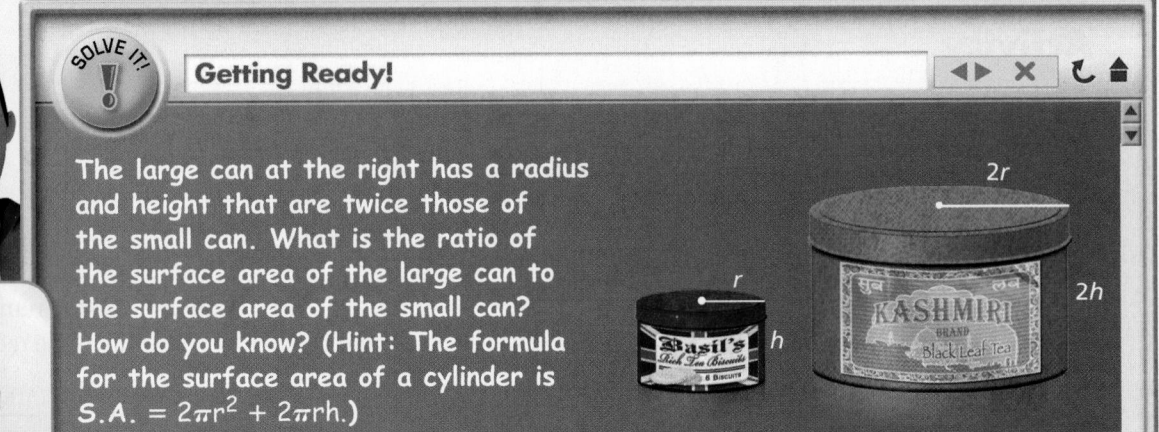

Getting Ready!

The large can at the right has a radius and height that are twice those of the small can. What is the ratio of the surface area of the large can to the surface area of the small can? How do you know? (Hint: The formula for the surface area of a cylinder is S.A. $= 2\pi r^2 + 2\pi rh$.)

© **MATHEMATICAL PRACTICES** In the Solve It, finding the ratio of the cans' surface areas involves dividing one polynomial by another.

Essential Understanding You can divide polynomials using techniques similar to the techniques used for dividing real numbers, including long division.

Plan

How can you change this problem into one you know how to solve?
Change the division to multiplication so that you can use the Distributive Property.

© **Problem 1** Dividing by a Monomial

What is $(9x^3 - 6x^2 + 15x) \div 3x^2$?

$(9x^3 - 6x^2 + 15x) \div 3x^2 = (9x^3 - 6x^2 + 15x) \cdot \dfrac{1}{3x^2}$ Multiply by $\dfrac{1}{3x^2}$, the reciprocal of $3x^2$.

$= \dfrac{9x^3}{3x^2} - \dfrac{6x^2}{3x^2} + \dfrac{15x}{3x^2}$ Use the Distributive Property.

$= 3x^1 - 2x^0 + 5x^{-1}$ Subtract exponents when dividing powers with the same base.

$= 3x - 2 + \dfrac{5}{x}$ Simplify.

The answer is $3x - 2 + \dfrac{5}{x}$.

 Got It? **1.** Divide.

    a. $(4a^3 + 10a^2 + 3a) \div 2a^2$

    b. $(5b^4 - 15b^2 + 1) \div 5b^3$

    c. $(12c^4 + 18c^2 + 9c) \div 6c$

The process of dividing a polynomial by a binomial is similar to long division of real numbers. You write the answer as quotient $+ \frac{\text{remainder}}{\text{divisor}}$.

 Problem 2 Dividing by a Binomial

What is $(3d^2 - 4d + 13) \div (d + 3)$?

Step 1 Begin the long division process.

> Align terms by their degrees. Put $3d$ above $-4d$ of the dividend.

$$
\begin{array}{r}
3d \phantom{{}+13} \\
d + 3 \overline{)3d^2 - 4d + 13} \\
\underline{3d^2 + 9d} \phantom{{}+13} \\
-13d + 13
\end{array}
$$

Divide: $3d^2 \div d = 3d$.
Multiply: $3d(d+3) = 3d^2 + 9d$. Then subtract.
Bring down 13.

Plan

How do you get started?
Divide the first term in the dividend by the first term in the divisor. Here, you divide $3d^2$ by d.

Step 2 Repeat the process: divide, multiply, subtract, and bring down.

$$
\begin{array}{r}
3d - 13 \\
d + 3 \overline{)3d^2 - 4d + 13} \\
\underline{3d^2 + 9d} \\
-13d + 13 \\
\underline{-13d - 39} \\
52
\end{array}
$$

> Align terms by their degrees. Put -13 above 13 of the dividend.

Divide: $-13d \div d = -13$.
Multiply: $-13(d+3) = -13d - 39$. Then subtract.
The remainder is 52.

The answer is $3d - 13 + \frac{52}{d + 3}$.

 Got It? **2.** What is $(2m^2 - m - 3) \div (m + 1)$?

When the dividend has a missing term, add the missing term with a coefficient of zero.

Ⓒ **Problem 3** Dividing Polynomials With a Zero Coefficient

Geometry The width w of a rectangle is $3z - 1$. The area A of the rectangle is $18z^3 - 8z + 2$. What is an expression for the length of the rectangle?

Know	**Need**	**Plan**
Area: $18z^3 - 8z + 2$ Width: $3z - 1$	The length of the rectangle	Use the formula for the area of a rectangle, $A = \ell w$. Divide A by w to solve for ℓ.

Think

Why add a term with a coefficient of 0?
If the dividend is missing a term when written in standard form, you must add the term with a coefficient of 0 to act as a placeholder.

$$
\begin{array}{r}
6z^2 + 2z - 2 \\
3z - 1 \overline{)18z^3 + 0z^2 - 8z + 2} \\
\underline{18z^3 - 6z^2} \\
6z^2 - 8z \\
\underline{6z^2 - 2z} \\
-6z + 2 \\
\underline{-6z + 2} \\
0
\end{array}
$$

> The dividend has no z^2-term. So rewrite the dividend to include a z^2-term with coefficient 0.

An expression for the length of the rectangle is $6z^2 + 2z - 2$.

 **Got It? 3.** Divide.

    a. $(q^4 + q^2 + q - 3) \div (q - 1)$ **b.** $(h^3 - 4h + 12) \div (h + 3)$

To divide polynomials using long division, you must write the divisor and the dividend in standard form before you divide.

© Problem 4 **Reordering Terms and Dividing Polynomials**

Think

How can you eliminate choices?
If the product of the divisor and choice A equals the dividend, then choice A is correct. Here, the product does not equal the dividend, so eliminate choice A.

Multiple Choice What is $(-10x - 1 + 4x^2) \div (-3 + 2x)$?

  Ⓐ $2x - 2$ Ⓒ $2x - 2 + \dfrac{7}{2x - 3}$

  Ⓑ $2x - 2 - \dfrac{7}{2x - 3}$ Ⓓ $2x - 2 + \dfrac{7}{2x + 2}$

$$
\begin{array}{r}
2x - 2 \\
2x - 3 \overline{)\,4x^2 - 10x - 1} \\
\underline{4x^2 - 6x} \\
-4x - 1 \\
\underline{-4x + 6} \\
-7
\end{array}
$$

> You must rewrite $-10x - 1 + 4x^2$ and $-3 + 2x$ in standard form before you divide.

The answer is $2x - 2 - \dfrac{7}{2x - 3}$. The correct answer is B.

© Got It? 4. In parts (a) and (b), divide.

    a. $(-7 - 10y + 6y^2) \div (4 + 3y)$ **b.** $(21a + 2 + 18a^2) \div (5 + 6a)$

    c. Reasoning How can you check the answer to Problem 4? Show your work.

---

take note   **Concept Summary**   **Dividing a Polynomial by a Polynomial**

Step 1   Arrange the terms of the dividend and divisor in standard form. If a term is missing from the dividend, add the term with a coefficient of 0.

Step 2   Divide the first term of the dividend by the first term of the divisor. This is the first term of the quotient.

Step 3   Multiply the first term of the quotient by the whole divisor and place the product under the dividend.

Step 4   Subtract this product from the dividend.

Step 5   Bring down the next term.

Repeat Steps 2–5 as necessary until the degree of the remainder is less than the degree of the divisor.

Lesson Check

Do you know HOW?

Divide.

1. $(20m^3 + 10m^2 - 5m - 3) \div 5m^2$

2. $(20c^2 + 23c - 7) \div (c - 1)$

3. $(25n^3 - 11n + 4) \div (5n + 4)$

4. $(-16a - 15 + 15a^2) \div (3 + 5a)$

Do you UNDERSTAND?

5. Vocabulary How is dividing polynomials like dividing real numbers? How is it different?

6. Writing What are the steps that you repeat when performing polynomial long division?

7. Reasoning How would you rewrite $1 - x^4$ before dividing it by $x - 1$?

 **Practice and Problem-Solving Exercises**

 Divide.

See Problems 1, 2, and 3.

8. $(x^6 - x^5 + x^4) \div x^2$

9. $(12x^8 - 8x^3) \div 4x^4$

10. $(9c^4 + 6c^3 - c^2) \div 3c^2$

11. $(n^5 - 18n^4 + 3n^3) \div n^3$

12. $(8q^2 - 32q) \div 2q^2$

13. $(7t^5 + 14t^4 - 28t^3 + 35t^2) \div 7t^2$

14. $(6x^4 - 5x^3 + 6x^2) \div 2x^2$

15. $(21t^5 + 3t^4 - 11t^3) \div 7t^3$

16. $(n^2 - 5n + 4) \div (n - 4)$

17. $(y^2 - y + 2) \div (y + 2)$

18. $(3x^2 - 10x + 3) \div (x - 3)$

19. $(-4q^2 - 22q + 12) \div (2q + 1)$

20. $(5t^2 - 500) \div (t + 10)$

21. $(2w^3 + 3w - 15) \div (w - 1)$

22. $(3b^3 - 10b^2 + 4) \div (3b - 1)$

23. $(c^3 - c^2 - 1) \div (c - 1)$

Write an expression for the missing dimension in each figure.

24.

$\ell = \blacksquare$

$A = r^3 - 24r - 5$ $w = r - 5$

25.

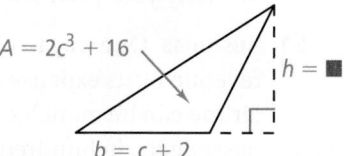

$A = 2c^3 + 16$ $h = \blacksquare$

$b = c + 2$

Divide.

See Problem 4.

26. $(49 + 16b + 2b^2) \div (2b + 4)$

27. $(4a^2 - 6 + 3a) \div (7 + 4a)$

28. $(39w + 14 + 3w^2) \div (9 + 3w)$

29. $(4t + 2t^2 - 9) \div (-6 + 2t)$

30. $(-13x + 6x^3 - 6 - x^2) \div (3x - 5)$

31. $(6 - q + 8q^3 - 4q^2) \div (2q - 2)$

32. $(6x^4 + 4x^3 - x^2) \div (6 + 2x)$

33. $(12c^3 + 11c^2 - 15c + 8) \div (-4 + 3c)$

34. $(7b + 16b^3) \div (-1 + 8b)$

35. $(4y + 9y^3 - 7) \div (-5 + 3y)$

B Apply

36. Open-Ended Write a binomial and a trinomial using the same variable. Divide the trinomial by the binomial.

37. Think About a Plan The area A of a trapezoid is $x^3 + 2x^2 - 2x - 3$. The lengths of its two bases b_1 and b_2 are x and $x^2 - 3$, respectively. What is an expression for the height h of the trapezoid? Write your answer in the form quotient $+ \frac{remainder}{divisor}$.
- What formula can you use to find the area of a trapezoid?
- How can you use the formula to write an expression for h?

Divide.

38. $(56a^2 + 4a - 12) \div (2a + 1)$

39. $(5t^4 - 10t^2 + 6) \div (t + 5)$

40. $(3k^3 - 0.9k^2 - 1.2k) \div 3k$

41. $(-7s + 6s^2 + 5) \div (2s + 3)$

42. $(64c^3 - 125) \div (5 - 4c)$

43. $(21 - 5r^4 - 10r^2 + 2r^6) \div (r^2 - 3)$

44. $(2t^4 - 2t^3 + 3t - 1) \div (2t^3 + 1)$

45. $(z^4 + z^2 - 2) \div (z + 3)$

46. $(-2z^3 - z + z^2 + 1) \div (z + 1)$

47. $(6m^3 + 3m + 70) \div (m + 4)$

48. Writing Suppose you divide a polynomial by a binomial. How do you know if the binomial is a factor of the polynomial?

49. Geometry The volume of the rectangular prism shown at the right is $m^3 + 8m^2 + 19m + 12$. What is the area of the shaded base of the prism?

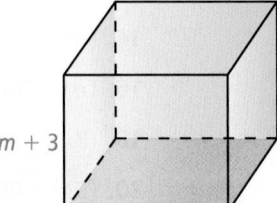

50. Look for a Pattern Find a pattern by dividing the polynomials.
  a. What is $(d^2 - d + 1) \div (d + 1)$?
  b. What is $(d^3 - d^2 + d - 1) \div (d + 1)$?
  c. What is $(d^4 - d^3 + d^2 - d + 1) \div (d + 1)$?
  d. What do you think would be the result of dividing $d^5 - d^4 + d^3 - d^2 + d - 1$ by $d + 1$?
  e. Verify your prediction by dividing the polynomials.

51. Business One way to measure a business's efficiency is by dividing the business's revenue by its expenses. The annual revenue, in millions of dollars, of a certain airline can be modeled by $200s^3 - s^2 + 400s + 1500$, where s is the number of passengers, in hundreds of thousands. The expenses, in millions of dollars, of the airline can be modeled by $200s + 300$. What is the airline's revenue divided by its expenses? Write your answer in the form quotient $+ \frac{remainder}{divisor}$.

52. Reasoning If $x + 3$ is a factor of $x^2 - x - k$, what is the value of k?

STEM 53. Physics Consider the formula for distance traveled, $d = rt$.
  a. Solve the formula for t.
  b. Use your answer from part (a). What is an expression for the time it takes to travel a distance of $t^3 - 6t^2 + 5t + 12$ miles at a rate of $t + 1$ miles per hour?

STEM 54. Packaging Three tennis balls with radius r are packed into a cylindrical can with radius r and height $6r + 1$. What fraction of the can is empty? Write your answer in the form quotient $+ \frac{remainder}{divisor}$.

55. Simplify $\frac{x^{16} - 1}{x - 1}$ by long division and by factoring. Which method do you prefer? Explain your answer.

Divide.

56. $(4a^3b^4 - 6a^2b^5 + 10a^2b^4) \div 2ab^2$

57. $(15x^2 + 7xy - 2y^2) \div (5x - y)$

58. $(90r^6 + 28r^5 + 45r^3 + 2r^4 + 5r^2) \div (9r + 1)$

59. $(2b^6 + 2b^5 - 4b^4 + b^3 + 8b^2 - 3) \div (b^3 + 2b^2 - 1)$

Standardized Test Prep

60. Which of the following is true for $(2x^2 + 4x + 2) \div 2x$?

I. The remainder is negative.

II. The dividend is in standard form.

III. The quotient is greater than the divisor for positive values of x.

    Ⓐ I only   Ⓑ II only   Ⓒ I and II   Ⓓ II and III

61. Which equation represents the line that passes through $(5, -8)$ and is parallel to the line at the right?

    Ⓕ $y = 2x + 2$ Ⓗ $y = -2x$

    Ⓖ $y + 2x = 2$ Ⓘ $y - 2x = 2$

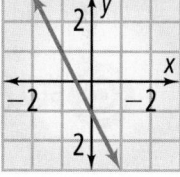

62. What are the factors of the expression $x^3 - 4x$?

    Ⓐ $x^3, -4x$ Ⓑ $x, x^2 - 4$ Ⓒ $x - 2, x + 2$ Ⓓ $x, x - 2, x + 2$

63. A theater has 18 rows of seats. Each row has 28 seats. Tickets cost $4 for adults and $2.50 for children. The Friday night show was sold out and the revenue from ticket sales was $1935. Barbara says that 445 adults were at the show. Is her statement reasonable? Explain your answer.

Mixed Review

Multiply or divide.   ◀ See Lesson 11-2.

64. $\dfrac{n^2 + 7n - 8}{n - 1} \cdot \dfrac{n^2 - 4}{n^2 + 6n - 16}$ **65.** $\dfrac{6t^2 - 30t}{2t^2 - 53t - 55} \cdot \dfrac{6t^2 + 35t + 11}{18t^2}$

66. $\dfrac{3c^2 - 4c - 32}{2c^2 + 17c + 35} \div \dfrac{c - 4}{c + 5}$ **67.** $\dfrac{x^2 + 9x + 20}{x^2 + 5x - 24} \div \dfrac{x^2 + 15x + 56}{x^2 + x - 12}$

Get Ready!   **To prepare for Lesson 11-4, do Exercises 68–71.**

Simplify each expression.   ◀ See p. 803.

68. $\dfrac{4}{9} + \dfrac{2}{9}$ **69.** $\dfrac{1}{4} - \dfrac{1}{3}$ **70.** $\dfrac{7x}{8} + \dfrac{x}{8}$ **71.** $\dfrac{7}{12y} - \dfrac{1}{12y}$

11-4 Adding and Subtracting Rational Expressions

© **Common Core State Standards**

A-APR.D.7 . . . add, subtract, multiply, and divide rational expressions.

MP 1, MP 2, MP 3, MP 4

Objective To add and subtract rational expressions

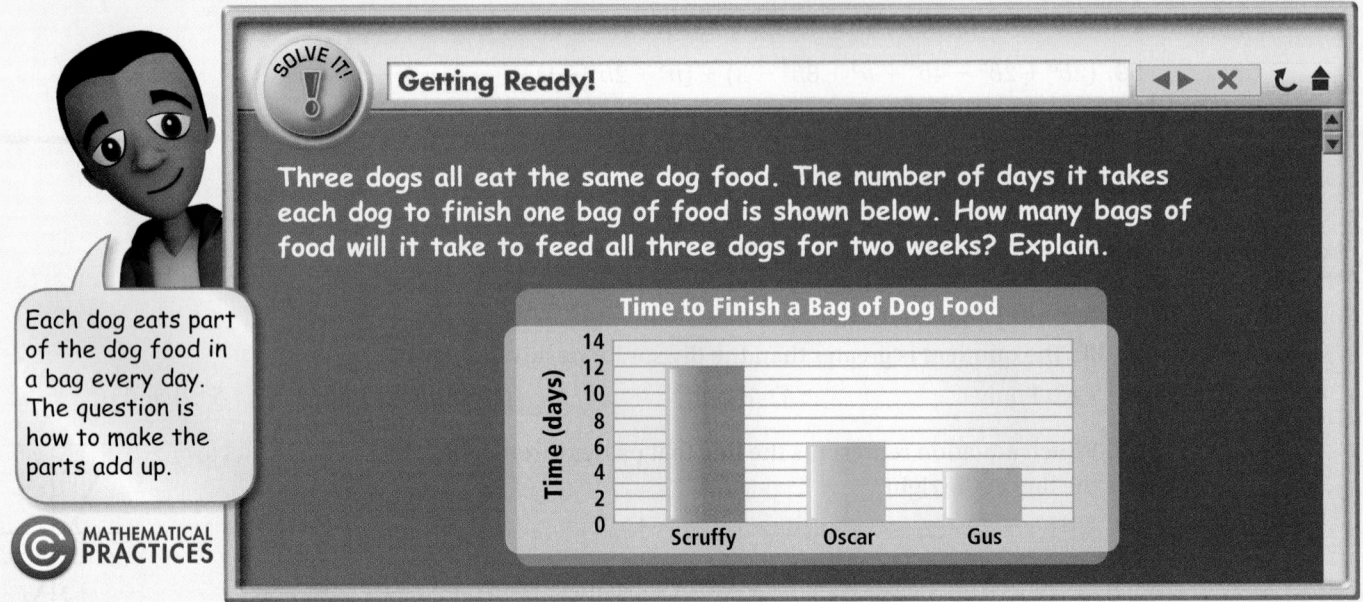

Getting Ready!

Three dogs all eat the same dog food. The number of days it takes each dog to finish one bag of food is shown below. How many bags of food will it take to feed all three dogs for two weeks? Explain.

Each dog eats part of the dog food in a bag every day. The question is how to make the parts add up.

© **MATHEMATICAL PRACTICES**

Essential Understanding You can use the same rules to add and subtract rational expressions that you use to add and subtract numerical fractions.

You can add the numerators of rational expressions with like denominators. If a, b, and c represent polynomials (with $c \neq 0$), then $\frac{a}{c} + \frac{b}{c} = \frac{a+b}{c}$.

 Problem 1 **Adding Expressions With Like Denominators**

What is the sum?

Think

Once you are comfortable adding rational expressions with like denominators, you can add the numerators and simplify all in one step.

A $\dfrac{4}{3y} + \dfrac{7}{3y}$

$\dfrac{4}{3y} + \dfrac{7}{3y} = \dfrac{4+7}{3y}$ Add the numerators.

$= \dfrac{11}{3y}$ Simplify the numerator.

B $\dfrac{3x}{x-2} + \dfrac{x}{x-2}$

$\dfrac{3x}{x-2} + \dfrac{x}{x-2} = \dfrac{3x+x}{x-2}$ Add the numerators.

$= \dfrac{4x}{x-2}$ Simplify the numerator.

 Got It? **1.** What is the sum $\dfrac{2a}{3a-4} + \dfrac{3a}{3a-4}$?

Similarly, you can subtract rational expressions with like denominators.

 Problem 2 Subtracting Expressions With Like Denominators

Think

Why put parentheses around $4x + 3$?
You want to subtract the entire numerator $4x + 3$, and parentheses are needed to indicate that. Without the parentheses, you would only be subtracting $4x$.

What is the difference $\dfrac{7x + 5}{3x^2 - x - 2} - \dfrac{4x + 3}{3x^2 - x - 2}$?

$$\dfrac{7x + 5}{3x^2 - x - 2} - \dfrac{4x + 3}{3x^2 - x - 2} = \dfrac{7x + 5 - (4x + 3)}{3x^2 - x - 2}$$ Subtract the numerators.

$$= \dfrac{7x + 5 - 4x - 3}{3x^2 - x - 2}$$ Distributive Property

$$= \dfrac{3x + 2}{3x^2 - x - 2}$$ Simplify the numerator.

$$= \dfrac{3x + 2^{\,1}}{{}_1(3x + 2)(x - 1)}$$ Factor the denominator. Divide out the common factor $3x + 2$.

$$= \dfrac{1}{x - 1}$$ Simplify.

 Got It? **2.** What is the difference?

a. $\dfrac{2}{z + 3} - \dfrac{7}{z + 3}$ b. $\dfrac{9n - 3}{10n - 4} - \dfrac{3n + 5}{10n - 4}$ c. $\dfrac{7q - 3}{q^2 - 4} - \dfrac{6q - 5}{q^2 - 4}$

To add or subtract rational expressions with different denominators, you can write the expressions with the least common denominator (LCD).

 Problem 3 Adding Expressions With Different Denominators

What is the sum $\dfrac{5}{6x} + \dfrac{3}{2x^2}$?

Step 1 Find the LCD of $\dfrac{5}{6x}$ and $\dfrac{3}{2x^2}$. First write the denominators $6x$ and $2x^2$ as products of prime factors. To form the LCD, list each factor the greatest number of times it appears in a denominator.

Think

Why is the LCD $6x^2$ instead of $6x$?
One of the denominators has two factors of x. So the LCD must also have two factors of x.

$6x = 2 \cdot 3 \cdot x$ Factor each denominator.

$2x^2 = 2 \cdot \quad x \cdot x$

$\text{LCD} = 2 \cdot 3 \cdot x \cdot x = 6x^2$ The LCD is the LCM of $6x$ and $2x^2$.

Step 2 Rewrite each rational expression using the LCD and then add.

$$\dfrac{5}{6x} + \dfrac{3}{2x^2} = \dfrac{5 \cdot x}{6x \cdot x} + \dfrac{3 \cdot 3}{2x^2 \cdot 3}$$ Rewrite each fraction using the LCD.

$$= \dfrac{5x}{6x^2} + \dfrac{9}{6x^2}$$ Simplify numerators and denominators.

$$= \dfrac{5x + 9}{6x^2}$$ Add the numerators.

 Got It? **3.** What is the sum $\dfrac{3}{7y^4} + \dfrac{2}{3y^2}$?

Problem 4 Subtracting Expressions With Different Denominators

What is the difference $\dfrac{3}{d-1} - \dfrac{2}{d+2}$?

Step 1 Find the LCD of $\dfrac{3}{d-1}$ and $\dfrac{2}{d+2}$.

Since there are no common factors, the LCD is $(d-1)(d+2)$.

Step 2 Rewrite each rational expression using the LCD and then subtract.

$$\dfrac{3}{d-1} - \dfrac{2}{d+2} = \dfrac{3(d+2)}{(d-1)(d+2)} - \dfrac{2(d-1)}{(d-1)(d+2)}$$ Rewrite each fraction using the LCD.

$$= \dfrac{3d+6}{(d-1)(d+2)} - \dfrac{2d-2}{(d-1)(d+2)}$$ Simplify each numerator.

$$= \dfrac{3d+6-(2d-2)}{(d-1)(d+2)}$$ Subtract the numerators.

$$= \dfrac{d+8}{(d-1)(d+2)}$$ Simplify the numerator.

Think

Should you multiply the denominator or leave it in factored form?
There might be common factors to divide out later. So leave the denominator in factored form.

Got It? **4.** What is the difference $\dfrac{c}{3c-1} - \dfrac{4}{c-2}$?

Problem 5 Using Rational Expressions

Gas Mileage A certain truck gets 25% better gas mileage when it holds no cargo than when it is fully loaded. Let m be the number of miles per gallon of gasoline the truck gets when it is fully loaded. The truck drops off a full load and returns empty. What is an expression for the number of gallons of gasoline the truck uses?

Gas mileage = 1.25m

Gas mileage = m

Think

How can unit analysis help you?
You can use unit analysis to verify that gallons of gasoline used equals distance traveled divided by miles per gallon.
$\dfrac{\text{mi}}{\text{mi/gal}} = \text{mi} \cdot \dfrac{\text{gal}}{\text{mi}} = \text{gal}$

Step 1 Write expressions for the amount of gasoline used on the outward trip and on the return trip.

Outward trip: $\text{gasoline used} = \dfrac{\text{distance traveled}}{\text{miles per gallon}} = \dfrac{80}{m}$

Return trip: $\text{gasoline used} = \dfrac{\text{distance traveled}}{\text{miles per gallon}} = \dfrac{80}{1.25m}$

80-mi trip outward

80-mi return trip

Step 2 Add the expressions to find the total amount of gasoline the truck uses.

$$\text{total gasoline used} = \dfrac{80}{m} + \dfrac{80}{1.25m}$$

$$= \dfrac{80(1.25)}{1.25m} + \dfrac{80}{1.25m}$$ Rewrite using the LCD, 1.25m.

$$= \dfrac{100}{1.25m} + \dfrac{80}{1.25m}$$ Simplify the first numerator.

$$= \dfrac{180}{1.25m}$$ Add the numerators.

$$= \dfrac{144}{m}$$ Simplify.

Got It? 5. a. A bicyclist rides 5 mi out and then rides back. His speed returning is reduced 20% because it is raining. Let r be his speed in miles per hour riding out. What is an expression that represents his total time in hours riding out and back?

b. Reasoning In Problem 5, suppose m represents the number of miles per gallon of gasoline the truck gets when it holds no cargo. What expression represents the number of miles per gallon of gasoline the truck gets when fully loaded? Explain.

Lesson Check

Do you know HOW?

Add or subtract.

1. $\dfrac{4}{x-7} + \dfrac{7}{x-7}$

2. $\dfrac{9}{2y+4} - \dfrac{5}{2y+4}$

3. $\dfrac{4}{6b^2} + \dfrac{5}{8b^3}$

4. A runner practices running 2 mi up a slope and 2 mi down. She runs down the slope 50% faster than she runs up it. Let r be the runner's speed, in miles per hour, when running up the slope. What expression represents the time she spends running?

Do you UNDERSTAND?

5. Writing Suppose your friend was absent today. How would you explain to your friend how to add and subtract rational expressions?

6. Compare and Contrast How is finding the LCD of two rational expressions similar to finding the LCD of two numerical fractions? How is it different?

7. Reasoning Your friend says she can always find a common denominator for two rational expressions by finding the product of the denominators.
a. Is your friend correct? Explain.
b. Will your friend's method always give you the LCD? Explain.

Practice and Problem-Solving Exercises

 **Practice**

Add or subtract.

See Problems 1 and 2.

8. $\dfrac{5}{2m} + \dfrac{4}{2m}$

9. $\dfrac{5}{c-5} + \dfrac{9}{c-5}$

10. $\dfrac{3}{b-3} - \dfrac{b}{b-3}$

11. $\dfrac{5c}{2c+7} + \dfrac{c-28}{2c+7}$

12. $\dfrac{1}{2-b} - \dfrac{4}{2-b}$

13. $\dfrac{n}{n^2+4n+4} + \dfrac{2}{n^2+4n+4}$

14. $\dfrac{2y+1}{y-1} - \dfrac{y+2}{y-1}$

15. $\dfrac{3n+2}{n+4} - \dfrac{n-6}{n+4}$

16. $\dfrac{2t}{2t^2-t-3} - \dfrac{3}{2t^2-t-3}$

Find the LCD of each pair of expressions.

See Problems 3 and 4.

17. $\dfrac{1}{2}; \dfrac{4}{x^2}$

18. $\dfrac{b}{6}; \dfrac{2b}{9}$

19. $\dfrac{1}{z}; \dfrac{3}{7z}$

20. $\dfrac{8}{5b}; \dfrac{12}{7b^3c}$

21. $\dfrac{3}{5}; \dfrac{x}{x+2}$

22. $\dfrac{2}{ab}; \dfrac{a-b}{b^2c}$

23. $\dfrac{3m}{m+n}; \dfrac{3n}{m-n}$

24. $\dfrac{1}{k}; \dfrac{3}{k^2-2}$

Add or subtract.

25. $\dfrac{7}{3a} + \dfrac{2}{5}$

26. $\dfrac{4}{x} - \dfrac{2}{3}$

27. $\dfrac{27}{n^3} - \dfrac{9}{7n^2}$

28. $\dfrac{6}{5x^8} + \dfrac{4}{3x^6}$

29. $\dfrac{a}{a+3} - \dfrac{4}{a+5}$

30. $\dfrac{9}{m+2} + \dfrac{8}{m-7}$

31. $\dfrac{a}{a+3} + \dfrac{a+5}{4}$

32. $\dfrac{5}{t^2} - \dfrac{4}{t+1}$

33. Exercise Jane walks one mile from her house to her grandparents' house. Then she returns home, walking with her grandfather. Her return rate is 70% of her rate walking alone. Let r represent her rate walking alone.

   a. Write an expression for the amount of time Jane spends walking.

   b. Simplify your expression.

   c. Suppose Jane's rate walking alone is 3 mi/h. About how much time does she spend walking?

 **See Problem 5.**

 **Apply**

ⓒ **34. Error Analysis** A student added two rational expressions as shown. What error did the student make?

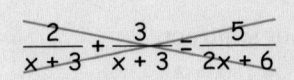

ⓒ **35. Writing** When you use the LCD to add or subtract rational expressions, will the answer always be in simplest form if you use the LCD? Explain.

ⓒ **36. Open-Ended** Write two rational expressions with different denominators. Find the LCD and add the two expressions.

Add or subtract.

37. $\dfrac{y^2 + 2y - 1}{3y + 1} - \dfrac{2y^2 - 3}{3y + 1}$

38. $\dfrac{h^2 + 1}{2t^2 - 7} + \dfrac{h}{2t^2 - 7}$

39. $\dfrac{r - 5}{9 + p^3} - \dfrac{2k + 1}{9 + p^3}$

40. $\dfrac{2 - x}{xy^2z} - \dfrac{5 + z}{xy^2z}$

41. $9 + \dfrac{x - 3}{x + 2}$

42. $\dfrac{t}{2t - 3} - 11$

ⓒ **43. Think About a Plan** The groundspeed for jet traffic from Los Angeles to New York City can be about 100 mi/h faster than the groundspeed from New York City to Los Angeles. This difference is due to a strong westerly wind at high altitudes. If r is a jet's groundspeed from New York City to Los Angeles, write and simplify an expression for the round-trip air time. The two cities are about 2500 mi apart.

   • Can you write an expression for the air time from New York City to Los Angeles?

   • In terms of r, what is the jet's groundspeed from Los Angeles to New York City? Can you use this speed to write an expression for the air time from Los Angeles to New York City?

ⓒ **44. Rowing** A rowing team practices rowing 2 mi upstream and 2 mi downstream. The team can row downstream 25% faster than they can row upstream.

   a. Let u represent the team's rate rowing upstream. Write and simplify an expression involving u for the total amount of time they spend rowing.

   b. Let d represent the team's rate rowing downstream. Write and simplify an expression involving d for the total amount of time they spend rowing.

   c. Reasoning Do the expressions you wrote in parts (a) and (b) represent the same time? Explain.

For $f(x) = 8x$, $g(x) = \frac{1}{x}$, and $h(x) = \frac{4}{x-5}$, perform the indicated operation.

Example $f(x) \div g(x) = 8x \div \frac{1}{x} = 8x \cdot \frac{x}{1} = 8x^2$

45. $f(x) + g(x)$ **46.** $f(x) \cdot g(x)$ **47.** $g(x) - h(x)$ **48.** $h(x) \div f(x)$

 **Challenge**   Simplify each complex fraction.

49. $\dfrac{3 + \frac{x}{2}}{2 + \frac{x}{3}}$ **50.** $\dfrac{x + y}{1 + \frac{x}{y}}$ **51.** $\dfrac{-4}{\frac{3}{x} + y}$

52. $\dfrac{\frac{1}{x} - \frac{4}{x}}{\frac{3}{y} + \frac{5}{y}}$ **53.** $\dfrac{\frac{3}{x} + \frac{4}{y}}{\frac{2}{x} - \frac{3}{y}}$ **54.** $\dfrac{\frac{7}{c+1} + 4}{3 - \frac{2}{c+1}}$

 Apply What You've Learned

MATHEMATICAL
PRACTICES
MP 2

Look back at the diagram of the lunch box on page 663. In part (d) of the Apply What You've Learned in Lesson 11-1, you found an expression in terms of x for the surface area of the lunch box.

  a. What is the least common denominator for the two terms of your expression for the surface area of the lunch box?

  b. Write the expression for the surface area of the lunch box as a single rational expression.

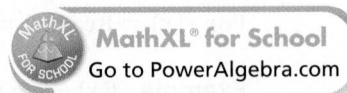
Do you know HOW?

Simplify each expression. State any excluded values.

1. $\dfrac{6x^2 - 24}{x + 2}$

2. $\dfrac{3c + 9}{3c - 9}$

3. $\dfrac{k - 2}{k^2 + 2k - 8}$

4. $\dfrac{2x^2 + 13x + 15}{2x + 10}$

5. $\dfrac{9 - x^2}{x^2 + x - 12}$

6. **Geometry** The height of a rectangular prism is 3 more than twice its width w. The volume of the prism is $2w^3 + 7w^2 + 6w$. Write a simplified expression for the length of the prism.

Multiply or divide.

7. $\dfrac{4}{y^3} \cdot \dfrac{-3}{5y}$

8. $\dfrac{z - 3}{3z} \cdot \dfrac{z + 8}{z + 2}$

9. $\dfrac{x^2 - 4}{x + 3} \cdot \dfrac{x^2 + 7x + 12}{x - 2}$

10. $\dfrac{z + 5}{z} \div \dfrac{3z + 15}{4z}$

11. $\dfrac{2a - 1}{a - 3} \div (a^2 - a - 6)$

12. $\dfrac{4d^2 - 3d}{7d} \div (4d^2 + d - 3)$

13. $(6x^3 - 4x^2 + 2x) \div 4x^2$

14. What is the simplified form of $\dfrac{\frac{1}{x + 5}}{\frac{3x}{x^2 - 25}}$?

15. The length of a rectangle is $4x + 1$ and the area is $12x^3 + 23x^2 + 13x + 2$. What is an expression for the width?

Add or subtract.

16. $\dfrac{3}{8x} + \dfrac{5}{8x}$

17. $\dfrac{5y}{y + 3} - \dfrac{7y}{y + 3}$

18. $\dfrac{3}{5x^2} + \dfrac{5}{2x}$

19. $\dfrac{4}{t - 3} - \dfrac{1}{t - 2}$

20. $\dfrac{2x}{x - 5} + \dfrac{9}{x + 4}$

Do you UNDERSTAND?

21. **Reasoning** The expression $\dfrac{p}{x^2 + x - 12}$ simplifies to $\dfrac{x + 5}{x - 3}$. Write the expression p represents.

22. **Error Analysis** Your friend says that the first step in simplifying $\dfrac{x - 3}{x + 4} \cdot \dfrac{x}{3 - x}$ is to divide out the common factors $x - 3$ and $3 - x$.
    a. Explain your friend's error.
    b. What is a possible correct first step?

23. **Writing** A student's first step in finding the product $\dfrac{7}{x} \cdot x^3$ was to rewrite the expression as $\dfrac{7}{x} \cdot \dfrac{x^3}{1}$. Why do you think the student did this?

24. **Compare and Contrast** When you are dividing a polynomial by a monomial, you can multiply by the reciprocal or use long division. How are these two methods the same? How are they different? Which method do you prefer? Explain your answer.

25. **Reasoning** You are dividing a polynomial in one variable with a degree of 5 by a monomial in the same variable with a degree of 2. Would you expect the quotient to have a degree greater than or less than 5? Explain your answer.

11-5 Solving Rational Equations

Common Core State Standards

A-CED.A.1 Create equations . . . in one variable and use them to solve problems. *Include equations arising from . . . simple rational . . . functions.* **Also A-REI.A.2**

MP 1, MP 2, MP 3, MP 4

Objective To solve rational equations and proportions

MATHEMATICAL PRACTICES

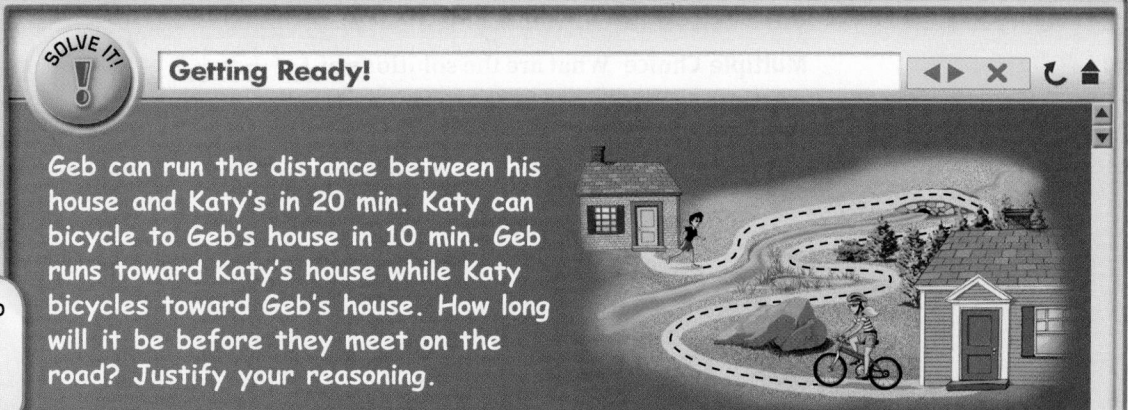

SOLVE IT!

Getting Ready!

Geb can run the distance between his house and Katy's in 20 min. Katy can bicycle to Geb's house in 10 min. Geb runs toward Katy's house while Katy bicycles toward Geb's house. How long will it be before they meet on the road? Justify your reasoning.

A diagram can help you understand this situation. Use a straight path.

A **rational equation** is an equation that contains one or more rational expressions.

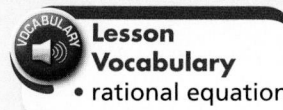
Lesson Vocabulary
• rational equation

Essential Understanding You can solve a rational equation by first multiplying each side of the equation by the LCD. When each side of a rational equation is a single rational expression, you can solve the equation using the Cross Products Property.

Problem 1 Solving Equations With Rational Expressions

Plan

Have you seen an equation like this before?
Yes. In Lesson 2-3, you solved equations that contained fractions. As you did there, you can clear the fractions from the equation by multiplying by a common denominator.

What is the solution of $\frac{5}{12} - \frac{1}{2x} = \frac{1}{3x}$? Check the solution.

$$\frac{5}{12} - \frac{1}{2x} = \frac{1}{3x}$$ The denominators are 12, 2x, and 3x. The LCD is 12x.

$$12x\left(\frac{5}{12} - \frac{1}{2x}\right) = 12x\left(\frac{1}{3x}\right)$$ Multiply each side by 12x.

$$12^1x\left(\frac{5}{{}_112}\right) - 12x^6\left(\frac{1}{{}_12x}\right) = 12x^4\left(\frac{1}{{}_13x}\right)$$ Distributive Property

$$5x - 6 = 4$$ Simplify.

$$5x = 10$$ Add 6 to each side.

$$x = 2$$ Divide each side by 5.

Check $\frac{5}{12} - \frac{1}{2(2)} \stackrel{?}{=} \frac{1}{3(2)}$ See if $x = 2$ makes $\frac{5}{12} - \frac{1}{2x} = \frac{1}{3x}$ true.

$$\frac{1}{6} = \frac{1}{6} \ ✔$$

Got It? 1. What is the solution of each equation? Check your solution.

  a. $\frac{1}{3} + \frac{3}{x} = \frac{2}{x}$

  b. $\frac{4}{7x} + \frac{1}{3} = \frac{7}{3x}$

To solve some rational equations, you need to factor a quadratic expression.

 Problem 2 Solving by Factoring

Multiple Choice What are the solutions of $1 - \frac{1}{x} = \frac{12}{x^2}$?

  (A) $-11, 12$ (B) $-4, 3$ (C) $-3, 4$ (D) $12, 13$

$$1 - \frac{1}{x} = \frac{12}{x^2}$$ The denominators are x and x^2. The LCD is x^2.

$$x^2\left(1 - \frac{1}{x}\right) = x^2\left(\frac{12}{x^2}\right)$$ Multiply each side by x^2.

$$x^2(1) - {}^{x}x^2\left(\frac{1}{x_1}\right) = {}^{1}x^2\left(\frac{12}{x^2_{1}}\right)$$ Distributive Property

$$x^2 - x = 12$$ Simplify.

$$x^2 - x - 12 = 0$$ Collect terms on one side.

$$(x - 4)(x + 3) = 0$$ Factor the quadratic expression.

$$x - 4 = 0 \text{ or } x + 3 = 0$$ Zero-Product Property

$$x = 4 \text{ or } \quad x = -3$$ Solve for x.

Think

Is there a different way to solve this equation?
Yes. Because it's a quadratic equation, you can also solve it by using the quadratic formula, by completing the square, or by graphing.

Check Determine whether 4 and -3 both make $1 - \frac{1}{x} = \frac{12}{x^2}$ a true statement.

When $x = 4$:

$$1 - \frac{1}{x} = \frac{12}{x^2}$$

$$1 - \frac{1}{4} \overset{?}{=} \frac{12}{(4)^2}$$

$$1 - \frac{1}{4} \overset{?}{=} \frac{12}{16}$$

$$\frac{3}{4} = \frac{3}{4} ✔$$

When $x = -3$:

$$1 - \frac{1}{x} = \frac{12}{x^2}$$

$$1 - \frac{1}{(-3)} \overset{?}{=} \frac{12}{(-3)^2}$$

$$1 + \frac{1}{3} \overset{?}{=} \frac{12}{9}$$

$$\frac{4}{3} = \frac{4}{3} ✔$$

The solutions are 4 and -3. The correct answer is C.

  Got It? 2. What are the solutions of each equation in parts (a) and (b)? Check your solutions.

  a. $\frac{5}{y} = \frac{6}{y^2} - 6$

  b. $d + 6 = \frac{d + 11}{d + 3}$

  c. Reasoning How can you tell that the rational equation $\frac{2}{x^2} = -1$ has no solutions just by looking at the equation?

To solve a work problem, find the fraction of the job each person does in one unit of time (for example, in 1 h or 1 min). The sum of the fractions for everyone working is the fraction of the job completed in one unit of time.

Problem 3 Solving a Work Problem

Painting Amy can paint a loft apartment in 7 h. Jeremy can paint a loft apartment of the same size in 9 h. If they work together, how long will it take them to paint a third loft apartment of the same size?

Know
- Amy's painting time is 7 h.
- Jeremy's painting time is 9 h.

Need
Amy and Jeremy's combined painting time

Plan
Find what fraction of a loft each person can paint in 1 h. Then write and solve a rational equation.

Relate   fraction of loft Amy can paint in 1 h $+$ fraction of loft Jeremy can paint in 1 h $=$ fraction of loft painted in 1 h

Define   Let t = the painting time, in hours, if Amy and Jeremy work together.

Think

Where have you seen a problem like this before?
In Problem 1 of this lesson, you solved a similar equation containing rational expressions.

Write $\dfrac{1}{7}$ $+$ $\dfrac{1}{9}$ $=$ $\dfrac{1}{t}$

$63t\left(\dfrac{1}{7} + \dfrac{1}{9}\right) = 63t\left(\dfrac{1}{t}\right)$ Multiply each side by the LCD, 63t.

$9t + 7t = 63$ Distributive Property

$16t = 63$ Simplify.

$t = \dfrac{63}{16}$, or $3\dfrac{15}{16}$ Divide each side by 16.

It will take Amy and Jeremy about 4 h to paint the loft apartment together.

Got It? 3. One hose can fill a pool in 12 h. Another hose can fill the same pool in 8 h. How long will it take for both hoses to fill the pool together?

Some rational equations are proportions. You can solve them by using the Cross Products Property.

 Problem 4 Solving a Rational Proportion

Think

Can you use the LCD to solve this equation?
Yes, but when each side of a rational equation is a single rational expression, using cross products is often easier. Otherwise, you have to multiply each side of the equation by the LCD, $(x + 2)(x + 1)$.

What is the solution of $\frac{4}{x + 2} = \frac{3}{x + 1}$**?**

$$\frac{4}{x + 2} = \frac{3}{x + 1}$$

$4(x + 1) = 3(x + 2)$ Cross Products Property

$4x + 4 = 3x + 6$ Distributive Property

$x = 2$ Solve for x.

Check $\frac{4}{2 + 2} \overset{?}{=} \frac{3}{2 + 1}$

$1 = 1$ ✔

Got It? **4.** Find the solution(s) of each equation. Check your solutions.

a. $\frac{3}{b + 2} = \frac{5}{b - 2}$ **b.** $\frac{c}{3} = \frac{7}{c - 4}$

The process of solving a rational equation may give a solution that is extraneous because it makes a denominator in the original equation equal 0. An extraneous solution is a solution of an equation that is derived from the original equation, but is not a solution of the original equation itself. So you must check your solutions.

 Problem 5 Checking to Find an Extraneous Solution

Think

What extraneous solutions are possible?
Since $\frac{6}{x + 5}$ and $\frac{x + 3}{x + 5}$ are undefined when $x = -5$, a possible extraneous solution is -5.

What is the solution of $\frac{6}{x + 5} = \frac{x + 3}{x + 5}$**?**

$$\frac{6}{x + 5} = \frac{x + 3}{x + 5}$$

$6(x + 5) = (x + 3)(x + 5)$ Cross Products Property

$6x + 30 = x^2 + 8x + 15$ Simplify each side of the equation.

$0 = x^2 + 2x - 15$ Collect terms on one side.

$0 = (x - 3)(x + 5)$ Factor.

$x - 3 = 0$ or $x + 5 = 0$ Zero-Product Property

$x = 3$ or $x = -5$ Solve for x.

Check $\frac{6}{3 + 5} \overset{?}{=} \frac{3 + 3}{3 + 5}$ $\frac{6}{-5 + 5} \overset{?}{=} \frac{-5 + 3}{-5 + 5}$

$\frac{6}{8} = \frac{6}{8}$ ✔ $\frac{6}{0} = \frac{-2}{0}$ ✗   Undefined!

The equation has one solution, 3.

Got It? **5.** What is the solution of $\frac{x - 4}{x^2 - 4} = \frac{-2}{x - 2}$? Check your solution.

Lesson Check

Do you know HOW?

Solve each equation. Check your solutions.

1. $\frac{1}{2x} + \frac{3}{10} = \frac{1}{5x}$

2. $\frac{5}{x^2} = \frac{6}{x} - 1$

3. $\frac{-2}{x+2} = \frac{x+4}{x^2-4}$

4. Sarah picks a bushel of apples in 45 min. Andy picks a bushel of apples in 75 min. How long will it take them to pick a bushel together?

Do you UNDERSTAND?

5. Vocabulary How is an extraneous solution of a rational equation similar to an excluded value of a rational expression? How is it different?

6. Open-Ended Write a rational equation that has one solution and one extraneous solution.

7. Error Analysis In the work shown at the right, what error did the student make in solving the rational equation?

$$1 + \frac{1}{m} = \frac{1}{5}$$
$$\frac{2}{m} = \frac{1}{5}$$
$$m = 10$$

Practice and Problem-Solving Exercises

 **Practice**

Solve each equation. Check your solutions.

See Problems 1 and 2.

8. $\frac{1}{2} + \frac{2}{x} = \frac{1}{x}$

9. $5 + \frac{2}{p} = \frac{17}{p}$

10. $\frac{3}{a} - \frac{5}{a} = 2$

11. $y - \frac{6}{y} = 5$

12. $\frac{5}{2s} + \frac{3}{4} = \frac{9}{4s}$

13. $7 + \frac{3}{x} = \frac{7}{x} + 9$

14. $\frac{2}{c-2} = 2 - \frac{4}{c}$

15. $\frac{5}{3p} + \frac{2}{3} = \frac{5+p}{2p}$

16. $\frac{8}{x+3} = \frac{1}{x} + 1$

17. $\frac{1}{t-2} = \frac{t}{8}$

18. $\frac{v+2}{v} + \frac{4}{3v} = 11$

19. $\frac{4}{3(c+4)} + 1 = \frac{2c}{c+4}$

20. $\frac{3+a}{2a} = \frac{1}{3} + \frac{5}{6a}$

21. $\frac{a}{a+3} = \frac{2a}{a-3} - 1$

22. $\frac{z}{z+2} - \frac{1}{z} = 1$

23. Gardening Marian can weed a garden in 3 h. Robin can weed the same garden in 4 h. If they work together, how long will the weeding take them?

See Problem 3.

24. Trucking David can unload a delivery truck in 20 min. Allie can unload the same delivery truck in 35 min. If they work together, how long will the unloading take?

Solve each equation. Check your solutions. If there is no solution, write *no solution*.

See Problems 4 and 5.

25. $\frac{5}{x+1} = \frac{x+2}{x+1}$

26. $\frac{4}{c+4} = \frac{c}{c+25}$

27. $\frac{3}{m-1} = \frac{2m}{m+4}$

28. $\frac{2x+4}{x-3} = \frac{3x}{x-3}$

29. $\frac{30}{x+3} = \frac{30}{x-3}$

30. $\frac{x+2}{x+4} = \frac{x-2}{x-1}$

 **Apply**

31. Writing How could you use cross products to solve $\frac{1}{x-2} = \frac{2x-6}{x+6} + 1$?

32. Open-Ended Write a rational equation that has 5 as a solution.

Solve each equation. Check your solutions.

33. $\dfrac{2r}{r-4} - 2 = \dfrac{4}{r+5}$

34. $\dfrac{r+1}{r-1} = \dfrac{r}{3} + \dfrac{2}{r-1}$

35. $\dfrac{3}{s-1} + 1 = \dfrac{12}{s^2-1}$

36. $\dfrac{d}{d+2} - \dfrac{2}{2-d} = \dfrac{d+6}{d^2-4}$

37. $\dfrac{s}{3s+2} + \dfrac{s+3}{2s-4} = \dfrac{-2s}{3s^2-4s-4}$

38. $\dfrac{u+1}{u+2} = \dfrac{-1}{u-3} + \dfrac{u-1}{u^2-u-6}$

ⓒ **39. Think About a Plan** Two pipes fill a storage tank with water in 9 h. The smaller pipe takes three times as long to fill the tank as the larger pipe. How long would it take the larger pipe to fill the tank alone?
- What variable should you define for this situation?
- In terms of your variable, what fraction of the tank is filled in 1 h by the larger pipe alone? By the smaller pipe alone?

40. Running You take 94 min to complete a 10-mi race. Your average speed during the first half of the race is 2 mi/h greater than your average speed during the second half. What is your average speed during the first half of the race?

41. a. Graphing Calculator Write two functions using the expressions on the two sides of the equation $\dfrac{6}{x^2} + 1 = \dfrac{(x+7)^2}{6}$. Graph the functions.
b. What are the coordinates of the points of intersection?
ⓒ **c. Reasoning** Are the x-coordinates of the points of intersection solutions of the equation? Explain.

STEM **Electricity** Two lamps can be connected to a battery in a circuit in series or in parallel. You can calculate the total resistance R_T in a circuit if you know the resistance in each lamp. Resistance is measured in ohms (Ω). For a circuit connected in series, $R_T = R_1 + R_2$. For a circuit connected in parallel, $\dfrac{1}{R_T} = \dfrac{1}{R_1} + \dfrac{1}{R_2}$.

42. The lamps are connected in series. $R_T = 20\ \Omega$. Find R_2.

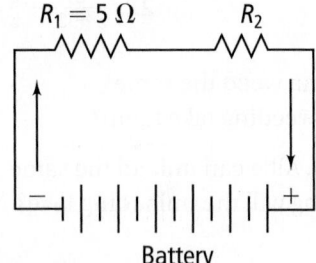

43. The lamps are connected in parallel. $R_T = 12\ \Omega$. Find R_2.

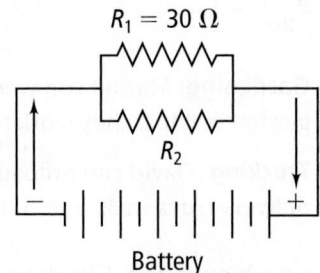

44. Travel A plane flies 450 mi/h. It can travel 980 mi with a tailwind in the same amount of time as it travels 820 mi against the wind. Solve the equation $\dfrac{980}{450+s} = \dfrac{820}{450-s}$ to find the speed s of the wind.

ⓒ **Challenge**

45. Window Washing Sumi can wash the windows of an office building in $\frac{3}{4}$ the time it takes her apprentice. One day they worked on a building together for 2 h 16 min, and then Sumi continued alone. It took her 4 h 32 min more to complete the job. How long would it take her apprentice to wash all the windows alone?

Solve each equation. Check your answers.

46. $\dfrac{x-6}{x+3} + \dfrac{2x}{x-3} = \dfrac{4x+3}{x+3}$

47. $\dfrac{n}{n-2} + \dfrac{n}{n+2} = \dfrac{n}{n^2-4}$

48. $\dfrac{2}{r} + \dfrac{1}{r^2} + \dfrac{r^2+r}{r^3} = \dfrac{1}{r}$

49. $\dfrac{3}{t} - \dfrac{t^2-2t}{t^3} = \dfrac{4}{t^2}$

50. Painting To paint a room, it takes Mike 75 min, Joan 60 min, and Kyle 80 min when each person works alone. If all three work together, how long will the painting take?

STEM 51. Chemistry A chemist has one solution that is 80% acid and a second solution that is 30% acid. How many liters of each solution will the chemist need in order to make 50 L of a solution that is 62% acid?

Standardized Test Prep

SAT/ACT

52. Which inequality contains both solutions of $x = \dfrac{1}{2} + \dfrac{3}{x}$?

(A) $-1 < x < 3$ (B) $-2 < x \le 2$ (C) $-2 \le x < 0$ (D) $-3 \le x \le -1$

53. Which expression is equivalent to $\dfrac{\frac{4}{x+3}}{\frac{2x-6}{x^2-9}}$?

(F) 2 (G) -2 (H) $\dfrac{8}{x^2+6x+9}$ (I) $\dfrac{2x+6}{x-3}$

54. Which is the least common denominator of $\dfrac{1}{x}$, $\dfrac{x}{3}$, and $\dfrac{3}{2x}$?

(A) $2x$ (B) $3x$ (C) $6x$ (D) $6x^2$

Short Response

55. A grizzly bear can run as fast as 30 mi/h. At that rate, how many feet would a grizzly bear travel in 1 s? Explain your answer.

Mixed Review

Add or subtract.   ◀ **See Lesson 11-4.**

56. $\dfrac{5}{x^2y^2z} - \dfrac{8}{x^2y^2z}$

57. $\dfrac{3h^2}{2t^2-8} + \dfrac{h}{t-2}$

58. $\dfrac{k-11}{k^2+6k-40} - \dfrac{5}{k-4}$

Graph each function, either by translating the graph of $y = \sqrt{x}$ or by making a table of values.   ◀ **See Lesson 10-5.**

59. $f(x) = -2\sqrt{x}$ **60.** $y = \sqrt{x+7}$ **61.** $f(x) = \sqrt{x-2} - 8$ **62.** $y = \sqrt{0.25x}$

Get Ready! **To prepare for Lesson 11-6, do Exercises 63–66.**

Determine whether each equation represents a direct variation. If it does, find the constant of variation.   ◀ **See Lesson 5-2.**

63. $y - 3x = 0$ **64.** $y + 7 = x$ **65.** $x + 4y + 1 = 1$ **66.** $8x = 3y$

11-6 Inverse Variation

 Common Core State Standards

F-IF.B.5 Relate the domain of a function to its graph and, where applicable, to the quantitative relationship it describes . . . **Also A-CED.A.2**

MP 1, MP 2, MP 3, MP 4

Objectives To write and graph equations for inverse variations
To compare direct and inverse variations

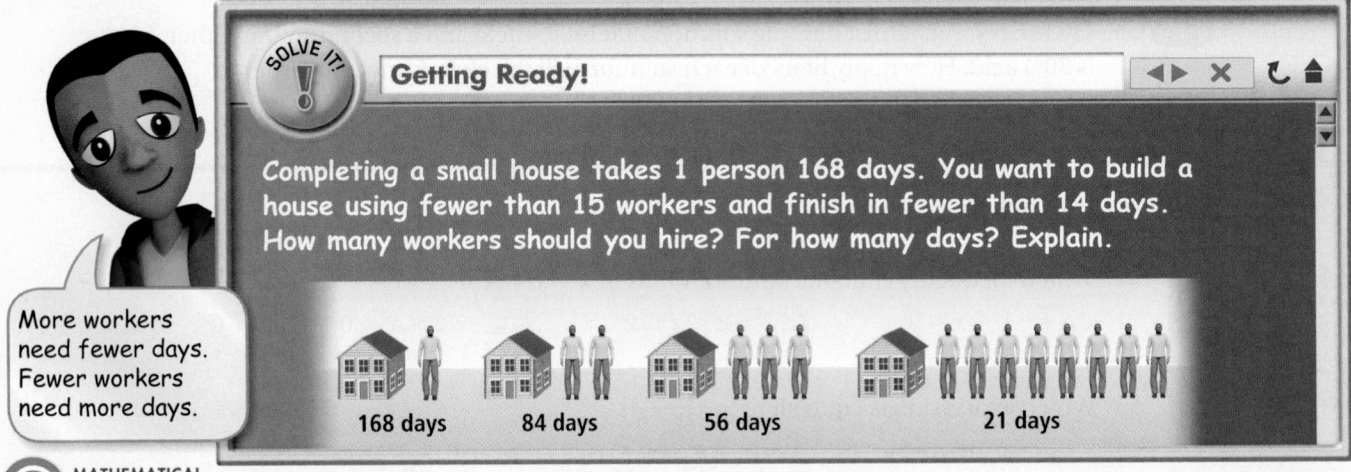

SOLVE IT!

Getting Ready!

Completing a small house takes 1 person 168 days. You want to build a house using fewer than 15 workers and finish in fewer than 14 days. How many workers should you hire? For how many days? Explain.

168 days   84 days   56 days   21 days

More workers need fewer days. Fewer workers need more days.

MATHEMATICAL PRACTICES

In the Solve It, the number of construction days decreases as the number of workers increases. The product of crew size and construction days is constant.

Essential Understanding If the product of two variables is a nonzero constant, then the variables form an inverse variation.

**Lesson Vocabulary**
• inverse variation
• constant of variation for an inverse variation

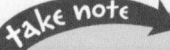 **take note**

Key Concept   Inverse Variation

An equation of the form $xy = k$ or $y = \frac{k}{x}$, where $k \neq 0$, is an **inverse variation.**

The **constant of variation for an inverse variation** is k, the product $x \cdot y$ for an ordered pair (x, y) that satisfies the inverse variation.

© **Problem 1** **Writing an Equation Given a Point**

Suppose y varies inversely with x, and $y = 8$ when $x = 3$. What is an equation for the inverse variation?

$xy = k$	Use the general form of an inverse variation.
$3(8) = k$	Substitute 3 for x and 8 for y.
$24 = k$	Simplify.
$xy = 24$	Write an equation. Substitute 24 for k in $xy = k$.

Think

Make sure you don't stop at $24 = k$. To write the inverse variation equation, you have to substitute 24 for k in $xy = k$.

An equation for the inverse variation is $xy = 24$, or $y = \frac{24}{x}$.

Got It? **1.** Suppose y varies inversely with x, and $y = 9$ when $x = 6$. What is an equation for the inverse variation?

 **Problem 2** Using Inverse Variation (STEM)   GRIDDED RESPONSE

Physics The weight needed to balance a lever varies inversely with the distance from the fulcrum to the weight. How far away from the fulcrum should the person sit to balance the lever?

160 lb

 1000 lb

x

7 ft

Relate   The 1000-lb elephant is 7 ft from the fulcrum. The 160-lb person is x ft from the fulcrum. Weight and distance vary inversely.

Define   Let weight$_1$ = 1000 lb. Let distance$_1$ = 7 ft. Let weight$_2$ = 160 lb. Let distance$_2$ = x ft.

Write   weight$_1$ · distance$_1$ = weight$_2$ · distance$_2$

$\qquad$ 1000 · 7 = 160 · x $\qquad$ Substitute.

$\qquad\qquad$ $7000 = 160x$ $\qquad$ Simplify.

$\qquad\qquad\qquad$ $43.75 = x$ $\qquad$ Divide each side by 160.

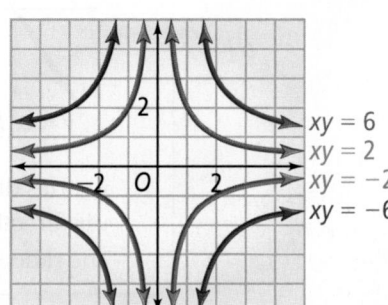

The person should sit 43.75 ft from the fulcrum to balance the lever.

Think

Is your answer reasonable?
The heavier object must be closer to the fulcrum to balance the lever. Since the elephant weighs more than the person, the person should sit more than 7 ft from the fulcrum.

 Got It? **2.** A 120-lb weight is placed on a lever, 5 ft from the fulcrum. How far from the fulcrum should an 80-lb weight be placed to balance the lever?

Several graphs of inverse variations $xy = k$ are shown at the right. Notice that each graph has two unconnected parts. When $k > 0$, the graph lies in the first and third quadrants. When $k < 0$, the graph lies in the second and fourth quadrants. Since k is a nonzero constant, $xy \neq 0$. So neither x nor y can equal 0.

As it moves away from the origin, the graph of an inverse variation equation approaches the x-axis and the y-axis without actually intersecting them.

$xy = 6$
$xy = 2$
$xy = -2$
$xy = -6$

You can graph an inverse variation $xy = k$ or $y = \frac{k}{x}$ by making a table of values and plotting points.

Problem 3 **Graphing an Inverse Variation**

What is the graph of $y = \frac{8}{x}$?

Step 1 Make a table of values.

Plan

How do you know which x-values to choose?
Choose positive and negative values. Choose x-values that divide easily into 8 to get ordered pairs that are easy to graph.

x	−8	−4	−2	−1	0	1	2	4	8
y	−1	−2	−4	−8	undefined	8	4	2	1

When $x = 0$, there is no y-value.

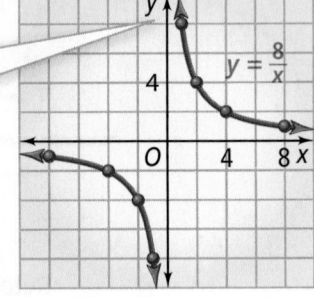

Step 2 Plot the points from the table. Connect the points in Quadrant I with a smooth curve. Do the same for the points in Quadrant III.

Got It? **3. a.** What is the graph of $y = \frac{-8}{x}$?
    b. Reasoning For $k > 0$, how are the graphs of $y = \frac{k}{x}$ and $y = \frac{-k}{x}$ alike? How are they different?

Recall that a direct variation is an equation of the form $y = kx$. The following summary will help you recognize and use direct and inverse variations.

take note

Concept Summary   Direct and Inverse Variations

Direct Variation

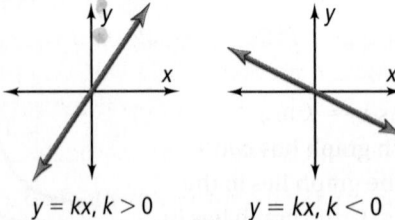

$y = kx, k > 0$ $y = kx, k < 0$

y varies directly with x.
y is directly proportional to x.
The ratio $\frac{y}{x}$ is constant.

Inverse Variation

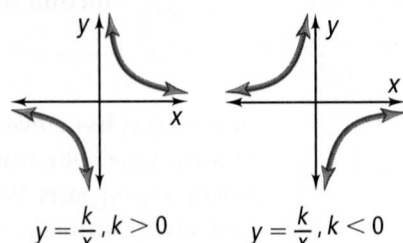

$y = \frac{k}{x}, k > 0$ $y = \frac{k}{x}, k < 0$

y varies inversely with x.
y is inversely proportional to x.
The product xy is constant.

Problem 4 Determining Direct or Inverse Variation

Do the data in each table represent a *direct variation* or an *inverse variation*? For each table, write an equation to model the data.

A

x	y
3	−15
4	−20
5	−25

The values of y seem to vary directly with the values of x. Check each ratio $\frac{y}{x}$.

$$\frac{-15}{3} = -5 \qquad \frac{-20}{4} = -5 \qquad \frac{-25}{5} = -5$$

The ratio $\frac{y}{x}$ is the same for all data pairs. So this is a direct variation, and $k = -5$.

An equation is $y = -5x$.

Think

How can you check the reasonableness of your answers?
Substitute each x-value from the table into the equation and find the corresponding value of y. The y-values given by the equation should match the y-values in the table.

B

x	y
2	9
4	4.5
6	3

The values of y seem to vary inversely with the values of x. Check each product xy.

$$2(9) = 18 \qquad 4(4.5) = 18 \qquad 6(3) = 18$$

The product xy is the same for all data pairs. So this is an inverse variation, and $k = 18$.

An equation is $xy = 18$, or $y = \frac{18}{x}$.

 Got It? **4.** Do the data in each table represent a *direct variation* or an *inverse variation*? For each table, write an equation to model the data.

a.

x	y
4	−12
6	−18
8	−24

b.

x	y
4	−12
6	−8
8	−6

Problem 5 Identifying Direct or Inverse Variation

Does each situation represent a *direct variation* or an *inverse variation*? Explain your reasoning.

Think

To answer these problems, you may find it helpful to first make a table of values. In part (A), for instance, let x be the number of friends and let y be the cost per person.

A **Boating** The cost of a $120 boat rental is split among several friends.

The cost per person times the number of friends equals the total cost of the boat rental. Since the total cost is a constant product of $120, the cost per person varies inversely with the number of friends. This is an inverse variation.

B **Entertainment** You download several movies for $14.99 each.

The cost per download times the number of movies downloaded equals the total cost of the downloads. Since the ratio $\frac{\text{total cost}}{\text{number of movies downloaded}}$ is constant at $14.99, the total cost varies directly with the number of movies downloaded. This is a direct variation.

Got It? **5.** Does each situation represent a *direct variation* or an *inverse variation*? Explain your reasoning.

a. You buy sweaters in a clothing store for $35 each.

b. You walk 5 mi each day. Your speed and time spent walking vary each day.

Lesson Check

Do you know HOW?

1. Suppose y varies inversely with x, and $y = -3$ when $x = 17$. What is an equation for the inverse variation?

2. An 80-lb weight is placed on a lever, 9 ft from the fulcrum. What amount of weight should you put 6 ft from the fulcrum to balance the lever?

3. What is the graph of $y = \frac{10}{x}$?

4. Do the data in the table represent a *direct variation* or an *inverse variation*? Write an equation that models the data.

x	y
−3	6
−6	12
−9	18

Do you UNDERSTAND?

5. Vocabulary Is the equation $\frac{xy}{3} = 5$ an inverse variation? If so, what is the constant of variation?

6. Does the graph of an inverse variation *always*, *sometimes*, or *never* pass through the origin? Explain.

7. Reasoning Suppose you place two different weights on a lever. Which weight must be closer to the fulcrum in order for the lever to balance? Explain.

8. Reasoning Suppose the price per pencil at an office supply store decreases as the number of pencils you buy increases. Does the price per pencil necessarily vary inversely with the number of pencils bought? Explain.

Practice and Problem-Solving Exercises

 Practice   Suppose y varies inversely with x. Write an equation for the inverse variation.   ◀ See Problem 1.

9. $y = 6$ when $x = 3$ **10.** $y = 1$ when $x = -2$ **11.** $y = 7$ when $x = 8$

12. $y = 3$ when $x = 0.5$ **13.** $y = -10$ when $x = -2.4$ **14.** $y = 3.5$ when $x = 2.2$

15. Travel A family takes $2\frac{1}{2}$ h to drive from their house to a lake at 48 mi/h. The travel time varies inversely with the speed of the car. How long will the return trip take at 40 mi/h?   ◀ See Problem 2.

16. Bicycling A camper takes 2 h to ride a bike around a reservoir at 10 mi/h at the beginning of the summer. By the end of the summer, she can ride around the reservoir in $1\frac{1}{2}$ h. The time to travel around the reservoir varies inversely with the speed she pedals. What is her speed at the end of the summer?

Graph each inverse variation.   ◀ See Problem 3.

17. $y = \frac{9}{x}$ **18.** $xy = 12$ **19.** $y = \frac{-15}{x}$ **20.** $\frac{14}{x} = y$

21. $20 = xy$ **22.** $y = \frac{7.5}{x}$ **23.** $xy = -24$ **24.** $y = \frac{-1}{x}$

Do the data in each table represent a *direct variation* or an *inverse variation*? Write an equation to model the data in each table.

See Problem 4.

25.

x	y
2	1
5	2.5
8	4

26.

x	y
4	15
6	10
10	6

27.

x	y
−3	−24
9	8
12	6

Tell whether each situation represents a *direct variation* or an *inverse variation*. Explain your reasoning.

See Problem 5.

28. You buy some chicken for $1.79/lb.

29. An 8-slice pizza is shared equally by a group of friends.

30. You find the length and width of several rectangles. Each has an area of 24 cm^2.

 **Apply**

Suppose y varies inversely with x. Find the constant of variation k for each inverse variation. Then write an equation for the inverse variation.

31. $y = -8$ when $x = -32$

32. $x = \frac{1}{2}$ when $y = 5$

33. $y = 25$ when $x = 0.04$

Each pair of points is on the graph of an inverse variation. Find the missing value.

34. $(3, 5)$ and $(1, y)$

35. $(2.5, 4)$ and $(x, 2)$

36. $\left(x, \frac{1}{2}\right)$ and $\left(\frac{1}{3}, \frac{1}{4}\right)$

Measurement Does each formula represent a *direct variation* or an *inverse variation*? Explain your reasoning.

37. the perimeter P of an equilateral triangle with side length s: $P = 3s$

38. the time t to travel 150 mi at a rate of r mi/h: $t = \frac{150}{r}$

39. the circumference C of a circle with radius r: $C = 2\pi r$

40. Think About a Plan Suppose 4 people can paint a house if they work 3 days each. How long would it take a crew of 5 people to paint the house?
- Can you determine whether this situation represents a direct variation or an inverse variation?
- How can you write an equation that will help you solve the problem?

41. Writing Explain how the variable y changes in each situation.
  a. y varies directly with x. The value of x is doubled.
  b. y varies inversely with x. The value of x is doubled.

42. Surveying Both of the two rectangular building lots shown at the right have the same area. Write an equation to find the length of the second lot.

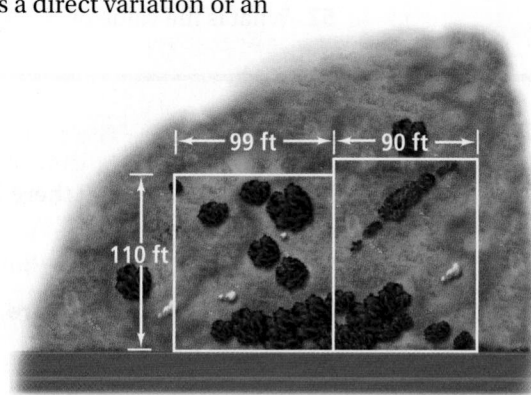

Tell whether each table represents a *direct variation* or an *inverse variation*.
Write an equation to model the data. Then complete the table.

43.

x	y
10	4
20	■
8	3.2

44.

x	y
0.4	28
1.2	84
■	63

45.

x	y
1.6	30
4.8	10
■	96

STEM **46. Physics** Boyle's Law states that volume V varies inversely with pressure P for any gas at a constant temperature in an enclosed space. Suppose a gas at constant temperature occupies 15.3 L at a pressure of 40 mm of mercury. What equation models this situation?

Ⓒ 47. Error Analysis When graphing a certain function, Pedro sees that the value of y decreases by 2 whenever the value of x increases by 1. Pedro says that the graph represents an inverse variation. Is he correct? Explain.

Ⓒ Challenge **48.** Write an equation to model each situation.
  a. y varies inversely with the fourth power of x.
  b. y varies inversely with the fourth power of x and directly with z.

STEM **49. Physics** The intensity of a sound s varies inversely with the square of the distance d from the sound. This can be modeled by the equation $sd^2 = k$, where k is a constant. If you decrease your distance from the source of a sound by half, by what factor will the intensity of the sound increase? Explain your reasoning.

Standardized Test Prep

SAT/ACT

50. What is the value of $\dfrac{1}{(64)^{-\frac{1}{3}}}$?

51. The diagram shows two squares. The area of the nonshaded region is $4x^2 + 16x + 16$. The area of the shaded region is $5x^2 + 14x + 9$. What is $|a + b|$?

52. What is the value of $\dfrac{7^3 \cdot 2^5}{7 \cdot 2^3}$?

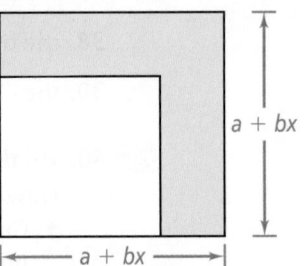

$a + bx$

$a + bx$

Mixed Review

Solve each equation. If there is no solution, write *no solution*.

◀ **See Lesson 11-5.**

53. $\dfrac{2}{d+5} = \dfrac{3}{d-5}$

54. $\dfrac{-1}{y} + \dfrac{1}{y} = 1$

55. $\dfrac{3}{m-4} + 2 = \dfrac{5m}{m-4}$

Get Ready! **To prepare for Lesson 11-7, do Exercises 56–59.**

Graph each function.

◀ **See Lessons 4-4, 7-6, and 9-1.**

56. $f(x) = x - 8$

57. $g(x) = x^2 + 3$

58. $y = 3^x$

59. $f(x) = 2x + 1$

11-7 Graphing Rational Functions

Common Core State Standards

F-IF.B.4 For a function that models a relationship between two quantities, interpret key features of graphs and tables . . . and sketch graphs showing key features . . .
Also A-CED.A.2

MP 1, MP 2, MP 3, MP 4, MP 5

Objective To graph rational functions

SOLVE IT!

Getting Ready!

◄► ✕ ↻ ⬆

On any trip, the time you travel in a car varies inversely with the car's average speed. The function $t = \frac{60}{r}$ represents the time it takes to travel 60 mi at different rates. Will the graph ever intersect the horizontal axis? The vertical axis? Explain your reasoning.

Time (hours), t

Rate (miles per hour), r

What does the graph tell you about the relationship between speed and the time needed to make the trip?

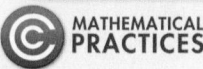
MATHEMATICAL PRACTICES

Inverse variations are examples of *rational functions.* A **rational function** can be written in the form $f(x) = \frac{\text{polynomial}}{\text{polynomial}}$, where the denominator cannot be 0.

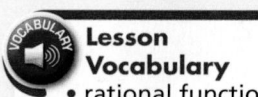
Lesson Vocabulary
• rational function
• asymptote

Essential Understanding To graph a rational function $f(x)$, you need to understand the graph's behavior near values of x where the function is undefined.

Any value of the variable that makes the denominator of a rational function equal to 0 is an excluded value.

Problem 1 Identifying Excluded Values

What is the excluded value for each function?

A $f(x) = \frac{5}{x - 2}$

B $y = \frac{-3}{x + 8}$

$x - 2 = 0$ ← Set the denominator equal to 0. → $x + 8 = 0$

$x = 2$ ← Solve for x. → $x = -8$

The excluded value is $x = 2$.

The excluded value is $x = -8$.

Think

Why are some values of x excluded?
Division by 0 is undefined. So any value of x that makes the denominator equal to 0 is excluded.

Got It? **1.** What is the excluded value for $y = \frac{3}{x + 7}$?

The graphs of many rational functions are related to each other. Compare the graphs below of $y = \frac{1}{x}$ and $y = \frac{1}{x-3}$.

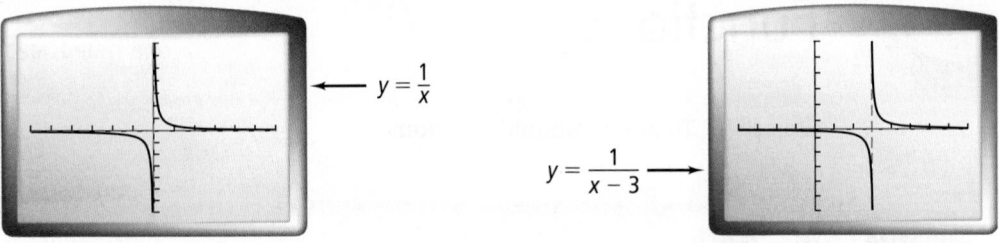

$\longleftarrow y = \frac{1}{x}$

$y = \frac{1}{x-3} \longrightarrow$

The graphs are identical in shape, but the second graph is translated 3 units right.

Notice that the graph of $y = \frac{1}{x}$ approaches both axes but does not cross either axis. The axes in this graph function as *asymptotes*. A line is an **asymptote** of a graph if the graph gets closer to the line as x or y gets larger in absolute value. In the graph of $y = \frac{1}{x-3}$ above, the x-axis and the line $x = 3$ are asymptotes.

When the numerator and denominator of a rational function have no common factors other than 1, there is a vertical asymptote at each excluded value.

 Problem 2 Using a Vertical Asymptote

What is the vertical asymptote of the graph of $y = \frac{5}{x+2}$? Graph the function.

Think

The numerator and denominator have no common factors. To find the vertical asymptote, find the excluded value.

To graph the function, first make a table of values. Use values of x near -2, where the asymptote occurs.

Use the points from the table to make the graph. Draw a dashed line for the vertical asymptote.

Write

$x + 2 = 0$
$\quad x = -2$

The vertical asymptote is the line $x = -2$.

x	−7	−4	−3	−1	0	3
y	−1	−2.5	−5	5	2.5	1

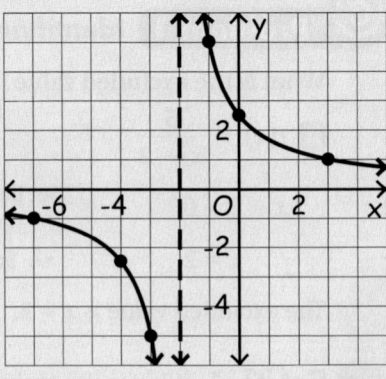

 Got It? **2.** What is the vertical asymptote of the graph of $h(x) = \frac{-3}{x-6}$? Graph the function.

Compare the graphs and asymptotes below of $y = \frac{1}{x}$ and $y = \frac{1}{x} + 3$.

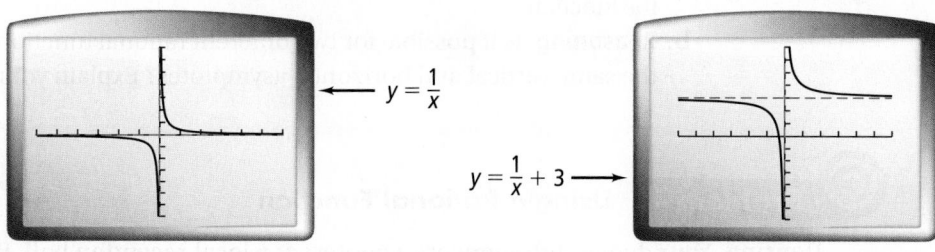

$\leftarrow y = \frac{1}{x}$

$y = \frac{1}{x} + 3 \longrightarrow$

vertical asymptote at $x = 0$
horizontal asymptote at $y = 0$

vertical asymptote at $x = 0$
horizontal asymptote at $y = 3$

The graphs are identical in shape, but notice in the second graph that both the graph and the horizontal asymptote of $y = \frac{1}{x}$ have been translated 3 units up.

For a rational function of the form $y = \frac{a}{x - b} + c$, there is a horizontal asymptote at $y = c$.

take note

Concept Summary   Identifying Asymptotes

Words

The graph of a rational function of the form $y = \frac{a}{x - b} + c$ has a vertical asymptote at $x = b$ and a horizontal asymptote at $y = c$.

Example

$y = \frac{1}{x + 4} + 1$

$y = \frac{1}{x - (-4)} + 1$

vertical asymptote: $x = -4$
horizontal asymptote: $y = 1$

Ⓒ **Problem 3** Using Vertical and Horizontal Asymptotes

What are the asymptotes of the graph of $f(x) = \frac{3}{x - 1} - 2$? Graph the function.

Step 1   From the form of the function, you can see that there is a vertical asymptote at $x = 1$ and a horizontal asymptote at $y = -2$.

Think

How do you choose x-values for the table?
The vertical asymptote is $x = 1$. So you should choose x-values on either side of 1. That way, your sketch will show both parts of the graph.

Step 2   Make a table of values using values of x near 1.

x	−5	−2	−1	0	2	3	4
y	−2.5	−3	−3.5	−5	1	−0.5	−1

Step 3   Sketch the asymptotes. Graph the function.

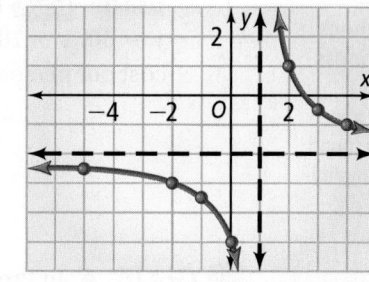

Got It? 3. a. What are the asymptotes of the graph of $y = \frac{-1}{x+3} - 4$? Graph the function.

b. Reasoning Is it possible for two different rational functions to have the same vertical and horizontal asymptotes? Explain your reasoning.

Ⓒ **Problem 4** **Using a Rational Function**

Dancing Your dance club sponsors a contest at a local reception hall. Reserving a private room costs \$350, and the cost will be divided equally among the people who enter the contest. Each person also pays a \$30 entry fee.

A What equation gives the total cost per person y of entering the contest as a function of the number of people x who enter the contest?

Relate $\boxed{\text{total cost per person}}$ = $\dfrac{\boxed{\text{cost of renting private room}}}{\boxed{\text{number of people entering contest}}}$ + $\boxed{\text{entry fee per person}}$

Write $\boxed{y}$ = $\boxed{\dfrac{350}{x}}$ + $\boxed{30}$

The equation $y = \frac{350}{x} + 30$ models the situation.

B What is the graph of the function in part (A)? Use the graph to describe the change in the cost per person as the number of people who enter the contest increases.

Use a graphing calculator to graph $y = \frac{350}{x} + 30$.

Since both y and x must be nonnegative numbers, use only the part of the graph in the first quadrant.

You can see from the graph that as the number of people who enter the contest increases, the cost per person decreases. Because the graph has a horizontal asymptote at $y = 30$, the cost per person will eventually approach \$30.

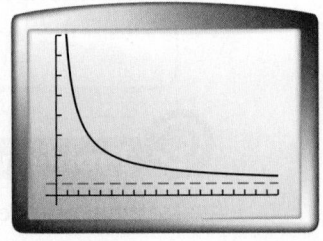

C Approximately how many people must enter the contest in order for the total cost per person to be about \$50?

Use the (trace) key or the **TABLE** feature. When $y \approx 50$, $x \approx 18$. So if 18 people enter the contest, the cost per person will be about \$50.

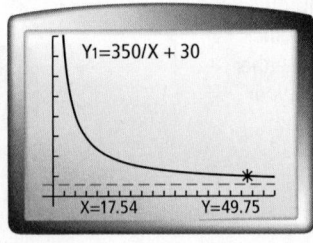

Y₁=350/X + 30

X=17.54   Y=49.75

Think

How can you check the reasonableness of your answer?
Substitute 18 for x in the equation you found in part (A) and simplify. If y is approximately \$50, your answer is reasonable.

Got It? 4. In Problem 4, suppose the cost to rent a private room increases to \$400. Approximately how many people must then enter the contest in order for the total cost per person to be about \$50?

You can think of functions whose graphs have similar features as families of functions. You have studied six families of functions in this book. Their properties and graphs are shown in the summary.

Concept Summary Families of Functions

Linear function

$y = mx + b$

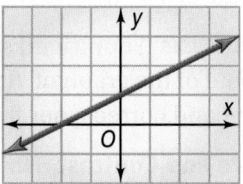

parent function: $f(x) = x$
slope $= m$
y-intercept $= b$
The greatest exponent is 1.

Quadratic function

$y = ax^2 + bx + c$

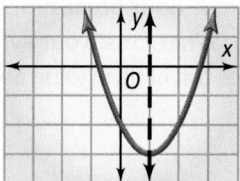

parent function: $f(x) = x^2$
parabola with axis of
symmetry at $x = \frac{-b}{2a}$
The greatest exponent is 2.

Absolute value function

$y = |x - a| + b$

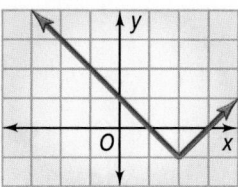

parent function: $f(x) = |x|$
Shift $y = |x|$ horizontally a units.
Shift $y = |x|$ vertically b units.
vertex at (a, b)
The greatest exponent is 1.

Exponential function

$y = ab^x$

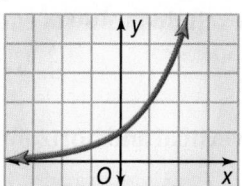

growth where $b > 1$
decay where $0 < b < 1$
The variable is the exponent.

Square root function

$y = \sqrt{x - b} + c$

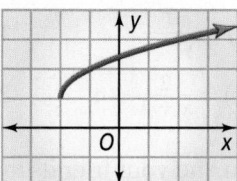

Shift $y = \sqrt{x}$ horizontally b units.
Shift $y = \sqrt{x}$ vertically c units.
The variable is under the radical.

Rational function

$y = \frac{a}{x - b} + c$

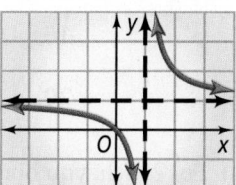

vertical asymptote at $x = b$
horizontal asymptote at $y = c$
The variable is in the denominator.

Lesson Check

Do you know HOW?

1. What is the excluded value for $y = \frac{4}{x+1}$?

2. What are the asymptotes of $f(x) = \frac{8}{x-2} + 3$? Graph the function.

3. The function $t = \frac{240}{r} + 0.5$ models the total time t, in hours, it will take you to travel 240 mi at r mi/h, assuming you stop for a half-hour break along the way. Graph this function. What must your average speed be in order for your travel time to be about 4 h?

Do you UNDERSTAND?

4. **Vocabulary** Find the excluded value and the vertical and horizontal asymptotes of the function $y = \frac{7}{x-5} + 1$.

5. **Reasoning** Write an example of a rational function with a vertical asymptote at $x = -2$ and a horizontal asymptote at $y = 4$.

6. **Error Analysis** Your friend says that the vertical asymptote of the graph of $f(x) = \frac{1}{x+5} + 2$ is $x = 5$. Describe and correct your friend's error.

7. **Compare and Contrast** How are an excluded value and a vertical asymptote of a rational function alike? How are they different?

Practice and Problem-Solving Exercises

 Identify the excluded value of each rational function.

See Problem 1.

8. $f(x) = \frac{3}{x}$

9. $y = \frac{1}{x-2}$

10. $y = \frac{x}{x+2}$

11. $h(x) = \frac{-3}{2x-6}$

Identify the vertical and horizontal asymptotes of each graph.

See Problems 2 and 3.

12.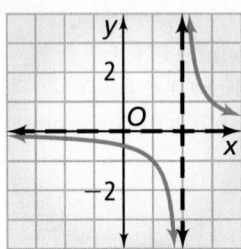

13.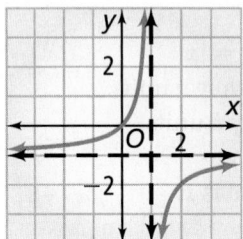

14.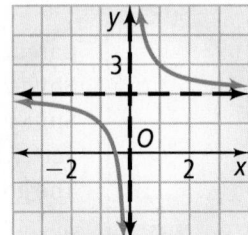

Identify the asymptotes of the graph of each function. Then graph the function.

15. $y = \frac{3}{x}$

16. $y = \frac{-10}{x}$

17. $f(x) = \frac{1}{x-5}$

18. $g(x) = \frac{4}{x+4}$

19. $y = \frac{1}{x} - 5$

20. $y = \frac{-3}{x} + 6$

21. $h(x) = \frac{2}{x+1} + 4$

22. $f(x) = \frac{-1}{x-3} - 5$

23. **Nutrition** For lunch, you bought two veggie pizzas for you and your friends to divide evenly. Each pizza contains 960 Calories. In addition, each person eats a banana, which contains 100 Calories.

See Problem 4.

   a. Write and graph an equation that gives the number of Calories C consumed by each person as a function of the total number of people n.

   b. Approximately how many people must share the pizzas in order for each person to consume about 500 Calories?

24. **Event Planning** You have a budget of $1200 to pay the musicians who will play a charity benefit. Two musicians have agreed to perform without charge.
   a. Write and graph an equation that gives the cost c of hiring one paid musician as a function of the number of musicians m who play the benefit.
   b. Suppose you use your entire budget and get 18 musicians to play the benefit. What is the cost of hiring each paid musician?

 **Apply**

Describe how the graph of each function is a translation of the graph of $f(x) = \frac{7}{x}$.

25. $g(x) = \frac{7}{x+1}$

26. $y = \frac{7}{x} - 15$

27. $h(x) = \frac{7}{x} + 1$

28. $y = \frac{7}{x+3} - 2$

29. $g(x) = \frac{7}{x-3}$

30. $f(x) = \frac{7}{x+12}$

31. **Think About a Plan** In the formula $I = \frac{445}{x^2}$, I is the intensity of light, in lumens, at a distance of x feet from a light bulb of 445 watts. At about what distance is the intensity 25 lumens?
   • How can you use the graph of the function to determine the answer?
   • How can you check the reasonableness of your answer?

32. **Open-Ended** Write equations of two rational functions with graphs that are identical except that one is shifted vertically 3 units with respect to the other.

33. **a.** Graph $y = \frac{1}{x}$ and $y = \frac{1}{x^2}$.
   b. What are the vertical and horizontal asymptotes of the graph of each function?
   c. What is the range of $y = \frac{1}{x}$? Of $y = \frac{1}{x^2}$?

Describe the graph of each function.

34. $y = 4x + 1$

35. $h(x) = |x - 4|$

36. $y = 0.4^x$

37. $f(x) = \frac{x}{4}$

38. $y = \frac{4}{x} + 1$

39. $h(x) = \sqrt{x - 4} + 1$

40. $g(x) = x^2 - 4$

41. $f(x) = \frac{4}{x+4} - 1$

42. $g(x) = \frac{3}{x} - 12$

43. **Writing** Describe the similarities and differences in the graphs of $y = \frac{3}{x+2}$ and $y = \frac{-3}{x+2}$.

STEM 44. **Physics** As radio signals move away from a transmitter, they become weaker. The function $s = \frac{1600}{d^2}$ gives the strength s of a signal at a distance of d miles from a transmitter.
   a. **Graphing Calculator** Graph the function. For what distances is $s \leq 1$?
   b. Find the signal strength at 10 mi, 1 mi, and 0.1 mi.
   c. **Reasoning** Suppose you drive by the transmitter for one radio station while your car radio is tuned to a second station. The signal from the transmitter can interfere and come through your radio. Use your results from part (b) to explain why.

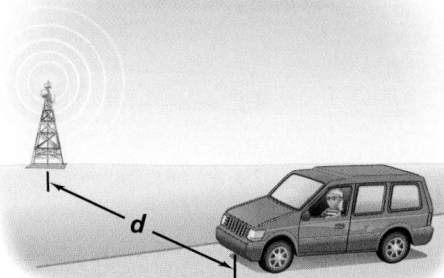

 **Graph each function. Include a dashed line for each asymptote.**

45. $g(x) = \dfrac{x}{x-1}$

46. $y = \dfrac{1}{(x-1)^2}$

47. $y = \dfrac{2}{(x-2)(x+2)}$

48. $y = \dfrac{1}{x^2 - 2x}$

49. Graph $f(x) = \dfrac{(x+2)(x+1)}{x+2}$ and $g(x) = x + 1$. Are the graphs the same? Explain.

Apply What You've Learned

MATHEMATICAL
PRACTICES
MP 2, MP 5

In the Apply What You've Learned in Lesson 11-4, you wrote a rational expression for the surface area of the lunch box described on page 663.

a. Write the equation of a rational function that gives the surface area $S(x)$ of the lunch box in terms of x.

b. Graph the function on a graphing calculator. Describe a viewing window that shows the full shape of the graph for $x > 0$.

c. Use your graphing calculator to find the coordinates of the minimum point of the function when $x > 0$. Round to the nearest hundredth.

d. What does the minimum point tell you?

Graphing Rational Functions

Common Core State Standards

A-CED.A.2 Create equations in two or more variables to represent relationships between quantities; graph equations on coordinate axes with labels and scales.

MP 5

MATHEMATICAL PRACTICES

Functions such as $y = \frac{1}{x}$, $y = \frac{1}{x+2}$, and $y = \frac{1}{x} - 4$ are examples of rational functions. When you use a graphing calculator to graph a rational function, false connections may appear on the screen. When this happens, you need to make adjustments to see the true shape of the graph.

Graph the function $y = \frac{1}{x+2} - 4$. You can enter this as $y = 1 \div (x+2) - 4$. The graph on your screen may look like the one at the right. The highest point and the lowest point on the graph that appear on the screen are not supposed to connect. If you use the **trace** key on the calculator, you can see that no point on the graph lies on this connecting line. So this is a false connection.

False connection

Here's how you can graph a rational function and avoid false connections.

Step 1 Press the **mode** key. Then scroll down and right to highlight the word **DOT**. Then press **enter**.

Step 2 Graph the function $y = \frac{1}{x+2} - 4$ again. Now the false connection is gone.

Step 3 Use the **trace** key or **TABLE** feature to find some points on the graph. Sketch the graph.

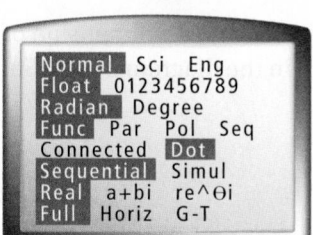

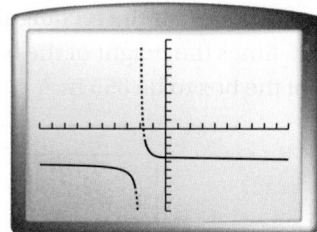

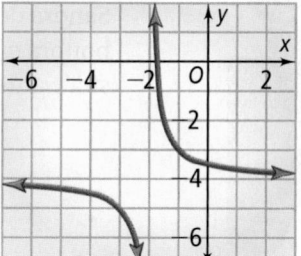

Exercises

Use a graphing calculator to graph each function. Then sketch the graph.

1. $y = \frac{3}{x}$

2. $y = -\frac{4}{x}$

3. $y = \frac{1}{x+2}$

4. $y = \frac{1}{x-4}$

5. $y = \frac{1}{x} + 2$

6. $y = \frac{1}{x} - 3$

7. $y = \frac{1}{x-1} + 2$

8. $y = \frac{3}{x-2} - 4$

9. a. Graph $y = \frac{1}{x}$, $y = \frac{1}{x-4}$, and $y = \frac{1}{x+3}$.

    b. Make a Conjecture How does adding or subtracting a positive number in the denominator of $y = \frac{1}{x}$ translate the graph?

10. a. Graph $y = \frac{1}{x}$, $y = \frac{1}{x} - 4$, and $y = \frac{1}{x} + 3$.

    b. Make a Conjecture How does adding or subtracting a positive number on the right side of $y = \frac{1}{x}$ translate the graph?

Pull It **All Together**

Completing the Performance Task

Look back at your results from the Apply What You've Learned sections in Lessons 11-1, 11-4, and 11-7. Use the work you did to complete the following.

To solve these problems you will pull together many concepts and skills that you have studied about rational expressions and functions.

1. Solve the problem in the Task Description on page 663 by finding the dimensions Sandra should use for the lunch box. Round the dimensions to the nearest hundredth of an inch. Show all your work and explain each step of your solution.

2. Reflect Choose one of the Mathematical Practices below and explain how you applied it in your work on the Performance Task.

MP 2: Reason abstractly and quantitatively.

MP 4: Model with mathematics.

MP 5: Use appropriate tools strategically.

On Your Own

Sandra decides to alter the design of the rectangular lunch box so that one dimension of the bottom of the box is 1.25 times the height of the box, as shown in the diagram below. She still wants the volume of the box to be 355 in.^{3}.

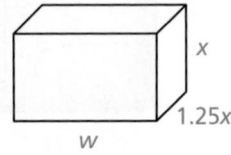

a. Find the minimum amount of cardboard needed to make the box. Round to the nearest square inch.

b. What are the dimensions of the box that uses the minimum amount of cardboard? Round the dimensions to the nearest hundredth of an inch.

11 Chapter Review

Connecting **BIG** ideas and Answering the Essential Questions

1 Equivalence
Rational expressions can be represented many ways. When a rational expression is simplified, the numerator and denominator have no common factors except 1.

Simplifying Rational Expressions (Lesson 11-1)
$$\frac{7y + 21}{y + 3} = \frac{7(y + 3)^1}{_1 y + 3}$$
$$= 7$$

Multiplying, Dividing, Adding, and Subtracting Rational Expressions (Lessons 11-2, 11-3, and 11-4)
$$\frac{7}{3x} - \frac{5}{3x} = \frac{7 - 5}{3x}$$
$$= \frac{2}{3x}$$

2 Functions
Rational functions have equations of the form $f(x) = \frac{\text{polynomial}}{\text{polynomial}}$. The graph of a rational function may have vertical and horizontal asymptotes.

Graphing Rational Functions (Lesson 11-7)
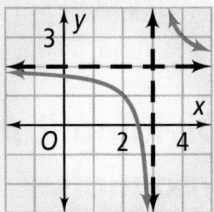

Inverse Variation (Lesson 11-6)
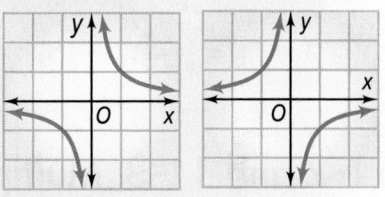

3 Solving Equations and Inequalities
To isolate the variable in a rational equation, multiply by the LCD and then solve the resulting equation. Check for extraneous solutions.

Solving Rational Equations (Lesson 11-5)
$$\frac{1}{2} + \frac{3}{t} = \frac{5}{8}$$
$$8t\left(\frac{1}{2} + \frac{3}{t}\right) = 8t\left(\frac{5}{8}\right)$$
$$4t + 24 = 5t$$
$$24 = t$$

🔊 Chapter Vocabulary

- asymptote (p. 706)
- constant of variation for an inverse variation (p. 698)
- excluded value (p. 664)
- inverse variation (p. 698)
- rational equation (p. 691)
- rational expression (p. 664)
- rational function (p. 705)

Choose the correct term to complete each sentence.

1. A value of x for which a rational function $f(x)$ is undefined is a(n) ? .

2. A line that the graph of a function gets closer to as x or y gets larger in absolute value is a(n) ? .

3. A(n) ? is a ratio of two polynomial expressions.

11-1 Simplifying Rational Expressions

Quick Review

A **rational expression** is an expression that can be written in the form $\frac{\text{polynomial}}{\text{polynomial}}$. A rational expression is in simplified form when the numerator and denominator have no common factors other than 1.

Example

What is the simplified form of $\frac{x^2 - 9}{x^2 - 2x - 15}$?

$$\frac{x^2 - 9}{x^2 - 2x - 15} = \frac{(x+3)(x-3)}{(x+3)(x-5)}$$ Factor the numerator and denominator.

$$= \frac{(x+3)^1(x-3)}{1(x+3)(x-5)}$$ Divide out the common factor.

$$= \frac{x-3}{x-5}$$ Simplify.

Exercises

Simplify each expression. State any excluded values.

4. $\frac{2x^2 + 6x}{10x^3}$

5. $\frac{m-3}{3m-9}$

6. $\frac{x^2 + 6x + 9}{5x + 15}$

7. $\frac{2a^2 - 4a + 2}{3a^2 - 3}$

8. $\frac{2s^2 - 5s - 12}{2s^2 - 9s + 4}$

9. $\frac{4-c}{2c-8}$

10. Geometry What fraction of the rectangle is shaded? Write your answer as a rational expression in simplified form.

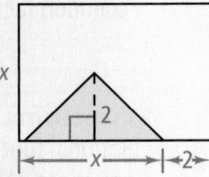

11-2 and 11-3 Multiplying and Dividing Rational Expressions and Dividing Polynomials

Quick Review

You can multiply and divide rational expressions using the same properties you use to multiply and divide numerical fractions.

$$\frac{a}{b} \cdot \frac{c}{d} = \frac{ac}{bd}, \text{ where } b \neq 0 \text{ and } d \neq 0.$$

$$\frac{a}{b} \div \frac{c}{d} = \frac{a}{b} \cdot \frac{d}{c} = \frac{ad}{bc}, \text{ where } b \neq 0, c \neq 0, \text{ and } d \neq 0.$$

To divide a polynomial by a monomial, divide each term of the polynomial by the monomial. To divide a polynomial by another polynomial, use long division. When dividing polynomials, write the answer as quotient $+ \frac{\text{remainder}}{\text{divisor}}$.

Example

What is the quotient $\frac{y}{y+3} \div \frac{y-3}{y-2}$?

$$\frac{y}{y+3} \div \frac{y-3}{y-2} = \frac{y}{y+3} \cdot \frac{y-2}{y-3}$$

$$= \frac{y(y-2)}{(y+3)(y-3)}$$

Exercises

Multiply or divide.

11. $\frac{4x+12}{x^2-2x} \cdot \frac{x}{6x+18}$

12. $\frac{a^2 + 5a + 4}{a^3} \div \frac{a^2 + 3a + 2}{a^2 - 2a}$

13. $\frac{x^2 + 13x + 40}{x-7} \div \frac{x+8}{x^2-49}$

14. $(12x^2 + 9x - 7) \div 3x$

15. $(3d^2 + 2d - 29) \div (d+3)$

16. Geometry The width and area of a rectangle are shown in the figure at the right. What is the length of the rectangle?

$(2b - 1)$ in.

$A = (4b^3 + 5b - 3)$ in.^{2}

11-4 Adding and Subtracting Rational Expressions

Quick Review

You can add and subtract rational expressions. To add or subtract expressions with like denominators, add or subtract the numerators and write the result over the common denominator. To add or subtract expressions with different denominators, write the expressions with the LCD and then add or subtract the numerators.

Example

What is $\frac{1}{a+7} + \frac{a}{a-5}$?

$$\frac{1}{a+7} + \frac{a}{a-5} = \frac{1(a-5)}{(a+7)(a-5)} + \frac{a(a+7)}{(a+7)(a-5)}$$

$$= \frac{a-5}{(a+7)(a-5)} + \frac{a^2+7a}{(a+7)(a-5)}$$

$$= \frac{a-5+a^2+7a}{(a+7)(a-5)}$$

$$= \frac{a^2+8a-5}{(a+7)(a-5)}$$

Exercises

Add or subtract.

17. $\frac{8x}{x+1} - \frac{3}{x+1}$

18. $\frac{6}{7x} + \frac{1}{4}$

19. $\frac{5}{2+x} + \frac{x}{x-4}$

20. $\frac{9}{3x-1} - \frac{5x}{2x+3}$

21. Air Travel The distance between Atlanta, Georgia, and Albuquerque, New Mexico, is about 1270 mi. The groundspeed for jet traffic from Albuquerque to Atlanta can be about 18% faster than the groundspeed from Atlanta to Albuquerque. Let r be the speed from Atlanta to Albuquerque in miles per hour. What is a simplified expression for the round-trip flying time?

11-5 Solving Rational Equations

Quick Review

You can solve a **rational equation** by multiplying each side by the LCD. Check possible solutions to make sure each satisfies the original equation.

Example

What is the solution of $\frac{3}{8} + \frac{4}{x} = \frac{7}{x}$?

$$\frac{3}{8} + \frac{4}{x} = \frac{7}{x}$$

$$8x\left(\frac{3}{8} + \frac{4}{x}\right) = 8x\left(\frac{7}{x}\right)$$

$$8^1x\left(\frac{3}{8_1}\right) + 8x^1\left(\frac{4}{x_1}\right) = 8x^1\left(\frac{7}{1x}\right)$$

$$3x + 32 = 56$$

$$3x = 24$$

$$x = 8$$

Check $\frac{3}{8} + \frac{4}{8} \overset{?}{=} \frac{7}{8}$

$\frac{7}{8} = \frac{7}{8}$ ✔

Exercises

Solve each equation. Check your solutions.

22. $\frac{1}{2} + \frac{3}{t} = \frac{5}{8}$

23. $\frac{3}{m-4} + \frac{1}{3(m-4)} = \frac{6}{m}$

24. $\frac{2c}{c-4} - 2 = \frac{4}{c+5}$

25. $\frac{5}{2x-3} = \frac{7}{3x}$

26. Business A new photocopier can make 72 copies in 2 min. When an older photocopier is operational, the two photocopiers together can make 72 copies in 1.5 min. How long would it take the older photocopier to make 72 copies working alone?

11-6 Inverse Variation

Quick Review

When the product of two variables is constant, the variables form an **inverse variation**. You can write an inverse variation in the form $xy = k$ or $y = \frac{k}{x}$, where k is the constant of variation.

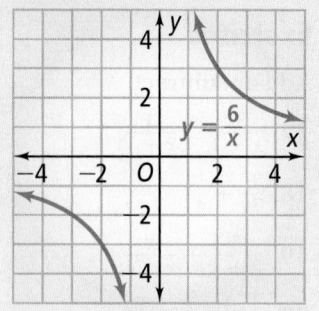

Example

Suppose y varies inversely with x, and $y = 8$ when $x = 6$. What is an equation for the inverse variation?

$xy = k$	General form of an inverse variation
$6(8) = k$	Substitute 6 for x and 8 for y.
$48 = k$	Simplify.
$xy = 48$	Write an equation.

Exercises

Suppose y varies inversely with x. Write an equation for the inverse variation.

27. $y = 7$ when $x = 3$

28. $y = 4$ when $x = 2.5$

29. $y = -9$ when $x = 2$

30. $y = 5$ when $x = -5$

Graph each inverse variation.

31. $xy = 15$

32. $y = \frac{-18}{x}$

33. Running Suppose a runner takes 45 min to run a route at 8 mi/h at the beginning of training season. By the end of training season, she can run the same route in 38 min. What is her speed at the end of training season?

11-7 Graphing Rational Functions

Quick Review

A **rational function** can be written in the form $f(x) = \frac{\text{polynomial}}{\text{polynomial}}$. The graph of a rational function in the form $y = \frac{a}{x - b} + c$ has a vertical asymptote at $x = b$ and a horizontal asymptote at $y = c$. A line is an **asymptote** of a graph if the graph gets closer to the line as x or y gets larger in absolute value.

Example

What is the graph of $f(x) = \frac{1}{x - 1} + 2$?

From the form of the function, you can see that there is a vertical asymptote at $x = 1$ and a horizontal asymptote at $y = 2$. Sketch the asymptotes.

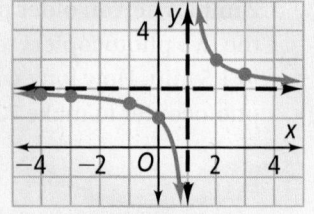

Make a table of values. Then graph the function.

x	−4	−3	−1	0	2	3
y	1.8	1.75	1.5	1	3	2.5

Exercises

Identify the excluded value for each function.

34. $f(x) = \frac{5}{x}$

35. $y = \frac{3}{x + 4}$

Identify the asymptotes of the graph of each function. Then graph the function.

36. $y = \frac{1}{x + 2}$

37. $f(x) = \frac{-2}{x + 3}$

38. $y = \frac{5}{x - 4} + 1$

39. $f(x) = \frac{3}{x - 5} - 1$

40. Physics For a 225-watt bulb, the intensity I of light in lumens at a distance of x feet is $I = \frac{225}{x^2}$.
   a. What is the intensity of light 5 ft from the bulb?
   b. Suppose your distance from the bulb doubles. How does the intensity of the light change? Explain.

Do you know HOW?

Write an equation of the inverse variation that includes the given point.

1. $(2, 2)$

2. $(-8, -4)$

Identify the excluded value for each rational function.

3. $f(x) = \dfrac{19 + x}{x - 5}$

4. $y = \dfrac{2x}{8x - 12}$

Identify the asymptotes of each function. Then graph the function.

5. $y = \dfrac{6}{x}$

6. $y = \dfrac{1}{x} + 3$

7. $f(x) = \dfrac{4}{x - 2}$

Simplify each expression. State any excluded values.

8. $\dfrac{6p - 30}{3p - 15}$

9. $\dfrac{n^2 + 4n - 5}{n + 5}$

Multiply or divide.

10. $\dfrac{3}{x - 2} \cdot \dfrac{x^2 - 4}{12}$

11. $\dfrac{5x}{x^2 + 2x} \div \dfrac{30x^2}{x + 2}$

Divide.

12. $(12x^4 + 9x^3 - 10x^2) \div 3x^3$

13. $(4x^4 - 6x^3 - 2x^2 - 2x) \div (2x - 1)$

Find the LCD of each pair of expressions.

14. $\dfrac{5}{h}, \dfrac{6}{3h}$

15. $\dfrac{4}{a^2 b^3}, \dfrac{3}{9ab^4}$

Add or subtract.

16. $\dfrac{4b - 2}{3b} + \dfrac{b}{b + 2}$

17. $\dfrac{9}{n} - \dfrac{8}{n + 1}$

Solve each equation. Check your solutions.

18. $\dfrac{v}{3} + \dfrac{v}{v + 5} = \dfrac{-4}{v + 5}$

19. $\dfrac{16}{x + 10} = \dfrac{8}{2x - 1}$

20. Cleaning Mark can clean his father's office in 30 min. His younger sister Lynn can clean the office in 40 min. How long will it take the two of them together to clean the office?

Do you UNDERSTAND?

© 21. Open-Ended Write a rational expression for which 6 and 3 are excluded values.

22. Geometry The height of a square prism is $3n + 1$. The volume of the prism is $3n^3 + 13n^2 + 16n + 4$. What is the area of the square base of the prism?

© 23 Reasoning Rosa divided a polynomial $p(x)$ by $x - 4$ and obtained this result: $2x + 13 + \dfrac{59}{x - 4}$. What is $p(x)$?

© 24. Error Analysis Your friend says the solution of the rational equation $\dfrac{m}{m - 3} + \dfrac{1}{4} = \dfrac{3}{m - 3}$ is 3. Explain the error that your friend may have made.

© 25. Reasoning Consider the equation $\dfrac{3}{x - a} = \dfrac{x}{x - a}$. For what value(s) of a does the equation have exactly one solution? No solution? Explain.

Common Core Cumulative Standards Review

Ⓣ Ⓘ Ⓟ Ⓢ Ⓕ Ⓞ Ⓡ Ⓢ Ⓤ Ⓒ Ⓒ Ⓔ Ⓢ Ⓢ

Some questions on tests ask you to simplify an expression. Read the question at the right. Then follow the tips to answer it.

Which expression is equivalent to $\dfrac{20x^3y^5 - 30x^6y^4}{5x^3y^3}$?

Ⓐ $4x^6y^8 - 6x^9y^7$

Ⓑ $4y^2 - 6x^3y$

Ⓒ $-2x^6y^6$

Ⓓ $15y^2 - 25x^3y$

TIP 2

When you divide powers that have the same base, you subtract the exponents.

Think It Through

Write the expression as a difference of two fractions. Then simplify each fraction using the laws of exponents.

$$\dfrac{20x^3y^5 - 30x^6y^4}{5x^3y^3}$$

$$= \dfrac{20x^3y^5}{5x^3y^5} - \dfrac{30x^6y^4}{5x^3y^3}$$

$$= 4x^{3-3}y^{5-3} - 6x^{6-3}y^{4-3}$$

$$= 4x^0y^2 - 6x^2y^1$$

$$= 4y^2 - 6x^3y$$

TIP 1

Use the fact that a fraction $\dfrac{a+b}{c}$ can be written in the form $\dfrac{a}{c} + \dfrac{b}{c}$.

Vocabulary Builder

As you solve test items, you must understand the meanings of mathematical terms. Choose the correct term to complete each sentence.

A. The quantity $b^2 - 4ac$ is the (*vertex, discriminant*) of the equation $ax^2 + bx + c = 0$.

B. Two lines are (*parallel, perpendicular*) if their slopes are negative reciprocals of each other.

C. A (*linear, quadratic*) equation is an equation that can be written in the form $Ax + By = C$, where A, B, and C are real numbers, and A and B are not both 0.

D. A(n) (*rational, exponential*) expression is a ratio of two polynomials.

E. When you (*solve, evaluate*) an equation, you are finding the value or values that make the equation true.

Selected Response

Read each question. Then write the letter of the correct answer on your paper.

1. Which function describes the tables of values?

x	−2	−1	0	1
f(x)	−3	−1	1	3

Ⓐ $f(x) = x - 1$ Ⓒ $f(x) = x + 1$

Ⓑ $f(x) = 2x$ Ⓓ $f(x) = 2x + 1$

2. What is the factored form of $6w^4 + 15w^2$?

Ⓕ $w^2(6w^2 + 15)$

Ⓖ $3w^2(2w^2 + 5)$

Ⓗ $3w(2w^3 + 5w)$

Ⓘ $3w^2(2w^2 + 5w)$

3. Which expression is equivalent to $\frac{x+2}{x+4} - \frac{x+1}{x-3}$?

Ⓐ $\dfrac{-2(3x-5)}{(x+4)(x-3)}$

Ⓑ $\dfrac{-2(3x+5)}{(x+4)(x-3)}$

Ⓒ $\dfrac{-2(3x+5)}{(x-4)(x+3)}$

Ⓓ $\dfrac{2(3x-5)}{(x+4)(x-3)}$

4. Which is equivalent to $\dfrac{18x^2y + 24x^3y^4 - 12x^7y^2}{6x^2y}$?

Ⓕ $12 + 18xy^3 - 6x^5y$

Ⓖ $4xy^3 - 2x^5y$

Ⓗ $3 + 4xy^3 - 2x^5y$

Ⓘ $3x^2y + 4x^3y^4 - 2x^7y^2$

5. Which expression is equivalent to $\dfrac{x-4}{\frac{x+3}{x-1}}$?

Ⓐ $\dfrac{x^2 + 5x - 4}{x + 3}$

Ⓑ $\dfrac{x + 4}{x^2 + 2x - 3}$

Ⓒ $\dfrac{x^2 + 7x + 12}{x - 1}$

Ⓓ $\dfrac{x^2 - 5x + 4}{x + 3}$

6. Which of the following points are on the graph of $y = -2x + 3$?

Ⓕ $(0, -2)$ and $(1, 1)$

Ⓖ $(0, 3)$ and $(1, -1)$

Ⓗ $(1, 1)$ and $(0, 3)$

Ⓘ $(-1, 1)$ and $(0, -2)$

7. Which real-number property is illustrated below?
$$2x^2 + 3x^2 = (2 + 3)x^2 = 5x^2$$

Ⓐ Associative Property of Addition

Ⓑ Commutative Property of Addition

Ⓒ Distributive Property

Ⓓ Identity Property of Addition

8. What is (are) the solution(s) of the equation $\dfrac{2x+1}{5x} = \dfrac{4x-5}{3x}$?

Ⓕ 0

Ⓖ 2

Ⓗ 0 and 2

Ⓘ no solution

9. About 8 babies are born in the United States each minute. Using this estimate, about how many babies are born each year?

Ⓐ 70,000

Ⓑ 200,000

Ⓒ 4,000,000

Ⓓ 300,000,000

10. Which expression is equivalent to $\left(27m^6n\right)^{\frac{1}{3}}$?

Ⓕ $3m^2\sqrt[3]{n}$

Ⓖ $3m\sqrt[3]{n}$

Ⓗ $3m^2n$

Ⓘ $3m^2\sqrt{n}$

11. Which statement below about the function $y = 2x^2 - 3$ is correct?

Ⓐ The value of y is never less than -3.

Ⓑ The value of y is never greater than 2.

Ⓒ The value of x is always greater than the value of y.

Ⓓ The value of y is always greater than the value of x.

12. The length s of one edge of a cube is given by $s = \sqrt{\frac{A}{6}}$, where A represents the cube's surface area. Suppose a cube has an edge length of 10 cm. What is its surface area?

Ⓕ 60 cm^2

Ⓖ 600 cm^2

Ⓗ 6000 cm^2

Ⓘ $60,000 \text{ cm}^2$

13. What is the x-intercept of the graph of $-5x + y = -20$?

Ⓐ -20

Ⓑ -4

Ⓒ 4

Ⓓ 20

14. Davis bought 2 candy bars and 3 bags of chips for $5.45. Reese bought 5 bags of chips for $6.25. How much did each candy bar cost?

Ⓕ $.85

Ⓖ $.95

Ⓗ $1.25

Ⓘ $1.70

Constructed Response

15. A dinner party at a restaurant had 37 people. Each person ordered one of two entrées. One entrée cost $15, and the other entrée cost $18. The total cost of all the entrées was $606. How many $15 entrées were ordered?

16. A chemistry student needs to make 20 liters of a solution that is 60% acid. She plans to make the solution by mixing a solution that is 70% acid with another solution that is 45% acid. How many liters of the 45% acid solution will she need?

17. What is the negative solution of $2x^2 + x = 3$?

18. Karen can mow the lawn in 15 min. Her friend Kim can mow the lawn in 10 min. If they work together, how many minutes will they take to mow the lawn?

19. Sandra takes 6 h to drive 300 mi. If she increases her speed by 5 mi/h, how many hours will she take to drive 440 mi?

20. The graph of $f(x) = x + 3$ is shown. What is the y-intercept of the function $f(x) - 6$?

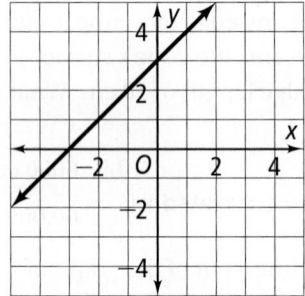

21. A roof on a house has a triangular cross section with at least two angles of equal measure. One angle of the triangle measures 120°. What is the measure, in degrees, of one of the other two angles?

22. Line p passes through points $(5, -4)$ and $(2, 7)$. What is the slope of a line that is perpendicular to line p?

23. A cylinder has a height of 20 cm and a diameter of 6 cm. What is the volume, in cubic centimeters, of the cylinder? Use 3.14 for π.

24. What is the simplified form of $\frac{x^2 - 81}{2x^2 + 23x + 45}$?

25. Phillip works at a grocery store after school and on weekends. He earns $8.50 per hour. What is a function rule for his total earnings $f(h)$ for working h hours?

26. What is the simplified form of $\frac{x^2 + 3x - 18}{6x + 36}$? Show your work.

27. Jordyn has three test grades of 95, 84, and 85, so far. If the final exam counts for two test scores and she needs at least 450 points for an A, what is the lowest score she can get on the final exam and still get an A for the course?

28. Rewrite the expression $\sqrt[4]{(81x^3)}$ using rational exponents.

29. The graph below shows the piecewise function for the total cost for x hours of labor at an automotive repair center. What will be the total cost of labor for a repair that takes $4\frac{1}{2}$ hours?

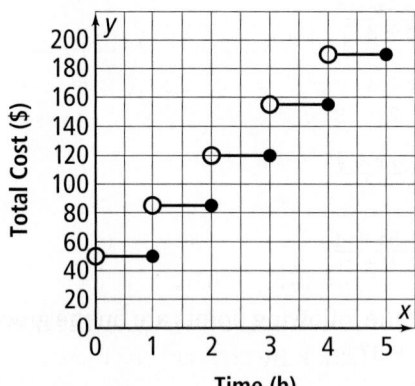

30. What are the solution(s) of the system?

$$y = x^2 - x - 6$$
$$y = 2x - 2$$

Extended Response

31. The formula $C = \frac{5}{9}(F - 32)$ can be used to find the Celsius temperature C if you know the Fahrenheit temperature F.

  a. Transform the equation to find the Fahrenheit temperature F in terms of the Celsius temperature C.

  b. Use the formula in part (a) to find the Fahrenheit temperature equivalent to 35°C.

Get Ready!

Skills
Handbook,
p. 803

Adding and Subtracting Fractions

Add or subtract. Write each answer in simplest form.

1. $\frac{2}{3} + \frac{1}{2}$　　　　**2.** $\frac{7}{12} - \frac{5}{8}$　　　　**3.** $\frac{16}{25} + \frac{3}{10}$　　　　**4.** $\frac{5}{9} - \frac{5}{36}$

Lesson 1-6

Multiplying and Dividing Real Numbers

Simplify each fraction.

5. $\frac{6 + 4 + 7 + 9}{4}$　　　　**6.** $\frac{1.7 + 4.2 + 3.1}{3}$　　　　**7.** $\frac{11 + 16 + 9 + 12 + 7}{5}$

Lesson 1-7

Distributive Property

Simplify each expression.

8. $6(x - 7)$　　　　**9.** $\frac{1}{2}(4x + 6)$　　　　**10.** $-2(5 - x)$　　　　**11.** $0.5(5 + 4x)$

Lesson 3-8

Unions and Intersections of Sets

Let $X = \{x \mid x$ is an odd whole number less than $16\}$, $Y = \{2, 6, 9, 10, 16\}$, and $Z = \{z \mid z$ is an even whole number less than $19\}$. Find each union or intersection.

12. $X \cup Y$　　　　**13.** $X \cap Y$　　　　**14.** $Y \cap Z$　　　　**15.** $X \cup Y \cup Z$

Lesson 5-7

Scatter Plots

For each table, make a scatter plot of the data. Describe the type of correlation that the scatter plot shows.

16.

Messenger Bag Sales				
Price ($)	30	45	60	75
Number Sold	150	123	85	50

17.

Driving Distances and Times				
Distance (mi)	5	38	15	8
Time (min)	15	56	28	22

Looking Ahead Vocabulary

18. There are three *outcomes* for a hockey team during a game: win, lose, or tie. What are the possible *outcomes* for flipping a coin?

19. On a highway, the *median* is the strip of land that divides the two sides of opposing traffic. How would you expect a *median* to divide a data set?

20. The color purple is a *combination* of the colors red and blue. Does the order in which the colors are combined change the result of the *combination*?

CHAPTER 12

Data Analysis and Probability

Download videos connecting math to your world.

Interactive! Vary numbers, graphs, and figures to explore math concepts.

The online Solve It will get you in gear for each lesson.

Math definitions in English and Spanish

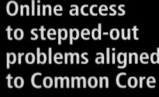

Online access to stepped-out problems aligned to Common Core

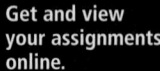

Get and view your assignments online.

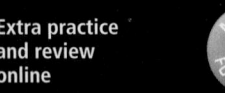

Extra practice and review online

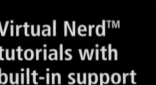

Virtual Nerd™ tutorials with built-in support

Chapter Preview

Vocabulary

English/Spanish Vocabulary Audio Online:

English	Spanish
combination, *p. 765*	combinación
event, *p. 769*	suceso
matrix, *p. 726*	matriz
measure of central tendency, *p. 738*	medida de tendencia central
outcome, *p. 769*	resultado
outlier, *p. 738*	valor extremo
permutation, *p. 763*	permutación
probability, *p. 769*	probabilidad
quartile, *p. 746*	cuartiles
sample space, *p. 769*	espacio de muestra

BIG ideas

1 Data Collection and Analysis
Essential Question How can collecting and analyzing data help you make decisions or predictions?

2 Data Representation
Essential Question How can you make and interpret different representations of data?

3 Probability
Essential Question How is probability related to real-world events?

 DOMAINS
• Interpreting Categorical and Quantitative Data
• Making Inferences and Justifying Conclusions
• Conditional Probability and the Rules of Probability

Common Core Performance Task

Choosing a Location for a Tournament

Luis manages a youth baseball league. He has to choose a location for the league's tournament for the next two years. The tournament takes place in August each year.

The ideal location is warm, with little rain. Luis has narrowed down the choices to two cities: Oakville and Fairview. Each city is in an area that is prone to hurricanes, so Luis will also take into account the likelihood that the city will not have a hurricane in August two years in a row.

Luis collects the following data about the cities.

Oakville Climate Data for August

Year	2004	2005	2006	2007	2008	2009	2010	2011	2012	2013
Rainfall (in.)	2.4	4.2	1.8	15.1	2.6	2.3	2.0	4.2	3.8	2.1
Avg. Temp. (°F)	78	84	89	72	74	77	82	87	76	78
Hurricane?	no	yes	no	yes	no	no	no	yes	yes	no

Fairview Climate Data for August

Year	2005	2006	2007	2008	2009	2010	2011	2012	2013
Rainfall (in.)	4.5	1.8	2.2	5.0	5.1	4.5	2.3	3.8	4.5
Avg. Temp. (°F)	83	77	82	80	87	86	86	82	83
Hurricane?	no	no	no	yes	no	yes	no	no	no

Task Description

Decide whether the tournament should be held in Oakville or Fairview, and justify your decision.

Connecting the Task to the Math Practices

MATHEMATICAL PRACTICES

As you complete the task, you'll apply several Standards for Mathematical Practice.

- You'll calculate and analyze measures of central tendency and dispersion. (MP 6)
- You'll create a box-and-whisker plot to represent data. (MP 4)
- You'll use probability to help you construct an argument. (MP 3)

12-1 Organizing Data Using Matrices

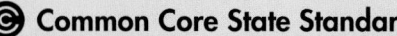
Common Core State Standards

Prepares for N-VM.C.6 Use matrices to represent and manipulate data, e.g., to represent payoffs or incidence relationships in a network.

MP 1, MP 3, MP 4, MP 6

Objectives To organize data in a matrix
To add and subtract matrices and multiply a matrix by a scalar

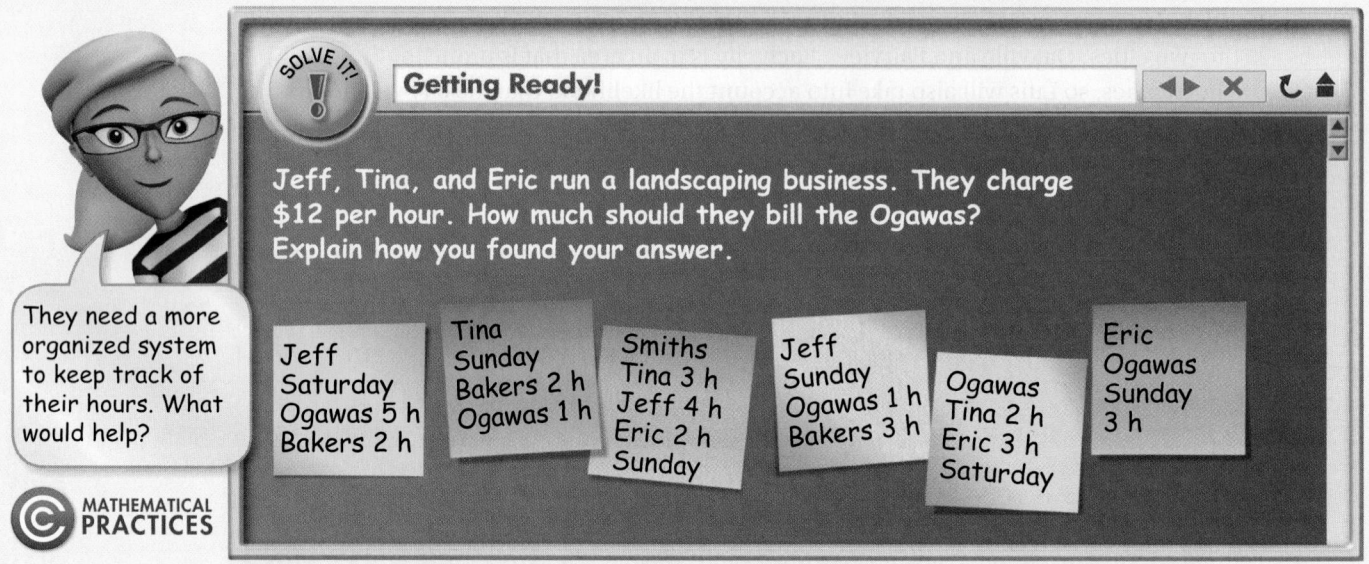

Getting Ready!

Jeff, Tina, and Eric run a landscaping business. They charge $12 per hour. How much should they bill the Ogawas? Explain how you found your answer.

They need a more organized system to keep track of their hours. What would help?

Jeff
Saturday
Ogawas 5 h
Bakers 2 h

Tina
Sunday
Bakers 2 h
Ogawas 1 h

Smiths
Tina 3 h
Jeff 4 h
Eric 2 h
Sunday

Jeff
Sunday
Ogawas 1 h
Bakers 3 h

Ogawas
Tina 2 h
Eric 3 h
Saturday

Eric
Ogawas
Sunday
3 h

MATHEMATICAL PRACTICES

Lesson Vocabulary
• matrix
• element
• scalar
• scalar multiplication

A **matrix** is a rectangular arrangement of numbers in rows and columns. The plural of *matrix* is *matrices* (pronounced MAY truh seez). The matrix below shows the hours Jeff, Tina, and Eric worked on Saturday.

$$
\begin{array}{c}
 \text{Ogawas} \quad \text{Bakers} \\
\begin{array}{c} \text{Jeff} \\ \text{Tina} \\ \text{Eric} \end{array}
\left[\begin{array}{cc} 5 & 2 \\ 2 & 0 \\ 3 & 0 \end{array} \right] \leftarrow \text{Row}
\end{array}
$$

$\uparrow$
Column

You identify the size of a matrix by the number of rows and the number of columns. The matrix above has 3 rows and 2 columns, so it is a 3 × 2 matrix.

Each number in a matrix is an **element**. Matrices are equal if they are the same size and the elements in corresponding positions are equal.

$$
\begin{bmatrix} -1 & 2 \\ 4 & 0 \end{bmatrix} = \begin{bmatrix} -1 & \frac{4}{2} \\ (5-1) & 0 \end{bmatrix}
$$

Essential Understanding You can use matrices to organize data. This may make it easier to perform calculations on the data.

You may need to add or subtract matrices in order to solve problems. You can only add or subtract matrices that are the same size. You add or subtract matrices by adding or subtracting the corresponding elements.

 Problem 1 Adding and Subtracting Matrices

What is each sum or difference?

A $\begin{bmatrix} -5 & 2.7 \\ 7 & -3 \end{bmatrix} + \begin{bmatrix} -3 & -3.9 \\ -4 & 2 \end{bmatrix} = \begin{bmatrix} -5 + (-3) & 2.7 + (-3.9) \\ 7 + (-4) & -3 + 2 \end{bmatrix}$ Add corresponding elements.

$= \begin{bmatrix} -8 & -1.2 \\ 3 & -1 \end{bmatrix}$ Simplify.

B $\begin{bmatrix} 2 & 11 \\ -4 & 3.2 \\ 1.5 & -5 \end{bmatrix} - \begin{bmatrix} -1 & 8 \\ -6.5 & 4 \\ 0 & -3 \end{bmatrix} = \begin{bmatrix} 2 - (-1) & 11 - 8 \\ -4 - (-6.5) & 3.2 - 4 \\ 1.5 - 0 & -5 - (-3) \end{bmatrix}$ Subtract corresponding elements.

$= \begin{bmatrix} 3 & 3 \\ 2.5 & -0.8 \\ 1.5 & -2 \end{bmatrix}$ Simplify.

Got It? **1.** What is each sum or difference in parts (a) and (b)?

a. $\begin{bmatrix} 5 \\ 3.2 \\ -4.9 \end{bmatrix} + \begin{bmatrix} -9 \\ -1.7 \\ -11.1 \end{bmatrix}$ **b.** $\begin{bmatrix} -4 & 0 \\ 3 & 7 \end{bmatrix} - \begin{bmatrix} -5 & -1 \\ 0.5 & -3 \end{bmatrix}$

c. Reasoning Explain why you cannot add or subtract matrices that are not the same size.

Think

Can you add the matrices?
Yes, you can add the matrices because they are the same size. Each matrix has 2 rows and 2 columns.

You may also need to multiply a matrix by a real number in order to solve problems. The real-number factor is called a **scalar.** Multiplying a matrix by a scalar is called **scalar multiplication.** To use scalar multiplication, multiply each element in the matrix by the scalar.

 Problem 2 Multiplying a Matrix by a Scalar

What is the product $3 \begin{bmatrix} 4 & -1.5 \\ 1 & -6 \end{bmatrix}$**?**

$3 \begin{bmatrix} 4 & -1.5 \\ 1 & -6 \end{bmatrix} = \begin{bmatrix} 3(4) & 3(-1.5) \\ 3(1) & 3(-6) \end{bmatrix}$ Multiply each element by the scalar, 3.

$= \begin{bmatrix} 12 & -4.5 \\ 3 & -18 \end{bmatrix}$ Simplify.

Think

Which factor is the scalar?
The scalar is the real-number factor, 3.

Got It? **2.** What is each product?

a. $-2\begin{bmatrix} -3 & 7.1 & 5 \end{bmatrix}$ **b.** $1.5\begin{bmatrix} -11 & 3 \\ 0 & -1.5 \end{bmatrix}$

You can use matrices to organize real-world data.

 Problem 3 **Using Matrices**

Weather Use the weather chart below. Which city has the greatest average number of clear days in a full year?

Average Number of Clear and Cloudy Days

September – February	March – August
Phoenix: 102 clear, 41 cloudy	Phoenix: 110 clear, 27 cloudy
Miami: 43 clear, 58 cloudy	Miami: 31 clear, 59 cloudy
Portland: 55 clear, 82 cloudy	Portland: 45 clear, 83 cloudy

Portland, ME

Phoenix, AZ

Miami, FL

Plan

What size matrices should you use?
There are three cities and two types of weather represented by the data. So you can use 3×2 matrices or 2×3 matrices.

Step 1 Use matrices to organize the information.

September–February

               Clear Cloudy

$$\begin{matrix} \text{Phoenix} \\ \text{Miami} \\ \text{Portland} \end{matrix} \begin{bmatrix} 102 & 41 \\ 43 & 58 \\ 55 & 82 \end{bmatrix}$$

March–August

               Clear Cloudy

$$\begin{matrix} \text{Phoenix} \\ \text{Miami} \\ \text{Portland} \end{matrix} \begin{bmatrix} 110 & 27 \\ 31 & 59 \\ 45 & 83 \end{bmatrix}$$

Step 2 Add the matrices to find the average numbers of clear and cloudy days in a full year for each city. The matrices are the same size, so you can add them.

$$\begin{bmatrix} 102 & 41 \\ 43 & 58 \\ 55 & 82 \end{bmatrix} + \begin{bmatrix} 110 & 27 \\ 31 & 59 \\ 45 & 83 \end{bmatrix} = \begin{bmatrix} 212 & 68 \\ 74 & 117 \\ 100 & 165 \end{bmatrix}$$ Add corresponding elements.

Step 3 Find the greatest average number of clear days in a full year. The first column of the matrix represents the average number of clear days in a full year for each city. The greatest number in that column is 212, which corresponds to Phoenix. So Phoenix has the greatest average number of clear days in a full year.

$$\begin{bmatrix} 212 & 68 \\ 74 & 117 \\ 100 & 165 \end{bmatrix}$$

 Got It? **3.** Which city in Problem 3 has the greatest average number of cloudy days in a full year?

Lesson Check

Do you know HOW?

Find each sum or difference.

1. $\begin{bmatrix} 0 & 7 \\ -4 & 5 \end{bmatrix} + \begin{bmatrix} -3 & 2 \\ 4 & -1 \end{bmatrix}$ **2.** $\begin{bmatrix} 5 & 4 \\ -1 & 0 \end{bmatrix} - \begin{bmatrix} 3 & 1 \\ -3 & 3 \end{bmatrix}$

Find each product.

3. $2\begin{bmatrix} 4 & 0 & 5 \\ -2 & 1 & 2 \end{bmatrix}$ **4.** $-6\begin{bmatrix} 5 & 0 \\ 2 & -3 \end{bmatrix}$

Do you UNDERSTAND?

5. Vocabulary How many elements are there in a 3×3 matrix?

6. Error Analysis A student added two matrices as shown at the right. Describe and correct the mistake.

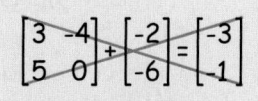

7. Open-Ended Write two different 3×3 matrices. Then add your matrices.

Practice and Problem-Solving Exercises

 **Practice** Find each sum or difference. **See Problem 1.**

8. $\begin{bmatrix} 1 & -1 \\ 0 & 1 \end{bmatrix} + \begin{bmatrix} 0 & 1 \\ 1 & -1 \end{bmatrix}$ **9.** $\begin{bmatrix} -3 & 6 \\ 2 & 0 \end{bmatrix} - \begin{bmatrix} -2 & 5 \\ 2 & 0 \end{bmatrix}$ **10.** $\begin{bmatrix} 5 & 2 \\ -1 & 8 \end{bmatrix} - \begin{bmatrix} 7 & -4 \\ 0 & 2 \end{bmatrix}$

11. $\begin{bmatrix} 4 & -1 \\ 2 & 0 \\ 3 & 5 \end{bmatrix} + \begin{bmatrix} -2 & 0 \\ 3 & -1 \\ -3 & 5 \end{bmatrix}$ **12.** $\begin{bmatrix} 0 & 0.4 \\ -2 & 5.3 \\ 1.2 & 3.7 \end{bmatrix} + \begin{bmatrix} 1.8 & -5 \\ 7.1 & 0 \\ 0.3 & 2.3 \end{bmatrix}$ **13.** $\begin{bmatrix} 4.7 & -0.3 \\ 2.9 & 0.7 \\ -3.5 & 1.3 \end{bmatrix} - \begin{bmatrix} 2.3 & 7.3 \\ -5.1 & 0.4 \\ 4.2 & 0 \end{bmatrix}$

Find each product. **See Problem 2.**

14. $4\begin{bmatrix} 6 & -3 \\ 0 & 5 \end{bmatrix}$ **15.** $-2\begin{bmatrix} 3 & -1 \\ 7 & -2 \end{bmatrix}$ **16.** $0\begin{bmatrix} 5.3 & -7.2 \\ -1.8 & 0.6 \end{bmatrix}$ **17.** $-5\begin{bmatrix} 3.8 & 2.1 & 7 \\ 9.4 & -6 & 0 \end{bmatrix}$

18. $2.7\begin{bmatrix} 3 & 4.7 \\ 0 & -3 \\ 5.7 & 2.7 \end{bmatrix}$ **19.** $-3.1\begin{bmatrix} 4 & 7.5 \\ 9 & -5 \\ 1 & 4.6 \end{bmatrix}$ **20.** $8.3\begin{bmatrix} -1 & 8.2 \\ 0.3 & -4.1 \\ 6.2 & 9.5 \end{bmatrix}$ **21.** $-0.2\begin{bmatrix} 8.3 & -3 & 0 \\ 4.5 & 5.6 & 1 \\ -1 & 2.9 & 7 \end{bmatrix}$

22. Sports For a certain city, the tables below show the numbers of participants in various sports in 2005 and 2010. Which sport had the greatest numerical increase in student participation between 2005 and 2010? Find your answer using matrices. **See Problem 3.**

Sports Participation, 2005

Sport	Students	Adults
Baseball	739	215
Basketball	1023	437
Football	690	58
Soccer	1546	42

Sports Participation, 2010

Sport	Students	Adults
Baseball	892	351
Basketball	1114	483
Football	653	64
Soccer	1712	37

23. Manufacturing A furniture company has two factories. During the first shift, Factory A made 250 chairs and 145 tables, and Factory B made 300 chairs and 75 tables. During the second shift, Factory A made 275 chairs and 90 tables, and Factory B made 240 chairs and 120 tables. Which factory made more chairs during the two shifts? Find your answer using matrices.

24. Sales The weekly sales records below show the numbers of different colors and models of shoes sold in two weeks. Which is the color and model shoe with the highest sales between February 2 and 15? Find your answer using matrices.

Shoe Sales, Feb. 2–8

Color	Model 73	Model 84
Black	153	79
White	241	116
Blue	58	32
Brown	95	47

Shoe Sales, Feb. 9–15

Color	Model 73	Model 84
Black	172	82
White	278	130
Blue	65	29
Brown	103	54

 **Apply**

Simplify each expression. (*Hint:* Multiply before adding or subtracting.)

25. $2\begin{bmatrix} 6 & 0 & -2 \\ -5 & 3 & 1 \end{bmatrix} - \begin{bmatrix} 3 & -1 & -6 \\ 0 & 4 & 2 \end{bmatrix}$

26. $\begin{bmatrix} 0 & 3.4 & 5 \\ 4.1 & -2 & 1 \end{bmatrix} + 0.5\begin{bmatrix} -8 & 6.4 & 0 \\ 0.2 & -2.8 & 4.2 \end{bmatrix}$

27. $-3\begin{bmatrix} 4.2 & -7.3 & 0.7 \\ 2.7 & -9.3 & 11.8 \\ 3.6 & 8.2 & -4.8 \end{bmatrix} - 2\begin{bmatrix} 7.8 & -4.1 & 9.4 \\ -8 & 0 & 0.8 \\ -1.4 & 5.9 & 3.3 \end{bmatrix}$

28. $\begin{bmatrix} -3.7 & 2.5 & -7.5 \\ 2.2 & -6.2 & 0.3 \\ 1.5 & -3.1 & 4.9 \end{bmatrix} + (-5)\begin{bmatrix} 8.7 & 1.5 & 4.5 \\ -4 & 0.1 & -7.3 \\ 5.8 & 4.1 & 7.3 \end{bmatrix}$

29. Think About a Plan Use the table at the right that shows nutrition information for 1 serving of each type of food. For which item(s) do 6 servings have less than 1000 Calories?
- What matrix represents the nutrition information for 1 serving?
- How can you find the nutrition information for 6 servings?

FOOD ITEM		Serving	Calories	Protein (g)	Fat (g)
	Chicken	1	148	29	3.5
	Fruit salad	1	221	1	0
	Spaghetti & meatballs	1	273	11	13

Source: U.S. Department of Agriculture

30. Politics The results of an election for mayor are shown below. The town will hold a runoff election between the top two candidates if no one received more than 50% of the votes. Should the town hold a runoff? If so, which candidates should be in the runoff? Explain your reasoning.

Votes by Precinct

Candidate	Precinct 1	2	3	4
Greene	373	285	479	415
Jackson	941	871	114	97
Voigt	146	183	728	682

Find the values of x and y that make each equation true.

31. $\begin{bmatrix} 0 & x \\ 2x & -4 \end{bmatrix} + \begin{bmatrix} 3 & 4y \\ y & 8 \end{bmatrix} = \begin{bmatrix} 3 & 18 \\ 1 & 4 \end{bmatrix}$

32. $\begin{bmatrix} x & -1 \\ 4 & 3x \end{bmatrix} + \begin{bmatrix} -3y & 5 \\ -6 & 2y \end{bmatrix} = \begin{bmatrix} 7 & 4 \\ -2 & 10 \end{bmatrix}$

Standardized Test Prep

SAT/ACT

33. Which matrix is equal to $-3 \begin{bmatrix} 5.5 & -1 \\ -3 & 2 \end{bmatrix}$?

Ⓐ $\begin{bmatrix} 8.5 & 2 \\ 0 & 5 \end{bmatrix}$　　Ⓑ $\begin{bmatrix} 2.5 & -4 \\ -6 & -1 \end{bmatrix}$　　Ⓒ $\begin{bmatrix} 16.5 & -3 \\ -9 & 6 \end{bmatrix}$　　Ⓓ $\begin{bmatrix} -16.5 & 3 \\ 9 & -6 \end{bmatrix}$

34. Which equation represents a line parallel to the graph of $y = 3x + 6$?

Ⓕ $x - \frac{1}{3}y = 0$　　　　　　　　　　　Ⓗ $y = \frac{1}{3}x + 2$

Ⓖ $y = -3x + 2$　　　　　　　　　　　Ⓘ $y = 2x + 6$

35. What is the simplified form of $2\sqrt{108}$?

Ⓐ $12\sqrt{3}$　　　　Ⓑ $6\sqrt{12}$　　　　Ⓒ $3\sqrt{26}$　　　　Ⓓ $2\sqrt{6}$

Short Response

36. Carlos does his homework at a rate of 25 problems per hour. Cecelia does her homework at a rate of 30 problems per hour. Carlos started his homework 12 min before Cecelia. How many hours after Carlos started his homework will they have done the same number of problems? Show your work.

Mixed Review

See Lesson 11-7.

Identify the excluded value of each rational function.

37. $y = \frac{3}{x - 5}$　　　　　　**38.** $y = \frac{-1}{x}$　　　　　　**39.** $f(x) = \frac{5x}{x - 4}$

Get Ready! To prepare for Lesson 12-2, do Exercises 40 and 41.

For each table, make a scatter plot of the data. Tell whether a correlation exists. If so, tell whether the correlation reflects a causal relationship. Explain your reasoning.

See Lesson 5-7.

40. Shoe Sizes and Test Scores

Name	Shoe Size	Test Score
Baker	9	87
Johns	11	94
Rivera	8	96
Samuels	7	75

41. Sales Commissions

Employee	Products Sold	Commission Earned ($)
Andrews	38	310
Garcia	24	250
Jordan	47	448
Walker	53	495

12-2 Frequency and Histograms

Common Core State Standards

S-ID.A.1 Represent data with plots on the real number line (dot plots, histograms, and box plots). **Also N-Q.A.1**

MP 1, MP 2, MP 3, MP 4, MP 6

Objective To make and interpret frequency tables and histograms

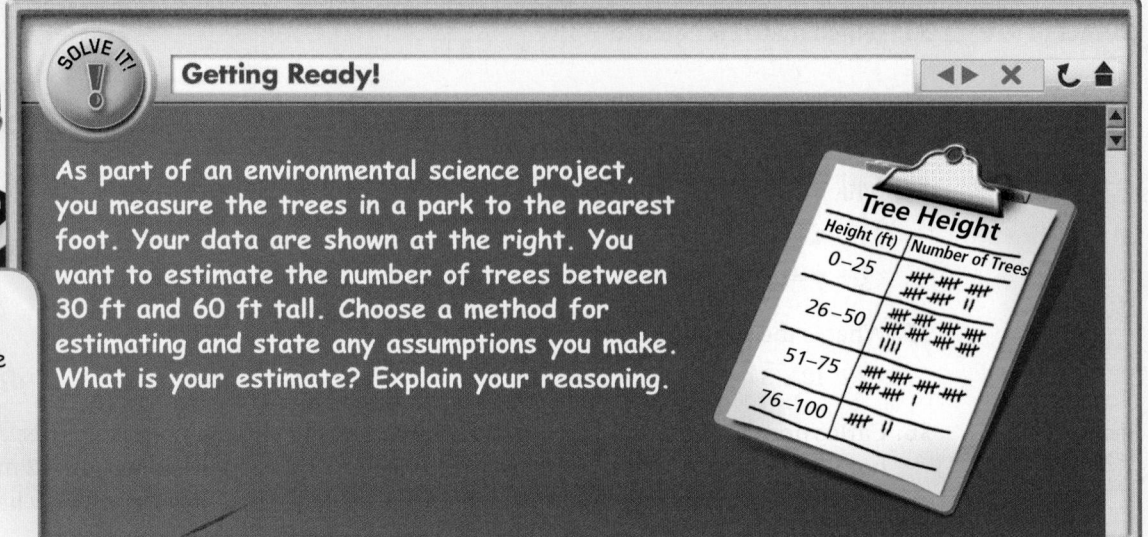

Getting Ready!

As part of an environmental science project, you measure the trees in a park to the nearest foot. Your data are shown at the right. You want to estimate the number of trees between 30 ft and 60 ft tall. Choose a method for estimating and state any assumptions you make. What is your estimate? Explain your reasoning.

You can make assumptions to help you estimate so long as you realize that you may need to change your assumptions if you get better information.

Tree Height

Height (ft)	Number of Trees
0–25	𝍸𝍸𝍸 𝍸𝍸𝍸 𝍸𝍸
26–50	𝍸𝍸𝍸 𝍸𝍸𝍸 𝍸𝍸𝍸 𝍸𝍸𝍸 𝍸𝍸𝍸 𝍸𝍸𝍸
51–75	𝍸𝍸𝍸 𝍸𝍸𝍸 𝍸𝍸𝍸 𝍸𝍸𝍸
76–100	𝍸𝍸𝍸 𝍸𝍸

Essential Understanding There are many ways to organize and visually display data. Sometimes it is helpful to organize numerical data into intervals.

The **frequency** of an interval is the number of data values in that interval. A **frequency table** groups a set of data values into intervals and shows the frequency for each interval. Intervals in frequency tables do not overlap, do not have any gaps, and are usually of equal size.

Lesson Vocabulary
• frequency
• frequency table
• histogram
• cumulative frequency table

 Problem 1 Making a Frequency Table

Baseball The numbers of home runs by the batters in a local home run derby are listed below. What is a frequency table that represents the data?

7 17 14 2 7 9 5 12 3 10 4 12 7 15

The minimum data value is 2 and the maximum is 17. Intervals of 4 seem reasonable. In the first column of the table, list the intervals. Count the number of data values in each interval and list the number in the second column.

Home Run Results

Home Runs	Frequency
2–5	4
6–9	4
10–13	3
14–17	3

Plan

How do you choose intervals?
The data values range from 2 to 17, so there are a total of 16 possible values. You can divide these 16 values into 4 intervals of size 4.

 Got It? **1.** What is a frequency table for the data in Problem 1 that uses intervals of 5?

A **histogram** is a graph that can display data from a frequency table. A histogram has one bar for each interval. The height of each bar shows the frequency of data in the interval it represents. There are no gaps between bars. The bars are usually of equal width.

Problem 2 Making a Histogram

Television The data below are the numbers of hours per week a group of students spent watching television. What is a histogram that represents the data?

7 10 1 5 14 22 6 8 0 11 13 3 4 14 5

Know	Need	Plan
A set of data values	A histogram of the data values	Make a frequency table. This will help you construct the histogram.

Use the intervals from the frequency table for the histogram. Draw a bar for each interval. Make the height of each bar equal to the frequency of its interval. The bars should touch but not overlap. Label each axis.

Watching Television

Hours	Frequency
0–5	6
6–11	5
12–17	3
18–23	1

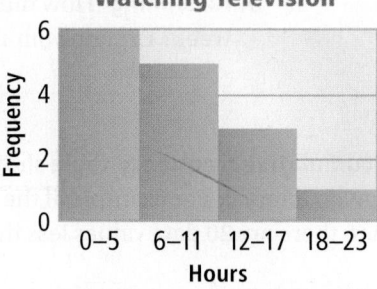

Watching Television

 Got It? **2.** The finishing times, in seconds, for a race are shown below. What is a histogram that represents the data?

95 105 83 80 93 98 102 99 82 89 90 82 89

You can describe histograms in terms of their shape. Three types are shown below.

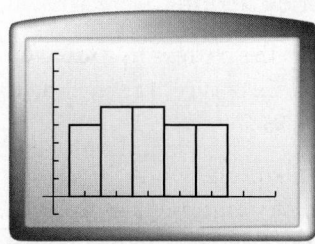

If the bars are roughly the same height, the histogram is *uniform*.

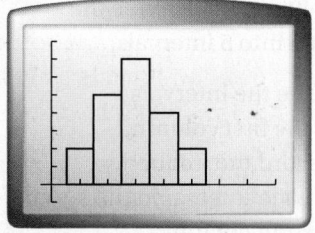

If a vertical line can divide the histogram into two parts that are close to mirror images, then the histogram is *symmetric*.

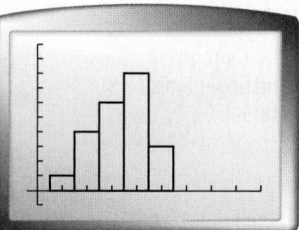

If the histogram has one peak that is not in the center, the histogram is *skewed*.

Think

Where have you seen symmetry before?
The parabolas you graphed in Chapter 9 are symmetric with respect to their axis of symmetry.

© **Problem 3** Interpreting Histograms

Is each histogram *uniform*, *symmetric*, or *skewed*?

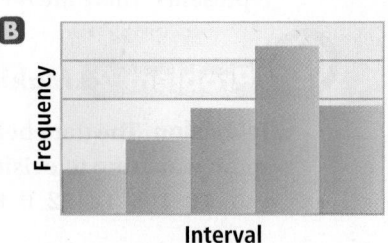

A

This histogram is symmetric because the halves are close to mirror images.

B

This histogram is skewed because the peak is not in the center.

© ✓ **Got It?** **3. a.** The following set of data shows the numbers of dollars Jay spent on lunch over the last two weeks. Make a histogram of the data. Is the histogram *uniform, symmetric,* or *skewed*?

17 1 4 11 14 14 5 16 6 5 9 10 13 9

b. Reasoning How much money should Jay plan to bring for lunch next week? Explain your reasoning.

A **cumulative frequency table** shows the number of data values that lie in or below a given interval. For example, if the cumulative frequency for the interval 70–79 is 20, then there are 20 data values less than or equal to 79.

© **Problem 4** Making a Cumulative Frequency Table

Text Messaging The numbers of text messages sent on one day by different students are shown below. What is a cumulative frequency table that represents the data?

17 3 1 30 11 7 1 5 2 39 22 13 2 0 21 1 49 41 27 2 0

Think

What does a cumulative frequency table tell you?
A cumulative frequency table tells you the number of data values that are less than or equal to the upper limit of each interval.

Step 1 Divide the data into intervals. The minimum is 0 and the maximum is 49. You can divide the data into 5 intervals.

Step 2 Write the intervals in the first column. Record the frequency of each interval in the second column.

Daily Text Messaging

Number of Text Messages	Frequency	Cumulative Frequency
0–9	11	11
10–19	3	14
20–29	3	17
30–39	2	19
40–49	2	21

11 + 3 = 14
14 + 3 = 17
17 + 2 = 19
19 + 2 = 21

Step 3 For the third column, add the frequency of each interval to the frequencies of all the previous intervals.

✓ **Got It?** **4.** What is a cumulative frequency table that represents the data below?

12 13 15 1 5 7 10 9 2 2 7 11 2 1 0 15

Lesson Check

Do you know HOW?

The data below show battery life, in hours, for different brands of batteries.

12 9 10 14 10 11 10 18 21 10 14 22

1. Make a frequency table of the data.

2. Make a histogram of the data.

3. Make a cumulative frequency table of the data.

Do you UNDERSTAND?

4. **Vocabulary** How might a frequency table help a store owner determine the busiest business hours?

5. **Compare and Contrast** What is the difference between a symmetric histogram and a skewed histogram?

6. **Writing** How can you use a frequency table of a data set to construct a cumulative frequency table?

Practice and Problem-Solving Exercises

Use the data to make a frequency table. ◀ See Problem 1.

7. wing spans (cm): 150 126 139 144 125 149 133 140 142 149 150 127 130

8. marathon times (min): 135 211 220 180 175 161 246 201 192 167 235 208

9. top speeds (mi/h): 108 90 96 150 120 115 135 126 165 155 130 125 100

Use the data to make a histogram. ◀ See Problem 2.

10. costs of items: $11 $30 $22 $8 $15 $28 $17 $17 $1 $19 $29 $21 $12 $25

11. ages of relatives: 18 5 27 34 56 54 9 14 35 22 78 94 47 52 2 16 17 10

12. restaurant waiting times (min): 20 35 15 25 5 10 40 30 10 50 20 60 10 8

13. points per game: 10 2 13 18 22 20 8 9 12 33 10 13 21 18 5 16 17 13

Tell whether each histogram is *uniform*, *symmetric*, or *skewed*. ◀ See Problem 3.

14.
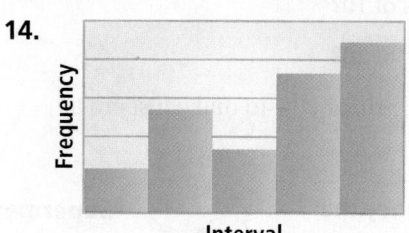

15.
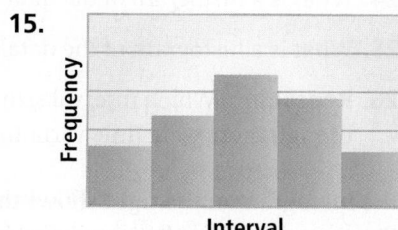

16.
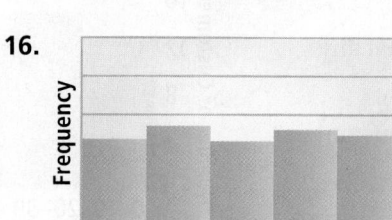

17.
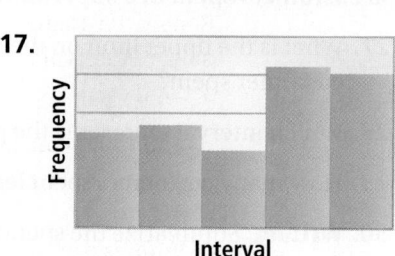

See Problem 4.

Use the data to make a cumulative frequency table.

18. trail lengths (mi): 4 1 5 2 1 3 7 12 6 3 11 9 2 1 3 4 1 2 5 3 1 1

19. heights of buildings (ft): 105 245 300 234 225 156 180 308 250 114 150 285

20. earthquake magnitudes: 2.1 5.4 6.7 3.2 4.5 2.7 2.6 3.1 4.4 8.1 4.1 2.9 2.1

B Apply

21. **Music** The Perpendicular Bisectors' new CD is shown at the right.
   a. Make a cumulative frequency table that represents the lengths of the songs in seconds.
   b. About what percent of the songs are under 4 min? How do you know?

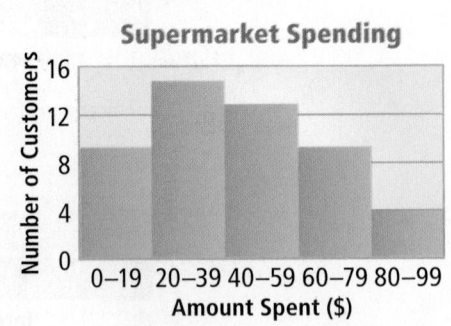

Add It (intro)	1:25
A Fraction of My Love	3:30
Common Denominator	4:14
Always, Sometimes, Never	2:56
Factorial	3:15
Transitive Property	4:20
All You Need Is Math	4:58
SAS	3:51
Frequency	3:32
Subtract It (outro)	1:56

22. **Think About a Plan** A travel agent conducted a survey to find out how many times people go to the beach each year. The results of the survey are shown in the histogram below. About how many people were surveyed?

Annual Beach Trips

(histogram: Number of Responses vs. Number of Trips; intervals 0–24, 25–49, 50–74, 75–99)

- What does the height of each bar represent?
- How can you use the bar heights to find the number of people surveyed?

Use the test scores below.
   81 70 73 89 68 79 91 59 77 73 80 75 88 65 82 94 77 67 82

23. What is a histogram of the data that uses intervals of 5?

24. What is a histogram of the data that uses intervals of 10?

25. What is a histogram of the data that uses intervals of 20?

26. **Reasoning** Which interval size would you use—5, 10, or 20—to make it seem as though there were little variation in the test scores?

The histogram at the right shows the amounts of money that 50 customers spent in a supermarket.

Supermarket Spending

(histogram: Number of Customers vs. Amount Spent ($); intervals 0–19, 20–39, 40–59, 60–79, 80–99)

27. What is the upper limit on the amount of money that any customer spent?

28. Which interval represents the greatest number of customers?

29. How many customers spent less than $20?

30. **Writing** Summarize the spending of the 50 customers represented in the histogram.

31. Error Analysis A student made the frequency table at the right using the data below. Describe and correct the error.

40 21 28 53 24 48 50 55 42 29 22 52 43 26 44

Interval	Frequency
20–29	6
40–49	5
50–59	4

Challenge **32.** Make a histogram for a set of 200 data values. The histogram must have 40% of the values lie in the interval 20–29. The remaining values should be evenly divided among the intervals 0–9, 10–19, 30–39, and 40–49.

33. Copy and complete the cumulative frequency table at the right.

Interval	Frequency	Cumulative Frequency
0–9	■	6
10–19	■	17
20–29	■	26
30–39	■	35

Standardized Test Prep

SAT/ACT **34.** What is the shape of the histogram at the right?

Ⓐ symmetric   Ⓒ skewed

Ⓑ proportional   Ⓓ uniform

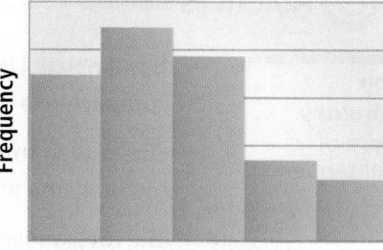

35. What is the solution of $(-4x - 6) + (6x + 1) = -13$?

Ⓕ -4 Ⓗ 6

Ⓖ 5   Ⓘ 9

36. What is the factored form of $x^2 - 6x - 16$?

Ⓐ $(x + 2)(x + 8)$ Ⓑ $(x - 2)(x + 8)$ Ⓒ $(x + 2)(x - 8)$ Ⓓ $(x - 2)(x - 8)$

Short Response **37.** Between what two integer values of x do the graphs of $y = 20(0.5)^x$ and $y = 0.5 \cdot 4^x$ intersect? Show your work.

Mixed Review

Find each sum or difference.   ◆ See Lesson 12-1.

38. $\begin{bmatrix} 4 & 6 \\ 5 & 7 \end{bmatrix} + \begin{bmatrix} 8 & 10 \\ 9 & 11 \end{bmatrix}$ **39.** $\begin{bmatrix} 0.2 & 0.6 \\ 0.8 & 0.5 \end{bmatrix} - \begin{bmatrix} 2.3 & 5.9 \\ 7.5 & 1.0 \end{bmatrix}$

Get Ready!   **To prepare for Lesson 12-3, do Exercises 40 and 41.**

Order the numbers in each exercise from least to greatest.   ◆ See Lesson 1-3.

40. $13, \frac{5}{4}, -4, -16, 0, 2, 16, \frac{1}{2}$ **41.** $0.9, -0.2, 1.2, 5, -1, 0, 0.1, 2$

12-3 Measures of Central Tendency and Dispersion

Common Core State Standards

S-ID.A.2 Use statistics appropriate to the . . . data distribution to compare center . . . and spread . . . of two or more different data sets. **Also S-ID.A.3, N-Q.A.2**

MP 1, MP 2, MP 3, MP 4, MP 6

Objective   To find mean, median, mode, and range

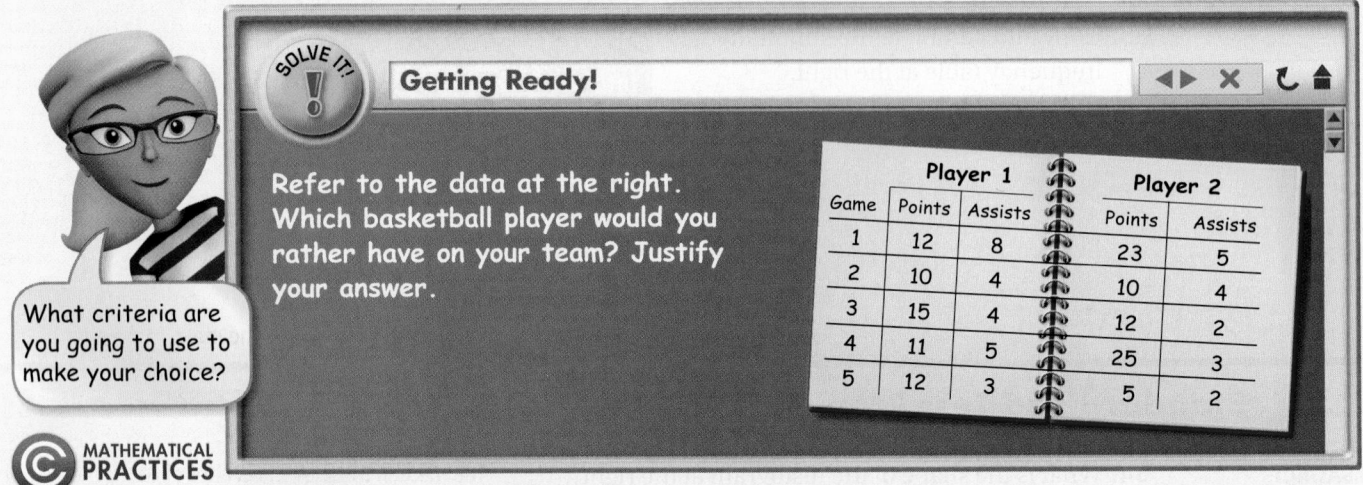

Getting Ready!

Refer to the data at the right. Which basketball player would you rather have on your team? Justify your answer.

What criteria are you going to use to make your choice?

Game	Player 1 Points	Player 1 Assists	Player 2 Points	Player 2 Assists
1	12	8	23	5
2	10	4	10	4
3	15	4	12	2
4	11	5	25	3
5	12	3	5	2

MATHEMATICAL PRACTICES

Lesson Vocabulary
- measure of central tendency
- outlier
- mean
- median
- mode
- measure of dispersion
- range of a set of data

Essential Understanding   You can use different measures to interpret and compare sets of data.

One way to summarize a set of data is to use a *measure of central tendency*. Mean, median, and mode are all **measures of central tendency.**

The measure of central tendency that best describes a data set may depend on whether the data set has an *outlier*. An **outlier** is a data value that is much greater or less than the other values in the set. Below is a review of mean, median, and mode, and when to use each as the measure of central tendency.

Key Concept   Mean, Median, and Mode

Measure	When to Use
The **mean** equals $\frac{\text{sum of the data values}}{\text{total number of data values}}$. The mean is often referred to as the *average*.	Use mean to describe the middle of a set of data that *does not* have an outlier.
The **median** is the middle value in a data set when the values are arranged in order. For a set containing an even number of data values, the median is the mean of the two middle data values.	Use median to describe the middle of a set of data that *does* have an outlier.
The **mode** is the data item that occurs the most times. A data set can have no mode, one mode, or more than one mode.	Use mode when the data are nonnumeric or when choosing the most popular item.

Problem 1 Finding Measures of Central Tendency

Bowling What are the mean, median, and mode of the bowling scores below? Which measure of central tendency best describes the scores?

Bowler 1: 104
Bowler 2: 117
Bowler 3: 104
Bowler 4: 136

Bowler 5: 189
Bowler 6: 109
Bowler 7: 113
Bowler 8: 104

Think

Is there an outlier in the data set?
Yes, the score 189 is much higher than the other scores.

Mean: $\dfrac{104 + 117 + 104 + 136 + 189 + 109 + 113 + 104}{8} = 122$

The mean is the sum of the scores divided by the number of scores.

Median: 104 104 104 109 113 117 136 189   List the data in order.

$\dfrac{109 + 113}{2} = 111$

The median of an even number of data values is the mean of the two middle data values.

Mode: 104

The mode is the data item that occurs the most times.

Because there is an outlier, 189, the median is the best measure to describe the scores. The mean, 122, is greater than most of the scores. The mode, 104, is the lowest score. Neither the mean nor the mode describes the data well. The median best describes the data.

 Got It? **1.** Consider the scores from Problem 1 that do not include the outlier, 189. What are the mean, median, and mode of the scores? Which measure of central tendency best describes the data?

You can use an equation to find a value needed to achieve a given average.

Problem 2 Finding a Data Value

Grades Your grades on three exams are 80, 93, and 91. What grade do you need on the next exam to have an average of 90 on the four exams?

Plan

What information is unknown?
The grade on the fourth exam is unknown. Use a variable to represent this grade.

$\dfrac{80 + 93 + 91 + x}{4} = 90$ Use the formula for the mean. Let $x =$ the grade on the fourth exam.

$\dfrac{264 + x}{4} = 90$ Simplify the numerator.

$264 + x = 360$ Multiply each side by 4.

$x = 96$ Subtract 264 from each side.

Your grade on the next exam must be 96 for you to have an average of 90.

Got It? 2. a. The grades in Problem 2 were 80, 93, and 91. What grade would you need on your next exam to have an average of 88 on the four exams?

   b. Reasoning If 100 is the highest possible score on the fourth exam, is it possible to raise your average to 92? Explain.

A **measure of dispersion** describes how *dispersed*, or spread out, the values in a data set are. One measure of dispersion is *range*. The **range of a set of data** is the difference between the greatest and least data values.

Problem 3 Finding the Range

Finance The closing prices, in dollars, of two stocks for the first five days in February are shown below. What are the range and mean of each set of data? Use the results to compare the data sets.

Think

How do the purposes of the range and the mean differ?
The range helps you find how spread out the data values are. The mean helps you find a typical data value.

Stock A: 25 30 30 47 28

range: $47 - 25 = 22$

mean: $\dfrac{25 + 30 + 30 + 47 + 28}{5}$

$= \dfrac{160}{5} = 32$

Stock B: 34 28 31 36 31

range: $36 - 28 = 8$

mean: $\dfrac{34 + 28 + 31 + 36 + 31}{5}$

$= \dfrac{160}{5} = 32$

Both sets of stock prices have a mean of 32. The range of the prices for Stock A is 22, and the range of the prices for Stock B is 8. Both stocks had the same average price during the 5-day period, but the prices for Stock A were more spread out.

 Got It? 3. For the same days, the closing prices, in dollars, of Stock C were 7, 4, 3, 6, and 1. The closing prices, in dollars, of Stock D were 24, 15, 2, 10, and 5. What are the range and mean of each set of data? Use your results to compare Stock C with Stock D.

Problem 4 Finding Measures of Central Tendency and Ranges

The results of a survey on the number of televisions in students' households are shown in the line plot.

Think

Why can multiplication be used when finding the mean?
Multiplication is equivalent to repeated addition. Rather than adding 2 four times, you can multiply 4 times 2.

Televisions per Household

```
                    X
                    X
          X   X   X
          X   X   X
      X   X   X   X   X
      X   X   X   X   X
      1   2   3   4   5
```

A Calculate the mean, median, and range of the data.

Mean: $\dfrac{(2 \cdot 1) + (4 \cdot 2) + (6 \cdot 3) + (4 \cdot 4) + (2 \cdot 5)}{18} = \dfrac{54}{18} = 3$

Median: 1, 1, 2, 2, 2, 2, 3, 3, ③, ③, 3, 3, 4, 4, 4, 4, 5, 5; $\dfrac{3 + 3}{2} = \dfrac{6}{2} = 3$

Range: $5 - 1 = 4$

The mean is 3, the median is 3, and the range is 4.

B How can you tell from the graph that the mean and median are equal?

When the graph is symmetric, the mean and median will be equal.

Got It? 4. The line plot shows the number of students in each homeroom at Jefferson High School.

Number of Students

```
                        X
                    X   X
            X       X   X
            X       X   X
            X   X   X   X   X
            X   X   X   X   X   X
           19  20  21  22  23  24
```

    a. Find the mean, median, and range of the data.

    b. How can you use the line plot to determine whether the mean and median are equal?

 Problem 5 **Comparing Measures of Central Tendency**

The results from the same quiz given to two different classes are shown in the line plots.

Class A

```
        X   X
        X   X
    X   X   X   X
X   X   X   X   X   X
X   X   X   X   X   X
X   X   X   X   X   X
1   2   3   4   5   6
```

Quiz Scores

Class B

```
                X   X
            X   X   X
            X   X   X
            X   X   X
    X   X   X   X   X
X   X   X   X   X   X
1   2   3   4   5   6
```

Quiz Scores

A **Which class has a higher standard for being in the top half of the quiz scores?**

In order to be in the top half of the quiz scores, a student must have a greater quiz score than 50% of the class. The median is the middle value, therefore 50% of the data are less than the median and 50% of the data are greater than the median. You need to calculate the median of each data set to determine which class has a higher standard for being in the top half of the quiz scores.

Class A:

    Median: $\dfrac{3+4}{2} = \dfrac{7}{2} = 3.5$

Class B:

    Median: 5

Class B has a higher standard for being in the top half of the quiz scores.

B **By comparing line plots, how can you tell which mean is greater?**

The data for Class B are shifted right when compared to the data for Class A. Therefore the mean will be greater.

Think

What must be the same in order to compare the shapes of the line plots?
The intervals on the number line must be exactly the same.

 Got It? 5. Results from a third class are shown here.

    a. Is the mean for Class C greater than or less than the mean for Class A?

    b. Is the median for Class C greater than or less than the median for Class A?

    c. How can you tell which data set has a greater mean by comparing the graphs?

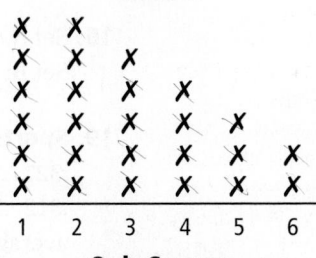

Class C

```
X   X
X   X   X
X   X   X   X
X   X   X   X   X
X   X   X   X   X   X
X   X   X   X   X   X
1   2   3   4   5   6
```

Quiz Scores

Lesson Check

Do you know HOW?

Find the mean, median, and mode of each data set. Explain which measure best describes the data.

1. 1 29 33 31 30 33

2. 8.2 9.3 8.5 8.8 9.0

3. A student has gotten the following grades on his tests: 87, 95, 86, and 88. He needs to have an average of 90 to receive an A for the class. What is the minimum grade he must get on the last test in order to have an average of 90?

Do you UNDERSTAND?

4. Vocabulary How do mean, median, and mode describe the central tendency of a data set? Why are three different measures needed?

5. Error Analysis One student said 10 was the range of the data set 2, 10, 8, and 3. Another student said the range was 8. Which student is correct? Explain.

6. Reasoning How is the range of a data set affected by an outlier?

Practice and Problem-Solving Exercises

Find the mean, median, and mode of each data set. Tell which measure of central tendency best describes the data.

◀ See Problem 1.

7. weights of books (oz): 12 10 9 15 16 10

8. golf scores: 98 96 98 134 99

9. time spent on Internet (min/day): 75 38 43 120 65 48 52

10. ages of students on math team: 14 14 15 15 16 15 15 16

Find the value of x such that the data set has the given mean.

◀ See Problem 2.

11. 3.8, 4.2, 5.3, x; mean 4.8

12. 99, 86, 76, 95, x; mean 91

13. 100, 121, 105, 113, 108, x; mean 112

14. 31.7, 42.8, 26.4, x; mean 35

15. Sales The line plot at the right shows the numbers of weekly sales a salesperson made in the first nine weeks of a ten-week sales period. The salesperson's target is an average of 14 sales each week. How many sales does the salesperson need in the tenth week to meet the target average?

Number of Weekly Sales

```
                  X    X
             X    X    X
        X    X    X    X
        12   13   14   15
```

Find the range and mean of each data set. Use your results to compare the two data sets.

◀ See Problem 3.

16. Set A: 0 12 7 19 21
Set B: 13 16 15 17 12

17. Set C: 4.5 7.1 8.3 6.9
Set D: 2.1 29.5 1.2 3.3

18. Set E: 113 183 479 120 117
Set F: 145 129 153 135 142

19. Sports Over the past 6 seasons, one baseball player's batting averages were .265, .327, .294, .316, .281, and .318. A second player's batting averages were .304, .285, .312, .291, .303, and .314. What are the range and mean of each player's batting averages? Use your results to compare the players' batting skills.

Determine which data set has a greater mean and a greater median.

See Problems 4 and 5.

20.

Company A	Company B

Company A:
```
X  X
X  X  X  X
X  X  X  X  X  X
50 51 52 53 54 55
```
**Monthly Earnings
(thousands of dollars)**

Company B:
```
      X  X  X
      X  X  X
X  X  X  X  X  X
50 51 52 53 54 55
```
**Monthly Earnings
(thousands of dollars)**

21.

Student A:
```
                  X
                  X
            X     X
      X  X  X     X
   X  X  X  X     X
   X  X  X  X     X
X  X  X  X  X     X
X  X  X  X  X     X
30 31 32 33 34 35
```
Student A
Text Messages per Day

Student B:
```
X
X  X
X  X  X  X
X  X  X  X
X  X  X  X  X
X  X  X  X  X
X  X  X  X  X
30 31 32 33 34 35
```
Student B
Text Messages per Day

Apply

22. Reasoning The mean of a data set is 7.8, the mode is 6.6, and the median is 6.8. What is the least possible number of data values in the set? Explain.

23. Manufacturing Two manufacturing plants make sheets of steel for medical instruments. The back-to-back stem-and-leaf plot at the right shows data collected from the two plants.
  a. What are the mean, median, mode, and range of each data set?
  b. Which measure of central tendency best describes each data set? Explain.
  c. How can you use the shape of the back-to-back stem-and-leaf plot to determine which data set has the greater mean? Explain.

Width of Steel (mm)		
Manufacturing Plant A		**Manufacturing Plant B**
	4	3 5 9
8 7 4 4 2	5	2 7
4 3 1	6	3 4
	7	2

Key: 6 | 3 means 6.3
1 | 6 | 3
1 | 6 means 6.1

24. Think About a Plan The diameters of 5 circles are given below. What are the mean, median, mode, and range of the circumferences of the circles?
  6.5 in. 3.2 in. 7.4 in. 6.5 in. 5.8 in.
  • What are the mean, median, mode, and range of the diameters?
  • How do the mean, median, mode, and range change when the data change from diameters to circumferences?

25. Reasoning How does subtracting the same amount from each value in a data set affect the mean, median, mode, and range? Explain.

26. Reasoning How does dividing each value in a data set by the same nonzero amount affect the mean, median, mode, and range? Explain.

27. Wildlife Management A wildlife manager measured and tagged twelve adult male crocodiles. The data he collected are at the right. He estimates the crocodiles will grow 0.1 m each year. What will be the mean, median, mode, and range of the crocodiles' lengths after 4 yr?

Crocodile Lengths (m)			
2.4	2.5	2.5	2.3
2.8	2.4	2.3	2.4
2.1	2.2	2.5	2.7

 28. Reasoning A friend tells you to apply for a sales job at a certain company because the salespeople earned an average of $47,500 last year. Last year, 6 salespeople earned $33,000, 3 earned $46,000, 2 earned $42,000, and 1 earned $150,000. Would you apply for the job based on what your friend says? Explain.

Challenge

29. Travel During the first 6 h of a car trip, your average speed is 44 mi/h. During the last 4 h of your trip, your average speed is 50 mi/h. What is your average speed for the whole trip? (*Hint:* First find the total number of miles traveled.)

30. Find the mean, median, mode, and range of the following algebraic expressions: $9x, 4x, 11x, 7x, 5x, 4x$. Assume that $x > 0$.

Apply What You've Learned

MATHEMATICAL
PRACTICES
MP 6

Look back at the August rainfall data on page 725. Choose from the following words and numbers to complete the sentences below.

mean	median	mode	range
outlier	2.4	2.5	3.3
3.74	4.05	4.2	4.5

For Oakville, the mean August rainfall is **a.** ? in., and the median August rainfall is **b.** ? in. The **c.** ? of this data set is 4.2 in. The data value 15.1 is a(n) **d.** ? . The measure of central tendency that best describes this data set is the **e.** ? .

For Fairview, the mean August rainfall is approximately **f.** ? in., and the median August rainfall is **g.** ? in. The **h.** ? of this data set is 3.3 in.

Standard Deviation

© **Common Core State Standards**

S-ID.A.2 Use statistics appropriate to the . . . data distribution to compare center . . . and spread . . . of two or more different data sets.

MP 2

You have learned about one measure of dispersion, range. Another measure of dispersion is *standard deviation*. **Standard deviation** is a measure of how the values in a data set vary, or deviate, from the mean.

Statisticians use several special symbols in the formula for standard deviation.

The Greek letter sigma (σ) represents standard deviation.

x is a value in the data set.
$\bar{x}$ is the mean of the data set.

$$\sigma = \sqrt{\frac{\Sigma(x - \bar{x})^2}{n}}$$

The capital sigma (Σ) represents the sum of a series of numbers.

n is the number of values in the data set.

Example

Find the mean and standard deviation of each data set. Which data set has a greater standard deviation? Use tables to help organize your work.

Step 1 Find the mean, $\bar{x}$.

Step 2 Find the difference between each data value and the mean, $x - \bar{x}$.

Step 3 Square each difference, $(x - \bar{x})^2$.

Step 4 Find the average (mean) of these squares, $\dfrac{\Sigma(x - \bar{x})^2}{n}$.

Step 5 Take the square root to find the standard deviation, $\sqrt{\dfrac{\Sigma(x - \bar{x})^2}{n}}$.

Data Set 1				Data Set 2			
x_1	$\bar{x}_1$	$x_1 - \bar{x}_1$	$(x_1 - \bar{x}_1)^2$	x_2	$\bar{x}_2$	$x_2 - \bar{x}_2$	$(x_2 - \bar{x}_2)^2$
12.6	15	−2.4	5.76	13.4	14.5	−1.1	1.21
15.1	15	0.1	0.01	11.7	14.5	−2.8	7.84
11.2	15	−3.8	14.44	18.3	14.5	3.8	14.44
17.9	15	2.9	8.41	14.8	14.5	0.3	0.09
18.2	15	3.2	10.24	14.3	14.5	−0.2	0.04
$\dfrac{\Sigma(x_1 - \bar{x}_1)^2}{n}$		7.772		$\dfrac{\Sigma(x_2 - \bar{x}_2)^2}{n}$		4.724	
$\sqrt{\dfrac{\Sigma(x_1 - \bar{x}_1)^2}{n}}$		≈ 2.79		$\sqrt{\dfrac{\Sigma(x_2 - \bar{x}_2)^2}{n}}$		≈ 2.17	

Data set 1 has a greater standard deviation at 2.79.

Exercises

Find the mean and standard deviation of each data set. Round to the nearest hundredth. Which data set has a greater standard deviation?

1. Data set 1: 4, 8, 5, 12, 3, 9, 5, 2
Data set 2: 5, 9, 11, 4, 6, 11, 2, 7

2. Data set 1: 102, 98, 103, 86, 101, 110
Data set 2: 90, 89, 100, 97, 102, 97

3. Data set 1: 8.2, 11.6, 8.7, 10.6, 9.4, 10.1, 9.3
Data set 2: 9.3, 10.2, 8.1, 12.3, 8.7, 9.9, 10.1

4. Data set 1: 32, 40, 35, 28, 42, 32, 44
Data set 2: 40, 38, 51, 39, 46, 40, 52

12-4 Box-and-Whisker Plots

Common Core State Standards

S-ID.A.2 Use statistics appropriate to the ... data distribution to compare center ... and spread ... of two or more different data sets. **Also N-Q.A.1, S-ID.A.1**

MP 1, MP 2, MP 3, MP 4, MP 6

Objectives To make and interpret box-and-whisker plots
To find quartiles and percentiles

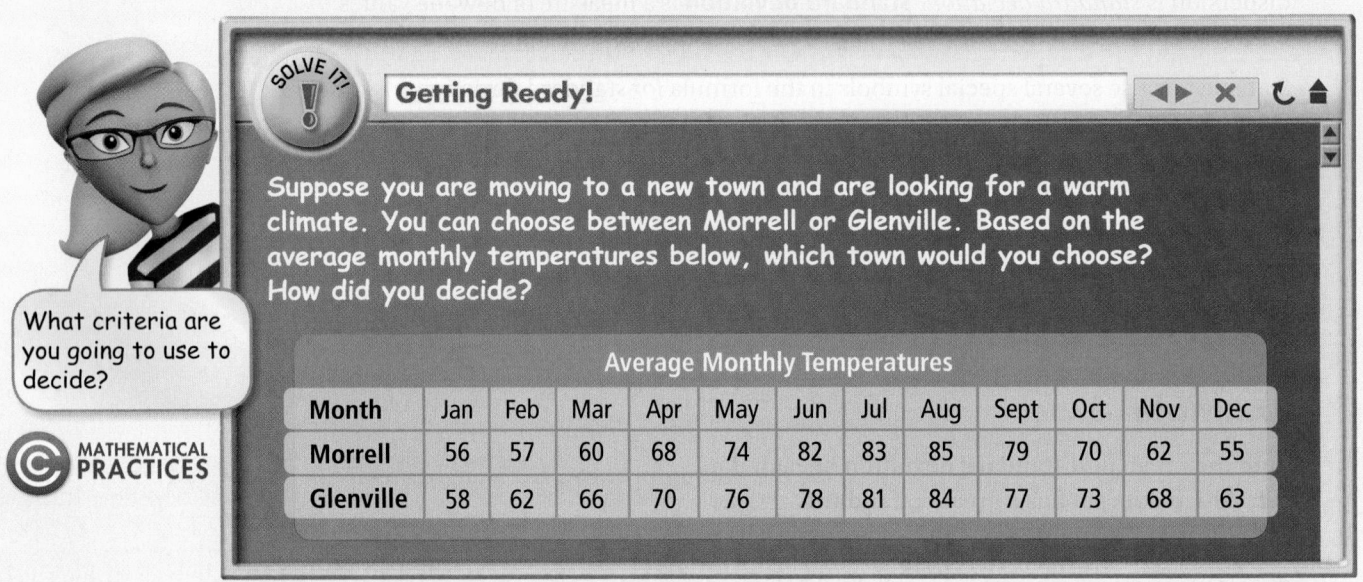

SOLVE IT!

Getting Ready!

Suppose you are moving to a new town and are looking for a warm climate. You can choose between Morrell or Glenville. Based on the average monthly temperatures below, which town would you choose? How did you decide?

What criteria are you going to use to decide?

MATHEMATICAL PRACTICES

Average Monthly Temperatures												
Month	Jan	Feb	Mar	Apr	May	Jun	Jul	Aug	Sept	Oct	Nov	Dec
Morrell	56	57	60	68	74	82	83	85	79	70	62	55
Glenville	58	62	66	70	76	78	81	84	77	73	68	63

In the Solve It, you may have looked at different parts of each data set in order to compare the two data sets.

Essential Understanding Separating data into subsets is a useful way to summarize and compare data sets.

Quartiles are values that divide a data set into four equal parts. The median (or second quartile, Q_2) separates the data into upper and lower halves. The first quartile (Q_1) is the median of the lower half of the data. The third quartile (Q_3) is the median of the upper half of the data. The **interquartile range** is the difference between the third and first quartiles.

Lesson Vocabulary
• quartile
• interquartile range
• box-and-whisker plot
• percentile
• percentile rank

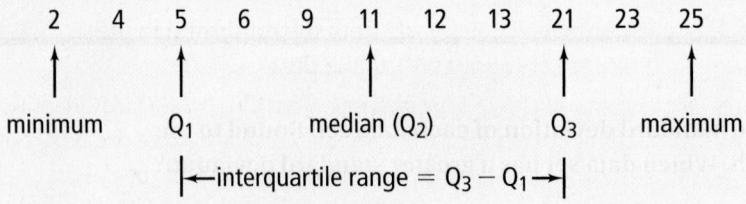

For a set of data that has an odd number of values, you do not include the median in either half when finding the first and third quartiles.

What are the minimum, first quartile, median, third quartile, and maximum of the data set below?

125 80 140 135 126 140 350 75

Step 1 Arrange the data in order from least to greatest.

75 80 125 126 135 140 140 350

Step 2 Find the minimum, maximum, and median.

75 80 125 126 135 140 140 350

$$\text{median } (Q_2) = \frac{126 + 135}{2} = 130.5$$

The minimum is 75. The maximum is 350. The median is 130.5.

Think

How do you find the first quartile for an even number of values?
The first quartile is the median of the lower half of the data, so you find the mean of the middle two values in the lower half.

Step 3 Find the first quartile and the third quartile.

75 80 125 126 135 140 140 350

$$\text{first quartile } (Q_1) = \frac{80 + 125}{2} = 102.5$$

$$\text{third quartile } (Q_3) = \frac{140 + 140}{2} = 140$$

The first quartile is 102.5. The third quartile is 140.

✓ **Got It?** **1.** What are the minimum, first quartile, median, third quartile, and maximum of each data set?
   a. 95 85 75 85 65 60 100 105 75 85 75
   b. 11 19 7 5 21 53

A **box-and-whisker plot** is a graph that summarizes a set of data by displaying it along a number line. It consists of three parts: a box and two whiskers.

Box-and-Whisker Plot

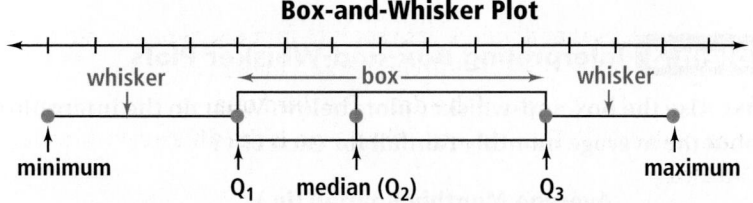

- The left whisker extends from the minimum to the first quartile. It represents about 25% of the data.
- The box extends from the first quartile to the third quartile and has a vertical line through the median. The length of the box represents the interquartile range. It contains about 50% of the data.
- The right whisker extends from the third quartile to the maximum. It represents about 25% of the data.

Problem 2 Making a Box-and-Whisker Plot

Agriculture The table at the right shows the amount of crops harvested in the United States for a certain period. What box-and-whisker plot represents the data?

Crops Harvested

Year	Acres (millions)	Year	Acres (millions)
0	314	6	307
1	321	7	316
2	315	8	312
3	316	9	314
4	314	10	303
5	311		

SOURCE: U.S. Department of Agriculture

Know
A set of data

Need
A box-and-whisker plot

Plan
Find the minimum, maximum, and quartiles of the data. Use these numbers to make the box-and-whisker plot.

Step 1 Order the data to find the minimum, maximum, and quartiles.

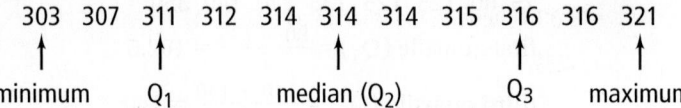

303 307 311 312 314 314 314 315 316 316 321

minimum Q_1 median (Q_2) Q_3 maximum

Step 2 Draw the box-and-whisker plot.

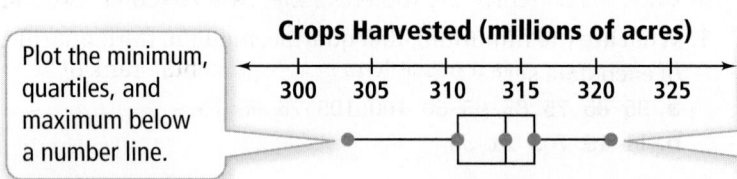

Plot the minimum, quartiles, and maximum below a number line.

Crops Harvested (millions of acres)

300   305   310   315   320   325

Draw a box from Q_1 to Q_3. Draw a vertical line through the median. Draw line segments from the box to the minimum and maximum.

 Got It? **2.** What box-and-whisker plot represents the following monthly sales, in millions of dollars, of audio devices: 15 4 9 16 10 16 8 14 25 34?

Problem 3 Interpreting Box-and-Whisker Plots

Weather Use the box-and-whisker plots below. What do the interquartile ranges tell you about the average monthly rainfall for each city?

Think

Why is the interquartile range useful?
It represents the middle of the data set, so it is not affected by the minimum, maximum, or any outliers.

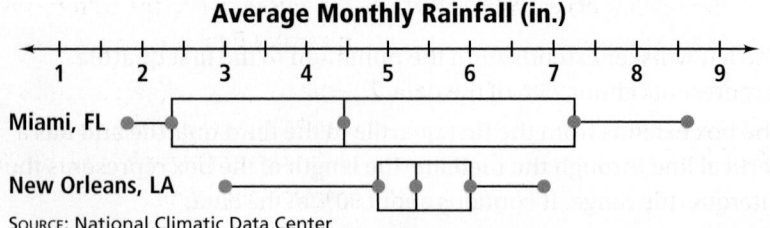

Average Monthly Rainfall (in.)

1   2   3   4   5   6   7   8   9

Miami, FL

New Orleans, LA

SOURCE: National Climatic Data Center

The box for Miami is longer, so Miami has the greater interquartile range.
This greater range means the middle 50% of Miami's monthly rainfalls vary more widely than those of New Orleans.

Got It? 3. What do the medians tell you about the average monthly rainfalls for Miami and New Orleans?

Percentiles separate data sets into 100 equal parts. The **percentile rank** of a data value is the percentage of data values that are less than or equal to that value.

 Problem 4 Finding a Percentile Rank

Multiple Choice Of 25 test scores, eight are less than or equal to 75. What is the percentile rank of a test score of 75?

Ⓐ 8   Ⓑ 17   Ⓒ 32   Ⓓ 75

Think

How else could you find the percentile rank?
You could solve the proportion $\frac{8}{25} = \frac{p}{100}$ for p.

$\frac{8}{25}$ Write the ratio of the number of test scores less than or equal to 75 compared to the total number of test scores.

$\frac{8}{25} = 0.32$ Rewrite the fraction as a percent.

$= 32\%$

The percentile rank of 75 is 32. The correct answer is C.

  Got It? 4. a. Of the 25 scores in Problem 4, there are 15 scores less than or equal to 85. What is the percentile rank of 85?

     b. Reasoning Is it possible to have a percentile rank of 0? Explain.

 Lesson Check

Do you know HOW?

Identify the minimum, first quartile, median, third quartile, and maximum of each data set. Then make a box-and-whisker plot of each data set.

1. file sizes (megabytes): 54 100 84 124 188 48 256

2. daily attendance: 29 24 28 32 30 31 26 33

3. In the box-and-whisker plots below, which class has the greater interquartile range of arm spans?

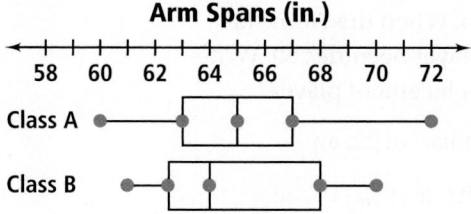

Arm Spans (in.)

58 60 62 64 66 68 70 72

Class A

Class B

Do you UNDERSTAND?  **MATHEMATICAL PRACTICES**

4. Vocabulary Which portion of a box-and-whisker plot represents the interquartile range?

5. Students taking a make-up test receive the following grades: 77, 89, 88, 67, 91, 95, 83, 79, 81, and 65. Which grade has a percentile rank of 70?

6. Reasoning About what percent of the data in a data set falls between the minimum value and the third quartile? Explain.

7. Error Analysis A test is graded on a scale from 0 to 100. Your friend says that if you score a 78, your percentile rank must be 78. Is your friend correct? Explain.

Practice and Problem-Solving Exercises

MATHEMATICAL
PRACTICES

 **Practice**

Find the minimum, first quartile, median, third quartile, and maximum of each data set.

See Problem 1.

8. 12 10 11 7 9 10 5

9. 4.5 3.2 6.3 5.2 5 4.8 6 3.9 12

10. 55 53 67 52 50 49 51 52 52

11. 101 100 100 105 101 102 104

Make a box-and-whisker plot to represent each set of data.

See Problem 2.

12. song lengths (s): 227 221 347 173 344 438 171 129 165 333

13. movie ratings: 1 5 1 2.5 3 2 3.5 2 3 1.5 4 2 4 1 3 4.5

14. weekly museum visitors: 531 469 573 206 374 421 505 489 702

15. camera prices: $280 $220 $224 $70 $410 $90 $30 $120

16. Fuel Use Use the box-and-whisker plots below. What do they tell you about the fuel efficiencies for each type of vehicle? Explain.

See Problem 3.

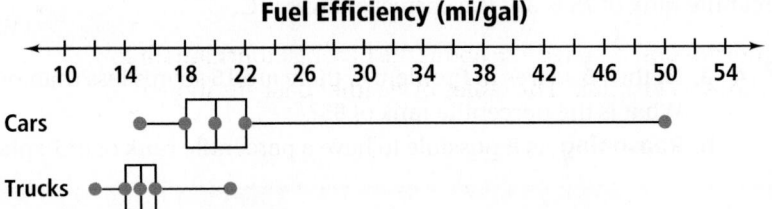

17. Of 10 test scores, six are less than or equal to 80. What is the percentile rank of a test score of 80?

See Problem 4.

18. Of 35 judges' scores awarded during a gymnastics event, 28 are less than or equal to 7.5. What is the percentile rank of a score of 7.5?

B Apply

19. Think About a Plan You are one of the finalists at a science fair. The scores of the other finalists are 87, 89, 81, 85, 87, 83, 86, 94, 90, 97, 80, 89, 85, and 88. Write an inequality that represents your possible scores if your percentile rank is 80.
- What percent of the scores must be less than or equal to your score?
- What is the total number of finalists' scores?

20. Writing Explain the difference between *range* and *interquartile range*.

21. Basketball The heights of the players on a basketball team are 74 in., 79 in., 71.5 in., 81 in., 73 in., 76 in., 78 in., 71 in., 72 in., and 73.5 in. When the 76-in.-tall player is replaced, the percentile rank of the 73.5-in.-tall player becomes 60. Write an inequality that represents the possible heights of the replacement player.

22. Open-Ended Make a data set of 10 numbers that has a median of 22, an interquartile range of 10, and a minimum less than 4.

23. Reasoning Must the third quartile of a data set be less than the maximum value? Explain.

STEM 24. **Packaging** A cereal company is choosing between two devices to package their cereal into bags. The box-and-whisker plots at the right show the weights of the bags packed by each device.

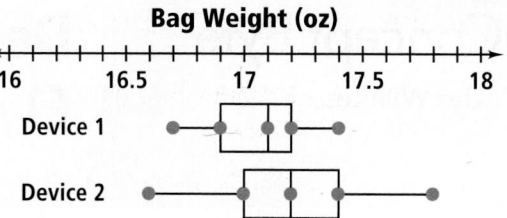

Bag Weight (oz)

a. Which device produces packages with a more consistent weight? Explain.

b. Which device should be chosen if the manufacturer wants to minimize the number of packages with weights less than 17 oz? More than 17.2 oz? Explain.

 25. **Reasoning** Can you find the mean, median, and mode of a data set by looking at a box-and-whisker plot? Explain.

26. Of 100 people that take a test, nine have scores greater than 93. What is the percentile rank of a score of 93?

Apply What You've Learned

MATHEMATICAL PRACTICES

MP 4

Look back at the information on page 725 about the baseball tournament for which Luis must choose a location. The tables of weather data are shown again below.

Oakville Climate Data for August

Year	2004	2005	2006	2007	2008	2009	2010	2011	2012	2013
Rainfall (in.)	2.4	4.2	1.8	15.1	2.6	2.3	2.0	4.2	3.8	2.1
Avg. Temp. (°F)	78	84	89	72	74	77	82	87	76	78
Hurricane?	no	yes	no	yes	no	no	no	yes	yes	no

Fairview Climate Data for August

Year	2005	2006	2007	2008	2009	2010	2011	2012	2013
Rainfall (in.)	4.5	1.8	2.2	5.0	5.1	4.5	2.3	3.8	4.5
Avg. Temp. (°F)	83	77	82	80	87	86	86	82	83
Hurricane?	no	no	no	yes	no	yes	no	no	no

a. Make box-and-whisker plots to represent the temperature data for Oakville and Fairview.

b. What conclusions can you make about the temperatures in August in the two cities?

c. Luis finds that the average August temperature in Fairview in 2004 was 73°. How would including this additional data value change the box-and-whisker plot you made in part (a)? Would it change the conclusions you made in part (b)?

PowerAlgebra.com | **Lesson 12-4** Box-and-Whisker Plots | 751

Designing Your Own Survey

Common Core State Standards

Prepares for S-IC.B.3 Recognize the purposes of and differences among sample surveys, experiments, and observational studies; explain how randomization relates to each.

MP 2

You have learned how to organize, display, and summarize data. In this activity you will explore methods of collecting data.

Suppose a statistician is trying to predict how a town will vote in an upcoming election. She could ask every person in the town, but this method takes too much time and work. Instead, she might rely on an information-gathering survey that is sent to only some people in the town. She can then use the results to predict how other people in the town might vote.

When you design a survey, you need to make sure that the people you survey are representative of the group you want to study.

Activity 1

Suppose you want to find out how many hours of exercise the students at your school get each week. At the school gym you ask everybody you see, "How many hours of exercise do you get every week?"

1. Will the results of your survey be representative of your entire school? Explain.

2. Is there a better location to conduct your survey?

3. Suppose you asked, "Do you work out every day like a healthy person, or are you a lazy couch potato who only works out once in a while?" Do you think the results of your survey would change? Explain your reasoning.

Activity 2

In this activity, you will design and conduct a survey.

4. Select a topic for your survey. You could ask about favorite sporting events, snacks, musical instruments, or another topic of your choice.

5. **Writing** What question will you ask? Will your question influence the opinion of the people you are surveying?

6. What group of people do you want to study? Are you going to ask the entire group, or just a portion of the whole group?

7. **Data Collection** Complete your survey.

8. **Writing** Summarize your results with a graph and a brief description.

9. **Reasoning** Are the people you surveyed representative of the group you want to study? Explain.

Samples and Surveys

Common Core State Standards

S-IC.B.3 Recognize the purposes of and differences among sample surveys, experiments, and observational studies . . .

MP 1, MP 2, MP 3, MP 4, MP 6

Objective To classify data and analyze samples and surveys

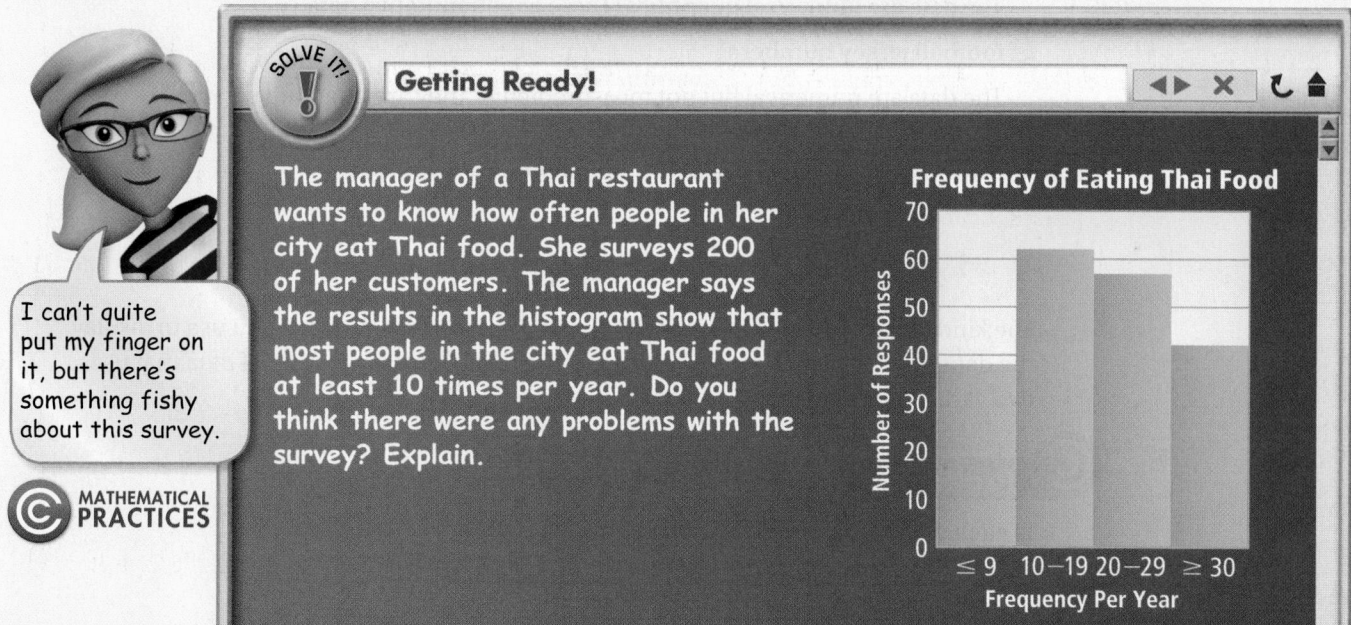

Getting Ready!

The manager of a Thai restaurant wants to know how often people in her city eat Thai food. She surveys 200 of her customers. The manager says the results in the histogram show that most people in the city eat Thai food at least 10 times per year. Do you think there were any problems with the survey? Explain.

I can't quite put my finger on it, but there's something fishy about this survey.

MATHEMATICAL PRACTICES

Frequency of Eating Thai Food

(histogram: y-axis "Number of Responses" 0 to 70; x-axis "Frequency Per Year" with categories ≤ 9, 10–19, 20–29, ≥ 30)

In the Solve It, the restaurant manager collected data from the customers of the restaurant. In this lesson, you will learn about ways to collect data.

Lesson Vocabulary
• quantitative
• qualitative
• univariate
• bivariate
• population
• sample
• bias

Essential Understanding When collecting data to solve a problem, you need to make sure that your methods are fair and that you accurately represent the results.

You can collect data using measurements or categories. **Quantitative** data measure quantities and can be described numerically, such as test scores and ages. **Qualitative** data name qualities and can be words or numbers, such as sports or ZIP codes.

Types of Data	Description	Examples
Quantitative	Has units and can be measured and numerically compared	**Age:** 13 yr **Weight:** 214 g **Time:** 23 min
Qualitative	Describes a category and cannot be measured or numerically compared	**Hair color:** brown **Attitude:** optimistic **ZIP code:** 02125

 **Problem 1** **Classifying Data**

 **Think**

Are the data numerical measurements?
Movie titles and jersey numbers are not numerical measurements, but a number of students is.

Is each data set *qualitative* or *quantitative*?

A **favorite movies**

The data are not numerical quantities. These are qualitative data.

B **numbers of students in different schools who take Spanish**

The data are numerical quantities. These are quantitative data.

C **football jersey numbers**

The data are numerical but not measurements. They are qualitative data.

 Got It? **1.** Is each data set *qualitative* or *quantitative*? Explain.
     a. costs of CDs   **b.** eye colors

The kind of data you are working with determines the type of graph you use to display the data. A set of data that uses only one variable is **univariate.** A set of data that uses two variables is **bivariate.**

 Problem 2 **Identifying Types of Data**

Think

Does the data set involve one or two variables?
One variable means the data set is univariate. Two variables means the data set is bivariate.

Is each data set *univariate* or *bivariate*?

A **the atomic weights of the elements in the periodic table**

There is only one variable, atomic weight. The data set is univariate.

B **the edge lengths and volumes of cubes**

There are two variables, edge length and volume. The data set is bivariate.

 Got It? **2.** Is each data set *univariate* or *bivariate*? Explain.
     a. heights and weights of mammals
     b. the cost of Internet service from several different providers

---

Statisticians collect information about specific groups of objects or people. The entire group that you want information about is called a **population.** When a population is too large to survey, statisticians survey a part of it to find characteristics of the whole. The part that is surveyed is called a **sample.**

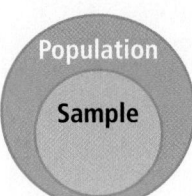

Three sampling methods are shown on the next page. When designing a survey, you should choose a sample that reflects the population.

Name	Sampling Method	Example
Random	Survey a population at random.	Survey people whose names are drawn out of a hat.
Systematic	Select a number *n* at random. Then survey every *n*th person.	Select the number 5 at random. Survey every fifth person.
Stratified	Separate a population into smaller groups, each with a certain characteristic. Then survey at random within each group.	Separate a high school into four groups by grade level. Survey a random sample of students from each grade.

 Problem 3 Choosing a Sample

DVD Rentals **You want to find out how many DVDs students at your school rent in a month. You interview every tenth teenager you see at a mall. What sampling method are you using? Is this a good sample?**

Since you are interviewing every tenth teenager, this method is systematic. This is not a good sample because it will likely include teenagers who do not attend your school.

Think

What population are you trying to represent with this sample?
You want to collect information about the students at your school.

 Got It? **3.** You revise your plan and interview all students leaving a school assembly who are wearing the school colors. Will this plan give a good sample? Explain.

A survey question has **bias** when it contains assumptions that may or may not be true. Bias can influence opinion and can make one answer seem better than another. Survey questions must be carefully worded to avoid bias.

Problem 4 Determining Bias in a Survey Question

Movies **A reporter wants to find out what kinds of movies are most popular with local residents. The reporter asks, "Do you prefer exciting action movies or boring documentaries?" Is the question biased? Explain.**

Know

The survey question

Need

To determine whether the question is biased

Plan

Check the question for adjectives or phrases that make one category seem more appealing.

The question is biased because the words *exciting* and *boring* make action films sound more interesting than documentaries.

  Got It? **4. Reasoning** How can the question in Problem 4 be reworded so that it is not biased?

Samples can also be biased. For example, all voluntary-response samples are biased because you cannot be sure that the people who choose to respond are representative of the population. The location where a survey is conducted can also cause a sample to be biased.

 Problem 5 Determining Bias in a Sample

Sports You want to determine what percent of teens ages 14 to 18 watch wrestling on TV. At a high school wrestling match, you ask every third teenager whether he or she watches wrestling on TV. How might this cause bias in the results of your survey?

The sample chosen is not representative of the population. People who attend a high school wrestling match may be more likely to watch wrestling on TV.

Think

Ask yourself whether the sample and the population have similar characteristics. If not, the sample is biased.

Got It? 5. You want to know how many of your classmates have cell phones. To determine this, you send every classmate an e-mail asking, "Do you own a cell phone?" How might this method of gathering data affect the results of your survey?

Lesson Check

Do you know HOW?

Determine whether each sampling method is *random*, *systematic*, or *stratified*.

1. You survey every tenth student who enters the cafeteria.

2. You draw student ID numbers out of a hat and survey those students.

3. You survey two students at random from each class.

Do you UNDERSTAND?

4. **Vocabulary** Is a data set of your class's test scores *qualitative* or *quantitative* data?

5. **Writing** Explain why "Do you prefer delicious fruit or plain vegetables for a snack food?" is a biased survey question.

6. **Compare and Contrast** What is the difference between univariate data and bivariate data? Give an example of each type of data.

 ## Practice and Problem-Solving Exercises

 Practice Determine whether each data set is *qualitative* or *quantitative*.

See Problem 1.

7. favorite recording stars

8. best-selling DVDs

9. numbers of gigabytes in memory cards

10. prices of TVs

Determine whether each data set is *univariate* or *bivariate*.

See Problem 2.

11. numbers of CDs your classmates own

12. ages and heights of your friends

13. ZIP codes of your relatives

14. circumferences and radii of circles

Determine whether the sampling method is *random, systematic,* or *stratified.* Tell whether the method will produce a good sample.

See Problem 3.

15. A pollster randomly selects 100 people from each town in a certain candidate's district to see if they support the candidate.

16. A factory tests the quality of every thirtieth shirt made.

17. A printing company randomly selects 10 of 450 books it printed to see if all the books were printed properly.

Determine whether each question is biased. Explain your answer.

See Problem 4.

18. Since global warming is a big problem, do you support government funding of studies on global warming?

19. Where would you most like to go on vacation?

20. Do you prefer shopping online or the excitement of going to stores with friends?

21. You want to find out how much time people in your town spend doing volunteer work. You call 100 homes in the community during the day. Of those surveyed, 85% are over the age of 60. How might this create bias in your survey results?

See Problem 5.

22. You want to find out how many people in your neighborhood have pets in their homes. You ask every fourth person at the local dog park. How might this create bias in your survey results?

Ⓑ Apply

Ⓒ 23. Reasoning You review the results of survey questions given to two random samples of students from your school. The results are shown in the table below. Why are the results not the same?

Favorite Color

Color	Red	Blue	Green	Yellow	Pink	Purple	Black
Group A	8	6	4	2	5	4	1
Group B	7	7	3	0	6	5	2

Ⓒ 24. Think About a Plan You want to find out what types of music students would like to listen to at the next school dance. How would you conduct a survey to find the music preferences of your entire school?
- What sampling method can you use to choose an unbiased sample?
- How can you write survey questions that are not biased?

25. Travel A travel agent wants to determine whether a trip to France is a popular vacation for young adults. How could each factor described below create bias in the survey results?
a. The agent interviews people at an international airport.
b. The agent asks, "Would you prefer to vacation in France or in Italy?"
c. Of the people interviewed, 86% took a French class in high school.

26. **Error Analysis** Malik is conducting a survey about the legal voting age in the United States. His question is, "Isn't the legal voting age too high?" When his friends suggested that his question was biased, he revised it to be, "Don't you think the legal voting age should be lower?" Describe and correct the error in his rewritten survey question.

In each situation, identify the population and sample. Tell whether each sample is a *random*, *systematic*, or *stratified* sample.

27. For one month, the owner of a sporting goods store asks every fifteenth customer which sport he or she most enjoys watching on TV.

28. One student from each club is chosen at random to represent the school at the school fair.

29. At a high school football game, every spectator places his or her ticket stub in a bowl. After the game, the coach chooses ten people to march in the victory parade.

30. A restaurant asks every third customer to complete an evaluation form.

Classify the data as *qualitative* or *quantitative* and as *univariate* or *bivariate*.

31. average number of visitors per day at each of six different theme parks

32. monthly low temperatures in Rochester, New York

33. names of U.S. presidents and the states they were born in

34. favorite color and a person's gender

35. **Sports** A student posts a survey on a Web site asking readers to choose their favorite sport to play from a list of five sports. The results are shown at the right.
   a. What biases might exist as a result of the design of this survey?
   b. Do you believe the results of this survey are valid? Explain your answer.

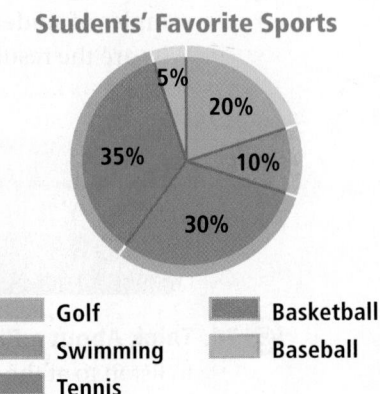
Students' Favorite Sports

5%
20%
35%
10%
30%

■ Golf   ■ Basketball
■ Swimming   ■ Baseball
■ Tennis

36. **Writing** You are writing an article for the school newspaper about support for the mayor's proposal for bike paths. For each situation below, determine whether the data collection method will result in an unbiased sample of town residents. Explain your answer.
   a. You survey every tenth person leaving a bicycle repair store.
   b. You call homes in your neighborhood every morning Monday through Friday for one week.
   c. You send an e-mail to 100 classmates chosen at random.
   d. You poll every fifth person at a popular local sandwich shop.

37. **Market Research** A perfume company sends a sample of a new scent to 500 homes. Each responder who sends back a response card saying how much she likes the scent will have a chance to win a bottle of perfume. How will this affect the results?

38. Elections A radio station asks its listeners to call and tell who their favorite candidate is in an upcoming election. Sixty-eight percent of the callers prefer a certain candidate, so the radio station announces that the candidate will win the election. Is the conclusion valid? Explain.

 Challenge

39. Data Collection You want to find out what kinds of pets the families of students attending your school have.

   a. Write an unbiased question for your survey. Will you be collecting quantitative or qualitative data?

   b. Choose a population and sampling method. Describe them both.

   c. Collect the data as you described and display the results in a graph.

40. Writing A toothpaste company reports that four out of five dentists recommend their toothpaste. What information do you need to know about the survey to determine whether the results are unbiased?

Standardized Test Prep

SAT/ACT

41. What is the solution of the equation $\frac{x}{2} - 11 = 19$?

   (A) 8 (B) 16 (C) 30 (D) 60

42. What is 0.0000212 written in scientific notation?

   (F) 2.12×10^5 (G) 2.12×10^{-5} (H) 21.2×10^{-6} (I) 2.12×10^{-6}

43. 40% of what number is 50?

   (A) 155 (B) 125 (C) 20 (D) 2

Short Response

44. A reporter is trying to predict who will win an open seat on the city council. Her plan is to ask 20 coworkers who they think will win. Will this plan give a good sample? Explain.

Mixed Review

45. Of 30 test scores, 12 are less than or equal to 85. What is the percentile rank of a test score of 85?

◀ See Lesson 12-4.

46. There are 15 bands in a competition. The judges give 9 bands a score of 7.5 or lower. What is the percentile rank of 7.5?

Solve each inequality.

◀ See Lesson 3-4.

47. $4 - 3a < 3a - 2$ **48.** $3(x - 2) \le 6x + 3$ **49.** $2.7 + 2b > 3.4 - 1.5b$

Get Ready! To prepare for Lesson 12-6, do Exercises 50–52.

Write each fraction in simplest form.

◀ See p. 801.

50. $\frac{5 \cdot 4 \cdot 3 \cdot 2 \cdot 1}{3 \cdot 2 \cdot 1}$ **51.** $\frac{7 \cdot 6 \cdot 5 \cdot 4 \cdot 3 \cdot 2 \cdot 1}{5 \cdot 4 \cdot 3 \cdot 2 \cdot 1}$ **52.** $\frac{6 \cdot 5 \cdot 4 \cdot 3 \cdot 2 \cdot 1}{5 \cdot 4 \cdot 3 \cdot 2 \cdot 1}$

Concept Byte

Use With Lesson 12-5

ACTIVITY

Two-Way Frequency Tables

 Common Core State Standards

S-ID.B.5 Summarize categorical data for two categories in two-way frequency tables . . . Recognize possible associations and trends in the data.

MP 2

Two-way frequency tables are a convenient way to show data.

Activity 1

The table at the right gives information about ticket sales for two movies. The table also separates those sales into ticket purchases by men and ticket purchases by women.

Of the 103 tickets sold for *Story of Love*, 78 tickets, or 75.7%, were sold to men. Of the 90 men who purchased tickets, 78 of them, or 86.7%, purchased a ticket for *Story of Love*.

Calculate the ratio and percent for each of the following.

1. Men who purchased tickets to *Martial Arts Champ* to all men.

2. Men who purchased tickets to *Martial Arts Champ* to all who purchased tickets to *Martial Arts Champ*.

3. Women who purchased tickets to *Martial Arts Champ* to all who purchased tickets to *Martial Arts Champ*.

4. Women who purchased tickets to *Story of Love* to all who purchased tickets to *Story of Love*.

5. Which movie is more popular with women? With men?

Movie Ticket Sales

Gender	Movie	
	Story of Love	*Martial Arts Champ*
Men	78	12
Women	25	86

Activity 2

You can use two-way frequency tables to make better predictions.

The citizens of Parkdale are preparing to vote on a bond issue to fund an expansion of the public library. The table at the right records data about support for the bond issue.

For each of the following, calculate the ratio and percent in relation to all people in the given age group.

6. The people between 18 and 25 who support the bond issue.

7. The people between 26 and 64 who support the bond issue.

8. The people 65 or older who oppose the bond issue.

9. The people between 26 and 64 who oppose the bond issue.

10. An expert predicts that 10% of the voters will be between 18 and 25, 40% will be between 26 and 64, and 50% will be 65 or older. Based on her predictions, she can calculate the result of the election from the expression $0.1a + 0.4b + 0.5c$ where a, b, and c are the decimal forms of the ratio of people supporting the bond issue in the three groups. Predict the percent of votes in favor of the bond issue.

Support for Bond Issue

	Age		
	18–25	26–64	≥ 65
Support	79	55	33
Oppose	21	45	67

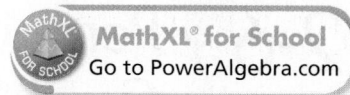

Do you know HOW?

Find each sum or difference.

1. $\begin{bmatrix} -2 & 3 \\ 0 & 4 \\ -1 & 1 \end{bmatrix} + \begin{bmatrix} 4 & -1 \\ 3 & 0 \\ -3 & 2 \end{bmatrix}$

2. $\begin{bmatrix} 0 & -2 \\ 3 & 1 \\ -4 & 3 \end{bmatrix} - \begin{bmatrix} -1 & 0 \\ 2 & 5 \\ -4 & 3 \end{bmatrix}$

Find each product.

3. $-2\begin{bmatrix} 3 & 0 \\ -2 & 1 \end{bmatrix}$ 4. $3\begin{bmatrix} -1 & 3 \\ 0 & 2 \end{bmatrix}$

Tell whether each histogram is *uniform*, *symmetric*, or *skewed*.

5.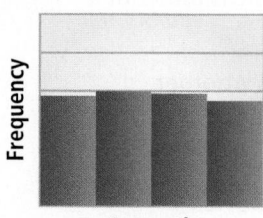

6.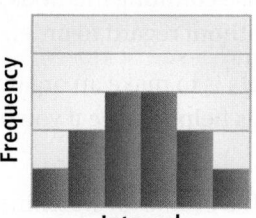

7. **Gymnastics** A gymnast's scores from his tryouts are listed below. Make a frequency table and a histogram that represent the data.
8.8 9.1 3.5 6.9 7.3 9.6 9.0 5.7 7.2 4.3 8.9 9.5

8. **Basketball** A basketball player's points per game are listed below. Make a cumulative frequency table that represents the data.
16 8 19 12 9 10 11 9 12 23 5 20 13 6 17

9. **Music** The hours per week that a school band practiced are listed below. What are the mean, median, mode, and range of their practice times? Which measure of central tendency best describes their practice times?
7 5 9 7 4 6 10 8 5 7 8 7 3 12 15 13 8

Identify the minimum, first quartile, median, third quartile, and maximum of each data set. Then make a box-and-whisker plot of each data set.

10. daily visitors: 34 29 32 25 97 93 112 108 90

11. commute (mi): 8 33 28 7 42 9 30 38 22 6 37

12. **Movies** Of the ratings for ten movies, eight ratings are less than or equal to 7. What is the percentile rank of a rating of 7?

Determine whether each data set is *qualitative* or *quantitative*.

13. favorite books   14. prices of DVDs

15. **Business** A software business e-mails every thousandth name on an e-mail list to find out what software the people are using. Is the survey plan *random*, *systematic*, or *stratified*? Will it give a good sample? Explain.

Do you UNDERSTAND?

16. **Reasoning** When you compare two sets of data, will the set with the greater interquartile range always have the greater range? Explain and give an example.

17. **Writing** When is each measure of central tendency most useful?

18. **Error Analysis** A student wrote the matrix equation at the right. Describe and correct the mistake.

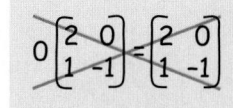

19. **Open-Ended** Describe a problem that you could solve by conducting a survey. Write an unbiased survey question, and explain how to choose a good sample for your survey.

20. **Reasoning** Which measure of central tendency would be most appropriate for qualitative data? Explain your answer.

12-6 Permutations and Combinations

Common Core State Standards

Prepares for S-CP.B.9 Use permutations and combinations to compute probabilities of compound events and solve problems.

MP 1, MP 2, MP 3, MP 4, MP 6

Objective To find permutations and combinations

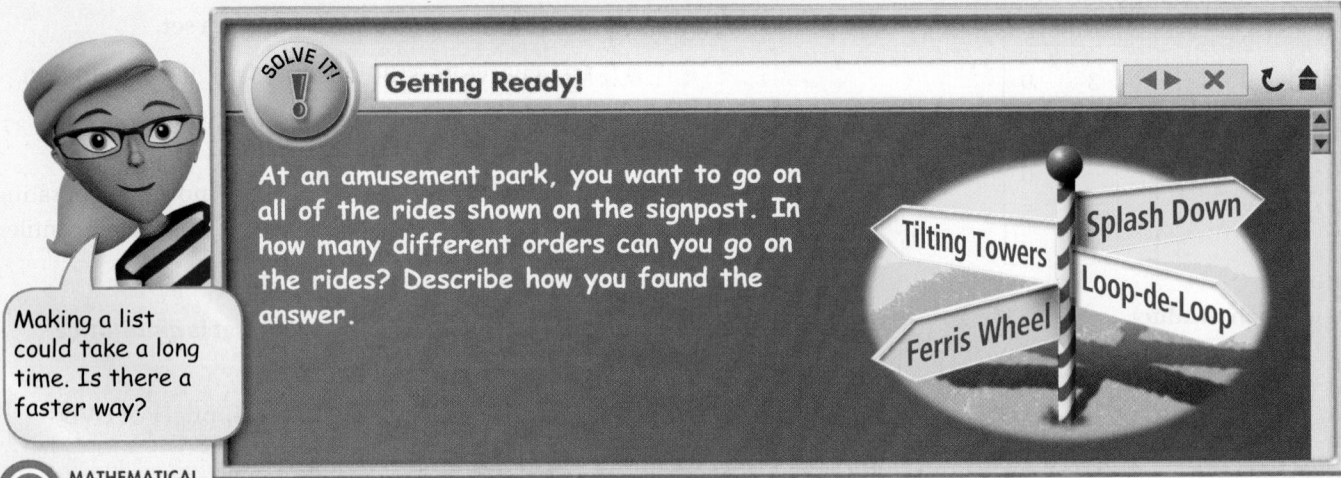

Getting Ready!

At an amusement park, you want to go on all of the rides shown on the signpost. In how many different orders can you go on the rides? Describe how you found the answer.

Making a list could take a long time. Is there a faster way?

MATHEMATICAL PRACTICES

Lesson Vocabulary
• Multiplication Counting Principle
• permutation
• *n* factorial
• combination

Essential Understanding You can use counting methods to find the number of possible ways to choose objects with and without regard to order.

One way to find the possible orders of objects is to make an organized list. Another way is to make a tree diagram. Both methods help you see if you have thought of all the possibilities.

The tree diagram below shows all the possible orders for watching three movies (a comedy, a drama, and an action film).

First Movie	Second Movie	Third Movie	Order of Movies
comedy	drama	action	comedy, drama, action
	action	drama	comedy, action, drama
drama	comedy	action	drama, comedy, action
	action	comedy	drama, action, comedy
action	comedy	drama	action, comedy, drama
	drama	comedy	action, drama, comedy

There are six possible orders for watching the three movies.

When one event does not affect the result of a second event, the events are *independent*. When events are independent, you can find the number of outcomes using the Multiplication Counting Principle.

Key Concept   Multiplication Counting Principle

If there are *m* ways to make a first selection and *n* ways to make a second selection, then there are *m* • *n* ways to make the two selections.

Example

For 5 shirts and 8 pairs of shorts, the number of possible outfits is 5 • 8 = 40.

 Problem 1 Using the Multiplication Counting Principle

Shopping Use the diagram below. How many ways are there to get from the first floor to the third floor using only escalators?

Think

What is another way to solve this problem?
You can draw a diagram like the tree diagram on the previous page to show all of the possible escalator routes.

$2 \cdot 3 = 6$

Routes by escalator from first floor to second floor

Routes by escalator from second floor to third floor

Routes by escalator from first floor to third floor

There are 6 possible ways to get from the first floor to the third floor using only escalators.

Got It? **1. a.** A pizza shop offers 8 vegetable toppings and 6 meat toppings. How many different pizzas can you order with one meat topping and one vegetable topping?

b. Reasoning Is a tree diagram a convenient way to find the answer to part (a)? Explain.

A **permutation** is an arrangement of objects in a specific order. Here are the possible permutations of the letters A, B, and C without repeating any letters.

ABC   ACB   BAC   BCA   CAB   CBA

Problem 2 Finding Permutations

Plan

How do you use the Multiplication Counting Principle to find the number of permutations?
Multiply the number of ways to make each selection.

Baseball How many different batting orders can you have with 9 players?

There are 9 choices for the first batter, 8 for the second, and so on.

$$9 \cdot 8 \cdot 7 \cdot 6 \cdot 5 \cdot 4 \cdot 3 \cdot 2 \cdot 1 = 362{,}880 \qquad \text{Use a calculator.}$$

There are 362,880 possible batting orders.

 Got It? 2. A swimming pool has 8 lanes. In how many ways can 8 swimmers be assigned lanes for a race?

A short way to write the product in Problem 2 is 9!, read "nine factorial." For any positive integer n, the expression **n factorial** is written as $n!$ and is the product of the integers from n down to 1. The value of 0! is defined to be 1.

You can use factorials to write a formula for the number of permutations of n objects arranged r at a time.

---

take note

Key Concept Permutation Notation

The expression $_nP_r$ represents the number of permutations of n objects arranged r at a time.

$$_nP_r = \frac{n!}{(n-r)!}$$

Example $_8P_2 = \frac{8!}{(8-2)!} = \frac{8!}{6!} = \frac{8 \cdot 7 \cdot 6 \cdot 5 \cdot 4 \cdot 3 \cdot 2 \cdot 1}{6 \cdot 5 \cdot 4 \cdot 3 \cdot 2 \cdot 1} = 56$

 Problem 3 Using Permutation Notation

Think

How can you think about this problem in a different way?
You can use the Multiplication Counting Principle. There are 7 choices for the first song, 6 for the second, 5 for the third, 4 for the fourth, and 3 for the fifth.

Music A band has 7 new songs and wants to put 5 of them on a demo CD. How many arrangements of 5 songs are possible?

To find the number of possible arrangements, find the value of $_7P_5$.

Method 1 Use the formula for permutations.

$$_7P_5 = \frac{7!}{(7-5)!} = \frac{7!}{2!} = \frac{7 \cdot 6 \cdot 5 \cdot 4 \cdot 3 \cdot 2 \cdot 1}{2 \cdot 1} \qquad \text{Write using factorials.}$$

$$= 2520 \qquad \text{Simplify.}$$

Method 2 Use a graphing calculator.
Press **7** **math** ◀ **2** **5** **enter** .

$$_7P_5 = 2520$$

There are 2520 possible arrangements of 5 songs.

Got It? **3.** There are 6 students in a classroom with 8 desks. How many possible seating arrangements are there?

A **combination** is a selection of objects without regard to order. For example, if you are selecting two side dishes from a list of five, the order in which you choose the side dishes does not matter.

Key Concept Combination Notation

The expression $_nC_r$ represents the number of combinations of n objects chosen r at a time.

$$_nC_r = \frac{n!}{r!(n-r)!}$$

Example $_8C_2 = \frac{8!}{2!(8-2)!} = \frac{8!}{2!6!} = \frac{8 \cdot 7 \cdot 6 \cdot 5 \cdot 4 \cdot 3 \cdot 2 \cdot 1}{(2 \cdot 1)(6 \cdot 5 \cdot 4 \cdot 3 \cdot 2 \cdot 1)} = 28$

Problem 4 Using Combination Notation

Multiple Choice Twenty people report for jury duty. How many different 12-person juries can be chosen?

Ⓐ 20   Ⓑ 240   Ⓒ 125,970   Ⓓ 479,001,600

Plan

Do you use a permutation or a combination?
The order of the people on the jury does not matter, so use a combination.

You need the number of combinations of 20 jurors chosen 12 at a time. Find $_{20}C_{12}$.

$_{20}C_{12} = \dfrac{20!}{12!(20-12)!} = \dfrac{20!}{12!8!}$ Write using factorials.

$= 125,970$ Simplify using a calculator.

There are 125,970 different 12-person juries. The correct answer is C.

 Got It? **4.** In how many different ways can you choose 3 types of flowers for a bouquet from a selection of 15 types of flowers?

 Lesson Check

Do you know HOW?

Find the value of each expression.

1. 7!   **2.** 13!   **3.** $_6P_3$

4. $_{10}P_4$ **5.** $_5C_3$ **6.** $_7C_3$

7. How many outfits can you make with 6 shirts and 4 pairs of pants?

Do you UNDERSTAND?   MATHEMATICAL PRACTICES

Ⓒ **8. Vocabulary** Would you use permutations or combinations to find the number of possible arrangements of 10 students in a line? Why?

Ⓒ **9. Compare and Contrast** How are permutations and combinations similar? How are they different?

Ⓒ **10. Reasoning** Explain why $_nC_n$ is equal to 1.

Practice and Problem-Solving Exercises

 MATHEMATICAL PRACTICES

 Practice

11. Telephones A seven-digit telephone number can begin with any digit except 0 or 1. There are no restrictions on digits after the first digit.

    a. How many possible choices are there for the first digit? For each digit after the first digit?

    b. How many different seven-digit telephone numbers are possible?

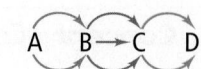 **See Problem 1.**

12. Use the diagram and the Multiplication Counting Principle to find each of the following:

    a. the number of routes from A to C

    b. the number of routes from A to D

13. Sports In an ice-skating competition, the order in which competitors skate is determined by a drawing. Suppose there are 10 skaters in the finals. How many different orders are possible for the final program?

See Problem 2.

14. Photography Suppose you are lining up with 4 cousins for a photo. How many different arrangements are possible?

Find the value of each expression.

See Problem 3.

15. $_8P_4$ **16.** $_9P_3$ **17.** $_7P_6$ **18.** $_8P_5$ **19.** $_7P_2$

20. $_5P_5$ **21.** $_6P_1$ **22.** $_{11}P_0$ **23.** $_{10}P_2$ **24.** $_{12}P_9$

25. Reading You have 10 books on your bookshelf. In how many orders can you read 4 of the books on a summer vacation?

26. Student Government A student council has 24 members. The council is selecting a 3-person committee to plan a car wash. Each person on the committee will have one task: one person will find a location, another person will organize publicity, and the third person will schedule volunteers. In how many different ways can 3 students be chosen and given a task?

Find the value of each expression.

See Problem 4.

27. $_6C_6$ **28.** $_5C_4$ **29.** $_9C_1$ **30.** $_7C_2$ **31.** $_8C_5$

32. $_3C_0$ **33.** $_8C_6$ **34.** $_7C_5$ **35.** $_{10}C_9$ **36.** $_{15}C_4$

37. Law For some civil cases, at least 9 of 12 jurors must agree on a verdict. How many combinations of 9 jurors are possible on a 12-person jury?

38. Gift Certificates For your birthday you received a gift certificate from a music store for 3 CDs. There are 8 CDs you would like to have. How many different groups of 3 CDs can you select from the 8 you want?

39. Quilting There are 30 fabrics available at a quilt store. How many different groups of 5 fabrics can you choose for a quilt?

 **Apply**

Determine which value is greater.

40. $_8P_6$ or $_6P_2$

41. $_9P_7$ or $_9P_2$

42. $_{10}P_3$ or $_8P_4$

43. $_9C_6$ or $_9P_6$

44. $_{11}C_5$ or $_{11}C_8$

45. $_7C_4$ or $_8C_5$

 46. Think About a Plan Draw four points like those in Figure 1. Draw line segments so that every point is joined to every other point. How many line segments did you draw? How many segments would you need to join each point to all the others in Figure 2?
- How many points are there in Figure 2?
- Should you use combinations or permutations to find the number of segments that join pairs of points?

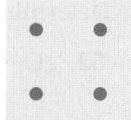   

Figure 1   Figure 2

47. a. Lena wants a password that uses the 4 letters of her name. How many permutations are possible using each letter only once?
  b. Writing Is creating a password based on your name a good idea? Explain your reasoning.

48. License Plates In one state, a regular license plate has a two-digit number that is fixed by county, then one letter, and then four one-digit numbers.
  a. How many different license plates are possible in each county?
  b. Suppose there are 92 counties in the state. How many license plates are possible in the entire state?

Find the number of arrangements of letters taken three at a time that can be formed from each set of cards.

49. A B C D E

50. P Q R

51. E F G H I J K

52. M N O P

Reasoning Explain whether each situation is a permutation problem or a combination problem.

53. A locker contains 8 books. You select 3 books at random. How many different sets of books can you select?

54. You take 4 books out of the school library to read during spring vacation. In how many different orders can you read the 4 books?

55. Media The call signs of radio and television stations in the United States generally begin with the letter W east of the Mississippi River and the letter K west of the Mississippi. Repetition of letters is allowed.
  a. How many different call signs are possible if each station uses a W or K followed by 3 letters?
  b. How many different call signs are possible if each station uses a W or K followed by 4 letters?

Find the value of each expression.

56. $\dfrac{_5P_3}{_5P_2}$

57. $\dfrac{_4P_3}{_4P_2}$

58. $\dfrac{_7P_3}{_7P_2}$

59. $_2C_2 + {}_2C_1 + {}_2C_0$

60. $_3C_3 + {}_3C_2 + {}_3C_1 + {}_3C_0$

61. $_{90}C_{90}$

 **Challenge** **Determine whether each statement is *always*, *sometimes*, or *never* true. Assume $n \neq 0$.**

62. $_nC_1 = n$

63. $_3C_x > x$

64. $_nC_{(n-1)} = n$

65. A test has 10 questions. You must answer a total of 7 questions, including exactly 4 of the first 6 questions.
   a. In how many ways can you choose 4 of the first 6 questions?
   b. How many questions are left after you have answered 4 of the first 6 questions? How many must you still answer?
   c. In how many ways can you choose questions to finish the test?
   d. How many different ways are there of completing the test (meeting all of its requirements)?

Standardized Test Prep

GRIDDED RESPONSE

 SAT/ACT

66. The school cafeteria serves lunches consisting of 1 main dish, 1 vegetable, 1 salad, and 1 dessert. The menu has choices of 2 main dishes, 3 vegetables, 3 salads, and 4 desserts. How many different lunches are possible?

67. What is 7.3×10^{-2} written in standard form?

68. How many elements are in the union of the two sets $M = \{4, 5, -6, 7, 8\}$ and $N = \{-4, 5, 6, 7, -8\}$?

69. You deposit $500 in an account earning 5.25% annual interest. You make no further deposits to the account and the interest is compounded annually. What is the balance in dollars after 10 yr? Round to the nearest dollar.

Mixed Review

Determine whether each data set is *qualitative* or *quantitative*.   ◀ **See Lesson 12-5.**

70. ZIP codes

71. race times

72. heights of people

73. emotions

Use the quadratic formula to solve each equation. If necessary, round answers to the nearest hundredth.   ◀ **See Lesson 9-6.**

74. $2x^2 + 12x - 11 = 0$

75. $x^2 - 7x + 2 = 0$

76. $x^2 + 4x - 8 = 0$

77. $3x^2 + 8x + 5 = 0$

Get Ready! **To prepare for Lesson 12-7, do Exercises 78–81.**

Rewrite each decimal or fraction as a percent.   ◀ **See page 805.**

78. 0.32

79. 0.09

80. $\dfrac{45}{200}$

81. $\dfrac{9}{50}$

12-7 Theoretical and Experimental Probability

© Common Core State Standards

S-CP.A.1 Describe events as subsets of a sample space (the set of outcomes) using characteristics (or categories) of the outcomes, or as . . . complements of other events. . . . **Also S-CP.A.4**

MP 1, MP 2, MP 3, MP 4, MP 6

Objective To find theoretical and experimental probabilities

Getting Ready! ◀▶ ✕ ↻ ⌂

On one game show, you get one chance to spin the wheel at the right. If the spinner stops on a red section, you win a prize of your choice. On another game show, you choose one of 15 envelopes. Three of the envelopes contain a prize that you chose. Which game show would you rather be on? Explain your reasoning.

> I want to win a prize. What's the best decision?

MATHEMATICAL PRACTICES In the Solve It, spinning red and choosing the right envelope are desired outcomes. An **outcome** is the result of a single trial, such as spinning a wheel. The **sample space** is all the possible outcomes. An **event** is any outcome or group of outcomes. The outcomes that match a given event are favorable outcomes.

Here is how these terms apply to rolling an even number on a number cube.

event	sample space	favorable outcomes
↓	↓	↓
rolling an even number	1, 2, 3, 4, 5, 6	2, 4, 6

Lesson Vocabulary
- outcome
- sample space
- event
- probability
- theoretical probability
- complement of an event
- odds
- experimental probability

Essential Understanding The **probability** of an event, or *P*(event), tells you how likely it is that the event will occur. You can find probabilities by reasoning mathematically or by using data collected from an experiment.

In the number-cube example above, the outcomes in the sample space are equally likely to occur. When all possible outcomes are equally likely, you can find the *theoretical probability* of an event using the following formula.

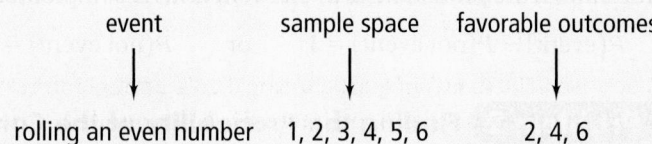

theoretical probability $P(\text{event}) = \dfrac{\text{number of favorable outcomes}}{\text{number of possible outcomes}}$

$$P(\text{rolling an even number}) = \frac{3}{6} = \frac{1}{2}$$

You can write the probability of an event as a fraction, a decimal, or a percent. The probability of an event ranges from 0 to 1.

equally likely to occur

impossible   or not occur   certain

0 ←— less likely   0.5   more likely —→ 1

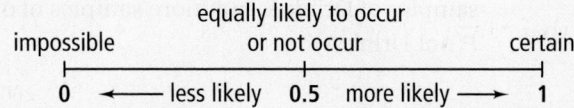

Problem 1 Finding Theoretical Probability STEM

Astronomy Our solar system's 8 planets, in order of least to greatest distance from the sun, are Mercury, Venus, Earth, Mars, Jupiter, Saturn, Uranus, and Neptune. You will randomly draw one of the names of the planets and write a report on that planet. What is the theoretical probability that you will select a planet whose distance from the sun is less than Earth's?

Think

Does a "favorable outcome" always mean that something good happens?
No. For example, if you are determining the probability of losing a game, the "favorable" outcomes are the outcomes where you lose.

$$P(\text{event}) = \frac{\text{number of favorable outcomes}}{\text{number of possible outcomes}}$$

$$= \frac{2}{8}$$ Two planets out of 8 are nearer to the sun than Earth: Mercury and Venus.

$$= \frac{1}{4}$$ Simplify.

The probability of selecting a planet whose distance from the sun is less than Earth's is $\frac{1}{4}$.

 Got It? **1.** In Problem 1, what is the theoretical probability that you will select a planet whose distance from the sun is greater than Earth's?

The **complement of an event** consists of all outcomes in the sample space that are not in the event. The possible outcomes for rolling a number cube are 1, 2, 3, 4, 5, and 6. The outcomes for rolling an even number are 2, 4, and 6. The outcomes for the complement of rolling an even number are 1, 3, and 5.

The sum of the probabilities of an event and its complement is 1.

$$P(\text{event}) + P(\text{not event}) = 1 \quad \text{or} \quad P(\text{not event}) = 1 - P(\text{event})$$

 Problem 2 Finding the Probability of the Complement of an Event

Consumer Research In a taste test, 50 participants are randomly given a beverage to sample. There are 20 samples of Drink A, 10 samples of Drink B, 10 samples of Drink C, and 10 samples of Drink D. What is the probability of a participant not getting Drink A?

Think

How else can you find P(not Drink A)?
You can divide the number of other drink samples by the total number of samples.
P(not Drink A)
$= \frac{10 + 10 + 10}{50}$
$= \frac{30}{50} = \frac{3}{5}$

$$P(\text{Drink A}) = \frac{\text{number of samples of Drink A}}{\text{total number of samples}} = \frac{20}{50} = \frac{2}{5} \quad \text{Find } P(\text{Drink A}).$$

$$P(\text{not Drink A}) = 1 - P(\text{Drink A}) \quad\quad\quad\quad\quad \text{Use the complement formula.}$$

$$= 1 - \frac{2}{5} = \frac{3}{5} \quad\quad\quad\quad\quad\quad\quad \text{Substitute and simplify.}$$

The probability of not getting Drink A is $\frac{3}{5}$.

  Got It? **2. Reasoning** Suppose a taste test is repeated with the same number of samples of Drink A, but more samples of other drinks. What happens to $P(\text{not Drink A})$?

Odds describe the likelihood of an event as a ratio comparing the number of favorable and unfavorable outcomes.

$$\text{odds in favor of an event} = \frac{\text{number of favorable outcomes}}{\text{number of unfavorable outcomes}}$$

$$\text{odds against an event} = \frac{\text{number of unfavorable outcomes}}{\text{number of favorable outcomes}}$$

© Problem 3 Finding Odds

Think

How is finding odds different from finding probability?
To find odds, you compare favorable and unfavorable outcomes. To find probability, you compare favorable outcomes and all possible outcomes.

What are the odds in favor of the spinner landing on a number greater than or equal to 6?

Favorable outcomes: 6, 7, 8   Total: 3
Unfavorable outcomes: 1, 2, 3, 4, 5   Total: 5

The odds in favor of the event are $\frac{3}{5}$, or 3 : 5.

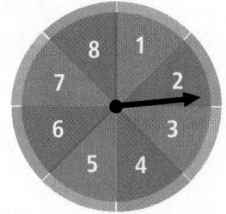

Got It? 3. What are the odds against the spinner landing on a number less than 3?

Experimental probability is based on data collected from repeated trials.

experimental probability $P(\text{event}) = \dfrac{\text{number of times the event occurs}}{\text{number of times the experiment is done}}$

© Problem 4 Finding Experimental Probability STEM

Think

How is the formula for experimental probability similar to the formula for theoretical probability?
In each formula, you divide a number of items corresponding to an event by a total number of items.

Quality Control After receiving complaints, a skateboard manufacturer inspects 1000 skateboards at random. The manufacturer finds no defects in 992 skateboards. What is the probability that a skateboard selected at random has no defects? Write the probability as a percent.

$P(\text{no defects}) = \dfrac{\text{number of skateboards with no defects}}{\text{number of skateboards examined}}$

$= \dfrac{992}{1000}$ Substitute.

$= 0.992$ Write as a decimal.

$= 99.2\%$ Change to percent.

The probability that a skateboard selected at random has no defects is 99.2%.

Got It? 4. Suppose the manufacturer in Problem 4 inspects 2500 skateboards. There are 2450 skateboards with no defects. What is the probability that a skateboard selected at random has no defects? Write the probability as a percent.

You can use experimental probability to make a prediction. Predictions are not exact, so round your results.

 **Problem 5** Using Experimental Probability

Pets You ask 500 randomly selected households in your town if they have a dog. Of the 500 households, 197 respond that they do have a dog. If your town has 24,800 households, about how many households are likely to have a dog?

Know
- 197 of 500 respondents own a dog
- Your town has 24,800 households

Need
Likely number of households that own a dog

Plan
Find the experimental probability that a household owns a dog. Then multiply it by the total number of households.

$$P(\text{own dog}) = \frac{\text{number of respondents that own a dog}}{\text{number of households surveyed}} = \frac{197}{500} = 0.394$$

households with dog = $P(\text{own dog}) \cdot$ total number of households

= 0.394 · 24,800   Substitute.

= 9771.2   Simplify.

It is likely that approximately 9770 households in your town own a dog.

 Got It? **5.** A manufacturer inspects 700 light bulbs and finds that 692 of the light bulbs work. There are about 35,400 light bulbs in the manufacturer's warehouse. About how many of the light bulbs in the warehouse are likely to work?

 Lesson Check

Do you know HOW?

Find the theoretical probability of each event when rolling a number cube.

1. $P(4)$

2. $P(\text{less than 3})$

3. $P(\text{not 3})$

4. $P(\text{not greater than 4})$

5. What are the odds in favor of rolling a 4 on a number cube?

6. You toss a dart at a dartboard 500 times. You hit the bull's-eye 80 times. What is the experimental probability that you hit the bull's-eye?

Do you UNDERSTAND?  MATHEMATICAL PRACTICES

7. Vocabulary What is the difference between theoretical probability and experimental probability?

8. Error Analysis Eric calculated the probability of getting a number less than 3 when randomly choosing an integer from 1 to 10. Describe and correct his error.

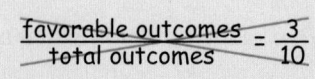

9. Open-Ended Describe a real-world situation in which one event is nearly certain to occur and another event is highly unlikely.

Practice and Problem-Solving Exercises

MATHEMATICAL PRACTICES

**Practice**

The spinner at the right is divided into six equal parts. Find the theoretical probability of landing on the given section(s) of the spinner.

◀ **See Problems 1 and 2.**

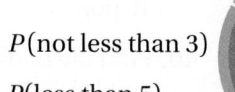

10. P(blue)   **11.** P(white)   **12.** P(5)   **13.** P(not less than 3)

14. P(8)   **15.** P(even)   **16.** P(not 2)   **17.** P(less than 5)

18. P(not green)   **19.** P(not red)   **20.** P(even or odd)   **21.** P(greater than 4)

Use the spinner at the right above. Find the odds.

◀ **See Problem 3.**

22. odds in favor of even number   **23.** odds against 2   **24.** odds against a factor of 6

25. odds against green   **26.** odds in favor of blue   **27.** odds in favor of a multiple of 5

The results of a survey of 100 randomly selected students at a 2000-student high school are shown at the right. Find the experimental probability that a student selected at random has the given plans after graduation.

◀ **See Problem 4.**

Plans for After Graduation

Response	Number of Responses
Go to community college	24
Go to 4-year college	43
Take a year off before college	12
Go to trade school	15
Do not plan to go to college	6

28. P(community college)

29. P(4-year college)

30. P(trade school)

31. P(not trade school)

32. P(trade school or community college)

33. A park has about 500 trees. You find that 27 of 67 randomly chosen trees are oak trees. About how many trees in the entire park are likely to be oak trees?

◀ **See Problem 5.**

**Apply**

34. Error Analysis A spinner has 3 red and 5 blue sections of equal size. A friend says the odds in favor of spinning blue are 3 : 5. Describe and correct the error.

35. Think About a Plan The United States has a land area of about 3,536,278 mi^2. Illinois has a land area of about 57,918 mi^2. What is the probability that a location in the United States chosen at random is not in Illinois? Give your answer to the nearest tenth of a percent.
- How can you solve this problem using the complement of an event?
- How do you write a fraction as a percent?

36. Transportation Out of 80 workers surveyed at a company, 17 walk to work.
- **a.** What is the experimental probability that a randomly selected worker at that company walks to work?
- **b.** Predict about how many of the 3600 workers at the company walk to work.

37. Open-Ended Suppose your teacher chooses a student at random from your algebra class. What is the probability that a boy is not selected?

38. Reasoning The odds in favor of Event A are equal to the odds against Event A. What is the probability of Event A? Explain.

Football The stem-and-leaf plot at the right shows the difference between the points scored by the winning and losing teams in the Super Bowl during one 20-yr period.

39. Find the probability that the winning team won by less than 10 points.

40. Find the odds that the winning team won by 10 to 15 points.

41. Find the probability that the winning team won by more than 20 points.

Difference Between Winning and Losing Super Bowl Scores	
0	1 3 3 3 3 4 7 7
1	0 1 2 3 4 5 7
2	3 7 7
3	5
4	5

Key: 1 | 0 means 10 points

 **Challenge**

42. Reasoning The odds in favor of choosing a red marble from a bag of red and blue marbles are 7 : 3. What is the probability of choosing a blue marble? Explain.

Geometry Use the figure at the right. Assume that the white square is centered in the large square. If you randomly choose a point inside the figure, what is the probability that it will be in the region described?

43. $P(\text{red})$

44. $P(\text{blue})$

45. $P(\text{not blue})$

46. $P(\text{green or white})$

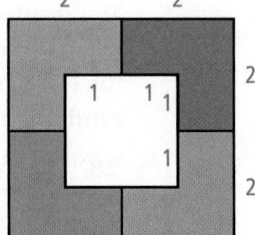

Standardized Test Prep

47. What is the median of the following class sizes: 29, 31, 28, 25, 27, 33, 33, 26?

    Ⓐ 28　　　　　　Ⓑ 28.5　　　　　　Ⓒ 29　　　　　　Ⓓ 33

48. If $y = 10$ when $x = 5$, and y varies inversely with x, which equation relates x and y?

    Ⓕ $xy = 5$　　　　Ⓖ $y = \frac{50}{x}$　　　　Ⓗ $xy = 2$　　　　Ⓘ $y = \frac{2}{x}$

Short Response

49. A basketball team has 11 players. How many different 5-player groups can the coach choose to play during a game? Show your work.

Mixed Review

Find the number of permutations or combinations.

◀ **See Lesson 12-6.**

50. $_7P_4$　　　　**51.** $_3P_3$　　　　**52.** $_6P_2$　　　　**53.** $_9C_1$　　　　**54.** $_5C_4$

Get Ready! To prepare for Lesson 12-8, do Exercises 55–59.

Find each union or intersection. Let $J = \{4, 5, 6, 7\}$, $K = \{1, 4, 7, 10\}$, and $L = \{x \mid x \text{ is an even whole number less than } 12\}$.

◀ **See Lesson 3-8.**

55. $J \cup K$　　　**56.** $J \cap L$　　　**57.** $J \cup L$　　　**58.** $L \cap K$　　　**59.** $K \cup L$

Conducting Simulations

 Common Core State Standards

S-IC.B.5 Use data from a randomized experiment to compare two treatments; use simulations to decide if differences between parameters are significant.

MP 5

A *simulation* is a model of a real-life situation. One way to do a simulation is to use random numbers generated by a graphing calculator or computer program.

On a graphing calculator, the command **RANDINT** generates random integers. To create a list of random integers, press (math) ◁ (5). The calculator will display **RANDINT(.** After the parenthesis, type (0) (,) (9) (9), and press (enter) repeatedly to create random 1- and 2-digit numbers from 0 to 99.

Activity 1

About 40% of people in the United States have type A blood. Estimate the probability that the next two people who donate blood in a blood drive have type A blood.

Step 1 To simulate this situation, let a 2-digit number represent 2 people. Use a calculator to generate 40 random 2-digit numbers, like the example at the right.

Step 2 Since about 40% of people in the United States have type A blood, 40% of the digits 0–9 can be used to represent these people. Let 0, 1, 2, and 3 represent people with type A blood, and let 4, 5, 6, 7, 8, and 9 represent people without type A blood. So, the 2-digit number 53 represents one person without type A blood (the digit 5) and one person with type A blood (the digit 3).

Step 3 In the example at the right, the six numbers in red represent two consecutive people who have type A blood. The other 2-digit numbers have at least one digit that represents a person of a blood type other than type A.

$$P(\text{two consecutive people of blood type A}) = \frac{\text{number of times the event occurs}}{\text{number of times the experiment is done}}$$

$$= \frac{6}{40} = 0.15$$

53	18	33	75
93	34	36	45
25	71	47	46
66	13	63	36
21	59	27	07
83	25	72	24
73	52	59	81
14	09	40	64
81	72	02	38
21	09	92	10

Convert 1-digit numbers like 9 into 2-digit numbers by adding a leading zero.

You can also simulate situations using other methods, such as rolling number cubes, spinning spinners, or flipping coins.

Activity 2

A cereal company has a promotion in which 1 in every 6 boxes contains a movie ticket.

Step 1 Roll two number cubes to represent two boxes of the cereal. Let 1 represent a winning box and let 2, 3, 4, 5, and 6 represent a nonwinning box.

Step 2 Record the result. Repeat this process 30 times. Use your results to estimate the probability that both boxes contain a movie ticket.

Probability of Compound Events

© Common Core State Standards

S-CP.B.7 Apply the Addition Rule, $P(A \text{ or } B) = P(A) + P(B) - P(A \text{ and } B)$, and interpret the answer in terms of the model. **Also S-CP.B.8**

MP 1, MP 2, MP 3, MP 4, MP 6

Objectives To find probabilities of mutually exclusive and overlapping events
To find probabilities of independent and dependent events

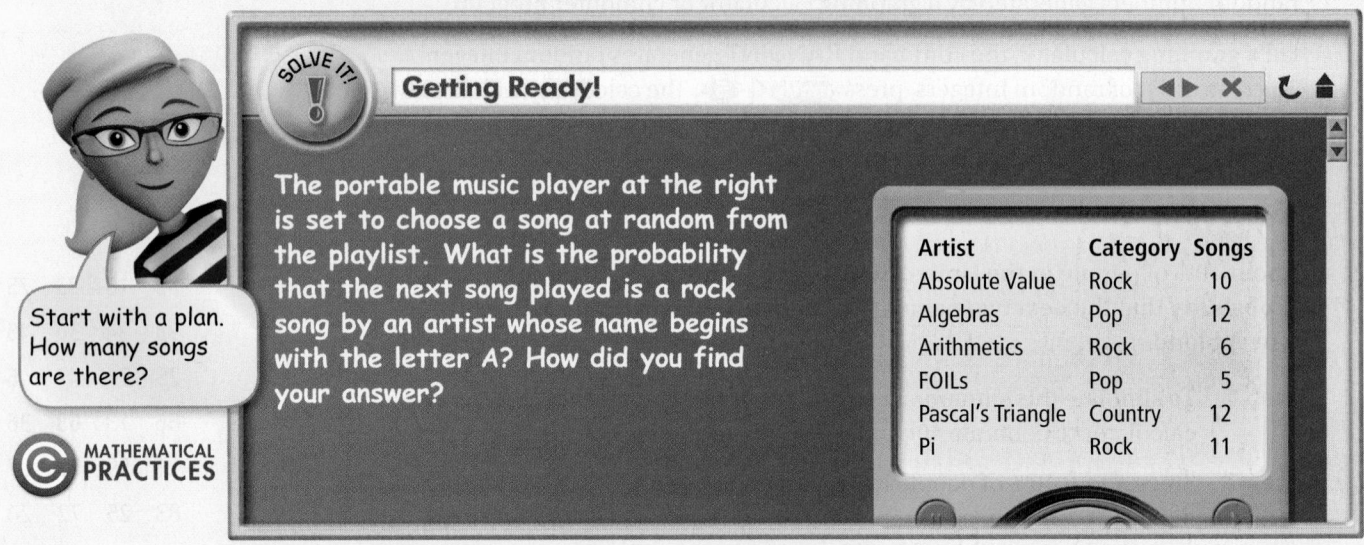

SOLVE IT!

Getting Ready!

The portable music player at the right is set to choose a song at random from the playlist. What is the probability that the next song played is a rock song by an artist whose name begins with the letter A? How did you find your answer?

Start with a plan. How many songs are there?

Artist	Category	Songs
Absolute Value	Rock	10
Algebras	Pop	12
Arithmetics	Rock	6
FOILs	Pop	5
Pascal's Triangle	Country	12
Pi	Rock	11

© MATHEMATICAL PRACTICES

In the Solve It, you found the probability that the next song is both a rock song and also a song by an artist whose name begins with the letter A. This is an example of a **compound event,** which consists of two or more events linked by the word *and* or the word *or*.

Essential Understanding You can write the probability of a compound event as an expression involving probabilities of simpler events. This may make the compound probability easier to find.

When two events have no outcomes in common, the events are **mutually exclusive events.** If A and B are mutually exclusive events, then $P(A \text{ and } B) = 0$. When events have at least one outcome in common, they are **overlapping events.**

You need to determine whether two events A and B are mutually exclusive before you can find $P(A \text{ or } B)$.

Lesson Vocabulary
- compound event
- mutually exclusive events
- overlapping events
- independent events
- dependent events

take note

Key Concept Probability of *A* or *B*

Probability of Mutually Exclusive Events
If A and B are mutually exclusive events, $P(A \text{ or } B) = P(A) + P(B)$.

Probability of Overlapping Events
If A and B are overlapping events, $P(A \text{ or } B) = P(A) + P(B) - P(A \text{ and } B)$.

Problem 1 Mutually Exclusive and Overlapping Events

Suppose you spin a spinner that has 20 equal-sized sections numbered from 1 to 20.

Ⓐ What is the probability that you spin a 2 or a 5?

Because the spinner cannot land on both 2 and 5, the events are mutually exclusive.

$$P(2 \text{ or } 5) = P(2) + P(5)$$

$$= \frac{1}{20} + \frac{1}{20} \quad \text{Substitute.}$$

$$= \frac{2}{20} = \frac{1}{10} \quad \text{Simplify.}$$

The probability that you spin a 2 or a 5 is $\frac{1}{10}$.

Ⓑ What is the probability that you spin a number that is a multiple of 2 or 5?

Since a number can be a multiple of 2 and a multiple of 5, such as 10, the events are overlapping.

$$P(\text{multiple of 2 or multiple of 5})$$

$$= P(\text{multiple of 2}) + P(\text{multiple of 5}) - P(\text{multiple of 2 and 5})$$

$$= \frac{10}{20} + \frac{4}{20} - \frac{2}{20} \quad \text{Substitute.}$$

$$= \frac{12}{20} = \frac{3}{5} \quad \text{Simplify.}$$

The probability that you spin a number that is a multiple of 2 or a multiple of 5 is $\frac{3}{5}$.

Think

How many multiples are there?
There are 10 multiples of 2: 2, 4, 6, 8, 10, 12, 14, 16, 18, and 20. There are 4 multiples of 5: 5, 10, 15, and 20. There are 2 multiples of 2 and 5: 10 and 20.

Got It? 1. Suppose you roll a standard number cube.

    a. What is the probability that you roll an even number or a number less than 4?

    b. What is the probability that you roll a 2 or an odd number?

A standard set of checkers has equal numbers of red and black checkers. The diagram at the right shows the possible outcomes when randomly choosing a checker, putting it back, and choosing again. The probability of getting a red on either choice is $\frac{1}{2}$. The first choice, or event, does not affect the second event. The events are *independent*.

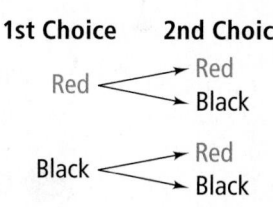

Two events are **independent events** if the occurrence of one event does not affect the probability of the second event.

take note

Key Concept   Probability of Two Independent Events

If A and B are independent events, $P(A \text{ and } B) = P(A) \cdot P(B)$.

Problem 2 Finding the Probability of Independent Events

Suppose you roll a red number cube and a blue number cube. What is the probability that you will roll a 3 on the red cube and an even number on the blue cube?

$$P(\text{red 3}) = \frac{1}{6}$$ Only one of the six numbers is a 3.

$$P(\text{blue even}) = \frac{3}{6} = \frac{1}{2}$$ Three of the six numbers are even.

$$P(\text{red 3 and blue even}) = P(\text{red 3}) \cdot P(\text{blue even})$$

$$= \frac{1}{6} \cdot \frac{1}{2} = \frac{1}{12}$$ Substitute and then simplify.

The probability is $\frac{1}{12}$.

Think

Are the events independent?
Yes. The outcome of rolling one number cube does not affect the outcome of rolling another number cube.

 Got It? **2.** You roll a red number cube and a blue number cube. What is the probability that you roll a 5 on the red cube and a 1 or 2 on the blue cube?

 Problem 3 Selecting With Replacement

Games You choose a tile at random from the game tiles shown. You replace the first tile and then choose again. What is the probability that you choose a dotted tile and then a dragon tile?

Because you replace the first tile, the events are independent.

$$P(\text{dotted}) = \frac{4}{15}$$ 4 of the 15 tiles are dotted.

$$P(\text{dragon}) = \frac{3}{15} = \frac{1}{5}$$ 3 of the 15 tiles are dragons.

$$P(\text{dotted and dragon}) = P(\text{dotted}) \cdot P(\text{dragon})$$

$$= \frac{4}{15} \cdot \frac{1}{5}$$ Substitute.

$$= \frac{4}{75}$$ Simplify.

The probability that you will choose a dotted tile and then a dragon tile is $\frac{4}{75}$.

Plan

Why are the events independent when you select with replacement?
When you replace the tile, the conditions for the second selection are exactly the same as for the first selection.

 Got It? **3.** In Problem 3, what is the probability that you randomly choose a bird and then, after replacing the first tile, a flower?

Two events are **dependent events** if the occurrence of one event affects the probability of the second event. For example, suppose in Problem 3 that you do *not* replace the first tile before choosing another. This changes the set of possible outcomes for your second selection.

 **Key Concept   Probability of Two Dependent Events**

If A and B are dependent events, $P(A \text{ then } B) = P(A) \cdot P(B \text{ after } A)$.

Problem 4 **Selecting Without Replacement** GRIDDED RESPONSE

Games Suppose you choose a tile at random from the tiles shown in Problem 3. Without replacing the first tile, you select a second tile. What is the probability that you choose a dotted tile and then a dragon tile?

Because you do not replace the first tile, the events are dependent.

$$P(\text{dotted}) = \frac{4}{15} \qquad \text{4 of the 15 tiles are dotted.}$$

$$P(\text{dragon after dotted}) = \frac{3}{14} \qquad \text{3 of the 14 remaining tiles are dragons.}$$

$P(\text{dotted then dragon}) = P(\text{dotted}) \cdot P(\text{dragon after dotted})$

$$= \frac{4}{15} \cdot \frac{3}{14} = \frac{2}{35} \qquad \text{Substitute and then simplify.}$$

The probability that you will choose a dotted tile and then a dragon tile is $\frac{2}{35}$.

Think

How is *P*(dragon after dotted) different from *P*(dragon)?
After selecting the first tile without replacement, there is one less tile to choose from for the second choice.

 Got It? **4.** In Problem 4, what is the probability that you will randomly choose a flower and then, without replacing the first tile, a bird?

 Problem 5 **Finding the Probability of a Compound Event**

Essay Contest One freshman, 2 sophomores, 4 juniors, and 5 seniors receive top scores in a school essay contest. To choose which 2 students will read their essays at the town fair, 2 names are chosen at random from a hat. What is the probability that a junior and then a senior are chosen?

Know	**Need**	**Plan**
Grade levels of the 12 students	*P*(junior then senior)	Determine whether the events are dependent or independent and use the formula that applies.

The first outcome affects the probability of the second. So the events are dependent.

$$P(\text{junior}) = \frac{4}{12} = \frac{1}{3} \qquad \text{4 of the 12 students are juniors.}$$

$$P(\text{senior after junior}) = \frac{5}{11} \qquad \text{5 of the 11 remaining students are seniors.}$$

$P(\text{junior then senior}) = P(\text{junior}) \cdot P(\text{senior after junior})$

$$= \frac{1}{3} \cdot \frac{5}{11} = \frac{5}{33} \qquad \text{Substitute and then simplify.}$$

The probability that a junior and then a senior are chosen is $\frac{5}{33}$.

Got It? **5. a.** In Problem 5, what is the probability that a senior and then a junior are chosen?

b. Reasoning Is P(junior then senior) different from P(senior then junior)? Explain.

 ## Lesson Check

Do you know HOW?

Use the cards below.

1. You choose a card at random. What is each probability?

  a. P(B or number)   **b.** P(red or 5)

  c. P(red or yellow)   **d.** P(yellow or letter)

2. What is the probability of choosing a yellow card and then a D if the first card *is not* replaced before the second card is drawn?

3. What is the probability of choosing a yellow card and then a D if the first card is replaced before the second card is drawn?

Do you UNDERSTAND?

MATHEMATICAL PRACTICES

4. Vocabulary What is an example of a compound event composed of two overlapping events when you spin a spinner with the integers from 1 through 8?

5. Reasoning Are an event and its complement mutually exclusive or overlapping? Use an example to explain.

6. Open-Ended What is a real-world example of two independent events?

7. Error Analysis Describe and correct the error below in calculating P(yellow or letter) from Exercise 1, part (d).

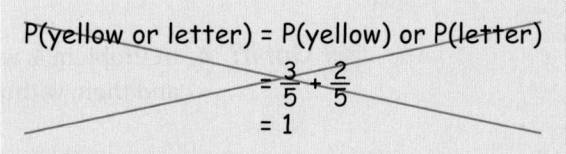

$$P(\text{yellow or letter}) = P(\text{yellow}) \text{ or } P(\text{letter})$$
$$= \frac{3}{5} + \frac{2}{5}$$
$$= 1$$

 ## Practice and Problem-Solving Exercises

MATHEMATICAL PRACTICES

 **Practice** You spin the spinner at the right, which is divided into equal sections. Find each probability.

See Problem 1.

  8. P(4 or 7)   **9.** P(even or red)   **10.** P(odd or 10)

  11. P(3 or red)   **12.** P(red or less than 3)   **13.** P(odd or multiple of 3)

  14. P(7 or blue)   **15.** P(red or more than 8)   **16.** P(greater than 6 or blue)

You roll a blue number cube and a green number cube. Find each probability.   **See Problem 2.**

  17. P(blue even and green even)   **18.** P(blue and green both less than 6)

  19. P(green less than 7 and blue 4)   **20.** P(blue 1 or 2 and green 1)

You choose a tile at random from a bag containing 2 A's, 3 B's, and 4 C's. You replace the first tile in the bag and then choose again. Find each probability.   **See Problem 3.**

  21. P(A and A)   **22.** P(A and B)   **23.** P(B and B)   **24.** P(C and C)   **25.** P(B and C)

You pick a coin at random from the set shown at the right and then pick a second coin without replacing the first. Find each probability.

◀ **See Problem 4.**

26. *P*(dime then nickel)　　　**27.** *P*(quarter then penny)

28. *P*(penny then dime)　　　**29.** *P*(penny then quarter)

30. *P*(penny then nickel)　　　**31.** *P*(dime then penny)

32. *P*(dime then dime)　　　**33.** *P*(quarter then quarter)

34. Cafeteria Each day, you, Terry, and 3 other friends randomly choose one of your 5 names from a hat to decide who throws away everyone's lunch trash. What is the probability that you are chosen on Monday and Terry is chosen on Tuesday?

◀ **See Problem 5.**

35. Free Samples Samples of a new drink are handed out at random from a cooler holding 5 citrus drinks, 3 apple drinks, and 3 raspberry drinks. What is the probability that an apple drink and then a citrus drink are handed out?

B Apply

Are the two events *dependent* or *independent*? Explain.

36. Toss a penny. Then toss a nickel.

37. Pick a name from a hat. Without replacement, pick a different name.

38. Pick a ball from a basket of yellow and pink balls. Return the ball and pick again.

ⓒ **39. Writing** Use your own words to explain the difference between independent and dependent events. Give an example of each.

ⓒ **40. Reasoning** A bag holds 20 yellow mints and 80 other green or pink mints. You choose a mint at random, eat it, and choose another.
　a. Find the number of pink mints if *P*(yellow then pink) = *P*(green then yellow).
　b. What is the least number of pink mints if
　　 P(yellow then pink) > *P*(green then yellow)?

ⓒ **41. Think About a Plan** An acre of land is chosen at random from each of the three states listed in the table at the right. What is the probability that all three acres will be farmland?
　• Does the choice of an acre from one state affect the choice from the other states?
　• How must you rewrite the percents to use a formula from this lesson?

Percent of State That Is Farmland	
Alabama	27%
Florida	27%
Indiana	65%

42. Phone Poll A pollster conducts a survey by phone. The probability that a call does not result in a person taking this survey is 85%. What is the probability that the pollster makes 4 calls and none result in a person taking the survey?

ⓒ **43. Open-Ended** Find the number of left-handed students and the number of right-handed students in your class. Suppose your teacher randomly selects one student to take attendance and then a different student to work on a problem on the board.
　a. What is the probability that both students are left-handed?
　b. What is the probability that both students are right-handed?
　c. What is the probability that the first student is right-handed and the second student is left-handed?

 **Challenge**

44. Suppose you roll a red number cube and a yellow number cube.
  a. What is P(red 1 and yellow 1)?
  b. What is P(red 2 and yellow 2)?
  c. What is the probability of rolling any matching pair of numbers? (*Hint:* Add the probabilities of each of the six matches.)

45. A two-digit number is formed by randomly selecting from the digits 1, 2, 3, and 5 without replacement.
  a. How many different two-digit numbers can be formed?
  b. What is the probability that a two-digit number contains a 2 or a 5?
  c. What is the probability that a two-digit number is prime?

Apply What You've Learned

MATHEMATICAL PRACTICES

MP 3

Look back at the information on page 725 about the baseball tournament for which Luis must choose a location. The tables of weather data are shown again below.

Oakville Climate Data for August

Year	2004	2005	2006	2007	2008	2009	2010	2011	2012	2013
Rainfall (in.)	2.4	4.2	1.8	15.1	2.6	2.3	2.0	4.2	3.8	2.1
Avg. Temp. (°F)	78	84	89	72	74	77	82	87	76	78
Hurricane?	no	yes	no	yes	no	no	no	yes	yes	no

Fairview Climate Data for August

Year	2005	2006	2007	2008	2009	2010	2011	2012	2013
Rainfall (in.)	4.5	1.8	2.2	5.0	5.1	4.5	2.3	3.8	4.5
Avg. Temp. (°F)	83	77	82	80	87	86	86	82	83
Hurricane?	no	no	no	yes	no	yes	no	no	no

a. For each city, determine the probability that there is a hurricane in August in any given year.

b. Did you use theoretical probability or experimental probability in part (a)? Explain.

c. Which city has a greater probability of having no hurricanes in August for two years in a row? Use the probability of compound events to help you give an argument that justifies your answer.

Concept Byte

Use With Lesson 12-8

TECHNOLOGY

Normal Distributions

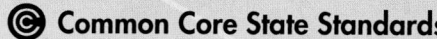 **Common Core State Standards**

S-ID.A.4 Use the mean and standard deviation of a data set to fit it to a normal distribution and to estimate population percentages . . .

MP 5

A **normal distribution** shows data that vary randomly from the mean in a pattern of a symmetric, bell-shaped curve called a *normal curve*. A normal distribution has the following properties.

 MATHEMATICAL PRACTICES

- About 68% of the data fall within one standard deviation of the mean.
- About 95% of the data fall within two standard deviations of the mean.
- About 99.7% of the data fall within three standard deviations of the mean.

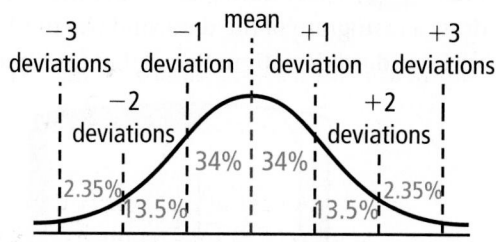

Example 1

The weights of pumpkins a farmer harvests one year are normally distributed with a mean of 40 lb and a standard deviation of 5 lb.

A **Find the percent of the pumpkins that weigh between 35 lb and 50 lb.**

Draw a normal curve for the distribution. Note that 35 lb is 1 standard deviation below the mean and 50 lb is 2 standard deviations above the mean.

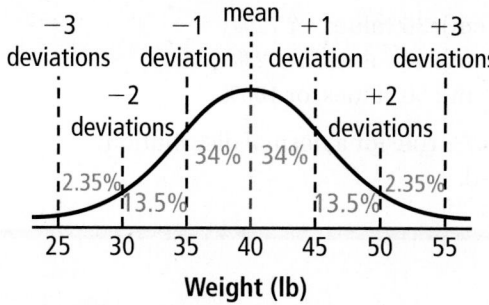

Weight (lb)

Add the percents between 35 lb and 50 lb on the normal curve.

34% + 34% + 13.5% = 81.5%

About 81.5% of the pumpkins weigh between 35 lb and 50 lb.

B **Find the percent of the pumpkins that weigh between 33 lb and 43 lb.**

Neither 33 lb nor 43 lb is a whole number of standard deviations from the mean, so you cannot use the normal curve drawn in part (A). Instead, use a graphing calculator that computes percents associated with normal distributions. One model of calculator uses the following command.

normalcdf(*lower bound, upper bound, mean, standard deviation*)

For this problem, enter **normalcdf(33, 43, 40, 5)**. The calculator returns a percent expressed as a decimal: about 0.645. This means that about 64.5% of the pumpkins weigh between 33 lb and 43 lb.

Example 2

The heights (in centimeters) of 50 women in a movie theater are shown below. Use a graphing calculator to make a histogram of the data, and find the mean and standard deviation. Then determine whether the data are approximately normally distributed.

162, 170, 173, 163, 157, 168, 162, 153, 158, 177, 162, 159, 169, 161, 170, 160, 156, 183, 166, 152, 174, 160, 157, 163, 158, 154, 146, 167, 165, 153, 160, 162, 161, 154, 165, 167, 170, 158, 159, 167, 166, 156, 161, 163, 158, 161, 161, 166, 163, 148

Press **stat** , select **Edit...**, and enter the data into list L1. Use the **stat plot** feature to draw a histogram of the data, and use the **1-Var Stats** feature to calculate the mean and standard deviation. Recall that the Greek letter σ represents standard deviation.

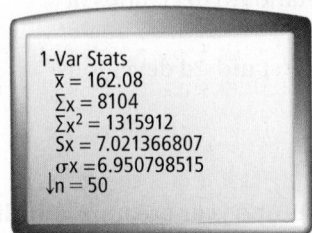

1-Var Stats
$\bar{x}$ = 162.08
Σx = 8104
Σx^2 = 1315912
Sx = 7.021366807
σx = 6.950798515
$\downarrow n$ = 50

The histogram is bell-shaped and symmetric about the mean, which is one characteristic of a normal distribution. The mean is about 162.1 cm and the standard deviation is about 7.0 cm. Find the percent of the data values that lie within one, two, and three standard deviations of the mean.

Within 1σ of mean (between 155.1 cm and 169.1 cm): 36 values, or 72%
Within 2σ of mean (between 148.1 cm and 176.1 cm): 46 values, or 92%
Within 3σ of mean (between 141.1 cm and 183.1 cm): 50 values, or 100%

The data come close to following the 68%-95%-99.7% rule for a normal distribution. So the data are approximately normally distributed.

Exercises

1. Boxes of cereal are filled by a machine. The weights of cereal in the boxes are normally distributed with a mean of 16 oz and a standard deviation of 0.25 oz.

  a. What percent of boxes contain between 15.5 oz and 16 oz of cereal?
  b. What percent of boxes contain more than 16.25 oz of cereal?
  c. What percent of boxes contain between 15.8 oz and 16.15 oz of cereal?

2. The prices of 50 TVs sold at an electronics store are shown below. Use a graphing calculator to make a histogram of the data, and find the mean and standard deviation. Are the data approximately normally distributed? Explain.

$880, $205, $945, $230, $355, $540, $365, $600, $200, $615, $825, $860, $745, $730, $790, $945, $205, $220, $600, $665, $835, $390, $880, $590, $460, $900, $430, $835, $280, $920, $835, $570, $710, $265, $895, $270, $380, $565, $515, $520, $465, $425, $555, $585, $255, $750, $725, $330, $905, $280

12

Pull It **All Together**

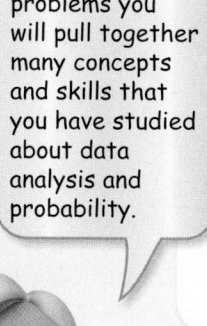

To solve these problems you will pull together many concepts and skills that you have studied about data analysis and probability.

Completing the Performance Task

Look back at your results from the Apply What You've Learned sections in Lessons 12-3, 12-4, and 12-8. Use the work you did to complete the following.

1. Solve the problem in the Task Description on page 725 by deciding whether the tournament should be held in Oakville or Fairview, and justify your decision. Show all your work and explain each step of your solution.

 2. **Reflect** Choose one of the Mathematical Practices below and explain how you applied it in your work on the Performance Task.

MP 3: Construct viable arguments and critique the reasoning of others.

MP 4: Model with mathematics.

MP 6: Attend to precision.

On Your Own

Luis prefers to hold the tournament in the city where the residents are more likely to attend baseball games. To gather data, he surveys a random sample of 10 residents of Oakville and 10 residents of Fairview.

Luis asks how many sporting events each resident attends in a typical year. He also asks each resident the following question: "Do you prefer the excitement and strategy of a baseball game to the experience of watching other sports?" The responses for residents of the two cities are shown below.

Decide which city Luis should choose based on the data in these tables, and justify your decision. Include a critique of Luis's survey questions.

Oakville Residents' Survey Responses

Resident	A	B	C	D	E	F	G	H	I	J
Number of Events	4	12	15	4	0	8	10	20	2	4
Prefer Baseball?	yes	yes	yes	no	no	yes	no	yes	no	no

Fairview Residents' Survey Responses

Resident	A	B	C	D	E	F	G	H	I	J
Number of Events	6	11	15	14	8	8	13	15	7	13
Prefer Baseball?	no	yes	yes	yes	no	no	yes	yes	no	yes

12 Chapter Review

Connecting **BIG** ideas and Answering the Essential Questions

1. Data Collection and Analysis

When you collect data, you should use a sampling technique free of bias. You can use standard measures to describe data sets and make estimates, decisions, or predictions.

Data Analysis (Lessons 12-3 and 12-4)

11 12 14 16 11 10 13 7

Mean: 11.75   Median: 11.5

Mode: 11   Range: 9

Samples and Surveys (Lesson 12-5)

Data Types: qualitative, quantitative, univariate, bivariate

Sample Types: random, systematic, stratified

2. Data Representation

You can use matrices, frequency tables, histograms, box-and-whisker plots, tree diagrams, and other representations to describe different types of data sets.

Data Displays (Lessons 12-1, 12-2, 12-4, and 12-6)

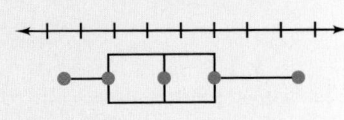

3. Probability

You can find theoretical and experimental probabilities to make decisions or predictions about future events.

Theoretical and Experimental Probability (Lesson 12-7)

Theoretical: $\dfrac{\text{number of favorable outcomes}}{\text{number of possible outcomes}}$

Experimental: $\dfrac{\text{number of times event occurs}}{\text{number of times experiment is done}}$

Probability of Compound Events (Lesson 12-8)

Independent:
$P(A \text{ and } B) = P(A) \cdot P(B)$

Dependent:
$P(A \text{ then } B) = P(A) \cdot P(B \text{ after } A)$

Chapter Vocabulary

- bias (p. 755)
- bivariate (p. 754)
- box-and-whisker plot (p. 747)
- combination (p. 765)
- complement of an event (p. 770)
- compound event (p. 776)

- dependent events (p. 778)
- element (p. 726)
- frequency (p. 732)
- histogram (p. 733)
- independent events (p. 777)
- interquartile range (p. 746)
- matrix (p. 726)

- measure of central tendency (p. 738)
- outcome (p. 769)
- outlier (p. 738)
- overlapping events (p. 776)
- percentile (p. 749)
- permutation (p. 763)
- population (p. 754)

- probability (p. 769)
- qualitative (p. 753)
- quantitative (p. 753)
- quartile (p. 746)
- range of a set of data (p. 740)
- sample (p. 754)
- scalar multiplication (p. 727)
- univariate (p. 754)

Choose the correct term to complete each sentence.

1. Each numerical item of data in a matrix is called a(n) ? .

2. The number of data values in an interval is the ? of the interval.

3. A(n) ? is a data value much greater or less than the other values in a data set.

4. The median of the lower half of an ordered data set is the first ? .

12-1 Organizing Data Using Matrices

Quick Review

You can use **matrices** to organize data. To add or subtract matrices that are the same size, add or subtract the corresponding **elements**. To multiply a matrix by a **scalar**, multiply each element by the scalar.

Example

What is the difference?

$$\begin{bmatrix} 3 & 2 \\ -1 & 5 \\ 2 & -2 \end{bmatrix} - \begin{bmatrix} 2 & 4 \\ 4 & -3 \\ 1 & 0 \end{bmatrix} = \begin{bmatrix} 3-2 & 2-4 \\ -1-4 & 5-(-3) \\ 2-1 & -2-0 \end{bmatrix}$$

$$= \begin{bmatrix} 1 & -2 \\ -5 & 8 \\ 1 & -2 \end{bmatrix}$$

Exercises

Find each sum, difference, or product.

5. $\begin{bmatrix} -5 & 1 \\ 0 & 8 \end{bmatrix} - \begin{bmatrix} 7 & -6 \\ -4 & 2 \end{bmatrix}$

6. $\begin{bmatrix} 0.4 & 1.5 \\ 3.2 & -3 \\ 1.5 & -2.1 \end{bmatrix} + \begin{bmatrix} 4 & 3 \\ 6.3 & -7.2 \\ 1.9 & -0.5 \end{bmatrix}$

7. $-4.2 \begin{bmatrix} 3 & 1.1 \\ 3 & -2 \\ -1 & 2.9 \end{bmatrix}$

12-2 Frequency and Histograms

Quick Review

The **frequency** of an interval is the number of data values in that interval. A **histogram** is a graph that groups data into intervals and shows the frequency of values in each interval.

Example

Below are the prices of the television models sold at an electronics store. What is a histogram of the data?

$1399 $1349 $999 $2149 $149 $279 $449 $379 $1379
$799 $3199 $1099 $499 $899 $949 $1799 $1699 $3499

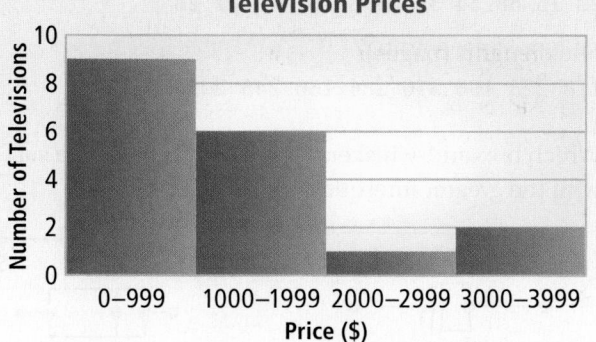

Exercises

Use the data to make a histogram.

8. customers: 141 128 132 141 152 169 121 133 131
   156 142 136 135 144 135 153

9. workout times (min): 41 29 46 39 37 44 33 51 42 30

Tell whether each histogram is *uniform*, *symmetric*, or *skewed*.

10.
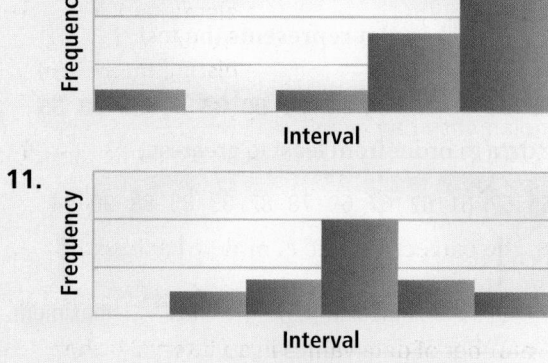

11.

12-3 Measures of Central Tendency and Dispersion

Quick Review

The **mean** of a data set equals $\frac{\text{sum of the data values}}{\text{total number of data values}}$. The **median** is the middle value in the data set when the values are arranged in order. The **mode** is the data item that occurs the most times. The **range of a set of data** is the difference between the greatest and least data values.

Example

The quality ratings of 9 movies showing at a movie theater near you are 5.6, 7.9, 7.0, 5.9, 7.8, 6.2, 6.4, 5.2, and 5.6. What are the mean, median, mode, and range of the data?

mean:

$$\frac{5.6 + 7.9 + 7.0 + 5.9 + 7.8 + 6.2 + 6.4 + 5.2 + 5.6}{9} = 6.4$$

5.2 5.6 5.6 5.9 6.2 6.4 7.0 7.8 7.9   Order the data.

median: 6.2   6.2 is the middle value.

mode: 5.6   5.6 occurs most often.

range: $7.9 - 5.2 = 2.7$ Find difference between greatest and least values.

Exercises

Find the mean, median, mode, and range of each data set.

12. points scored by a football team: 23 31 26 27 25 28 23 23 25 29 29 29 25 22 30

13. clips per package: 12 12 13 12 12 12 12 12 12 13 12 11 12 12 12 12 12

14. Cats A veterinarian examines 9 cats. The weights of the cats are 13.4 lb, 13.1 lb, 10.4 lb, 6.8 lb, 11.4 lb, 10.8 lb, 13.4 lb, 11.3 lb, and 9.3 lb. Find the mean, median, and mode of the data. Which measure of central tendency best describes the data?

15. Basketball A basketball player scores 22, 19, 25, and 17 points in four games. How many points does the basketball player need to score in the fifth game to average 22 points scored per game?

12-4 Box-and-Whisker Plots

Quick Review

A **box-and-whisker plot** organizes data values into four groups using the minimum value, the first quartile, the median, the third quartile, and the maximum value.

Example

What box-and-whisker plot represents the test scores below?

62 57 78 69 85 43 94 82 61 90 83 51 67 88 55

Arrange the data in order from least to greatest.

43 51 55 57 61 62 67 69 78 82 83 85 88 90 94

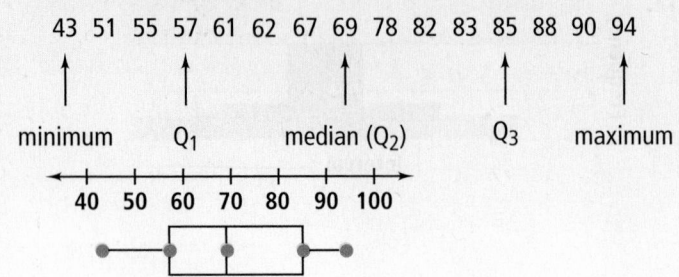

Exercises

Make a box-and-whisker plot of each data set.

16. movie lengths (min):
125 117 174 131 142 108 188 162 155 167 129 133 147 175 150

17. dog weights (lb):
23 15 88 34 33 49 52 67 42 71 28

18. book lengths (pages):
178 223 198 376 284 156 245 202 315 266

19. Which box-and-whisker plot represents the data set with the greater interquartile range? Explain.

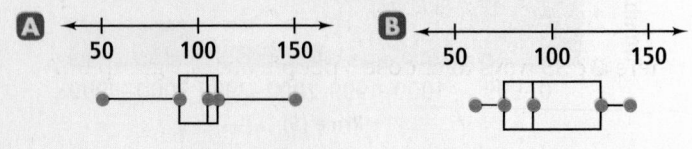

12-5 Samples and Surveys

Quick Review

You can obtain information about a **population** of people by surveying a smaller part of it, called a **sample**. The sample should be representative of the population. An unrepresentative sample or a poorly worded question can result in **bias**.

Example

A survey asks, "Should Plainville make itself proud by building a beautiful new library?" Is the question biased?

The question is biased. The words *proud* and *beautiful* make it clear that the answer is expected to be yes.

Exercises

Determine whether the sampling method is *random*, *systematic*, or *stratified*. Tell whether the method will give a good sample. Then write an unbiased survey question for the situation.

20. **Movies** An interviewer outside a movie theater asks every third person in line whether he or she will see more or fewer movies in the coming year.

21. **Student Government** Ten randomly chosen students in each class (freshman, sophomore, junior, and senior) are asked whom they support for student council president.

12-6 Permutations and Combinations

Quick Review

If there are m ways to make a first selection and n ways to make a second selection, then there are $m \cdot n$ ways to make the two selections.

A **permutation** is an arrangement of objects in a specific order. The number of permutations of n objects arranged r at a time, $_nP_r$, equals $\frac{n!}{(n-r)!}$.

A **combination** is a selection of objects without regard to order. The number of combinations of n objects chosen r at a time, $_nC_r$, equals $\frac{n!}{r!(n-r)!}$.

Example

In how many ways can you choose 3 people to serve on a committee out of a group of 7 volunteers?

The order does not matter, so this is a combination problem.

$$_7C_3 = \frac{7!}{3!(7-3)!} = \frac{7!}{3!4!}$$ Write using factorials.

$$= \frac{7 \cdot 6 \cdot 5 \cdot 4 \cdot 3 \cdot 2 \cdot 1}{(3 \cdot 2 \cdot 1)(4 \cdot 3 \cdot 2 \cdot 1)}$$ Write the factorials as products.

$$= 35$$ Simplify.

There are 35 ways to choose 3 people out of a group of 7.

Exercises

Find the number of permutations.

22. $_9P_5$
23. $_3P_2$
24. $_8P_3$
25. $_5P_2$
26. $_6P_4$
27. $_7P_2$

Find the number of combinations.

28. $_8C_2$
29. $_9C_4$
30. $_5C_3$
31. $_6C_3$
32. $_7C_3$
33. $_5C_4$

34. **Side Dishes** You can choose any 2 of the following side dishes with your dinner: mashed potatoes, cole slaw, french fries, applesauce, or rice. How many different combinations of side dishes can you choose?

35. **Talent Show** There are 8 groups participating in a talent show. In how many different orders can the groups perform?

36. **Clothing** You have 6 shirts, 7 pairs of pants, and 3 pairs of shoes. How many different outfits can you wear?

12-7 Theoretical and Experimental Probability

Quick Review

An **event** is an **outcome** or group of outcomes. The **probability** of an event, which indicates how likely it is to occur, is written $P(\text{event})$. When all possible outcomes are equally likely, the **theoretical probability** of an event is given by $P(\text{event}) = \dfrac{\text{number of favorable outcomes}}{\text{number of possible outcomes}}$.

Example

What is the theoretical probability that a randomly chosen date is a day beginning with a T?

There are 2 favorable outcomes, Tuesday and Thursday.

There are 7 possible outcomes, the 7 days of the week.

$P(\text{day beginning with a T}) = \dfrac{\text{number of favorable outcomes}}{\text{number of possible outcomes}}$
$= \dfrac{2}{7}$

The probability of a day beginning with a T is $\dfrac{2}{7}$.

Exercises

The spinner at the right is divided into six equal sections. Find the theoretical probability of landing on the given sections of the spinner.

37. $P(\text{even})$ **38.** $P(\text{odd})$

39. $P(5)$ **40.** $P(\text{not } 3)$

41. $P(7)$ **42.** $P(\text{more than } 4)$

43. Apples An apple farmer finds that he has to throw out 15 bad apples from the 225 he has picked. What is the experimental probability that the next apple he picks will be good?

12-8 Probability of Compound Events

Quick Review

You can use a formula to find the probability of a **compound event** involving two events A and B.

Mutually exclusive events: $P(A \text{ or } B) = P(A) + P(B)$

Overlapping events:
$P(A \text{ or } B) = P(A) + P(B) - P(A \text{ and } B)$

Independent events: $P(A \text{ and } B) = P(A) \cdot P(B)$

Dependent events: $P(A \text{ then } B) = P(A) \cdot P(B \text{ after } A)$

Example

You roll a number cube and flip a coin. What is the probability that you roll a 5 and the coin comes up heads?

Rolling a 5 and flipping heads are independent events.

$P(5 \text{ and heads}) = P(5) \cdot P(\text{heads}) = \dfrac{1}{6} \cdot \dfrac{1}{2} = \dfrac{1}{12}$

The probability of rolling a 5 and flipping heads is $\dfrac{1}{12}$.

Exercises

You randomly pick two marbles from a bag containing 3 yellow marbles and 4 red marbles. You pick the second marble without replacing the first marble. Find each probability.

44. $P(\text{red then red})$ **45.** $P(\text{yellow then red})$

You roll a number cube twice. Find each probability.

46. $P(6 \text{ then } 3)$ **47.** $P(\text{odd then even})$

Are the two events *dependent* or *independent*? Explain.

48. You pick one of 7 names from a hat and then pick a second name without replacing the first one.

49. You spin a spinner with 5 equal sections and pick a marble from a bag containing 2 green marbles and 4 blue marbles.

Do you know HOW?

Simplify.

1. $\begin{bmatrix} 0 & -3 \\ 2 & 0 \\ 1 & -1 \end{bmatrix} - \begin{bmatrix} 2 & 0 \\ -1 & 1 \\ -2 & 3 \end{bmatrix}$ 2. $-3\begin{bmatrix} 1 & 2 & -1 \\ 0 & -2 & 3 \\ -3 & 1 & 0 \end{bmatrix}$

Tell whether each histogram is *uniform, symmetric,* or *skewed*.

3.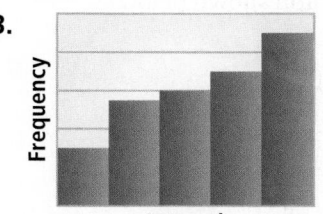

4.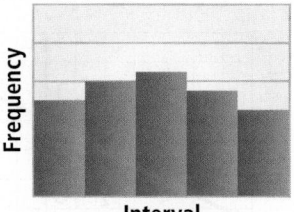

5. **Sports** The 400-m race times (in seconds) for a track team are listed below. Make a frequency table and a histogram that represent their times.

    58 54 63 56 60 58 72 61 60 59 57 52 66 68

6. **Landscaping** The hours a gardener worked over the past 14 weeks are listed below. What are the mean, median, mode, and range of the hours the gardener worked? Which measure of central tendency best describes the data?

    39 52 41 44 47 36 51 44 50 40 53 46 44 35

7. **Diving** The weights of 8 scuba divers, without tanks, are 85, 103, 94, 97, 88, 91, 104, and 95 kg. A tank weighs 15 kg. What are the mean, median, mode, and range of the divers' weights with tanks?

Identify the minimum, first quartile, median, third quartile, and maximum of each data set. Then make a box-and-whisker plot of each data set.

8. test scores: 87 52 91 66 79 56 73 90 78 51 83

9. speeds (mi/h): 41 19 31 13 48 22 61 30 34 37

10. Out of 10 dogs, 4 weigh no more than 12.5 kg. What is the percentile rank of the weight 12.5 kg?

11. **Cafeteria** A teacher asks a student chosen at random from each table in the cafeteria for his or her opinion of school food. Will this survey method give a good sample? Explain.

12. **Security** Suppose a password contains 4 lowercase letters. How many permutations are possible if no letters are repeated?

13. What is the value of $_6C_3$?

The spinner at the right is divided into four equal sections. Find the theoretical probability of landing on the given section(s) of the spinner.

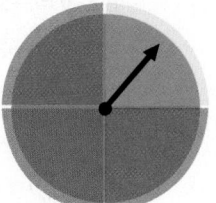

14. $P(\text{orange})$

15. $P(\text{blue})$

16. $P(\text{not green})$

17. Suppose you choose a tile at random from a bag containing 5 X's, 4 Y's, and 3 Z's. You replace the first tile in the bag and choose again. What is the probability of choosing 2 Y's?

18. Suppose you choose a marble at random from a bag containing 3 blue, 5 yellow, and 7 red marbles. You choose a second marble without replacing the first. What is the probability of choosing 2 blue marbles?

Do you UNDERSTAND?

19. **Reasoning** Could a student use the formula $P(A \text{ or } B) = P(A) + P(B) - P(A \text{ and } B)$ to solve a problem about mutually exclusive events and get the correct answer? Explain.

20. **Writing** How do you calculate interquartile range? How is this measure useful?

21. **Open-Ended** Give examples of univariate and bivariate data. How do these types of data differ?

22. **Reasoning** Is it possible for r to be greater than n in $_nC_r$? Explain.

Common Core
End-of-Course Assessment

 **ASSESSMENT**

Selected Response

Read each question. Then write the letter of the correct answer on your paper.

1. Which equation represents a line with a greater slope and lesser y-intercept than the line shown?

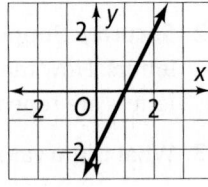

  (A) $y = x - 1$

  (B) $y = -x - 1$

  (C) $y = -2x - 2$

  (D) $y = 3x - 3$

2. Which expression is equivalent to $3(x^2 + 1) - 5x(x^2 + x + 1)$?

  (F) $-5x^3 + 8x^2 + 5x + 3$

  (G) $-5x^3 - 2x^2 - 5x + 3$

  (H) $-10x^3 + x^2 - 7x + 6$

  (I) $5x^3 - 2x^2 - 5x + 3$

3. You roll a pair of number cubes. What is the probability of rolling odd numbers on both cubes?

  (A) $\dfrac{1}{12}$

  (B) $\dfrac{1}{6}$

  (C) $\dfrac{1}{4}$

  (D) $\dfrac{2}{3}$

4. What is the greatest value in the range of $f(x) = x^2 - 3$ for the domain $\{-3, 0, 1, 2\}$?

  (F) -3 (H) 2

  (G) 0 (I) 6

5. Which equation best represents the graph at the right?

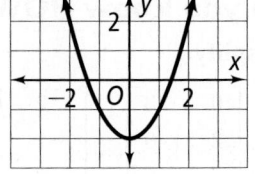

  (A) $y = x^2$

  (B) $y = -x^2$

  (C) $y = x^2 - 2$

  (D) $y = x^2 + 2$

6. Which table models the graph shown below?

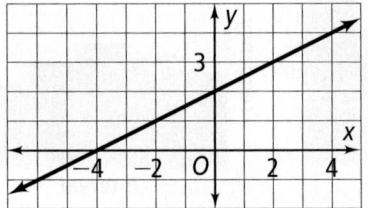

  (F)

x	-2	0	1	4
y	1	2	3	4

  (G)

x	-6	-3	0	6
y	-1	0.5	2	5

  (H)

x	-1	0	3	4
y	-6	-4	2	4

  (I)

x	0	0.5	1	2
y	-4	-3	-2	0

7. Which of the graphs below represents the solution set of $-3 < x + 3 \le 7$?

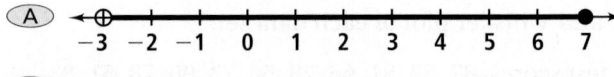

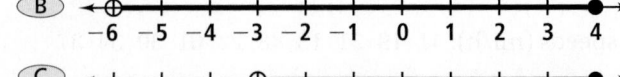

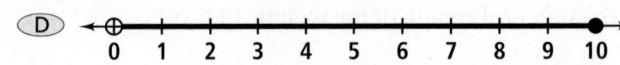

8. Consider the graph shown below. Which statement is always a correct conclusion about the coordinates of the points on the graph?

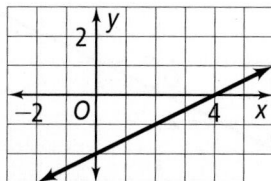

- **F** The *x*-values are always 2 less than the *y*-values.
- **G** The *y*-values are always 4 more than the *x*-values.
- **H** For positive values of *x*, the *x*-values are always greater than the *y*-values.
- **I** For positive values of *x*, the *y*-values are always greater than the *x*-values.

9. Which expression is equivalent to $\dfrac{4x^2 - 9}{6x^2 + 9x}$?

- **A** $\dfrac{2x - 3}{x + 3}$
- **B** $\dfrac{2}{3 + x}$
- **C** $\dfrac{2x + 3}{3x}$
- **D** $\dfrac{2x - 3}{3x}$

10. Which ordered pair is a solution of the given system?
$$2x + 5y = -11$$
$$10x + 3y = 11$$

- **F** $(3, -2)$
- **H** $(-2, 3)$
- **G** $(-3, 2)$
- **I** $(2, -3)$

11. What is the slope-intercept form of the equation $-3x + 4y = 8$?

- **A** $y = 3x + 2$
- **B** $y = 3x + 8$
- **C** $y = \dfrac{3}{4}x + 2$
- **D** $y = -\dfrac{3}{4}x + 2$

12. What is a linear inequality that describes the graph below?

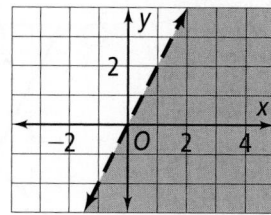

- **F** $y \le 2x$
- **H** $y > 2x$
- **G** $y < 2x$
- **I** $y \ge 2x$

13. What equation do you get when you solve $2x^2y - 4y = -24$ for *y*?

- **A** $y = -\dfrac{12}{x^2 - 2}$
- **B** $y = \dfrac{12}{x^2 + 2}$
- **C** $y = \dfrac{12}{x^2 - 2}$
- **D** $y = -x^2 - 22$

14. What is the minimum point of the parabola graphed below?

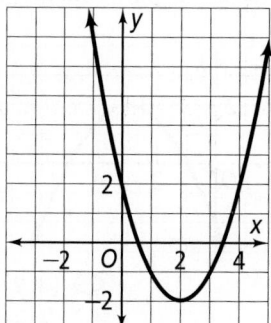

- **F** $(-2, 2)$
- **G** $(2, -2)$
- **H** $(0, 2)$
- **I** There is no minimum.

15. What is the graph of the given system of equations?

$$2x + y = -3$$
$$-x + y = -1$$

A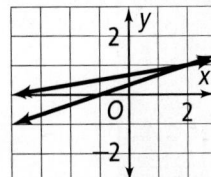

C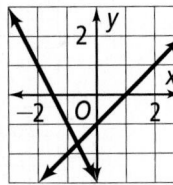

B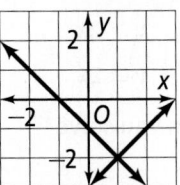

D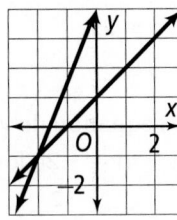

16. What is $\sqrt{81n^3}$ in exponential form?

F $9n^{\frac{1}{2}}$

G $9n^{\frac{3}{2}}$

H $81n^{\frac{3}{2}}$

I $81n^{\frac{1}{2}}$

17. What is the vertex of the parabola graphed below?

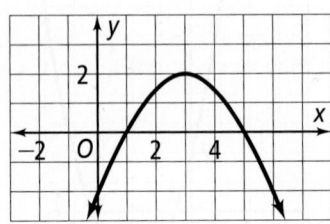

A $(0, -1)$ C $(3, 2)$

B $(1, 0)$ D $(5, 0)$

18. A line passes through the point $(-3, -2)$ and has slope 2. What is an equation of the line?

F $y = 2x - 0.5$

G $y = 2x + 0.5$

H $y = 2x + 1$

I $y = 2x + 4$

19. What equation describes a line that is parallel to the line below and passes through the point $(-2, 1)$?

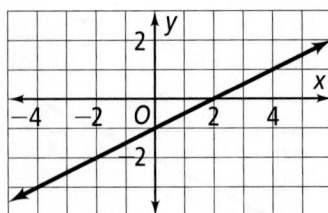

A $y = 2x + 2$

B $y = \frac{1}{2}x + 2$

C $y = \frac{1}{2}x + 1$

D $y = 2x + 3$

20. What is an equation of the axis of symmetry for the graph of the function $f(x) = 2x^2 + 4x - 5$?

F $x = -1$

G $x = 1$

H $x = -2$

I $x = 2$

21. What is the solution of the equation
$\frac{4x + 3}{3} - \frac{2x - 1}{2} = 3$?

A 0

B 4.5

C 7

D 8

22. Which polynomial represents the volume of the triangular prism?

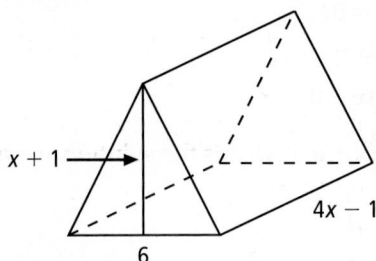

F $24x^2 + 18x - 6$

G $12x^2 + 9x - 3$

H $4x^2 + 5x - 1$

I $4x^2 + 3x - 1$

23. What are the solutions of the equation
$3x^2 + 11x - 4 = 0$?

Ⓐ $\frac{1}{3}, 4$

Ⓑ $\frac{1}{3}, -4$

Ⓒ $-\frac{1}{3}, 4$

Ⓓ $3, -4$

24. What are the solutions of $x + 2 = \sqrt{2x^2 - x - 2}$?

Ⓕ $6, 1$

Ⓖ $-6, -1$

Ⓗ $6, -1$

Ⓘ $-6, 1$

25. Simplify the expression $\dfrac{27a^{\frac{5}{2}}b^{\frac{4}{3}}}{9a^2b}$.

Ⓐ $3ab$

Ⓑ $18a^{\frac{1}{4}}b^{\frac{1}{6}}$

Ⓒ $3a^{\frac{1}{2}}b^{\frac{1}{3}}$

Ⓓ $27a^{\frac{1}{4}}b^{\frac{1}{6}}$

26. How does the mean of the data set below change if each value is increased by 8?
105 110 104 107 102 106 133 81

Ⓕ The mean increases by 1.

Ⓖ The mean increases by 8.

Ⓗ The mean decreases by 8.

Ⓘ The mean does not change.

27. What is $(2x^2 - 4x + 8) - (3x^2 + 10x + 2)$?

Ⓐ $-x^2 - 14x - 6$

Ⓑ $-x^2 + 6x + 6$

Ⓒ $-x^2 - 14x + 6$

Ⓓ $5x^2 + 6x + 10$

28. Which of the following is the solution set for the equation $|p - 2| = 7$?

Ⓕ $\{-5, 9\}$

Ⓖ $\{-9, 9\}$

Ⓗ $\{-5\}$

Ⓘ $\{9\}$

29. Keysha randomly surveyed 150 people at a football game last weekend to find out whether they like hot dogs, hamburgers, or nachos. She recorded her results in the Venn diagram below. Of the 850 people at the game, how many should she expect to like both hot dogs and hamburgers?

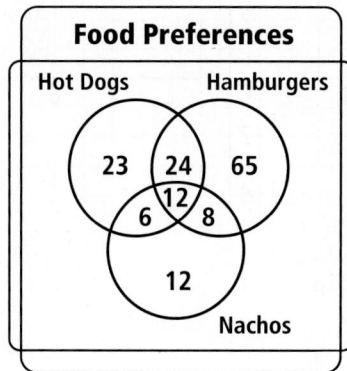

Ⓐ 204

Ⓑ 281

Ⓒ 306

Ⓓ 782

30. What is the simplified form of $\dfrac{5x^2y^3}{3x^3y^4}$?

Ⓕ $\dfrac{5x^5y^7}{3}$

Ⓖ $\dfrac{5}{3xy}$

Ⓗ $\dfrac{5x^2y^3}{3x^3y^4}$

Ⓘ $\dfrac{5y^7}{3x^5}$

31. Line p passes through points $(5, -4)$ and $(2, 7)$. What is the slope of a line that is perpendicular to line p?

Ⓐ $-\dfrac{11}{3}$

Ⓑ $-\dfrac{3}{11}$

Ⓒ $\dfrac{3}{11}$

Ⓓ $\dfrac{11}{3}$

32. Which of the following is an equation of a reasonable trend line for the scatter plot shown?

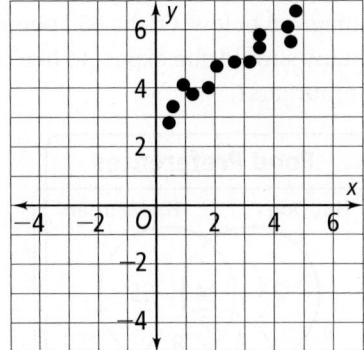

- Ⓕ $y = \frac{1}{3}x + 8$

- Ⓖ $y = \frac{2}{3}x + 3$

- Ⓗ $y = \frac{1}{2}x - 3$

- Ⓘ $y = 3x + 3$

33. The sides of a square are all increased by 2 in. The area of the new square is 49 in.². What is the length of a side of the original square?

- Ⓐ 2 in.
- Ⓑ 4.5 in.
- Ⓒ 5 in.
- Ⓓ 9 in.

34. Which of the following sets of points does NOT represent a function?

- Ⓕ $\{(-2, 0), (-1, 1), (0, 4), (1, -2), (2, -6)\}$
- Ⓖ $\{(-5, 0), (-4, 0), (-3, 0), (-2, 0), (-1, 0)\}$
- Ⓗ $\{(0, 1), (1, 10), (1, 100), (10, 100), (100, 1000)\}$
- Ⓘ $\{(2, 4), (3, 9), (4, 16), (5, 25), (6, 36)\}$

35. Ricardo's art class is making a tile mosaic using similar right triangles.

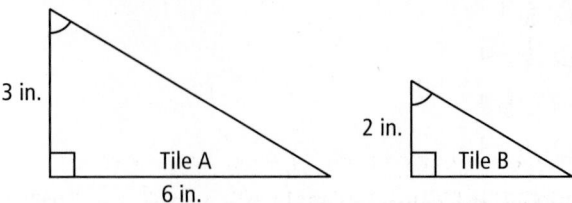

Tile A and Tile B are similar. What is the area of Tile B?

- Ⓐ 4 in.²
- Ⓑ 5 in.²
- Ⓒ 6 in.²
- Ⓓ 12 in.²

36. What type of histogram is shown below?

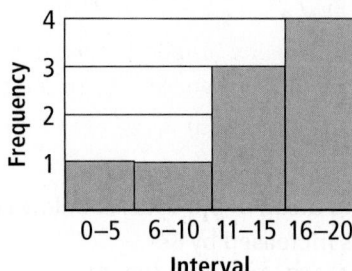

- Ⓕ skewed
- Ⓖ uniform
- Ⓗ symmetric
- Ⓘ none of these

37. How much shorter would it be to travel from point A to point B diagonally than to travel from point A through point C and up to point B along the perimeter of the rectangle?

- Ⓐ 1268 ft
- Ⓑ 1446 ft
- Ⓒ 2044 ft
- Ⓓ 2543 ft

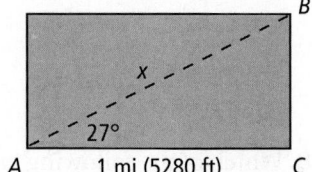

38. What is the solution of $3x + 7 = 25$?

    (F) $x = 11$

    (G) $x = 8$

    (H) $x = 7$

    (I) $x = 6$

39. The volume of a cylinder is given by the formula $V = \pi r^2 h$, where V represents the volume, r represents the radius of the base, and h represents the height of the cylinder. Which equation can be used to find r in terms of V and h?

    (A) $r = \sqrt{\dfrac{V}{\pi h}}$

    (B) $r = \dfrac{V}{\pi h}$

    (C) $r = \sqrt{V \pi h}$

    (D) $r = \sqrt{\dfrac{\pi h}{V}}$

40. Which of the following functions can be used to find the nth term of the sequence 6, 11, 16, 21, 26, . . . ?

    (F) $A(n) = 5 + (n - 1)(6)$

    (G) $A(n) = 6 + (n + 1)(5)$

    (H) $A(n) = 6 + (n - 1)(5)$

    (I) $A(n) = 5 + (n + 1)(6)$

41. Which of the following is equivalent to $\sqrt[3]{64a^2b}$?

    (A) $4a^{\frac{2}{3}}b^{\frac{1}{3}}$

    (B) $64a^2b^{\frac{1}{3}}$

    (C) $4a^2b$

    (D) $64a^2b$

42. What is a solution to the system?

$$y = x^2 + 2x - 15$$
$$y - 4x = -12$$

    (F) $(0, 3)$

    (G) $(3, 0)$

    (H) $(4, 5)$

    (I) $(-5, 3)$

Constructed Response

43. What is the y-coordinate of the vertex of the function $y = 2x^2 + 5x - 8$?

44. Lisa is driving a car at an average speed of 55 mi/h.
    a. What is Lisa's average speed in feet per second?
    b. How many feet will Lisa travel in 40 min?

45. The width of a rectangle is 10 in. less than its length. If the perimeter of the rectangle is 36 in., what is its width in inches?

46. Is the question "Do you prefer delicious steak or ordinary meatloaf for dinner?" biased? Explain.

47. A new toy store is opening next week, and the owner is deciding how to price one of the toys. The equation $S = -32p^2 + 960p$ predicts the total sales S as a function of the toy's price p, where S and p are in dollars. What price will produce the highest total sales?

48. A rectangular prism has a volume of $6x^4 - 13x^3 - 5x^2$. What expressions can represent the dimensions of the prism? Use factoring.

Extended Response

49. The box-and-whisker plots below show the points scored by two college football teams in games over the course of one season.

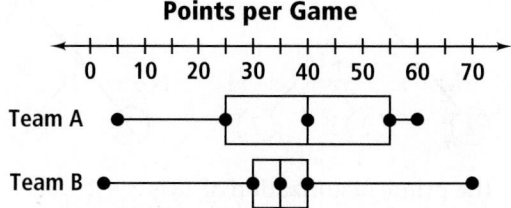

Points per Game

What do the medians tell you about each team's points per game?

50. Natalia spent $153 of her savings at the mall. She bought clothes, a few paperback novels, and an $18 DVD. She spent 4 times as much on clothes as she did on the paperbacks.
    a. Write an equation that can be used to determine how much money Natalia spent on the paperback novels.
    b. Use the equation to determine how much Natalia spent on paperbacks.

Skills **Handbook**

Prime Numbers and Composite Numbers

A prime number is a whole number greater than 1 that has exactly two factors, the number 1 and itself.

Prime number	2	5	17	29
Factors	1, 2	1, 5	1, 17	1, 29

A composite number is a number that has more than two factors. The number 1 is neither prime nor composite.

Composite number	6	15	48
Factors	1, 2, 3, 6	1, 3, 5, 15	1, 2, 3, 4, 6, 8, 12, 16, 24, 48

Example 1

Is 51 prime or composite?

51 = 3 • 17   Try to find factors other than 1 and 51.

51 is a composite number.

You can use a factor tree to find the prime factors of a number. When all the factors are prime numbers, it is called the prime factorization of the number.

Example 2

Use a factor tree to write the prime factorization of 28.

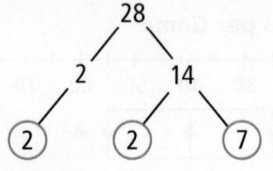   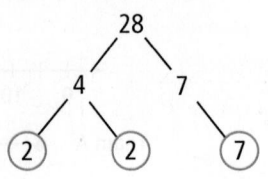

The order of listing the factors may be different, but the prime factorization is the same.

The prime factorization of 28 is 2 • 2 • 7.

Exercises

Is each number prime or composite?

1. 9 C   **2.** 16 C   **3.** 34 C   **4.** 61 P   **5.** 7 P   **6.** 13 p

7. 12 C   **8.** 40 C   **9.** 57 C   **10.** 64 C   **11.** 120 C   **12.** 700 C

List all the factors of each number.

13. 46   **14.** 32   **15.** 11   **16.** 65   **17.** 27   **18.** 29

1,2,23,46   1,2,4,8,16,32   1,11   1,5,13,65   1,3,9,27   1,29

Use a factor tree to write the prime factorization of each number.

19. 18 2•3•3   **20.** 20 2•2•5   **21.** 27 3•3•3   **22.** 54 2•3•3•3   **23.** 64 2•2•2•2•2•2   **24.** 96 2•2•2•2•2•3

Factors and Multiples

A common factor is a number that is a factor of two or more numbers. The greatest common factor (GCF) is the greatest number that is a common factor of two or more numbers.

Example 1

Find the GCF of 24 and 64.

Method 1 List all the factors of each number.

Factors of 24	1, 2, 3, 4, 6, 8, 12, 24	Find the common factors: 1, 2, 4, 8.
Factors of 64	1, 2, 4, 8, 16, 32, 64	The greatest common factor is 8.

The GCF of 24 and 64 is 8.

Method 2 Use the prime factorization of each number.

$24 = 2 \cdot 2 \cdot 2 \cdot 3$ Find the prime factorization of each number.

$64 = 2 \cdot 2 \cdot 2 \cdot 2 \cdot 2 \cdot 2$

$GCF = 2 \cdot 2 \cdot 2 = 8$ The product of the common prime factors is the GCF.

A common multiple is a number that is a multiple of two or more numbers. The least common multiple (LCM) is the least number that is a common multiple of two or more numbers.

Example 2

Find the LCM of 12 and 18.

Method 1 List the multiples of each number.

Multiples of 12	12, 24, 36, . . .	List the multiples of each number until you find the first common multiple.
Multiples of 18	18, 36, . . .	

The LCM of 12 and 18 is 36.

Method 2 Use the prime factorization of each number.

$12 = 2 \cdot 2 \cdot 3$

$18 = 2 \cdot 3 \cdot 3$

$LCM = 2 \cdot 2 \cdot 3 \cdot 3 = 36$ Use each prime factor the greatest number of times it appears in either number.

Exercises

Find the GCF of each set of numbers.

1. 12 and 22   **2.** 7 and 21   **3.** 24 and 48   **4.** 42, 63, and 105

Find the LCM of each set of numbers.

5. 16 and 20   **6.** 14 and 21   **7.** 11 and 33   **8.** 6, 7, and 12

Using Estimation

To make sure the answer to a problem is reasonable, you can estimate before you calculate. If the answer is close to your estimate, the answer is probably correct.

Example 1

Estimate to find whether each calculation is correct.

a. Calculation		Estimate
$126.91	≈	$130
$14.05	≈	$10
+$25.14	≈	+$30
$266.10		$170

The answer is not close to the estimate. It is not reasonable. The calculation is incorrect.

b. Calculation		Estimate
372.85	≈	370
−227.31	≈	−230
145.54		140

The answer is close to the estimate. It is reasonable. The calculation is correct.

For some situations, like estimating a grocery bill, you may not need an exact answer. A *front-end estimate* will give you a good estimate that is usually closer to the exact answer than an estimate you would get by rounding alone. Add the front-end digits, estimate the sum of the remaining digits by rounding, and then combine sums.

Example 2

Tomatoes cost $3.54, squash costs $2.75, and lemons cost $1.20. Estimate the total cost of the produce.

Add the	3.54	→	0.50	Estimate by rounding. Then add.
front-end digits.	2.75	→	0.80	
	+1.20	→	+0.20	
	6		1.50	

Since 6 + 1.50 = 7.50, the total cost is about $7.50.

Exercises

Estimate by rounding.

1. the sum of $15.70, $49.52, and $278.01 *≈ 350.*

2. 563 − 125 *≈ 430*

3. the sum of $163.90, $107.21, and $33.56 *≈ 300*

4. 824 − 467 *≈ 350*

Use front-end estimation to find each sum or difference.

5. $1.65 + $5.42 + $9.89 *≈ 17.00*

6. 1.369 + 7.421 + 2.700 *≈ 11.490*

7. 9.563 − 2.480 *≈ 7.080*

8. 1.17 + 3.92 + 2.26 *≈ 7.40*

9. 8.611 − 1.584 *≈ 10.190*

10. $2.52 + $3.04 + $5.25 *≈ 10.80*

11. Ticket prices at an amusement park cost $11.25 for adults and $6.50 for children under 12. Estimate the cost for three children and one adult. *≈ $30.80*

Simplifying Fractions

A fraction can name a part of a group or region. The region below is divided into 10 equal parts and 6 of the equal parts are shaded.

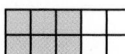 $\dfrac{6}{10}$ ← Numerator
← Denominator Read as "six tenths."

Two fractions that represent the same value are called equivalent fractions. You can find a fraction that is equivalent to a given fraction by multiplying the numerator and the denominator of the given fraction by the same nonzero number.

Example 1

Write five fractions that are equivalent to $\frac{3}{5}$.

$$\frac{3}{5} = \frac{3 \cdot 2}{5 \cdot 2} = \frac{6}{10} \qquad \frac{3}{5} = \frac{3 \cdot 3}{5 \cdot 3} = \frac{9}{15} \qquad \frac{3}{5} = \frac{3 \cdot 4}{5 \cdot 4} = \frac{12}{20} \qquad \frac{3}{5} = \frac{3 \cdot 5}{5 \cdot 5} = \frac{15}{25} \qquad \frac{3}{5} = \frac{3 \cdot 6}{5 \cdot 6} = \frac{18}{30}$$

The fraction $\frac{3}{5}$ is in simplest form because its numerator and denominator are relatively prime, which means their only common factor is 1. To write a fraction in simplest form, divide its numerator and its denominator by their greatest common factor (GCF).

Example 2

Write $\frac{6}{24}$ in simplest form.

Step 1 Find the GCF of 6 and 24.

$6 = 2 \cdot 3$ Multiply the common prime factors, 2 and 3.
$24 = 2 \cdot 2 \cdot 2 \cdot 3$ GCF = $2 \cdot 3 = 6$.

Step 2 Divide the numerator and the denominator of $\frac{6}{24}$ by the GCF, 6.

$$\frac{6}{24} = \frac{6 \div 6}{24 \div 6} = \frac{1}{4} \qquad \text{Simplify.}$$

Exercises

Write five fractions that are equivalent to each fraction.

1. $\frac{4}{7}$ $\frac{8}{14}, \frac{12}{21}, \frac{16}{28}, \frac{20}{35}, \frac{24}{42}$ 2. $\frac{9}{16}$ $\frac{18}{32} \frac{27}{48} \frac{36}{64}, \frac{45}{80}, \frac{54}{96}$ 3. $\frac{3}{8}$ $\frac{6}{16} \frac{9}{24}, \frac{12}{32} \frac{15}{40}, \frac{18}{48}$ 4. $\frac{8}{17}$ $\frac{16}{34} \frac{24}{51}, \frac{32}{68}, \frac{40}{85}, \frac{48}{102}$ 5. $\frac{5}{6}$ $\frac{10}{12}, \frac{15}{18}, \frac{20}{24}, \frac{25}{30}, \frac{30}{36}$ 6. $\frac{7}{10}$ $\frac{14}{20} \frac{21}{30} \frac{28}{40}, \frac{35}{50}, \frac{42}{60}$

Complete each statement.

7. $\frac{3}{7} = \frac{\blacksquare}{21}$ 9   8. $\frac{5}{8} = \frac{20}{\blacksquare}$ 32   9. $\frac{11}{12} = \frac{44}{\blacksquare}$ 48   10. $\frac{12}{16} = \frac{\blacksquare}{4}$ 3   11. $\frac{50}{100} = \frac{1}{\blacksquare}$ 2

Is each fraction in simplest form? If not, write the fraction in simplest form.

12. $\frac{4}{12}$ $\frac{1}{3}$ 13. $\frac{3}{16}$ yes   14. $\frac{5}{30}$ $\frac{1}{6}$ 15. $\frac{9}{72}$ $\frac{1}{8}$ 16. $\frac{11}{22}$ $\frac{1}{2}$ 17. $\frac{24}{25}$ yes

Write each fraction in simplest form.

18. $\frac{8}{16}$ $\frac{1}{2}$ 19. $\frac{7}{14}$ $\frac{1}{2}$ 20. $\frac{6}{9}$ $\frac{2}{3}$ 21. $\frac{20}{30}$ $\frac{2}{3}$ 22. $\frac{8}{20}$ $\frac{2}{5}$ 23. $\frac{12}{40}$ $\frac{3}{10}$

Fractions and Decimals

You can write a fraction as a decimal.

Example 1

Write $\frac{3}{5}$ as a decimal.

$$\begin{array}{r} 0.6 \\ 5\overline{)3.0} \end{array}$$ Divide the numerator by the denominator.

So $\frac{3}{5} = 0.6$.

You can write a decimal as a fraction.

Example 2

Write 0.38 as a fraction.

$0.38 = 38 \text{ hundredths} = \frac{38}{100} = \frac{19}{50}$

Some fractions can be written as decimals that repeat, but do not end.

Example 3

Write $\frac{3}{11}$ as a decimal.

Divide the numerator by the denominator, as shown at the right. The remainders 8 and 3 keep repeating. Therefore 2 and 7 will keep repeating in the quotient.

$\frac{3}{11} = 0.2727\ldots = 0.\overline{27}$

$$\begin{array}{r} 0.2727\ldots \\ 11\overline{)3.0000\ldots} \\ \underline{2.2} \\ 80 \\ \underline{77} \\ 30 \\ \underline{22} \\ 80 \\ \underline{77} \\ 3 \end{array}$$

You can write a repeating decimal as a fraction.

Example 4

Write 0.363636 . . . as a fraction.

Let $x = 0.363636\ldots$

$100x = 36.36363636\ldots$ When 2 digits repeat, multiply by 100.

$99x = 36$ Subtract $x = 0.363636$.

$x = \frac{36}{99} \text{ or } \frac{4}{11}$ Divide each side by 99.

Exercises

Write each fraction or mixed number as a decimal.

1. $\frac{3}{10}$ 0.3   **2.** $\frac{13}{12}$ $1.08\overline{3}$ **3.** $\frac{4}{20}$ 0.2   **4.** $\frac{25}{75}$ $0.\overline{3}$ **5.** $\frac{5}{7}$ $0.7142857\ldots$ **6.** $4\frac{3}{25}$ 4.12

Write each decimal as a fraction in simplest form.

7. 0.07 $\frac{7}{100}$ **8.** 0.25 $\frac{1}{4}$ **9.** 0.875 $\frac{7}{8}$ **10.** 0.4545 $\frac{5}{99}$ **11.** 6.3336 $6\frac{1}{3}$ **12.** 7.2626 $7\frac{26}{99}$

Adding and Subtracting Fractions

You can add and subtract fractions when they have the same denominator.
Fractions with the same denominator are called like fractions.

Example 1

a. Add $\frac{4}{5} + \frac{3}{5}$.

$$\frac{4}{5} + \frac{3}{5} = \frac{4+3}{5} = \frac{7}{5} = 1\frac{2}{5} \quad \leftarrow \quad$$ Add or subtract the numerators and keep the same denominator.

b. Subtract $\frac{5}{9} - \frac{2}{9}$.

$$\rightarrow \quad \frac{5}{9} - \frac{2}{9} = \frac{5-2}{9} = \frac{3}{9} = \frac{1}{3}$$

Fractions with unlike denominators are called unlike fractions. To add or subtract unlike
fractions, find the least common denominator (LCD) and write equivalent fractions with
the same denominator. Then add or subtract the like fractions.

Example 2

Add $\frac{3}{4} + \frac{5}{6}$.

$$\frac{3}{4} + \frac{5}{6} = \frac{9}{12} + \frac{10}{12}$$

Find the LCD. The LCD is the least common multiple (LCM) of the denominators.
The LCD of 4 and 6 is 12. Write equivalent fractions.

$$= \frac{9+10}{12} = \frac{19}{12}, \text{ or } 1\frac{7}{12}$$

Add like fractions and simplify.

To add or subtract mixed numbers, add or subtract the fractions. Then add or
subtract the whole numbers. Sometimes when subtracting mixed numbers you
have to regroup so that you can subtract the fractions.

Example 3

Subtract $5\frac{1}{4} - 3\frac{2}{3}$.

$$5\frac{1}{4} - 3\frac{2}{3} = 5\frac{3}{12} - 3\frac{8}{12}$$

Write equivalent fractions with the same denominator.

$$= 4\frac{15}{12} - 3\frac{8}{12}$$

Write $5\frac{3}{12}$ as $4\frac{15}{12}$ so you can subtract the fractions.

$$= 1\frac{7}{12}$$

Subtract the fractions. Then subtract the whole numbers.

Exercises

Add or subtract. Write each answer in simplest form.

1. $\frac{2}{7} + \frac{3}{7}$ $\frac{5}{7}$

2. $\frac{3}{8} + \frac{7}{8}$ $1\frac{1}{4}$

3. $\frac{6}{5} + \frac{9}{5}$ 3

4. $\frac{4}{9} + \frac{8}{9}$ $1\frac{1}{3}$

5. $6\frac{2}{3} + 3\frac{4}{5}$ $10\frac{7}{15}$

6. $1\frac{4}{7} + 2\frac{3}{14}$ $3\frac{11}{14}$

7. $4\frac{5}{6} + 1\frac{7}{18}$ $6\frac{2}{9}$

8. $2\frac{4}{5} + 3\frac{6}{7}$ $6\frac{23}{35}$

9. $4\frac{2}{3} + 1\frac{6}{11}$ $6\frac{7}{33}$

10. $3\frac{7}{9} + 5\frac{4}{11}$ $9\frac{14}{99}$

11. $8 + 1\frac{2}{3}$ $9\frac{2}{3}$

12. $8\frac{1}{5} + 3\frac{3}{4}$ $11\frac{19}{20}$

13. $11\frac{3}{8} + 2\frac{1}{16}$ $13\frac{7}{16}$

14. $\frac{7}{8} - \frac{3}{8}$ $\frac{1}{2}$

15. $\frac{9}{10} - \frac{3}{10}$ $\frac{3}{5}$

16. $\frac{17}{5} - \frac{2}{5}$ 3

17. $\frac{11}{7} - \frac{2}{7}$ $1\frac{2}{7}$

18. $\frac{5}{11} - \frac{4}{11}$ $\frac{1}{11}$

19. $8\frac{5}{8} - 6\frac{1}{4}$ $2\frac{3}{8}$

20. $3\frac{2}{3} - 1\frac{8}{9}$ $1\frac{7}{9}$

21. $8\frac{5}{6} - 5\frac{1}{2}$ $3\frac{1}{3}$

22. $12\frac{3}{4} - 4\frac{5}{6}$ $7\frac{11}{12}$

23. $17\frac{2}{7} - 8\frac{2}{9}$ $9\frac{4}{63}$

24. $7\frac{3}{4} - 3\frac{3}{8}$ $4\frac{3}{8}$

25. $4\frac{1}{12} - 1\frac{11}{12}$ $2\frac{1}{6}$

Multiplying and Dividing Fractions

Skills Handbook

To multiply two or more fractions, multiply the numerators, multiply the denominators, and simplify the product, if necessary.

Example 1

Multiply $\frac{3}{7} \cdot \frac{5}{6}$.

Method 1 Multiply the numerators and the denominators. Then simplify.

$$\frac{3}{7} \cdot \frac{5}{6} = \frac{3 \cdot 5}{7 \cdot 6} = \frac{15}{42} = \frac{15 \div 3}{42 \div 3} = \frac{5}{14}$$

Method 2 Simplify before multiplying.

$$\frac{1\cancel{3}}{7} \cdot \frac{5}{\cancel{6}2} = \frac{1 \cdot 5}{7 \cdot 2} = \frac{5}{14}$$

To multiply mixed numbers, change the mixed numbers to improper fractions and multiply the fractions. Write the product as a mixed number.

Example 2

Multiply $2\frac{4}{5} \cdot 1\frac{2}{3}$.

$$2\frac{4}{5} \cdot 1\frac{2}{3} = \frac{14}{\cancel{5}_1} \cdot \frac{\cancel{5}^1}{3} = \frac{14}{3} = 4\frac{2}{3}$$

To divide fractions, change the division problem to a multiplication problem. Remember that $8 \div \frac{1}{4}$ is the same as $8 \cdot 4$. To divide mixed numbers, change the mixed numbers to improper fractions and divide the fractions.

Example 3

a. Divide $\frac{4}{5} \div \frac{3}{7}$.

$$\frac{4}{5} \div \frac{3}{7} = \frac{4}{5} \cdot \frac{7}{3} \qquad \text{Multiply by the reciprocal of the divisor.}$$

$$= \frac{28}{15} \qquad \text{Simplify.}$$

$$= 1\frac{13}{15} \qquad \text{Write as a mixed number.}$$

b. Divide $4\frac{2}{3} \div 7\frac{3}{5}$.

$$4\frac{2}{3} \div 7\frac{3}{5} = \frac{14}{3} \div \frac{38}{5} \qquad \text{Change to improper fractions.}$$

$$= \frac{14^7}{3} \cdot \frac{5}{38_{19}} \qquad \text{Simplify.}$$

$$= \frac{35}{57} \qquad \text{Multiply.}$$

Exercises

Multiply or divide. Write your answers in simplest form.

1. $\frac{2}{5} \cdot \frac{3}{4}$

2. $\frac{3}{7} \cdot \frac{4}{3}$

3. $1\frac{1}{2} \cdot 5\frac{3}{4}$

4. $3\frac{4}{5} \cdot 10\frac{2}{1}$

5. $5\frac{1}{4} \cdot \frac{2}{3}$

6. $4\frac{1}{2} \cdot 7\frac{1}{2}$

7. $3\frac{2}{3} \cdot 6\frac{9}{10}$

8. $6\frac{1}{2} \cdot 7\frac{2}{3}$

9. $2\frac{2}{5} \cdot 1\frac{1}{6}$

10. $4\frac{1}{9} \cdot 3\frac{3}{8}$

11. $\frac{3}{5} \div \frac{1}{2}$

12. $\frac{4}{5} \div \frac{9}{10}$

13. $2\frac{1}{2} \div 3\frac{1}{2}$

14. $1\frac{4}{5} \div 2\frac{1}{2}$

15. $3\frac{1}{6} \div 1\frac{3}{4}$

16. $5 \div \frac{3}{8}$

17. $\frac{4}{9} \div \frac{3}{5}$

18. $\frac{5}{8} \div \frac{3}{4}$

19. $2\frac{1}{5} \div 2\frac{1}{2}$

20. $6\frac{1}{2} \div \frac{1}{4}$

Fractions, Decimals, and Percents

Percent means per hundred. 50% means 50 per hundred. $50\% = \frac{50}{100} = 0.50$.

You can write a fraction as a percent by writing the fraction as a decimal first. Then move the decimal point two places to the right and write a percent sign.

Example 1

Write each number as a percent.

a. $\frac{3}{5}$

$\frac{3}{5} = 0.6$

$0.6 = 60\%$

b. $\frac{7}{20}$

$\frac{7}{20} = 0.35$

$0.35 = 35\%$

c. $\frac{2}{3}$

$\frac{2}{3} = 0.66\overline{6}$

$0.66\overline{6} = 66.\overline{6}\% \approx 66.7\%$

You can write a percent as a decimal by moving the decimal point two places to the left and removing the percent sign. You can write a percent as a fraction with a denominator of 100. Then simplify the fraction, if possible.

Example 2

Write each percent as a decimal and as a fraction or mixed number.

a. **25%**

$25\% = 0.25$

$25\% = \frac{25}{100} = \frac{1}{4}$

b. $\frac{1}{2}\%$

$\frac{1}{2}\% = 0.5\% = 0.005$

$\frac{1}{2}\% = \frac{\frac{1}{2}}{100} = \frac{1}{2} \div 100$

$= \frac{1}{2} \cdot \frac{1}{100} = \frac{1}{200}$

c. **360%**

$360\% = 3.6$

$360\% = \frac{360}{100} = \frac{18}{5} = 3\frac{3}{5}$

Exercises

Write each number as a percent. If necessary, round to the nearest tenth.

1. 0.56

2. 0.09

3. 6.02

4. 5.245

5. 8.2

6. 0.14

7. $\frac{1}{7}$

8. $\frac{9}{20}$

9. $\frac{1}{9}$

10. $\frac{5}{6}$

11. $\frac{3}{4}$

12. $\frac{7}{8}$

Write each percent as a decimal.

13. 7%

14. 8.5%

15. 0.9%

16. 250%

17. 83%

18. 110%

19. 15%

20. 72%

21. 0.03%

22. 36.2%

23. 365%

24. 101%

Write each percent as a fraction or mixed number in simplest form.

25. 19%

26. $\frac{3}{4}\%$

27. 450%

28. $\frac{4}{5}\%$

29. 64%

30. $\frac{2}{3}\%$

31. 24%

32. 845%

33. $\frac{3}{8}\%$

34. 480%

35. 60%

36. 350%

Exponents

Skills Handbook

You can express $2 \cdot 2 \cdot 2 \cdot 2 \cdot 2$ as 2^5. The raised number 5 shows the number of times 2 is used as a factor. The number 2 is the base. The number 5 is the exponent.

$2^5 \leftarrow$ **exponent**
$\uparrow$
base

Factored Form: $2 \cdot 2 \cdot 2 \cdot 2 \cdot 2$ 　　　Exponential Form: 2^5 　　　Standard Form: 32

A number with an exponent of 1 is the number itself: $8^1 = 8$.
Any number, except 0, with an exponent of 0 is 1: $5^0 = 1$.

Example 1

Write each expression using exponents.

a. $8 \cdot 8 \cdot 8 \cdot 8 \cdot 8$ 　　　**b.** $2 \cdot 9 \cdot 9 \cdot 9 \cdot 9 \cdot 9 \cdot 9$ 　　　**c.** $6 \cdot 6 \cdot 10 \cdot 10 \cdot 10 \cdot 6 \cdot 6$

Count the number of times each number is used as a factor.

$= 8^5$ 　　　　　　　$= 2 \cdot 9^6$ 　　　　　　　$= 6^4 \cdot 10^3$

Example 2

Write each expression in standard form.

a. 2^3 　　　　　　　**b.** $8^2 \cdot 3^4$ 　　　　　　　**c.** $10^3 \cdot 15^2$

Write each expression in factored form and multiply.

$2 \cdot 2 \cdot 2 = 8$ 　　　$8 \cdot 8 \cdot 3 \cdot 3 \cdot 3 \cdot 3 = 5184$ 　　　$10 \cdot 10 \cdot 10 \cdot 15 \cdot 15 = 225{,}000$

For powers of 10, the exponent tells how many zeros are in the number in standard form.

$10^1 = 10$ 　　　$10^3 = 10 \cdot 10 \cdot 10 = 1000$ 　　　$10^5 = 10 \cdot 10 \cdot 10 \cdot 10 \cdot 10 = 100{,}000$

You can use powers of 10 to write numbers in expanded form.

Example 3

Write 739 in expanded form using powers of 10.

$739 = 700 + 30 + 9 = (7 \cdot 100) + (3 \cdot 10) + (9 \cdot 1) = (7 \cdot 10^2) + (3 \cdot 10^1) + (9 \cdot 10^0)$

Exercises

Write each expression using exponents.

1. $6 \cdot 6 \cdot 6 \cdot 6$ 　　　**2.** $7 \cdot 7 \cdot 7 \cdot 7 \cdot 7$ 　　　**3.** $5 \cdot 2 \cdot 2 \cdot 2 \cdot 2$

4. $3 \cdot 3 \cdot 3 \cdot 3 \cdot 3 \cdot 14 \cdot 14$ 　　　**5.** $4 \cdot 4 \cdot 3 \cdot 3 \cdot 2$ 　　　**6.** $3 \cdot 5 \cdot 5 \cdot 7 \cdot 7 \cdot 7$

Write each number in standard form.

7. 4^3 　　　**8.** 9^4 　　　**9.** 12^2 　　　**10.** $6^2 \cdot 7^1$ 　　　**11.** $11^2 \cdot 3^3$

Write each number in expanded form using powers of 10.

12. 658 　　　**13.** 1254 　　　**14.** 7125 　　　**15.** 83,401 　　　**16.** 294,863

Scientific Notation and Significant Digits

In *scientific notation*, a number has the form $a \times 10^n$, where n is an integer and $1 \le |a| < 10$.

Example 1

Write 5.59×10^6 in standard form.

$5.59 \times 10^6 = 5\,590\,000 = 5{,}590{,}000$

A positive exponent indicates a value greater than 1.
Move the decimal point six places to the right.

Example 2

Write 0.0000318 in scientific notation.

$0.0000318 = 3.18 \times 10^{-5}$

Move the decimal point to create a number between 1 and 10.
Since the original number is less than 1, use a negative exponent.

When a measurement is in scientific notation, all the digits of the number between 1 and 10 are *significant digits*. When you multiply or divide measurements, your answer should have as many significant digits as the least number of significant digits in any of the numbers involved.

Example 3

Multiply $(6.71 \times 10^8 \text{ mi/h})$ and $(3.8 \times 10^4 \text{ h})$.

$(6.71 \times 10^8 \text{ mi/h})(3.8 \times 10^4 \, h) = (6.71 \cdot 3.8)(10^8 \cdot 10^4)$ Rearrange factors.

$= 25.498 \times 10^{12}$ Add exponents when multiplying powers of 10.

$= 2.5498 \times 10^{13}$ Write in scientific notation.

$\approx 2.5 \times 10^{13} \text{mi}$ Round to two significant digits.

three significant digits   two significant digits

Exercises

Change each number to scientific notation or to standard form.

1. 1,340,000   **2.** 6.88×10^{-2} **3.** 0.000775   **4.** 0.0072   **5.** 1.113×10^5

6. 8.0×10^{-4} **7.** 1895   **8.** 2.3×10^3 **9.** 123,400   **10.** 7.985×10^4

Write each product or quotient in scientific notation. Round to the appropriate number of significant digits.

11. $(1.6 \times 10^2)(4.0 \times 10^3)$ **12.** $(2.5 \times 10^{-3})(1.2 \times 10^4)$ **13.** $(4.237 \times 10^4)(2.01 \times 10^{-2})$

14. $\dfrac{7.0 \times 10^5}{2.89 \times 10^3}$ **15.** $\dfrac{1.4 \times 10^4}{8.0 \times 10^2}$ **16.** $\dfrac{6.48 \times 10^6}{3.2 \times 10^5}$

17. $(1.78 \times 10^{-7})(5.03 \times 10^{-5})$ **18.** $(7.2 \times 10^{11})(5 \times 10^6)$ **19.** $(8.90 \times 10^8) \div (2.36 \times 10^{-2})$

20. $(3.95 \times 10^4) \div (6.8 \times 10^8)$ **21.** $(4.9 \times 10^{-8}) \div (2.7 \times 10^{-2})$ **22.** $(3.972 \times 10^{-5})(4.7 \times 10^{-4})$

Perimeter, Area, and Volume

The perimeter of a figure is the distance around the figure. The area of a figure is the number of square units contained in the figure. The volume of a three-dimensional figure is the number of cubic units contained in the figure.

Example 1

Find the perimeter of each figure.

a.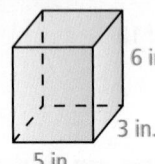

Add the measures of the sides.
$3 + 4 + 5 = 12$
The perimeter is 12 in.

3 in. 5 in. 4 in.

b.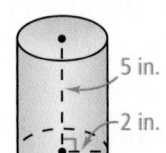

Use the formula $P = 2\ell + 2w$.
$P = 2(3) + 2(4)$
$= 6 + 8 = 14$
The perimeter is 14 cm.

3 cm 4 cm

Example 2

Find the area of each figure.

a.

Use the formula $A = bh$.
$A = 6 \cdot 5 = 30$
The area is 30 in.^{2}.

5 in. 6 in.

b.

Use the formula $A = \frac{1}{2}(bh)$.
$A = \frac{1}{2}(7 \cdot 6) = 21$
The area is 21 in.^{2}.

6 in. 7 in.

Example 3

Find the volume of each figure.

a.

Use the formula $V = Bh$.
$B =$ area of the base
$= 3 \cdot 5 = 15$
$V = 15 \cdot 6 = 90$ in.^{3}
The volume is 90 in.^{3}.

6 in. 3 in. 5 in.

b.

Use the formula $V = \pi r^2 h$.
$V = 3.14 \cdot 2^2 \cdot 5$
$= 3.14 \cdot 4 \cdot 5 = 62.8$ in.^{3}
The volume is 62.8 in.^{3}.

5 in. 2 in.

Exercises

For Exercises 1–2, find the perimeter of each figure. For Exercises 3–4, find the area of each figure. For Exercises 5–7, find the volume of each figure.

1.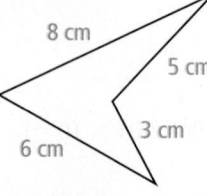

8 cm 5 cm 3 cm 6 cm

2.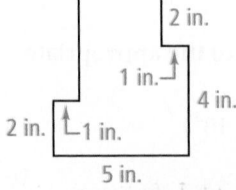

2 in. 1 in. 4 in. 2 in. 1 in. 5 in.

3.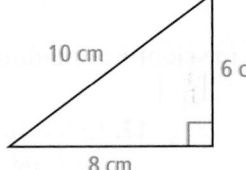

10 cm 6 cm 8 cm

4.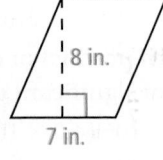

8 in. 7 in.

5.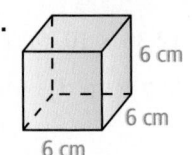

6 cm 6 cm 6 cm

6.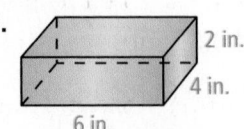

2 in. 4 in. 6 in.

7.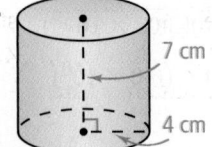

7 cm 4 cm

Line Plots

A line plot is created by placing a mark above a number line corresponding to each data value. Line plots have two main advantages:

- You can see the frequency of data values.

- You can see how the data values compare.

Example

The table at the right gives the heights, in inches, of a group of 25 adults. Display the data in a line plot. Describe the data shown in the line plot.

Heights of Adults (in.)				
59	60	63	63	64
64	64	65	65	65
67	67	67	67	68
68	68	69	70	70
71	72	73	73	77

The data are graphed on a number line.

The title describes the data.

An **X** represents one element of the data set.

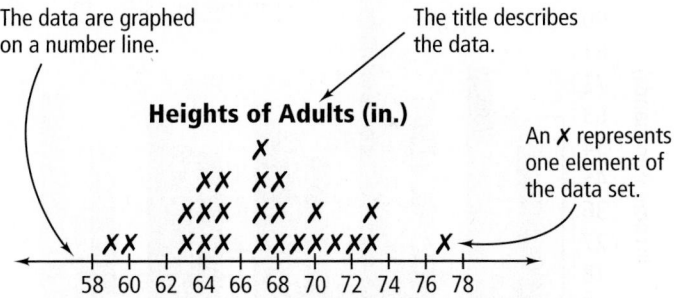

The line plot shows that most of the heights are concentrated around 67 in., the maximum value is 77 in., and the minimum value is 59 in.

Exercises

Display each set of data in a line plot.

1. 3, 6, 4, 3, 6, 0, 4, 5, 0, 4, 6, 1, 5, 1, 0, 5, 5, 6, 5, 3

2. 19, 18, 18, 18, 19, 20, 19, 18, 18, 17, 18, 20, 19, 17

Draw a line plot for each frequency table.

3.

Number	1	2	3	4	5	6
Frequency	4	1	0	5	7	2

4.

Number	12	13	15	16	18	19
Frequency	2	5	1	3	6	3

5. Olympics The numbers of gold medals won by different countries during the 2002 Winter Olympics are listed below.

1, 1, 1, 2, 2, 2, 3, 3, 3, 3, 4, 4, 4, 5, 7, 10, 12, 13

Display the data in a line plot. Describe the data shown in the line plot.

Bar Graphs

Bar graphs are used to display and compare data. The horizontal axis shows categories and the vertical axis shows amounts. A multiple bar graph includes a key.

Example

Draw a bar graph for the data in the table below.

Median Household Income

Town	2 person	3 person	4 person
Mason	$62,690	$68,070	$77,014
Barstow	$68,208	$82,160	$99,584
York	$51,203	$58,902	$67,911
Rexford	$52,878	$54,943	$63,945
Onham	$54,715	$61,437	$69,260

The categories (in the first column) are placed on the horizontal scale. The amounts (in the second, third, and fourth columns) are used to create the scale on the vertical scale and to draw each bar.

Graph the data for each town. Use the values in the top row to create the key.

The highest median income is $99,584. A reasonable range for the vertical scale is $0 to $108,000.

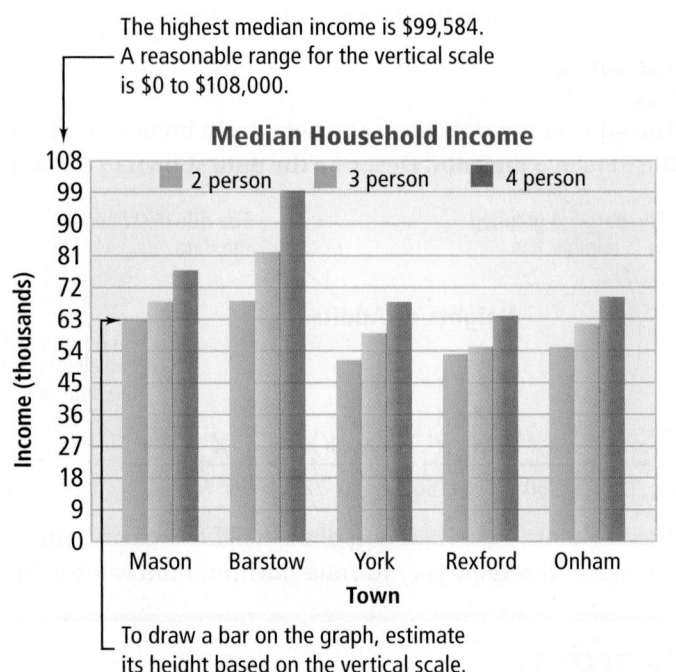

To draw a bar on the graph, estimate its height based on the vertical scale.

Exercises

1. Draw a bar graph for the data in the table below.

Highest Temperatures (°F)

Town	March	June	August
Mason	61	86	83
Barstow	84	104	101
York	89	101	102
Rexford	88	92	93
Onham	81	104	100

2. a. Reasoning If one more column of data were added to the table in the example, how would the bar graph be different?

    b. If one more row of data were added to the table in the example, how would the bar graph be different?

Line Graphs

Line graphs are used to display the change in a set of data over a period of time. A multiple-line graph shows change in more than one category of data over time. You can use a line graph to look for trends and make predictions.

Example

The data in the table below show the number of households, in thousands, that have cable TV and the number of households that subscribe to newspapers in a certain city. Graph the data.

Households With Cable TV and Newspapers (thousands)

Year	1980	1990	1995	2000	2005
Cable TV	15.2	51.9	60.5	68.6	73.9
Newspapers	62.2	62.3	58.2	55.8	53.3

Since the data show changes over time for two sets of data, use a double line graph. The horizontal scale displays years. The vertical axis shows the number of households for each category.

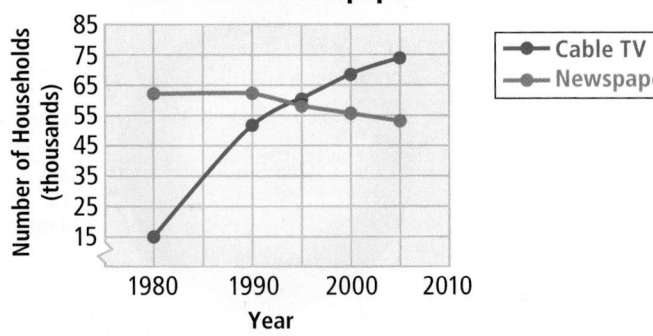

Notice that there is a *break* in the vertical axis. You can use a zigzag line to indicate a break from 0 to 15 since there is no data less than 15 to graph.

Exercises

Graph the data in each table.

1.   **Market Share (percent)**

Year	2004	2005	2006	2007
Rap/Hip Hop	12.1	13.3	11.4	10.8
Pop	10.0	8.1	7.1	10.7

SOURCE: Recording Industry of America

2.   **Percent of Schools With Internet Access**

Year	1997	1999	2001	2003
Elementary	75	94	99	100
Secondary	89	98	100	100

SOURCE: National Center for Education Statistics

Circle Graphs

A circle graph is an efficient way to present certain types of data. The entire circle represents all of the data. Each section of the circle represents a part of the whole and can be labeled with the actual data or the data expressed as a fraction, decimal, or percent. The angles at the center are central angles, and each angle is proportional to the percent or fraction of the total.

Example

Students at a high school were asked to pick their favorite instrument. The table at the right shows the number of students who chose each instrument. Draw a circle graph for the data.

Favorite Musical Instruments

Instrument	Number of Students
Bass	35
Drums	103
Piano	150
Guitar	182

Step 1 Add to find the total number.

$$35 + 103 + 150 + 182 = 470$$

Step 2 For each central angle, set up a proportion to find the measure. Use a calculator to solve each proportion.

$$\frac{35}{470} = \frac{a}{360°} \qquad \frac{103}{470} = \frac{b}{360°} \qquad \frac{150}{470} = \frac{c}{360°} \qquad \frac{182}{470} = \frac{d}{360°}$$

$$a \approx 27° \qquad\qquad b \approx 79° \qquad\qquad c \approx 115° \qquad\qquad d \approx 139°$$

Step 3 Use a compass to draw a circle. Draw the approximate central angles using a protractor.　　**Step 4** Label each sector.

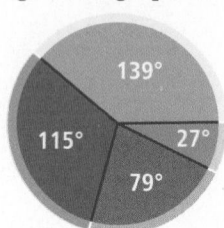

Favorite Musical Instruments

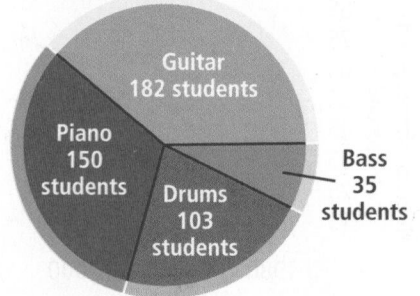

Exercises

1. **a.** Use the data in the table to draw a circle graph.
   b. Approximately what percent of students ride the bus?
   c. Approximately how many times more students walk than ride in a car?

Methods of Transportation

Transportation Method	Walk	Bicycle	Bus	Car
Number of Students	252	135	432	81

2. **Data Collection** Survey your class to find out how they get to school. Use the data to draw a circle graph.

Stem-and-Leaf Plots

A stem-and-leaf plot is a display of data that uses the digits of the data values. To make a stem-and-leaf plot, separate each number into a stem and a leaf. A stem and leaf for the number 2.39 is shown at the right.

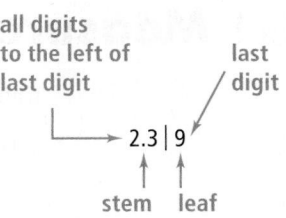

all digits
to the left of
last digit
last
digit

2.3 | 9

stem   leaf

You can use a stem-and-leaf plot to organize data. The data below describe the price for the same notebook at several stores.

Notebook Prices: $2.39 $2.47 $2.43 $2.21 $2.33 $2.28 $2.26

2.2	1 6 8
2.3	3 9
2.4	3 7

Key: 2.4 | 3 means 2.43

Use the first two digits for the "stems."

Use the corresponding last digits for the "leaves." Arrange the numbers in order.

You can use a back-to-back stem-and-leaf plot to display two related data sets. The stems are between two vertical bars, and the leaves are on each side. Leaves are in increasing order from the stems. In the back-to-back stem-and-leaf plot below, 3|4|1 represents a commute time of 43 min in Town A and a commute time of 41 min in Town B.

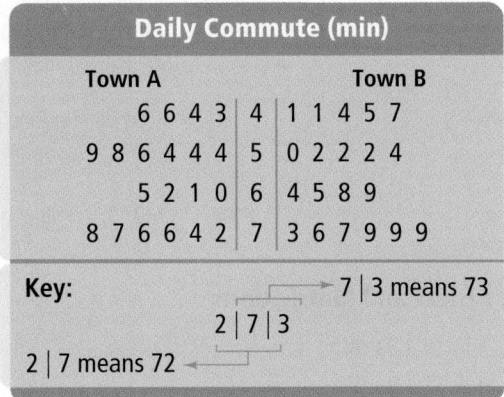

Daily Commute (min)

Town A		Town B
6 6 4 3	4	1 1 4 5 7
9 8 6 4 4 4	5	0 2 2 2 4
5 2 1 0	6	4 5 8 9
8 7 6 6 4 2	7	3 6 7 9 9 9

Key: → 7 | 3 means 73

2 | 7 | 3

2 | 7 means 72 ←

Exercises

Make a stem-and-leaf plot for each set of data.

1. 18 35 28 15 36 10 25 22 15

2. 18.6 18.4 17.6 15.7 15.3 17.5

3. 785 776 788 761 768 768 785

4. 0.8 0.2 1.4 3.5 4.3 4.5 2.6 2.2

5. Make a back-to-back stem-and-leaf plot of the test scores of the two classes below.
   Class A: 98 78 85 72 94 81 68 83
   Class B: 87 91 79 75 90 81 82 100

Reference

Table 1 **Measures**

	United States Customary	Metric
Length	12 inches (in.) = 1 foot (ft) 36 in. = 1 yard (yd) 3 ft = 1 yard 5280 ft = 1 mile (mi) 1760 yd = 1 mile	10 millimeters (mm) = 1 centimeter (cm) 100 cm = 1 meter (m) 1000 mm = 1 meter 1000 m = 1 kilometer (km)
Area	144 square inches (in.^{2}) = 1 square foot (ft^2) 9 ft^2 = 1 square yard (yd^2) 43,560 ft^2 = 1 acre (a) 4840 yd^2 = 1 acre	100 square millimeters (mm^2) = 1 square centimeter (cm^2) 10,000 cm^2 = 1 square meter (m^2) 10,000 m^2 = 1 hectare (ha)
Volume	1728 cubic inches (in.^{3}) = 1 cubic foot (ft^3) 27 ft^3 = 1 cubic yard (yd^3)	1000 cubic millimeters (mm^3) = 1 cubic centimeter (cm^3) 1,000,000 cm^3 = 1 cubic meter (m^3)
Liquid Capacity	8 fluid ounces (fl oz) = 1 cup (c) 2 c = 1 pint (pt) 2 pt = 1 quart (qt) 4 qt = 1 gallon (gal)	1000 milliliters (mL) = 1 liter (L) 1000 L = 1 kiloliter (kL)
Weight or Mass	16 ounces (oz) = 1 pound (lb) 2000 pounds = 1 ton (t)	1000 milligrams (mg) = 1 gram (g) 1000 g = 1 kilogram (kg) 1000 kg = 1 metric ton
Temperature	32°F = freezing point of water 98.6°F = normal human body temperature 212°F = boiling point of water	0°C = freezing point of water 37°C = normal human body temperature 100°C = boiling point of water

Customary Units and Metric Units		
Length	1 in. = 2.54 cm 1 mi ≈ 1.61 km 1 ft ≈ 0.305 m	
Capacity	1 qt ≈ 0.946 L	
Weight and Mass	1 oz ≈ 28.4 g 1 lb ≈ 0.454 kg	

Time		
60 seconds (s) = 1 minute (min) 60 minutes = 1 hour (h) 24 hours = 1 day (d) 7 days = 1 week (wk)	4 weeks (approx.) = 1 month (mo) 365 days = 1 year (yr) 52 weeks (approx.) = 1 year	12 months = 1 year 10 years = 1 decade 100 years = 1 century

Table 2 **Reading Math Symbols**

Symbols	Words
•	multiplication sign, times ($\times$)
$=$	equals
$\stackrel{?}{=}$	Are the statements equal?
$\approx$	is approximately equal to
$\neq$	is not equal to
$<$	is less than
$>$	is greater than
$\leq$	is less than or equal to
$\geq$	is greater than or equal to
$\cong$	is congruent to
$\pm$	plus or minus
( )	parentheses for grouping
[ ]	brackets for grouping
{ }	set braces
%	percent
$|a|$	absolute value of a
. . .	and so on
$-a$	opposite of a
π	pi, an irrational number, approximately equal to 3.14
$\circ$	degree(s)
a^n	nth power of a
$\sqrt{x}$	nonnegative square root of x
$\frac{1}{a}, a \neq 0$	reciprocal of a
a^{-n}	$\frac{1}{a^n}, a \neq 0$
$\overleftrightarrow{AB}$	line through points A and B
$\overline{AB}$	segment with endpoints A and B
AB	length of $\overline{AB}$; distance between points A and B

Symbols	Words
$\angle A$	angle A
$m\angle A$	measure of angle A
$\triangle ABC$	triangle ABC
(x, y)	ordered pair
$x_1, x_2, \ldots$	specific values of the variable x
$y_1, y_2, \ldots$	specific values of the variable y
$\bar{x}$	mean of data values of x
σ	standard deviation
$f(x)$	f of x; the function value at x
m	slope of a line
b	y-intercept of a line
$a:b$	ratio of a to b
$\begin{bmatrix} 1 & 3 \\ 2 & 4 \end{bmatrix}$	matrix
$\sin A$	sine of $\angle A$
$\cos A$	cosine of $\angle A$
$\tan A$	tangent of $\angle A$
$n!$	n factorial
$_nP_r$	permutations of n objects arranged r at a time
$_nC_r$	combinations of n objects chosen r at a time
$P(event)$	probability of an event
$\wedge$	raised to a power (in a spreadsheet formula)
*	multiply (in a spreadsheet formula)
/	divide (in a spreadsheet formula)

Properties and Formulas

Chapter 1 Foundations for Algebra

Order of Operations
1. Perform an operation(s) inside grouping symbols.
2. Simplify powers.
3. Multiply and divide from left to right.
4. Add and subtract from left to right.

Commutative Property of Addition
For every real number a and b, $a + b = b + a$.

Commutative Property of Multiplication
For every real number a and b, $a \cdot b = b \cdot a$.

Associative Property of Addition
For every real number a, b, and c,
$(a + b) + c = a + (b + c)$.

Associative Property of Multiplication
For every real number a, b, and c,
$(a \cdot b) \cdot c = a \cdot (b \cdot c)$.

Identity Property of Addition
For every real number a, $a + 0 = a$.

Identity Property of Multiplication
For every real number a, $1 \cdot a = a$.

Multiplication Property of -1
For every real number a, $-1 \cdot a = -a$.

Zero Property of Multiplication
For every real number a, $a \cdot 0 = 0$.

Inverse Property of Addition
For every real number a, there is an additive inverse
$-a$ such that $a + (-a) = 0$.

Inverse Property of Multiplication
For every nonzero number a, there is a multiplicative inverse
such that $a \cdot \frac{1}{a} = 1$.

Distributive Property
For every real number a, b, and c:
$a(b + c) = ab + ac$
$(b + c)a = ba + ca$
$a(b - c) = ab - ac$
$(b - c)a = ba - ca$

Chapter 2 Solving Equations

Addition Property of Equality
For every real number a, b, and c, if $a = b$, then
$a + c = b + c$.

Subtraction Property of Equality
For every real number a, b, and c, if $a = b$, then
$a - c = b - c$.

Multiplication Property of Equality
For every real number a, b, and c, if $a = b$, then $a \cdot c = b \cdot c$.

Division Property of Equality
For every real number a, b, and c, where $c \neq 0$, if $a = b$,
then $\frac{a}{c} = \frac{b}{c}$.

Cross Products of a Proportion
If $\frac{a}{b} = \frac{c}{d}$, then $ad = bc$.

Percent Proportion
$\frac{a}{b} = \frac{p}{100}$, where $b \neq 0$.

Percent Equation
$a = p\% \cdot b$, where $b \neq 0$.

Simple Interest Formula
$I = prt$

Percent of Change
$p\% = \frac{\text{amount of increase or decrease}}{\text{original amount}}$
amount of increase = new amount − original amount
amount of decrease = original amount − new amount

Relative Error
relative error $= \frac{|\text{measured or estimated value} - \text{actual value}|}{\text{actual value}}$

Chapter 3 Solving Inequalities

The following properties of inequality are also true for
$\geq$ and $\leq$.

Addition Property of Inequality
For every real number a, b, and c,
if $a > b$, then $a + c > b + c$;
if $a < b$, then $a + c < b + c$.

Subtraction Property of Inequality
For every real number a, b, and c,
if $a > b$, then $a - c > b - c$;
if $a < b$, then $a - c < b - c$.

Multiplication Property of Inequality
For every real number a, b, and c, where $c > 0$,
if $a > b$, then $ac > bc$;
if $a < b$, then $ac < bc$.
For every real number a, b, and c, where $c < 0$,
if $a > b$, then $ac < bc$;
if $a < b$, then $ac > bc$.

Division Property of Inequality
For every real number a, b, and c, where $c > 0$,
if $a > b$, then $\frac{a}{c} > \frac{b}{c}$;
if $a < b$, then $\frac{a}{c} < \frac{b}{c}$.
For every real number a, b, and c, where $c < 0$,
if $a > b$, then $\frac{a}{c} < \frac{b}{c}$;
if $a < b$, then $\frac{a}{c} > \frac{b}{c}$.

Reflexive Property of Equality
For every real number a, $a = a$.

Symmetric Property of Equality
For every real number a and b,
if $a = b$, then $b = a$.

Transitive Property of Equality
For every real number a, b, and c,
if $a = b$ and $b = c$, then $a = c$.

Transitive Property of Inequality
For every real number a, b, and c,
if $a < b$ and $b < c$, then $a < c$.

Chapter 4 An Introduction to Functions

Arithmetic Sequence
The explicit form for the rule of an arithmetic sequence is
$A(n) = A(1) + (n - 1)d$, where $A(n)$ is the nth term,
$A(1)$ is the first term, n is the term number, and
d is the common difference.

The recursive form for the rule of an arithmetic sequence is
$A(n) = A(n - 1) + d$; $A(1) = a$, where $A(n)$ is the nth term,
a is the first term, n is the term number, and d is the
common difference.

Chapter 5 Linear Functions

Slope
$$\text{slope} = \frac{\text{vertical change}}{\text{horizontal change}} = \frac{\text{rise}}{\text{run}}$$

Direct Variation
A direct variation is a relationship that can be represented by
a function of the form $y = kx$, where $k \neq 0$.

Slope-Intercept Form of a Linear Equation
The slope-intercept form of a linear equation is
$y = mx + b$, where m is the slope and b is the
y-intercept.

Point-Slope Form of a Linear Equation
The point-slope form of the equation of a nonvertical line
that passes through the point (x_1, y_1) with slope m is
$y - y_1 = m(x - x_1)$.

Standard Form of a Linear Equation
The standard form of a linear equation is $Ax + By = C$,
where A, B, and C are real numbers and A and B are not
both zero.

Slopes of Parallel Lines
Nonvertical lines are parallel if they have the same slope and
different y-intercepts. Any two vertical lines are parallel.

Slopes of Perpendicular Lines
Two lines are perpendicular if the product of their slopes is
-1. A vertical line and horizontal line are perpendicular.

Residual
A residual is the difference between the y-value of a data
point and the corresponding y-value of a model for the data
set. You can find a residual by calculating $y - \hat{y}$, where y
represents the y-value of the data set and y represents the
corresponding y-value predicted from the model.

Chapter 6 Systems of Equations and Inequalities

Solutions of Systems of Linear Equations
A system of linear equations can have one solution, no
solution, or infinitely many solutions:
- If the lines have different slopes, the lines intersect, so
  there is one solution.
- If the lines have the same slopes and different
  y-intercepts, the lines are parallel, so there are no
  solutions.
- If the lines have the same slopes and the same
  y-intercepts, the lines are the same, so there are infinitely
  many solutions.

Chapter 7 Exponents and Exponential Functions

Zero as an Exponent
For every nonzero number a, $a^0 = 1$.

Negative Exponent
For every nonzero number a and rational number n,
$a^{-n} = \frac{1}{a^n}$.

Multiplying Powers With the Same Base
For every nonzero number a and rational numbers m and n,
$a^m \cdot a^n = a^{m+n}$.

Dividing Powers With the Same Base
For every nonzero number a and rational numbers m and n,
$\frac{a^m}{a^n} = a^{m-n}$.

Raising a Power to a Power
For every nonzero number a and rational numbers m and n,
$(a^m)^n = a^{mn}$.

Raising a Product to a Power
For every nonzero number a and b and rational number n,
$(ab)^n = a^n b^n$.

Raising a Quotient to a Power
For every nonzero number a and b and rational number n,
$\left(\frac{a}{b}\right)^n = \frac{a^n}{b^n}$.

Properties of Rational Exponents
If the nth root of a is a real number and m is an integer, then
$\frac{1}{a^n} = \sqrt[n]{a}$ and $\frac{m}{a^n} = \sqrt[n]{a^m} = \left(\sqrt[n]{a}\right)^m$. If m is negative,
$a \neq 0$.

Exponential Growth and Decay
An exponential function has the form $y = a \cdot b^x$, where a is a nonzero constant, b is greater than 0 and not equal to 1, and x is a real number.

- The function $y = a \cdot b^x$, where b is the growth factor, models exponential growth for $a > 0$ and $b > 1$.
- The function $y = a \cdot b^x$, where b is the decay factor, models exponential decay for $a > 0$ and $0 < b < 1$.

Geometric Sequence
The explicit form for the rule of a geometric sequence is
$A(n) = a \cdot r^{n-1}$, where $A(n)$ is the nth term, a is the first term, n is the term number, and r is the common ratio.

The recursive form for the rule of a geometric sequence is
$A(n) = A(n-1) \cdot r$; $A(1) = a$, where $A(n)$ is the nth term, a is the first term, n is the term number, and r is the common ratio.

Chapter 8 Polynomials and Factoring

Factoring Special Cases
For every nonzero number a and b:
$a^2 - b^2 = (a + b)(a - b)$
$a^2 + 2ab + b^2 = (a + b)(a + b) = (a + b)^2$
$a^2 - 2ab + b^2 = (a - b)(a - b) = (a - b)^2$

Chapter 9 Quadratic Functions and Equations

Graph of a Quadratic Function
The graph of $y = ax^2 + bx + c$, where $a \neq 0$, has the line
$x = \frac{-b}{2a}$ as its axis of symmetry. The x-coordinate of the vertex is $\frac{-b}{2a}$.

Zero-Product Property
For every real number a and b, if $ab = 0$, then
$a = 0$ or $b = 0$.

Quadratic Formula
If $ax^2 + bx + c = 0$, where $a \neq 0$, then
$x = \frac{-b \pm \sqrt{b^2 - 4ac}}{2a}$.

Property of the Discriminant
For the quadratic equation $ax^2 + bx + c = 0$, where $a \neq 0$, the value of the discriminant $b^2 - 4ac$ tells you the number of solutions.

- If $b^2 - 4ac > 0$, there are two real solutions.
- If $b^2 - 4ac = 0$, there is one real solution.
- If $b^2 - 4ac < 0$, there are no real solutions.

Chapter 10 Radical Expressions and Equations

The Pythagorean Theorem
In a right triangle, the sum of the squares of the lengths of the legs is equal to the square of the length of the hypotenuse: $a^2 + b^2 = c^2$.

The Converse of the Pythagorean Theorem
If a triangle has sides of lengths a, b, and c, and $a^2 + b^2 = c^2$, then the triangle is a right triangle with hypotenuse of length c.

Multiplication Property of Square Roots
For every number $a \geq 0$ and $b \geq 0$, $\sqrt{ab} = \sqrt{a} \cdot \sqrt{b}$.

Division Property of Square Roots

For every number $a \geq 0$ and $b > 0$, $\sqrt{\frac{a}{b}} = \frac{\sqrt{a}}{\sqrt{b}}$.

Trigonometric Ratios

sine of $\angle A = \dfrac{\text{length of leg opposite } \angle A}{\text{length of hypotenuse}}$

cosine of $\angle A = \dfrac{\text{length of leg adjacent to } \angle A}{\text{length of hypotenuse}}$

tangent of $\angle A = \dfrac{\text{length of leg opposite } \angle A}{\text{length of leg adjacent to } \angle A}$

Chapter 11 Rational Expressions and Functions

Inverse Variation

An inverse variation is a relationship that can be represented by a function of the form $y = \frac{k}{x}$, where $k \neq 0$.

Chapter 12 Data Analysis and Probability

Mean

The mean of a set of data values $= \dfrac{\text{sum of the data values}}{\text{total number of data values}}$.

Standard Deviation

Standard deviation is a measure of how the values in a data set vary, or deviate from the mean.

$$\sigma = \sqrt{\frac{\Sigma(x - \bar{x})^2}{n}}$$

Multiplication Counting Principle

If there are m ways to make a first selection and n ways to make a second selection, there are $m \cdot n$ ways to make the two selections.

Permutation Notation

The expression $_nP_r$ represents the number of permutations of n objects arranged r at a time.

$$_nP_r = \frac{n!}{(n - r)!}$$

Combination Notation

The expression $_nC_r$ represents the number of combinations of n objects chosen r at a time.

$$_nC_r = \frac{n!}{r!(n - r)!}$$

Theoretical Probability

$P(\text{event}) = \dfrac{\text{number of favorable outcomes}}{\text{number of possible outcomes}}$

Probability of an Event and Its Complement

$P(\text{event}) + P(\text{not event}) = 1$, or
$P(\text{not event}) = 1 - P(\text{event})$

Odds

Odds in favor of an event $= \dfrac{\text{number of favorable outcomes}}{\text{number of unfavorable outcomes}}$

Odds against an event $= \dfrac{\text{number of unfavorable outcomes}}{\text{number of favorable outcomes}}$

Experimental Probability

$P(\text{event}) = \dfrac{\text{number of times the event occurs}}{\text{number of times the experiment is done}}$

Probability of Mutually Exclusive Events

If A and B are mutually exclusive events, then
$P(A \text{ or } B) = P(A) + P(B)$.

Probability of Overlapping Events

If A and B are overlapping events, then
$P(A \text{ or } B) = P(A) + P(B) - P(A \text{ and } B)$.

Probability of Two Independent Events

If A and B are independent events, then
$P(A \text{ and } B) = P(A) \cdot P(B)$.

Probability of Two Dependent Events

If A and B are independent events, then
$P(A \text{ then } B) = P(A) \cdot P(B \text{ after } A)$.

Formulas of **Geometry**

You will use a number of geometric formulas as you work through your algebra book. Here are some perimeter, area, and volume formulas.

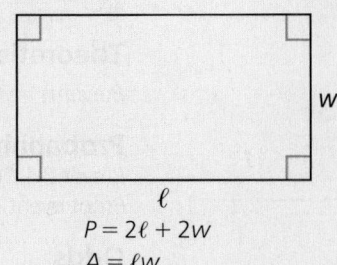

$P = 2\ell + 2w$
$A = \ell w$

Rectangle

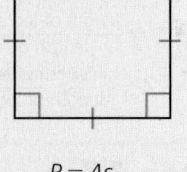

$P = 4s$
$A = s^2$

Square

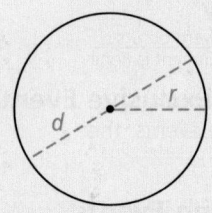

$C = 2\pi r$ or $C = \pi d$
$A = \pi r^2$

Circle

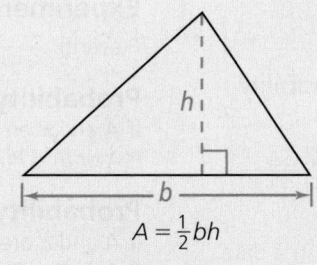

$A = \frac{1}{2}bh$

Triangle

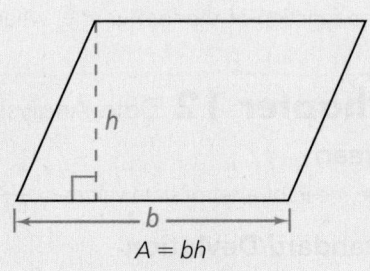

$A = bh$

Parallelogram

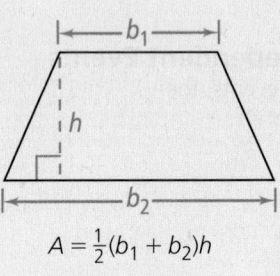

$A = \frac{1}{2}(b_1 + b_2)h$

Trapezoid

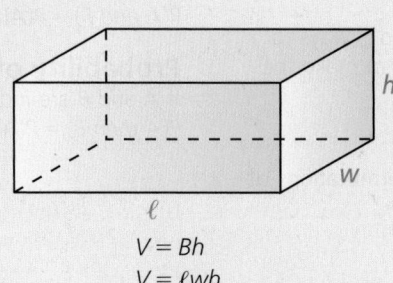

$V = Bh$
$V = \ell wh$

Right Prism

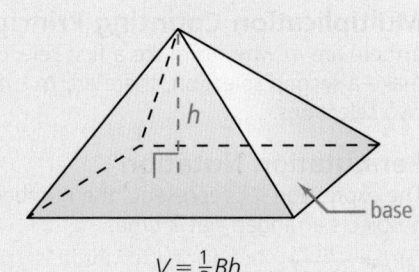

$V = \frac{1}{3}Bh$

Pyramid

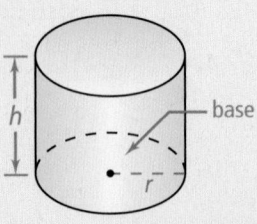

$V = Bh$
$V = \pi r^2 h$

Right Cylinder

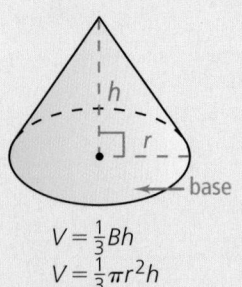

$V = \frac{1}{3}Bh$
$V = \frac{1}{3}\pi r^2 h$

Right Cone

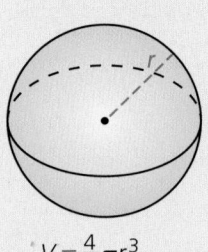

$V = \frac{4}{3}\pi r^3$

Sphere

Visual **Glossary**

English

A

Absolute value (p. 31)   The distance that a number is from zero on a number line.

> **Example**   −7 is 7 units from 0, so
> $|-7| = 7$.

Absolute value function (p. 346)   A function with a V-shaped graph that opens up or down. The parent function for the family of absolute value functions is $y = |x|$.

> **Example**

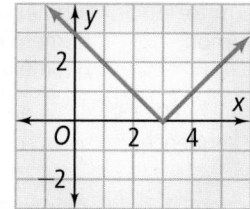

Additive inverse (p. 32)   The opposite or additive inverse of any number a is $-a$. The sum of opposites is 0.

> **Example**   −5 and 5 are additive inverses
> because $-5 + 5 = 0$.

Algebraic expression (p. 4)   A mathematical phrase that includes one or more variables.

> **Example** $7 + x$ is an algebraic expression.

Angle of depression (p. 648)   An angle from the horizontal down to a line of sight. It is used to measure heights indirectly.

> **Example**

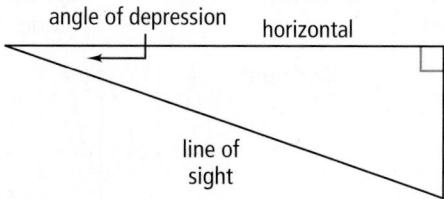

Spanish

Valor absoluto (p. 31)   La distancia a la que un número está del cero en una recta numérica.

Función de valor absoluto (p. 346)   Función cuya gráfica forma una V que se abre hacia arriba o hacia abajo. La función madre de la familia de funciones de valor absoluto es $y = |x|$.

Inverso aditivo (p. 32)   El opuesto o inverso aditivo de cualquier número a es $-a$. La suma de los opuestos es 0.

Expresión algebraica (p. 4)   Frase matemática que contiene una o más variables.

Ángulo de depresión (p. 648)   Un ángulo de la horizontal hacia la línea de vista. Ángulo con que se miden indirectamente las alturas.

English

Spanish

Angle of elevation (p. 648)   An angle from the horizontal up to a line of sight. It is used to measure heights indirectly.

Ángulo de elevación (p. 648)   Ángulo de la horizontal hacia la línea de vista. Ángulo con que se miden las alturas indirectamente.

Example

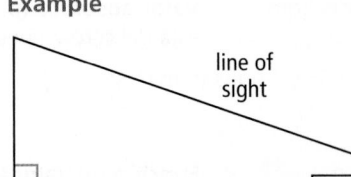

line of sight

horizontal   angle of elevation

Arithmetic sequence (p. 275)   A number sequence formed by adding a fixed number to each previous term to find the next term. The fixed number is called the common difference.

Progresión aritmética (p. 275)   En una progresión aritmética la diferencia entre términos consecutivos es un número constante. El número constante se llama la diferencia común.

Example   4, 7, 10, 13, . . . is an arithmetic sequence.

Asymptote (p. 700)   A line that the graph of a function gets closer to as *x* or *y* gets larger in absolute value.

Asíntota (p. 700)   Línea recta a la que la gráfica de una función se acerca indefinidamente, mientras el valor absoluto de *x* o *y* aumenta.

Example

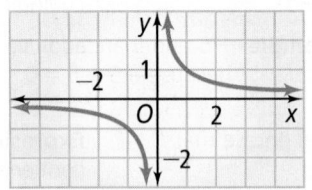

The *y*-axis is a vertical asymptote for $y = \frac{1}{x}$. The *x*-axis is a horizontal asymptote for $y = \frac{1}{x}$.

Axis of symmetry (p. 546)   The line that divides a parabola into two matching halves.

Eje de simetría (p. 546)   El eje de simetría es la línea que divide una parábola en dos mitades exactamente iguales.

Example

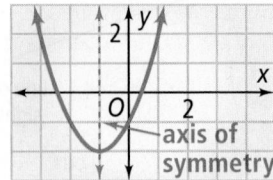

axis of symmetry

English

B

Base (p. 10)   A number that is multiplied repeatedly.

Example $4^5 = 4 \cdot 4 \cdot 4 \cdot 4 \cdot 4$. The base 4 is used as a factor 5 times.

Bias (p. 755)   A sampling error that causes one option to seem better than another. Survey questions or samples can be biased.

Binomial (p. 487)   A polynomial of two terms.

Example $3x + 7$ is a binomial.

Bivariate (p. 754)   A set of data that uses two variables is bivariate.

Box-and-whisker plot (p. 747)   A graph that summarizes data along a number line. The left whisker extends from the minimum to the first quartile. The box extends from the first quartile to the third quartile and has a vertical line through the median. The right whisker extends from the third quartile to the maximum.

Example

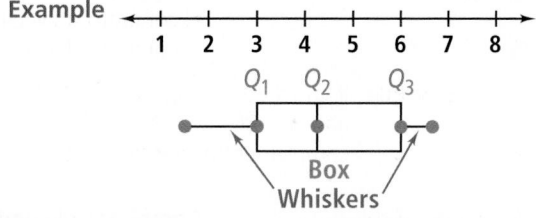

Spanish

Base (p. 10)   El número que se multiplica repetidas veces.

Parcialidad (p. 755)   Error de muestreo que hace que una opción parezca mejor que otra. Preguntas en una encuesta o muestras pueden ser parciales.

Binomio (p. 487)   Polinomio compuesto de dos términos.

Bivariado (p. 754)   Un conjunto de datos que usa dos variables es bivariado.

Gráfica de cajas (p. 747)   Gráfica que resume los datos a lo largo de una recta numérica. El brazo izquierdo se extiende desde el valor mínimo del primer cuartil. La caja se extiende desde el primer cuartil hasta el tercer cuartil y tiene una línea vertical que atraviesa la mediana. El brazo derecho se extiende desde el tercer cuartil hasta el valor máximo.

C

Causation (p. 340)   When a change in one quantity causes a change in a second quantity. A correlation between quantities does not always imply causation.

Coefficient (p. 48)   The numerical factor when a term has a variable.

Example   In the expression $2x + 3y + 16$, 2 and 3 are coefficients.

Combination (p. 765)   Any unordered selection of r objects from a set of n objects is a combination. The number of combinations of n objects taken r at a time is $_nC_r = \frac{n!}{r!(n-r)!}$ for $0 \leq r \leq n$.

Causalidad (p. 340)   Cuando un cambio en una cantidad causa un cambio en una segunda cantidad. Una correlación entre las cantidades no implica siempre la causalidad.

Coeficiente (p. 48)   Factor numérico de un término que contiene una variable.

Combinación (p. 765)   Cualquier selección no ordenada de r objetos tomados de un conjunto de n objetos es una combinación. El número de combinaciones de n objetos, cuando se toman r objetos cada vez, es $_nC_r = \frac{n!}{r!(n-r)!}$ para $0 \leq r \leq n$.

Example   The number of combinations of seven items taken four at a time is $_7C_4 = \frac{7!}{4!(7-4)!} = 35$.

There are 35 ways to choose four items from seven items without regard to order.

English

Spanish

Visual Glossary

Common difference (p. 275)   The difference between consecutive terms of an arithmetic sequence.

Diferencia común (p. 275)   La diferencia común es la diferencia entre los términos consecutivos de una progresión aritmética.

Example   The common difference is 3 in the arithmetic sequence 4, 7, 10, 13, . . .

Common ratio (p. 467)   The fixed number used to find terms in a geometric sequence.

Razón común (p. 467)   Número constante que se usa para hallar los términos en una progresión geométrica.

Example   The common ratio is $\frac{1}{3}$ in the geometric sequence 9, 3, 1, $\frac{1}{3}$, . . .

Complement of an event (p. 770)   All possible outcomes that are not in the event.
$P(\text{complement of event}) = 1 - P(\text{event})$

Complemento de un suceso (p. 770)   Todos los resultados posibles que no se dan en el suceso.
$P(\text{complemento de un suceso}) = 1 - P(\text{suceso})$

Example   The complement of rolling a 1 or a 2 on a number cube is rolling a 3, 4, 5, or 6.

Complement of a set (p. 196)   The set of all elements in the universal set that are not in a given set.

Complemento de un conjunto (p. 196)   Conjunto de todos los elementos en el conjunto universal que no se incluyen en el conjunto dado.

Example   If $U = \{ \ldots , -3, -2, -1, 0, 1, 2, 3, \ldots \}$ and $A = \{0, 1, 2, 3, \ldots \}$, then the complement of A is $A' = \{ \ldots , -3, -2, -1 \}$.

Completing the square (p. 576)   A method of solving quadratic equations. Completing the square turns every quadratic equation into the form $x^2 = c$.

Completar el cuadrado (p. 576)   Método para solucionar ecuaciones cuadráticas. Cuando se completa el cuadrado, se transforma la ecuación cuadrática a la fórmula $x^2 = c$.

Example $x^2 + 6x - 7 = 9$ is rewritten as $(x + 3)^2 = 25$ by completing the square.

Complex fraction (p. 528)   A fraction that has a fraction in its numerator or denominator or in both its numerator and denominator.

Fracción compleja (p. 528)   Una fracción compleja es una fracción que contiene otra fracción en el numerador o en el denominador, o en ambos.

Example $\dfrac{\frac{2}{7}}{\frac{3}{2}}$

Compound event (p. 776)   An event that consists of two or more events linked by the word *and* or the word *or*.

Suceso compuesto (p. 776)   Suceso que consiste en dos o más sucesos unidos por medio de la palabra *y* o la palabra *o*.

Example   Rolling a 5 on a number cube and then rolling a 4 is a compound event.

English

Spanish

Compound inequalities (p. 200) Two inequalities that are joined by *and* or *or*.

Desigualdades compuestas (p. 200) Dos desigualdades que están enlazadas por medio de una *y* o una *o*.

    Examples $5 < x$ and $x < 10$
                    $14 < x$ or $x \le -3$

Compound interest (p. 461) Interest paid on both the principal and the interest that has already been paid.

Interés compuesto (p. 461) Interés calculado tanto sobre el capital como sobre los intereses ya pagados.

    Example For an initial deposit of $1000 at a
              6% interest rate with interest
              compounded quarterly, the function
              $y = 1000\left(\frac{0.06}{4}\right)^x$ gives the account
              balance y after x years.

Conclusion (p. 616) The conclusion is the part of an *if-then* statement (conditional) that follows *then*.

Conclusión (p. 616) La conclusión es lo que sigue a la palabra *entonces* en un enunciado condicional.

    Example In the conditional "If an animal
              has four legs, then it is a horse,"
              the conclusion is "it is a horse."

Conditional (p. 616) A conditional is an *if-then* statement.

Condicional (p. 616) Un enunciado condicional es del tipo *si . . ., entonces . . .*

    Example If an animal has four legs, then it
              is a horse.

Conditional probability (p. 783) A probability that contains a condition that may limit the sample space for an event. The notation $P(B|A)$ is read "the probability of event B, given event A."

Probabilidad condicional (p. 783) Probabilidad que contiene una condición que puede limitar el espacio de muestra de un suceso. La notación $P(B|A)$ se lee "la probabilidad del suceso B, dado el suceso A."

Conjugates (p. 627) The sum and the difference of the same two terms.

Valores conjugados (p. 627) La suma y resta de los mismos dos términos.

    Example $(\sqrt{3} + 2)$ and $(\sqrt{3} - 2)$ are
              conjugates.

Consistent system (p. 365) A system of equations that has at least one solution is consistent.

Sistema consistente (p. 365) Un sistema de ecuaciones que tiene por lo menos una solución es consistente.

    Example

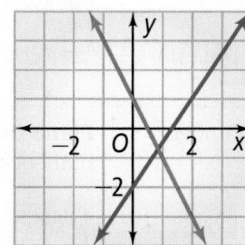

English

Spanish

Constant (p. 48) A term that has no variable factor.

Constante (p. 48) Término que tiene un valor fijo.

Example In the expression $4x + 13y + 17$, 17 is a constant term.

Constant of variation for direct variation (p. 301) The nonzero constant k in the function $y = kx$.

Constante de variación en variaciones directas (p. 301) La constante k cuyo valor no es cero en la función $y = kx$.

Example For the direct variation $y = 24x$, 24 is the constant of variation.

Constant of variation for inverse variation (p. 692) The nonzero constant k in the function $y = \frac{k}{x}$.

Constante de variación en variaciones inversas (p. 692) La constante k cuyo valor no es cero en la función $y = \frac{k}{x}$.

Example For the inverse variation $y = \frac{8}{x}$, 8 is the constant of variation.

Continuous graph (p. 255) A graph that is unbroken.

Gráfica continua (p. 255) Una gráfica continua es una gráfica ininterrumpida.

Example

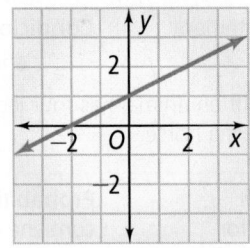

Converse (p. 616) The statement obtained by reversing the hypothesis and conclusion of a conditional.

Expresión recíproca (p. 616) Enunciado que se obtiene al intercambiar la hipótesis y la conclusión de un enunciado condicional.

Example The converse of "If I was born in Houston, then I am a Texan" is "If I am a Texan, then I was born in Houston."

Conversion factor (p. 117) A ratio of two equivalent measures in different units.

Factor de conversión (p. 117) Razón de dos medidas equivalentes en unidades diferentes.

Example The ratio $\frac{1 \text{ ft}}{12 \text{ in.}}$ is a conversion factor.

Coordinate plane (p. 60) A plane formed by two number lines that intersect at right angles.

Plano de coordenadas (p. 60) Se forma cuando dos rectas numéricas se cortan formando ángulos rectos.

Example

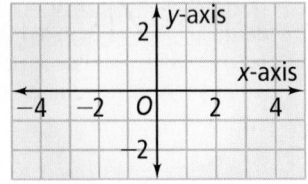

English

Spanish

Coordinates (p. 60)   The numbers that make an ordered pair and identify the location of a point.

Coordenadas (p. 60)   Números ordenados por pares que determinan la posición de un punto sobre un plano.

Example

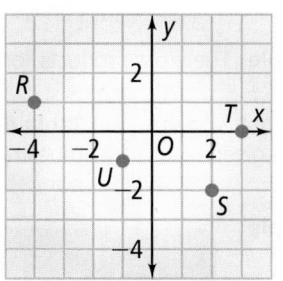

The coordinates of
R are $(-4, 1)$.

Correlation coefficient (p. 339)   A number from -1 to 1 that tells you how closely the equation of the line of best fit models the data.

Coeficiente de correlación (p. 339)   Número de -1 a 1 que indica con cuánta exactitud la línea de mejor encaje representa los datos.

Example

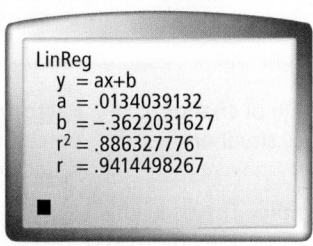

The correlation coefficient is
approximately 0.94.

Cosine (p. 645)   In a right triangle, such as $\triangle ABC$ with right $\angle C$,

cosine of $\angle A = \dfrac{\text{length of side adjacent to } \angle A}{\text{length of hypotenuse}}$, or $\cos A = \dfrac{b}{c}$.

Coseno (p. 645)   En un triángulo rectángulo tal que $\triangle ABC$ con $\angle C$ recto, el coseno de

$\angle A = \dfrac{\text{longitud del lado adyacente a } \angle A}{\text{longitud de la hipotenusa}}$, o $\cos A = \dfrac{b}{c}$.

Example

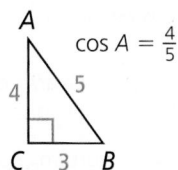

$\cos A = \dfrac{4}{5}$

Counterexample (p. 25)   An example showing that a statement is false.

Contraejemplo (p. 25)   Ejemplo que demuestra que un enunciado es falso.

Example Statement   All apples are red.
Counterexample   A Granny Smith apple is green.

Cross product (of sets) (p. 220)   The cross product of two sets A and B, denoted by $A \times B$, is the set of all ordered pairs with the first element in A and with the second element in B.

Producto cruzado (de dos conjuntos) (p. 220)   El producto cruzado de dos conjuntos A y B, definido por $A \times B$, es el conjunto de todos los pares ordenados cuyo primer elemento está en A y cuyo segundo elemento está en B.

English

Spanish

Cross products (of a proportion) (p. 125)   In a proportion $\frac{a}{b} = \frac{c}{d}$, the products ad and bc. These products are equal.

Productos cruzados (de una proporción) (p. 125)   En una proporción $\frac{a}{b} = \frac{c}{d}$, los productos ad y bc. Estos productos son iguales.

Example   The cross products for $\frac{3}{4} = \frac{6}{8}$ are $3 \cdot 8$ and $4 \cdot 6$.

Cumulative frequency table (p. 734)   A table that shows the number of data values that lie in or below the given intervals.

Tabla de frecuencia cumulativa (p. 734)   Tabla que muestra el número de valores de datos que están dentro o por debajo de los intervalos dados.

Example

Interval	Frequency	Cumulative Frequency
0–9	5	5
10–19	8	13
20–29	4	17

D

Decay factor (p. 462)   1 minus the percent rate of change, expressed as a decimal, for an exponential decay situation.

Factor de decremento (p. 462)   1 menos la tasa porcentual de cambio, expresada como decimal, en una situación de reducción exponencial.

Example   The decay factor of the function $y = 5(0.3)^x$ is 0.3.

Deductive reasoning (p. 25)   A process of reasoning logically from given facts to a conclusion.

Razonamiento deductivo (p. 25)   El razonamiento deductivo es un proceso de razonamiento lógico que parte de hechos dados hasta llegar a una conclusión.

Example   Based on the fact that the sum of any two even numbers is even, you can deduce that the product of any whole number and any even number is even.

Degree of a monomial (p. 486)   The sum of the exponents of the variables of a monomial.

Grado de un monomio (p. 486)   La suma de los exponentes de las variables de un monomio.

Example $-4x^3y^2$ is a monomial of degree 5.

Degree of a polynomial (p. 487)   The highest degree of any term of the polynomial.

Grado de un polinomio (p. 487)   El grado de un polinomio es el grado mayor de cualquier término del polinomio.

Example   The polynomial $P(x) = x^6 + 2x^3 - 3$ has degree 6.

English	Spanish

Dependent events (p. 778) When the outcome of one event affects the probability of a second event, the events are dependent events.

Sucesos dependientes (p. 778) Dos sucesos son dependientes si el resultado de un suceso afecta la probabilidad del otro.

Example You have a bag with marbles of different colors. If you pick a marble from the bag and pick another without replacing the first, the events are dependent events.

Dependent system (p. 365) A system of equations that does not have a unique solution.

Sistema dependiente (p. 365) Sistema de ecuaciones que no tiene una solución única.

Example The system $\begin{cases} y = 2x + 3 \\ -4x + 2y = 6 \end{cases}$ represents two equations for the same line, so it has many solutions. It is a dependent system.

Dependent variable (p. 240) A variable that provides the output values of a function.

Variable dependiente (p. 240) Variable de la que dependen los valores de salida de una función.

Example In the equation $y = 3x$, y is the dependent variable.

Difference of squares (p. 525) A difference of two squares is an expression of the form $a^2 - b^2$. It can be factored as $(a + b)(a - b)$.

Diferencia de dos cuadrados (p. 525) La diferencia de dos cuadrados es una expresión de la forma $a^2 - b^2$. Se puede factorizar como $(a + b)(a - b)$.

Examples $25a^2 - 4 = (5a + 2)(5a - 2)$
$m^6 - 1 = (m^3 + 1)(m^3 - 1)$

Direct variation (p. 301) A linear function defined by an equation of the form $y = kx$, where $k \neq 0$.

Variación directa (p. 301) Una función lineal definida por una ecuación de la forma $y = kx$, donde $k \neq 0$, representa una variación directa.

Example $y = 18x$ is a direct variation.

Discrete graph (p. 255) A graph composed of isolated points.

Gráfica discreta (p. 255) Una gráfica discreta es compuesta de puntos aislados.

Example

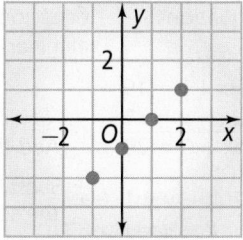

Discriminant (p. 585) The discriminant of a quadratic equation of the form $ax^2 + bx + c = 0$ is $b^2 - 4ac$. The value of the discriminant determines the number of solutions of the equation.

Discriminante (p. 585) El discriminante de una ecuación cuadrática $ax^2 + bx + c = 0$ es $b^2 - 4ac$. El valor del discriminante determina el número de soluciones de la ecuación.

Example The discriminant of $2x^2 + 9x - 2 = 0$ is 97.

Disjoint sets (p. 215)   Sets that do not have any elements in common.

Conjuntos ajenos (p. 215)   Conjuntos que no tienen elementos en común.

Example The set of positive integers and the set of negative integers are disjoint sets.

Distributive Property (p. 46)   For every real number a, b, and c:

$a(b + c) = ab + ac$ $(b + c)a = ba + ca$

$a(b - c) = ab - ac$ $(b - c)a = ba - ca$

Propiedad Distributiva (p. 46)   Para cada número real a, b y c:

$a(b + c) = ab + ac$ $(b + c)a = ba + ca$

$a(b - c) = ab - ac$ $(b - c)a = ba - ca$

Examples $3(19 + 4) = 3(19) + 3(4)$

$(19 + 4)3 = 19(3) + 4(3)$

$7(11 - 2) = 7(11) - 7(2)$

$(11 - 2)7 = 11(7) - 2(7)$

Domain (of a relation or function) (p. 268)   The possible values for the input of a relation or function.

Dominio (de una relación o función) (p. 268)   Posibles valores de entrada de una relación o función.

Example In the function $f(x) = x + 22$, the domain is all real numbers.

 E

Element (of a matrix) (p. 726)   An item in a matrix.

Elemento (de una matriz) (p. 726)   Componente de una matriz.

Example $\begin{bmatrix} 5 & -2 \\ 7 & 3 \end{bmatrix}$

5, 7, -2, and 3 are the four elements of the matrix.

Elements (of a set) (p. 17)   Members of a set.

Elementos (p. 17)   Partes integrantes de un conjunto.

Example Cats and dogs are elements of the set of mammals.

Elimination method (p. 378)   A method for solving a system of linear equations. You add or subtract the equations to eliminate a variable.

Eliminación (p. 378)   Método para resolver un sistema de ecuaciones lineales. Se suman o se restan las ecuaciones para eliminar una variable.

Example $3x + y = 19$

$\underline{2x - y = 1}$

$5x + 0 = 20$ Add the equations to get $x = 4$.

$2(4) - y = 1$ $\rightarrow$ Substitute 4 for x in the second equation.

$8 - y = 1$

$y = 7$ $\rightarrow$ Solve for y.

Empty set (p. 195)   A set that does not contain any elements.

Conjunto vacío (p. 195)   Conjunto que no contiene elementos.

Example The intersection of the set of positive integers and the set of negative integers is the empty set.

English

Equation (p. 53) A mathematical sentence that uses an equal sign.

Example $x + 5 = 3x - 7$

Equivalent equations (p. 81) Equations that have the same solution.

Example $\frac{9}{3} = 3$ and $\frac{9}{3} + a = 3 + a$ are equivalent equations.

Equivalent expressions (p. 23) Algebraic expressions that have the same value for all values of the variable(s).

Example $3a + 2a$ and $5a$ are equivalent expressions.

Equivalent inequalities (p. 171) Inequalities that have the same set of solutions.

Example $x + 4 < 7$ and $x < 3$ are equivalent inequalities.

Evaluate (p. 12) To substitute a given number for each variable, and then simplify.

Example To evaluate $3x + 4$ for $x = 2$, substitute 2 for x and simplify. $3(2) + 4 = 6 + 4 = 10$

Event (p. 769) Any group of outcomes in a situation involving probability.

Example When rolling a number cube, there are six possible outcomes. Rolling an even number is an event with three possible outcomes, 2, 4, and 6.

Excluded value (p. 664) A value of x for which a rational expression $f(x)$ is undefined.

Experimental probability (p. 771) The ratio of the number of times an event actually happens to the number of times the experiment is done.

$$P(\text{event}) = \frac{\text{number of times an event happens}}{\text{number of times the experiment is done}}$$

Example A baseball player's batting average shows how likely it is that a player will get a hit, based on previous times at bat.

Spanish

Ecuación (p. 53) Enunciado matemático que tiene el signo de igual.

Ecuaciones equivalentes (p. 81) Ecuaciones que tienen la misma solución.

Expresiones equivalentes (p. 23) Expresiones algebraicas que tienen el mismo valor para todos los valores de la(s) variable(s).

Desigualdades equivalentes (p. 171) Las desigualdades equivalentes tienen el mismo conjunto de soluciones.

Evaluar (p. 12) Método de sustituir cada variable por un número dado para luego simplificar la expresión.

Suceso (p. 769) En la probabilidad, cualquier grupo de resultados.

Valor excluido (p. 664) Valor de x para el cual una expresión racional es indefinida.

Probabilidad experimental (p. 771) La razón entre el número de veces que un suceso sucede en la realidad y el número de veces que se hace el experimento.

$$P(\text{suceso}) = \frac{\text{número de veces que sucede un suceso}}{\text{número de veces que se hace el experimento}}$$

Visual **Glossary**

English

Spanish

Explicit formula (p. 276)   An explicit formula expresses the nth term of a sequence in terms of n.

Fórmula explícita (p. 276)   Una fórmula explícita expresa el n-ésimo término de una progresión en función de n.

Example   Let $a_n = 2n + 5$ for positive integers n. If $n = 7$, then
$a_7 = 2(7) + 5 = 19$.

Exponent (p. 10)   A number that shows repeated multiplication.

Exponente (p. 10)   Denota el número de veces que debe multiplicarse.

Example $3^4 = 3 \cdot 3 \cdot 3 \cdot 3$
The exponent 4 indicates that 3 is used as a factor four times.

Exponential decay (p. 462)   A situation modeled with a function of the form $y = ab^x$, where $a > 0$ and $0 < b < 1$.

Decremento exponencial (p. 462)   Para $a > 0$ y $0 < b < 1$, la función $y = ab^x$ representa el decremento exponencial.

Example $y = 5(0.1)^x$

Exponential function (p. 453)   A function that repeatedly multiplies an initial amount by the same positive number. You can model all exponential functions using $y = ab^x$, where a is a nonzero constant, $b > 0$, and $b \neq 1$.

Función exponencial (p. 453)   Función que multiplica repetidas veces una cantidad inicial por el mismo número positivo. Todas las funciones exponenciales se pueden representar mediante $y = ab^x$, donde a es una constante con valor distinto de cero, $b > 0$ y $b \neq 1$.

Example

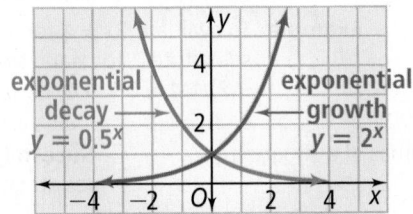

Exponential growth (p. 460)   A situation modeled with a function of the form $y = ab^x$, where $a > 0$ and $b > 1$.

Incremento exponencial (p. 460)   Para $a > 0$ y $b > 1$, la función $y = ab^x$ representa el incremento exponencial.

Example $y = 100(2)^x$

Extraneous solution (p. 635)   A solution of an equation derived from an original equation that is not a solution of the original equation.

Solución extraña (p. 635)   Una solución extraña es una solución de una ecuación derivada que no es una solución de la ecuación original.

Example $\dfrac{b}{b + 4} = 3 - \dfrac{4}{b + 4}$

$b = 3(b + 4) - 4$ Multiply by $(b + 4)$.
$b = 3b + 12 - 4$
$-2b = 8$
$b = -4$

Replace b with -4 in the original equation. The denominator is 0, so -4 is an extraneous solution.

English

Spanish

Extrapolation (p. 337) The process of predicting a value outside the range of known values.

Extrapolación (p. 337) Proceso que se usa para predecir un valor por fuera del ámbito de los valores dados.

 F

Factor by grouping (p. 529) A method of factoring that uses the Distributive Property to remove a common binomial factor of two pairs of terms.

Factor común por agrupación de términos (p. 529) Método de factorización que aplica la propiedad distributiva para sacar un factor común de dos pares de términos en un binomio.

Example The expression $7x(x - 1) + 4(x - 1)$ can be factored as $(7x + 4)(x - 1)$.

Formula (p. 110) An equation that states a relationship among quantities.

Fórmula (p. 110) Ecuación que establece una relación entre cantidades.

Example The formula for the volume V of a cylinder is $V = \pi r^2 h$, where r is the radius of the cylinder and h is its height.

Frequency (p. 732) The number of data items in an interval.

Frecuencia (p. 732) Número de datos de un intervalo.

Example In the data set 4, 7, 12, 4, 5, 8, 11, 2, the frequency of the interval 5–9 is 3.

Frequency table (p. 732) A table that groups a set of data values into intervals and shows the frequency for each interval.

Tabla de frecuencias (p. 732) Tabla que agrupa un conjunto de datos en intervalos y muestra la frecuencia de cada intervalo.

Example

Interval	Frequency
0–9	5
10–19	8
20–29	4

Function (p. 241) A relation that assigns exactly one value in the range to each value of the domain.

Función (p. 241) La relación que asigna exactamente un valor del rango a cada valor del dominio.

Example Earned income is a function of the number of hours worked. If you earn $4.50/h, then your income is expressed by the function $f(h) = 4.5h$.

Function notation (p. 269) To write a rule in function notation, you use the symbol $f(x)$ in place of y.

Notación de una función (p. 269) Para expresar una regla en notación de función se usa el símbolo $f(x)$ en lugar de y.

Example $f(x) = 3x - 8$ is in function notation.

Function rule (p. 262)   An equation that describes a function.

Regla de función (p. 262)   Ecuación que describe una función.

Example $y = 4x + 1$ is a function rule.

 G

Geometric sequence (p. 467)   A number sequence formed by multiplying a term in a sequence by a fixed number to find the next term.

Progresión geométrica (p. 467)   Tipo de sucesión numérica formada al multiplicar un término de la secuencia por un número constante, para hallar el siguiente término.

Example $9, 3, 1, \frac{1}{3}, \ldots$ is an example of a geometric sequence.

Growth factor (p. 460)   1 plus the percent rate of change for an exponential growth situation.

Factor incremental (p. 460)   1 más la tasa porcentual de cambio en una situación de incremento exponencial.

Example   The growth factor of $y = 7(1.3)^x$ is 1.3.

 H

Histogram (p. 733)   A special type of bar graph that can display data from a frequency table. Each bar represents an interval. The height of each bar shows the frequency of the interval it represents.

Histograma (p. 733)   Tipo de gráfica de barras que muestra los datos de una tabla de frecuencia. Cada barra representa un intervalo. La altura de cada barra muestra la frecuencia del intervalo al que representa.

Example

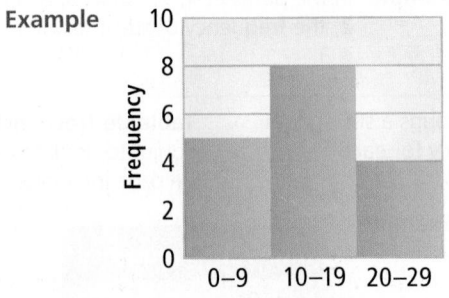

Hypotenuse (p. 614)   The side opposite the right angle in a right triangle. It is the longest side in the triangle.

Hipotenusa (p. 614)   En un triángulo rectángulo, el lado opuesto al ángulo recto. Es el lado más largo del triángulo.

Example

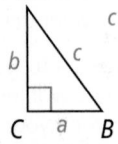

c **is the hypotenuse.**

Hypothesis (p. 615)   In an *if-then* statement (conditional), the hypothesis is the part that follows *if*.

Hipótesis (p. 615)   En un enunciado *si. . . entonces. . .* (condicional), la hipótesis es la parte del enunciado que sigue el *si*.

Example   In the conditional "If an animal has four legs, then it is a horse," the hypothesis is "an animal has four legs."

English | Spanish

I

Identity (p. 104) An equation that is true for every value.

Identidad (p. 104) Una ecuación que es verdadera para todos los valores.

Example $5 - 14x = 5\left(1 - \frac{14}{5}x\right)$ is an identity because it is true for any value of x.

Inconsistent system (p. 365) A system of equations that has no solution.

Sistema incompatible (p. 365) Un sistema incompatible es un sistema de ecuaciones para el cual no hay solución.

Example $\begin{cases} y = 2x + 3 \\ -2x + y = 1 \end{cases}$ is a system of parallel lines, so it has no solution. It is an inconsistent system.

Independent events (p. 777) When the outcome of one event does not affect the probability of a second event, the two events are independent.

Sucesos independientes (p. 777) Cuando el resultado de un suceso no altera la probabilidad de otro, los dos sucesos son independientes.

Example The results of two rolls of a number cube are independent. Getting a 5 on the first roll does not change the probability of getting a 5 on the second roll.

Independent system (p. 365) A system of linear equations that has a unique solution.

Sistema independiente (p. 365) Un sistema de ecuaciones lineales que tenga una sola solución es un sistema independiente.

Example $\begin{cases} x + 2y = -7 \\ 2x - 3y = 0 \end{cases}$ has the unique solution $(-3, -2)$. It is an independent system.

Independent variable (p. 240) A variable that provides the input values of a function.

Variable independiente (p. 240) Variable de la que dependen los valores de entrada de una función.

Example In the equation $y = 3x$, x is the independent variable.

Index (p. 448) With a radical sign, the index indicates the degree of the root.

Índice (p. 448) Con un signo de radical, el índice indica el grado de la raíz.

Example index 2   index 3   index 4
$$\sqrt{16} \qquad \sqrt[3]{16} \qquad \sqrt[4]{16}$$

Inductive reasoning (p. 63) Making conclusions based on observed patterns.

Razonamiento inductivo (p. 63) Sacar conclusiones a partir de patrones observados.

Inequality (p. 19) A mathematical sentence that compares the values of two expressions using an inequality symbol.

Desigualdad (p. 19) Expresión matemática que compara el valor de dos expresiones con el símbolo de desigualdad.

Example $3 < 7$

English

Input (p. 240) A value of the independent variable.

Example The input is any value of x you substitute into a function.

Integers (p. 18) Whole numbers and their opposites.

Example ... $-3, -2, -1, 0, 1, 2, 3, ...$

Interpolation (p. 337) The process of estimating a value between two known quantities.

Interquartile range (p. 746) The interquartile range of a set of data is the difference between the third and first quartiles.

Example The first and third quartiles of the data set 2, 3, 4, 5, 5, 6, 7, and 7 are 3.5 and 6.5. The interquartile range is $6.5 - 3.5 = 3$.

Intersection (p. 215) The set of elements that are common to two or more sets.

Example If $C = \{1, 2, 3, 4\}$ and $D = \{2, 4, 6, 8\}$, then the intersection of C and D, or $C \cap D$, is $\{2, 4\}$.

Interval notation (p. 203) A notation for describing an interval on a number line. The interval's endpoint(s) are given, and a parenthesis or bracket is used to indicate whether each endpoint is included in the interval.

Example For $-2 \leq x < 8$, the interval notation is $[-2, 8)$.

Inverse function (p. 329) If function f pairs a value b with a then its inverse, denoted f^{-1}, pairs the value a with b. If f^{-1} is also a function, then f and f^{-1} are inverse functions.

Example If $f(x) = x + 3$, then $f^{-1}(x) = x - 3$.

Inverse operations (p. 82) Operations that undo one another.

Example Addition and subtraction are inverse operations. Multiplication and division are inverse operations.

Spanish

Entrada (p. 240) Valor de una variable independiente.

Números enteros (p. 18) Números que constan exclusivamente de una o más unidades, y sus opuestos.

Interpolación (p. 337) Proceso que se usa para estimar el valor entre dos cantidades dadas.

Intervalo intercuartil (p. 746) El rango intercuartil de un conjunto de datos es la diferencia entre el tercero y el primer cuartiles.

Intersección (p. 215) El conjunto de elementos que son comunes a dos o más conjuntos.

Notación de intervalo (p. 203) Notación que describe un intervalo en una recta numérica. Los extremos del intervalo se incluyen y se usa un paréntesis o corchete para indicar si cada extremo está incluido en el intervalo.

Funcion inversa (p. 329) Si la función f empareja un valor b con a, entonces su inversa, cuya notación es f^{-1}, empareja el valor a con b. Si f^{-1} también es una función, entonces f y f^{-1} son funciones inversas.

Operaciones inversas (p. 82) Las operaciones que se cancelan una a la otra.

English

Spanish

Inverse variation (p. 692) An equation of the form $xy = k$ or $y = \frac{k}{x}$, where $k \neq 0$, is an inverse variation with constant of variation k.

Variación inversa (p. 692) La ecuación $y = \frac{k}{x}$, ó $xy = k$, donde $k \neq 0$, es una variación inversa con una constante de variación k.

Example The length x and the width y of a rectangle with a fixed area vary inversely. If the area is 40, $xy = 40$.

Irrational number (p. 18) A number that cannot be written as a ratio of two integers. Irrational numbers in decimal form are nonterminating and nonrepeating.

Número irracional (p. 18) Número que no puede expresarse como razón de dos números enteros. Los números irracionales en forma decimal no tienen término y no se repiten.

Example $\sqrt{11}$ and π are irrational numbers.

Isolate (p. 82) Using properties of equality and inverse operations to get a variable with a coefficient of 1 alone on one side of the equation.

Aislar (p. 82) Usar propiedades de igualdad y operaciones inversas para poner una variable con un coeficiente de 1 sola a un lado de la ecuación.

Example
$$x + 3 = 7$$
$$x + 3 - 3 = 7 - 3$$
$$x = 4$$

L

Leg (p. 614) Each of the sides that form the right angle of a right triangle.

Cateto (p. 614) Cada uno de los dos lados que forman el ángulo recto en un triángulo rectángulo.

Example 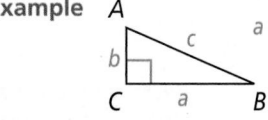 a **and** b **are legs.**

Like radicals (p. 626) Radical expressions with the same radicands.

Radicales semejantes (p. 626) Expresiones radicales con los mismos radicandos.

Example $3\sqrt{7}$ and $25\sqrt{7}$ are like radicals.

Like terms (p. 48) Terms with exactly the same variable factors in a variable expression.

Términos semejantes (p. 48) Términos con los mismos factores variables en una expresión variable.

Example $4y$ and $16y$ are like terms.

Linear equation (p. 308) An equation whose graph forms a straight line.

Ecuación lineal (p. 308) Ecuación cuya gráfica es una línea recta.

Example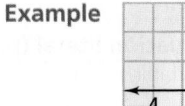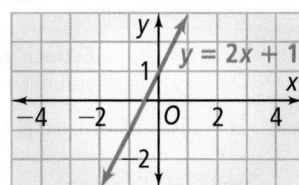

English

Spanish

Linear function (p. 241)   A function whose graph is a line is a linear function. You can represent a linear function with a linear equation.

Función lineal (p. 241)   Una función cuya gráfica es una recta es una función lineal. La función lineal se representa con una ecuación lineal.

Example

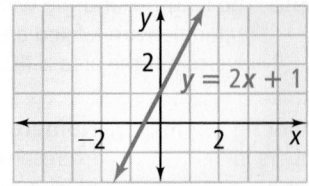

$y = 2x + 1$

Linear inequality (p. 394)   An inequality in two variables whose graph is a region of the coordinate plane that is bounded by a line. Each point in the region is a solution of the inequality.

Desigualdad lineal (p. 394)   Una desigualdad lineal es una desigualdad de dos variables cuya gráfica es una región del plano de coordenadas delimitado por una recta. Cada punto de la región es una solución de la desigualdad.

Example

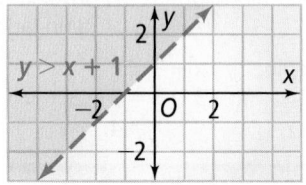

$y > x + 1$

Linear parent function (p. 308)   The simplest form of a linear function.

Función lineal elemental (p. 308)   La forma más simple de una función lineal.

Example $y = x$

Line of best fit (p. 339)   The most accurate trend line on a scatter plot showing the relationship between two sets of data.

Recta de mayor aproximación (p. 339)   La línea de tendencia en un diagrama de puntos que más se acerca a los puntos que representan la relación entre dos conjuntos de datos.

Example

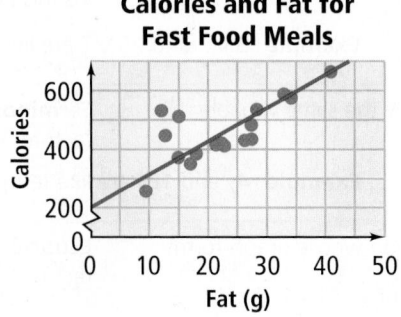

Calories and Fat for Fast Food Meals

Literal equation (p. 109)   An equation involving two or more variables.

Ecuación literal (p. 109)   Ecuación que incluye dos o más variables.

Example $4x + 2y = 18$ is a literal equation.

Matrix (p. 726) A matrix is a rectangular array of numbers written within brackets. A matrix with m horizontal rows and n vertical columns is an $m \times n$ matrix.

Matriz (p. 726) Una matriz es un conjunto de números encerrados en corchetes y dispuestos en forma de rectángulo. Una matriz que contenga m filas y n columnas es una matriz $m \times n$.

Example $\begin{bmatrix} 2 & 5 & 6.3 \\ -8 & 0 & -1 \end{bmatrix}$ is a 2×3 matrix.

Maximum (p. 547) The y-coordinate of the vertex of a parabola that opens downward.

Máximo (p. 547) La coordenada y del vértice en una parábola que se abre hacia abajo.

Example

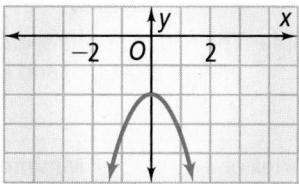

Since the parabola opens downward, the y-coordinate of the vertex is the function's maximum value.

Mean (p. 738) To find the mean of a set of data values, find the sum of the data values and divide the sum by the number of data values. The mean is $\frac{\text{sum of the data values}}{\text{total number of data values}}$.

Media (p. 738) Para hallar la media de un conjunto de datos, halla la suma de los valores de los datos y divide la suma por el total del valor de los datos. La media es $\frac{\text{la suma de los datos}}{\text{el número total de valores de datos}}$.

Example In the data set 12, 11, 12, 10, 13, 12, and 7, the mean is $\frac{12 + 11 + 12 + 10 + 13 + 12 + 7}{7} = 11$.

Measure of central tendency (p. 738) Mean, median, and mode. They are used to organize and summarize a set of data.

Medida de tendencia central (p. 738) La media, la mediana y la moda. Se usan para organizar y resumir un conjunto de datos.

Example For examples, see *mean*, *median*, and *mode*.

Measure of dispersion (p. 740) A measure that describes how dispersed, or spread out, the values in a data set are. Range is a measure of dispersion.

Medida de dispersión (p. 740) Medida que describe cómo se dispersan, o esparcen, los valores de un conjunto de datos. La amplitud es una medida de dispersión.

Example For an example, see *range*.

Median (p. 738) The middle value in an ordered set of numbers.

Mediana (p. 738) El valor del medio en un conjunto ordenado de números.

Example In the data set 7, 10, 11, 12, 12, 12, and 13, the median is 12.

Visual **Glossary**

English

Spanish

Midpoint (p. 114) The point M that divides a segment $\overline{AB}$ into two equal segments, $\overline{AM}$ and $\overline{MB}$.

Punto medio (p. 114) El punto M que divide un segmento $\overline{AB}$ en dos segmentos iguales, $\overline{AM}$ y $\overline{MB}$.

Example M is the midpoint of $\overline{XY}$.

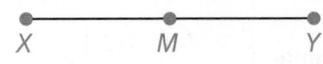

Midpoint Formula (p. 114) The midpoint M of a line segment with endpoints $A(x_1, y_1)$ and $B(x_2, y_2)$ is $\left(\dfrac{x_1 + x_2}{2}, \dfrac{y_1 + y_2}{2}\right)$.

Fórmula del punto medio (p. 114) El punto medio M de un segmento con puntos extremos $A(x_1, y_1)$ y $B(x_2, y_2)$ es $\left(\dfrac{x_1 + x_2}{2}, \dfrac{y_1 + y_2}{2}\right)$.

Example The midpoint of a segment with endpoints $A(3, 5)$ and $B(7, 1)$ is $(5, 3)$.

Minimum (p. 547) The y-coordinate of the vertex of a parabola that opens upward.

Mínimo (p. 547) La coordenada y del vértice en una parábola que se abre hacia arriba.

Example

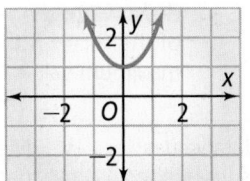

Since the parabola opens upward, the y-coordinate of the vertex is the function's minimum value.

Mode (p. 738) The mode is the most frequently occurring value (or values) in a set of data. A data set may have no mode, one mode, or more than one mode.

Moda (p. 738) La moda es el valor o valores que ocurren con mayor frequencia en un conjunto de datos. El conjunto de datos puede no tener moda, o tener una o más modas.

Example In the data set 7, 7, 9, 10, 11, and 13, the mode is 7.

Monomial (p. 486) A real number, a variable, or a product of a real number and one or more variables with whole-number exponents.

Monomio (p. 486) Número real, variable o el producto de un número real y una o más variables con números enteros como exponentes.

Example 9, n, and $-5xy^2$ are examples of monomials.

Multiplication Counting Principle (p. 763) If there are m ways to make the first selection and n ways to make the second selection, then there are $m \cdot n$ ways to make the two selections.

Principio de Conteo en la Multiplicación (p. 763) Si hay m maneras de hacer la primera selección y n maneras de hacer la segunda selección, quiere decir que hay $m \cdot n$ maneras de hacer las dos selecciones.

Example For 5 shirts and 8 pairs of shorts, the number of possible outfits is $5 \cdot 8 = 40$.

English

Spanish

Multiplicative inverse (p. 40)   Given a nonzero rational number $\frac{a}{b}$, the multiplicative inverse, or reciprocal, is $\frac{b}{a}$. The product of a nonzero number and its multiplicative inverse is 1.

Inverso multiplicativo (p. 40)   Dado un número racional $\frac{a}{b}$ distinto de cero, el inverso multiplicativo, o recíproco, es $\frac{b}{a}$. El producto de un número distinto de cero y su inverso multiplicativo es 1.

Example $\frac{4}{3}$ is the multiplicative inverse of $\frac{3}{4}$ because $\frac{3}{4} \times \frac{4}{3} = 1$.

Mutually exclusive events (p. 776)   When two events cannot happen at the same time, the events are mutually exclusive. If A and B are mutually exclusive events, then $P(A \text{ or } B) = P(A) + P(B)$.

Sucesos mutuamente excluyentes (p. 776)   Cuando dos sucesos no pueden ocurrir al mismo tiempo, son mutuamente excluyentes. Si A y B son sucesos mutuamente excluyentes, entonces $P(A \text{ o } B) = P(A) + P(B)$.

Example   Rolling an even number E and rolling a multiple of five M on a standard number cube are mutually exclusive events.

$$P(E \text{ or } M) = P(E) + P(M)$$
$$= \frac{3}{6} + \frac{1}{6}$$
$$= \frac{4}{6}$$
$$= \frac{2}{3}$$

Natural numbers (p. 18)   The counting numbers.

Números naturales (p. 18)   Los números que se emplean para contar.

Example $1, 2, 3, \ldots$

Negative correlation (p. 336)   The relationship between two sets of data, in which one set of data decreases as the other set of data increases.

Correlación negativa (p. 336)   Relación entre dos conjuntos de datos en la que uno de los conjuntos disminuye a medida que el otro aumenta.

Example

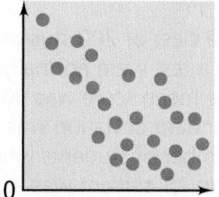

0

Negative square root (p. 39)   A number of the form $-\sqrt{b}$, which is the negative square root of b.

Raíz cuadrada negativa (p. 39) $-\sqrt{b}$ es la raíz cuadrada negativa de b.

Example -7 is the negative square root of $\sqrt{49}$.

***n* factorial (p. 764)**   The product of the integers from n down to 1, for any positive integer n. You write n factorial as $n!$. The value of $0!$ is defined to be 1.

***n* factorial (p. 764)**   Producto de todos los enteros desde n hasta 1, de cualquier entero positivo n. El factorial de n se escribe $n!$. El valor de $0!$ se define como 1.

Example $4! = 4 \times 3 \times 2 \times 1 = 24$

Visual **Glossary**

English

Spanish

No correlation (p. 336) There does not appear to be a relationship between two sets of data.

Sin correlación (p. 336) No hay relación entre dos conjuntos de datos.

Example

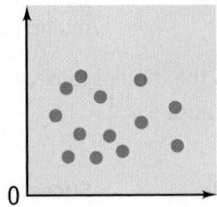

Nonlinear function (p. 246) A function whose graph is not a line or part of a line.

Función no lineal (p. 246) Función cuya gráfica no es una línea o parte de una línea.

Example

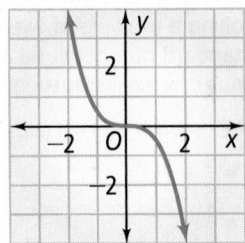

Normal distribution (p. 783) A normal distribution shows data that vary randomly from the mean in the pattern of a bell-shaped curve.

Distribución normal (p. 783) Una distribución normal muestra, con una curva en forma de campana, datos que varían alcatoriamento respecto de la media.

Example

Distribution of Test Scores

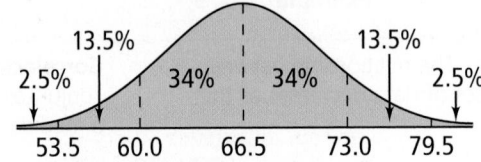

In a class of 200 students, the scores on a test were normally distributed. The mean score was 66.5 and the standard deviation was 6.5. The number of students who scored greater than 73 percent was about 13.5% + 2.5% of those who took the test.
16% of 200 = 32
About 32 students scored 73 or higher on the test.

Null set (p. 195) A set that has no elements.

Conjunto vacío (p. 195) Conjunto que no tiene elementos.

Example { } or ∅

Numerical expression (p. 4) A mathematical phrase involving numbers and operation symbols, but no variables.

Expresión numérica (p. 4) Frase matemática que contiene números y operaciones con símbolos, pero no variables.

Example 2 + 4

English

Odds (p. 771)   A ratio that compares the number of favorable and unfavorable outcomes. Odds in favor are number of favorable outcomes : number of unfavorable outcomes. Odds against are number of unfavorable outcomes : number of favorable outcomes.

Example   You have 3 red marbles and 5 blue marbles. The odds in favor of selecting red are 3 : 5.

Open sentence (p. 53)   An equation that contains one or more variables and may be true or false depending on the value of its variables.

Example $5 + x = 12$ is an open sentence.

Opposite (p. 32)   A number that is the same distance from zero on the number line as a given number, but lies in the opposite direction.

Example -3 and 3 are opposites.

Opposite reciprocals (p. 331)   A number of the form $-\frac{b}{a}$, where $\frac{a}{b}$ is a nonzero rational number. The product of a number and its opposite reciprocal is -1.

Example $\frac{2}{5}$ and $-\frac{5}{2}$ are opposite reciprocals because $\left(\frac{2}{5}\right)\left(-\frac{5}{2}\right) = -1$.

Ordered pair (p. 60)   Two numbers that identify the location of a point.

Example   The ordered pair $(4, -1)$ identifies the point 4 units to the right on the x-axis and 1 unit down on the y-axis.

Order of operations (p. 11)
1. Perform any operation(s) inside grouping symbols.
2. Simplify powers.
3. Multiply and divide in order from left to right.
4. Add and subtract in order from left to right.

Example $6 - (4^2 - [2 \cdot 5]) \div 3$
$= 6 - (16 - 10) \div 3$
$= 6 - 6 \div 3$
$= 6 - 2$
$= 4$

Spanish

Probabilidad a favor (p. 771)   Razón que compara el número de resultados favorables y no favorables. Las posibilidades a favor son el número de resultados favorables : número de resultados no favorables. Las posibilidades en contra son el número de resultados no favorables : número de resultados favorables.

Enunciado abierto (p. 53)   Una ecuación es un enunciado abierto si contiene una o más variables y puede ser verdadera o falsa dependiendo del valor de sus variables.

Opuestos (p. 32)   Dos números son opuestos si están a la misma distancia del cero en la recta numérica, pero en sentido opuesto.

Recíproco inverso (p. 331)   Número en la forma $-\frac{b}{a}$, donde $\frac{a}{b}$ es un número racional diferente de cero. El producto de un número y su recíproco inverso es -1.

Par ordenado (p. 60)   Un par ordenado de números que denota la ubicación de un punto.

Orden de las operaciones (p. 11)
1. Se hacen las operaciones que están dentro de símbolos de agrupación.
2. Se simplifican todos los términos que tengan exponentes.
3. Se hacen las multiplicaciones y divisiones en orden de izquierda a derecha.
4. Se hacen las sumas y restas en orden de izquierda a derecha.

English	Spanish

Origin (p. 60)   The point at which the axes of the coordinate plane intersect.

Origen (p. 60)   Punto de intersección de los ejes del plano de coordenadas.

Example

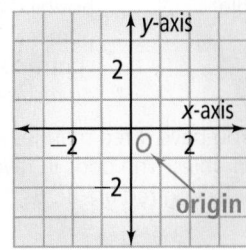

Outcome (p. 769)   The result of a single trial in a probability experiment.

Resultado (p. 769)   Lo que se obtiene al hacer una sola prueba en un experimento de probabilidad.

Example   The outcomes of rolling a number cube are 1, 2, 3, 4, 5, and 6.

Outlier (p. 738)   An outlier is a data value that is much higher or lower than the other data values in the set.

Valor extremo (p. 738)   Un valor extremo es el valor de un dato que es mucho más alto o mucho más bajo que los otros valores del conjunto de datos.

Example   For the set of values 2, 5, 3, 7, 12, the data value 12 is an outlier.

Output (p. 240)   A value of the dependent variable.

Salida (p. 240)   Valor de una variable dependiente.

Example   The output of the function $f(x) = x^2$ when $x = 3$ is 9.

Overlapping events (p. 776)   Events that have at least one common outcome. If A and B are overlapping events, then $P(A \text{ or } B) = P(A) + P(B) - P(A \text{ and } B)$.

Sucesos traslapados (p. 776)   Sucesos que tienen por lo menos un resultado en común. Si A y B son sucesos traslapados, entonces $P(A \text{ ó } B) = P(A) + P(B) - P(A \text{ y } B)$.

Example   Rolling a multiple of 3 and rolling an odd number on a number cube are overlapping events.

$$P(\text{multiple of 3 or odd}) = P(\text{multiple of 3}) + P(\text{odd}) - P(\text{multiple of 3 and odd})$$
$$= \frac{1}{3} + \frac{1}{2} - \frac{1}{6}$$
$$= \frac{2}{3}$$

P

Parabola (p. 546)   The graph of a quadratic function.

Parábola (p. 546)   La gráfica de una función cuadrática.

Example

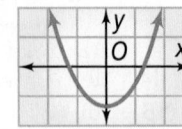

Visual **Glossary**

English

Spanish

Parallel lines (p. 330) Two lines in the same plane that never intersect. Parallel lines have the same slope.

Rectas paralelas (p. 330) Dos rectas situadas en el mismo plano que nunca se cortan. Las rectas paralelas tienen la misma pendiente.

Example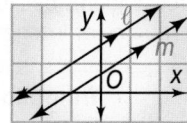

Parent function (p. 308) A family of functions is a group of functions with common characteristics. A parent function is the simplest function with these characteristics.

Función elemental (p. 308) Una familia de funciones es un grupo de funciones con características en común. La función elemental es la función más simple que reúne esas características.

Example $y = x$ is the parent function for the family of linear equations of the form $y = mx + b$.

Percent change (p. 144) The ratio of the amount of change to the original amount expressed as a percent.

Cambio porcentual (p. 144) La razón de la cantidad de cambio y la cantidad original, expresada como un porcentaje.

Example The price of a sweater was $20. The price increases $2. The percent change is $\frac{2}{20} = 10\%$.

Percent decrease (p. 144) The percent change found when the original amount decreases.

Disminución porcentual (p. 144) Cambio porcentual que se encuentra cuando la cantidad original disminuye.

Example The price of a sweater was $22. The price decreases $2. The percent change is $\frac{2}{22} \approx 9\%$.

Percent error (p. 146) The ratio of the absolute value of the difference of the measured (or estimated) value and an actual value compared to the actual value, expressed as a percent.

Error porcentual (p. 146) Razón del valor absoluto de la diferencia de un valor medido (o estimado) y un valor actual en comparación con el valor actual, expresada como un porcentaje.

Example The diameter of a CD is measured as 12.1 cm. The greatest possible error is 0.05 cm. The percent error is $\frac{0.05}{12.1} \approx 0.4\%$.

Percentile (p. 749) A value that separates a data set into 100 equal parts.

Percentil (p. 749) Valor que separa el conjunto de datos en 100 partes iguales.

Percentile rank (p. 749) The percentage of data values that are less than or equal to a given value.

Rango percentil (p. 749) Porcentaje de valores de datos que es menos o igual a un valor dado.

Percent increase (p. 144) The percent change found when the original amount increases.

Aumento porcentual (p. 144) Cambio porcentual que se encuentra cuando la cantidad original aumenta.

Visual **Glossary**

Visual Glossary

Perfect squares (p. 17)   Numbers whose square roots are integers.

Cuadrado perfecto (p. 17)   Número cuya raíz cuadrada es un número entero.

Example   The numbers 1, 4, 9, 16, 25, 36, . . . are perfect squares because they are the squares of integers.

Perfect square trinomial (p. 523)   Any trinomial of the form $a^2 + 2ab + b^2$ or $a^2 - 2ab + b^2$.

Trinomio cuadrado perfecto (p. 523)   Todo trinomio de la forma $a^2 + 2ab + b^2$ ó $a^2 - 2ab + b^2$.

Example $(x + 3)^2 = x^2 + 6x + 9$

Permutation (p. 763)   An arrangement of some or all of a set of objects in a specific order. You can use the notation $_nP_r$ to express the number of permutations, where n equals the number of objects available and r equals the number of selections to make.

Permutación (p. 763)   Disposición de algunos o de todos los objetos de un conjunto en un orden determinado. El número de permutaciones se puede expresar con la notación $_nP_r$, donde n es igual al número total de objetos y r es igual al número de selecciones que han de hacerse.

Example   How many ways can you arrange 5 objects 3 at a time?
$$_5P_3 = \frac{5!}{(5-3)!} = \frac{5!}{2!} = \frac{5 \cdot 4 \cdot 3 \cdot 2 \cdot 1}{2 \cdot 1} = 60$$

There are 60 ways to arrange 5 objects 3 at a time.

Perpendicular lines (p. 331)   Lines that intersect to form right angles. Two lines are perpendicular if the product of their slopes is -1.

Rectas perpendiculares (p. 331)   Rectas que forman ángulos rectos en su intersección. Dos rectas son perpendiculares si el producto de sus pendientes es -1.

Example

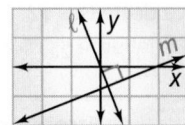

Piecewise function (p. 348)   A piecewise function has different rules for different parts of its domain.

Función de fragmentos (p. 348)   Una función de fragmentos tiene reglas diferentes para diferentes partes de su dominio.

Point-slope form (p. 315)   A linear equation of a nonvertical line written as $y - y_1 = m(x - x_1)$. The line passes through the point (x_1, y_1) with slope m.

Forma punto-pendiente (p. 315)   La ecuación lineal de una recta no vertical que pasa por el punto (x_1, y_1) con pendiente m está dada por $y - y_1 = m(x - x_1)$.

Example   An equation with a slope of $-\frac{1}{2}$ passing through $(2, -1)$ would be written $y + 1 = -\frac{1}{2}(x - 2)$ in point-slope form.

English

Spanish

Polynomial (p. 487) A monomial or the sum or difference of two or more monomials. A quotient with a variable in the denominator is not a polynomial.

Polinomio (p. 487) Un monomio o la suma o diferencia de dos o más monomios. Un cociente con una variable en el denominador no es un polinomio.

Example $2x^2$, $3x + 7$, 28, and $-7x^3 - 2x^2 + 9$ are all polynomials.

Population (p. 754) The entire group that you are collecting information about.

Población (p. 754) El grupo entero del cual juntas información.

Positive correlation (p. 336) The relationship between two sets of data in which both sets of data increase together.

Correlación positiva (p. 336) La relación entre dos conjuntos de datos en la que ambos conjuntos incrementan a la vez.

Example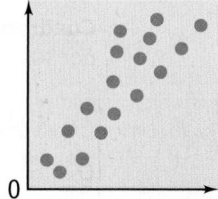

Power (p. 10) The base and the exponent of an expression of the form a^n.

Potencia (p. 10) La base y el exponente de una expresión de la forma a^n.

Principal square root (p. 16) A number of the form $\sqrt{b}$. The expression $\sqrt{b}$ is called the principal (or positive) square root of b.

Raíz cuadrada principal (p. 16) La expresión $\sqrt{b}$ se llama raíz cuadrada principal (o positiva) de b.

Example 5 is the principal square root of $\sqrt{25}$.

Probability (p. 769) How likely it is that an event will occur (written formally as P(event)).

Probabilidad (p. 769) La posibilidad de que un suceso ocurra, escrita formalmente P(suceso).

Example You have 4 red marbles and 3 white marbles. The probability that you select one red marble, and then, without replacing it, randomly select another red marble is $P(\text{red}) = \frac{4}{7} \cdot \frac{3}{6} = \frac{2}{7}$.

Properties of equality (p. 81) For all real numbers a, b, and c:

   Addition: If $a = b$, then $a + c = b + c$.

   Subtraction: If $a = b$, then $a - c = b - c$.

   Multiplication: If $a = b$, then $a \cdot c = b \cdot c$.

   Division: If $a = b$, and $c \neq 0$, then $\frac{a}{c} = \frac{b}{c}$.

Propiedades de la igualdad (p. 81) Para todos los números reales a, b y c:

   Suma: Si $a = b$, entonces $a + c = b + c$.

   Resta: Si $a = b$, entonces $a - c = b - c$.

   Multiplicación: Si $a = b$, entonces $a \cdot c = b \cdot c$.

   División: Si $a = b$, y $c \neq 0$, entonces $\frac{a}{c} = \frac{b}{c}$.

Visual **Glossary**

English   # Spanish

Proportion (p. 124)   An equation that states that two ratios are equal.

Proporción (p. 124)   Es una ecuación que establece que dos razones son iguales.

Example $\dfrac{7.5}{9} = \dfrac{5}{6}$

Pythagorean Theorem (p. 614)   In any right triangle, the sum of the squares of the lengths of the legs is equal to the square of the length of the hypotenuse: $a^2 + b^2 = c^2$.

Teorema de Pitágoras (p. 614)   En un triángulo rectángulo, la suma de los cuadrados de los catetos es igual al cuadrado de la hipotenusa: $a^2 + b^2 = c^2$.

Example

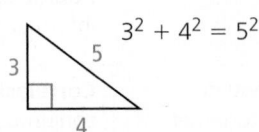

$3^2 + 4^2 = 5^2$

Q

Quadrants (p. 60)   The four parts into which the coordinate plane is divided by its axes.

Cuadrantes (p. 60)   El plano de coordenadas está dividido por sus ejes en cuatro regiones llamadas cuadrantes.

Example

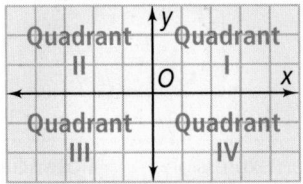

Quadratic equation (p. 561)   A quadratic equation is one that can be written in the standard form $ax^2 + bx + c = 0$, where $a \neq 0$.

Ecuación cuadrática (p. 561)   Ecuación que puede expresarse de la forma normal como $ax^2 + bx + c = 0$, en la que $a \neq 0$.

Example $4x^2 + 9x - 5 = 0$

Quadratic formula (p. 582)   If $ax^2 + bx + c = 0$ and $a \neq 0$, then $x = \dfrac{-b \pm \sqrt{b^2 - 4ac}}{2a}$.

Fórmula cuadrática (p. 582)   Si $ax^2 + bx + c = 0$ y $a \neq 0$, entonces $x = \dfrac{-b \pm \sqrt{b^2 - 4ac}}{2a}$.

Example $2x^2 + 10x + 12 = 0$

$$x = \frac{-b \pm \sqrt{b^2 - 4ac}}{2a}$$

$$x = \frac{-10 \pm \sqrt{10^2 - 4(2)(12)}}{2(2)}$$

$$x = \frac{-10 \pm \sqrt{4}}{4}$$

$$x = \frac{-10 + 2}{4} \text{ or } \frac{-10 - 2}{4}$$

$$x = -2 \text{ or } -3$$

Quadratic function (p. 546)   A function of the form $y = ax^2 + bx + c$, where $a \neq 0$. The graph of a quadratic function is a parabola, a U-shaped curve that opens up or down.

Función cuadrática (p. 546)   La función $y = ax^2 + bx + c$, en la que $a \neq 0$. La gráfica de una función cuadrática es una parábola, o curva en forma de U que se abre hacia arriba o hacia abajo.

Example $y = 5x^2 - 2x + 1$ is a quadratic function.

English

Quadratic parent function (p. 546) The simplest quadratic function $f(x) = x^2$ or $y = x^2$.

Example $y = x^2$ is the parent function for the family of quadratic equations of the form $y = ax^2 + bx + c$.

Qualitative (p. 753) Data that name qualities are qualitative.

Example The data red, blue, red, green, blue, and blue are qualitative data.

Quantitative (p. 753) Data that measure quantity and can be described numerically are quantitative.

Example The data 5 ft, 4 ft, 7 ft, 4 ft, 8 ft, and 10 ft are quantitative.

Quantity (p. 4) Anything that can be measured or counted.

Example A dozen is another way to describe a quantity of 12 eggs.

Quartile (p. 746) A quartile is a value that separates a finite data set into four equal parts. The second quartile (Q_2) is the median of the data set. The first and third quartiles (Q_1 and Q_3) are the medians of the lower half and upper half of the data, respectively.

Example For the data set 2, 3, 4, 5, 5, 6, 7, 7, the first quartile is 3.5, the second quartile (or median) is 5, and the third quartile is 6.5.

R

Radical (p. 16) An expression made up of a radical symbol and a radicand.

Example $\sqrt{a}$

Radical equation (p. 633) An equation that has a variable in a radicand.

Example $\sqrt{x} - 2 = 12$
$\sqrt{x} = 14$
$(\sqrt{x})^2 = 14^2$
$x = 196$

Radical expression (p. 619) Expression that contains a radical.

Example $\sqrt{3}$, $\sqrt{5x}$, and $\sqrt{x - 10}$ are examples of radical expressions.

Spanish

Función cuadrática madre (p. 546) La función cuadrática más simple $f(x) = x^2$ ó $y = x^2$.

Cualitativo (p. 753) Los datos que indican cualidades son cualitativos.

Cuantitativo (p. 753) Los datos que miden cantidades y pueden ser descritos numéricamente son cuantitativos.

Cantidad (p. 4) Cualquier cosa que se puede medir o contar.

Cuartil (p. 746) Un cuartil es el valor que separa un conjunto de datos finitos en cuatro partes iguales. El segundo cuartil (Q_2) es la mediana del conjunto de datos. El primer cuartil y el tercer cuartil (Q_1 y Q_3) son medianas de la mitad inferior y de la mitad superior de los datos, respectivamente.

Radical (p. 16) Expresión compuesta por un símbolo radical y un radicando.

Ecuación radical (p. 633) Ecuación que tiene una variable en un radicando.

Expresión radical (p. 619) Expresiones que contienen radicales.

Radicand (p. 16) The expression under the radical sign is the radicand.

Radicando (p. 16) La expresión que aparece debajo del signo radical es el radicando.

Example The radicand of the radical expression $\sqrt{x+2}$ is $x+2$.

Range (of a relation or function) (p. 268) The possible values of the output, or dependent variable, of a relation or function.

Rango (de una relación o función) (p. 268) El conjunto de todos los valores posibles de la salida, o variable dependiente, de una relación o función.

Example In the function $y = |x|$, the range is the set of all nonnegative numbers.

Range of a set of data (p. 740) The difference between the greatest and the least data values for a set of data.

Rango de un conjunto de datos (p. 740) Diferencia entre el valor mayor y el menor en un conjunto de datos.

Example For the set 2, 5, 8, 12, the range is $12 - 2 = 10$.

Rate (p. 116) A ratio of a to b where a and b represent quantities measured in different units.

Tasa (p. 116) La relación que existe entre a y b cuando a y b son cantidades medidas con distintas unidades.

Example Traveling 125 miles in 2 hours results in the rate $\frac{125 \text{ miles}}{2 \text{ hours}}$ or 62.5 mi/h.

Rate of change (p. 294) The relationship between two quantities that are changing. The rate of change is also called slope.

$$\text{rate of change} = \frac{\text{change in the dependent variable}}{\text{change in the independent variable}}$$

Tasa de cambio (p. 294) La relación entre dos cantidades que cambian. La tasa de cambio se llama también pendiente.

$$\text{tasa de cambio} = \frac{\text{cambio en la variable dependiente}}{\text{cambio en la variable independiente}}$$

Example Video rental for 1 day is $1.99.
Video rental for 2 days is $2.99.

$$\text{rate of change} = \frac{2.99 - 1.99}{2 - 1}$$
$$= \frac{1.00}{1}$$
$$= 1$$

Ratio (p. 116) A ratio is the comparison of two quantities by division.

Razón (p. 116) Una razón es la comparación de dos cantidades por medio de una división.

Example $\frac{5}{7}$ and 7 : 3 are ratios.

Rational equation (p. 685) An equation containing rational expressions.

Ecuación racional (p. 685) Ecuación que contiene expresiones racionales.

Example $\frac{1}{x} = \frac{3}{2x-1}$ is a rational equation.

Rational expression (p. 664) A ratio of two polynomials. The value of the variable cannot make the denominator equal to 0.

Expresión racional (p. 664) Una razón de dos polinomios. El valor de la variable no puede hacer el denominador igual a 0.

Example $\frac{3}{x^3 + x}$, where $x \neq 0$

English

Rational function (p. 699)   A function that can be written in the form $f(x) = \frac{\text{polynomial}}{\text{polynomial}}$. The value of the variable cannot make the denominator equal to 0.

Example $y = \dfrac{x}{x^2 + 2}$

Rationalize the denominator (p. 622)   To rationalize the denominator of an expression, rewrite it so there are no radicals in any denominator and no denominators in any radical.

Example $\dfrac{2}{\sqrt{5}} = \dfrac{2}{\sqrt{5}} \cdot \dfrac{\sqrt{5}}{\sqrt{5}} = \dfrac{2\sqrt{5}}{\sqrt{25}} = \dfrac{2\sqrt{5}}{5}$

Rational number (p. 18)   A real number that can be written as a ratio of two integers. Rational numbers in decimal form are terminating or repeating.

Example $\frac{2}{3}$, 1.548, and 2.292929 . . . are all rational numbers.

Real number (p. 18)   A number that is either rational or irrational.

Example 5, -3, $\sqrt{11}$, $0.666\ldots$, $5\frac{4}{11}$, 0, and π are all real numbers.

Reciprocal (p. 41)   Given a nonzero rational number $\frac{a}{b}$, the reciprocal, or multiplicative inverse, is $\frac{b}{a}$. The product of a nonzero number and its reciprocal is 1.

Example $\frac{2}{5}$ and $\frac{5}{2}$ are reciprocals because
$\frac{2}{5} \times \frac{5}{2} = 1$.

Recursive formula (p. 275)   A recursive formula defines the terms in a sequence by relating each term to the ones before it.

Example   Let $a_n = 2.5a_{n-1} + 3a_{n-2}$.

If $a_5 = 3$ and $a_4 = 7.5$, then
$a_6 = 2.5(3) + 3(7.5) = 30$.

Relation (p. 268)   Any set of ordered pairs.

Example $\{(0, 0), (2, 3), (2, -7)\}$ is a relation.

Spanish

Función racional (p. 699)   Función que puede expresarse de forma $f(x) = \frac{\text{polinomio}}{\text{polinomio}}$. El valor de la variable no puede hacer el denominador igual a 0.

Racionalizar el denominador (p. 622)   Para racionalizar el denominador de una expresión, ésta se escribe de modo que no haya radicales en ningún denominador y no haya denominadores en ningún radical.

Número racional (p. 18)   Número real que puede expresarse como la razón de dos números enteros. Los números racionales en forma decimal son exactos o periódicos.

Número real (p. 18)   Un número que es o racional o irracional.

Recíproco (p. 41)   El recíproco, o inverso multiplicativo, de un número racional $\frac{a}{b}$ cuyo valor no es cero es $\frac{b}{a}$. El producto de un número que no es cero y su valor recíproco es 1.

Fórmula recursiva (p. 275)   Una fórmula recursiva define los términos de una secuencia al relacionar cada término con los términos que lo anteceden.

Relación (p. 268)   Cualquier conjunto de pares ordenados.

Relative error (p. 146)   The ratio of the absolute value of the difference of a measured (or estimated) value and an actual value compared to the actual value.

Error relativo (p. 146)   Razón del valor absoluto de la diferencia de un valor medido (o estimado) y un valor actual en comparación con el valor actual.

Example   You estimated that a plant would be 5 in. tall 3 months after it was planted. The plant was actually 5.5 in. tall 3 months after it was planted. The relative error is

$$\frac{|5 - 5.5|}{5.5} = \frac{|-0.5|}{5.5} = \frac{0.5}{5.5} = \frac{1}{11},$$

or about 9%.

Residual (p. 344)   The difference between the y-value of a data point and the corresponding y-value of a model for the data set.

Residuo (p. 344)   La diferencia entre el valor de y de un punto y el valor de y correspondiente a ese punto en el modelo del conjunto de datos.

Root of the equation (p. 561)   A solution of an equation.

Ráiz de la ecuación (p. 561)   Solucion de una ecuación.

Roster form (p. 194)   A notation for listing all of the elements in a set using set braces and commas.

Lísta (p. 194)   Una notación en la que se enlistan todos los elementos en un conjunto usando llaves y commas.

Example   The set of prime numbers less than 10, expressed in roster form, is {2, 3, 5, 7}.

S

Sample (p. 754)   The part of a population that is surveyed.

Muestra (p. 754)   Porción que se estudia de una población.

Example   Let the set of all males between the ages of 19 and 34 be the population. A random selection of 900 males between those ages would be a sample of the population.

Sample space (p. 769)   All possible outcomes in a situation.

Espacio muestral (p. 769)   Todos los resultados posibles de una ecuación.

Example   When you roll a number cube, the sample space is {1, 2, 3, 4, 5, 6}.

Scalar (p. 727)   A real number is called a scalar for certain special uses, such as multiplying a matrix. See *Scalar multiplication*.

Escalar (p. 727)   Un número real se llama escalar en ciertos casos especiales, como en la multiplicación de una matriz. Ver *Scalar multiplication*.

Example
$$2.5\begin{bmatrix} 1 & 0 \\ -2 & 3 \end{bmatrix} = \begin{bmatrix} 2.5(1) & 2.5(0) \\ 2.5(-2) & 2.5(3) \end{bmatrix}$$
$$= \begin{bmatrix} 2.5 & 0 \\ -5 & 7.5 \end{bmatrix}$$

English

Spanish

Scalar multiplication (p. 727) Scalar multiplication is an operation that multiplies a matrix A by a scalar c. To find the resulting matrix cA, multiply each element of A by c.

Multiplicación escalar (p. 727) La multiplicación escalar es la que multiplica una matriz A por un número escalar c. Para hallar la matriz resultante cA, multiplica cada elemento de A por c.

Example
$$2.5 \begin{bmatrix} 1 & 0 \\ -2 & 3 \end{bmatrix} = \begin{bmatrix} 2.5(1) & 2.5(0) \\ 2.5(-2) & 2.5(3) \end{bmatrix}$$
$$= \begin{bmatrix} 2.5 & 0 \\ -5 & 7.5 \end{bmatrix}$$

Scale (p. 132) The ratio of any length in a scale drawing to the corresponding actual length. The lengths may be in different units.

Escala (p. 132) Razón de cualquier longitud de un dibujo a escala a la longitud real correspondiente. Las longitudes pueden tener diferentes unidades.

Example For a drawing in which a 2-in. length represents an actual length of 18 ft, the scale is 1 in. : 9 ft.

Scale drawing (p. 132) An enlarged or reduced drawing similar to an actual object or place.

Dibujo a escala (p. 132) Dibujo que muestra de mayor o menor tamaño un objeto o lugar dado.

Example

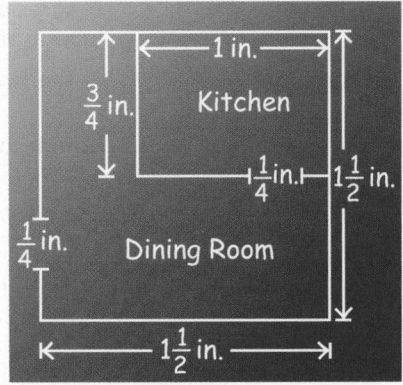

Scale model (p. 132) A three-dimensional model that is similar to a three-dimensional object.

Modelo de escala (p. 132) Modelo tridimensional que es similar a un objeto tridimensional.

Example A ship in a bottle is a scale model of a real ship.

English

Spanish

Scatter plot (p. 336) A graph that relates two different sets of data by displaying them as ordered pairs.

Diagrama de puntos (p. 336) Gráfica que muestra la relación entre dos conjuntos. Los datos de ambos conjuntos se presentan como pares ordenados.

Example

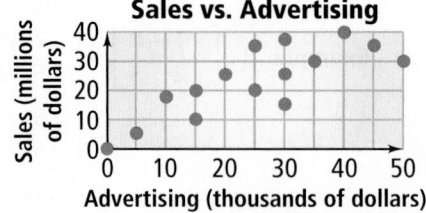

Sales vs. Advertising

The scatter plot displays the amount spent on advertising (in thousands of dollars) versus product sales (in millions of dollars).

Scientific notation (p. 427) A number expressed in the form $a \times 10^n$, where n is an integer and $1 < |a| < 10$.

Notación científica (p. 427) Un número expresado en forma de $a \times 10^n$, donde n es un número entero y $1 < |a| < 10$.

Example 3.4×10^6

Sequence (p. 274) An ordered list of numbers that often forms a pattern.

Progresión (p. 274) Lista ordenada de números que muchas veces forma un patrón.

Example $-4, 5, 14, 23$ is a sequence.

Set (p. 17) A well-defined collection of elements.

Conjunto (p. 17) Un grupo bien definido de elementos.

Example The set of integers:
$$Z = \{\ldots, -3, -2, -1, 0, 1, 2, 3, \ldots\}$$

Set-builder notation (p. 194) A notation used to describe the elements of a set.

Notación conjuntista (p. 194) Notación que se usa para describir los elementos de un conjunto.

Example The set of all positive real numbers in set-builder notation is $\{x \mid x \in \mathbb{R}$ and $x > 0\}$. This is read as "the set of all values of x such that x is a real number and x is greater than 0."

Similar figures (p. 130) Similar figures are two figures that have the same shape, but not necessarily the same size.

Figuras semejantes (p. 130) Dos figuras semejantes son dos figuras que tienen la misma forma pero no son necesariamente del mismo tamaño.

Example

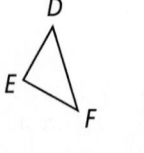 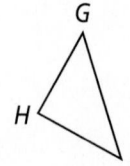

$\triangle DEF$ and $\triangle GHI$ are similar.

English

Spanish

Simple interest (p. 139) Interest paid only on the principal.

Interés simple (p. 139) Intéres basado en el capital solamente.

Example The interest on $1000 at 6% for 5 years is $1000(0.06)5 = $300.

Simplify (p. 10) To replace an expression with its simplest name or form.

Simplificar (p. 10) Reemplazar una expresión por su versión o forma más simple.

Example $\dfrac{3+5}{8}$

Sine (p. 645) In a right triangle, such as $\triangle ABC$, with right $\angle C$,

sine of $\angle A = \dfrac{\text{length of side opposite } \angle A}{\text{length of hypotenuse}}$ or $\sin A = \dfrac{a}{c}$.

Seno (p. 645) En un triángulo rectángulo tal que $\triangle ABC$ con $\angle C$ recto,

el seno de $\angle A = \dfrac{\text{longitud del lado opuesto a } \angle A}{\text{longitud de la hipotenusa}}$, o $\operatorname{sen} A = \dfrac{a}{c}$.

Example 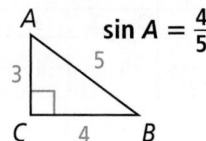 $\sin A = \dfrac{4}{5}$

Slope (p. 295) The ratio of the vertical change to the horizontal change.

slope $= \dfrac{\text{vertical change}}{\text{horizontal change}} = \dfrac{y_2 - y_1}{x_2 - x_1}$, where $x_2 - x_1 \neq 0$

Pendiente (p. 295) La razón del cambio vertical al cambio horizontal.

pendiente $= \dfrac{\text{cambio vertical}}{\text{cambio horizontal}} = \dfrac{y_2 - y_1}{x_2 - x_1}$, donde $x_2 - x_1 \neq 0$

Example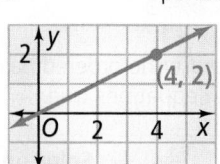

The slope of the line above is $\dfrac{2}{4} = \dfrac{1}{2}$.

Slope-intercept form (p. 308) The slope-intercept form of a linear equation is $y = mx + b$, where m is the slope of the line and b is the y-intercept.

Forma pendiente-intercepto (p. 308) La forma pendiente-intercepto es la ecuación lineal $y = mx + b$, en la que m es la pendiente de la recta y b es el punto de intersección de esa recta con el eje y.

Example $y = 8x - 2$

Solution of an equation (one variable) (p. 54) Any value or values that make an equation true.

Solución de una ecuación (una variable) (p. 54) Cualquier valor o valores que hagan verdadera una ecuación.

Example 3 is the solution of the equation $4x - 1 = 11$.

Solution of an equation (two variables) (p. 61) A solution of a two-variable equation with the variables x and y is any ordered pair (x, y) that makes the equation true.

Solución de una ecuación (dos variables) (p. 61) La solución de una ecuación con dos variables que tiene las variables x e y es cualquier par ordenado que hace que la ecuación sea verdadera.

Example (4, 1) is one solution of the equation $x = 4y$.

English

Spanish

Solution of an inequality (one variable) (p.165)
Any value or values of a variable in the inequality that makes
an inequality true.

Solución de una desigualdad (una variable) (p. 165)
Cualquier valor o valores de una variable de la desigualdad
que hagan verdadera la desigualdad.

Example The solution of the inequality
$x < 9$ is all numbers less than 9.

Solution of an inequality (two variables) (p. 394)
Any ordered pair that makes the inequality true.

Solución de una desigualdad (dos variables) (p. 394)
Cualquier par ordenado que haga verdadera la desigualdad.

Example Each ordered pair in the yellow
area and on the solid red line is a
solution of $3x - 5y \le 10$.

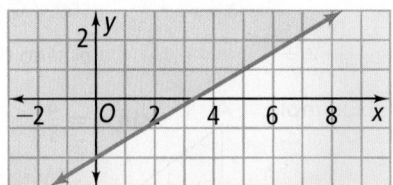

Solution of a system of linear equations (p. 364)
Any ordered pair in a system that makes all the equations
of that system true.

Solución de un sistema de ecuaciones lineales (p. 364)
Todo par ordenado de un sistema que hace verdaderas todas
las ecuaciones de ese sistema.

Example (2, 1) is a solution of the system
$y = 2x - 3$
$y = x - 1$
because the ordered pair makes
both equations true.

Solution of a system of linear inequalities (p. 400)
Any ordered pair that makes all of the inequalities in the
system true.

Solución de un sistema de desigualdades lineales (p. 400)
Todo par ordenado que hace verdaderas todas las
desigualdades del sistema.

Example

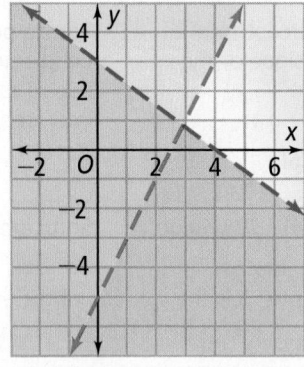

The shaded green area shows the
solution of the system $\begin{array}{l} y > 2x - 5 \\ 3x + 4y < 12 \end{array}$.

English

Spanish

Square root (p. 16)   A number a such that $a^2 = b$. $\sqrt{b}$ is the principal square root. $-\sqrt{b}$ is the negative square root.

Raíz cuadrada (p. 16)   Si $a^2 = b$, entonces a es la raíz cuadrada de b. $\sqrt{b}$ es la raíz cuadrada principal. $-\sqrt{b}$ es la raíz cuadrada negativa.

Example -3 and 3 are square roots of 9.

Square root function (p. 642)   A function that contains the independent variable in the radicand.

Función de raíz cuadrada (p. 642)   Una función que contiene la variable independiente en el radicando.

Example $y = \sqrt{2x}$ is a square root function.

Standard deviation (p. 745)   A measure of how data varies, or deviates, from the mean.

Desviación típica (p. 745)   Medida de cómo los datos varían, o se desvían, de la media.

Example   Use the following formula to find the standard deviation.

$$\sigma = \sqrt{\frac{\sum (x - \bar{x})^2}{n}}$$

Standard form of a linear equation (p. 322)   The standard form of a linear equation is $Ax + By = C$, where A, B, and C are real numbers and A and B are not both zero.

Forma normal de una ecuación lineal (p. 322)   La forma normal de una ecuación lineal es $Ax + By = C$, donde A, B y C son números reales, y donde A y B no son iguales a cero.

Example $6x - y = 12$

Standard form of a polynomial (p. 487)   The form of a polynomial that places the terms in descending order by degree.

Forma normal de un polinomio (p. 487)   Cuando el grado de los términos de un polinomio disminuye de izquierda a derecha, está en forma normal, o en orden descendente.

Example $15x^3 + x^2 + 3x + 9$

Standard form of a quadratic equation (p. 561)   The standard form of a quadratic equation is $ax^2 + bx + c = 0$, where $a \neq 0$.

Forma normal de una ecuación cuadrática (p. 561)   Cuando una ecuación cuadrática se expresa de forma $ax^2 + bx + c = 0$.

Example $-x^2 + 2x - 9 = 0$

Standard form of a quadratic function (p. 546)   The standard form of a quadratic function is $f(x) = ax^2 + bx + c$, where $a \neq 0$.

Forma normal de una función cuadrática (p. 546)   La forma normal de una función cuadrática es $f(x) = ax^2 + bx + c$, donde $a \neq 0$.

Example $f(x) = 2x^2 - 5x + 2$

Stem-and-leaf plot (p. 734)   A display of data made by using the digits of the values.

Diagrama de tallo y hojas (p. 734)   Un arreglo de los datos que usa los dígitos de los valores.

Example

Number of Points				
0	1	7		
1	0	0	2	
2	3	3	7	7	8
3	2	1	5	9	9

Key: $2 \mid 3$ means 23

Step function (p. 348)   A step function pairs every number in an interval with a single value. The graph of a step function can look like the steps of a staircase.

Función escalón (p. 348)   Una función escalón empareja cada número de un intervalo con un solo valor. La gráfica de una función escalón se puede parecer a los peldaños de una escalera.

Subset (p.17)   A subset of a set consists of elements from the given set.

Subconjunto (p. 17)   Un subconjunto de un conjunto consiste en elementos del conjunto dado.

Example   If $B = \{1, 2, 3, 4, 5, 6, 7\}$
and $A = \{1, 2, 5\}$, then A is a
subset of B.

Substitution method (p. 372)   A method of solving a system of equations by replacing one variable with an equivalent expression containing the other variable.

Método de sustitución (p. 372)   Método para resolver un sistema de ecuaciones en el que se reemplaza una variable por una expresión equivalente que contenga la otra variable.

Example   If $y = 2x + 5$ and
$x + 3y = 7$, then
$x + 3(2x + 5) = 7$.

System of linear equations (p. 364)   Two or more linear equations using the same variables.

Sistema de ecuaciones lineales (p. 364)   Dos o más ecuaciones lineales que usen las mismas variables.

Example $y = 5x + 7$
$y = \frac{1}{2}x - 3$

System of linear inequalities (p. 400)   Two or more linear inequalities using the same variables.

Sistema de desigualdades lineales (p. 400)   Dos o más desigualdades lineales que usen las mismas variables.

Example $y \leq x + 11$
$y < 5x$

T

Tangent (p. 645)   In a right triangle, such as $\triangle ABC$ with right $\angle C$,
tangent of $\angle A = \dfrac{\text{length of side opposite } \angle A}{\text{length of side adjacent to } \angle A}$, or $\tan A = \dfrac{a}{b}$.

Tangente (p. 645)   En un triángulo rectángulo tal que $\triangle ABC$, con $\angle C$ recto,
la tangente de $\angle A = \dfrac{\text{longitud del lado opuesto a } \angle A}{\text{longitud del lado adyacente a } \angle A}$,
o la $\tan A = \dfrac{a}{b}$.

Example   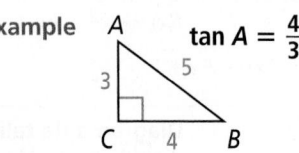 $\tan A = \dfrac{4}{3}$

Term (p. 48)   A number, variable, or the product or quotient of a number and one or more variables.

Término (p. 48)   Un número, una variable o el producto o cociente de un número y una o más variables.

Example   The expression $5x + \frac{y}{2} - 8$ has
three terms: $5x$, $\frac{y}{2}$, and -8.

Term of a sequence (p. 274)   A term of a sequence is any number in a sequence.

Término de una progresión (p. 274)   Un término de una secuencia es cualquier número de una secuencia.

Example -4 is the first term of the
sequence $-4, 5, 14, 23$.

English

Theoretical probability (p. 769)   The ratio of the number of favorable outcomes to the number of possible outcomes if all outcomes have the same chance of happening.

$$P(\text{event}) = \frac{\text{number of favorable outcomes}}{\text{number of possible outcomes}}$$

Spanish

Probabilidad teórica (p. 769)   Si cada resultado tiene la misma probabilidad de darse, la probabilidad teórica de un suceso se calcula como la razón del número de resultados favorables al número de resultados posibles.

$$P(\text{suceso}) = \frac{\text{numero de resultados favorables}}{\text{numero de resultados posibles}}$$

Example   In tossing a coin, the events of getting heads or tails are equally likely. The likelihood of getting heads is $P(\text{heads}) = \frac{1}{2}$.

Translation (p. 346)   A transformation that shifts a graph horizontally, vertically, or both.

Translación (p. 346)   Proceso de mover una gráfica horizontalmente, verticalmente o en ambos sentidos.

Example

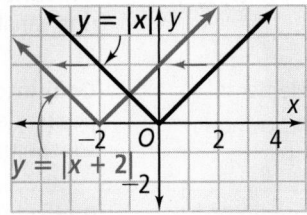

$y = |x + 2|$ is a translation of $y = |x|$.

Trend line (p. 337)   A line on a scatter plot drawn near the points. It shows a correlation.

Línea de tendencia (p. 337)   Línea de un diagrama de puntos que se traza cerca de los puntos para mostrar una correlación.

Example

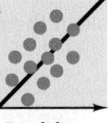 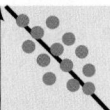

Positive   **Negative**

Trigonometric ratios (p. 645)   The ratios of the sides of a right triangle. See *cosine*, *sine*, and *tangent*.

Razones trigonométricas (p. 645)   Las razones de los lados de un triángulo rectángulo. Ver *coseno*, *seno*, y *tangente*.

Trinomial (p. 487)   A polynomial of three terms.

Trinomio (p. 487)   Polinomio compuesto de tres términos.

Example $3x^2 + 2x - 5$

U

Union (p. 214)   The set that contains all of the elements of two or more sets.

Unión (p. 214)   El conjunto que contiene todos los elementos de dos o más conjuntos.

Example   If $A = \{1, 3, 6, 9\}$ and $B = \{1, 5, 10\}$, then the union of A and B, or $A \cup B$, is $\{1, 3, 5, 6, 9, 10\}$.

English

Spanish

Unit analysis (p. 117) Including units for each quantity in a calculation to determine the unit of the answer.

Análisis de unidades (p. 117) Incluir unidades para cada cantidad de un cálculo como ayuda para determinar la unidad que se debe usar para la respuesta.

Example To change 10 ft to yards, multiply by the conversion

factor $\frac{1 \text{ yd}}{3 \text{ ft}}$.

$10 \text{ ft} \left(\frac{1 \text{ yd}}{3 \text{ ft}} \right) = 3\frac{1}{3} \text{ yd}$

Unit rate (p. 117) A rate with a denominator of 1.

Razón en unidades (p. 117) Razón cuyo denominador es 1.

Example The unit rate for 120 miles driven in 2 hours is 60 mi/h.

Univariate (p. 754) A set of data that uses only one variable is univariate.

Univariado (p. 754) Un conjunto de datos que tiene sólo una variable es univariado.

Universal set (p. 196) The set of all possible elements from which subsets are formed.

Conjunto universal (p. 196) Conjunto de todos los posibles elementos específicos del cual se forma un subconjunto.

Unlike radicals (p. 626) Radical expressions that do not have the same radicands.

Radicales no semejantes (p. 626) Expresiones radicales que no tienen radicandos semejantes.

Example $\sqrt{2}$ and $\sqrt{3}$ are unlike radicals.

Variable (p. 4) A symbol, usually a letter, that represents one or more numbers.

Variable (p. 4) Símbolo, generalmente una letra, que representa uno o más valores de una cantidad.

Example x is the variable in the equation
$9 - x = 3$.

Vertex (p. 547) The highest or lowest point on a parabola. The axis of symmetry intersects the parabola at the vertex.

Vértice (p. 547) El punto más alto o más bajo de una parábola. El punto de intersección del eje de simetría y la parábola.

Example

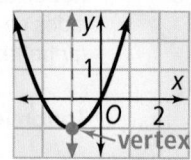

English

Vertical-line test (p. 269)   The vertical-line test is a method used to determine if a relation is a function or not. If a vertical line passes through a graph more than once, the graph is not the graph of a function.

Spanish

Prueba de la recta vertical (p. 269)   La prueba de recta vertical es un método que se usa para determinar si una relación es una función o no. Si una recta vertical pasa por el medio de una gráfica más de una vez, la gráfica no es una gráfica de una función.

Example

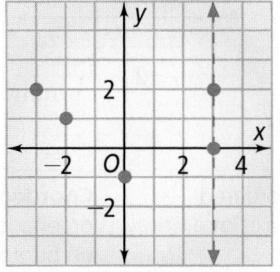

A line would pass through (3, 0) and (3, 2), so the relation is not a function.

W

Whole numbers (p. 18)   The nonnegative integers.

Números enteros positivos (p. 18)   Todos los números enteros que no son negativos.

Example   0, 1, 2, 3, . . .

X

x-axis (p. 60)   The horizontal axis of the coordinate plane.

Eje x (p. 60)   El eje horizontal del plano de coordenadas.

Example

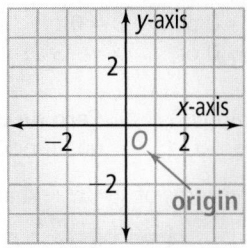

x-coordinate (p. 60)   The first number in an ordered pair, specifying the distance left or right of the y-axis of a point in the coordinate plane.

Coordenada x (p. 60)   El primer número de un par ordenado, que indica la distancia a la izquierda o a la derecha del eje y de un punto en el plano coordenadas.

Example   In the ordered pair (4, −1), 4 is the x-coordinate.

x-intercept (p. 322)   The x-coordinate of a point where a graph crosses the x-axis.

Intercepto en x (p. 322)   Coordenada x por donde la gráfica cruza el eje de las x.

Example   The x-intercept of $3x + 4y = 12$ is 4.

English   ## Spanish

y-axis (p. 60)   The vertical axis of the coordinate plane.

Eje y (p. 60)   El eje vertical del plano de coordenadas.

Example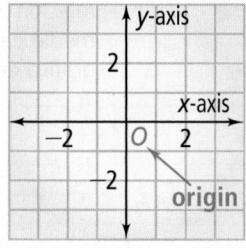

y-coordinate (p. 60)   The second number in an ordered pair, specifying the distance above or below the x-axis of a point in the coordinate plane.

Coordenada y (p. 60)   El segundo número de un par ordenado, que indica la distancia arriba o abajo del eje x de un punto en el plano coordenadas.

Example   In the ordered pair (4, −1), −1 is the y-coordinate.

y-intercept (p. 308)   The y-coordinate of a point where a graph crosses the y-axis.

Intercepto en y (p. 308)   Coordenada y por donde la gráfica cruza el eje de las y.

Example   The y-intercept of $y = 5x + 2$ is 2.

Zero-Product Property (p. 568)   For all real numbers a and b, if $ab = 0$, then $a = 0$ or $b = 0$.

Propiedad del producto cero (p. 568)   Para todos los números reales a y b, si $ab = 0$, entonces $a = 0$ ó $b = 0$.

Example $x(x + 3) = 0$
$x = 0$ or $x + 3 = 0$
$x = 0$ or $x = -3$

Zero of a function (p. 561)   An x-intercept of the graph of a function.

Cero de una función (p. 561)   Intercepto x de la gráfica de una función.

Example   The zeros of $y = x^2 - 4$ are ± 2.

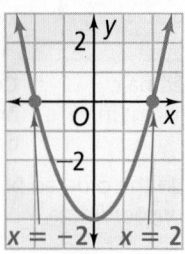

Visual **Glossary**

Selected Answers

Chapter 1

Get Ready! p. 1

1. 6 **2.** 5 **3.** 1 **4.** 20 **5.** 15 **6.** 44 **7.** 72 **8.** 150 **9.** 400
10. 8 **11.** $294 **12.** $\frac{4}{5}$ **13.** $\frac{5}{7}$ **14.** $\frac{1}{7}$ **15.** $\frac{12}{13}$ **16.** 0.7
17. 0.6 **18.** 0.65 **19.** 0.93 **20.** $0.4\overline{6}$ **21.** $\frac{11}{14}$
22. $10\frac{7}{15}$ **23.** $\frac{1}{10}$ **24.** $3\frac{11}{12}$ **25.** Answers may vary.
Sample: $20 + 15$ **26.** Answers may vary. Sample: A
simplified expression is one that is briefer or easier to
work with than the original expression. **27.** Answers
may vary. Sample: To evaluate an expression means to find
its numeric value for given values of the variables.

Lesson 1-1 pp. 4–9

Got It? 1. $n + 18$ **2a.** $6n$ **b.** $\frac{18}{n}$ **c.** No; 6 less a number
y means $6 - y$ and 6 less than a number y means
$y - 6$. **3a.** $4x - 8$ **b.** $2(x + 8)$ **c.** $\frac{5}{12 + x}$ **4a.** the sum of a
number x and 8.1 **b.** the sum of ten times a number x
and 9 **c.** the quotient of a number n and 3 **d.** five times
a number x less 1 **5.** subtract 2 from the number
of sides in the polygon; $n - 2$
Lesson Check 1a. numerical **b.** algebraic **c.** numerical
2a. $9t$ **b.** $x - \frac{1}{2}$ **c.** $m + 7.1$ **d.** $\frac{207}{n}$ **3.** six times a number
c **4.** one less than a number x **5.** the quotient of a
number t and 2 **6.** 4 less than the product of 3 and a
number t **7.** Numerical expressions are mathematical
phrases involving only numbers and operations. Algebraic
expressions are mathematical phrases that include one or
more variables. An algebraic expression includes at least
one variable. A numerical expression does not include any
variables. **8.** $49 + 0.75n$
Exercises 9. $p + 4$ **11.** $\frac{n}{8}$ **13.** $\frac{t}{82}$ **15.** $5n + 6.7$
17. 5 more than a number q **19.** the product of 12 and x
21. one more than the product of 9 and a number n
23. the difference of 15 and the quotient of 1.5 and d
25. 5 more than the product of 9 and a number n;
$9n + 5$ **27.** $8 - 9r$ **29.** $\frac{3}{7}y - 4$ **31.** It should be "the
quotient of 5 and n." **33a.** $4.50n$ **b.** $40.50 **35.** A
37. Answers may vary. Sample: An umpire picks up b
baseballs for a game in addition to the three he had.
39. Answers may vary. Sample: Yes; sometimes you cannot
be sure from a verbal description what order is intended for
the operations. **41.** $2x + 6$ or $6 + 2x$ **43.** G **45.** $\frac{3}{4}$
46. $\frac{5}{14}$ **47.** $\frac{7}{10}$ **48.** $\frac{1}{6}$ **49.** 3 **50.** 3 **51.** 1 **52.** 4

Lesson 1-2 pp. 10–15

Got It? 1a. 81 **b.** $\frac{8}{27}$ **c.** 0.125 **2a.** 27 **b.** 7 **c.** 17 **d.** A
fraction bar acts as a grouping symbol since you simplify
numerator and denominator before you divide.

3a. 3 **b.** 11 **4.** $c + \frac{1}{10}c$; $47.30, $86.90, $104.50,
$113.30
Lesson Check 1. 25 **2.** 8 **3.** $\frac{9}{16}$ **4.** 23 **5.** 1728 **6.** 0
7. exponent 3; base 4 **8.** The student subtracted before
multiplying; $23 - 8 \cdot 2 + 3^2 = 23 - 8 \cdot 2 + 9$
$= 23 - 16 + 9 = 7 + 9 = 16$
Exercises 9. 243 **11.** 16 **13.** $\frac{8}{27}$ **15.** 0.004096 **17.** 2
19. 4.5 **21.** 53 **23.** 16 **25.** 1728 **27.** 4 **29.** 1024
31. 496 **33.** 3458 **35.** mv; 15,000, 20,000, 25,000
37. 256 **39.** 5 **41.** 12

Lesson 1-3 pp. 16–22

Got It? 1a. 8 **b.** 5 **c.** $\frac{1}{6}$ **d.** $\frac{9}{11}$ **2.** about 6 **3a.** rational
numbers, natural numbers, whole numbers, integers
b. rational numbers **c.** rational numbers **d.** irrational
numbers **4a.** $\sqrt{129} < 11.52$ **b.** Yes; $4\frac{1}{3} > \sqrt{17}$ also
compares the two numbers.
5. $-\frac{7}{2}, -2.1, \sqrt{5}, \sqrt{9}, 3.5$
Lesson Check 1. irrational numbers **2.** rational
numbers, integers **3.** $-5, \sqrt{16}, 4.1, \frac{47}{10}$ **4.** about 4 in.
5. rational numbers and irrational numbers **6.** Answers
may vary. Sample: 0.5 **7.** Rational; its value is 10, which
can be written as a ratio of two integers, $\frac{10}{1}$. **8.** Irrational;
$\sqrt{0.29}$ is a nonrepeating, nonterminating number.
Exercises 9. 6 **11.** 4 **13.** $\frac{6}{7}$ **15.** $\frac{1}{3}$ **17.** 1.4 **19.** about 4
21. about 16 **23.** about 18 **25.** about 13 in. **27.** rational
numbers **29.** rational numbers, integers **31.** irrational
numbers **33.** rational numbers **35.** irrational numbers
37. $5\frac{2}{3} > \sqrt{29}$ **39.** $\frac{4}{3} < \sqrt{2}$ **41.** $-\frac{7}{11} < -0.63$
43. $-\frac{22}{25} < -0.\overline{8}$ **45.** $-2, -\frac{7}{4}, \frac{1}{2}, \sqrt{5}, 2.4$ **47.** $-\frac{59}{9}, -6,$
4.3, $\sqrt{20}$ **49.** $-\frac{9}{4}, -\frac{13}{6}, -2.1, -\frac{26}{13}$ **51.** about 12 ft
53. True; Answers may vary; any integer can be expressed
as a rational number. **55.** False; Answers may vary; 2 is a
positive number and an integer. **57.** $\frac{417}{1}$ **59.** $\frac{201}{100}$
61. $\frac{306}{100}$ **63.** about 12 ft **65.** $\frac{864}{275}$; its value 3.14181 . . . is
closer to the value of π than $\sqrt{10}$, which is 3.16227 . . .
67. no; no the real number line extends indefinitely in
both the positive and negative direction. **69.** It is true for
products involving two numbers greater than 0 and less
than 1. **71a.** 4 **b.** 10 **c.** 7 **d.** 13 **73.** I **75.** 16 **76.** 78
77. 512 **78.** $14 + x$ **79.** $4(y + 1)$ **80.** $\frac{3880}{z}$ **81.** $\frac{19}{3}t$
82. 18 **83.** 72 **84.** 442 **85.** 9

Lesson 1-4 pp. 23–28

Got It? 1a. Identity Prop. of Mult. **b.** Commutative
Prop. of Add. **2.** 720 tennis balls **3a.** $9.45x$ **b.** $9 + 4h$
c. $\frac{2}{3n}$ **4a.** True; Commutative Prop. of Mult. and Identity

Prop. of Add. **b.** False; answers may vary. Sample: $4(2 + 1) \neq 4(2) + 1$ **c.** No; it is true when a and b are both either 0 or 2.

Lesson Check 1. Comm. Prop. of Add. **2.** Assoc. Prop. of Mult. **3.** $4.45 **4.** $24d$ **5a.** no **b.** yes **6.** Comm. Prop. of Mult.; Assoc. Prop. of Mult.; multiply; multiply

Exercises 7. Comm. Prop. of Add. **9.** Ident. Prop. of Add. **11.** Comm. Prop. of Mult. **13.** 36 **15.** 9.7 **17.** 80 **19.** $110 **21.** $18x$ **23.** $110p$ **25.** $11 + 3x$ **27.** $1.2 + 7d$ **29.** $1.5n$ **31.** $11y$ **33.** False; answers may vary. Sample: $8 \div 4 \neq 4 \div 8$ **35.** true; Mult. Prop. of -1

37a. 497 mi **b.** 497 mi **c.** The Commutative Property of Addition applies to this situation. **39.** no **41.** yes **43.** yes **45.** no **47.** Hannah can only afford to give all her friends the same gift. **49.** 390 **51.** 0 **53.** no; $(a - b) - c \neq a - (b - c)$ **55.** no; $(a \div b) \div c \neq a \div (b \div c)$ **57.** $(b + c)a = a(b + c)$ and $ba + ca = ab + ac$ by the Comm. Prop. of Mult. **59.** H **61.** F **62.** $-6, 1.6, \sqrt{6}, 6^3$ **63.** $-17, 1.4, \frac{8}{5}, 10^2$ **64.** $-4.5, 1.75, \sqrt{4}, 14^1$ **65.** 14 **66.** 1 **67.** 1.1 **68.** $\frac{1}{18}$

Lesson 1-5   pp. 30–36

Got It? 1. -4 **2a.** -24 **b.** -2 **c.** -2 **d.** -8 **3a.** 13.5 **b.** any value where $a = b$ **4.** -2473 ft, or 2473 ft below sea level

Lesson Check 1. -3 **2.** -3 **3.** -3 **4.** -7 **5.** 2 **6.** -7 **7.** 0 **8.** Subtracting is the same as adding the opposite. **9.** The opposite of a number is the number that is added to it to equal 0. If a number is positive, its opposite is negative. However, if a number is negative, its opposite is positive.

Exercises

11. 5
$-3\ -2\ -1\ \ 0\ \ 1\ \ 2\ \ 3\ \ 4\ \ 5\ \ 6\ \ 7$

13. -5
$-7\ -6\ -5\ -4\ -3\ -2\ -1\ \ 0\ \ 1\ \ 2$

15. 3
$-5\ -4\ -3\ -2\ -1\ \ 0\ \ 1\ \ 2\ \ 3\ \ 4\ \ 5$

17. -12
$-14\ \ \ \ -12\ \ \ \ -10\ \ \ \ -8$

19. -11 **21.** 5 **23.** -11 **25.** 4.4 **27.** -3 **29.** $\frac{13}{36}$ **31.** -20 **33.** 48 **35.** -2 **37.** -20.3 **39.** 1.6 **41.** $\frac{15}{16}$ **43.** $48.54 **45.** -7.1 **47.** The sum of -4 and 5 is $+1$, not -1; $-4 - (-5) = -4 + 5 = 1$ **49.** $-\frac{1}{12}$ **51.** 1 **53.** positive **55.** negative **57.** Find the absolute value of each number. The sign of the number with the larger absolute value will be the sign of the sum. **59.** False; if both numbers are negative, the difference is larger than the sum. If the absolute values are equal, the sum is 0. **61.** 29.62 in. **63.** -2 **65.** Sometimes; only true when $m = 0$, the result will be $-m = m$ **67.** $\frac{W}{10}$ **69a.** Yes; check students' work. Sample: $|3 - 1| = |2| = 2$ and

$|1 - 3| = |-2| = 2$ **b.** No; check students' work. Sample: $|3 + (16)| = |-3| = 3$ but $|3| + |-6| = 3 + 6 = 9$ **71.** H **73.** F **75.** yes **76.** no **77.** yes **78.** rational numbers **79.** rational numbers **80.** rational numbers, whole numbers, natural numbers, and integers **81.** rational numbers **82.** irrational numbers **83.** 18.75 **84.** 17 **85.** 318

Lesson 1-6   pp. 38–44

Got It? 1a. -90 **b.** 2.4 **c.** $-\frac{21}{50}$ **d.** 16 **2a.** 8 **b.** ± 4 **c.** -11 **d.** $\pm\frac{1}{6}$ **3.** $-$72 **4a.** $-\frac{3}{10}$ **b.** Yes; a positive divided by a negative is negative and the opposite of a positive divided by a positive is also negative.

Lesson Check 1. 36 **2.** $-\frac{5}{32}$ **3.** -16 **4.** $\frac{9}{8}$ **5.** -5

6.
$-15\ \ \ \ -10\ \ \ \ -5\ \ \ \ \ 0$

7a. 2; a positive number has a positive and negative square root. **b.** 1; $\sqrt{0} = 0$, so there is one square root.

Exercises 9. 96 **11.** 20.5 **13.** -25 **15.** $\frac{1}{12}$ **17.** 1 **19.** 1.44 **21.** 13 **23.** -30 **25.** $-\frac{5}{9}$ **27.** $-\frac{11}{4}$ **29.** ± 0.5 **31.** -6 **33.** -3 **35.** -0.9 **37.** -250 **39.** $115 **41.** 3 **43.** -1 **45.** $-\frac{25}{18}$ **47.** $\frac{1}{2}$ **49.** $-94\frac{1}{2}$ bushels **55.** -180 **57.** $38\frac{2}{5}$ **59.** $-13°F$ **61.** First change $-2\frac{1}{2}$ to the improper fraction $-\frac{5}{2}$. Then multiply $-1\frac{2}{3}$ by the reciprocal of $-\frac{5}{2}$, which is $-\frac{2}{5}$. **63.** $\frac{800}{63}$, or $12\frac{44}{63}$ **65a.** If $0 \div x = y$, then $xy = 0$. Since $x \neq 0$, then $y = 0$ by the Zero Property of Multiplication. **b.** Suppose there is a value of y such that $x \div 0 = y$. Then $x = 0 \cdot y$, so $x = 0$. But this is a contradiction, since $x \neq 0$. So there is no value of y such that $x \div 0 = y$. **67.** Always; the quotient is -1. **69.** -8 **71.** 1 **73.** 30 **74.** -10 **75.** -10 **76.** Ident. Prop. of Add. **77.** Comm. Prop. of Mult. **78.** Assoc. Prop. of Mult.

Lesson 1-7   pp. 46–52

Got It? 1a. $5x + 35$ **b.** $36 - 2t$ **c.** $1.2 + 3.3c$ **d.** $-2y^2 + y$ **2a.** $\frac{4}{3}x - \frac{16}{3}$ **b.** $\frac{11}{6} + \frac{1}{2}x$ **c.** $\frac{5}{4} + \frac{1}{2}x$ **d.** $\frac{1}{2} - \frac{1}{4}x$ **3a.** $-a - 5$ **b.** $x - 31$ **c.** $-4x + 12$ **d.** $-6m + 9n$ **4.** $29 **5a.** $2y$ **b.** $-12mn^4$ **c.** $8y^3z - 6yz^3$ **d.** No; it is already simplified since there are no like terms to combine.

Lesson Check 1a. $7j + 14$ **b.** $-8x + 24$ **c.** $-4 + c$ **d.** $-11 - 2b$ **2.** $-8x^2 + 3xy + (-9x) + (-3)$ **3.** $2ab + (-5ab^2) + (-9a^2b)$ **4.** yes **5.** no **6a.** yes **b.** no; Commutative Prop. of Mult. **c.** yes **d.** no; Associative Prop. of Add. **7.** $500 - 1$; answers may vary. Sample: These numbers are easily multiplied by 5, making it possible to use the Distr. Prop. to solve this using mental math. **8a.** yes; no like terms **b.** This expression can be simplified by using the Distr. Prop. **c.** No; $12xy$ and $3yx$ are like terms.

Exercises 9. $6a + 60$ **11.** $25 + 5w$ **13.** $90 - 10t$ **15.** $112b + 96$ **17.** $4.5 - 12c$ **19.** $f - 2$ **21.** $12z + 15$

23. $\frac{3}{11} - \frac{7d}{17}$ **25.** $\frac{2}{5}x + \frac{7}{5}$ **27.** $\frac{8}{3} - 3x$ **29.** $5 - \frac{8}{5}t$
31. $11 - n$ **33.** $-20 - d$ **35.** $-9 + 7c$ **37.** $-18a + 17b$
39. $m - n - 1$ **41.** 40.8 **43.** 897 **45.** 23.4
47. 24.6 **49.** \$49.50 **51.** \$4725 **53.** $20x$ **55.** $-2t$
57. $17w^2$ **59.** $5y^2$ **61.** $-3x + y + 11$
63. $3h^2 - 11h - 3$ **65.** the product of 3 and the
difference of t and 1; $3t - 3$ **67.** one-third the difference
of 6 times x and 1; $2x - \frac{1}{3}$ **69.** The sum, not the product,
of the terms should be found; $4(x + 5) = 4x + 4 \cdot 5 = 4x + 20$. **71.** $33x + 22$ **73.** $35n - 63$ **75.** 0
77. $-5m^3n + 5mn$ **79.** $23x^2y - 8x^2y^2 - 4x^3y^2 - 9xy^2$
81. $\frac{1}{3}(9 + 12n) = \frac{9}{3} + \frac{12n}{3} = 3 + 4n$ **83.** Answers
may vary. Sample: $3(m - 2n - 5)$. **85.** $45d + 26$
87. $24 + 2t$ **89.** $-m - 9n + 12$

Lesson 1-8   pp. 53–58

Got It? 1a. open **b.** true **c.** false **2.** yes **3.** $49 = 14h$
4. 9 **5a.** -10 **b.** Answers may vary. Sample: -5 **6.** The
solution is between -8 and -9.
Lesson Check 1. no **2.** 15 **3.** $p = 1.5n$ **5.** Answers
may vary. Sample: $\frac{x}{3} = 15$. **6.** 9
Exercises 7. false **9.** true **11.** false **13.** open **15.** open
17. no **19.** yes **21.** no **23.** yes **25.** $4x + (-3) = 8$
27. $115d = 690$ **29.** 13 **31.** 6 **33.** 12 **35.** 6 **37.** 2
39. 4 **41.** 6 **43.** 4 **45.** 8 **47.** between -5 and -4
49. 2004 **51.** An expression describes the relationship
between numbers and variables. An equation shows that
two expressions are equal. An expression can be simplified
but has no solution. **53.** -6 **55.** between 3 and 4
57. between -3 and -2 **59.** 0 **61.** Check students'
work. **63.** 120 lb **65.** Answers may vary. Sample: The
friend knows an odd number divided by an even number
cannot be an integer.

Review   p. 60

1. Answers may vary. Sample: For the sum -3 for the
x-coordinate, you could roll a 4 on the negative cube and a
1 on the positive cube. For the sum 4 for the y-coordinate,
you could roll a 1 on the negative cube and a 5 on the
positive cube. **3.** Answers may vary. The number on the
negative cube must be greater than the number on the
positive cube.

Lesson 1-9   pp. 61–66

Got It? 1a. yes **b.** yes **c.** no **d.** yes
2a.

Megan's and Will's Laps					
Megan's laps	1	2	3	4	5
Will's laps	7	8	9	10	11

$y = x + 6$

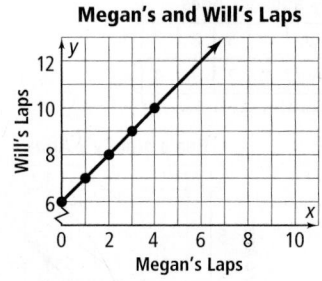

Megan's and Will's Laps

b. The graph would start at (0, 5) instead of (0, 2) and y
would always be 5 greater than x.

3a.

Orange tiles	4	8	12	16
Total tiles	9	18	27	36

54 tiles

b.

Blue tiles	1	2	3	4
Yellow tiles	2	4	6	8

48 yellow tiles

Lesson Check 1. no **2.** yes
3.

Drink Cost				
Drinks bought	1	2	3	4
Cost (\$)	2.50	5	7.50	10

$y = 2.50x$

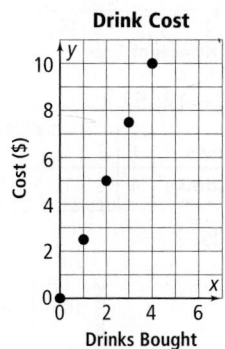

Drink Cost

4. 110 Calories **5.** With inductive reasoning, conclusions
are reached by observing patterns. With deductive
reasoning, conclusions are reached by reasoning logically
from given facts. **6.** Answers may vary. Sample: Both
equations contain unknown values. An equation in
one variable represents a situation with one unknown
quantity. An equation in two variables represents a
situation where two variable quantities have a
relationship. **7.** All; y is 2 more than x.
Exercises 9. no **11.** no **13.** yes **15.** yes

17.

Bea's and Ty's Ages				
Bea's age	4	5	6	7
Ty's age	1	2	3	4

$y = x - 3$

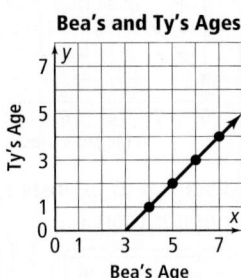

Bea's and Ty's Ages

19.

Sides and Triangles				
Number of sides	3	6	9	12
Number of triangles	1	2	3	4

$y = \frac{1}{3}x$

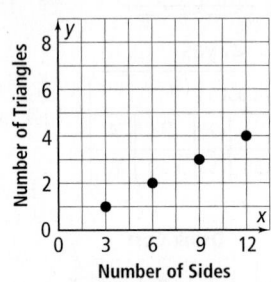

21. 56 in. **23.** $y = x - 12$; 52 in.

25.

Number of Houses	1	2	3	4	5
Number of Windows	4	8	12	16	20

a. 36 windows **b.** $k + 4$

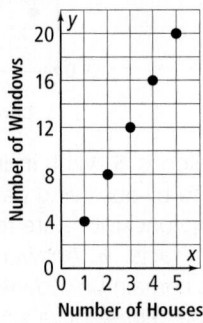

27. yes **29.** no **31.** 11 h **33.** Check students' work.
35. $y = -x - 3.5$; the graph is of a line, which passes through $(0, -3.5)$, $(3.5, 0)$ **37.** H **39.** F **40.** no **41.** yes
42. yes **43–48.** Check students' work. **47.** 9 **48.** −3
49. −14 **50.** −27 **51.** 40 **52.** −30 **53.** −1 **54.** −81

Chapter Review   pp. 68–72

1. irrational **2.** opposite **3.** like terms **4.** absolute value
5. inductive reasoning **6.** 737w **7.** $q - 8$ **8.** $x + 84$

9. $51t + 9$ **10.** $\frac{63}{h} - 14$ **11.** $b - \frac{k}{5}$ **12.** the sum of 12 and
a number a **13.** 31 less than a number r **14.** the product
of 19 and a number t **15.** the quotient of b
and 3 **16.** 3 less than the product of 7 and c **17.** the sum
of 2 and the quotient of x and 8 **18.** 6 less than the
quotient of y and 11 **19.** 13 more than the product of 21
and d **20.** 81 **21.** 125 **22.** $\frac{1}{36}$ **23.** 9.8 **24.** 100
25. 48 **26.** $8\frac{1}{3}$ **27.** 40 **28.** 79 **29.** 123 **30a.** 216
b. The surface area is reduced to a fourth of its
previous value. **31.** 615 mi **32.** irrational **33.** rational
34. irrational **35.** rational **36.** 10 **37.** 7 **38.** 5
39. rational numbers, integers **40.** rational numbers
41. irrational numbers **42.** rational numbers, whole
numbers, natural numbers, integers **43.** rational numbers
44. rational numbers **45.** $-1\frac{4}{5}, -1\frac{2}{3}, 1.6$ **46.** $-0.8, \frac{7}{9}, \sqrt{3}$
47. $9w - 31$ **48.** −96 **49.** 0 **50.** $41 - 4t$ **51.** 1
52. yes **53.** no **54.** no **55.** no **56.** 5 **57.** −5 **58.** −9
59. 1.8 **60.** −144 **61.** 40 **62.** −3 **63.** −19 **64.** 3
65. −8 **66.** 60 **67.** 16 **68.** 12 **69.** −11 **70.** 19
71. −100 **72.** −56 **73.** 225 **74.** $-\frac{3}{10}$ **75.** $10x - 15$
76. $-14 + 2a$ **77.** $-\frac{1}{2}j + 4$ **78.** v^2 **79.** $6y - 6$
80. $\frac{3}{2}y - \frac{1}{4}$ **81.** $6 - 6y$ **82.** $y - 3$ **83.** $-\frac{1}{3}y + 6$
84. $-2ab^2$ **85.** $2850 **86.** Yes; the variable parts of the
terms are the same. **87.** yes **88.** no **89.** no **90.** yes
91. 10 **92.** between 12 and 13 **93.** between 2 and 3
94. between 3 and 4 **95.** yes **96.** no **97.** no **98.** no
99. y is 5 more than the product of 10 and x;
$y = 10x + 5$.
55, 65, 75

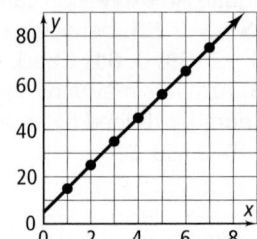

Chapter 2

Get Ready!   p. 77

1. Answers may vary. Sample: For each lawn mowed,
$7.50 is earned; $y = 7.50x$. **2.** Answers may vary. Sample:
30 pages are read each hour; $y = 30x$. **3.** 3
4. −10 **5.** 8 **6.** −8 **7.** 7.14 **8.** 16.4 **9.** $-\frac{9}{20}$ **10.** $-\frac{7}{15}$
11. 17 **12.** −3 **13.** 576 **14.** −2.75 **15.** $16k^2$ **16.** $13xy$
17. $2t + 2$ **18.** $12x - 4$ **19.** Answers may vary. Sample:
The shirts might look the same but be different sizes or
different colors; the triangles will be the same shape but
different sizes. **20.** Answers may vary. Sample: The model
ship is the same shape but just a smaller size than the
actual ship.

Lesson 2-1   pp. 81–87

Got It? 1a. -8 **b.** The Subtr. Prop. of Eq. states that subtracting the same number from each side of an equation produces another equation that is equivalent. **2a.** -6 **b.** 2 **3a.** $\frac{2}{3}$ **b.** -4.375 **4a.** 57 **b.** -72 **5a.** 16 **b.** Yes; multiplying each side of the second equation by the reciprocal of $\frac{2}{3}$ produces the first equation. **6.** 6 months
Lesson Check 1. -4 **2.** 13 **3.** $4\frac{4}{5}$ **4.** $\frac{1}{3}b = 117$; 351 pages **5.** Subtr. Prop. of Eq. **6.** Div. Prop. of Eq. **7.** Add. Prop. of Eq. **8.** Mult. Prop. of Eq. **9.** Check students' work.
Exercises 11. 19 **13.** -9 **15.** 26 **17.** 7.5 **19.** 132 **21.** 13.5 **23.** 2 **25.** -4 **27.** -4 **29.** 0.16 **31.** 5 **33.** $-\frac{1}{2}$ **35.** 175 **37.** -117 **39.** 81 **41.** -34 **43.** 12 **45.** -25 **47.** 81 **49.** 24 **51.** p = city's population at start of three-year period; $p - 7525 = 581,600$; 589,125 **53.** \$4500 **55.** $-\frac{1}{21}$ **57.** $7\frac{1}{3}$ **59.** $31\frac{1}{4}$ **61.** $\frac{1}{3}$ **63.** 0.8 **65.** $2\frac{1}{2}$ **67.** -25 **69.** $-\frac{1}{2}$ **71.** Each side of the equation should be multiplied by 9, not $\frac{1}{9}$; $(9)(-36) = (9)\left(\frac{x}{9}\right)$, so $x = -324$. **73.** 21 aces **75.** 2450 letters **77.** $\frac{1}{2}s = 12$ **79.** A **81.** B **82.** 10,000 **83.** $52x$ **84.** $6 - x$ **85.** $m + 4$ **86.** 2 **87.** $\frac{25}{36}$ **88.** 1

Lesson 2-2   pp. 88–93

Got It? 1. 16 **2.** 56 ads **3a.** 26 **b.** $6 = \frac{x}{4} - \frac{2}{4}$; 26; answers may vary. Sample: The equation in part (a) is easier because it uses fewer fractions.
4. $\frac{x}{3} - 5 + 5 = 4 + 5$ Add. Prop. of Eq.

$\frac{x}{3} = 9$ Use addition to simplify.

$\frac{x}{3} \cdot 3 = 9 \cdot 3$ Mult. Prop. of Eq.

$x = 27$ Use multiplication to simplify.

Lesson Check 1. -5 **2.** 63 **3.** -7 **4.** -13 **5.** \$.62 **6.** Subtr. Prop. of Eq. and Mult. Prop. of Eq.; subtr. **7.** Add. Prop. of Eq. and Div. Prop. of Eq.; add. **8.** Add. Prop. of Eq. and Mult. Prop. of Eq.; add. **9.** Subtr. Prop. of Eq. and Div. Prop. of Eq.; subtr. **10.** Answers may vary. Sample: No, you must either multiply both sides by 5 first or write the left side as the difference of two fractions and then add $\frac{3}{5}$ to both sides.
Exercises 11. -12 **13.** -1 **15.** -2 **17.** -27 **19.** 126 **21.** -3 **23.** 16 boxes **25.** \$1150 **27.** 29 **29.** -2 **31.** -8 **33.** 8 **35.** 6 **37.** -15 **39.** 2.7 **41.** 5 **43.** -3.8 **45.** 0.449
47. $15 - 9 = 9 - 3p - 9$ Subt. Prop. of Eq.

$6 = -3p$ Use subtraction to simplify.

$\frac{6}{-3} = \frac{-3p}{-3}$ Div. Prop of Eq.

$-2 = p$ Use division to simplify.

49. $9 + \frac{c}{-5} - 9 = -5 - 9$ Sub. Prop. of Eq.

$\frac{c}{-5} = -14$ Use subtraction to simplify.

$\frac{c}{-5} \cdot -5 = -14 \cdot -5$ Mult. Prop. of Eq.

$c = 70$ Use multiplication to simplify.

51. 4 should be added to each side; $2x - 4 + 4 = 8 + 4$ so $2x = 12$ and $x = 6$. **53a.** 4 **b.** yes **c.** Answers may vary. Sample: The method in part (a) is easier because it doesn't involve fractions. **55.** 10.5 **57.** 4 **59.** about 2 km **61.** 2 in. **63.** No; the left side of the equation is 0 and the right side of the equation is 4. **65.** No; division by 0 is not allowed. **67.** 46 **69.** 5 **70.** 3.8 **71.** 144 **72.** 6.5 **73.** false; sample: $|-5| - |2| \ne -5 - 2$ **74.** false; sample: $-4 + 1 = -3$, $|-4| = 4$ and $|-3| = 3$ **75.** $35 - 7t$ **76.** $4x - 10$ **77.** $-6 + 3b$ **78.** $10 - 25n$

Lesson 2-3   pp. 94–100

Got It? 1a. 6 **b.** 3 **2.** \$14 **3a.** 6 **b.** Yes; divide both sides of the equation by 3 first. **4a.** $2\frac{14}{23}$ **b.** $2\frac{1}{6}$ **5.** 12.55
Lesson Check 1. $4\frac{11}{15}$ **2.** -7 **3.** 2 **4.** 2 **5.** 16 ft **6.** Answers may vary. Sample: Subtract 1.3 from each side, and then divide each side by 0.5. **7.** Answers may vary. Sample: Apply the Distr. Prop., and then add 28 to each side and divide each side by 21. **8.** Answers may vary. Sample: Multiply each side by the common denominator 18 to clear the fractions. Add 72 to each side and then divide by -4. **9.** Answers may vary. Sample: Amelia's method; it does not involve working with fractions until the end.
Exercises 11. $2\frac{6}{7}$ **13.** 6 **15.** $5\frac{4}{7}$ **17.** -10 **19.** $3x + 6x + 20 = 92$; \$8 per h **21.** 6 **23.** 3.75 or $3\frac{3}{4}$ **25.** $7\frac{3}{7}$ **27.** $\frac{1}{6}$ **29.** 9.75 or $9\frac{3}{4}$ **31.** $\frac{7}{25}$ **33.** $2\frac{1}{3}$ **35.** $56\frac{5}{8}$ **37.** $\frac{1}{5}$ **39.** 3.5 **41.** 5 **43.** 4.27 **45.** $43\frac{3}{7}$ **47.** $3\frac{5}{16}$ **49.** 1.5 or $1\frac{1}{2}$ **51.** 2 **53.** $6\frac{2}{3}$ **55.** \$15 **57.** Answers may vary. Sample: Combine the like terms on the left side of the equation. **59.** 3 games **61.** 25 **63.** 20 **65.** 4 weeks **67.** 4 c

Lesson 2-4   pp. 102–108

Got It? 1a. -4 **b.** The answer is the same, -4. **2.** about 27 months **3a.** -5 **b.** 4 **4a.** infinitely many solutions **b.** no solution
Lesson Check 1. 7 **2.** -3 **3.** infinitely many solutions **4.** no solution **5.** 100 business cards **6.** C **7.** A **8.** B **9.** If the numeric values are the same on both sides, it is an identity. If they are different, there is no solution.
Exercises 11. -9 **13.** 6 **15.** -4 **17.** $-1\frac{3}{4}$ **19.** 22 ft **21.** 25 **23.** -37 **25.** 18 **27.** no solution **29.** no solution **31.** identity **33.** $\frac{2}{63}$ **35.** -19 **37.** no solution **39.** -9 **41a.** $\frac{d}{60}$ **b.** $\frac{d}{40}$ **c.** $\frac{d}{60} + 1 = \frac{d}{40}$; 120 mi; 48 mi/h **43.** Subtraction should be used to isolate the variable, not division by the variable. $2x = 6x$, so $0 = 4x$, and $x = 0$. **45.** 2 months **47.** about 857 bottles **49a.** always true **b.** sometimes true **c.** sometimes true **51.** Check students' work. **53.** Check students' work. **55.** Check students' work. **57.** B **59.** A **60.** 5 **61.** -6 **62.** 1 **63.** 0.9 m **64.** 22 **65.** 9 **66.** 11.2

Lesson 2-5   pp. 109–114

Got It? 1a. $\frac{4+5n}{2}$; -3; 2, 7 **b.** $y = 10$; $y = 4$
2. $x = \frac{-t-r}{p}$ **3.** 6 in. **4.** about 55 days
Lesson Check 1. $y = \frac{2x+12}{5}$ **2.** $b = \frac{a+10}{2}$
3. $x = \frac{p}{m+2n}$ **4.** $F = \frac{9}{5}C + 32$ **5.** 40 yd **6.** literal
equation **7.** literal equation **8.** both **9.** both
10. Answers may vary. Sample: They are the same in each
case since you are isolating a variable by using inverse
operations. They are different because, in an equation in
one variable, to isolate the variable, inverse operations are
used on numbers only. In a literal equation, inverse operations
are used on variables as well as numbers.
Exercises 11. $y = -2x + 5$; 7; 5; -1 **13.** $y = \frac{3x-9}{5}$;
$-\frac{12}{5}$; $-\frac{9}{5}$; $-\frac{6}{5}$ **15.** $y = -\frac{5x-4}{4}$; $-\frac{1}{4}$; $-\frac{3}{2}$; $-\frac{11}{4}$
17. $y = \frac{x+4}{4}$; $\frac{1}{2}$; 2; $\frac{5}{2}$ **19.** $x = \frac{p}{m+n}$ **21.** $x = \frac{t}{r+s}$
23. $x = \frac{S-C}{C}$ **25.** $x = \frac{A-C}{Bt}$ **27.** $x = 2y - 4$ **29.** 4.5 in.
31. 7 cm **33.** 0.4 h **35.** $h = \frac{n}{7\ell}$; 8 ft **37.** $x = \frac{ay}{b} + a$
39. $h = \frac{3V}{\pi r^2}$ **41.** $a = 2b - x$ **43.** $-108.4°F$ **45.** 3 was
added to the left side of the equation instead of
subtracted; $2m - 3 = -6n$, $\frac{2m-3}{-6} = n$. **47.** 5 cm³
49a. $A = 2s^2 + 4sh$ **b.** $h = \frac{A-2s^2}{4s}$; 14 cm
c. $A = 6s^2$ **51.** 6 **53.** 92 chirps **54.** 5 **55.** 3 **56.** -4
57. 3 **58.** identity **59.** no solution **60.** 147 **61.** -40
62. 567 **63.** 100 **64.** 3 **65.** $\frac{8}{5}$ **66.** $\frac{7}{45}$

Lesson 2-6   pp. 116–121

Got It? 1. No; Store C is still the lowest. **2.** 12.5 m
3a. about 442 m **b.** about 205 euros **4a.** about 22 mi/h
b. Yes; $\frac{60\,s}{1\,min} \cdot \frac{60\,min}{1\,h}$ is the same as $\frac{3600\,s}{1\,h}$.
Lesson Check 1. 8 bagels for $4.15 **2.** 116 oz **3.** 12 m
4. $80\frac{2}{3}$ ft/s **5.** not a unit rate **6.** unit rate **7.** No; a
conversion factor is a ratio of two equivalent measures in
different units and is always equal to 1. **8.** Greater; to
convert you multiply by 16.
Exercises 9. Olga **11.** 189 ft **13.** 40 oz **15.** 240 s
17. about 8.2 m **19.** 7900 cents **21.** about 35 in.
23. 1.875 gal/h **25.** 87 **27.** 150 **29.** 18 **31.** 0.5 mi
33. 5 oz **35.** recipe B **37.** Miles; kilometers; kilometers
cancel out and miles are left. **39.** 1580.82 INR; 19.98 GBP
41. Answers may vary. Sample: Estimating the size to the
nearest inch is appropriate because the carpenter is leaving
an estimated amount on either side of the television, not
an exact amount. **43.** 2255.6 mm

Lesson 2-7   pp. 124–129

Got It? 1. 5.6 **2a.** 1.8 **3.** -5 **4.** 145.5 mg
Lesson Check 1. 4.8 **2.** 27 **3.** 3 **4.** 5 **5.** 6.75 h **6.** m

and q **7.** n and p **8.** mq and np **9.** Yes; sample: One
method creates an equation using the fact that the cross
products are equal, and the other method creates an
equivalent equation using the Mult. Prop. of Eq. to clear
the denominators.
Exercises 11. -19.5 **13.** 4.2 **15.** 112.5 **17.** $16\frac{2}{3}$
19. 10 **21.** 14 **23.** $26\frac{2}{3}$ **25.** -15 **27.** 4.75 **29.** 11
31. $-6\frac{2}{3}$ **33.** -5 **35.** 8 dozen **37.** about 14 people
39. $\frac{\$.07}{1\,kWh} = \frac{\$143.32}{x\,kWh}$; 2047.4 kWh **41.** at the same time as
you **43.** 1.8 **45.** 2.7 **47.** 4.2 **49.** $-\frac{2}{3}$ **51.** 3 was not
fully distributed when multiplying 3 and $x + 3$; $16 =$
$3x + 9$, $7 = 3x$, $x = \frac{7}{3}$. **53.** Check students' work.
55. $\frac{-4}{3}$ **57.** $\frac{-5}{7}$ **59.** 22 h **61.** H **63.** 1.5 **64.** 7 **65.** 90
66. 190 **67.** no solution **68.** $\frac{1}{5}$ **69.** identity **70.** $2\frac{4}{5}$ or 2.8
71. $2\frac{2}{15}$ or $2.1\overline{3}$ **72.** $6\frac{2}{3}$ or $6.\overline{6}$ **73.** $\frac{3}{5}$ or 0.6

Lesson 2-8   pp. 130–136

Got It? 1. 24 **2.** 30 ft **3a.** about 66 mi **b.** Write and
solve the proportion $\frac{2}{250} = \frac{1}{x}$; 1 in. represents 125 mi.
4. 300 ft
Lesson Check 1a. 32.5 cm **b.** 1 : 2.5 **2.** 225 km
3. The order of the letters in each triangle tells which parts
are corresponding. **4a.** yes **b.** no **c.** yes **5.** Answers may
vary. Sample: No, it is greater than 100 times since 100 mi
is more than 100 times greater than 1 in.
Exercises 7. $\angle F \cong \angle K$, $\angle G \cong \angle L$, $\angle H \cong \angle M$,
$\angle I \cong \angle N$, $\frac{FG}{KL} = \frac{GH}{LM} = \frac{HI}{MN} = \frac{FI}{KN}$ **9.** 40 **11.** 100
13. 37.5 km **15.** 225 km **17.** 67.5 ft **19.** $6\frac{1}{2}$ ft × $2\frac{1}{2}$ ft
21. no **23a.** The student used CJ instead of AJ.
b. $\frac{BC}{AJ} = \frac{GH}{FN}$ **25.** 39,304 times **27.** Yes; all squares will
have sides that are in proportion (the same length), and
the measures of corresponding $\angle$s are equal (90°).
29. Answers may vary. Sample: No; the finished table
could have been a parallelogram with different angles
than the parallelogram in the sketch. The angle measures
were not given.

Lesson 2-9   pp. 137–143

Got It? 1. 60% **2.** 75%; the answers are the same.
3. $3600 **4.** $41\frac{2}{3}$ **5.** 4 yr
Lesson Check 1. 30% **2.** 120% **3.** 28 **4.** 48 **5.** $180
6. 100 **7.** $75 **8.** Answers may vary. Sample: 12 is what
percent of 10?
Exercises 9. 20% **11.** 62.5% **13.** $41\frac{2}{3}$% **15.** 36
17. 13 **19.** 16 **21.** $52 **23.** 400 **25.** 22.5 **27.** $22\frac{2}{3}$
29. $108 **31.** part; 5.04 **33.** part; 142.5 **35.** percent;
$1333\frac{1}{3}$ **37.** 66,000 mi² **39.** 16 **41.** 75 **43.** B **45.** 121%;
it costs more to make a penny than the penny is worth.

47. The values for a and b are reversed; $\frac{3}{1.5} = \frac{p}{100}$, $1.5p = 300$, $p = 200\%$. **49.** \$181 **51.** $29\frac{1}{6}\%$
53. 25 students **55.** F **57.** 14.4 cm **58.** 18 cans
59. $c = 1.75 + 2.4\left(m - \frac{1}{8}\right)$; $2\frac{5}{8}$ mi **60.** 1250%
61. 0.6 **62.** 175%

Lesson 2-10   pp. 144–150

Got It? 1. about 32% **2.** about 17% **3.** about 16%
4. 65.5 in. and 66.5 in. **5.** It would be smaller since the measurement of each dimension is closer to the actual value of each dimension.
Lesson Check 1. about 2% **2.** about 61% **3.** 7.25 ft and 7.75 ft **4a.** percent decrease **b.** percent decrease
c. percent increase **5.** 0.05 m **6.** A percent increase involves an increase of the original amount and a percent decrease involves a decrease of the original amount.
Exercises 7. increase; 50% **9.** decrease; 7%
11. decrease; 4% **13.** increase; 54% **15.** increase; 27%
17. about 55% **19.** about 13% **21.** 1.05 kg; 1.15 kg
23. about 28% **25.** 175% increase **27.** 42% decrease
29. 39% increase **31.** 48.75 m^2; 63.75 m^2
33. 505.25 ft^2; 551.25 ft^2 **37.** The original amount is 12, not 18; $\frac{18 - 12}{12} = \frac{6}{12} = 0.5 = 50\%$. **39.** 12.63
41a. 21% **b.** 21% **c.** 21%; sample: the new length is 1.1 times as great as the original length. $1.1^2 = 1.21$ or 121%, which shows a 21% increase over the original amount of 100%. **43.** I **45.** $66\frac{2}{3}\%$ **46.** 64.75 **47.** 21
48–51.

$-3, -2.8, \frac{1}{2}, 2$

Chapter Review   pp. 152–156

1. inverse operations **2.** identity **3.** rate **4.** scale
5. cross products **6.** -7 **7.** 7 **8.** 14 **9.** 65 **10.** 3.5
11. -4 **12.** -5 **13.** -8 **14.** \$6.50 **15.** Add. Prop. of Eq.; Simplify.; Div. Prop. of Eq.; Simplify. **16.** 11 **17.** 8
18. -7.5 **19.** $3\frac{18}{85}$ **20.** 28 **21.** 14.7 **22.** $4h + 8h + 50 = 164$; \$9.50 **23.** $37t + 8.50t + 14.99 = 242.49$; 5 tickets **24.** -90 **25.** 7.2 **26.** identity **27.** no solution
28. $8h = 16 + 6h$; 8 ft **29.** $\frac{d}{65} = \frac{d}{130} + 3$; 390 mi
30. $x = \frac{-c}{a + b}$ **31.** $x = -t - r$ **32.** $x = \frac{m - p}{5}$
33. $x = \frac{pqs}{p + q}$ **34.** 40 cm **35.** 15 mm **36.** 16 in.
37. 78 in. **38.** 71 oz **39.** 2.25 min **40.** 3960 yd
41. 240 loaves **42.** about 6 lb **43.** $\frac{5}{11}$ s or about 0.45 s
44. 21 **45.** -4 **46.** 1.6 **47.** 21 **48.** 39 **49.** -1
50. 12 in. **51.** 42 in. **52.** 300% **53.** 108 **54.** 170
55. 60 seeds **56.** 30% **57.** 72 students **58.** increase;

11% **59.** decrease; 20% **60.** decrease; 11% **61.** increase; 32% **62.** about 47% **63.** about 39% **64.** Yes; 50% of 38° is 19° and 38° + 19° = 57°.

Chapter 3

Get Ready!   p. 161

1. > **2.** = **3.** > **4.** < **5.** 7 **6.** -4 **7.** 1 **8.** 2 **9.** 3
10. -12 **11.** 32.4 **12.** 23 **13.** 29.5 **14.** -28 **15.** -12
16. 48 **17.** 5 **18.** -24 **19.** -10 **20.** 1.85 **21.** -24
22. -2 **23.** 3 **24.** 60 **25.** -4 **26.** 3 **27.** $\frac{1}{2}$ **28.** 2.5
29. 4.1 **30.** 24 **31.** Answers may vary. Sample: Two inequalities are joined together. **32.** Answers may vary. Sample: the part that the two groups of objects have in common

Lesson 3-1   pp. 164–170

Got It? 1a. $p \geq 1.5$ **b.** $t + 7 < -3$ **2a.** 1 and 3
b. The solution of the equation is -2. The solution of the inequality is all real numbers greater than -2.
3a.

b.

c.

4a. $x < -3$ **b.** $x \geq 0$ **5.** No; the speed limit can only be nonnegative real numbers.

Lesson Check 1. $y \geq 12$ **2a.** no **b.** no **c.** yes **d.** yes
3.

4. $x \leq -3$

5. Substitute the number for the variable and simplify. If the number makes the inequality true, then it is a solution of the inequality. **6.** Answers may vary. Sample: $x \geq 0$, whole numbers, a baseball team's score during an inning, amount in cubic centimeters of liquid in a chemistry beaker; $x > 0$, counting numbers, length of a poster, distance in blocks between your house and a park
7. Check students' work.

Exercises 9. $b < 4$ **11.** $\frac{k}{9} > \frac{1}{3}$ **13a.** yes **b.** no **c.** yes
15a. yes **b.** no **c.** no **17.** D **19.** A
21.

23.

25.

27.

29. $x > -4$ **31.** $x \geq 2$ **33.** $x \geq 5$ **35.** Let $p = $ the number of people seated; $p \leq 172$. **37.** Let $w = $ number of watts of the light bulb; $w \leq 75$. **39.** Let $m = $ amount of money earned; $m > 20{,}000$. **41.** Check students' work. **43.** $x \leq 186{,}000$ **45.** b is greater than 0. **47.** z is greater than or equal to 25.6. **49.** 21 is greater than or equal to m. **51.** 2 less than g is less than 7. **53.** r more than 6 is greater than -2. **55.** 1.2 is greater than k. **57.** Answers may vary. Sample: *No more than* means "is less than or equal to," since the amount cannot be greater than the given number. *No less than* means "is greater than or equal to," since the amount cannot be less than the given number. **59.** $998 > 978$, so Option A > Option B. **61.** Answers may vary. Sample: Use reasoning or guess and check to see that the values of x that are less than 3 make the inequality true. **63.** line graph that shows an open circle at -3 stretching to shaded circle at 3 **65.** C **67.** A **69.** increase; 20% **70.** decrease; 10% **71.** decrease; 67% **72.** 44 **73.** $-\frac{5}{24}$ **74.** -3 **75.** $-1\frac{3}{7}$ **76.** 11 **77.** -2 **78.** -11 **79.** $-\frac{1}{9}$

Lesson 3-2   pp. 171–177

Got It? 1. $n < 2$

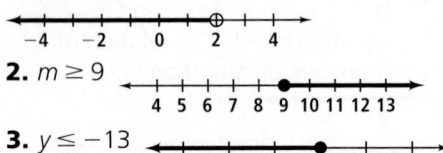

2. $m \geq 9$

3. $y \leq -13$

4a. $p \geq 8$ **b.** Yes. The $\geq$ symbol can be used to represent all 3 phrases.

Lesson Check

1. $p < 5$

2. $d \leq 10$

3. $y < -12$

4. $c > 3$

5. $w \leq 524$ **6.** Add or subtract the same number from each side of the inequality. **7a.** Subtract 4 from each side. **b.** Add 1 to each side. **c.** Subtract 3 from each side. **d.** Add 2 to each side. **8.** They are similar in that 4 is being added to or subtracted from each side of the inequalities. They are different in that one inequality adds 4 and the other subtracts 4.

Exercises 9. 6 11. 3.3

13. $y > 13$

15. $c < -4$

17. $t \geq -3$

19. $p > 12$

21. $f > \frac{1}{3}$

23. $r < 0$

25. $s < 4.7$

27. $c < 1\frac{3}{7}$

29. 3 **31.** 4.2

33. $x \leq 5$

35. $c > -7$

37. $a \geq -1$

39. $n > -2\frac{2}{3}$

41. $d \geq -1$

43. $3 + 4 + g \geq 10$; $g \geq 3$ **45.** Add 4 to each side.
47. Add $\frac{1}{2}$ to each side. **49.** yes

51.

51	
17	x

53.

3 ⊢ 13
m

55. $d \leq 2$ **57.** $-4\frac{4}{5} > p$ **59.** $-1.2 > z$ **61.** $p > 12$
63. $h \geq -\frac{7}{8}$ **65.** $5\frac{7}{16} \geq m$ **67a.** yes **b.** No; in the first inequality, r is greater than or equal to the amount. In the second inequality, r is less than or equal to the amount. **c.** In part (a), these are equations with only one solution. In part (b), because the inequality relationship is different, there is no relationship between the two inequalities.
69. Answers may vary. Sample: 94, 95, or 96. **71.** The graph should be shaded to the right, not the left.

73a. No; the solution should be $a \geq 8.6 - 3.2$, or $a \geq 5.4$. **b.** Answers may vary. Sample: Other numbers that are not substituted could also be solutions to the inequality. **75.** at least $88.74 **77.** True **79.** Not true; sample: $x = 5$, $y = 3$, $w = 4$

Lesson 3-3   pp. 178–183

Got It? 1. $c > 2$

2. $n > 3$

3a. 1, 2, 3, or 4 cases **b.** $\frac{75}{4.50} = 16\frac{2}{3}$, but you cannot walk $\frac{2}{3}$ of a dog. If you round down to 16, you will only make \$72. So round up to 17.
4. $x < 2$

Lesson Check 1. D **2.** B **3.** A **4.** C **5a.** Multiplication by -2; it is the inverse of division by -2. **b.** Addition of 4; it is the inverse of subtraction of 4. **c.** Division by -6; it is the inverse of multiplication by -6. **6.** The inequality symbol was not reversed when multiplying by a negative.
$-5\left(-\frac{n}{5}\right) < -5(2)$, $n < -10$

Exercises

7. $x \geq -10$

9. $p < 32$

11. $v \leq -3$

13. $x \geq -3$

15. $m \leq 0$

17. $m < 2$

19. $m \geq 2$

21. $c > 6$

23. $z > -3$

25. $b \leq -\frac{1}{6}$

27. $h > -13$

29. $q \leq 9$

31. no more than 66 text messages **33–35.** Answers may vary. Samples are given. **33.** $-5, -4, -3, -2$
35. $-6, -5, -4, -3$ **37.** Multiply each side by -4 and reverse the inequality symbol. **39.** Divide each side by 5.
41. -2 **43.** 4 **45.** Sometimes true; sample: It is true when $x = 4$ and $y = 0.5$ but false when $x = 4$ and $y = -2$. **47.** Sometimes true; sample: It is true when $x = 4$ and $y = 2$ but false when $x = 0$ and $y = 2$.
49. at least 0.08 mi per min

51. $3(-1) \geq 3\left(\frac{t}{3}\right)$ Mult. Prop. of Ineq.
    $-3 \geq t$ Simplify.

53. $2(0.5) \leq 2\left(\frac{1}{2}c\right)$ Mult. Prop. of Ineq.
    $1 \leq c$ Simplify.

55. $5\left(\frac{n}{5}\right) \leq 5(-2)$ Mult. Prop. of Ineq.
    $n \leq -10$ Simplify.

57. $-\frac{7}{5}(1) > -\frac{7}{5}\left(-\frac{5}{7}s\right)$ Mult. Prop. of Ineq.
    $-\frac{7}{5} > s$ Simplify.

59. If the most expensive sandwiches and drinks are ordered, the cost is $3(7) + 3(2) = 27$, leaving \$3. If the most expensive snack is bought, the least number of snacks you can afford is 1. If the least expensive sandwiches and drinks are ordered, the cost is $3(4) + 3(1) = 15$, leaving \$15. If the least expensive snack is bought, the greatest number of snacks you can afford is 15. **61.** $x < 20$, $x < 30$, $x < 40$, . . . ; any inequality following the one that a is a solution to. This is because each following inequality has the same solutions as the previous inequalities, with more values as solutions.
63. $3.14d > 29.5$ and $d > 9.4$, so the men's basketballs need a 10-in. box; $3.14d > 27.75$, $d > 8.8$ so the youth basketballs need a 9-in. box. **65.** D **67.** $w = \ell - 3$, $18 = 2\ell + 2(\ell - 3)$, $18 = 4\ell - 6$, $24 = 4\ell$, so $\ell = 6$ (Length is 6 in.). **68.** $x \leq -11$ **69.** $y \geq 13.6$ **70.** $q < 5$
71. $-\frac{1}{4} > c$ **72.** $-1 < b$ **73.** $y \leq 75$ **74.** 2 **75.** -2
76. 1

Lesson 3-4   pp. 186–192

Got It? 1a. $a \geq -4$ **b.** $n < 3$ **c.** $x < 25$ **2.** any width greater than 0 ft and less than or equal to 6 ft **3.** $m \leq -3$
4a. $b > 3$ **b.** Answers may vary. Sample: adding 1 to each side. This would gather the constant terms onto one side of the inequality. **5a.** no solution **b.** all real numbers
Lesson Check 1. $a > 2$ **2.** $t \leq 5$ **3.** $z < 13$ **4.** no solution **5.** greater than 0 cm and less than or equal to 8 cm **6.** The variable terms cancel each other out and a false inequality results. **7.** Yes; each side can be divided by 2 first. **8.** No; there is no solution, since -6 is not greater than itself. If the inequality symbol were $\geq$, your friend would be correct.
Exercises 9. $f \leq 3$ **11.** $y > -2$ **13.** $r \geq 3.5$
15. $5s \geq 250$; $s \geq 50$ mph **17.** $k \geq 1$ **19.** $j < -1$
21. $z < 9$ **23.** $x < 3$ **25.** $f \leq 6$ **27.** $m \geq -5$ **29.** all real numbers **31.** all real numbers **33.** all real numbers
35. $x \geq -4$ **37.** $t \geq \frac{9}{5}$ **39.** $n \geq -2$ **41.** $a \geq 0.5$
43. $k \leq \frac{13}{6}$ **45.** 5.5 h **47.** D **49a.** $v \geq 4$ **b.** $4 \leq v$
c. They are equivalent. **d.** Check students' work. **51.** at least \$3750 **53.** $3y$ was subtracted from instead of added to each side; $7y \leq 2$, $y \leq \frac{2}{7}$. **55.** $-5, -4, -3, -2, -1, 0,$ 1, 2, 3, 4, 5, and 6 **57a.** 73 boxes **b.** 4 trips

Lesson 3-5   pp. 194–199

Got It? 1. $N = \{2, 4, 6, 8, 10, 12\}$; $N = \{x \mid x$ is an even natural number, $x \leq 12\}$ **2.** $\{n \mid n < -3\}$
3a. $\{\}$ or $\varnothing$, $\{a\}$, $\{b\}$, $\{a, b\}$; $\{\}$ or $\varnothing$, $\{a\}$, $\{b\}$, $\{c\}$, $\{a, b\}$, $\{a, c\}$, $\{b, c\}$, $\{a, b, c\}$ **b.** Yes; every element of set A is part of set B, since $-3 < 0$. **4.** $A' = \{$February, April, June, September, November$\}$

Lesson Check 1. $G = \{1, 3, 5, 7, 9, 11, 13, 15, 17\}$;
$G = \{x \mid x \text{ is an odd natural number}, x < 18\}$
2. $\{d \mid d \leq 3\}$ **3.** $\{\}$ or $\varnothing$, $\{4\}$, $\{8\}$, $\{12\}$, $\{4, 8\}$, $\{4, 12\}$,
$\{8, 12\}$, $\{4, 8, 12\}$ **4.** $W' = \{\text{spring, summer, fall}\}$ **5.** A; its
complement is the set of all elements in the universal set
that are not in A'. **6a.** Yes; the empty set is a subset of
every set. **b.** No; the number 5 in the first set is not an
element of the second set. **c.** Yes; the element in the first
set is also an element of the second set. **7.** sometimes
8. The student forgot that 0 is also a whole number.
Exercises 9. $\{0, 1, 2, 3\}$; $\{m \mid m \text{ is an integer}, -1 <$
$m < 4\}$ **11.** $\{1, 2, 3, 4, 5, 6, 7, 8, 9, 10\}$; $\{p \mid p \text{ is a}$
natural number, $p < 11\}$ **13.** $\{y \mid y \geq 4\}$ **15.** $\{m \mid m >$
$-5\}$ **17.** $\{p \mid p \geq 1\}$ **19.** $\{\}$ or $\varnothing$, $\{a\}$, $\{e\}$, $\{i\}$, $\{o\}$, $\{a, e\}$,
$\{a, i\}$, $\{a, o\}$, $\{e, i\}$, $\{e, o\}$, $\{i, o\}$, $\{a, e, i\}$, $\{a, e, o\}$, $\{a, i, o\}$, $\{e,$
$i, o\}$, $\{a, e, i, o\}$ **21.** $\{\}$ or $\varnothing$, $\{dog\}$, $\{cat\}$, $\{fish\}$, $\{dog, cat\}$,
$\{dog, fish\}$, $\{cat, fish\}$, $\{dog, cat, fish\}$ **23.** $\{\}$ or $\varnothing$, $\{1\}$
25. $\{1, 4, 5\}$ **27.** $\{\ldots, -4, -2, 0, 2, 4, \ldots\}$
29. $A' = \{\text{Tuesday, Thursday, Friday, Saturday}\}$ **31.** False;
some elements of U are not elements of B. **33.** True; the
empty set is a subset of every set. **35.** $M = \{m \mid m \text{ is odd}$
integer, $1 \leq m \leq 19\}$ **37.** $G = \{g \mid g \text{ is an integer}\}$
39. $\{\text{Mercury, Venus, Earth}\}$ **41.** $\{\}$ or $\varnothing$ **43.** $\{x \mid x \leq 0\}$
45. $\{\}$ or $\varnothing$ **47.** $T' = \{x \mid x \text{ is an integer}, x \leq 0\}$ **49.** 1
51. 512 **53.** A **55.** D **57.** Mum's Florist: $\frac{\$26.40}{24} = \$1.025$
each. First Flowers Florist: $\frac{\$750}{6} = \$1.25$ each. Mum's
Florist has a lower cost per rose. **58.** $b > 8$ **59.** $t \leq 5$
60. $z < 13$ **61.** 6 **62.** -3 **63.** 3
64.
65.
66.

Lesson 3-6   pp. 200–206

Got It? 1a. $-4 \leq x < 6$
b. $x \leq 2\frac{1}{2}$ or $x > 6$

c. *x is between* -5 *and* 7 *does not include* -5 *or* 7.
Inclusive means that -5 *and* 7 *are included*.
2. $\frac{2}{3} < y < 6$

3. Answers may vary. Sample: No, to get a B, the average
of the 4 tests must be at least 84. If x is the 4th test score,
$\frac{78 + 78 + 79 + x}{4} \geq 84$, $235 + x \geq 336$, and $x \geq 101$,
which is impossible.
4. $y > 3$ or $y \leq -2$

5a. $-2 < x \leq 7$
b. $(7, \infty)$

Lesson Check 1. $0 \leq x < 8$

2. $1 \leq r < 4$

3. $85 \leq x \leq 100$ **4.** $x \leq 6$; $(-\infty, 6)$ **5.** A, C, and D
6. Answers may vary. Sample: The bracket indicates a
specific number is part of the solution. The symbol ∞
means that the numbers continue without end. So a
parenthesis should follow. **7.** $x \leq 7$ or $x > 7$; $(-\infty, \infty)$
8. The graph of a compound inequality with the word *and*
contains the overlap of the graphs that form the inequality.
The graph of a compound inequality with the word *or*
contains both of the graphs that form the inequality.
Exercises 9. $-5 < x < 7$

11. $-7 < k < 5$

13. $2 < p \leq 5$

15. $3\frac{3}{4} < x < 8\frac{1}{2}$

17. $b < -1$ or $b > 2$

19. $d \geq 2$ or $d < 2$

21. $y \leq -2$ or $y \geq 5$

23. $x \leq 2$

25. $x \leq -1$ or $x > 3$

27. $(-2, \infty)$

29. $(-\infty, -2)$ or $[1, \infty)$

31. $(1, 6]$ **33.** $(-\infty, -5)$ or $[5, \infty)$ **35.** $-3 < x < 4$
37. $3 \leq x < 6$ **39.** $2\frac{2}{3} \leq v \leq 6$ **41.** $-4\frac{1}{12} \leq w < 12\frac{1}{4}$
43. $4 < x < 14$ **45.** any length greater than 6 ft and
less than 36 ft **47.** any length greater than 11 m and
less than 23 m **49.** any real number except 4
51a. $102.5 \leq R \leq 184.5$ **b.** 22 years old **53.** B
55. $35 \leq 10.4 + 0.0059g \leq 50$, $24.6 \leq 0.0059g \leq 39.6$,
$4169.49 \leq g \leq 6711.86$; minimum water consumption is
4169 gal and maximum water consumption is about
6712 gal. **56.** $\{\}$ or $\varnothing$, $\{1\}$, $\{3\}$, $\{5\}$, $\{7\}$, $\{1, 3\}$, $\{1, 5\}$, $\{1, 7\}$,

{3, 5}, {3, 7}, {5, 7}, {1, 3, 5}, {1, 3, 7}, {1, 5, 7}, {3, 5, 7}, {1, 3, 5, 7} **57.** $B' = \{1, 2, 3, 5, 7, 15\}$ **58.** no **59.** $\frac{1}{3} < b$
60. $n \leq 3$ **61.** $7 \geq r$ **62.** $=$ **63.** $>$ **64.** $>$

Lesson 3-7   pp. 207–213

Got It? 1. $n = 3$ and $n = -3$

2. The 80 represents your friend's starting distance from you. The 5 represents your friend's constant speed of 5 ft/s. She is 60 ft away at 4 s and 28 s. **3.** no solution
4. $x \geq 0.5$ or $x \leq -4.5$

5a. $|w - 32| \leq 0.05$; $31.95 \leq w \leq 32.05$ **b.** No; 213 is part of the absolute value expression. You cannot add 213 until after you write the absolute value inequality as a compound inequality.
Lesson Check 1. $x = 5$ or $x = -5$

2. $n = 7$ or $n = -7$

3. $t = 3$ or $t = -3$

4. $-2 < h < 8$

5. $x \leq -3$ or $x \geq -1$

6. 2; there are two values on a number line that are the same distance from 0. **7.** The absolute value cannot be equal to a negative number since distance from 0 on a number line must be nonnegative. **8.** Answers may vary. Sample: The equation is set equal to 2 and −2. The first inequality is set to be ≤ 2 and ≥ -2. The second inequality is set to be ≥ 2 or ≤ -2.
Exercises 9. $b = -\frac{1}{2}$ or $b = \frac{1}{2}$

11. $n = 4$ or $n = -4$

13. $x = 8$ or $x = -8$

15. $m = 3$ or $m = -3$

17. $r = 13$ or $r = 3$ **19.** $g = -1$ or $g = -5$ **21.** no solution **23.** $v = 6$ or $v = 0$ **25.** $f = 1.5$ or $f = -2$
27. $y = 3$ or $y = 0$ **29.** no solution **31.** no solution
33. $-5 < x < 5$

35. $y \leq -11$ or $y \geq -5$

37. $4 \leq p \leq 10$

39. $t < -3$ or $t > \frac{7}{3}$

41. $t \leq -2.4$ or $t \geq 4$

43. $-4 \leq v \leq 5$

45. $-11 \leq f \leq 2$

47. any length between 89.95 cm and 90.05 cm, inclusive **49.** $d = 9$ or $d = -9$ **51.** no solution **53.** $y = 3.4$ or $y = -0.6$ **55.** $c = 8.2$ or $c = -0.2$ **57.** $-6\frac{1}{4} < n < 6\frac{1}{4}$
59. $-8 < m < 4$ **61.** $49°F \leq T \leq 64°F$ **63.** The 200 represents your friend's starting distance from you. The 18 represents your friend's constant speed of 18 ft/s. $t = 4\frac{4}{9}$ s and $17\frac{7}{9}$ s **65.** $-1 \leq y + 7 \leq 1$, $-8 \leq y \leq -6$
67. Answers may vary. Sample: To be more than 1 unit away from −5 on a number line means $x + 5 > 1$ or $x + 5 < -1$. **69a.** between 193.74 g and 209.26 g, inclusive **b.** Yes; answers may vary. Sample: Some nickels could weigh more and some could weigh less, and their average could be the official amount. **71.** $|x| < 4$
73. $|x - 6| > 2$ **75.** between 89.992 mm and 90.008 mm, inclusive **77.** 2 **79.** 3 **81.** always
83. 4.265 **85.** 5 **87.** 120 **88.** $-282 \leq e \leq 20{,}310$
89. $36.9 \leq T \leq 37.5$ **90.** $2x + 10$ **91.** $-3y + 21$
92. $4\ell + 5$ **93.** $-m + 12$ **94.** $A = \{x \mid x$ is a whole number, $x < 10\}$ **95.** $B = \{x \mid x$ is an odd integer, $1 \leq x \leq 7\}$ **96.** $C = \{-14, -12, -10, -8, -6\}$
97. $D = \{8, 9, 10, 12, 14, 15, 16\}$

Lesson 3-8   pp. 214–220

Got It? 1a. $P = \{0, 1, 2, 3, 4\}$; $Q = \{2, 4\}$; $P \cup Q = \{0, 1, 2, 3, 4\}$ **b.** Answers may vary. Sample: If $B \subseteq A$, then $A \cup B$ will contain the same elements as A. **2a.** $A \cap B = \{2, 8\}$ **b.** $A \cap C = \varnothing$ **c.** $C \cap B = \{5, 7\}$ **3.** A and E **4.** 10 **5a.** $\{x \mid x \geq 3\} \cap \{x \mid x < 6\}$
b. $\{x \mid x < -2\} \cup \{x \mid x > 5\}$
Lesson Check 1. $X \cup Y = \{1, 2, 3, 4, 5, 6, 7, 8, 9, 10\}$
2. $X \cap Y = \{2, 4, 6, 8, 10\}$ **3.** $X \cap Z = \varnothing$ **4.** $Y \cup Z = \{1, 2, 3, 4, 5, 6, 7, 8, 9, 10\}$ **5.** 31 people **6.** $A \cup B$ contains more elements because it contains all the elements in both sets. **7.** The union of sets is the set that contains all elements of each set. The intersection of sets is the set of elements that are common to each set. **8.** true
9. false
Exercises 11. $A \cup C = \{1, 2, 3, 4, 5, 7, 10\}$
13. $B \cup C = \{0, 2, 4, 5, 6, 7, 8, 10\}$ **15.** $C \cup D = \{1, 2, 3, 5, 7, 9, 10\}$ **17.** $A \cap C = \varnothing$ **19.** $B \cap C = \{2\}$
21. $C \cap D = \{5, 7\}$

Selected Answers

23.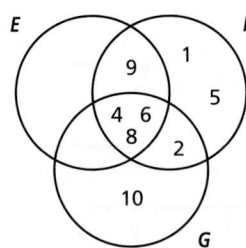

25. 10 girls **27.** $\{x|x > -3\} \cap \{x|x < \frac{19}{3}\}$
29. $\{w|w \le -\frac{3}{4}\} \cup \{w|w \ge 1\}$ **31.** $\{x|x < -7\}$
$\cup \{x|x > 21\}$ **33.** $W \cup Y \cup Z = \{0, 2, 3, 4, 5, 6, 7, 8\}$
35. $W \cap X \cap Z = \{6\}$ **37.** 62 patients **39.** $A \cap B = A$
41. $\{(\pi, 2), (\pi, 4), (2\pi, 2), (2\pi, 4), (3\pi, 2), (3\pi, 4),$
$(4\pi, 2), (4\pi, 4)\}$ **43.** {(reduce, plastic), (reuse, plastic),
(recycle, plastic)} **45.** Sometimes; when $A = B = C$,
the statement is true. When A, B, and C are distinct sets
the statement is false. **47.** F **49.** $x = 4$ or $x = -4$
50. $n = 2$ or $n = -2$ **51.** $f = 2$ or $f = 8$ **52.** $y = \frac{4}{3}$ or
$y = -\frac{8}{3}$ **53.** $-5 \le d \le 5$ **54.** $x \le -4$ or $x \ge 10$
55. $w < -15$ or $w > 9$ **56.** $x = \frac{4}{3}$ or $x = -\frac{4}{3}$ **57.** yes
58. no **59.** yes

Chapter Review   pp. 222–226

1. roster form **2.** union **3.** empty set **4.** solution of an
inequality **5.** equivalent inequalities

6.

7.

8.

9.

10. $x > 5$ **11.** $x \le -2$ **12.** $x > -5.5$ **13.** $w > 6$

14. $v < 10$

15. $-12 < t$

16. $n \ge \frac{5}{4}$

17. $8.6 \le h$

18. $q > -2.5$

19. $4.25 + x \le 15.00$; $x \le 10.75$

20. $x < 3$

21. $t < -3$

22. $y \le 6$

23. $h > -24$

24. $g > 4$

25. $n \le 15$

26. $d \ge 16\frac{13}{27}$

27. $m > -1\frac{67}{171}$

28. $7.25h \ge 200$; at least 28 full hours **29.** $k \ge -0.5$
30. $c < -2$ **31.** $t < -6$ **32.** $y \le -56$ **33.** $x < 2\frac{2}{3}$
34. $x \le -13$ **35.** $a \le 5.8$ **36.** $w > 0.35$ **37.** $200 +$
$0.04s \ge 450$; $s \ge 6250$ **38.** $\{\}$ or $\varnothing$, $\{s\}$, $\{t\}$, $\{s, t\}$
39. $\{\}$ or $\varnothing$, $\{5\}$, $\{10\}$, $\{15\}$, $\{5, 10\}$, $\{5, 15\}$, $\{10, 15\}$, $\{5, 10, 15\}$
40. $A = \{0, 2, 4, 6, 8, 10, 12, 14, 16\}$; $A = \{x|x$ is an
even whole number less than 18$\}$ **41.** $B' = \{1, 3, 5, 7\}$
42. $-2\frac{1}{2} \le d < 4$ **43.** $-1.5 \le b < 0$ **44.** $t \le -2$
or $t \ge 7$ **45.** $m < -2$ or $m > 3$ **46.** $2 \le a \le 5$
47. $6.5 > p \ge -4.5$ **48.** $65 \le t \le 88$ **49.** $y = 3$
or $y = -3$ **50.** $n = 2$ or $n = -6$ **51.** $r = 1$ or
$r = -5$ **52.** no solution **53.** $-3 \le x \le 3$ **54.** no
solution **55.** $x < 3$ or $x > 4$ **56.** $k < -7$ or $k > -3$
57. any length between 19.6 mm and 20.4 mm, inclusive
58. $A \cup B = A$

59.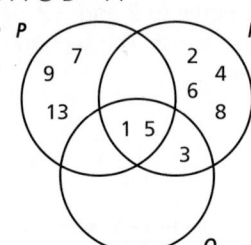

60. $N \cap P = \{x|x$ is a
multiple of 6$\}$ **61.** 5 cats

Chapter 4
Get Ready!   p. 231

1. -7 **2.** -18 **3.** 2 **4.** -1

5.

Bob's and His Dog's Ages (years)										
Dog's Age	0	1	2	3	4	5	6	7	8	9
Bob's Age	9	10	11	12	13	14	15	16	17	18

Bob's and His Dog's Ages

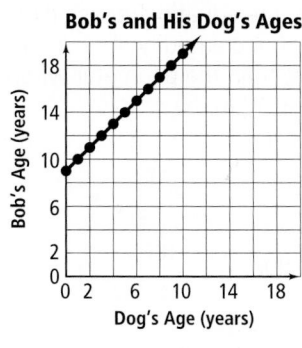

$B = 9 + d$, where B is Bob's age and d is his dog's age.

6.

Sue's Number of Laps per Minute										
Number of Minutes	0	1	2	3	4	5	6	7	8	9
Number of Laps	0	1.5	3	4.5	6	7.5	9	10.5	12	13.5

Sue's Number of Laps per Minute

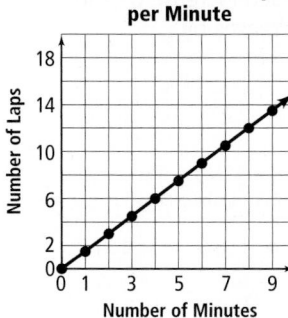

$\ell = 1.5m$, where m is the number of minutes and ℓ is the number of laps.

7.

Total Cost for Cartons of Eggs										
Number of Cartons	0	1	2	3	4	5	6	7	8	9
Total Cost (dollars)	0	3	6	9	12	15	18	21	24	27

Total Cost for Cartons of Eggs

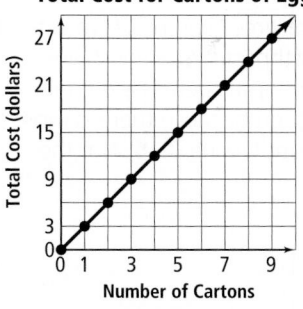

$C = 3n$, where C is the cost and n is the number of cartons.

8–11.

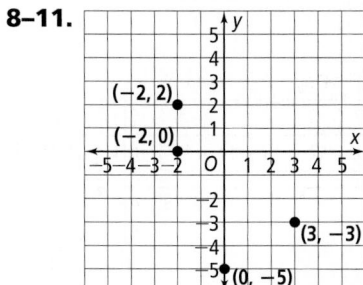

12. -3 **13.** 66 **14.** 6 **15.** 4 **16.** 0, -4 **17.** 3, 7
18. no solution **19.** $\frac{11}{2}, \frac{3}{2}$ **20.** Its value is based on the first value. **21.** 4 **22.** There are no breaks in the graph.

Lesson 4-1   pp. 234–239

Got It? 1a. Time, length; the length of the board remains constant for a time before another piece is cut off. **b.** Time, cost; the cost remains constant for a certain number of minutes. **2.** C
3a. Answers may vary. Sample:

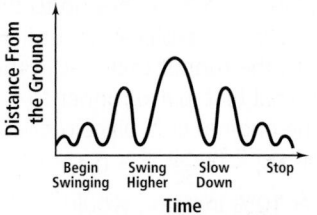

b. The end of the graph would decrease sharply.
Lesson Check 1. Car weight, fuel used; the heavier the car, the more fuel is used. **2.** The temperature rises slightly in the first 2 h and then falls over the next 4 h.
3. rising slowly: B; constant: C; falling quickly: D
4. Answers may vary. Sample: the depth of water in a stream bed over time
Exercises 5. Number of pounds, total cost; as the number of pounds increases, the total cost goes up, at first quickly and then more slowly. **7.** Area painted, paint in can; the more you paint, the less paint left in the can. You are using the paint at a constant rate. **9.** A
11. Answers may vary. Sample:

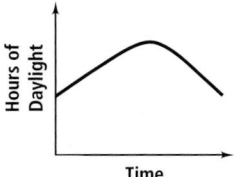

13. Answers may vary. Sample:

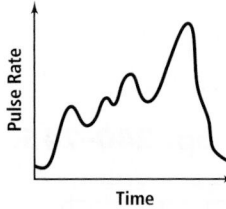

15. The graph shown represents the relationship between the number of shirts and the cost per shirt, not the total cost.

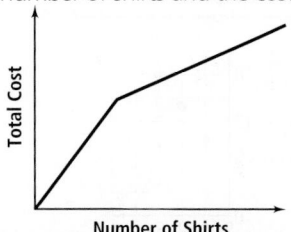

17. No, they are not the same. Your speed on the ski lift is constant. Your speed going downhill is not.

a.

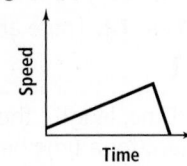

b.

19. The three runners start at the same time. At time A, one runner has a fast start, and the other two are a little slower. At B, the second–place runner catches up to the first–place runner and passes the first–place runner in order to win at time C. At C, the runner that was in third place catches up to the original first–place runner to finish second. At D, only the original first–place runner remains in the race. **21.** B **23.** $\frac{9.35 - 8.50}{8.50} = 0.10$, or a 10% increase. Another 10% increase would bring your hourly wage to 1.1(9.35) = 10.285, or $10.29. One further 10% increase would bring your rate to 1.1(10.29) = 11.3135, or $11.32.

24. $\{-3, -1, 1, 3, 4, 5, 7, 9\}$ **25.** $\{1\}$
26. $\{-1, 1, 3, 4, 5, 7, 9, 12\}$ **27.** $\{1, 4\}$

28.

Connie's Age	Donald's Age
0	4
1	5
2	6
3	7

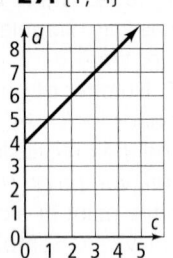

$d = c + 4$

29.

Time (hours)	Number of Cards
0	0
1	3
2	6
3	9

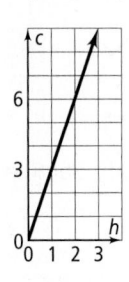

$c = 3h$

Lesson 4-2   pp. 240–245

Got It? 1a.

Number of Triangles	1	2	3	4
Perimeter	10	14	18	22

Multiply the number of triangles by 4 and add 6; $y = 4x + 6$.

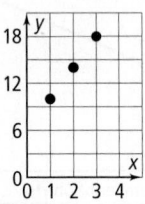

b. Add 4. **c.** The 4x part of the equation means that for each triangle the perimeter is increased by 4. If you know the perimeter of n triangles, then the perimeter when 1 more triangle is added will increase by 4.
2a. Yes; the value of y is 8 more than twice the value of x; $y = 2x + 8$.
b. No; the input value 1 has more than one output value.

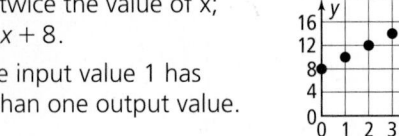

Lesson Check

1a.

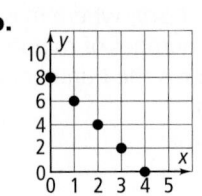

y increases by 1 for each increase of 1 for x.

b.

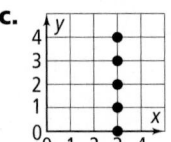

For each increase of 1 in x, y decreases by 2.

c.

x is 3 for any value of y.

2.

Number of Squares	1	2	3	4	10	30	n
Perimeter	4	6	8	10	22	62	2n + 2

3. independent: number of times you brush your teeth; dependent: amount of toothpaste **4.** a and b are functions because for each input there is a unique output, but c is not a function because there is more than one output value for the input value 3. **5.** No; the graph is not a line.

Exercises

7.

Number of Pentagons	1	2	3
Perimeter	5	8	11

Multiply the number of pentagons by 3 and add 2; $y = 3x + 2$.

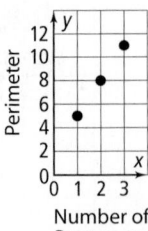

Number of Pentagons

9. Start with −3 and add 5 for each increase of 1 for x; $y = 5x − 3$.

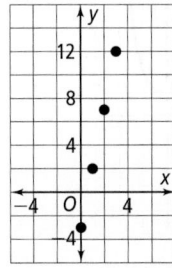

11. Yes; for each additional hour of climbing, you gain 92 ft of elevation; $y = 92x + 1127$.

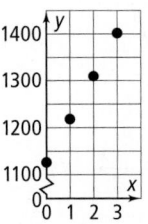

13. Yes; for every 17 mi traveled, the amount of gas in your tank goes down by 1 gallon; $y = −\frac{1}{17}x + 11.2$.

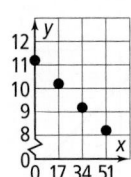

15.

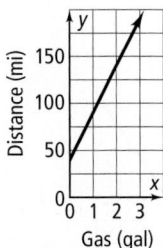

No; all points are not on a straight line.

17.

Gas Used, x	Distance, y
0	40
1	90
2	140
3	190

$y = 50x + 40$

Either distance or gas could be the independent variable, depending on what information is supplied and what is to be calculated.

19. graph of a line that goes through (0, 0); (1, 6), (2, 12); the horizontal axis is labeled Distance and the vertical axis is labeled Time.

Lesson 4-3   pp. 246–251

Got It?

1a. 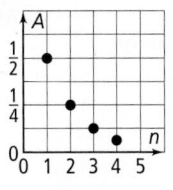   nonlinear

b. No; you can always multiply a number by $\frac{1}{2}$. The denominator of the fraction will get larger and larger, so the value of the fraction will approach 0 but never reach it.

2. The number of branches is 3 raised to the xth power; $y = 3^x$; 81, 243.

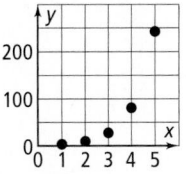

3. $y = x^2$

Lesson Check

1. 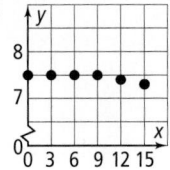   linear

2. $y = 3x − 2$ **3.** C **4a.** linear function **b.** nonlinear function **5.** Only the first two pairs fit this rule. The rule that fits all the pairs is $y = x^2 + 1$.

Exercises

7. 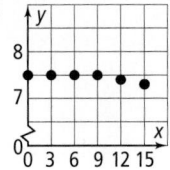   **9.**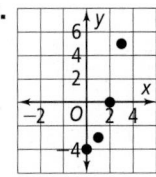

nonlinear   nonlinear

11. 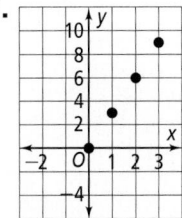   linear

13. $y = 4x^2$ **15.** $y = 2x^3$ **17.** Independent: r, dependent: V; volume depends on the length of the radius. **19.** Let y = number of bags, and $y = 6\pi r^2$; 3 bags; 4 bags; 5 bags. **21.** $y = x^2 + \frac{2}{19}$; the value of y is $\frac{2}{19}$ more than the square of x. **23.** B **25.** [2] $\frac{\$.89}{15}$ oz is nearly $.0593, \frac{\$1.69}{29}$ oz is nearly $.0583; the 29–oz can has the lower cost per ounce. [1] one minor computational error

26. The value of y is 3 more than twice x; $y = 2x + 3$.

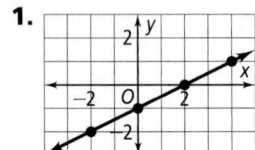

27. $-24, -3, 14.5$ **28.** $-11, 1, 11$ **29.** $-18, 0, -12.5$

Lesson 4-4   pp. 253–259

Got It?

1.

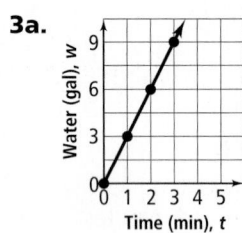

2a.

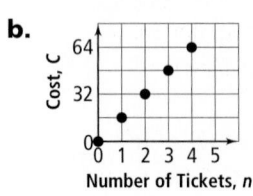

b. 700 lb; when $g = 0$, the spa is empty, and $W = 700$.

3a.

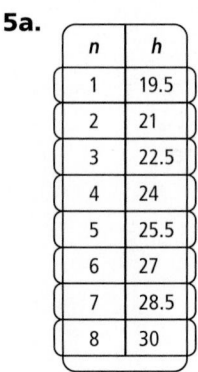

continuous because you can have any amount of water

b.

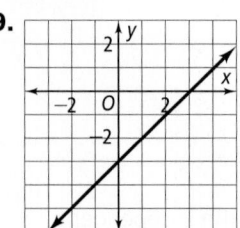

discrete because you can only have a whole number of tickets

4.

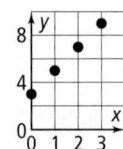

Lesson Check

1.

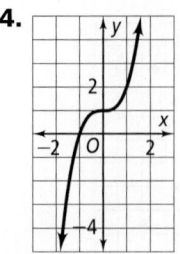

2.

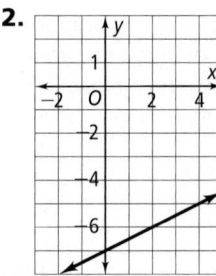

3.

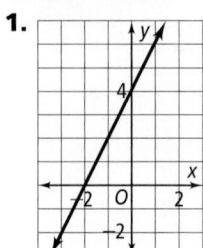

4.

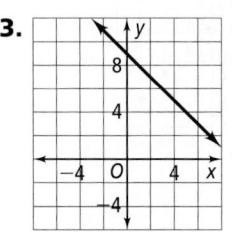

5a.

n	h
1	19.5
2	21
3	22.5
4	24
5	25.5
6	27
7	28.5
8	30

b.

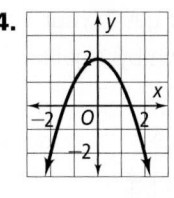

6. discrete **7.** continuous **8.** The graph should not be discrete; connect the points with a line so the graph is continuous.

Exercises

9.

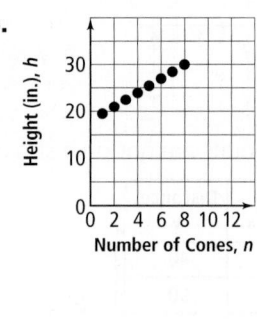

11.

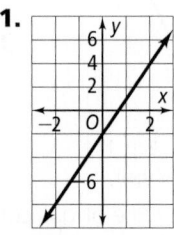

13.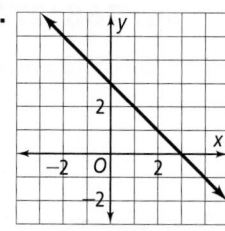

15.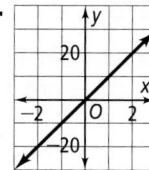

17.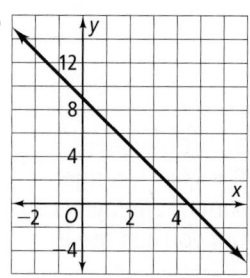

19.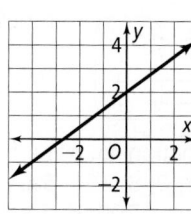

21.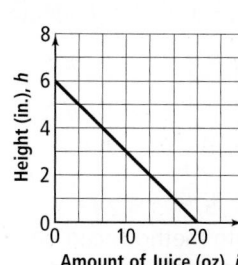

After you drink 20 oz of juice, the height is 0, so the interval $0 \le j \le 20$ makes sense. The height goes from $0 \le h \le 6$; continuous, because you can have juice in any amount.

23.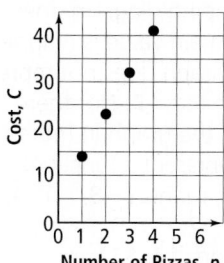

The number of pizzas can be any whole number, except zero, so $0 < p$. 1 pizza costs $14, so $14 \le C$.

25.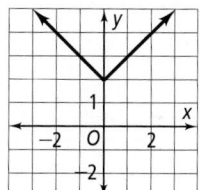

27.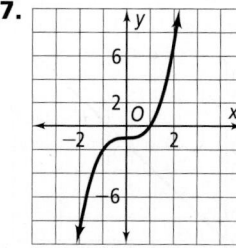

29.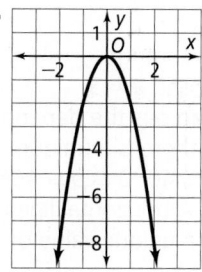

31.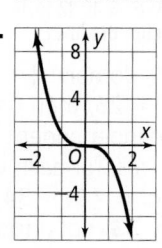

33. No; the graph is still continuous over the appropriate values of d and t.

35.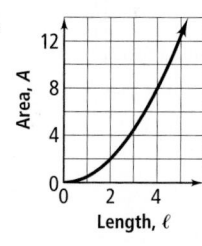

Continuous; lengths and areas can be any number.

37a.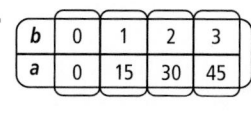

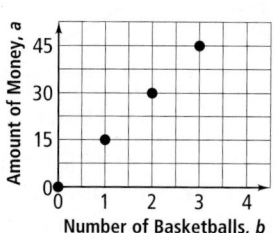

b	0	1	2	3
a	0	15	30	45

Discrete; you can only have whole numbers of basketballs.
b. 8 **39.** between 2 and 3 s **41.** Table for $y = 2x$ has x values -1, 0, 1, 2, 3 and corresponding y-values -2, 0, 2, 4, 6; graph of the line $y = 2x$; graph passes through (0, 0) and (1, 2). Table for $y = 2x^2$ has x values -1, 0, 1, 2, 3 and corresponding y-values -2, 0, 2, 8, 18; graph of $y = 2x^2$ is U-shaped going through $(-1, -2)$, (0, 0), (1, 2), (2, 8).

Lesson 4-5   pp. 262–267

Got It? 1. $W = 50,000 + 420m$
2a. $C = 12 + 15n$; $162 **b.** No; making the stay shorter only halves the daily charge, not the bath charge.
3a. $A = b^2 + 2b$; 288 in.^{2}
b. 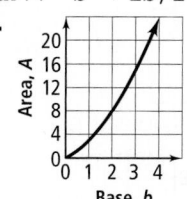   The graph is not a line.

Lesson Check 1. $C = 3.57p$ **2.** $f = \frac{h}{12}$
3. $y = x + 2$ **4.** $V = (d + 1)^3$ **5.** dependent, a; independent, b **6.** You can't add holes and minutes. The correct rule is $t = 15n$. **7.** Continuous; side length and area can be any positive real numbers.
Exercises 9. $C = 8 + \frac{1}{2}n$ **11.** $\frac{h}{3} + 2.5 = w$
13. $p = 6.95 + 0.95t$ **15.** $a = 8 - \frac{1}{6}b$
17. $d = -10 - 50t$; -160 ft **19.** $A = \frac{3}{2}h + \frac{5}{2}h^2$; 99 cm^2 **21.** $A = 3w^2 - 2w$; 8 ft^2 **23.** Answers may vary. Sample: The rule covers all values, whereas the table only represents some of the values.
25. $d = -3.5 - 108m$; -435.5 m

27a.

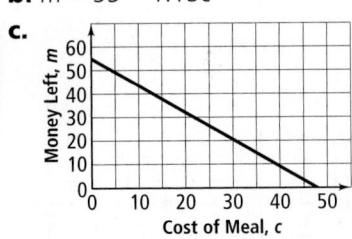

Cost of Meal	$15	$21	$24	$30
Money Left	$37.75	$30.85	$27.40	$20.50

b. $m = 55 - 1.15c$

c.

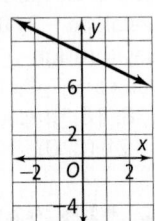

29a. $d = 1.8w$ **b.** No; the room is not wide enough.
c. $6\frac{2}{3}$ ft **31.** Table has x-values $-4, -3, -2, -1, 0, 1, 2,$ $3, 4$ and corresponding y-values $7, 6, 5, 4, 3, 2, 1, 0, -1$; the graph is a line that passes through $(0, 3)$ and $(3, 0)$; the function rule is $y = -x + 3$ **33.** B **35.** C

37.   **38.**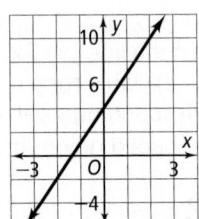

39. 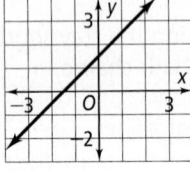   **40.**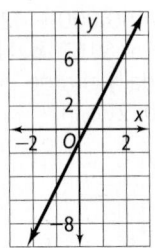

41. 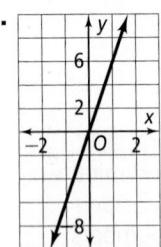   **42.**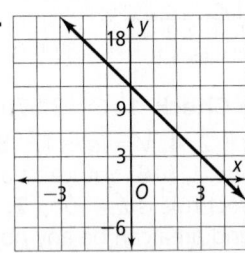

43. 132 oz **44.** 4.5 m **45.** 51 ft **46.** 1.5 min **47.** 9 days
48. 9500 m **49.** -36 **50.** 21 **51.** 111.6 **52.** -9 **53.** 14
54. 1 **55.** $\frac{5}{3}$ **56.** $\frac{21}{16}$

Lesson 4-6   pp. 268–273

Got It? 1a. domain: {4.2, 5, 7}; range: {0, 1.5, 2.2, 4.8}

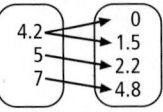

not a function

b. domain: {$-2, -1, 4\ 7$}; range: {$1, 2, -4, -7$}

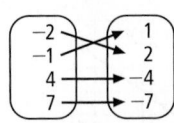

function

2a. function **b.** not a function **3.** 1500 words
4. {$-8, 0, 8, 16$} **5a.** domain: $0 \le q \le 7$, range: $0 \le A(q) \le 700$ **b.** The least amount of paint you can use is 0 quarts. The greatest amount you can use is 3 quarts.

Lesson Check 1. domain: {$-2, -1, 0, 1$}, range: {3, 4, 5, 6}

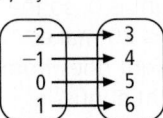

function

2. yes **3.** 9 **4.** {$-2, -1, 0, 1, 2$} **5.** $f(x) = 2x + 7$
6. Answers may vary. Sample: Both methods can be used to determine whether there is more than one output for any given input. A mapping diagram does not represent a function if any domain value is mapped to more than one range value. A graph does not represent a function if it fails the vertical line test. **7.** No; there exists a vertical line that intersects the graph in more than one point, so the graph does not represent a function.
Exercises 9. domain {1, 5, 6, 7}, range {$-8, -7, 4, 5$}; yes **11.** domain {0, 1, 4}, range {$-2, -1, 0, 1, 2$}; no **13.** not a function **15.** function **17.** $11
19. {$-39, -7, 1, 5, 21$} **21.** {$-7, -2, -1, 3$}
23. $0 \le c \le 16, 0 \le D(c) \le 1568$

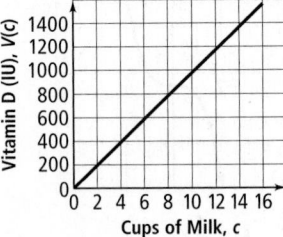

25. function; domain: {$-4, -1, 0, 3$}, range: {-4}
27. 5; if $f(a) = 26$, then $6a - 4 = 26$ and $a = 5$.
29a. c is the independent variable and p is the dependent variable. **b.** Yes; for each value of c, there is a unique value of p. **c.** $p = 5c - 34$ **d.** $0 \le c \le 40, 0 \le p \le 166$
31. function **33.** not a function **35.** A horizontal line is a function because each value of x has a unique value of y; a

vertical line is not a function because the *x*-value has more than one *y*-value associated with it. **37.** 23 **39.** 6 **41.** 5.25 **43.** 11 stamps **45.** $E = 5h + 7$ **46.** $a = 4.5s + 10$ **47a.** time and distance

b.

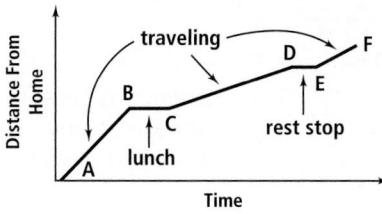

A Trip to the Mountains

48. 9, 12, 15, 18 **49.** 8, 15, 22, 29 **50.** 0.4, −2.6, −5.6, −8.6

Lesson 4-7   pp. 274–281

Got It? 1a. Add 6 to the previous term; 29, 35.
b. Multiply each previous term by $\frac{1}{2}$; 25, 12.5.
c. Multiply each previous term by −2; 32, −64.
d. Add 4 to the previous term; 1, 5. **2a.** not an arithmetic sequence **b.** arithmetic sequence; 2 **c.** arithmetic sequence; −6 **d.** not an arithmetic sequence **3a.** $A(n) = A(n − 1) + 6$; $A(9) = 51$ **b.** $A(n) = A(n − 1) + 12$; $A(9) = 119$ **c.** $A(n) = A(n − 1) + 0.5$; $A(9) = 11.3$
d. $A(n) = A(n − 1) − 9$; $A(9) = 25$ **e.** Answers may vary. Sample answer: It depends on which term you are trying to find. If you are trying to find the 2nd or 3rd term, then yes, a recursive formula is useful. If you are trying to find the 100th term, then no, a recursive formula is not useful. **4a.** $A(n) = 100 − (n − 1)1.75$; $73.75 **b.** 57 **5a.** $A(n) = 21 + (n − 1)(2)$
b. $A(n) = 2 + (n − 1)(7)$ **6a.** $A(n) = A(n − 1) + 10$
b. $A(n) = A(n − 1) + 3$
Lesson Check 1. Add 8 to the previous term; 35, 43.
2. Multiply the previous term by −2; 48, −96. **3.** not an arithmetic sequence **4.** arithmetic sequence; 9
5. $A(n) = A(n − 1) − 2$, $A(1) = 9$; $A(n) = 9 − 2(n − 1)$
6. −6; the pattern is "add −6 to the previous term."
7. Evaluate $A(n) = 4 + (n − 1)8$ for $n = 10$; $A(10) = 4 + (10 − 1)8 = 76$. **8.** Yes; $A(n) = A(1) + (n − 1)d = A(1) + nd − d$ by the Distributive Property.
Exercises 9. Add 7 to the previous term; 34, 41.
11. Add 4 to the previous term; 18, 22. **13.** Add −2 to the previous term; 5, 3. **15.** Add 1.1 to the previous term; 5.5, 6.6. **17.** Multiply the previous term by 2; 72, 144. **19.** not an arithmetic sequence **21.** not an arithmetic sequence **23.** yes; 1.3 **25.** not an arithmetic sequence **27.** yes; −0.5 **29.** not an arithmetic sequence **31.** $A(n) = A(n − 1) − 11$, $A(1) = 99$ **33.** $A(n) = A(n − 1) − 3$; $A(1) = 13$ **35.** $A(n) = A(n − 1) + 0.1$; $A(1) = 4.6$ **37.** $A(n) = 50 − 3.25(n − 1)$; $11 **39.** $A(n) = 7.3 + (n − 1)(3.4)$ **41.** $A(n) = 0.3 + (n − 1)(−0.3)$ **43.** $A(n) = A(n − 1) − 5$, $A(1) = 3$

45. $A(n) = A(n − 1) + 1$, $A(1) = 4$ **47.** 2, 12, 47
49. 17, 33, 89 **51.** −2, 8, 43 **53.** −3.2, −5.4, −13.1
55. Yes; the common difference is −4; $A(n) = A(n − 1) − 4$, $A(1) = −3$; $A(n) = −3 + (n − 1)(−4)$.
57. No; there is no common difference. **59.** Yes; the common difference is −0.8; $A(n) = A(n − 1) − 0.8$, $A(1) = 0.2$; $A(n) = 0.2 + (n − 1)(−0.8)$. **61.** 10, 11.2, 12.4; $A(n) = 8.8 + (n − 1)(1.2)$ **63.** −2, −4, −6; $A(n) = (n − 1)(−2)$ **65.** Answers may vary. Sample: $A(n) = 15 + 2(n − 1)$ **67.** 350, 325, 300, 275, 250, 225; you owe $225 at the end of six weeks.
69a. 1, 6, 15, 20, 15, 6, 1 **b.** 1, 2, 4, 8, 16; 64
71a. 11, 14 **b.**   **c.** The points all lie on a line.

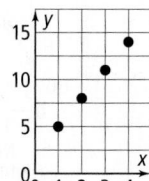

73. x; $4x + 4$ **75a.** The next figure is a drawing of a blue pentagon. **b.** Blue. The colors rotate red, blue, and purple. Every third figure is purple, so the 21st figure is purple. The figure just before that is blue. **c.** 10 sides; figure 23 is in the 8th group of three figures; the number of sides in each group of three figures is $3 + (n − 1)$; substitute 8 for n.

Chapter Review   pp. 283–286

1. independent variable **2.** linear **3.** range
4. Answers may vary. Sample:

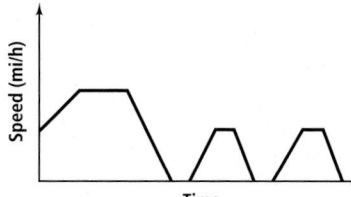

5. Answers may vary. Sample:

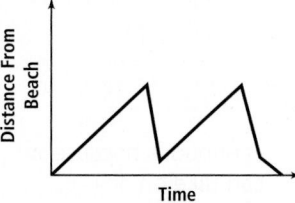

6. Chairs painted, paint left; each time p increases by 1, L decreases by 30; $L = 128 − 30p$.

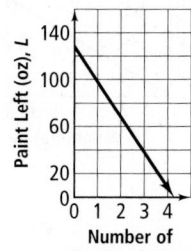

7. Snacks purchased, total cost; for each additional snack, total cost goes up by 3; $C = 18 + 3s$.

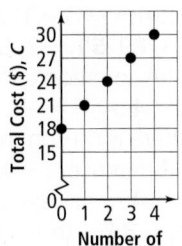

Total Cost ($), C
Number of Snacks Purchased, s

8. Independent n, dependent E; the elevation is 311 more than 15 times the number of flights climbed; $E = 15n + 311$.

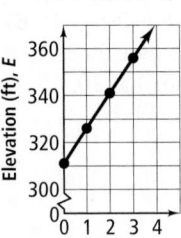

Elevation (ft), E
Number of Flights Climbed, n

9.
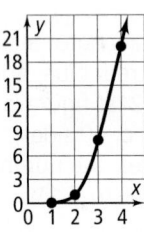
nonlinear

10.
linear

11.
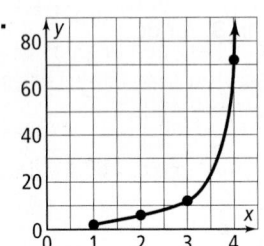
nonlinear

12.
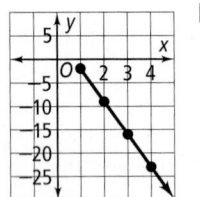
linear

13.
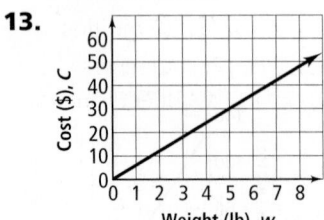
continuous because w can take on any nonnegative value

Cost ($), C
Weight (lb), w

14.
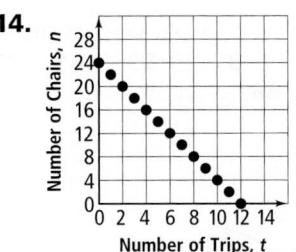
discrete because the number of trips must be a whole number

Number of Chairs, n
Number of Trips, t

15.
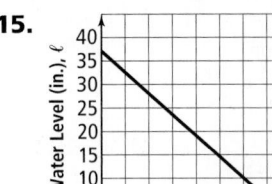
continuous because t can take on any nonnegative value

Water Level (in.), ℓ
Time (h), t

16.
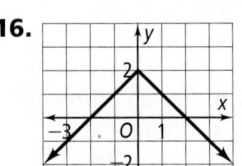

17. $V = 243 - 0.2s$ **18.** $C = 200 + 45h$ **19.** not a function **20.** function **21.** -4; 6 **22.** 53; 33

23. $\{7.2, 1.12, -4.2, -34.6\}$ **24.** $A(n) = A(n - 1) + 5$, $A(1) = 3$; $A(n) = 3 + (n - 1)(5)$

25. $A(n) = A(n - 1) - 3$, $A(1) = -2$; $A(n) = -2 + (n - 1)(-3)$

26. $A(n) = A(n - 1) + 2.5$, $A(1) = 4$; $A(n) = 4 + (n - 1)(2.5)$ **27.** $A(n) = A(n - 1) - 7$, $A(1) = 18$; $A(n) = 18 + (n - 1)(-7)$

28. $A(n) = 4 + (n - 1)(3)$ **29.** $A(n) = 13 + (n - 1)(11)$

30. $A(n) = 19 + (n - 1)(-1)$

31. $A(n) = 5 + (n - 1)(-2)$

Chapter 5

Get Ready!   p. 291

1. yes **2.** no **3.** yes **4.** $y = \frac{1}{2}x + 2$ **5.** $y = 3x - 2$

6. $y = -x - 2$ **7.** boat **8.** bean plant

9.

x	f(x)
-2	1
0	3
2	5

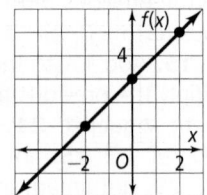

10.

x	f(x)
-1	2
0	0
1	-2

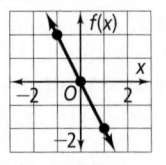

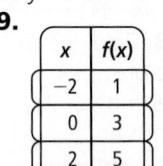

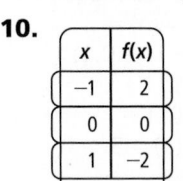

882

11.

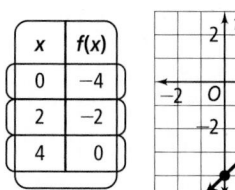

x	f(x)
0	−4
2	−2
4	0

12. $A(n) = 2 + (n − 1)3$ **13.** $A(n) = 13 + (n − 1)(−3)$
14. $A(n) = −3 + (n − 1)2.5$ **15.** the steepness of the line
16. Two lines are parallel if they lie in the same plane and
do not intersect. **17.** A y-intercept is the y-coordinate of
the point where the line crosses the y-axis.

Lesson 5-1   pp. 294–300

Got It? 1. Yes; the rate of change is constant. **2a.** $\frac{2}{5}$
b. $−\frac{1}{3}$ **c.** yes **3a.** $−\frac{4}{3}$
b. Yes, because the slope is $−\frac{4}{3}$
and the line slopes downward
from left to right.

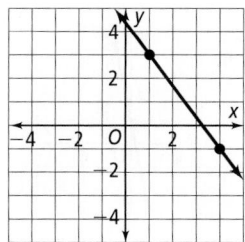

4a. undefined **b.** 0
Lesson Check 1. Yes; the rate of change between any
two points is the same. **2.** $−\frac{1}{5}$ **3.** $−\frac{5}{3}$ **4.** Slope; slope is
the ratio of vertical change to horizontal change. **5.** 0;
the slope of a horizontal line is 0. **6.** Answers may vary.
Sample: Both methods give the same result. You need
the graph to count the units of change. You need the
coordinates of the points to use the slope formula.
7. The student calculated the ratio of horizontal change
to vertical change, but slope is the ratio of vertical change
to horizontal change; $\frac{1}{2}$.
Exercises 9. Yes; 1; there is one bun per hot dog.
11. −2 **13.** 4 **15.** $\frac{3}{4}$ **17.** 1 **19.** −1 **21.** $\frac{7}{10}$ **23.** 0
25. 0 **27.** positive; 9 **29.** positive; 12 **31.** independent:
number of people; dependent: cost; $12/person

33. 0; yes, because the
slope is 0 and the
line is horizontal.

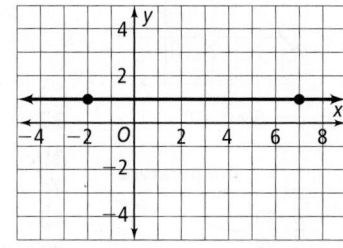

35. 0; yes, because the
slope is 0 and the line
is horizontal.

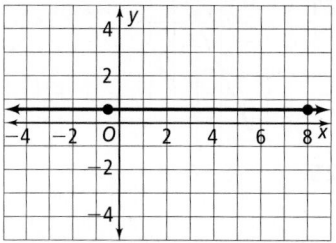

37. −0.048352; yes,
because the slope
is approximately −0.05
and the line slopes
downward from left
to right.

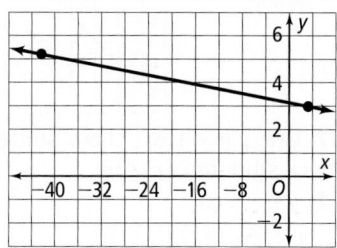

39. horse; mouse **41.** $2050 per month **43.** 6 **45.** 4 **47.** 3
49a. 5 **b.**

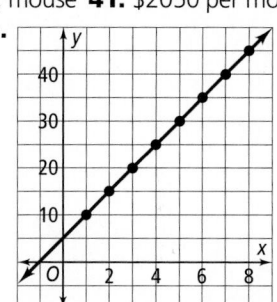

c. The slope is equal
to the common
difference.

51. Yes; the slopes from G to H, from H to I, and from G
to I all equal $\frac{1}{2}$ **53.** No; the slopes between all pairs of
points are not the same. **55.** No; the slopes between all
pairs of points are not the same. **57.** $\frac{−n}{2m}$

Lesson 5-2   pp. 301–306

Got It? 1. yes; $−\frac{4}{5}$ **2.** $y = −5x$; 75
3a. $y = 0.166x$

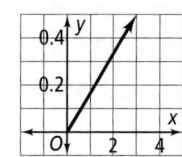

b. 0.38; the slope is the coefficient of the x-term.
4. yes; $y = −0.75x$
Lesson Check 1. yes; 3 **2.** $y = 10x$ **3.** 30 muffins
4. yes; $y = −\frac{1}{2}x$ **5.** always **6.** never **7.** sometimes
8. Yes; if $q = kp$, then $p = \frac{1}{k}q$, which is a direct variation
with constant of variation $\frac{1}{k}$.
Exercises 9. no **11.** yes; −2 **13.** yes; $\frac{7}{3}$ **15.** $y = −5x$;
−60 **17.** $y = \frac{5}{2}x$; 30 **19.** $y = 2.6x$; 31.2

21. 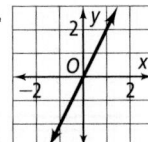 **23.**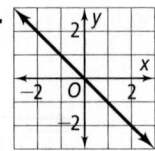

25. $d = 10.56t$

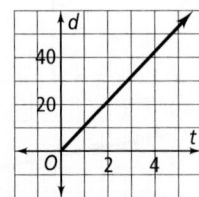

27. yes; $y = -1.5x$; check students' graphs **29.** no; check students' graphs

31. $y = -20x$

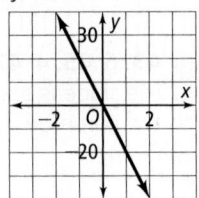

33. $y = 6x$

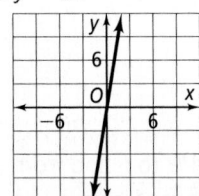

35a. 48 volts **b.** 0.75 ohm **37.** No; as the rate increases, the time decreases. **39.** No; as the number of items you purchase increases, the amount of money you have left decreases. **41.** y does not vary directly with x because $y \neq 0$ when $x = 0$. **43a.** $\frac{2}{5}$ **b.** $y = \frac{2}{5}x$; 52 lb **45.** -6

47a. $c = 3.85g$; yes; the constant of variation is 3.85

b. c is about $0.12m$ **c.** about $28.80 **49.** 165.6

51. 280.50 **52.** 1 **53.** 0 **54.** 6 **55.** $-\frac{5}{3}$ **56.** 15

57. -11 **58.** 6 **59.** -7

Lesson 5-3   pp. 308–314

Got It? 1a. $-\frac{1}{2}, \frac{2}{3}$ **b.** The graph moves down 3 units; the equation of the line changes to $y = -\frac{1}{2}x + \frac{2}{3} - 3 = -\frac{1}{2}x - \frac{7}{3}$. **2.** $y = \frac{3}{2}x - 1$ **3a.** The graph slants down from left to right, so the slope of the line should be negative. The slope is -1. **b.** $y = -x + 2$ **c.** No; the slope is constant, so it is the same between any two points on the line. **4.** $y = \frac{1}{2}x - \frac{7}{2}$

5a. 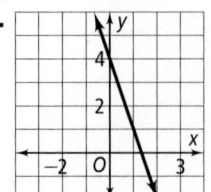 **b.**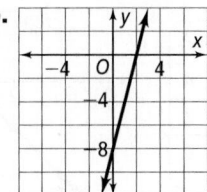

6. $y = 35x + 65$

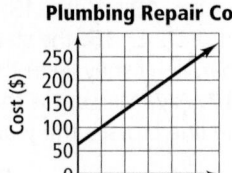

Lesson Check 1. $y = 6x - 4$ **2.** $y = -x + 1$

3.

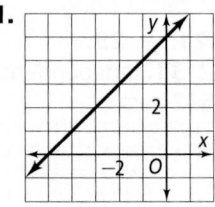

4. Yes; it is a horizontal line with a y-intercept of 5.
5. Sometimes; answers may vary. Sample: $y = 3x$ represents direct variation, but $y = 3x + 1$ does not.
6. Answers may vary. Sample: You can plot points or you can use the slope-intercept form to plot the y-intercept and then use the slope to find a second point.

Exercises 7. 3, 1 **9.** 2, -5 **11.** 5, -3 **13.** 0, 4

15. $\frac{1}{4}, -\frac{1}{3}$ **17.** $y = 3x + 2$ **19.** $y = 0.7x - 2$

21. $y = -2x + \frac{8}{5}$ **23.** $y = 2x - 3$ **25.** $y = -2x + 4$

27. $y = \frac{5}{2}x - \frac{1}{2}$ **29.** $y = -x + 2$

31. 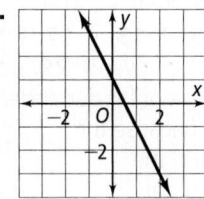 **33.**

35. $y = 5x + 65$ **37.** $-3, 2$

39. $9, \frac{1}{2}$

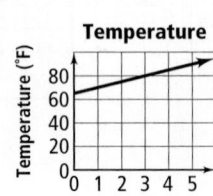

41. $9, -15$

43. $2 - a, a$

45. 2030

47a. $y = 35x + 50$

b.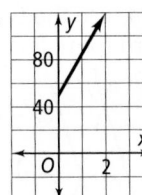

c. The amount of time the repair takes and the cost must be positive.

49. 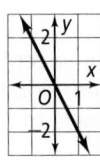 **51.** 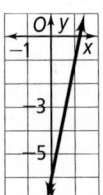 **53.**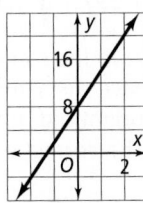

55. $a_1 = -1$, $a_n = a_{n-1} + 4$; $y = 4x - 5$; the common difference of 4 is equal to the slope of the line in slope-intercept form. **57.** Answers may vary. Samples: graph the line, determine whether the equation can be rewritten in the form $y = mx + b$. **59.** $\frac{-1}{2}$ **61.** $\frac{3}{4}$ **63.** B **65.** D **67.** Sometimes true; if $a > 0$ then $ab > ac$; otherwise $ab < ac$. **68.** $y = 5x$; 50 **69.** $y = 2x$; 20 **70.** $y = 3x$; 30 **71.** $t = -9$ **72.** $q = 27$ **73.** $x = 7$ **74.** $-3x + 15$ **75.** $5x + 10$ **76.** $-\frac{4}{9}x + \frac{8}{3}$ **77.** $1.5x + 18$

Lesson 5-4   pp. 315–320

Got It? 1. $y + 4 = \frac{2}{3}(x - 8)$ **2.**

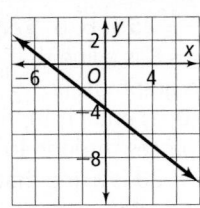

3a. $y + 3 = \frac{7}{3}(x + 2)$ **b.** They are both equal to $y = \frac{7}{3}x + \frac{5}{3}$; you can use any point on a line to write an equation of the line in point-slope form. **4a.** Answers may vary. Sample: $y - 3320 = 1250(x - 2)$; the rate at which water is being added to the tank, in gallons per hour **b.** $y = 1250x + 820$; the initial number of gallons of water in the tank

Lesson Check 1. $\frac{4}{9}$; $(-7, 12)$ **2.** $y + 8 = -2(x - 3)$

3.

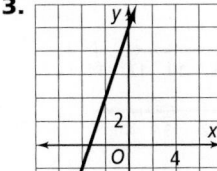

4. Answers may vary. Sample: $y + 2 = 2(x + 1)$
5. the slope m of the line and a point (x_1, y_1) on the line

6. yes; $1 - 4 = 3(-2 + 1)$ **7.** Yes; answers may vary. Sample: $y - a = m(x - b)$, $y = mx - mb + a$, $y = mx + (a - mb)$

Exercises 9. $y - 2 = -\frac{5}{3}(x - 4)$
11. $y = -1(x - 4)$

13. 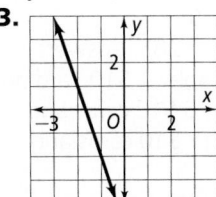 **15.**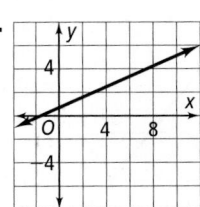

17. Answers may vary. Sample: $y - 1 = -\frac{3}{4}(x - 1)$
19–21. Point-slope forms may vary. Samples are given.
19. $y - 4 = \frac{3}{2}(x - 1)$; $y = \frac{3}{2}x + \frac{5}{2}$ **21.** $y - 6 = -\frac{1}{3}(x + 6)$; $y = -\frac{1}{3}x + 4$ **23.** $y = 8.5x$; the slope 8.5 represents the hourly wage in dollars; the y-intercept 0 represents the amount earned for working 0 h.

25.

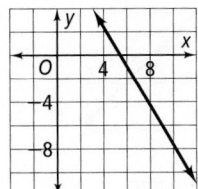

27. Answers may vary. Sample: $C - 10 = \frac{5}{9}(F - 50)$; $15°C$ **29.** $b = -0.0018a + 212$; $207.5°F$
31a. $j(x) = 2x - 2$; check students' drawings.
b. $k(x) = 2x + 1$; check students' drawings. **c.** Sample answer: Adding a number to a function changes the y-intercept, and the slope remains the same. Adding a number to the x-value of a function changes the y-intercept and the slope remains the same.

Lesson 5-5   pp. 322–328

Got It? 1a. 12; −10 **b.** 4; $\frac{3}{2}$ **2.**

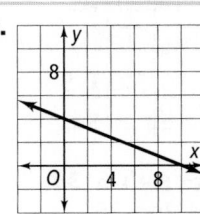

3a. 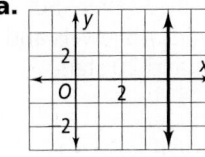 **b.**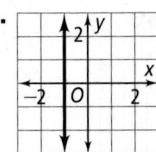

c. 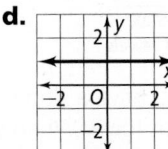 **d.**

4. $x + 3y = 0$ **5a.** $x + 15y = 60$ **b.** domain:
nonnegative integers less than or equal to 60; range:
$\{0, 1, 2, 3, 4\}$
Lesson Check 1. $3, -\frac{9}{4}$

2.

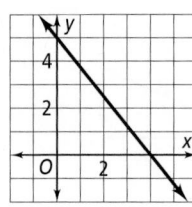

3. horizontal line
4. $x - 2y = -6$
5. $10x + 25y = 285$; answers
may vary. Sample: 1 $10 card and
11 $25 cards, 6 $10 cards and
9 $25 cards, 11 $10 cards and
7 $25 cards

6a. point-slope form **b.** slope-intercept form **c.** point-slope
form **d.** standard form **7.** Answers may vary. Sample:
slope-intercept form; it is easy to find the y-intercept
and calculate the slope from the graph.

Exercises 9. $2, -1$ **11.** $-\frac{20}{3}, 4$ **13.** $1.5, -2.5$

15.

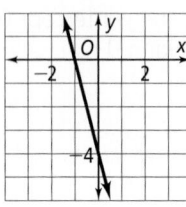

17.

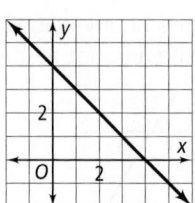

19.

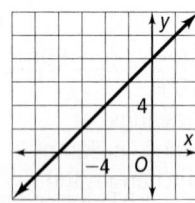

21.

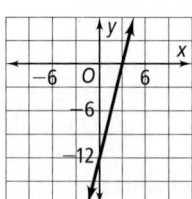

23. horizontal **25.** horizontal

27.

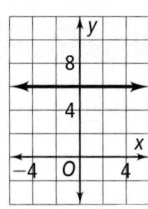

29.

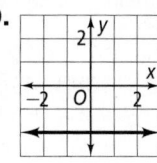

31. $2x - y = -5$ **33.** $2x + y = 10$ **35.** $2x + 3y = -3$
37. $5j + 2s = 250$

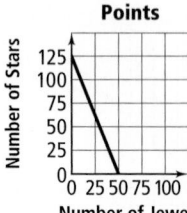

Answers may vary. Sample: 50
jewels and 0 stars, 48 jewels and 5
stars, 42 jewels and 20 stars

39. When you have a slope and the y-intercept, use the
slope-intercept form. When you have two points or a

slope and a point, use the point-slope form. When you
have the standard form, it is easy to graph.
41.

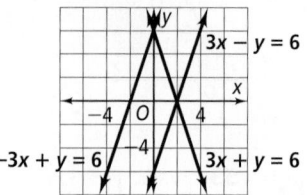

Two lines have the same slope but different y-intercepts.
Two lines have the same y-intercept but different slopes.
43. The student did not subtract 1 from each side of the
equation. The correct equation is $4x - y = -1$.

45.

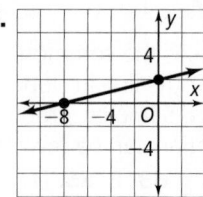

47.

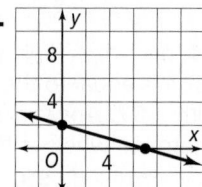

49.

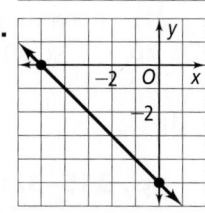

51. Both functions have a
y-intercept at $(0, 3)$. Both
functions have a negative slope.
The first function has a slope of
$-\frac{3}{4}$ and the second function has
a slope of $-\frac{1}{2}$.

53. $10, -\frac{10}{3}$ **55.** $6, 6$ **57.** $4, -\frac{8}{5}$ **59.** square; the graph
of $x + 4y = 8$ is a line that passes through $(0, 2)$ and
$(8, 0)$; the graph of $4x - y = -1$ is a line that passes
through $(0, 1)$ and $(1, 5)$; the graph of $x + 4y = -12$ is a
line that passes through $(0, -3)$ and $(-4, -2)$; the graph
of $4x - y = 20$ is a line that passes through $(5, 0)$ and
$(4, -4)$. **61.** $4x - y = -2$ **63a.** $200s + 150a = 1200$
b. Answers may vary. Sample: student $1.50 and adult
$6, student $2.25 and adult $5, student $3 and adult $4.
b. Check students' work. **65.** H **67.** H

69–71. Point-slope forms may vary. Samples are given.
69. $y + 1 = -\frac{5}{8}(x - 5)$; $y = -\frac{5}{8}x + \frac{17}{8}$
70. $y + 2 = \frac{4}{3}x$; $y = \frac{4}{3}x - 2$
71. $y + 1 = x + 2$; $y = x + 1$
72. $-2 < t \le 3$

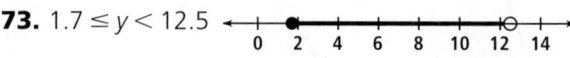

73. $1.7 \le y < 12.5$
74. $x \le -1$ or $x > 3$
75. 2 **76.** 3 **77.** 0

Lesson 5-6   **pp. 330–335**

Got It? 1. $y = 2x + 5$ **2a.** Neither; the slopes are not
equal or opposite reciprocals. **b.** Parallel; the slopes are

equal. **3.** $y = -\frac{1}{2}x + \frac{17}{2}$ **4.** $y = -\frac{2}{3}x + 10$

Lesson Check 1. $y = 6x$ and $y = 6x - 2$; $y = -\frac{1}{6}x$ and $y = 6x$, $y = -\frac{1}{6}x$ and $y = 6x - 2$ **2.** $y = -4x + 11$ **3.** $y = -x - 1$ **4a.** yes **b.** no **c.** no **6.** In both cases, you compare the slopes of the lines. If the slopes are equal, then the lines are parallel. If the slopes are opposite reciprocals, the lines are perpendicular.

Exercises 7. $y = 3x$ **9.** $y = 4x - 7$ **11.** $y = \frac{2}{3}x$

13. Perpendicular; the slopes are opposite reciprocals.

15. Parallel; the slopes are equal. **17.** Perpendicular; one line is vertical and the other line is horizontal. **19.** $y = \frac{1}{3}x$ **21.** $y = -\frac{1}{5}x - \frac{9}{5}$ **23.** $y = -\frac{1}{2}x + \frac{5}{2}$ **25.** $y = -\frac{1}{2}x + 4$

27. a and f; b and d, c and e **29.** Sometimes; if the slopes are equal and the y-intercepts are not equal, then the lines are parallel. **31.** 2; the common difference of an arithmetic sequence represents the slope of the linear graph. Since the graphs of the sequences are parallel, their slopes must be equal.

33. $x = 3$ **35.** $y = -100x + 600$, $y = -100x + 1000$; parallel; the slopes are the same. **37.** No; the slope of segment PQ is 2, the slope of segment QR is -1, and the slope of segment PR is $\frac{1}{2}$. No two slopes are opposite reciprocals, so no angle of the triangle is a right angle. **39.** G

41. 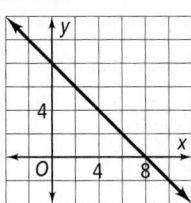 **42.**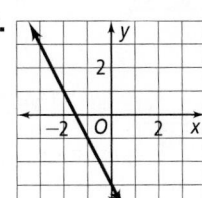

43. 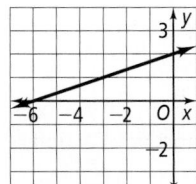 **44.** $y = 3x - 2$
45. $y = -\frac{2}{5}x + \frac{29}{5}$
46. $y = 0.25x + 1.875$
47. $y = -\frac{40}{7}x + \frac{660}{7}$

Lesson 5-7   pp. 336–343

Got It? 1a. 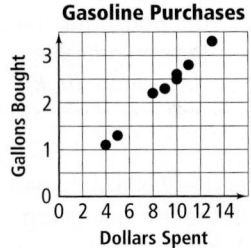 positive correlation

b. No correlation; the length of a city's name and the population are not related. **2a.** Answers may vary. Sample:

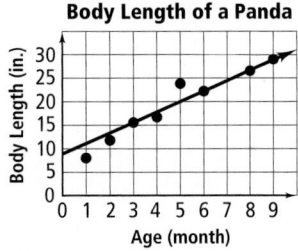

$y = 2.23x + 8.8$; about 24.4 in. **b.** No; an adult panda does not grow at the same rate as a young panda.

3a. about $9964 **b.** The slope tells you that the cost increases at a rate of about $409.43 per year. **4a.** There may be a positive correlation, but it is not causal because a more expensive vacation does not cause a family to own a bigger house. **b.** There is a positive correlation and a causal relationship. The more time you spend exercising, the more Calories you burn.

Lesson Check

1. 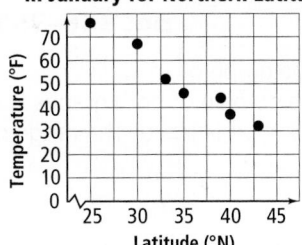 negative correlation

2–3. Answers may vary. Samples are given.
2. $y = -2x + 120$ **3.** about 20°F **4.** You use interpolation to estimate a value between two known values. You use extrapolation to predict a value outside the range of the known values. **5.** Both the trend line and the line of best fit show a correlation between two sets of data. The line of best fit is the most accurate trend line. **6.** If y decreases as x decreases, then there is a positive correlation because a trend line will have a positive slope.

Exercises 7.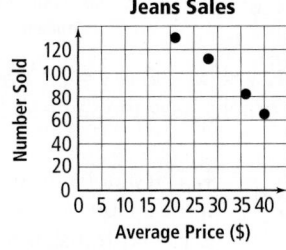

negative correlation

9. Answers may vary. Sample:

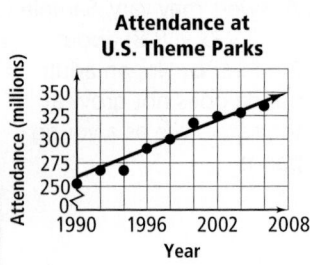

$y = 5x - 9690$; about 335 million

11. $y = 21.4x - 41557$; 0.942; 1542.6 million tickets
13. no correlation likely **15.** There is likely a correlation and a possible causal relationship, because the higher the price of hamburger, the less people are likely to buy.
17. Check students' answers. **19.** about 7 cm
21a. $y = 10.5x + 88.2$ **b.** 10.5; the sales increase by about 10.5 million units each year. **c.** 88.2; the estimated number of units sold in the year 1990 **23.** A **25.** D

27. $y = 5x - 13$ **28.** $y = -x + 5$ **29.** $y = -\frac{2}{3}x + \frac{10}{3}$
30. 5 **31.** 0 **32.** 18 **33.** 12

Lesson 5-8   pp. 346–351

Got It? 1a. The graph is the graph of $y = |x|$ translated 4 units up. **b.** The domain of both graphs is all real numbers. The range of $y = |x|$ is $y \geq 0$. The range of $y = |x| - 2$ is $y \geq -2$.

2.

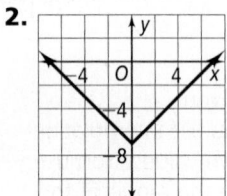

3.

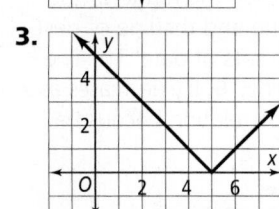

4.

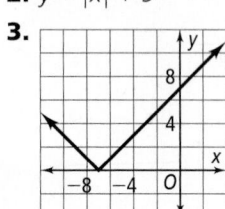

Lesson Check 1. $y = |x| - 8$ is $y = |x|$ translated 8 units down; the graphs have the same shape.
2. $y = |x| + 9$

3.

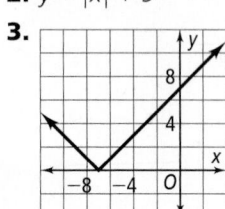

4. The graphs have the same shape; $y = |x| - 4$ is $y = |x|$ translated 4 units down and $y = |x - 4|$ is $y = |x|$ translated 4 units right.

5. The student should translate the graph 10 units to the right.

Exercises 7. It is a translation of $y = |x|$ left 4 units.
9.

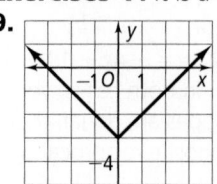

11.

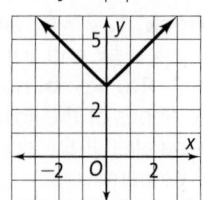

13.

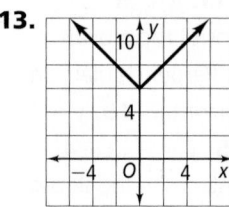

15.

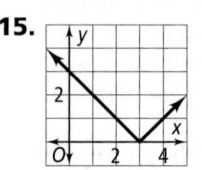

17.

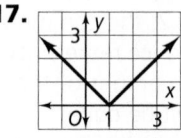

19.

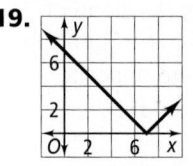

21.

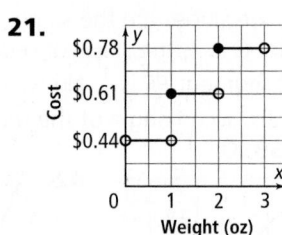

23.

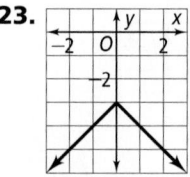

25.

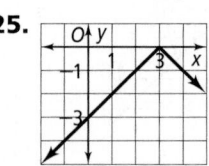

27. $y = -|x + 2.25|$ **29.** $y = -|x - 4|$
31. $(-1, 3)$

33.

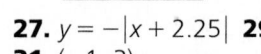

It is a translation of $y = |x|$ up 2 units and right 1 unit.

35a.

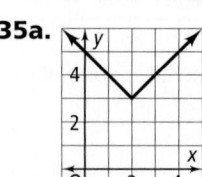

b. $(2, 3)$ **c.** The x-coordinate is the horizontal translation and the y-coordinate is the vertical translation; (h, k).

37. Graph of $y = -|x + 4| - 7$ is a V-shaped graph opening downward with the left side going through $(-6, -9)$ and $(-4, -7)$ and the right side going through $(-4, -7)$ and $(-2, -9)$. **39.** $\frac{-3}{8}$ **41.** $\frac{1}{2}$

42–43. Answers may vary. Samples are given.
42. $y = 0.25x + 5.05$ **43.** $y = 12.5x$

44. 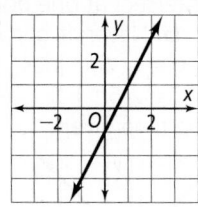 **45.**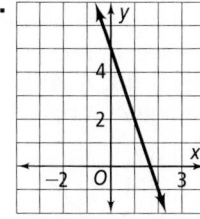

46. 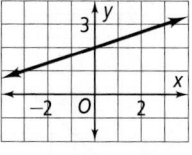 **47.**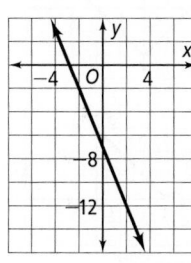

Chapter Review pp. 353–356

1. interpolation **2.** rate of change **3.** point-slope form
4. opposite reciprocals **5.** line of best fit **6.** -1 **7.** 0 **8.** 3
9. undefined **10.** 3 **11.** $-\frac{1}{2}$ **12.** $y = -2x$; -14
13. $y = \frac{5}{2}x$; $\frac{35}{2}$ **14.** $y = \frac{1}{3}x$; $\frac{7}{3}$ **15.** $y = -x$; -7 **16.** no
17. yes; $y = -2.5x$ **18.** $y = 4$ **19.** $y = x - 5$
20. $y = \frac{2}{3}x + 1$ **21.** $y = -x - 1$

22. 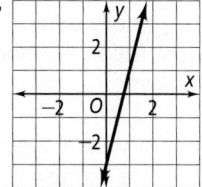 **23.**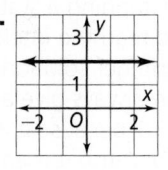

24. 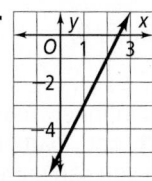 **25.**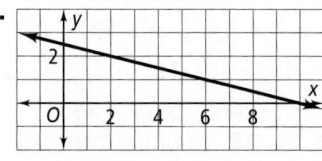

26. $y = 5x - 11$ **27.** $y = 9x - 5$ **28.** Parallel;
the slopes are equal. **29.** Neither; the slopes are not
equal or opposite reciprocals. **30.** $y = \frac{1}{3}x + 4$
31. $y = -\frac{1}{8}x + \frac{21}{2}$ **32.** negative correlation
33. no correlation **34.** positive correlation

35a.

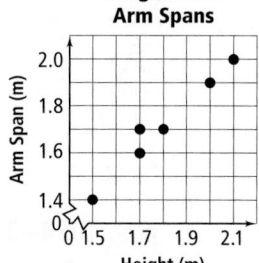

Heights and Arm Spans

b–d. Answers may vary. Samples are given.
b. $y = 0.96x - 0.01$ **c.** about 1.5 m **d.** about 2.1 m

36.  **37.**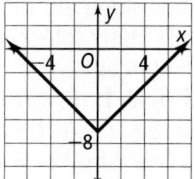

38. 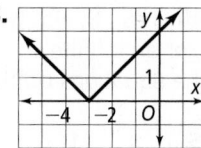 **39.**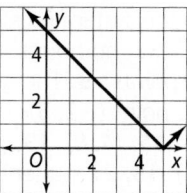

40.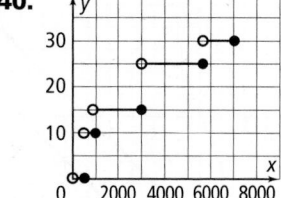

Chapter 6

Get Ready! p. 361

1. identity **2.** 1 **3.** no solution **4.** 3 **5.** 1.5 **6.** no solution
7. $x < 3$ **8.** $r \leq 35$ **9.** $t > -13$ **10.** $f \geq -2$ **11.** $s > \frac{5}{23}$
12. $x \geq -18$ **13a.** $2x - 1$ **b.** $A = \frac{1}{2}x(2x - 1)$
c. 248 cm^2
14.

15. 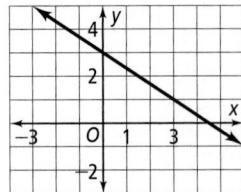 **16.**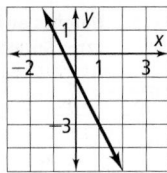

17. inconsistent **18.** deletes

Lesson 6-1   pp. 364–370

Got It? 1. $(-2, 0)$ **2.** 5 months **3a.** no solution
b. infinitely many solutions **c.** Systems with one solution
have lines with different slopes. Systems with no solutions
have the same slope but different y-intercepts. Systems
with infinitely many solutions have the same slope and
the same y-intercept.
Lesson Check 1. $(6, 13)$ **2.** $(16, 14)$ **3.** $(-1, 0)$
4. $(-1, -3)$ **5a.** $c = 10t + 8$; $c = 12t$ **b.** $(4, 48)$; the
cost is the same whether you buy 4 tickets for a cost of
$48 online or at the door. **6.** A, III; B, II; C, I **7.** No; a
solution to the system must be on both lines. **8.** No; two
lines intersect in no points, one point, or an infinite
number of points. **9.** The graphs of the equations both
contain the point $(-2, 3)$.
Exercises 11. $(4, 9)$ **13.** $(2, -2)$ **15.** $(-3, -11)$
17. $(-1, 3)$ **19.** 27 students; 3 students **21.** 10 classes
23. no solution   **25.** no solution

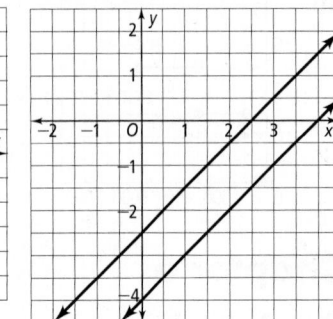

27. infinitely many solutions **29.** infinitely many solutions

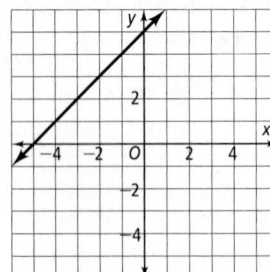 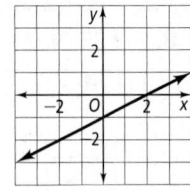

31. 13 h
33. You should substitute the values of x and y into both
equations to make sure that true statements result.
35. No solution; the lines have the same slope and
different y-intercepts so they are parallel.
37. Infinitely many solutions; the lines are the same.

39. $b = 2.5t + 40$
    $b = 5t$; 16 weeks
41a. Sometimes; if $g > h$, the lines intersect at one point,
but if $g = h$, the lines never intersect. **b.** Never; if $g < h$,
the lines intersect at one point, but if $g = h$, the lines
never intersect. **43.** A **45a.** $C = 20$, $C = 2.5h + 5$
b. 6 h **c.** Garage A; it costs less for the time given.

46. 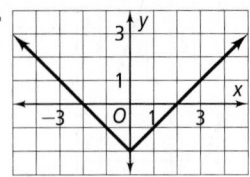 **47.**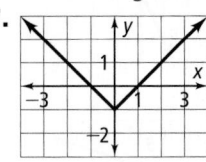

48. 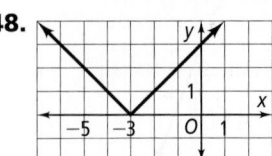 **49.**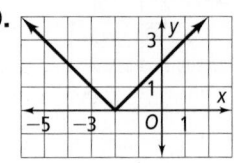

50. 1 **51.** $-\frac{1}{2}$ **52.** $-\frac{2}{3}$ **53.** $\frac{3}{5}$ **54.** $y = -2x + 19$
55. $y = -\frac{3}{2}x + 15$ **56.** $y = \frac{8}{15}x$ **57.** $y = \frac{1}{3}x - \frac{14}{3}$

Lesson 6-2   pp. 371–377

Got It? 1. $(-8, -9)$ **2a.** $\left(7\frac{1}{3}, -4\frac{7}{9}\right)$ **b.** x; $x + 3y = -7$
3. 5 new games **4.** infinitely many
Lesson Check 1. $\left(25\frac{5}{11}, 6\frac{4}{11}\right)$ **2.** $(3, 5)$ **3.** no solution
4. no solution **5.** 7 singing, 5 comedy **6.** Answers may
vary. Sample: Graphing a system can be inexact, and it is
very difficult to read the intersection, especially when
there are noninteger solutions. The substitution method is
better, as it can always give an exact answer.
7. $-2x + y = -1$ because it is easily solved for y.
8. $6x - y = 1$ because it is easily solved for y. **9.** False; it
has infinitely many solutions. **10.** False; you can use it,
but the arithmetic may be harder.
Exercises 11. $(2, 6)$ **13.** $\left(-\frac{5}{7}, 2\frac{2}{7}\right)$ **15.** $(3, 0)$
17. $(-11, -19)$ **19.** $(-12, -5)$ **21.** $\left(0, -\frac{1}{2}\right)$
23. 2 children, 9 adults **25.** 18°, 72° **27.** infinitely many
solutions **29.** infinitely many solutions **31.** one solution
33. Solve $1.2x + y = 2$ for y because then you can solve
the system using substitution. **35.** The student solved an
equation for x but then substituted it into the same
equation, not the other equation.
    $x + 8y = 21$, so $x = 21 - 8y$
    $7(21 - 8y) + 5y = 14$
    $147 - 56y + 5y = 14$
          $-51y = -133$
        $y = \frac{-133}{-51} = 2\frac{31}{51}$
So, $x = 21 - 8\left(2\frac{31}{51}\right) = 21 - \frac{1064}{51} = \frac{7}{51}$
The solution is $\left(\frac{7}{51}, 2\frac{31}{51}\right)$.
37. 20 more girls **39.** 2.75 s **41.** Answers may vary.

Sample: Solve the first equation, $y + x = x$, for y, so $y = x - x = 0$. But the second equation is not defined for $y = 0$; therefore, there is no solution. **43a.** 25 s after Pam starts, 26 s after Michelle starts **b.** Yes; 26 s after Michelle starts, both runners will be at 195 m. Pam, who is running at a faster rate, will go on to win.

Lesson 6-3   pp. 378–386

Got It? 1a. (2, 7) **b.** (−1, −2) **2.** car: 20 min; truck: 30 min **3a.** Sample answer: You can multiply the first equation by 3 to eliminate the y.
b. Sample answer: $-15x - 6y = 18$; (−2, 2)
$$3x + 6y = 6$$
c. $-5(-2) - 2(2) = 6;$ $3(-2) + 6(2) = 6$
         $10 - 4 = 6$ $-6 + 12 = 6$
4a. Sample answer: You can multiply the first equation by 3 and multiply the second equation by −4 to eliminate x.
b. Sample answer: $\dfrac{12x + 9y = -57}{-12x + 8y = 40}$; (−4, −1)
c. $\dfrac{4(-4) + 3(-1) = -19}{-16 - 3 = -19}$ and $\dfrac{3(-4) - 2(-1) = -10}{-12 + 2 = -10}$
5. no solution

Lesson Check 1. (2, 3) **2.** (1, 4) **3.** $\left(\frac{7}{25}, -\frac{2}{25}\right)$
4. Elimination; the objective of the elimination method is to add (or subtract) two equations to eliminate a variable. **5.** The Addition Property of Equality says that adding equals to equals gives you equals. This is what you are doing in the elimination method. **6.** Answers may vary. Sample: Decide which variable to eliminate, and then multiply, if necessary, one or both equations so that the coefficients of the variable are the same (or opposites). Then subtract (or add) the two equations. This will result in one equation with a single variable that you can solve. Then substitute to find the value of the other variable.

Exercises 7. (4, 5) **9.** (1, 5) **11.** (3, 15)
13a. $12x + 2y = 90$ **b.** solo act: 5 min;
         $6x + 2y = 60$ ensemble act: 15 min
15. (3, 1) **17.** (5, 3) **19.** (2, −1) **21.** no solution
23. one solution **25.** infinitely many solutions **27.** $12; $7
29. The student forgot to multiply the constant in the second equation by 4.
$15x + 12y = 6$
$12x + 12y = -12$
   so, $3x = 18$
      $x = 6$
31. Answers may vary. Sample:
$3x - 2y = 7$
$5x + 2y = 33$
Because the coefficients of the y-terms are already opposites, simply add the two equations to get $8x = 40$, or $x = 5$. Substitute $x = 5$ into either equation to get $y = 4$. The solution is (5, 4).

33. (2, 0); answers may vary. Sample: Substitution; the first equation is easily solved for y. **35.** (6, 5); answers may vary. Sample: Substitution; the first equation is already solved for y. **37.** (6, −4); answers may vary. Sample: Elimination; you can multiply each equation by the LCD of the denominators to eliminate the fractions. Then you can use elimination. **39.** parasailing: $51; horseback riding: $30 **41.** $\left(2, \frac{1}{2}\right)$ **43.** (5, 3, −1) **45.** 7 **47.** 5.46
49. 390 **50.** (7, 3.5) **51.** (34, 27) **52.** (5, −3) **53.** $a > 1$
54. $x \geq 7$ **55.** $b > 0.2$ **56.** 2.75 h

Lesson 6-4   pp. 387–392

Got It? 1. 720 books **2.** The tanks will never have the same amount of water because the solution to the system is (−2, 14), which is not a viable solution because it is not possible to have time be −2 hours. **3a.** 3.5 mi/h; 1.5 mi/h **b.** You will be pushed backward.
Lesson Check 1. 300 copies **2.** 1 kg of 30% gold, 3 kg of 10% gold **3.** 2.25 mi/h; 0.75 mi/h **4.** Before the break-even point, expenses exceed income. After the break-even point, income exceeds expenses. **5.** Answers may vary. Sample: elimination; neither equation is easily solved for a variable. **6.** You would need more of the 15% brand, since 25% is closer to 15% than 40%.
Exercises 7. 40 bicycles **9.** $950 at 5% and $550 at 4%; Let x represent the amount of money invested at 5% and let y represent the amount of money invested at 4%. The solution to the system is (950, 550).
11. 4 ft/s; 2 ft/s
13a. Let x = the number of pennies and let y = the number of quarters.
$x + y = 15$
$0.01x + 0.25y = 4.35$
The solution is 17.5 quarters and −2.5 pennies.
b. No; you cannot have a negative number of coins.
15. (−3, −2); substitution because the second equation is already solved for y **17.** $A = -3$ and $B = -2$.
19–21. Answers may vary. Samples are given.
19. Substitution; both equations are already solved for y, so you can set them equal. **21.** Substitution; the second equation is already solved for y. **23.** $66\frac{2}{3}$ mL of the 5% mixture; $133\frac{1}{3}$ mL of the 6.5% mixture **25.** It can also be solved by the elimination method because the variables are lined up and the coefficients of the y-terms are the same. So one would simply have to subtract the second equation. **27.** 37 **29.** C **31.** The slope of the line is $\frac{3-1}{4-3} = 2$. So $y - 1 = 2(x - 3)$, or $y - 1 = 2x - 6$. The equation of the line passing through the points (3, 1) and (4, 3) is $y = 2x - 5$. **32.** (−7, 6) **33.** (−2, −2)
34. (4, 2.5) **35.** $a > 5$ **36.** $d \leq -2.5$ **37.** $q \leq -4$

Lesson 6-5   pp. 394–399

Got It? 1a. yes **b.** No; it could be on the line $y = x + 10$.

2.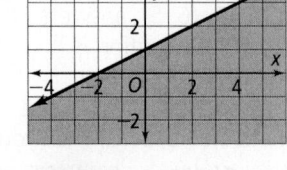

3a. 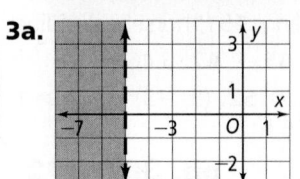 **b.**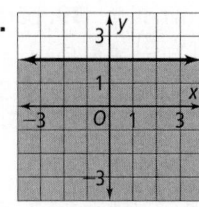

4. Answers may vary. Sample: 0 lb of peanuts and 3 lb of cashews; 6 lb of peanuts and 0 lb of cashews; 1 lb of peanuts and 1 lb of cashews

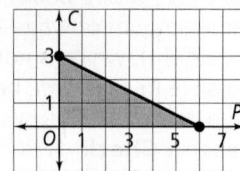

5. $y > \frac{1}{3}x - 2$
Lesson Check 1. no

2. 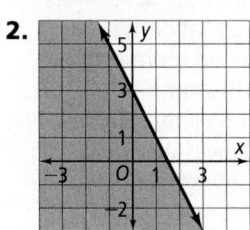 **3.**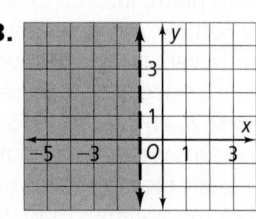

4. $y < \frac{1}{2}x - 1$ **5.** Answers will vary. Sample: The solutions of a linear equation and a linear inequality are coordinates of the points that make the equation or inequality true. The graph of a linear equation is a line, but the graph of a linear inequality is a region of the coordinate plane. **6.** Since the inequality is already solved for y, the $<$ symbol means you should shade below the boundary line. All of these shaded points will make the inequality true. **7.** $y \geq 5x + 1$

Exercises 9. solution **11.** solution **13.** solution

15. 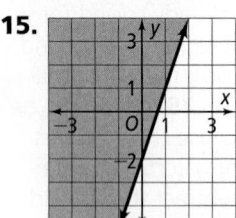 **17.**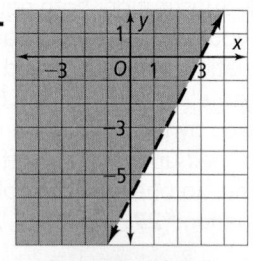

19. 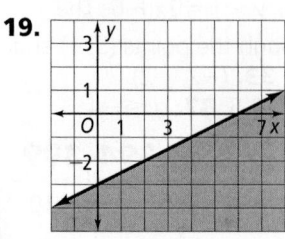 **21.**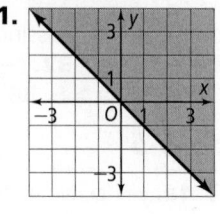

23. 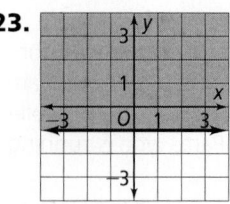 **25.**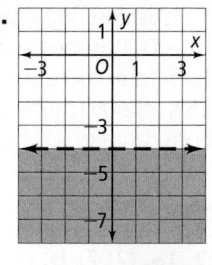

27. 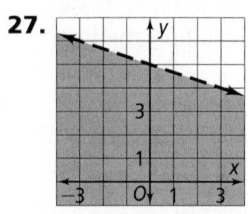 **29.**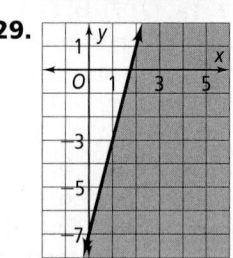

31. $9x + 12y \geq 120$

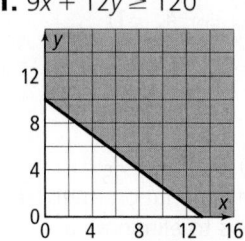

Answers may vary. Sample: 4 lb of cod and 12 lb of flounder; 10 lb of cod and 10 lb of flounder; 12 lb of cod and 4 lb of flounder

33. $y > \frac{3}{2}x - 3$ **35.** $250x + 475y \leq 6400$, where x represents the number of refrigerators and y represents the number of pianos

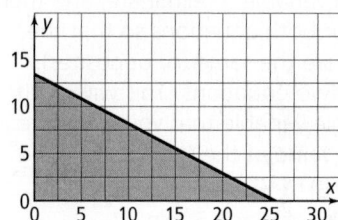

Yes; the point (12, 8) is not in the shaded region.
37. The student graphed $y \leq 2x + 3$ instead of $y \geq 2x + 3$. The other side of the line should be shaded.

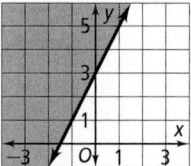

39. $-5x + 1.5y \geq -10$, where x is the number of CDs bought and y is the number sold; actual solutions include only points representing whole numbers of CDs bought and sold. The graph is a line in the first quadrant; passing through (2, 0) and (5, 10) and is shaded to the left.
41. The slope must be negative; in order for the point (3, 2) to be above the line and the point (1, 2) to be below the line, the boundary line must be sloping

downward. If the line had a positive slope, sloping upward, then the point (1, 2) would be above the line and would satisfy $y > mx + b$, which is not what is given. **43.** G **45.** 96 days

46. $2 < x \le 7$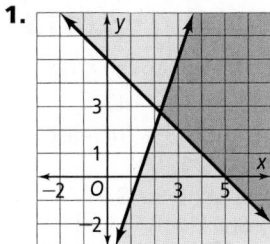

47. one solution: $(-6, -9)$ **48.** one solution: $(2, 0)$
49. no solution

Lesson 6-6   pp. 400–405

Got It?

1.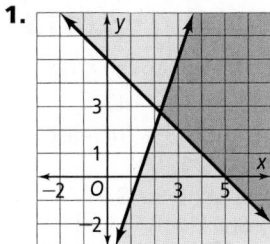

2a. $y < -\frac{1}{2}x + 1$
$\qquad y \le \frac{1}{2}x + 1$

b. No; the red line is dashed so points on that line are not included in the solution.

3.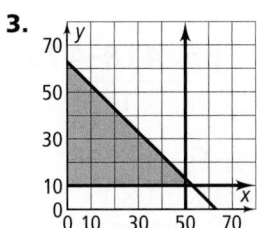

$2x + 2y \le 126$,
$x \le 50$, $y \ge 10$

Lesson Check 1.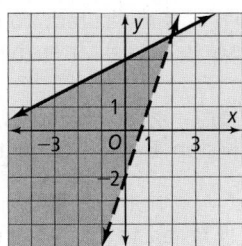

2. $y \ge 3x + 3$
$\quad y < -x - 2$

3.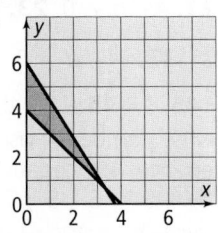

4. You can substitute the ordered pair into each inequality to make sure that it makes each true. **5.** Not necessarily; as long as there is some overlap of the half-planes, then the system will have a solution. **6.** You need to find the intersection of each of the two systems, but the intersections of lines will be a point or line and the intersections of inequalities will be a line or a planar section.

Exercises 7. yes **9.** no

11.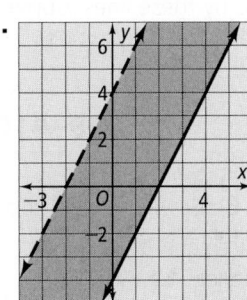

13.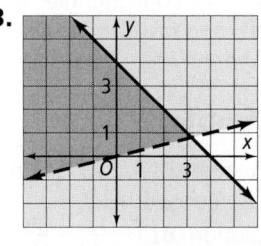

15.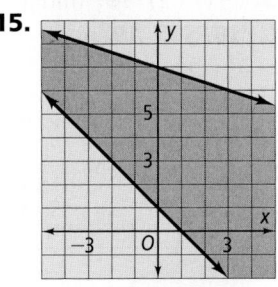

17.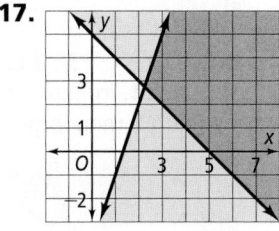

19.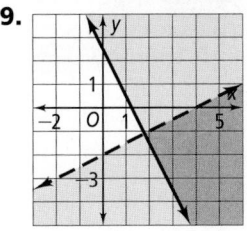

21.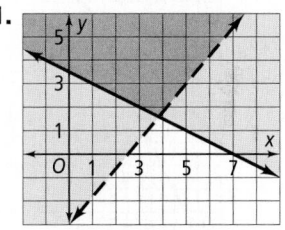

23. $y \le x + 2$, $y < -\frac{1}{3}x$ **25.** $y \ge 2$, $y > x + 1$
27. Let x = hours driven by slower driver, let y = hours driven by faster driver.

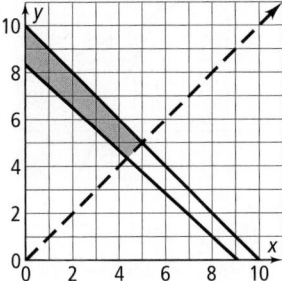

29a.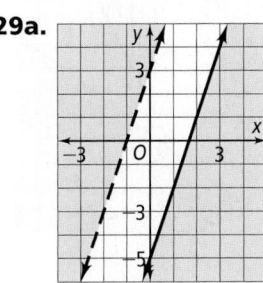

b. No; they have the same slope and different y-intercepts, so they will never intersect. **c.** no
d. No; there are no points that satisfy both inequalities.

31. You can buy 5 T-shirts and 1 dress shirt or 2 T-shirts and 3 dress shirts. **33.** C **35.** Check students' work.
37. The graph shows two lines, one passing through (1, 1)

and $(-1, -1)$ and the other passing through $(-1, 1)$ and $(1, -1)$. Four triangles are formed by these lines; upper, left, and lower ones are shaded. Right triangle is not shaded.

Chapter Review pp. 408–410

1. inconsistent **2.** elimination **3.** system of linear equations **4.** $(-8, -11)$ **5.** $(-2, 6)$ **6.** $(-3, -3)$ **7.** no solution **8.** $\left(-\frac{14}{3}, -\frac{35}{3}\right)$ **9.** infinitely many solutions **10.** 4 yr **11.** The lines will be parallel. **12.** $(4, 7)$ **13.** $(3, -10)$ **14.** no solution **15.** $(-1, -2)$ **16.** infinitely many solutions **17.** $\left(-\frac{11}{17}, -\frac{188}{17}\right)$ **18.** \$55 **19.** no solution **20.** $(-1, 13)$ **21.** $(-11, -7)$ **22.** $(5, 12)$ **23.** $(4.5, 3)$ **24.** infinitely many solutions **25.** small centerpiece: 25 min, large centerpiece: 40 min

26. 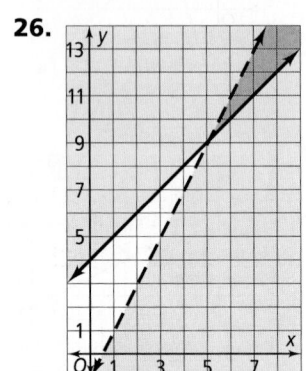 **27.**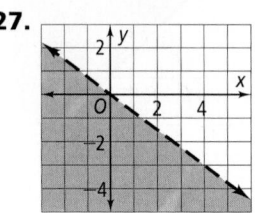

28. 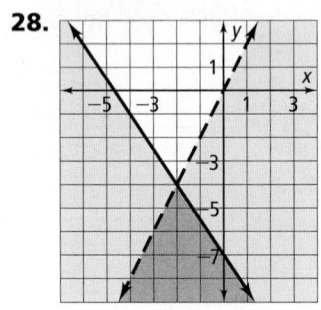 **29.**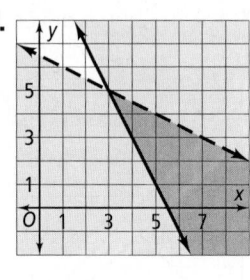

30. 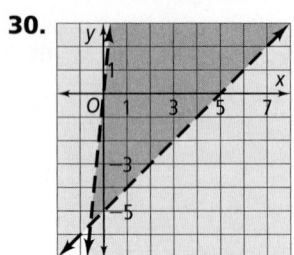 **31.**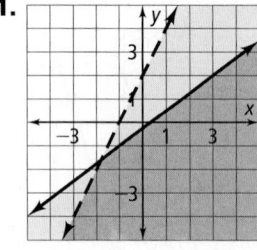

32.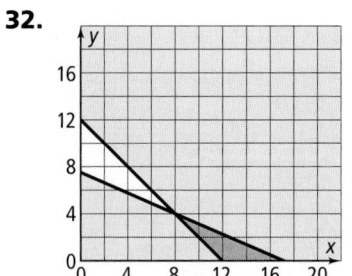

Chapter 7

Get Ready! p. 415

1. 0.7 **2.** 6.4 **3.** 0.008 **4.** 3.5 **5.** $0.\overline{27}$ **6.** 49 **7.** 5.09 **8.** 0.75 **9.** 4 **10.** 16 **11.** 4 **12.** 2000 **13.** -147 **14.** 100 **15.** 49 **16.** 117 **17.** -31 **18.** 33% increase **19.** 25% decrease **20.** 17% decrease **21.** 5% increase **22.** $\{-8, 0, -24.5\}$ **23.** $\{18, 10, -32.875\}$ **24.** $\{-11, -1, 16.5\}$ **25.** yes; how quickly the plant grows **26.** The quantity would increase rapidly. **27.** decreasing

Lesson 7-1 pp. 418–423

Got It? 1a. $\frac{1}{64}$ **b.** 1 **c.** $\frac{1}{9}$ **d.** $\frac{1}{6}$ **e.** $\frac{1}{16}$ **2a.** $\frac{1}{x^9}$ **b.** n^3 **c.** $\frac{4b}{c^3}$ **d.** $2a^3$ **e.** $\frac{1}{m^2 n^5}$ **3a.** $\frac{1}{16}$ **b.** $-\frac{1}{50}$ **c.** $\frac{1}{15,625}$ **d.** $-\frac{5}{2}$ **e.** It is easier to simplify first. That gives you, $1 \times 1 = 1$. **4.** 600 represents the number of insects 2 weeks before the population was measured; 5400 represents the population when it was measured; 16,200 represents the number of insects 1 week after the population was measured.

Lesson Check 1. $\frac{1}{32}$ **2.** 1, $m \neq 0$ **3.** $\frac{5s^2}{t}$ **4.** $4x^3$ **5.** -2 **6.** $\frac{1}{8}$ **7.** division **8.** b^0 is equal to 1, not 0; $\frac{x^n}{a^{-n}b^0} = \frac{a^n x^n}{1} = a^n x^n$

Exercises 9. $\frac{1}{9}$ **11.** $\frac{1}{25}$ **13.** $\frac{1}{16}$ **15.** -1 **17.** 1 **19.** $0.\overline{4}$ or $\frac{4}{9}$ **21.** $4a$, $b \neq 0$ **23.** $\frac{5}{x^4}$ **25.** $\frac{1}{9n}$ **27.** $\frac{3}{x^2 y}$ **29.** $\frac{1}{c^5 d^7}$ **31.** $4s^3$ **33.** $\frac{6}{ac^3}$, $d \neq 0$ **35.** $\frac{t^7}{u^{11}}$ **37.** $-\frac{1}{27}$ **39.** -225 **41.** $\frac{4}{5}$ **43.** $\frac{25}{81}$ **45.** 100; there were 100 visitors 4 months before the number of visitors was measured. **47.** negative **49.** negative **51.** 10^{-1} **53.** 10^{-3} **55a.** $5^{-2}, 5^{-1}, 5^0, 5^1, 5^2$ **b.** 5^4 **c.** a^n **57.** $4gh^{-3}$ **59.** $\frac{8c^5 d^{-4} e^2}{11}$ **61.**

n	3	$\frac{1}{6}$	7	$\frac{5}{8}$	2
n^{-1}	$\frac{1}{3}$	6	$\frac{1}{7}$	$\frac{8}{5}$	0.5

63. Answers may vary. Sample: Let $a = \frac{2}{3}$, then $a^{-1} = \frac{3}{2}$, $a^2 = \frac{4}{9}$, and $a^{-2} = \frac{9}{4}$. **65.** No; answers may vary. Sample: $3x^{-2} = \frac{3}{x^2}$ which is not the reciprocal of $3x^2$.

67. 21 **69.** $8 - 48m^2$ **71.** -1 and 1 **73.** 1 **75.** 4.5 **77.** 4

78. 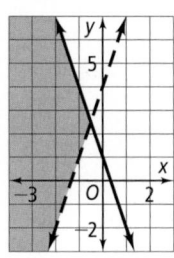 **79.**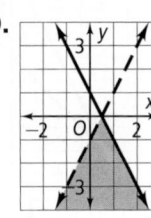

80.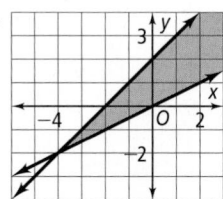

81. $y = -x + 4$
82. $y = 5x - 2$
83. $y = \frac{2}{5}x - 3$
84. $y = -\frac{3}{11}x - 17$
85. $y = \frac{5}{9}x + \frac{1}{3}$
86. $y = 1.25x - 3.79$
87. 60,000

88. 0.07 **89.** 820,000 **90.** 0.003 **91.** 340,000

Lesson 7-2　　　　　　　　　　pp. 425–431

Got It? 1a. 8^9 **b.** $(0.5)^{-11}$ **c.** 9^5 **2a.** $15x^{14}$
b. $-56cd^2$ **c.** $\frac{12j^3}{k^2}$ **d.** Since they have like bases,
you keep the same base and add the exponents;
$x^a \cdot x^b \cdot x^c = x^{(a+b+c)}$ **3.** 6.7×10^{30} molecules of
water **4a.** 2 **b.** 3 **c.** 8 **5a.** 125 **b.** 9 **c.** 8 **6a.** $4c^{\frac{4}{5}}$
b. $n^{\frac{5}{3}}$ **c.** $b^{\frac{10}{9}}c^{\frac{13}{10}}$ **d.** $441j^{\frac{5}{6}}m^{\frac{7}{4}}$

Lesson Check 1. 8^{12} **2.** $6n^{\frac{17}{12}}$ **3.** 2.4×10^{10} **4.** 39,900
km **5.** No; x and y are not like bases and they do not
share a common factor. **6.** Sometimes; if the product ab
is greater than 10, then the number will not be in
scientific notation. **7.** No; $4 \times 3 = 12$ and $\frac{1}{2} + \frac{1}{5} = \frac{7}{10}$ so
the correct result is $12a^{\frac{7}{10}}$.
Exercises 9. $(-6)^{19}$ **11.** 2^9 **13.** $(-8)^0$
15. $5c^{10}$ **17.** $\frac{y^3}{x}$ **19.** $\frac{-240m^3}{r}$ **21.** 8.84×10^7 mi
23. 5 **25.** 8 **27.** 16,384 **29.** $196d^{\frac{7}{3}}g^{\frac{7}{3}}$ **31.** 9 **33.** $\frac{1}{2}$
35. $\frac{1}{6}$ **37.** 3.42×10^{34} molecules **39.** 2.7×10^{-8}
41. 8×10^{-8} **43.** $\frac{1}{a}$ **45.** $-12x^6 + 40x^4$ **47.** 3^4
49. $(2^{x+y})\left(3^{\frac{5}{4}}\right)$ **51.** $(t+3)^{\frac{6}{5}}$ **53.** 22.5 times **55.** H
57. H **59.** (3, 2) **60.** $(-4, -5)$ **61.** (4, 7) **62.** 18, 34, 46
63. $-1, 7, 13$ **64.** $-6.8, -22.8, -34.8$ **65.** $\frac{1}{16}$ **66.** $5x$
67. $\frac{4n^2}{m}$ **68.** $\frac{-3x^3z^6}{y^2}$

Lesson 7-3　　　　　　　　　　pp. 432–438

Got It? 1a. p^{20} **b.** p^{20} **c.** $p^{\frac{1}{8}}$ **d.** $p^{\frac{1}{8}}$ **e.** yes;
$(a^m)^n = a^{mn} = (a^n)^{(m)}$ **2a.** $\frac{1}{x^{22}}$ **b.** w^3 **c.** s^4

3a. $343m^{27}$ **b.** $\frac{1}{16z^4}$ **c.** $\frac{1}{9g^8}$ **4a.** $81y^{20}$ **b.** $81c^{16}$
c. $\frac{5400b^3}{a^3}$ **5.** about 1.125×10^{10} joules of energy
Lesson Check 1. n^{18} **2.** $\frac{1}{b^{21}}$ **3.** $81a^2$ **4.** $81x^{20}$
5. 1.6×10^{11} **6.** 3.2×10^{-14} **7.** Answers may vary.
Sample: When you raise a power to a power you multiply
the exponents. When you multiply powers with the same
base, you add the exponents. **8.** The second student;
when you add like terms you add the coefficients and
keep the same variable part. **9.** Answers may vary.
Sample: x^2, $(x^3)^{\frac{2}{3}}$, $\left(x^{\frac{2}{5}}\right)^5$, $(x^5)^{\frac{2}{5}}$

Exercises 11. n^{32} **13.** x^4 **15.** $\frac{1}{x^{\frac{3}{10}}}$ **17.** $z^{\frac{1}{2}}$ **19.** $c^{\frac{1}{3}}$

21. $\frac{x^{\frac{1}{12}}}{m^3}$ **23.** $\frac{1}{49a^2}$ **25.** $\frac{1}{6g^2}$ **27.** $\frac{1}{8y^{\frac{7}{3}}}$ **29.** $\frac{y^{\frac{19}{3}}}{z^{\frac{1}{2}}}$ **31.** $32j^{35}k^{11}$

33. $\frac{j^{32}}{32k^{26}}$ **35.** 1.024×10^{13} **37.** 8×10^{-9}

39. 2.56×10^{22} **41.** 1.3312053×10^{25}

43. 4 **45.** $\frac{6}{7}$ **47.** $-\frac{1}{8}$ **49.** -2 **51.** -3 **53.** $243x^3$

55. $b^{\frac{2}{3}}$ **57.** $-8a^5b^4$ **59.** 0 **61.** 9 **63a.** The student did
not simplify the expression inside the parentheses first.
b. 25 **65.** yes; $(7xyz)^2$ **67.** 3 **69.** 1 **71.** 4 **73.** 10; $(2x)^4$,
$(4x^2)^2$, $(16x^4)^1$, $(-2x)^4$, $(-4x^2)^2$, $\left(\frac{1}{2}x\right)^{-4}$, $\left(\frac{1}{4}x^2\right)^{-2}$,
$\left(\frac{1}{16}x^4\right)^1$, $\left(\frac{1}{-2x}\right)^{-4}$, $\left(\frac{1}{-4x^2}\right)^{-2}$

Lesson 7-4　　　　　　　　　　pp. 439–445

Got It? 1a. $y^{\frac{1}{4}}$ **b.** $d^{\frac{1}{2}}$ **c.** $\frac{k^5}{j^3}$ **d.** $\frac{b^5}{a^8}$ **e.** y^4z^7
2. about 169 people per square mile **3a.** $\frac{16}{x^6}$ **b.** Answers
may vary. Sample: You can simplify within the parentheses
first to give you $\left(a^{-\frac{17}{4}}\right)^4 = a^{-17}$ or you can raise the
quotient to a power first, $\left(\frac{a^3}{a^{20}}\right) = a^{-17}$. **4.** $\frac{25b^2}{a^2}$

Lesson Check 1. $\frac{1}{y^7}$ **2.** $\frac{x^{12}}{27}$ **3.** $\frac{n^3}{m^3}$ **4.** $\frac{625y^{16}}{81x^8}$
5. 27 cubes **6.** In raising a quotient to a power, the
exponent goes to all the factors of both the numerator and
the denominator and in raising a product to a power, the
exponent goes to all the factors.
7a. Answers may vary. Sample: g^3 can be rewritten as
$\frac{1}{g^{-3}}$, so $\frac{g^3}{g^7} = \frac{1}{g^7} \cdot \frac{1}{g^{-3}}$.
Exercises 9. $\frac{1}{3}$ **11.** 0 **13.** 3 **15.** n^3 **17.** y^2 **19.** $\frac{2m^4}{n^4}$
21. $\frac{t^{11}}{27m^2}$ **23.** $\frac{3b^7}{a^6c^8}$ **25.** 4×10^{-5} **27.** 4.2×10^3
29. 7×10^{-3} **31.** about 4.4×10^{-2} deer per acre
33. $\frac{9}{64}$ **35.** $\frac{81x^4}{y^4}$ **37.** $\frac{216}{15,625}$ **39.** $\frac{262,144}{n^{30}}$ **41.** $\frac{5}{2}$ **43.** $\frac{25y^8}{49x^3}$

45. $\frac{x}{25}$ **47.** b^{31} **49.** 5^3 should be 125. **51.** Each factor should be raised to the fourth power and simplified.
53. The base d should only appear once.
55a. about 1636 h **b.** about 31 h **57.** dividing powers with the same base, definition of negative exponent
59. raising a power to a power, dividing powers with the same base, definition of negative exponent **61.** $\frac{1}{16m^8}$
63. a^4 **65.** $\frac{1}{a^9}$ **67.** $\frac{y^{10}}{2x^5}$ **69.** Answers may vary. Samples are given.

I. $\left(\frac{3}{x^2}\right)^{-3} = \left(\frac{x^2}{3}\right)^3$ Rewrite using the reciprocal.

$= \frac{(x^2)^3}{3^3}$ Raise the numerator and denominator to the third power.

$= \frac{x^6}{27}$ Simplify.

II. $\left(\frac{3}{x^2}\right)^{-3} = \frac{3^{-3}}{(x^2)^{-3}}$ Raise a quotient to a power rule

$= \frac{3^{-3}}{x^{-6}}$ Power to a power rule

$= \frac{x^6}{3^3}$ Definition of negative exponent

$= \frac{x^6}{27}$ Simplify.

III. $\left(\frac{3}{x^2}\right)^{-3} = \left(\frac{x^2}{3}\right)^3$ Rewrite using the reciprocal.

$= \frac{x^2}{3} \cdot \frac{x^2}{3} \cdot \frac{x^2}{3}$ Definition of an exponent

$= \frac{x^6}{27}$ Simplify.

71. $\frac{x^6}{9y^8}$ **73.** $\frac{2}{27}$ **75.** $\frac{c^6}{a^{18}b^6}$ **77.** $\frac{y^6}{256x^2}$ **79.** about $3\frac{1}{3}$ m
81. $x = 7$ and $y = 4$; use the two given expressions to find the system of equations, $x - y = 3$ and $x - 3y = -5$. Solve the system to find the values of x and y. **83.** $\left(\frac{m}{n}\right)^7$ **85.** $\left(\frac{3x}{2y}\right)^3$ **87a.** a^{-n} **b.** $\frac{1}{a^n}$
c. Since $\frac{a^0}{a^n}$ equals both a^{-n} and $\frac{1}{a^n}$, a^{-n} must equal $\frac{1}{a^n}$, which is the definition of a negative exponent.

89. n^{4x} **91.** $\frac{1}{m^3}$ **93.** About 1.6×10^6 g/m³ **95.** H
97. The domain is $0 \le b \le 8$ because you can use between 0 and 8 bags. The range is $0 \le A(b) \le 9600$ because $A(0) = 0$ and $A(8) = 9600$.

98. $8m^2$ **99.** $\frac{2s^6}{27}$ **100.** $2c^{\frac{1}{3}}$ **101.** $9r^{\frac{1}{2}}$ **102.** n^{15}

103. $(0, 0)$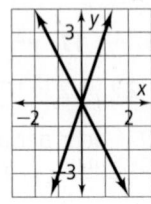

104. $(-4, -7)$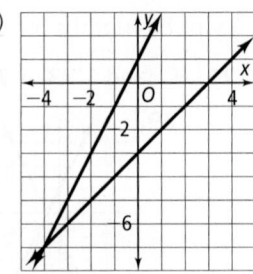

105. $(3, 5)$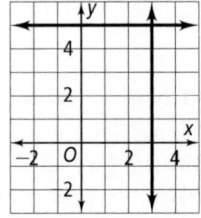

106. no solution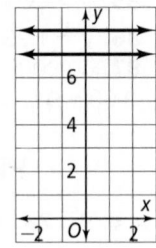

107. 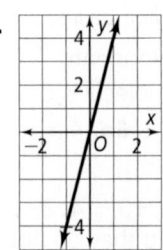 **108.**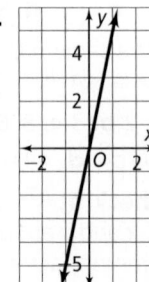

109. 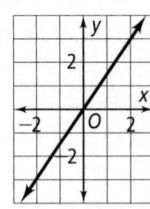 **110.**

Lesson 7-5   pp. 448–452

Got It? 1a. 3 **b.** 2 **c.** 4 **d.** 6 **2a.** $\sqrt[6]{a^5}$ **b.** $5\sqrt[3]{x}$
c. $9\sqrt[3]{2y^2}$ **3a.** $s^{\frac{2}{3}}$ **b.** $12x^{\frac{4}{3}}$ **c.** $32y^{\frac{5}{2}}$ **d.** $256a^2$ **4.** about 1868.1 Calories per day

Lesson Check 1. 2 **2.** 3 **3.** 625 **4.** $x^{\frac{1}{2}}$ **5.** $\sqrt[5]{c}$ **6.** $4\sqrt[3]{d^2}$
7. $2y^{\frac{3}{4}}$ **8.** Sample answer: The exponent $\frac{2}{3}$ needs to be applied to both 27 and y. Therefore the radical should be written as $\sqrt[3]{(27y)^2}$ and then simplified to $9\sqrt[3]{y^2}$.

9. Sample answer: To multiply two radicals with the same radicand, first rewrite the expression in exponential form. Then add the exponents. **10.** Sample answer: No; $\sqrt{4^3} - \sqrt{4} = 6$

Exercises 11. 7 **13.** 5 **15.** 6 **17.** $\sqrt[3]{a^2}$ **19.** $25\sqrt{x}$
21. $5\sqrt{x}$ **23.** $7\sqrt{2d}$ **25.** $4\sqrt[3]{(3c)^2}$ **27.** $4c^2$ **29.** $4x^{\frac{2}{3}}$
31. $5y^{\frac{3}{4}}$ **33.** $x^{\frac{3}{4}}$ **35.** \$6062.20 **37.** $\sqrt[4]{x^5}$ **39.** $\sqrt{c}\,\sqrt[6]{d^5}$
41. $42x$ **43.** $b^{\frac{2}{3}} - b^{\frac{1}{3}}$ **45.** $2b^{\frac{5}{3}} - 4a^{\frac{3}{4}}$ **47.** y **49.** about
1.17 in. **51.** $3\sqrt{x^3} = 3x^{\frac{3}{2}}$; yes; $4x^{\frac{3}{2}} + 3x^{\frac{3}{2}} = 7x^{\frac{3}{2}}$; yes,
$7x^{\frac{3}{2}} = 7\sqrt{x^3}$ **53.** \$7.15 **55.** C **57.** $7s^{\frac{5}{2}}$ **58.** $5t^6$
59. $-32x^{20}$ **60.** -6 **61.** $27d^{\frac{3}{2}}$ **62.** $-12c^2$
63. $100a^6$ **64.** $-4y^8$ **65.** $9t^{\frac{2}{3}}$ **66.** $4x - y = -7$
67. $2x - y = 13$ **68.** $7x + 6y = 12$
69. $6x - 3y = -17$ **70.** $x - 6y = 3$
71. $9x - 36y = -108$ **72.** Add 3; 12, 15, 18.
73. Subtract 6; $-8, -14, -20$. **74.** Increase the
denominator by one; $\frac{1}{5}, \frac{1}{6}, \frac{1}{7}$. **75.** Add 5; 17, 22, 27.
76. Subtract 4; $-9, -13, -17$. **77.** Take next perfect
square; 16, 25, 36.

Lesson 7-6   pp. 453–459

Got It? 1a. Linear; the x-values have a common
difference of 1 and the y-values have a common difference
of 2. **b.** Yes; the independent variable x is an exponent.
2. 14,580 rabbits

3a. 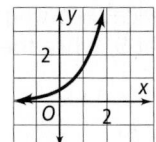   **b.**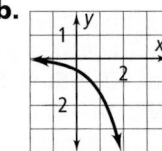

4a. 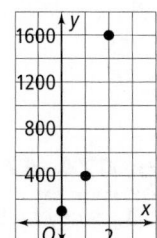   **b.** 300%

5a. about -1.34 **b.** about -0.45 **c.** about -0.45
Lesson Check 1. 48 **2.** 5

3. 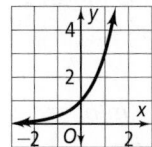   **4.**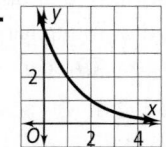

5. Answers may vary. Linear functions have a constant
rate of change, while an exponential function has a
constant finite ratio. **6.** No; the value of the base cannot

be negative. **7.** The student did not use the order of
operations correctly. You must evaluate the exponent
before you multiply: $f(-1) = 3 \cdot 4^{-1} = 3 \cdot \frac{1}{4} = \frac{3}{4}$.
Exercises 9. Linear; the x-values have a common
difference of 1 and the y-values have a common difference
of 3. **11.** Linear; the independent variable x is not an
exponent. **13.** Linear; the independent variable x is not an
exponent. **15.** 12.5 **17.** -3.44×10^{10}
19. 4800 foxes

21. 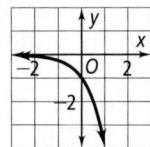   **23.**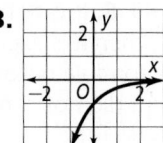

25. 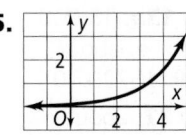   **27.**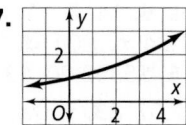

29.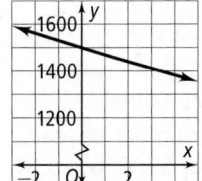

31. about 1.34 and about -2.96
33. $\{0.16, 0.4, 1, 2.5, 6.25, 15.625\}$; increase
35. $\{0.3125, 1.25, 5, 20, 80, 320\}$; increase
37. $\{0.015625, 0.125, 1, 8, 64, 512\}$; increase
39. $\{1111.\overline{11}, 333.\overline{33}, 100, 30, 9, 2.7\}$; decrease
41a. $y = 15 \times 2^{\frac{n}{3}}$ **b.** $y = 15 \times 3^{\frac{n}{4}}$

43a. 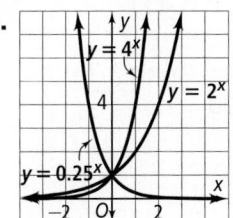   **b.** $(0, 1)$ **c.** No; the values of
y are always positive.
d. When $0 < b < 1$, the
graph decreases to the right,
but when $b > 1$, the graph
rises to the right. The larger
the value of b, the faster it
rises.

45. $f(x) = 200x^2$ **47.** $f(x) = 100x^2$
49a.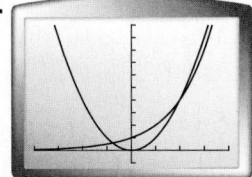

b. Answers may vary. Sample: the values are close
though the exponential function is greater from 1 to 2,
the two functions are equal at $x = 2$, and then the
quadratic function is greater from 2 to 3.

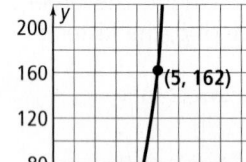
c. Answers may vary. Sample: The function values increase more rapidly. **51.** 6 **53.** 3 **55a.** 4 **b.** 3 **c.** $y = 4 \cdot 3^x$ **d.** $\frac{4}{9}$; 324

Lesson 7-7   pp. 460–466

Got It? 1. about 43,872 subscribers; 1.05^m
2. $4489.01 **3a.** about 55 kilopascals **b.** The decimal equivalent of 100% is 1.
Lesson Check 1. 4 **2.** 15 **3.** 0.2 **4.** 0.94
5. $32,577.89 **6.** If $b > 1$, then it is exponential growth. If $0 < b < 1$, then it is exponential decay. **7.** The value of $n = 1$ so the formula becomes $A = P(1 + r)^t$.
8. The student did not convert 3.5% to a decimal; $A = 500\left(1 + \frac{0.035}{4}\right)^{(4 \cdot 2)} = 500(1.00875)^8 \approx 536.09$.

Exercises 9. 14, 2 **11.** 25,600, 1.01 **13a.** 15,000 **b.** 0.04, 1.04 **c.** 1.04 **d.** 15,000, 1.04, x **e.** about 39,988 **15.** $5352.90 **17.** $634.87 **19.** $5229.70
21. $1277.07 **23.** 5, 0w.5 **25.** 100, $\frac{2}{3}$ **27.** about 33,236 **29.** exponential decay **31.** exponential decay **33.** No; the value of the car is about $5243.
35. Answers may vary. Sample: $y = -4 \cdot 1.05^x$; this is an exponential function, but it models neither exponential growth nor decay because $a < 0$. **37.** neither
39a. $P = 400(1.05)^n$, where n is the number of years and P is the profit. **b.** $5031.16 **41a.** $220 **b.** $3.96 **c.** $223.96 **d.** $193.96 **e.** 9 months **f.** $18.07

Lesson 7-8   pp. 467–472

Got It? 1a. geometric **b.** arithmetic **c.** geometric **d.** neither geometric nor arithmetic **2a.** $a_n = a_{n-1} + 2$, $a_1 = 2$; $a_n = 2 + (n - 1)(2)$
b. $a_n = a_{n-1} \cdot \left(\frac{1}{2}\right)$, $a_1 = 40$; $a_n = 40 \cdot \left(\frac{1}{2}\right)^{n-1}$
3a. $a_n = a_{n-1} \cdot 6$, $a_1 = 14$; $a_n = 14 \cdot 6^{n-1}$; $a_8 = 3{,}919{,}104$ **b.** $a_n = a_{n-1} \cdot \frac{1}{2}$, $a_1 = 648$; $a_n = 648 \cdot \left(\frac{1}{2}\right)^{n-1}$; $a_8 \approx 5.06$
4. $f(x) = 2 \cdot 3^{x-1}$;

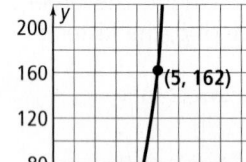

Lesson Check 1. yes; 3 **2.** yes; $\frac{1}{4}$ **3.** no
4. $a_n = 5 \cdot 4^{n-1}$; $a_n = a_{n-1} \cdot 4$, $a_1 = 5$
5. $a_n = 4 \cdot (-2)^{n-1}$; $a_n = a_{n-1} \cdot (-2)$, $a_1 = 4$

6. $a_n = 162 \cdot \left(\frac{2}{3}\right)^{n-1}$; $a_n = a_{n-1} \cdot \left(\frac{2}{3}\right)$, $a_1 = 162$
7. $a_n = 3 \cdot (2)^{n-1}$; $a_n = a_{n-1} \cdot (2)$, $a_1 = 3$ **8.** Answers will vary. Sample answer: This is the explicit formula. The recursive formula is $a_1 = 1$, $a_n = a_{n-1} \cdot (-1)$. **9.** Both arithmetic and geometric sequences can increase or decrease. Geometric sequences increase or decrease by a constant ratio. Arithmetic sequences increase or decrease by a constant difference.

Exercises 11. not geometric; no constant ratio
13. geometric; constant ratio of $\frac{3}{4}$ **15.** geometric; constant ratio of 2 **17.** $\frac{1}{3}$ **19.** 4 **21.** -3
23. $a_n = 3 \cdot (2)^{n-1}$ **25.** $a_n = 3 \cdot (-4)^{n-1}$
27. $a_n = 686 \cdot \left(\frac{1}{7}\right)^{n-1}$ **29.** $a_1 = 1$, $a_n = a_{n-1} \cdot 5$
31. $a_1 = 2$, $a_n = a_{n-1} \cdot (-4)$
33. $a_1 = 192$, $a_n = a_{n-1} \cdot \left(\frac{2}{3}\right)$
35. $a_n = 48 \cdot \left(\frac{3}{4}\right)^{n-1}$; $a_n = a_{n-1} \cdot \frac{3}{4}$, $a_1 = 48$
37. $f(x) = 8 \cdot 2^{x-1}$; The graph of the function passes through the points (1, 8), (2, 16), (3, 32), (4, 64). **39.** not geometric **41.** geometric; $\frac{1}{7}$; $a_n = 98 \cdot \left(\frac{1}{7}\right)^{n-1}$; $a_1 = 98$, $a_n = a_{n-1} \cdot \frac{1}{7}$
43. geometric; $-\frac{1}{2}$; $a_n = 200 \cdot \left(-\frac{1}{2}\right)^{n-1}$; $a_1 = 200$, $a_n = a_{n-1} \cdot \left(-\frac{1}{2}\right)$ **45.** arithmetic

47. arithmetic **49.** geometric **51.** Check students' answers. **53.** Both sequences triple for each following term. However, the first sequence starts at 5, while the second starts at 10. **55.** G **57.** I
59. $a_n = 0 + 9n$; $a_1 = 0$, $a_n = a_{n-1} + 9$
60. $a_n = 5 + -2n$; $a_1 = 0$, $a_n = a_{n-1} + (-2)$
61. $a_n = -7 + 4n$; $a_1 = -7$, $a_n = a_{n-1} + 4$
62. $x = -8$ **63.** $y = -2$ **64.** $a = \frac{35}{4}$ **65.** 75% increase **66.** 37.5 **67.** $2x + 5y$ **68.** $4a + 2b$
69. $-4c + 5d$

Chapter Review   pp. 474–478

1. geometric sequence **2.** growth factor **3.** decay factor **4.** exponential growth **5.** exponential decay **6.** 1
7. $\frac{1}{49}$ **8.** $\frac{4y^8}{x^2}$ **9.** $\frac{q^4}{p^2}$ **10.** 9 **11.** $\frac{9}{16}$ **12.** 1 **13.** 45 **14.** $\frac{25}{9}$
15. $-\frac{20}{9}$ **16.** No; -3 should be raised to the fourth power instead of multiplying it by 4. **17.** $3^2 \cdot 3^8 = 3^{10}$
18. $a^6 \cdot a^2 = a^8$ **19.** $x^2y^5 \cdot x^3y^6 = x^5y^{11}$
20. $a^{\frac{1}{2}} \cdot a^{\frac{1}{2}} = a$ **21.** $x^{\frac{2}{3}} \cdot x^{\frac{3}{4}} = x^{\frac{11}{12}}$ **22.** $m^{\frac{3}{4}}n^{\frac{1}{2}} \cdot m^{\frac{1}{2}}n^{\frac{1}{2}} = m^{\frac{5}{4}}n$ **23.** $2d^5$ **24.** x^7 **25.** $-x^4y^{12}$ **26.** $s^{\frac{19}{15}}$ **27.** $p^{\frac{4}{3}}q^{\frac{3}{2}}$
28. $6mn^3$ **29.** 7.8×10^3 pores **30.** 3 **31.** -5 **32.** 2
33. $\left(x^{\frac{2}{3}}\right)^2 = x^2$ **34.** $\left(a^{\frac{1}{2}}\right)^{\frac{1}{2}} = a^{\frac{1}{4}}$ **35.** $\left(2x^2y^{\frac{1}{4}}\right)^2 = 4x^4y^{\frac{1}{2}}$

36. $q^{12}r^4$ **37.** 1.7956 **38.** $\frac{243x^3y^{11}}{16}$ **39.** $-\frac{4}{3r^{10}z^8}$ **40.** x^4

41. $a^3b^{\frac{7}{2}}$ **42.** $\frac{1}{w^3}$ **43.** $7x^4$ **44.** $\frac{n^{35}}{v^{21}}$ **45.** $\frac{e^{20}}{81c^{12}}$

46. 2×10^{-3} **47.** 2.5×10^2 **48.** 5×10^{-5}
49. 3×10^3 **50.** Answers may vary. Sample:
 1) Simplify the expression within the parentheses.
 2) Take the reciprocal of the rational expression raised to the third power.
 3) Use the quotient raised to a power rule by applying the exponent to both the numerator and denominator.
 4) Simplify the numerator.
 5) Simplify the denominator using the power rule.

51. $\sqrt{m}$ **52.** $\sqrt[3]{p^2}\sqrt[5]{r^4}$ **53.** $6x^2$ **54.** $5\sqrt[3]{x}$

55. $8\sqrt[4]{x^3}$ **56.** $x\sqrt[3]{25}\sqrt{y}$ **57.** $(xy)^{\frac{1}{2}}$ **58.** $a^{\frac{1}{4}}$ **59.** $b^{\frac{2}{3}}$

60. x^2y^3 **61.** $3x^{\frac{1}{2}}$ **62.** $x^{\frac{2}{5}}y^{\frac{3}{5}}$ **63.** 4, 16, 64
64. 0.01, 0.0001, 0.000001 **65.** 20, 10, 5
66. 6, 12, 24

67. 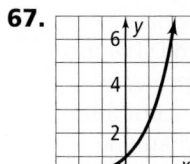 **68.**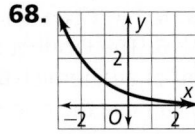

69. 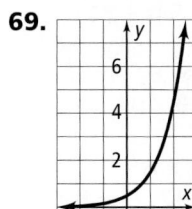 **70.**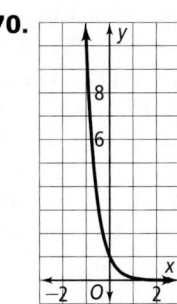

71a. 800 bacteria **b.** about 1.4×10^{16} bacteria
72. exponential growth; 3 **73.** exponential decay; 0.32
74. exponential growth; $\frac{3}{2}$ **75.** exponential decay; $\frac{1}{4}$
76. $2697.20 **77.** 463 people **78.** 2 **79.** 10 **80.** $\frac{1}{5}$
81. $\frac{1}{3}$ **82.** $a_1 = 20$, $a_n = a_{n-1} \cdot 3$
83. $a_1 = 5$, $a_n = a_{n-1} \cdot \frac{1}{2}$ **84.** $a_1 = 3$, $a_n = a_{n-1} \cdot 4$
85. $a_1 = 10$, $a_n = a_{n-1} \cdot \frac{1}{10}$

Chapter 8

Get Ready! p. 483

1. 1, 2, 3, 4, 6, 12 **2.** 1, 2, 3, 6, 9, 18 **3.** 1, 2, 4, 5, 10, 20, 25, 50, 100 **4.** 1, 3, 9, 27, 81 **5.** 1, 2, 3, 4, 6, 8, 9, 12, 18,

24, 36, 72 **6.** 1, 2, 3, 4, 5, 6, 10, 12, 15, 20, 25, 30, 50, 60, 75, 100, 150, 300 **7.** 1, 2, 5, 10, 25, 50, 125, 250
8. 1, 3, 9, 23, 69, 207 **9.** $x^2 - 9x$ **10.** $3d + 15$
11. $24r^2 - 15r$ **12.** $34m - 29$ **13.** $-36a^2 - 6a$
14. $-s^2 - 7s - 2$ **15.** $25x^2$ **16.** $9v^{\frac{5}{2}}$ **17.** $64c^6$
18. $56m^{\frac{28}{5}}$ **19.** $81b^6$ **20.** $36p^2q^2$ **21.** $7n$ **22.** $-125t^{12}$
23. p^2q^3 **24.** $5x$ **25.** $-\frac{1}{8n^5}$ **26.** $3y^2$ **27.** 3
28. A binomial is an expression with two terms.
29. b; $(x + 4)(x + 4) = (x + 4)^2$, which is a square, and $(x + 4)(x + 4) = x^2 + 8x + 16$, which is a trinomial.

Lesson 8-1 pp. 486–491

Got It? 1a. 2 **b.** 5 **c.** 0 **2.** $5x^4$, $-5x^2y^4$
3a. $8x^2 + 2x - 3$, quadratic trinomial **b.** Answers may vary. Sample: Writing a polynomial in standard form allows you to see which monomial term has the greatest degree and how many terms the polynomial has.
4. $-12x^3 + 120x^2 - 255x + 6022$
5. $-4m^3 - 4m^2 - 2m + 21$

Lesson Check 1. 4 **2.** 5 **3.** $11r^3 + 11$
4. $x^2 - 3x - 7$ **5.** quadratic trinomial **6.** linear binomial **7.** The coefficient of the sum of like monomials is the sum of the coefficients. To add polynomials, you group like terms and add their coefficients. A monomial has only one term and a polynomial can have more than one term.

Exercises 9. 3 **11.** 10 **13.** 0 **15.** no degree
17. $11m^3n^3$ **19.** $14t^4$ **21.** $18v^4w^3$
23. $-8bc^4$ **25.** $-2q + 7$; linear binomial
27. $-7x^2 - 4x + 4$; quadratic trinomial
29. $3z^4 - 2z^2 - 5z$; fourth degree trinomial
31. $9x^2 + 8$ **33.** $20x^2 + 5$ **35.** $-18x^2 + 228x + 2300$
37. $2x^3 + 8$ **39.** $5h^4 + h^3$ **41.** $9x - 1$
43. The student forgot to distribute the negative sign to all the terms in the second set of parentheses.
$\left(4x^2 - x + 3\right) - \left(3x^2 - 5x - 6\right) =$
$4x^2 - x + 3 - 3x^2 - (-5x) - (-6) =$
$4x^2 - 3x^2 - x + 5x + 3 + 6 =$
$x^2 + 4x + 9$ **45.** $-5y^3 + 2y^2 - 6$
47. $3z^3 + 15z^2 - 10z - 5$ **49.** No. Answers may vary. Sample: $\left(x^2 - x + 3\right) + \left(x - x^2 + 1\right) = 4$, which is a monomial. **51.** $14pq^6 - 11p^4q - p^4q^4$

Lesson 8-2 pp. 492–496

Got It? 1. $15n^4 - 5n^3 + 40n$ **2.** $3x$
3a. $3x^2\left(3x^4 + 5x^2 + 4\right)$ **b.** $-6x^2\left(x^2 + 3x + 2\right)$
4. $9x^2(4 - \pi)$

Lesson Check 1. $12x^4 + 42x^2$ **2.** $2a^2$ **3.** $3m(2m - 5)$
4. $4x\left(x^2 + 2x + 3\right)$ **5.** B **6.** C **7.** A **8.** Answers may vary. Sample: $18x^3 + 27x^2$

Exercises 9. $7x^2 + 28x$ **11.** $30m^2 + 3m^3$ **13.** $8x^4 -$ $28x^3 + 4x^2$ **15.** 4 **17.** 9 **19.** 4 **21.** $3(3x - 2)$
23. $7(2n^3 - 5n^2 + 4)$ **25.** $2x(7x^2 - x + 4)$
27. $25x^2(9 - \pi)$ **29.** $-10x^3 + 8x^2 - 26x$
31. $-60a^3 + 20a^2 - 70a$ **33.** $-t^3 + t^2 + t$
35. $20x^2 + 5x$; $5x(4x + 1)$ **37.** $17xy^3(y + 3x)$
39. $a^5(31ab^3 + 63)$ **41.** 49; $p = 7a$ and $q = 7b$, where a and b have no common factors other than 1, so $p^2 = 49a^2$ and $q^2 = 49b^2$. Since a^2 and b^2 have no common factors other than 1, the GCF of p^2 and q^2 is 49. **43a.** $V = 64s^3$ **b.** $V = 48(\pi)s^2$
c. $V = 64s^3 - 48(\pi)s^2$ **d.** $V = 16s^2(4s - 3\pi)$ **e.** about 182,088 in.^{3} **45.** $\frac{1}{3}$ **47.** $16x^5$; 5 **49.** $8x^2 + 4x + 5$
50. $7x^4 + 3x^2 - 1$ **51.** $-5x^3 - 6x$
52. $7x^4 + 2x^3 - 8x^2 + 4$
53. $y \le \frac{4}{5}x - 2$ **54.** $y \ge \frac{7}{2}x - 4$

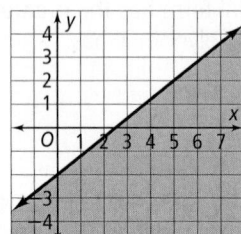   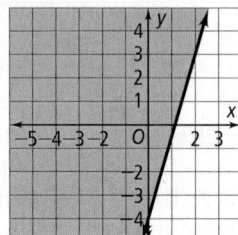

55. $y < -\frac{1}{3}x - 3$

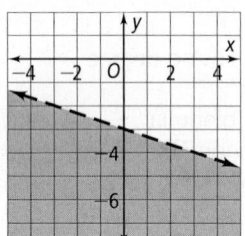

56. $8x - 40$ **57.** $-3w - 12$ **58.** $1.5c + 4$

Lesson 8-3   pp. 498–503

Got It? 1. $4x^2 - 21x - 18$ **2.** $3x^2 + 13x + 4$
3a. $3x^2 + 2x - 8$ **b.** $4n^2 - 31n + 42$
c. $4p^3 - 10p^2 + 6p - 15$ **4.** $4\pi x^2 + 20\pi x + 24\pi$
5a. $2x^3 - 9x^2 + 10x - 3$ **b.** Answers may vary.
Sample: Distribute the trinomial to each term of the binomial. Then continue distributing and combining like terms as needed.

Lesson Check 1. $x^2 + 9x + 18$ **2.** $2x^2 + x - 15$
3. $x^3 + 5x^2 + 2x - 8$ **4.** $x^2 + 2x - 15$ **5.** Find the sum of the products of the FIRST terms, OUTER terms, INNER terms, and LAST terms. **6.** $3x^2 + 11x + 8$ **7.** The degree of the product is the sum of the degrees of the two polynomials.

Exercises 9. $y^2 + 5y - 24$ **11.** $c^2 - 15c + 50$
13. $6x^2 + 13x - 28$ **15.** $a^2 - 12a + 11$

17. $2h^2 + 11h - 63$ **19.** $6p^2 + 23p + 20$
21. $4x^2 + 11x - 20$ **23.** $b^2 - 12b + 27$
25. $45z^2 - 7z - 12$ **27.** $4w^2 + 21w + 26$
29. $4\pi x^2 + 22\pi x + 28\pi$ **31.** $x^3 + 2x^2 - 14x + 5$
33. $10a^3 + 12a^2 + 9a - 20$ **35.** $x^2 + 200x + 9375$
37. $-n^3 - 3n^2 - n - 3$ **39.** $2m^3 + 10m^2 + m + 5$
41. $12z^4 + 4z^3 + 3z^2 + z$ **43.** Yes, when you multiply two polynomials you get a sum of monomials. A sum of monomials is always a polynomial. **45a. i.** $x^2 + 2x + 1$, 121 **ii.** $x^2 + 3x + 2$, 132 **iii.** $x^2 + 4x + 3$, 143
b. The digits in the product of the two integers are the coefficients of the terms in the product of the two binomials. **47.** $6x^2 + 24x + 24$ **49.** $24c^4 + 72c^2 + 54$

Lesson 8-4   pp. 504–509

Got It? 1a. $n^2 - 14n + 49$ **b.** $4x^2 + 36x + 81$
2. $(16x + 64)$ ft^2 **3a.** 7225 **b.** Answers may vary.
Sample: You could write 85 as $(80 + 5)$ or as $(100 - 15)$.
4a. $x^2 - 81$ **b.** $36 - m^4$ **c.** $9c^2 - 16$ **5.** 2496
Lesson Check 1. $c^2 + 6c + 9$ **2.** $g^2 - 8g + 16$
3. $4r^2 - 9$ **4.** $4x^2 + 12x + 9$ in.^{2} **5.** The Square of a Binomial **6.** The Product of a Sum and Difference
7. The Square of a Binomial **8.** Answers may vary.
Sample: You can use the rule for the product of a sum and difference to multiply two numbers when one number can be written as $a + b$ and the other number can be written as $a - b$.

Exercises 9. $w^2 + 10w + 25$ **11.** $9s^2 + 54s + 81$
13. $a^2 - 16a + 64$ **15.** $25m^2 - 20m + 4$
17. $(10x + 15)$ units^2 **19.** $36 - x^2$ in.^{2} **21.** 6241
23. 162,409 **25.** $v^2 - 36$ **27.** $z^2 - 25$ **29.** $100 - y^2$
31. 1596 **33.** 3591 **35.** 89,991 **37.** $4a^2 + 4ab + b^2$
39. $g^2 - 14gh + 49h^2$ **41.** $64r^2 - 80rs + 25s^2$
43. $p^8 - 18p^4q^2 + 81q^4$ **45.** $a^2 - 36b^2$ **47.** $r^4 - 9s^2$
49. $9w^6 - z^4$ **51.** $8x^2 + 32x + 32$
53. Answers may vary. Sample:
   $a^2 = b(a - b) + b^2 + (a - b)^2 + b(a - b)$ Area of big square = sum of areas of the 4 interior rectangles
   $= 2b(a - b) + b^2 + (a - b)^2$ Combine like terms.
   $= 2ab - 2b^2 + b^2 + (a - b)^2$ Distributive Property
   $= 2ab - b^2 + (a - b)^2$ Combine like terms.
   So, $(a - b)^2 = a^2 - 2ab + b^2$ by the Add. and Subtr. Prop. of =.
55. No; $\left(3\frac{1}{2}\right)^2 = \left(3 + \frac{1}{2}\right)^2 = \left(3 + \frac{1}{2}\right)\left(3 + \frac{1}{2}\right) = 3^2 + 2(3)\left(\frac{1}{2}\right) + \left(\frac{1}{2}\right)^2 = 9 + 3 + \frac{1}{4} = 12\frac{1}{4} \ne 9\frac{1}{4}$
57a. $(3m + 1)^2 = 9m^2 + 6m + 1 = 3(3m^2 + 2m) + 1$
Since $3(3m^2 + 2m)$ is a multiple of 3, the expression on the right is 1 more than a multiple of 3. **b.** no; $(3m + 2)^2 = 3(3m^2 + 4m) + 4$ **59.** C **61.** The graph shows a line passing through (4, 0) and (0, 5). Both sides of the graph are shaded, but there is no overlap.

Selected Answers

The solutions are the coordinates of the points on the line with equation $5x + 4y = 20$.
62. $6x^2 - 11x - 10$ **63.** $24m^2 - 34m + 7$
64. $5x^2 + 53x + 72$ **65.** decrease of 25% **66.** increase of 25% **67.** increase of 25% **68.** decrease of 12.5%
69. $6x(2x^3 + 5x^2 + 7)$ **70.** $9(8x^3 + 6x^2 + 3)$
71. $7x(5x^2 + x + 9)$

Lesson 8-5   pp. 512–517

Got It? 1. $(r + 8)(r + 3)$ **2a.** $(y - 4)(y - 2)$
b. No. There are no factors of 2 with sum -1.
3a. $(n + 12)(n - 3)$ **b.** $(c - 7)(c + 3)$ **4.** $x + 8$ and $x - 9$ **5.** $(m + 9n)(m - 3n)$

Lesson Check 1. $(x + 4)(x + 3)$ **2.** $(r - 7)(r - 6)$
3. $(p + 8)(p - 5)$ **4.** $(a + 4b)(a + 8b)$ **5.** $n - 7$ and $n + 4$ **6.** positive **7.** positive **8.** negative **9.** when the constant term is positive and the coefficient of the second term is negative

Exercises 11. 2 **13.** 2 **15.** $(t + 2)(t + 8)$
17. $(n - 7)(n - 8)$ **19.** $(q - 6)(q - 2)$ **21.** 6 **23.** 1
25. $(w + 1)(w - 8)$ **27.** $(x + 6)(x - 1)$
29. $(n + 2)(n - 5)$ **31.** $r - 4$ and $r + 1$ **33.** A
35. $(r + 9s)(r + 10s)$ **37.** $(m - 7n)(m + 4n)$
39. $(w - 10z)(w - 4z)$ **41a.** p and q must have the same sign. **b.** p and q must have opposite signs.
43. $x - 12$ **45.** $4x^2 + 12x + 5$; $(2x + 5)(2x + 1)$
47a. They are opposites. **b.** Since the coefficient of the middle term is negative, the number with the greater absolute value must be negative. So, p must be a negative integer. **49.** $(x + 25)(x + 2)$ **51.** $(k - 21)(k + 3)$
53. $(s + 5t)(s - 15t)$ **55.** $(x^6 + 7)(x^6 + 5)$
57. $(r^3 - 16)(r^3 - 5)$ **59.** $(x^6 - 24)(x^6 + 5)$ **61.** C
63. A **65.** $c^2 + 8c + 16$ **66.** $4v^2 - 36v + 81$
67. $9w^2 - 49$ **68.** $\frac{ad}{b}$ **69.** $\frac{8d}{7}$ **70.** $mn - c$ **71.** $7x$
72. 6 **73.** 3

Lesson 8-6   pp. 518–522

Got It? 1a. $(3x + 5)(2x + 1)$ **b.** The factors are both negative. **2.** $(2x + 7)(5x - 2)$ **3.** $2x + 3$ and $4x + 5$
4. $4(2x + 1)(x - 5)$

Lesson Check 1. $(3x + 1)(x + 5)$ **2.** $(5q + 2)(2q + 1)$
3. $(2w - 1)(2w + 3)$ **4.** $3x + 8$ and $2x - 9$ **5.** There are no factors of 20 with sum 7. **6.** 24 **7.** Answers may vary. Sample: If $a = 1$, you look for factors of c whose sum is b. If $a \neq 1$, you look for factors of ac whose sum is b.

Exercises 9. $(3d + 2)(d + 7)$ **11.** $(4p + 3)(p + 1)$
13. $(2g - 3)(4g - 1)$ **15.** $(2k + 3)(k - 8)$
17. $(3x - 4)(x + 9)$ **19.** $(2d + 5)(2d - 7)$ **21.** $5x + 2$ and $3x - 4$ **23.** $2(4v - 3)(v + 5)$ **25.** $5(w - 2)(4w - 1)$
27. $3(3r - 5)(r + 2)$ **29–33.** Answers may vary. Samples are given. **29.** -31, $(5v + 3)(3v - 8)$; 31,

$(5v - 3)(3v + 8)$ **31.** 20, $(3g + 2)(3g + 2)$; 15, $(3g + 1)(3g + 4)$ **33.** 41, $(8r - 7)(r + 6)$; -5, $(8r - 21)(r + 2)$ **35.** $6x + 4$ **37a.** $(2x + 2)(x + 2)$; $(x + 1)(2x + 4)$ **b.** yes **c.** Answers may vary. Sample: Neither factoring is complete. Each one has a common factor, 2. **39.** $3(11k + 4)(2k + 1)$ **41.** $28(h - 1)(h + 2)$
43. $(11n - 6)(5n - 2)$ **45.** $(9g - 5)(7g - 6)$ **47.** 2; explanations may vary. Sample: $ax^2 + bx + c$ factors to $(ax + 1)(x + c)$ or $(ax + c)(x + 1)$ so $b = ac + 1$ or $b = a + c$. **49.** $(7p - 3q)(7p + 12q)$ **51a.** -2, -3
b. $(x + 2)(x + 3)$ **c.** Answers may vary. Sample: if you set each factor equal to 0 and solve the resulting equations, you get the x–intercepts.

Lesson 8-7   pp. 523–528

Got It? 1a. $(x + 3)^2$ **b.** $(x - 7)^2$ **2.** $4m - 9$
3a. $(v - 10)(v + 10)$ **b.** $(s - 4)(s + 4)$
4a. $(5d + 8)(5d - 8)$ **b.** No; $25d^2 + 64$ is not a difference of two squares. **5a.** $12(t + 2)(t - 2)$
b. $3(2x + 1)^2$

Lesson Check 1. $(y - 8)^2$ **2.** $(3q + 2)^2$
3. $(p + 6)(p - 6)$ **4.** $6w + 5$ **5.** perfect-square trinomial
6. perfect-square trinomial **7.** difference of two squares
8. In a difference of two squares, both terms are perfect squares separated by a subtraction symbol.

Exercises 9. $(h + 4)^2$ **11.** $(d - 10)^2$ **13.** $(q + 1)^2$
15. $(8x + 7)^2$ **17.** $(3n - 7)^2$ **19.** $(5z + 4)^2$
21. $10r - 11$ **23.** $5r + 3$ **25.** $(a + 7)(a - 7)$
27. $(t + 5)(t - 5)$ **29.** $(m + 15)(m - 15)$
31. $(9r + 1)(9r - 1)$ **33.** $(8q + 9)(8q - 9)$
35. $(3n + 20)(3n - 20)$ **37.** $3(3w + 2)(3w - 2)$
39. $(x^2)^2 - (y^2)^2$; $(x - y)(x + y)(x^2 + y^2)$ **41.** Answers may vary. Sample: Rewrite the absolute value of both terms as squares. The factorization is the product of two binomials. The first is the sum of square roots of the squares. The second is the difference of the square roots of the squares. Example 1: $x^2 - 4 = (x + 2)(x - 2)$; Example 2: $4y^2 - 25 = (2y + 5)(2y - 5)$
43. [1] Subtract by combining like terms.
$(49x^2 - 56x + 16) - (16x^2 + 24x + 9) =$
$(49x^2 - 16x^2) + (-56x - 24x) + (16 - 9) =$
$33x^2 - 80x + 7$
[2] Factor each expression, then use the rule for factoring the difference of two squares. $(49x^2 - 56x + 16) - (16x^2 + 24x + 9) = (7x - 4)^2 - (4x + 3)^2 =$
$[(7x - 4) - (4x + 3)] - [(7x - 4) + (4x + 3)] =$
$(3x - 7)(11x - 1) = 33x^2 - 80x + 7$
45. 11, 9 **47.** 14, 6 **49a.** Answers may vary. Sample: $x^2 + 6x + 9$ **b.** because the first term x^2 is a square, the last term 3^2 is a square, and the middle term is $2(x)(3)$ **51.** $(8r^3 - 9)^2$ **53.** $(6m^2 + 7)^2$ **55.** $(x^{10} - 2y^5)^2$

57a. $(4 + 9n^2)(2 + 3n)(2 - 3n)$ **b.** They are squares of square terms. **c.** Answers may vary. Sample: $16x^4 - 1$ **59.** H **61a.** $c = 190 - 2p$ **b.** graph of a line through (0, 200), (1, 198), (2, 196), (3, 194), (4, 192), (5, 190)

62. $(6x + 7)(3x - 2)$ **63.** $(2x + 3)(4x + 3)$

64. $(4x - 7)(3x - 5)$ **65.** 2 **66.** $3m$ **67.** $4h^2$

Lesson 8-8   pp. 529–533

Got It? 1a. $(2t^2 + 5)(4t + 7)$ **b.** Answers may vary. Sample: In Lesson 8-6, you rewrote the middle term as the sum of two terms and then factored by grouping. In this problem, there were already two middle terms.

2. $3h(h^2 + 2)(2h + 3)$ **3.** Answers may vary. Sample: $2x, 5x + 2,$ and $6x + 1$

Lesson Check 1. $(4r^2 + 3)(5r + 2)$

2. $(3d^2 - 5)(2d + 1)$ **3.** $6(2x^2 + 3)(2x + 5)$

4. Answers may vary. Sample: $4x, 3x + 1,$ and $3x + 2$ **5.** No; the polynomial is a perfect square. **6.** Yes; when you write $23w$ as $20w + 3w$ the resulting two groups of terms have the same factor, $w + 5$. **7.** Yes; two groups of terms have the same factor, $4t - 7$. **8.** No; when you factor out the GCF from each pair of terms, there is no common factor.

Exercises 9. $2z^2, 3$ **11.** $2r^2, -5$ **13.** $(5q^2 + 1)(3q + 8)$

15. $(7z^2 + 8)(2z - 5)$ **17.** $(2m + 1)(2m - 1)(2m + 3)$

19. $(4v^2 - 5)(5v + 6)$ **21.** $(4y^2 - 3)(3y + 1)$

23. $w(w^2 + 6)(3w - 2)$ **25.** $3q(q + 2)(q - 2)(2q + 1)$

27. $2(d^2 + 4)(2d - 3)$ **29.** Answers may vary. Sample: $4c, c + 8,$ and $c + 5$ **31.** $9t(t - 8)(t - 2)$

33. $8(m^2 + 5)(m + 4)$ **35.** The factorization is correct, but it is not complete. The GCF of all the terms is $4x$, not 4. $4x^4 + 12x^3 + 8x^2 + 24x = 4x(x^3 + 3x^2 + 2x + 6) = 4x[x^2(x + 3) + 2(x + 3)] = 4x(x^2 + 2)(x + 3)$

37. Answers may vary. Sample: Split the expression into three binomials. Find the GCF of each binomial, then factor again. **39.** Answers may vary. Sample: $30x^3 + 36x^2 + 40x + 48 = 2(3x^2 + 4)(5x + 6)$

41. $(y + 2)(y - 2)(y + 11)$ **43.** $(6g^3 - 7h^2)(5g^2 + 4h)$

45. $(2^3 + 2^0)(2^2 + 2^1 + 2^0)$; 9(7) **47.** D **49.** B

51. $5r(2r^2 + 1)(r + 3)$ **52.** $(m + 6)^2$ **53.** $(8x - 9)^2$

54. $(7p + 2)(7p - 2)$ **55.** not a function

56. function **57.** function

58.

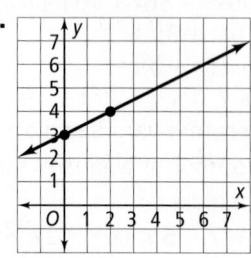

59.

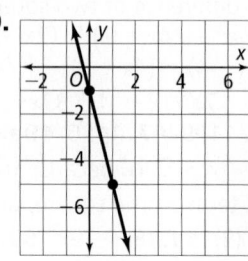

60.

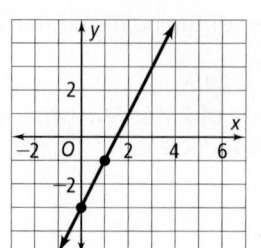

61.

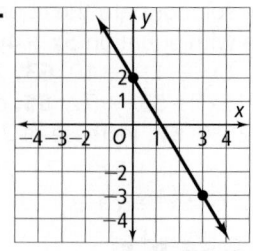

Chapter Review   pp. 535–538

1. binomial **2.** polynomial **3.** monomial **4.** perfect-square trinomial **5.** degree of the monomial

6. $-9r^2 + 11r + 3$; quadratic trinomial **7.** $b^3 + b^2 + 3$; cubic trinomial **8.** $8t^2 + 3$; quadratic binomial

9. $4n^5 + n$; fifth degree binomial **10.** $6x + 8$; linear binomial **11.** p^3q^3; sixth degree monomial **12.** $v^3 + 5$

13. $14s^4 - 4s^2 + 9s + 7$ **14.** $9h^3 - 3h + 3$

15. $7z^3 - 2z^2 - 16$ **16.** $-20k^2 + 15k$

17. $36m^3 + 8m^2 - 24m$ **18.** $6g^3 - 48g^2$

19. $3d^3 + 18d^2$ **20.** $-8n^4 - 10n^3 + 18n^2$

21. $-2q^3 + 8q^2 + 11q$ **22.** $4p(3p^3 + 4p^2 + 2)$

23. $3b(b^3 - 3b + 2)$ **24.** $9c(5c^4 - 7c^2 + 3)$

25. $4g(g + 2)$ **26.** $3(t^4 - 2t^3 - 3t + 4)$

27. $3h^3(10h^2 - 2h - 5)$ **28.** 30; if the GCF of p and q is 5, then the GCF of $6p$ and $6q$ is 6(5) = 30.

29. $w^2 + 13w + 12$ **30.** $10s^2 - 7s - 12$

31. $9r^2 - 12r + 4$ **32.** $6g^2 - 41g - 56$

33. $21q^2 + 62q + 16$ **34.** $12n^4 + 20n^3 + 15n + 25$

35. $t^2 + 6t - 27$ **36.** $36c^2 + 60c + 25$

37. $49h^2 - 9$ **38.** $3y^2 - 11y - 42$

39. $32a^2 - 44a - 21$ **40.** $16b^2 - 9$

41. $(3x + 5)(x + 7)$; $3x^2 + 26x + 35$

42. $(g - 7)(g + 2)$ **43.** $(2n - 1)(n + 2)$

44. $2(3k - 2\ell)(k - \ell)$ **45.** $(p + 6)(p + 2)$

46. $(r + 10)(r - 4)$ **47.** $(2m + n)(3m + 11n)$

48. $(t + 2)(t - 15)$ **49.** $(2g - 1)(g - 17)$

50. $3(x + 2)(x - 1)$ **51.** $(d - 3)(d - 15)$

52. $(w + 3)(w - 18)$ **53.** $7(3z - 7)(z - 1)$

54. $-2(h - 7)(h + 5)$ **55.** $(x + 2)(x + 19)$

56. $(5v + 8)(2v - 1)$ **57.** $5(g + 2)(g + 1)$ **58.** Answers may vary. Sample: If the expression is factorable then there must be factors of 18 whose sum is $b = 15$. The factors of 18 are 1 and 18, 2 and 9, 3 and 6. None of these have a sum equal to 15, so the expression is not factorable. **59.** $(s - 10)^2$

60. $(4q + 7)^2$ **61.** $(r + 8)(r - 8)$ **62.** $(3z + 4)(3z - 4)$

63. $(5m + 8)^2$ **64.** $(7n + 2)(7n - 2)$

65. $(g + 15)(g - 15)$ **66.** $(3p - 7)^2$ **67.** $(6h - 1)^2$

68. $(w + 12)^2$ **69.** $8(2v + 1)(2v - 1)$

70. $(5x - 6)(5x + 6)$ **71.** $3n + 9$ **72.** It is a perfect-square trinomial. **73.** $3y^2$; 1 **74.** $8m^2$; 3
75. $2d(d + 1)(d - 1)(3d + 2)$ **76.** $(b^2 + 1)(11b - 6)$
77. $(5z^2 + 1)(9z + 4)$ **78.** $3(a^2 + 2)(3a - 4)$

Chapter 9

Get Ready!   p. 543

1. -13 **2.** -3.5 **3.** -9 **4.** -0.5 **5.** -23 **6.** -3

7. 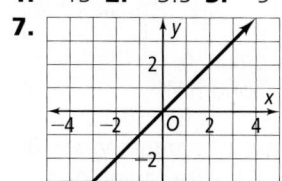 **8.**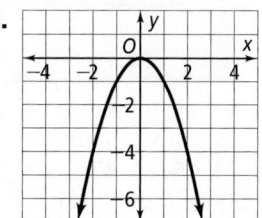

9. 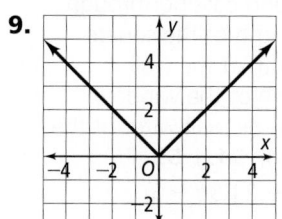 **10.**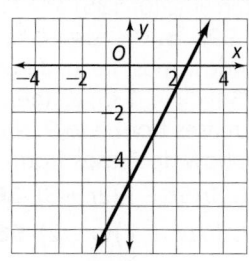

11. 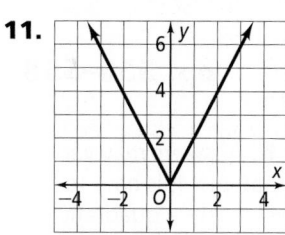 **12.**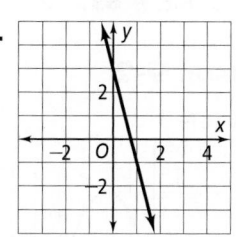

13. -108 **14.** 0 **15.** 49 **16.** 25 **17.** 24 **18.** 144
19. $(2x + 1)^2$ **20.** $(5x - 3)(x + 7)$
21. $(4x - 3)(2x - 1)$
22. $(x - 9)^2$ **23.** $(6y - 5)(2y + 3)$
24. $(m - 9)(m + 2)$
25. A quadratic function is of the form
$f(x) = ax^2 + bx + c$, where $a \neq 0$. **26.** Answers will vary.
Sample: You can fold the graph along the axis of symmetry
and the two halves of the graph will match. **27.** Answers
will vary. Sample: the product of two factors can only be
zero if at least one of the factors is zero.

Lesson 9-1   pp. 546–552

Got It? 1. $(-2, -3)$; minimum

2. 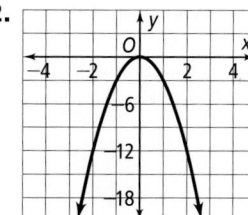 domain: all real numbers,
range: $y \leq 0$

3. $f(x) = -\frac{1}{3}x^2$, $f(x) = -x^2$, $f(x) = 3x^2$

4. 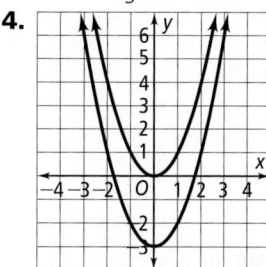 Answers will vary. Sample:
They have the same shape,
but the second parabola is
shifted down 3 units.

5a. 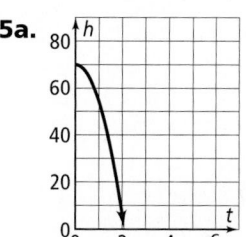 about 2 s

b. domain: $0 \leq t \leq 1.2$; range: $0 \leq h \leq 20$
Lesson Check

1.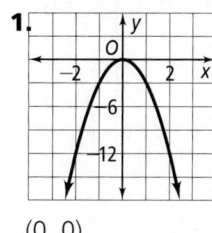

(0, 0)

2.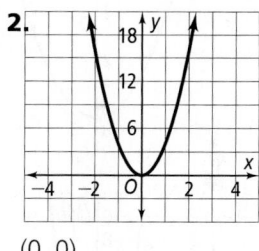

(0, 0)

3.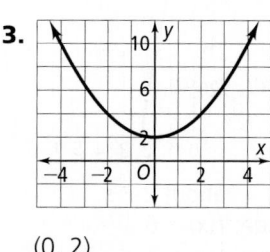

(0, 2)

4.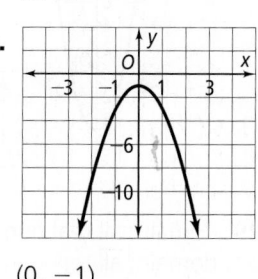

(0, −1)

5. If $a > 0$, the vertex is a minimum. If $a < 0$, the vertex
is a maximum. **6.** Answers will vary. Sample: They have
the same shape, but the second graph is shifted up 1 unit.

Exercises 7. (2, 3); maximum **9.** (2, 0); minimum

11. 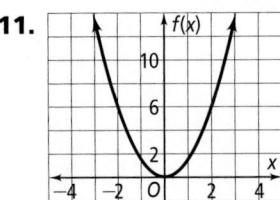 domain: all real numbers; range: $f(x) \geq 0$

13. 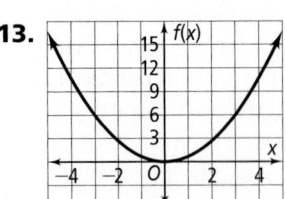 domain: all real numbers; range: $f(x) \geq 0$

15. 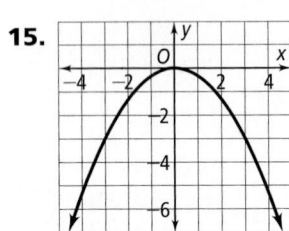 domain: all real numbers; range: $y \leq 0$

17. $f(x) = x^2$, $f(x) = -3x^2$, $f(x) = 5x^2$

19. $f(x) = -\frac{2}{3}x^2$, $f(x) = -2x^2$, $f(x) = -4x^2$

21. 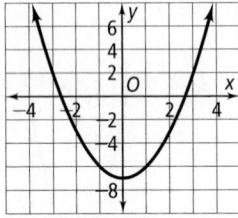   **23.**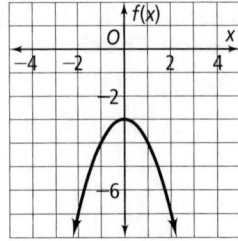

25. 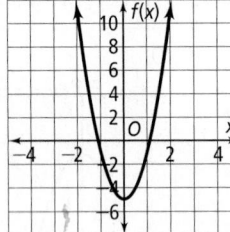   **27.**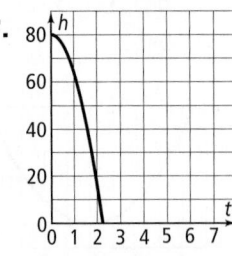

about 2.2 s

29. domain: all real numbers; range: $f(x) \geq 6$

31. domain: all real numbers; range: $y \leq -9$

33. Answers will vary. Sample: If $a > 0$, the parabola opens upward. If $a < 0$, the parabola opens downward. The vertex of the parabola is (0, c). **35.** A

37a. $g(x) = 3x^2 + 6$; the graph of $g(x)$ is shifted up 4 units and is narrower than the graph of $f(x)$.

b. $h(x) = 9x^2 + 2$; the graph of $h(x)$ is narrower than the graph of $f(x)$. **c.** Multiplying a quadratic function by a number shifts the graph up or down and changes the width of the parabola. Multiplying the x value of a quadratic function by a number only changes the width of the parabola.

39. 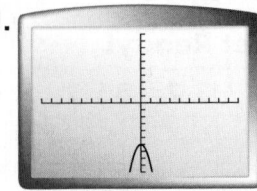   **41.**

vertex: (0, 3)   vertex: (0, −6)
axis of symmetry: $x = 0$ axis of symmetry: $x = 0$

43. M **45.** M **47a.** $a > 0$ **b.** $|a| > 1$ **49a.** graph of a parabola in the first quadrant, pointing down, with intercepts (0, 135) and (11.6, 0) and passing through (6, 99). **b.** $0 < x < 9$; the side length of the square window must be less than the width of the wall.

c. $54 < y < 135$; as the side length of the window increases from 0 to 9, the area of the wall without the window decreases from 135 to 54. **51.** I **53.** F

55. $3r(5r + 1)(2r + 3)$ **56.** $(3q^2 - 2)(5q - 6)$

57. $(7b^3 + 1)(b + 2)$ **58.** 0.75 **59.** −0.4 **60.** $-\frac{3}{8}$

61. $\frac{7}{20}$ **62.** $\frac{1}{8}$ **63.** −2

Lesson 9-2   pp. 553–558

Got It?

1a.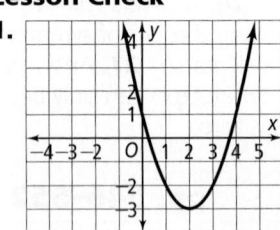

b. Answers may vary. Sample: It is easy to evaluate a quadratic function in the form $y = ax^2 + bx + c$ when $x = 0$.

2. 2 s; 69 ft; $5 \leq h \leq 69$

Lesson Check

1.   **2.**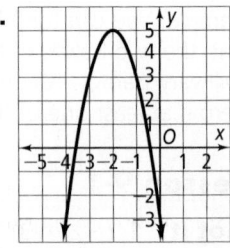

3.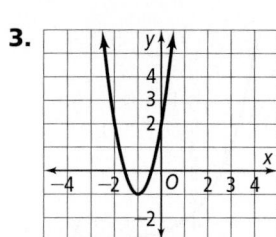

4.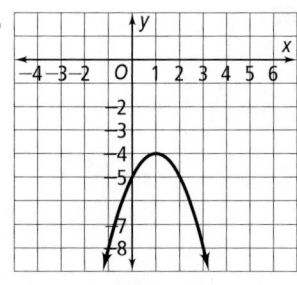

5. If $a > 0$, the graph opens upward and the vertex is a minimum. If $a < 0$, the graph opens downward and the vertex is a maximum. The greater the value of $|a|$, the narrower the parabola is. The axis of symmetry is the line $x = -\frac{b}{2a}$. The x-coordinate of the vertex is $-\frac{b}{2a}$. The y-intercept of the parabola is c. **6.** First graph the vertex and then graph the y-intercept. Reflect the y-intercept over the axis of symmetry to get a third point. Then sketch the parabola through these three points.

Exercises 7. $x = 0$; $(0, 3)$ **9.** $x = -1$; $(-1, -3)$
11. $x = 1.5$; $(1.5, -4.75)$ **13.** $x = 0.3$; $(0.3, 2.45)$
15. $x = -0.5$; $(-0.5, -6.5)$ **17.** B **19.** A

21.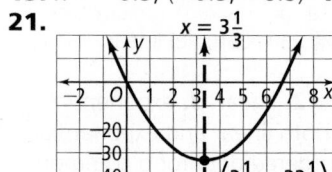

23. 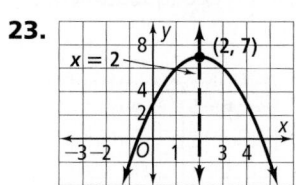 **25.**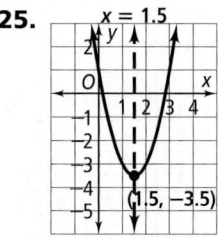

27. 25 ft; 625 ft²; $0 < A \leq 625$

29a. $(-1, 19)$ **b.** $(-2, -5)$ **31.** \$50

33. The value of b is -6, so
$-\frac{b}{2a} = -\left(\frac{-6}{2(-1)}\right) = -\left(\frac{-6}{-2}\right) = -3$. **35a.** 0.4 s **b.** No, the ball does not start at height 0 m.

Lesson 9-3   pp. 561–566

Got It? 1a. ± 4 **b.** no solution **c.** 0 **2a.** ± 6 **b.** no solution **c.** 0 **3a.** 7.9 ft **b.** The solutions of the equation in Problem 3 are irrational numbers, which are difficult to approximate on a graph.
Lesson Check 1. ± 5 **2.** ± 2 **3.** ± 12 **4.** ± 15 **5.** The zeros of a function are the x-intercepts of the function. Example: $y = x^2 - 25$ has zeros ± 5. **6.** Answers will vary. Sample: When an equation has noninteger solutions,

it is almost always easier to use square roots to find its solutions. **7.** a and c have opposite signs; $c = 0$; a and c have the same sign.
Exercises 9. no solution **11.** ± 2 **13.** ± 3 **15.** 0
17. no solution **19.** ± 3 **21.** ± 18 **23.** 0 **25.** $\pm \frac{5}{2}$
27. ± 2 **29.** ± 4 **31.** ± 3 **33.** Let $x = $ length of side of a square, then $x^2 = 75$; 8.7 ft **35.** 7.1 ft **37.** 0 **39.** 1
41. $n > 0$; $n = 0$; $n < 0$ **43.** no solution **45.** $\pm \frac{1}{6}$
47. ± 0.4 **49.** 144 **51.** When you subtract 100 from each side, you get $x^2 = -100$, which has no solution. **53.** 6.3 ft **55a.** $= 6(A2)^2 - 24$
b. ± 2; the solution(s) of the quadratic equation is (are) the x-value(s) in column A that make(s) the value in column B equal 0. **c.** Answers may vary. Sample: Find each instance of a sign change in column B. The solution(s) lie(s) between the corresponding x-values in column A. **57.** 28 cm

Lesson 9-4   pp. 568–572

Got It? 1a. $-1, 5$ **b.** $-\frac{3}{2}, 4$ **c.** $-\frac{1}{2}, -14$ **d.** $\frac{2}{7}, \frac{4}{5}$

2a. $-2, 7$ **b.** $-5, 4$ **c.** $\frac{3}{2}, 6$ **3a.** -7 **b.** The quadratic polynomials are perfect squares. **4.** 17 in. by 23 in.
Lesson Check 1. $4, 7$ **2.** $-9, 6$ **3.** $\frac{8}{3}, 3$ **4.** 2.5 ft by 4 ft
6. To solve the equation, you first factor the quadratic expression, then set each factor equal to 0, and solve.
7. No, if $ab = 8$, then there are infinitely many possible values of a and b, such as $a = 2$ and $b = 4$ or $a = -1$ and $b = -8$.

Exercises 9. $-\frac{5}{4}, -7$ **11.** $0, 2.5$ **13.** $\frac{7}{4}, -\frac{8}{3}$ **15.** $-8, 4$
17. $-1.5, 12$ **19.** $-\frac{5}{4}, 8$ **21.** $-3, 7$ **23.** $1.5, 4$ **25.** $\pm \frac{4}{3}$
27. 4 ft by 6 ft **29.** $\{-4, -2\}$ **31.** $\{-5, -2\}$ **33.** $q^2 + 7q - 18 = 0$; $-9, 2$ **35.** $x = 2$ and $x = 1$; the x-intercepts of the parabola are the same as the zeros of the function. **37.** 2; $\pm k$ **39.** $0, 4, 6$ **41.** $0, 3$ **43.** $-5, -1, 1$ **45.** $-3, -2, 3$

Lesson 9-5   pp. 576–581

Got It? 1. 100 **2a.** $-2.21, -6.79$ **b.** No, there are no factors of 15 with a sum of 9. **3a.** $(-2, 6)$ **b.** $(-6, 2)$
4. 5.77 ft
Lesson Check 1. $-18, 10$ **2.** $-11, 15$ **3.** $-21, 14$
4. $-9, 7.5$ **5.** Answers will vary. Samples are given.
a. factoring; $k^2 - 3k - 304 = (k - 19)(k + 16)$
b. completing the square **6.** Answers will vary. Sample: You have to know how to solve using square roots in order to solve by completing the square. There are more steps involved in completing the square.

Exercises 7. 81 **9.** 225 **11.** $\frac{289}{4}$ **13.** $-16, 9$
15. $-10.24, -5.76$ **17.** $-10.12, -1.88$ **19.** $(-2, -20)$

21. $(1, -324)$ **23.** $(-1, -29)$ **25.** $-1.65, 3.65$
27. $-1.96, 2.56$ **29.** $-7, 1$ **31.** about 13.3
33a. $75 - 2w$ **b.** 11.6 ft or 25.9 ft **c.** 51.9 ft or 23.1 ft
35. no solution **37.** $2.27, 5.73$ **39.** no solution
41. $-0.11, 9.11$ **43.** She forgot to divide each side by 4 to make the coefficient of the x^2-term 1.
47. $-0.45, 4.45$ **49a.** $3 \pm \sqrt{5}$ **b.** $(3, -5)$ **c.** Answers will vary. Sample: p is the x–coordinate of the vertex and $-q$ is the y-coordinate of the vertex. **51.** 0.0215 **53.** 2
55. 4.5 **57.** $-6, -5$ **58.** $\pm\frac{8}{3}$ **59.** $-\frac{1}{6}, \frac{5}{2}$
60. m^{12} **61.** $-\frac{1}{b}$ **62.** t^{13} **63.** y^{29} **64.** 81 **65.** 0 **66.** -15

Lesson 9-6   pp. 582–588

Got It? 1. $-3, 7$ **2.** 144.8 ft **3a.** Factoring; the equation is easily factorable. **b.** Square roots; there is no x-term. **c.** Quadratic formula, graphing; the equation cannot be factored. **4a.** 2 **b.** 2; if $a > 0$ and $c < 0$, then $-4ac > 0$ and $b^2 - 4ac > 0$.
Lesson Check 1. $-4, \frac{1}{3}$ **2.** $-0.94, 1.22$ **3.** 2 **4.** If the discriminant is positive, there are 2 x-intercepts. If the discriminant is 0, there is 1 x-intercept. If the discriminant is negative, there are no x-intercepts. **5.** Factoring because the equation is easily factorable; quadratic formula or graphing because the equation cannot be factored. **6.** If you complete the square for $ax^2 + bx + c = 0$, you will get the quadratic formula.

Exercises 7. $-1.5, -1$ **9.** $-3, 1.25$ **11.** $-\frac{5}{6}, \frac{10}{3}$
13. $-11, 4\frac{2}{3}$ **15.** $-2.6, 12$ **17.** $-2.56, 0.16$
19. $-0.47, 1.34$ **21.** $-2.26, 0.59$ **23.** Quadratic formula, completing the square, or graphing; the coefficient of the x^2-term is 1, but the equation cannot be factored. **25.** Quadratic formula, graphing; the equation cannot be factored. **27.** Factoring; the equation is easily factorable. **29.** 0 **31.** 0 **33.** 2 **35.** ± 4 **37.** ± 1.73
39. 2 **41.** No, there are no real-number solutions of the equation $(14 - x)(50 + 5x) = 750$. **43.** Find values of a, b, and c such that $b^2 - 4ac > 0$. **45a.** 16; 1, 5
b. 81; $-5, 4$ **c.** 73; $-0.39, 3.89$ **d.** Rational; if the discriminant is a perfect square, then its square root is an integer, and the solutions are rational. **47.** never
49. always **51.** I **53.** G **55.** 1.54, 8.46
56. $-2, -1$ **57.** $-6.06, 0.06$

58.
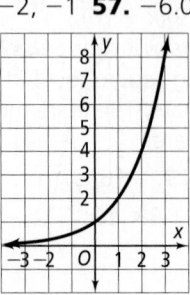
59.
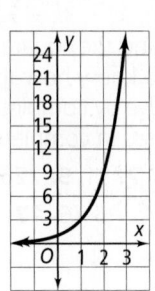

60.
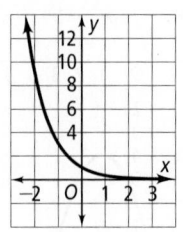
61.
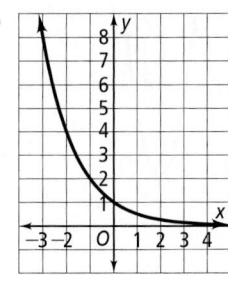

Lesson 9-7   pp. 589–594

Got It?
1a.
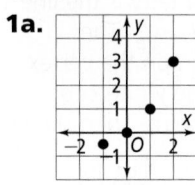
exponential

b.
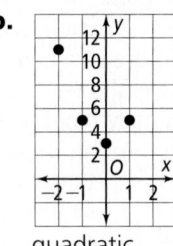
quadratic

2. exponential **3.** Answers will vary. Sample: linear; $y = 480.7x + 18,252.4$
Lesson Check 1. quadratic **2.** linear **3.** exponential
4. No, a function cannot be both linear and exponential.
5. Graph the points, or test ordered data for a common difference (linear function), a common ratio (exponential function), or a common second difference (quadratic function).

Exercises
7.
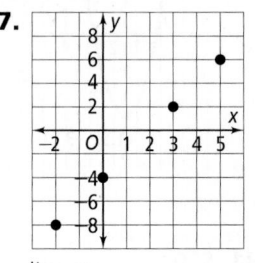
linear

9.
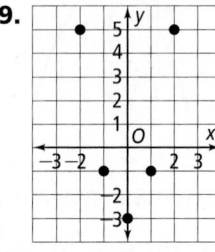
quadratic

11.
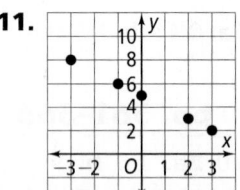
linear

13. linear
15. quadratic; $y = 3x^2$
17. linear; $y = -0.5x + 2$
19. exponential; $y = 540(1.03)^x$

21b. The second common difference is twice the coefficient of the x^2-term. **c.** When second differences are the same, the data are quadratic. The coefficient of the x^2-term is one-half the second difference.

23. Answers will vary. Sample: (0, 5), (2, 13), (4, 29), (6, 53)

25a. 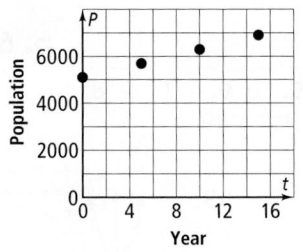 linear

b. The population changes by 600 every 5 years; the *y*-values have a common difference, so a linear model works best. **c.** $p = 120t + 5100$ **d.** 8700 **e.** $70t + 3800$ **27a.** 6, 12, 18, 24; 6, 6, 6 **b.** 6 **c.** Yes, the first differences are constant for linear functions, the second differences are constant for quadratic functions, and the third differences are constant for cubic functions.
29. I **31.** $(5x + 2)(2x - 1)$ **32.** −1.5, 0.5
33. −3.83, 1.83 **34.** 0.13, 2.54 **35.** (6, 4) **36.** (2, 7)
37. (1, −2)

Lesson 9-8   pp. 596–601

Got It? 1a. (−2, 9), (1, 3) **b.** no solution **2.** Day 5; 234 people **3.** (−6, −42), (7, 114) **4a.** (−2, 2), (1, −1)
b. Substitution; substitute −*x* for *y* in the first equation.

Lesson Check

1. 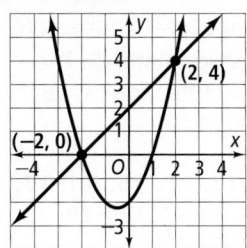 (2, 4), (−2, 0)

2. (6, 10), (−7, 192) **3.** (1, 4), (4, 1) **4.** (1, 4) **5.** (−3, −3), (−1.5, −1.5) **6a.** Answers may vary. Sample:
$y = x^2 + x - 2$, $y = -x + 1$ **b.** Answers may vary.
Sample: $y = x^2 - x$, $y = x - 1$ **c.** Answers may vary.
Sample: $y = x^2 + x - 2$, $y = x - 5$
7. In both cases, you can use graphing, substitution, or elimination. If you don't use graphing, you must know how to solve a quadratic equation in order to solve a linear-quadratic system.

Exercises

9. 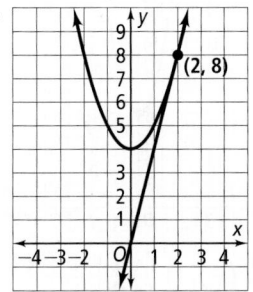 (2, 8)

11. 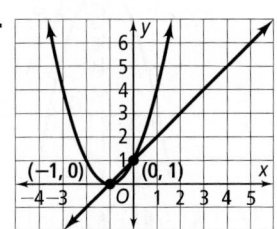 (0, 1), (−1, 0)

13.

(0, 4), (−3, −5)
15. (2, 4), (−1, 1)
17. Day 13, 2451 players of each type
19. (6, −2), (−9, −47)
21. (9, −71), (−11, −91)
23. $(-4, -41), \left(\frac{1}{3}, \frac{7}{3}\right)$
25. no solution
27. (2, −5), (−4, 1)

29. (−3, 0), (−6, −3)
31. $y = 2x + 2$ **33.** The system has no solution.
35a. 7.4 **b.** 7.8 **c.** (1.61, 0), (1.61, 3.22), (−1.61, 3.22), (−1.61, 0) **d.** 10.38 **37.** B **39.** B **41.** Given (*x*, *y*), where *x* is the number of balls and *y* is the weight of the box, you have the points (4, 5) and (10, 11). The slope of the line that passes through these two points is
$\frac{11-5}{10-4} = \frac{6}{6} = 1$. An equation of the line is
$y - 5 = 1(x - 4)$, or $y = x + 1$. The equation of the line in standard form is $x - y = -1$. **42.** quadratic;
$y = 0.2x^2$ **43.** exponential; $y = 4(2.5)^x$ **44.** linear;
$y = -4.2x + 7$ **45.** 14 **46.** $\frac{5}{7}$ **47.** 1.2 **48.** 9 **49.** 0.6
50. 20

Chapter Review   pp. 603–606

1. parabola **2.** axis of symmetry **3.** discriminant **4.** vertex
5.

6.

7.
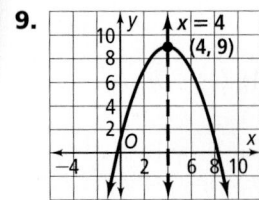

8.
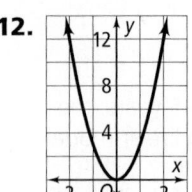

9.
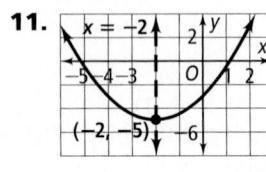

10. $\left(-\frac{3}{4}, 11\frac{1}{8}\right)$
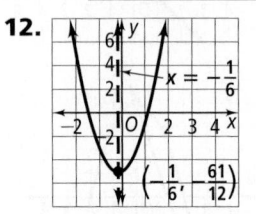

11.
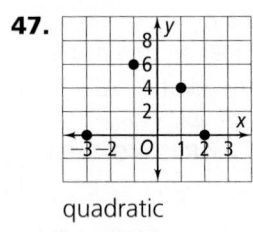

12.
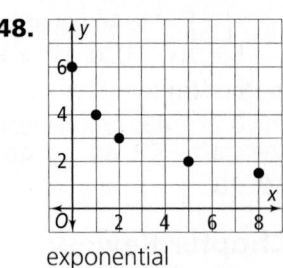

13. Answers will vary. Sample: $y = -x^2$ **14.** Answers will vary. Sample: $y = x^2$ **15.** Answers will vary. Sample: $y = x^2$ **16.** Answers will vary. Sample: $y = 0.5x^2$ **17.** ± 2 **18.** ± 5 **19.** 0 **20.** no solution **21.** $\pm\frac{2}{3}$ **22.** ± 4 **23.** -3, -4 **24.** 0, 2 **25.** 4, 5 **26.** $-3, \frac{1}{2}$ **27.** $-\frac{2}{3}, \frac{3}{2}$ **28.** 1, 4 **29.** 2.3 in. **30.** -6.74, 0.74 **31.** 0.38, 2.62 **32.** -2, -1.5 **33.** -9.12, -0.88 **34.** -1.65, 3.65 **35.** 1.26, 12.74 **36.** 7.6 ft by 15.8 ft **37.** 6.4 in. by 13.8 in. **38.** two **39.** two **40.** -1.84, 1.09 **41.** -2.5, 4 **42.** 7.87, 0.13 **43.** -0.25, 0.06 **44.** ± 5; square roots because there is no x-term **45.** 3; factoring because it is easy to factor **46.** 1.5 s

47.
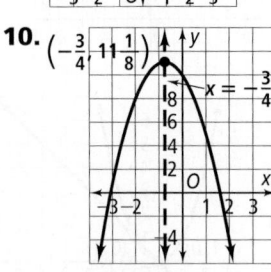
quadratic

48.

exponential

49. $y = 3x - 2$ **50.** $y = 5(2)^x$ **51.** $(-1, 8), (2, -1)$ **52.** $(0, -1), (1, -2)$ **53.** $(-1, -1), (1, 1)$ **54.** $(-2, -4)$, $(3, 6)$ **55.** $(-8, 3), (12, 123)$ **56.** $(7, -2), (9, 6)$ **57.** $(-7, -45), (-4, -21)$ **58.** $(-13, 64), (3, -16)$ **59.** $(6, 69) (10, 145)$ **60.** $(-9, 33), (-12, 63)$ **61.** If you look at the graph and see how many times the graphs intersect, that is how many solutions the system will have.

Chapter 10

Get Ready! p. 611

1. 6 **2.** 18 **3.** 4.5 **4.** 8 **5.** 10 **6.** 4 **7.** 12 **8.** 14
9. $-2h^2 + 5h + 12$ **10.** $9b^4 - 49$
11. $-15x^2 - 11x - 2$

12.
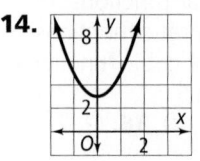

13.
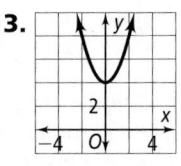

14.

15. 2 **16.** 2 **17.** 0
18. 1 **19.** 2 **20.** 2
21. They both contain the same radical expression, $\sqrt{3}$.

22. I would be rich.

Lesson 10-1 pp. 614–618

Got It? 1. 15 cm **2.** 9 **3a.** no; $20^2 + 47^2 \neq 52^2$
b. yes; $(2a)^2 + (2b)^2 = 4a^2 + 4b^2 = 4\left(a^2 + b^2\right) = 4c^2 = (2c)^2$

Lesson Check 1. 39 **2.** 7 **3.** yes; $12^2 + 35^2 = 37^2$
4. If you are a student, then you study math. **5.** The value of 13 should have been substituted for c since it is the hypotenuse. The correct equation is $12^2 + x^2 = 13^2$; $x = 5$.
Exercises 7. 8 **9.** 12 **11.** 17 **13.** 4.5 **15.** 6.1 **17.** 41 **19.** 8.5 **21.** 1.2 mi **23.** yes **25.** no **27.** yes **29.** 10 ft **31.** yes **33.** yes **35.** yes **37.** 719 ft **39.** Yes; $50^2 + 120^2 = 130^2$, so the triangle formed by the forces is a right triangle. **41a.** $a^2 + 2ab + b^2$ **b.** c^2 **c.** $\frac{1}{2}ab$ **d.** $a^2 + 2ab + b^2 = 4\left(\frac{1}{2}ab\right) + c^2$; $a^2 + b^2 = c^2$; it is the Pythagorean Theorem.

Lesson 10-2 pp. 619–625

Got It? 1. $6\sqrt{2}$ **2.** $-4m^5\sqrt{5m}$ **3a.** $18\sqrt{3}$ **b.** $3a^2\sqrt{2}$ **c.** $210x^3$ **d.** yes; $\sqrt{14t^2} = t\sqrt{14}$ **4.** $w\sqrt{17}$ **5a.** 4 **b.** $\frac{3}{a}$ **c.** $\frac{5y\sqrt{y}}{z}$ **6a.** $\frac{\sqrt{6}}{3}$ **b.** $\frac{\sqrt{10m}}{6m}$ **c.** $\frac{\sqrt{21s}}{3}$
Lesson Check 1. $7\sqrt{2}$ **2.** $4b^2\sqrt{b}$ **3.** $12m^2$ **4.** $\frac{\sqrt{15}}{x}$ **5.** $\frac{\sqrt{15}}{3}$ **6.** $\frac{\sqrt{3n}}{n}$ **7a.** Yes; there are no perfect-square factors in 31, there are no fractions in the radicand, and there are no radicals in the denominator. **b.** No; there is a fraction in the radicand. **c.** No; 25 is a perfect-square factor of 175. **8.** Answers may vary. Sample:
$\frac{3}{\sqrt{12}} = \frac{3}{2\sqrt{3}} \cdot \frac{\sqrt{3}}{\sqrt{3}} = \frac{3\sqrt{3}}{6} = \frac{\sqrt{3}}{2}$;

$\frac{3}{\sqrt{12}} = \frac{3}{\sqrt{12}} \cdot \frac{\sqrt{12}}{\sqrt{12}} = \frac{3\sqrt{12}}{12} = \frac{\sqrt{12}}{4} = \frac{2\sqrt{3}}{4} = \frac{\sqrt{3}}{2}$

9. A radical expression is in simplified form if the radicand has no perfect-square factors other than 1, the radicand contains no fractions, and no radicals appear in the denominator of a fraction.

Exercises 11. $3\sqrt{11}$ **13.** $-2\sqrt{15}$ **15.** $50\sqrt{7}$
17. $5t^2\sqrt{2t}$ **19.** $-63x^4\sqrt{3x}$ **21.** $-18y\sqrt{3y}$ **23.** 4
25. 30 **27.** $42n^2$ **29.** $16y^3$ **31.** $-126a\sqrt{a}$ **33.** $24c^7$
35. $w\sqrt{26}$ **37.** $\frac{7\sqrt{3}}{4}$ **39.** $\frac{\sqrt{3x}}{8}$ **41.** $\frac{77a}{2}$ **43.** $\frac{\sqrt{10x}}{4x}$
45. $2\sqrt{11}$ **47.** $\frac{4}{5}$ **49.** $2\sqrt{6}$ in. **51.** not simplest form; radical in the denominator of a fraction **53.** Simplest form; radicand has no perfect-square factors other than 1.
55a. $f\sqrt{3f}$ **b.** $\frac{1}{x^2}$ **c.** $\frac{\sqrt{2a}}{2a}$ **d.** $\frac{\sqrt{2m}}{4m}$ **57a.** $\sqrt{18 \cdot 10} = \sqrt{180} = \sqrt{36} \cdot \sqrt{5} = 6\sqrt{5}$ **b.** Answers may vary.
Sample: 4 and 45 **59.** $2\sqrt{13}$ **61.** $\frac{-2\sqrt{a}}{a^2}$ **63.** $\frac{x\sqrt{y}}{y^2}$
65. $4\sqrt{5}$ **67.** $ab^2c\sqrt{abc}$ **69.** $\frac{8\sqrt{6a}}{3a}$ **71.** $1 \pm \sqrt{5}$
73. Answers may vary. Sample: 12, 27, 48 **75.** $10b^2$
77a. $5\left(\frac{\sqrt{2\pi}}{\pi}\right)$ ft, 3.99 ft **b.** $4\left(\frac{\sqrt{2\pi}}{\pi}\right)$, 3.19 in.
c. $\left(\frac{\sqrt{10\pi}}{\pi}\right)$ m, 1.78 m

Lesson 10-3   pp. 626–631

Got It? 1a. $-\sqrt{2}$ **b.** $7\sqrt{5}$ **2a.** $8\sqrt{7}$ **b.** $8\sqrt{2}$
c. No; if they are unlike and have no common factors other than 1, even if they can be simplified, they still will not be like. **3a.** $2\sqrt{3} + 5\sqrt{2}$ **b.** $15 - 4\sqrt{11}$
c. $-6\sqrt{2} - 6$ **4.** $\frac{-3\sqrt{10} + 3\sqrt{5}}{5}$ **5.** $(6\sqrt{5} - 6)$ in., or about 7.4 in.
Lesson Check 1. $5\sqrt{3}$ **2.** $\sqrt{6}$ **3.** $\sqrt{21} - 2\sqrt{7}$
4. $41 - 12\sqrt{5}$ **5.** $3\sqrt{5} - \sqrt{10}$ **6.** $2\sqrt{7} - 4$
7a. $\sqrt{13} + 2$ **b.** $\sqrt{6} - \sqrt{3}$ **c.** $\sqrt{5} + \sqrt{10}$
8. $\sqrt{3} \cdot \sqrt{3} \ne 9$; $\frac{\sqrt{3} + 1}{3 - 1} = \frac{\sqrt{3} + 1}{2}$
Exercises 9. $7\sqrt{5}$ **11.** $8\sqrt{3}$ **13.** 0 **15.** $-7\sqrt{5}$
17. $9\sqrt{10}$ **19.** $\frac{19\sqrt{5}}{2}$ **21.** $2\sqrt{3} + 3\sqrt{2}$ **23.** $3\sqrt{7} - 21$
25. $5\sqrt{33} - 15\sqrt{22}$ **27.** -6 **29.** $62 - 20\sqrt{6}$
31. $\frac{3\sqrt{7} + 3\sqrt{3}}{4}$ **33.** $-2\sqrt{5} - 5$ **35.** $\frac{7\sqrt{13} - 7\sqrt{5}}{8}$
37. $\frac{23\sqrt{5} - 23}{2}$ ft, or about 14.2 ft **39.** $-\frac{4}{3}$; -1.3
41. $\frac{-1 + \sqrt{7}}{4}$; -0.4 **43.** $9 + 6\sqrt{2} + 4\sqrt{5} + 3\sqrt{10}$; 35.9 **45.** No; yes; you can simplify $\sqrt{12}$ to $2\sqrt{3}$ and then combine the like radicals. **47.** $5\sqrt{10}$
49. $22\sqrt{3} - 6$ **51.** $\frac{13 + \sqrt{65} + \sqrt{130} + 5\sqrt{2}}{8}$ **53.** -24
55. $4\sqrt{3} + 4\sqrt{2} + 3\sqrt{6} + 6$ **57.** $s\sqrt{3}$ **59a.** $x^{\frac{n}{2}}$
b. $x^{\frac{n-1}{2}}\sqrt{x}$ **61.** $\frac{n\sqrt{5} - n}{2}$ **63a.** $3\sqrt{2}$ **b.** $2\sqrt{7}$
c. $\sqrt{2}(p + q)$ **65.** H **67.** The graph of the function $y = |x|$ is V–shaped with the vertex at the origin. The domain is all real numbers and the range is $\{y \mid y \ge 0\}$,

because no matter what value of x you input, the output will always be nonnegative. **68.** $6\sqrt{3}$ **69.** $15\sqrt{6}$
70. $\frac{2\sqrt{2}}{3c}$ **71.** 15 **72.** 8^{16} **73.** 2^{11} **74.** 5^{27} **75.** 3^3
76. -1 **77.** $-4, 3$ **78.** $-5, 3$ **79.** $-3, \frac{2}{3}$ **80.** $-2, \frac{1}{2}$ **81.** -7

Lesson 10-4   pp. 633–638

Got It? 1. 9 **2.** 0.825 ft **3.** 7 **4.** -2 **5a.** no solution
b. The principal root of a number is never negative.
Lesson Check 1. 12 **2.** 3 **3.** 1 **4.** no solution **5.** C
6. If $x^2 = y^2$, then $x = y$; no, if $x = -1$ and $y = 1$, then $x^2 = y^2$, but $x \ne y$.
Exercises 7. 4 **9.** 36 **11.** 8 **13.** 16 **15.** -2 **17.** about 5.2 ft **19.** 4.5 **21.** 7 **23.** 4 **25.** 2 **27.** none **29.** -7
31. 3 **33.** no solution **35.** no solution **37.** The student did not check the solutions in the original equations. Both of those solutions are extraneous, so the equation has no solution. **39a.** 25 **b.** 11.25 **41.** Add $\sqrt{y + 2}$ to each side of the equation. Square each side of the equation. Solve for y. Check each apparent solution in the original equation. **43.** 3 **45.** no solution **47.** 1.5 **49.** 1600 ft
51. The square of $\sqrt{x - 1}$ will have only two terms, while the square of $\sqrt{x} - 1$ will have three terms.
53. D **55.** B **57.** $5\sqrt{2}$ **58.** -24 **59.** $-\frac{2\sqrt{3} - 4\sqrt{2}}{5}$
60. no solution **61.** $-2, 2$ **62.** $-\frac{3}{2}, -\frac{2}{3}$

63.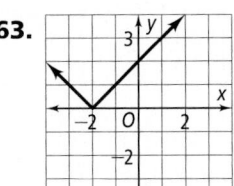

64.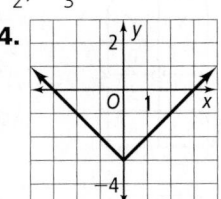

65.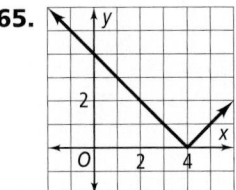

Lesson 10-5   pp. 639–644

Got It? 1. $x \le 2.5$ **2a.** when the power is more than 56.25 watts **b.** 4

3.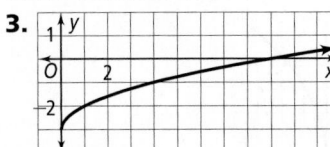

4.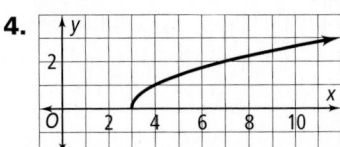

Lesson Check 1. $x \geq -3$

2.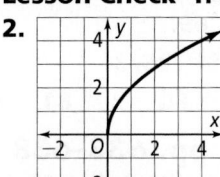

3.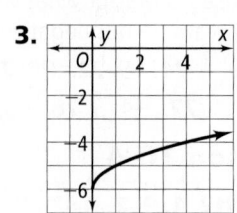

4. No; there is no variable in the radicand. **5.** The graph of $y = \sqrt{x-1}$ is the graph of $y = \sqrt{x}$ shifted to the right 1 unit. **6.** Yes; the domain includes all the values of x such that the radicand has a value greater than or equal to zero, so for $b > 0$, the domain of $y = \sqrt{x+b}$ is $x \geq -b$, which includes negative values.

Exercises 7. $x \geq 0$ **9.** $x \geq 7$ **11.** $x \geq -2$
13. $x \leq 18$ **15.** $x \geq 4$

17.

x	f(x)
0	0
1	4
4	8

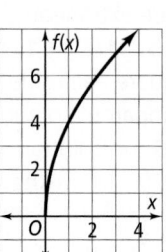

19.

x	y
0	0
3	3
5.3	4

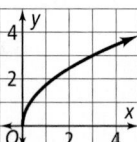

21.

x	y
0	0
1	-3
4	-6

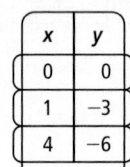

23.

x	y
0	0
2	1
8	2

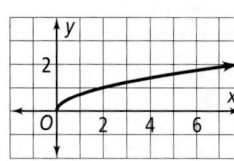

25.

h	v
0	0
1	4.4
6	10.8

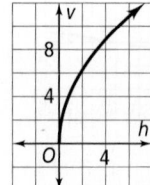

$h > 5.1$ m
27. A **29.** B

31.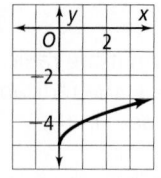

33.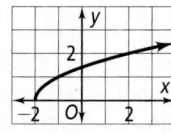

35.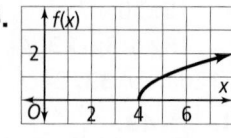

37.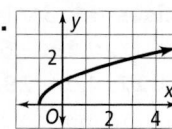

39. $x \geq 4$; $y \geq 0$

41a. 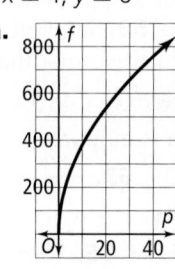   **b.** about 45 lb/in.^{2}

43. about 2800 m/s

45.

x	f(x)
0	0
1	4
2	5.7
4	8

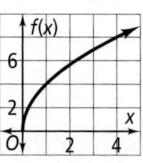

47.

x	y
0	0
2	1
4	1.4
8	2

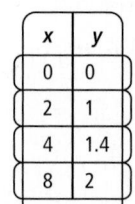

49.

x	f(x)
-2	-4
-1	-3
2	-2

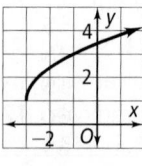

51.

x	y
-3	1
-2	2.4
-1	3
0	3.4

53a. No; the graph does not pass the vertical-line test.
b. The graph of $y = \sqrt{x}$ is the first-quadrant portion of the graph of $x = y^2$. **c.** $y = -\sqrt{x}$

55.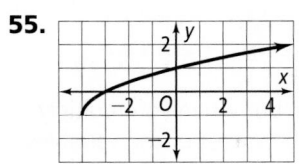

57.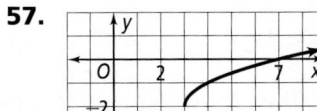

59.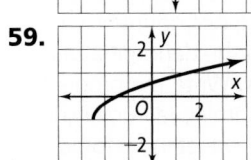

61a. The graph is V–Shaped with vertex at (0, 5) and passing through (1, 6) and (–1, 6). **b.** $y = |x| + 5$

Lesson 10-6   pp. 645–651

Got It? 1. $\frac{3}{5}$; $\frac{4}{5}$; $\frac{3}{4}$ **2a.** 0.9848 **b.** 1 **c.** 0.9659
d. 0.1564 **e.** sin 45° = cos 45°; a 45°-45°-90° triangle is an isosceles right triangle, so the legs have the same length, and the sine and cosine are the same ratio. **3.** 1.9
4. 41.8° **5.** about 130 ft

Lesson Check 1. $\frac{4}{5}$ **2.** $\frac{3}{5}$ **3.** $\frac{4}{3}$ **4.** about 6.4 cm
5. 73.7° **6.** To find the sine of an angle, you find the ratio of the length of the opposite leg to the length of the hypotenuse. To find the cosine of an angle, you find the ratio of the length of the adjacent leg to the length of the hypotenuse. **7.** The student should use the $\sin^{-1}$ key; $\sin^{-1}(0.9) = 64.15806724.$

Exercises 9. $\frac{5}{13}$ **11.** $\frac{8}{17}$ **13.** $\frac{8}{17}$ **15.** $\frac{5}{13}$ **17.** 0.1736
19. 0.0872 **21.** 0.9397 **23.** 0.9455 **25.** 5.5 **27.** 19.2
29. 66.0 **31.** 60° **33.** 37° **35.** about 47.7 ft **37.** Divide the length of the adjacent side by the cosine of the acute angle. **39.** 514.3 **41.** 78.4 **43a.** about 1,720,000 ft
b. about 326 mi **45.** 550 ft **47a.** sin A **b.** cos A **c.** tan A
49. F **51.** The number line has a filled circle on 0.5 and points to the left.

52.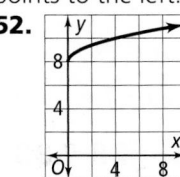

53.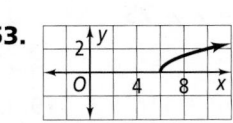

54.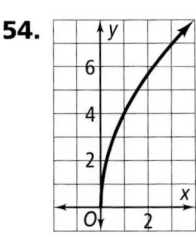

55. yes **56.** yes **57.** no
58. $(x - 3)(x + 4)$
59. $(x + 2)(x + 4)$
60. $(x + 3)(x - 5)$
61. $(x + 3)(x + 6)$

Chapter Review   pp. 653–656

1. trigonometric ratios **2.** extraneous solution **3.** unlike radicals **4.** rationalize the denominator **5.** conjugates
6. 6.5 **7.** 12.5 **8.** 6.1 **9.** 84 **10.** 17.5 **11.** 0.7 **12.** 6.6
13. 2.4 **14.** yes **15.** yes **16.** no **17.** yes **18.** no **19.** yes
20. no **21.** no **22.** yes **23.** $-42\sqrt{6}$ **24.** $\sqrt{3}$ **25.** $\frac{5}{2}a$
26. $\frac{2}{3s}$ **27.** $-\frac{28}{3}x^2\sqrt{x}$ **28.** $30t^4\sqrt{3}$ **29.** Answers may vary. Sample: $\sqrt{32s}$, $\frac{8s}{\sqrt{2s}}$, $8\sqrt{\frac{s}{2}}$; they all have the s and the factor 2 under the radical. **30.** $s\sqrt{10}$ **31.** $2\sqrt{6}$
32. $4 + 2\sqrt{3}$ **33.** $4 - 2\sqrt{10}$ **34.** $\frac{-3\sqrt{2} + 9}{7}$
35. $-2 + \sqrt{3}$ **36.** $\frac{-3 + 3\sqrt{5}}{2}$ in. **37.** 169 **38.** 9 **39.** 18
40. 21 **41.** 2 **42.** 1 **43.** 1.5 **44.** $\frac{1}{2}$ **45.** 56.5 cm³
46. $x \geq 0$ **47.** $x \geq -4$

48.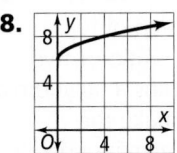

49.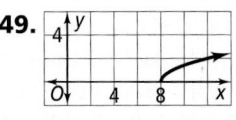

50.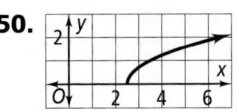

51.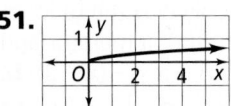

52.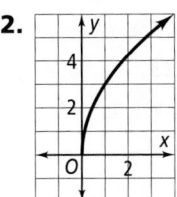

53. sin $A = \frac{8}{17}$, cos $A = \frac{15}{17}$, tan $A = \frac{8}{15}$
54. sin $A = \frac{\sqrt{5}}{5}$, cos $A = \frac{2\sqrt{5}}{5}$, tan $A = \frac{1}{2}$
55. sin $A = \frac{\sqrt{7}}{4}$, cos $A = \frac{3}{4}$, tan $A = \frac{\sqrt{7}}{3}$
56. length of $\overline{AC} \approx 9.9$, length of $\overline{BC} \approx 6.7$
57. length of $\overline{AB} \approx 10.2$, length of $\overline{BC} \approx 6.3$
58. length of $\overline{AB} \approx 26.9$, length of $\overline{AC} \approx 20.0$
59. length of $\overline{AC} \approx 24.5$, length of $\overline{BC} \approx 5.2$

Chapter 11

Get Ready!   p. 661

1. $2\frac{1}{30}$ **2.** $3\frac{1}{4}$ **3.** $-\frac{73}{120}$ **4.** $\frac{11}{35}$ **5.** $\frac{q^6}{p^5}$ **6.** $6\frac{30}{49}$ **7.** $\frac{64}{729}$
8. $\frac{8yz^6}{5x^6}$ **9.** $-7, 9$ **10.** $-\frac{5}{3}, \frac{7}{4}$ **11.** -13 **12.** 0, 3
13. $-\frac{4}{3}, 5$ **14.** $-5, -\frac{2}{3}$ **15.** $-10, -1$ **16.** $-3, 7$
17. $-\frac{1}{2}, \frac{5}{3}$ **18.** no solution **19.** 1 **20.** 4 **21.** The excluded

values are not allowed. **22.** A rational expression involves a ratio. **23.** One is decreasing as the other increases.

Lesson 11-1　　pp. 664–669

Got It? 1a. $\frac{3}{a}$, $a \neq 0$　**b.** $\frac{9d^2}{2d+4}$, $d \neq -2$　**c.** $\frac{1}{3}$, $n \neq \frac{3}{2}$
d. $13c$, none　**2a.** $\frac{2}{x+2}$; $x \neq -2$, $x \neq 4$　**b.** $\frac{a-2}{3}$; $a \neq 1$
c. $\frac{6}{2z+3}$; $z \neq -2$, $z \neq -\frac{3}{2}$　**d.** $\frac{c-3}{c+3}$; $c \neq -3$, $c \neq -2$
3a. -1; $x \neq 2.5$　**b.** $-y - 4$; $y \neq 4$　**c.** $-\frac{3}{2d+1}$; $d \neq -\frac{1}{2}$,
$d \neq \frac{1}{3}$　**d.** $-\frac{3}{2z+2}$; $z \neq \pm 1$　**4a.** $12x + 4$　**b.** No, h must
be greater than 2π in order for the value of a to be
greater than 0. If h is less than or equal to 2π, then a will
be negative, and length cannot be negative.

Lesson Check 1. 3; $x \neq -3$　**2.** $-\frac{1}{x+3}$; $x \neq -3$, $x \neq 5$
3. $4x$　**4a.** No, the expression is not the ratio of two
polynomials.　**b.** Yes, the expression is the ratio of two
polynomials.　**5.** If the denominator contains a polynomial,
there may be values of the variable that make the
denominator equal to zero, and division by zero is undefined.
6. The only way the rational expression is not in simplest
form is if the numerator and the denominator are equal.
7a. yes, $3 - x = -(x - 3)$　**b.** no, $2 - y = -(y - 2)$

Exercises 9. $\frac{1}{7x}$, $x \neq 0$　**11.** $\frac{1}{2}$, $p \neq 12$　**13.** $\frac{x+2}{x^2}$, $x \neq 0$
15. $\frac{2}{b+4}$, $b \neq \pm 4$　**17.** $\frac{w}{w-7}$, $w \neq \pm 7$　**19.** $\frac{m+3}{m+2}$,
$m \neq -4$, $m \neq -2$　**21.** $b + 3$, $b \neq -5$　**23.** -1, $n \neq \frac{5}{4}$
25. -2, $m \neq 2$　**27.** $\frac{-1}{v+5}$, $v \neq \pm 5$　**29.** $w + 1$
31. $\frac{2r-1}{r+5}$, $r \neq -5$　**33.** $\frac{5t-4}{3t-1}$, $t \neq -2$, $t \neq \frac{1}{3}$
35. $\frac{3(z+4)}{z^3}$, $z \neq 0$　**37.** $-\frac{2a+1}{a+3}$, $a \neq -3$, $a \neq \frac{5}{2}$
39. $-\frac{c(3c+5)}{5c+4}$, $c \neq -\frac{4}{5}$, $c \neq 2$　**41.** No, $y = \frac{x^2-9}{x+3}$ is not
defined for $x = -3$ but $x - 3$ is.　**43.** The student
canceled terms instead of factors;
$\frac{x^2+2x}{2x} = \frac{x(x+2)}{2x} = \frac{x+2}{2}$.　**45.** Answers may vary.
Sample: $\frac{1}{(x-4)(x+3)}$　**47.** $\frac{5w}{5w+6}$　**49.** $\frac{a-3b}{a+4b}$,
$a \neq -4b$, $a \neq 2b$　**51.** Sometimes; it is true for all
values of b except 0.　**53.** Sometimes; it is true for all
values of a except -1.

Lesson 11-2　　pp. 670–676

Got It? 1a. $\frac{15}{y^4}$, $y \neq 0$　**b.** $\frac{x(x+1)}{(x-2)(x-3)}$, $x \neq 3$, $x \neq 2$
2a. $3x(x+1)$　**b.** Yes, but you will have to simplify the
resulting expression.　**3a.** $(x-7)(3x-2)$
b. $(x+1)(x+3)$　**4a.** $\frac{1}{y}$　**b.** $\frac{6}{k+4}$　**5.** $\frac{z-1}{z^2+2}$　**6.** $\frac{1}{q^2}$

Lesson Check 1. $\frac{6}{5t^6}$　**2.** $\frac{(2x+5)(x-5)}{4}$　**3.** $3k^2(k+1)$
4. $\frac{4x}{(x+7)(2x+3)}$　**5.** $\frac{(a-2)^2}{3a}$　**6.** x^2　**7.** no;

$\frac{\frac{a}{b}}{c} = \frac{a}{b} \div c = \frac{a}{b} \cdot \frac{1}{c} = \frac{a}{bc}$, where $\frac{a}{\frac{b}{c}} = a \div \frac{b}{c} = a \cdot \frac{c}{b} = \frac{ac}{b}$

8. The procedures are the same, but when you multiply
rational expressions, there may be values of the variables
for which the rational expressions are not defined.
9. The variables b, c, and d appear in the denominators,
and division by 0 is not defined.　**10a.** Write the product of
the rational expression and the polynomial, factor, divide
out common factors, and write the product in factored
form.　**b.** Rewrite the quotient of the rational expression
and the polynomial as the product of the rational
expression and the reciprocal of the polynomial. Factor the
numerators and denominators, divide out common factors,
and write the answer in factored form.

Exercises 11. $\frac{35x}{36}$　**13.** $\frac{40}{3a^5}$　**15.** $\frac{2x(x-1)}{3(x+1)}$　**17.** $\frac{2c(c+2)}{c-1}$
19. $\frac{(r+2)(r-2)}{2r}$　**21.** $t - 4$　**23.** $4(t+1)(t+2)$
25. $\frac{(x-1)(x-2)}{3}$　**27.** $\frac{(h-1)(h+4)}{3}$　**29.** $\frac{x+1}{2}$
31. $\frac{1}{c^2-1}$　**33.** 6　**35.** $-\frac{1}{2}$　**37.** $\frac{n-3}{4n+5}$　**39.** $\frac{11}{7k-15}$
41. $\frac{b-1}{3(b+1)}$　**43.** 18　**45.** $\frac{1}{2(x+1)}$　**47.** $\frac{2(3g+1)}{g(3g-1)}$
49. $\frac{1}{3z(z+10)}$　**51.** $t + 3$　**53.** $\frac{3t-5}{7t^2}$　**55.** $\frac{x-2}{x-3}$
57. \$88.71　**59.** \$518,011.65　**61.** The student forgot to
rewrite the divisor as its reciprocal before canceling.
$\frac{3a}{a+2} \div \frac{(a+2)^2}{a-4} = \frac{3a}{a+2} \cdot \frac{a-4}{(a+2)^2} = \frac{3a(a-4)}{(a+2)^3}$
63. 0, 4, and -4 make the denominators equal 0.
65. $\frac{2m^2(m+2)}{(m-1)(m+4)}$　**67.** 1　**69.** $-\frac{(2a+3b)(a+2b)}{(5a+b)(2a-3b)}$　**71.** G
73. $0 = -16t^2 + 35t + 2.5$ or $16t^2 - 35t - 2.5 = 0$;
use the quadratic formula to solve for t.
$t = \frac{35 \pm \sqrt{35^2 + 4 \cdot 16 \cdot 2.5}}{32} \approx \frac{35 \pm 37.2}{32}$, $t \approx 2.26$ s
74. $\frac{7}{3}$, $m \neq 2$　**75.** $\frac{1}{2a^2-3}$, $a \neq 0$, $a \neq \pm\frac{\sqrt{6}}{2}$
76. $\frac{2c-9}{2c+8}$, $c \neq -4$, $c \neq 4.5$　**77.** $2x^2 + 10x + 12$
78. $-3n^2 + 11n + 20$　**79.** $6a^3 - 21a^2 + 2a - 7$

Lesson 11-3　　pp. 678–683

Got It? 1a. $2a + 5 + \frac{3}{2a}$　**b.** $b - \frac{3}{b} + \frac{1}{5b^3}$
c. $2c^3 + 3c + \frac{3}{2}$　**2.** $2m - 3$　**3a.** $q^3 + q^2 + 2q + 3$
b. $h^2 - 3h + 5 - \frac{3}{h+3}$　**4a.** $2y - \frac{19}{3} + \frac{55}{3(3y+4)}$
b. $3a + 1 - \frac{3}{6a+5}$　**c.** Check whether
$(2x-3)(2x+2) - 7$ equals $4x^2 - 10x - 1$.
Lesson Check 1. $4m + 2 - \frac{1}{m} - \frac{3}{5m^2}$
2. $20c + 43 + \frac{36}{c-1}$　**3.** $5n^2 - 4n + 1$　**4.** $3a - 5$
5. Both processes involve dividing, multiplying, and
subtracting, then "bringing down," and repeating as
needed. When dividing polynomials you may need to

insert a term with a coefficient of 0 as a placeholder.
6. Divide, multiply, subtract, bring down, and repeat as necessary. **7.** $-x^4 + 0x^3 + 0x^2 + 0x + 1$

Exercises 9. $3x^4 - \frac{2}{x}$ **11.** $n^2 - 18n + 3$
13. $t^3 + 2t^2 - 4t + 5$ **15.** $3t^2 + \frac{3t}{7} - \frac{11}{7}$
17. $y - 3 + \frac{8}{y+2}$ **19.** $-2q - 10 + \frac{22}{2q+1}$
21. $2w^2 + 2w + 5 - \frac{10}{w-1}$ **23.** $c^2 - \frac{1}{c-1}$
25. $4c^2 - 8c + 16$ **27.** $a - 1 + \frac{1}{4a+7}$
29. $t + 5 + \frac{21}{2t-6}$ **31.** $4q^2 + 2q + \frac{3}{2} + \frac{9}{2q-2}$
33. $4c^2 + 9c + 7 + \frac{36}{3c-4}$
35. $3y^2 + 5y + \frac{29}{3} + \frac{124}{3(3y-5)}$ **37.** $2x + 2$
39. $5t^3 - 25t^2 + 115t - 575 + \frac{2881}{t+5}$
41. $3s - 8 + \frac{29}{2s+3}$ **43.** $2r^4 + r^2 - 7$
45. $z^3 - 3z^2 + 10z - 30 + \frac{88}{z+3}$
47. $6m^2 - 24m + 99 - \frac{326}{m+4}$ **49.** $m^2 + 5m + 4$
51. $s^2 - \frac{301}{200}s + \frac{1703}{400} + \frac{891}{400(2s+3)}$ **53a.** $t = \frac{d}{r}$
b. $(t^2 - 7t + 12)$ h **55.** $(x^8 + 1)(x^4 + 1)(x^2 + 1)(x + 1)$; factoring is much simpler and faster, since long division requires writing a polynomial with 17 terms. **57.** $(3x + 2)$
59. $2b^3 - 2b^2 + 3$ **61.** G **63.** There are $18 \cdot 28 = 504$ seats in the theater. If 445 adults were at the theater, the revenue would be $445 \cdot 4 = 1780$. That means the revenue for the children's tickets is $1935 - 1780 = 155$. So the number of children's seats sold is $155 \div 2.5 = 62$. The total number of seats sold would be $62 + 445 = 507$. Since $507 > 504$, Barbara's answer is not reasonable.
64. $n + 2$ **65.** $\frac{(t-5)(3t+1)(2t+11)}{3t(2t-55)(t+1)}$ **66.** $\frac{3c+8}{2c+7}$
67. $\frac{(x+5)(x+4)^2}{(x+7)(x+8)^2}$ **68.** $\frac{2}{3}$ **69.** $-\frac{1}{12}$ **70.** x **71.** $\frac{1}{2y}$

Lesson 11-4   pp. 684–689

Got It? 1. $\frac{5a}{3a-4}$ **2a.** $\frac{-5}{z+3}$ **b.** $\frac{3n-4}{5n-2}$ **c.** $\frac{1}{q-2}$
3. $\frac{9+14y^2}{21y^4}$ **4.** $\frac{c^2-14c+4}{(3c-1)(c-2)}$ **5a.** $\frac{45}{4r}$ **b.** $\frac{4m}{5}$; if n is the miles per gallon when the truck is full, then $m = 1.25n$ and therefore $n = \frac{m}{1.25}$ or $\frac{4m}{5}$.

Lesson Check 1. $\frac{11}{x-7}$ **2.** $\frac{2}{y+2}$ **3.** $\frac{16b+15}{24b^3}$ **4.** $\frac{10}{3r}$
5. If the expressions have like denominators, add or subtract numerators as indicated and place over the denominator. If they have unlike denominators, factor if needed, find the LCD, rewrite the expressions with the common denominator, add or subtract as indicated, and simplify. **6.** The procedure is the same. The LCD is the LCM of the denominators. **7a.** yes **b.** No, it will give you a common denominator, but not necessarily the least common denominator.

Exercises 9. $\frac{14}{c-5}$ **11.** $\frac{6c-28}{2c+7}$ **13.** $\frac{1}{n+2}$ **15.** 2
17. $2x^2$ **19.** $7z$ **21.** $5(x+2)$ **23.** $(m+n)(m-n)$

25. $\frac{35+6a}{15a}$ **27.** $\frac{189-9n}{7n^3}$ **29.** $\frac{(a+4)(a-3)}{(a+3)(a+5)}$
31. $\frac{a^2+12a+15}{4(a+3)}$ **33a.** $\frac{1}{r} + \frac{1}{0.7r} = \frac{1.7}{0.7r}$ **b.** $\frac{17}{7r}$
c. about 0.81 h or 48.6 min **35.** Not always; the numerator may contain a factor of the LCD.
37. $\frac{-y^2+2y+2}{3y+1}$ **39.** $\frac{r-2k-6}{9+p^3}$ **41.** $\frac{10x+15}{x+2}$
43. $\frac{5000r+250,000}{r(r+100)}$ **45.** $\frac{8x^2+1}{x}$ **47.** $\frac{-3x-5}{x(x-5)}$
49. $\frac{3}{2}$ **51.** $\frac{-4x}{3+xy}$ **53.** $\frac{3y+4x}{2y-3x}$

Lesson 11-5   pp. 691–697

Got It? 1a. -3 **b.** $\frac{37}{7}$ **2a.** $-\frac{3}{2}, \frac{2}{3}$ **b.** $-7, -1$ **c.** The expression $\frac{2}{x^2}$ cannot be negative. **3.** 4.8 h **4a.** -8
b. $-3, 7$ **5.** 0
Lesson Check 1. -1 **2.** 1, 5 **3.** 0 **4.** about 28 min
5. An extraneous solution of a rational equation is an excluded value of the associated rational function.
6. Answers may vary. Sample: $\frac{x^2}{x-1} = \frac{1}{x-1}$
7. The student forgot to first multiply both sides of the equation by the LCD, $5m$.
Exercises 9. 3 **11.** $-1, 6$ **13.** -2 **15.** 5 **17.** $-2, 4$
19. $\frac{16}{3}$ **21.** -1 **23.** $1\frac{5}{7}$ h **25.** 3 **27.** $-\frac{3}{2}, 4$ **29.** no solution
31. You could rewrite the right side of the equation as $\frac{3x}{x+6}$ and then cross multiply. **33.** -14 **35.** $-5, 2$
37. $-\frac{6}{5}, -1$ **39.** 12 h

41a.
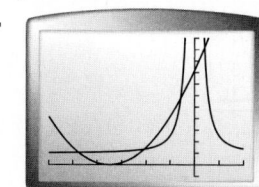
b. $(-9.53, 1.07)$, $(-4.16, 1.35)$, $(-1.12, 5.76)$, $(0.81, 10.16)$

c. Yes; the x-values are solutions to the original equation since both sides are equal. **43.** 20 Ω **45.** $11\frac{1}{3}$ h **47.** $0, \frac{1}{2}$
49. 1 **51.** 32 L of 80% solution, 18 L of 30% solution
53. F **55.** $\frac{30 \text{ m}}{1 \text{ h}} \cdot \frac{1 \text{ h}}{3600 \text{ s}} \cdot \frac{5280 \text{ ft}}{1 \text{ mi}} = 44$ ft/s **56.** $-\frac{3}{x^2y^2z}$
57. $\frac{3h^2+2ht+4h}{2(t-2)(t+2)}$ **58.** $\frac{-4k-61}{(k-4)(k+10)}$
59.
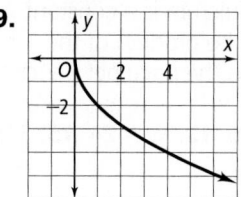
60.
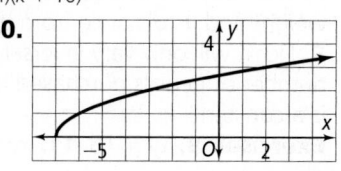

61.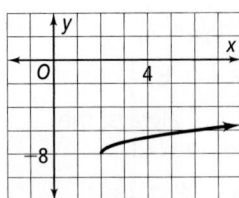

62.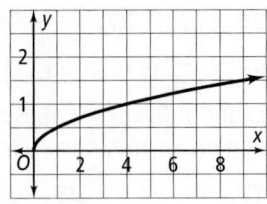

63. yes; 3 **64.** no **65.** yes; $-\frac{1}{4}$ **66.** yes; $\frac{8}{3}$

Lesson 11-6   pp. 698–704

Got It? 1. $xy = 54$ **2.** 7.5 ft

3a.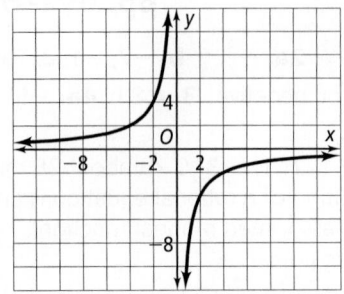

b. They are the same shape. They are reflections of each other over the *y*-axis. **4a.** direct; $y = -3x$ **b.** inverse; $xy = -48$ **5a.** Direct; the ratio of the total cost to the number of sweaters bought is a constant, 35. **b.** Inverse; the product of your speed and the time spent walking is a constant, 5.

Lesson Check 1. $xy = -51$ **2.** 120 lb

3.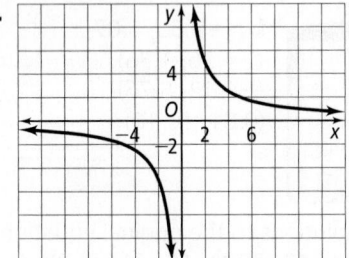

4. direct; $y = -2x$ **5.** yes; 15 **6.** Never; the equation is of the form $y = \frac{k}{x}$, and 0 is not in the domain of the function.

7. The heavier must be closer because the product of the weight and its distance from the fulcrum is a constant.
8. No; it will only vary inversely if the product of the number of pencils purchased times the price per pencil is a constant.

Exercises 9. $xy = 18$ **11.** $xy = 56$ **13.** $xy = 24$ **15.** 3 h

17.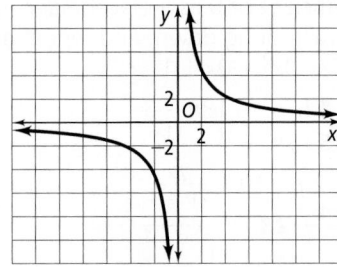

19.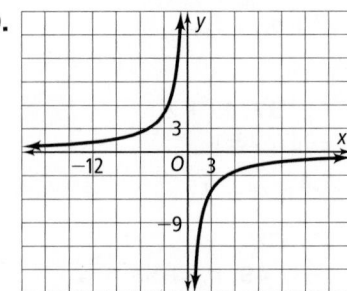

21.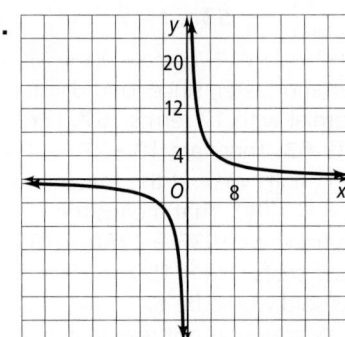

23.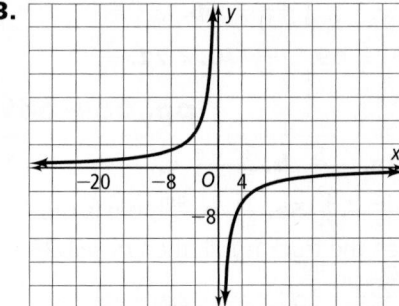

25. direct; $y = \frac{x}{2}$ **27.** inverse; $xy = 72$ **29.** Inverse variation; the product of cost per person times the number of people is a constant. **31.** 256; $xy = 256$
33. 1; $xy = 1$ **35.** 5 **37.** Direct; the ratio $\frac{P}{s}$ is a constant, 3. **39.** Direct; the ratio $\frac{C}{r}$ is a constant, 2π.
41a. The value of *y* doubles. **b.** The value of *y* is cut in half. **43.** direct; $y = 0.4x$; 8 **45.** inverse; $xy = 48$; 0.5
47. No; the equation of the graph is of the form
$y = -2x + b$. **49.** 4; $s\left(\frac{d}{2}\right)^2 = \frac{sd^2}{4} = k$, so $s = \frac{4k}{d^2}$.
51. 8 **53.** −25 **54.** no solution **55.** $-\frac{5}{3}$

56.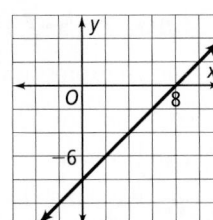

57.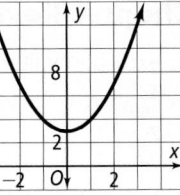

58.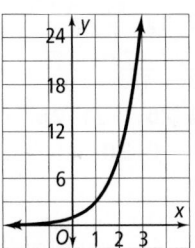

59.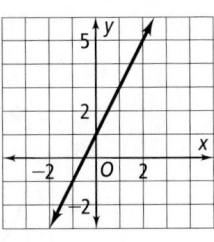

Lesson 11-7   pp. 705–713

Got It? 1. -7

2. $x = 6$

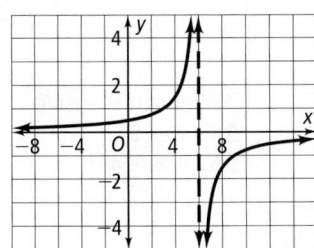

3a. $x = -3, y = -4$

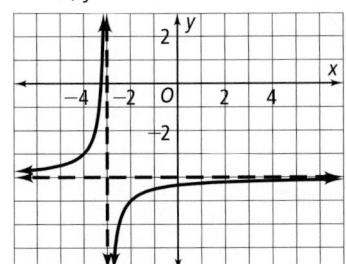

b. Yes; for example, $y = \frac{1}{x}$ and $y = -\frac{1}{x}$ have the same vertical and horizontal asymptotes. **4.** about 20 people

Lesson Check 1. -1

2. $x = 2, y = 3$

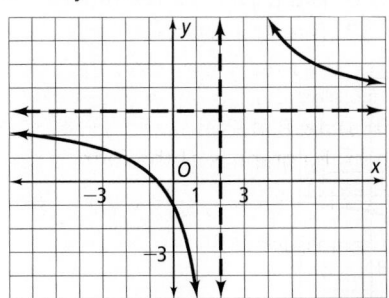

3. 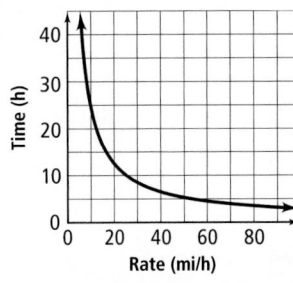   about 68.6 mi/h

4. 5; $x = 5, y = 1$ **5.** Answers will vary. Sample: $y = \frac{1}{x + 2} + 4$ **6.** The vertical asymptote is $x + 5 = 0$, or $x = -5$.   **7.** If the excluded value is a, then the vertical asymptote is $x = a$.

Exercises 9. 2   **11.** 3   **13.** $x = 1, y = -1$

15. $x = 0, y = 0$

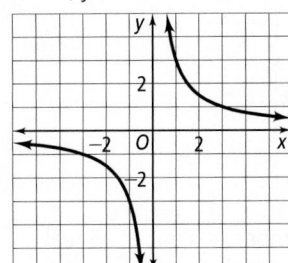

17. $x = 5, y = 0$

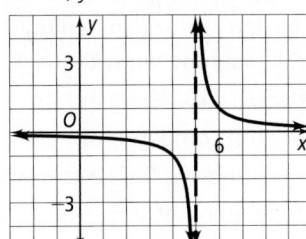

19. $x = 0, y = -5$

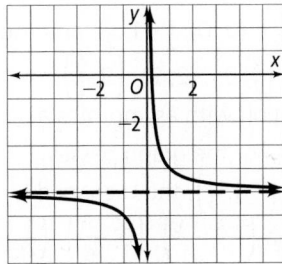

21. $x = -1, y = 4$

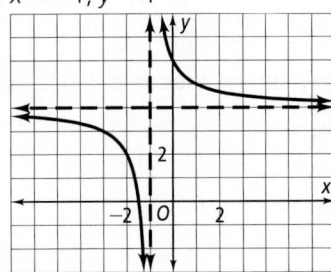

23a. $C = \frac{1920}{n} + 100$

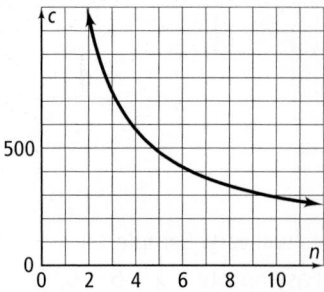

b. 5 people **25.** translates the graph 1 unit to the left **27.** translates the graph 1 unit up **29.** translates the graph 3 units to the right **31.** about 4.2 ft

33a.

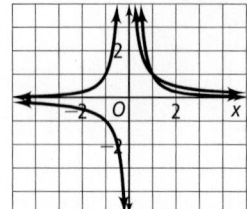

b. $x = 0$, $y = 0$ **c.** all real numbers except 0; all real numbers greater than 0 **35.** absolute value function with vertex (4, 0) **37.** line with slope $\frac{1}{4}$ through origin **39.** translation of radical function $y = \sqrt{x}$ shifted right 4 units and up 1 unit **41.** rational function with asymptotes $x = -4$ and $f(x) = -1$ **43.** The graph of $y = \frac{3}{x+2}$ and $y = -\frac{3}{x+2}$ are both composed of two curves with asymptotes $x = -2$ and $y = 0$. The graph of $y = -\frac{3}{x+2}$ is a reflection of the graph of $y = \frac{3}{x+2}$ across the x-axis. **45.** Graph of a rational function with asymptotes at $x = 1$ and $g(x) = 1$; the left section of the graph passes through $\left(-5, \frac{5}{6}\right)$, (0, 0), $\left(-1, \frac{1}{2}\right)$ and the right section passes through $\left(\frac{3}{2}, 3\right)$, (2, 2), $\left(3, \frac{3}{2}\right)$.
47. Graph of a rational function with asymptotes at $x = -2$, $x = 2$; the left section of the graph passes through $\left(-6, \frac{1}{16}\right)$, $\left(-4, \frac{1}{6}\right)$, $\left(-3, \frac{2}{5}\right)$, the U-shaped middle section passes through $\left(\frac{-3}{2}, \frac{-8}{7}\right)$, $\left(0, \frac{-1}{2}\right)$, $\left(\frac{3}{2}, \frac{-8}{7}\right)$, and the right section passes through $\left(3, \frac{2}{5}\right)$, $\left(4, \frac{1}{6}\right)$, $\left(6, \frac{1}{16}\right)$. **49.** Both graphs pass through (−1, 0) and (0, 1), but they are not the same; $f(x)$ is not defined when $x = -2$.

Chapter Review   pp. 715–718

1. excluded value **2.** asymptote **3.** rational expression
4. $\frac{x+3}{5x^2}$, $x \neq 0$ **5.** $\frac{1}{3}$, $m \neq 3$ **6.** $\frac{x+3}{5}$, $x \neq -3$
7. $\frac{2(a-1)}{3(a+1)}$, $a \neq -1$, $a \neq 1$ **8.** $\frac{2s+3}{2s-1}$, $x \neq \frac{1}{2}$, $x \neq 4$
9. $-\frac{1}{2}$, $c \neq 4$ **10.** $\frac{1}{x+2}$ **11.** $\frac{2}{3(x-2)}$ **12.** $\frac{(a+4)(a-2)}{a^2(a+2)}$
13. $(x+5)(x+7)$ **14.** $4x - 3 - \frac{7}{3x}$
15. $3d - 7 - \frac{8}{d+3}$ **16.** $2b^2 + b + 3$ **17.** $\frac{8x-3}{x+1}$
18. $\frac{24+7x}{28x}$ **19.** $\frac{x^2+7x-20}{(x+2)(x-4)}$ **20.** $\frac{-15x^2+23x+27}{(3x-1)(2x+3)}$
21. $\frac{138,430}{59r}$ **22.** 24 **23.** 9 **24.** −14 **25.** −21 **26.** 6 min
27. $xy = 21$ **28.** $xy = 10$ **29.** $xy = -18$ **30.** $xy = -25$
31.

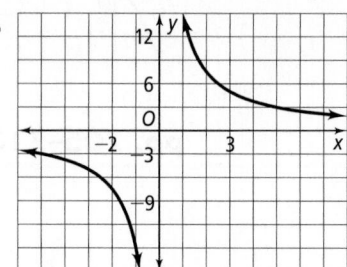

32.

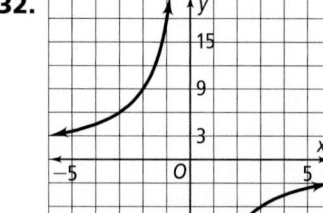

33. about 9.5 mi/h
34. $x \neq 0$
35. $x \neq -4$

36. $x = -2$, $y = 0$

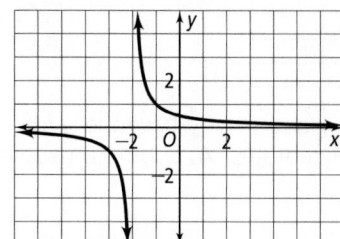

37. $x = -3$, $y = 0$

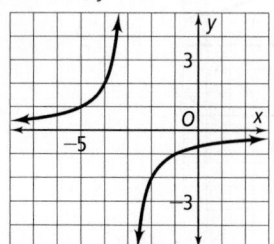

38. $x = 4, y = 1$

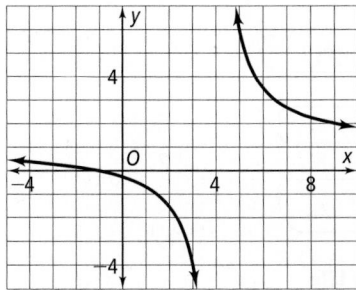

39. $x = 5, y = -1$

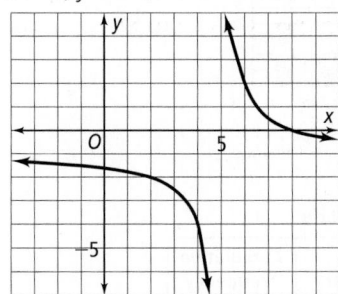

40a. 9 lumens **b.** Intensity is inversely related to the square of the distance, so at twice the distance the intensity is $\frac{1}{4}$ as great.

Chapter 12

Get Ready! p. 723

1. $\frac{7}{6}$ **2.** $-\frac{1}{24}$ **3.** $\frac{47}{50}$ **4.** $\frac{5}{12}$ **5.** $\frac{13}{2}$ **6.** 3 **7.** 11 **8.** $6x - 42$
9. $2x + 3$ **10.** $-10 + 2x$ **11.** $2.5 + 2x$ **12.** {1, 2, 3, 5, 6, 7, 9, 10, 11, 13, 15, 16} **13.** {9} **14.** {2, 6, 10, 16}
15. {0, 1, 2, 3, 4, 5, 6, 7, 8, 9, 10, 11, 12, 13, 14, 15, 16, 18}
16.

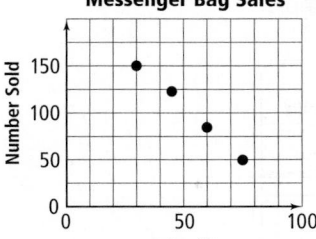

negative

17.

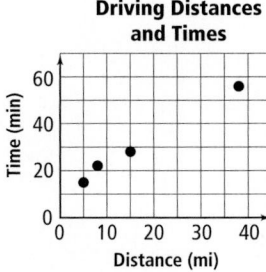

positive

18. heads or tails **19.** into two parts with an equal number of data values **20.** no

Lesson 12-1 pp. 726–731

Got It?

1a. $\begin{bmatrix} -4 \\ 1.5 \\ -16 \end{bmatrix}$ **b.** $\begin{bmatrix} 1 & 1 \\ 2.5 & 10 \end{bmatrix}$

c. You add or subtract matrices by adding or subtracting the corresponding elements. If matrices are not the same size they will not have corresponding elements in each case.
2a. $[6 \quad -14.2 \quad -10]$ **b.** $\begin{bmatrix} -16.5 & 4.5 \\ 0 & -2.25 \end{bmatrix}$
3. Portland

Lesson Check

1. $\begin{bmatrix} -3 & 9 \\ 0 & 4 \end{bmatrix}$ **2.** $\begin{bmatrix} 2 & 3 \\ 2 & -3 \end{bmatrix}$

3. $\begin{bmatrix} 8 & 0 & 10 \\ -4 & 2 & 4 \end{bmatrix}$ **4.** $\begin{bmatrix} -30 & 0 \\ -12 & 18 \end{bmatrix}$

5. 9 **6.** The student added entries across the rows, but the matrices are not the same size so they cannot be added.

Exercises

9. $\begin{bmatrix} -1 & 1 \\ 0 & 0 \end{bmatrix}$ **11.** $\begin{bmatrix} 2 & -1 \\ 5 & -1 \\ 0 & 10 \end{bmatrix}$ **13.** $\begin{bmatrix} 2.4 & -7.6 \\ 8 & 0.3 \\ -7.7 & 1.3 \end{bmatrix}$

15. $\begin{bmatrix} -6 & 2 \\ -14 & 4 \end{bmatrix}$ **17.** $\begin{bmatrix} -19 & -10.5 & -35 \\ -47 & 30 & 0 \end{bmatrix}$

19. $\begin{bmatrix} -12.4 & -23.25 \\ -27.9 & 15.5 \\ -3.1 & -14.26 \end{bmatrix}$ **21.** $\begin{bmatrix} -1.66 & 0.6 & 0 \\ -0.9 & -1.12 & -0.2 \\ 0.2 & -0.58 & -1.4 \end{bmatrix}$

23. Factory B **25.** $\begin{bmatrix} 9 & 1 & 2 \\ -10 & 2 & 0 \end{bmatrix}$

27. $\begin{bmatrix} -28.2 & 30.1 & -20.9 \\ 7.9 & 27.9 & -37 \\ -8 & -36.4 & 7.8 \end{bmatrix}$

29. chicken **31.** $x = -2, y = 5$ **33.** D **35.** A **37.** 5
38. 0 **39.** 4
40.

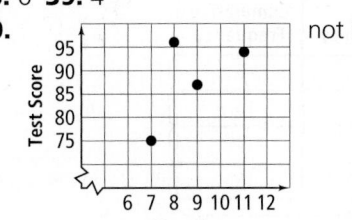

not likely

41. 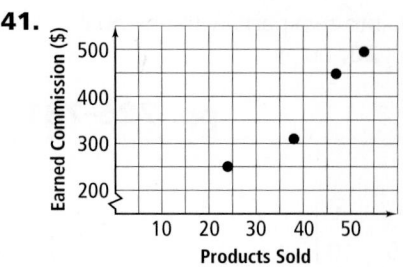 Causal; the amount of sales is related to earnings.

Lesson 12-2 pp. 732–737

Got It?

1. Answers may vary. Sample:

Home Runs	Frequency
2–6	4
7–11	5
12–16	4
17–21	1

2. Answers may vary. Sample:

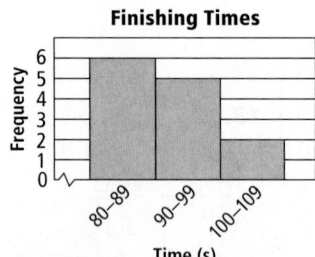

3a. 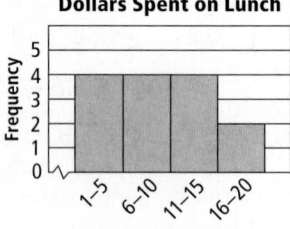 uniform

b. Answers may vary. Sample: $70 for the week; the data are fairly uniform, so on average he spends about $10 per day.

4.

Interval	Frequency	Cumulative Frequency
0–4	6	6
5–9	4	10
10–14	4	14
15–19	2	16

Lesson Check

1.

Battery Life

Hours	Frequency
9–12	7
13–16	2
17–20	1
21–24	2

2.

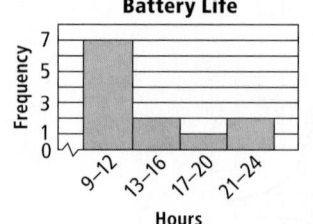

3.

Battery Life

Hours	Frequency	Cumulative Frequency
9–12	7	7
13–16	2	9
17–20	1	10
21–24	2	12

4. The store owner could look at the frequency column to pick out the busiest hours. **5.** A symmetric histogram has roughly the same shape if you fold it down the middle. A skewed histogram has a peak that is not in the center. **6.** Add the frequency of each interval to the frequencies of all the previous intervals.

Exercises

7. Answers may vary. Sample:

Wing Spans

Number of Centimeters	Frequency
125–134	5
135–144	4
145–154	4

9. Answers may vary. Sample:

Top Speeds

Miles per Hour	Frequency
90–109	4
110–129	4
130–149	2
150–169	3

11. Answers may vary. Sample:

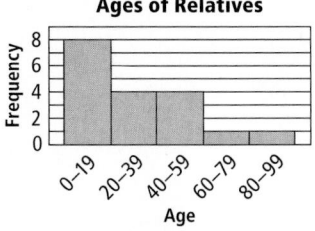

Ages of Relatives

13. Answers may vary. Sample:

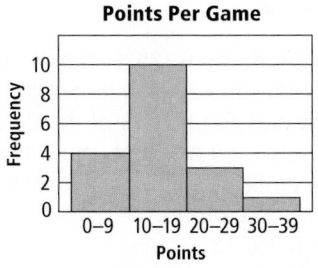

Points Per Game

15. symmetric **17.** skewed
19. Answers may vary. Sample:

Heights of Buildings

Feet	Frequency	Cumulative Frequency
100–149	2	2
150–199	3	5
200–249	3	8
250–299	2	10
300–349	2	12

21a. **The Perpendicular Bisectors**

Time/Song (min)	Frequency	Cumulative Frequency
0–1:19	0	0
1:20–2:39	2	2
2:40–3:59	5	7
4:00–5:19	3	10

b. 70%; 7 out of 10 songs are shorter than 4 min.
23. Answers may vary. Sample:

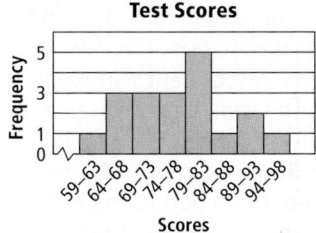

Test Scores

25. Answers may vary. Sample:

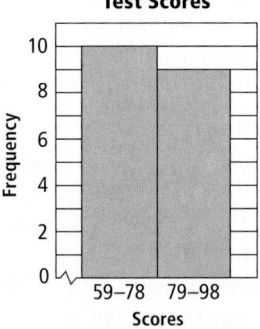

Test Scores

27. $99 **29.** 9 customers **31.** There were no numbers in the range of 30 to 39 so the student just left out this interval. The intervals in a frequency table should not have any gaps, so the student should have included the interval 30–39.

Interval	Frequency
20–29	6
30–39	0
40–49	5
50–59	4

33. Frequencies in the second column are 6, 11, 9, 9 **35.** F
37. Methods may vary. Sample: Graph the two functions using a graphing calculator. Use the trace and intersect features to find the intersection. Since $x \approx 1.77$, the x value where the two graphs intersect is between 1 and 2.

38. $\begin{bmatrix} 12 & 16 \\ 14 & 18 \end{bmatrix}$ **39.** $\begin{bmatrix} -2.1 & -5.3 \\ -6.7 & -0.5 \end{bmatrix}$ **40.** $-16, -4, 0, \frac{1}{2}, \frac{5}{4},$
2, 13, 16 **41.** $-1, -0.2, 0, 0.1, 0.9, 1.2, 2, 5$

Lesson 12-3   pp. 738–744

Got It? 1. 112.4, 109, 104; mean **2a.** 88% **b.** No; you would need a grade of 104. **3.** Stock C: 6, 4.2; Stock D: 22, 11.2; Stock C had a range of 6 and a mean of 4.2, while Stock D had a range of 22 and a mean of 10.8 for this 5-day period. **4a.** mean: 20.8; median: 21; range: 5 **b.** You can use the line plot to see whether the data are symmetric. If they are, then the mean and median are equal; if they are not, then the mean and median are not equal. **5a.** less than **b.** less than **c.** The data for Class C are shifted left when compared to the data for Class A. Therefore the mean will be less.

Lesson Check 1. 26.2, 30.5, 33; the median, since there is an outlier in this set **2.** 8.76, 8.8, no mode; the mean, since there is no outlier **3.** 94 **4.** All are describing the data set by finding a representative measure of central tendency. The mean can be influenced by outliers, which can overstate or understate the measure. The median is the middle value of the ranked data, and the mode is the most commonly occurring piece of data. **5.** The correct range is 8 because the range is defined as the difference between the highest and lowest values. **6.** Since an outlier is either much larger or much smaller than most of the data, it causes the range to become larger.

Exercises 7. 12, 11, 10; mean **9.** 63, 52, no mode; median **11.** 5.9 **13.** 125 **15.** 15 **17.** Set C: 3.8, 6.7; Set D: 28.3, 9.0; the range of Set C is 3.8 with a mean of 6.7, while Set D has a range of 28.3 and a mean of 9. **19.** First player: .062, .300; Second player: .029, .302; the second player had a slightly higher mean over the six seasons and was more consistent as shown by the smaller range. **21.** Student A has a greater mean and a greater median. **23a.** Plant A: 5.8, 5.8, 5.4, 1.2; Plant B: 5.6, 5.5, no mode; 2.9 **b.** Plant A: mean as there is no outlier; Plant B: either mean or median, if you consider 7.2 to be an outlier **c.** The greater data values are in the bottom rows of a stem-and-leaf plot. Since more of the data is concentrated near the bottom of the plot for Plant A than for Plant B, Plant A has the greater mean. **25.** The mean, median, and mode will each decrease by that amount, while the range will stay the same. If you subtract the same number d from each set then the sum will decrease by nd where n is the number of data values. Therefore when you divide the total by n, the mean will decrease by d. $\frac{S - nd}{n} = \frac{S}{n} - d$. For the median, the middle number will decrease by d. The mode will decrease by d. The range, on the other hand, will remain the same since (highest value $- d) - ($lowest value $- d) =$ highest $-$ lowest. **27.** mean: 2.8 m, median: 2.8 m, mode: 2.8 m and 2.9 m, range: 0.7 m **29.** 46.4 mi/h

Lesson 12-4   pp. 746–751

Got It? 1a. 60, 75, 85, 95, 105 **b.** 5, 7, 15, 21, 53
2.

Monthly Sales (millions of $)

3. The median tells you the middle value of the data. So in Miami the monthly rainfall is below 4.5 in. for half the months and above 4.5 in. for half the months. For New Orleans the monthly rainfall is below about 5.3 in. for half the months and above 5.3 in. for the other half of the months. **4a.** 60 **b.** No; since the percentile rank is the percent of scores that fall at or below a given score there is always at least 1 value associated with a given value. There is no 0 percentile; the lowest score is the first percentile.

Lesson Check
1. 48, 54, 100, 188, 256

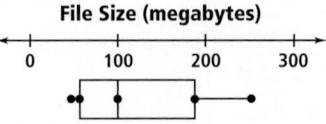
File Size (megabytes)

2. 24, 27, 29.5, 31.5, 33

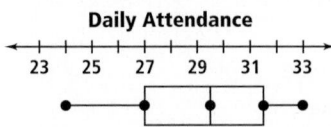
Daily Attendance

3. Class B **4.** the middle box **5.** 88 **6.** 75%; the third quartile is the value that divides the data so that about 75% of the data lies below and about 25% of the data lies above. **7.** No; the test is scored on point values from 0 to 100, whereas the percentile rank tells you how you did in reference to the rest of the group.

Exercises 9. 3.2, 4.2, 5, 6.15, 12
11. 100, 100, 101, 104, 105
13.

Movie Ratings

15.

Camera Prices ($)

17. 60 **19.** $90 \le x < 94$ **21.** $0 < h \le 73.5$ **23.** It could also be equal to the maximum value, which could happen if the top quarter of the scores all have the same value. **25.** You can only find the median, which is the value at the line in the box.

Lesson 12-5   pp. 753–759

Got It? 1a. quantitative; numerical quantities **b.** qualitative; not numerical **2a.** Bivariate; there are two variables. **b.** Univariate; there is only one variable. **3.** No; if you are using a stratified sampling method, you should sample at random from each group. **4.** Answers may vary. Sample: Do you prefer action movies or documentaries? **5.** Students who have e-mail may be more likely to have a cell phone.
Lesson Check 1. systematic **2.** random **3.** stratified **4.** quantitative **5.** The words *delicious* and *plain* are biased and might influence a respondent's answer. **6.** Univariate data involve one variable and bivariate data involve two variables.
Exercises 7. qualitative **9.** quantitative **11.** univariate **13.** univariate **15.** stratified; not a good sample as it assumes each town has a similar number of voters

17. random; good sample **19.** not biased; respondent is not influenced by question **21.** During the day many people are at work so your sample is not representative of the population. **23.** Because each sample is random, it would not be expected to be exactly the same.
25a. People at an airport are more likely to be travelers.
b. Your question is influencing the result. Respondents might prefer "neither." **c.** The sample is biased as it includes mostly people who might prefer France.
27. people who are customers at the store; every fifteenth customer; systematic **29.** attendees at the game; random attendees; random **31.** quantitative; univariate
33. qualitative; bivariate **35a.** Responses are voluntary and there are sports that are not listed. **b.** no for the reasons listed in part (a) **37.** Response is voluntary and only those who like the scent are probably going to return the card. **39a.** Answers may vary. Sample: Does your family have a pet? If so, what kind of pet is it?; qualitative
b. Check students' work. **c.** Check students' work.
41. D **43.** B **45.** 40 **46.** 60 **47.** $a > 1$ **48.** $x \geq -3$
49. $b > 0.2$ **50.** 20 **51.** 42 **52.** 6

Lesson 12-6   pp. 762–768

Got It? 1a. 48 **b.** No; the tree diagram would be very large, so using the Multiplication Counting Principle would be easier. **2.** 40,320 ways **3.** 20,160 **4.** 455 ways
Lesson Check 1. 5040 **2.** 6,227,020,800 **3.** 120
4. 5040 **5.** 10 **6.** 35 **7.** 24 outfits **8.** permutations
9. Permutations are used to count in situations where order is important. Combinations are used to count in situations where selection, not order, is important.
10. There is only one way to take n things, n at a time.
Also, $_nC_n = \frac{n!}{n!(n-n)!} = \frac{1}{0!} = \frac{1}{1} = 1$.
Exercises 11a. 8, 10 **b.** 8×10^6 or 8,000,000
13. 3,628,800 **15.** 1680 **17.** 5040 **19.** 42 **21.** 6
23. 90 **25.** 5040 ways **27.** 1 **29.** 9 **31.** 56 **33.** 28
35. 10 **37.** 220 ways **39.** 142,506 groups **41.** $_9P_7$
43. $_9P_6$ **45.** $_8C_5$ **47a.** 24 ways **b.** No; there is a limited number of ways that you can arrange the letters so someone can figure it out. **49.** 60 **51.** 210
53. Combination; the order of the books does not matter. **55a.** 35,152 call signs **b.** 913,952 call signs
57. 2 **59.** 4 **61.** 1 **63.** sometimes **65a.** 15 **b.** 4; 3 **c.** 3
d. 60 **67.** 0.073 **70.** qualitative **71.** quantitative
72. quantitative **73.** qualitative **74.** 0.81, −6.81
75. 6.70, 0.30 **76.** 1.46, −5.46 **77.** −1, −1.67
78. 32% **79.** 9% **80.** 22.5% **81.** 18%

Lesson 12-7   pp. 769–774

Got It? 1. $\frac{5}{8}$ **2.** It will be $1 - \frac{20}{50 + x}$, where x is the number of other samples added. The probability will increase. **3.** 3 : 1 **4.** 98% **5.** about 34,995 light bulbs

Lesson Check 1. $\frac{1}{6}$ **2.** $\frac{1}{3}$ **3.** $\frac{5}{6}$ **4.** $\frac{2}{3}$ **5.** 1 : 5 **6.** 16%
7. Theoretical probability is based on the number of favorable outcomes when all of the outcomes are equally likely. Experimental probability is based on the results of an experiment. **8.** There are only two outcomes that are favorable, getting a 1 or a 2, therefore the probability is $\frac{2}{10}$, or $\frac{1}{5}$.
Exercises 11. 0 **13.** $\frac{2}{3}$ **15.** $\frac{1}{2}$ **17.** $\frac{2}{3}$ **19.** $\frac{2}{3}$ **21.** $\frac{1}{3}$
23. 5 : 1 **25.** 5 : 1 **27.** 1 : 5 **29.** 43% **31.** 85%
33. about 201 trees **35.** 98.4% **39.** 40%
41. 25% **43.** $\frac{3}{16}$ **45.** $\frac{5}{8}$ **47.** B **49.** Since order does not make a different group, this is a combination problem. $_{11}C_5 = \frac{11!}{5!(11-5)!} = 462$. There are 462 different groups the coach can choose. **50.** 840
51. 6 **52.** 30 **53.** 9 **54.** 5 **55.** {1, 4, 5, 6, 7, 10}
56. {4, 6} **57.** {0, 2, 4, 5, 6, 7, 8, 10} **58.** {4, 10}
59. {0, 1, 2, 4, 6, 7, 8, 10}

Lesson 12-8   pp. 776–782

Got It? 1a. $\frac{5}{6}$ **b.** $\frac{2}{3}$ **2.** $\frac{2}{225}$ **3.** $\frac{1}{18}$ **4.** $\frac{1}{105}$ **5a.** $\frac{5}{33}$ **b.** No; the numerators and the denominators are the same, so the product is the same.
Lesson Check 1a. $\frac{4}{5}$ **b.** $\frac{3}{5}$ **c.** 1 **d.** $\frac{4}{5}$ **2.** $\frac{3}{20}$ **3.** $\frac{3}{25}$
4. Answers may vary. Sample: find the probability of spinning a number less than 5 that is even. **5.** Mutually exclusive; answers may vary. Sample: The complement of being even on a number cube is being odd, and even and odd are mutually exclusive. **7.** Because a tile can be both yellow and a letter, the formula should be
$P(\text{yellow or letter}) = P(\text{yellow}) + P(\text{letter}) - P(\text{yellow and letter}) = \frac{3}{5} + \frac{2}{5} - \frac{1}{5} = \frac{4}{5}$.
Exercises 9. $\frac{4}{5}$ **11.** $\frac{1}{2}$ **13.** $\frac{3}{5}$ **15.** $\frac{7}{10}$ **17.** $\frac{1}{4}$ **19.** $\frac{1}{6}$
21. $\frac{4}{81}$ **23.** $\frac{1}{9}$ **25.** $\frac{4}{27}$ **27.** $\frac{1}{36}$ **29.** $\frac{1}{36}$ **31.** $\frac{1}{12}$ **33.** 0
35. $\frac{3}{22}$ **37.** Dependent; the outcome of the first event affects the outcome of the second. **39.** For independent events, the outcome of the first event does not affect the outcome of the second event, while for dependent events, the outcome is affected. An example of two independent events is the rolling of two number cubes. An example of two dependent events is picking two cards from a deck without replacing the first one. **41.** about 4.7% **43a–c.** Check students' work. **45a.** $\frac{1}{36}$ **b.** $\frac{1}{36}$
c. $\frac{1}{6}$

Chapter Review   pp. 786–790

1. element **2.** frequency **3.** outlier **4.** quartile
5. $\begin{bmatrix} -12 & 7 \\ 4 & 6 \end{bmatrix}$ **6.** $\begin{bmatrix} 4.4 & 4.5 \\ 9.5 & -10.2 \\ 3.4 & -2.6 \end{bmatrix}$

7. $\begin{bmatrix} -12.6 & -4.62 \\ -12.6 & 8.4 \\ 4.2 & -12.18 \end{bmatrix}$ **8.**

Customers

9.

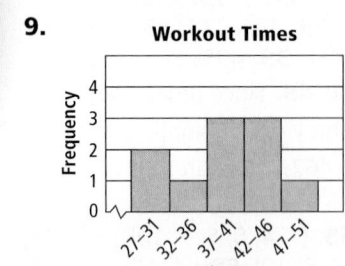

Workout Times

10. skewed
11. symmetric
12. 26.3, 26, 23 and 25 and 29, 9
13. 12.1, 12, 12, 2
14. 11.1, 11.3, 13.4; mean or median
15. 27

16.

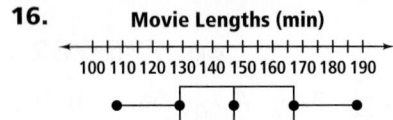

Movie Lengths (min)

17.

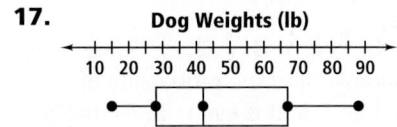

Dog Weights (lb)

18.

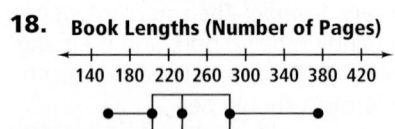

Book Lengths (Number of Pages)

19. B; the box in A is from about 90 to 110, where the box in B is from about 75 to 125. **20.** Systematic; good sample; do you plan on seeing more or fewer movies in the coming year? **21.** Stratified; good sample; who do you support for student council president? **22.** 15,120 **23.** 6 **24.** 336 **25.** 20 **26.** 360 **27.** 42 **28.** 28 **29.** 126 **30.** 10 **31.** 20 **32.** 35 **33.** 5 **34.** 10 **35.** 40,320 ways **36.** 126 outfits **37.** $\frac{1}{2}$ **38.** $\frac{1}{2}$ **39.** $\frac{1}{6}$ **40.** $\frac{5}{6}$ **41.** 0 **42.** $\frac{1}{3}$ **43.** about 93.3% **44.** $\frac{2}{7}$ **45.** $\frac{2}{7}$ **46.** $\frac{1}{36}$ **47.** $\frac{1}{4}$ **48.** Dependent; the outcome of the first event affects the outcome of the second event. **49.** Independent; the outcome of the spinner does not affect the outcome of the pick.

Skills Handbook

p. 798 1. composite **3.** composite **5.** prime **7.** composite **9.** prime **11.** composite **13.** 1, 2, 23, 46 **15.** 1, 11 **17.** 1, 3, 9, 27 **19.** $2 \cdot 3 \cdot 3$ **21.** $3 \cdot 3 \cdot 3$ **23.** $2 \cdot 2 \cdot 2 \cdot 2 \cdot 2 \cdot 2$

p. 799 1. 2 **3.** 24 **5.** 80 **7.** 33

p. 800 1–11. Answers may vary. Samples are given. **1.** $350 **3.** $300 **5.** $17 **7.** 6.90 **9.** 7 **11.** $30.80

p. 801 1. $\frac{8}{14}, \frac{12}{21}, \frac{16}{28}, \frac{20}{35}, \frac{24}{42}$ **3.** $\frac{6}{16}, \frac{9}{24}, \frac{12}{32}, \frac{15}{40}, \frac{18}{48}$ **5.** $\frac{10}{12}, \frac{15}{18}, \frac{20}{24}, \frac{25}{30}, \frac{30}{36}$ **7.** 9 **9.** 48 **11.** 2 **13.** yes **15.** no; $\frac{1}{8}$ **17.** yes **19.** $\frac{1}{2}$ **21.** $\frac{2}{3}$ **23.** $\frac{3}{10}$

p. 802 1. 0.3 **3.** 0.2 **5.** $0.\overline{714285}$ **7.** $\frac{7}{100}$ **9.** $\frac{7}{8}$ **11.** $6\frac{1}{3}$

p. 803 1. $\frac{5}{7}$ **3.** 3 **5.** $10\frac{7}{15}$ **7.** $6\frac{2}{9}$ **9.** $6\frac{7}{33}$ **11.** $9\frac{2}{3}$ **13.** $13\frac{7}{16}$ **15.** $\frac{3}{5}$ **17.** $1\frac{2}{7}$ **19.** $2\frac{3}{8}$ **21.** $3\frac{1}{3}$ **23.** $9\frac{4}{63}$ **25.** $2\frac{1}{6}$

p. 804 1. $\frac{3}{10}$ **3.** $8\frac{5}{8}$ **5.** $3\frac{1}{2}$ **7.** $25\frac{3}{10}$ **9.** $2\frac{4}{5}$ **11.** $1\frac{1}{5}$ **13.** $\frac{5}{7}$ **15.** $1\frac{17}{21}$ **17.** $\frac{20}{27}$ **19.** $\frac{22}{25}$

p. 805 1. 56% **3.** 602% **5.** 820% **7.** 14.3% **9.** 11.1% **11.** 75% **13.** 0.07 **15.** 0.009 **17.** 0.83 **19.** 0.15 **21.** 0.0003 **23.** 3.65 **25.** $\frac{19}{100}$ **27.** $4\frac{1}{2}$ **29.** $\frac{16}{25}$ **31.** $\frac{6}{25}$ **33.** $\frac{3}{800}$ **35.** $\frac{3}{5}$

p. 806 1. 6^4 **3.** $5 \cdot 2^4$ **5.** $4^2 \cdot 3^2 \cdot 2$ **7.** 64 **9.** 141 **11.** 3267 **13.** $(1 \cdot 10^3) + (2 \cdot 10^2) + (5 \cdot 10^1) \cdot (4 \cdot 10^0)$ **15.** $(8 \cdot 10^4) + (3 \cdot 10^3) + (4 \cdot 10^2) + (0 \cdot 10^1) + (1 \cdot 10^0)$

p. 807 1. 1.34×10^6 **3.** 7.75×10^{-4} **5.** 111,300 **7.** 1.895×10^3 **9.** 1.234×10^5 **11.** 6.4×10^5 **13.** 8.52×10^2 **15.** 17.5 **17.** 8.95×10^{-12} **19.** 3.77×10^{10} **21.** 1.8×10^{-6}

p. 808 1. 22 cm **3.** 24 cm² **5.** 216 cm³ **7.** 352 cm³

p. 809 1.

3.

```
                      X                    X
                    X X                    X
        X         X X X X               X X
      X X         X X X X         X     X X
      X X         X X X X         X     X X
      ─────────────────────      X     X X
      0 1 2 3 4 5 6               X     X X X
                                 X X   X X X
                                 ───────────────
                                 1 2 3 4 5 6
```

5. Gold Medals Won

```
      X
  X X X X
  X X X X
  X X X X X   X       X       X
  ───────────────────────────────
  0 1 2 3 4 5 6 7 8 9 10 11 12 13
```

The line plot shows that most of the countries won about 3 gold medals. The maximum number of gold medals that a country won was 13, and the minimum was 1.

p. 810 1.

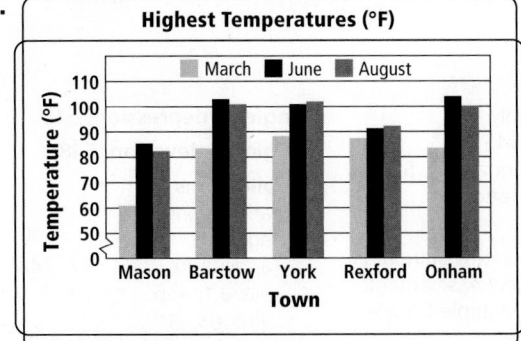

Highest Temperatures (°F)

Legend: March | June | August

p. 811 1.

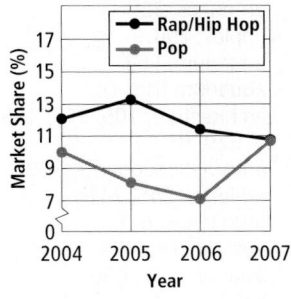

Market Share

Legend: Rap/Hip Hop | Pop

p. 812 1a. Transportation Mode

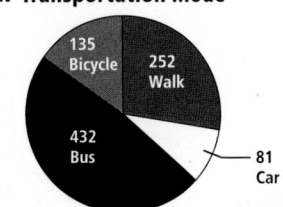

135 Bicycle | 252 Walk | 432 Bus | 81 Car

b. 48%
c. 3 times

p. 813 1.

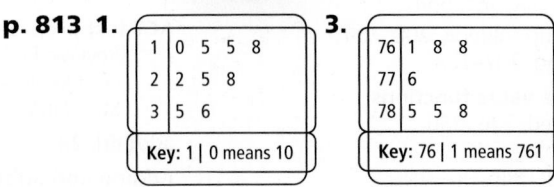

1	0 5 5 8
2	2 5 8
3	5 6

Key: 1 | 0 means 10

3.

76	1 8 8
77	6
78	5 5 8

Key: 76 | 1 means 761

5.

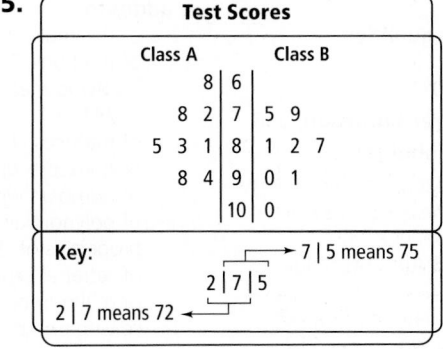

Test Scores

Class A		Class B
8	6	
8 2	7	5 9
5 3 1	8	1 2 7
8 4	9	0 1
	10	0

Key: 7 | 5 means 75

2 | 7 | 5

2 | 7 means 72

Index

A

absolute value, 31, 71

absolute value equations
graphing, 207–208
with no solution, 208–209
solving, 207–208

absolute value functions
defined, 346, 356
graphing, 346
parent, 346
vertex of, 350

absolute value inequalities
graphing, 209–210
solving, 209–210

absolute value parent function, 346

absolute value symbol, 31

Activity. *See also* Extension; Technology
Always, Sometimes, Never, 37
Analyzing Residual Plots, 595
Characteristics of Absolute Value
  Graphs, 351
Conducting Simulations, 775
Designing Your Own Survey, 752
Dividing Polynomials Using Algebra
  Tiles, 677
Finding Roots, 567
Graphing Functions and Solving
  Equations, 260–261
Graphing Linear Inequalities, 406
Graphing Rational Functions, 713
Inverse of a Linear Function, 329
Investigating $y = mx + b$, 307
Matrices and Solving Systems,
  385–386
Modeling Equations With Variables on
  Both Sides, 101
Modeling Multi-Step Inequalities, 185
Modeling One-Step Equations, 80
More Algebraic Properties, 184
Multiplying Powers, 424
Operations With Rational and Irrational
  Numbers, 45
Powers of Powers and Powers of
  Products, 432
Rates of Increase, 559–560
Relating Radicals to Rational
  Exponents, 447
Solving Systems Using Algebra Tiles,
  371
Solving Systems Using Tables and
  Graphs, 370
Standard Deviation, 733
Two-Way Frequency Tables, 760
Unit Analysis, 122–123
Using Models to Factor, 511

Using Models to Multiply, 497
Using Residuals, 344–345
Using Tables to Solve Equations, 59
Writing Quadratic Equations,
  573–574

ACT test prep. *See* Cumulative Standards
  Review; End-of-Course Assessment;
  Gridded Response; Multiple Choice;
  Standardized Test Prep

addend, 23

Adding and Subtracting Fractions, 803

addition
of decimals, 24
of fractions, 31, 803
involving measures of central tendency,
  741
of matrices, 727
of numbers with different signs, 31
of numbers with same sign, 31
of polynomials, 487, 488
properties of. *See* property(ies)
of rational expressions, 684, 685
of real numbers, 30–31, 33
solving equations using, 80, 82
solving inequalities using, 171, 172
solving systems of linear equations
  using, 378

Addition Property
of Equality, 81, 153
of Inequality, 171

additive inverse, 32

algebraic expressions
defined, 4, 69
dividing, 440
evaluating, 12
multiplying powers in, 425
simplifying, 48–49
writing, 4–5

algebra tiles
modeling equations, 80, 101
modeling factoring, 511
modeling multiplication, 497
modeling multi-step inequalities, 185
modeling quadratic equations, 576
solving systems, 371

alpha key, of graphing calculator, 406

Always, Sometimes, Never, 37

analysis
of data, 725, 785, 786
of errors. *See* Error Analysis exercises
of graphs, 234

Analyzing Residual Plots, 595

***and*, compound inequalities
containing,** 200, 201, 217–218

angle of depression, 648

angle of elevation, 648

applications
admissions, 457
ages, 62
agriculture, 335, 377, 748
aircraft, 436
airports, 391
air travel, 65, 169, 717
allowance, 223
antennas, 22
apples, 790
aquarium, 563
aquarium fish, 182
architecture, 106, 117, 135, 154, 333,
  629, 650
arithmetic sequences, 300
athletics, 245, 741
auto loans, 675
automobiles, 479
aviation, 265, 650
bakery, 128
baking, 265, 287
banking, 12, 177, 212, 368, 479,
  593, 668
baseball, 113, 732, 764
basketball, 57, 183, 211, 750,
  761, 788
beverages, 257
bicycle sales, 57
bicycling, 157, 321, 702
bike path, 334
biking, 212
biology, 390
birds, 157
bird watching, 34
boating, 392, 701
boiling point, 319
books, 85
bowling, 99, 739
bridges, 134
buffet, 252
business, 106, 321, 342, 388, 390,
  391, 393, 398, 404, 409, 465, 557,
  600, 682, 717, 761
cafeteria, 277, 781, 791
camping, 216, 219, 539
carpentry, 398, 515, 521, 532, 570
car rental, 266
cars, 148
car-sharing program, 93
car value, 465
car wash, 272
cats, 143, 226, 788
cell phone plans, 368
cells, 452
check for reasonableness, 324

Mid-Chapter Quiz, 29, 115, 193, 252, 321, 393, 446, 510, 575, 632, 690, 761

Mixed Review, 15, 22, 28, 36, 44, 66, 87, 93, 108, 114, 129, 143, 150, 170, 183, 199, 213, 239, 251, 267, 273, 306, 314, 328, 335, 350, 369, 384, 392, 399, 423, 431, 445, 452, 472, 496, 509, 517, 528, 533, 552, 581, 588, 594, 601, 631, 638, 651, 676, 683, 697, 704, 731, 737, 759, 768, 774

Open-Ended exercises, 9, 14, 21, 43, 52, 56, 57, 66, 86, 100, 108, 114, 128, 141, 142, 149, 157, 167, 169, 176, 183, 191, 198, 212, 227, 238, 250, 252, 261, 265, 272, 278, 279, 297, 299, 328, 333, 341, 357, 368, 383, 391, 393, 404, 411, 423, 430, 436, 442, 444, 451, 466, 471, 508, 510, 521, 527, 528, 532, 539, 565, 566, 575, 580, 593, 599, 604, 607, 624, 632, 637, 654, 657, 668, 675, 682, 688, 695, 711, 719, 729, 750, 761, 772, 773, 780, 781, 791

Quick Review, 69–72, 153–156, 223–226, 284–286, 354–356, 409–410, 475–478, 536–538, 604–606, 654–656, 716–718, 788–790

Standardized Test Prep, 15, 22, 28, 36, 44, 66, 87, 93, 108, 114, 129, 143, 150, 170, 183, 199, 213, 239, 251, 267, 273, 306, 314, 328, 335, 350, 369, 384, 392, 399, 423, 431, 445, 452, 472, 496, 509, 517, 528, 533, 552, 581, 588, 594, 601, 631, 638, 651, 676, 683, 697, 704, 731, 737, 759, 768, 774

Associative Property
of Addition, 23
of Multiplication, 23

astronomy, 156, 430, 443, 445, 770

asymptote
defined, 706, 718
horizontal, 707
identifying, 707
vertical, 706–707

average, 738. *See also* mean

axes, 60, 234

axis of symmetry, 546, 604

B

Bar Graphs, 810

base
defined, 10
of exponent, 425
finding, 139

multiplying powers with same, 425

best fit, line of. *See* line of best fit

bias
defined, 755, 789
in samples, 756
in survey questions, 755

Big Ideas
Data Collection and Analysis, 725, 785, 786
Data Representation, 725, 785, 786
Equivalence, 79, 151, 152, 163, 221, 222, 417, 473, 474, 485, 534, 535, 613, 652, 653, 663, 714, 715
Functions, 233, 282, 283, 293, 352, 353, 417, 473, 545, 602, 603, 613, 653, 663, 714, 715
Modeling, 233, 282, 283, 293, 352, 353, 363, 407, 408, 545, 602, 603
Probability, 725, 785, 786
Properties, 3, 67, 68, 417, 473, 474, 534, 535
Proportionality, 79, 151, 152, 293, 352, 353
Solving Equations and Inequalities, 79, 151, 152, 163, 221, 363, 407, 408, 545, 602, 603, 613, 652, 653, 663, 714, 715
Variable, 3, 67, 68, 163, 221, 222

binomials
dividing polynomials by, 679
modeling multiplication of, 497
multiplying, 498, 499
squaring, 504–505

biology, 17, 84, 111, 128, 191, 212, 338, 365, 390, 429, 450, 477, 628, 629

bivariate, 754

box-and-whisker plot
defined, 747, 788
interpreting, 748
making, 748

braces, 17, 194

brackets, 11, 203

break-even point, 388

C

calc key, of graphing calculator, 261, 339, 370, 456, 555, 567, 595, 598

calculator, 675. *See also* graphing calculator
degree mode, 646
equations in slope-intercept form, 307
exercises that use, 457, 458, 465, 551, 556, 649
histograms, 733

linear inequalities, 406
line of best fit, 339
permutations, 764
rational functions, 707, 708, 713
regressions, 595
roots, 567
systems of quadratic equations, 598
trigonometric ratios, 646
vertical motion model, 555

cards, 45

causation, 340

Challenge exercises, 9, 15, 22, 28, 36, 44, 52, 58, 66, 87, 93, 100, 108, 114, 121, 129, 136, 143, 150, 170, 177, 183, 192, 199, 206, 213, 220, 239, 245, 251, 259, 267, 273, 279, 300, 306, 313, 320, 327, 335, 343, 369, 377, 383, 392, 398, 404, 423, 431, 438, 452, 459, 471, 491, 496, 503, 509, 517, 522, 528, 533, 548, 552, 566, 572, 581, 588, 594, 600, 618, 625, 631, 638, 643, 651, 668, 676, 683, 689, 696, 712, 731, 737, 745, 751, 759, 768, 774, 782

change
percent decrease, 145
percent increase, 145
percent of, 144–147
rate of, 182, 212, 294, 354

Chapter Review, 68–72, 152–156, 222–226, 283–286, 353–356, 408–410, 474–478, 535–538, 603–606, 653–656, 715–718, 787–790

Chapter Test, 73, 157, 227, 287, 357, 411, 479, 539, 607, 657, 719, 791

Characteristics of Absolute Value Graphs, 351

check for reasonableness, 324

chemistry, 35, 123, 205, 206, 391, 411, 427, 430, 630, 697

Choose a Method exercises, 120

circle
area of, 110
circumference of, 110, 111

Circle Graphs, 812

circumference, 110, 111, 183, 211

classifying
data, 753–754
equations, 53
functions as linear or nonlinear, 247
lines, 332
numbers, 17–18
real numbers, 18
relation as function, 268–269

Index

horizontal asymptote, 707

horizontal lines, 296, 323, 331, 395

horizontal translations, 348

hypotenuse
defined, 614
finding length of, 615

hypothesis, 615

I

identity, 104, 154

Identity Property
of Addition, 24
of Multiplication, 24, 25

if-then statement, 615

inclusive, 200

inconsistent systems of linear equations, 365–366

increase, percent, 145

independent events, 777–778, 790

independent systems of linear equations, 365–366

independent variables, 240, 241, 249, 255, 294, 454

index of radical expression, 448

indirect measurement, 131

INDPNT feature, of graphing calculator, 567

inductive reasoning, 63

INEQUAL feature, of graphing calculator, 406

inequality(ies). *See also* solving inequalities
absolute value, 209–210
comparing real numbers using, 19
compound, 200–204, 217–218
defined, 19, 164
equivalent, 171
graphing, 167
graphs of, 165, 166, 172–173, 179, 181, 200–204, 209–210, 400
linear. *See* linear inequalities
multiple ways of representing, 167
multi-step, 185, 186–189
solution as union or intersection of sets, 218
solving using Addition Property of Inequality, 171, 172
solving using Division Property of Inequality, 180–181
solving using Multiplication Property of Inequality, 178–179
solving using Subtraction Property of Inequality, 173
with special solutions, 189
symbols for, 19, 166, 173
Triangle Inequality Theorem, 205

with variables on both sides, 188
writing, 164, 187, 201–203, 218
writing from a graph, 166

inequality, properties of. *See* property(ies)

input, 240

input value, 284

integers
square of, 17
in standard form, 324
as subset of rational numbers, 18

intercepts. *See* x-intercept; y-intercept

interdisciplinary
archaeology, 451
art, 143, 376, 495, 532, 539, 579, 621
astronomy, 156, 430, 443, 445, 446, 770
biology, 17, 84, 111, 128, 191, 212, 338, 365, 390, 429, 450, 477, 628, 629
chemistry, 35, 123, 205, 206, 391, 411, 427, 430, 630, 697
earth science, 93
economics, 142, 461
geography, 142, 438
geometry, 14, 15, 21, 51, 92, 99, 107, 113, 115, 143, 149, 150, 176, 187, 190, 192, 258, 264, 279, 304, 319, 327, 335, 375, 376, 383, 393, 404, 437, 444, 446, 490, 496, 502, 507, 510, 514, 519, 531, 533, 537, 538, 539, 565, 566, 571, 581, 600, 604, 607, 618, 625, 631, 636, 637, 654, 655, 657, 667, 676, 682, 690, 716, 719, 774
government, 175
history, 43, 617, 630
language, 86
music, 71, 85, 126, 127, 478, 736, 761, 764
physics, 169, 205, 271, 306, 311, 444, 463, 551, 565, 618, 642, 682, 699, 704, 711, 718
reading, 56, 269, 766
science, 113, 133, 470, 471
statistics, 128
U.S. history, 86

interest
compound, 139, 461, 462
simple, 139, 140

interpolation, 337, 356

interquartile range, 746

INTERSECT feature, of graphing calculator, 261, 370, 456, 598

intersection
defined, 215, 226
point, of system of linear equations, 364

symbol for, 215

interval notation, 203

inverse
additive, 32
multiplicative, 40
of a relation, 273
of linear functions, 329

inverse function, 329

Inverse of a Linear Function, 329

inverse operations, 82, 153

Inverse Property
of Addition, 32
of Multiplication, 40–41

inverse variation
comparing with direct variation, 700–701, 703
constant of variation for, 698
defined, 698, 718
equation, 698
graphing, 699–700
identifying, 701
using in real-world problems, 699

Investigating $y = mx + b$, 307

irrational numbers, 18

isolate, 82

K

Key Concepts
Adding Real Numbers, 31
Addition Property of Inequality, 171
Combination Notation, 765
Continuous and Discrete Graphs, 255
Dividing Real Numbers, 40
Division Property of Inequality, 180
Equivalence of Radicals and Rational Exponents, 449
Exponential Decay, 462, 478
Exponential Function, 453
Exponential Growth, 460, 478
Factoring a Difference of Two Squares, 525
Factoring Perfect-Square Trinomials, 523
Geometric Sequence, 467
Graph of a Quadratic Function, 554
Inverse Variation, 698
Mean, Median, and Mode, 738
Multiplication Counting Principle, 763
Multiplication Property of Inequality, 178
Multiplying Real Numbers, 39
Order of Operations, 11
Percent Change, 144
The Percent Equation, 138
The Percent Proportion, 137
Permutation Notation, 764
Point-Slope Form of a Linear Equation, 315

Index

Acknowledgments

Staff Credits

The people who made up the High School Mathematics team—representing composition services, core design digital and multimedia production services, digital product development, editorial, editorial services, manufacturing, marketing, and production management—are listed below.

Emily Allman, Dan Anderson, Scott Andrews, Christopher Anton, Carolyn Artin, Michael Avidon, Margaret Banker, Charlie Bink, Niki Birbilis, Suzanne Biron, Beth Blumberg, Tim Breeze-Thorndike, Kyla Brown, Rebekah Brown, Judith Buice, Sylvia Bullock, Stacie Cartwright, Carolyn Chappo, Christia Clarke, Mary Ellen Cole, Tom Columbus, Andrew Coppola, AnnMarie Coyne, Bob Craton, Nicholas Cronin, Patrick Culleton, Damaris Curran, Steven Cushing, Sheila DeFazio, Cathie Dillender, Emily Dumas, Patty Fagan, Frederick Fellows, Jorgensen Fernandez, Mandy Figueroa, Suzanne Finn, Sara Freund, Matt Frueh, Jon Fuhrer, Andy Gaus, Mark Geyer, Mircea Goia, Andrew Gorlin, Shelby Gragg, Ellen Granter, Jay Grasso, Lisa Gustafson, Toni Haluga, Greg Ham, Marc Hamilton, Chris Handorf, Angie Hanks, Scott Harris, Cynthia Harvey, Phil Hazur, Thane Heninger, Aun Holland, Amanda House, Chuck Jann, Linda Johnson, Blair Jones, Marian Jones, Tim Jones, Gillian Kahn, Matthew Keefer, Brian Keegan, Jim Kelly, Jonathan Kier, Jennifer King, Tamara King, Elizabeth Krieble, Meytal Kotik, Brian Kubota, Roshni Kutty, Mary Landry, Christopher Langley, Christine Lee, Sara Levendusky, Lisa Lin, Wendy Marberry, Dominique Mariano, Clay Martin, Rich McMahon, Eve Melnechuk, Cynthia Metallides, Hope Morley, Christine Nevola, Michael O'Donnell, Michael Oster, Ameer Padshah, Stephen Patrias, Jeffrey Paulhus, Jonathan Penyack, Valerie Perkins, Brian Reardon, Wendy Rock, Marcy Rose, Carol Roy, Irene Rubin, Hugh Rutledge, Vicky Shen, Jewel Simmons, Ted Smykal, Emily Soltanoff, William Speiser, Jayne Stevenson, Richard Sullivan, Dan Tanguay, Dennis Tarwood, Susan Tauer, Tiffany Taylor-Sullivan, Catherine Terwilliger, Maria Torti, Mark Tricca, Leonid Tunik, Ilana Van Veen, Lauren Van Wart, John Vaughan, Laura Vivenzio, Samuel Voigt, Kathy Warfel, Don Weide, Laura Wheel, Eric Whitfield, Sequoia Wild, Joseph Will, Kristin Winters, Allison Wyss, Dina Zolotusky

Additional Credits: Michele Cardin, Robert Carlson, Kate Dalton-Hoffman, Dana Guterman, Narae Maybeth, Carolyn McGuire, Manjula Nair, Rachel Terino, Steve Thomas

Illustration

Kevin Banks: 333; **Jeff Grunewald:** 238, 265, 266, 546, 568, 581, 619, 621, 639, 645, 693; **Christopher Wilson:** 253, 268, 276, 323, 372, 394, 486, 504, 563, 675, 686, 726, 730, 732, 736, 738, 762, 763, 767, 769, 776, 778; **XNR Productions:** 4, 132, 142, 151, 169, 171, 389, 455

Technical Illustration

Aptara, Inc.; GGS Book Services

Photographs

Every effort has been made to secure permission and provide appropriate credit for photographic material. The publisher deeply regrets any omission and pledges to correct errors called to its attention in subsequent editions.

Unless otherwise acknowledged, all photographs are the property of Pearson Education, Inc.

Photo locators denoted as follows: Top (T), Center (C), Bottom (B), Left (L), Right (R), Background (Bkgd)

Cover
Gary Bell/Corbis

Front Matter
ix, x Stan Liu/Getty Images

Page 43 (BR) The Art Gallery Collection/Alamy Images; **54** (CR) Satellite Imaging Corp./GeoEye Inc.; **84** (CR) Livio Soares/BrazilPhotos, (BR) Island Effects/iStockphoto, (CC) Wildlife Bildagentur GmbH/Kimball Stock; **113** (CR) Reuters/Corbis; **133** (TR) Courtesy of the Historical and Interpretive Collections of the Franklin Institute, (CC) Ingram Publishing/SuperStock, (TC) Medi-Mation Ltd /Photo Researchers, Inc.; **164** (CR) Google, Inc.; **167** (TR) ©Shubroto Chattopadhyay/Corbis, (TL) Macduff Everton/Getty Images; **196** (C) acilo/iStockphoto; **221** (BR) ©DK Images, (TR) ©Ned Frisk Photography/Corbis; **255** (CC) Ian O'Leary/©DK Images, (CL) iStockphoto, (CR) Taylor S. Kennedy/National Geographic Image Collection; **302** (TCR) Friedrich Saurer/Photo Researchers, Inc., (CR) GSFC/NASA, (BR) NASA/©AP Images; **311** (T) David Joyner/iStockphoto, (TR) Tobias Bernhard/Corbis; **365** (TL) Ilian Animal/Alamy Images, (TR) James Carmichael Jr./Photoshot; **422** (TR) Kevin Schafer/Photoshot; **458** (CR) Biophoto Associates /Photo Researchers, Inc.; **494** (TR) brt PHOTO/Alamy Images, (TCR) Paulo Fridman/Corbis; **512** (TCR) iStockphoto; **518** (TCR) iStockphoto, (CR) wingmar/iStockphoto; **524** (CR) Brandon Alms/Shutterstock; **570** (TR) Jxpfeer/Dreamstime LLC; **579** (BR) ©DK Images; **615** (TR) Rob Belknap/iStockphoto; **617** (BR) Geoffrey Morgan/Alamy Images; **624** (TR) Laure Neish/iStockphoto; **628** (BR) Art Wolfe/Getty Images; **630** (TC) Thomas Sakoulas/Greeklandscapes; **675** (CR) Scott Krycia/iStockphoto; **686** (C) Theo Allofs/PhotoLibrary Group/Getty Images.